ELEMENTS OF WRITING

Annotated Teacher's Edition

JAMES L. KINNEAVY
JOHN E. WARRINER

First Course

Holt, Rinehart and Winston
Harcourt Brace Jovanovich

HBJ

Austin • Orlando • San Diego • Chicago • Dallas • Toronto

Critical Readers

Virginia Ruth Anderson
Westridge Middle School
Austin, Texas

Nancy Beesley
Westfield Junior High School
Bloomingdale, Illinois

Beth Deluzain
Bay County Public Schools
Panama City, Florida

Linda George
Durant Middle School
Durant, Oklahoma

Linda Lewis
Battlefield Middle School
Fredericksburg, Virginia

Mary Felice Ray
Drexel Hills Middle School
Drexel Hills, Pennsylvania

Lynne Rice
Beverly Hills Middle School
Upper Darby, Pennsylvania

Sandy White
Lyman Gilmore Jr. High School
Grass Valley, California

Requests for permission to make copies of any part of the work should be mailed to: Permissions Department, Holt, Rinehart and Winston, Inc., 8th Floor, Orlando, Florida 32887.

Some material previously published in: ENGLISH COMPOSITION AND GRAMMAR, FIRST COURSE, Annotated Teacher's Edition copyright © 1988 by Harcourt Brace Jovanovich, Inc.; WARRINER'S ENGLISH GRAMMAR AND COMPOSITION, FIRST COURSE, Annotated Teacher's Edition copyright © 1986 by Harcourt Brace Jovanovich, Inc.; WARRINER'S ENGLISH GRAMMAR AND COMPOSITION, FIRST COURSE, Teacher's Manual copyright © 1982, 1977, 1973, 1969, 1965, 1960 by Harcourt Brace Jovanovich, Inc. Copyright renewed 1988 by Jean W. McLemore, Allison Warriner, Richard Treanor and John H. Treanor, Jr. All rights reserved.

Acknowledgments: See pages 935–944, which are an extension of the copyright page.

Printed in the United States of America

ISBN 0-03-047153-2   1 2 3 4 5 6   062   94 93 92

James L. Kinneavy, the Jane and Roland Blumberg Centennnial Professor of English at The University of Texas at Austin, directed the development and writing of the composition strand in the program. He is the author of *A Theory of Discourse* and coauthor of *Writing in the Liberal Arts Tradition.* Professor Kinneavy is a leader in the field of rhetoric and composition and a respected educator whose teaching experience spans all levels—elementary, secondary, and college. He has continually been concerned with teaching writing to high school students.

John E. Warriner developed the organizational structure for the Handbook of Grammar, Usage, and Mechanics in the book. He coauthored the *English Workshop* series, was general editor of the *Composition: Models and Exercises* series, and editor of *Short Stories: Characters in Conflict.* He taught English for thirty-two years in junior and senior high school and college.

Professional Essays

Donald M. Murray is Professor Emeritus of English at The University of New Hampshire, where he served as director of Freshman English and as English Department Chairperson. As a journalist, he won a number of awards including the Pulitzer Prize for editorial writing on the *Boston Globe* in 1954.

Lee Odell has a Ph.D. in English and Education from The University of Michigan. A former middle school and high school teacher of English, he now teaches writing at Rensselaer Polytechnic Institute. He has published frequently on the teaching of writing and is interested in the processes of writing, talking, and thinking.

Maxine C. Hairston has a Ph.D. in English from the The University of Texas at Austin, where she served as Director of Freshman English. She is the author of several texts on writing theory and the teaching of writing, including *A Contemporary Composition.*

Barbara J. Shade has a Ph.D. in Educational Psychology from The University of Wisconsin-Madison. She is a Professor and Dean of the School of Education at The University of Wisconsin-Parkside. She specializes in the social and psychological attributes of people with high academic achievement with an emphasis on African American. She has written extensively on culture and its impact on learning and achievement.

Wanda B. Schindley has an Ed.D. in Composition and Rhetoric from East Texas State University. She teaches at Northeast Texas Community College and serves as coordinator and curriculum specialist for the Workplace Partnership program. She coauthored an eleven-volume teacher's resource series, *The English Teacher's Guide to the Essential Elements.*

Charles W. Leftwich has an Ed.D. in Educational Administration from Harvard University. He is a professor in the Department of Educational Administration at East Texas State University. He worked in public schools for over twenty-five years as a teacher, a vice-principal, a principal, and a superintendent.

Patricia G. Tweeddale has an Ed.D. in Educational Administration from East Texas State University. She has taught at-risk students in high school and has written about the impact of public education policy on such students. She is a partner in an educational consulting service that focuses on helping teachers to teach at-risk student populations successfully.

Norbert Elliot has a Ph.D. in English from The University of Tennessee. A director of the writing program at New Jersey Institute of Technology, he is a specialist in test development and writing assessment.

Karen L. Greenberg has a Ph.D. in Linguistics from New York University. She is an Associate Professor of English at Hunter College of The City University of New York, where she directs the Developmental English Program and teaches courses in writing and linguistics. She is the director of the National Testing Network in Writing, and she has authored numerous books and essays on writing instruction and assessment.

David A. England has a Ph.D. in English from Indiana University. He is the Associate Dean of Teacher Education at Louisiana State University. A former high shool English teacher, he has been active in the National Council of Teachers of English and was active in the National Writing Project.

Writers and Editors

Mary Hynes-Berry has a Ph.D. in English from The University of Wisconsin-Madison. She is an educational consultant for public schools in Chicago, Illinois. She has been a writer of educational materials for over fifteen years.

Mary Katherine Kuykendall has an M.A. in English from Baylor University. She taught in secondary schools in the Dallas area for ten years and taught composition and literature courses at Southern Methodist University for seven years, where she was named Outstanding Professor in 1976. She has been writing educational materials for five years and currently creates high school correspondence courses at The University of Texas Telelearning Center and teaches composition at Austin Community College.

Ann Moseley has a Ph.D. in American literature from The University of Oklahoma at Norman. She has co-authored two developmental freshman reading and composition textbooks. She currently teaches at East Texas State University in Commerce, Texas.

Mary Elizabeth Podhaizer has an M.Ed. from the University of Vermont. She has been a writer of educational materials in literature and composition for fifteen years. She is currently engaged in research on secondary students' responses to literature.

Sylvia Teague has an M.A. in economics from The University of Texas, where she also taught economics for two years. She has been writing educational materials in composition and literature for five years.

David Young has an M.A. in literature from The University of Florida. He is the technical editor for KBN Engineering and Applied Sciences, Inc., and he also owns a small publishing company in Gainesville, Florida.

Acknowledgments

We wish to thank the following teachers who participated in field testing of pre-publication materials for this series:

Susan Almand-Myers
Meadow Park Intermediate
  School
Beaverton, Oregon

Theresa L. Bagwell
Naylor Middle School
Tucson, Arizona

Ruth Bird
Freeport High School
Sarver, Pennsylvania

Joan M. Brooks
Central Junior High School
Guymon, Oklahoma

Candice C. Bush
J. D. Smith Junior High School
N. Las Vegas, Nevada

Mary Jane Childs
Moore West Junior High School
Oklahoma City, Oklahoma

Brian Christensen
Valley High School
West Des Moines, Iowa

Lenise Christopher
Western High School
Las Vegas, Nevada

Mary Ann Crawford
Ruskin Senior High School
Kansas City, Missouri

Linda Dancy
Greenwood Lakes Middle
  School
Lake Mary, Florida

Elaine A. Espindle
Peabody Veterans Memorial
  High School
Peabody, Massachusetts

Joan Justice
North Middle School
O'Fallon, Missouri

Beverly Kahwaty
Pueblo High School
Tucson, Arizona

Lamont Leon
Van Buren Junior High School
Tampa, Florida

Susan Lusch
Fort Zumwalt South High
  School
St. Peters, Missouri

Michele K. Lyall
Rhodes Junior High School
Mesa, Arizona

Belinda Manard
McKinley Senior High School
Canton, Ohio

Nathan Masterson
Peabody Veterans Memorial
  High School
Peabody, Massachusetts

Marianne Mayer
Swope Middle School
Reno, Nevada

Penne Parker
Greenwood Lakes Middle
  School
Lake Mary, Florida

Amy Ribble
Gretna Junior-Senior
  High School
Gretna, Nebraska

Kathleen R. St. Clair
Western High School
Las Vegas, Nevada

Carla Sankovich
Billinghurst Middle School
Reno, Nevada

Sheila Shaffer
Cholla Middle School
Phoenix, Arizona

Joann Smith
Lehman Junior High School
Canton, Ohio

Margie Stevens
Raytown Middle School
Raytown, Missouri

Mary Webster
Central Junior High School
Guymon, Oklahoma

Susan M. Yentz
Oviedo High School
Oviedo, Florida

Contents in Brief

Table of Contents

▶ A TEACHER'S GUIDE TO ELEMENTS OF WRITING

CHAPTER 2 ▸ LEARNING ABOUT PARAGRAPHS

TEACHING CHAPTER 2 57A-57D

► CHAPTER 3 LEARNING ABOUT COMPOSITIONS

CHAPTER 6 CREATIVE WRITING

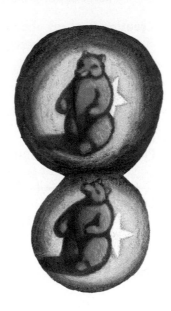

CHAPTER 8 WRITING TO PERSUADE

► CHAPTER **10** **WRITING A REPORT**

▶ CHAPTER *12* **ENGLISH: ORIGINS AND USES**

PART TWO **HANDBOOK**

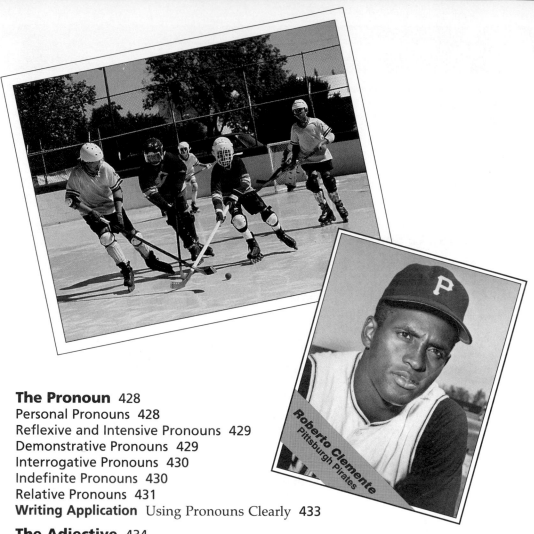

► CHAPTER *17* THE PHRASE   489

Prepositional and Verbal Phrases

▶ CHAPTER 18 THE CLAUSE   514

Independent and Subordinate Clauses

▶ CHAPTER 19 KINDS OF SENTENCE STRUCTURE 532

Simple, Compound, and Complex Sentences

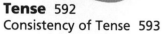

▶ CHAPTER 22 USING PRONOUNS CORRECTLY 604

Nominative and Objective Case Forms

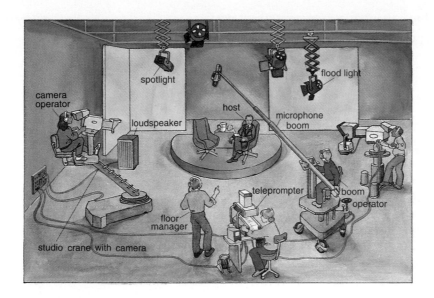

spotlight
flood light
camera operator
host
microphone boom
loudspeaker
teleprompter
boom operator
floor manager
studio crane with camera

▶ CHAPTER 30 LISTENING   808

Strategies for Active Listening

Listening with a Purpose 808

Using Skills and Strategies

Fiction

Arna Bontemps, *Chariot in the Sky: A Story of the Jubilee Singers*

Mona Gardner, "The Dinner Party"

Virginia Hamilton, *A White Romance, Willie Bea and the Time the Martians Landed*

Rudyard Kipling, "Rikki-tikki-tavi"

Barry Lopez, "Coyote Places the Stars"

Gary Paulsen, *Hatchet*

Marjorie Kinnan Rawlings, *The Yearling*

Mari Sandoz, "Winter Thunder"

George Shannon, "A Drink for Crow," *Stories to Solve*

Virginia Driving Hawk Sneve, "The Medicine Bag"

Gary Soto, "The Jacket," "The Marble Champ"

Mildred Taylor, *Roll of Thunder, Hear My Cry*

Yoshiko Uchida, *A Jar of Dreams*

Nonfiction

"A Doll Made to Order," *Newsweek*

"Ubuhlali and Umnaka—Beaded Necklaces and Bangles," *African Crafts*

Dan Carlinsky, "Kites"

Michael DiLeo, "Dream of the Blue Dolphins," *American Way*

Lonnie Dyer, "Kachinas: Sacred Drama of the Hopis"

Wallace H. Black Elk and William S. Lyon, *Black Elk: The Sacred Ways of a Lakota*

Delia Ephron, "How to Eat Like a Child"

Anthony Glass, *Journal of an Indian Trader*

Whitney Hair, "Cures from the Jungle," *Ranger Rick*

Fred Johnson, *Meet-a-Cheetah*

Gary Johnson, "A Son's Challenge"

Marjorie Lamb, "One Day a Month, Go Without Meat," *2 Minutes a Day for a Greener Planet*

Gary Larson, *The PreHistory of the Far Side*

John G. Neihardt, *Black Elk Speaks*

Dudley Randall, "Questions and Answers"

Sally Ride with Susan Okie, "Weightless in Space," *To Space and Back*

Carson I. A. Ritchie, *Insects, The Creeping Conquerors and Human History*

Louise L. Sherman, "A Review of Lois Lowry's *Number the Stars*"

Monica Sone, *Nisei Daughter*

James P. Terzian and Kathryn Cramer, *Mighty Hard Road*

Greg Walz-Chojnacki, "The Spaceport Mermaids," *Odyssey*

Eudora Welty, *One Writer's Beginnings*

Eliot Wigginton, *I Wish I Could Give My Son a Wild Raccoon*

Elizabeth Yates, *My Diary—My World*

Poetry

Matsuo Basho, *Haiku*

Robert Frost, "Stopping by Woods on a Snowy Evening"

Ted Hughes, "My Aunt"

A Teacher's Guide to

ELEMENTS OF WRITING

CONTENTS

JAMES L. KINNEAVY

DONALD MURRAY

KAREN GREENBERG

BARBARA
SHADE

LEE ODELL

MAXINE
HAIRSTON

NORBERT
ELLIOT

PATRICIA TWEEDDALE
CHARLES LEFTWICH

WANDA
SCHINDLEY

T37

HOW DARE THEY?

. . . IN THE SPIRIT OF MAINTAINING THE LASTING VALUES AND STANDARDS OF THE SERIES . . .

Certainly when teachers saw a new name listed as a coauthor with John E. Warriner, some of you must have said, "How can the editors dare do this?" Like the editors, I am fully aware that Warriner has been a legendary name in high school English composition and grammar books since 1941, the year of the first edition of his series, till the present. His high school textbooks have changed somewhat through the decades, but they have stood the test of half of a century—despite many educational trends and fashions—because they have incorporated important values and standards. I am aware of all of this, aware that Warriner's texts have almost a biblical authority.

But even the Bible is translated anew for different generations. So it is in the spirit of maintaining the lasting values and standards of the series while bringing a few further changes that this new edition of the series is published with a new name listed as coauthor. I was properly flattered when the company's editors asked me to be the consultant for the composition sections of the books in the new series. But I was also in awe of this long tradition of excellence and can only hope that this tradition can be upheld.

Like John E. Warriner, I have a long and varied experience as a teacher. He taught in junior high, high school, and college. I have taught in elementary school, high school, and college. He taught for many years; I have been teaching since 1941 and continue to teach today. For the past twenty-five years I have given workshops to high school students involved in state-wide competitive contests in extemporaneous writing. Like Warriner, I have attempted to keep up with the profession and to reflect in my writings what we have learned and continue to learn about teaching the language arts. I have trained students to teach at all grade levels from elementary school through graduate school. I have also observed student teachers for years at the high school and college levels.

You will find in this series, therefore, an attempt to maintain the best values of the Warriner series and to add to it a few new features that teachers, administrators, scholars, and editors think will make it an even better set of books.

THE TEACHER'S EDITION IS A *GREAT* HELP

I know that teaching school combines the blue and white collar syndromes: You're there at 8:00 and leave at 4:00; then you take on extra-hour professional chores in the evening and on weekends of correcting papers, reading to keep up professionally (which you are doing right now), working on extracurricular activities,

attending conventions, etc. You need all of the timesavers you can find.

You will find many of them in this edition. On each page you will find that your objectives, your lesson plan, and your resources are packed around the student text. Questions you can ask the students are provided (with answers). Vocabulary items are defined. Adaptations to more-advanced students, to less-advanced students, and to ESL students are suggested. Special exercises supplementing those in the textbook are provided. Student responses to questions are foreseen and reactions suggested. Applications to critical thinking and to cooperative learning are continually provided.

All in all these helps are a treasure trove. Before spending hours looking up supplementary materials for a class, look in your teacher's edition. Someone else may have done your work already and saved you hours. When I look at the wealth of all of these materials and contrast them to what I had to teach with in my early teaching years in both elementary and high school, I am green with envy.

Beginning teachers especially should exploit these materials, built upon the experiences of hundreds of their predecessors. These experiences can help new teachers avoid some all-too-common problems. Let me point out some of them.

RELATIONSHIP BETWEEN COMPOSITION AND GRAMMAR

You will find in the new series the same close relationship between composition and grammar that has characterized the series since its inception. You can see this by simply looking at the table of contents.

Such a look makes quite clear that the primacy and the preponderance of attention is given to writing, and that grammar is a handmaid to writing. But both are covered extensively.

Given the increasing importance of rhetoric in public schools and in college, you will find more depth in the composition section

of this textbook. There is a more discernible structure to the various chapters on writing. These chapters reflect the concern for certain important kinds of writing—concerns that are reflected in many state writing tests. Thus, there is a chapter devoted to each of the major aims of writing: to inform, to persuade, to explain, to prove, to entertain, and to allow the students to express themselves. Each of the modes of writing usually gets a chapter at each grade level: narrating, describing, classifying and defining, and evaluating. This structure is more explicit in the new series than it was in the earlier ones.

In each of these chapters, however, the close relationship between composition and grammar

WHAT THIS TEXTBOOK DOES NOT WANT TO DO IS TO ENCOURAGE THE ISOLATED TEACHING OF GRAMMATICAL SKILLS IN A ROTE MANNER.

is maintained. There is a grammatical issue covered in each chapter, particularly relevant to the kind of writing being covered. Thus, a chapter on persuasion can consider the problem of fragments, often seen in advertisements. A chapter on description can consider the importance of adjectives and adverbs. Finally, nearly all of these chapters refer to the grammar chapters for coverage of issues that relate to the kind of writing under consideration.

This careful attempt to relate grammar to composition was explicit in the longtime title of this series, which has linked grammar to composition for years.

This linkage is confirmed by seventy years of *empirical research*. Studies at all levels, from elementary school through college, confirm that grammar is learned best when taught in conjunction with composition, as well as with speaking and with literature. These studies have been made in the United States, in Canada, in the British Isles, and in Australia. What this textbook does not want to do is to encourage the isolated teaching of grammatical skills in a rote manner. This is called the formal teaching of grammar. Sometimes, it has to be done. But most of the time, the grammar is linked to a writing assignment and even motivated by it. For instance, consistent fragments in a formal paper suggest a lesson in the sentence, emphasizing its elements and its completeness. This improves the composition and also teaches the grammar in a manner that gives it meaning.

THE PROCESSES OF COMPOSING

In keeping with the emphasis in the schools and in college writing courses, you will find a continuation of the unremitting concern with the processes of writing in every writing chapter of the series—a concern begun several years ago. The stress on process will be evident in the structuring of the chapters by the stages of the writing process; in the frequent

The students are usually divided into *peer support groups* of three or four, all working on similar projects, and all trying to help each other turn out better work. The members of the groups help one another plan the papers, critique each other's rough drafts, and provide a real audience for the final version. The members of the group are like a miniature research group working on a common project.

*T*HIS *DOMINANCE OF THE WHOLE OVER THE PARTS* EXPLAINS THE GENERAL STRUCTURE OF THE BOOK. THE WRITING CHAPTERS COME AT THE BEGINNING OF THE BOOK, AND THE GRAMMAR, USAGE, AND MECHANICS MAKE UP THE LAST SECTION OF THE BOOK.

use of support groups of students to react to each other's plans, drafts, and papers; and in teacher and peer interventions in the writing process. The idea that writing is a solitary, sedentary process, as a poet once said, is not at all adhered to in this textbook. Rather writing is viewed as a collaborative and cooperative action.

A COOPERATIVE ATMOSPHERE

The process view of writing that sees the writing place as a happy, cooperative workshop rather than a silent dungeon enables the students to get support and help from one another and from the teacher.

The *teacher* moves from group to group, helping in the planning, discussing problems, critiquing rough drafts, and grading the final drafts. Like the members of the peer support groups, the teacher fulfills different functions: at times the teacher is a motivator, a source of ideas, a theorist who has general ideas that apply to the current situation, a careful listener, a constructive critic of plans and rough drafts, a sympathetic reader and grader of the final version, and above all, a fellow writer.

With this view of the writing process, the teacher with a *heavy paper load* can find help from the students. The teacher isn't the only person who reads a student's paper. The other members of the support group can assist the teacher with useful feedback to the author at any level of the writer's concerns with mechanics, with word choice, with organization, with ideas, and with style. If the teacher trains support groups to be helpful and constructively critical, a good deal of the drudgery of grading papers can be avoided.

Finally, the writing process often results in some kind of *publication*, possibly in a public speech (or in a performance in the case of creative writing), sometimes in a class newspaper put out by desktop publishing on a computer, sometimes in a school newspaper, or maybe just in a permanent portfolio that the student keeps of his or her better work.

THE WHOLE AND THE PARTS

Another motif that you will see given more prominence from the very beginning and running through all of the writing chapters is the insistence on the relationship between the whole and the parts in the composing process. A theme is like a sentence: It is made up of parts that are uttered in a chronological sequence, but the whole is greater than the parts because it also includes the relationships among the parts and with the whole. We don't begin a sentence with no idea where it is going to end or what it is going to say; we begin with a whole and choose the parts to articulate it. We may change our minds halfway through a sentence and adjust to our new idea; the same phenomenon often happens with a whole theme.

In other words, a theme begins with a vague but somewhat distinct idea of a whole and looks around for the parts that will embody that idea. The parts are single words, phrases, sentences, paragraphs, even large sections of the theme.

Consequently, in the writing chapters, each of these parts is treated as a part of a whole. A composition is not an expanded word or phrase or paragraph. An expanded paragraph is a big paragraph, just as an expanded wheel is just a big wheel, not suddenly a complete automobile. To use another metaphor, a student setting out to write a composition is like an architect who draws up a plan of the whole building; it's going to be a home or a department store or a restaurant or a sports coliseum or whatever. But the architect doesn't haphazardly gather bricks and steel and staircases and chimneys and just throw them together.

With this idea of the dominance of the whole over the parts, each of the writing chapters pursues the writing process through to the production of a complete theme. There are writing activities throughout addressing the parts, but they are all orchestrated to the final whole.

This *dominance of the whole over the parts* explains the general structure of the textbook. The writing chapters come at the beginning, and the grammar, usage, and mechanics make up the last section.

In fact, the suggested treatment for writing encourages the students to write rapidly and enthusiastically in their first plans, sketches, and drafts, without stopping to check spelling, word choice, or grammatical purity. The idea is to

*T*HE IDEA IS TO SUPPORT THE WRITING PROCESS AS A CREATIVE SURGE IN THE BEGINNING. THE MECHANICAL MATTERS ARE OFTEN BETTER HANDLED IN THE REVISION.

support the writing process as a creative surge in the beginning. The mechanical matters are often better handled in revision.

AIMS AND MODES AS WAYS OF THINKING

The close connections among the aims and modes of writing and rather different ways of thinking have been emphasized in the introduction to the student's edition, so these will not be repeated here in any detail. But at the heart of the series is the notion that writing involves thinking all of the time; and different ways of writing involve different ways of thinking. Expressive writing is quite different from expository writing, and some students can do one type better than another. Nevertheless, a minimum competence in each aim and mode is necessary to the development of a full mental life. You are encouraged to reread the **"Introduction to Writing"** chapter to see the development of this notion.

THE AIMS OF WRITING AND DIFFERENT DIALECTS

You will undoubtedly notice that different levels of formality are suggested with the different aims of writing. In the chapters on expres-

sive writing, a casual, personal, and familiar style is suggested. At the other extreme, in the chapters on information and proof, a more formal sense of grammar and word choice is expected. This is true in real life and in the classroom. In between self-expression and these types of expository writing, there are various shades of formality in persuasive, creative, and exploratory writing.

The model adopted here is that of Martin Joos, whose book *The Five Clocks* distinguishes five different levels of formality that nearly all of us use, depending on the circumstances. Joos calls these the intimate, the colloquial, the consultative, the formal, and the ritual levels. We speak to our family members (and sometimes our pets) in the familiar dialect. We speak to our friends in an ordinary conversation on the colloquial level. We adopt the consultative tone usually when we are teaching class. We use our formal dialect when we are giving speeches at a convention. And we use the ritual level of formality when we are at church or are graduating or are being initiated into a society.

But teachers are not the only people who have their five levels of

formality. Teenagers also have their own dialects for intimacy—I say dialects because girls have a different intimate dialect than do boys. Teenagers also have their own colloquial, consultative, formal, and ritual dialects. Mature people have their own five levels. Finally, the elderly have their own five dialects, often quite different from the other age levels.

Being aware of the different purposes for writing and the various levels of formality also helps the teacher be more aware of *minority dialects*, such as those used by Hispanic, Asian, and African Americans. The use of these dialects in expressive and sometimes in creative writing is often to be encouraged. On the other hand, the dialect of the targeted audience is to be encouraged in persuasion. In expository writing, there is more emphasis on the standard dialect.

WRITING AND LITERATURE

While you are teaching this book on handling writing and grammar, you are also using a separate textbook for literature. But the necessity of putting the major readings in different literary genres covered in the ninth grade in a special book should not at all imply a separation of the study of literature from that of writing or grammar. All through the literature book, there are writing assignments that cover the same purposes that are taught in the writing book. Students are asked to react expressively, persuasively, creatively, and informatively to literary selections. Thus the literature textbook resonates the same tones and rhythms as the writing textbook.

lection. These questions are usually answered in an oral forum. The oral emphasis continues throughout the chapter because each stage of the writing process is carried out by means of small support groups of three or four students helping each other in planning, organizing, writing, and revising, as explained above. Frequently the publication of the paper takes an oral form. Thus persuasive speeches are delivered in front of the class.

The support group is clearly as much of a listening group as it is a speaking group. Students learn to listen carefully to each other in order to make constructive suggestions for improvement.

Thus the four language arts are carefully interwoven into the structure of each chapter at each stage of the writing process.

WRITING AND NEW TECHNOLOGIES

Whenever possible, teachers should take advantage of the new technologies that are increasingly becoming available at the high school level. Consequently, throughout this edition, there are continual reminders of these possibilities. Let us mention a few of them.

Networking with Computers

Some high schools have word processors available for use in teaching some writing classes. A few of these are even networked to allow student interactions with each other, either with the entire class or with selected support groups. The simultaneous writing reactions of all members of the class to a common reading assign-

ment is one of the most effective methods to insure one hundred percent participation in group discussions, especially if the right questions are asked. And the use of computers to set up small support groups for the different stages of the writing process is also an exceptionally efficient technique of using small groups in teaching writing.

Revising and Word Processors

Even without networking, however, the use of word processors is to be commended whenever possible, particularly because of the manner in which revising is accomplished on computers. Students who formerly hated to revise now see revision as an easy and enjoyable manner to improve their work, not just at the level of vocabulary or mechanics, but even at the level of full discourse changes.

Spelling, Vocabulary, Grammar, and Word Processors

Word processors also bring substantial help to the poor speller and to the student having trouble finding the right word. Nearly all word-processing programs have some type of spell-check feature that shows students which words are incorrectly spelled. Thus each student can keep a list of his or her own problem words. This is acknowledged by nearly all spelling research as the single best way to improve spelling. Most spell-check programs are accompanied by programs that properly hyphenate words at the end of a line. This is an additional bonus for students who use word processors.

Conversely, this series is permeated with reading and literature. Each writing chapter includes models of the type of writing that is being studied. Many samples are drawn from the literary canon. In one of the textbooks, for instance, to illustrate the aims of writing, there is an excellent poem by William Stafford. Nearly every chapter in the student's edition contains similar material. Of course, all of these selections are annotated.

Further, in this edition, in each chapter of the book there are **Literature Links**, which take common literary selections and relate them to the material being studied in the chapter. Besides the **Literature Links**, there is the **Quotation for the Day**, a writing prompt drawn from literature.

Some writing chapters are almost completely devoted to literary writing, especially the chapters on creative writing, narration, and description.

Thus writing and literature are highly integrated by a common underlying philosophy of language.

WRITING AND THE OTHER LANGUAGE ARTS

In addition to being highly integrated with literature, this writing textbook is also tightly integrated with reading, speaking, and listening.

Each chapter contains several reading samples of the type of writing being studied. These are carefully analyzed by the students by means of questions after each se-

In addition, most word processors now come with a thesaurus of some size. This enables the students to look for options in vocabulary, even while working at the computer.

Thirdly, some word processors now have grammar programs that can check tense, case, subject-verb agreement, fragments, etc. These are not as common as spell-check features or thesauruses, but they are becoming available.

Publishing and Word Processors

Even if there is not a full classroom of word processors, it is possible to use a word processor as a desktop publisher to enable students to see some of their writings in elegant print and format. These can be put into portfolios for permanent records. Frequently throughout the annotated teacher's edition you are reminded of this option as one method of publishing the students' papers.

A FINAL WORD: USE YOUR OWN PERSONAL STAFF

Possibly after reading this essay, which brings together many of the rather complex tasks of the writing teacher, you may have been somewhat intimidated. But luckily you don't have to solve all of these problems overnight. The teaching of writing is a slow and cumulative process. Each chapter of this textbook focuses on a very specific issue and tries to teach just that particular skill. Following chapters build on the skill just learned. The student is slowly building up a range of abilities, not suddenly moving from barbarism to literacy.

Of course, in the preceding grades, your predecessors have worked with the students whom you now face, just as your colleagues will pick up where you leave off. And you are not alone at the present time: Your current colleagues are working with the same students in other classes.

In other words, just as writing is a cooperative endeavor among the students with each other and with you in your classroom, so also is it a cooperative endeavor among a sequence of teachers from year to year and among a group of teachers one year at a time. In many cases, parents are also willing cooperators.

Put Your Staff to Work

This textbook adds several more dimensions of helpmates. The authors are seasoned professionals who have faced many of the issues of these chapters before. These authors draw on other textbooks with which they are familiar. They also draw heavily on scholars that they have consulted. Thus, when I said earlier that the best way for a poor speller to improve spelling skills was to keep a journal list of personal mistakes, add to it when new mistakes are made, and consult this personal list regularly, this statement was drawing on ten years of research at two major universities with thousands of students. The marketing staff of this series is also made up of seasoned professionals who make it their business to find out what teachers want in a textbook. The teaching consultants who tried out the materials for these chapters were chosen because of their experience and knowledge. Finally, the editors of

this series are acknowledged masters in their field—they have marketed the best-selling series in writing and grammar for almost half of a century.

Thus, you the teacher are backed by a phalanx of authors, scholars, market experts, teacher consultants, and editors all trying to assist you as you work with your students and other teachers. They are really your own personal staff. Use this book intelligently and this staff springs to life at your command. Donne's statement particularly can be applied to teachers: "No teacher is an island."

This textbook tries to put you in touch with all of these other helpers in the business of education. It can take a good deal of the loneliness out of teaching.

No One Does A More Important Job

Finally, you should be assured that your task is at the top of educational priorities. No one does a more important job than the teacher of writing. Throughout history, people who can write have been considered educated. Writing, in fact, has been the hallmark of the educated person in antiquity, in the Middle Ages (they were called clerks at that time), and in the modern period as well. A person who teaches students how to write is at the forefront of the educational enterprise. Such a person is also teaching students how to think in ways that will enable them to cope with a complex modern society as full human beings. 🍎

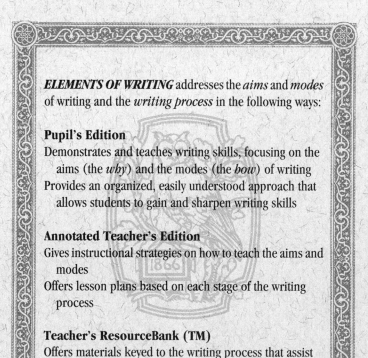

ELEMENTS OF WRITING addresses the *aims* and *modes* of writing and the *writing process* in the following ways:

Pupil's Edition
Demonstrates and teaches writing skills, focusing on the aims (the *why*) and the modes (the *how*) of writing
Provides an organized, easily understood approach that allows students to gain and sharpen writing skills

Annotated Teacher's Edition
Gives instructional strategies on how to teach the aims and modes
Offers lesson plans based on each stage of the writing process

Teacher's ResourceBank (TM)
Offers materials keyed to the writing process that assist students in achieving the aims and modes

By Donald M. Murray

Use Genre as Lens

"We write about what we don't know about what we know."

Students are usually introduced to each genre—essay, narrative, poem—in isolated units, as if one form of writing would contaminate another. But each genre is a lens, a way to observe, record, and examine the world. Students should be encouraged to use each genre to explore a single important experience.

Student writers and their teachers should begin the exploration with a personal experience—an event, a person, a place—that holds a significant mystery for them. Mystery is the starting place for most writing, what Grace Paley described when she said, "We write about what we don't know about what we know." Invite your students to explore a moment in their lives to which they keep returning in memory, the way the tongue seeks the missing tooth.

Encourage your students to play with the fragments of language connected with that experience in their minds and on paper to discover a line, a phrase, or a word that contains a tension or conflict within the experience. The "line" might be a word—*Christmas*—that

might have special implications for a student with a Catholic mother and a Jewish father. It might be a phrase—*the debts of Christmas*—to a person whose family spends too much money to make up for their true family feelings. The "line" could be a sentence—"Each Christmas I remember my sister who will never grow old"—for someone who lost a sister years before. Each "line" has a tension and mystery the writer needs to understand by writing.

Before your students begin, it is important to remind them that all writing is experimental, that experimentation implies failure, and that failure is instructive. It is not possible they will fail; it is imperative that they fail. We do not improve our writing by avoiding failure, but by making use of it.

To guarantee failure, urge students to write the first draft fast. Velocity is as important in writing as it is in bicycle racing. Speed will produce the accidents of language, connection, and insight that will propel the draft forward towards meaning. And velocity allows students to escape, for the moment,

the censor that demands premature correctness.

They should allow their drafts to instruct them. The evolving text will take its own course, exploring the experience as it is relived. If they are patient, receptive, and open to surprise, the text will tell them what they have to say. You may want to write two statements by E. M. Forster on the chalkboard:

Think before you speak is criticism's motto; speak before you think creation's.

and

How do I know what I think until I see what I say?

Students should write out loud, hearing the text as they write it. They may actually do this—it is your classroom—or read silently but *listen* to the text. As they tune their voices to the story being told, the voice—angry, nostalgic, humorous, sad, analytical, instructive, argumentative, poetic, even narrative—will reveal the meaning of the draft to the writer.

I invite you to stand beside me at my workbench and to observe me

as I use genre to explore an experience of mine.

THE ESSAY

I prefer the term *reflective essay* to *personal essay* because the writer reflects on personal experience, or on a topic of personal interest. The essay is neither a simple narrative of experience nor of thought unanchored by experience, but a combination of thought and experience, an effort to discover and share meaning in experience. The essay is a demonstration of critical thinking.

Some notes on the craft of the essay.

• Narrow the territory to be explored so you can achieve depth.
• Be specific. The specific will instruct. The more specific you are, the more universal your audience will be.
• Work locally; the paragraph you have just written contains the seed of the next paragraph. For example, if you have said the experience was important, show how it was important in the next paragraph.
• Answer the reader's questions. Writing is a conversation between reader and writer.
• When the draft surprises you, pay attention. Develop the surprise to discover its meaning.

On April 21, while visiting a daughter and her husband in their new home, I got up early without the alarm, as is my habit, and ended up sitting at the top of the stairs waiting for my family to wake, and I found mystery in the experience. It was a moment full of emotion, and I needed—not wanted, but needed—to explore that moment through writing.

I made a few notes in my daybook:

I can remember myself as a small boy in Doctor Denton's trying to be quiet sitting at the head of the stairs (night) waiting for the family to get up

I can remember my own daughter's impatient waiting

Sunday morning I sit at the head of the stairs a good place to read, a good place legs waiting, wife, behind me in the room, my wife

The next day I wrote the column that was published in *The Boston Globe*, April 30, 1991:

I am once again a small boy in Dr. Denton's sitting at the top of the stairs waiting for the snoring to stop and another day to begin.

I am, at the same time, an old man sitting at the top of the stairs in the new home of a daughter and her husband, waiting once more for the snoring to stop and a new day to begin.

Minnie Mae and I, on our first visit, have taken their bed, and they sleep on the hide-a-bed in the living room. They work in the theatre and have agreed to get up early—at 9 o'clock on Sunday morning—because the old folks are here.

But I followed the custom of many old men and was up at 5:33 AM. I tiptoed downstairs, went out to the car, explored Mount Kisco, sipped a cup of coffee at Dunkin Donuts—yes, and had a doughnut, and yes, juice to get down my six pills I take because of previous doughnuts—bought the Sunday "New York Times," sat in the car reading it, and now, at eight AM sit at the head of the stairs where I can stretch my legs, flex my football knee, and read my book and wait.

It has been a good morning, and I feel little guilt that I have not been able to sleep in. They will laugh at my compulsion to be up and doing, and I will tease them for their laziness, but they will not understand the joy I, like many over sixties, experience when I am up in the lonely hours of dawn.

I ruminate—early morning is ideal for rumination—on the fact that as a child I was always up early when I could lose myself in a book —no TV then—explore the backyard or the vacant lot where the morning glories grew.

Awake before the grown-ups, I could be what I needed to be:

T HIS MORNING I DIDN'T GET UP UNTIL 5:45, BECAUSE I STAYED UP UNTIL 11:15 WATCHING THE NCAA BASKETBALL. BUT IN SUMMER I'LL BE UP AT 4:30, MAKE COFFEE, LET OUT THE DOG, GO PICK UP *THE BOSTON GLOBE*. THEN I WRITE."

Lindbergh crossing the Atlantic alone, Admiral Byrd isolated in his tiny room under the Antarctic ice, the unnamed Indian scout watching the palefaces land on the Maine coast.

As a teenager I bicycled my route for Gallagher's News Agency in Quincy finishing before the sun was up, drove Miller's grocery truck to market in Boston or cleaned the vegetables and laid them out in rows on the boxes balanced in front of the small store on Beach street.

Only now I confess that when I nicked myself trimming the lettuce that was packed in ice, my hands numb and clumsy, I would turn that lettuce head so the blood did not show. I was apprentice to Miller's game: profit through deceit.

I still remember playing grown-up early in the morning, the grocer's apron twice tucked so it did not sweep the sawdust strewn floor. The profit would be Miller's not mine, but I anticipated the customers who might, this Depression Saturday, pay cash. That anticipation would last until midnight when Mr. Miller would go out and scan the street right and left and reluctantly, when no one was on the street, give the command to close.

In combat I preferred the early morning patrols, guard duty when I was alone to watch the theatre of morning's change from dark to light, the promise of a new day even when the landscape was littered with last night's dead.

After college I worked for a morning newspaper and liked the mystery and companionship of the night worker, enjoyed the coming home at dawn. Eventually I returned to days, and morning became my best writing time as it is for most writers.

Goethe advised, "Use the day before the day. Early morning hours have gold in their mouth."

John Hersey testified that "To be a writer is to sit down at one's desk in the chill portion of every day, and to write." A few years ago poet Donald Hall said, "I get up at 5 without an alarm. This morning I didn't get up until 5:45, because I stayed up until 11:15 watching the NCAA basketball. But in summer I'll be up at 4:30, make coffee, let out the dog, go pick up *The Boston Globe*. Then I write."

In retirement I, like so many other over sixties, still get up early when there are no cows to milk, no commuter train to meet, no factory shift to join. It is habit, but for me a habit built not from compulsion but delight.

Sitting at the top of the stairs waiting for the young—and the not-so-young Minnie Mae—to wake, I try to define the strange emotion I feel. At last it comes to me. I am, after a lifetime of chasing the carrot, content.

I have another day to celebrate. Sitting here alone, I can enjoy the feeling of this house that is turning so quickly into a home. I am comfortable in this home and know that soon my wife will wake with a groan and a smile, and downstairs I will hear conversation and music, smell coffee and we will all make plans for the day not too far off when a grandchild will sit where I sit, perhaps beside me, waiting for another day to begin.

The grandchild has arrived. His name is Joshua. I have not yet sat beside him at the top of the stairs but I will.

THE NARRATIVE

There are many wonderful ways to tell stories, but I suggest student fiction writers begin with the scene.

Conrad is supposed to have said that a novel is a series of scenes of confrontation. The writer experienced in nonfiction tells *about* the story; the fiction writer *reveals* the story. That is an enormous difference, and the writing of a scene is the best way to cross the divide. Students can draw on their experiences with TV and film. The reader observes a room with the fourth wall removed; the action within the room tells the story and the reader discovers its meaning. As the short-story writer Becky Rule points out, students think that fiction has no rules, but the rules come from the story, and they are established early; if Hamlet is an indecisive prince he can suddenly become a king but not a decisive one.

Some notes on the craft of narrative.

• Start with character, not theme. The story and its meaning are revealed through the interaction of the characters.

• Write in the third person. It gives you more room and detachment.

• Dialogue is action, what the characters do to each other. Joan Didion says, "I don't have a very clear idea of who the characters are until they start talking."

• Point of view is where the camera is positioned to record the scene. In the beginning, stick with one point of view, perhaps entering into one head but not jumping in and out of every head. If you are in one sister's head, you don't know Frank is in the freezer; in the other sister's head, you do.

• Kurt Vonnegut counsels, "Don't put anything in a story that does not reveal character or advance the action."

In writing a draft of my novel, I found myself stealing the experience from my own essay and began a scene:

Melissa found Iain sitting in the shadows at the top of the stairs, "It's 5:30 in the morning."

He nodded.

"On guard duty?"

"In a way. I often sit herein winter, watch the light just before dawn, the woods, the field that goes down to the lake."

She thought for a moment of what it would be like to be a spy to your life, always on guard and asked, "You said last night that wherever you are, you see a field of fire, are aware of where to dig in, put the machine guns, even after all there years?"

"I'm not proud of it, Melissa. It's just my geography, an infantryman's geography."

"Do you always see a geography of war?"

"Always first, then I can make it go away. Most times. It's natural, just the way I

see things. The doctor sees you as kidney or a colon; I'm an old soldier, I see a field of fire, where the attack would come from."

"That's sad."

"Tedd's a soldier too, Melissa."

They hear the key probe for the lock, at last find it, and hurried down the stairs....

That is just a small fragment of narrative, and yet you can see how the story is revealing itself dramatically to the writer and the reader.

THE POEM

Poetry is the most disciplined and difficult form of writing. It is also the most fun. Experience is distilled by the writing of poetry. Poetry is always play—play with image and language so that meaning is revealed directly without rhetoric getting between the writer and reader or between experience and reader. Inexperienced poets often write with adjectives and adverbs, trying to describe their own feelings. The experienced poet writes with information, revealing specifics, provocative details, and compelling images that make the reader feel and think. The meaning is rarely stated but always there. In the poem, even more than fiction, the meaning is implied. The poem is the stimulus to the reader's thinking.

Some notes on the craft of poetry.

• Forget, for the moment, rhyme, meter, and traditional verse forms.

- Brainstorm images and other specifics, creating a list that may become a poem.
- Draft lines—not sentences but fragments of language—that capture an event, person, or place.
- Rearrange the lines until they reveal a meaningful pattern.
- Pay attention to the line breaks, trying to end on a strong word that causes the reader to read on.

The morning I wrote the column, I also wrote, on the computer, what might become a poem for my poetry group that was meeting that Thursday evening. I pasted this in my daybook:

Sitting at the top of the stairs
I listen to the silences
to understand Grandma's war with Mother

Sitting at the top of the stairs
I tune
        train myself to 1 elinesss

Later that day I made a handwritten note I also cut out and pasted in the daybook:

I lived at the top of the stairs, behind the living room couch, under the dining room table, the tent of tablecloth—in the apple tree, under the porch,

And still later I drafted a poem that went through one radical and three or four extensive revisions (periods of word play) until it became the following completed poem:

Childhood Espionage

Spy to my life, I lived at the top of the stairs, recorded silence, mapped how hurt was done. Under the porch, at the bedroom door, behind living room

sofa, I filled notebooks with what was not said, not done, escaped to the sidewalk, tried to read the shades drawn against my life. It must be Mother's shadow

sitting on the edge of the double bed, must be father's kneeling to pray. I cannot be sure, circle the block, listen to the neighbor's opera of argument , stand under

an open window where conversation will pour over me Once I saw my friend's older sister. She never pulled the shade. The dogs learned my smell

and let me patrol back yard, alley, vacant lot, in silence. I found the room where the Beckers kept the boy with the enormous head, watched comfort flow

from a priest's dancing hands as he gave the last rites to Vinnie's grandma, swayed to the rhythm of the Mitchells' bedroom dancing, lying down. Late, I returned to the home

of closed doors where we passed each other without touching. We never raised our voices, never stood between

light and shade, never let a secret fall out a window.

Students should be encouraged to take central experiences from their lives—Willa Cather said, "Most of the basic material a writer works with is acquired before the age of fifteen"—and explore them with an array of genre, using each lens—essay, narrative, poem—and then examining the subject through other genre, perhaps argument, report, screenplay, or news story, to discover the many meanings in their lives. ❦

Sources quoted include Grace Paley, Joan Didion, and Kurt Vonnegut cited in the following work: Donald M. Murray, *Shoptalk: Learning to Write with Writers*, Boynton/ Cook Publishers, Inc., 1990.

ELEMENTS OF WRITING addresses the *aims* and *modes* of writing and the *writing process* in the following ways:

Pupil's Edition
Demonstrates and teaches writing skills, focusing on the aims (the *why*) and the modes (the *how*) of writing
Provides an organized, easily understood approach that allows students to gain and sharpen writing skills

Annotated Teacher's Edition
Gives instructional strategies on how to teach the aims and modes
Offers lesson plans based on each stage of the writing process

Teacher's ResourceBank (TM)
Offers materials keyed to the writing process that assist students in achieving the aims and modes

BY JAMES L. KINNEAVY

MEET THE AIMS AND MODES OF WRITING

THE PLACE TO START (AND END) THE TEACHING OF WRITING IS TO HAVE STUDENTS SEE WHAT WRITTEN LANGUAGE CAN DO FOR THEM.

WHY WRITE? WHERE DO I BEGIN?

Writing is a very complex activity, and so is the teaching of writing. I admit these facts, and I have been teaching writing for fifty years. You may be teaching your first class this year, and you probably have the same problem: In the face of this complex process, where do you start?

Some teachers recommend what may seem to be a very simple and logical approach: Start with the simple building blocks of writing and gradually work up to more complex blocks. In other words, teach students some elementary things about words, then move up to phrases, afterwards teach sentences, eventually work up to paragraphs, and finally, have students write full themes. Some say that this is how children learn to use language orally. At first blush this theory has a kind of plausible simplicity to it. Years of research, however, have shown that it doesn't work and that it isn't the way children learn language.

LANGUAGE GETS THINGS DONE

Babies see that family members around them accomplish things by using language, and they quickly learn to use it themselves to get food, drink, or attention. This is the motivation behind all language acquisition and usage, from cradle to grave—language gets things done.

Consequently, if we can keep this elementary driving force behind our attempts to teach writing (or any language art for that matter), we can draw on a basic incentive that even babies understand. But when language teaching is divorced from getting things done, students rightly find it boring and uninteresting.

For this reason, the place to start (and end) the teaching of writing is to have students see what written language can do for them. What can writing do? In one introductory chapter, we attempt to get students to look around and see what language is getting done. We call language-users the hidden agents behind many of the

miracles of our age, we say that language is where the action is, and we call language-users the movers and shakers of the world.

We focus the student's attention on the different kinds of things that language accomplishes, using very concrete examples. But the principle is the same at every grade-level and on into the college educations, careers, and adult lives of our graduates: The central concept in the teaching of writing at every level is an awareness of the aims or purposes of writing.

THE FOUR MAJOR AIMS OF WRITING

Luckily for you, as well as for the students, these aims are not infinite, unpredictable, and unmanageable. They can be reduced to a few basic categories, and both you and the students have a good deal of practical experience with the categories in general. For example, one kind of language experience with which you are very familiar has to do with attempts to explain to or inform an audience about something of which it is partially or totally ignorant. You do this daily in the classroom and the students are the targets of this use of language. Other examples of this kind of writing are news stories in newspapers and magazines, encyclopedia articles, reports, textbooks, discussions, proposed solutions to problems, research studies, etc. The emphasis is always on the subject matter, considered more or less objectively. *This kind of writing is generically referred to as expository writing.*

As a teacher, you are only too aware of a second kind of writing that places more emphasis on the writer. In this case, the writing reveals the feelings of the writer, allows the writer to voice his or her aspirations or reactions to something in a quite personal way, or gives the writer a chance to articulate important beliefs. Examples of this kind of writing are journals, diaries, myths, prayers, credos, and protests. Of course, some of this writing may also overlap with other kinds. The major emphasis in this kind of writing is on the writer. *This kind of writing is often called expressive writing.*

As a teacher, you often try to convince your students of the importance of an education and of their duties as citizens. As a matter of fact, in our culture we are bombarded with attempts to get read-

ers to vote a certain way, to change attitudes or beliefs, to buy certain products, to switch allegiances, etc. Examples of such writing are advertising, political speeches, legal oratory, editorials, and religious sermons. In all of these cases, the focus of the use of language is on the receiver of the message. *Usually, this kind of writing is called rhetorical or persuasive writing.*

A fourth kind of writing, probably your favorite, is literature. This type of writing is given an honored place in English classes. We read selections of literature. They are intended to delight us and sometimes to teach us lessons. Examples of literature range from simple jokes, funny stories, ballads, small poems, and TV sitcoms to serious dramas, movies, novels, and epics. We try to get students to write this way when we teach creative writing. *Although all writing involves originality, we usually reserve the term* creative writing *for this kind of writing.*

THE COMMUNICATION BASIS OF THE AIMS OF WRITING

As a perceptive reader, you may have noticed as we went through the four major aims of writing that each one emphasized a different element of the communication process. It is not accidental that the major purposes of writing gener-

ally can be reduced to four. The structure of the written communication process is based on a writer, a reader, a language, and the subject matter; you may have seen these elements presented in a graphic form, such as the communication triangle shown below.

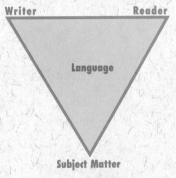

The major parts of the communication process.

You will find that students usually recognize that these four elements all play an important role in the writing process, but it is more difficult to get them to see that the role of each element changes in the different aims of writing.

CHANGING ROLES OF ELEMENTS IN DIFFERENT AIMS

In the expressive aim, as we pointed out above, the major focus of the attention is on the writer; the reader, language, and subject matter take on secondary roles. In persuasion, on the other hand, the reader takes center stage; the writer, though present, wants to get the message acted upon and uses language and subject matter to achieve this end.

In expository writing, the subject matter is given the lead role in the communication drama; the writer, reader, and language are

subordinate to the explanation, proof, or communication of information that is involved. In literature, finally, the emphasis is on the beauty of the literary craftsmanship as an object of delight to the reader; the subject matter and the author, though present, are not as important as the literary object. When we are studying *Huck Finn*, the novel is more important than either Mark Twain or life on the Mississippi as experienced by a young white boy and a black man.

To assist you to get students to see these differing roles, the relationship between the elements of the communication process and those of the aims of discourse is expressed graphically below. (The major aims of writing and the main parts of the communication process).

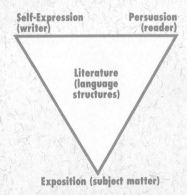

The major aims of writing.

Consequently, from aim to aim there is a continual shifting of roles in the communication process. The lead role determines the major purpose of the writing and the other roles become subordinate. Many teachers have found that this simple diagram enables students to grasp the changing dynamics of language use.

AS A TEACHER, YOU OFTEN TRY TO CONVINCE YOUR STUDENTS OF THE IMPORTANCE OF AN EDUCATION . . .

DOMINANT AIMS AND OVERLAP

As a teacher, you have probably written one or two of these different kinds of writing, but you may not have written all of them. In your own writing you are certainly aware that most writing does not attempt to achieve all of these aims at the same time. A specific piece of writing usually has a single dominant aim, subordinating the others to avoid conflicts and confusion. Though subordinate, the other aims are still present. Thus, movie ads in the newspaper contain important information about actors, actresses, directors, titles, show times, etc., but the information is there to persuade people to come to the movies.

Similarly, a scientific report proving that smelters of Sudbury, Ontario, affect the ecology of the area emphasizes in an objective way the evidence for this hypothesis. But there is clearly the implicit notion that something ought to be done about it (a persuasive strain). Indeed, all the aims overlap each other.

WHY ARE THE BASIC AIMS IMPORTANT?

Despite overlaps, however, it is quite important to distinguish the various aims. It is crucial that both teachers and students understand why.

As a teacher, you are very aware that the criteria by which one kind of discourse is judged are different from the criteria by which another kind of discourse is judged. You know and try to impress upon your students that expository writing is judged on the basis of objective evidence; the appeal of the writer

JAMES L. KINNEAVY
AUTHOR OF
ELEMENTS OF WRITING

as such is not relevant to the final proof or explanation, nor is the use of emotion or humor. For this reason, you know that when you teach expository writing, it is important to discourage the use of these other kinds of appeal—they are, in fact, considered inappropriate in news stories, scientific reports, or textbooks. Thus the pedagogy of expository writing follows from the nature of this kind of writing.

But when you switch to teaching other kinds of writing, these other appeals are positive and important. In persuasion, for example, the emphasis is on the appeal of the writer and the appeal to the interests of the audience. The differences among exposition, persuasion, literature, and self-expression force you to emphasize different criteria when

teaching these different kinds of writing. There is no single criterion of aim which makes all writing good. That is why the different aims are taught separately.

THE MODES OF WRITING

After all this talk about the aims of writing, you, as a teacher, might very well say to me, "Well, Mr. Kinneavy, all this may be very true. But are you maintaining that if I get students to pay attention to the aims of their writing, all other problems will disappear? There are many other facets of the process of writing to which we teachers have to pay attention. Grammar is clearly a persistent concern, as are spelling, vocabulary, sentence structure, paragraphing, genres of writing (letter, report, story, poem, speech, ad, etc.), subject matter,

and last but not least, the modes. What do you propose to do with all of these issues?"

I recognize all of these concerns and reply that they will be given close and continuous attention throughout the entire course, but in this introduction I would like to stress the last dimension, that of the modes of writing.

This dimension bridges the two mentioned just before it—genre and subject matter, and it implicates a major concern of all writing teachers—organization. More than any other aspect of writing, modes determine overall organization. This particular essay, for example, is a series of classifications and definitions.

At times in the history of writing, modes have been given almost as much attention as the aims, but most of the time they have been a serious second candidate. The modes are listed differently in various books. In this textbook we call narration, description, classification, and evaluation the modes. They could be called the genres of writing, and they could be called ways of looking at subject matter.

USE THE NEWSPAPER TO DISPLAY THE MODES

When I want to introduce students to the modes, I use a newspaper. I ask students to find examples of news stories (narratives). I ask them to find classifications, especially in the classifieds, as they are called. I ask the students to examine individual items within each section of the classifieds and to tell me what the details are. It becomes clear to them that there are hundreds of specific descriptions of cars, houses, lost dogs, jobs, etc., in the classifieds. Finally, I have the students check reviews of books, movies, television programs, concerts, football games, etc. These are all evaluations. Modes are as ubiquitous as the aims of writing.

Like the aims, the modes have to be taught separately. What makes a good narrative is not what makes a good evaluation or a good description or a good classification. The rules of defining are not at all the rules of narrating. As with the aims of writing, the modes of writing are different in nature and require different pedagogies. Consequently, the modes are given careful consideration in the following chapters.

THE PHILOSOPHIC BASIS OF THE MODES

You are probably wondering if there is a neat graphic structure that you can use to help students with the modes. Yes, there is. But, before it can be presented, let us ask the preliminary question, "What is a mode?"

WHAT IS A MODE?

A mode is a different perspective on a given subject matter. Take George Washington or a razor, two very different kinds of subject matter. I can write a history of George Washington or a history of the development of a given razor. I can describe the individuating characteristics of a given razor. I can

classify George Washington or a razor from several different viewpoints. Finally, I can evaluate George Washington, and I can evaluate the razor. Each of these discourses is a very different kind of writing.

What explains the differences? In other words, what differentiates narration from description, for example? Narration is always dynamic; it is concerned with change, whereas description is static. A narrator looks at the changing aspects of something, whereas a describer looks at the static aspects of the same thing.

When you are trying to get students to see the difference between description and classification, ask them what a description of Washington entails and what a classification of Washington would require. In description, the individuating characteristics of his personality are stressed (the father of our country, for example), but a classification of Washington pays attention to the different roles he assumed (president, general, husband, etc.). Both pay attention to Washington as static, and are therefore not like narration.

When you are trying to get students to differentiate narration from evaluation, first have someone tell a little of the history of Washington at Valley Forge. Then have someone evaluate Washington as a general. They will see that narration as such, simply details change in something, whereas evaluation considers that thing's performance against some norm and makes a judgment of approval or disapproval. Both narration and evaluation are dynamic: Narration details change, and evaluation considers performance.

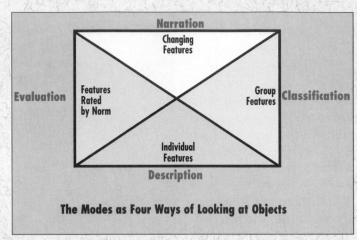

The Modes as Four Ways of Looking at Objects

These differences are shown above in **The Modes as Four Ways of Looking at Objects**.

In the textbook, these four modes will be continuously related to the aims. Anything that is written will always involve both an aim and a mode. Together, they solve nearly all of the organizational problems of writing, for either the aim or the mode determines the way the theme is laid out, as the following chapters will show. The aim especially determines the style, as will be made clear in each chapter. Thus, the aim and the mode of a given piece largely determine the main ideas, the overall organization, and the direction of the style. 🦅

ELEMENTS OF WRITING addresses the *aims* and *modes* of writing in the following ways:

Pupil's Edition
Demonstrates and teaches writing skills, focusing on the aims (the *why*) and the modes (the *how*) of writing

Provides an organized, easily understood approach that allows students to gain and sharpen writing skills

Annotated Teacher's Edition
Gives instructional strategies on how to teach the aims and modes

Teacher's ResourceBank (TM)
Offers materials keyed to the writing process that assist students in achieving the aims and modes

By Lee Odell

Showing vs. Telling:
Using Models in Teaching Writing

MAKE US SEE WHAT YOU'RE TALKING ABOUT.

For some time now, teachers of writing have made a point of exhorting students to make their writing "show, not tell." Don't just tell us your reactions or opinions, we say to them. Make us see what you're talking about. If you're trying to describe a person, let us see facial expressions, details of clothing, mannerisms, actions; let us hear exactly what the person says. Or, if students are trying to write persuasively, we insist: Don't just give us your generalized conclusions. Give us some specific information that lets us see what you base your judgment on and that lets us decide for ourselves whether your judgment makes sense.

This advice is not an infallible, inflexible rule. Writers can't elaborate on everything. Furthermore, readers sometimes let a generali-zation pass unchallenged because it seems to ring true or because writers have sufficient authority for us simply to take their word on the matter. But if we are judicious in asking students to "show, not tell," the phrase constitutes good advice for writers and excellent advice for teachers. If we want students to make significant progress as writers, we will have to show them—not just tell them, *show*

LEE ODELL OPENS HIS CLASSROOM DOOR AT RENSSELAER POLYTECHNIC INSTITUTE.

them—what we mean. In effect, we need to make sure they have models, not just of the kinds of writing they will do but of the writing processes.

There is, of course, a long history to the practice of working with models. For centuries, teachers of rhetoric and writing have required students to study the works of great writers, sometimes having students copy model texts word for word or asking students to imitate the sentence structures they found in these works. Indeed, a version of this practice persisted through the middle 1980s in the form of sentence combining. This system did not ask students to emulate one specific writer, but it did show them frequently used sentence patterns in the works of highly admired professional writers so students could construct their own sentences based on a wide variety of these patterns.

Traditional approaches to using models have their uses, but these approaches are not what I'm talking about here. I'm suggesting that we depart from traditional practice in several ways. For one thing, the model should come not solely from famous authors but rather from books and magazines students read willingly and have readily accessible. Also, teachers don't have to provide all the models; students should be asked to bring in articles or excerpts from books that they personally find engaging and effective. Finally, these models should not be treated as though they are sacred; they are, instead, objects for analysis—for criticism as well as for praise. We and our students need to examine entire models where writ-

ers have used successful strategies that students might incorporate into their own writing, as the occasion warrants. But we and our students also need to identify things that don't work and maybe even to collaborate on devising ways to improve the model.

There are several ways we might use models, but my favorite is to use them to help students solve their own writing difficulties. For example, a number of my students can't figure out how to begin a piece of writing, what Donald Murray would refer to as a "lead." When this is a problem, I ask students to bring in copies of the first pages of articles that they somehow found themselves reading,

I DON'T WANT STUDENTS TO THINK THERE IS JUST ONE WAY TO BEGIN A PIECE OF WRITING.

~~~~~

even though the topics might not normally have concerned them.

For example, one student brought in an article entitled "Hell on Wheels," which began this way:

Almost from the time the downtown No. 4 subway train began its 21-mile run below New York City at 11:38 p.m. on the night of Tuesday, Aug. 27, something seemed amiss. Heading from the Bronx to Manhattan, the train overshot the platform at a couple of stations. At times it slowed to a crawl and then accelerated to breakneck speeds. The conductor contacted the motorman, Robert Ray, 38, several

times on the intercom to find out if everything was all right. Ray replied that he was fine. But that was clearly not the case....

This article begins, of course, with a claim about a specific event ("something seemed amiss") and then illustrates this claim with a series of incidents. It mentions specific, troubling things that happened (for example, the train "slowed to a crawl and then accelerated to breakneck speeds"); it reports what people said to each other; and then it challenges what one of the people said ("But that clearly was not the case...."). In this last sentence, the author creates a conflict that engages the reader and lets the reader know

what the rest of the article will be about (i.e., it will show how the driver's claim was "not the case").

Other articles brought in by the students began quite differently—by citing troubling statistics, for example, or by describing general trends in society that a reader was almost certain to know and be concerned about. These differences are important. I don't want students to think there is just one way to begin a piece of writing. Consequently, I photocopied a variety of examples and asked students to talk them through to identify the strategies writers had used to engage readers. My goal was to

help students recognize some of the options that are open to them in doing their own writing.

In addition to bringing in models written by professionals, it can be extremely useful for us to bring in copies of our own efforts to do the same kind of writing students are working on. And once we have developed an atmosphere of trust, it can be useful to bring in effective examples of student work, continually asking such questions as these: What did the writer do here? How did he or she go about capturing our interest and letting us know what to expect in the rest of the text? Is there anything that this writer is doing that you might profitably do? Again, the goal is not to provide recipes or rules chiseled on tablets of stone but to get students to see what is possible.

MODELING THE COMPOSING PROCESS

Thus far, I have been describing ways we might use written products as models. In addition, we also need models of the composing processes of writers. This modeling can be as sophisticated or as rudimentary as our students need. It can focus on the work of an individual writer as Donald Murray shows in his "Use Genre as Lens" essay or on the efforts of peers as they revise their initial drafts. That is, we need to let students see the processes professional writers and students go through in doing their own writing and even in responding to classmates' writing.

There are several activities teachers can use that allow students to observe their peers' writing processes. For example, a colleague was concerned that her tenth-graders would have difficulty passing the state basic competency test that is required for high school graduation. Knowing that one of the questions on that test was likely to require students to report information in a well-organized form, she could have concentrated on paragraph form and the proper use of transitions. But suspecting that her students' difficulties were more profound than that, she decided that her students weren't paragraphing because they did not understand that certain kinds of expository paragraphs require writers to group facts by setting up categories that the paragraphs would be about.

Consequently, she asked students to watch a videotape of a movie that she was fairly certain they would find moving, an account of the difficulties encountered by a child who had been classified as mentally retarded but who had, nonetheless, a number of good traits and who was personally likable. After students had watched the videotape, she asked them to write down every fact they could remember from the movie and to collaborate as a class to make the list as complete as possible. That night she typed a complete list of facts, made an overhead transparency of them, and then cut the transparency into strips, each strip containing one fact.

The next day, she asked students to collaborate on ways to group these facts. For instance, students noticed that many of the facts pertained to ways people reacted to the young boy, while others could be grouped under such headings

as the boy's reactions to other people or his abilities. As students discussed ways of grouping facts, the teacher reflected what they were saying by moving the transparency strips around on the overhead projector. She was showing, not telling, her students about the basic process they needed to create one type of organized paragraph.

Another approach to modeling the composing process comes from a ninth-grade teacher concerned that her students' descriptive writing was bland. She believed their real problem was not a lack of descriptive adjectives and adverbs but that students weren't really looking closely at the people or objects they were describing.

She also knew that television programs routinely provide excellent examples of the process of observing. That is, as a rule, television cameras do not stay in one spot to observe everything from the same angle and distance. Instead, the cameras change position to vary the angles and the distances from which they view things. For example, one detective program began with a close-up shot of a ringing phone. Then the camera moved back so that the viewers could see a well-dressed man hurrying across an elegant apartment toward the phone. Next, the camera moved in to focus on the man's trembling hands as he nervously dried his sweaty palms on his handkerchief before picking up the phone. Finally, the camera shifted focus again, to show the head and shoulders of a burly, unshaven man speaking into a pay phone. These shifts in focus set the scene for the entire episode.

To help students understand this process of observing by shifting focus, the teacher asked students, as part of their homework, to watch one of their favorite TV programs and to count the number of times the camera shifted its focus in a two-minute period. She also asked them to make notes about the different things they saw every time the camera shifted focus. The next day they discussed these episodes and concluded that a program in which the camera did not shift focus would almost certainly be dull.

To help students see how this process applied to writing, the teacher gave students the following description:

She probably has false teeth and wears glasses. She wears her hair up in a bun and wears dresses from the 1930s. She has a habit of tapping her pencil on her desk.

Students readily agreed that this passage was uninteresting. To help them see why, the teacher asked students to think of the grammatical subject of each sentence as the visual focus of the sentence. (In response to the predictable question, the teacher told students that, for this passage, they could think of the grammatical subject as "how the writer begins each sentence.") Students saw readily that this writer's "camera" was standing in one place, not shifting at all. So the teacher asked students to work in groups to revise the passage so that the grammatical focus reflected changes in visual focus.

As one group collaborated on revising the passage, the following discussion took place:

"OK. Let's start with her false teeth—yeah—write that down."

She has false teeth.

"No, dummy. We gotta start the sentence with 'her false teeth'."

Her false teeth.

"OK, now what?"

"Oh, no. If we start with that we gotta add stuff. Like....'Her false teeth look funny'."

"Yeah, put that down."

"No, you gotta tell what 'funny' means. She'll [the teacher] only ask 'What's funny mean?' "

"I got it." Her false teeth look yellow. *"My grandma's are."*

"Yeah, 'cause they're old, like her."

"Hey. Who's writing?"

"I am." Her false teeth are yellow because they're old.

"That's good."

"OK, now the stuff on glasses. Oh, gosh. We're gonna have to add stuff to everything!"

Indeed, they would. And that was just the point. Their teacher wanted them to see that as they shifted visual focus, they would have to explore their subject further. Not only was their teacher showing these students a fundamental process of observing, but also she was showing them how the process of observing translated into the process of writing.

In addition to modeling the writing process, we also need to model the process of responding to writing. It is true that students can learn to make very helpful comments about their peers' writing. But the important phrase here is *learn to*. As Karen Spear has pointed out in her excellent book *Sharing Writing*, working in response groups is a complex process. It requires that students be able to go beyond uninformative, global comments ("Yeah, it's pretty good." "I guess it's OK.") and do two things: pay attention to specific words, phrases, or ideas and explain why and how they personally react to those things. The ninth-grade class I've just described illustrates one way to model the process of responding. When the teacher asked students to revise the bland description, she was showing them a process they could use in responding to each other's drafts. That is, she was helping them see that when they responded to a classmate's descriptive writing, they might consider whether the student had shifted focus and whether the shifts in focus helped give the reader a clearer visual picture of the person, object, or place being described. Indeed, the teacher made sure students worked as a class to give this sort

of response to one or two students' subsequent drafts.

But modeling the response process may not be enough. It may also be necessary to model the processes of listening to and using those responses. Listening can be especially difficult when the response implies that a writer's work is unclear or in need of further effort. In such cases, any writer—and students are no exception—may well become defensive, more eager to prove that responses are invalid or irrelevant than to listen to those responses and consider the uses they might have. In other words, students may need to learn how to respond to responses.

If so, teachers may need to model the way we want student writers to react to their classmates' comments. Specifically, we should bring in our own efforts to do some of the same writing students are doing and ask students to respond to it. Where is it clear or unclear? What sort of personality or attitude is our writ-

ing conveying? At what points have we said things that seem appropriate or inappropriate for the audience we are addressing? My experience in doing this sort of work with students is that if they trust us, they can be very perceptive and painfully direct. If they don't get it, they can tell us so in no uncertain terms. In doing so, they give us a chance to show how a writer listens to readers, not by arguing but by attempting to find out why readers react as they do and then using that information to revise a subsequent draft.

The process of modeling is, like everything else about teaching writing, a slow business. One example rarely does the trick. But if we are persistent in showing students what is involved in producing good writing through the writing process, we can usually count on results. But if we don't model, we should expect our distinction between *showing* and *telling* to fall on deaf ears. If we don't follow our own advice, why should they? ❧

ELEMENTS OF WRITING addresses the *writing process* and *cooperative learning* in the following ways:

Pupil's Edition
Provides students with detailed instruction for each stage of the writing process
Provides numerous activities and exercises in the writing chapters for students to work cooperatively

Annotated Teacher's Edition
Offers lesson plans based on each stage of the writing process
Offers *COOPERATIVE LEARNING* features that suggest activities for teaching writing and grammar

Teacher's ResourceBank (TM)
Furnishes materials that can be used for peer evaluation

BY MAXINE HAIRSTON

THE JOY OF WRITING

STUDENTS NEED TO GET SOME FUN OUT OF WHAT THEY'RE DOING.

MAXINE HAIRSTON TAKES A BREAK FROM CLASSES.

In recent years I have come to believe that the most important job I can do as a writing teacher is to help my students enjoy writing. I say this because I'm convinced that unless students find some pleasure in their writing classes, most of them will not be willing to invest the time and energy required to turn out work that they—and we, as their teachers—can be proud of. Few adults are disciplined and determined enough to drudge away at some project—whether it's exercising or learning Spanish verbs—simply because someone else tells us that it will be good for us in the long run. We just won't stay with such projects unless there's some satisfaction in the process itself. How much harder it is, then, for youngsters to whom college or even next fall seems light years away to subject themselves to the hard work of learning to write if they get no pleasure from it at the time. Deficit motivation, working to avoid penalties or simply for a passing grade, isn't enough; students need to get some fun out of what they're doing. Fortunately, given what we now know about teaching the writing process, it's quite possible to create a writing classroom in which many students work from growth motivation; that is, they work at their writing because they enjoy doing it for its own sake.

Cognitive studies, ethnographic studies about writing, and the national projects argue that four characteristics define the congenial writing classroom, the kind in which students are likely to enjoy writing and to flourish as writers.

First, teachers provide a low-risk environment that encourages students to write without fear. Second, teachers have students develop their papers through a series of drafts and revisions. Third, teachers honor the students' right to their own writing, allowing students to choose their own topics and encouraging them to write about their interests. Fourth, teachers create and support a collaborative learning environment.

ESTABLISHING A LOW-RISK CLASSROOM

Creating a low-risk environment in the writing classroom may seem like a formidable challenge, and indeed it can be at the beginning of a new term when many students are as wary as stray cats. They're nervous for fear someone is going to try to trap them. In the first week of a writing class sometimes I feel as if I want to wear a banner across my chest, emblazoned with "Trust me! It's going to be all right!" But I can understand students' anxiety. Students who have come from writing courses with a heavy emphasis on rules and form, courses in which they did badly, have good reason to see a composition course as a high-risk situation. No wonder they start out by trying to stay in the safety zone of rules and formulas.

The humanistic psychologist Abraham Maslow theorizes that all people have two sets of forces operating within them: a need for safety and a fear of risk on one hand and an urge toward growth

and autonomy on the other hand. Maslow also believes that every individual has an innate urge to create, to grow, to discover new abilities and talents. I agree; I think all children want to communicate, to write something that catches the interest and attention of others, but most will hesitate if they think they will be punished for breaking rules. As Maslow points out, "Safety needs are prepotent over growth needs....[and] in general, only a child who feels safe dares to grow forward healthily" (49). He adds, "Only the [teacher] who respects fear and defense can teach; . . . " (53).

The writing teacher's challenge is to foster the low-risk environment that will encourage creativity and expression but at the same time to work toward helping students master the writing conventions that they must know to be accepted as writers. There are several ways teachers can do this. First, of course, is to emphasize that we write in stages; we plan, we draft, we read and reread, and we revise. Final details matter when a writer gets ready to publish, but the most-productive writers learn how to suspend their error monitors in the early stages.

I have found it helps me to suspend my own error monitor when reading early drafts if I can put down my pencil and force myself to read strictly for content, good practice for trying to become a courteous reader. I ask myself, what is this writer trying to express? Why? How? Then I make only a large-scale response, focus-

I N THE FIRST WEEK OF A WRITING CLASS SOMETIMES I FEEL AS IF I WANT TO WEAR A BANNER ACROSS MY CHEST, EMBLAZONED WITH "TRUST ME! IT'S GOING TO BE ALL RIGHT!"

~~~~~

ing on being positive and on asking questions that could help the next draft. I emphasize that I hope to see substantial change and development in that draft. It would waste time even to mention error at this stage. When students realize that I really am not looking for mistakes in their drafts, they begin to relax and become more venturesome.

On second drafts, I still try to avoid writing on the paper, but focus on more specific suggestions for improvement. I also make checks in the margins to indicate potential trouble spots that the writers need to be aware of when they begin to polish their papers, sometimes adding a comment that the writer should be alert for problems with commas, subject-verb agreement, or whatever area seems most troublesome. This gives the writer specific areas to concen-

trate on at proofreading/editing time.

Probably one of the best ways to reduce risk in the writing classroom is to set up a portfolio system that allows students to draft a variety of papers over a period of time and then to choose a limited number to develop fully and submit for final evaluation. This method has become increasingly popular for a number of reasons. For one, student writers can work more as adult working writers do. They can attempt different kinds of writing, can stay with those projects that go well and, putting the others aside, they can invest as much as they like in them. It also gives students more control over the evaluation process. They decide which pieces they want evaluated; the teacher doesn't even have to see the others. There is considerable literature on the portfolio system if you find it an attractive option. (See also Elliot and Greenberg's essay "The Direct Assessment of Writing: Notes for Teachers.")

A final specific suggestion for reducing your students' anxieties is to establish a hierarchy of errors. We know from research that not all errors are created equal. Some are truly damaging, for instance, wrong verb forms, egregious sentence fragments, double negatives, and faulty parallelism. Errors like these set off alarms for most readers. Others, such as split infinitives, comparison of absolutes, or misusing *lie* and *lay* cause scarcely a riffle with most audiences. We should be lenient about such lapses and reduce the number of things our students have to worry about.

We should also remember that the more a writer attempts, the more mistakes he or she is likely to make. But if we are encouraging growth, we need to let student writers know that we regard such mistakes as the natural accompaniment of growth and as less important than the students' fresh ideas.

TEACHING THE WRITING PROCESS THROUGH A SYSTEM OF DRAFTS

Because this textbook so strongly emphasizes that drafting, evaluating, and revising are essential parts of the writing process, I don't feel I need to build an elaborate case for having students develop their papers in drafts. Fortunately, with most writing teachers and curriculum supervisors embracing the concept of writing as a process, students accept drafting as a routine practice. I hope so, because students write more freely and more confidently when they know that their readers view their drafts as "work in progress," not as finished products to be critiqued and judged. Under such a system, knowing they're not irrevocably committed to what they've written, writers can afford experiments. Writing tentatively, they can count on getting help from their readers to help them work out their ideas. That's very reassuring, particularly to students who haven't written much and aren't sure they have anything to say.

The less articulate, inexperienced writers are probably those who get the most out of numerous drafts because they have the opportunity to improve first attempts

WRITING CAN BECOME A GENUINE JOY FOR GOOD WRITERS WORKING AT THEIR PEAK.

substantially before they must submit the papers for evaluation. They also have the chance to get feedback *during* the writing process, feedback that is far more valuable than comments on a paper that has already been graded. We know that many students, perhaps even most, pay scant attention to comments written on graded papers, especially negative comments. But when they get comments—both written and oral—on drafts, they are likely to pay attention because they use them to real advantage.

Good students also benefit from drafts, although sometimes they may resist doing them because the system requires more work than they've usually had to do in order to get good grades. But for some good writers, developing a paper through drafts can be a heady experience as they tap into talent they didn't know they had and then earn new recognition from their peers. Writing can become a genuine joy for good writers working at their peak.

In my opinion, the worse possible system for having students write papers is to give a fresh assignment each week, have everyone write the paper only once and turn it in for a grade, and then return the graded papers and repeat the process. Under such circumstances, the anxiety level skyrockets for all but the most able

students, writers get no help during the process (when they need it most), and teachers never learn what most students can really do. Even when students write in class, those papers should be drafts that they can work on again during the next class periods. Only then are students likely to develop their potential.

LETTING STUDENTS CHOOSE THEIR OWN TOPICS FOR WRITING

After several years of having students choose their own writing topics I am committed to the practice because it has several invaluable benefits. First, most students have never had an opportunity to write about matters they're genuinely interested in and can write about with authority. Too often they see traditional assignments that ask everyone to write on the same topic as meaningless exercises in which the teacher seems to be forgetting that students are individuals.

Second, students are more likely to put time and energy into their writing when they can explore topics that interest them. When students are writing on their own topics, they may also discover a potent truth: Writing is a powerful tool for learning, one that will serve them well.

Third, when students choose their own topics, a rich diversity

can develop as they write about their own special interests. Some students may write about family rituals that come from their ethnic heritages or about unusual people in their families; others may write about living in another country or on a military base; others may write about hobbies—bicycling or scuba diving or canoeing. The possibilities are almost endless. In many schools, a rich multicultural tapestry can emerge as students from diverse backgrounds and cultures read each other's work and share stories.

Fourth, students will become more-confident writers because they have more control over their writing. As they develop their expertise in some area, they begin to realize how much they know about something, whether it's car stereos or cooking hamburgers. They can take on a new identity in the class and find that people pay attention to what they have to say. That's good for all of us.

Finally, when students choose their own writing topics, the class simply becomes more interesting for everyone. Students may cover a remarkable range of subjects, and even those writing on similar topics bring different perspectives to them. Boredom drops quickly because everyone is constantly learning directly from other people's experiences. Perhaps the greatest bonus is to teachers, who not only garner a wealth of information about their students, but also over a period of years become mini-experts on numerous topics. Furthermore, they are spared trying to think up a good writing topic and then having to read fifty papers on that topic.

I BELIEVE STRONGLY IN PEER GROUPS AND COLLABORATIVE LEARNING IN WRITING CLASSES.

It does take considerable class time to help select topics, since many students will protest that they have nothing to write about, but such obstacles can be overcome in a few days of brainstorming and group work in class. As teacher, you can come in with a list of possible topics and then work with the class to generate subtopics. Or ask everyone to bring in a list of fifteen things to write about, encouraging the concrete and specific rather than large, abstract categories.

I have had good success with asking students to choose a general topic to write on for the whole term and then to pick subtopics for individual papers. That way they get into their topics in some depth and eliminate the process of having to work through choosing a fresh topic for each paper. You may want to specify the kinds of papers students write within their topics—informative, expressive, persuasive, and so on—to focus the class within the formats they're learning from the textbook.

ESTABLISHING A COLLABORATIVE-LEARNING CLASSROOM

I believe strongly in peer groups and collaborative learning in writing classes. Perhaps their greatest advantage is that they give students an immediate sense of audience, something that's hard to achieve when the teacher is the only reader for the drafts. Usually they respect each other's opinions; in fact, they may take their peers' responses more seriously than they do the teacher's because they feel closer to peers and they genuinely want to communicate.

Students also begin to see how useful collaboration can be for generating ideas. Most students in writing groups readily admit how much their classmates have contributed to the final versions of their papers. Each class period when I hand back graded papers, I pick two or three of the best ones to read aloud and then ask the writer and the writer's group to comment on how the paper developed through drafts. Their accounts are revealing, and the investment they feel in each other's work is truly gratifying.

I favor randomly chosen groups of at least four students so if someone is absent, the discussion doesn't break down. I reorganize groups to allow working with as many writers as possible. This arrangement also enhances every student's exposure to diverse cultural experiences as they get to know other students more closely. Managing groups in the classroom may not be easy, although I suspect trained secondary teachers know considerably more about it than most college teachers do. For the teacher who doesn't feel comfortable with groups, there is considerable literature on the concept. (See the professional bibliography on p. T74.)

Ultimately, groups help to establish the whole class as a community of writers who work together, feel a common sense of purpose, and see writing as a shared enterprise that's important to everyone. We all know intuitively that the most important element for achieving a congenial writing classroom is the teacher's attitude, and for that reason it's important for the teacher to be a part of that community, not to be an outside authority and a judge. Teachers need to write with students during writing workshops and share writing with them—its joys and frustrations. With luck and time, I am convinced that both teachers and students will enjoy being in a writing classroom more than they might have thought possible.

Work Cited

Maslow, Abraham. Toward a Psychology of Being, 2nd ed. New York: D. Van Nostrand Company. 1968.

ELEMENTS OF WRITING addresses students' understanding of the *writing process*, acceleration of learning through *cooperative group work*, and feedback to students through effective *assessment* in the following ways:

Pupil's Edition

Provides detailed instruction for each stage of the writing process

Provides numerous activities and exercises in the writing chapters for students to work cooperatively

Annotated Teacher's Edition

Provides students with detailed instruction for each stage of the writing process

Offers *COOPERATIVE LEARNING* features that suggest activities for teaching writing and grammar

Gives helpful assessment ideas in the *TIMESAVER*, *A DIFFERENT APPROACH*, and *ASSESSMENT* features

Teacher's ResourceBank (TM)

Offers materials keyed to the writing process that assist students in achieving the aims and modes

Furnishes materials that can be used for peer evaluation

Provides an **Assessment Portfolio** section and **Holistically Graded Composition Models** for the writing chapters

BY BARBARA J. SHADE

TEACHING FOR LEARNING'S SAKE

THIS APPROACH TO TEACHING WILL EMPOWER STUDENTS AS LEARNERS.

Helping students incorporate ideas, skills, and concepts that will improve their ability to perform tasks and to solve problems is the ultimate goal of teaching. Teachers who achieve this goal effectively find ways to accommodate students' different learning styles so that the teaching-learning process works more efficiently.

What do we mean by *learning styles*? Over the years, researchers have identified three dimensions in which students have specific learning preferences: (1) their preferences for various environmental factors that influence the learning climate; (2) their preferences about the ways they choose to engage in the learning process (motivational style); and (3) their preferences for the various ways in which they process information (cognitive style).

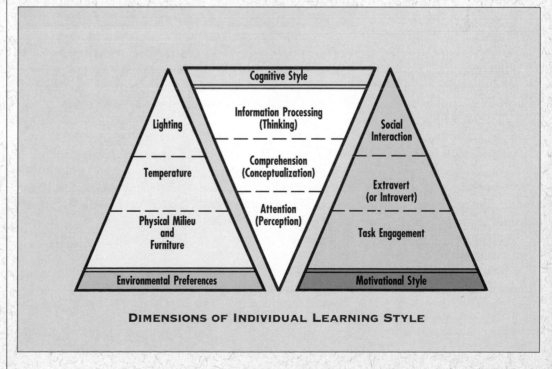

DIMENSIONS OF INDIVIDUAL LEARNING STYLE

ENVIRONMENTAL PREFERENCES

Individual environmental preferences focus on the lighting, temperature, and furniture used in the learning process. For example, some individuals might prefer bright light while others prefer it muted; some might prefer a warm room while others like it cool. A variation in studying postures has also been noted, with some individuals preferring to sit in a traditional classroom desk while others prefer to stand or recline when engaged in a learning task.[1]

MOTIVATIONAL STYLE

The second dimension of learning style focuses upon the extent to which students take responsibility for their own learning. Teachers often incorrectly assume that students' desire to engage in work is inherent. As with other aspects of learning, the extent to which individuals become involved in work depends upon how they have been socialized to respond to work. Some students, for example, have been taught to rely on others for assistance, to follow directions as given, and to perform the task as modeled. Others have been made more independent of others and have been taught to work alone, to find their own solutions, and to decide whether or not they can complete the work before asking for assistance. Corno and Mandinach refer to this stylistic dimension as

---

[1] For a more detailed description of the social and physical environment preferences of students, the reader should examine the writings of Kenneth and Rita Dunn.

BARBARA SHADE AT UNIVERSITY OF WISCONSIN-PARKSIDE CAMPUS.

a preference for resource management, and students tend to use the approach that makes them feel the most comfortable and the most competent.

The teaching-learning process involves human interaction, and students prefer different levels of involvement with others, depending upon the social and personality development that emanates from their families and communities. Families stressing prosocial behavior encourage children to help, to share, and to work toward benefiting others.

These students are more likely to give and receive assistance in the learning process and to like cooperative-learning ventures.

Children trained to be highly individualistic and self-oriented are less likely to cooperate and offer help. Learners with this orientation function well in a competitive setting because they prefer to work alone and are less likely to enjoy cooperative-learning activities unless there is a reward or a method of accommodating their need for individuality.

COGNITIVE STYLE

The least discussed dimension of learning style—that of cognitive style—represents individually preferred ways of perceiving, organizing, and evaluating information so that it can be learned.

Three cognitive processes influence the way individuals acquire and produce knowledge. These are the perceptual, the conceptual, and the evaluative processes.

1. Perceptual Processes: The most recognized area in learning-style literature, this area focuses on the sensory modalities. Through cultural socialization, learners develop a preference for either the visual modality (photographs, graphs, art, texts); the aural modality (records, tapes, lectures); the haptic/kinesthetic modality (group discussions, interactive debates, drama); or some combination of these. Instruction delivered through the preferred modality establishes an instant rapport that allows students to process information more easily.

Different cultures socialize their children to attend to different cues in the environment; therefore, students have selective attention. Some students focus their attention on the task or idea being presented. For others, the people, their peers, their self-evaluation, or even the teacher's reaction to them are the most important elements on which to focus. How children choose to attend to cues is an important dimension of learning, and teachers who wish to ensure cognitive engagement find ways to influence the perceptive focus of the students.

2. Conceptual Processes: Having focused on an idea that must be learned, students must then classify it based upon prior experiences. The techniques involved include assessing similarities and differences to prior knowledge, as well as determining how best to define or describe the concepts. Again, the extent to which students can manipulate various concepts depends upon whether or not the ideas can be communicated to them using a common language with commonly accepted images.

Some students prefer to have ideas presented in a hierarchical manner, beginning with the big picture followed by the details involved (whole to part). Other students prefer to have the information presented in a more sequential approach, beginning with the minute details and building toward the larger concept (part to whole). Regardless of the technique used, teachers must include methods of helping learners make connections with prior knowledge.

3. Evaluative Processes: The third aspect of cognitive style focuses on the processes of thinking about the information. *Thinking* is difficult to define, but many researchers define it as "comprehension monitoring." The major focus of thinking centers on the individual's ability to plan, monitor, and evaluate his or her learning and understanding about the information he or she is seeking to learn.

Again, teachers should look for variations in the way individuals approach thinking. On one hand, individuals may spend time using their imaginations to create ideas based upon personal views or beliefs. On the other hand, some individuals will engage in a more formal logic, which requires familiarity with the rules in order to select the correct problem-solving strategies. In the first type of information processing, individuals seem to arrive at their decisions rather intuitively, using a process that seems to be generated from an internalized logic. In the second type, the one most influenced by instruction, students learn to organize and review their approach to information or problems through an analytical process.

ACCOMMODATING VARIATIONS IN LEARNING STYLES

When teachers are first introduced to the concept of learning styles, they immediately conjure up visions of having to construct thirty different learning plans to accommodate their students. Learning styles is not another euphemism for individually guided education. Instead, it is an entreaty to teachers to provide different approaches and strategies that individuals can use as they work at learning.

In today's classrooms, there are basically *two distinct modes of learning*: the *traditional orientation*, the one to which most instruction is geared; and the *community orientation*, the one more likely to be displayed by African American, Hispanic American, Native American, and immigrant Asian students who identify closely with the culture of their ethnic communities.

Particular suggestions to enhance the instructional process for the community-oriented students who are often ignored in instructional delivery system include the following ones:

Environment Style Accommodation: For the community-oriented students, the classroom should become inviting and supportive as an experiential setting in which students can use various media to explore concepts that may be foreign to them because they are not prevalent in their communities or because their economic situation does not permit the type of travel or involvement in enrichment activities that is true of the more successful, economically affluent students. Being able to see an enlarged picture of the Eiffel Tower in the classroom can provide an important conceptual image that might be needed to foster comprehension. Because learning centers permit self-exploration, they should also become important aspects of the classroom design for all levels of students in all types of classes.

Motivational Style Accommodation: Having the opportunity to participate in a good class discussion on lesson content motivates community-oriented students, satisfying their needs to share information with others and to obtain feedback. Moreover, it provides them an opportunity to listen to different perspectives. Teachers should note, however, that group discussion is not the same as class recitation in which students are asked to recite facts and information to the teacher from a textbook. For example, it is not enough to discuss nouns as a part of speech without leading students through the concept of a complete sentence and of the purpose of using nouns within sentences and paragraphs. Moreover, students need to be able to identify nouns within the framework of their own speech and written narratives as well as to determine how and why they have used a particular word as a noun.

The key to a good group discussion is a teacher who is an excellent questioner, who is reflective, who can lead students to reflect and inquire, and who has an excellent understanding of the broad structure and relationships within the lesson content.

Information Processing Style Accommodation: Teachers can facilitate the processing of information by students through the use of some of the following techniques:

1. Present concepts with multimedia using a variety of modalities.

*T*HE KEY TO A GOOD GROUP DISCUSSION IS A TEACHER WHO IS AN EXCELLENT QUESTIONER, WHO IS REFLECTIVE, WHO CAN LEAD STUDENTS TO REFLECT AND INQUIRE, . . .

✺✺✺✺✺

*T*EACHERS MUST REMEMBER THAT STUDENTS HAVE DIFFERENT PERCEPTIONS OF THE WORLD AND TEACH TO THESE PERCEPTIONS.

❦❦❦

2. Assist the students in identifying the relationships of concepts through cognitive mapping, brainstorming, or reciprocal teaching in which you ask them to predict possible answers in stories.

3. Take time to ensure there is a common understanding of words, concepts, or ideas. Bilingual students should be encouraged to interpret the words in their languages. Students should also be encouraged to develop art projects as representations of the ideas and to use new words in their oral interactions with you.

4. Model the thinking processes that are needed to complete tasks successfully. Most importantly, provide students the time to think about a problem or to complete an assignment so that they grasp the underlying meaning. Students learn best when they can perform a task with the teacher available to provide feedback.

Teachers must remember that students have different perceptions of the world and teach to these perceptions. Assisting students in

The stylistic differences of these two preferences seem to lie along the following continuum:

School-Oriented Students	Community-Oriented Students
Environmental Preferences: Prefer less intense, perhaps earth-oriented colors or plain whites Seem able to work well in classrooms in which seats are in rows.	*Environmental Preferences:* Prefer warm, bright colors— blues and yellows are particularly soothing. Seem to prefer groupings of desks or tables, which perpetuate cooperation.
Motivational Style: Are individualistic and prefer to work alone on tasks. Are competitive and self-regulated in resource management.	*Motivational Style:* Are prosocial, more cooperative, and prefer to work with others on tasks. Are more dependent and like to have help from peers with constant reinforcement from the teacher or adult.
Cognitive Style: Learn well through auditory senses and function well with print media. Are able to focus attention on a specific task or object. Can focus on a single task for a sustained period of time. Understand American English used in textbooks, magazines, newspapers, and television, which facilitates comprehension. Backgrounds are closer to the writers of the curriculum materials, which facilitates meaning. Prefer or can handle material well when presented in a linear-sequential manner. Have been taught to use formal logic, algorithms, and analytical thinking. Are more likely to present written and spoken thoughts in a sequential manner. Are likely to function in a low-context fashion and to explain all variations of meanings because they assume the meaning is not shared.	*Cognitive Style:* Prefer visual material to emphasize oral presentation. Like group discussions, debates, and projects. Prefer to constantly scan room or object for new features, nonverbal cues, or contextual features. Prefer a variety of tasks in a relatively short time to maintain attention. Can focus on several tasks at one time. Likely to speak dialect or community-oriented language or are bilingual, which creates different orientation to words and meanings. Backgrounds usually differ from that of texts, requiring reinterpretation of the material within the context of the communities from which students come. Prefer to have material presented in a holistic, relational, or contextual manner, a presentation from whole to part. Are more intuitive and synergistic and may not have been taught to use formal logic to approach objects and problems. Have been exposed to more observational learning. Are more likely to present thoughts in a spiral or episodic fashion. Are likely to function in a high-context fashion and to assume that the meaning is shared by all individuals with whom they are communicating

learning requires lots of talking—talking between students and teachers and between students. Expressing ideas orally allows better processing and comprehension.

When considering the use of learning styles, teachers must confront three important perceptions. First, teachers should understand that the identified style preference should not and cannot be used as evidence of deficiencies. Being different does not mean that the child is deficient in ability. Second, teachers should not think that the community-oriented style reflects all members of a group. It is merely behavior that is most likely to be found within the community. Third, teachers who use the concept of learning styles should do so as indicators of approaches to lesson design and to the selection of methods of instruction, not as the basis for judging intellectual potential.

A FINAL CAVEAT

Developing a successful learner is the ultimate goal of a successful teacher, and ensuring that children become successful learners requires that teachers see themselves not as the ultimate purveyors of knowledge, but as guides through the learning process. This approach to teaching will empower students as learners. By incorporating various learning-style approaches in the classroom and in the curriculum, teachers will assist students to maximize the energy they spend in the learning process. This permits students to approach the learning process in their own words and to use the information as a bridge. When learners grasp the ideas and really know that they know, their sense of self-worth and confidence and their intellectual strength improve tremendously. It is at this point teachers know they, too, have been successful. What a great sense of accomplishment!

Additional Readings

Grossman, Herbert. *Educating Hispanic Students.* Springfield, Illinois: Charles C. Thomas Publisher, 1984.

Henson, Kenneth T. *Theory Into Practice: Matching Teaching and Learning Styles.* Columbus, Ohio: Ohio State University, 1984.

Shade, Barbara J. *Culture, Style, and the Educative Process.* Springfield, Illinois: Charles C. Thomas Publisher, 1989.

Tharp, Roland and Ronald Gallimore. *Rousing Minds to Life.* New York: Cambridge University Press, 1988.

Trueba, Henry T., Lila Jacobs and Elizabeth Kirton. *Cultural Conflict and Adaptation: The Case of Hmong Children in American Society.* New York: Falmer Press, 1990.

ELEMENTS OF WRITING addresses the needs of America's diverse student populations and the range of students' *learning styles* in the following ways:

Pupil's Edition
Represents a wide range of ethnically diverse cultures in the literary models and a broad selection of topics in the exercises and examples

Accomodates a range of learning styles by providing a variety of student activities

Offers teachers a flexible program that can be easily adapted to suit a variety of situations

Annotated Teacher's Edition
Provides specific *MEETING INDIVIDUAL NEEDS* features such as *Learning Styles, Less-Advanced, Advanced, Students with Special Needs, LEP/ESL,* and *At-Risk*

Suggests ways for language teachers to address language diversity in the multicultural classroom

Teacher's ResourceBank (TM)
Meets individual needs of students with graphic organizers and reinforcement practice activities

WANDA B. SCHINDLEY

INTEGRATING THE LANGUAGE ARTS

INTEGRATING THE TEACHING OF THE LANGUAGE ARTS CREATES THE MAGIC THAT HELPS STUDENTS LEARN.

Thirty-five years ago in a rural classroom, a creative woman integrated the teaching of reading, writing, speaking, listening, and even math. Her second-graders built a playhouse-size cardboard post office, made block-letter signs, wrote and read letters, counted tokens to buy and sell stamps, and spoke and listened as postmaster and customer. That teacher had not read research on the integration of skills or on using whole-language methodologies, but she knew intuitively what worked. I don't remember much about my experiences in kindergarten, first grade, third grade, or even fourth grade, but I remember well that second-grade classroom; I remember the magic of learning.

Integrating the teaching of the language arts creates the magic that helps students learn. It cre-ates a context for developing language proficiency and relevancy for reading, writing, speaking, and listening activities. Students grow through active participation in language activities. Although categorizing the language arts may be necessary for describing curricula, in the classroom language skills are best learned through doing—through seeking meaning from texts, through writing and revising, and through sharing ideas and opinions.

WANDA SCHINDLEY IS A SPECIALIST FOR THE WORKPLACE PARTNERSHIP.

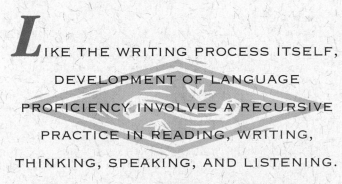

SUGGESTIONS FOR INTEGRATING THE LANGUAGE ARTS

• Involve students in prereading activities such as discussion, writing, research, and sometimes, vocabulary development. Creating a context for reading involves discussing themes and related issues, making predictions, recalling prior knowledge and related experiences, and searching out related information.

• Involve students in prewriting activities such as discussion of possible topics and details, reading model essays, searching out and reading informative pieces, reading literary writing, interviewing others, and sentence-combining or sentence-revision activities. Like the writing process itself, development of language proficiency involves a recursive practice in reading, writing, thinking, speaking, and listening.

• Make writing assignments relevant by having students write for and share with real audiences for meaningful purposes. Have students share their writing with peers.

• Relate correctness—development of conventional usage, spelling, grammar, and punctuation—to the revising and proofreading stages of the writing process. Correctness becomes important to students when it helps them communicate their ideas clearly. Class review of grammar, usage, and mechanics can be done with sentences from student papers and with sentence-combining, sentence-manipulation, and vocabulary activities.

• Approach standard usage in speech as appropriate for use in business and academic situations, not as a replacement for all vernacular expression.

• Encourage student involvement in class discussion, team study groups, cooperative research projects and presentations, group creative writing, and role playing.

• Foster an atmosphere in which students feel free to respond to, to evaluate, and to critique literature.

• Act as facilitator in students' discovery processes through activities that encourage creative and critical thinking—decision making and problem solving—and allow students to take more responsibility for their own learning.

• Create an atmosphere of cooperation, caring, and high expectations.

USING THE TEXTBOOK IN AN INTEGRATED APPROACH

Literature selections are provided in each chapter to give students opportunities to read before writing. However, this book can be used in a literature-driven approach as the springboard to writing by incorporating into the study of each chapter ample readings from literature anthologies, magazines, and student papers. The features in each chapter of the *Teacher's Edition* contain suggestions for integrating additional literature selections (**Integrating the Language Arts: Literature Link**), using a

*L*IKE THE WRITING PROCESS ITSELF, DEVELOPMENT OF LANGUAGE PROFICIENCY INVOLVES A RECURSIVE PRACTICE IN READING, WRITING, THINKING, SPEAKING, AND LISTENING.

variety of group activities (Cooperative Learning), and encouraging students to use higher-level thinking skills to contribute to class discussion (Critical Thinking).

Throughout, the textbook guides students through the prewriting, writing, evaluating, revising, proofreading, and publishing phases of the writing process. It also instructs students in the dynamics and behavior involved in group work with ample opportunities for group writing, revising, speaking, and listening activities. The chapters on speaking and listening help students develop skills that will serve them throughout their school years and later as citizens.

The **Common Error** and **Integrating the Language Arts** features in each chapter of the *Teacher's Edition* contain suggestions for integrating the teaching of grammar, usage, and mechanics into the stages of the writing process, as do the suggestions for integrating the language arts in the introduction of each composition chapter.

Sample Integrated Lesson Plan

A lesson on creative writing might begin with a class discussion about stories and poems.

Guiding questions encourage students to share attitudes (What kinds of stories/poems do you like?)

—in order to recall prior knowledge about the structure of stories (What happened toward the end of a favorite story? How did you feel as you read? What name do we use for the most exciting or scary part of the story?)

—and of poems (Can you think of a favorite poem? What do you like about the poem?)

—and to synthesize knowledge about fiction and poetry (What characteristics do stories and poems have in common? What other forms might a writer use to tell about an event or to express an idea?)

Students might then read the stories and poems and discuss their responses and evaluations of each. Volunteers might bring their favorite stories, poems, or lyrics to share with the class before beginning to write original stories and poems.

Teachers can use group stories and poems as guided practice and as a non-threatening introduction to creative writing. Students working in groups to create story lines and to describe characters and setting will quickly learn literary terminology to use within the group. A group activity in which students write noun poems might begin informal grammar instruction as the class brainstorms a list of words that name people, places, things, or ideas. Small groups can then choose from the list of topics for noun-metaphor poems.

Example: Dreams are
    Envelopes of hope,
    Fluffy clouds that
      disappear in daylight,
    Stars to reach for.

As groups begin to revise and proofread their poems for class presentation, teachers might focus on the use of commas and end marks.

When students begin the creative writing assignments, they are

again given opportunities to write, discuss, read, think, talk, revise, and so on. Instruction in usage and mechanics can be provided to the class as the need arises, to partners as they debate an issue of correctness, and to individuals in one-on-one conferences.

Finally, students share their work with the class—perhaps anonymously at first, but eventually as accomplished and proud authors who share a firsthand knowledge of the creation of literature and a greater understanding of language. 🍂

ELEMENTS OF WRITING addresses the *integration* of the various aspects of language in the following ways:

Pupil's Edition
Connects the study of writing to reading, speaking, listening, grammar, usage, and mechanics
Reinforces in the language-structure chapters the fundamentals of effective communication, stressing application and proficiency

Annotated Teacher's Edition
Provides features that give a variety of strategies to link every aspect of language diversity instruction—*INTEGRATING THE LANGUAGE ARTS: Literature Link, Library Skills Link, Mechanics Link, Grammar Link, Usage Link, Technology Link*

Teacher's ResourceBank (TM)
Offers supplemental materials on every aspect of the language arts

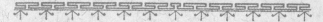

By Charles W. Leftwich & Patricia G. Tweeddale

Accepting the Differences:
Teaching the At-Risk Student

...IT IS UNLIKELY THAT AT-RISK STUDENTS WILL LEAVE SCHOOL WITH THE BASIC SKILLS OUR EDUCATION SYSTEM SHOULD PROVIDE.

Teachers are facing a growing population of students for whom a minimal success such as completing high school is not probable. These students comprise the group known as at-risk, a label that can be acquired for reasons ranging from race and socioeconomic background to being a teenage parent or coming from a single-parent home, from having a parent or sibling incarcerated to being a latchkey child. Whatever the reason for the categorization, it is unlikely that at-risk students will leave school with the basic skills our education system should provide.

The task of teaching the at-risk student must begin with knowledge of individual student characteristics that are relevant to the instructional objective at hand. A focus upon stereotypical characteristics denies attention to the in-

PATRICIA TWEEDDALE AND CHARLES LEFTWICH IN THEIR OFFICE.

"FEAR OF DIFFERENCE IS DREAD OF LIFE ITSELF."

- mary parker follett

dividual learner and what that student brings to the classroom. Because teaching and learning are highly interactive social encounters, the efficacy of any given encounter may be dependent upon the emotional response of both parties to their first contact.

The initial response by a teacher is often conditioned by previous exposure to learners similar to the one in question. Positive previous exposure leads to a sense of confidence in the ability to successfully foster and facilitate learning. However, if a teacher has had negative previous exposure, the quality of the initial encounter may be tainted by the teacher's lack of confidence in effecting learning or establishing a positive social interaction.

There are at least two sources for interference in the initial interaction between the teacher and the at-risk student, the vicarious and the real. Vicarious sources are grounded in images created by other teachers, the school organization, and community expectations, as well as portrayal in print and electronic media by editorial and entertainment entities.

The real source of interference in the initial interaction may well be so subtle as to escape recognition, and yet it seems to be pervasive. It is a fundamental rejection of differences. The nonverbal language exhibited by the at-risk stu-

dent is different or at least unfamiliar, and this may reinforce the teacher's sense of being called upon to do an impossible task. The student's verbal language may also be unfamiliar, and the clash between assumptions of what students ought to sound like and what the teacher actually hears further frustrates and impedes the teaching process.

Interaction between the teacher and the learner should focus upon the individual student's character-

istics with the intention of discovering what sets that individual apart from others. New learning is built upon old learning, and new knowledge is supported by old; therefore, the teacher of the at-risk student must concentrate on discovering what the student knows. Often this can be a difficult task since that knowledge may be communicated in a different mode. The teacher should be aware of some characteristics of the at-risk student: negative self-image, a

heavy dependence upon and rigid adherence to a distinct mode of concrete thinking, a unique dialect of spoken language, low motivation, and a lack of positive response to constructive criticism. Any at-risk student may exhibit one or all of these characteristics in varying degrees. What is important is to recognize and appreciate the student as an individual. Whatever the individual's characteristics, they are an integral part of the learner and as such must be taken

FOR THE TEACHER TO INTERACT SUCCESSFULLY WITH THE AT-RISK STUDENT, A SENSE OF TRUST AND ACCEPTANCE MUST BE ESTABLISHED.

into account in structuring interaction. And that structuring is solely the responsibility of the teacher; the structure must be the product of informed assessment rather than reactive judgment.

For the teacher to interact successfully with the at-risk student, a sense of trust and acceptance must be established. The student must suspend any suspicions of the teacher's intentions, which is no small accomplishment given the student's probable historical experience with schools. The teacher must overcome any negative preconceptions of the nature of the at-risk student that may stem from some students' appearance. In fact, teacher response to the appearance of the at-risk student may be a much larger barrier to a positive interaction than any of the student's other characteristics. The student cannot help but sense rejection by the teacher and will respond in kind. The student, being less sophisticated, frequently manifests inner anger and frustration by overt, socially unacceptable behavior. Administrators and teachers may deal with this behavior as if it were the real problem rather than a symptom. However, if the teacher is well aware of the differ-

ences that are brought to the classroom and can accept them, there can develop an interaction in which the teacher and the student are focused on, rather than distracted from, their respective tasks— teaching and learning.

Another difficulty in developing meaningful interaction is overcoming the sense of hopelessness that at-risk students feel. At-risk students know they are at-risk; they have been told this from the beginning. Innumerable sights and sounds reinforce an absence of control over their environment. Hopelessness often pervades the neighborhoods in which they live. Past experience has probably taught them that high hopes and effort more often than not lead to disappointment and heartbreak. The challenge for the teacher is to identify the students' strengths though they be disguised or denied beneath the protective facade of bravado and coolness, and to try to inspire and motivate students who have little or no expectation of success and who outwardly signal an intense desire to be left alone. To meet this challenge, the teacher more than ever before must be a thinker, a planner, and a decision maker. Then, drawing on

a rich professional knowledge base, the teacher can serve as a model and mediator.

It is one thing to understand intellectually that at-risk students bring to the classroom with them entirely different bents and behaviors. It is another, however, to confront these differences and to view them as starting points for teaching. If we are to succeed in teaching this segment of our student body, we have to understand and accept

these differences and to exercise our expertise as planners and implementers of instruction.

Successful teaching continues to hinge on the characteristics of the learner, the material to be learned, the specific tasks to be mastered, and the strategies utilized by the teacher. No one ever said it would be easy. Surprisingly though, many have found it to be professionally fulfilling and personally rewarding.

ELEMENTS OF WRITING addresses the needs of America's diverse student populations and the range of student *learning styles* in the following ways:

Pupil's Edition
Represents a wide range of ethnically diverse cultures in the literary models and a broad selection of topics in the exercises and examples
Accomodates a range of learning styles by providing a variety of student activities
Offers teachers a flexible program that can be easily adapted to a variety of situations

Annotated Teacher's Edition
Provides specific *MEETING INDIVIDUAL NEEDS* features such as *Learning Styles*, *Less-Advanced, Advanced, Students with Special Needs, LEP/ESL*, and *At-Risk*
Suggests ways for language teachers to address diversity in the multicultural classroom

Teacher's ResourceBank (TM)
Meets individual needs of students with graphic organizers and reinforcement practice activities

By NORBERT ELLIOT & KAREN GREENBERG

THE DIRECT ASSESSMENT OF WRITING:

Notes For Teachers

HOW CAN ASSESSMENT STRATEGIES BE MODIFIED TO HELP BOTH TEACHERS AND STUDENTS?

Teachers spend a great deal of time assessing students' writing; they correct errors, offer suggestions, and assign grades. This process can be exhausting to teachers and discouraging for students. How can assessment strategies be modified to help both teachers and students?

Instruction and assessment can be aligned so that the two work together. To enable instruction and assessment to complement each other, teachers have turned to two relatively new methods of direct assessment: holistic scoring and portfolio assessment.

HOLISTIC SCORING

One of the most common methods of scoring writing samples is holistic scoring, a procedure based on the responses of concerned readers to a meaningful whole composition. Holistic scoring involves reading a writing sample for an overall impression of the writing and assigning the sample a score based on a set of consistent scoring criteria. Most holistic scoring systems use a scoring scale, or guide, that describes papers at six or eight different levels of competence.

Holistic scoring has many advantages:

1. It communicates to students that writing is a process leading to a unified, synergistic piece of writing.
2. Writing samples that have been holistically scored provide students with clear information about the quality of their writing, but they are less intimidating than grades or written critiques.

NORBERT ELLIOT, DIRECTOR OF THE WRITING PROGRAM AT THE NEW JERSEY INSTITUTE OF TECHNOLOGY.

3. Holistic scoring is rapid. Readers spend only minutes judging the total effect of a paper.

4. The criteria on a holistic scoring scale give teachers a vocabulary to use in discussing essays with students and their parents.

5. The process of developing holistic scoring guides and scoring writing samples enables teachers to share their unique responses to writing, as well as their evaluative criteria. If an entire department uses the same scoring guide, students will realize that effective writing has definable features upon which all of their English teachers agree.

Nevertheless, there are weaknesses to this method. It alone cannot, for instance, provide diagnostic information about specific writing proficiencies and deficiencies. The score cannot substitute for a teacher's detailed responses to an essay—the provocative notes in the margin, the encouraging comments at the end, etc. This weakness, however, can be overcome if teachers review papers with their students in light of the scoring criteria.

Another weakness is more serious. Using holistic scoring, teachers often consider only one piece of writing during assessment. If only one sample of writing is evaluated, then teachers may not get a representative idea of students' writing ability, because this ability does not exist in a vacuum but varies from day to day and across the aims and modes of writing. In response to this concern, teachers have investigated a second method of direct assessment.

KAREN GREENBERG, DIRECTOR OF THE NATIONAL TESTING NETWORK IN WRITING.

PORTFOLIO ASSESSMENT

Portfolio assessment allows writing teachers to evaluate various samples of students' work, taken at various times under various conditions. Consequently, portfolio assessment can provide a fuller portrait of writing abilities.

To begin portfolio assessment, teachers develop a series of writing assignments that express the goals of a course. For instance, a group of teachers might require their students to write papers based on each of James Kinneavy's aims: expressive writing (a journal entry), informative writing (a summary of a news article), literary writing (a short story), and persuasive writing (an editorial). Over time, students work on these papers both at home and in class. Portfolios can include other forms of communication that students have produced, such as artwork, audio recordings, or videotapes.

Teachers need not assess everything that is included in a portfolio. In fact, it is often preferable not to evaluate every piece of a student's writing. This strategy allows teachers to separate instruction and response from formed evaluation. Portfolio assessment, therefore, can be based on samples that the teacher, the student, or both consider to be the student's best writing.

Clearly, there are advantages to this method:

1. Because multiple samples are assessed, portfolio assessment is a valid, authentic evaluation.

2. Because the authenticity of the assessment is increased, the curriculum becomes enriched.

As teachers plan tasks, they debate curricular values and strategies, devise workable instructional schemes for the classroom, and design thoughtful evaluative criteria for assignments.

With portfolio assessment, students gain a more positive attitude toward writing. Because they invest in their writing, students seek both teacher and peer response, create multiple drafts, and revise for their readers. Over time, a school's entire writing program can become an exciting adventure in communication and critical thinking.

CONCLUSION

There is still much to be investigated about the evaluation of writing. What kind of assessment best suits the multiple literacies on which our democratic society rests? What kind of local assessments will best supplement large-scale assessment? How can assessment reveal more about effective teaching? Answers will have to come from those who know students best: their teachers. 🍎

ELEMENTS OF WRITING addresses *holistic evaluation* and *portfolio assessment* in the following ways:

Annotated Teacher's Edition
Offers a wide variety of assessment ideas in the *TIMESAVER, A DIFFERENT APPROACH*, and *ASSESSMENT* features

Teacher's ResourceBank (TM)
Provides an **Assessment Portfolio** section and **Holistically Graded Composition Models** for the writing chapters

BY DAVID A. ENGLAND

PROFESSIONAL BIBLIOGRAPHY

COMPOSING PROCESSES

Bellanoff, Pat, Peter Elbow, and Sheryl Fontaine I, eds. *Nothing Begins with N*. Carbondale and Edwardsville, IL: Southern Illinois University Press, 1991. An overview of what we know about the uses of freewriting in the classroom, with major sections on strategies and benefits for teachers and students.

Berthoff, Anne E. *The Making of Meaning*. Upper Montclair, NJ: Boynton/Cook Publishers, Inc., 1991. Suggesting that classrooms can become philosophical laboratories, Berthoff shows the way to practical approaches for thoughtful teachers.

Brannon, Lil, and C.H. Knoblauch. *Rhetorical Traditions and the Teaching of Writing*. Upper Montclair, NJ: Boynton/Cook Publishers, Inc., 1984. Staying with the theory and history provided in this book's early chapters rewards readers who come to understand better the basis and rewards of teaching in nontraditional ways.

Caplan, Rebekah. *Showing-Writing: A Training Program to Help Students to be Specific*. The University of California, Berkeley, CA: Bay Area Writing Project Publications. This nicely focused monograph is itself a good illustration of "showing, not telling," and it explains how the author tested her program for helping students learn to be more specific in their writing.

Dellinger, Dixie Gibbs. *Out of the Heart: How to Design Writing Assignments for High School Courses*. The University of California, Berkeley, CA: Bay Area Writing Project Publications. The author provides several examples of assignment sequences, each reflecting a solid discourse theory, for teachers who want to move beyond disconnected assignments in writing classes.

Kinneavy, James L., William J. McCleary, and Neil Nakadate. *Writing in the Liberal Arts Tradition* (2nd ed.). New York, NY: Harper & Row, 1990. This book is the basis for the writing chapters in the *Elements of Writing* series.

Kirby, Dan, and Tom Liner. *Inside Out: Developmental Strategies for Teaching Writing*. Upper Montclair, NJ: Boynton/Cook Publishers, Inc., 1981. *Developmental* aptly describes the authors' approach as they explain and demonstrate teaching strategies designed to help writers at all levels of sophistication improve their writing processes.

Kutz, Elanor, and Hephzibah Roskelly. *An Unquiet Pedagogy: Transforming Practice in the English Classroom*. Upper Montclair, NJ: Boynton/Cook Publishers, Inc., 1991. This seminal book will challenge traditional assumptions about learners and literacy as it explores how imagination and learner-constructed knowledge undergird any meaningful writing in classes where the development of true literacy is the goal.

Mohr, Marian M. *Revision: The Rhythm of Meaning*. Upper Montclair, NJ: Boynton/Cook Publishers, Inc., 1984. This book defines and exemplifies revision in terms that teachers will understand, adapt, and use as they help their students improve initial drafts.

Murray, Donald M. *Learning by Teaching*. Upper Montclair, NJ: Boynton/Cook Publishers, Inc., 1982. The author connects his process model for writing his thoughts on the processes of teaching writing in a readable text with useful examples and illustrations from the author's experiences as a teacher and writer.

————. *A Writer Teaches Writing* (2nd ed.). Boston, MA: Houghton-Mifflin, 1974. This early "writing process" work was designed to show how real writers write and to make that knowledge useful and powerful for teachers of writing.

Romano, Tom. *Clearing the Way: Working with Teenage Writers*. Portsmouth, NH: Heinemann, 1987. Especially helpful chapters on conferencing and evaluation distinguish this book, which is written in a lively style and which is supported with examples of students' writing and clear insights into a writing teachers' learning.

Willis, Meredith Sue. *Personal Fiction Writing: A Guide for Writing from Real Life for Teachers, Students, and Writers*. New York, NY: Teachers & Writers Collaborative. An experienced writer and teacher shares classroom-tested ideas on helping students to describe places, people, and action; to write dialogues and monologues; to create structure; and to revise what they have written.

Ziegler, Alan. *The Writing Workshop*, Vol. 1. New York, NY: Teachers & Writers Collaborative, 1981. This description of a workshop method for individualizing writing instruction includes ample references to students' work and sharp observations by the author.

————. Vol. 2. New York, NY: Teachers & Writers Collaborative, 1984. This is an excellent catalog of assignments exemplified by students' responses to them, along with the author's observations—a sequel to Vol. 1, which describes a writing environment conducive to such assignments and approaches.

COOPERATIVE LEARNING

Elbow, Peter. *Writing Without Teachers*. New York, NY: Oxford University Press, 1973. The title of the book should not suggest that teachers are not necessary, but rather that they assume different roles in nurturing students' group processes and peer-response activities.

Eubanks, Ilona M. "Nonstandard Dialect Speakers and Collaborative Learning." *The Writing Instructor* Vol. 10 (Spring 1991): 143-147. This article examines features of the traditional language-and-writing classroom that leads to difficulty, frustration, and often failure for speakers of nonstandard dialects.

Golub, Jeff, ed. *Focus on Collaborative Learning: Classroom Practices in the Teaching of English 1988*. Urbana, IL: National Council of Teachers of English, 1988. In compiling this collection of best practices, the editor includes pieces from teachers who describe general collaborative-learning skills before moving to others who discuss how these skills are applied in literature study and various writing activities, from prewriting through revision.

Healey, Mark K. *Using Students' Writing Response Groups in the Classroom*. The University of California, Berkeley, CA: Bay Area Writing Project Publications. In a monograph that realistically assesses problems often associated with response groups, the author provides practical suggestions on how to help students become more helpful in fostering growth in peers' writing.

Rabkin, Eric S., and Macklin Smith. *Teaching Writing That Works*. Ann Arbor, MI: The University of Michigan Press, 1990. In a step-by-step process for breaking the cycle of one individual student writing for a teacher, the authors move from the development of ideas in group settings through group editing and evaluation. Writing designed to help students accomplish "real work" is central to all group activities.

Spear, Karen. *Sharing Writing*. Upper Montclair, NJ: Boynton/Cook Publishers, Inc., 1988. This most practical guide to forming and nurturing response groups could only have been written with the benefit of this teacher's broad and thoughtful experience with response groups in writing courses. The book begins with an honest and promising appraisal of "challenges in peer response groups."

INDIVIDUAL NEEDS/LANGUAGE DIVERSITY

Brooks, Charlotte K., ed. *Tapping Potential: English and the Language Arts for the Black Learner*. Urbana, IL: National Council of Teachers of English, 1985. In addition to explaining why many African American children have not responded to the standard curriculum taught in traditional ways, contributors to this collection offer specific suggestions for classroom practices.

Cleary, Linda Miller. "A Profile of Carlos: Strengths of a Nonstandard Dialect Writer." *English Journal* 77 (September 1988): 59-64. A case study in which the language barriers and biases faced by one writer prove instructive for his teachers and for all teachers.

Connor, Ulla Maija, and Sara Allaei Kurtz. "Exploring the Dynamics of Cross-Cultural Collaboration in Writing Classrooms." *The Writing Instructor* 10 (Fall 1990): 19-28. After reviewing what is known about cross-cultural writing, the authors provide guidelines and recommendations for establishing collaborative groups in multicultural writing classes.

Daniels, Harvey, and Marcia Farr. *Language Diversity and Writing Instruction*. New York, NY: ERIC Clearinghouse on Reading and Communication Skills, National Council of Teachers of English: 1986. This book succeeds in providing just enough theory and background of teachers seeking to improve the writing of students who are native speakers of nonstandard dialects.

Gonzales, Roseann Ducnas. "When Minority Becomes Majority: The Changing Face of English Classrooms." *English Journal* 79 (January 1990): 16-23. Even though the recommendations in this article are for all the language arts, applications to writing instruction will be easy and crucial to teachers in multicultural classes.

Marik, Ray. *Special Education Students Write: Classroom Activities and Assignments*. The University of California, Berkeley, CA: Bay Area Writing Project Publications. Case studies of students with special learning needs are the bases for the author's advocacy of well-sequenced, developmentally appropriate writing activities for all learners.

Rose, Mike. *Lives on the Boundary*. New York, NY: Penguin Books, 1989. The author's experiences as a remedial student contributed to his sensitive understanding of the educational underclass about which he writes so effectively.

Shade, Barbara J. Robinson, ed. *Culture, Style and the Educative Process*. Springfield, IL: Charles C.Thomas, 1989. This book provides insight into various cultures' learning styles as well as methods for enhancing students' retention by addressing their learning styles.

Shaughnbessy, M.P. *Errors and Expectations: A Guide for the Teacher of Basic Writing*. New York, NY: Oxford University Press, 1977. The author's strategies for unlocking expression and clarity for basic college writers are helpful to high school writers as well.

Sottlar, James, ed. *Teaching the Gifted*. Urbana, IL: National Council of Teachers of English, 1988. Ways to identify students with special talents in the language arts, to individualize instruction to meet their needs, and to encourage independent thinking in academically advanced students are among topics in this collection.

Urzua, Carole. "'You Stopped Too Soon': Second Language Children Composing and Revising." *TESOL Quarterly* 21 (June 1987): 279-304. This research report shares what six months of careful observations of Southeast Asian students' writing taught teachers about how second-language children learn to write.

ASSESSMENT

Belanoff, Pat, and Marcia Dickson. *Portfolio Grading: Process and Product*. Portsmouth, NH: Heinemann, 1991. In a good blending of theory and practice in how to use writing portfolios for assessment in many settings, this book allows teachers to plan strategies unique to their own purposes.

Clay, Marie M. "Research Currents: What Is and What Might Be in Education." *Language Arts* 67 (March 1990): 288-298. After discussing problems and limitations of standardized testing, the author makes recommendations toward more useful assessment models and philosophies across the language arts and into high school.

Holmes, Ken. *Perspectives on Teaching and Assessing the Language Arts*. Urbana, IL: National Council of Teachers of English, 1990. These essays include a rationale for multiculturalism in reading materials as well as a timely consideration of assessment in whole-language approaches.

Najimy, Norman C. *Measure to Measure: A Guidebook for Evaluating Students' Expository Writing*. Urbana, IL: National Council of Teachers of English, 1981. By using examples of students' writing, this guide suggests how teachers' responses can enhance instruction instead of threatening students.

Posner, Richard. "Life Without Scan-Tron: Tests as Thinking." *English Journal* 76 (February 1987): 35-38. This author demonstrates how six types of written, in-class tests improve his students' writing, thinking, and mastery of subject matter.

Robinson, Joy L., et al. *Creating Writers: Linking Assessment and Writing Instruction*. White Plains, NY: Longman, 1990. This book helps students and teachers agree on attributes of good writing and has scoring guides that help link instruction to assessment.

RESPONDING TO WRITING

Belanoff, Pat, and Peter Elbow. *Sharing and Responding*. New York, NY: Random House, 1989. This book provides useful examples of students' responses to peers' writing along with clear rationales and activities designed to increase the value of peer responses.

Freedman, Sarah Warhauer. Response to Student Writing. Urbana, IL: National Council of Teachers of English, 1987. This research report on the state of the art in response to writing not only indicates what teachers do and how students feel about it, but offers clear ideas on best practices in providing students with feedback.

Harris, Muriel. *Teaching One-to-One: The Writing Conference*. Urbana, IL: National Council of Teachers of English, 1986. The author provides a strong justification for one-on-one conferencing in the writing classroom and provides useful strategies and insights that can help writing teachers at all levels.

Sommers, Nancy. "Responding to Student Writing." *College Composition and Communication* 32 (May 1982): 148-56. The author encourages teachers to respond to the ideas, meanings, and purposes in students' papers before error hunting in order for students to engage in meaningful revision.

Sullivan, Patrick. "Responding to Student Writing: The Consequences of Some Common Remarks." *English Journal* 75 (February 1986). The author describes the hidden messages behind four types of comments teachers frequently make in responding to students' writing.

WHOLE LANGUAGE/INTEGRATION

Cronin, Hines, David Meadows, and Richard Sinatra. "Integrating Computers, Reading, and Writing Across the Curriculum." *Educational Leadership* 48 (September 1990): 57-60. Good illustrations suggest how visual maps can be constructed via computers to enhance students' thinking and organizational skills in all school subjects.

Kroll, Barry M., and Roberta J. Vann. *Exploring Speaking-Writing Relationships: Connections and Contracts*. Urbana, IL: National Council of Teachers of English, 1981. A precursor of many whole-language texts and approaches, these essays provide instructive analysis of how speaking and writing can be composed and contrasted toward better understanding and teaching of both.

Martin, Nancy, et al. *Writing Across the Curriculum*. Portsmouth, NH: Boynton/Cook Publishers, Inc., 1983. Each pamphlet in this series suggests ways to integrate the teaching of writing by "writing to learn" in various school subjects.

Newkirk, Thomas. *Only Connect: Uniting Reading and Writing*. Upper Montclair, NJ: Boynton/Cook Publishers, Inc., 1986. An excellent middle section on "Reading, Writing, and Interpreting" will help teachers see possibilities for reading in the writing classroom and vice versa.

Peterson, Bruce T, ed. *Convergences: Transactions in Reading and Writing*. Urbana, IL: National Council of Teachers of English, 1986. This collection of essays cuts across several fields in contemporary writing theory and research to explain the logic of integrating reading and writing in the classroom.

Schuman, Baird R., and Denny Wolfe. *Teaching English Through the Arts*. Urbana, IL: National Council of Teachers of English, 1990. In this "Theory and Research into Practice" (TRIP) booklet, the authors provide teachers with classroom-tested ways to connect reading and writing in English classes to popular culture and traditional art forms.

Self, Judith. *Plain Talk About Learning and Writing Across the Curriculum*. Urbana, IL: National Council of Teachers of English, 1987. Teachers of different subjects demonstrate how writing can provide a helpful way for students to think about content and experiences in all subjects.

WRITING ACROSS THE CURRICULUM

Fulwiler, Toby. *Teaching with Writing*. Upper Montclair, NJ: Boynton/Cook Publishers, Inc., 1987. An especially strong chapter on writing and testing helps make this treatment of process writing in the content areas valuable for teachers in all subject areas.

Gere, Anne Ruggles, ed. *Roots in the Sawdust: Writing to Learn Across the Disciplines*. Urbana, IL: National Council of Teachers of English, 1985. The editor has compiled essays on how writing can improve thinking and enhance learning in all the traditionally included subjects such as science and math with the added bonus of thoughtful essays on writing in art and foreign-language classes.

Kiniry, Malcolm, and Ellen Strenski. "Sequencing Expository Writing: A Recursive Approach." *College Composition and Communication* 36 (May 1985): 191-202. Though the model described here is based on a college program, the rhetorical strategies and discipline-specific approaches to writing are applicable to high school writers.

Talbot, Bill. "Writing for Learning in School: Is It Possible?" *Language Arts* 67 (January 1990): 47-57. The author describes his experiences in observing students who were learning how to use writing for learning and raises both concerns and hopes based on his observations.

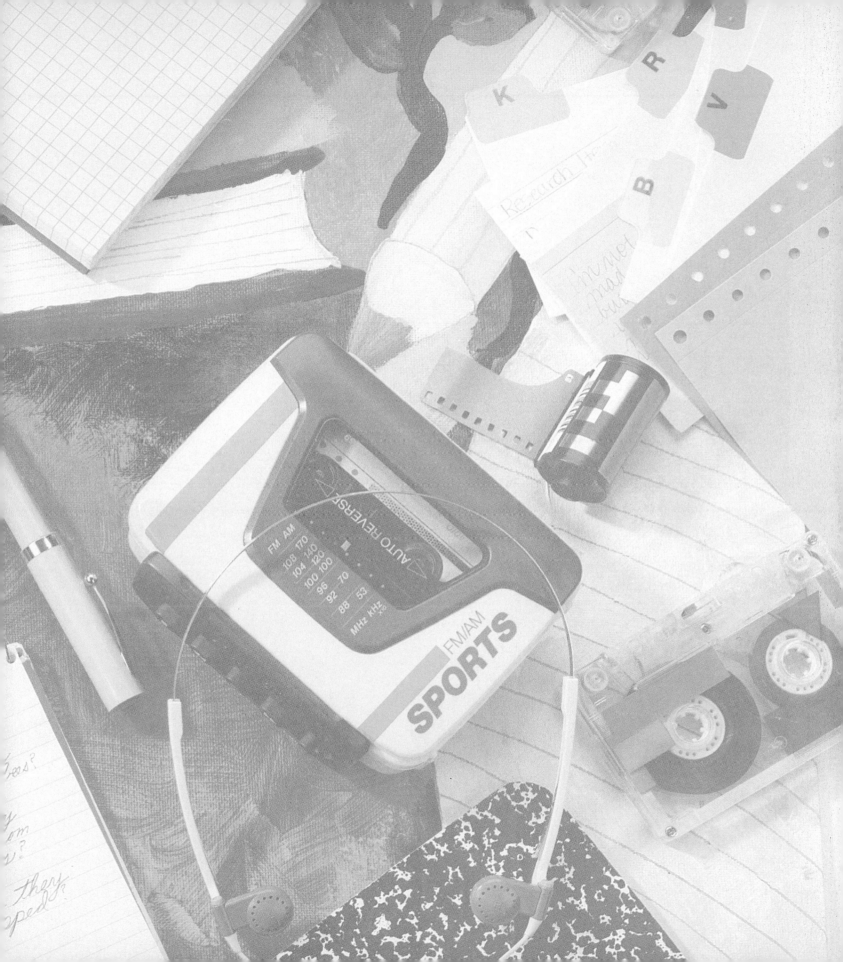

ELEMENTS OF

WRITING

JAMES L. KINNEAVY
JOHN E. WARRINER

First Course

  Holt, Rinehart and Winston

Harcourt Brace Jovanovich

Austin • Orlando • San Diego • Chicago • Dallas • Toronto

Critical Readers

Grateful acknowledgment is made to the following critical readers who reviewed pre-publication materials for this book:

John Algeo
University of Georgia
Athens, Georgia

Alice Bartley
Byrd Middle School
Henrico County, Virginia

Elaine A. Espindle
Peabody Veterans Memorial High
    School
Peabody, Massachusetts

Merry Anne Hilty
Heskett Middle School
Bedford, Ohio

Janet Hoeltzel
Union Seventh Grade Center
Broken Arrow, Oklahoma

Carolyn Kavanagh
East Flagstaff Junior High School
Flagstaff, Arizona

Rebecca Hight Miller
Westridge Middle School
Orlando, Florida

Patty Sais
Truman Middle School
Albuquerque, New Mexico

Martha Teague Weaver
Cullman Middle School
Cullman, Alabama

Requests for permission to make copies of any part of the work should be mailed to: Permissions Department, Holt, Rinehart and Winston, Inc., 8th Floor, Orlando, Florida 32887.

Some material previously published in: ENGLISH COMPOSITION AND GRAMMAR, FIRST COURSE, Pupil's Edition, copyright © 1988, 1986, 1982, 1977, 1973, 1969, 1965, 1963, 1958 by Harcourt Brace Jovanovich, Inc.

Acknowledgments: See pages 935–940, which are an extension of the copyright page.

Printed in the United States of America

ISBN 0-03-047142-7

1 2 3 4 5 6 7 8 9   062   95 94 93 92

Authors

James L. Kinneavy, the Jane and Roland Blumberg Centennial Professor of English at The University of Texas at Austin, directed the development and writing of the composition strand in the program. He is the author of *A Theory of Discourse* and coauthor of *Writing in the Liberal Arts Tradition.* Professor Kinneavy is a leader in the field of rhetoric and composition and a respected educator whose teaching experience spans all levels—elementary, secondary, and college. He has continually been concerned with teaching writing to high school students.

John E. Warriner developed the organizational structure for the Handbook of Grammar, Usage, and Mechanics in the book. He coauthored the *English Workshop* series, was general editor of the *Composition: Models and Exercises* series, and editor of *Short Stories: Characters in Conflict.* He taught English for thirty-two years in junior and senior high school and college.

Writers and Editors

Ellen Ashdown has a Ph.D. in English from the University of Florida. She has taught composition and literature at the college level. She is a professional writer of educational materials and has published articles and reviews on education and art.

Norbert Elliot has a Ph.D in English from the University of Tennessee. A director of the writing program at New Jersey Institute of Technology, he is a specialist in test development and writing assessment.

Mary Hix has an M.A. in English from Wake Forest University. She has taught freshman composition courses. She is a professional writer and editor of educational materials in language arts.

Madeline Travers-Hovland has a Master of Arts in Teaching from Harvard University. She has taught English in elementary and secondary school and has been an elementary school librarian. She is a professional writer of educational materials in literature and composition.

Alice M. Sohn has a Ph.D. in English Education from Florida State University. She has taught English in middle school, secondary school, and college. She has been a writer and editor of educational materials in language arts for twelve years.

Patricia Street was an honor's major in English Expression at Brown University. A professional writer for twenty-five years and a writer/editor of educational materials in language arts for five years, she is currently compiling a reference book for writers.

PART ONE

WRITING

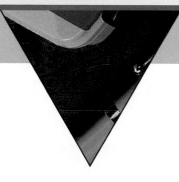

INTRODUCTION TO WRITING
Calling the Signals

OBJECTIVES

- To explore the ways that writers and writing affect the world
- To identify and analyze the aims of writing
- To compare and contrast the aims of writing

USING THE INTRODUCTION TO WRITING

This introduction to writing is just that—an introduction. It starts by talking briefly about the power of writing in peoples' lives rather than by talking about writing as schoolwork. Next, it touches upon the two central focuses of the writing chapters in the

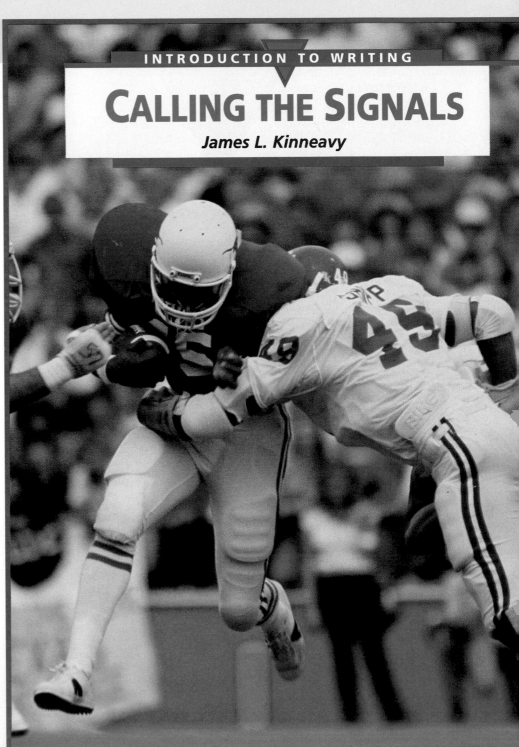

INTRODUCTION TO WRITING

CALLING THE SIGNALS
James L. Kinneavy

textbook—the "how" of writing (modes) and the "why" of writing (aims).

The communication triangle graphically reflects the four major aims of James Kinneavy's theory of discourse. For more information, refer to the essay in the front of this book, **"Meet the Aims and Modes of Writing,"** or to Dr. Kinneavy's two books, *A Theory of Discourse* and *Writing in the Liberal Arts Tradition.* ■

The quarterback looks up at the game clock. Nine seconds to go. An anxious buzz fills the stands as the fans desperately hope for a last-minute miracle. "22!" the quarterback calls out, quickly glancing around to make sure that the team is in place. "Red—44—Hup!" The defensive line digs in, pawing the ground like a herd of raging bulls. A running back moves quickly across the field behind the line. "Hup! Hup!" the quarterback yells. He takes the ball from the center. Helmets and pads crash as both teams struggle for precious ground.

The quarterback set the play in motion. But he was just the instrument. Where did it all really begin? Who was really **calling the signals**?

The Signal Callers

Long before football season opened, players and coaches labored over the hundreds of pages that make up the team's playbook. The big play didn't begin on the field. Someone planned it. Someone wrote it down. And then—at long last—the players put all that writing into action on the playing field.

It's this way with almost everything that happens in life—from the very simplest things to the most complicated. Writers call many of the signals.

Movie actors and TV stars act out what someone else has first written. Singers sing notes and lyrics that are scored on paper. Scientists record the results of their experiments on paper. Politicians are elected because they make convincing speeches—speeches that are often written by someone else. And the laws they help pass after they're elected are all written down. Even most of the world's religions are based on the written word.

Is writing calling your signals? Probably. Have you ever bought anything after seeing it advertised? Somebody wrote the words that persuaded you. How did you learn that new computer game? Did you read the instructions? Somebody wrote them. Have you ever tried out for a sport? Somebody wrote the announcement about the time and place of the tryouts. Somebody wrote the words you're reading now!

Writers are people with power. They call the signals.

What's the Power?

All *writers* share the same power—the power of communication. They all have something to say (a *subject*), someone to say it to (an *audience*), and a way to say it (a *language*). You can have this power of communication, too. Try to think of communication as a triangle. Language—both written and spoken—is at the center.

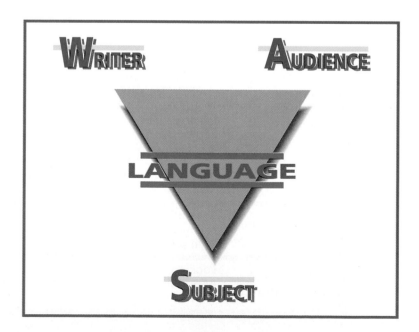

How Do Writers Communicate?

The Writing Process

Powerful communicators know that planning is the key to good writing. Planning helps writers develop their ideas and then communicate them in a way that readers will understand and enjoy. Planning is an important part of a *writing process* that includes some basic steps, or stages. In one way or another, all writers use these basic steps.

⊕ **Prewriting**	Thinking and planning—coming up with a subject to write about, a purpose, and an audience; gathering ideas and details, making a plan for presenting ideas and details
⊕ **Writing**	Writing a first draft—using sentences and paragraphs to get ideas across; following a plan for presenting ideas
⊕ **Evaluating and Revising**	Reading over the draft to see what changes are needed; making changes to improve the draft
⊕ **Proofreading and Publishing**	Looking for and fixing mistakes; writing or printing out a final copy; sharing it with an audience

Why Do Writers Write?

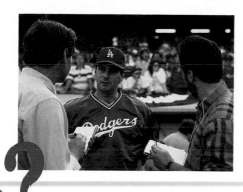

The Aims of Writing

Writers almost always have some purpose in mind for writing. They know what they want to accomplish before they start. All writing has one or more of four basic *aims*, or purposes. These are to inform, to persuade, to express yourself, and to be creative.

To Inform	Writers may give facts and other kinds of information, or they may explain something.
To Persuade	Writers sometimes try to persuade other people. They want readers to think about something differently or to take action.
To Express Themselves	Often, writers write just to express their own feelings and thoughts.
To Be Creative	Writers may also write to be creative. They create stories, poems, songs, and plays.

On the next few pages are four models. Each one is about a girl named Lupe. However, the models are all different because each has a different aim. Notice how the aim shapes what the writers say and how they say it.

PERSUASIVE WRITING

Dear Lupe,

What's this I hear about your being down in the dumps because you think you're no good at sports? If you want to be a sports champion, moping won't get you there. But I can tell you what will.

First of all, think what you do best. What are your strong points? Find a sport that'll let you use your talents. You're intelligent. You think out your problems and overcome them. You've got a lot of determination. And, you've never minded competing. These are all talents that make you a winner.

Remember, Lupe, champions aren't all muscle and sweat. There are sports that need smart, spirited people like you. Look around. Find one that suits your talents. Then everyone will know what I know. Lupe's a winner!

Keep me posted. There's a sport out there that's just right for you. Use your talents. Go for it.

Love,
Grandpa

READER'S RESPONSE

1. Do you think that anyone can become good in at least one sport by trying hard enough? Why or why not?
2. What reasons does Grandpa use to convince Lupe she can be good at a sport? Do his reasons convince you?

ANSWERS
Reader's Response

1. Responses will vary. Students should support their opinions with reasons and evidence.
2. Grandpa tries to convince Lupe that she can be good at a sport by reminding her that she is intelligent, that she can solve problems, that she is determined, and that she likes to compete. Students may or may not be convinced by these reasons.

EXPRESSIVE WRITING

I did it! I won! I'm the new playground marble champion. My ba killing me and my thumb's so sore can hardly write., but I guess I've found my sport.

I did it! I won! I'm the new playground marble champion. My back's killing me and my thumb's so sore I can hardly write, but I guess I've found my sport.

I felt pretty good in all the matches except the last girls' match. The girl looked really tough to beat. She was. I'm not sure how I did it. Then I had to face the boys' winner.

Was I ever scared! It wasn't as bad as I thought it would be, though.

I got two big trophies. A guy from the newspaper took my picture and wrote down some things about me. It's supposed to be in the paper tomorrow. I can't wait. Grandpa'll be so proud. People kept congratulating me, even when we went out for pizza to celebrate. It was kind of embarrassing to get so much attention, but it was fun.

It was a great day. I won two <u>sports</u> trophies and met some nice people and even made new friends. Everybody was super nice to me. It was one of the best days ever.

READER'S RESPONSE

1. How would you feel if you won a tournament, as Lupe did?
2. Who is writing this journal entry? What are Lupe's thoughts and feelings about her victory?

ANSWERS
Reader's Response

1. Responses will vary. To help students answer this question, encourage them to visualize themselves winning a tournament.

2. Lupe is writing this journal entry. Students might say Lupe thinks about winning the tournament, her sore back, her trophies, the forthcoming newspaper article about her victory, her grandpa, going out for pizza, and people she met. Lupe seems to feel very happy and excited.

INFORMATIVE WRITING

Local girl wins marble tournament

Twelve-year-old Lupe Medrano of 127 Broad Street is this year's winner of the annual Playground Marble Tournament. The tournament, sponsored by the Fresno Marble Association, was held yesterday at the city playground.

Lupe, a seventh-grade student at Central Middle School, first defeated a long series of opponents to win the girls' division. She then played and defeated the winner of the boys' division to win the championship.

Lupe admitted she had never played marbles until two weeks ago. She said she trained by doing fingertip push-ups to strengthen her wrists, and by squeezing an eraser to strengthen her thumb. "I also practiced for hours every day," she said.

The head referee and the president of the Fresno Marble Association presented Lupe with her two trophies.

FIRST PLACE
MARBLES CHAMPIONSHIP

FIRST PLACE
GIRLS DIVISION

READER'S RESPONSE

1. Have you ever been in any kind of tournament? Can you tell your classmates something about tournaments that this article doesn't tell?
2. Does this article mostly give facts about Lupe and the tournament, or does it express the writer's feelings? How can you recognize the writer's aim?

ANSWERS

Reader's Response

1. Responses will vary. Encourage students to share their experiences.
2. The article gives facts. The writer's aim — informative — is recognizable because of the many facts included in the article.

CREATIVE WRITING

The Marble Champ

by Gary Soto

Lupe Medrano, a shy girl who spoke in whispers, was the school's spelling bee champion, winner of the reading contest at the public library three summers in a row, blue ribbon awardee in the science fair, the top student at her piano recital, and the playground grand champion in chess. She was a straight-A student and—not counting kindergarten, when she had been stung by a wasp—never missed one day of elementary school. She had received a small trophy for this honor and had been congratulated by the mayor.

But though Lupe had a razor-sharp mind, she could not make her body, no matter how much she tried, run as fast as the other girls'. She begged her body to move faster, but could never beat anyone in the fifty-yard dash.

The truth was that Lupe was no good in sports. She could not catch a pop-up or figure out in which direction to kick the soccer ball. One time she kicked the ball at her own goal and scored a point for the other team. She was no good at baseball or basketball either, and even had a hard time making a hula hoop stay on her hips.

It wasn't until last year, when she was eleven years old, that she learned how to ride a bike. And even then she had to use training wheels. She could walk in the swimming pool but couldn't swim, and chanced roller skating only when her father held her hand.

"I'll never to be good at sports," she <u>fumed</u> one rainy day as she lay on her bed gazing at the shelf her father had made to hold her awards. "I wish I could win something, anything, even marbles."

At the word "marbles," she sat up. "That's it. Maybe I could be good at playing marbles." She hopped out of bed and rummaged through the closet until she found a can full of her brother's marbles. She poured the rich glass treasure on her bed and picked five of the most beautiful marbles.

She smoothed her bedspread and practiced shooting, softly at first so that her aim would be accurate. The marble rolled from her thumb and clicked against the targeted marble. But the target wouldn't budge. She tried again and again. Her aim became accurate, but the power from her thumb made the marble move only an inch or two. Then she realized that the bedspread was slowing the marbles. She also had to admit that her thumb was weaker than the neck of a newborn chick.

She looked out the window. The rain was letting up, but the ground was too muddy to play. She sat cross-legged on the bed, rolling her five marbles between her palms. Yes, she thought, I could play marbles, and marbles is a sport. At that moment she realized that she had only two weeks to practice. The playground championship, the same one her brother had entered the previous year, was coming up. She had a lot to do.

To strengthen her wrists, she decided to do twenty push-ups on her fingertips, five at a time. "One, two, three . . ." she groaned. By the end of the first set she was breathing hard, and her muscles burned from exhaustion. She did one more set and decided that was enough push-ups for the first day.

She squeezed a rubber eraser one hundred times, hoping it would strengthen her thumb. This seemed to work because the next day her thumb was sore. She could hardly hold a marble in her hand, let alone send it flying with power. So Lupe rested that day and listened to her brother, who gave her tips on how to shoot: get low, aim with one eye, and place one knuckle on the ground.

"Think 'eye and thumb'—and let it rip!" he said.

After school the next day she left her homework in her backpack and practiced three hours straight, taking time only to eat a candy bar for energy. With a popsicle stick, she drew an odd-shaped circle and tossed in four marbles. She used her shooter, a milky <u>agate</u> with <u>hypnotic</u> swirls, to blast them. Her thumb *had* become stronger.

After practice, she squeezed the eraser for an hour. She ate dinner with her left hand to spare her shooting hand and said nothing to her parents about her dreams of athletic glory.

Practice, practice, practice. Squeeze, squeeze, squeeze. Lupe got better and beat her brother and Alfonso, a neighbor kid who was supposed to be a champ.

"Man, she's bad!" Alfonso said. "She can beat the other girls for sure. I think."

The weeks passed quickly. Lupe worked so hard that one day, while she was drying dishes, her mother asked why her thumb was swollen.

"It's muscle," Lupe explained. "I've been practicing for the marbles championship."

"You, honey?" Her mother knew Lupe was no good at sports.

"Yeah. I beat Alfonso, and he's pretty good."

That night, over dinner, Mrs. Medrano said, "Honey, you should see Lupe's thumb."

"Huh?" Mr. Medrano said, wiping his mouth and looking at his daughter.

"Show your father."

"Do I have to?" an embarrassed Lupe asked.

"Go on, show your father."

Reluctantly, Lupe raised her hand and flexed her thumb. You could see the muscle.

The father put down his fork and asked, "What happened?"

"Dad, I've been working out. I've been squeezing an eraser."

"Why?"

"I'm going to enter the marbles championship."

Her father looked at her mother and then back at his daughter. "When is it, honey?"

"This Saturday. Can you come?"

The father had been planning to play racquetball with a friend Saturday, but he said he would be there. He knew his daughter thought she was no good at sports and he wanted to encourage her. He even rigged some lights in the backyard so she could practice after dark. He squatted with one knee on the ground, <u>entranced</u> by the sight of his daughter easily beating her brother.

The day of the championship began with a cold <u>blustery</u> sky. The sun was a silvery light behind slate clouds.

"I hope it clears up," her father said, rubbing his hands together as he returned from getting the newspaper. They ate breakfast, paced nervously around the house waiting for 10:00 to arrive, and walked the two blocks to the playground (though Mr. Medrano wanted to drive so Lupe wouldn't get tired). She signed up and was assigned her first match on baseball diamond number three.

Lupe, walking between her brother and her father, shook from the cold, not nerves. She took off her mittens, and everyone stared at her thumb. Someone asked, "How can you play with a broken thumb?" Lupe smiled and said nothing.

She beat her first opponent easily, and felt sorry for the girl because she didn't have anyone to cheer for her. Except for her sack of marbles, she was all alone. Lupe invited the girl, whose name was Rachel, to stay with them. She smiled and said, "OK." The four of them walked to a card table in the middle of the outfield, where Lupe was assigned another opponent.

She also beat this girl, a fifth-grader named Yolanda, and asked her to join their group. They proceeded to more matches and more wins, and soon there was a crowd of people following Lupe to the finals to play a girl in a baseball cap. This girl seemed dead serious. She never even looked at Lupe.

"I don't know, Dad, she looks tough."

Rachel hugged Lupe and said, "Go get her."

"You can do it," her father encouraged. "Just think of the marbles, not the girl, and let your thumb do the work."

The other girl broke first and earned one marble. She missed her next shot, and Lupe, one eye closed, her thumb quivering with energy, blasted two marbles out of the circle but missed her next shot. Her opponent earned two more before missing. She stamped her foot and said "Shoot!" The score was three to two in favor of Miss Baseball Cap.

The referee stopped the game. "Back up, please, give them room," he shouted. Onlookers had gathered too tightly around the players.

Lupe then earned three marbles and was set to get her fourth when a gust of wind blew dust in her eyes and she missed badly. Her opponent quickly scored two marbles, tying the game, and moved ahead six to five on a lucky shot. Then she missed, and Lupe, whose eyes felt scratchy when she blinked, relied on instinct and thumb muscle to score the tying point. It was now six to six, with only three marbles left. Lupe blew her nose and studied the angles. She dropped to one knee, steadied her hand, and shot so hard she cracked two marbles from the circle. She was the winner!

"I did it!" Lupe said under her breath. She rose from her knees, which hurt from bending all day, and hugged her father. He hugged her back and smiled.

Everyone clapped, except Miss Baseball Cap, who made a face and stared at the ground. Lupe told her she was a great player, and they shook hands. A newspaper photographer took pictures of the two girls standing shoulder-to-shoulder, with Lupe holding the bigger trophy.

Lupe then played the winner of the boys' division, and after a poor start beat him eleven to four. She blasted the marbles, shattering one into sparkling slivers of glass. Her opponent looked on glumly as Lupe did what she did best—win!

The head referee and the President of the Fresno Marble Association stood with Lupe as she displayed her trophies for the newspaper photographer. Lupe shook hands with everyone, including a dog who had come over to see what the <u>commotion</u> was all about.

That night, the family went out for pizza and set the two trophies on the table for everyone in the restaurant to see. People came up to congratulate Lupe, and she felt a little embarrassed, but her father said the trophies belonged there.

Back home, in the privacy of her bedroom, she placed the trophies on her shelf and was happy. She had always earned honors because of her brains, but winning in sports was a new experience. She thanked her tired thumb. "You did it, thumb. You made me champion." As its reward, Lupe went to the bathroom, filled the bathroom sink with warm water, and let her thumb swim and splash as it pleased. Then she climbed into bed and drifted into a hard-won sleep.

READER'S RESPONSE

1. How do you think this story might have ended if Lupe had lost the marble tournament?
2. Most people like to read short stories like this. Do you? Why or why not? What do you like best about this story?

ANSWERS
Reader's Response

1. Responses will vary. You could have students write alternative endings for the story.
2. Responses will vary. Students should give reasons for liking or not liking to read short stories. If students do not like the story, you could allow them to tell what they dislike most about the story.

Writing and Thinking Activities

1. Get together with two or three other students. Then discuss these questions about the four models you've just read.
   a. Which model mostly tells the writer's thoughts and feelings?
   b. Which one tries to convince its reader to do something? What does the writer want the reader to do?
   c. Which one mostly tells readers facts and details about the event?
   d. Which model makes you feel that you're actually at the event? How has the writer been creative?
2. When you communicate with other people, what are your aims? During two hours of a typical day, keep track of each time you use language. Think about the times you write, read, speak, and listen. How often is your aim to inform? to persuade? to express yourself? to be creative? Share what you found out with two or three classmates. What aims do each of you most often have?
3. Which type of writing do you think is used most often? Is it informative, persuasive, self-expressive, or creative? Pick out a magazine or newspaper to bring to class. Work with some other students to find examples of all four types of writing. Then decide which one is used most. Do some publications have just one type of writing?
4. What is creative writing? To be creative is the main purpose of writing that creates literature, such as novels, short stories, poems, and plays. But isn't all writing creative in some way? What about letters, book reports, and newspaper articles? Would you call them creative? Find some examples of writing that is creative, even though the basic purpose or aim is informative, persuasive, or self-expressive.

ANSWERS
Writing and Thinking Activities

1. a. the journal entry (expressive)
   b. the letter (persuasive)—Grandpa wants Lupe to keep trying to find a sport at which she can be successful.
   c. the newspaper article
   d. the short story—The writer has created believable characters and a detailed plot.

Questions 2 and 4 can be assigned at various times throughout the year.

Question 3 is a group project that could serve as a good motivational activity.

WRITING AND THINKING

OBJECTIVES

- To find ideas for writing by using a variety of prewriting techniques
- To analyze the audience and purpose of a composition
- To arrange ideas in a logical order appropriate for the purpose, audience, and topic of a composition
- To write a first draft of a composition
- To evaluate and revise a composition for content, organization, and style
- To proofread a composition and to prepare it for publication

Motivation

Many seventh-graders may be unfamiliar with the writing process. They may also have unrealistic expectations about writing; for example, some students may expect that their first drafts will serve as final drafts. One way to motivate students is to ask them if any student has ever done a task or chore only to discover later that there was a more efficient way to do it. Allow volunteers to tell about their experiences. Then discuss how the better ways of doing the tasks differed from the old methods. Point out how the stages in the writing process can make writing easier and more manageable.

Introduction

This chapter introduces the writing process as a thinking and decision-making tool. This process, with appropriate modification, works for any mode of writing (narration, description, classification, or evaluation) and with any aim (expressive, informative, persuasive, or literary).

The chapter explores and explains the writing process from beginning to end. It introduces six different prewriting techniques that are useful for generating ideas and gathering information. A discussion of drafting follows, and instruction continues with an explanation of evaluating and revising. The chapter concludes with material on proofreading and publishing.

Integration

Techniques and explanations given in this chapter can be applied to the writing situations presented in **Chapters 2-11**. You will also find that the writing process has applications to other content areas. For example, prewriting techniques can be used to generate ideas and to gather information for formal and informal speaking and to prepare for listening. When using the library, students can use brainstorming to create lists of words to look up in the on-line or card catalog. Employing the writing process can improve a student's answers on essay tests. Finally, during the revising and proofreading stage, you can demonstrate how useful the study of grammar, usage, and mechanics is to clear communication.

The chart on the next page illustrates the strands of language arts as they are integrated into this chapter. For vocabulary study, glossary words are underlined in some writing models.

QUOTATIONS
All **Quotations for the Day** are chosen because of their relevance to instructional material presented in that segment of the chapter and for their usefulness in establishing student interest in writing.

INTEGRATING THE LANGUAGE ARTS

Selection	Reading and Literature	Writing and Critical Thinking	Language and Syntax	Speaking, Listening, and Other Expression Skills
"Questions and Answers" by Dudley Randall 20-22 from "Rikki-tikki-tavi" by Rudyard Kipling 40 "Stopping by Woods on a Snowy Evening" by Robert Frost 56	Responding personally to literature 23 Reading to evaluate a writer's revisions 57 Reading critically to evaluate 36	Generating ideas by writing a journal entry 28, 29 Generating ideas by freewriting 29 Generating ideas by brainstorming 30 Generating and linking ideas by clustering 31 Collecting and writing sensory details 33 Generating ideas by asking the 5W-How? questions 35 Generating ideas by asking "What if?" questions 35 Writing a plot outline 35 Writing for specific purpose and audience 28, 38, 45 Selecting information with purpose and audience in mind 38 Analyzing details to choose appropriate orders for different audiences, purposes 41 Making a chart to show comparison 43 Making a sequence chain to show chronological order 43 Writing a first draft 45 Evaluating and revising a draft 52 Evaluating and revising a paragraph 48, 54 Proofreading a paragraph 54 Using brainstorming to generate ideas for publishing 55 Writing a journal entry to analyze the revision process 57	Defining and identifying clichés 23 Adjusting language to suit audience and purpose 52 Proofreading a paragraph for errors in capitalization, punctuation, spelling, and sentence run-ons and fragments 54 Proofreading for errors in usage and mechanics 54 Analyzing language and syntax changes in a poem 55	Brainstorming in a small group 30, 35, 55 Listening to collect sensory details 33 Listening with a focus 33, 36 Reading aloud to a group 45 Discussing an evaluation with a partner 52 Listening attentively to record important details 36 Using visual aids to locate and interpret information 36

SEGMENT PLANNING GUIDE

Whether you are planning for a quick review of a writing concept or preparing an extended lesson on composition you can use the following Planning Guide to adapt the chapter material to the individual needs of your class.

SEGMENT	PAGES	CONTENT	RESOURCES
1 Looking at the Process	19-23		
Literary Model **"Questions and Answers"**	20-22	Guided reading: a professional writer's advice on how to write	
Reader's Response	23	Model evaluation: responding to literature and listing clichés	
2 Aim and Process	24-25		
3 Prewriting	26-43		Freewriting
Finding Ideas For Writing	26	Explanation: using prewriting techniques	Brainstorming and Clustering
Chart: Prewriting Techniques	26	Guidelines: examining prewriting techniques	Asking Questions
Exercise 1	28	Applied practice: making a journal entry	Reading and Listening with a Focus
Exercise 2	29	Applied practice: freewriting in a journal entry	
Exercise 3	30	Cooperative learning: listing ideas	Thinking About Purpose
Exercise 4	31	Applied practice: using clustering	Audience
Critical Thinking: Observing with Your Five Senses	32	Guidelines: collecting sensory information	Chronological Order
Critical Thinking Exercise	33	Applied practice: observing sensory details	Spatial Order
Asking Questions	33-35	Introduction: asking the *5W-How?* and "What if" questions	Order of Importance
Exercise 5	35	Applied practice: listing *5W-How?* questions	
Exercise 6	35	Cooperative learning: brainstorming "What if?" questions and writing a plot outline	
Reading and Listening	35-36	Guidelines: reading and listening critically	
Exercise 7	36	Applied practice: reading and listening	
Thinking About Purpose and Audience	37-38	Guidelines: relating purpose and audience to aim	
Chart: Purpose	37	Guidelines: examining main purpose and form	
Exercise 8	38	Applied practice: choosing appropriate statements	
Chart: Ways to Organize	39	Guidelines: examining types of order	
Literary Model from **"Rikki-tikki-tavi"**	40	Guided reading: examining chronological order in a model	
Critical Thinking: Arranging Ideas	40	Guidelines: identifying methods of arranging information	
Critical Thinking Exercise	41	Applied practice: choosing an order for ideas	
Using Visuals to Organize	41-43	Guidelines: using charts to organize ideas	

SEGMENT	PAGES	CONTENT	RESOURCES
Exercise 9	43	Applied practice: making a chart to organize information	
Exercise 10	43	Applied practice: creating a sequence chain	
4 *Writing*	*44-45*		Writing a First Draft
Writing a First Draft	44-45	Guidelines: using criteria to write a first draft	
Exercise 11	45	Applied practice: writing a first draft	
5 *Evaluating and Revising*	*46-52*		Practicing Peer Evaluation
Self-Evaluation	46	Guidelines: examining criteria for self-evaluation	Revising: Adding and Cutting
Chart: Peer Evaluation	47	Guidelines: examining criteria for peer evaluation	Revising: Replacing and Reordering
Critical Thinking: Evaluating Writing	47	Guidelines: applying evaluation criteria	
Critical Thinking Exercise	48	Cooperative learning: evaluating statements	
Chart: Revision Techniques	49	Guidelines: examining techniques in examples	
Chart: Guidelines for Evaluating and Revising	51	Guidelines: applying evaluation and revision techniques	
Exercise 12	52	Cooperative learning: evaluating and revising	
6 *Proofreading and Publishing*	*53-55*		Proofreading
Proofreading	53	Guidelines: using proofreading criteria	Publishing and Manuscript Form
Chart: Proofreading	53	Guidelines: examining proofreading criteria	
Exercise 13	54	Applied practice: proofreading a paragraph	
Publishing	54	Publishing ideas: reaching an audience	
Chart: Guidelines for Form	55	Guidelines: examining criteria	
Exercise 14	55	Cooperative learning: brainstorming ideas	
Chart: Symbols for Revising and Proofreading	55	Guidelines: examining symbol, example, and meaning of symbol	
7 *Making Connections*	*56-57*		
A Writer's Revisions	56-57	Applied practice: writing a journal entry	
Literary Model **"Stopping by Woods on a Snowy Evening"**	56	Guided reading: comparing an author's revisions to published writing	
Reflecting on the Process	57	Applied practice: recording uses of writing	
WHOLE-CHAPTER RESOURCE Chapter Review			

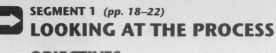

LOOKING AT THE PROCESS

OBJECTIVES

- To analyze personal reading habits
- To analyze personal feelings about criticism and writing
- To express clichés in a fresh way

TEACHING THE LESSON

You may wish to read the introductory paragraphs to students before you begin working on the model. Give students a chance to respond before you proceed.

Because some students may be puzzled by parts of the model, you could also read the model to the class as students read along. Explain difficult vocabulary and

VISUAL CONNECTIONS
The False Mirror

About the Artist. Belgian artist René Magritte was born in 1898. He studied at Académic de Beaux-Arts in Brussels and later served in the Belgian Army. In addition to painting, Magritte did photography and graphic design. He also worked as a writer and an editor.

Magritte's surreal paintings challenge the viewer by placing extremely realistic images in unreal juxtapositions.

Ideas for Writing. Discuss *The False Mirror* with the class. Ask students to free associate with the word *eve, vision, mirror,* and *sky.* Have them consider the possible relationships between their ideas. Then have each student write and expressive paragraph inspired by the picture and by the ideas mentioned in the discussion.

1 WRITING AND THINKING

unfamiliar concepts as you go and add additional background information where necessary with the help of the annotations. Finally, have students reread the model independently to get the flow.

After students are thoroughly familiar with the model, you can generate further discussion by returning to the **As You Read** feature on this page. Encourage students to suggest other kinds of writing to which they think Randall's advice applies.

Use the questions in **Reader's Response** to generate discussion by recording the answers to questions 1 and 2 as if they were part of a survey. Question 1 can lead to discussion of both individual preferences and class trends, while question 2 can lead to an assessment of what students hope to gain

Looking at the Process

Did you ever stop and think about what happens when you write? You actually go through an amazing **process**. It begins with thoughts and feelings that grow in your brain until they finally flow out as written words on paper.

Writing and You. Do you find that it's sometimes easy to write, but at other times the words just won't cooperate? Is your brain brimming with ideas? Or is it often hard to think of something to write about? Professional writers have the same problems. Sometimes they can't come up with a good idea. The words just won't come out right. What is the hardest part of writing for you?

As You Read. As you read what editor Dudley Randall says about writing poetry, see if you think his advice applies to other kinds of writing besides poetry.

The False Mirror, Rene Magritte (1928). Oil on canvas, 21¾ × 31⅞". Collection, The Museum of Modern Art, New York. Purchase. © 1992 C. Herscovici/ARS, N.Y. Photograph © 1992 The Museum of Modern Art, New York.

QUOTATION FOR THE DAY

"A creative artist works on his next composition because he was not satisfied with his previous one." (Dimitri Shostakovich, 1906–   , Soviet musical composer)

Write the quotation on the chalkboard and ask students to freewrite for a few minutes about the quotation's meaning. Ask students what might happen if all people were so satisfied with their first great achievements that they didn't attempt new projects.

MEETING INDIVIDUAL NEEDS

LEP/ESL

General Strategies. Because clichés are closely tied to the culture that produces them, one cannot expect this information to be transferable to all students. It is important to remain sensitive to this fact and to realize that students will need a literal definition of *cliché*. Part of the explanation provided, "expressions that have been worked to death," is far too idiomatic. You may want to have students offer examples of clichés from their native languages.

19

from the course. Model revising a cliché before students finish question 3.

ASSESSMENT

You can use students' written or oral responses to the questions at the end of the interview to evaluate how well they have analyzed their personal reading habits and their feelings about writing. The group answers to question 3 will give you an impression of students' thinking and interests.

Q & A
Questions & Answers
by Dudley Randall

The following questions are asked frequently in letters from beginning poets to Broadside Press. The answers are by Dudley Randall, Broadside Press editor.

1 Q. I am a fifteen year old high school student and have been writing poetry for one year. How do I go about having a book published?

A. How fortunate that you became a poet so early! You have many years of writing ahead of you, so it's not necessary to rush into the permanence of book <u>format</u>. Some poets, Robert Hayden among them, published books very young, and now they don't want their <u>juvenile</u> publications to be seen. I asked Hayden for permission to reprint a poem from his first book, *Heartshape in the Dust,* and he said, "No, *no,* No, NO, *NO!* I wrote those poems in my <u>apprentice</u> years, when I was learning to write, and I don't want any of them reprinted."

This period of learning how to write, discovering new poets, experimenting with new forms, can be one of your most enjoyable. Don't <u>terminate</u> it <u>prematurely</u>. Read, read, read. And write, write, write.

USING THE SELECTION
Questions and Answers

1

Robert Hayden was the first black poet chosen as Consultant in Poetry to the Library of Congress. Born Asa Bundy Sheffey, his name was legally changed by his foster parents. He died in 1980.

2

Randall himself wrote his first poem at age 4 and had poetry published in the *Detroit Free Press* at age 13.

CLOSURE

To bring closure to this segment, have student volunteers give their interpretations of Randall's statement, "Read, read, read. And write, write, write."

ENRICHMENT

You may want to suggest that students find and read some of the mentioned works by Robert Hayden, Mari Evans, and Karl Shapiro. Then have students report to the class their evaluations of these authors' works. ■

21

Don't try for book publication until you have published
3 extensively in magazines and newspapers. Mari Evans was
4 well-known for her contributions to magazines and anthologies before she published her first book. Such publication will be an indication that many different editors have found your work acceptable. Then publishers, perhaps, will have seen your poems somewhere, and will be more willing to risk from $500 to $10,000 on a first book by you, than on a book by an unknown poet.

5 All the poems you sent me were in rimed couplets, which are only one of many forms and which have their limitations.
6 Master the scores of other forms which you will find in Karl Shapiro's *A Prosody Handbook* or in any handbook on writing poetry. Also, learn correct spelling and grammar. When you have learned the rules, you can break them, if you have good reasons to.

After you have done these things, you can start sending your poems to magazines. Choose publications where the competition is not too tough, like your local newspaper, your school newspaper or yearbook, literary magazine, or your church bulletin. After mastering spelling, grammar, and forms, you will be ready to be published, but try ephemeral publications first, not the permanence of books, which you may regret later. Have fun!

"*This period of learning how to write, discovering new poets, experimenting with new forms, can be one of your most enjoyable.*"

3
Mari Evans was a professor of Black literature and the producer, director, and writer for the television program "The Black Experience." She wrote poems and novels for young people.

4
anthologies: collections of poems chosen by the compiler

5
Rimed (another spelling of *rhymed*) couplets are two successive lines of poetry of the same length that rhyme.

6
Karl Shapiro, a professor of English, won the Pulitzer Prize for poetry in 1945.

VISUAL CONNECTIONS

Exploring the Subject. Dudley Randall was born in 1914 in Washington, D.C., the son of a Congregational minister and a teacher. He studied in Michigan and at the University of Ghana. His first job was at a foundry, and he then worked as a mail clerk, carrier, and librarian. In 1963 he founded the Broadside Press, which published the work of many African American poets. In 1980, Randall founded Broadside Poets Theater and Broadside Poetry Workshop.

7

flatters your ego: makes you feel good about yourself

8

Amerikkka: ironic spelling of America, used by the Black Panthers to include the initials of the Ku Klux Klan

SELECTION AMENDMENT
Description of change: words changed, mechanics corrected, excerpted
Rationale: to focus on the concept of the writing process presented in this chapter

2
Q. I have a teacher who reads and criticizes my poems. He says they are full of clichés. What can I do?

A. One of the best ways to learn to write is to have your work read and criticized by a <u>competent</u> person. You must develop a thick skin to criticism, and the ability to evaluate it <u>objectively</u> and apply it to your work to make it better. Praise

7 only flatters your ego, but searching criticism exposes your flaws and points out what you must do to write better.

Clichés are expressions which have been worked to death and have lost their freshness, surprise, and power, like "right

8 on," "pigs," "Queen of the Nile," "Amerikkka," "sweet as a rose." Perhaps the reason you use clichés is that you have not read enough to observe their repetition. Read more widely and develop the <u>knack</u> of spotting over-used expressions and eliminate them from your writing.

READER'S RESPONSE

1. In his first answer, Randall advises the fifteen year old poet, "Read, read, read. And write, write, write." How much reading do you do? What kinds of reading do you enjoy most?
2. Randall says that criticism helps you learn to write better. How do you feel when someone criticizes your writing? How do you think you can learn to be a better writer?
3. Clichés are hard to overcome. List some familiar clichés ("tough as nails," "fresh as a daisy," and so on). Then see if you can think of a fresh way to express each idea. You can work with a partner or several classmates.

LOOKING AHEAD

In this chapter you'll practice a general approach or process that applies to all types of writing. As you work through the chapter, remember that

- careful thinking is part of writing
- the planning that you do before you write is crucial
- the writing process can be adapted to fit your own writing style

smooth as silk

green as grass

ANSWERS
Reader's Response

Responses will vary. Question 1, part one, should include a daily or weekly amount of time. Part two should include specific titles, as well as genres.

For question 2, part one, in addition to describing in general how they deal with criticism, students should suggest what kinds of criticism they find particularly helpful. For part two, students should suggest the kinds of help that might be given through the course. Answers might include hearing poetry read by real poets, getting guidance and feedback, and seeing more examples of kinds of writing that are less familiar.

Question 3 has three parts. First, students must list expressions that are actually clichés. Second, they must correctly interpret the idea expressed by each clichés. Third, they must provide an appropriate, fresh substitute.

THE "WHY" AND "HOW" OF WRITING

TEACHING THE AIMS

Before they look at these pages, ask students to think about why they write. Specifically, they should focus on the last pieces of writing they have done and identify the purposes they had in mind when they wrote. Then have students read the information on the aims of writing so they can identify which of the four purposes (or combination thereof) stated there best fits their situations.

Ask students to try to recall how they thought and made decisions for those same pieces of writing. Have them independently

LESS-ADVANCED STUDENTS

Students might have trouble linking what they perceive as their aims for writing with the four aims listed on the page. For example, students might protest that the four aims do not apply to their own. They might cite alternative aims, such as "I did my homework assignment to get a good grade; I wrote down my new friend's phone number so I wouldn't forget it; I wrote my name in my notebook so other people would know it was mine."

Help students to see that these are all examples of the informative aim (probably the hardest for them to distinguish). Doing homework informs the teacher that the assignment was understood; recording a phone number enables a person to use it later; writing a name in a notebook informs others whom it belongs to. Help students work through other specific examples that may be bothering them by identifying which of the four aims applies.

24

Aim—The "Why" of Writing

People write because they have something to say, someone to say it to, and a purpose for saying it. That's the general *why* for communicating. But what are the specific purposes people have for writing?

Maybe you think there are many, many purposes for writing. But there are really only a few.

WHY PEOPLE WRITE	
To express themselves	To get to know themselves better; to find meaning in their lives
To share information	To give information other people need or want; to share special knowledge
To persuade	To convince other people to do something or believe something
To create literature	To be creative; to say something in a unique way

Everything people write has one of these four purposes—sometimes more than one at the same time. For example, a writer may want to share information *and* to persuade, to express himself or herself *and* to create literature.

Like all the other writers in the world, you'll be writing for at least one of these four purposes.

Process—The "How" of Writing

Writing is a skill that improves with practice. It's also part of a *process*, a series of steps that lead to an end result. The following diagram shows the steps that usually take place

read through the material on process, and then you can go over the pie chart below with them. Ask students to identify the most basic order of the writing process—where on the chart they would start, which directions they would move in, and where they would stop [start at prewriting, move clockwise to proofreading and publishing]. Then explain that every writer has a different process—

that's why the chart is circular. A writer may move recursively. ■

in the writing process. But every writer is different. You may spend less time prewriting than the person sitting next to you. And that person may spend much more time revising than you do. As you review the writing process, notice how every stage requires thinking. Writing and thinking happen together whenever you write.

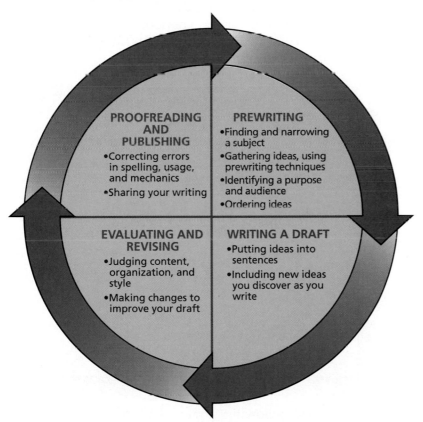

PROOFREADING AND PUBLISHING
• Correcting errors in spelling, usage, and mechanics
• Sharing your writing

PREWRITING
• Finding and narrowing a subject
• Gathering ideas, using prewriting techniques
• Identifying a purpose and audience
• Ordering ideas

EVALUATING AND REVISING
• Judging content, organization, and style
• Making changes to improve your draft

WRITING A DRAFT
• Putting ideas into sentences
• Including new ideas you discover as you write

Unlike a chiseler working in stone, you can make changes easily when you write. At any point in the writing process, you can go back to an earlier stage or even start all over again. Suppose you're writing a committee report about a food drive your scout troop will sponsor. As you write your first draft, you may realize you don't know enough about the kinds of food you need to collect. So you go back to prewriting to gather more information.

 INTEGRATING THE LANGUAGE ARTS

Literature Link. Divide the class into pairs. Give each group a literature book with a wide variety of fiction and nonfiction selections. Have each group find one example of each of the aims. Then have groups explain their choices.

A DIFFERENT APPROACH

You may want to use another diagram to illustrate the writing process for students. One possibility is to compare writing a story, essay, or poem to playing a championship game. The players must plan carefully, gather and organize the players and equipment, and keep their purpose in mind to win. Writers, like the players, may have to adjust their plans and go back to a previous stage before proceeding to their goals.

Use pictures of sports players in each stage of their process to parallel how writers journey through the writing process.

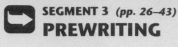

SEGMENT 3 *(pp. 26–43)*
PREWRITING
OBJECTIVES
- To find ideas for writing by using writers' journals, freewriting, brainstorming, clustering, asking questions, and reading and listening with a focus
- To identify purpose and audience for writing
- To arrange information by using charts and sequence chains

26   *Writing and Thinking*

Finding Ideas for Writing

Have you ever complained, "I can't think of anything to write about"? Locked inside your mind are thousands of ideas for writing—your experiences, interests, and observations. You can unlock ideas for writing by practicing the following prewriting techniques.

PREWRITING TECHNIQUES		
Writer's Journal	Keeping a record of personal experiences, observations, and ideas	Page 27
Freewriting	Writing for a few minutes about whatever comes to mind	Page 28
Brainstorming	Listing all ideas as quickly as you think of them	Page 29
Clustering	Brainstorming ideas and using circles and lines to show connections	Page 31
Asking Questions	Asking the *5W–How?* and "What if?" questions	Page 33
Reading and Listening with a Focus	Reading and listening to find specific information	Page 35

In the following pages, you will experiment with different prewriting techniques. Some will probably feel more comfortable and work better for you than others. And often you'll use more than one prewriting technique at a time. For example, you might browse through your writer's journal and decide to write about being in an emergency room after breaking your wrist. Then you might brainstorm to recall specific details about this experience.

MOTIVATION

Ask each student to list ten writing topics. Many students won't have enough ideas. Explain that coming up with good ideas is sometimes difficult, but that this lesson will show students new methods to discover topics.

TEACHING THE LESSON

After students read the introduction and journal section independently, point out that some journal entries may be fairly polished, while others may be scribblings that can be worked on later. Encourage flexibility in students' entries. Some students might be familiar only with journals that record the day's events in a fairly formal style, and this

Prewriting **27**

Writer's Journal

In your *writer's journal* you'll write about things that happen and things that interest you. Journal entries can be very short or go on for several pages. You can include "Things I Like"—a special section of quotations, articles, and cartoons. Soon your journal will become a good sourcebook for writing ideas.

- For your writer's journal, use a special notebook or folder. Set aside a time to write every day.
- Forget about grammar, spelling, and punctuation at this stage. Just get your thoughts down on paper.
- Encourage your imagination. Write about dreams and daydreams. Try creating songs, poems, or stories. If you enjoy drawing, include pictures and cartoons.

HERE'S HOW

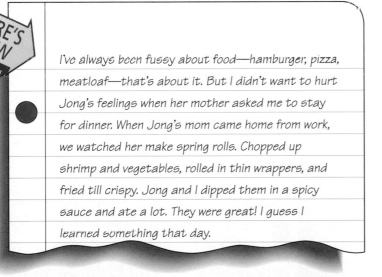

I've always been fussy about food—hamburger, pizza, meatloaf—that's about it. But I didn't want to hurt Jong's feelings when her mother asked me to stay for dinner. When Jong's mom came home from work, we watched her make spring rolls. Chopped up shrimp and vegetables, rolled in thin wrappers, and fried till crispy. Jong and I dipped them in a spicy sauce and ate a lot. They were great! I guess I learned something that day.

MEETING INDIVIDUAL NEEDS

LEP/ESL

General Strategies. For LEP students, a writer's journal may prove to be an effective tool for developing creative expression because it does not demand the student be overly anxious about correct grammar. Additionally, writers' journals may serve to reinforce students' self-worth. Encourage students to draw upon their backgrounds and stress that they do have something valuable to say. Suggest that they begin by copying fragments of favorite songs, poems, quotations, or stories.

ADVANCED STUDENTS

You may wish to encourage advanced students to try each of the six prewriting techniques for two purposes so the students can better grasp the scope of what the techniques can do for them.

All six techniques do double duty: They can be used to generate ideas for writing and to gather information. Different techniques work better for different writing situations, and students should learn to use each strategy effectively.

idea of what a journal should be could inhibit students' expressiveness when they are completing **Exercise 1**.

After students read **Freewriting** independently, have them discuss how freewriting differs from the journal writing they've already done. Then point out that freewriting can be done in their journals, as it will be in **Exercise 2**.

You may wish to model freewriting on an overhead projector by using a student-supplied subject to give the class a sense of how to generate freewriting. Then have students complete **Exercise 1** independently.

Because **Brainstorming** focuses on cooperative learning, you may want to divide the class into groups of four before they even read the section. Have groups read

ANSWERS
Exercise 1

Entries will vary. As the chapter indicates, length will also vary. Remember, students are not to be concerned about grammar, spelling, and punctuation. Instead, evaluate students on fluency—getting their thoughts down on paper.

LEARNING STYLES

Auditory Learners. Students might benefit from freetalking in addition to freewriting. Allow students to record their ideas on audio tapes. Have them use the same directions, but students should keep talking, rather than writing, if they get stuck. Model the process first, and then show students how to use a tape recorder, how to protect their tapes when they're finished, and how to play their ideas back to transcribe.

E X E R C I S E 1 ▶   **Keeping a Writer's Journal**

Ten years from now, what will you remember about your life? Your ideas, feelings, and experiences are worth recording. Write a journal entry that you can share with your classmates. Write about something important that happened yesterday or something you're looking forward to.

Freewriting

Freewriting is writing down whatever ideas pop into your head about a subject. Set a time limit of three to five minutes, and go!

- Write about something that's important to you.
- Write whatever your subject makes you think of or remember. Don't worry about complete sentences, spelling, or punctuation.
- If you get stuck, write anything. Don't let your pen or pencil stop, just continue writing down all your ideas. Keep writing until the time is up.

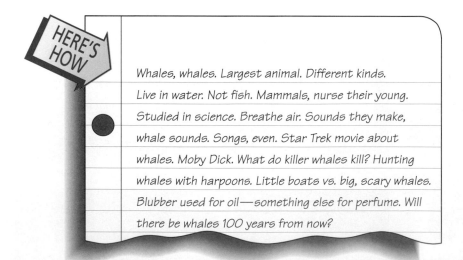

HERE'S HOW

Whales, whales. Largest animal. Different kinds.

Live in water. Not fish. Mammals, nurse their young.

Studied in science. Breathe air. Sounds they make,

whale sounds. Songs, even. Star Trek movie about

whales. Moby Dick. What do killer whales kill? Hunting

whales with harpoons. Little boats vs. big, scary whales.

Blubber used for oil—something else for perfume. Will

there be whales 100 years from now?

independently, and then you can discuss any problems they have.

For **Exercise 3,** suggest that students choose one group member to record each group's ideas. Point out that other students must respect the recorder's role and not speak too quickly. Suggest that each student keep a piece of scrap paper to record his or her own ideas in case the recorder falls behind.

This method will prevent the loss of good ideas.

If students are unfamiliar with visual organizers, they may be uncomfortable with clustering as a method of organization. If this is the case, point out that the key to making a good cluster is to find different connecting principles. For example, in the model cluster the writer has broken the language into smaller parts (dialects), shown where the ☞

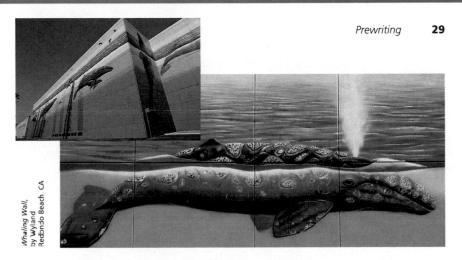

Whaling Wall,
by Wyland
Redondo Beach, CA

Focused freewriting, or *looping,* helps you narrow your topic and gather details. Choose a word or phrase from freewriting you've already done. (You might choose "hunting whales," for example.) Then freewrite for several minutes on this limited topic.

EXERCISE 2 ▶ **Using Freewriting**

Where do you go to have fun? Where do you go when you want to think? Where do you feel most at home? Think of a place that's special to you. How would you describe the place and your feelings about it? Freewrite in your journal for three minutes about the place. Or freewrite about another topic that's important to you.

Brainstorming

You can *brainstorm* alone, but it's more fun with a partner or a group. Then you can bounce ideas off each other.

- Write a subject—any subject—at the top of a piece of paper or on a chalkboard.
- Write down every single thought about the subject that comes to mind. Don't stop to judge ideas. (You can do that later.)
- Keep going until you run out of ideas.

A DIFFERENT APPROACH
Some further examples might help students understand how idiosyncratic and flexible a journal can be. Show students a copy of *The Book of Lists* and suggest that they keep their own lists— books they've read, things they'd like to buy, birds they've seen, or states they've visited. They might list family records (such as family trees or genealogies); ideas for stories; or favorite jokes, puns, or riddles.

ANSWERS
Exercise 2

Responses will vary. Tell students that if they can think of nothing to write, they should write "I have nothing to say" over and over. In most cases, they'll soon start writing something other than that one sentence.

INTEGRATING THE LANGUAGE ARTS
Test-taking Link. As students move into middle school or junior high, they start having more essay questions on tests. Show students how brainstorming, as well as some of the other prewriting techniques, can be a useful first step in writing an extended answer to a test question. If you know that students will in fact have such tests, you may want to provide opportunities for them to practice using prewriting techniques in testing simulations.

language is used (bilingual information), and suggested applications (media and education). Other categories that could be added include "famous Hispanic Americans," or "American-English words with Spanish origins."

To introduce **Asking Questions** on p. 33 ask students if they've ever been scolded for asking too many questions. After a brief discussion, tell them that this is their chance to ask as many questions as they want.

Point out that, like other types of writing, questions can fit different aims. They can have an expressive aim (Why did this have to happen to me?), an informative aim (What is the diameter of Pluto?), a persuasive aim (Don't you want to have hair that is clean and manageable with less fuss?), or a cre-

---

![icon] **CRITICAL THINKING**
Categorizing

Knowing something about standard categories and how they are used to analyze a subject by parts can prove useful for most students. Students need to recognize that not every category will work for every subject and that more than one category may work for some subjects.

Some categories to use as the basis of analysis are time periods; examples; people, places, and things associated with the subject; features of the subject; applications or uses of the subject; causes of the subject; effects of the subject; and types of the subject. Model each category that you want to present and encourage students to use this knowledge in conjunction with brainstorming and clustering.

ANSWERS
Exercise 3

Responses will vary. The trick here is to treat all responses equally, no matter how silly or seemingly unrelated they are. Everything should be listed in the order in which it is said. Members of a group are to make no judgments of the responses of other members.

Here are some brainstorming notes on the subject "shopping mall." Notice that the list includes some silly ideas that will be thrown out later.

Shopping Mall	
place to meet friends	non-shopping mall, don't
spend most of Saturday there	shop much
people watching, make up	walk around—talk
stories	record stores, video games
shopping mall on Mars?	some adults grouchy with us
underwater shopping mall?	everyone who's anyone
saw a movie star at the mall	great food—yogurt bar,
	potato bar

EXERCISE 3   **Using Brainstorming**

Brainstorming is more fun in a group. Team up with two or three classmates for a brainstorming session on one of the following subjects or on one of your own. Brainstorm as long a list of ideas as you can.

1. UFOs
2. fears
3. rock groups
4. video games
5. community problems
6. heroes

ative aim (What if there really were a man in the moon?). In this section they will focus on questions with informative and creative aims.

As you teach the *5W-How? Questions* on p. 33, you may want to provide students with some appropriate lead paragraphs of newspaper stories to illustrate how the questions correspond with the actual writing.

As you encourage students to think creatively, suggest that they use dreams and daydreams as sources of "What if?" questions.

Students who do not follow rock music can be given an alternative topic for **Exercise 5**. For **Exercise 6** students will need extra guidance.

Cont. on p. 33

Clustering

Clustering is sometimes called *webbing* or may be called *making connections.* When you make a cluster diagram, you break a topic into its smaller parts.

- Write your subject in the center of your paper and circle it.
- Around the subject, write related ideas as you think of them. Circle these ideas, and draw lines to connect them with the subject.
- An idea may make you think of other ideas. Connect these with circles and lines, too.

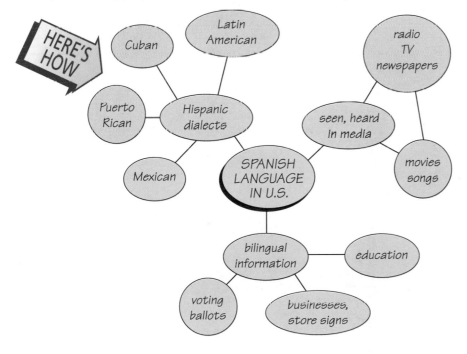

EXERCISE 4 ▶ **Using Clustering**

Make a cluster diagram for a subject you didn't use from Exercise 3 (page 30), or pick a subject of your own. Use circles and lines to show how ideas are connected.

MEETING INDIVIDUAL NEEDS

LESS-ADVANCED STUDENTS

Because clustering requires higher-level thinking skills to organize the ideas generated, it is more complicated than brainstorming. To make clustering easier, begin by putting a copy of the cluster diagram from the textbook on an overhead transparency. Make each category from the **Critical Thinking** feature in a different color to show how the cluster works. Give students a chance to add new categories and connections to the diagram. As students suggest additions, discuss the new categories and relationships in the diagram. If students are still having trouble with the concept of clustering, have them work in groups to complete **Exercise 4**.

ANSWERS
Exercise 4

Responses will vary. Many students find clustering more useful than outlining. Clustering involves a step beyond freewriting and brainstorming: It involves both generating and organizing material to show relationships.

OBSERVING WITH YOUR FIVE SENSES OBJECTIVES

- To use the five senses to observe details
- To record sensory details categorized by the sense used

TEACHING *OBSERVING WITH YOUR FIVE SENSES*

For students who have difficulty, you may want to suggest focusing on one sense at a time. Students who are uncomfortable with the supercomputer scenario in the exercise might have an easier time if they observe from their own perspectives. The students need to be given ample time to make the observations.

LEP/ESL

General Strategies. If possible, group students in pairs prior to introducing the **Critical Thinking Exercise** and provide them with a bilingual dictionary. Give groups two study sheets, one with the sample grouping of sensory details from the **Here's How** in random order and a second study sheet with the headings *Sight, Sound, Smell, Taste,* and *Touch* listed vertically on the page. Ask students to look up the meanings of any words they don't understand and to group the expressions under the appropriate headings. This activity will prepare students to enter more actively into a class discussion of the material.

 CRITICAL THINKING

Observing with Your Five Senses

While you're awake, you receive steady input from each of your five senses (sight, sound, smell, taste, touch). Most of the time you ignore these *sensory details.* But as a writer you need to *observe* the world around you with all five senses alert and ready to receive information.

Here are a writer's notes on a Cuban American New Year's Eve celebration.

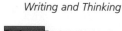

SIGHT:	dark night; brightly lit house; about thirty family members and friends; children playing; men tending the backyard barbecue
SOUND:	record player; singing; people talking, telling jokes, laughter; children's shouts; TV in living room
SMELL:	slow-roasting pig; spicy smells; freshly ground coffee
TASTE:	crisp barbecued pork; black beans and rice; yucca; fried plantains; guava pastries; bitter orange
TOUCH:	warm night; breezes through open windows; embroidered tablecloth; paper plates and plastic forks and knives

Cont. from p. 31

Although the textbook presents reading and listening with a focus primarily as ways to gather information, students should not neglect reading and listening as ways to get ideas. Information-gathering skills will become increasingly important to students as they write compositions to inform and persuade. For this reason, you may wish to introduce **Reference Notes** on p. 36 now and review this material again just before you assign an informative or persuasive composition. Students should complete **Exercise 7** independently.

Students might have trouble grasping that the forms of writing suggested in the **Purposes and Forms** chart on p. 37 are not the only forms for the purpose listed and that

 CRITICAL THINKING EXERCISE:
Observing Sensory Details

Imagine yourself as a supercomputer designed to record every sensory detail. You're collecting details for a description that will go into a time capsule to be opened in the year 3000. Collect details for all five senses as you observe one of the following.

1. a basketball or football game
2. a pizza parlor or other restaurant
3. the school cafeteria
4. a dance
5. a birthday party
6. a city street or highway

Asking Questions

Practice asking yourself two different kinds of questions. One kind helps you find facts. The other kind exercises your imagination.

5W-How? Questions. News reporters track down information by asking the ***5W-How? questions:*** *Who? What? Where? When? Why?* and *How?* For some topics, some question words won't apply. And with other topics, you may think of several good questions for a question word.

ANSWERS
Critical Thinking Exercise

Responses will vary, but each student should make observations of a real event and record details for all five senses. You may wish to instruct students to group their observations according to the senses they used to obtain them, as in the **Here's How** model.

A DIFFERENT APPROACH

Your students will probably need to use brainstorming to complete the **Critical Thinking Exercise.** Besides the guidelines they have already been given, you may want to give your students these hints:

1. Brainstorm in a group.
2. Make your goal quantity.
3. Try to build off others' ideas.
4. Try using a tape recorder so you don't have to give attention to writing.
5. Wait for a period of time after the brainstorming session to evaluate your ideas.

those forms may fit other purposes as well. Make sure students understand that expressive writing, for example, is not limited to journal entries, letters, and personal essays, nor are journal entries, letters, and personal essays necessarily expressive. Sharing concrete examples of a variety of expressive forms and a variety of letters fitting all four aims would help students see this point.

While students might sometimes find it useful to judge how formally or informally to write by how they would speak to their audiences, it is important to emphasize the differences between oral and written language. Each has its own conventions and contexts, and students should not take the comparison too far. On the other hand, reading one's own writing aloud can be an

Here are some questions one writer asked when preparing to write a school newspaper article about new automobile designs.

MEETING INDIVIDUAL NEEDS

ADVANCED STUDENTS

Students who can work comfortably with the *5W-How?* and *What if?* questions might be ready to expand into new areas. You could give the following additional question words to help students gather even more information about their topics:

If, then . . .?
Which . . .?
Has . . .?
Is (Isn't) . . .?
Won't . . .?
Does (Doesn't) . . .?
Will . . .?

You may wish to have students identify situations in which these different kinds of questions (present, future, negative) are most useful.

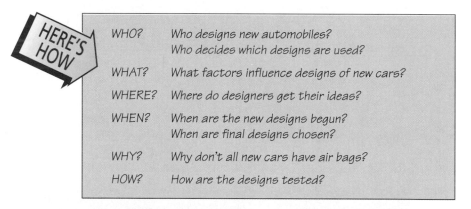

HERE'S HOW

WHO?	Who designs new automobiles? Who decides which designs are used?
WHAT?	What factors influence designs of new cars?
WHERE?	Where do designers get their ideas?
WHEN?	When are the new designs begun? When are final designs chosen?
WHY?	Why don't all new cars have air bags?
HOW?	How are the designs tested?

"What if?" Questions. What if you could become invisible? What if you could fly? *"What if?" questions* will help you find ideas for creative writing. The following are some "What if?" questions you might ask to spark your imagination.

excellent check on whether it sounds too stuffy, too informal, or too scattered. Encourage students to use reading aloud as a technique to help them complete **Exercise 8.**

Students might never have given much thought to different possibilities of organization. For this reason, read the **Arranging Ideas** section on p. 39 to the class and define vocabulary that may be diffi-cult (chronological, narrative poem, biography, explanation, persuasive, spatial, description, definition, importance, logical, related, and classification); finally, supplement the material with examples.

Explain that *visual* means "having to do with sight." A visual aid helps the writer see the relationships between ideas. Tell students that clustering, which they've already

- *What if I could change one thing in my life?* (What if I were a genius? What if I lived on a ranch?)
- *What if some common thing did not exist?* (What if there were no telephones? What if Earth had no water?)
- *What if one situation in the world could be changed?* (What if everyone lived forever? What if everyone spoke the same language?)

EXERCISE 5 ▶ Asking the *5W-How?* Questions

As a reporter for your local newspaper, you have been assigned to write an article about a popular music group that's coming to town. Choose a real group, and make a list of *5W-How?* questions that you'd like to ask the musicians.

EXERCISE 6 ▶ Asking "What if?" Questions

You and a partner are planning a short story for your class magazine. Brainstorm as many "What if?" questions as you can. (This is the way movie producers get their ideas: What if a family went on a vacation and left their son home alone?) Then write a brief plot outline for your story.

EXAMPLES   What if the person on TV could hear what you say?
What if two of your classmates were actually aliens from another planet?

Reading and Listening with a Focus

Suppose you're writing about what America was like before Columbus arrived in the New World. How can you find out? For a topic you can't observe directly, find information by reading and listening with a focus—with something specific in mind.

ANSWERS
Exercise 5

Answers may vary. Here are some possibilities:

Who? — Who listens to this group?
What? — What particular songs will they perform here?
Where? — Where is the group from?
When? — When did the group begin playing?
Why? — Why is the group popular?
How? — How did the group get started?

ANSWERS
Exercise 6

Responses will vary. Remember that recent book and movie plots have shown that "What if?" questions can include fantasy and science fiction. Encourage students to make their plot outlines brief. At this point, do not allow students to go into detail.

EXERCISE 6

Teaching Note. Students will need additional guidance about what to include in a plot outline. You may want to give them a chart such as the following one:

Beginning: main characters' names, situation (where are they and what is happening? what do they want or what problem do they have?)

Middle: (what happens?)

End: (how is the problem resolved?)

done, is a kind of visual aid because it organizes information in a visual way to show how ideas are related to each other.

In the **Using Visual Aids to Organize Ideas** section on p. 41 students will learn how to create two kinds of visual aids: charts and sequence chains. Before students independently work through **Exercises 9** and **10,** show them that sequence chains can also be drawn vertically to look like flow charts.

INTEGRATING THE LANGUAGE ARTS

Technology Link. Another source that students might find useful, but which has its own rules for finding specific information, is databases. Because these are being used more and more in classrooms, some guidelines are given here for finding specific information in them.

1. Keep a piece of paper and a pencil with you while you search. Copy the name of the database and the categories or types of categories that were used to construct it.
2. Scan the categories horizontally and the records vertically to see how the database is built.

ANSWERS
Exercise 7

Responses will vary. Students are likely to find the programs on public broadcasting stations or, if they get cable, on Arts & Entertainment or the Discovery Channel. If they do not have television sets, students can probably view nature programs in their public library.

Reading.   Reading sources include such items as books, magazines, newspapers, and pamphlets. Here are some techniques you can use to find specific information.

- Check a book's table of contents and index. Go directly to the pages on your topic.
- Don't read everything. Skim the text quickly. Look only for information on your topic. Don't forget to check photos and captions, too.
- When you find information on your topic, read carefully. Take notes on main ideas and important details.

☞ REFERENCE NOTE: For more information on reading, see page 846 and pages 848–853.

Listening.   Some people learn better by listening than by reading. You can gather information on a specific topic by listening to speeches, interviews, radio and TV programs, audiotapes, and videotapes. You can use the following techniques whenever you listen for information.

- Get ready ahead of time by thinking of questions on your topic.
- Listen for main ideas and important details. Take notes to help you remember.

☞ REFERENCE NOTE: For more information on listening, see pages 808–813.

EXERCISE 7 ▶   **Practicing Reading and Listening**

Look through a TV program listing for this week (most newspapers publish a daily guide) and make a list of all the programs you can find about nature. (Nature programs include such areas as plants, animals, weather, astronomy, earth sciences, oceanography, and geology.) Choose one program on your list, and watch it. Jot down at least five facts you learned from watching the program.

To review this section, begin by asking each student to identify his or her favorite prewriting technique and explain why he or she likes it. Then have the class look at **Chapters 4–10** in the **Table of Contents** of their textbooks. Have volunteers tell which prewriting techniques they think would be most useful for each chapter and have them explain their choices.

 *Prewriting*

Thinking About Purpose and Audience

Purpose.   Before you write, always ask yourself, *"Why am I writing?"* This chart shows the basic *purposes* for writing and some forms you might use for each purpose.

MAIN PURPOSE	FORMS OF WRITING
To express your feelings	Journal entry, letter, personal essay
To explain or inform	Science or history report, news story, biography, autobiography, travel essay
To persuade	Persuasive essay, letter to the editor, advertisement, political speech
To be creative	Short story, poem, play

Audience.   You also need to identify your *audience,* or readers. Think about how you'll adapt your writing to a specific audience. Ask yourself these questions:

- What do my readers already know about my topic?
- What will I need to explain? What will they find most interesting?
- What kinds of words and sentences (simple or more difficult and complex) should I use?

Perhaps your hobby is collecting arrowheads. If you're writing a letter to a relative in Juneau, Alaska, your cousin may have no idea what arrowheads are. You'll need to explain what they look like, how they're made, and where they're found. You'll probably use the kind of vocabulary

To help students better understand purpose, you can play a guessing game in which students are given a developing writing situation, and then they identify the purpose(s) involved. Explain the following two situations:

1. An angry consumer is unhappy with a purchase and is writing to the company to complain. (This situation may combine expressive, informative, and persuasive purposes, depending on how it is viewed.)
2. A novelist riding a bus has a brilliant idea and doesn't want to forget it. (This situation may combine creative and informative purposes.)

As students discuss each scenario, ask them to identify how they knew which purposes were present. Afterwards, you may wish to allow students to present scenarios so their classmates can guess the purposes.

EXTENSION

Have students come up with ideas of how they can use freewriting, brainstorming, or visualizing for purposes other than generating ideas for writing.

ENRICHMENT

You could have students write letters to favorite authors to ask them how they think of ideas for writing. When the answers come in, they can serve as the bases for articles for the school newspaper or for a booklet that can be shared with other classes. Authors can usually be reached through their publishers. ■

ANSWERS
Exercise 8

1 and **2** belong in the report; **3** (unrelated to topic, purely personal), **4** (about Italian, not Hawaiian volcano), and **5** (knowledge classmates probably would already have, not specifically about Hawaiian volcanoes) do not belong in the report.

COOPERATIVE LEARNING

Have the class work in pairs to expand **Exercise 8**. First, groups should complete **Exercise 8** as described. Second, groups should consider each omitted statement and work together to identify a writing context in which the sentence would be appropriate. Finally, they should rewrite the sentence so that it fits the context given in the exercise.

---

38   *Writing and Thinking*

and language that you would use if you were speaking directly to your cousin.

But suppose you're writing a report on arrowheads for your history class. You may still need to supply some background information, but your report will sound more formal than the language you use when writing a letter to someone you know well.

EXERCISE 8 ▶ **Thinking About Purpose and Audience**

You're writing a science report about active volcanoes in Hawaii. Your purpose is to inform, and your readers are your classmates. Which of these statements belong in your report? Which ones don't?

1. Two active volcanoes in Hawaii Volcanoes National Park are Mauna Loa and Kilauea.
2. The town of Volcano, Hawaii, where many scientists live, is built right next to an active volcano.
3. I'm really afraid to even think about volcanoes ever since I saw a late-night movie about a killer volcano.
4. Mount Vesuvius in Italy is a steep-sided, symmetrical cinder cone volcano.
5. When volcanoes erupt, they can cause a lot of damage.

 *Prewriting*

Arranging Ideas

How you present your ideas is just as important as what you have to say. So after you find a topic and gather information about it, you need to plan the order of ideas. This chart shows four common ways of ordering, or arranging, information.

WAYS TO ORGANIZE IDEAS		
TYPE OF ORDER	**DEFINITION**	**EXAMPLES**
Chronological	Describe events in the order they happen.	Story, narrative poem, explanation of a process, history, biography, play
Spatial	Describe objects according to location (near to far, left to right, and so on).	Description, directions, explanation
Importance	Give details from least to most important or the reverse.	Persuasive writing, description, explanation, evaluative writing
Logical	Group related details together.	Definition, classification

 REFERENCE NOTE: For more information on arranging ideas, see pages 74–75.

LOOK, MOM, I PUT ALL MY CLOTHES FOR TOMORROW ON THE STAIRS.

THEN IN THE MORNING, I'LL RUN OUT IN MY UNDERWEAR AND SLIDE DOWN AT TOP SPEED!

IF I AIM GOOD, I GO RIGHT INTO MY PANTS WHILE I'M PUTTING ON MY SHIRT, AND BY THE BOTTOM, I'M ALL DRESSED FOR SCHOOL!

AND IF YOU PUT MY CEREAL ON THE STAIRS TOO, I WON'T HAVE TO GET UP UNTIL 30 SECONDS BEFORE THE BUS COMES.

FORGET IT, CALVIN.

 **MEETING INDIVIDUAL NEEDS**

LESS-ADVANCED STUDENTS

Students might be overwhelmed by the vocabulary in the **Ways to Organize Ideas** chart. You may want to provide a simplified version, such as the one below:

Type of Order	**Definition**
Time Order (Chronological)	tells what happened first, next, and last
Location (Spatial)	groups descriptions or organizes directions
Importance	works from least to most important or vice versa
Logical	places the subject in the appropriate class and provides details showing how the term is alike or different from others in the same class

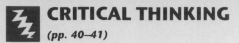
OBJECTIVE

- To create and order details for specific writing situations

TEACHING *ARRANGING IDEAS*

Tell students that it is not unusual for a piece of writing to move back and forth between two or more organizing principles. Sometimes, works must be analyzed by paragraph, as well as by overall structure, to discover how they are organized. The short story "Rikki-tikki-tavi" is a good example.

MEETING INDIVIDUAL NEEDS

LEP/ESL

General Strategies. Students might not be able to conceptualize the chronological sequence in this exercise because some of the vocabulary in the Kipling excerpt may be problematic. To help students, write the following verbs on the chalkboard: *bounding, gathered, flung out, struck, came, danced, to get behind.* Discuss these actions so that students can visualize what is happening.

INTEGRATING THE LANGUAGE ARTS

Literature Link. Have students read and discuss Kipling's short story "Rikki-tikki-tavi." Explain that Kipling uses several types of ordering to further his story. Copy the second and fifth paragraphs of the short story on the chalkboard, and ask students to identify the order used in each. [The second paragraph is an example of spatial order, and the fifth uses order of importance.] Discuss how a single piece of writing can incorporate multiple organizations.

SELECTION AMENDMENT

Description of change: excerpted
Rationale: to focus on the concept of chronological order presented in this chapter

---

CRITICAL THINKING
Arranging Ideas

Your topic, purpose, and details will give you a clue about which order to use. For example, you're writing a description of Skylab, the U.S. space station launched in 1973. Your purpose is to inform; your audience is your classmates. You've collected information about each room. So you decide to use spatial order, moving from one end of the space station to the other end.

In the following story of a mongoose fighting a cobra named Nagaina, a natural order is chronological. What happens first? What happens last?

> Rikki-tikki was bounding all round Nagaina, keeping just out of reach of her stroke, his little eyes like hot coals. Nagaina gathered herself together, and flung out at him. Rikki-tikki jumped up and backward. Again and again and again she struck, and each time her head came with a whack on the matting of the veranda and she gathered herself together like a watch spring. Then Rikki-tikki danced in a circle to get behind her, and Nagaina spun around to keep her head to his head, so that the rustle of her tail on the matting sounded like dry leaves blown along by the wind.
>
> Rudyard Kipling, "Rikki-tikki-tavi"

The exercise is fairly straightforward, but many writing situations require much more complex decision making than is presented here.

CRITICAL THINKING EXERCISE:
Choosing an Order for Ideas

For each of the following writing situations, think about the kinds of details you would use. Then choose an appropriate order for those details. Look at the chart on page 39, Ways to Organize Ideas, for a description of each of the types of order.

1. In a letter to a pen pal, you describe what your room looks like.
2. You are writing a letter to the editor of the local newspaper. To persuade readers to approve a new park tax, you give three reasons why your town needs more parks.
3. You enjoy creative writing. For your little sister's birthday present, you plan to write an adventure story about dragons.
4. For an English assignment, you are going to review a new book that you have just read, telling whether you think it's worth recommending to your classmates.

Using Visuals to Organize Ideas

Visuals—such as charts, graphs, maps, sequence chains, time lines, drawings, or diagrams—can turn messy, disorganized prewriting notes into neat packages of ideas and details. Charts and sequence chains can help you organize your ideas.

Charts.   Think about the details you have gathered, and look for ways to group ideas. Then decide on the headings that will cover most of your information. Write your details under those headings. In the following chart, for example, one writer gives three types of information about the Ojibwas and the Seminoles.

INTEGRATING THE LANGUAGE ARTS

Literature Link. The autobiographical excerpt from *Sound-Shadows of the New World* by Ved Mehta provides examples of the four organizations. Have students read the selection to discuss the overall organization [chronological]. Then draw their attention to the paragraphs noted below, and have them identify the organization of each. Discuss how the writer of a narrative may incorporate several types of organizations to further the purpose.

1. the paragraph about the gymnasium [logical]
2. the paragraph in which Miss Harper talks about obstacles [importance]
3. the paragraph in which Mehta goes through the obstacle course [chronological]
4. the paragraph that starts with Mehta at the trolley stop [spatial]

VISUAL CONNECTIONS

Exploring the Subject. The Ojibwas, also called the Chippewa (as distinguished from the Chippewayan from western Canada), were natives of eastern Canada and lived along the northern border of Lake Superior.

The Seminoles were Creeks who settled in Florida. The name means "runaways," perhaps to designate their break from the main group.

HERE'S HOW

	OJIBWAS 1600s	SEMINOLES 1700s
WHERE THEY LIVED	Around the Great Lakes	Florida
KIND OF HOUSE	Wigwam	Open-sided houses on stilts
SOURCES OF FOOD	Hunted, fished, farmed, and gathered wild plants	Hunted, fished, and farmed

Sequence Chains. A *sequence chain* organizes events in chronological order. You can use a sequence chain to show the main events in a story or the steps in a process. The following is a sequence chain for a short story.

HERE'S HOW

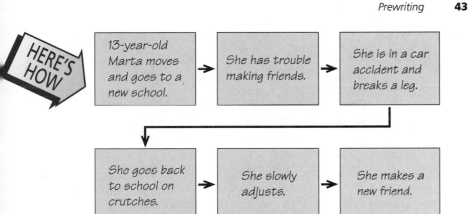

EXERCISE 9 ▶ **Making a Chart**

How can you show a comparison of two countries? Make a chart to organize the following notes about the United States and China. What headings will you use?

> The United States has a total area of 3,600,000 square miles.
> It has over 250,000,000 people.
> Its form of government is a democracy.
> China has a population of over 1,100,000,000 people.
> It is governed by a communist regime.
> It has a total area of over 3,690,000 square miles.

EXERCISE 10 ▶ **Making a Sequence Chain**

Create a sequence chain for one of these assignments. (Do one or the other, not both.)

1. Show the main events in a story. You can create a plot for a short story, or show the events in a story that you have read or in a movie or TV show that you have seen.
2. Show the stages in the writing process. Use the information in the pie-shaped diagram on page 25.

ANSWERS
Exercise 9

	U. S.	China
area (sq. mi.)	3,600,000	3,690,000
population	over 250 million	over 1.1 billion
government	democracy	communist regime

ANSWERS
Exercise 10

Responses will vary. Here is a possibility for number 2:

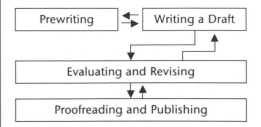

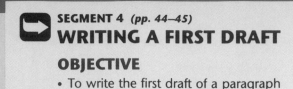

OBJECTIVE

- To write the first draft of a paragraph

TEACHING THE LESSON

Have students read the introductory material and the **Writing Note.** Then discuss how writing is a very personal matter—people have different styles and unique ways of enacting the writing process. Explain that part of what students will be doing in this textbook is working on discovering their own writing processes and voices.

Writing a First Draft

Once you've completed the final step in prewriting—planning the organization of your ideas—you'll be ready to put your ideas down on paper. Each person has a slightly different way of drafting a paper. Some people write quickly, going with the flow of their ideas. Others draft slowly, carefully thinking about each sentence and paragraph that they write. Trust your own style, and do whatever works best for you.

- Use your prewriting plans to guide you as you write your first draft.
- As you write, you may come up with new ideas. Include these ideas in your draft.
- Don't worry about spelling and grammar errors. You can correct them later.

WRITING NOTE

In writing, *voice* is the way the words sound. As you put your ideas into sentences and paragraphs, try to express your ideas simply and naturally. Don't use words just because they sound "important." Your writing should have your own voice—and sound like you.

On page 45 is the first draft of a paragraph about Mary McLeod Bethune, an African American educator from South Carolina who lived from 1875 to 1955. Notice the writer's questions that appear in brackets. These show that the writer will later return to the prewriting stage to find more information before writing the final draft. Notice, also, that the writing in this draft does not sound as polished as the final draft will. In this first draft there are problems with both content and organization that the writer will fix later.

QUOTATION FOR THE DAY

"When once the itch of literature comes over a man, nothing can cure it but the scratching of a pen." (Samuel Lover, 1797–1868, Irish novelist, painter, and musician)

Students might discuss the quotation and create a sentence telling what the quotation says about writing. Ask students to give examples of times that they felt a need to share their thoughts or feelings.

MEETING

INDIVIDUAL

NEEDS

LEP/ESL

General Strategies. Give students the option of writing about some skill they do not have, one that seems very important to them. Have them imagine how their lives would be different if they could get the requisite instruction, guidance, and practice to master this skill. The more personally meaningful the subject matter, the more successful the writing task is likely to be for students.

Have a volunteer read the **Here's How** paragraph aloud. Ask how the writer of the model has used the writing process to write a first draft [included notes; didn't worry about flow or transitions; concentrated on ideas instead of correctness]. Model for students how you would start a paragraph about not being able to read, and ask the class for suggestions as you compose. Have students complete **Exercise 11** independently.

For closure, have students discuss the question "What is a first draft?" ■

Mary McLeod Bethune was the first in her family to go to school. She started when she was eleven. [Twelve? Check this.] The school was a mission school for black children. [Where? Go back for details.] Mary was a fast learner. She had to walk a long way to and from school. Mary's family sacrificed to let her attend school. When she was in school, she couldn't help with all the chores on the family farm. Mary liked to plow. When she started her third year, she helped the teacher. She also began teaching her brothers and sisters at home to read. Mary was good at math. She helped people with their accounts so the big planters couldn't cheat them.

 VISUAL CONNECTIONS
Exploring the Subject. Mary McLeod Bethune (1875–1955) is known as a leader in improving educational opportunities for African Americans. The school she started for girls in 1904 in Daytona Beach, Florida, merged in 1923 with a college to become Bethune-Cookman College. Serving in that capacity until 1942, Bethune was its first president.

EXERCISE 11▶ **Writing a First Draft**

Many children and adults in the world today don't know how to read any language. Imagine that you were never taught to read. What would you miss? How would it change your life? Get ready to write a draft of a paragraph telling how you'd feel if you couldn't read. Use one or more of the prewriting techniques on pages 26–36 to explore your thoughts on this topic. Arrange your ideas in a way that makes sense. For this topic, logical order or order of importance might work well. Draft your paragraph and share it with your classmates.

ANSWERS
Exercise 11

Drafts will vary. Drafts should address the topic and show evidence that prewriting has been employed. Ignore errors in grammar, punctuation, spelling, and usage. Instead of grades, you might want to supply process suggestions. For example: This draft could have been better if you'd done some organizing during prewriting.

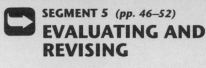

EVALUATING AND REVISING

OBJECTIVE

- To evaluate and revise the first draft of a paragraph

TEACHING THE LESSON

Tell students that there are times—when they are taking a test, for example—when there may not be time for evaluating and revising. Usually, though, this stage is a chance to broaden the focus of their writing to include questions of form, as well as of content. When students reach this stage,

Cont. on p. 48

RESOURCES

EVALUATING AND REVISING
- Practicing Peer Evaluation
- Revising: Adding and Cutting
- Revising: Replacing and Reordering

QUOTATION FOR THE DAY

"Great critics, of whom there are piteously few, build a home for the truth." (Raymond Chandler, 1888–1959, American novelist)

Share the quotation with students and lead them to understand that evaluation and revision are sometimes difficult processes because they involve being honest with oneself and one's peers about the quality of a piece of writing.

MEETING INDIVIDUAL NEEDS

LEP/ESL

General Strategies. At this critical stage of the writing process, you may want to spend a short amount of time with each of your ESL students to emphasize the positive aspects of his or her draft. Most students want and need to know if they are headed in the right direction; however, they may feel too shy to ask for guidance.

Evaluating and Revising

You can't fix a TV set—or anything else—until you figure out what's wrong with it. In the same way, after you've finished your first draft and are looking over what you've written, you'll need to figure out what parts aren't working so that you can fix them. *Evaluating* and *revising* are really two separate steps in the writing process, but most people do them together.

Evaluating

When you *evaluate* your writing, you judge what's good about it and what needs to be improved. You evaluate writing more often than you realize. Each time you decide whether you like a book or magazine, you're evaluating.

Self-Evaluation. It's often harder to judge your own writing than someone else's. Use these tips to evaluate your own writing.

- Put your draft aside for awhile. Rest your brain.
- Read your paper carefully at least three times. Each time focus on something different. For example, you might ask yourself questions like these:
    Are the ideas clear?
    Are the ideas in the most effective order?
    Are sentences well worded and smoothly connected to each other?
- Read your paper aloud to yourself. Listen for awkward or unclear spots.

Peer Evaluation. You can get some feedback on your writing from a partner or several classmates. (A peer is someone who is your equal—in this case, your classmate.) When you use peer evaluation, get ready to play two roles: (1) a writer whose work is being evaluated, and (2) a reader who is evaluating a classmate's writing.

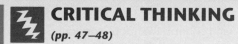
EVALUATING WRITING OBJECTIVE

• To evaluate a paragraph

TEACHING *EVALUATING WRITING*

This feature provides students with four criteria to help them evaluate writing. To help students complete the **Critical Thinking Exercise**, you should go over the more detailed list of criteria in the **Revision Techniques** chart on p. 49.

GUIDELINES FOR PEER EVALUATION

Tips for the Writer

1. Make a list of questions for the reader. Ask what the reader thinks about parts of your paper you're not sure about.
2. Keep an open mind. Take all of the comments that your reader makes seriously, and don't be offended by any criticism. Even professional writers get suggestions for improvement from their editors.

Tips for the Reader

1. Always tell the writer something good about the paper.
2. Focus on content and organization. Don't point out spelling and grammar errors.
3. Put your suggestions into helpful questions: "Can you say this in easier words?" or "Can you add some specific details?"
4. Suggest something specific the writer can do to improve the paper.

MEETING INDIVIDUAL NEEDS

LEP/ESL

Spanish. It is important to note that the strategy of having students work in small groups reinforces the value that some Spanish-speaking cultures — for example the Mexican-American culture — places on collective, cooperative efforts rather than on individual, competitive ones. In assigning the **Critical Thinking Exercise**, you may want to pair students, encourage them to compare their ideas about the paragraph, and have them complete the evaluation as a team.

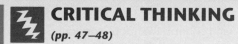 CRITICAL THINKING

Evaluating Writing

Whenever you evaluate, you judge something by measuring it against established standards. Here are some basic standards for judging good writing. (See page 51 for a more detailed list of standards.)

1. The writing is interesting. It grabs and holds your attention.
2. The writing has a clear main idea.
3. The main idea is supported with enough details.
4. The ideas are presented in a clear and reasonable order.

Because this exercise is complex, you may want to allow students to work in groups.

Cont. from p. 46

they will probably be more confident about what they want to say and have a clearer idea of how they are going to say it.

Have student volunteers read **Evaluating and Revising.** Point out that the benefits of self-evaluation are different from those of peer evaluation. Ask students why both kinds of evaluation are valuable.

ANSWERS
Critical Thinking Exercise

Responses will vary. You may wish to require a minimum of four statements. Following are examples of statements students might make:

1. The writing is interesting.
2. The organization needs work.
3. The voice in the next to the last sentence is inappropriate to the purpose and audience.
4. The first sentence has too much information for a lead.

CRITICAL THINKING EXERCISE:
Evaluating a Paragraph

If you think octopuses are scary, wait till you meet the giant squid. With one or two classmates, evaluate the following paragraph. Use the standards for good writing given on page 47. Write at least one comment on what's good about the paragraph. Then write at least one comment on what needs to be improved.

A strange sea creature that people rarely see because it lives in deep waters is the giant squid. Giant squids can grow up to sixty feet long. There are old sea stories about giant squids attacking boats. They wrap their tentacles around them. Rows of sucking disks line the arms. The giant squid's eyes are huge, up to 15 inches wide. Boy, I wouldn't want to meet one, would you? Old sailors called giant squids sea monsters.

Students should understand that an objective opinion can be useful for assessment.

Encourage students to finish their first drafts early so they can take a break before evaluating. You may wish to reiterate that a little break lets a writer see his or her work much more clearly.

Because there are so many possible ways to change a given sentence, revision requires a great deal of decision making. Students who excel at evaluation may have a hard time revising, and students who can fix any problem once it is pointed out to them may be unable to identify problems by themselves.

To help students quickly become familiar with revision symbols, you may want to have each student make a personal

Revising

When you *revise,* you make changes to improve your writing. You can make your changes by hand or on a typewriter or word processor. Whatever you use as your writing tool, to revise your writing you'll use just four basic revision techniques: *adding, cutting, replacing,* and *reordering.* (To understand the examples, see the chart of symbols on page 55.)

REVISION TECHNIQUES

TECHNIQUE	EXAMPLE
1. **Add.** Add new information and details. Add words, sentences, or paragraphs.	The book *Lovey: A Very Special Child* is written by a [with severe emotional problems] woman who teaches children.
2. **Cut.** Take out repeated, unnecessary, or related ideas.	The children have serious problems. One of the children, Hannah, hides in a closet at first.
3. **Replace.** Replace weak or awkward wording with precise words or details.	Hannah doesn't talk to the teacher or other kids, but she acts up when she's upset. [cries and screams]
4. **Reorder.** Move information, sentences, and paragraphs for clear order.	In time, Hannah joins the class and begins to talk and learn. The teacher patiently works with Hannah.

In the following revised paragraph (you read it earlier as a first draft, page 45), the writer has used these four revision techniques. Do you think the changes improve the paragraph? How?

MEETING INDIVIDUAL NEEDS

LESS-ADVANCED STUDENTS

It might be helpful to begin with a class discussion differentiating the two terms *evaluating* and *criticizing.* If the term *evaluation* is not clearly understood, students may unwittingly sabotage each other's writing efforts, as well as their own. Create two columns on the chalkboard and ask students to give examples from daily life of each of these behaviors. The idea is to emphasize that evaluation is helpful in seeing a situation more clearly. The evaluation process involves getting new information and making intelligent decisions based on that information. Reading food labels, checking one's heart rate after exercise, reviewing a consumer report before purchasing a car or motorbike—all are examples of evaluating facts to make well-informed decisions. The connotation of *criticism,* on the other hand, especially when given in a negative manner, can cause hurt feelings and block the learning process.

reference card. They can copy the symbols and their meanings along with examples.

Work with students to evaluate the paragraph in **Exercise 12.** Then have them revise a paragraph for which an evaluation is provided. This procedure will help you assess students' understanding.

CLOSURE

Ask students if they have ever revised without evaluating. Students might suggest that sometimes writers change things without troubling about analysis. Point out that the sense of what sounds good and what doesn't is a valuable part of evaluating.

CRITICAL THINKING
Analysis

You may wish to have the class analyze the changes made in the model paragraph. Here are some notes on the changes:

1. The first changes use sentence combining to make the sentences more succinct and more specific.
2. The third change involves reorganizing material to follow chronological order.
3. The fourth change adds specific details.
4. The fifth change eliminates unnecessary material.
5. The sixth change adds necessary detail the writer knew was missing from the first draft.

VISUAL CONNECTIONS
Exploring the Subject.
Bethune-Cookman College in Daytona Beach, Florida, offers training in the liberal arts and education. Both A.B. and B.S. degrees are offered. The school is co-educational.

Mary McLeod Bethune was the first in her family to go to school. She started when she was eleven. [Twelve? Check this.] The school was a ⟨Presbyterian⟩ mission school for black children. [Where? Go back for ⟨in Mayesville, South Carolina⟩ details.] (Mary was a fast learner.) She had to walk ⟨three miles⟩ a long way to and from school. Mary's family sacrificed to let her attend school. When she was in school, she couldn't help with all the chores on the family farm. Mary liked to plow. When she started her third year, she helped the teacher. She also began teaching her brothers and sisters at home to read. Mary was good at math. She helped ⟨both black and white neighbors⟩ people with their accounts so the big planters couldn't cheat them.

cut/add
add/cut
cut/reorder
replace
cut
replace

Mary McLeod Bethune at the college she founded in 1904 in Daytona Beach, Florida.

EXTENSION

Besides body paragraphs that develop the main idea of a paper, compositions also often include function paragraphs. These paragraphs are not for development; rather, they have several other purposes. Share the following uses of function paragraphs with your students and then have them find and bring examples of function paragraphs to class:

1. to get the reader's attention
2. as a transition from one topic to another
3. to use conversation for illustrating a point
4. to break up long paragraphs
5. to emphasize a point ■

GUIDELINES FOR EVALUATING AND REVISING

EVALUATION GUIDE	REVISION TECHNIQUE
CONTENT	
1 Is the writing interesting?	**Add** specific examples, a brief story, dialogue, or details. **Cut** repeated or boring details.
2 Are there enough details?	**Add** details, facts, statistics, or examples to support the main idea.
3 Is the main idea clear?	**Add** a sentence that clearly states your main idea.
4 Are there unrelated ideas?	**Cut** the ideas that are not related to your topic.
ORGANIZATION	
5 Are ideas and details arranged in a clear order?	**Reorder** ideas and details to make the meaning more easily understood.
6 Are the connections between ideas and sentences clear?	**Add** transitional words and phrases, such as *first, next, finally, similarly, because, for example*, and so on. (See pages 74–75.)
STYLE	
7 Does the language fit the audience and purpose?	**Replace** slang and contractions in formal writing. Use *I* and *me* when you need to create a relaxed feeling.
8 Do sentences read smoothly?	**Reorder** words to vary sentence beginnings. Reword to vary sentence structure.

A DIFFERENT APPROACH

Here are some additional guidelines for self-evaluation:

1. Remember your weak spots. People tend to make the same mistakes. Look back at your old papers and get to know what problems you often have.
2. Try different techniques. Try reading just the topic sentences of body paragraphs. Do they flow well?
3. Try looking at body paragraphs one at a time starting from the end. Do the detail sentences support the main ideas?
4. Try comparing your draft with your prewriting organizer. You may have made some changes as you wrote, but you should also be able to match up the two versions.

INTEGRATING THE LANGUAGE ARTS

Technology Link. Revising is far easier on a word-processed manuscript than on a handwritten or typed manuscript. To add, use the insert mode and the words you type will be added neatly to the text. The delete key will remove material you wish to cut. Replacing can be done by first deleting and then inserting. Reordering can be done with functions that mark a block of text and move it. If possible, demonstrate these capabilities on a computer attached to an overhead projector.

EXERCISE 12 ▶ **Evaluating and Revising a Paragraph**

With a partner, evaluate the following first draft. Then, revise the paragraph. Use the Guidelines for Evaluating and Revising on page 51. You may add, cut, reorder, or replace words and details.

Many Arab Americans live in the United States. Syrians arrived first in the late nineteenth century. They taught their heritage to their American-born children. Syrian American-born children learn to read and write the Arabic language. In Detroit, there is a large Arab American population. In Detroit, the people hold an Arab World Festival every year. They dance traditional dances like the <u>debke</u>, eat traditional foods, sell traditional Old World crafts. Doug Flutie, an Arab American, won the Heisman Trophy in 1984. There are many Arabic-language newspapers and journals in the United States. Many people from Egypt, Lebanon, and Jordan came to the United States after World War II.

Islamic Center of Greater Toledo, Ohio

PROOFREADING AND PUBLISHING

OBJECTIVES

- To proofread a given paragraph
- To brainstorm and list publishing ideas

TEACHING THE LESSON

After a volunteer reads through the introductory paragraphs and **Guidelines for Proofreading,** reinforce that students should use these guidelines as they proofread. You may want to model proofreading for your students on a sample paragraph that includes the types of problems listed in the guidelines. Have students complete

Proofreading and Publishing

One last step to finish your writing, then you'll need to find a way to share what you've written with an audience.

Proofreading

Remember puzzle pictures that asked, "What's wrong with this picture?" You had to search carefully to find mistakes—a cat wearing one plaid sock, a man writing with a fish, a woman wearing a reversed coat. Think of *proofreading* as solving a puzzle—searching out and fixing all the mistakes in grammar, spelling, capitalization, and punctuation.

Be sure to allow enough time to put your paper aside for awhile. It's easier to find mistakes when you've had a break. Try peer proofreading, too. Exchange papers with a partner and see if you can find errors in each other's papers.

GUIDELINES FOR PROOFREADING

1. Is every sentence a complete sentence, not a fragment or run-on? (See pages 354–360.)
2. Does every sentence begin with a capital letter? Does every sentence end with the correct punctuation mark? Are punctuation marks used correctly within sentences? (See pages 675–676 and pages 701–761.)
3. Do plural subjects have plural verbs? And do singular subjects have singular verbs? (See pages 551–569.)
4. Are verb forms and verb tenses used correctly? (See pages 580–599.)
5. Are adjective and adverb forms used correctly in comparisons? (See pages 629–636.)
6. Are the forms of personal pronouns used correctly? (See pages 606–621.)
7. Does every pronoun agree with its antecedent (the word it refers to) in number and gender? Are pronoun references clear? (See pages 572–574.)
8. Is every word spelled correctly? (See pages 764–793.)

RESOURCES

PROOFREADING AND PUBLISHING
- Proofreading
- Publishing and Manuscript Form

QUOTATION FOR THE DAY

"The chief glory of every people arises from its authors." (Samuel Johnson, 1709–1784, English writer)

Write the quotation on the chalkboard and use it as a prompt for a journal entry. Students might write about the ways authors contribute to society. Encourage students to remember that proofreading is their last opportunity to prepare their work for its reading audience.

MEETING INDIVIDUAL NEEDS

LEP/ESL

General Strategies. Although proofreading is an integral part of the writing process, you may find that placing too much emphasis on perfect spelling, mechanics, and usage can block students' abilities to take risks with creative expression and to believe that they have something valuable to say. Instead of marking each error on students' papers, you may just want to note the kinds of errors a student consistently makes.

Exercise 13 independently. By the proofreading stage, students have usually spent so much time with their writing that they are tired of it. For a change of pace and to overcome the negative effects of reading the same prose so many times, have students read their works aloud and backwards, either word by word, if they are looking for spelling and capitalization errors, or sentence by sentence if they are searching for usage and punctuation errors. (If they employ the second method, pronouns and antecedents will have to be checked separately by reading forwards.)

Only on very rare occasions will students not have had a reader or listener in mind from the very beginning. This practice is part of the prewriting choice of audience. Students should not be allowed to think

ANSWERS
Exercise 13
1. *thinked* should be *thought*
2. *surprized* should be *surprised*
3. *blocks* should be *block*
4. *easy* should be *easily*
5. *jungles. Thick* should be *jungles,* [or —] *thick*
6. *Grow* should be *Jungles grow*

INTEGRATING THE LANGUAGE ARTS

Technology Link. A variety of techniques can be used on word processors to find proofreading errors. A spell-check feature can both identify misspelled or questionable words and suggest possible corrections. A find-and-replace function can help check consistency. Print options can help provide a footer with a page number, and special commands enable a word processor to double space so the writer doesn't have to do it manually after each line.

EXERCISE 13 ▶ Proofreading a Paragraph

Can you find and correct the mistakes in this paragraph? (You should find six.) You can use a dictionary and the **Handbook of Grammar** on pages 394–793.

> When she heard the words <u>tropical rain forest</u>, Janet always thinked of a jungle. She was surprized to learn that few bushes grow in most parts of a tropical rain forest. The crowns of trees blocks the sunlight from the ground, so you can easy walk through most areas of a rain forest. Only where enough sunlight hits the ground do you find jungles. Thick, tangled masses of plants. Grow by rivers and in places where the land was once cleared.

Publishing

After proofreading your paper, find yourself a reader—or a listener. Remember that the purpose of most writing is to communicate with a reader. You may want to try one of the following ideas.

- Submit your writing to the school newspaper, yearbook, or magazine. Your local newspaper might publish a letter to the editor.
- Read aloud what you've written to your classmates or family or friends.
- Post book and movie reviews. You could use your class bulletin board, or you could use a library bulletin board for reviews that are written by the whole school.
- Make a class booklet. Each student should submit one piece of writing. You can also include original drawings and cartoons. Lend your booklet to other classes and to the school library.
- Keep a folder that contains your best writing. Share it with your family and friends or a trusted adult.

Follow the guidelines on the next page when making the final copy of your paper.

that finding an audience is generally something writers do only when they're finished writing. You may want to complete **Exercise 14** with the class.

CLOSURE

Have a volunteer explain the difference between revising and proofreading. ■

GUIDELINES FOR THE FORM OF A PAPER

1. Use only one side of a sheet of paper.
2. Write in blue or black ink, type, or use a word processor.
3. Leave margins of about one inch at the top, sides, and bottom of each page.
4. Follow your teacher's instructions for placing your name, the date, your class, and the title on your paper.
5. Double-space if you type. Don't skip lines if you write.
6. Indent the first line of each paragraph.
7. Keep your paper neat and clean.

E X E R C I S E 14 ▶ **Identifying Ways to Publish**

What are other ways to publish your writing? Think about all the types of writing (stories, poems, letters, essays, and reports) that can be shared in different ways. Brainstorm with your classmates to list other publishing ideas.

SYMBOLS FOR REVISING AND PROOFREADING

SYMBOL	EXAMPLE	MEANING OF SYMBOL
☰	San juan	Capitalize a lowercase letter.
/	Ruth's Father	Lowercase a capital letter.
⋀	the name of ʌschool *(the)*	Insert a missing word, letter, or punctuation mark.
℘	Take it it back.	Leave out a word, letter, or punctuation mark.
∿	bel(ei)f	Change the order of letters or words.
¶	¶"Help!" he called.	Begin a new paragraph.
⊙	Dr⊙Chiang Woo	Add a period.
⋏	Oh⌄I don't know.	Add a comma.

LESS-ADVANCED STUDENTS

Students who are unfamiliar with proofreading symbols might be overwhelmed by the list in the textbook. To give students a chance to integrate new information, you may wish to introduce the symbols a few at a time.

ANSWERS
Exercise 14

Responses will vary. Possible additional ways to publish include reading poetry, staging a reader's theater using scripts, and presenting reports as slide shows or videotapes.

MAKING CONNECTIONS

A WRITER'S REVISIONS
OBJECTIVES
- To analyze a writer's revisions
- To write a journal entry that explains one's own revision procedure

A WRITER'S REVISIONS
Teaching Strategies

Read the introductory paragraphs and Frost's poem aloud. Then allow students to work in pairs to answer the questions on Frost's revisions. Finally, let groups share their responses with the class. This activity will give students some ideas about their own revision processes.

USING THE SELECTION
Stopping by Woods on a Snowy Evening

1

Explain that the horse is probably not accustomed to stopping without reason, particularly at night.

2

These two sounds represent the two forces in conflict in the man's life, his desires and his obligations.

3

Note the alliteration of the words *dark* and *deep*. They enhance the poem's musical quality.

56

56

MAKING CONNECTIONS

A Writer's Revisions

Here's a chance to peek over the shoulder of Robert Frost, one of America's best-known poets. You can watch as he hesitates, changes his mind, scratches an idea out, starts over, gets a line just right. On the left is Frost's poem "Stopping by Woods on a Snowy Evening." Read the poem, then compare it with Frost's original handwritten version. It shows the changes he made in his first draft. What changes did Frost make?

Stopping by Woods on a Snowy Evening
by Robert Frost

Whose woods these are I think I know.
His house is in the village, though;
He will not see me stopping here
To watch his woods fill up with snow.

1 My little horse must think it queer
To stop without a farmhouse near
Between the woods and frozen lake
The darkest evening of the year.

2 He gives his harness bells a shake
To ask if there is some mistake.
The only other sound's the sweep
Of easy wind and downy flake.

3 The woods are lovely, dark, and deep,
But I have promises to keep,
And miles to go before I sleep,
And miles to go before I sleep.

Do you think the horse is better as a he or a she? Frost seems to have changed his mind at least twice. Which lines in the poem seem to have given him the most trouble? Originally (in Stanza 2), Frost wrote "Between a forest and a lake." Why do you suppose he changed those words to "Between the woods and frozen lake" in the final version of the poem?

Write a journal entry about how you revise. Describe what you do when you revise and how you feel about revising. Do you spend a great deal of time revising, or a little? Can you remember a time when you made some great improvements as you revised?

Reflecting on the Writing Process

If writing is a "basic skill for getting through life," in what ways do you use writing in your daily life? For two or three days, keep a record in your journal listing each time you write and the reason you write. For example, you might jot down a class assignment, write a note to a friend, make a list of things you must do after school, or take a phone message. Record each and every time you write and the reason.

You may be surprised at the many ways you and your classmates use writing! Share examples from your writing record with the rest of the class.

GUIDELINES

Students' journal entries should address all the points mentioned. The answers should be complete and thoughtful. Because it is a journal entry, you should allow for some variations in style and not expect a revised and proofread product.

REFLECTING ON THE WRITING PROCESS
Teaching Strategies

You may wish to plan the assignment of this exercise in conjunction with your students' other teachers to ensure an interesting variety of writing opportunities.

This activity might also be a good opportunity to review the aims of writing discussed in the introductory chapter, **"Calling the Signals."** Challenge students to analyze the aim of each type of writing they have recorded.

GUIDELINES

Students' journal listings should include a variety of writing situations. Students should be able to identify the purpose and audience for each writing occasion.

Chapter
2 LEARNING ABOUT PARAGRAPHS

OBJECTIVES

- To analyze the effect of paragraph length
- To identify main ideas and topic sentences
- To collect three types of supporting details: sensory details, facts, and examples
- To identify sentences that destroy unity
- To identify transitional words and phrases
- To collect descriptive details
- To use narration to develop paragraphs
- To use comparison/contrast to develop paragraphs
- To use evaluation to develop paragraphs
- To write an expressive paragraph
- To write a persuasive paragraph
- To write an informative paragraph
- To write a creative paragraph

Motivation

You may want to demonstrate the value of logically planned paragraphs by taking a long paragraph and arbitrarily changing the sentence order. Students will probably see that lack of logical planning creates confusion. Let the students try to rearrange the sentences in logical order.

Introduction

Students have already written paragraphs in earlier grades, but this chapter shows them how to better plan their paragraphs. At the same time, their reading comprehension will increase as they better understand how paragraphs work. They will first review the modes that can be used to develop paragraphs: description, narration, comparison and contrast, and evaluation. Then they will be given the opportunity to use these modes in paragraphs with the expressive, informative, persuasive, and creative aims.

Elements that have been added for this grade level are unity and coherence. Because of the abstract quality of these concepts, you may want to provide numerous examples of paragraphs illustrating unity and coherence to help students master these concepts.

Integration

The chapter can serve as a resource in the teaching of reading as well as in the teaching of writing. By understanding how paragraphs work, students can improve their ability to identify main ideas and supporting details. In addition, whenever they write, they can be reminded of the aims and modes they may choose from. They will also become aware of the significance of very short paragraphs.

You may want to stress the usefulness of these new understandings by urging students to use the strategies on reading and writing assignments in other classes. Examples from their social studies, science, or math textbooks can help improve their reading comprehension in various academic disciplines.

This chapter also presents an opportunity to address some of the most fundamental aspects of grammar—sentence structure and punctuation—when you teach identification and use of transitions. Students need to know how to correctly use sentence structure and punctuation in their writing, and they will be ready for grammar instruction as it relates to their own paragraphs.

The chart on the next page illustrates the strands of language arts as they are integrated into this chapter. For vocabulary study, glossary words are underlined in some writing models.

QUOTATIONS

All **Quotations for the Day** are chosen because of their relevance to instructional material presented in that segment of the chapter and for their usefulness in establishing student interest in writing.

INTEGRATING THE LANGUAGE ARTS

Selection	Reading and Literature	Writing and Critical Thinking	Language and Syntax	Speaking, Listening, and Other Expression Skills
FROM **Black Elk Speaks** as told through John G. Neihardt **60-62** **"Kachinas: Sacred Drama of the Hopis"** by Lonnie Dyer **64** **A White Romance** by Virginia Hamilton **66** **Hatchet** by Gary Paulsen **67** **"A Doll Made to Order"** from **Newsweek 68** **A Jar of Dreams** by Yoshiko Uchida **68** **"Winter Thunder"** by Mari Sandoz **72** **Black Elk: The Sacred Ways of a Lakota** by Wallace H. Black Elk and William S. Lyon **75** **One Writer's Beginnings** by Eudora Welty **77-78** **Chariot in the Sky: A Story of the Jubilee Singers** by Arna Bontemps **79-80** **"Kites"** by Dan Carlinsky **80** **Insects, The Creeping Conquerors and Human History** by Carson I. A. Ritchie **81**	Analyzing paragraph lengths **63** Analyzing characters' relationships **63** Responding personally to writing **63** Finding main idea **63, 67-68, 72-73** Finding the topic sentence **67-68** Finding details **70** Recognizing unity of supporting details **72-73** Identifying details that destroy unity **72-73** Identifying transitions **76** Identifying sensory details and spatial order **78** Analyzing elements of comparison/contrast **83** Identifying supporting reasons in an evaluative paragraph **85**	Writing a journal entry **63, 86** Collecting supporting details **70, 78** Identifying unity in a paragraph **72-73** Identifying sentences that destroy unity **72-73** Collecting descriptive details **78** Arranging events in chronological order **81-82** Composing events to support a story topic **81-82** Listing steps in a process **81-82** Determining cause and effect **81-82** Writing statements of comparison and contrast **83** Developing an evaluation **85** Supporting an opinion **85** Writing for different purposes **86** Writing an expressive paragraph **86-87** Using the writing process **86-91** Writing a persuasive paragraph **87-88** Using freewriting as a prewriting technique **86, 91** Revising paragraphs **87, 88, 90, 91** Writing an informative paragraph **88-90** Writing a creative paragraph **90-91**	Checking for unity and coherence **72-73** Proofreading for errors in usage and mechanics **87, 88, 90, 91** Beginning new paragraphs when writing dialogue **67**	Sharing statements of comparison and contrast in a small group **83** Brainstorming ideas with peers **83**

SEGMENT PLANNING GUIDE

Whether you are planning for a quick review of a writing concept or preparing an extended lesson on composition you can use the following Planning Guide to adapt the chapter material to the individual needs of your class.

SEGMENT	PAGES	CONTENT	RESOURCES
1 *Looking at the Parts*	*59-63*		
Literary Model from **Black Elk Speaks**	60-62	Guided reading: a model of paragraph writing	
Reader's Response/Writer's Craft	63	Model evaluation: responding to literature and analyzing paragraph writing	
2 *The Parts of a Paragraph*	*64-70*		The Main Idea The Topic Sentence Sensory Details Facts and Examples
The Main Idea	64	Guidelines: finding the main idea in a model paragraph	
The Topic Sentence	65-66	Guidelines: finding the topic sentence in a model paragraph	
Writing Note	67	Writing suggestion: starting new paragraphs	
Exercise 1	67-68	Applied practice: identifying main ideas and topic sentences in model paragraphs	
Supporting Sentences	69	Guidelines: identifying sensory details, facts, and examples	
Chart: Supporting Sentences	69	Guidelines: examining various details used to support main ideas	
Exercise 2	70	Applied practice: listing supporting details	
3 *Unity and Coherence*	*71-76*		Unity in Paragraphs Coherence in Paragraphs Using Transitions
Unity	71-72	Explanation: relating supporting details to the main idea in a model paragraph	
Exercise 3	72-73	Applied practice: identifying sentences in model paragraphs that destroy unity	
Coherence	74-76	Guidelines: examining the use of transitional words and phrases in a model	
Chart: Transitional Words and Phrases	74	Guidelines: examining transitional words used in various modes of writing	
Exercise 4	76	Applied practice: listing transitional words and phrases in a model paragraph	
4 *Description*	*77-78*		Description: Spatial Order
Chart: Ways of Developing Paragraphs	77	Guidelines: examining description, narration, comparison and contrast, and evaluation	
Using Description	77-78	Guidelines: examining spatial order in a model	
Exercise 5	78	Applied practice: collecting and ordering descriptive details	

SEGMENT	PAGES	CONTENT	RESOURCES
5 *Narration*	*78-82*		Chronological Order
Telling a Story	79-80	Example: examining the use of narration in a model paragraph	
Explaining a Process	80	Example: examining the use of order in a model paragraph	
Explaining Causes and Effects	80-81	Example: examining how events relate in a model paragraph	
Exercise 6	81-82	Applied practice: using narration to develop paragraphs	
6 *Comparison and Contrast*	*82-83*		Comparing and Contrasting
Logical Order in Comparing and Contrasting	82-83	Guidelines: examining comparison and contrast in a model	
Exercise 7	83	Cooperative learning: writing statements that contrast and compare subjects	
7 *Evaluation*	*84-85*		Evaluating
Writing an Evaluation	84	Guidelines: examining order of importance in a model	
Exercise 8	85	Applied practice: developing an evaluation	
8 *Making Connections*	*86-91*		
Writing a Paragraph to Express Yourself	86-87	Guidelines: using a sentence to get started Applied practice: writing an expressive paragraph	
Writing a Paragraph to Persuade	87-88	Guidelines: writing a persuasive paragraph Applied practice: writing a persuasive paragraph	
Writing a Paragraph to Inform	88-90	Guidelines: writing a paragraph to inform Applied practice: writing an informative paragraph	
Writing a Paragraph That Is Creative	90-91	Guidelines: using criteria to write a creative paragraph Applied practice: writing a creative paragraph	
WHOLE-CHAPTER RESOURCE Chapter Review			

⬛ LOOKING AT THE PARTS

OBJECTIVES

- To analyze purposes for paragraphs
- To write a journal entry about a personal experience

MOTIVATION

You could focus on the lesson by giving students a piece of writing without paragraph indentions. Ask students to place a slash mark wherever they think a new paragraph should begin. Students will see that paragraphing makes writing easier to understand.

👁 VISUAL CONNECTIONS
Senegalese Fishing Village

About the Artist. Frank Frazier, an African American artist, has been painting for over 25 years. A major theme of his work is African American heritage—from scenes of the streets of Harlem, where he was raised, to the *Tribal Series,* a series of collages about Africa. Frazier's stylized paintings emphasize the importance of pride, social justice, and community.

Ideas for Writing. Discuss Frazier's work with the class. Ask students to write expressive paragraphs inspired by the picture. Students can respond to the style and colors used, or they can write about the subject of the collage. Some students might want to write from the point of view of one of the characters shown. Emphasize the importance of paragraph unity: every sentence should relate directly to the main idea.

2 LEARNING ABOUT PARAGRAPHS

TEACHING THE LESSON

Students could read the introductory paragraphs silently. Ask one or two students to summarize the ideas.

You will probably want to read the selection from *Black Elk Speaks* aloud and stop at the end of each paragraph for discussion. Use the annotations to give students additional information.

GUIDED PRACTICE

Discuss the first question under **Reader's Response** with the class. Have students give specific reasons from the selection to support their answers. This question prepares students for writing their journal entries.

Next, ask students to find the short paragraphs mentioned in question 4 in the **Writer's Craft** section. Answer the first part

Looking at the Parts

Have you ever thought about the **parts** of a bicycle? A bike has handlebars, wheels, and a seat, but not all bikes are alike. Some are bigger than others; some have more parts than others.

You can think of paragraphs that way, too. They all have words, and they all say something. But some are bigger than others and some have more parts than others.

Writing and You. Some paragraphs stand alone, but most of them work together like links in a chain. Have you ever noticed that paragraphs can be very short—even a single word or sentence, and that other paragraphs go on and on?

As You Read. The following paragraphs are from a book about the life of a Native American, Black Elk. What do you notice about the sizes of the paragraphs?

Senegalese Fishing Village, Frank Frazier (1989), Visions in Black Gallery.

QUOTATION FOR THE DAY

"Writing has laws of perspective, of light and shade, just as painting does, or music. If you are born knowing them, fine. If not, learn them. Then rearrange the rules to suit yourself." (Truman Capote, 1924–1984, American writer)

This quotation mentions laws as they relate to rules and structure. Explain to students that this chapter is about an important structure in writing, the paragraph.

MEETING **INDIVIDUAL** NEEDS

LEP/ESL

General Strategies. In order for students to understand fully the narrative in this segment, discuss the following vocabulary items:

1. *Wasichus* — "white man"
2. *big shining wagon* — "train"
3. *very big house with sharp pointed towers* — "castle"
4. *yellow and white metal* — "gold and silver"
5. *got sick and fell over* — "fainted"

of the question by showing students the transitions in the paragraph. Then find evidence in the other paragraph to respond to the second part of the question.

INDEPENDENT PRACTICE

After you have completed questions 1 and 4 with the students, they should be prepared to do the journal entry (question 2) and question 3 independently.

"They put us in some of those shining wagons and took us to a very beautiful place..."

FROM

► Black Elk ◄

Speaks

as told through

JOHN G. NEIHARDT

(Flaming Rainbow)

Black Elk (at left) and his friend, Elk, participating in Buffalo Bill's Wild West Show, touring England.

ASSESSMENT

You will be able to assess students' understanding during the class discussion of questions in **Reader's Response** and **Writer's Craft.** Or you could have students find one very long paragraph and one very short paragraph from some selection in the textbook, and then have the class explain the purposes of both paragraphs.

CLOSURE

Ask for volunteers to explain why writing is divided into paragraphs and how long paragraphs should be. [Students should know that there are no set rules for paragraphing, but that the paragraphing will be long or short for a purpose.]

☛

One day we were told that Majesty was coming. I did not know what that was at first, but I learned afterward. It was Grandmother England (Queen Victoria), who owned Grandmother's Land [Canada] where we lived awhile after the Wasichus murdered <u>Crazy Horse</u>.

1   She came to the show in a big shining wagon, and there were soldiers on both sides of her, and many other shining wagons came too. That day other people could not come to the show—

2   just Grandmother England and some people who came with her.

3   Sometimes we had to shoot in the show, but this time we did not shoot at all. We danced and sang, and I was one of the dancers chosen to do this for the Grandmother, because I was young and limber then and could dance many ways. We stood right in front of Grandmother England. She was little but fat and we liked her, because she was good to us. After we had danced, she spoke to us. She said something like this: "I am sixty-seven years old. All over the world I have seen all kinds of people; but today I have seen the best-looking people I know. If

4   you belonged to me, I would not let them take you around in a show like this." She said other good things too, and then she said we must come to see her, because she had come to see us. She shook hands with all of us. Her hand was very little and soft.

5   We gave a big cheer for her, and then the shining wagons came in and she got into one of them and they all went away.

In about a half-moon after that we went to see the Grandmother. They put us in some of those shining wagons and took us to a very beautiful place where there was a very big house with sharp, pointed towers on it. There were many seats built high in a circle, and these were just full of Wasichus who were all

6   pounding their heels and yelling: "<u>Jubilee</u>! Jubilee! Jubilee!" I never heard what this meant.

7   They put us together in a certain place at the bottom of the seats. First there appeared a beautiful black wagon with two

USING THE SELECTION
from Black Elk Speaks

1

This refers to Buffalo Bill's Wild West Show that toured England for Queen Victoria's jubilee.

2

Why do you think he calls her *Grandmother?* [It's a familiar, friendly term. He is honoring her as an elder, a wise woman.]

3

Describe the show. [There is shooting, dancing, and singing.]

4

Why do you think she "would not let them take you around in a show like this"? [A possible response is that they are being exploited.]

5

Point out that this long paragraph has described one event—Queen Victoria's visit to the show.

6

jubilee: a special anniversary; here, the 50th year of Queen Victoria's reign

7

This paragraph describes the jubilee festivities, giving many supporting details. Have students name these details ["beautiful black wagon," "two black horses," "four gray horses"].

Have students bring a textbook from another class, such as science or social studies, and help them analyze a paragraph in the chapter they are currently studying. Ask a volunteer to read a short paragraph. You can summarize the main idea of that paragraph for the class. Then ask students to choose two paragraphs from their books and to find the main ideas. ■

62

black horses, and it went all around the show place. I heard that the Grandmother's grandson, a little boy, was in that wagon. Next came a beautiful black wagon with four gray horses. On each of the two right hand horses there was a rider, and a man walked, holding the front left hand horse. I heard that some of Grandmother's relatives were in this wagon. Next came eight buckskin horses, two by two, pulling a shining black wagon. There was a rider on each right hand horse and a man walked, holding the front left hand horse. There were soldiers, with bayonets, facing outward all around this wagon. Now all the people in the seats were roaring and yelling "Jubilee!" and "Victoria!" Then we saw Grandmother England again. She was sitting in the back of the wagon and two women sat in the front, facing her. Her dress was all shining and her hat was all shining and her wagon was all shining and so were the horses. She looked like a fire coming.

Afterward I heard that there was yellow and white metal all over the horses and the wagon.

8 When she came to where we were, her wagon stopped and she stood up. Then all those people stood up and roared and bowed to her; but she bowed to us. We sent up a great cry and our women made the tremolo. The people **9** in the crowd were so excited that we heard some of them got sick and fell over. Then when it was quiet, we sang a song to the Grandmother.

That was a very happy time.

10 We liked Grandmother England, because we could see that she was a fine woman, and she was good to us. Maybe if she had been our Grandmother, it would have been better for our people.

8

Why do you think she bowed to them? [Students might respond that she had respect for them.]

9

Why were the people so excited? [They may have thought the yells meant they were going to attack.]

10

Why did the Black Elk's people think Queen Victoria was a "fine woman"? [A possible response is that she honored and respected them.]

SELECTION AMENDMENT
Description of change: excerpted
Rationale: to focus on the concept of paragraphs as presented in this chapter

READER'S RESPONSE

1. Why did Black Elk like "Grandmother" England?
2. Have you ever met anyone you liked as much as Black Elk liked the Queen of England, someone who was very different from you? Write a brief journal entry about the experience.

WRITER'S CRAFT

3. There are two very long paragraphs in this passage. Each one has at least eighteen lines. What is the first of these long paragraphs about? the second?
4. Neihardt uses two very short paragraphs here. Which of these paragraphs do you think moves the reader from one idea to another? Which makes an idea stand out?

LOOKING AHEAD

In this chapter, you'll study the form and structure of paragraphs. Even though most paragraphs are a part of a longer piece of writing, keep in mind that

- most paragraphs have a central, or main, idea
- sensory details, facts, and examples may be used to support the main idea
- description, narration, comparison and contrast, and evaluation are four ways of developing paragraphs

ANSWERS

Reader's Response

1. He liked her because she was good to him and his people. The queen seems to imply that if they were her people, she wouldn't let them be exploited as they were in the show. Later, after the ceremonies she showed them respect by bowing.

2. A satisfactory entry will describe someone the student admires, but who is very different from the student.

Writer's Craft

3. The first long paragraph is about Queen Victoria's visit to Buffalo Bill's Wild West Show. The second very long paragraph is a description of the parade that Black Elk and his people watched.

4. In the sixth paragraph, the sentence "Afterward I heard that there was yellow and white metal all over the horses and the wagon," emphasizes the grandeur of the parade.

   Then, in the eighth paragraph, the sentence "That was a very happy time" moves the reader from one idea to another—from the tribe's admiration for Queen Victoria to the idea that their lives could have been better had she been their Grandmother.

OBJECTIVES

- To identify main ideas and topic sentences
- To list at least two supporting details

MOTIVATION

Using the first example in this section, read the paragraph without the topic sentence. Ask the students the main idea. Then give them the topic sentence, which makes the idea clear.

RESOURCES

THE PARTS OF A PARAGRAPH

- The Main Idea
- The Topic Sentence
- Sensory Details
- Facts and Examples

QUOTATION FOR THE DAY

"The beginning is easy; what happens next is much harder." (Mavis Gallant, 1922–   , Canadian author)

Ask students if they agree with Gallant's idea. Is it easy to begin a paragraph? Explain to students that writing a clear paragraph starts with writing a strong main idea.

SELECTION AMENDMENT
Description of change: excerpted
Rationale: to focus on the concept of the parts of a paragraph as presented in this chapter

---

The Parts of a Paragraph

The Main Idea

Paragraphs that stand alone almost always have a main idea. So do paragraphs that are part of a longer piece of writing. The *main idea* is the big idea in the paragraph. In the following paragraph, you will find the main idea in the first sentence. It tells you that this paragraph is about how Hopis use Kachina dolls.

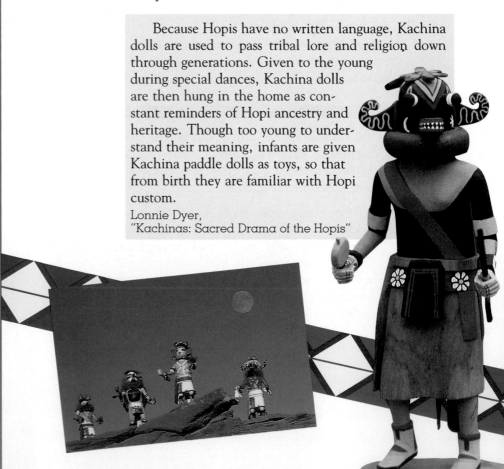

Because Hopis have no written language, Kachina dolls are used to pass tribal lore and religion down through generations. Given to the young during special dances, Kachina dolls are then hung in the home as constant reminders of Hopi ancestry and heritage. Though too young to understand their meaning, infants are given Kachina paddle dolls as toys, so that from birth they are familiar with Hopi custom.

Lonnie Dyer,
"Kachinas: Sacred Drama of the Hopis"

First, ask for definitions of *topic sentence, main idea,* and *supporting details.* You could use paragraphs in the selection by Black Elk to illustrate these elements. Ask students to read silently the explanations in the textbook and then ask the students to restate the definitions in their own words.

You could use two of the example paragraphs—preparing for battle and a runner's plans for a race—to help students identify the structure of paragraphs. In the first paragraph, identify the spatial order of the supporting details. In the second paragraph, emphasize the chronological order of the sentences.

The Topic Sentence

Location of the Topic Sentence. The *topic sentence* states the main idea of the paragraph. You may find it at the beginning of the paragraph, in the middle, or even at the end. Then it's like a surprise ending. In the paragraph on page 64, the topic sentence is the first sentence of the paragraph: *Because Hopis have no written language, Kachina dolls are used to pass tribal lore and religion down through generations.*

In the paragraph below, the topic sentence is last. This sentence makes clear that the villagers are preparing for a battle. The other sentences lead up to that point.

> Quickly, quickly we gathered the sheep into the pens. Children rushed through the village gathering firewood to pile inside the homes. Men and women scooped up pots and pots of water, filling cisterns and containers as rapidly as possible. People pulled the last ears of corn from the fields and turned their backs on the dry stalks. Finally, we all stood together in the plaza in the center of the village for just a moment before the fighters went to stand near the walls and the wide-eyed children were coaxed inside the houses. And so we prepared for the coming battle.

MEETING
INDIVIDUAL
NEEDS

LEP/ESL

General Strategies. Exercise 1 is a cognitively demanding activity, requiring analysis, logic, and discrimination. Not all students will have had sufficient opportunity to practice these skills. Therefore, instead of requiring that this exercise be approached independently, you may want to pair ESL students with native speakers. When the exercise is completed, ask several pairs of students to share their findings with the class.

ADVANCED STUDENTS

Students who quickly master the objectives in this lesson can be encouraged to apply their skills to other written material—books, magazines, and pamphlets. Ask students to find a specified number of paragraphs and to identify the topic sentences and supporting details in those paragraphs. Each student could copy one or two of those paragraphs, label them, and display them on the bulletin board.

Analyze the first paragraph in **Exercise 1** with the class. Be sure to identify the main idea and the types of supporting details in each paragraph.

You could model the skills required for **Exercise 2** in a similar manner.

After you have done the first question in both **Exercise 1** and **2**, students can complete the other questions independently.

CRITICAL THINKING
Synthesis

You may want to take literally the phrase *build a paragraph* and give your students squares of paper, all the same size except for one longer one for the foundation of the paragraph. Ask each student to write the topic sentence of a paragraph on the foundation piece of paper. Then ask students to build the paragraphs by adding blocks of supporting details. They can paste these component parts on a sheet of paper, and you could display their creations.

CRITICAL THINKING
Evaluation

Have students evaluate paragraphs in their writing folders. (Or you may want to provide the class with student samples from your own files.) Ask students to find the topic sentence in each paragraph, and then have them number the supporting details. Also, have them answer the following two questions on a separate sheet of paper:

1. Is the topic sentence or main idea clear?
2. Do the supporting details provide enough information?

SELECTION AMENDMENT
Description of change: excerpted
Rationale: to focus on the concept of the topic sentence as presented in this chapter

Importance of a Topic Sentence. Paragraphs that relate a series of events or that tell a story often don't have a topic sentence. Read the following paragraph. It doesn't have a topic sentence. But all the sentences are about one main idea—the runner's plans for a race.

> She dug her running shoe into the cracked sidewalk in front of her. She pictured the broken sidewalk along a fairly empty thoroughfare where she must run. That highway snaking through the city was wide and black. If anyone was going to block her path, try to mug her, it would happen there. Out there, the sky above her would look gray-purple. And by the time she got there, it would most likely start to rain. She could *perform* in rain. She ran almost truer when it rained. Maybe it was that she was more conscious of slippery surfaces and compensated.
>
> Virginia Hamilton, *A White Romance*

Although all paragraphs don't have to have topic sentences, it is helpful to use them when you are writing. They may help you focus on your main idea. They also help the reader find the main idea.

ASSESSMENT

Have students bring examples of paragraphs from self-selected reading or from any textbook. Ask them to underline the topic sentence or main idea in each paragraph and to identify the types of supporting details. These examples could be displayed for other students.

RETEACHING

You may want to approach this lesson from another angle by typing several paragraphs. Be sure to place each sentence on a new line. Cut the paragraphs apart, and then ask students to arrange the sentences in the proper order. You can help the class identify the topic sentence and supporting details.

The Topic Sentence **67**

WRITING NOTE

In a longer piece of writing, start a new paragraph when you change ideas. Also, if you are writing dialogue (the actual words of people), start a new paragraph when you change speakers.

EXERCISE 1 ▶ **Identifying Main Ideas and Topic Sentences**

Finding a main idea is like detective work. In each of the following paragraphs search out the main idea. If there's a topic sentence, identify it. If there is no topic sentence, look at all the details in the paragraph and tell in your own words the main idea of the paragraph.

1.   He turned and looked back at the stand of raspberries. The bear was gone, the birds were singing, he saw nothing that could hurt him. <u>There was no danger here that he could sense, could feel</u>. In the city, at night, there was sometimes danger. You could not be in the park at night, after dark, because of the danger. But here, the bear had looked at him and had moved on and—this filled his thoughts—the berries were so good.

                        Gary Paulsen, from *Hatchet*

MEETING INDIVIDUAL NEEDS

STUDENTS WITH SPECIAL NEEDS

It is important for the teacher of any learning disabled student to utilize the tactile-kinesthetic approach as much as possible. Divide the class into groups of four or five. Give each group a different paragraph from any literary genre. Have each student in the group take one of the sentences in its paragraph and write it in large letters on notebook paper. The sheets of sentences should then be mixed up. Each group will then take its turn going to the front of the room and holding up its sentences while the class determines which is the topic sentence and which are supporting sentences.

SELECTION AMENDMENT
Description of change: excerpted
Rationale: to focus on the concept of the topic sentence as presented in this chapter

Make a transparency or a worksheet that features a paragraph with the sentences out of order. Let the class tell you how to change the order of the paragraph so that the topic sentence is clear and the supporting details are in proper order.

Try typing several paragraphs of students' writing from a previous year, and ask your class to evaluate these paragraphs in terms of clear topic sentences and adequate supporting details. ■

INTEGRATING THE LANGUAGE ARTS

Literature Link. You may want to ask students to find examples of sensory details in their literature textbooks. Refer students first to a piece of writing such as "Survive the Savage Sea" by Dougal Robertson, a journal describing Robertson's terrifying struggle to survive after his boat was sunk by killer whales. Analyze this writing with the class. Then have students select other literature. After reading, they can give short, oral summaries to the class and explain the sensory details they have found.

A DIFFERENT APPROACH

Place different objects in paper bags and give one bag to each student. Ask each student to describe his or her object by using as many different types of sensory details as possible. After each student reads his or her description aloud, let the class guess what the object is. You could use such common objects as a paper clip, an apple, a tennis ball, or a bar of soap.

SELECTION AMENDMENTS
Description of changes: excerpted
Rationale: to focus on the concept of the topic sentence as presented in this chapter

2. m.i.—In spite of the disabilities associated with spina bifida, Auralea Moore leads an active life.

2.　　Like lots of other kids her age, eight-year-old Auralea Moore plays baseball, swims and skis. She also has a favorite plaything: a 19-inch doll named Susan, who was handcrafted to look like her. Auralea was born with spina bifida, a birth defect that has left her paralyzed from the waist down. Her look-alike doll, equipped with a pair of blue and silver "designer" braces, helps her remember that although she may be handicapped, she is definitely not out of the action.

"A Doll Made to Order," *Newsweek*

3.　　Personally, I thought Maxwell was just about the homeliest dog I'd ever seen in my entire life. He looked like a little old man draped in a piece of brown velvet that was too long, with the leftover cloth hanging in thick folds under his chin. Not only that, his long droopy ears dragged on the ground, he had sad wet eyes and huge thick paws with splayed toes. I mean, who could love a dog like that, except my brother Joji, aged nine, who is a bit on the homely side himself.

Yoshiko Uchida, *A Jar of Dreams*

Supporting Sentences

Supporting sentences give details that explain or prove th main idea. These sentences are called *supporting sentences* because they contain *sensory details*, *facts*, or *examples* that support the main idea of the paragraph.

Sensory details are words that describe one of the five senses—sight, sound, touch, taste, and smell. *Facts* give information that can be proved true in a concrete way. For instance, it's a fact that sea gulls drop clams on rocks to break them open. It's also a fact that great herds of buffalo once roamed the western plains. *Examples* give typical instances of an idea. A manatee is an example of a mammal that lives in the water. A chameleon is a lizard whose changes in coloring are an example of protective coloration. This chart shows the kinds of details you can use to support the main idea of the paragraph.

SUPPORTING SENTENCES	
Sensory Details	**Examples**
Sight	The bright sun glared off the front windshield of the car.
Sound	Thunder boomed down the canyon, echoing off the walls.
Touch	My hands felt frozen to the cold, steel handlebars.
Taste	Thirstily, she gulped down the sweet orange juice.
Smell	The sharp, unpleasant odor of fresh asphalt met his nose.
Facts	In 1961, Roger Maris slammed sixty-one home runs to break the old record of sixty held by Babe Ruth.
Examples	Fierce windstorms occur throughout the world. In the central United States, tornadoes have wind speeds over two hundred miles per hour.

EXERCISE 2 ▶ **Collecting Supporting Details**

When you write paragraphs, you have to collect (find or think up) details of support. You can practice with the following topic sentences. For each, one kind of supporting detail is suggested—sensory details, facts, or examples. List at least two details to support each topic sentence.

EXAMPLE
1. **The appliance that toasts our bread has changed over the years. (facts)**
1. *Details: It originated in the early 1900s. It consisted of bare wires with no thermostat. The first pop-up toaster appeared in 1926.*

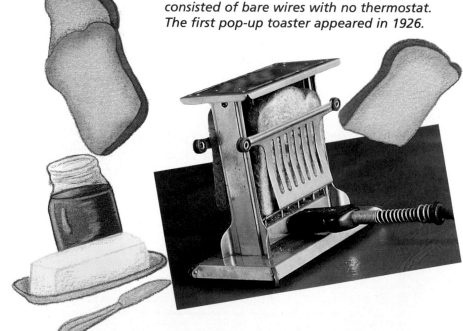

1. The time I spend getting ready for school in the mornings is not my favorite part of the day. (sensory details)
2. My dream is to spend two days in a shopping mall. (examples)
3. One person's actions can make a difference in the lives of others. (facts)
4. When I'm hungry, I can just imagine my favorite meal. (sensory details)

UNITY AND COHERENCE

OBJECTIVES

- To identify sentences that destroy unity in a paragraph
- To identify transitional words and phrases in a paragraph

MOTIVATION

Create a collage of an animal that has, for example, a lion's head, a horse's legs, and an alligator's tail. Ask the students what's wrong with your creature. Then explain that all the parts in a piece of writing need to go together, too.

☞

Unity and Coherence

A paragraph is a little like a car. It has to have *unity*—you don't want one blue fender on a red car. And it has to have *coherence*—the back of the car has to be connected to the front.

Unity

A paragraph has **unity** when all the sentences support, or tell something about, one main idea. A paragraph that doesn't have unity may confuse your readers. For example, in a paragraph about Bonnie St. John, you might tell how she became a skiing champion despite losing a leg. But if you mentioned a friend who is also a skier, you would destroy the unity. That information wouldn't be related to your main idea.

People Weekly © 1986 Richard Howard

In the paragraph on the following page, the first sentence states the main idea. Notice how all the other sentences tell something more about the heavy snow.

RESOURCES

UNITY AND COHERENCE
- Unity in Paragraphs
- Coherence in Paragraphs
- Using Transitions

QUOTATION FOR THE DAY

"The discipline of the writer is to be still and listen to what his subject has to tell him." (Rachel Carson, 1907–1964, American marine biologist)

Write the quotation on the chalkboard, and ask students to explore the quotation in journal entries. Students might write about a time when they learned something new by writing or reading, or they might write about a conversation or a letter in which the speaker or writer lost sight of his or her subject. Explain that paragraphs that center around a main subject or idea are effective and unified.

MEETING INDIVIDUAL NEEDS

LEP/ESL

Spanish. *Unity* is similar to the Spanish word *unidad,* but the concept may not be familiar even though the word is a cognate.

Write a definition for *unity* on the chalkboard. Ask the class to suggest examples of unity that do not pertain to writing. [Some possibilities include "the unity of members of a family," "the unity of states to form a nation," and "the unity of nations as a global community."]

INTEGRATING THE LANGUAGE ARTS

Literature Link. You may want to show your students how understanding paragraph unity can help comprehension. Have them use their literature textbooks to find examples of paragraphs that demonstrate unity. They might read "Guess What? I Almost Kissed My Father Good Night" by Robert Cormier.

Students will also notice that some paragraphs are very short and that some paragraphs have main ideas rather than topic sentences.

The snow began quietly this time, like an afterthought to the gray Sunday night. The moon almost broke through once, but toward daylight, a little wind came up and started white curls, thin and lonesome, running over the old drifts left from the New Year storm. Gradually the snow thickened, until around eight-thirty the two ruts of the winding trails were covered and undisturbed, except down in the Lone Tree district, where an old, yellow bus crawled heavily along, feeling out the ruts between the choppy sand hills.

Mari Sandoz, "Winter Thunder"

EXERCISE 3 ▶ **Identifying Sentences That Destroy Unity**

Each of the following paragraphs has one <u>sentence that destroys the unity</u>. Try your skill at finding the sentences that don't belong. [Hint: First, decide what the main idea is. Next, decide whether each supporting sentence is **closely** connected to the main idea.]

INDEPENDENT PRACTICE

Students can complete **Exercises 3** and **4** independently, or you could assign students to check the unity and coherence in their own writing.

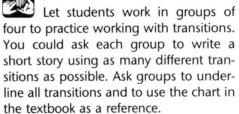

Unity and Coherence   **73**

1. It felt like an oven to Tamara as she walked up the street toward the park. It was a hot day for baseball practice. <u>She wondered if the Cardinals game would be on television that evening</u>. Tamara told herself she couldn't let the heat slow her down, though. The coach would be deciding today who would start in the season's first game. And she wanted to be playing third.

2. Canoes are made for many different purposes. White-water canoes are for use in fast, rock-filled streams. They're made to turn quickly to avoid obstacles. Other canoes are made for lakes and quiet rivers. They don't turn too quickly, so they won't be your first choice for use on a river with lots of rapids. On the other hand, they're easy to paddle in a straight line. The white-water canoe can't be paddled in a straight line no matter what you do. <u>You can also find canoes that are made to carry either one or two people</u>. Before choosing a canoe, think about what kind of water you'll be using it in.

COOPERATIVE LEARNING

Let students work in groups of four to practice working with transitions. You could ask each group to write a short story using as many different transitions as possible. Ask groups to underline all transitions and to use the chart in the textbook as a reference.

To help the groups function smoothly, assign duties to each student. A discussion leader can call on different students to add sentences to the story, and a writer can record the story while a timer makes sure the group finishes on time. Finally, a reporter can share the group's efforts with the class.

SELECTION AMENDMENT
Description of change: excerpted
Rationale: to focus on the concept of unity as presented in this chapter

ASSESSMENT

You can use students' performance on the exercises to assess mastery. Or students can show that they understand this lesson by putting it to use. You could ask each student to write a unified and coherent paragraph. Ask each student to underline all transitions and to explain how the paragraph has unity.

RETEACHING

To help students identify sentences that destroy unity, review how to identify a topic sentence. Take a paragraph from the opening selection by Black Elk. Underline the transitions, and then help students change the transitions to change the meaning.

INTEGRATING THE LANGUAGE ARTS

Technology Link. If the equipment is available, let students use word processors to make final drafts of paragraphs that they write. Using the machine to underline or boldface transitions and topic sentences will reinforce students' knowledge. Groups also work especially well with word processors, with one student using the keyboard and the others dictating the story or paragraph.

Mechanics Link. You may want to teach punctuation of transitional words and phrases at this point. You could review the punctuation of introductory transitional phrases and transitions that interrupt a sentence. Refer students to **Chapter 26** for more information.

Coherence

A paragraph has ***coherence*** when readers can tell how and why ideas are connected.

To create coherence you can do two things. First, you can arrange your details in an *order* that makes sense to the reader. In the section Ways of Developing Paragraphs (page 77), you'll learn more about how to organize details.

The second way of creating coherence in paragraphs is to use *transitional words* or *phrases* to connect ideas. These are words and phrases like *for example, mainly,* and *in addition.* They not only connect ideas, but also tell why and how they're related.

The following chart shows examples of some of the common words and phrases used for transitions that help to create coherence.

TRANSITIONAL WORDS AND PHRASES		
COMPARING AND CONTRASTING IDEAS		
also	another	similarly
although	but	too
and	however	yet
SHOWING CAUSE AND EFFECT / NARRATION		
as a result	for	so that
because	since	therefore
SHOWING TIME / NARRATION		
after	first, second, etc.	then
before	next	until
finally	often	when
SHOWING PLACE / DESCRIPTION		
above	down	next
around	here	over
before	in	there
beside	into	under

EXTENSION

Students could evaluate their own writing by selecting paragraphs from their writing folders to check for unity and for use of transitions. Ask students to revise when necessary.

The following paragraph tells how Native Americans are recognized everywhere. The writer uses transitional words to show how ideas are connected. Notice, for example, how the writer says that at "first" kids pretend they don't see him. "Then" they turn and look.

> <u>When</u> I go someplace, most of the time those little people see me. At <u>first</u> they'll pretend not to see me. They go past me a little ways, <u>and then</u> they will turn back <u>and</u> look at me. <u>Then</u> they'll nudge their mama or daddy or grandma or grandpa, <u>and</u> I'll hear them say, "There's an Indian back there." <u>So</u> the Indians are <u>still</u> here. We never phased away. We didn't just blend <u>into</u> society <u>and</u> vanish. In fact, we're appearing more <u>and</u> more <u>and</u> more. We get <u>around</u> more now, <u>too</u>. Indians are not just confined only to the United States or one state or one county or one city or one house. They know us <u>all over</u> this Earth.
>
> Wallace H. Black Elk and William S. Lyon,
> *Black Elk: The Sacred Ways of a Lakota*

MEETING INDIVIDUAL NEEDS

ADVANCED STUDENTS

Students who grasp the concept of transitions quickly could change the transitions of one of the example paragraphs to alter its meaning.

LESS-ADVANCED STUDENTS

Less-advanced students can practice using transitions by filling in the blanks of a paragraph. You can provide a paragraph with blanks left where transitions had been provided. Work with students to complete the paragraph.

SELECTION AMENDMENT
Description of change: excerpted
Rationale: to focus on the concept of coherence as presented in this chapter

A DIFFERENT APPROACH

Have students compose a story orally. Seat students in a circle and give them a beginning sentence such as "It was a camping trip I'll never forget" or "You won't believe what happened to me in the video store." Then point to a student and give a transition to begin the next sentence. That student must continue the story, using the transition you give. When that student finishes, he or she chooses a student to continue the story and gives another transition to that student. Each student should have a turn. The last student should give his or her transition to you so you can end the story.

EXERCISE 4 ▶ **Identifying Transitional Words and Phrases**

Identifying transitional words and phrases can help you see how they work when they are used in paragraphs. Using the chart on page 74 as a guide, make a list of all the <u>transitional words and phrases</u> in the following paragraph.

<u>When</u> she was elected to be chief of the Cherokee Nation <u>in</u> 1987, Wilma Mankiller took on a huge job. <u>But</u> she was used to challenges. She had <u>already</u> had to overcome great handicaps <u>because</u> of serious injuries she suffered in a head-on auto accident <u>in</u> 1979. <u>So while</u> others were impressed by the new chief's dedication, no one who really knew her well found her leadership ability surprising. The new chief developed many needed projects. <u>First</u>, she planned new water supply lines. <u>Second</u>, she set up a new job training program. <u>Next</u>, she started new rural health clinics. <u>Finally</u>, she planned a health and nutrition program. These were only a few of the programs that this ambitious new Cherokee chief set in motion during her first term in office. <u>Then</u>, <u>in</u> 1991, Wilma Mankiller was re-elected for a second term as chief.

OBJECTIVE
- To list descriptive details that describe a particular subject

TEACHING THE LESSON
Ask students to describe a favorite hangout. Write their descriptions on the chalkboard. Show the class how to order the points spatially and add sensory details as needed. Then discuss Eudora Welty's use of spatial order and sensory details in *One Writer's Beginnings* on p. 77 and 78. Students should then complete **Exercise 5.**

Ways of Developing Paragraphs

What you're writing about, your subject or topic, usually determines the way you develop it. Here are four ways of writing a paragraph.

WAYS OF DEVELOPING PARAGRAPHS	
Description	Looking at parts of a person, place, or thing
Narration	Looking at changes in a person, place, or thing over time
Comparison and Contrast	Finding likenesses and differences between people, places, or things
Evaluation	Judging the person, place, or thing's value or worth

Description

How would you describe your favorite hangout to one of your friends? What does the Ninja Turtle Michelangelo look like?

In answering either of these questions, you're *describing* something. That means you're picking out specific details, or features, to tell about that will help someone else recognize it.

In describing something, you often use *spatial order.* Spatial order organizes details according to their location. In the following paragraph, notice how the writer uses sensory details and spatial order to describe her father's farm.

> The farm my father grew up on, where Grandpa Welty and Grandma lived, was in southern Ohio in the rolling hills of Hocking County, near the small town of Logan. It was one of the neat, narrow-porched, two-story farmhouses, painted white, of the Pennsylvania-German country. Across its front grew feathery cosmos and barrel-sized peony bushes with stripy heavy-scented blooms pushing out of the leaves. There was a springhouse to one side, down a little

DESCRIPT
- Descriptio   er

QUOTATI   THE DAY
"Noth   comes real till it is experien   " (John Keats, 1795–1821,   t)

Ask   recall a time when some   bed junior high school, or a   class or teacher. Then have   give several sensory detail   their classmates experience

LEP/ESL
General Strategies. To clarify the concept of spatial order, ask a volunteer to come to the chalkboard to make a rough drawing of the farm described by Eudora Welty. Giving your students an opportunity to see Welty's paragraph graphically represented will further their understanding of the importance of descriptive details.

ASSESSMENT

Assess students' performance on **Exercise 5** or evaluate students' use of details in their own writing.

CLOSURE

Point to some object in the classroom and have students list as many details about it as possible. Then ask for volunteers to explain which type of spatial order would be the best to use if they were to write a descriptive paragraph of that object. ∎

INTEGRATING THE LANGUAGE ARTS

Literature Link. There are some especially good examples of descriptive paragraphs in "Rikki-Tikki-Tavi" by Rudyard Kipling. The second paragraph, for instance, vividly describes Rikki-Tikki-Tavi. After students have read this paragraph, have them search through stories that they have enjoyed reading to find paragraphs that contain vivid descriptions. Then have volunteers share their findings.

ANSWERS
Exercise 5

This exercise will be satisfactorily completed if the students list sensory details in a logical spatial order—from far away to near, from left to right, from top to bottom. There should be enough details to leave the reader with a clear picture of the subject described.

SELECTION AMENDMENT
Description of change: excerpted
Rationale: to focus on the concept of descriptive details as presented in this chapter

walk only one brick in width, and an old apple orchard in front, the barn and the pasture and fields of corn and wheat behind. Periodically there came sounds from the barn, and you could hear the crows, but everything else was still.

Eudora Welty, *One Writer's Beginnings*

EXERCISE 5 ▶ Collecting Descriptive Details

How would you describe an insect, a rock star, or a movie set? Work in a group of two or three classmates. Choose one of the subjects below and list sensory details that describe it. Then, arrange them in spatial order.

1. the creepiest animal you've ever seen
2. your favorite car
3. the best setting for a science fiction movie
4. your classroom, moments before a holiday break
5. your favorite season

Narration

What happened when a character lost in the frigid arctic wilderness couldn't build a fire? How is soccer played? What caused the ocean liner *Titanic* to sink?

SEGMENT 5 *(pp. 78–82)*

NARRATION

OBJECTIVES

- To create a story in chronological order
- To explain a process in chronological order
- To explain causes and effects

TEACHING THE LESSON

You may want to ask a different student to read each part of the explanations while the other students read along silently.

Explain chronological order by giving students an example. Make a list of several things you do when you rise each morning. Place these events in a scrambled order. Then show this list to students and have

When you answer any of these questions, you are *narrating*. That means you are telling about an event or an action as it changes over time. Because narrating tells about changes in time, you usually use *chronological*, or time, *order*.

You can use narration to tell a story (what happened to the character in the Arctic), to explain a process (how to play soccer), or to explain causes and effects (what caused the *Titanic* to sink).

Telling a Story. Everybody loves a good story. You've probably listened to one or told one today. It may have been made up, or it may have been about something that really happened.

The following is a story slaves told many years ago about some strange escapes from slavery.

Uncle Mingo's forehead wrinkled like a mask in the moonlight. "Don't make light of what old folks tell you, son," he warned. "If the old folks say they seen slaves pick up and fly back to Africa, like birds, just don't you dispute them. If they tell you about a slave preacher what led his whole flock to the beach and sat down on the sand with them, looking across the ocean

---

▼ **RESOURCES**

NARRATION
- Narration: Chronological Order

QUOTATION FOR THE DAY

"The only obligation to which in advance we may hold a novel . . . . is that it be interesting." (Henry James, 1843–1916, American novelist)

Use the quotation to prompt students to write journal entries about interesting novels or stories they have read. Explain that most novels and stories are forms of narration.

MEETING INDIVIDUAL NEEDS

AFRICAN AMERICAN

The excerpt from Arna Bontemps's *Chariot in the Sky* deals with escape from slavery and may be sensitive material to some students. You may find it useful to underscore the sobriety of the passage. Point out that the passage is written in dialect and therefore certain expressions differ from standard English.

them decide on the proper order. Lead students to understand that chronological order involves a time sequence.

GUIDED PRACTICE

You could use the example paragraphs to illustrate the three kinds of narration. Have a volunteer read each paragraph. Then work with the class to identify chronological order and transitions in each paragraph.

![hands icon] **COOPERATIVE LEARNING**
Organize the class into groups of four students to find and analyze examples of the three types of narration. Groups can use magazines, newspapers, and so on. Have each group find an example of each of the three types and explain how each example illustrates its type of narration. You could put these examples on a bulletin board and categorize them as storytelling, explaining a process, and explaining causes and effects.

toward home, don't ask no questions. Next morning nobody could find trace of that preacher or his people. And no boat had been there neither. One day when I was chopping cotton in the field, I looked up and the old fellow working in the row next to mine was gone. He was too feeble to run away, and I couldn't see no place for him to hide. None of the others in the field saw him leave either, but later on an old woman drinking water at a well, told us she noticed something pass in front of the sun about that time, like a hawk or a buzzard maybe, but she didn't pay it much mind."

Arna Bontemps, *Chariot In the Sky: A Story of the Jubilee Singers*

Explaining a Process. When you tell how to do something or how something works, you're *explaining a process.* Often, this means telling how to do something step by step—what is done first, then next, and so on. This is chronological order.

The following paragraph tells how kites may have been developed.

Like a lot of very old activities, no one is quite sure how kite flying started. Perhaps an ancient Chinese first noticed big leaves of certain plants fluttering at the end of long vines. Then, after watching "leaf-kites" for a while, he tied his straw hat to a string just for fun and happily found that the wind kept it flying. Later, he may have stretched a piece of animal skin over a bamboo frame and flown that from the end of a line.

Dan Carlinsky, "Kites"

SELECTION AMENDMENTS
Description of changes: excerpted
Rationale: to focus on the concept of narration as presented in this chapter

Explaining Causes and Effects. Narrating is also used to *explain causes and effects.* In other words, narrating can be used to tell how one event is a result of an earlier event.

INDEPENDENT PRACTICE

Exercise 6 will allow the students to work independently. Students could share their lists orally. Ask the other students to respond by telling the writer whether or not more information is needed and if the steps are presented in chronological order.

ASSESSMENT

Have students write one paragraph from the three outlines created for **Exercise 6.** These paragraphs will be acceptable if they are complete and presented in chronological order.

Ways of Developing Paragraphs **81**

The following paragraph tells what causes crickets to stop chirping. It also tells one helpful effect of their sudden silence.

Effect
Cause

Cause

Effect

> As you walk along the sidewalk, the tree crickets keep up their song until you are quite close; then they stop. They can sense your presence and fall silent. If, as sometimes happens in Blantyre, there is a leopard prowling around among the trash cans a few blocks away, then the tree crickets near to it will stop singing, and you will be warned of its presence in time to turn back. So singing insects are excellent watchdogs.
>
> Carson I. A. Ritchie, *Insects, The Creeping Conquerors and Human History*

EXERCISE 6 ▶ **Using Narration to Develop Paragraphs**

Can you tell a story about the time you were most frightened? Can you explain how to tie your shoes? Can you tell the causes and effects of not cleaning up your room for a month? The following exercises will give you some practice in telling about events in the order in which they happen. Follow the directions for each item.

CRITICAL THINKING
Analysis

To reinforce that professional writers write narrative paragraphs following chronological order, ask each student to bring to class one example of a narrative paragraph from a book or a magazine. In class, ask students to circle the transitions that indicate time (chronological order) and to number each new step in their narratives.

SELECTION AMENDMENT
Description of change: excerpted
Rationale: to focus on the concept of narration as presented in this chapter

ANSWERS

Exercise 6

Responses will vary.

1. The list should contain three or more events, in chronological order, that tell the story indicated.

2. The list should contain three or more steps, in chronological order, that explain the chosen process.

3. The list should contain at least three possible causes or three possible effects.

▼ **RESOURCES** ▼

COMPARISON AND CONTRAST

• Comparing and Contrasting

QUOTATION FOR THE DAY

"Fiction is a removing activity. The ghost that haunts all writers is, 'Am I betraying reality?'" (John Fowles, 1926–   , English novelist)

Ask students to freewrite for a few minutes about how their lives differ from the fictional lives of characters their age in books or on television programs or in movies. Explain that students have just participated in comparing and contrasting.

82

1. Each of the topics below could be the subject of a story. Select one of these topics and make up three or more events that might be in the story. Arrange all of the events in chronological order. Don't forget to use your imagination.
   a. A mysterious light follows your family's car down a lonesome, country road one night.
   b. A tall, shy, new student enters your school. He doesn't really fit in at first, but soon the situation changes.

2. Pick one of the following activities. Then list three or more steps you'd need to take in order to perform this activity. Arrange the steps in chronological order— that is, the order in which they should happen.
   c. how to boot up (start) a computer
   d. how to clean up your room

3. Choose one of the following. Give at least three possible causes or three possible effects.
   e. missing the school bus (give causes)
   f. a water shortage in your town or region (give effects)

Comparison and Contrast

How are ice skates like roller blades? In what ways are they different?

If you can answer these questions, you can compare and contrast ice skates and roller blades. Whenever you *compare,* you tell how things are alike. Whenever you *contrast,* you tell how things are different from one another.

When you compare and contrast, you can use *logical order.* Something that is logical is something that makes sense. When you compare and contrast, it is logical to group related ideas together.

Read the following paragraph. The writer compares and contrasts her two sisters. How are the sisters alike? How are they different?

SEGMENT 6 *(pp. 82–83)*
COMPARISON AND CONTRAST
OBJECTIVE
- To write statements that compare and contrast two subjects and to share these statements with a group

TEACHING THE LESSON

After reading the lesson, use two objects, perhaps an apple and an orange and guide students by comparing and contrasting these objects. Write all descriptions on the chalkboard. Then assign **Exercise 6** and use students' responses to assess their progress. To close, have volunteers read their answers to **Exercise 6.** ■

Comparison

Contrast

> My sisters may be twins, but they are very different. Sara and Sally look exactly alike. They both have long, braided black hair and big black eyes with eyelashes out to there. But the resemblance stops with looks. If they just stand still, they can pretend to be each other. If they talk or move, the joke is over. Sara talks all the time and bounces just like Winnie the Pooh's friend Tigger. Sally never says anything except "Pass the peanut butter," and she moves like a sick snail. How can they be twins?

LEP/ESL

General Strategies. Some students may be confused by the concept of comparing and contrasting. Try a demonstration for the class. List two related topics on the chalkboard and have students suggest likenesses and differences and write these. Then rearrange this information into separate categories. Emphasize that you are grouping ideas so that they relate more closely.

E X E R C I S E 7 ▶ **Speaking and Listening: Comparison and Contrast**

Remember the ice skates and roller blades? Now it's your turn to think about two subjects that are enough alike to be compared and different enough to be interesting. Write one statement that tells how these subjects are alike and one statement that tells how they are different. Share your statements with a small group. With the help of the group, think of some other similarities and differences.

You might compare and contrast the following items:

1. being a child and being a teenager
2. good horror movies and bad horror movies
3. living in a large city and living in a small community

ANSWERS
Exercise 7

Responses will vary. Each group member should develop at least one valid comparison statement and one valid contrast statement.

EVALUATION

OBJECTIVES

- To write an evaluation of a given subject
- To list reasons in the order of importance

TEACHING THE LESSON

Try to motivate students by asking them first to evaluate a current movie, by giving reasons why it is good or bad. Then read the textbook information aloud to the students, pausing for discussion after each paragraph. You can also analyze the example about Yellowstone Park with the class. Then model **Exercise 8** for students. They can

---

RESOURCES

EVALUATION
- Evaluating

QUOTATION FOR THE DAY

"You are just a puzzled man making notes about what you think." (Walter Lippmann, 1899–1974, American journalist)

Explain to students that most people are making notes when they develop opinions. Then tell the class that writing a good evaluation involves organizing one's opinions in the order of their importance. Have students choose a subject and practice defining their opinions in journal entries.

MEETING INDIVIDUAL NEEDS

LEP/ESL

General Strategies. Allowing students to work in small groups to complete **Exercise 8** may help students who are having difficulty in finding specific details to use as support in their writing. Find out which students have seen the same movies recently or have regularly viewed the same programs. Group these students and ask groups to list a specified number of reasons for their evaluations.

Evaluation

Do you like broccoli? Did you enjoy Robert M. Service's poem "The Cremation of Sam McGee"?

Whenever you answer questions like these, you're *evaluating.* In other words, you're telling whether you think broccoli and the poem are good or bad. You'd want to give reasons for your answer. For example, you might say you gagged on cooked broccoli, but you love raw broccoli with cheese dip. You might say you enjoyed the poem because of its rhyme or because of its humor.

When writing an evaluation, you will probably organize it by *order of importance.* For example, you might place your most important information first. Then you'd put your next most important information, and so on. Or, you might arrange your most important information last, so that you gradually lead up to your biggest point.

The following paragraph was written to persuade people not to build more buildings in Yellowstone National Park. Notice the reasons the writer gives for the evaluation.

	I don't think that more hotels, campgrounds, and restaurants should be built in Yellowstone National Park. The park is set aside to protect the animals and plants that live there and to allow people to experience the wilderness. When more buildings
Reason	go up, more people crowd into the park. And the more people there are, the less room there is for wildlife and for wilder-
Reason	ness. People don't just take up space. They also scare the animals and keep them from living as they would naturally live in the wild. In Yellowstone National Park, I think
Evaluation	the most important thing is to protect the animals and the natural wilderness. If this means putting a stop to more building, then the building should be stopped.

complete the exercise independently. To assess progress, have students use their responses to **Exercise 8** and develop these responses into evaluative paragraphs.

CLOSURE

Have volunteers read their evaluations aloud. After each paragraph has been read, have other students list on the chalkboard what information they heard in the evaluation. ■

EXERCISE 8 ▶ **Developing an Evaluation**

What's your evaluation? Why do you think so? Choose one of the following subjects and write your evaluation of it. Give at least two reasons for your opinion. List first the reason you think is more important.

→ EXAMPLE **1.** our school's basketball team

    1. *Evaluation:* It's a very good team.
         Reasons: (1) Our center is five foot ten.
               (2) Our guards are very quick.
               (3) Players who are not even starting are also good shooters.

1. the street you live on

2. a book you've read lately or movie you've seen recently

3. the newest fad in clothes

ANSWERS
Exercise 8

Responses will vary, but are considered acceptable if they follow the example's structure, state an opinion, and offer at least two reasons supporting that opinion.

MAKING CONNECTIONS

WRITING A PARAGRAPH TO EXPRESS YOURSELF OBJECTIVE

- To use the writing process to write an expressive paragraph

WRITING A PARAGRAPH TO EXPRESS YOURSELF

Teaching Strategies

Help students begin by asking them to write possible completions to each of the suggested beginning sentences. Ask for volunteers to read their ideas for each topic to help other students think of similar incidents or feelings.

Students can give feedback about the unity and coherence in the paragraphs. You may want to display students' completed paragraphs.

GUIDELINES

If you give students the option of not sharing their expressive writing with others, then just completing the assignment is acceptable. If you haven't given them that option, the paragraph should meet these criteria:

1. There is a topic sentence.

2. All sentences develop the main idea.

3. Transitions make the organization clear.

4. There is a conclusion.

MAKING CONNECTIONS

Now that you know the form and structure of paragraphs, how do you use your knowledge? Try applying what you've learned as you write paragraphs for different purposes. Remember that the basic purposes of writing are self-expression, information, persuasion, and creativity.

WRITING PARAGRAPHS FOR DIFFERENT PURPOSES

Writing a Paragraph to Express Yourself

Have you ever thought about writing as a way to think problems through? as a way to explore an idea you're puzzling over? or maybe as just a way to decide what you really do think about something? Writing can help you sort out your thoughts.

On a separate sheet of paper—or in your journal or diary if you keep one—write an expressive paragraph. Use one of the following sentences to get started. See where it leads you.

1. My closest friend means so much to me because ____.
2. I'm happiest when I'm ____ because ____.
3. One thing I'd like to change about myself is ____.
4. I get sad when I think about ____.
5. Something I'd really like to do within the next year is ____.

 Prewriting.   Sometimes you don't really know what you think until you sit down to write about it. Then the ideas may come out in a rush and all out of order. That's okay. Just start writing. Don't worry about complete sentences, picking the right word, or even correct spelling.

- To use the writing process to write a persuasive paragraph

Writing, Evaluating, and Revising. Expressive writing is often a very personal kind of writing. You may not want to share this writing with others. In that case, just write a draft. You may not need to revise it. If you want to share it with others, though, you should reread it. Check it for unity and coherence. Are the sentences organized so the ideas are clear?

Proofreading and Publishing. If you have decided to share your writing with others, be sure that you proofread it carefully. Check your usage and mechanics. You may want to make a clean copy for others to read.

Writing a Paragraph to Persuade

One of the earliest skills you learned was persuasion. You may have used it to get your mom or dad to buy a certain cereal in the supermarket. Sometimes parents are easy to persuade. Sometimes they aren't. Convincing other people can be just as hard or harder. You need to have reasons that support the point you want to make.

Look at the photographs. One shows an abandoned railroad track. The other shows a bike path that was built along a strip of land that was once a railroad. Imagine that a railroad that runs through your county has been abandoned. The railroad company is willing to give it to the county, but the county doesn't know what to do with it.

WRITING A PARAGRAPH TO PERSUADE
Teaching Strategies

Explain the imaginary situation presented in the textbook and encourage students to give their ideas orally, either in support of the proposal or in opposition to it. Then let students work in groups, each group producing one letter to a county official. After the letters are finished, ask each group to read its letter to the class. As a follow-up, or for extra credit, encourage students to take positions on a controversy in your community and to write letters to the appropriate officials or to a local newspaper.

GUIDELINES
Use the following criteria for evaluating students' paragraphs:

1. The writer's opinion was clear.
2. The arguments were convincing.
3. Every sentence supports the topic sentence (opinion).
4. The arguments are arranged in logical order.

Some people want to turn it into a bikeway, like the one in the photograph. But many people, especially people who own land along the railway, oppose the bikeway. They are afraid that they'd lose their privacy and that the county can't afford to build and maintain the bikeway.

Write a paragraph in which you try to persuade county leaders either to support the bikeway or to oppose it. Think about the advantages and disadvantages of your proposal and organize your reasons carefully. You may want to review the section on Evaluating (page 84) before you begin writing.

Prewriting. You may want to begin by listing your reasons for supporting or opposing the bikeway. Choose the best two or three reasons for your paragraph.

Writing, Evaluating, and Revising. You'll want to begin your paragraph with a clear topic sentence that states your opinion. You can use one of these topic sentences or make up your own.

> The county government should support making a bikeway where the railroad used to run.

> The county government should oppose making a bikeway where the railroad used to run.

After completing your draft, review it carefully. Do you have two or three reasons? Do they support your topic sentence? Have you arranged them in the best order? Revise your paragraph to make it more convincing.

Proofreading and Publishing. Proofread your final draft and correct any errors in usage and mechanics. Then share your paragraph with classmates, your parents, or neighbors. Ask them if it persuaded them.

Writing a Paragraph to Inform

In school and out, you'll be asked to write paragraphs that inform. Your teachers want to see what you have learned

---

- To use the writing process to write an informative paragraph

WRITING A PARAGRAPH TO INFORM

Teaching Strategies

To make sure that students understand how to plan an informative paragraph, discuss the chart on the San Francisco earthquake and explain how to organize the facts given. Then ask students to write their paragraphs individually. Students can read and evaluate their rough drafts in groups of four or five students. While in groups, students should respond to the readings by answering the questions in the section on **Writing, Evaluating, and Revising** on p. 90.

in class. A friend may want your recipe for making a pizza. A relative in another state may want to know what you did on vacation.

The chart below gives information about the 1989 San Francisco earthquake. Use the information to write an informative paragraph. Here's a topic sentence to get you started.

> Topic Sentence: The 1989 San Francisco earthquake caused a great deal of damage.

THE SAN FRANCISCO EARTHQUAKE OF 1989

Occurred October 17, 1989, with many aftershocks
Measured 7.1 on the Richter scale
Collapsed $1\frac{1}{4}$-mile section of double-decker Nimitz Freeway (I-880)
Caused delay of third game of World Series
Hundreds of buildings destroyed; thousands damaged
Damage of approximately six billion dollars
Official death toll of 63
More than 3,000 injured

GUIDELINES

A paragraph is acceptable if it includes a clear topic sentence, two or three sentences using information from the chart, unity with all sentences directly supporting the topic sentence, and clear transitions that show the organization of the paragraph. Each student should underline the topic sentence, circle transitions, number supporting facts, and question any information not directly related to the topic sentence.

WRITING A PARAGRAPH
THAT IS CREATIVE
OBJECTIVE
- To use the writing process to write a creative paragraph

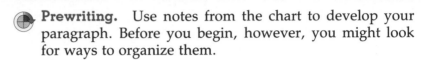

Prewriting. Use notes from the chart to develop your paragraph. Before you begin, however, you might look for ways to organize them.

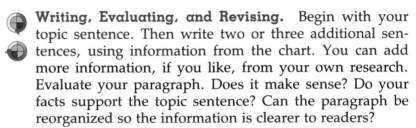

Writing, Evaluating, and Revising. Begin with your topic sentence. Then write two or three additional sentences, using information from the chart. You can add more information, if you like, from your own research. Evaluate your paragraph. Does it make sense? Do your facts support the topic sentence? Can the paragraph be reorganized so the information is clearer to readers?

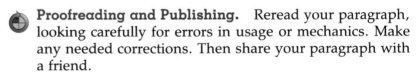

Proofreading and Publishing. Reread your paragraph, looking carefully for errors in usage or mechanics. Make any needed corrections. Then share your paragraph with a friend.

Writing a Paragraph That Is Creative

Try to visualize this scene. It's a dark, moonless night. You've been walking along a sandy beach for more than an hour. You're all alone, and this part of the beach is isolated. There are no lights anywhere to be seen. The wind is getting stronger and stronger. Waves are crashing against the beach. Suddenly, you hear the sound of horse hooves pounding into the sand. Then you hear a dog barking. You turn and look toward the sounds. You can't

WRITING A PARAGRAPH
THAT IS CREATIVE
Teaching Strategies

Read the first paragraph of this section aloud to help students visualize the scene. Ask them to respond orally to the questions given in the textbook before continuing the story. Have students work with partners to evaluate the endings. You may also want to ask students to prepare their final drafts—complete with illustrations—for publishing on the bulletin board.

GUIDELINES

These paragraphs will be acceptable if they provide a logical continuation of the scene, include at least three or four sentences of information, and tell the story clearly.

see anything at first. But then, the sounds draw closer. You can just make out the dark shape of a rider and horse coming toward you. A large dog races alongside, occasionally barking.

What happens next? Make it up. Write a paragraph that tells about the next event. Your paragraph doesn't have to tell the rest of the story. Just add some information about what occurs next. Use the following questions to help you write the paragraph.

- Is the rider a stranger or a friend?
- Is the dog chasing the horse and rider or running along with them?
- Do you feel threatened or relieved that the rider has come?
- Does the rider stop in front of you or go on past? If the rider stops, what do you say first?

Prewriting. Think about possible answers to the questions. You might try freewriting about the situation for a few minutes. Just let your ideas develop as you go. See where they lead you.

When you finish, read what you've written. Pick out one or two ideas and use them to develop your paragraph.

Writing, Evaluating, and Revising. Using the ideas from freewriting, write three or four sentences that tell what happens next. Remember, your paragraph doesn't have to complete the story. It only needs to tell the next part.

When you've finished your paragraph, review it. Does it leave the reader wanting to know more? Revise your paragraph to improve any weaknesses you've noticed.

Proofreading and Publishing. Read your final draft again and correct any errors in usage or mechanics. Then share your paragraph with a group of classmates. Discuss your ideas about how the story ends.

Chapter 3 LEARNING ABOUT COMPOSITIONS

OBJECTIVES

- To give personal responses to a work of literature
- To identify and analyze the characteristics of a composition
- To write a main idea based on a set of notes
- To organize notes for an early plan of composition
- To utilize various orderings in composition
- To analyze and identify types of introductions
- To use transitional words and phrases effectively
- To write a conclusion
- To analyze conclusions
- To write an informative composition

Motivation

As your seventh-grade students begin to study composition form, they might experience anxiety about writing. To allay their worries, provide several examples of compositions. For instance, you may choose an article on skateboarding or a profile on a popular music group. By showing students that compositions encompass many aspects of daily life, you can encourage them to be receptive to the information in this chapter. Once you have shown students the examples, initiate a discussion of the structural components of these compositions. Have students identify the ways the compositions begin and end. Depending on the compositions used, students might be able to identify a clear link between the introduction and the conclusion. Explain that well-written compositions share several characteristics.

Introduction

Through a discussion of the uses of composition form, help students see that the order in which information is presented is extremely important. A well-written composition must have a clear beginning, a well-ordered body, and a clear conclusion.

Show students that composition form is used to achieve all of the aims of discourse. A composition can be used to inform, to express, to create, or to persuade. For instance, if the subject of a composition were "football," it might inform its audience of the outcome of a game, express displeasure with the behavior of visiting fans, tell a story about what might have happened during the coach's pep talk, or persuade the audience to cheer for a specific team.

Integration

This chapter may be used to enhance other activities in your classroom. For example, if students are having difficulty organizing any type of writing, have them refer to the information about early plans and formal outlines in **Chapter 2**. This reinforcement will refresh students' memories about ordering information to achieve coherence and unity. The descriptions of chronological, spatial, and logical order may help students choose the most effective organization of their writing.

If you are beginning a creative-writing unit on short stories or poetry, the information on writing an introduction, body, and conclusion may be helpful to students. Alfred Noyes's "The Highwayman," Morley Callaghan's "Luke Baldwin's Vow," or Ernest Hemingway's "A Day's Wait" provide good examples.

The chart on the next page illustrates the strands of language arts as they are integrated into this chapter. For vocabulary study, glossary words are underlined in some writing models.

QUOTATIONS

All **Quotations for the Day** are chosen because of their relevance to instructional material presented in that segment of the chapter and for their usefulness in establishing student interest in writing.

INTEGRATING THE LANGUAGE ARTS

Selection	Reading and Literature	Writing and Critical Thinking	Language and Syntax	Speaking, Listening, and Other Expression Skills
"The Spaceport Mermaids" by Greg Walz-Chojnacki **94-95** **"A Son's Challenge"** by Gary Johnson **105**	Finding main idea **96** Identifying introduction **106** Analyzing introduction **96, 106** Analyzing conclusion **96, 110**	Analyzing composition form **96** Using reading to induce thought **96, 98** Choosing main ideas **98, 112** Grouping details **111-112** Ordering details **101, 111-112** Creating an early plan **101, 112** Analyzing introductions **96, 106** Understanding transitions **108-109** Writing a new conclusion **110** Analyzing information to organize for writing **101, 112** Writing a main idea **98, 112** Using writing process to write a composition to inform **111**	Organizing paragraphs to support a main idea **113** Using transitions **108-109** Proofreading for grammar, usage, and mechanics **113**	Sharing information and ideas in a small group **98, 110** Evaluating peer writing **110**

SEGMENT PLANNING GUIDE

Whether you are planning for a quick review of a writing concept or preparing an extended lesson on composition you can use the following Planning Guide to adapt the chapter material to the individual needs of your class.

SEGMENT	PAGES	CONTENT	RESOURCES
1 *Looking at the Whole*	*93-96*		
Literary Model **"The Spaceport Mermaids"**	94-95	Guided reading: a model of a composition	
Reader's Response/ Writer's Craft	96	Model evaluation: responding to literature and analyzing composition	
2 *What Makes a Composition*	*97-103*		The Main Idea of a Composition
What Makes a Composition	97	Introduction: learning about composition form	
The Composition Plan	98	Introduction: planning a composition	Grouping Details
The Main Idea	98	Explanation: focusing on a topic	Ordering Details
Exercise 1	98-99	Cooperative learning: writing the main ideas	
Early Plans	100	Introduction: grouping and ordering ideas	Formal Outlines
Grouping	100	Guidelines: using criteria to group details	
Ordering	100-101	Guidelines: learning chronological, spatial, and logical order	
Exercise 2	101	Cooperative learning: making an early plan	
Formal Outlines	101-102	Guidelines: examining a topic outline	
Writer's Model	102-103	Guided reading: examining a composition and an outline	
The Parts of a Composition	104	Introduction: examining the elements of a composition	
3 *The Introduction*	*104-106*		The Introduction
Capturing the Reader's Interest	104	Guideline: examining a good introduction	
Stating the Main Idea	104	Explanation: stating a main idea in an introduction	
Ways to Write Introductions	104	Guidelines: examining techniques	
Writer's Model	104	Guided reading: using a question as an introduction	
Literary Model from **"A Son's Challenge"**	105	Guided reading: using an anecdote as an introduction	
Writer's Model	105	Guided reading: using interesting facts as an introduction	
Exercise 3	106	Cooperative learning: identifying types of introductions	

SEGMENT	PAGES	CONTENT	RESOURCES
4 *The Body*	*107-109*		The Body Unity and Coherence
Unity	107	Explanation: using detail to unify a composition	
Chart: Framework for a Composition	107	Guidelines: structuring a unified composition	
Coherence	108	Guidelines: using order and transitional words for coherence	
Exercise 4	108-109	Applied practice: using transitions to connect sentences	
5 *The Conclusion*	*109-110*		The Conclusion
Ways to Write Conclusions	109	Examples: writing conclusions	
Writer's Models	109-110	Guided readings: examining interesting conclusions	
Exercise 5	110	Applied practice: rewriting a conclusion	
6 *Making Connections*	*111-113*		
A Composition to Inform	111-112	Guidelines: writing a composition to inform	
Writing a Composition to Inform	112-113	Applied practice: writing an informative composition	
WHOLE-CHAPTER RESOURCE Chapter Review			

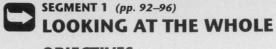

SEGMENT 1 *(pp. 92–96)*
LOOKING AT THE WHOLE

• To evaluate the composition structure of a literary model

OBJECTIVES
• To give personal responses to a work of literature
• To identify and analyze the characteristics of a composition

VISUAL CONNECTIONS
76 C-7

About the Artist. Al Held, born in 1928 in Brooklyn, New York, is a painter noted for his complex use of space. His abstract, geometrical work gives viewers a glimpse into a huge, multidimensional world. The forms in his paintings often seem to turn themselves inside out because of the optical illusion that results from a reversible perspective.

Related Expression Skills. Provide students with photocopies of optical illusions. Have them work in small groups to analyze the images to discover how the parts work together to create the illusion. Students might experiment by cutting and rearranging the images or simply by using different colors in them. Point out that the essential part of an optical illusion is intangible; the way the elements work together is what creates the effect. Relate this idea to the importance of arranging the elements of a written composition.

3 LEARNING ABOUT COMPOSITIONS

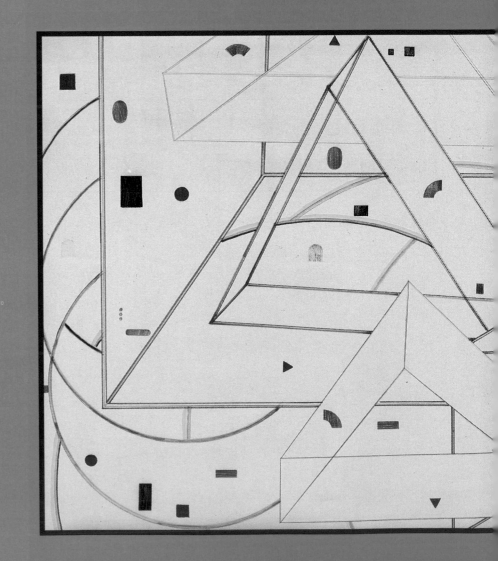

You may want to provide students with copies of a magazine, a newspaper, a literature book, or another source to look for similarities in form among different types of writing. Prompt students with questions about paragraph quantity, structure, and length.

Have a volunteer read the introductory paragraphs of the chapter, and discuss with the class why composition form is used so often.

Tell students to pay particular attention to the structure while they read the model. Because some of the language may be unfamiliar to students, you may want to read the article aloud to assess students' understanding more easily. ☞

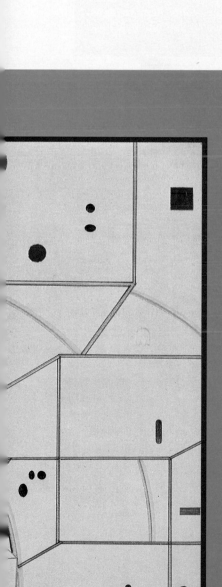

76 C-7, Al Held (1976). Colored pencil, graphite, crayon and felt-tip on paper. Sheet and image: 27 × 39 $\frac{13}{16}$ inches. Collection of Whitney Museum of American Art. Purchase with funds from the Drawing Committee. 86.2

Looking at the Whole

When you think about the volleyball team, do you think about the individual players? *Daniel has a strong serve, but Sarah is more accurate.* Or do you think about the whole team? *Our seventh-grade team is going to win the tournament.* In writing, you can think of words, sentences, or paragraphs as parts. A composition is a **whole** piece of writing.

Writing and You. A magazine article tells about a baseball superstar. A newspaper report tells about a teenager doing volunteer work. A student's history paper explains how the Civil War started. Each of these is a whole piece of writing, a kind of composition. Why do you think the composition form is used so often?

As You Read. On the next pages is a magazine article about manatees. What can you tell about composition form from reading this article?

QUOTATION FOR THE DAY

"Have common sense and . . . stick to the point." (Somerset Maugham, 1874–1965, British novelist and dramatist)

Write the quotation on the chalkboard and ask students to respond by freewriting for a few minutes on why Maugham's quotation is good advice for writers. You may want to tell students that most well-written compositions follow Maugham's directive, since they usually have one main idea and several paragraphs that support the main point.

MEETING
INDIVIDUAL
NEEDS

LEP/ESL

General Strategies. You may want to introduce students to composition form through group discussion. Bring the material to a more familiar level by asking students if they have ever written a personal letter. Emphasize that a personal letter is an example of composition. Ask the following questions: Do most personal letters have a beginning, a middle, and an end? Why is it important to follow this sequence? What objectives do we keep in mind when writing a letter? The idea here is to build on an experience (letter writing) that is likely to be familiar to the LEP/ESL student.

Discuss the **Reader's Response** questions with students. If they have never seen a manatee or a dolphin (question 1), they might describe incidents that they have read about or seen on television.

Answers to the **Writer's Response** questions may be used to assess students' mastery of composition structure.

RETEACHING

Find a composition with a well-defined introduction, body, and conclusion, and cut the composition apart by separating its three major sections. Then help students analyze the contents of the three sections so they can put the composition back together in the correct order.

USING THE SELECTION
The Spaceport Mermaids

1

Legends of mermaids have probably existed for thousands of years. A mermaid has the head and upper body of a woman and the tail of a fish instead of legs. Mariners believed mermaids to be signs of impending bad fortune.

94

"For centuries, sailors have told of the legendary mermaid which appeared to lonely mariners during their long sea voyages. Nowadays, astronauts, too, have the chance to see mermaids—at Kennedy Space Center in Florida."

the spaceport mermaids
by Greg Walz-Chojnacki

Mermaids?

1   Well, manatees, actually. Some people think these large, flippered creatures may have looked like <u>humanoids</u>—mermaids—to bored, superstitious seamen after months at sea.

Thousands of these gentle sea mammals live in the coastal waters of Florida, including the waterways of the Kennedy Space Center.

Unfortunately, these creatures, which have poor eyesight, are an endangered species. They are often injured by the propellers of power boats that cruise under the Florida sunshine. But the playful animals have been finding a safe <u>haven</u> in the waters surrounding the space center.

When NASA purchased 188,000 acres for the Apollo program, it set aside a large part of the land for the Merritt Island Wildlife Refuge. NASA has a policy of protecting many species there, including bald eagles, alligators, and sea turtles.

NASA has been protecting manatees since 1977. Although manatee deaths have been increasing in Florida, only two have died in space center waters since 1984, and those two died of natural causes.

CLOSURE

To reinforce the idea that composition is the most prevalent form of writing, have students brainstorm a list of places they see compositions. [Possible sources are magazines, newspapers, books, encyclopedias, textbooks, pamphlets, and other items.] To review, ask a volunteer to describe composition form.

ENRICHMENT

Students might want to learn more about manatees. Suggest that they research the topic and present their findings to the rest of the class. ■

95

NASA, in cooperation with state and federal wildlife agencies, has attached space-age radio monitors to some manatees to identify and protect their habitats. NASA also gives special training to space center personnel who operate boats, so they can avoid harming the creatures.

Even the boats used to recover the Shuttle's solid rocket boosters have been built with the manatees in mind. When retrieving the boosters in the Atlantic Ocean, the ships use ordinary propellers. But the ships are powered by water jets when they reach the waters inhabited by manatees.

The manatees seem to know a safe place when they find one. Their numbers have been increasing at the space center since 1984.

NASA's manatee protection policy has been a real success. Kennedy Space Center employees have many opportunities to see these fascinating creatures in the waterways of America's spaceport.

2   Now, if astronauts start seeing mermaids in orbit, that will be a completely different kind of problem!

"Some people think these large, flippered creatures may have looked like humanoids—mermaids—to bored, superstitious seamen after months at sea."

2
What would it mean if astronauts started seeing mermaids in orbit? [Responses will vary. Possibilities include that astronauts are seeing things that aren't there, or that there are creatures in space.]

👁 VISUAL CONNECTIONS
Ideas for Writing. You may want to have students use expressive/creative writing to compare manatees and mermaids or to describe an experience they have had with a manatee or a dolphin. Some possibilities include a short story in which a mariner finds a mermaid, a poem comparing manatees to mermaids, or a poem describing a personal encounter.

SELECTION AMENDMENT
Description of change: excerpted
Rationale: to focus on the concept of composition form presented in this chapter

ANSWERS

Reader's Response

Responses will vary.

1. Manatees and dolphins are liked because they are friendly, intelligent, and playful animals.

2. Students might mention the space shuttle, space exploration, or science. Manatees do not seem to have anything to do with the space center.

Writer's Craft

3. Each paragraph discusses the manatees in the waterways near the Kennedy Space Center. Walz-Chojnacki writes "NASA has a policy of protecting many species there . . ." and "NASA has been protecting manatees since 1977."

4. The mention of mermaids catches the reader's attention because it is startling. The Kennedy Space Center doesn't have obvious associations with mermaids.

5. The ending refers to the legends of sailors' seeing mermaids at sea and to the first paragraph's mention of mermaids at the Kennedy Space Center.

READER'S RESPONSE

1. If you have ever seen a manatee or a dolphin, tell about your experience with the animal. Why do you think people like these animals so much?

2. When you think of NASA and the Kennedy Space Center, what usually comes to your mind? Do you think of manatees?

WRITER'S CRAFT

3. How do you know that the main idea of the article is about NASA protecting the manatee?

4. The first paragraph talks about astronauts seeing mermaids. You know that mermaids don't exist. Why do you think the author begins the article this way?

5. How does the ending relate to the first paragraph?

LOOKING AHEAD

In this chapter, you'll learn about the parts of a composition. You'll find that most compositions are alike in certain ways. Most of them

- have one main idea
- have three main parts—an introduction, a body, and a conclusion
- have several paragraphs that work together to support the main idea

SEGMENT 2 *(pp. 97–103)*
WHAT MAKES A COMPOSITION?
OBJECTIVES
- To write a main idea based on a set of notes
- To organize notes for an early plan of a composition
- To determine the best order for a composition

Learning About Compositions **97**

What Makes a Composition?

Writing compositions probably isn't your favorite activity. Sometimes it's hard to think of something to write about. And then it may be hard to think of how to begin or end your composition.

In this chapter, you'll learn about composition form—how the different parts work together to create a whole piece of writing. Then you'll be able to use that form in other chapters to explain a process, to persuade, to write about literature, and to write a research report.

PEANUTS, reprinted by permission of UFS, Inc.

WHAT MAKES A COMPOSITION?
- The Main Idea of a Composition
- Grouping Details
- Ordering Details
- Formal Outlines

QUOTATION FOR THE DAY

"It you don't know where you are going, you will probably end up somewhere else." (Laurence J. Peter, 1919–   , Canadian educator)

Share this quotation with your students and use it to emphasize the importance of making early plans, arranging related groups of ideas, and constructing formal outlines.

MEETING
INDIVIDUAL
NEEDS

LEP/ESL

General Strategies. Instead of having students work independently to complete **Exercise 1**, create groups of three and have them brainstorm together. Then have one student from each group report its main idea. Write these ideas on the chalkboard as they are stated. Engage the class in a constructive analysis of each suggested main idea using the following questions. What factors contribute to a strong main idea? How can some of these main ideas be rewritten and strengthened?

To demonstrate the importance of organization to students, scramble the following group of sentences and write them on the chalkboard:

> Arnold walked down the street.
> First, he passed the grocery store.
> Next, he walked by the florist.

> Finally, he got to the theater at the end of the street.
> After buying his ticket, he went inside.
> The theater was dark.
> When the movie was over, he walked back home.

MEETING INDIVIDUAL NEEDS

LESS-ADVANCED STUDENTS

Some students might have difficulty focusing on specific main ideas or including appropriate information. To help students, give them several simple encyclopedia or magazine articles and have them find each article's main idea. Show students how each of the other sentences supports that main idea. You may want to point out information that the authors do not include because it is not relevant to the main idea.

ANSWERS

Exercise 1

Responses will vary.
One possible main idea is that recycling can save resources.

The Composition Plan

What are you doing this weekend? Will you work, play a sport, or take music lessons? You've probably already made some plans for this weekend and maybe for future ones. Compositions, like weekends, usually turn out much better when they are planned.

The Main Idea

When you have a topic for your composition, think what you want to say about it. What is most important and interesting? What you want to say about your topic is your *main idea.*

One writer wanted to write about competing in a skateboarding contest. He thought about the days of practicing, the new tricks, and the excitement. He finally decided to focus on how much fun the contest was. "Skateboard contests are fun" became his main idea.

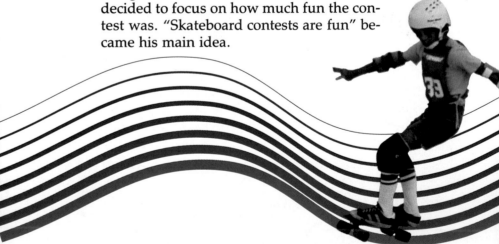

EXERCISE 1 ▶ **Writing the Main Idea**

Are you throwing away things that could be recycled instead? The writer who took the following notes became interested in recycling after hearing about the problems of too much trash. Read over the notes and decide on a main idea for a composition on recycling. Write down the main idea and then get together with two or three other students. Compare your ideas. Are they the same?

Ask students if they can determine the meaning of the sentences in their disorganized order. Have them put the sentences in an order that makes more sense. Point out that the order in which information is presented is extremely important to the meaning of a composition.

TEACHING THE LESSON

Have a volunteer read the introductory information. Discuss it as a class. Reassure students that learning composition form will make writing an easier, more understandable process. When they read **The Composition Plan,** have several students with plans for their weekends share

You can set up a recycling center in your home or school.

Try not to buy items in jars or boxes that can't be recycled.

Find out how to get a community recycling program started.

Don't accept food that's in plastic containers at fast-food restaurants.

Separate your trash, and throw away only what can't be recycled.

Don't waste paper—use both sides of your notebook and other writing paper.

Don't wrap your lunch in plastic.

Buy or make canvas or nylon grocery bags and lunch sacks that you can use again.

Don't buy things you don't really want or need.

INTEGRATING THE LANGUAGE ARTS

Literature Link. The short story "Last Cover" by Paul Annixter provides a good example of chronological order in a composition. Students could read this story and write down words or phrases that indicate time order. Then the class could discuss how the author uses time and its passage to frame the work. You may also want to have students locate sections of the story that use spatial or logical order to organize information. [An example of spatial organization that students might find is the description of Bandit's hiding place in the pool when the hunters are searching for him.]

MEETING **INDIVIDUAL** NEEDS

STUDENTS WITH SPECIAL NEEDS

Writing a composition can seem overwhelming to students with a visual motor deficit. You may want to have student helpers aid such students in organizing and in writing down ideas.

with the class to compare how each feels about making plans.

You may want to have the class generate a list of main ideas after you have gone over **The Main Idea** on p. 98. The list might include "Skateboard stunts are difficult," "Watching wrestling on television is enjoyable," or "We have the best football team in the state." Remind students that the topics "skateboarding," "wrestling," and "football" are too broad to be main ideas.

As you guide students through the information on early plans and formal outlines, stress that these are methods for organizing their work. The emphasis is not on any exact method of outlining as much as it is on the need to organize materials carefully. This is a good time to share other methods of

INTEGRATING THE LANGUAGE ARTS

Vocabulary Link. As students organize their compositions, emphasize the use of specific words as signposts. Explain that some words such as *however, but,* and *nevertheless* are used to indicate a reversal in thought. Words like *so, thus,* and *consequently* are used to summarize what an author is saying. Also, an author will sometimes use ordering words like *first, second, then,* and *finally* to organize information.

Keep a list of these signpost words on a bulletin board. Let students add words to the list and have them use the list when they write compositions.

TIMESAVER

At the end of this chapter, students are asked to write informative compositions. You may want to have them begin thinking about possible main ideas and the order of their compositions while the information is fresh in their minds. After referring to the **Making Connections** section, have students begin the writing process as you discuss composition features from main idea to conclusion. This method will give you more time to guide and evaluate students' application of the organizational material in this chapter.

WRITING NOTE   You can always change your main idea for your composition. As you find ideas and think about your topic, you may decide that you want to say something different. Then you can just rewrite your main idea.

Early Plans

An *early plan,* sometimes called an *informal outline,* is a way to organize your ideas. First, put your ideas into related groups. Then, arrange the groups in an order that makes sense to readers.

Grouping.   Look at the information you have. Which details belong together? Do you have several notes about one part of your topic? Follow these steps to group ideas.

1. Group notes that have something in common.
2. Write a heading for each group of notes.
3. Put the heading with that group of notes. (This will make it easier to organize your writing later.)
4. If you have notes that don't seem to fit, set them aside. Later, you may find a place to use them.

Ordering.   The order you use depends partly on your information. What should come first? What last? If your composition tells about how to perform skateboarding tricks, you're writing about a step-by-step process. Then it's natural to use *chronological* (time) *order.* Is your composition about a trip to see the giant redwoods? You might use *spatial order* and describe the trees in the order you see them.

The important thing is to arrange your ideas in an order that makes sense to readers. The writer of the composition on pet pigs (page 102) uses *logical order.* The writer tells first about the benefits of having a pet pig and then tells about the drawbacks. In logical order, related ideas are grouped together. This early plan shows how the writer grouped related ideas for the essay.

organizing such as graphic organizers.

Read **A Writer's Model** on p. 102 with students to compare the actual structure of the work with the outline.

Have students share their main ideas for **Exercise 1** with the class so that you can point out that there is more than one correct main idea for every topic; the main idea depends upon the composition's focus within the topic.

To prepare students to create early plans in **Exercise 2**, explain that differing main ideas might yield differing organizational plans. Use students' plans to demonstrate how the details and information can be organized to best support the main ideas.

TOPIC: PET PIGS	
BENEFITS	DRAWBACKS
clean easier than some other animals to housebreak don't shed or get fleas can communicate easy to train will play and do tricks easy to feed	can get very large can be lazy can be too playful not a good watch animal

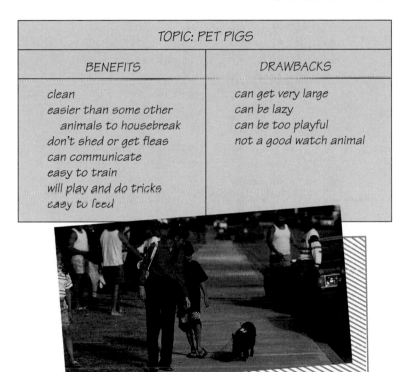

VISUAL CONNECTIONS
Exploring the Subject.
Knowing that pigs are intelligent animals, some scientists studied their language to see if the sounds were significant. They learned that the grunts have meanings like "Watch out," "Here I am," "Dinner is ready," and "Who are you?"

ANSWERS
Exercise 2

Responses will vary. Here is a possibility:

Logical Order

Ideas for your home:

You can set up a recycling center in your home.
Separate your trash, and throw away only what can't be recycled.
Don't waste paper—use both sides of your notebook and other writing paper.
Don't wrap your lunch in plastic.

Ideas for your community:

Find out how to get a community recycling program started.
Don't buy things you don't really want or need.
Buy or make canvas or nylon grocery bags and lunch sacks that you can use again.
Try not to buy items in jars or boxes that can't be recycled.
Don't accept food that's in plastic containers at fast-food restaurants.

EXERCISE 2 ▶ Making an Early Plan

Working with a partner, make an early plan for a composition based on the notes on recycling in Exercise 1. What will be the best order for the composition? After you decide, group the notes in that order. Then arrange the notes within the groups in a way that makes sense.

 REFERENCE NOTE: For more help in arranging ideas, see pages 77–84.

Formal Outlines

A *formal outline* is more structured than an early plan. It uses letters and numbers to label main headings and ideas that belong below those headings. A formal outline can have either topics (single words or phrases) or complete sentences.

As practice for organizing information, have students rewrite their early plans as formal outlines. They could do this rewriting independently before comparing their formal outlines with outlines of other students for **Exercise 2.**

To provide students an opportunity to demonstrate their understanding of the information, give them a list of details similar to the recycling notes in the text. Then have students use these details to develop main ideas, form early plans, and organize plans into formal outlines.

MEETING INDIVIDUAL NEEDS

ADVANCED STUDENTS

Students might already be well versed in organizing compositions. You may want to work with students on utilizing the organization of their essays to further support their main ideas. Give students short magazine or encyclopedia articles along with main ideas slightly different than those of the articles, and have students arrange the material to best support the new idea. Tell students they may make changes in content, if necessary. Also, remind them that the ordering of the material should be like an arrow pointing the reader's thoughts toward the main idea. Tell students to be prepared to defend the changes they make.

102   *Learning About Compositions*

Here's a topic outline for the essay on pet pigs. Compare it to the finished composition, below. Notice that the introduction and conclusion aren't a part of the outline.

Title: The Patter of Little Hooves
Main Idea: Pigs make great pets.

  I. Benefits
    A. Characteristics
      1. Cleanliness
      2. Ease of housebreaking
      3. Lack of fur and fleas
      4. Friendliness
    B. Enjoyment of games
      1. Fetching
      2. Swimming
      3. Rolling over
      4. Climbing stairs
  II. Drawbacks
    A. Playfulness
    B. Inability to protect

☞ **REFERENCE NOTE:** For more information about formal outlines, see pages 333–334.

A WRITER'S MODEL

Here's the composition on pet pigs. See how the paragraphs are based on the parts of the outline? Does every paragraph support the idea that pigs make great pets?

The Patter of Little Hooves

INTRODUCTION

What comes to mind when you think about pigs? Many people think of words like <u>dirty</u>, <u>smelly, unfriendly</u>, and even <u>stupid</u>. It may surprise you, but these words don't describe pigs at all. You may be even more surprised that

Main idea

many people think that pigs make great pets.

CLOSURE

Ask students to explain why good organization is so important in writing a composition. List possible topics on the chalkboard and discuss suitable main ideas for each topic. How would a composition be organized if students actually wrote one for one of the topics?

ENRICHMENT

Give students copies of a fairly short encyclopedia article and have them analyze its organization by creating outlines or maps of the article. This activity will help students see how professional writers also use organizational tools in writing compositions. ■

103

INTEGRATING THE LANGUAGE ARTS

Grammar Link. If you prefer that students use complete sentences in outlines, have them rewrite into complete sentences the words and phrases of the model outline.

Technology Link. Students who are using computers should become familiar with the outlining feature of some word processing programs. The feature serves as a tool for planning and organizing and allows the user to move blocks of text around easily.

BODY

Main topic: Characteristics

As a matter of fact, pig lovers will tell you that pigs are very pleasant. Many people say that pigs are much better pets than cats or dogs. They point out that pigs are really very clean and are more easily housebroken than most other pets. Pigs don't shed or get fleas. And they are friendly companions. They are happy to sit quietly and watch TV with you and never complain about your choice of programs.

Main topic: Enjoyment of games

Pigs learn quickly and enjoy playing games. They will happily fetch sticks that are thrown for them. They can also be taught to swim, roll over, climb stairs, or do just about any other pet trick.

Main topic: Playfulness and inability to protect

On the other hand, pet pigs have their drawbacks. For one thing, they can be too playful. One pig owner found that nothing could stop her pet pig from taking the phone off the hook. He liked to hear the dial tone! Also, they won't protect you. They're more likely to smile at a burglar than to run the criminal off.

CONCLUSION

Pigs have possibly been around for about thirty-five million years. Yet it's only recently that people have begun to use words like cuddly, sweet, and smart to describe them. The day of the pig has finally arrived. Who knows? Maybe someday you'll hear the patter of little hooves around your house.

THE PARTS OF A COMPOSITION: THE INTRODUCTION

OBJECTIVES

- To analyze several types of introductions
- To identify introduction types

TEACHING THE LESSON

To capture students' interest, discuss the beginnings of several movies. A movie director knows that the opening scenes must quickly capture the viewers' attention. For example, *Star Wars* begins with a battle scene between forces of the Rebel Alliance and the Imperial forces, and *Dances with*

RESOURCES

THE PARTS OF A COMPOSITION: THE INTRODUCTION

- The Introduction

QUOTATION FOR THE DAY

"The worst sin is dullness." (David H. C. Read, 1910–   , Scottish-born American, clergyman, author, and former POW)

Write the quotation on the chalkboard and have students write journal entries relating the quotation to the characteristics of good writing. Encourage students to remember Read's thought—especially when they write introductions.

MEETING
INDIVIDUAL
NEEDS

LEARNING STYLES

Auditory Learners. Have students read aloud the sample introductions, or allow students to read aloud quietly as they work. If students are still having difficulty understanding what they are reading, read the passage to them while they listen.

The Parts of a Composition

A composition may have several paragraphs, but it has three basic parts. The first part is the *introduction*. It's a little bit like the topic sentence in a paragraph. The second part may be much longer. It's called the *body*. The last part is the *conclusion*. It ends the composition.

The Introduction

Does the first paragraph of a book or an article sometimes capture your interest immediately? Do you keep reading to find out more?

Capturing the Reader's Interest. A good *introduction* grabs the reader's attention. It makes the reader want to read the rest of the composition. For example, the writer of the composition about pet pigs asks a question and follows it with a surprising statement. Just when the reader begins thinking about the usual bad words used to describe pigs, the writer says that pigs are not at all like most people think. Most readers will want to keep reading to find out why this is so.

Stating the Main Idea. A good introduction also states the main idea. This tells the reader what the composition will be about.

Ways to Write Introductions

You can use several different ways to make an introduction interesting. The following numbered examples show a few techniques you might try.

1. **Ask a question.** You've seen how a question works in the introduction to the composition on pigs. Here's another example. The writer asks a question and then immediately answers it.

   What's a top-notch sport that's rolling its way from coast to coast? Roller-blading!

As these opening movie scenes capture a viewer's interest, a good introduction should capture the reader's attention and prepare the reader for the main discussion of the subject.

Have a student read the introductory material to the class. As you explain each of the possible types of introductions, ask students if their sample introductions fit the type being presented. Have students share their introductions with the class. This activity could also be used as an aid in assessing students' understanding of the material.

Guide students through **Exercise 3** if they are having difficulty differentiating the types of introductions. If they seem to have a

The Introduction **105**

2. **Tell an anecdote.** An *anecdote* (a short, interesting, or even humorous story or incident) adds drama to your composition. Your reader will be caught by the humor or the human interest. Anecdotes add intriguing details to an introduction. This anecdote is from the introduction to a dramatic article about the son of a woman with multiple sclerosis.

> One Saturday afternoon in January 1989, Suzan Sharp, 43, and her eight-year-old son, David, were trudging across a snowy parking lot in Chippawa Falls, Wis., when Suzan's cane slid on an ice patch. She tumbled face-first into the slush. David rushed to his mother's side. "Are you all right, Mom?"
>
> Gary Johnson, "A Son's Challenge"

3. **State an interesting or startling fact.** Curiosity also makes a reader want to read on. An exciting statement of fact creates curiosity.

> Most people know about the huge Saint Bernards who save travelers lost in the mountains, but a tiny canary once saved its owner's life. As its elderly owner lay unconscious on the floor, the bird flew to a niece's house and got attention by tapping again and again on the window. It seems that pets of all kinds have saved human lives.

MEETING INDIVIDUAL NEEDS

ADVANCED STUDENTS

Students might not have difficulty identifying the different types of introductions, so you may not want them to follow the stated directions in **Exercise 3.** Instead, have them rewrite each of the introductions in a different way. For instance, number 1 states an interesting or startling fact. Have students rewrite it so that it begins with a question.

SELECTION AMENDMENT
Description of change: excerpted
Rationale: to focus on the concept of introductions presented in this chapter

CLOSURE

Locate introductions in two or three magazine, encyclopedia, or textbook articles. Have students classify the introductions by type and explain why the introductions are or are not effective. ■

ANSWERS

Exercise 3

1. stating an interesting or startling fact
2. asking a question
3. telling an interesting anecdote

 INTEGRATING THE LANGUAGE ARTS

Literature Link. Have students read the first three paragraphs of Mona Gardner's "The Dinner Party" or a similar work. Before allowing students to read further, ask what this introduction does. What do they already know about the story? Can they make any predictions about what will happen? Once students have finished reading the entire work, remind them of their responses to the above questions. How accurate were their predictions? Did the story's introduction have a connection to the ending? "The Dinner Party" could also be used as an example for the next two segments of this chapter (**The Body** and **The Conclusion**).

EXERCISE 3 ▶ **Identifying Types of Introductions**

Can you recognize the three ways of writing introductions? Working with two or three classmates, try to identify the technique used in each of these introductions.

1.   There's a mystery in the sky. Centuries ago, ancient astronomers wrote about it. But when later astronomers looked for it, most of them thought the ancient astronomers were wrong. The mystery in the sky is whether there is a tenth planet, out beyond Neptune and Pluto. Many scientists believe Planet X is lurking out there waiting to be rediscovered!

2.   *Do, re, mi, fa, sol, la, ti, do.* Did you ever wonder where in the world such words came from? An Italian monk named Guido d'Arezzo used the first syllable of each line of a Latin hymn to represent the music scale. Guido taught music in the monasteries, and the musical note system he developed made his work easier. Many people believe he is the inventor of written music.

3.   Susanne woke up early on the morning of her thirteenth birthday. Someone had tied a string to the foot of her bed. On the string was a note that said, "Follow me." She put her hand on the string and started walking. The string led first to her brother's room, where he and their parents were waiting to go with her while she followed the string. It was the beginning of the most exciting birthday Susanne ever had.

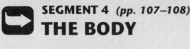
OBJECTIVE

- To use transitional words and phrases effectively

TEACHING THE LESSON

Using the same article or story that you used for **The Introduction**, analyze what happens in the middle paragraphs and emphasize how these paragraphs relate to the introduction.

Read with students the segment's introductory material and the material on unity. Refer to **"The Spaceport Mermaids"**

The Body **107**

The Body

The *body* of a composition usually contains several paragraphs, and every paragraph helps to support the main idea by developing a part of it.

All these paragraphs somehow have to stick together, too. Have you noticed that you lose interest if what you're reading never makes a point or connects ideas? Compositions that bore you probably don't have *unity* and *coherence*.

Unity.   *Unity* means that the paragraphs in the body of your paper all work together to support your main idea. Look at the model composition on pigs (page 102). Notice how each of the paragraphs has its own main idea (topic). Now look at each of the paragraph topics again. Notice how each of these paragraph topics ties in with the main idea of the whole composition—"Pigs make great pets."

In addition, as you read each paragraph, you'll see that the details in it tie directly to the paragraph topic. So every sentence in every paragraph leads back to the main idea of the composition.

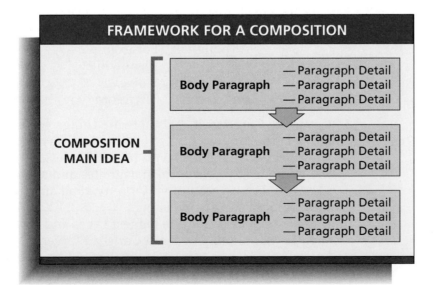

FRAMEWORK FOR A COMPOSITION

COMPOSITION MAIN IDEA

Body Paragraph
— Paragraph Detail
— Paragraph Detail
— Paragraph Detail

Body Paragraph
— Paragraph Detail
— Paragraph Detail
— Paragraph Detail

Body Paragraph
— Paragraph Detail
— Paragraph Detail
— Paragraph Detail

RESOURCES

THE BODY
- The Body
- Unity and Coherence

QUOTATION FOR THE DAY

"The trouble is, he jumbles his statements together—rather like a bag of eels in which you can't exactly see which are the heads and which are the tails." (John Dos Passos, 1896–1970, American writer)

Use the quotation to emphasize the importance of clarity and coherence in writing. Point out that transitions help guide the reader smoothly from the beginning to the end of a composition.

MEETING **INDIVIDUAL** NEEDS

LESS-ADVANCED STUDENTS

Students might have difficulty providing enough elaboration in the body paragraphs of their compositions. Give students three or four narrow, interesting topics. Work with students to provide at least three separate details that would support a main idea related to the topic. Emphasize the need to explain ideas so that readers will accept what is said.

and have students identify the details in each paragraph and explain how those details help to support the paragraph's and the composition's main ideas.

To help students understand the function of transitional words in achieving coherence, work with them to circle transitional words in a sample article. Discuss how the transitions function in the sentences and in the composition as a whole.

For closure, ask students the following questions:

1. How can you make certain that your composition is easy to follow?
2. What are some factors in making sure your paragraphs are easy to understand? ■

Coherence. Have you ever noticed how some things you read are easier to follow than others? One sentence leads easily into another, and one paragraph to the next. This type of writing has *coherence.*

You can do two things to make sure your composition has coherence. First, arrange your ideas in an order that makes sense. Second, make sure it's obvious to your readers how your ideas are connected. For example, you can let your readers know how your ideas are connected by using *transitional words and phrases* such as *for example, first, then, next,* and *finally.* In the composition on pigs, words and phrases such as *for one thing, on the other hand,* and *as a matter of fact* help the reader see the connections the writer is making.

☞ REFERENCE NOTE: See pages 74–75 for more information on transitional words and phrases.

EXERCISE 4 ▶ **Using Transitions**

Some transitional words and phrases are listed below. They are followed by some sentence sets that need them. Choose the best transition for each sentence set, but don't use the same word or phrase more than once.

Although	For example
Besides	Meanwhile
Eventually	However
As a result	Therefore

1. For example
1. Caves are fun to visit, but there are things you should know before you go. ___, you should always dress warmly and wear shoes with nonskid soles.
2. Many caves have beautiful stalagmites and stalactites. ___, some caves are not very pretty at all and just have smooth walls and ceilings. **2. However**
3. If you haven't been to the biggest caves and caverns, such as Mammoth Cave and Carlsbad Caverns, maybe you can go someday. ___, you might be able to visit a smaller cave close to where you live.
3. Meanwhile

THE CONCLUSION

OBJECTIVES

- To write a conclusion for a composition
- To analyze others' conclusions

TEACHING THE LESSON

By the time students reach the point of writing conclusions, they often feel as though they have already said all that they need to say. Remove the conclusion from an encyclopedia or magazine article (you may want to use an example you used with **The Introduction**), and have students read only the introduction and the body. Ask ☞

---

4. Caves are usually formed by water that flows underground and wears away rock over millions of years. ____, the water can form enormous rooms underground. **4. Eventually**

5. As a result *or* **Therefore**

5. When caves are formed in limestone, dripping water dissolves the rock. Over time, the drips harden into crystal formations. ____, limestone caves often have beautiful sparkling shapes in them.

The Conclusion

Your *conclusion* should let your readers feel that your composition is complete. It shouldn't stop suddenly so that they feel let down. Your conclusion needs to tie the ideas together and flow once again into your main idea.

Ways to Write Conclusions

1. **Refer to your introduction.** In the model composition on pigs (pages 102–103), the writer brings readers back to the idea of "words used to describe pigs."

> **Introduction:** Many people think of words like *dirty, smelly, unfriendly,* and even *stupid.*
>
> **Conclusion:** Yet it's only recently that people have begun to use words like *cuddly, sweet,* and *smart* to describe them.

RESOURCES

THE CONCLUSION
- The Conclusion

QUOTATION FOR THE DAY

"The best kind of showbiz is making your point." (Noel Coward, 1899–1973, British playwright)

Write the quotation on the chalkboard and ask students to freewrite for a moment about an instance when someone stated an opinion in a convincing way. Tell the class that the conclusion of a composition is the writer's final chance to make a convincing impression on the reader.

students if they feel as if the composition has ended. Do they want to know anything else? Is the article finished?

After students have read each conclusion type, ask them if they have ever seen a story or an article that ended in that way.

Before students complete **Exercise 5**, have them rewrite the conclusion for one of the articles you showed them previously.

For closure, ask the following question: What are three characteristics of a good conclusion? [It lets the reader feel the composition is complete. It doesn't stop suddenly. It ties the ideas and flows into the main idea.] ■

LEP/ESL

General Strategies. Making the concept of *conclusion* more concrete and encouraging the class to share appropriate examples is likely to interest and involve the LEP/ESL student more effectively than independent study would. Begin by explaining that people naturally like things to be completed. Ask students to share examples of conclusions in their daily environmemt and list these on the chalkboard.

ANSWERS
Exercise 5

Conclusions will vary. Here are two possibilities:

If you ever have the chance to visit the Kennedy Space Center, don't just look for the space shuttle. Include the manatees on your list of sights to see!

Pigs have no more drawbacks than more traditional pets such as dogs and cats. Also, they are friendly and playful. If you are considering getting a new pet, keep the pig in mind.

2. **Close with an interesting comment.** Another way to end your composition is to leave your readers with an interesting statement that clearly signals "the end."

> Roller-blading may not replace the bicycle as a way to travel, but for some people, it's the only way to roll!

3. **Restate your main idea.** One direct way to wrap up a composition is to restate your main idea *in different words*. This conclusion restates the idea that there is a mysterious planet somewhere out in space.

> Were the ancient astronomers right about a tenth planet? Is it orbiting far beyond Pluto and Neptune, waiting for astronomers to find it? Maybe someday soon there will be a tenth planet to learn about: the mysterious Planet X.

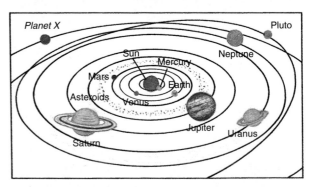

EXERCISE 5 ▶   Writing a Conclusion

The two models in this chapter—about manatees (page 94) and about pigs (page 102)—both use the same way of ending the composition. They both refer to the introduction. Write a new conclusion for one of these two models, using a different technique (pages 109–110). Then get together with two or three classmates and compare your conclusions.

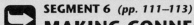
MAKING CONNECTIONS

A COMPOSITION TO INFORM
OBJECTIVE

- To write an informative composition

111

MAKING CONNECTIONS

A Composition to Inform

You write for different purposes. You write to express your feelings, to tell a story, to persuade, or to inform. You can use the composition form you learned in this chapter for all these purposes.

Here are some notes about Saint Augustine, Florida, one of the oldest cities in the United States. To help you get started, the information has been organized into three groups. Study the notes until you're familiar with the information. Then write a short composition to *inform* your readers about this historic city. You may not want to use all the information.

SAINT AUGUSTINE, FLORIDA
HISTORY
1. Ponce de León landed near the area in 1513, looking for the fountain of youth.
2. He claimed the land for Spain.
3. The settlement of Saint Augustine was established in 1565 by Pedro Menéndez de Avilés.
4. Saint Augustine is the oldest continuously settled site in the United States.
5. It was nearly destroyed by Sir Francis Drake and his English forces in 1586.
6. Spain sold Florida to the United States in 1821.

A COMPOSITION TO INFORM
Teaching Strategies

To help students begin, remind them that they have already written or evaluated introductions, bodies, and conclusions of compositions. Now they have only to put what they already know together.

Then answering any questions about the information, read the notes about Saint Augustine with your students. Reinforce that these are prewriting notes from which they can develop their main ideas.

You may need to lead students through the writing-process steps. Students can refer to the information in other segments of the chapter for help in writing the various parts of their compositions.

GUIDELINES

Use the questions for **Writing, Evaluating, and Revising** on p. 113 as a basis for grading students' compositions. Also, papers should be relatively free of grammar, usage, and mechanics errors.

LEP/ESL

General Strategies. Students who are new to the United States might need more information about Florida to complete their compositions. To remedy this situation, either provide books with more information on Florida or allow students to choose other more familiar locations.

SAINT AUGUSTINE, FLORIDA *(continued)*
LOCATION
1. Saint Augustine is located in northeastern Florida.
2. It is on a narrow peninsula formed by the Matanzas and San Sebastian rivers.
3. It is one-half mile from the Atlantic Ocean.
POINTS OF INTEREST
1. The Spanish fortress of Castillo de San Marcos was built in 1672 of coquina, a local shellrock. This is the oldest masonry fort in the United States.
2. The Cathedral of Saint Augustine was built in 1790. This is the seat of the oldest Catholic parish in the United States.
3. The Spanish Quarter is an area of reconstructed and restored buildings.

Writing a Composition to Inform

 Prewriting. After you've looked over the facts listed on page 111 and above, think about your main idea. What should it be? Write it down. Then use the three groups to create an early plan of your own.

Writing, Evaluating, and Revising. Think about some way to capture your reader's attention, and write your introduction.

Next, draft the body paragraphs of your composition. Remember that each paragraph must have a topic that ties into your main idea. Then write a conclusion that ties your information together and ends your composition in a satisfactory way.

When you have finished, look over your first draft, and see what can be done to improve it. You might trade papers with a classmate and evaluate each other's writing. Ask these questions about your paper:

1. Does the introduction grab the reader's attention?
2. Is the main idea stated clearly?
3. Does each body paragraph connect to the main idea?
4. Do the details in each paragraph connect to the paragraph topic?
5. Does the conclusion tie the composition together and make it seem complete?

Proofreading and Publishing. Set your paper aside for a while. Come back to it later and read over it again. Look for and correct any mistakes in grammar, usage, and mechanics. Then write or print out a clean copy. You could show your paper to your social studies teacher if you study the history of the United States. Or show it to your family as an idea for a place to visit.

TIMESAVER

To save time in grading the final compositions, have students use the sample questions for **Writing, Evaluating, and Revising** to complete peer evaluations.

To ensure objective evaluations, have students put code words instead of names on their papers. While you will have a list of names and code words, students will be unaware of whose papers they are reading.

Chapter 4

EXPRESSIVE WRITING

Motivation

You could begin by asking students to list all the kinds of writing they have done in the past six months. Then ask them to describe what they have written. Continue around the room until all students have given examples. After explaining the four aims of writing—expressive, persuasive, literary, and informative—have students attempt to classify each kind of writing they have done. They might discover that most of their writing is expressive—letters, notes, journals, or diaries. Explain that this will be the type of writing they will do in this chapter.

Introduction

Expressive writing is often the first type of writing students learn. You might emphasize that all writing involves a process and that skills learned in this chapter will be used in other kinds of writing as well. However, in expressive writing, students are writing about their personal experiences, while other writing has different aims. If they acquire these skills in this lesson, learning the other writing aims will probably be easier.

Integration

Students usually like to tell about what has happened to them. You could add a speaking or storytelling option to the assignments in this chapter. Students should prepare for speaking in the same way they prepare for a written personal narrative. Tell students they should use notes rather than read their essays.

In addition, explain to students that people have used expressive writing in subjects other than English. For example, scientists have kept journals about their research, and many historical figures have written extensive diaries. This chapter could accompany a unit on nonfiction, which would include some of these journals or diaries.

The chart on the next page illustrates the strands of language arts as they are integrated into this chapter. For vocabulary study, glossary words are underlined in some writing models.

QUOTATIONS

All **Quotations for the Day** are chosen because of their relevance to instructional material presented in that segment of the chapter and for their usefulness in establishing student interest in writing.

INTEGRATING THE LANGUAGE ARTS

Selection	Reading and Literature	Writing and Critical Thinking	Language and Syntax	Speaking, Listening, and Other Expression Skills
"The Jacket" by Gary Soto 116-121 "Dream of the Blue Dolphins" by Michael DiLeo 130-132 from **My Diary—My World** by Elizabeth Yates 143 from *Journal of an Indian Trader* by Anthony Glass 145-146	Experiencing vicariously the situations and events in a selection 121 Drawing conclusions and making inferences 121 Discovering reflections of personal values in literature 121 Evaluating main idea 121, 143 Responding creatively to writing 121 Identifying supporting details 121, 133, 145 Determining author's attitude 121, 138, 143 Analyzing an introduction 133 Identifying sensory details 121, 133, 138 Identifying author's opinion 121, 133	Evaluating a personal narrative 121, 139 Writing a journal entry 121, 143-144 Analyzing and identifying author's thoughts and feelings 121, 133 Using freewriting and clustering as prewriting techniques 124 Engaging in cooperative learning 124, 137, 139 Brainstorming 124 Choosing a topic 124 Collecting sensory details by visualizing 128 Arranging details in chronological order 128 Gathering and listing details 129, 146 Analyzing the parts of a personal narrative 133 Analyzing order of events 133, 145 Writing a first draft 135 Analyzing an author's revisions 137-138 Participating in peer evaluation 137, 139 Evaluating and revising a personal narrative 139 Proofreading and publishing a personal narrative 141 Writing a personal narrative 146 Writing a personal letter 147	Proofreading for usage and mechanics errors 141 Proofreading for punctuation 140	Telling stories 124 Listening to and responding to personal stories told by others 124 Relating ideas to personal experiences or prior knowledge 124 Listening attentively to record details 124 Discussing questions about a personal narrative with peers 133 Practicing peer evaluation with a partner 137-138

SEGMENT PLANNING GUIDE

Whether you are planning for a quick review of a writing concept or preparing an extended lesson on composition you can use the following Planning Guide to adapt the chapter material to the individual needs of your class.

SEGMENT	PAGES	CONTENT	RESOURCES
1 *Discovering Yourself*	*115-121*		
Literary Model **"The Jacket"**	116-121	Guided reading: a model of expressive writing	
Reader's Response/Writer's Craft	121	Model evaluation: responding to literature and analyzing expressive writing	
2 *Ways to Express Yourself*	*122*		
3 *Prewriting*	*123-129*		Writing a Personal Narrative Recalling Details
Choosing an Experience to Write About	123-124	Guidelines: selecting suitable topics for expressive writing	
Exercise 1	124	Cooperative learning: exploring topics for personal narratives	
Writing Assignment: Part 1	124	Applied practice: choosing a topic for a personal narrative	
Gathering and Organizing Your Ideas	125	Introduction: considering purpose and audience and recalling and arranging details	
Thinking About Purpose and Audience	125	Explanation: understanding purpose and audience	
Recalling Details	126-127	Guidelines: remembering events and sensory details	
Writing Note	127	Writing suggestion: using personal pronouns	
Critical Thinking: Visualizing Sensory Details	127	Guidelines: collecting details by visualizing	
Critical Thinking Exercise	128	Applied practice: listing sensory details	
Arranging Details	128-129	Guidelines: charting details in chronological order	
Writing Assignment: Part 2	129	Applied practice: charting events, sensory details, dialogue, thoughts, and feelings	
4 *Writing*	*130-135*		Ending a Personal Narrative
The Parts of a Personal Narrative	130	Explanation: learning the three basic parts of a narrative	
Literary Model **"Dream of the Blue Dolphins"**	130-132	Guided reading: examining a model of personal narrative	
Exercise 2	133	Cooperative learning: analyzing the organization of a personal narrative	
A Writer's Model for You	133	Introduction: examining techniques in a model	
Writer's Model	133-134	Guided reading: examining a sample essay	

SEGMENT	PAGES	CONTENT	RESOURCES
Chart: Framework for a Personal Narrative	135	Guidelines: structuring a personal narrative	
Writing Assignment: Part 3	135	Applied practice: writing a draft of a personal narrative	
5 *Evaluating and Revising*	*136-139*		Writing a Personal Narrative
Evaluating and Revising	136	Introduction: evaluating and revising a personal narrative	
Chart: Evaluating and Revising Personal Narrative	137	Guidelines: applying evaluation and revision techniques	
Exercise 3	137-138	Applied practice: analyzing a writer's revisions	
Writing Note	138	Writing suggestion: using dialogue	
Writing Assignment: Part 4	139	Cooperative learning: evaluating and revising personal narratives	
6 *Proofreading and Publishing*	*140-141*		Writing a Personal Narrative
Mechanics Hint	140	Writing suggestion: using dialogue	
Publishing	140-141	Publishing ideas: reaching an audience	
Writing Assignment: Part 5	141	Applied practice: proofreading and publishing	
7 *Writing Workshop*	*142-144*		All the resources in this chapter may be used in this segment.
A Journal Entry	142	Explanation: exploring through a journal	
Literary Model from **My Diary—My World**	143	Guided reading: examining a journal entry	
Writing a Journal Entry	143-144	Guidelines: applying skills to the writing process	
8 *Making Connections*	*145-149*		
Writing Across the Curriculum: Expressive Writing and History	145	Guidelines: identifying details in a model journal entry Applied practice: writing a personal narrative about an experience	
Literary Model from **Journal of an Indian Trader**	145-146	Guided reading: examining a model of a journal entry	
Expressive Writing and Personal Letters	146	Introduction: writing personal letters	
Writer's Model	147	Sample: examining thoughts and feelings in a personal letter	

WHOLE-CHAPTER RESOURCES
A Writing Process Log, A Writing Prompt, Holistically Graded Models, Assessment Portfolio Materials

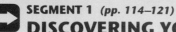

DISCOVERING YOURSELF

OBJECTIVES

- To respond to a personal narrative
- To write an expressive journal entry
- To identify sensory details in a personal narrative

- To analyze the author's purpose in a piece of expressive writing

 VISUAL CONNECTIONS
Pas de Deux

About the Artist. Miriam Schapiro was born in Toronto, Ontario, in 1923. She received her B.A., M.A., and M.F.A. degrees from the State University of Iowa. She became a full-time artist in 1955. In 1971 Schapiro co-founded the Feminist Art Program with Judy Chicago at the California Institute of Arts in Valencia. Schapiro's style evolved into a distinctive form of collage that includes fabrics, paints, and other materials in lively compositions.

Related Expression Skills. Schapiro used the name *femmage* to describe her collages. The term refers to using techniques and materials traditionally associated with women to create art that expresses a feminine point of view. Discuss with the class how the point of view of seventh-grade students is unique. What objects and activities are associated with early adolescence? Have interested students work together to incorporate their ideas into an expressive collage.

4 EXPRESSIVE WRITING

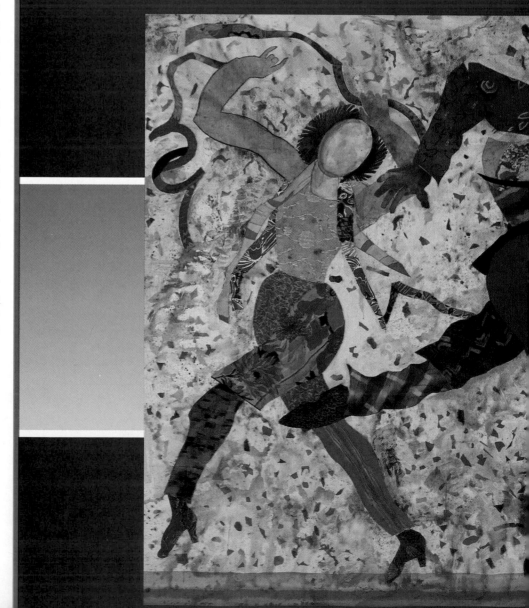

MOTIVATION

To help your students realize that they all have stories to tell, begin by asking these questions:

1. Can you remember a time when you felt embarrassed?

2. Have you ever had any clothes that you especially disliked?

Have students elaborate on both questions. You can use the second question as an introduction to the literary model that begins on p. 116.

Discovering Yourself

You've already discovered many things about yourself. You hate math, but not English. You like to sit in your room and listen to all kinds of music. But you hate green peas and liver. Yet there is still more you can **discover about yourself,** through expressive writing.

Writing and You. A teenager writes to his cousin about how excited he is to be going away to basketball camp this summer. A famous actress writes a book telling her life story. A young girl tells her diary how much she likes her new bike. When have you expressed your personal feelings in writing?

As You Read. Here's a narrative in which a man expresses his feelings about a jacket he had to wear as a boy. What are his feelings?

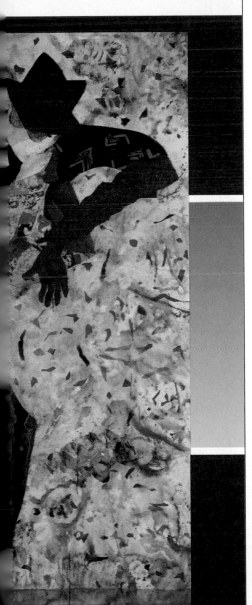

Pas de Deux, Miriam Schapiro (1986). Acrylic and fabric on canvas. 90" × 96". Collection of Dr. & Mrs. Acinapura. Courtesy Bernice Steinbaum Gallery, NYC.

QUOTATION FOR THE DAY

"I keep learning that if I am willing to go deep into my own heart, I am able, miraculously, to touch other people at the core." (Katherine Paterson, 1932–   , American children's story writer)

Ask students what events in their lives might have been shared by others. Then tell them to write about these events in their journals. They can later review their thoughts and possibly use this exercise as the basis of a longer work.

LEP/ESL

General Strategies. Gary Soto's use of figurative language in the model on pp. 116–121 may create difficulties for many students. You could write the following expressions on the chalkboard and discuss them with the class: *bitter as a penny, my arms feeling like braille from goose bumps, my teeth chattering like a cup of crooked dice, their heads like bookends pressing air together.*

You might provide some questions for students to think about as they read. Here are a few possibilities:

1. Why do you think the author chose to write about this subject?
2. If you were to write about something you owned, what would it be?
3. Describe some event in your life that has made your feelings change about yourself.
4. Why doesn't the writer's mother sympathize with his feelings?
5. Why does the writer call the jacket his "green ugly brother" near the end of the narrative?

After students have read the selection, you can lead a class discussion, using the

USING THE SELECTION
The Jacket

1

The first sentence gives the main idea.

2

Point out how the use of similes makes the author's feelings clearer. Ask students to look for other similes. [Two examples are "thin as a young tree" and "arms feeling like braille from goose bumps."]

3

Point out that the description "enough belts to hold down a small town" is an example of hyperbole.

4

Notice the bitter humor.

5

Point out that later the jacket is described as a "brother."

116

116

THE JACKET
by Gary Soto

1 My clothes have failed me. I remember the green coat that I wore in fifth and sixth grades when you either **2** danced like a champ or pressed yourself against a greasy wall, bitter as a penny toward the happy couples.

When I needed a new jacket and my mother asked what kind I wanted, I described something like bikers **3** wear: black leather and silver studs with enough belts to hold down a small town. We were in the kitchen, steam on the windows from her cooking. She listened so long while stirring dinner that I thought she understood for sure the kind I wanted. The next day when I got home from school, I discovered draped on my bedpost a **4** jacket the color of day-old guacamole. I threw my books on the bed and approached **5** the jacket slowly, as if it were a stranger whose hand I had to shake. I touched the vinyl sleeve, the collar, and peeked at the mustard-colored lining.

From the kitchen mother yelled that my jacket was in the closet. I closed the door

INDEPENDENT PRACTICE

You can use the questions in **Reader's Response** and in **Writer's Craft** for independent practice.

☞

117

> "From my bed, I stared at the jacket. I wanted to cry because it was so ugly and so big that I knew I'd have to wear it a long time."

to her voice and pulled at the rack of clothes in the closet, hoping the jacket on the bedpost wasn't for me but my mean brother. No luck. I gave up. From my bed, I stared at the jacket. I wanted to cry because it was so ugly and so big that I knew I'd have to wear it a long time. I was a small kid, thin as a young tree, and it would be years before I'd have a new one. I stared at the jacket, like an enemy, thinking bad things before I took off my old jacket whose sleeves climbed halfway to my elbow.

I put the big jacket on. I zipped it up and down several times, and rolled the cuffs up so they didn't cover my hands. I put my hands in the pockets and flapped the jacket like a bird's wings. I stood in front of the mirror, full face, then profile, and then looked over my shoulder as if someone had called me. I sat on the bed, stood against the bed, and combed my hair to see what I would look like doing something natural. I looked ugly. I threw it on my brother's bed and looked at it

6
How is the jacket personified throughout the story? [It is described as a stranger, an enemy, and an ugly brother.]

117

ASSESSMENT

You may want to ask students what a good personal narrative should include. As students answer, write their responses on the chalkboard. Students should list such criteria as numerous specific and sensory details, a clear main idea, and a clear explanation of the writer's feelings.

RETEACHING

Work with students in a small group to identify supporting details. Analyze **"The Jacket"** one paragraph at a time and help pick out the details. Students could list the types of sensory details by looking for one sense at a time.

118

7

Although the author seems critical of his mom at first, here he shows that he knows she's doing the best she can.

8

Studying the tear "as I would a cut on my arm" might show how he begins to identify with the jacket.

9

Did he know exactly what they were saying? Is it possible they were laughing about other things? [He didn't actually hear their words. They could have been talking about anything.]

10

Why do you think he took off his jacket to play kickball? [He probably felt ashamed of it.]

7 for a long time before I slipped it on and went out to the backyard, smiling a "thank you" to my mom as I passed her in the kitchen. With my hands in my pockets I kicked a ball against the fence, and then climbed it to sit looking into the alley. I hurled orange peels at the mouth of an open garbage can and when the peels were gone I watched the white puffs of my breath thin to nothing.

I jumped down, hands in my pockets, and in the backyard on my knees I teased my dog, Brownie, by swooping my arms while making bird calls. He jumped at me and missed. He jumped again and again, until a tooth sunk deep, ripping an L-shaped **8** tear on my left sleeve. I pushed Brownie away to study the tear as I would a cut on my arm. There was no blood, only a few loose pieces of fuzz. Damn dog, I thought, and pushed him away hard when he tried to bite again. I got up from my knees and went to my bedroom to sit with my jacket on my lap, with the lights out.

That was the first afternoon with my new jacket. The next day I wore it to sixth grade and got a D on a math quiz. During the morning recess Frankie T., the playground terrorist, pushed me to the ground and told me to stay there until recess was over. My best friend, Steve Negrete, ate an apple while looking at me, and the girls turned away to whisper on the monkey bars. The **9** teachers were no help: they looked my way and talked about how foolish I looked in my new jacket. I saw their heads bob with laughter, their hands half-covering their mouths.

10 Even though it was cold, I took off the jacket during lunch and played kickball in a thin shirt, my arms feeling like braille from goose bumps. But when I returned to class I slipped the jacket on and shivered until I was warm. I sat on my hands, heating them up, while my teeth chattered like a cup of crooked dice. Finally warm, I slid out of the jacket but a few minutes later put it back on when the fire bell rang. We paraded out into the yard where we, the sixth graders, walked past all the other grades to stand against the back fence. Everybody saw me. Although they didn't say out loud, "Man, that's ugly," I heard the buzz-buzz of gossip and even laughter that I knew was meant for me.

And so I went, in my guacamole jacket. So embarrassed, so

CLOSURE

You may want to ask students why they think people write personal narratives. Their responses might include that writers want to understand themselves better or want to share their experiences with others.

EXTENSION

Have students retell the story from the perspective of the author's brother or mother. Have students discuss how the change in perspective affects the story's effectiveness. ■

119

hurt, I couldn't even do my homework. I received Cs on quizzes, and forgot the state capitals and the rivers of South America, our friendly neighbor. Even the girls who had been friendly blew away like loose flowers to follow the boys in neat jackets.

I wore that thing for three years until the sleeves grew short and my forearms stuck out like the necks of turtles. All during that time no love came to me—no little dark girl in a Sunday dress she wore on Monday. At lunchtime I stayed with the ugly boys who leaned against the chainlink fence and looked around with propellers of grass spinning in our mouths. We saw girls walk by alone, saw couples, hand in hand, their heads like bookends pressing air together. We saw them and spun our propellers so fast our faces were blurs.

11   I blame that jacket for those bad years. I blame my mother for her bad taste and her cheap ways. It was a sad time for the heart. With a friend I spent my sixth-grade year in a tree in the alley waiting for something good to happen to me in that jacket, which had become the ugly brother who tagged along wherever I went. And it was about that time that I began to grow. My chest puffed up with muscle and, strangely, a few more ribs. Even my hands, those fleshy hammers, showed bravely through

11
The author restates the main idea.

the cuffs, the fingers already hardening for the coming fights. But that L-shaped rip on the left sleeve got bigger; bits of stuffing coughed out from its wound after a hard day of play. I finally scotch-taped it closed, but in rain or cold weather the tape **12** peeled off like a scab and more stuffing fell out until that sleeve shriveled into a <u>palsied</u> arm. That winter the elbows began to crack and whole chunks of green began to fall off. I showed the **13** cracks to my mother, who always seemed to be at the stove with steamed-up glasses, and she said that there were children in Mexico who would love that jacket. I told her that this was America and yelled that Debbie, my sister, didn't have a jacket like mine. I ran outside, ready to cry, and climbed the tree by the alley to think bad thoughts and watch my breath puff white and disappear.

12
Why do you think the author describes the tear in the jacket as being "like a scab"? [The jacket has become a part of his body.]

13
Soto respects the fact that his mother is hard-working, but it still upsets him that she does not seem to understand his feelings.

But whole pieces still casually flew off my jacket when I played hard, read quietly, or took <u>vicious</u> spelling tests at school.

14 When it became so spotted that my brother began to call me "camouflage," I flung it over the fence into the alley. Later, however, I swiped the jacket off the ground and went inside to drape it across my lap and mope.

I was called to dinner: steam <u>silvered</u> my mother's glasses as she said grace; my brother and sister with their heads bowed made ugly faces at their glasses of powdered milk. I gagged too, but eagerly ate big rips of buttered tortilla that held scooped up beans. Finished, I went outside with my jacket across my arm. It was a cold sky. The faces of clouds were piled up, hurting. I climbed the fence, jumping down with a grunt. I started up the alley and soon slipped into my jacket, that green ugly brother who breathed over my shoulder that day and ever since.

READER'S RESPONSE

1. The narrator blames his ugly jacket for the bad things that happen to him for three years while he wears it. Do you agree with this way of looking at things? How could a piece of clothing be responsible?
2. Have you ever had to wear a piece of clothing that you thought was ugly? In a short journal entry, write about how the experience made you feel.

WRITER'S CRAFT

3. Writers of personal narratives use sensory details—details of sight, sound, taste, touch, and smell—to make experiences seem real. What details of sight does the narrator use to make the jacket seem real to readers?
4. Personal narratives are about experiences that the writers think are important. Where does Gary Soto reveal that this experience was important to him? What do you think he discovered about himself?

14

Why do you think his brother called him "camouflage"? [The pattern of missing vinyl resembled military camouflage print. The name could also be symbolic of Soto's attempts to be less visible while wearing the jacket.]

ANSWERS

Reader's Response

Responses will vary.

1. Some students may identify with the author's dismay while others may conclude that the jacket seems to have little to do with what happens.
2. Help students think of an experience to write about by brainstorming with the class and listing possible topics on the chalkboard.

Writer's Craft

Answers may vary.

3. One detail is that the jacket is "the color of day-old guacamole." Also, it has vinyl sleeves, a mustard-colored lining, and sleeves so long that before he rolls them up, they cover his hands.
4. Gary Soto states, "My clothes have failed me," a conclusion that attempts to explain much of what has happened in his life. Later he writes, "I blame that jacket for those bad years." Soto believes that the jacket caused all his problems and his lack of success in school. It is "that green ugly brother who breathed over my shoulder that day and ever since."

TEACHING THE MODES

This lesson can make students aware of the possibilities in developing their personal narratives. Their work will be primarily in the narrative mode, but description, classification, or evaluation may be employed.

Take a single subject, such as popular music, and discuss what kind of personal essay could be written using each mode. Assess students' understanding by their contributions to this activity. ■

COOPERATIVE LEARNING

Divide the class into groups of three or four and assign each group a different topic, such as clothes, family vacations, or friends. Ask each group to plan four approaches to this topic—narration, description, classification, and evaluation—but to remember also that the essay should treat a personal experience. Students can refer to the introductory chapter, **"Calling the Signals,"** for explanations and examples of each mode.

CRITICAL THINKING
Analysis

Explain to students that few pieces of writing use only one mode. Ask them to look at **"The Jacket"** again and to find examples of all four modes. [The author uses narration to tell how he got the jacket, description to help the reader envision the jacket, classification to explain how he felt different from his peers, and evaluation to express his opinion of the jacket. Students may find other examples.]

Ways to Express Yourself

You'll find expressive writing all around you. You'll read it in magazines and newspapers and write it in journals and letters. Your writing is expressive when the focus is on you—what you experience, think, and feel. Here are some ways that you can develop expressive writing.

▶ **Narration:** writing in your journal about an event that happened to you because you're in a wheelchair; writing the story of your childhood for the school's time capsule.

Description: describing your grandparents' house to show how you feel about it; writing a funny description of the broccoli served in the lunchroom.

Classification: in a letter to your cousin, comparing your two best friends; in your journal, exploring which you enjoy more, tennis or basketball.

Evaluation: writing an essay about the water quality in the park's drinking fountains; explaining to your friend why the Miami Dolphins are the best NFL team.

LOOKING AHEAD

In the main assignment in this chapter, you'll use the strategy of narration to write about a personal experience. As you work through the chapter, keep in mind that a good personal narrative

- tells about the events in the order that they happened
- gives details about the events
- explains the meaning of the experience to the writer

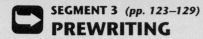
PREWRITING

OBJECTIVES

- To describe an experience to classmates
- To list different sensory details about an experience
- To choose a topic for a personal narrative

- To gather and organize ideas for a personal narrative

Writing a Personal Narrative

Prewriting

Choosing an Experience to Write About

A personal narrative is a true story about yourself. You often tell your good friends about your experiences. How do you decide which experiences are worth telling?

Start by thinking about events that meant something special to you: they touched your feelings. Your narrative could be about an experience that was funny, sad, amazing, or scary. Even a painful experience can make a good personal narrative. Did you ever break your leg? How did it happen? What did it feel like? A good friend would be eager to know. So would the audience for your narrative.

Keep these points in mind when you choose a topic for a personal narrative.

- *Write about something you remember well.* You want to *tell* about and *show* your experience to readers. You can't if you don't remember details about it.
- *Write about an experience that was important to you.* It doesn't have to be a big adventure, but it should have meaning for you.

RESOURCES

PREWRITING
- Recalling Details

QUOTATION FOR THE DAY

"If every time you sat down, you expected something great, writing would always be a great disappointment." (Natalie Goldberg, American writer, poet, and teacher)

Ask students to discuss their reactions to this quotation. Remind students that even writing efforts that don't produce great literary masterpieces can give valuable practice in writing.

MEETING INDIVIDUAL NEEDS

LEP/ESL

General Strategies. To help students focus on a specific event, have them work in pairs to interview each other and ask the following questions:

1. What is the event?
2. Where is the event?
3. Who was involved?
4. When did the event occur?
5. Why choose this event?

Students should then give short oral reports detailing their partners' intentions.

MOTIVATION

You could begin the lesson by asking students to tell something about themselves that most people don't know. Ask for volunteers and then continue calling on students until all have contributed.

TEACHING THE LESSON

Have each student write the following possible topics on a sheet of paper. Then provide an example for each of the topics and ask students to list examples of their own.
1. funny experiences
2. sad experiences
3. scary experiences
4. exciting experiences

124   *Expressive Writing*

- *Write about an experience you're willing to share.* You want to be comfortable sharing the experience with others.

ANSWERS
Exercise 1

Responses will vary.
To help students participate, explain the instructions for the exercise first, and then have students write one example and one sentence about the example.

STUDENTS WITH SPECIAL NEEDS

Students with emotional problems may be uncomfortable with self-expression. Using tactile activities can help students stay focused. Have students make collages depicting their favorite activities or hobbies. They can use magazines or newspapers and cut out pictures of activities that they enjoy. Once finished, students can write about their experiences in activities similar to those depicted in the collages.

| EXERCISE 1 | **Speaking and Listening: Exploring Topics for Personal Narratives** |

Get together with a partner or a few classmates and read the statements below. Can you remember an experience that fits each description? Tell each other the best stories you remember. Discuss what makes them interesting as stories.

1. You and a friend disagreed.
2. Something happened that was embarrassing (at the time) but funny (later).
3. An event made strangers notice or hear about you.
4. You won a contest or some other honor.
5. You spent a frightening night, perhaps when the lights went out after a storm.

 **WRITING ASSIGNMENT**   PART 1:
Choosing a Topic for a Personal Narrative

What experiences have you had that you want to explore in your writing? Choose one of those experiences to write about. Try looking through the list you made with your classmates for Exercise 1. If you find no ideas there, look through your journals, talk to your friends, or do a little private brainstorming.

Next, discuss the three points on pp. 123–124 that give advice on choosing a topic and advise students to use these guidelines. After students have chosen their topics, have a volunteer read aloud the **Thinking About Purpose and Audience** section. Discuss the concepts of purpose and audience. After asking for volunteers to give topics, you can work with the class to determine a purpose and audience for each topic.

After going over the list of types of details in the textbook on pp. 126–127, you can guide students in preparation for the final exercise in the segment by creating a chart on the chalkboard which lists ideas and details that could be used in a draft.

Direct the students to **Exercise 1** for the group activity.

Prewriting

Gathering and Organizing Your Ideas

In talking with friends, you often just start a story and hope to remember it as you go along. You write better, however, when you plan what to say and how to say it.

Thinking About Purpose and Audience

The *purpose* for writing a personal narrative is to discover your own thoughts and feelings and to learn a little about yourself. You also write to share the experience, and what it meant to you, with others.

Your *audience* is probably made up of your classmates and teacher and perhaps other adults you trust. Try to make your narrative interesting for them. Remember to give them the background information they may need to understand your narrative. Did you take a trip to the Grand Canyon? Explain its awesome beauty to them. Ask yourself what your audience will need to know in order to "be there" with you.

LESS-ADVANCED STUDENTS

Some students need to do extensive prewriting, but they might not be willing to make notes and lists. You could have them start by drawing pictures of the different events to be included in their narratives. Ask students to include as many details as possible. If available, supply colored pens or pencils so that students can include colors in their details.

Tell students that they could think of the pictures as a comic-book story, and draw a panel for each action. You could ask them to supply exact words in balloons above the characters' heads.

After they have finished drawing the pictures, ask students to write about what they have drawn.

Finally, have students work independently on **Writing Assignment: Parts 1** and **2** to prepare for writing a first draft.

ASSESSMENT

Assess quickly by asking students to exchange papers and check for gaps in the lists of events and a lack of details about any event. Have evaluators write their observations on separate sheets of paper and attach them to the papers.

Cont. on p. 128

A DIFFERENT APPROACH

Some students have trouble thinking about details for an entire narrative. You could guide the class in listing details by having the students work on one event at a time.

First, ask students to tell briefly what happened. Then, ask them to add several sensory details to each step of the events. After they have added the sensory details, ask students to add descriptive details of characters and places in their narratives. Have students include any dialogue that they remember. Finally, tell them to record any thoughts and feelings they had as the events happened.

You could follow this same procedure for each main event in the narrative.

INTEGRATING THE LANGUAGE ARTS

Literature Link. You could suggest that students read professional expressive pieces such as "My Grandmother Would Rock Quietly and Hum" by Leonard Adame or "The Night the Bed Fell" by James Thurber. These models of expressive writing might give students ideas for topics.

Recalling Details

A personal narrative is different from many other types of writing. That's because many of the details and events are stored inside your memory. You'll need to recall these details to make your experiences seem real for readers. Did you win a kite-designing contest? What sights and sounds will help you *tell* the experience so that readers can share it? What did people say and do? How did you feel?

As you plan your narrative, try to remember the following kinds of details.

1. **Events.** What happened? Make notes about all the little individual events that made up the whole event. You were chased by a huge dog! *The dog came bounding down the stairs; I turned; it took off from the bottom step . . .* and so on.

2. **Sensory details.** What did you hear, see, feel, and maybe even smell and taste? *That scratchy growl; that red glint in the dog's eye; the hot, moist smell of its breath . . .*

3. **Characters and places.** Were other people involved in your experience? What places were important? *Matt chased the dog down the stairs of the apartment building. Then I saw the dog dart between cars, cross the street, and run into Mr. Chang's market.*

TEACHING *VISUALIZING SENSORY DETAILS*

Model this activity by asking students to help you brainstorm for details that would describe the first few minutes of a typical class. Give a few details first and then ask for student replies.

After modeling, you can assign the **Critical Thinking Exercise.**

Prewriting **127**

4. **Dialogue and quotations.** Did you and others say anything interesting during the experience? *"Help! Somebody! Stop that dog!" "Aw, he won't bite—least, I've never known him to . . ."*
5. **Thoughts and feelings.** How did you think and feel? *I was terrified that the dog would bite me; I could feel the tingle of fear rushing up my back.*

WRITING NOTE

A personal narrative is a first-person story, so the words *I* and *me* play an important part. Even though others shared the experience, you're writing from your point of view. As you jot down details, stress what *you* saw and heard and felt, what *you* did, what *you* thought, and what the event meant to *you*.

CRITICAL THINKING

Visualizing Sensory Details

Collecting sensory details is easy when you can observe the subject. In a personal narrative, however, your subject is an event in the past. Instead of observing it, you have to rely on memory. You have to *visualize* (see) the event in your mind before you can collect sensory details.

For example, you're trying to remember details about a lightning storm. Pick a specific moment during the storm and picture the moment in your mind. Then, note what you observe with all your senses, not just your eyes. What do you see? What sounds are present? What do you feel, both in your skin and in your emotions? Does anything have a taste or smell?

Don't give up too quickly. Collecting details by visualizing is like the poem about shaking the ketchup bottle—none'll come and then a lot'll, but you have to keep at it.

Cont. from p. 126
RETEACHING

Provide students with a short piece of expressive writing, perhaps a magazine article, and ask them to prepare a prewriting chart like the one in the textbook for the article. Then, having volunteers provide the details, work through the chart on the chalkboard.

CLOSURE

Assure students that they have completed what many writers think is the hardest part of writing—the planning. Ask students to tell you what elements of writing they need to include in their work [a detailed topic, an organizational plan].

ANSWERS
Critical Thinking Exercise

Responses will vary.

To help students organize their work for this activity, tell them to make columns on their papers, with a different sense named at the top of each column. Have them list as many details as they can for each sense. Give them a minimum number of details as a goal. When students are finished, ask them to share their details with the class.

 CRITICAL THINKING EXERCISE:
Visualizing Details

Think of an event or occasion that was special to you. Maybe you spent a perfect day with friends at the beach last summer. Maybe you made your first A on a test. Close your eyes and visualize until you get a mental picture of the experience. Then, list as many details as you can for each sense. If possible, compare your notes with those of another person who experienced the event with you.

Arranging Details

The next step in planning your personal narrative is to arrange the details you've recalled. You need to put them in an order that will make sense to your readers. Many writers begin with background information and then use chronological order for the other details. Using *chronological order* (time order) means telling events in the order they happened. You begin with the event that happened first, then go on to the second, and so on.

☞ REFERENCE NOTE: For more information on chronological order, see pages 79 and 100.

As you arrange your details, list them in a chart. On the next page you can see how one writer organized details for a personal narrative.

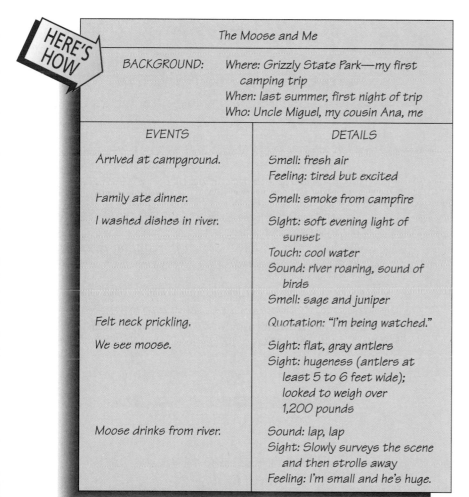

The Moose and Me	
BACKGROUND:	Where: Grizzly State Park—my first camping trip When: last summer, first night of trip Who: Uncle Miguel, my cousin Ana, me

EVENTS	DETAILS
Arrived at campground.	Smell: fresh air Feeling: tired but excited
Family ate dinner.	Smell: smoke from campfire
I washed dishes in river.	Sight: soft evening light of sunset Touch: cool water Sound: river roaring, sound of birds Smell: sage and juniper
Felt neck prickling.	Quotation: "I'm being watched."
We see moose.	Sight: flat, gray antlers Sight: hugeness (antlers at least 5 to 6 feet wide); looked to weigh over 1,200 pounds
Moose drinks from river.	Sound: lap, lap Sight: Slowly surveys the scene and then strolls away Feeling: I'm small and he's huge.

WRITING ASSIGNMENT

PART 2:
Gathering and Organizing Ideas

You chose an experience to write about in Writing Assignment, Part 1. Now, make a chart like the one above and list each event in the order it happened. Then, jot down details about each event, including sensory details, dialogue, and thoughts or feelings. Save your work.

MEETING INDIVIDUAL NEEDS

LESS-ADVANCED STUDENTS
Some students might have difficulty using a chart to structure the details of their experiences. You could have these students start with a timeline marked *Background, Beginning, Middle, End* to establish the narrative flow. Then have them transfer the information to the charts and complete the *Sensory details* and the *Thoughts and feelings* columns. This procedure should reduce the task to manageable proportions.

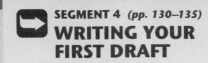

WRITING YOUR FIRST DRAFT

OBJECTIVES

- To analyze the organization and details of a personal narrative
- To write a draft of a personal narrative

MOTIVATION

Tell students to review their prewriting notes. Reassure them that writing this first draft should be easier because they have already done so much thinking and organizing.

RESOURCES

WRITING YOUR FIRST DRAFT
- Ending a Personal Narrative

QUOTATION FOR THE DAY

"The facts are always less than what really happened." (Nadine Gordimer, 1923– , South African novelist)

Discuss with students what they think Gordimer means by the phrase "what really happened." Encourage students to include more than just facts in their expressive writing. Challenge them to include details, thoughts, feelings, and the personal meaning of their experiences.

USING THE SELECTION
from Dream of the Blue Dolphins

1

Ask students how old they think the writer was when he swam with the dolphins and make sure students support their answers.

130

Writing Your First Draft

The Parts of a Personal Narrative

No two personal narratives are just alike, but they all have three basic parts.

- a *beginning* that grabs the reader's interest; sometimes gives background information and a hint about the importance of the experience
- a *middle* that tells about important events, describes people and places, and tells the writer's thoughts and feelings
- an *ending* in which the writer explains the outcome and shows the meaning of the experience

Here's how one professional writer, Michael DiLeo, uses these parts to create a personal narrative. Notice how he uses background information, dialogue, and sensory details to tell readers about his experience.

A MAGAZINE ARTICLE

Dream of the Blue Dolphins
by Michael DiLeo

BEGINNING
Attention grabber

Hint of meaning

Background information

In our dreams, there are certain just-out-of-reach experiences—like flying with eagles or running with wild horses—that promise to take us beyond the physical limitations of our bodies, to give us a glimpse of the full breadth of creation. Ten years ago, I was given the opportunity to make such a dream come true.

It all began at a party in San Francisco for the famed <u>neurobiologist</u> John Lilly. . . . At

Before they begin writing their narratives, read the two example narratives found in the textbook. In discussing **"Dream of the Blue Dolphins"** by Michael DiLeo, ask students to find the specific phrases or sentences to which the side glosses refer. For example, the first paragraph is labeled "Attention grabber." Have students tell exactly what in the paragraph will grab the reader's attention. Continue with the other labels in the same way, both for **"Dream of the Blue Dolphins"** and for **"The Moose and Me"** on pp. 133–134.

Writing Your First Draft **131**

Quotation

the time, Lilly was working with two dolphins, named Joe and Rosie, at a California oceanarium. In the middle of our conversation, Lilly said, "Would you like to swim with Joe and Rosie?" I quickly said yes.

MIDDLE

Event 1

Sensory details

Sensory details

Thoughts and feelings

Quotation

Event 2

The back tank at Marine World where Lilly kept Joe and Rosie was small and circular, perhaps fifteen yards across. As I slipped into the cool water, Joe, the male, swam up, his dorsal fin slicing the surface, while Rosie kept her distance. He was a sleek, silver-gray bullet, whose size and fluid quickness were breathtaking. I felt an odd push-pull: I was drawn to him, and yet there was in my mouth a taste of fear, bitter as the chlorine in the pool, the pure anxiety of feeling completely out of my league. As instructed by Lilly, I took hold of Joe's dorsal fin with one hand. Instantly, I was swept under the water.

"He'll test you to see if you're a good swimmer," Lilly had told me, "and if he decides you are, you'll get a great ride." I must have passed, for Joe took me on a series of shallow, stone-skip soundings, then

2
sleek: glossy and smooth

3
fluid: flowing smoothly

4
anxiety: uneasy thoughts or fears; worry

GUIDED PRACTICE

After discussing **"Dream of the Blue Dolphins,"** divide the class into groups of three or four to discuss the questions in **Exercise 2.** After the groups have agreed on responses to the five questions, lead a class discussion of each question.

INDEPENDENT PRACTICE

Students can work independently on **Writing Assignment: Part 3.** Explain to students that they don't have to restrict themselves to what's in their plans; if they think of other details, they can include them.

Sensory details

dove straight down. Just before we reached the bottom, he turned and shot for the surface. As my lungs tightened and my arm felt like giving way, we exploded out of the water together in an astonishing leap. I was riding a dolphin in midair.

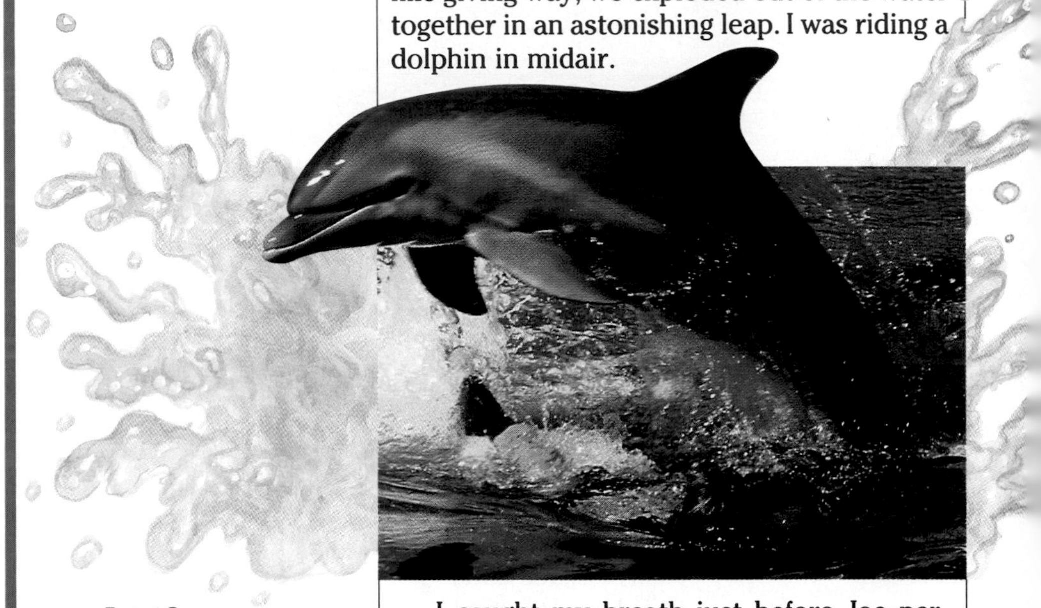

Event 3

Sensory details

ENDING

Outcome—meaning of experience

I caught my breath just before Joe performed another dive and jump. And another. His strength and control were beyond my comprehension. The line between air and water blurred as Joe kept up his crash course in the dolphin way of living in two worlds. He
9 circled the tank, corkscrewing through the water, testing my grip and my supply of air at every turn. Variations on this <u>repertoire</u> continued for some time, until suddenly Joe did a quick flip and left me bobbing in the water, my heart pounding with excitement. It was years before it occurred to me to wonder whether Joe was expressing, not his excitement at <u>interspecies</u> contact, but simply the frustration of total confinement.

American Way

9
corkscrewing: moving in a spiral course

SELECTION AMENDMENT
Description of change: excerpted
Rationale: to focus on the concept of writing a draft as presented in this chapter

Assessment should be based only on whether or not a first draft of approximately the assigned length has been completed. Have students annotate their first drafts as illustrated in the textbook so that you can readily see their ideas.

RETEACHING

One way to help students during this stage is to let them talk about the subject while you write their words. Try this for the first few sentences. Students should then be able to continue alone. You could pair students to begin **Writing Assignment: Part 3** in this way.

☞

EXERCISE 2 ▶ **Analyzing the Organization of a Personal Narrative**

Read and think about the article "Dream of the Blue Dolphins." Then, meet with two or three classmates to discuss the following questions.

1. Does the first sentence grab your attention? Explain why or why not.
2. What background information do you get in the introduction? Do you need this information to understand the narrative? Why?
3. In what order are the events organized?
4. What are some sensory details that DiLeo uses to describe his experience with Joe?
5. How does DiLeo let his readers know what he felt about the experience? the meaning he thought it had?

A Writer's Model for You

Michael DiLeo has written narratives for many years. He has a few fancy writing techniques, but he starts with a basic framework. The model below follows that basic framework, without some of the fancy techniques. You may want to use it as a model for your own personal narrative.

ANSWERS
Exercise 2

Answers may vary.

1. The two details of "flying with eagles" and "running with wild horses" are used as attention-grabbers.
2. The background information tells how the writer came to swim with the two dolphins. Without it, there would be puzzling gaps.
3. Events are listed in chronological order.
4. Sensory details include "a taste of fear, bitter as the chlorine in the pool," "my lungs tightened and my arm felt like giving way," and "I caught my breath."
5. DiLeo tells how he felt by including the details of his reactions, such as "bobbing in the water, my heart pounding with excitement." He reveals the meaning of his experience in the last sentence.

A WRITER'S MODEL

The Moose and Me

BEGINNING
Attention grabber

Background information

Hint of importance

What would you do if you came face to face with one of the biggest animals in the United States? I'm a city kid, but last summer Uncle Miguel and my cousin Ana took me camping in the woods for a whole week in Montana's Grizzly State Park. My best memory comes from the first night we were there.

CLOSURE

Ask students to name the three basic parts of a personal narrative [a beginning, a middle, and an ending]. Then ask students which part was the easiest and which was the most difficult to write.

EXTENSION

After their first drafts are finished, have students look for places where inserting a simile or a metaphor might make an event clearer to the reader, especially in describing feelings. Ask for volunteers to share their changes. ■

INTEGRATING THE LANGUAGE ARTS

Technology Link. If you have access to a computer lab, students can build their essays gradually on the computers. Ask students to include one kind of information at a time. For example, first ask them to write a summary of what happened, including characters and places. Then ask them to insert sensory details, perhaps even adding them one sense at a time. After this text has been included, tell students to insert dialogue. Finally, ask them to add their own thoughts and feelings.

---

134   *Expressive Writing*

MIDDLE
Event 1
Sensory details

Thoughts and feelings

Event 2

Sensory details

Quotation

Feelings

ENDING
Outcome—meaning of experience

We had just eaten supper, and I was alone down at the river, washing dishes. The sun was setting, and its soft evening light was streaming through the trees. The only sounds were those of the birds and the roar of the river.

Suddenly my neck began to prickle. I had a strange feeling I was being watched. I looked up and—wow! Right across the river, twenty feet away, stood a moose. You wouldn't believe his size! He had flat, gray and brown antlers that would have scraped a ceiling. I wasn't scared, though—in fact, I said to him, "Hey, moose, what's going on?" It was just as if I were talking to someone. That's the way I felt just then, a part of nature. The moose just looked at me, dipped his head, took a drink, looked around, and then walked off, calm as you please.

I'm still a city kid, but I'll tell you one thing. I have a new respect for nature. That moose was so big and I'm so small. Yet I felt I could talk to him.

If you decide to model your personal narrative after the one you've just read about the moose, you can use the following framework.

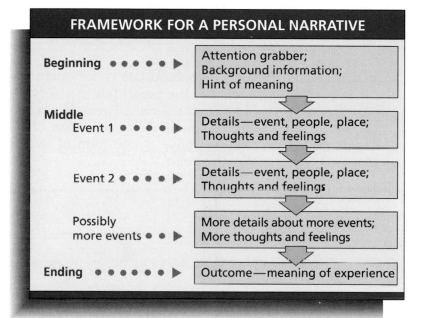

FRAMEWORK FOR A PERSONAL NARRATIVE

Beginning ● ● ● ● ● ▶	Attention grabber; Background information; Hint of meaning
Middle Event 1 ● ● ● ● ▶	Details—event, people, place; Thoughts and feelings
Event 2 ● ● ● ● ▶	Details—event, people, place; Thoughts and feelings
Possibly more events ● ● ▶	More details about more events; More thoughts and feelings
Ending ● ● ● ● ● ● ▶	Outcome—meaning of experience

Reminder

As you write your personal narrative

- arrange details about the events in chronological order
- include sensory details about each event
- include dialogue, thoughts, and feelings to make the experience come alive
- help your readers see the meaning of the experience

WRITING ASSIGNMENT

PART 3:
Writing a Draft of Your Personal Narrative

Now it's time to write. Use the chart you developed in Writing Assignment, Part 2 (page 129). Then just write the whole story as if you were telling it to a friend. Don't forget to end your narrative by telling its outcome and showing what the experience meant to you.

COOPERATIVE LEARNING
To provide an opportunity for students to receive feedback on their writing, divide the class into groups of four in which students can read their drafts aloud. After the readings, the listeners can respond by asking questions about anything that is unclear or by indicating any part of the narrative that seems to need more details. The writer doesn't have to respond, but he or she should take notes.

For the group work to proceed smoothly, assign the following titles and duties: to the left of the first reader, the timer can make sure the group finishes hearing all of the drafts in the allotted time; to the right of the reader, the discussion leader can make sure that everybody gets to participate and can decide when each student will read.

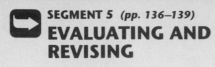
OBJECTIVES

- To analyze a writer's revisions
- To evaluate and revise a personal narrative

MOTIVATION

Ask students if a musician is ready to perform after first evaluating a piece of music. Why not? [The reply will probably be that musicians need to practice the piece to play it well.] Tell the class that writing requires practice as well.

QUOTATION FOR THE DAY

"I don't write easily or rapidly. My first draft usually has only a few elements worth keeping. I have to find out what those are and build from them and throw out what doesn't work, or what simply is not alive." (Susan Sontag, 1933–   , American writer)

Ask volunteers to explain how Sontag's quotation relates to evaluating and revising. Question other students to see if they have developed their own ideas for evaluation and revision. [Some writers draft in pencil so they can erase easily. Some writers use thick, black markers to cut lines. Some writers like to wait awhile before evaluating so the work will seem fresh and mistakes will be more apparent.]

136   *Expressive Writing*

Evaluating and Revising

In some kinds of writing—business letters, for example—it's important to get right to the point. But in a personal narrative, you need to fill in the details. These details help draw your readers in and make them feel a part of the experience. A personal narrative is one form of writing that isn't "short and to the point."

Reprinted by permission of UFS, Inc.

Use the chart on the next page to help you evaluate and revise your writing. First, ask yourself a question in the left-hand column. Then, if you find a weakness in your narrative, use the revision technique suggested in the right-hand column.

TEACHING THE LESSON

To emphasize the importance of knowing not only what's wrong in an essay but also how to fix it, go over the **Evaluating and Revising Personal Narratives** chart. You may want to model evaluating and revising by writing a short personal narrative and asking the class to evaluate it and suggest revisions.

Then complete **Exercise 3** as a class. You could guide students by answering half of the questions and having volunteers answer the other half.

EVALUATING AND REVISING PERSONAL NARRATIVES

EVALUATION GUIDE	REVISION TECHNIQUE
1 Does the writer grab the reader's interest in the introduction?	**Add** an interesting statement or question.
2 Has the writer given enough background information?	**Add** important details about where and when the experience happened. Tell who was there.
3 Are the events told in an order that makes sense?	**Reorder** events in the order they happened.
4 Has the writer used details that make events, people, and places seem real?	**Cut** dull or needless details. **Add** sensory details, quotations, and details about your thoughts and feelings.
5 Are the outcome and meaning of the experience clear?	**Add** a sentence or two that tells the outcome. **Add** information to show the importance of the experience to you.

MEETING INDIVIDUAL NEEDS

LEP/ESL

General Strategies. Although **Writing Assignment: Part 4** suggests that students evaluate each other's narratives, it may be more effective for you to meet with students individually. If possible, photocopy their narratives, so that each of you has a copy to refer to. Pull specific examples from their narratives to help them understand if they are meeting the necessary criteria.

As much as possible, emphasize the positive aspects of their drafts and make encouraging comments.

ADVANCED STUDENTS

If some students finish quickly, you can ask them to help any classmates who have questions. Or you could schedule an extra day for revising and allow students to use that time to help others.

EXERCISE 3 ▶ **Analyzing a Writer's Revisions**

Now's your chance to see inside an editor's mind. Working with a partner or a small group, study these revisions from the third paragraph of the writer's model on pages 133–134, and then answer the questions that follow. Get together with another group to compare your answers.

INDEPENDENT PRACTICE

Have students complete **Writing Assignment: Part 4** as independent practice.

ASSESSMENT

Ask students to turn in brief plans for revision of their rough drafts. This would also be an opportunity to meet with any students who aren't sure of how they want to revise their papers.

138   *Expressive Writing*

I had a strange feeling I was being watched. I looked up and—wow! Right across the river, ~~a few~~ *twenty* feet away, stood a   **replace**

moose. You wouldn't believe his size! He had antlers *flat, gray and brown* that would have scraped a   **add**

ceiling. I wasn't scared, though—in fact, I ~~talked~~ *said* to him *"Hey, moose, what's going on?" It was* just as if I were talking to   **replace/add**

~~some guy~~ *someone*. That's the way I felt then, *just* a part   **replace/add**

of nature. The moose just looked at me, dipped his head, took a drink, looked around, and then walked off. *calm as you please* Suddenly my   **add**

neck began to prickle.   **reorder**

1. Why does the writer move the last sentence? What does this do to the order of events?
2. In the third and fifth sentences, how does adding the words *twenty* and *flat, gray* improve the narrative?
3. In the sixth sentence, why does the writer add the quotation? How would the narrative have been different without it?
4. In the next-to-last sentence, why does the writer add the words *calm as you please*? What picture do these words give you of the moose?

WRITING NOTE   Dialogue—words people actually say—can bring a personal narrative to life. For example, read the following two passages. Both express the same information. Isn't the second one much livelier?

1.   Mario had called the National Weather Service and learned from a man there that it was snowing in the pass. Carmen thought we should go anyway and asked for my opinion. I agreed that we should try.

ANSWERS
Exercise 3

Answers may vary. Students should explain their answers.

1. This sentence lets the reader know what the writer is feeling. It makes the main point of the paragraph clear immediately.
2. These details make the picture clearer.
3. The quotation clarifies the relationship between the narrator and the moose at this time—friendly, informal, nonthreatening.
4. The words indicate the unexpectedly peaceful confrontation of the narrator and the moose, neither feeling threatened by the other.

INTEGRATING THE LANGUAGE ARTS

Literature Link. You may want to let students practice evaluating a piece of expressive writing by applying the **Evaluating and Revising Personal Narratives** chart to a selection such as "The Miraculous Phonograph Record" by William Saroyan or "The Courage That My Mother Had" by Edna St. Vincent Millay.

Evaluating and Revising   **139**

2.   "I just called the National Weather Service," Mario announced. "The guy says it's snowing in the pass."
         "Oh, let's go anyway," said Carmen. "We can make it. What do you think, Ginny?"
         "I'm game," I replied.

PART 4:
Evaluating and Revising Your Personal Narrative

You've seen how someone else improved a narrative. Now it's time to decide how to evaluate and improve your own narrative. Read your personal narrative with a partner and evaluate each other's work. As you work, use the evaluating and revising chart on page 137. (You might also want to use the peer-evaluation guidelines on page 47.) When you get your paper back, think about your partner's suggestions. Then, revise your narrative.

TIMESAVER
To evaluate quickly, you can use a checklist similar to the guide on p. 137. Repeat the fourth question for each paragraph so that you can indicate which paragraphs need more details. To give feedback, you can check a *yes* or *no* box. You could also include a place to check whether or not you need a conference with the student before he or she goes on to the next step in the writing process.

PROOFREADING AND PUBLISHING

OBJECTIVE

- To proofread and publish a final draft

TEACHING THE LESSON

You may need to discuss the seeming contradiction between writing expressively—for one's own self—and the idea of publication. Explain to students that even if the writer is the only audience, writing should be clear, neat, and easy to follow. Problems in grammar, usage, or mechanics can cause writing to be hard to read.

QUOTATION FOR THE DAY

"Every fine story must leave in the mind of the sensitive reader . . . a quality of voice that is exclusively the writer's own, individual, unique." (Willa Cather, 1876–1947, American writer, poet, and journalist)

Share the quotation with the class and explain that mechanical errors distract the reader from the story and keep the writer's individual voice from being heard.

MEETING
INDIVIDUAL
NEEDS

LEP/ESL

General Strategies. In creating personal narratives, it is crucial that students learn to trust their own abilities to convey feelings and perceptions. Instead of marking every grammatical and usage error in their compositions, you could focus on one type of error only and offer individual students extra practice in order to correct that error.

---

140 *Expressive Writing*

Proofreading and Publishing

Proofreading. Even simple mistakes in usage or mechanics can make your personal narrative hard to understand. It's important to proofread carefully and correct any mistakes you find.

MECHANICS HINT

Using Dialogue

You may often use dialogue in your narrative. The correct punctuation of dialogue is important so that readers know who is talking. In the first sentence below, you can't be sure who has called the National Weather Service. In the second sentence, punctuation makes the point clear.

EXAMPLES   Henry said I called the National Weather Service.
Henry said, "I called the National Weather Service."

☞ REFERENCE NOTE: For more help on punctuating dialogue, see pages 737–742.

Publishing. Once you have revised, proofread, and made corrections, make a clean copy. An audience always finds a clean, neat paper more interesting than a messy, difficult-to-read one. Here are two ways you can publish your narrative.

- One audience for your narrative may be your own future self. Start a scrapbook of memories, beginning

Guide students to check the types of errors that you have seen frequently in their rough drafts, such as subject-verb agreement, run-on sentences, and usage errors. Instruct students to check for one type of error at a time. Then they can do a comprehensive check. It is usually helpful to have a second reader repeat the process.

CLOSURE

Ask students to list possible means of publication for expressive writing. Beyond journals, they might also mention diaries, letters, and autobiographies. You could explain that there can even be expressive essays and speeches. ■

with this narrative. Years from now, you may be surprised at the picture you get of yourself.
- Make an anthology of personal narratives with your classmates. Create groupings of narratives on similar topics: outdoor adventures, conflicts with friends or family, school experiences, and so forth.

PART 5:
Proofreading and Publishing Your Personal Narrative

You've done a great deal of work, so reward yourself now with your best effort. Proofread your personal narrative carefully and correct the errors. (See page 53 for more help with proofreading.) Then publish your clean, corrected work. Try one of the suggestions above or any other way you'd like to share your narrative.

The Far Side cartoon by Gary Larson is reprinted by permission of Chronicle Features, San Francisco, CA.

COOPERATIVE LEARNING
You could divide the class into groups of five for this activity. Tell students to take their final drafts and a blank sheet of paper to their groups. Then provide the following instructions:

1. Pass your paper to the left (with the blank sheet on top) before each step. You should record on the blank sheets any mistakes you find. During this step, read the paper only to check general form. Is the student's name in the right place? Is there a title, and is it capitalized correctly? Are the margins correct?
2. During the next step you should check subject-verb agreement.
3. Next, check for correct punctuation of dialogue.
4. For the final step, read the paper backwards to check for spelling.

Note that these steps can be adapted to be used to proofread for any grammatical or mechanical concept you have been emphasizing.

"Wait! Wait! . . . Cancel that, I guess it says 'helf.'"

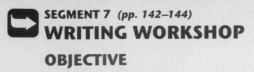

SEGMENT 7 *(pp. 142–144)*
WRITING WORKSHOP
OBJECTIVE
- To analyze and write a journal entry

MOTIVATION
Ask students how they work out problems or what they do when they feel confused. Explain that many people find that keeping a journal helps them to work things out without having to worry about grammar rules or what anybody else thinks.

RESOURCES

WRITING WORKSHOP: KEEPING A JOURNAL
- Recalling Details
- Ending a Personal Narrative
- Writing a Personal Narrative

QUOTATION FOR THE DAY

"Let your mind alone, and see what happens." (Virgil Thomson, 1896–1989, American composer and critic)

Write the quotation on the chalkboard and ask students to copy it onto the covers of their journals or notebooks. Explain that journal writing allows students to put their thoughts onto paper without worrying about mechanics or following a structured plan.

MEETING INDIVIDUAL NEEDS

LEP/ESL

General Strategies. Because of cultural differences, some students will have difficulty with self-disclosure. Strongly encourage students to submit their journals to you for periodic review. Give them the option of indicating which pages they would like you to read.

142

142

WRITING WORKSHOP

A Journal Entry

Some types of expressive writing, like the personal narrative, are meant to be shared. But other types of expressive writing are just for the writer.

A journal is a place where you can write just for yourself. You can write freely about events, reveal your thoughts, and express your anger and emotions.

Here, for once, you don't have to stick to one subject or plan what you think before you write. It's fine to let your words wander and see where they go. That's because a journal is not just a record of events; it's a tool for exploring what you think and feel.

Of course, every time you write something down, there's a chance someone else will read it. It's not unusual for people's journals and diaries to be published after they die!

Here is an excerpt from the diary of an author named Elizabeth Yates. This passage about her sister Jinny was written in 1918 when Elizabeth was in the sixth grade. As you read this entry, think about the value such writing may have had for Yates at the time and later in her life.

After students have read the journal entry by Elizabeth Yates, ask them why they think she wrote that particular entry. [She may have felt frustrated because her sister seemed to do everything well.] Then lead a discussion of the questions following the excerpt.

To help students begin writing, brainstorm with them to suggest situations that they might write about. After students have completed the first entry, ask them if writing helped them to think more clearly about the situations.

143

from My Diary—My World
by Elizabeth Yates

1   Jinny is seven years older than me. She's beautiful and brilliant. Her hair is long and fair, and now that she is doing it up in a knot, she looks more than ever like one of the Greek
2 goddesses in my mythology book. She can do everything well, even to tying the tie of her Peter Thomson suit, which I can never do with mine. And she doesn't get into trouble, which I do all the time. She writes not only the plays but other things, like a song for the Jugs and wonderful letters. She will be a very great writer someday, I know. I would do anything for her, and yet I can't seem to tell her, the way I can tell Brier, my secrets or
3 my dream of being a writer.

Thinking It Over

1. What do you see in this little passage that you probably wouldn't see in a formal biography of Jinny?
2. What impression do you get of Jinny? of Elizabeth's feelings about her?
3. What does Elizabeth "tell" her journal here that she probably didn't tell Jinny?

Writing a Journal Entry

Prewriting. You can write about any subject in your journal. Elizabeth Yates wrote about her sister Jinny. You might write your journal entry about someone interesting or important in your life. Maybe you'd like to write about a family member or a friend. Don't worry about coming up with something polished that you can show the world. Just write to explore what you think and remember.

USING THE SELECTION
from **My Diary—My World**

1

The writer is probably writing compliments she would never have said to her older sister.

2

Why do you think Jinny does these things so much better? [Perhaps it is because Jinny is seven years older and has had more time for trial and error.]

3

The writer reveals here that she wants to be like Jinny.

ANSWERS
Thinking It Over

Answers may vary.

1. It includes personal thoughts not only about the subject but also about the author.

2. Jinny is confident about herself. Elizabeth obviously is in awe of her sister.

3. Some details in the journal are that Elizabeth admires that Jinny can fix her tie properly, and write songs, plays, and letters. Elizabeth also thinks that Jinny looks like a Greek goddess.

SELECTION AMENDMENT
Description of change: excerpted
Rationale: to focus on the concept of keeping a journal as presented in this chapter

ASSESSMENT

Because writing a personal journal entry is often very difficult, you can give credit for students having completed the assignment.

CLOSURE

Ask students if they can think of any other journals by famous people. Then have volunteers explain why a journal would be categorized as expressive writing. ■

MEETING INDIVIDUAL NEEDS

AT-RISK STUDENTS

All students can learn from journal writing. Have students continue the activity throughout the year, with modifications. For example, when students are writing persuasive papers, they might write about things they disagree with; when they are studying literature, they can write personal responses to what they have read. This process may help students realize that writing isn't always for others; writing often helps people learn about themselves.

144

Writing. Write your journal entry. Then, reread it and think about what you've written. Is there anything else you want to say or explore? Don't forget that your only purpose in this kind of writing is to please yourself.

Publishing. After you've finished writing, go back and look at your entry. Did you discover anything new about yourself or your subject? Did you write anything you might use in another, more formal piece of writing, such as a personal narrative or a short story? Remember that you don't need to share your journal with anyone. However, saving what you've written to read again when you're older can be very interesting.

 **SEGMENT 8** *(pp. 145–147)*
MAKING CONNECTIONS

**WRITING ACROSS
THE CURRICULUM
OBJECTIVES**

- To analyze a journal entry for its historical
  value

- To write a journal entry that might have
  historical value

☞

145

MAKING CONNECTIONS

WRITING ACROSS THE CURRICULUM

Expressive Writing and History

Historians learn about the past from public documents, such as newspapers and treaties, as well as from private documents, such as letters and journals. In the following journal entry, a trader describes a meeting with a group of Native Americans in Texas in 1808. As you read the entry, look for details about the events, people, and places that were part of the trader's experience. Remember that the time is 1808. Some of the spelling and capitalization will seem strange to you.

> August 11th
>
> 1   The Messenger we sent to the Village returned early this Morning accompanied by six Indians and we were met by fifty men on Horseback, who Escorted us
> 2 into the Village   when in sight of the town we hoisted our flag and they immediately hoisted a similar one which they had received of Dr. Sibly of Nacki-
> 3 tosh. a man met us with an Invitation to the Chief's house. But we preferred encamping near the great spring and were conducted thither where I pitched my tent and hoisted my flag in front of it, about fifty yards
> 4 from the Chiefs house.—a band of Women came immediately [and] pulled up and cleared away the grass and weeds from about the camp and also cleared a path down to the spring. I then waited on the Great Chief and was received with every token of Friendship I informed him I would wait on him again the next day & inform[ed] him for what purpose we had come to his

WRITING ACROSS THE CURRICULUM
Teaching Strategies

After reading and discussing Anthony Glass's journal entry with students, you could discuss how the descriptive writing of a present-day author might sound confusing and strange to someone a hundred years from now. Ask students to brainstorm about events that reflect their lives. Then ask them to write journal entries and to exchange their finished papers for classmates to evaluate. Tell students to pretend they live in the future as they read and to tell what the journal entries tell the students about life in the past.

USING THE SELECTION
from **Journal of an Indian Trader**

1
Why do you think the trader sent a messenger? [Perhaps he didn't want to surprise the chief.]

2
The meetings seem to be formal but friendly.

3
The chief honors the trader with the invitation.

4
The women did very hard work in this Native American society.

EXPRESSIVE WRITING AND PERSONAL LETTERS
OBJECTIVES
- To analyze an expressive personal letter
- To write an expressive personal letter

5
Their hosts are generous with food. This shows hospitality and friendliness.

GUIDELINES

After students have chosen their topics, you may want to specify a minimum number of details to be included in their narratives. You could then suggest an organizational strategy like the one outlined in the **Framework for a Personal Narrative** chart on p. 135.

EXPRESSIVE WRITING AND PERSONAL LETTERS
Teaching Strategies

You can follow the instructions in the textbook, or you may want to alter this assignment to have students write letters to their friends in school. Students generally enjoy writing notes in class and thus might react enthusiastically to putting their thoughts and feelings in the form of personal letters.

SELECTION AMENDMENT

Description of change: excerpted
Rationale: to focus on the concept of keeping a journal as presented in this chapter

146

146

5 Country & returned to my tent   we found our Camp filled with a quantity of green Corn, Beans, Water and Mus Melons.

Anthony Glass, *Journal of an Indian Trader*

A personal narrative you write might one day become an important document about life today. Choose an event you remember—perhaps a hurricane or special trip—that might tell people a hundred years from now about life today. Write a personal narrative about your experience of the event. Include details that would help explain the experience to someone from a later time.

EXPRESSIVE WRITING AND PERSONAL LETTERS

Personal letters may be informative. For example, you might write to your aunt to tell her when you're arriving to visit. They also may be persuasive. You might write to a friend who moved away, trying to persuade him to come visit you in the summer. But often personal letters are expressive. We sometimes want to share our personal thoughts and feelings with good friends and close relatives, and a letter is one way to do that. In the following personal letter, a girl shares her feelings about her grandparents with a friend who lives some distance away.

December 2, 1993

Dear Joanna,

Thanks for the letter. It seems funny to think about you playing in the sun in Florida when it's already snowing here in Chicago. We got up early this morning to listen to the weather report. We were hoping the snow would be heavy enough that we wouldn't have to go to school. No such luck!

We had a great Thanksgiving. My grandparents cooked the meal, and we had Chinese food instead of turkey and dressing. While we were eating, they told me some stories about their life in China that I'd never heard before. It was kind of strange. I'd never thought much about China before. You know what I mean. The fact that my grandparents came from there didn't mean much to me.

Now I feel different. They made China sound so beautiful and so interesting. My grandfather says that Kweilin, where they lived, has lots of hills and rivers. I'd like to go there to visit when I get older. Want to go along?

Tell everybody I said hello, and tell your parents to let you come stay when school is out. You'll like Chicago, especially in the summer.

Your friend,
Amy

In this letter, Amy shares her thoughts and feelings about her experience with her grandparents. Do you have any thoughts or feelings you'd like to share with someone? Instead of calling, try writing a letter.

GUIDELINES

You may find that requiring a certain number of topics to be included in the letter will make it easier for students to organize their thoughts and for you to assess the assignment. You can then grade the letter based on how well it is organized and how many details are presented for each topic.

USING DESCRIPTION

OBJECTIVES

- To identify the uses of description
- To analyze the use of sensory details, exact words, and figures of speech in descriptions
- To select a subject and a particular feeling or mood for a description
- To collect and organize details for a description through observing, recalling, and imagining
- To write a draft of a description that uses sensory details, exact words, and figures of speech to create a particular feeling
- To evaluate and revise a description
- To proofread and publish a description

Motivation

You may be able to use a recent classroom activity to interest students in studying description. Think of a recent group activity such as a baseball game or a field trip. Then ask students if they have told anyone about their experiences. Tell them that they used description to tell about this event and explain that the more vivid their descriptions, the more interested their friends will be in hearing about their experiences.

Introduction

After relating description to students' everyday lives, explain that through description they can recreate pictures and images of objects, people, scenes, and events that they observe, recall, or imagine.

Then to help students understand the various uses of description, explain that four different students could each have a different purpose in describing a softball or baseball game. One student could describe how he or she felt about striking out in the bottom of the ninth

inning (self-expressive); another student could describe how the baseball field looked after the game to convince students to pick up litter (persuasive); a third student could write a news story describing the major events in the game (informative); and a fourth student could write a short story describing a space alien who becomes a baseball hero (creative).

Integration

This chapter can serve as an important resource for your class. For example, students can use description in creating characters in **Chapter 6: "Creative Writing"** or in analyzing characters in **Chapter 9: "Writing About Literature."**

In addition, you can help students to see how description applies to other studies. For example, a geographical explanation of a particular mountain range or a historical account of Abraham Lincoln would include description. Finally, the **Critical Thinking Exercise** titled **Observing Details** can be applied to scientific experiments and reports.

The chart on the next page illustrates the strands of language arts as they are integrated into this chapter. For vocabulary study, glossary words are underlined in some writing models.

QUOTATIONS
All **Quotations for the Day** are chosen because of their relevance to instructional material presented in that segment of the chapter and for their usefulness in establishing student interest in writing.

INTEGRATING THE LANGUAGE ARTS

Selection	Reading and Literature	Writing and Critical Thinking	Language and Syntax	Speaking, Listening, and Other Expression Skills
from **Nisei Daughter** by Monica Sone 150-151 from *Mighty Hard Road* by James P. Terzian and Kathryn Cramer 162 from *The Yearling* by Marjorie Kinnan Rawlings 164 from *Roll of Thunder, Hear My Cry* by Mildred Taylor 164 from **Willie Bea and the Time the Martians Landed** by Virginia Hamilton 166-167 Haiku by Matsuo Bashō 173	Identifying descriptive words 152, 165, 167, 170, 174, 175 Identifying sensory details 152, 158, 159, 161, 165, 167, 170, 174 Recognizing sensory details in literature 152, 165, 167 Keeping a word bank (list) of sensory words 158, 159, 161, 163 Recognizing an author's use of exact words 152, 163, 165, 167, 170, 174 Analyzing a description 152, 165, 167, 170 Appreciating descriptive poetry (haiku) 173	Writing a descriptive journal entry 152 Writing for an audience 156 Visualizing details 156 Selecting a subject for a description 156, 157, 159 Selecting and organizing details 160, 161 Determining feeling or mood in a description 156, 167 Analyzing figurative language, sensory details, and exact words 152, 165, 167, 174 Analyzing the organization of a description 161, 167 Writing a draft of a description that creates a particular feeling about a subject 168 Analyzing a writer's revisions 169-170 Evaluating and revising a draft of a description 170 Applying proofreading skills 171 Analyzing sensory details in a descriptive poem (haiku) 174 Writing a descriptive poem by using the writing process 174 Writing a classified advertisement 175-176 Writing a poem in two languages 176-177	Using positive (simple), comparative, and superlative forms of adjectives 165 Proofreading for errors in usage and mechanics 171, 174	Listening to and sharing personal experiences 152, 158 Listening to and sharing descriptions 171 Describing a subject orally 152, 158 Listening for sounds to be used as sensory details 158 Comparing lists orally 158, 161 Finding or creating a pictoral representation of a description 171 Reading a description orally 158, 171

CHAPTER 5

SEGMENT PLANNING GUIDE

Whether you are planning for a quick review of a writing concept or preparing an extended lesson on composition you can use the following Planning Guide to adapt the chapter material to the individual needs of your class.

SEGMENT	PAGES	CONTENT	RESOURCES
1 *Creating Pictures and Images*	*149-152*		
Literary Model from **Nisei Daughter**	150-151	Guided reading: a model of descriptive writing	
Reader's Response/ Writer's Craft	152	Model evaluation: responding to literature and analyzing descriptive writing	
2 *Uses of Description*	*153-154*		
3 *Prewriting*	*155-161*		Writing a Description
Planning a Description	155	Introduction: planning a description	Collecting Details
Thinking About Subject, Purpose, and Audience	155-156	Explanation: choosing subject, purpose, and audience	
Writing Assignment: Part 1	156-157	Applied practice: beginning a description	
Collecting Details	157-158	Guidelines: observing, recalling, and imagining details	
Exercise 1	158	Cooperative learning: collecting details	
Critical Thinking: Observing Details	159	Guidelines: becoming aware of sensory details	
Critical Thinking Exercise	159	Cooperative learning: listing and comparing details	
Writing Assignment: Part 2	160	Applied practice: charting details	
Selecting and Organizing Details	160	Guidelines: choosing and arranging details	
Exercise 2	161	Cooperative learning: listing and selecting details and order	
Writing Assignment: Part 3	161	Applied practice: listing details in order	
4 *Writing*	*162-168*		Creating Metaphors and Similes
The Basic Elements of Description	162-165	Guidelines: analyzing sensory details, exact words, and figures of speech	
Sensory Details	162	Introduction: using sensory details	
Literary Model from **Mighty Hard Road**	162	Guided reading: examining sensory details in a model	
Chart: A Word Bank	163	Example: creating a word bank	
Exact Words	163	Introduction: choosing exact words	
Literary Model from **The Yearling**	164	Guided reading: examining word usage in a model	

SEGMENT	PAGES	CONTENT	RESOURCES
Figures of Speech	164	Introduction: examining similes and metaphors	
Literary Model from *Roll of Thunder, Hear My Cry*	164	Guided reading: examining similes in a model	
Mechanics Hint	165	Writing suggestion: using noun plurals	
Literary Model from **Willie Bea and the Time the Martians Landed**	166-167	Guided reading: examining word usage in a model	
Exercise 3	167	Cooperative learning: analyzing description	
Writer's Model	167-168	Guided reading: examining details and exact words	
Writing Assignment: Part 4	168	Applied practice: writing a draft of a description	
5 *Evaluating and Revising*	*169-170*		Writing a Description
Chart: Evaluating and Revising Description	169	Guidelines: applying evaluation and revision techniques	
Exercise 4	169-170	Cooperative learning: analyzing a revision	
Writing Assignment: Part 5	170	Cooperative learning: evaluating and revising	
6 *Proofreading and Publishing*	*171-172*		Writing a Description
Publishing	171	Publishing ideas: reaching an audience	
Writing Assignment: Part 6	171	Cooperative learning: proofreading and publishing a description	
A Student Model	172	Guided reading: examining word usage	
7 *Writing Workshop*	*173-174*		All the resources in this chapter may be used in this segment.
A Descriptive Poem	173-174	Guidelines: reading and writing descriptive poems (haiku)	
Literary Model Haiku	173	Guided reading: examining a haiku	
Writing a Descriptive Poem	174	Applied practice: writing a descriptive poem	
8 *Making Connections*	*175-177*		
Mass Media and Description: A Classified Ad	175-176	Guidelines: writing a classified ad Applied practice: writing and presenting an ad	
Description and Literature: A Poem in Two Languages	176-177	Guidelines: using Spanish and English in a poem Applied practice: writing in two languages	
Charts: English and Spanish Nouns and Adjectives	177	Guidelines: selecting nouns and adjectives	

WHOLE-CHAPTER RESOURCES
A Writing Process Log, A Writing Prompt, Holistically Graded Models, Assessment Portfolio Materials

CREATING PICTURES AND IMAGES

OBJECTIVES

- To write personal responses to a short story
- To write a descriptive journal entry

- To identify and analyze the use of specific words and sensory details in a description

 VISUAL CONNECTIONS
Doubled Back

About the Artist. Bev Doolittle has been drawing since early childhood. While she was still in high school, she won a scholarship to study at the Art Center College of Design, then located in Los Angeles. She prepared for an advertising career and found a job at an agency. Later, she and her husband, Jay, left their jobs to tour the country as traveling artists, spending most of their time in the wilderness of the West and Northwest. After traveling, they settled in a small desert town and continued painting. Bev Doolittle began doing prints after her painting *Pintos* was discovered by a publisher of fine art prints.

Ideas for Writing. Discuss with students how this painting fools the viewer so that seeing the bear is a surprise. Suggest that they use chronological order instead of spatial order to write about their experiences of seeing this picture.

5 Using Description

TEACHING THE LESSON

Have a volunteer read aloud the opening paragraph. Emphasize the importance of description in creating pictures that appeal to all five senses. Because of the difficulty of both English and Japanese words in the selection by Monica Sone on pp. 150–151, you may want to read it to your students. Before addressing the **Writer's** **Craft** and **Reader's Response** questions, define difficult words such as *deprecatingly* and discuss how these words relate to Japanese customs, such as politely belittling oneself to avoid all appearance of pride.

Creating Pictures and Images

Doubled Back, Bev Doolittle (1988) © The Greenwich Workshop, Inc., Trumbull, CT 06611

Words are a writer's paintbrush. With words, a writer can create a **picture** so funny, so sad, or so frightening, that you feel like laughing, crying, or shuddering in fright at the "sight" of it.

Writing and You. A science fiction writer describes how the sun looks when it becomes a nova. A newspaper reporter describes the terrible damage left by a killer hurricane. With their vivid words, writers make you feel as though you were there—hearing, seeing, feeling, smelling, or tasting what they are writing about. Have you ever described something in writing?

As You Read. Here's an excerpt from a short story that describes a Japanese meal. As you read, look for words that make the meal seem real to you. Can you see or taste it?

QUOTATION FOR THE DAY

"I have always paid a good deal of attention to painting. . . . I tried to capture the same effect in words." (John Dos Passos, 1896–1970, American writer and poet)

Ask students to freewrite descriptions of several objects or scenes. Encourage them to include sensory details, descriptive words, and facts that make each object or scene unusual. Challenge students to write descriptions that create pictures in the reader's mind.

MEETING
INDIVIDUAL
NEEDS

LEP/ESL

General Strategies. Question one of **Reader's Response** offers a perfect opportunity for your ESL students to write about typical dishes that would be served at special occasions in their native countries. You may want to extend this writing activity and ask each ESL student to write a short composition about this meal. To reinforce acceptance and appreciation of cultural diversity, encourage each student to read his or her composition aloud and to answer questions from classmates.

Modeling your responses, guide students through the **Reader's Response** questions. After sharing your written response to question two, urge others to share their responses. Discuss examples given in question three with students by explaining how "magnificent black and silver lacquered tray" creates a picture and how "an enormous platter of *osushi*" helps the reader to visualize the platter.

USING THE SELECTION

from Nisei Daughter

1

Japanese custom requires a modest politeness.

2

Notice the use of words that appeal to the sense of hearing.

3

Why does Sone use the word *carmine* instead of *red*? [It's more specific.]

150

FROM **NISEI DAUGHTER**

BY MONICA SONE

150

While the Matsuis and our parents <u>reminisced</u> about the good old days, we thumbed through the worn photograph albums and old Japanese tourist magazines. Finally Mrs. Matsui excused herself and bustled feverishly around the dining

1 room. Then she invited us in. "*Sah,* I have nothing much to offer you, but please eat your fill."

"*Mah, mah,* such a wonderful assortment of *ogochi-soh,*" Mother

2 bubbled.

Balding Mr. Matsui snorted <u>deprecatingly</u>. Mrs. Matsui walked around the table with an enormous platter of *osushi,* rice cakes rolled in seaweed. We each took one and nibbled at it daintily, sipping tea. Presently she sailed out of the kitchen bearing a magnificent black and silver lacquered tray loaded with

3 <u>carmine</u> lacquer bowls filled with fragrant *nishime.* In pearly <u>iridescent</u>

INDEPENDENT PRACTICE

Have students independently answer the **Writer's Craft** questions in their journals.

ASSESSMENT

Your assessment of this introductory activity can be informal. Allow students to evaluate one another's journal entries, perhaps by reading them in small groups and then picking the best entry from each group to read to the class.

☞

china bowls, Mrs. Matsui served us hot chocolatey *oshiruko,* a sweetened bean soup dotted with tender white *mochi,* puffed up like oversized marshmallows.

4 **4**

This descriptive simile uses *like* to compare the "tender white *mochi*" to "oversized marshmallows."

5 ather and Mother murmured over the superb flavoring of each dish, while Mr. Matsui guffawed politely, "*Nani,* this woman isn't much of a cook at all."

I was fascinated with the *yakizakana,* barbecued perch, which, its head and tail raised saucily, looked as if it were about to flip out of the oval platter. Surrounding this centerpiece were lacquer boxes of desserts, neatly lined rows of red and green oblong slices of sweet bean cakes, a mound of crushed lima beans, tinted red and green, called *kinton.* There was a
6 vegetable dish called *kimpira* which looked like a mass of brown twigs. It turned out to be burdock, hotly seasoned with red pepper.

5

The author chooses words that help the reader hear as well as see the picture.

6

Another descriptive simile uses *like* to compare the dish of *kimpira,* or hot burdock, to "a mass of brown twigs."

SELECTION AMENDMENT
Description of change: excerpted
Rationale: to focus on the concept of descriptive writing presented in this chapter

Discuss the answers to questions 3 and 4 as a class and allow students to check their own work.

Conclude the lesson by asking five volunteers to give examples of sensory details from Sone's description. ■

ANSWERS

Reader's Response

Responses will vary.

1. Many students will have eaten Mexican, Chinese, and Italian food. Encourage students to be as descriptive as possible in their responses.
2. Students may describe lunching atop Mount Everest on Indian tea, rice, and frozen yogurt or having shark steak and fish eggs for breakfast on the ocean floor.

Writer's Craft

Answers may vary.

3. Some words and phrases that paint pictures are "pearly iridescent china bowls," "a sweetened bean soup dotted with tender white *mochi,* puffed up like oversized marshmallows," "neatly lined rows of red and green oblong slices of sweet bean cakes," "a mound of crushed lima beans, tinted red and green," and "a vegetable dish . . . which looked like a mass of brown twigs."

4. Some texture words are "rice cakes rolled in seaweed," "a mound of crushed lima beans," and "tender white *mochi,* puffed up like oversized marshmallows." Some taste words are "hot chocolate *oshiruko,* a sweetened bean soup," "barbecued perch," "sweet bean cakes," and "burdock, hotly seasoned with red pepper."

SELECTION AMENDMENT
Description of change: excerpted
Rationale: to focus on the concept of sensory details presented in this chapter

152

READER'S RESPONSE

1. Have you ever eaten a meal cooked by someone from a culture or country different than your own? Describe the meal for your classmates.
2. Imagine a meal in an unusual place. For example, perhaps you have lunch on Mount Everest or breakfast on the ocean floor. Write a short journal entry about the meal.

WRITER'S CRAFT

3. In this description, Monica Sone uses words like *enormous platter* and *magnificent black and silver lacquered tray* to create a picture of a Japanese meal. What are some other words she uses to paint a picture of the meal for you?
4. When they describe, writers often use *sensory details,* words that describe sights, sounds, tastes, textures, and smells. For example, "an enormous platter of *osushi*" helps you see the dish. What are some texture, or touch, words that Monica Sone uses? What are some taste words she uses?

"IN THE CHILDHOOD MEMORIES OF EVERY GOOD COOK, THERE'S A LARGE KITCHEN, A WARM STOVE, A SIMMERING POT AND A MOM."

BARBARA COSTIKYAN

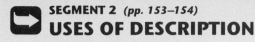
TEACHING THE AIMS

This section provides an overview of the different purposes for description. Bring to class examples of description used in the different aims—expressive, persuasive, informative, and creative. You can draw your examples from current tourist pamphlets, newspapers, magazines, literature anthologies, and textbooks. Divide students into groups and have them identify the aim (purpose) of each example.

Assess students' understanding of the aims of description by calling on individuals

Uses of Description

Writers of description always want to create a picture with words. But they don't always have the same purpose when they write. Here are four purposes the writers might have.

▶ **To Express Yourself:** in your journal, describing the emptiness in your old room as you pack and move to a new house; in a letter to a friend, describing the frightening characters in a horror movie.

To Persuade: describing the colorful, prize-filled piñata at a friend's birthday party so that your parents will let you have one at yours; describing the pitiful little puppy at the door to convince a friend to adopt it.

To Inform: describing your clothes so that an exchange student will recognize you at the train station; describing a missing bicycle so that a friend can help you look for it.

▶ **To Be Creative:** in a short story, describing the little alien from Mars who is the main character; in a school play, describing the horrible spider that falls from the ceiling.

If you stop at a tourist-information station on the interstate highway, you'll find descriptions of that state's special attractions. When you read your newspaper, you'll read descriptions of soccer or football games. Descriptions are also in ads on the veterinarian's bulletin board and in information pamphlets about computers

⛓ INTEGRATING THE LANGUAGE ARTS

Literature Link. Have students work in groups to find examples of description used to achieve each aim. Ask one group to look at a journal or autobiographical description such as "Rattlesnake Hunt" by Marjorie Kinnan Rawlings to examine examples of expressive description. Have a second group read Francisco Jimenez's story "The Circuit" to read and analyze a persuasive description about the difficult and discouraging life of the migrant worker. Tell a third group to analyze an informative description in an essay by a naturalist such as Edwin Way Teale or Edward Abbey. Finally, ask a group to examine a creative description of a character in a short story, perhaps in Morley Callaghan's "Luke Baldwin's Vow" or in Harper Lee's "One-Shot Finch."

to name one of the aims and to give a specific way that description could help to achieve that aim.

To conclude your discussion of the **Uses of Description,** refer students to the items in the **Looking Ahead** box below. Tell students that they will learn these skills as they study the chapter. ■

A DIFFERENT APPROACH

An alternate way to teach the examples of descriptive writing given on p. 153 is to write each example on a separate piece of paper, fold each piece, put the pieces in a container, and have students, individually or in groups, draw one and identify its use or aim. For example, if a student drew "in a short story, describing the little alien from Mars . . . ," he or she should identify the aim as creative.

in the computer store. And you can relax and enjoy description in stories, novels, poems, and plays. The purpose of the descriptions may be different, but they're all alike in one way. All the writers want you to form a picture or image of their subjects.

LOOKING AHEAD

In the main assignment in this chapter, you'll write a description. Your basic purpose will be to express yourself or to be creative. As you work through this chapter, keep in mind that an expressive or creative description

- is filled with details that create a picture or image of the subject
- uses sensory details, exact words, and figures of speech
- is clearly organized and easy to follow

Calvin & Hobbes, copyright 1986 Universal Press Syndicate. Reprinted with permission of Universal Press Syndicate. All rights reserved.

OBJECTIVES

- To select a subject and a mood for a description
- To practice listening skills by listening for details of sound
- To gather and organize details about a subject for a description

Writing a Description

Planning a Description

A good description doesn't just come out of thin air. It's the result of thinking and planning.

Thinking About Subject, Purpose, and Audience

A Subject.   You usually don't have to look around for a *subject* to describe. The subject is already there. For example, you need to describe a new jacket you want for your birthday. Or you need to describe your state capitol building in your history report. If you do have to think of a subject to write about, it helps to choose something you know well. You might think of an object in your own home or a place you know very well. If you don't know the subject well, you may have to use your imagination.

A Purpose.   Your *purpose* for writing can take you in two different directions. The first direction is to describe something *exactly as it is*. For example, if you've lost your pet dog, Flash, you need to describe his exact color, size, and markings. Otherwise you might get the wrong dog back.

The second direction is the one you take in expressive or creative descriptions. You describe something in a way that will *create a feeling or mood*. You may want to describe your day at the beach to make your readers feel how exciting it was. You could show that excitement by describing how it felt to surf in on a big wave or to catch and reel in a fifty-pound shark or to watch the volleyball soar across the net.

QUOTATION FOR THE DAY

"That pile of papers on his left side went on living like the watch on a dead soldier's wrist." (Jean Cocteau, 1889–1963, French poet, playwright, and film director)

Write the quotation on the chalkboard and ask students to discuss it. Each student could finish the sentence prompt "According to the quotation, writing . . . ." Encourage several volunteers to share their interpretations of the quotation with the class. Lead students to understand that writing a description is one way to immortalize something one sees, hears, feels, or experiences.

To illustrate the importance of details and mood in description, read aloud an effective descriptive beginning of a story or novel. Then ask students how the details set the mood and capture their interest. For example, read the first few lines of Madeline L'Engle's *A Wrinkle in Time* to illustrate how details create a mood of mystery and sus-pense. Tell students that they can also write effective description.

MEETING INDIVIDUAL NEEDS

LEP/ESL

General Strategies. Students might benefit from a class discussion that clearly discriminates among the terms *observe, recall,* and *imagine.* Create three columns on the chalkboard, using each of the above terms as headings. Ask students to suggest examples from daily life in which one is observing [combing one's hair in front of the mirror], recalling [trying to remember someone's name], and imagining [thinking about the future]. The more examples given for each category, the better. The idea is for students to realize that they use these skills every day.

A DIFFERENT APPROACH

Write on the chalkboard three or four words that indicate a mood or feeling. Then have students brainstorm vocabulary words and phrases that provide details that could support each mood. Here are some examples:

1. peaceful [quiet, soothing music, gentle breeze]
2. exciting [cheers, waving, heart beating]
3. frightening [screeching brakes, howling wolves, eerie screams]

156

---

156   *Using Description*

An Audience. Your *audience* will also make a difference in your description. Your best friend would remember that Flash was brown and white, but she might not remember the black spot on his ear. Always ask yourself what your audience will need to know to clearly see what you describe.

WRITING NOTE

When you want to show readers how you feel about a subject, put yourself into the picture. Use words like *I, me, my,* and *mine* when you talk about yourself. However, when you write a description for a formal report—like a science report—it may not be appropriate to use these words or to include your thoughts and feelings. You will have to decide which of these types of description—one that includes your feelings or one that is more focused on facts—better suits your purpose.

WRITING ASSIGNMENT

PART 1:
Beginning Your Description

In this chapter, you'll be writing a description of an object that expresses your feeling about it. First, you'll have to decide what you want to describe. You will be trying to create a feeling or mood, so you might want to choose something you have a specific feeling about. Also, make sure it's something you know well. Remember that your audience will include your teacher and classmates.

TEACHING THE LESSON

Since this lesson includes several related stages, you will want to be sure that students keep a sense of a unified goal as they develop separate but related prewriting skills. One way to keep this sense of purpose is for you to model each of the prewriting stages with a description of a single subject such as the eerie house pictured on p. 161.

Before asking the class to select their subjects and moods for **Writing Assignment: Part 1**, have students define the model subject [old house], purpose [to create a mood of mystery], and audience [classmates] of a description of the house.

Continue to model the lesson by showing students how you would observe, recall, and imagine details about the old

After you've finished doing all this thinking, write down the name of your subject. Then write two or three sentences that tell how you feel about it or how you want your readers to feel about it.

Collecting Details

Now that you have an interesting subject, how do you describe it? Where do you get the details to make it clear? You can observe, recall, or imagine it.

Observing. *Observing* a subject means paying close attention to it. It also means using all your senses. What do you see and hear? What do you feel, taste, and touch?

Recalling. Sometimes you can't observe a subject, but you can *recall* certain memories of it. You remember a pizza place because you had a good time there. Close your eyes and think about your subject. What do you see? What foods do you smell? What noises or music do you hear?

Imagining. You can *imagine* details about a subject you've never seen. This is especially important if you want to be creative. What's it like on the planet Saturn or inside a race car? What do you imagine you'd see? hear? smell? Or think about an alien from space. How does it look? walk? talk?

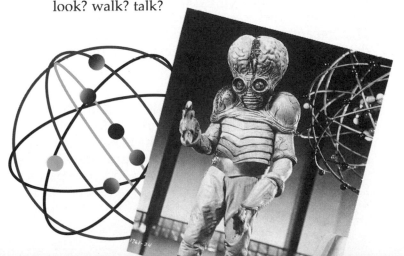

 INTEGRATING THE LANGUAGE ARTS

Literature Link. Read to your students two or three paragraphs from Mark Twain's description of Tom Sawyer's encounter with the cat in "The Cat and the Pain Killer." Ask students to identify the mood or feeling created by this exaggerated description [humor]. Then have students analyze what words and phrases contribute to the mood.

 VISUAL CONNECTIONS

Ideas for Writing. Have students write expressive/descriptive paragraphs describing the collage of space aliens, basing their prewriting on the following questions:

1. What details can be observed in the picture?
2. What details can students remember from movies they have seen about these creatures?
3. What details can they imagine about these creatures?

house before students follow these steps with their own subjects for **Writing Assignment: Part 2.** Write these details on the chalkboard as students identify them for you.

Finally, select and organize details about the old house, creating one or two different plans to be written on the chalkboard to serve as models for students as they begin to plan their descriptions in **Writing Assignment: Part 3.**

Cont. on p. 160

A DIFFERENT APPROACH

To increase students' skills in observing and describing, bring to class several different fruits for students to describe. Arrange students in groups of four, with each group focusing on a particular fruit such as an orange, a lemon, or a kiwi. (You may want to cut the fruits in half so students can observe the inside, too.)

Time students' responses, allowing three minutes for them to freewrite about what they observe, three minutes for them to freewrite about the related experiences that they can recall, and three minutes for them to freewrite about what they imagine.

After students finish their freewriting, have them compare their responses in small groups.

ANSWERS
Exercise 1

Responses will vary. Encourage students to be as specific as possible when explaining the sounds. Each group might select a recorder to make a group list of similar and different sounds that the group heard. Then groups can compare their lists.

Here are one writer's notes to describe the dark, scary experience she had the time she crawled under a house. Notice that the writer used two of the three ways of collecting details (page 157).

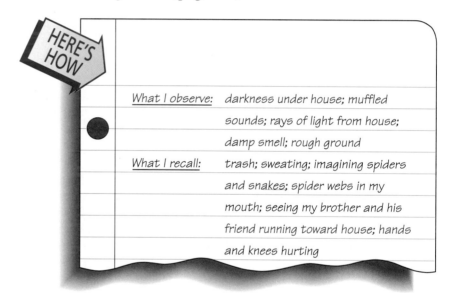

HERE'S HOW

What I observe:	*darkness under house; muffled sounds; rays of light from house; damp smell; rough ground*
What I recall:	*trash; sweating; imagining spiders and snakes; spider webs in my mouth; seeing my brother and his friend running toward house; hands and knees hurting*

EXERCISE 1 ▶ **Speaking and Listening: Collecting Details**

If you're describing a book, you don't have to worry too much about sounds. But you can't describe a herd of elephants or a rock concert without details about sound. That means you need to train your ears to listen for details. Use the following suggestions to practice your listening skills.

1. Take five minutes to listen for all the sounds in your home. Jot down notes as you listen. Can you hear a car motor outside? a creaky sound in the walls? the humming of the refrigerator? the ticking of a clock?
2. Get together with a partner. Take turns reading the list of sounds you heard. Did you and your partner hear similar sounds? What are some differences in your lists?

CRITICAL THINKING
(p. 159)

OBJECTIVE
- To list sensory details about a given subject

TEACHING *OBSERVING DETAILS*

Help your students to detect details through their various senses by modeling the process for them. Make five columns on the chalkboard, each column headed with one of the five senses. Then ask students to list words and phrases for each column that describe the pizza pictured below. ⚡

CRITICAL THINKING
Observing Details

You're eating a big slice of pizza, piled with melting cheese. You smell the spicy pepperoni and see the bright bits of green pepper. Vivid details like these make your readers experience what you describe.

You don't observe details with just your eyes. You also observe them by hearing, tasting, touching, and smelling. Make yourself aware of even the smallest details. Sit on a park bench. What strikes you first? Is the bench wooden or concrete? Are there names or initials carved or drawn on the bench? Can you smell flowers nearby or the fumes of traffic? What do you hear?

⚡ CRITICAL THINKING EXERCISE:
Observing Details

Practice your observing skills. Choose something you can observe directly, like the subjects listed below. Use all your senses to observe the subject. Make a list of as many details about it as you can. Compare with classmates who chose similar subjects. What details are different?

1. your bedroom closet
2. your back yard late at night or early in the morning
3. an aquarium
4. your favorite food
5. the refrigerator in your house

MEETING INDIVIDUAL NEEDS

LEP/ESL

General Strategies. It may be helpful to model the skills required for the **Critical Thinking Exercise** before requiring students to tackle it independently. Otherwise, students may not fully understand the objective of the exercise. Select one of the five listed subjects. Write it on the chalkboard. Have students brainstorm collectively and offer details appropriate to the subject. Write each of these details under the subject heading. Refrain from judging the suggestions offered; rather encourage full participation.

🖐 COOPERATIVE LEARNING

After students have selected their subjects, tell them to divide a piece of paper into five columns, to label each column for one of the five senses, and to try to have at least three details in each column.

Have students compare their lists in small groups. Form the groups based on the similarity of students' topics.

ANSWERS
Critical Thinking Exercise

Be sure students' responses are specific. You may want to require a certain number of details for each sense.

Cont. from p. 158
INDEPENDENT PRACTICE

Students will still need some guidance during the early stages of writing. Be available to answer questions and to check students' work informally as they work independently to select subjects and moods, to collect details about the subjects, and to select and arrange those details.

ASSESSMENT

Assess student mastery of prewriting concepts by monitoring their in-class work. Instead of evaluating on correctness, look for completion and fluency.

MEETING INDIVIDUAL NEEDS

LEARNING STYLES

Visual Learners. Suggest that students use graphic organizers to facilitate gathering and organizing information for descriptions given in spatial order. Share this example organizer with students and discuss the six different ways of arranging details in spatial order:

TOP

FAR		
LEFT	MIDDLE	RIGHT
NEAR		

BOTTOM

🏃 TIMESAVER

Because **Writing Assignment: Parts 1–3** build on each other, you will not need to check all three assignments for all of your students. Have students work in groups to check **Parts 1** and **2**, consulting you only when they encounter problems. Check **Part 3** yourself to ensure that students are ready to move on to the writing stage.

160

PART 2:
Collecting Details

Put your observing, recalling, and imagining skills into action! Collect the details for the subject you chose for Writing Assignment, Part 1 (page 156). Write your details in a chart like the one on page 158.

Selecting and Organizing Details

Sometimes, when you're going out, you choose everything you wear just to create a certain effect. You decide between a T-shirt and a shirt with buttons, or between a flashy belt and a plain one. You do the same kind of thing when you try to create a particular feeling or mood in a description. You use some details and leave out others. For example, if you want to show that the park was gloomy and depressing, you probably won't include details about the beautiful rose garden.

After you've chosen your details, you need to think about how to put them together. Here are two of the many ways you can arrange descriptive details.

spatial order: arrange details by location—good for describing places and objects
- from top to bottom or bottom to top
- from near to far or far to near
- from left to right or right to left

order of importance: arrange details by the importance you want to give them—good for describing people and animals
- from least to most important
- from most to least important

You don't have to use one of these organizations. Sometimes a description just won't work that way. However, it is important that you create a clear picture for your readers.

👉 **REFERENCE NOTE:** For more help on arranging information, see pages 77–84.

1. For what two reasons would you use description? [to describe something exactly as it is or to create a feeling or mood]

2. How do you collect details? [by observing, recalling, and imagining]

3. What are two ways to arrange details? [spatial order and order of importance] ■

Prewriting **161**

When you plan a description

- collect details by observing, recalling, or imagining
- select the details that will help you create a special feeling
- decide the best way to organize the details

EXERCISE 2 ▶ **Selecting and Organizing Details**

Write a description of the house pictured here to create a feeling of mystery and suspense. Make a list of all the details from the picture that would help create that feeling. Think how to arrange the details. Which would be better—spatial order or order of importance? Arrange your details in the order you've chosen. Next, work with two or three classmates to compare details and the order you used. Try to decide which details and which order work the best.

ANSWERS
Exercise 2
Students' descriptions should include details that appeal to each of the five senses.

WRITING ASSIGNMENT

PART 3:
Selecting and Organizing Details

Look over the details in the chart you made for Writing Assignment, Part 2 (page 160). Think about the feeling you want to create. Choose details and an order you think are best. Then list your details in that order.

WRITING YOUR FIRST DRAFT

OBJECTIVES

- To analyze a descriptive passage for the dominant feeling, sensory details, and order of arrangement

- To write a draft of a description that uses sensory details, exact words, and figures of speech

QUOTATION FOR THE DAY

"I even have loved spending an entire day seeking the buried treasure of one right word." (Ralph Schoenstein, Bill Cosby's ghostwriter)

Use the quotation to emphasize the importance of selecting precise words in descriptive writing. You can assign various subjects and ask each student to list a single word that best describes the person, place, thing, or idea.

SELECTION AMENDMENT
Description of change: excerpted
Rationale: to focus on the concept of sensory details presented in this chapter

---

Writing Your First Draft

An artist paints a picture with brushes and paint. These are the artist's tools. When you write a description, you're painting a picture, too. Your tools are words.

The Basic Elements of Description

Sensory details. Sensory details come from using your senses—sight, touch, hearing, smell, and taste. In this paragraph, many sensory details help create a strong picture of hard work.

> It was hot work, dusty work. Chemicals used for spraying the vines smelled bad and choked him. Spider webs got in his face. Broken vines scratched his arms. Grapes stained his hands. Sweat poured into his eyes, in spite of the handkerchief wrapped around his forehead.
>
> James P. Terzian and Kathryn Cramer, *Mighty Hard Road*

MOTIVATION

Tell students that you are going to read a descriptive passage. Then read aloud **A Writer's Model** on pp. 167–168. After explaining how this passage uses effective details in creating a feeling or mood, tell students it was written by a student.

TEACHING THE LESSON

First, focus on **The Basic Elements of Description**, pp. 162–165. As you focus on each element, read aloud (or have a student read) the selection from *Mighty Hard Road*. Then discuss the authors' specific sensory details, exact words, or figures of speech.

For example, you could address the sensory details of "hot work, dusty work," ☞

Writing Your First Draft **163**

Here's the beginning of a *word bank* for sensory details. You might start your own word bank in your journal. That way, you can add new words as you learn them.

A WORD BANK			
Sight	shiny faded broad	copper tall silvery	spotted rosy round
Touch	fuzzy scratchy	slippery cool	bumpy damp
Sound	screech mutter	murmur rumble	whisper roar
Smell	smoky rotten	fresh stale	spicy perfumy
Taste	warm sour	salty fresh	bitter sweet

Exact Words. Exact words make your description sharp. For example, an exact word for the color of your favorite sweater might be *turquoise* or *navy*, not *blue*. A duck doesn't *walk*, it *waddles*. In the following paragraph, a young boy finds a fawn, or young deer, that he has been looking for. As you read, notice how the writer uses exact words such as *startled*, *fawn*, and *stare*.

MEETING **INDIVIDUAL** NEEDS

LEP/ESL

General Strategies. When encouraging students to create word banks in their journals, it's imperative that they be instructed to record each word within a context. The students can define the words using either English or their native languages, use the words in sentences that indicate the words' meanings, or draw pictures or create visual cues that will suggest the words' meanings. Otherwise, students will end up with word banks that are lists of words totally out of context and, therefore, devoid of any meaning.

INTEGRATING THE LANGUAGE ARTS

Vocabulary Link. Tell students that using more exact verbs, nouns, and adjectives can make their descriptions more vivid. For example, more exact words for *walked* are *strutted, shuffled,* or *scurried*. Ask students to think of more exact words for the following verbs:

1. fell [tumbled, slipped, sprawled]
2. moved [shook, quivered, trembled]
3. looked [stared, peered, glanced]
4. talked [whined, mumbled, stuttered]

Students may need to use a dictionary or a thesaurus.

163

"smelled bad and choked him," "scratched his arms," "stained his hands," and "poured into his eyes."

You may want to review noun plurals as suggested in the **Mechanics Hint,** or you may discuss this concept only with your less-advanced students as needed.

Before you assign **Writing Assignment: Part 4,** you may want to continue the modeling you began in the **Prewriting** section of this chapter. Write on the chalkboard one set of notes created by your students for **Exercise 2.** Then using these notes and asking for suggestions from your students, write on a transparency a draft of a paragraph describing the creepy house from p. 161.

INTEGRATING THE LANGUAGE ARTS

Literature Link. The short story "Rikki-tikki-tavi" by Rudyard Kipling is an excellent example of an author's use of sensory details, exact words, and figures of speech. Have students follow along in their literature books or on a reproduced copy as you read several paragraphs. Then ask the following questions:

1. What sensory details does Kipling use?
2. What exact words does Kipling use?
3. What figures of speech does Kipling use?

Technology Link. If computers are available in your classroom or your school's library or learning center, encourage students to write their drafts on word processors so that they can use the comments command as a means of jotting notes about their drafts as they are composing.

164

> Movement directly in front of him startled him so that he tumbled backward. The fawn lifted its face to his. It turned its head with a wide, wondering motion and shook him through with the stare of its liquid eyes. It was quivering. It made no effort to rise or run. Jody could not trust himself to move.
>
> Marjorie Kinnan Rawlings, *The Yearling*

Figures of speech. *Figures of speech* compare two things that are very different. When you use a figure of speech, you don't mean exactly what you say. "This room is a pig pen" doesn't *really* mean that pigs live in the room. It just means the room is messy. *Similes* and *metaphors* are two figures of speech that are easy to use.

A *simile* compares two things using the word *like* or *as.*

> Little Man turned around and watched saucer-eyed as a bus bore down on him spewing clouds of red dust *like a huge yellow dragon breathing fire.*
>
> Mildred Taylor, *Roll of Thunder, Hear My Cry*

ASSESSMENT

Read drafts and give credit if students have clearly stated the feelings or moods they are trying to create and if they have included examples of sensory details, exact words, and figures of speech as support.

A *metaphor* compares two things directly. It doesn't use *like* or *as*.

> During the storm, the *sky was a cloudy sea.*

MECHANICS HINT

Noun Plurals

The exact words that you use in your descriptions are often nouns. Remember that nouns form their plurals in different ways.

Form the plural of many nouns by adding *s*.

EXAMPLES   Little *rays* of light helped me see.

I imagined hairy *spiders* and coiled *snakes* in the darkness.

Add *es* to nouns ending in *s*, *x*, *z*, *ch*, or *sh*.

EXAMPLE   In the dim light, I saw two small *foxes* hiding in the *bushes.*

Other nouns form their plurals in different ways. Use your dictionary to find the correct noun plurals.

☞ REFERENCE NOTE: For more about noun plurals, see pages 773–776.

Maybe you've seen someone for the first time who stood out in your mind. Could you describe that person vividly? Read the following description of an old doctor. As you read, look for details and words that make the doctor seem real.

MEETING INDIVIDUAL NEEDS

LEP/ESL

General Strategies. Because students will be using adjectives in descriptive writing, you may need to address potential problems with comparative adjectives. To form the comparative in Spanish, the word *más* ("more") is always used before the adjective. Your Spanish-speaking students might, therefore, adhere to the form *more happy* or *more loud* instead of making the shift to *happier* or *louder.* Another possible error may result from the fact that Spanish uses the word *que* (translated as "than" or "that"), resulting in sentences such as "My brother is more athletic that my sister." If necessary, offer students extra practice using the comparative forms.

If students are still having trouble with description, prepare a partial description like the following example and work with students to fill in the blanks:

At the back of the city park is a quiet spot that makes me feel . . . . The birds . . . and squirrels . . . like . . . . The wind blows gently through the trees. A little stream . . . .

CLOSURE

To conclude, divide the chalkboard into three columns. Label the first column "Sensory Details," the second "Exact Words," and the third "Figures of Speech." Then reread **A Writer's Model** to the class and ask volunteers to write examples from the story of each element of description in the appropriate column.

166   *Using Description*

USING THE SELECTION

from **Willie Bea and the Time the Martians Landed**

1

Moses, who lived to be one hundred and twenty years old, led the Israelites across the Red Sea and through the Wilderness to within sight of Canaan, the Promised Land.

2

A Homburg is a man's felt hat with a narrow, slightly rolled brim and a soft, dented crown.

VISUAL CONNECTIONS

Ideas for Writing. Ask students to study the picture of Dr. Taylor and to freewrite a description about him—using specific details—before reading Hamilton's description.

A PASSAGE FROM A NOVEL

from Willie Bea and the Time the Martians Landed
by Virginia Hamilton

Simile   1

Sensory details

Exact words

Dr. Taylor came in and he was old. To Willie Bea, he looked just like <u>Moses</u> on her Sunday School cards, but without a long beard. Wonderful white hair and sparkling eyes. Tall. Tall enough for heaven. Folks said he was eighty-seven, but to Willie Bea he looked closer to one hundred. His baby-fine snow-white hair reached to his shoulders. His black <u>greatcoat</u> came almost down to his ankles. He had on a green woolen scarf and he wore a black Homburg down low over his forehead. He wore old-fashioned leather <u>spats</u> that covered his feet from <u>instep</u> to

Give lists of objects, people, and places to students and ask them to use a simile or a metaphor to describe each. Here are some examples:

1. a watch [the heartbeat of time]
2. the highway at night [as shiny as a black ribbon]
3. a baby [the dawn of life]

Bring to class pictures of important people in history and science such as Abraham Lincoln, Harriet Tubman, and Marie Curie. Ask each student to select a picture to study and to write a one-paragraph description of his or her choice. Remind students to use sensory details, exact words, and figures of speech to create an overall mood. ■

Exact words

ankle. He came in and bowed in greeting and for Marva to take his Homburg hat. He had his black bag in one hand and his cane in the other, so he couldn't very well take off the hat himself.

E X E R C I S E 3 ▶ **Analyzing a Description**

After reading the description, can you see Dr. Taylor in your mind? Discuss the following questions about him with your class or small group.

1. What feeling do you get about Dr. Taylor from the passage? Think of a word that describes the feeling.
2. What simile does the writer use to describe him?
3. What are three sensory details the writer uses to describe the doctor's hair and coat? What are the exact words she uses about his spats and hat?
4. The writer seems to use both spatial order and order of importance. Where does she use spatial order? Where does she seem to use order of importance?

A Writer's Model for You

Virginia Hamilton is a skilled professional writer. If it makes you nervous to try to match her skill, look at the following paragraph. It is a little less complicated than the description of Dr. Taylor.

A WRITER'S MODEL

Simile
Exact words

Last summer I discovered a different world when I crawled under the house to look for a lost baseball. The crawl space was like a secret cave. Mostly it was dark, but little rays of light from the

ANSWERS
Exercise 3

Answers may vary.

1. Students might describe Dr. Taylor as old, dignified, or respectable.
2. Dr. Taylor "looked just like Moses on her Sunday School cards."
3. The doctor's hair is "baby-fine" and "snow-white." His coat is a "black greatcoat" that "came almost down to his ankles." He also "wore a black Homburg down low over his forehead," and "He wore old-fashioned leather spats that covered his feet from instep to ankle."
4. The first five lines of the text seem to be arranged in order of importance, concluding with the obviously important observation that Dr. Taylor seemed "tall enough for heaven" to the observer. The next few sentences seem to be arranged by spatial order, moving from Dr. Taylor's head (hair, hat) to his body (greatcoat) to his feet (spats).

SELECTION AMENDMENT
Description of change: excerpted
Rationale: to focus on the concept of drafting a description presented in this chapter

COOPERATIVE LEARNING

After students answer question 1 from **Exercise 3,** have them discuss their answers in small groups. Do they agree or disagree about the best word to describe the feeling created by the passage? What support can each student find for the word he or she chose?

Sensory details

Writer's feelings

Simile

house above helped me see. The ground smelled musty and damp, and it was rough on my hands and knees. Above me I could just barely hear music from the radio. Sticky cobwebs got in my mouth. It was cool, but I began to sweat. I imagined hairy spiders and coiled snakes in the darkness. I crawled quickly back to the front and poked my head out of the opening. Bright sunlight blinded my eyes. I felt like a bear coming out of its cave after a long winter's nap.

TIMESAVER

To save time as you check their drafts from **Writing Assignment: Part 4,** ask students to underline the sentences that express the feelings they want to create and to highlight sensory details in blue, exact words in pink, and figures of speech in yellow.

PART 4:
Writing a Draft of Your Description

Are you ready to paint a picture with words? Using the details that you've collected, write the first draft of your description. As you write, focus on the feeling you want to create about your subject. Remember to use sensory details, exact words, and figures of speech so that your description will seem real to your readers.

OBJECTIVES

- To analyze a writer's revisions
- To evaluate and revise a draft of a description

TEACHING THE LESSON

Model the techniques of evaluation and revision by applying the four questions from the **Evaluating and Revising Description** chart to the draft you wrote to model **Exercise 2.** Transfer the draft onto a transparency. Have a student read each evaluation question and then revise any problem ☞

 # Evaluating and Revising

On page 156 you saw how Calvin's mother helped him evaluate his description. Next, he must revise his work. This same process of evaluating and revising will help you improve your first draft. Use the following chart and ask yourself each question in the left-hand column. If you find a problem, use the ideas in the right-hand column to solve it.

EVALUATING AND REVISING DESCRIPTION

EVALUATION GUIDE	REVISION TECHNIQUE
1 Do details help readers "see" the subject?	**Add** sensory details and figures of speech.
2 Is the picture clear?	**Cut** words that are general or fuzzy. **Add** exact ones.
3 Do the details create a feeling about the subject?	**Cut** details that do not create the main feeling. **Add** details that support the feeling.
4 Are the details organized in a way that makes sense?	**Reorder** details in an order that helps the reader see the subject.

EXERCISE 4 ▶ **Analyzing a Writer's Revisions**

On the following page is part of the description you read on page 168. As you read, think about the changes the writer made during revision. With your class or in a small group, answer the questions that follow.

QUOTATION FOR THE DAY

"Apparent failure may hold in its rough shell the germs of a success that will blossom in time, and bear fruit throughout eternity." (Frances Ellen Watkins Harper, 1825–1911, American author, lecturer, and reformer)

Use the quotation to encourage students as they begin evaluating and revising their work. Lead students to understand that recognizing weak spots in their writing or having other students point out flaws in their work allows the writer to produce a successful and effective paper.

MEETING INDIVIDUAL NEEDS

LEP/ESL

General Strategies. You may want to pair ESL students who share the same native language. Before exchanging compositions, suggest that the students tell each other (using their native language) about the situation they have tried to describe. This strategy may relieve some of the pressure experienced in not being able to express precisely what they want to say.

areas with the class, asking for suggestions. You could use different-colored markers to make the changes on the draft.

CLOSURE

Using the **Evaluating and Revising Description** chart, write on the chalkboard the four questions for evaluation. Then ask students to write the appropriate techniques needed to solve the revision problems. ■

> Above me I could just barely hear
> ~~sounds~~ *music* from the radio. *Sticky* Cobwebs got in my   **replace/add**
> mouth. It was cool, but I began to sweat. I
> imagined *hairy* spiders and *coiled* snakes in the   **add**
> darkness. I crawled quickly back to the
> front and poked my head out of the
> opening. ~~The crawl space was about 4 1/2~~   **cut**
> ~~feet long.~~ Bright sunlight blinded my eyes.
> I felt like a bear coming out of its cave
> after a long winter's nap.

1. Why does the writer replace the word *sounds* in the first sentence with the word *music*? Which word is more exact?
2. In the second sentence, why does the writer add the word *Sticky* before the word *cobwebs*? How does this change make the sentence better?
3. In the fourth sentence, why does the writer add the words *hairy* and *coiled*?
4. Why does the writer cut the sentence *The crawl space was about 4 $\frac{1}{2}$ feet long*? [Hint: Read over the third guideline on the Evaluating and Revising Description chart on page 169.]

ANSWERS

Exercise 4

Responses will vary.

1. *Music* is more exact and, therefore, more effective.
2. The addition of *sticky* before *cobwebs* appeals more directly to the sense of touch.
3. The words *hairy* and *coiled* appeal to the reader's sense of sight.
4. This sentence does not appeal to the senses and does not fit the mood of a dark, frightening, cavelike place.

 INTEGRATING THE LANGUAGE ARTS

Technology Link. If students have access to computers, have them use the search command to find commonly used, weak descriptive words such as *good, very, big,* or *nice* so they can replace these words with stronger, more specific adjectives.

 **WRITING ASSIGNMENT**

PART 5:
Evaluating and Revising Your Description

It's a good idea to take advantage of other people's evaluations of your writing. Exchange papers with a partner or with a small group of classmates, and comment on each other's descriptions. (Don't forget to use the peer-evaluation guidelines on page 47.) Think about your own evaluations and your classmates' or partner's. Then revise your first draft.

PROOFREADING AND PUBLISHING

OBJECTIVES

- To use proofreading strategies to prepare a description for publication
- To share a description with an audience

TEACHING THE LESSON

To help your students become more effective proofreaders, write on a transparency a sample description with several errors in noun plurals, spelling, punctuation, and so forth. Then model proofreading with your class.

To help students understand the specific strengths and weaknesses of their ☞

Proofreading and Publishing

In proofreading, you add the finishing touches to your description. Now you can catch and correct errors in grammar, usage, and mechanics. When your description is as good as you can make it, share it with others. Here are two ideas:

- Make a classroom display of the places and objects everyone described. Draw, find, or create pictures, cartoons, or photos to go along with the descriptions.
- Play a guessing game with a small group of classmates. Read your description aloud. Then ask your classmates to identify the main feeling they get from the description. Is the feeling the same as or different from the one you wanted to create?

> **WRITING ASSIGNMENT**

PART 6:
Proofreading and Publishing Your Description

You've worked hard to create a clear picture with your description. Now get your picture ready for viewing by proofreading and correcting it carefully. Exchange papers with a partner. See if your partner can catch errors you missed. Then publish or share your description.

RESOURCES

PROOFREADING AND PUBLISHING
- Writing a Description

QUOTATION FOR THE DAY

"I can't write without a reader. It's precisely like a kiss—you can't do it alone." (John Cheever, 1912–1982, American author)

Write the quotation on the chalkboard and explain to students that when they publish their writing, they are sharing their work with an audience. Using Cheever's statement as a model, students might write original similes about writing.

MEETING INDIVIDUAL NEEDS

AFRICAN AMERICAN

It is possible that students will use the past tense when writing descriptions. There may be a tendency to omit the –ed marker for past tense regular verbs, as in "She miss the bus yesterday." As part of the proofreading process, you may want to work with students individually and scan their compositions for this omission. After the verb forms are changed, ask students to underline the past-tense suffixes and to read the compositions aloud. Listen carefully and model correct pronunciation.

descriptions, use the following grading system:

1. clearly stated mood (25%)
2. supported with sensory details, exact words, and figures of speech (25%)
3. arrangement of details (25%)
4. correctness of grammar, spelling, and punctuation (25%)

CLOSURE

Ask students the following questions:
1. Why is it important to proofread your description?
2. Why is it important to share your writing with an audience? ■

A STUDENT MODEL

Evaluation

1. Matt's description includes numerous sensory details and figures of speech that help the reader visualize Sherman. Some examples of sensory details are "black, small, compact dog"; "fox- or wolf-like face"; and "his bark . . . with a yip-brop-rorp." Matt uses several similes, such as "smells like a rotten onion" and "whines like a hungry seal."
2. The reader can easily see Matt's feeling about his subject with the inclusion of first-person pronouns and of phrases such as "a sweet, affectionate dog" and "I love him."
3. Matt organizes his details by the senses appealed to. His details are ordered by sights, smells, sounds, and actions.

A STUDENT MODEL

In the following paper, Matt Harris—a student at the University Laboratory School in Baton Rouge, Louisiana—writes about his dog, Sherman. Matt says it was hardest to "find the right words to describe Sherman, for he is difficult to describe." Even so, you'll probably notice that Matt finds just the right words to create a clear picture of Sherman.

No-Tail Sherman
by Matt Harris

Every time someone sees him, they ask what he is. We always tell them that Sherman is his name, and he is a Schipperke. He is a black, small, compact dog that is half fur. He has a fox- or wolf-like face, short fox ears, and no tail. Sherman weighs seventeen pounds and is a sweet, affectionate dog, although he is hyper and jumps up on everyone he sees. He doesn't smell bad too often; but when he does smell, he smells like a rotten onion just found on the bottom of an old grocery sack. Unfortunately, his bark can often be heard with a yip-brop-rorp and a bu-ru-ru-ru that is sharper than a razor blade. He prances lightly and with a bouncing motion, like a cat with springs on his feet. When he wants to go out, he whines like a hungry seal. If he gets the chance, he will get into the refrigerator and eat the peanut butter if the jar is left open. Sherman has a different attitude from most dogs. Most dogs lick the garbage can and attack the postman. Sherman licks the postman and attacks the garbage can.

Sherman is the most unusual dog I have ever known. I guess that is why I love him so much.

SEGMENT 7 *(pp. 173–174)*
WRITING WORKSHOP
OBJECTIVES
- To write personal responses to literature
- To analyze details of sight, sound, and touch in haiku
- To use the writing process to write a haiku

TEACHING THE LESSON
Begin your lesson by reading the sample haiku and perhaps other haiku from a literature book. Have students work in groups to answer the **Thinking It Over** questions on p. 174. Then have each group report its answers for each of the three questions.

Allow students time to experiment with language and to share their experimen- 👉

173

WRITING WORKSHOP

A Descriptive Poem

In this chapter, you've learned how to create a word-picture with sensory details, exact words, and figures of speech. You can use these same skills to write poetry. A kind of poetry that creates very small word-pictures is *haiku*.

Haiku is a Japanese form of poetry that describes one moment in nature. It has three lines with a certain number of syllables arranged in a pattern. As you read the following poems, notice how the writer captures a very simple but vivid scene in just three lines.

> The lightning flashes!
> And slashing through the darkness,
> A night-heron's screech.
> Matsuo Bashō, *translated by Earl Minor*

> An old silent pond . . .
> A frog jumps into the pond,
> splash! Silence again.
> Matsuo Bashō, *translated by Harry Behn*

RESOURCES

WRITING WORKSHOP
- Collecting Details
- Creating Metaphors and Similes
- Writing a Description

QUOTATION FOR THE DAY
"Keep going. Writing is finally play, and there's no reason why you should get paid for playing. If you're a real writer, you write no matter what." (Irwin Shaw, 1913–1984, German author)

Ask students to freewrite for a few minutes about some activities or hobbies they enjoy. You may wish to ask students to write about what motivates them to participate in difficult activities. Explain that writing, like playing a game or performing in a play or recital, can be difficult and fun at the same time.

tations with you and their classmates. If students have problems, suggest that they draw pictures first and then write about the pictures.

Consider awarding an A to any poem that meets the basic requirements, giving bonus points to those that are especially creative.

Write the following statements on the chalkboard and have students tell whether each is true or false:

1. A haiku is a three-line poem. [true]
2. The first and third lines in a haiku must rhyme. [false]
3. A haiku captures a particular scene or effect. [true] ■

174

ANSWERS
Thinking It Over

1. Responses will vary, but students should give reasons for their responses.
2. Details of sight in the first haiku are the "lightning flashes" and "slashing through the darkness." Details in the second haiku are the silent pond and the frog jumping.
3. A sound detail in the first poem is the "night-heron's screech." The frog's jumping into the pond in the second poem is a detail of sound and touch.

MEETING
INDIVIDUAL
NEEDS

LEP/ESL

General Strategies. Because the strength and beauty of haiku are in large part dependent on mastery of the language, keep in mind that this may be an especially challenging, if not frustrating, assignment for LEP/ESL students. You may want to allow students to write their descriptive poems in another verse form.

Thinking It Over

1. Which haiku do you like more? Why?
2. What details of sight does the poet use in each haiku?
3. What details of sound or touch do the poems include?

Writing a Descriptive Poem

Prewriting. Choose a scene in nature that you can observe, recall, or imagine clearly. You might choose the sun rising over the ocean, fireworks in a dark sky, a dog shaking off water after a swim. Visualize the subject, and jot down sensory details that describe it. Can you think of comparisons that might help you?

Writing, Evaluating, and Revising. As you write your haiku, listen to the sounds of words as well as to their meaning. In the first haiku, the word *screech* has a sharp sound. That kind of sound fits with the word *slashing*. Play with words to try out different sounds. Read your haiku to some classmates. Ask them if your description captures the feeling you want to give.

Proofreading and Publishing. Check spelling, punctuation, and capitalization before you write a final copy. Then decide how to arrange your poem on a page. Leave white space around it to draw attention to how brief it is. Sign your poem, and if you wish, illustrate it with a drawing or decoration.

175

MAKING CONNECTIONS

MASS MEDIA AND DESCRIPTION

A Classified Ad

Classified ads are another form of description. They are called *classified* because they are arranged in categories, such as "Jobs," "Cars," or "Yard Sales."

Classified ads are usually short, because newspapers charge by the word or line. Within a short space, the writer must make the item sound better than other, similar items. As you read this type of ad, look for words that might make you want to buy the item. Ads often use abbreviations such as *w/* for *with* and *inc.* for *includes*.

> Men's 10-speed bike. Black w/silver pin-stripe. Excellent condition, new tires; inc. pump, water bottle, wrench. $70. Call Ed. 555–1685.

MASS MEDIA AND DESCRIPTION
Teaching Strategies

The day before you plan to teach this lesson, ask students to look through the classified ads in a newspaper. Ask a few volunteers to bring several ads to read to the class.

Discuss with students the essential elements included in classified ads and list these elements on the chalkboard:

1. item for sale
2. description
3. condition
4. additional items included
5. price
6. name and telephone number

GUIDELINES

Remind students of the importance of audience in this assignment. Have students work in groups to check each other's ads for clarity and accuracy.

DESCRIPTION AND LITERATURE OBJECTIVE

- To write a descriptive poem that includes words from Spanish as well as from English

DESCRIPTION AND LITERATURE

Teaching Strategies

Explain to students that their poems do not need to rhyme. If they choose, they may write another haiku. Or students may write five-line poems called cinquains, as illustrated here:

River (one word for title)
Beautiful, tranquilo (two words describing title)
Flowing smoothly along (three words expressing action)
Dreams, hopes, beauty, peace (four words expressing feelings)
Shenandoah (one word that echoes title or related word)

If your literature book has one or more poems written in English and Spanish, read these poems to your class. Another source for such poems is *Mexican American Literature,* edited by Charles Tatum.

GUIDELINES

Have students work in groups of four to evaluate and revise their poems. Tell students to remember to underline the Spanish words. Have students practice reading their poems in groups before presenting them to the class. If possible, include a Spanish-speaking student in each group, or ask your Spanish-speaking students to circulate among the groups to help with pronunciation.

Cute, friendly gerbils. Clean, fun, easy to keep. No smells, little work. $5 each with week's food. Call Marin 555–5984.

Now try writing your own classified ad. Think of an object or pet you might sell someday and the way you would describe it. Then write a three- or four-line ad, making each line forty characters. (Each letter, number, space, and punctuation mark counts as a character.) Use abbreviations whenever possible. Later, exchange ads with your classmates.

DESCRIPTION AND LITERATURE

A Poem in Two Languages

Poets rely on the sounds of words as well as the meanings. Sometimes a word sounds very different in another language. Does a *perro* sound nicer than a *dog*? Does *agudo* sound as pointed as *sharp*?

Try writing a brief poem describing a scene in nature. Use any form you like. But don't write the whole poem in English. Instead, use some of the Spanish words in the following charts. If possible, have the words read aloud by someone who knows Spanish. Let your ear enjoy the sounds of these words.

The Spanish words that you can choose to use in your poem are shown in the two following charts. A collection of Spanish nouns is shown in the left-hand column of each chart, and a variety of Spanish adjectives is shown in the right-hand columns. You may use any of the nouns or any of the adjectives in your poem, or you can use noun and adjective combinations. However, there are a few important points to keep in mind when you use the words from these charts.

First, note that in Spanish, an adjective usually follows the noun it describes. For example, in English you would say "white flower," but in Spanish you would say *flor blanca*. Second, Spanish has a more complicated system than English for matching adjectives to the nouns they modify. For the purposes of this exercise, if you want to use a Spanish adjective to modify a Spanish noun, be sure to select the noun and adjective from the same numbered chart.

CHART #1	
NOUNS	ADJECTIVES
tree—*árbol* sun—*sol* sky—*cielo* day—*día* water—*agua*	dark—*oscuro* cool—*fresco* blue—*azul* red—*rojo* quiet—*tranquilo*

CHART #2	
NOUNS	ADJECTIVES
grass—*hierba* leaf—*hoja* flower—*flor* star—*estrella* night—*noche*	cool—*fresca* green—*verde* black—*negra* yellow—*amarilla* white—*blanca*

Chapter 6

CREATIVE WRITING

Motivation

Stir interest in stories by asking students to tell you about the best stories they know. Remind the students that a story need not be a book or a short story they have read, but might be a television show, a movie, or a story someone told them. Have the class share and discuss their responses. Did they name suspenseful stories or humorous stories? Do their ideas of good stories include stories that have messages as well as stories that just entertain? How many students mentioned family stories? Do most of the stories involve realistic events set in the familiar modern world? Do some students prefer the very different settings of science fiction, adventure, or fantasy? You can build enthusiasm about writing by pointing out that students will have a chance to write the kinds of stories they enjoy most.

Introduction

Through guided discussion, emphasize that opinions about what makes a good story vary enormously. Even so, all stories share the same major purposes—to give personal enjoyment and to offer insight into human behavior.

Ask students to brainstorm ideas for a story about a man and his dog. They should suggest two or three possibilities for science fiction, adventure, fantasy, satire, or mystery. Use the variety in responses to emphasize that the directions an interesting story can take are as unlimited as the author's imagination.

Integration

Students might compare and contrast myths and legends from their literature books with **"Coyote Places the Stars."** Have the class analyze whether each story explains a natural phenomenon, offers an explanation for mankind's behavior and experiences, or both. Students whose science curriculum includes an astronomy unit might report in more detail on the origins of constellations such as the Big Dipper.

This chapter offers many opportunities to reinforce students' multicultural awareness. Discuss how a culture's myths and legends are valuable and fascinating indications of what the culture believes about humans and the world. Students might be interested in researching features of the Plains Indians culture that celebrated Coyote. Students may want to research aspects of their ethnic heritages. Some may be inspired to work something they learn into their stories.

The chart on the next page illustrates the strands of language arts as they are integrated into this chapter. For vocabulary study, glossary words are underlined in some writing models.

QUOTATIONS
All **Quotations for the Day** are chosen because of their relevance to instructional material presented in that segment of the chapter and for their usefulness in establishing student interest in writing.

INTEGRATING THE LANGUAGE ARTS

Selection	Reading and Literature	Writing and Critical Thinking	Language and Syntax	Speaking, Listening, and Other Expression Skills
"Coyote Places the Stars" by Barry Lopez **180-182** **"The Dinner Party"** by Mona Gardner **195-197** **"My Aunt"** by Ted Hughes **206-207**	Analyzing character **183** Identifying conflict **183** Identifying supporting details **183** Using questions to analyze plot **197** Using questions to analyze story elements **197** Identifying theme in a short story **197** Finding main idea **197** Analyzing setting, plot, and character in a writer's model **197** Analyzing story elements in a narrative poem **208** Analyzing sound in a narrative poem **208**	Writing a journal entry **183** Gathering ideas for writing **187-188** Brainstorming **187** Planning character **191** Planning setting **191** Planning conflict and plot **191, 192** Using freewriting and clustering as prewriting techniques **191** Organizing information on a story map **192** Using detail and dialogue to develop character **194** Writing a first draft **201** Writing a story **201** Choosing an effective title **202** Evaluating and revising a draft of a story **203** Analyzing a writer's revisions **203** Publishing a story **205** Using story elements to write a narrative poem **208** Using the writing process to write a myth **209** Writing a new ending for a story **209**	Using dialogue **194** Proofreading for mechanics, grammar, and usage errors **205**	Talking to others about story ideas **187** Recreating natural speech through dialogue **194** Talking with others about story elements **197** Initiating and participating in discussions about literature **197** Talking with others to evaluate a writer's revisions **197, 203** Sharing stories **205**

SEGMENT PLANNING GUIDE

Whether you are planning for a quick review of a writing concept or preparing an extended lesson on composition you can use the following Planning Guide to adapt the chapter material to the individual needs of your class.

SEGMENT	PAGES	CONTENT	RESOURCES
1 *Imagining Other Worlds*	*179-183*		
Literary Model from **"Coyote Places the Stars"**	180-182	Guided reading: a model of creative writing	
Reader's Response/ Writer's Craft	183	Model evaluation: responding to literature and analyzing literary writing	
2 *Ways to Write Creatively*	*184*		
3 *Prewriting*	*185-192*		Writing a Story Finding a Story Idea Imagining Characters Describing a Setting Planning a Plot
Finding a Story Idea	185	Explanation: finding ideas for stories	
Thinking About Purpose and Audience	185	Explanation: keeping an audience interested	
Starting with Characters and Situations	186	Guidelines: creating characters and situations	
Character	186	Guidelines: imagining a character	
Situation	186	Guidelines: imagining a situation	
Exercise 1	187-188	Cooperative learning: building story ideas	
Writing Assignment: Part 1	188	Applied practice: finding a story idea	
Planning Your Story	189	Introduction: using details to describe characters and plot	
Imagining Characters	189	Guidelines: using criteria for describing characters	
Describing Setting	190	Guidelines: using criteria for describing setting	
Writing Assignment: Part 2	191	Applied practice: planning characters and setting	
Planning Your Plot	191	Guidelines: learning parts of a plot	
Creating a Story Map	191-192	Guidelines: examining a writer's story map	
Writing Assignment: Part 3	192	Applied practice: creating a story map	
4 *Writing*	*193-201*		Using Dialogue
Combining the Basic Elements of a Story	193	Introduction: learning criteria for a good story	
Making the Plot Move Along	193	Guidelines: structuring a story to hold interest	
Making Characters Seem Real	193-194	Guidelines: using details in description, action, and dialogue	
Exercise 2	194	Cooperative learning: creating realistic dialogue	
Looking at a Short Story	194	Introduction: examining a short story	
Literary Model **"The Dinner Party"**	195-197	Guided reading: examining a model of a short story	

SEGMENT	PAGES	CONTENT	RESOURCES
Exercise 3	197	Cooperative learning: analyzing the elements of a short story	
Using a Story Framework	198	Introduction: examining a model story for framework	
Writer's Model	198-200	Guided reading: examining a sample story	
Usage Hint	201	Writing suggestions: using verb tenses	
Writing Assignment: Part 4	201	Applied practice: writing a first draft	
5 *Evaluating and Revising*	*202-204*		Writing a Story
Evaluating and Revising	202	Introduction: making a story better	
Critical Thinking: Analyzing the Elements of a Story	202-203	Explanation: examining a writer's revisions	
Critical Thinking Exercise	203	Cooperative learning: analyzing a writer's revisions	
Writing Assignment: Part 5	203	Applied practice: evaluating and revising a story	
Chart: Evaluating and Revising Short Stories	204	Guidelines: applying evaluation and revision techniques	
6 *Proofreading and Publishing*	*205*		Writing a Story
Publishing	205	Publishing ideas: reaching an audience	
Writing Assignment: Part 6	205	Applied practice: proofreading and publishing a story	
7 *Writing Workshop*	*206-208*		All the resources in this chapter may be used in this segment.
A Narrative Poem	206	Explanation: learning story elements and poetic language in narrative poetry	
Literary Model/Questions **"My Aunt"**	206-207	Guided reading: analyzing story elements and language in a narrative poem	
Writing a Narrative Poem	208	Guidelines: writing a narrative poem Applied practice: applying story elements to poetry	
8 *Making Connections*	*209*		
Myths: Writing a Myth	209	Applied practice: making up a myth	
Creative Writing and Literature: Writing a New Ending for a Story	209	Applied practice: rewriting a story ending	

WHOLE-CHAPTER RESOURCE
A Writing Process Log, A Writing Prompt, Holistically Graded Models, Portfolio Assessment Materials

SEGMENT 1 *(pp. 178–183)*

IMAGING OTHER WORLDS

OBJECTIVES

- To write a personal response to literature
- To write a journal entry related to the plot of the literary model
- To analyze conflict and character in a story
- To determine an author's purpose

VISUAL CONNECTIONS
Persepol. 1980

About the Artwork. The first computer-generated art appeared in the late 1950s. As late as the 1980s, however, computers capable of producing art were rare, and few artists used them. Artists had either to write their own programs or adapt existing software.

About the Artist. David Em, a pioneer in computer art since the 1970s, studied painting at the Pennsylvania Academy of the Fine Arts. He has used traditional paints, but now uses computers to create a three-dimensional effect. Salvaging an old TV set with distorted color, he was inspired to look for ways to manipulate light electronically, and he soon discovered the potential of computer graphics.

6 CREATIVE WRITING

TEACHING THE LESSON

Explain that different cultures have different stories about the stars. These stories include details and explanations that help each story make sense. Have students look for details about Coyote's character that help explain what happens in **"Coyote Places the Stars."**

☞

Imagining Other Worlds

You probably like to go to the movies. Most people do. It's a chance to escape—for just a little while—to **other worlds**. Movies allow our **imaginations** to run wild. Anything can happen. And, best of all, things usually come out okay in the end.

Writing and You. Writers use their imagination to write movie scripts, novels, stories, plays, poems, and even comic strips. They tickle our own imagination by creating, and having us believe in, people and places that never were and never will be. They make us burst with excitement, fear, unreal expectations, and fun. Have you ever used your imagination to make up a story for a little child?

As You Read. As you read the following folk tale, you'll see how people can also use imagination to explain the world around them.

Persepol, 1980, © David Em/represented by Roberta Spieckerman Associates, San Francisco.

QUOTATION FOR THE DAY

"Dreams, books, are each a world; and books, we know, Are a substantial world . . . ." (William Wordsworth, 1770–1850, English Romantic poet)

Share the quotation with the class, and have students recall a book, story, or poem in which an author creates an alternative world. You may wish to have students write journal entries about the reading experiences they remember. Explain that an imagined world may be very realistic, as in a story about life in junior high school, or it may be very unrealistic, as in a science fiction or horror story.

MEETING INDIVIDUAL NEEDS

LEP/ESL

General Strategies. To help students build their vocabularies, give them a word list of the more difficult items in the selections, such as *coyote* and *grizzlies*. Have students skim the story looking for the words. Tell them to write the sentences in which the words are found and to underline the words. Students can look up the words before doing the reading to avoid stopping and losing their concentration. You may want students to keep their word lists (along with each word in context and its definition) for reviewing.

USING THE SELECTION
Coyote Places the Stars

1

Like many myths, this story is set in an indefinite but ancient time and features animals with both human and superhuman characteristics. Coyote is always shown as wily and clever, using his wits to benefit himself, often at the expense of others.

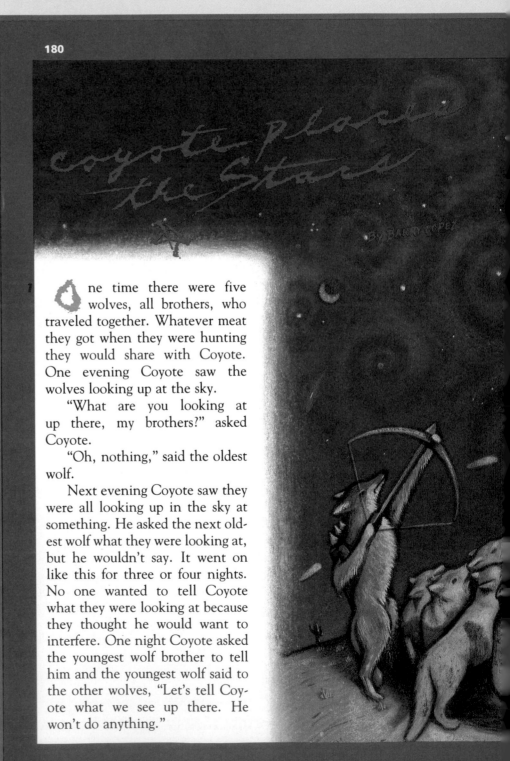

180

One time there were five wolves, all brothers, who traveled together. Whatever meat they got when they were hunting they would share with Coyote. One evening Coyote saw the wolves looking up at the sky.

"What are you looking at up there, my brothers?" asked Coyote.

"Oh, nothing," said the oldest wolf.

Next evening Coyote saw they were all looking up in the sky at something. He asked the next oldest wolf what they were looking at, but he wouldn't say. It went on like this for three or four nights. No one wanted to tell Coyote what they were looking at because they thought he would want to interfere. One night Coyote asked the youngest wolf brother to tell him and the youngest wolf said to the other wolves, "Let's tell Coyote what we see up there. He won't do anything."

GUIDED PRACTICE

You could provide your own reaction to one of the questions in the **Reader's Response** and **Writer's Craft** section as guided practice for students.

INDEPENDENT PRACTICE

Reader's Response and **Writer's Craft** can be used for independent practice. Allow students to make notes before they participate in class discussion. Explain that these notes will help them form better answers.

☞

181

VISUAL CONNECTIONS

Exploring the Subject. Discuss the character of Coyote as a representative of the trickster figure in folklore. Tricksters tend to be ambiguous characters. While they are always very clever and often amusing, their tricks can be cruel. Nonetheless, they often bring about valuable changes.

So they told him. "We see two animals up there. Way up there, where we cannot get to them."

"Let's go up and see them," said Coyote.

"Well, how can we do that?"

"Oh, I can do that easy," said Coyote. "I can show you how to get up there without any trouble at all."

Coyote gathered a great number of arrows and then began shooting them into the sky. The first arrow stuck in the sky and the second arrow stuck in the first. Each arrow stuck in the end of the one before it like that until there was a ladder reaching down to the earth.

"We can climb up now," said Coyote. The oldest wolf took his dog with him, and then the other four wolf brothers came, and then Coyote. They climbed all day and into the night. All the next day they climbed. For many days and nights they climbed until finally they reached the sky. They stood in the sky and looked over at the two animals the wolves had seen from down below. They were two grizzly bears.

"Don't go near them," said Coyote. "They will tear you apart." But the two youngest wolves were already headed over. And the next two youngest wolves followed them. Only the oldest wolf held back. When the wolves got near the grizzlies nothing happened. The wolves sat down and looked at the bears, and the bears sat there looking at the wolves. The oldest wolf, when he saw it was safe, came over with his dog and sat down with them.

2

Is Coyote showing off or is he right in saying that he has an easy way to get to the sky? [Coyote does not seem to have much trouble arranging the arrow ladder, but he clearly must have some kind of supernatural powers to do so. Some students might say even the ladder does not make it easy, because Coyote and the wolves climb for days and days.]

3

Do details about the setting suggest the natural world or an imaginary world? [The setting is left rather undefined, but the details suggest an imaginary place: creatures can move around the sky as they do on earth; nobody worries about natural needs like sleeping and eating during the long journey up the arrow ladder.]

ASSESSMENT

Although students' journals will not be graded, you will want to read and respond to them. Have students think about whether the new events they may have included in their versions change what the story explains.

CLOSURE

Read the following sentence and ask students if it describes a story or a science article:

"The hero Maui traps the sun to force it to move slowly across the sky."

[It describes a character and reflects imaginative thinking.] ■

4

How do you feel about the way Coyote abandons the wolves and the grizzlies in the sky? [Students might discuss whether or not Coyote and the wolves should be considered friends and what obligations they might have to each other.]

5

The apparently minor details, such as the number of wolf brothers and the way the oldest brings along his dog, become important when the story is seen as an explanation of the Big Dipper. The tale must account for the right number of stars and the relative brightness of each.

6

The meadowlark is a native bird found in prairie regions. Its clear, distinctive whistle is one of the first to be heard each spring.

SELECTION AMENDMENT
Description of change: excerpted
Rationale: to focus on the concept of creative writing presented in this chapter

Coyote wouldn't come over. He didn't trust the bears. "That makes a nice picture, though," thought Coyote. "They all look pretty good sitting there like that. I think I'll leave it that way for everyone to see. Then when people look at them in the sky they will say, 'There's a story about that picture,' and they will tell a story about me."

So Coyote left it that way. He took out the arrows as he <u>descended</u> so there was no way for anyone to get back. From down on the earth Coyote admired the arrangement he had left up there. Today they still look the same. They call those stars Big Dipper now. If you look up there you'll see three wolves make up the handle and the oldest wolf, the one in the middle, still has his dog with him. The two youngest wolves make up the part of the bowl under the handle and the two grizzlies make up the other side, the one that points toward the North Star.

When Coyote saw how they looked he wanted to put up a lot of stars. He arranged stars all over the sky in pictures and then made the Big Road across the sky with the stars he had left over.

When Coyote was finished he called Meadowlark over. "My brother," he said, "When I am gone, tell everyone that when they look up into the sky and see the stars arranged this way, that I was the one who did that. That is my work."

Now Meadowlark tells that story. About Coyote.

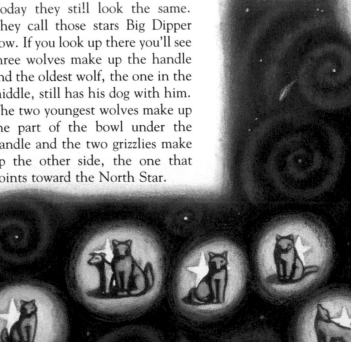

READER'S RESPONSE

1. Would you want Coyote for a friend? In a few words, describe his qualities—good and bad.
2. Were there places in the story where what happened was not what you expected? (What about those grizzlies?) In your journal, rewrite the story. Keep the same characters, but change the events of the story any way you want.

WRITER'S CRAFT

3. Item 1 above asked you to describe Coyote. What details in the story helped you know him?
4. Stories get set in motion because characters have problems and need to solve them. Who has a problem in this story? What is the problem? How is it solved?
5. How did the person who created this story use his imagination to explain a part of the world?

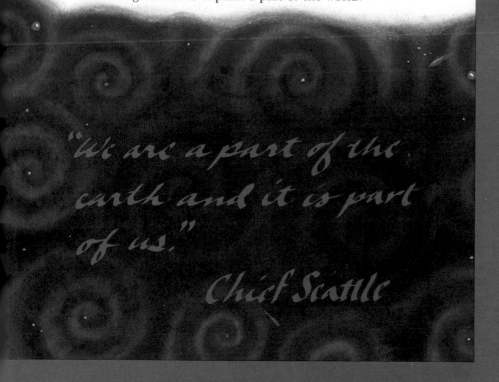

"We are a part of the earth and it is part of us."

Chief Seattle

ANSWERS

Reader's Response

Responses will vary.

1. Students might note different qualities. Coyote is curious and persistent. He has special powers and is cautious. He seeks admiration, but he does what he wants.

2. Students should use the same characters as the model, but the characters' actions will be different.

Writer's Craft

3. Coyote's character is shown in his persistence with the wolves and in his amazing ability to create the arrow ladder. Other qualities are revealed by his bragging and in details about others' reactions to Coyote, such as the way the wolves don't want to tell him what they are looking at and the way the younger wolves ignore his warning about the grizzlies.

4. The wolves have a problem with Coyote. They want to look at the animals and not have Coyote interfere; Coyote wants to know what they are doing. The problem is resolved when Coyote takes over, and the wolves are left in the sky with the bears.

5. This story uses familiar creatures and shows them acting in imaginary ways. You may want to extend the discussion to include some Greek myths.

SELECTION AMENDMENT

Description of change: excerpted
Rationale: to focus on the concept of creative writing as presented in this chapter

TEACHING THE MODES

After writing the words *narration, description, classification,* and *evaluation* on the chalkboard, demonstrate with examples. On the subject of baseball, for instance, dif-ferent modes could include a story about a key game, a song or poem describing the sights and sounds of a baseball park, a children's story about the differences between baseball and football, or a movie about an athlete who explains how he or she made the team. Have students name the mode to which each of the examples would belong. ■

CRITICAL THINKING
Analysis

Many teens relate to popular music better than to any other form of creative expression. Ask each student to name a song and then to analyze which of the four modes of development predominates in it. To clarify the modes, list on the chalkboard each mode and its characteristics as follows:

1. *narration* — tells what happened in the order it happened
2. *description* — tells how something looks, feels, tastes, or smells
3. *classification* — compares and contrasts or lists distinguishing qualities
4. *evaluation* — considers advantages and disadvantages and praises or condemns

---

Ways to Write Creatively

In this chapter you'll write a story and a poem, two types of creative writing. Other types are movie and play scripts, words for songs, children's books, and novels. Creative writing starts in the writer's imagination. Just as an artist uses paint, a writer uses words to create something special. Here are some ways of writing creatively.

▶ **Narration:**   in a television script, telling the story of a child genius and her longing for a normal life; telling a story about a Seminole boy who saves a panther cub in the Florida Everglades.

Description: in a song, describing a girl's hair and eyes; in a story about time travel, describing New York City in the year 4000.

Classification: in a poem, comparing envy to a wasp's sting; in a novel, contrasting a big-city girl with a boy from a small town.

Evaluation: in a poem, judging highways and billboards that interrupt and hide nature; in a play, showing how too much pride can drive away good friends.

LOOKING AHEAD

In this chapter, you'll use the strategy of narration to write a story. Keep in mind that an effective story

- entertains the reader
- solves a conflict, or problem
- holds the reader's attention with lifelike characters, an interesting plot, and a specific setting

OBJECTIVES

- To formulate a story idea
- To plan a story map with appropriate characters, setting, and plot

MOTIVATION

Have students look at the photographs below to identify the movies they come from [*Honey, I Shrunk the Kids* and *The Rocketeer*]. Then ask students if they could come up with ideas that are imaginative and entertaining.

☞

Writing a Story

Prewriting

Finding a Story Idea

Here's the big question: Where do you find a story idea? Here's the answer: Anywhere and everywhere. You might get an idea from a magazine or a photograph, from another story or a cartoon, or from a daydream or a nightmare.

As you look and listen around you, you can also play the "What if?" game: imagining any change or new thing that comes into your head. This is a way writers get some great ideas: *What if* a father shrank his kids? *What if* a man could strap a rocket to his back?

Thinking About Purpose and Audience

In writing a story, the one *purpose* you have is to entertain your readers. You may do it by making them laugh over the mistakes of a silly character. Or you may do it by involving them in a deep mystery. Just give your *audience* something that keeps them turning the pages.

RESOURCES

PREWRITING
- Finding a Story Idea
- Imagining Characters
- Describing a Setting
- Planning a Plot

QUOTATION FOR THE DAY

". . . To write about people you have to know people, to write about bloodhounds you have to know bloodhounds, to write about the Loch Ness monster, you have to find out about it." (James Thurber, 1894–1961, American humorist)

Lead students in a discussion of the subjects they know best. Would they like to write about those subjects? Could they build stories based on these subjects, or would they prefer to write straightforward reports?

To sharpen awareness of the terms *character* and *conflict,* call on students to read the material in the textbook. Then you could name the main character and the conflict in a recent episode of one of your favorite television shows as an example. You can facilitate students' participation by using a TV schedule to list a few shows on the chalk-board. Then call on students to name their favorite characters.

Playing a few rounds of another improvisation game may help students see that a story can be about anything. Have each student write on a slip of paper a sentence describing a character. Put the slips in a bag. Have a second bag that contains objects such as a pressed flower, a toy car, an

MEETING INDIVIDUAL NEEDS

LEP/ESL

General Strategies. The concepts of character, setting, and conflict are often difficult for ESL students to understand. If you think they might have problems, bring in a short cartoon and use it to write a story with the class. Ask students to tell you the conflict, the main character, and the setting of the cartoon story before beginning to write. They could also create a story map for the cartoon. If you work through a brief story with your students, they will get extra practice and a class-generated model for their writing assignments.

LESS-ADVANCED STUDENTS

For students who have difficulty with abstracting and summarizing, bring in a TV schedule with capsule summaries that describe conflicts and main characters of shows. Read several of these summaries aloud and call on students to identify the characters and to restate the conflicts.

186   *Creative Writing*

Starting with Characters and Situations

What keeps a reader turning pages? Almost always it's an interesting main *character* faced with a *conflict*—a situation that holds a problem or challenge. How will the brave princess rescue the prince from the tower? How will the class clown ever get the honor roll student to take her seriously?

Character. You can begin your story idea by thinking of a character. Suppose your little sister has a girlfriend who's very, very, *very* shy but amazingly sharp when you get her to talk. Or pretend that you see a newspaper photo of a ninety-year-old man from Jamaica. These people stick in your mind somehow—perhaps the girl has unusual eyes or the man has an interesting face. Could you put one in a situation with conflict? Of course you don't have to start with a real person. What kind of story could you build around a shy mouse from Jamaica?

Situation. Or you could begin in the opposite way. Think of an interesting situation or problem. It may be something you've seen on television, heard about from a friend, or actually experienced.

Maybe you know of someone hiding a cat in an apartment where animals are forbidden. Or you've always wondered what it would be like to be lost in a large city where you don't speak the language. From there, you can build a conflict and a story.

Here are just a few examples of how you might start with a character or a situation to build a story idea. A million other ideas are possible. Just feel free to let your imagination run wild!

STORY IDEAS

Character: Ninety-year-old man, born in Jamaica. Has lived almost all his life in New York City.
Situation: *What if . . .* he took his Social Security check, ran away from his niece's apartment, and stowed away on a cruise ship bound for Jamaica.

interesting stone, or a decorative box. Put students in small groups and have each group draw one character slip and one object. Allow two minutes for the group to improvise a story idea that puts the character into a situation involving the object.

Students should stay in these groups as they brainstorm ideas for **Exercise 1.** Emphasize that there is no single right story

idea. To illustrate how diverse ideas can be, have each group report on the suggestions they made.

After examining the model of the story map found on p. 192, you could further explain the concept by holding up a road map and asking what kind of help it can and can't provide. Point out that just as the road map guides the driver but doesn't transport ☞

Situation: Someone who can't speak English or Spanish is lost in Houston, Texas.

Character: *What if . . .* the person is a young boy who speaks Mayan, is visiting with a group of musicians, and has with him a wooden flute that he can play beautifully.

Reminder

When you're looking for story ideas, remember

- ideas can come from anywhere: your own experience, TV, newspapers, photographs, songs, and more
- your story needs a main character and a conflict
- try starting with a character or situation and asking "What if?" to build a story idea

EXERCISE 1 ▶ **Building Story Ideas**

Now try your hand (and imagination) at using the following characters and situations to come up with story ideas. Work with a small group, and brainstorm as many ideas as you want. [Remember: Your situations must hold a *conflict,* or *problem.*]

AT-RISK STUDENTS

This assignment provides students who face major problems in their personal lives with an opportunity to get a different perspective on their problems by turning these problems into stories. Emphasize that students are free to change any element they wish. Brainstorming about familiar situations may also suggest strategies for dealing with problems that students had not thought of before.

⇄ A DIFFERENT APPROACH

Some students might find it helpful to go from picture to language as they plan features of character and setting to use in their stories. Suggest using doodles or sketches as planning aids. Urge students to make their sketches full of details to enrich the characters. Show a few examples of portraits or caricatures and discuss how visual details often provide clues to personal qualities. To reinforce verbal expression, have students highlight important qualities and descriptive details in the finished sketches.

him or her, a planned story guides the writer but won't write itself. Extend the analogy to discuss different degrees of detail that might be included. Work through **Exercise 1** with students. You could display the following headings:
1. *WHO = Character*
2. *DOES WHAT = Action*
3. *WHY = Problem*

Ask different volunteers to include something under each heading.

To model the skills required in **Writing Assignment: Parts 1–3**, demonstrate how you would work through your own story ideas to produce a story map.

ANSWERS
Exercise 1

Answers may vary. You may want to set a time limit of 3–5 minutes for each item in the exercise. Have each group appoint a recorder to write down the ideas. Remind students that they should keep ideas flowing rather than developing one or two ideas in depth. For items 1 and 2, verify that each response involves a conflict rather than just a further statement of the condition given for the character. Have students test their suggestions by asking if the situation they think of triggers some action. For items 3 and 4, explain that the suggestion should include some specifics about a possible character such as gender, age, personality, background, and so on. At least some suggestions should include names.

1. **Character**: A young girl is extremely clever, but she's also painfully shy, always staying in the background.
   Situation: *What if* _____

2. **Character:** Ahmed Mostafa, with his elderly grandfather, takes care of dozens of homing pigeons on the roof of his building.
   Situation: *What if* _____

3. **Situation:** Someone is hiding a cat in an apartment where animals aren't allowed.
   Character: *What if* _____

4. **Situation:** All of the bicycles, roller skates, and skateboards disappear from a town.
   Character: *What if* _____

WRITING ASSIGNMENT

PART 1:
Finding a Story Idea

You may have gotten a great idea from the group brainstorming in Exercise 1. But if not, now you know how to go about getting one. Remember that you can use anything around you—from everyday experiences to space monsters on TV—to come up with characters and situations. Decide on your final story idea and write it down.

To complete **Writing Assignment: Parts 1–3**, students must make individual decisions about character, setting, and plot. Reassure them that ideas are never set in stone. They might even think of new twists as they begin to write.

Students will feel freer to experiment and plan if no grades are assigned to prewriting exercises. Use questions to help students develop their ideas thoroughly and effectively. For example, a response to a vague character description might be "Can you list three details that would help me pick this character out of a crowd?" ☞

 Prewriting

Planning Your Story

Professional writers plan their stories before they begin. Of course, that doesn't mean they don't make some changes along the way. Writers often surprise themselves!

Imagining Characters. If you want readers to pay attention to your story, your main character (and other important characters) should seem *alive*. The best way to get life into your characters is with specific, sharp *details*.

You can make up details: a lavender kitten with one orange eye and one purple eye. Or you can borrow details from real people: a Civil War general who has your own grandfather's twinkling green eyes. These questions will help you imagine your characters—make them solid.

- *What does the character look like?*
- *What is the character's name?*
- *How would you describe the character's personality?*
- *What does the character love and hate?*
- *What does the character sound like?*

One way to make notes on your characters is to keep the questions in mind and then freewrite a description.

HERE'S HOW

The boy in this story? Not a big handsome hero or anything—he's still a kid, maybe 11. Brown eyes, brown hair. Keeps flopping. Name? Two names—Matthew James. Yeah, no nicknames. But he's not a nerd—he likes to do kid things but also likes old people too cause they're always outdoors. And what does he hate? Well maybe not hate—he doesn't *like* people who are bullies.

COOPERATIVE LEARNING
Consider pairing students who are gifted artistically but who do not perform well in language arts with others who write well but who can't draw. Have the pairs pool their talents to produce the character sketches suggested in **A Different Approach** on p. 187. The artist will draw two portraits—one to express his or her ideas and one based on a verbal description provided by the partner. The partner will be responsible for labeling both sketches in precise, vivid language. The labeling can be especially helpful in creating word banks for the drawing partners that are not verbally proficient or whose vocabularies are limited. Each partner should look for feedback from the other to make sure the ideas are being transmitted accurately.

Or you could use a feedback technique. Review a student's planning sheets and then tell the student what you understood and ask if it matches the student's intentions.

Have students try to reconstruct plans for a finished story. Use a familiar story, perhaps even **"Coyote Places the Stars."** Put the outline for a story map on the chalkboard and work with students to make suggestions about how to fill it in.

INTEGRATING THE LANGUAGE ARTS

Literature Link. You may want to use a short story with a surprise ending to help students appreciate the differences between planning and writing. Have students read "After Twenty Years" by O. Henry. Ask them for examples of little details in the story that suddenly take on meaning when the final revelation is made. Point out that descriptive details about the appearance, career, and feelings of one man or the other emerge with no apparent pattern during the story. The full ironic force of how different they are as adults is felt only when it is revealed that Jimmy Wells did keep his appointment. At that point, it becomes clear that the writer had obviously planned a systematic contrast between the lifestyles, economic statuses, and personalities of the two boyhood friends.

VISUAL CONNECTIONS

Ideas For Writing. If you feel students need to practice descriptive writing, have them choose one of the two settings shown here and tell them to write one-paragraph descriptions that answer the planning questions. Alternatively, have two or three students read their planning notes for the setting. Then have others sketch what they think it would look like. Evaluate whether the descriptions provide enough details.

Describing Setting.   The *setting* is where and when the story takes place. A setting can be the corner of a room at night or a football stadium on Sunday afternoon. It can be the present or the age of dinosaurs.

The setting can give information about characters. A clean room, for example, shows readers that a character likes order and neatness. The setting can also create a mood. An abandoned house and a howling wind will make sure a scary story is scary.

Sometimes setting even creates a conflict. If you set your story in Alaska during a blizzard, your character might be trapped in the snow.

Here are some questions to help you plan your setting.

- *Where and when will my story take place?*
- *What places, weather, things, or times of day could be important in my story?*
- *What sensory details (smells, sights, sounds) can I use to describe these important parts of setting?*

CLOSURE

Call on students to identify story elements that need planning and that should be included in a story map [character, setting, and plot—including the conflict, the high point, and the outcome]

EXTENSION

Point out that critics will often attack a movie because of an inadequately developed story element, such as plot or character. Tell students to bring reviews of this kind to class and to write short explanations of which story elements are being criticized and why. ■

Prewriting   **191**

PART 2:
Planning Characters and Setting

To get a clearer picture of your characters and setting, use the questions on pages 189 and 190. You can jot down your responses, freewrite, or even use clustering. Write freely and let your ideas flow.

Planning Your Plot.   Suppose you have an interesting character, a girl named Tuyet Nguyen, and a good solid setting for her, an old two-story house in Myer's Cove, where she lives with her parents and grandmother. Now you need a *plot*, or series of events, for the story. While a plot is "what happens," it has these special parts:

- **A conflict:** As you've already learned, the main character must face some problem. *Tuyet wants piano lessons, but her family can't afford to pay for them.*
- **A series of events:** Your story must have action. The events must move forward as the character works on the conflict. *Tuyet may run errands to earn money, count her earnings daily, and dream of the lessons.*
- **A high point:** Your story also needs a moment, the high point, when the problem is going to be *settled* —one way or another. Readers' curiosity or suspense is at a high point. *Perhaps Tuyet's grandmother gets very sick. Will Tuyet have to sacrifice her piano lessons for her grandmother's medicine?*
- **An outcome:** The outcome shows how the problem is solved and what happens when it is. *Tuyet gives her savings to her parents and says she will forget the lessons. Her grandmother sees how much music means to her and promises to help Tuyet earn money when she is better.*

Creating a Story Map.   When you plan your plot, you can put it into a story map that outlines your character, setting, and plot all at once. The following example shows how one writer mapped her story about Matthew James and the gang.

LEP/ESL

General Strategies. To help ESL students think of ideas for characters with conflicts, encourage them to draw upon their experiences learning about American culture. You could suggest that they replace themselves with fictional characters in their stories, and embellish or expand upon the experiences to make them more entertaining and to follow a story format.

LESS-ADVANCED STUDENTS

If your less-advanced students have trouble thinking of story ideas independently, you may want to allow them to develop one of the suggested examples from **Story Ideas** on p. 186.

A DIFFERENT APPROACH

To help students develop their major characters, have them role-play the characters in small groups. One student might role-play a girl who doesn't speak the same language as her classmates, another might role-play a visitor from outer space, and so on. Encourage students to concentrate on how the characters would feel and act and what the characters would say and do.

HERE'S HOW

A STORY MAP	
CHARACTERS:	Matthew James, the gang (Chief, Corker, Dunce), Ms. Paglia
SETTING:	Woods, neighborhood, and park—summertime
PLOT:	Conflict: Matthew James wants to stop the gang from chopping down the roses.

Events:
 (1) Matthew James hears gang's plan.
 (2) Matthew worries about how to stop them. On a walk, he sees sprinklers: Idea!
 (3) The neighborhood goes to the picnic.

High point:
 (4) The gang sneaks to the roses.
 (5) Matthew soaks them with the sprinklers.

Outcome:
 (6) Ms. Paglia thinks the gang watered her roses and gives the boys flowers.

WRITING ASSIGNMENT

PART 3:
Creating a Story Map

Now it is time for the last stage of your planning. Exactly what will *happen* in your story? Remember that your plot needs certain elements: conflict, events, high point, and outcome. When you decide on the parts, put them into a story map like the one in the Here's How on this page. Don't forget to include characters and settings.

SEGMENT 4 *(pp. 193–201)*
WRITING YOUR FIRST DRAFT

OBJECTIVES
- To create dialogue for a character
- To analyze the elements of a short story
- To write a draft of a story

MOTIVATION

Explain to students that just as cooks reduce preparation time by having all the ingredients for a recipe ready ahead of time, writers who plan their characters and plot find it much easier to turn an idea into a story. Reassure students that with writing, as with meals, the finished product makes all the work worthwhile. ☞

Writing Your First Draft

Combining the Basic Elements of a Story

A map to a place isn't the place. And your story map isn't a story—yet. How do you turn the map into a bursting-with-life tale? Here are some tips.

Making the Plot Move Along.   A good *beginning* for a story hooks the reader's attention right away. You might start in the middle of an action—a burglar coming through the window, for example. Or you might describe the dark night and lonely street to set the mood.

In the *middle* of the story, keep your audience guessing. Make every event open up a possibility, create a surprise, or lead to the high point. What happens when Jowela sees the burglar? Don't let her stop to play a video game!

After your strong high point, make sure the *ending* is satisfying. Solve the problem but also tie up any loose ends. If Jowela traps the burglar and the police come, the conflict is over. But don't leave the burglar trapped in the shower stall. Get her out before Jowela and the police say good night.

Making Your Characters Seem Real.   You've learned that specific details make lifeless characters into lively ones. Here are three good ways to use details.

- Give clear descriptions of *appearance.* Don't say *She dressed oddly* when you can say *She wore purple felt overalls, green high-heeled sneakers, and a bright red cape.* (For more help with descriptions, see Chaper 4.)

RESOURCES

WRITING YOUR FIRST DRAFT
- Using Dialogue

QUOTATION FOR THE DAY

"When I actually sit down to write, I stop thinking. I am writing, I am listening to the story; I am not listening to myself." (Madeleine L'Engle, 1918–   , American science-fiction writer)

Ask students to freewrite for three minutes and encourage them to listen to their inner voices instead of thinking about what they write.

MEETING INDIVIDUAL NEEDS

AFRICAN AMERICAN

The writing stage allows students to use their dialects when writing their dialogues. It will give them an opportunity to use language creatively and to learn the situational appropriateness of language (dialect for the dialogue, standard English for the rest of the story). It can also emphasize the value of oral tradition, as stories they have heard may become subjects for their writing.

You may want to extend the analogy with cooking to introduce some of the strategies suggested for making characters seem real. Ask which of the following instructions seems more helpful:

1. Add flour and desired spices to liquid.
2. Slowly pour milk and beaten eggs into the flour, cinnamon, and nutmeg mixture.

Explain that just as a detailed recipe is easy to follow, using specific details in action, dialogue, and description makes it easy for a reader to imagine what is happening in a story.

"The Dinner Party" is so brief that it can be read aloud. Then students might read **A Writer's Model** on p. 198 independently. Have them form small groups to com-

---

194   *Creative Writing*

- Make *actions* specific. You could say *He sat down in the chair*. But readers would know this character much better if *He plopped down in the big recliner, dangling his legs over the arm.*
- Use *dialogue*. A summary of speech like *He refused to do it* will move action along. But *dialogue*—a character's own words—can also reveal emotion and personality. Use fragments, contractions, and slang if they're right for the character. *"No way! Are you nuts? I wouldn't call her if she was Queen of the World."*

EXERCISE 2 ▶ **Speaking and Listening: Creating Dialogue**

With a partner, create dialogues for the characters in the following situations. Try to make the dialogue natural—like real speech. Present your dialogues to another partner group. Then ask for feedback about whether you sound real—and why or why not.

1. An elderly woman calls the police to report that her cat is up in a tree. The police officer tries to convince her that the cat will be okay.
2. Two teenage boys try to decide how to spend the afternoon. Should they go to the mall or to the ice skating rink?

Looking at a Short Story

Every story is different. Writers combine plot, characters, and setting in different ways. The writer of the following short story makes sure you're aware of setting at the start. As you read, see if you can guess the surprise ending.

ANSWERS
Exercise 2

Narratives will vary. It is important that the dialogues be appropriate for the characters. The elderly lady and the policeman would not use teenage slang, but the boys probably would. The boys' language would depend on what kinds of motives they have for going to the museum or the mall, whether they really want to go to either place, and whether they want to go with each other.

pare the character sketches, the story map presented in **Here's How** on p. 192, and the completed draft. You can use the annotations to help students identify how the writer developed or changed elements of the plan in the actual writing.

To help students develop their characters, you could work with a volunteer to model **Exercise 2** for the other students.

After creating a brief dialogue, present it to the class with your chosen partner. Then ask students what details they learned about the character and what they still want to know.

☛

A SHORT STORY

The Dinner Party
by Mona Gardner

BEGINNING *1*
Setting

Situation and characters

The country is India. A colonial official and his wife are giving a large dinner party. They are seated with their guests— army officers and government <u>attachés</u> and their wives, and a visiting American <u>naturalist</u>—in their spacious dining room, which has a bare marble floor, open <u>rafters</u>, and wide glass doors opening onto a <u>veranda</u>.

Event 1 *2*

A spirited discussion springs up between a young girl who insists that women have outgrown the jumping-on-a-chair-at-the-sight-of-a-mouse era and a colonel who says that they haven't.

Dialogue *3*

"A woman's unfailing reaction in any crisis," the colonel says, "is to scream. And while a man may feel like it, he has that ounce more of nerve control than a woman has. And that last ounce is what counts."

USING THE SELECTION
The Dinner Party

1
One unusual feature of this short story is its use of the present tense. Discuss how this usage may help increase a sense of immediacy and suspense.

2
The conflict of the story—do women have self-control—is introduced here.

3
Ask students to describe how they imagine the colonel's tone of voice and facial expression as he speaks. Does he seem like someone with whom they would like to speak? [Most will have the impression that the colonel speaks and looks in a forceful and confident manner. Some may describe him as arrogant or self-satisfied.]

ASSESSMENT

Class discussion will allow you to evaluate how well students are able to analyze story elements such as plot, character, and dialogue. It's better not to distract or inhibit students by emphasizing mechanics and usage at this point. If possible, schedule conference times to review drafts, ask questions, or offer suggestions about story elements.

196   *Creative Writing*

4

By including this background information about cobras, the author makes sure the reader will understand why the hostess and the naturalist behave as they do.

5

With the American's exhibition of self-control here, it appears that the colonel's viewpoint is correct.

MIDDLE
Event 2
Hint of conflict—suspense

Specific action

The American does not join in the argument but watches the other guests. As he looks, he sees a strange expression come over the face of the hostess. She is staring straight ahead, her muscles contracting slightly. With a slight gesture she summons the native boy standing behind her chair and whispers to him. The boy's eyes widen: He quickly leaves the room.

Event 3

Of the guests, none except the American notices this or sees the boy place a bowl of milk on the veranda just outside the open doors.

Suspense   4

The American comes to with a start. In India, milk in a bowl means only one thing—bait for a snake. He realizes there must be a cobra in the room. He looks up at the rafters—the likeliest place—but they are bare. Three corners of the room are empty, and in the fourth the servants are waiting to serve the next course. There is only one place left—under the table.

Character
Setting

5

His first impulse is to jump back and warn the others, but he knows the commotion would frighten the cobra into striking. He speaks quickly, the tone of his voice so <u>arresting</u> that it <u>sobers</u> everyone.

Event 4

Dialogue

"I want to know just what control everyone at this table has. I will count to three hundred—that's five minutes—and not one of you is to move a muscle. Those who move will <u>forfeit</u> fifty <u>rupees</u>. Ready!"

Suspense

The twenty people sit like stone images while he counts. He is saying " . . . two hundred and eighty . . ." when, out of the corner of his eye, he sees the cobra emerge and make for the bowl of milk. Screams ring out as he jumps to slam the veranda doors safely shut.

Specific action
High point

If students are still unclear about how story elements fit together after discussing **"The Dinner Party"** and **A Writer's Model,** you could bring a short dramatic video to class. After students have viewed it, work with them to identify the setting and the characters. Then discuss whether the story begins at the beginning or in the middle of the action. Also identify the high point and the outcome. If students need more reinforcement, have them work as a class to construct a storyboard for the video.

ENDING
Dialogue

Outcome

Surprise ending

"You were right, Colonel!" the host exclaims. "A man has just shown us an example of perfect control."

"Just a minute," the American says, turning to his hostess. "Mrs. Wynnes, how did you know that cobra was in the room?"

A faint smile lights up the woman's face as she replies: "Because it was crawling across my foot."

EXERCISE 3 ▶ Analyzing the Elements of a Short Story

Think about the basic elements of "The Dinner Party." With a partner discuss the following questions.

1. Did you enjoy the story? How do you think you would have reacted if you'd been the American naturalist? or Mrs. Wynnes, the hostess?
2. How important is the story's setting? Could this story happen in your home? in some other setting in India?
3. How did the writer create suspense in the story?
4. Do you think the story has a message—an important idea? What is it?
5. Were you surprised by the story's ending? What clues does the writer give?

VISUAL CONNECTIONS

Exploring the Subject. The cobra is a highly poisonous snake found in Africa, India, and Asia. When excited or nervous, the snake's neck flattens into the characteristic hood shown in the picture. Cobras can spit their poison into the faces of small prey.

ANSWERS
Exercise 3

1. Most students will enjoy the story. How they say they would have reacted depends on the individual student's personality and honesty.

2. The setting is extremely important. Students should recognize that it could not have happened where there are no cobras. It could have happened in another setting in India, as long as similar characters were present.

3. The story's message seems to be that men do not necessarily have more control than women. The story concerns sexual stereotyping.

4. Students will probably be surprised by the ending, even though they might realize that Mrs. Wynnes is aware of the snake before the naturalist is. The way she is described when she becomes aware of the snake indicates that she must feel it, not see it.

SELECTION AMENDMENT
Description of change: excerpted
Rationale: to focus on the concept of writing a story as presented in this chapter

Ask students what story elements should be included in their rough drafts [characters, setting, and plot]. Next, ask them to identify these elements in **"The Dinner Party".** Tell them that readers should also be able to identify these features after reading the students' stories.

Show students how dialogue can indicate character. Extract several dialogues from short stories. Some good choices are *A Mother in Manville* by Marjorie Rawlings, *The Lost Beach* by Louise Hardeman, and *Charles* by Shirley Jackson. Read the dialogues and omit the narrative. Ask students how much

A DIFFERENT APPROACH

To give students practice in creating meaning and mood through dialogue, ask which of the following sentences creates the strongest image:

1. Ben asked Mr. Nikolin if he could go home.
2. Ben sadly asked Mr. Nikolin if he could go home.
3. "I can't take it any more," Ben said hoarsely. "Please Mr. Nikolin, let me go home now."

Discuss how it is much easier to imagine Ben when you know both what he said and how he said it. Challenge students to come up with other direct address statements in which Ben asks Mr. Nikolin to let him go home. The statements should demonstrate the following reactions: anger, embarrassment, hesitance, and laughter. Students can work independently or in pairs.

198   *Creative Writing*

Using a Story Framework

"The Dinner Party" has vivid descriptions, great suspense, and a surprise ending. It even has a serious message about mistaken ideas about women. It's polished and professional. But even if your story doesn't have all these elements (plus a high point with a cobra!), it can be just as entertaining.

Notice how the following writer starts with action and gets quickly to characters and conflict. You might want to follow this model for your story.

A WRITER'S MODEL

The Gang's Surprise

BEGINNING **Main character/** **Setting**	Matthew James scrambled over the wall and dashed to his hideout under the ivy. He hastily brushed his dark hair from his forehead. His brown eyes were sharp as he watched the gang
Situation	sneak through the woods and meet under the big willow tree. Chief, the gang leader, gave the orders.
Dialogue **Event 1**	"Tomorrow while everyone's at the cookout, we'll chop off all of old lady Paglia's roses," he said.
	Corker gave an approving whistle. Dunce nodded enthusiastically.
Dialogue	"Then we'll put the dumb roses on Mr. O'Brian's front steps, and it will look like he
Specific action	picked them," Chief added. The gang hollered and hooted. Chief and the gang had disliked the two elderly people ever since the day they made the boys pick up trash they'd thrown on the neighborhood lawns.
Conflict	Matthew James heard every word the gang said. He knew he had to stop them. He also knew

it wouldn't be easy. He sure couldn't fight them.

MIDDLE

Character

The next day was sunny and bright. Butterflies flitted and birds sang. But Matthew James was in a lousy mood. Time was running out, and he still had no plan.

Event 2

Specific action

He walked down the street and watched Ms. Paglia smell her roses. Her brown eyes twinkled with delight. He watched Ms. Dent pull out dandelions from her flower bed. Her brow was creased but she was singing. Then Mr. Mason

Suspense

hooked up his sprinkler system. There was a sudden shower. Matthew James had a brainstorm!

Event 3

At 5:00, the neighbors went to the park. At 5:45, the gang sneaked across the green back yards. "Okay, make it fast," said Chief. The boys took off at top speed toward Ms. Paglia's garden.

Event 4
High point

They reached the yellow rose bushes. They crouched down and pulled out pen knives. Then Matthew James turned the faucet behind Mr. Mason's garage. Water sprayed everywhere. The gang screamed and tried to run for cover, but there wasn't a dry spot anywhere. Matthew James had hooked up every sprinkler on the

Specific action

block. Water was shooting in all directions.

INTEGRATING THE LANGUAGE ARTS

Technology Link. Encourage students who have access to word processors to use them for drafting their stories. In general, writing on computers simplifies revising enormously. It can be especially helpful to dyslexics or students with motor-control problems because they often put so much energy into mechanics that they have little energy left for creating ideas.

You could introduce students to thesauruses to help them add specific details to their writing. If students are using computers for writing, remind them that there are many software programs that include user-friendly thesaurus features. Encourage them to take advantage of such features to find vivid and precise words.

A DIFFERENT APPROACH

Students who have access to video equipment might enjoy working as teams to produce a story as a short video. Discuss how the basic story elements and the planning stages for story development are very similar for print and video. However, you might remind students that actions need to be shown on the screen, not described in words. The team will also have to develop production details. Emphasize that it is important not to sacrifice the story to technical issues.

MEETING
INDIVIDUAL
NEEDS

ADVANCED STUDENTS

Put students into groups of four or five. Give each group a photocopy of a short story and have them annotate it, using as models the annotations for **"The Dinner Party"** and **A Writer's Model.** One of O. Henry's works would work well. Have groups exchange annotations to compare and evaluate.

Event 5

Dialogue

Luckily, Matthew James turned off the sprinklers just in time. Ms. Paglia suddenly appeared walking down the street. "I do believe I smell rain. Did it rain while I was in the park?" she asked herself. Then she noticed that her rose bushes were wet. "Well, my saints! Someone watered my roses," she said aloud. Suddenly, Ms. Paglia saw the gang huddled under a tree.

Suspense
Appearance details

ENDING

"Come here!" she shouted. The gang looked like drowned rats—*frightened* drowned rats—but they obeyed. Ms. Paglia patted each boy on the head and invited them all to the cookout for dessert.

Matthew James took a secret path and arrived at the park just as Ms. Paglia was telling everyone what happened. "These dear boys watered all our flowers and yards—as a surprise!" she exclaimed. The gang looked very confused. Matthew James smiled.

Outcome

"Good work," he said to himself and watched Ms. Paglia hand each soggy boy a yellow rose.

USAGE HINT

Using Verb Tenses

Story events are usually told in chronological order, using the past tense: *The villain* **grasped** *the prune. He* **thrust** *it fiercely toward my mouth.* To explain actions that happened before other past actions, use the past perfect tense.

EXAMPLE   **I had seen** [past perfect] an escape route before the villain grasped [past] the prune.

☞ **REFERENCE NOTE:** For more information on verb tenses, see pages 592–594.

PART 4:
Writing Your First Draft

Now it's time to begin your story. Go over the character and setting descriptions you wrote. Reread your story map, but remember that it's only a guide. You don't have to follow it exactly. Part of the fun of writing stories can be discovering new ideas. Begin writing and see what happens.

🖐 COOPERATIVE LEARNING

If your students have trouble writing their story drafts from their story maps, try having them work in small groups to analyze where the difficulties occurred. Students might compare their story maps to the stories they have written to see what elements need improvement. You might even set up three review groups to analyze one of the three elements of a story characters, setting, and plot. Each group could analyze one element of a story and pass the story to the next group for suggestions. You might want to be available to answer questions as they arise.

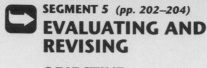

OBJECTIVE

- To evaluate and revise the elements of a story

TEACHING THE LESSON

Emphasize that the chart on p. 204 provides questions that will help students analyze their stories' organization. You could use a volunteer's paper and work through the chart with the class as guided practice before students make revisions independently.

(Cont. on p. 204)

RESOURCES

EVALUATING AND REVISING
- Writing a Story

QUOTATION FOR THE DAY

"Revising is when it may hit you. Revulsion. The feeling that all this stuff you have written is stupid, ugly, worthless—and cannot be fixed." (Peter Elbow, 1935–   , American author and professor of English)

Lead students in a discussion of the quotation. Tell them that it is common for writers to feel dissatisfied with their work. Have students make suggestions about what to do to get beyond that feeling. [A writer might need to put away his or her story for a time or ask a friend or a family member to read it and make suggestions.]

Evaluating and Revising

If you're like most writers, you feel a sense of accomplishment after you finish a draft. Part of you would like to quit. After all—you've written a story. But part of you knows the story could be better. And you want to make it as good as possible.

You need to read your story as a critic. Better yet, read it as a reader who wants to be entertained. To evaluate your story, use the guidelines on page 204 to find its strengths and weaknesses. If the answer to any question on the left-hand side of the chart is no, use the techniques on the right-hand side to make revisions.

WRITING NOTE The first thing readers see when they pick up a story is the title. Sometimes a title even *makes* them pick it up. Of course, not all titles are that exciting. But a good title isn't dull. Titles can come from an important character in the story, a significant plot event, or even the setting. What would be the best title for your story?

CRITICAL THINKING

Analyzing the Elements of a Story

All good writers *analyze* when they evaluate their writing. They examine their stories with a magnifying glass. They look at all the elements and how they fit together. When the writer of "The Gang's Surprise" analyzed her first paragraph, she made the following changes.

CRITICAL THINKING
(pp. 202–203)

OBJECTIVE

• To use questions to analyze a writer's revisions

TEACHING *ANALYZING THE ELEMENTS OF A STORY*

Remind students that they are likely to make revisions similar to those in **Exercise 3** in their stories. Emphasize that the questions and comments they receive should be thought of as helpful tools to improve their stories.

Evaluating and Revising   **203**

It was a June day in Burnside, before   **cut**
the neighborhood was going to have a big
picnic with lots of food. A boy named
                scrambled   and dashed
Matthew James went over the wall to his   **replace/add**
   (He hastily brushed his dark hair from his forehead)
hideout under the ivy. His brown eyes   **add**
were sharp as he watched the gang sneak
through the woods and meet under the
big willow tree. Chief, the gang leader,
           ¶ "Tomorrow while everyone's at the
gave the orders to meet during the   **replace**
cookout, we'll chop off all of old lady Paglia's roses," he said
cookout and cut Ms. Paglia's roses.

 CRITICAL THINKING EXERCISE:
Analyzing a Writer's Revisions

Work with a partner to analyze the revisions in the paragraph above. Use the following questions to guide your analysis. Also refer to the chart on page 204. It shows you the important elements of a short story.

1. Why did the writer cut so much from the beginning?
2. Why did the writer decide to use *scrambled* and *dashed* in the second sentence?
3. What's the reason for adding a whole sentence?
4. Do you think the replacement in the last sentence is a good revision? Why or why not?

 PART 5:
Evaluating and Revising Your Story

Use the chart on page 204 to help evaluate and revise your first draft. When you finish revising, swap stories with a classmate for feedback and suggestions.

MEETING
INDIVIDUAL
NEEDS

LEP/ESL

General Strategies. Help students improve their vocabularies by analyzing a passage and pointing out which common words could be replaced with more vibrant ones. Once you have indicated these words, have the class brainstorm to create replacements.

ANSWERS
Critical Thinking Exercise

Answers may vary. Here are some possibilities:

1. Phrases like "lots of food" and "a boy named" are uninteresting and unnecessary.
2. These words add detail and clarity.
3. The added sentence provides descriptive details.
4. Using Chief's exact words creates a more lifelike and believable sense of his character.

(Cont. from p. 202)

CLOSURE

To close the lesson, call on students to formulate questions about plot, conflict, setting, or character that they can use to evaluate their first drafts. ■

LEP/ESL

General Strategies. Before students write their first drafts, evaluate and revise **"The Gang's Surprise"** by employing the **Evaluating and Revising Short Stories** chart. This modeling will promote discussion about what strategies will help students' writing. It will also give students more guidance about what is expected from their writing and will clear up any uncertainties about the expressions used in the guide, including "strong high point," "vivid details," "keep readers wondering," and "catch reader's interest."

EVALUATING AND REVISING SHORT STORIES

EVALUATION GUIDE	REVISION TECHNIQUE
1 Does the beginning catch readers' interest?	**Add** (or **replace** other) sentences with vivid details of character, action, or setting.
2 Is the conflict clear early in the story?	**Add** or **reorder** sentences in which the main character faces a problem.
3 Do events create suspense or curiosity for readers?	**Cut** events that slow down action. **Add** events that keep readers wondering.
4 Does the plot have a strong high point and a satisfying outcome?	**Add** a tense scene that solves a conflict. **Add** details that explain how everything works out.
5 Are the characters lifelike and believable?	**Add** details about the characters' looks, actions, and thoughts. **Add** dialogue that sounds natural.
6 Is the setting clear? If possible, does it help set a mood?	**Add** specific details of time and place. **Add** vivid sensory details.

SELECTION REQUEST
Description of change: excerpted
Rationale: to focus on the concept of publishing a story as presented in this chapter

"Everyone you meet has a story,"

Madeleine L'Engle

SEGMENT 6 *(p. 205)*
PROOFREADING AND PUBLISHING

OBJECTIVES
- To proofread a story for errors in grammar, usage, and mechanics
- To publish a story

TEACHING THE LESSON

Read a passage aloud, deliberately mumbling and mispronouncing. Explain to students that they should not allow the effectiveness of their writing to suffer because of careless errors.

For closure, ask students to identify the kinds of mistakes they have made most often. ■

Proofreading and Publishing **205**

Proofreading and Publishing

Proofreading.   Now it's time to polish your story. To make it shine, double-check carefully to find and correct any errors in spelling, usage, and mechanics.

Publishing.   Don't be shy with your story. People *want* to be entertained. Let them see your special imagination. Here are two possibilities for publishing.

- Ask your principal if you may read some of the stories over the intercom during homeroom.
- Create giant comic-book murals of your stories and use them to decorate your classroom and the halls of your school.

WRITING ASSIGNMENT

PART 6:
Proofreading and Publishing Your Story

Make a neat, final copy of your story. Be sure to give that final copy one last good proofreading—and then share your story with an audience.

QUOTATION FOR THE DAY

"For several days after my first book was published I carried it about in my pocket, and took surreptitious peeps at it to make sure the ink had not faded." (James M. Barrie, 1860–1937, Scottish novelist and dramatist)

You may wish to share the quotation with the class and initiate a discussion of publication. Ask a few volunteers to tell how they reacted the first time they shared work with others. Remind students that people want to be entertained.

MEETING INDIVIDUAL NEEDS

LEP/ESL

General Strategies. Punctuating dialogue is a problem for many students. Because their stories must include dialogue, help students punctuate correctly by giving them a section of dialogue from the essay **"Coyote Places the Stars"** without the punctuation. Tell the class to put in the marks. Students can work in small groups and then check their work against the reading. Try to be available for students who need to ask questions after they have corrected their errors.

WRITING WORKSHOP

OBJECTIVES

- To analyze the elements of a narrative poem
- To use the writing process to write a narrative poem

TEACHING THE LESSON

Remind students that there are many ways to tell a story, and ask if anyone can think of a story that is sung. Next, discuss song lyrics as a form of poetry. Explain that songs have an established rhythm, use sound effects like rhyme or alliteration, and use figurative language. Then explain that narrative poems also tell stories.

RESOURCES

WRITING WORKSHOP
- Finding a Story Idea
- Imagining Characters
- Describing a Setting
- Planning a Plot
- Using Dialogue
- Writing a Story

QUOTATION FOR THE DAY

". . . the object of writing poetry is to make all poems sound as different as possible from each other. . . ." (Robert Frost, 1874–1963, American poet)

Ask students what elements of poetry can influence its sound. [Possibilities are words, rhythm, and rhyme.]

MEETING INDIVIDUAL NEEDS

LEP/ESL

General Strategies. Writing and reading poetry tends to be especially challenging to ESL students. You may want to ask them to locate and share narrative poems from their native languages. Ask them to introduce the poems in English, and to identify the story elements and sound effects.

206

WRITING WORKSHOP

A Narrative Poem

A poem that tells a story is called a ***narrative poem.*** A narrative poem is much like the story you just wrote. It has characters, plot, setting, and sometimes even dialogue.

But poetry adds other elements to storytelling—especially sounds and images. To create musical sounds, poets use rhythm, rhyme, and repeated sounds. The ***rhythm*** is created by the beats—the syllables that are stressed. The beat may be regular or it may be uneven and loose.

Rhyme is a regular pattern of similar vowel sounds (like *pop* and *top*). Rhyming words are often, but not always, at the end of the lines. Poets also create musical sounds by repeating the first letters of words ("*l*ovely *l*aughing *l*adies").

Poets create ***images,*** or word pictures, with words that appeal to the senses. For example, you might look for words that will help your readers see, or hear, or even feel what you are describing.

The following poem has rhythm, rhyme, great word pictures, and a hungry weed. Hungry? See for yourself.

My Aunt
by Ted Hughes

You've heard how a green thumb
Makes flowers come
Quite without toil
Out of any old soil.

Well, my Aunt's thumbs were green.
At a touch, she had blooms
Of prize Chrysanthemums—
The grandest ever seen.

For guided practice, use the questions about **"My Aunt"** to help students recognize story elements in narrative poetry. You can put a chart on the chalkboard listing the categories of characters, setting, conflict, and plot in one column. Using responses to the study questions, list details from the poem in another column.

Students will have the opportunity to work independently when they create their poems. Because many students find it difficult to write poetry, you may want to make this a credit/no-credit assignment in which you comment on the final results but dispense with letter grades.

People from miles around
Came to see those flowers
And were truly astounded
By her unusual powers.

One day a little weed
Pushed up to drink and feed
Among the pampered flowers
At her water-can showers.

Day by day it grew
With ragged leaves and bristles
Till it was tall as me or you—
It was a King of Thistles

"Prizes for flowers are easy,"
My aunt said in her pride.
"But was there ever such a weed
The whole world wide?"

She watered it, she tended it,
It grew alarmingly.
As if I had offended it,
It bristled over me.

"Oh Aunt!" I cried. "Beware of that!
I saw it eat a bird."
She went on polishing its points
As if she hadn't heard.

"Oh Aunt!" I cried. "It has a flower
Like a lion's beard—"
Too late! It was devouring her
Just as I had feared.

Her feet were waving in the air—
But I shall not proceed.
Here ends the story of my Aunt
And her ungrateful weed.

INTEGRATING THE LANGUAGE ARTS

Literature and Speaking. To stimulate interest and develop appreciation of narrative poetry, integrate this lesson with selections from your literature anthology. Poems like "The Cremation of Sam McGee" and "The Highwayman" make entertaining dramatic readings. You might have students present individual or choral readings of narrative poems.

A DIFFERENT APPROACH

You may want to offer students who feel overwhelmed at the thought of writing narrative poems the alternative of an oral presentation. They might prepare dramatic or choral readings of narrative poems from their literature books. Or let them present music videos that tell stories. In an introduction, they should identify story elements that can be seen in the narrative poems and in the videos.

SELECTION AMENDMENT
Description of change: excerpted
Rationale: to focus on the concept of narrative poetry as presented in this chapter

CLOSURE

Call on students to identify elements that can be found both in short stories and in narrative poems. [Character, conflict, setting, and plot are possibilities.] ■

208

ANSWERS
Thinking It Over

Answers may vary.

1. Characters in the poem include the speaker, the aunt, and the plant. The aunt enjoys a great reputation as a gardener (lines 5–12) and is so obsessed by the chance to do something new that she ignores suspicious signs (lines 21–24 and 29–32). The speaker is a bystander who is concerned by the way the weed "grew alarmingly" and "bristled" (lines 26–29).

2. The large bristling weed with a lion-like beard suggests some threat.

3. The obvious conflict in the poem is the weed's hunger for its cultivator.

4. The poem has a fairly strong beat, with two or three stresses in each short line. The metrical foot is roughly iambic.

5. Students might notice certain imagery, such as "waving in the air" or "polishing its points."

Thinking It Over

1. Who are the characters in this poem? (If you name only two, think again.) What can you tell about them—and how do you know it?
2. Gardens are usually peaceful settings. Is that true of this garden?
3. Do you see more than one problem or conflict in the poem? Explain.
4. How would you describe the beat of the poem? What syllables are stressed?
5. What examples of sounds and images do you hear and see?

Writing a Narrative Poem

Prewriting. Apply what you know about writing stories to writing a narrative poem. Try beginning with a character or with a situation. It can be fantastic (like "My Aunt") or realistic. After you've jotted down a few ideas, share them with a few classmates. Then choose an idea that you really like.

Writing, Evaluating, and Revising. Whether you rhyme the ends of lines is up to you. Experiment with a few lines to decide. And listen for rhythm with your ear. Notice where the beats, or stresses, are. Even if they aren't regular, the rhythm should be pleasing, not annoying. You can break your poem into lines and stanzas that seem natural to you. And don't forget other tools of the poet—repeated sounds and sensory images. (For more on sensory images, see Chapter 4.) After you've finished writing, read your poem aloud to hear how it sounds. Exchange poems with a classmate for feedback.

Proofreading and Publishing. Make a clean copy of your poem and proofread it carefully one last time. Your class might create a poem clothesline to hang your finished poems on, or you might perform some of your poems at the next parent-teacher organization meeting or Parent's Day.

SEGMENT 8 *(p. 209)*
MAKING CONNECTIONS

MYTHS
OBJECTIVE

• To write a myth explaining a natural phenomenon

CREATIVE WRITING AND LITERATURE OBJECTIVE

• To write a new ending for a story

209

MAKING CONNECTIONS

MYTHS

Writing a Myth

Myths are stories that people have told and passed down to others through the ages. Very often they try to explain something about the natural world. For example, the sun is a god's chariot driven across the sky, or the stars are the result of Coyote's magic handiwork, as in "Coyote Places the Stars" on pages 180–182.

People everywhere tell myths—in the Northern African desert, in the Central American jungle, and on the Canadian Plains. You can, too. Why is the sea salty? Why do people sneeze? Make up a myth to explain anything you like. Or, if you know a myth from your culture, retell it in your own words. That's how myths stay alive.

CREATIVE WRITING AND LITERATURE

Writing a New Ending for a Story

Sometimes when you read a story, it doesn't end quite like you imagine it will. Sometimes you want a different ending, the *right* one—yours. Here's your chance to step into the author's shoes. Pick one of the stories in this chapter—"Coyote Places the Stars," "The Dinner Party," or "The Gang's Surprise." Try your hand at writing a new ending for it. Begin at the story's high point.

MYTHS
Teaching Strategies

To help students generate ideas, brainstorm with the class about occurrences in nature that could be the basis for myths. Offer students the option of either telling or writing their myths.

GUIDELINES

Students' myths should contain explanations of natural events. Other criteria for assessment might include creativity and how well the different story elements are developed.

CREATIVE WRITING AND LITERATURE
Teaching Strategies

Ask students what was good about the endings of the selections in the textbook. List these comments on the chalkboard and then have students suggest alternative endings for the stories. Tell the students that they may now write new endings, based on their own preferences, provided that they include enough details and description to make their writing believable.

GUIDELINES

Story endings might be assessed in different ways. Detail of description, plausibility, and creativity are some points to consider.

Chapter 7

WRITING TO INFORM

OBJECTIVES

- To identify the informative aim and to analyze the characteristics of process writing
- To select an appropriate topic for a process essay and to write a thesis sentence introducing the process
- To analyze the intended audience of a process paper
- To list necessary steps chronologically
- To organize and draft a process essay
- To evaluate and revise a process essay
- To proofread a process essay and to prepare it for publication

Motivation

You may wish to lead a class discussion on the various ways process writing is used in everyday life. Begin by asking students how many times a day they receive instructions. Discuss what makes those instructions helpful. Have several students volunteer to give verbal instructions to the class—without demonstrations—on how to do simple classroom activities such as sharpening a pencil.

Introduction

In a class discussion, help students understand the importance of learning to give good directions. Help students see that directions are not given as commands but as helpful instructions. Have students identify factors that make directions hard to follow.

Discuss the difference between explaining a process, in which directions to complete a task are given, and informative writing, in which information is given but no directions are provided for achieving a goal. You may also wish to discuss directions that appear unclear to the students.

Integration

This chapter can be used as a resource for subjects across the curriculum. For example, students need to know how to follow directions to complete science projects, math problems, and literature assignments. You may choose to bring to class a variety of textbooks that explain processes and to allow students to identify examples of process instructions in each textbook.

If you assign demonstration speeches, you may want to use **Purposes for Explaining a Process** to assist students in analyzing audience. The **Prewriting** segment will also provide students with ideas for gathering their material so that they may present it in a well-organized manner.

While students are learning about process writing, encourage them to work cooperatively so that they can give each other feedback on the clarity of their instructions.

The chart on the next page illustrates the strands of language arts as they are integrated into this chapter. For vocabulary study, glossary words are underlined in some writing models.

QUOTATIONS
All **Quotations for the Day** are chosen because of their relevance to instructional material presented in that segment of the chapter and for their usefulness in establishing student interest in writing.

INTEGRATING THE LANGUAGE ARTS

Selection	Reading and Literature	Writing and Critical Thinking	Language and Syntax	Speaking, Listening, and Other Expression Skills
"How to Eat Like a Child" by Delia Ephron **212-214** from ***Ubuhlali and Umnaka-Beaded Necklaces and Bangles*** by Jane Kerina **226-227** **"Weightlessness in Space"** by Sally Ride with Susan Okie **236-237** **"A Drink for Crow"** told by George Shannon **239**	Finding details **215, 227, 238** Determining audience **215** Finding author's purpose **215** Analyzing details **238** Identifying cause and effect **238** Solving riddles **239**	Analyzing purposes of process essays **215** Choosing a topic **218** Analyzing audience **218** Brainstorming **218** Gathering ideas for writing **220** Analyzing steps in a process **227-228** Understanding chronological order **222, 228** Organizing information **222, 224** Evaluating details **223, 227-228** Writing a draft of a process paper that includes a thesis, a list of materials, and chronological steps **230** Analyzing a writer's revisions **233-234** Publishing a "how-to" paper **235, 238** Writing a cause-and-effect paper **238**	Proofreading for errors in word choice, spelling, capitalization, punctuation, and usage **235, 238**	Discussing possible topics for an informative essay **218** Discussing a work of non-fiction with peers **227** Following and giving oral directions **231** Applying good speaking and listening techniques **231** Sharing a story **238**

CHAPTER 7

SEGMENT PLANNING GUIDE

Whether you are planning for a quick review of a writing concept or preparing an extended lesson on composition you can use the following Planning Guide to adapt the chapter material to the individual needs of your class.

SEGMENT	PAGES	CONTENT	RESOURCES
1 *Working and Playing*	*211-215*		
Literary Model **"How to Eat Like a Child"**	212-214	Guided reading: a model of process writing	
Reader's Response/ Writer's Craft	215	Model evaluation: responding to literature and analyzing process models	
2 *Ways to Inform*	*216*		
3 *Prewriting*	*217-224*		Writing a "How-to" Paper
Choosing a Process	217-218	Guidelines: focusing on interest and audience	Listing Steps and Materials
Thinking About Interest	217	Guidelines: focusing on interest	
Thinking About Skill	218	Guidelines: knowing a subject	
Exercise 1	218	Applied practice: exploring possible topics	
Writing Assignment: Part 1	218	Applied practice: writing a topic sentence	
Gathering and Organizing Your Information	219	Introduction: organizing information	
Listing Steps and Materials	219	Guidelines: organizing information in a chart	
Writing Note	220	Writing suggestion: defining terms for readers	
Exercise 2	220	Cooperative learning: listing steps and material	
Organizing Your Information	220-221	Guidelines: explaining a process	
Critical Thinking: Arranging Steps in Order	222	Explanation: using chronological order in a "how-to" paper	
Critical Thinking Exercise	222-223	Cooperative learning: arranging steps chronologically	
Exercise 3	223-224	Applied practice: evaluating details	
Writing Assignment: Part 2	224	Applied practice: charting steps and materials	
4 *Writing*	*225-230*		Writing Your Introduction
Putting Your Ideas on Paper	225	Guidelines: structuring a "how-to" essay	
Introduction	225	Guidelines: catching readers' interest	
Body	225	Guidelines: giving clear instructions	
Conclusion	225	Guidelines: writing an interesting conclusion	
Literary Model from ***Ubuhlali and Umnaka—Beaded Necklaces and Bangles***	226-227	Guided reading: examining process writing	
Exercise 4	227-228	Cooperative learning: analyzing a "how-to" explanation	

SEGMENT	PAGES	CONTENT	RESOURCES
Following a Basic Framework for a "How-to" Paper	228	Guidelines: examining structure in process writing	
Writer's Model	228-229	Guided reading: examining a sample essay	
Writing Note	229	Writing suggestion: using drawings or diagrams	
Chart: Framework for a "How-to" Paper	230	Guidelines: examining framework for a process paper	
Writing Assignment: Part 3	230	Applied practice: writing a first draft	
5 *Evaluating and Revising*	*231-234*		Writing a "How-to" Paper
Evaluating and Revising	231	Guidelines: evaluating and revising a first draft	
Exercise 5	231	Cooperative learning: explaining and following a process	
Chart: Evaluating and Revising Process Essays	232	Applied practice: applying evaluation and revision techniques	
Usage Hint	233	Writing suggestion: using adjectives and nouns	
Exercise 6	233-234	Applied practice: analyzing a writer's revisions	
Writing Assignment: Part 4	234	Cooperative learning: evaluating and revising	
6 *Proofreading and Publishing*	*235*		Writing a "How-to" Paper
Publishing	235	Publishing ideas: reaching an audience	
Writing Assignment: Part 5	235	Applied practice: proofreading and publishing	
7 *Writing Workshop*	*236-238*		All the resources in this chapter may be used in this segment.
The Cause-and-Effect Paper	235	Introduction: writing cause-and-effect essays	
Literary Model from **"Weightless in Space"**	236-237	Examining techniques: analyzing cause and effect in a model	
Writing a Cause-and-Effect Paper	238	Applied practice: applying skills to the writing process	
8 *Making Connections*	*239-241*		
Process Across the Curriculum: Folk Tales, Riddles, and Brainteasers	239	Introduction: analyzing a brainteaser	
Literary Model from **"A Drink for Crow"**	239	Examining techniques: analyzing a process	
Speaking and Listening: Process in Social Studies	240-241	Guidelines: planning a treasure hunt Cooperative learning: creating a treasure map	

WHOLE-CHAPTER RESOURCES
A Writing Process Log, A Writing Prompt, Holistically Graded Models, Assessment Portfolio Materials

OBJECTIVES

- To write personal responses to literature
- To identify and analyze the characteristics of process writing
- To write instructions in response to a prompt

MOTIVATION

Ask students to follow your instructions for making a paper airplane or for completing some other hands-on process that can be easily explained. Then discuss with the class what made the instructions easy or difficult to follow.

 VISUAL CONNECTIONS
The Making of a Fresco, Showing the Building of a City

About the Artist. Diego Rivera, born in Mexico in 1886, is noted for his identification with the Mexican working class. His paintings often reflect his socialistic ideals by presenting a worker's view of the industrial world. Rivera's study of pre-Columbian art influenced his style, and he was inspired to work on murals after seeing relief friezes on the walls of ancient temples. Rivera's murals appear on government and public buildings in Mexico and in the United States. He died in 1957.

Exploring the Subject. This mural illustrates many of the steps involved in the process of making a fresco. In the background, the fresco itself portrays the process of building a city. Discuss the mural with the class. Ask students to identify the activities shown and to decide which process each scene illustrates.

7 WRITING TO INFORM

Have students silently read the first two paragraphs of **Working and Playing.** Discuss various situations that involve following instructions. Ask students what happens when they don't follow instructions. Encourage students to share funny anecdotes about times when they were embarrassed because they didn't follow instructions.

Then have students read the final paragraph on this page. Ask them to make predictions concerning the article. What are some special ways of eating that the author might discuss?

Ask several volunteers to take turns reading the sections of Ephron's essay aloud; allow time for responses after each section. Discuss whether or not the process in each

Working and Playing

Have dinosaur skeletons been found in the U.S.? How do you do an axel in ice skating? Where is the closest national park? Who wants to know? Someone somewhere does. We spend most hours **working or playing,** so the information we want is often about *processes:* how to do something or how something works.

Writing and You. You'd be surprised how much writing explains a process. A detective story explains how the murder weapon disappeared: it was an icicle. An article in *WaterSki* magazine gives tips for using a kneeboard. What process could you write about?

As You Read. Writers sometimes explain a special way of doing a familiar process. Do you think you know how to eat? Maybe not. As you read the following "how-to," notice the steps even a child could follow.

The Making of a Fresco Showing the Building of a City, Diego Rivera (1931), San Francisco Art Institute. Photo by Don Beatty © 1984.

QUOTATION FOR THE DAY

"Making movies is like playing baseball—the fun is the playing." (Robert Altman, 1922–   , American film director)

Write the quotation on the chalkboard and initiate a discussion about its meaning. Ask students to freewrite about the quotation, but to use writing instead of making movies as its subject.

MEETING INDIVIDUAL NEEDS

LEP/ESL

General Strategies. The eating methods listed in "**How to Eat Like A Child**" on pp. 212–214 refer to traditional American food. Students might have trouble visualizing eating these foods in the unusual ways described in the selection. For example, many Asians use different kinds of eating utensils.

After making sure students recognize the kinds of food, you may wish to have some native students act out common methods of eating the foods so that students can see why the descriptions given in the selection are humorous.

211

section is clear. Ask students if they can recreate the events.

You may need to discuss unfamiliar words with students before they read each section.

Guide students through the **Reader's Response** questions and through **Writer's Craft** question number 4 by discussing students' responses to Ephron's essay and her techniques of process writing.

How to

EAT

Like a Child

by Delia Ephron

Peas: Mash and flatten into thin sheet on plate. Press the back
1 of the fork into the peas. Hold fork vertically, prongs up, and lick off peas.

Mashed potatoes: Pat mashed potatoes flat on top. Dig several
2 little depressions. Think of them as ponds or pools. Fill the
3 pools with gravy. With your fork, sculpt rivers between pools and watch the gravy flow between them. Decorate with peas. Do not eat.

Alternative method: Make a large hole in center of mashed potatoes. Pour in ketchup. Stir until potatoes turn pink. Eat as you would peas.

Animal crackers: Eat each in this order—legs, head, body.

Sandwich: Leave the crusts. If your mother says you have to eat them because that's the best part, stuff the crusts into your pants pocket or between the cushions of the couch.

Spaghetti: Wind too many strands on the fork and make sure at least two strands dangle down. Open your mouth wide and stuff in spaghetti; suck noisily to inhale the dangling strands. Clean plate, ask for seconds, and eat only half. When carrying your plate to the kitchen, hold it tilted so that the remaining spaghetti slides off and onto the floor.

USING THE SELECTION
How To Eat Like a Child

1
vertically: in an upright position

2
How does the description of the depressions in the mashed potatoes as "ponds or pools" help the reader? [It gives the reader an idea of how they should look.]

3
sculpt: to shape into a form

INDEPENDENT PRACTICE

After discussing the techniques in the model, students should be ready to create their own special instructions as assigned in **Reader's Response** question 3.

ASSESSMENT

Students' lists of steps should be evaluated mainly on the basis of clarity and chronological order.

👈

Ice-cream cone: Ask for a double scoop. Knock the top scoop off while walking out the door of the ice-cream parlor. Cry. Lick the remaining scoop slowly so that ice cream melts down the outside of the cone and over your hand. Stop licking when the ice cream is even with the top of the cone. Be sure it is absolutely even. Eat a hole in the bottom of the cone and suck the rest of the ice cream out the bottom. When only the cone remains with ice cream coating the inside, leave on car dashboard.

4   **Ice cream in bowl:** Grip spoon upright in fist. Stir ice cream vigorously to make soup. Take a large helping on a spoon, place spoon in mouth, and slowly pull it out, sucking only the top layer of ice cream off. Wave spoon in air. Lick its back. Put in mouth again and suck off some more. Repeat until all ice cream is off spoon and begin again.

Cooked carrots: On way to mouth, drop in lap. Smuggle to garbage in napkin.

Spinach: Divide into little piles. Rearrange into new piles. After five or six <u>maneuvers</u>, sit back and say you are full.

Chocolate-chip cookies: Half-sit, half-lie on the bed, propped up by a pillow. Read a book. Place cookies next to you on the sheet so that crumbs get in the bed. As you eat the cookies,
5   remove each chocolate chip and place it on your stomach. When all the cookies are <u>consumed</u>, eat the chips one by one, allowing two per page.

4
Notice that these instructions begin almost every sentence with imperative verbs.

5
Do you think Ephron is serious when she instructs a person to put chocolate chips on the stomach? Why would she say this? [She is using verbal irony to create humor.]

RETEACHING

Give students copies of a short list of instructions. Then have students follow the list exactly. Ask them to explain to you how the list helped them achieve their goal.

CLOSURE

Discuss the purposes of process writing. Ask students to describe situations that might call for process papers.

 COOPERATIVE LEARNING
Pair students and place partners back-to-back. Have one student in each pair draw an object such as a square, a circle, or a triangle. The person who draws the picture must give his or her partner instructions on how to draw the exact same picture without revealing what is being drawn. Make sure partners take turns giving and following instructions. Have students display the pairs of drawings in the classroom and analyze the results of the exercise in a class discussion.

INTEGRATING THE LANGUAGE ARTS

Literature Link. Have students analyze and evaluate Edgar A. Guest's short story "Antaeus." Ask students to analyze the steps the narrator takes to achieve his goal. Have students pick out specific details that support these steps and the transitional expressions that help make the order of the procedure clear [helps the boys find good soil, shows them how to prepare the earth for planting, smooths the soil, sows the grass seed].

Library Link. Have students use the subject index in the card catalogue to find books similar to Ephron's in the library.

SELECTION AMENDMENT
Description of change: excerpted
Rationale: to focus on the concept of informative writing presented in this chapter

Milk shake: Bite off one end of the paper covering the straw. Blow through straw to shoot paper across table. Place straw in shake and suck. When the shake just reaches your mouth, place a finger over the top of the straw—the pressure will keep the shake in the straw. Lift straw out of shake, put bottom end in mouth, release finger, and swallow.

Do this until the straw is squished so that you can't suck through it. Ask for another. Open it the same way, but this time shoot the paper at the waitress when she isn't looking. Sip your shake casually—you are just minding your own business—until there is about an inch of shake remaining. Then blow through the straw until bubbles rise to the top of the glass. When your father says he's had just about enough, get a stomachache.

Chewing gum: Remove from mouth and stretch into spaghetti-like strand. Swing like a <u>lasso</u>. Put back in mouth. Pulling out one end and gripping the other end between teeth, have your gum meet your friend's gum and press them together. Think that you have just done something really disgusting.

Baked apple: With your fingers, peel skin off baked apple. Tell your mother you changed your mind, you don't want it. Later, when she is <u>harassed</u> and not paying attention to what she is doing, pick up the naked baked apple and hand it to her.

French fries: Wave one French fry in air for emphasis while you talk. Pretend to conduct orchestra. Then place four fries in your mouth at once and chew. Turn to your sister, open your mouth, and stick out your tongue coated with potatoes. Close mouth and swallow. Smile.

ENRICHMENT

Allow students to prepare three-to-five minute oral demonstrations of processes. If a video camera is available, you may want to videotape each student's speech and to allow students to borrow the videotapes to share with family members.

EXTENSION

Have students create a set of instructions that could be used to program a robot. For example, they can have the robot pick up a piece of chalk. Without knowing the goal, other students should act as robots and perform the instructions. ■

READER'S RESPONSE

1. You no doubt used a few of Delia Ephron's funny eating techniques when you were younger. Which one in her list was your specialty?
2. Now for the sequel: "How to Eat Like a Child II." Can you give special instructions for eating broccoli, cereal, two foods that no adult would combine, or something else? Share your technique.

WRITER'S CRAFT

3. The information you give in a "how-to" paper, even one about eating, usually includes equipment. Where does Ephron tell about equipment and how to use it?
4. Is Ephron writing for young children or for other readers? Is her article a real "how-to" paper or actually a "how-it-happens" paper? Does she want you to take her seriously? Give reasons for your answers.

ANSWERS

Reader's Response

Responses will vary.

1. Students should be able to explain what made their choices special.
2. Answers should include instructions and techniques.

Writer's Craft

3. Possible answers might include pressing fork into peas, winding strands of spaghetti onto fork, tilting plate, and using napkin to smuggle carrots to trash.
4. Some students who have younger brothers or sisters might be reminded of how their siblings eat ["how-it-happens paper"]. Other students might think they are being given instructions on how to eat like a child ["how-to" paper]. Students should support their answers with specific details from the selection.

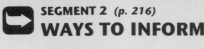
TEACHING THE MODES

This section is designed to explain to students one reason for writing "how-to" papers and the modes used in explaining processes. You may want to help students define and give examples of *narration*, *description, classification,* and *evaluation.* Ask the class to give further examples of how each mode might be used in process writing and speaking.

Assess students' understanding of the modes by having them give the mode of Ephron's essay [description]. ∎

INTEGRATING THE LANGUAGE ARTS

Technology Link. If word processors are available, students might use them to practice following and giving instructions. Have students work in pairs, with one student in each pair using the word processor's manual to learn about a special function, such as blocking text.

Then these students can tell their partners how to use the function. If time allows, students should switch roles to work with different functions.

---

216   *Writing to Inform*

Ways to Inform

You can share information in writing in four basic ways, or strategies. Which strategy do you use for explaining a process? It's the first one in the list below: *narration*—like narrating or telling a story. In a "how-to" process paper, for example, you're telling a step-by-step story of how to do something. Here are some specific examples of sharing information through the four basic writing strategies.

▶ **Narration:** telling a friend how you make tempura; explaining in a paper how a wooden drum makes sounds of different pitches.

Description: in a letter to your grandfather, describing the set you helped paint for a play; describing a hummingbird's nest to your class.

Classification: in science, explaining what the parts of a plant are for; telling your parents the differences between two bikes that you like.

Evaluation: in a report on a movie, telling whether the plot was interesting and logical; explaining how well a new "instant" camera works.

> ### LOOKING AHEAD
>
> In your main assignment in this chapter, you'll be writing a process paper explaining how to do something. Your purpose will be to give information. As you work through the exercises and the writing assignment, keep in mind that a "how-to" paper
>
> - includes all necessary materials and steps
> - presents the steps of the process in the order they're done

SEGMENT 3 *(pp. 217–224)*
PREWRITING

OBJECTIVES

- To generate possible topics for a process paper
- To select an appropriate topic and to compose a clear thesis for a process essay
- To analyze an audience for a process paper
- To list steps and materials for given processes
- To evaluate what details are necessary for a process paper
- To arrange steps in chronological order
- To use a chart to organize materials

Writing a "How-to" Paper

Choosing a Process to Explain

You can do many things that someone else might want to learn. Do you know how to keep your cat from getting fleas? Can you explain how to run a baby sitters' club? Are you good at racing dirt bikes? One way to look for a topic is to brainstorm a list of things you do well. Then, to narrow down the list, ask yourself these questions:

- What do I most like to spend time doing?
- What can I do best?

Thinking About Interest. To pick a topic, focus on interest—in two ways. Think about what interests you *and* what will interest your *audience*. A paper on how to get ready for school will bore an audience of teenagers—unless you make it funny! And most of your classmates already know how to heat up a pizza. But they might want to find out how to make a special food that you have at home, Navajo bread, for instance, or Japanese sushi. Or, you can write your paper for younger children. Just be sure that your topic and your audience match.

RESOURCES

PREWRITING
- Listing Steps and Materials

QUOTATION FOR THE DAY

"We are wiser than we know." (Ralph Waldo Emerson, 1803–1882, American author)

Write the quotation on the chalkboard and use the quotation to initiate a discussion. Remind students that each day they complete many processes that have become automatic. Have students work in small groups to brainstorm lists of processes that they go through regularly. The ideas that students list can be used later as the subjects of "how-to" papers.

MEETING
INDIVIDUAL
NEEDS

LEP/ESL

General Strategies. Students may have difficulty understanding what is meant by *self-expression.* You could help them understand the idea of self-expression by assigning or reading to them poems, excerpts from diaries, and expressive essays. Then discuss with students what ideas and feelings the writers might be expressing.

MOTIVATION

Have students share their answers to the questions in the opening paragraph of the chapter. You or a volunteer could write the responses on the chalkboard. Discuss the ideas that seem unusual to the class. Address why some topics would be of interest and others would not.

TEACHING THE LESSON

Have students copy the list from the chalkboard so they can use the ideas for prewriting. Then ask them to read the explanations in the textbook on interest and audience. You may wish to copy on the chalkboard the **Reminder** on this page to guide students as they choose their topics.

MEETING INDIVIDUAL NEEDS

LESS-ADVANCED STUDENTS

You may wish to have students work in pairs to ensure they are not omitting any necessary steps. Tell students to visualize themselves going through the steps. As one partner visualizes the steps and explains how to do the activity, the other partner can record the steps.

LEARNING STYLES

Visual Learners. Tell students to visualize each step of their processes and to fill in a flowchart like the one below:

My Process: ____

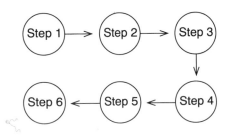

---

218   *Writing to Inform*

Thinking About Skill. The purpose of a "how-to" paper is to share information about a process so that your readers can do it themselves. This means you have to pick something you're good at. Writing about how to dance a hula might be a good idea. However, you have to be able to dance the hula well enough to explain it. Basically, the test of your explanation will be, "Does it work?" If your readers follow your directions on how to make a boomerang, the boomerangs they make should fly back.

To choose a "how-to" topic

- brainstorm a list of things you do well
- pick something that you really like to do
- pick a process that will interest your audience

| EXERCISE 1 | **Exploring Possible Topics** |

Meet with a few classmates to discuss possible topics for a "how-to" paper. You might brainstorm from broad areas like "the outdoors," "crafts," and "what I do on Saturday." As you come up with ideas, give each other feedback. Would you like to learn the process? Can an idea be covered in a paragraph or two?   Monitor the groups and assess how much each student participates in the discussion.

| **WRITING ASSIGNMENT** | PART 1: **Choosing a Process to Explain** |

You can pick a topic from your work in Exercise 1 or a topic of your own. Are you known for how well you can lip-sync the words to your favorite song? Can you explain how to do it? Will you write about how to twirl a baton? Would you like to tell younger children how to draw monsters? When you've decided on your topic, write one sentence telling what it is and who your audience will be.

GUIDED PRACTICE

Discuss your choice of a topic for a process paper with the class. (One possible topic is "How to Plan a Lesson.") Then list the steps and materials needed. Ask the class to help you put the steps in chronological order. Finally, make a list of details necessary for your process paper to be successful.

Prewriting **219**

 *Prewriting*

Gathering and Organizing Your Information

Planning your paper before you write will save time and make the writing easier. Since you know how to do the process, you probably have all the information you need. But if you have any questions, look for information in books, articles, or videotapes about the topic.

Listing Steps and Materials. Your readers need two kinds of information: (1) what steps to do and (2) what materials to use.

Here's a good technique for gathering information. Imagine yourself doing the process on a video screen. What steps do you see yourself going through? As you watch each step on your mental TV, think about the tools and materials you're using.

You can use a chart to organize your notes about steps and materials. Here's a chart one writer made for a "how-to" paper.

HERE'S HOW

How to Do a Magic Trick: Ballooney-Baloney	
Steps	Materials
1. Blow up some balloons.	Three or four balloons of ordinary colors (pink, blue, yellow). One balloon of unusual color (purple).
2. Stick two pieces of tape on one side of unusual balloon.	See-through tape, scissors.
3. Ask someone to stick pin into ordinary balloons.	Pins
4. Stick pin through center of tape on taped balloon.	

INTEGRATING THE LANGUAGE ARTS

Literature Link. Have students read and discuss J. Frank Dobie's autobiographical essay "When I Was a Boy on the Ranch." Ask students to use a chart like the one on this page to outline the steps Dobie gives in his explanation of how the children made play money.

Vocabulary Link. Help students understand the importance of using vocabulary that is familiar to their audiences. For example, some technical terms used in horseback riding may not be familiar to some members of the class. Discuss ways to handle this issue in writing. You might wish to have students make lists of possibly unfamiliar terms used in their hobbies. Then have students trade lists to look up the words in a dictionary or in another resource.

This way you will have modeled all the prewriting steps students will need to accomplish.

Have students work independently to choose topics to gather information, and to organize their details. Then place students in groups of three and have them discuss any problems they are having with these steps.

STUDENTS WITH SPECIAL NEEDS

Learning disabled students may have difficulty remembering and ordering every step in any activity done in the past. It may prove simpler for students to write about chronologically-ordered processes they have just completed.

ANSWERS
Exercise 2

Responses will vary. Students should include specific details such as the correct amount of shampoo, the proper kind of conditioner, and what size towel to use. Make sure students include all of the steps and materials of the processes.

WRITING NOTE As you take notes, jot down any terms that your readers might not know. This is especially important if you're writing for an audience younger than yourself. It's also important if you're writing about an unusual process. Your notes on terms like *karate chop, cakewalk,* and *D & D module* will remind you to define them in the paper.

EXERCISE 2 ▶ **Listing Steps and Materials**

Many processes you do every day have become almost as easy for you as breathing. Do you think you can break them into clear and separate steps? Get together with a group of classmates and divide each of the following processes into steps. Also, list materials you would need.

1. washing your hair
2. fixing your breakfast
3. doing the dishes
4. sharpening a pencil

Organizing Your Information. On the next page are one writer's directions for making a Huichol yarn painting. Can you follow them?

CLOSURE

Discuss with students the difficulties they had in their prewriting. Lead students to understand why prewriting is necessary and how it will help their final papers.

ENRICHMENT

Give the class copies of a page of cartoons. Ask students to circle the cartoons that show characters performing processes. Ask the students to write down in chronological order the steps of the process. Do the cartoon characters leave out any steps?

Cont. on p. 223

Prewriting   **221**

You put a little liquid glue along the outline of your design. Add more glue inside the design and press yarn into it. The Huichols use traditional designs, and they use beeswax, not glue. They live in a part of Mexico where there are mountains. Cut the yarn for the inside of the design in small pieces. Put the pieces of yarn as close together as possible. You put the long yarn on the outline first. The design should be drawn on cardboard.

 VISUAL CONNECTIONS
Exploring the Subject. The Huichol tribe is from the nearly inaccessible Sierra Madres in northern Mexico. These people are notable for having maintained to an exceptional degree their native speech, religion, and customs. Their religion is important in daily life, from considering dreams in decision making to consulting shamans (called *mara'akame*) for healing.

Suppose you tried to follow these directions the way they were written. Before you got to the end, you'd have to start over. And you would probably like to get your hands on the writer!

To make your process easy for readers to follow, first tell what materials are needed. Then give the steps in **chronological order,** the order that you'd do them.

As you're writing, many details may come into your mind. It's good to include details that relate directly to the process and help explain it. But don't use details that just get in the way (like the mountains in Mexico) or confuse your readers (like the beeswax).

OBJECTIVE

• To arrange steps in chronological order

Have students talk about times when they have received long and complicated explanations they could not understand. Discuss what might have been done to make the explanations easier to understand. Point out the importance of uncomplicated instructions. You might want to explain a

LEP/ESL

General Strategies. Some students may not understand the expressions *brainstorm* and *pick a process*. Once these concepts are explained, the students should be more at ease with them. However, if students are still having some trouble, you could demonstrate the various ways of brainstorming. For example, you could write ideas in circles on paper and connect the circles with lines to show how the ideas relate.

AT-RISK STUDENTS

Help students explore vocations or careers that interest them. Tell students to focus on the processes that people in these occupations complete daily to be successful at their jobs. You may want to have the class choose one type of job that it would like to know more about. Then invite a guest speaker who works in that field to discuss the importance of following instructions at work.

222   *Writing to Inform*

To plan a "how-to" paper

- list the steps that you want readers to follow
- note the materials needed for each step
- be sure the steps are in chronological order
- use only details that will help readers do the process

CRITICAL THINKING

Arranging Steps in Chronological Order

Has this ever happened to you?

You ask an expert a simple question. The expert gives you a long and complicated answer. By the end you've forgotten what your question was! You're also more confused than you were before you asked the question.

That's one way an explanation can be confusing. Another way is to have an explanation move back and forth in time—jumping from what to do first to what to do last to everything in between! This is especially frustrating in a "how-to" paper. You want to go straight forward in time, or *chronologically:* what comes first, second, and so on.

 CRITICAL THINKING EXERCISE:
Arranging Steps in Chronological Order

On the next page are out-of-order directions for making a kite into a "fighting kite" and for fighting other kites. Working with one or two classmates, put the steps into chronological order so that they're easy to follow. (You and your classmates might even enjoy actually following these directions.)

math problem as an example of a process that requires clear instructions.

Have students work in small groups to put the steps into chronological order. Then have each group write a topic sentence for this exercise.

Cont. from p. 221
EXTENSION

Have each student speak with a relative or other adult who knows how to do something like crocheting or whittling. Ask each student to have that person explain the steps needed to achieve the desired result. Students should record the steps. Then ask ☞

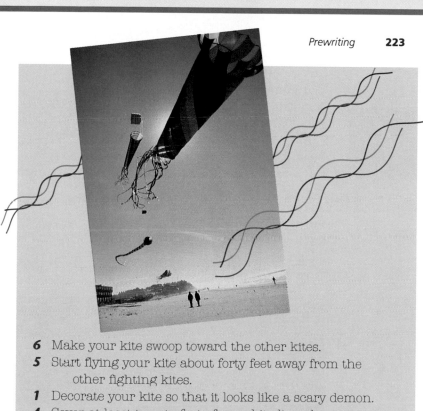

6 Make your kite swoop toward the other kites.

5 Start flying your kite about forty feet away from the other fighting kites.

1 Decorate your kite so that it looks like a scary demon.

4 Cover at least twenty feet of your kite line closest to your kite with this mixture, and let it dry.

3 Starting at the kite, put the mixture on the line. Make it as sharp and rough-edged as you can.

7 Try to saw other kite lines apart, or chase the other kites so that they dive down and crash.

2 Mix glue and sand together.

| EXERCISE 3 ▶ | Evaluating Details |

All of the details in your "how-to" paper should help readers do the process. If a detail doesn't help, take it out. Ask yourself *Could readers make a mistake if I leave this detail out? Is this detail something my audience already knows?* On the next page are some notes for a paper about making fried plantains or bananas. The audience is a class of seventh-graders. Which information would you cross out?

VISUAL CONNECTIONS
Related Expression Skills. Have your students research how to make a kite. Students should record the instructions and then make kites to display in class. Three of the most common and easily made kites are the Eddy Bow kite, the Coyne kite, and the butterfly kite. You could even have a contest with other teachers judging the best three kites.

ANSWERS
Exercise 3

Responses will vary, but students need to understand how easily a reader might make a mistake if a step is left out. This exercise is also a good reason to discuss what details are important and why. Students should leave out the following details:

1. Plantains are not as sweet as bananas.
2. You can't get plantains in most places in this country.

Buy ripe bananas or plantains.
Plantains are not as sweet as bananas.
You can't get plantains in most places in this country.
Peel bananas or plantains.
Cut them in half lengthwise and across.
Be sure you don't cut yourself.
Put butter or margarine in frying pan on medium heat.
Fry the fruit until it's golden brown.
Take bananas or plantains out of pan.
Sprinkle with sugar and cinnamon.
Eat now.
Clean up kitchen.
Save peelings for compost pile.

VISUAL CONNECTIONS

Exploring the Subject. The plantain is a kind of banana that grows in the tropics. Its appearance is much like the banana's, but it doesn't taste as sweet. Plantain flour is a mainstay in the diet of many people in tropical countries.

A DIFFERENT APPROACH

If it is available in a local library, you could refer students to the book *The Way Things Work* by David Macaulay, which has detailed explanations of processes with clear illustrations. Processes are grouped into four categories: the mechanics of movement, harnessing the elements, working with waves, and electricity automation. The author makes interesting connections; for example, the principle that makes a zipper work was used in building the pyramids.

WRITING
ASSIGNMENT

PART 2:
Gathering and Organizing Information

Fighting kites and fried bananas: That's enough practice. Now plan *your* "how-to" paper. Begin with a chart like the one on page 219. Be sure to list your steps in chronological order and jot down all materials. [Remember: You could find some terms to define.]

WRITING YOUR FIRST DRAFT

OBJECTIVES

- To analyze the principles of organization and the basic elements in a process essay
- To write a draft of a process essay

MOTIVATION

Ask students to create an origami bird, but don't give them instructions. Allow them to look only at the final product. Give students about five minutes to make the bird before you give them the instructions. Lead students to understand that clear instructions are important.

☞

Writing Your First Draft

Putting Your Ideas on Paper

Thinking and planning are important, but you've probably done enough for now. It's time to get down to the business of writing.

Introduction.   The introduction of a "how-to" paper can be just two or three sentences. As usual, you want to begin by catching your readers' interest. One way to do this is by giving the reader a reason for learning the process. Show that it's fun, challenging, or useful.

Body.   Begin the body of your paper by listing the materials. Then, give the steps in chronological order. You can explain steps when needed and give helpful tips, but include only information that's directly related to the process. Also use transitional words like *first, now,* and *after this* to make the steps clear and easy to follow.

☞ REFERENCE NOTE: For more information on transitional words and phrases, see pages 74–75.

Conclusion.   Your conclusion should be brief. Probably one or two sentences will do. You might repeat why learning the process is a good idea, give another reason, or end with a final tip.

In the following explanation, the writer tells you how to make beads the way young people in southern Africa do it. As you read, ask yourself if you could follow her directions.

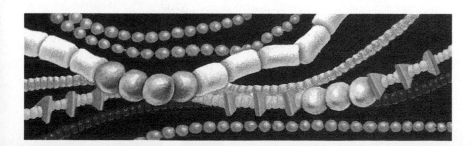

QUOTATION FOR THE DAY

"The perfect presence of mind, unconfused, unhurried by emotion, that any artistic performance requires. . . ." (Henry James, 1843–1916, American author)

You may wish to use the quotation to help students prepare for writing their first drafts. Explain that to produce good writing an author must have concentration, ideas about what he or she wants to say, and time to think clearly about the composition.

MEETING
INDIVIDUAL
NEEDS

LEP/ESL

General Strategies. Many students know how to get the attention of readers in their native languages. However, due to cultural and linguistic differences, students might be uncertain about how to catch the attention of people more familiar with American culture. Offer examples of attention-grabbing introductions and explain why they are effective.

Before students read the model essays, point out the **Framework for a "How-to" Process Paper** on p. 230 and ask students to keep these criteria in mind as they read.

Use the second model to guide students through an analysis of the elements of a process essay. It may be read silently or aloud. After students have finished reading, use the side glosses to initiate a discussion of the writer's clarity in giving instructions. When discussing the **Framework for a "How-To" Process Paper**, show students how to incorporate the lists of steps and materials they created in their prewriting into the framework.

MEETING INDIVIDUAL NEEDS

ADVANCED STUDENTS

Suggest that students find and analyze examples of process writing. Students can use the following questions as a guide:

1. Is the process identified early in the writing?
2. Are the steps in chronological order?
3. Does the writing appeal to a specific audience? Who?
4. Are the proper details for each step given?
5. What type of introduction is given?

LEARNING STYLES

Auditory Learners. Students might benefit from talking about their drafts. You may want to allow students to work in pairs to ask questions and record responses. Have one student in each pair read through the material while the other asks for clarification and points out any missed steps.

VISUAL CONNECTIONS

Related Expression Skills. Have students research the history of beadwork in Africa or on another continent. Then have them try making their own beads and bead chains. The students could use the instructions in the selection to decorate the beads in the styles of the cultures they've researched.

A PASSAGE FROM A BOOK

from Ubuhlali and Umnaka — Beaded Necklaces and Bangles

INTRODUCTION
Attention grabber
Reason for learning process

In the old days men and women as well as children wore beads; they were not simply decorations. In southern Africa, it was traditional to give beaded articles with special messages woven into them to loved ones and friends. . . .

The meanings of certain patterns and colors varied from place to place in southern Africa. Yellow usually symbolized wealth, and pink indicated poverty. Red showed anger and blue meant departure. White usually signified love. . . .

Process to be explained

Young people begin to learn beadwork by making simple necklaces of seeds and homemade beads. You can make your own beads as they were made long ago.

BODY
Step 1

For paste beads: Heat 3/4 cup of fine salt in a dry pan for a few minutes until it pops. Pour the salt into a bowl with 1/2 cup of flour.

Step 2

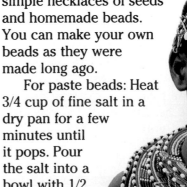

Many students have trouble deciding on attention-grabbers. To help them, give students sections from a newspaper. Ask them to look over the headlines and to choose articles that might interest them, based on the headlines. Have students brainstorm on what makes a headline good or weak.

INDEPENDENT PRACTICE

Have each student write answers to the questions for **Exercise 4** before they discussing the questions in groups. Have the groups share their responses with the class.

Students should write their drafts independently. Use student-teacher conferences if students need any help. At this point ☞

Step 3
Explanation

Add 1/2 cup of water to which you have added a few drops of food coloring if you want tinted beads. <u>Knead</u> this mixture thoroughly.

Step 4
Step 5

Roll out a snake of the paste and cut into equal pieces. Roll each of the pieces into a smooth round ball.

Step 6

To make flat beads, roll the paste out with a jar or rolling pin and cut beads into the desired shape.

Step 7
Helpful hint

Pierce each ball with a round toothpick. Stick toothpicks into a ball of soft clay or grapefruit rind to dry. Turn the beads periodically to prevent them from sticking to the toothpicks and allow them to dry thoroughly.

Step 8

Helpful hint

If you have not already tinted the paste, paint your beads with poster paint and cover with clear nail polish. For silver and gold beads use metallic nail polish.

from *African Crafts*

EXERCISE 4 ▶ **Analyzing a "How-to" Explanation**

Did you realize you could make beads using just salt, flour, and water? Take a closer look at this process by discussing the following questions with two or three classmates.

1. This passage is part of a chapter about African beadwork. How does the beginning introduce the topic? Do the first sentences grab your attention? Explain why or why not.
2. What are the basic steps in making both round and flat beads? What steps are different for round beads and flat beads?

TIMESAVER

Ask students to circle each step, to underline the materials needed, and to bracket the opening and closing statements in their drafts. This will help you quickly see if students need to add more information to their instructions.

ANSWERS
Exercise 4

1. The beginning is introduced with an attention-grabber about men and women wearing beads. Responses will vary, depending on whether the beginning grabs students' attention. Students should support their answers.
2. See the side glosses for steps. Steps 5, 6, and 7 give the different instructions for making flat or round beads.

SELECTION AMENDMENT
Description of change: wording changed and excerpted
Rationale: to focus on the concept of process writing presented in this chapter

in the process, stress the positive points of the students' writing.

ASSESSMENT

Before students begin evaluating, check their drafts to be sure each has a clear pattern of organization and that the steps are in chronological order.

3. Some students will want all of the materials listed beforehand so that they won't have to stop to look for a particular ingredient. Others may scan the steps and gather their materials before beginning the project.
4. The steps are in chronological order. Students who suggest rearranging the steps should show how their changes would improve the paper.
5. One possible conclusion is to give an idea for how to use the finished beads.

3. The writer doesn't list all materials before giving the steps. Do you think she should have? Explain.
4. Are the steps in chronological order? Would you change the order of any information to make the process easier to follow? If so, what and why?
5. Because this chapter goes on, the model does not have a conclusion. Make up one or two sentences that give the passage a good ending.

Following a Basic Framework for a "How-to" Paper

The explanation you've just read about making beads is part of a whole book about African crafts, so it isn't exactly like the paper you'll write. Your readers will want to know right away what materials they will need, and they may need more explanation of steps—not just a recipe approach. The following writer's model is an example of the kind of paper you'll write.

A WRITER'S MODEL

INTRODUCTION
Attention grabber
Reasons for learning process

Magic tricks are fun to do. This one will wake up anyone in your audience who's decided to take a little nap. It's sure to surprise your friends. To make sure it doesn't surprise you, practice before you do it for a real audience.

BODY
List of materials

Helpful hints

You need to buy three or four balloons that are ordinary in color and one balloon that's an unusual color. Pink, blue, or yellow will do for the ordinary balloons. Try to get purple or black for the unusual one—your magic balloon. You also need a roll of tape, two or three long pins, and a pair of scissors. (Be sure that you get see-through tape.)

Step 1

Before you do the trick for your audience, you have to prepare. First, blow up the balloons. Next,

RETEACHING

Ascertain from students' writing what they need more help understanding. Bring cookbooks or manuals from home and ask students to look at the instructions. With your students, analyze the methods the directions use. Explain to students that they can incorporate any ideas from the instructions that will help their writing.

CLOSURE

Ask students to share what has been difficult for them in the writing process. Next, have students share what they have found to be easiest about the process. List both types of responses on the chalkboard. Later, you could use the lists as a springboard for discussing individual learning styles and writing strategies. ■

Writing Your First Draft   **229**

Step 2
Explanation

Helpful hint

Step 3
Explanation

Step 4

Helpful hint
Step 5
Explanation
CONCLUSION
Final hints

cut two one-inch pieces of tape and stick them on the "magic" balloon. It's important that both pieces be on one side of the balloon, so that you can turn that side <u>away from</u> the audience. Also make sure the tape is perfectly smooth.

Now you're ready to show your trick. Ask volunteers from the audience to pop the ordinary balloons. Give each volunteer a pin and cover your ears for the big bang. Then, tell the audience you have a magic balloon. Say some "magic" words like "Fiddle-faddle, Ballooney-baloney" while you carefully stick a pin through the center of each tape. The tape keeps the "magic" balloon from popping.

After you've amazed your friends, you might want to show them how it's done. Otherwise, keep this trick a secret and add it to other tricks you can do.

CRITICAL THINKING
Synthesis

Ask students to choose poems from their literature textbooks and to imagine that as the poets, they must explain how the works were written. Encourage students to explain the purpose and audience of their poems and to describe the experiences of writing the poems.

A DIFFERENT APPROACH

You may want to work with the class to create a list of transitional words that students can use as a reference when drafting their process papers. Some words to include in the list are *first, second, next, after,* and *finally.*

WRITING NOTE
You may want to add drawings or diagrams to your paper. Pictures often help explain a process. A diagram showing foot patterns, for instance, might help you tell how to do a Native American ceremonial dance. (Remember, in some cases one picture is worth a thousand words.)

A DIFFERENT APPROACH

Another possible structure students could use to follow as they write is one that integrates materials with steps. Here is one possibility:

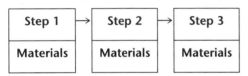

It's often helpful to have a pattern to follow when you write. You may want to model your "how-to" paper on the one you've just read about the magic trick. Here is the framework it follows:

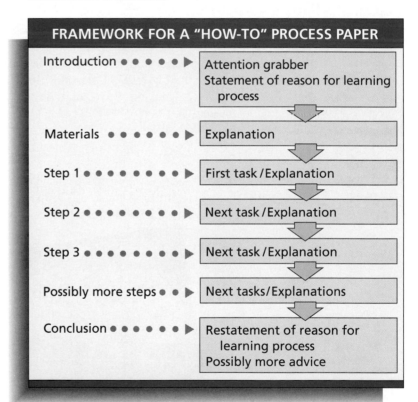

FRAMEWORK FOR A "HOW-TO" PROCESS PAPER

Introduction • • • • • ▶	Attention grabber Statement of reason for learning process
Materials • • • • • • ▶	Explanation
Step 1 • • • • • • • • ▶	First task / Explanation
Step 2 • • • • • • • • ▶	Next task / Explanation
Step 3 • • • • • • • • ▶	Next task / Explanation
Possibly more steps • • ▶	Next tasks / Explanations
Conclusion • • • • • • ▶	Restatement of reason for learning process Possibly more advice

WRITING ASSIGNMENT

PART 3:
Writing Your First Draft

Now you're ready to put your process on paper from beginning to end. Be sure to use the chart of steps and materials you created in Writing Assignment, Part 2 (page 224). Whenever you have a question about what to do, look back at the basic framework above.

EVALUATING AND REVISING

OBJECTIVES

- To distinguish between important and unnecessary information in a process paper
- To evaluate and revise a process essay

MOTIVATION

Ask students if they have ever tried to follow a cookie recipe and ended up with cookies that weren't very good. Were the instructions hard to follow? Did they ever get confused about what the author meant? Tell students that a poorly organized essay is like a bad recipe—it keeps the reader from achieving the goal. Explain that this is why

Evaluating and Revising

Don't be surprised when you find rough spots in your first draft. After all, *rough draft* is just another name for *first draft*!

For a "how-to" paper, evaluating with a partner is a big help. You know how to do your process, but someone who *doesn't* can see more quickly what's missing or confused. First, use Exercise 5 as a "test run" of your "how-to" paper with a partner.

Then, you can use the chart on the next page to take a closer look at your paper, find problems, and fix them. If your honest answer to a question in the left-hand column is *no*, use the revision technique in the right-hand column.

EXERCISE 5 **Speaking and Listening: Explaining and Following a Process** Be available to help students who have difficulty following the assignment.

Now you're going to read your draft out loud while a partner "acts out" the process. You'll need some imagination, but you have plenty—and this is a good test! First, read out your list of materials. Have your partner write each of the materials on a slip of paper. Then, read out the steps. Have your partner "use" the slips while pretending to do each step. Your partner can stop you and ask questions whenever something isn't clear. And *you* can call "Wait!" if there's a big mess. Make notes about problems right on your draft. Then, change roles.

"Oh, wait! Wait, Cory! ... Add the cereal *first* and *then* the milk!"

RESOURCES

EVALUATING AND REVISING

- Writing a "How-to" Paper

QUOTATION FOR THE DAY

"Don't think about style. Instead, think about writing clearly and simply and saying what you want to say as strongly as you can." (Bill Stout, professor of English, the University of Texas)

Copy this quotation on the chalkboard and ask students to discuss what they think style is. Lead students to understand that in revising they should, as Stout says, focus on making their writing clear.

MEETING INDIVIDUAL NEEDS

LEP/ESL

General Strategies. If they are unfamiliar with English grammar, some students might concentrate on having correct grammar in their sentences at the expense of giving adequate attention to content. However, other students might focus only on content and give insufficient attention to grammar. You could quickly glance at each student's draft and guide students to work on the necessary areas.

they need to evaluate their process essays and revise any weak spots.

TEACHING THE LESSON

The first part of the lesson is designed to show students how important it is to be specific. You may want to provide students with examples of how missing details can change the results of a process paper.

Remind students that they do not need to proofread at this stage, and then

LESS-ADVANCED STUDENTS

Students might have difficulty finding weaknesses in their drafts and in the drafts of other students, especially if they already know how to perform the tasks being explained. You may need to work closely with students to help them see the importance of chronological order and the problems of having even one step that is out of place.

EVALUATING AND REVISING PROCESS ESSAYS

	EVALUATION GUIDE	REVISION TECHNIQUE
1	Does the introduction grab the reader's attention and give reasons for learning the process?	**Add** interesting details to the beginning. **Add** a sentence that gives a reason for learning the process.
2	Does the paper list the materials before explaining the first step?	**Add** a list of all the materials needed before giving the first step.
3	Are the steps in chronological order? Are all the details necessary to explain the process?	**Reorder** the steps to put them in the order they must be done. **Cut** unnecessary details. **Add** any necessary details.
4	Do transitions help the reader follow the steps?	**Add** words like *first*, *then*, *before*, and *after*.
5	Does the paper end with a clear conclusion?	**Add** a sentence or two that restates the reason for learning the process or gives another reason. Offer a last hint.

As you evaluate and revise your "how-to" paper

- use specific words so your readers won't become confused by vague language
- vary sentence beginnings to keep your readers interested
- ask yourself if any part of your paper sounds complicated

discuss the differences between proofreading and editing. Make sure students understand that the revision stage is the time to make sure their ideas are clear and organized. A possible focus for stylistic revision is the **Usage Hint** on this page.

Show students a rough draft of a sample essay, such as "How to Plan a Lesson" from the **Guided Practice** of the prewriting segment. Discuss and model the changes that you would make in the sample essay.

Assign **Exercises 5** and **6** as independent practice. Then have students share their answers in a class discussion or in small groups.

USAGE HINT

Using Specific Adjectives and Nouns

It's especially important to use specific, exact adjectives and nouns in "how-to" papers. Specific adjectives and nouns answer the questions "How many?" or "What kind?" or "How much?" These kinds of words will make your paper more accurate and precise.

EXAMPLES   *Vague Adjectives and Nouns*:
Heat **some** salt in a **container**.

Specific Adjectives and Nouns:
Heat **3/4 cup** of **fine** salt in a **dry pan**.

👉 REFERENCE NOTE: For more information on specific adjectives and nouns, see pages 434–437 and 423–426.

EXERCISE 6 ▶   **Analyzing a Writer's Revisions**

Here's the way the writer revised the third paragraph in the model on pages 228–229. Study the changes. Then answer the questions that follow the paragraph.

Before you do the trick for your
audience, you have to prepare. ~~Your a~~   **cut**
~~audience may be made up of friends,~~
~~relatives, or neighbors.~~ (*Next*) Cut two (*one-inch*) pieces of   **add**
tape and stick them on the "magic"
balloon. But first blow up the balloons. It's   **reorder/cut/add**
important that both pieces be on one side
∧ *so that you can turn that side away from the audience*
of the balloon. Also make sure the tape is   **add**
perfectly smooth.

COOPERATIVE LEARNING
After students have completed **Exercise 5** and are familiar with the problems in their papers, they might create instructions that can be taken apart and put back together. Have students work in groups of three or four to create lists of instructions for making a product or completing a task. Then have students cut these instructions into strips and give the strips to another group. The second group should then work to put the instructions back in order.

You may want each student to revise one paragraph in class. Circulate through the room to monitor students' progress on all of this segment's assignments. This process should help you to assess the quality and quantity of changes and of suggestions that students make.

Have students answer the following questions about their essays:

1. Is my essay interesting to read?
2. Could I make this item or perform this task if I were a reader?
3. What could I do to improve my essay? ■

ANSWERS

Exercise 6

1. The writer deleted the second sentence because it had nothing to do with the process.

2. The sentence about blowing up the balloon was moved because it is the first step in the directions.

3. *Next* is used to indicate a new step. *One-inch* is a specific instruction telling how much tape to use.

4. It explains why the tape needs to be on one side of the balloon, and it also gives a hint that helps the reader successfully achieve the intended effect.

234   *Writing to Inform*

1. Why did the writer cut the second sentence?
2. What is the reason for moving the sentence about blowing up the balloons?
3. In the third sentence, why are *Next* and *one-inch* good additions?
4. How does the addition in the next-to-last sentence make the directions clearer for the reader?

 PART 4:
Evaluating and Revising Your Paper

Now it's time to use the chart on page 232 to evaluate and revise your paper. You can use it for a peer evaluation first. Then you can evaluate your own paper. When you're ready to make changes, look at what other students say about your paper. Which suggestions will you take? It's your paper, so the decision is up to you.

PEANUTS reprinted by permission of UFS, Inc.

PROOFREADING AND PUBLISHING

OBJECTIVE

- To use proofreading strategies to prepare a process essay for publication

TEACHING THE LESSON

You may choose to have students focus on one or two specific problem areas in grammar, usage, and mechanics, such as common errors students have made on the last papers they wrote.

For closure, have students discuss why proofreading is important to writing. ■

Proofreading and Publishing

Proofreading.   Every detail is important in a "how-to" paper. That's why you need to proofread carefully. Some mistakes, like writing "pain" instead of "pin" may just puzzle readers and make them laugh. But other proofreading errors can cause trouble. If you're telling how to make beads and write "1/4 cup salt" instead of "3/4 cup salt," your readers won't end up with beads. One last check can help you catch this kind of mistake.

Publishing.   Who was the audience you had in mind when you wrote your paper? Now you need to find a way to reach those readers. Here are three ways:

- Work with several classmates to produce a calendar. For each month, feature one "how-to" paper. Each paper might relate in some way to the weather or holidays in that month. Classmates who like to draw could do a diagram or picture to go with each process.
- If your paper is about a craft, give a copy to a store that sells craft supplies. The store could post your paper for its customers to read.
- Stage a class demonstration day. Some of your classmates can demonstrate how to do the processes they wrote about. Other classmates can pick a topic that sounds interesting and can follow the "how-to" paper's directions to do the process.

WRITING ASSIGNMENT

PART 5:
Proofreading and Publishing Your Paper

Proofread your "how-to" paper. Then, correct any mistakes you find in it. When your paper is as good as you can make it, find a way to share it. You may use one of the suggestions above or one of your own.

RESOURCES

PROOFREADING AND PUBLISHING
- Writing a "How-to" Paper

QUOTATION FOR THE DAY

"Sloppily prepared pieces, peppered with mechanical glitches that could easily have been caught and corrected by the writer, are rarely going to sell—and the few that do are bound to be heavily edited." (David Peterson, American author and editor)

Write this quotation on the chalkboard and ask students to discuss why they think writing with good content but with poor grammatical form might not sell.

MEETING **INDIVIDUAL** NEEDS

LEP/ESL

General Strategies. Many students do not recognize errors in English because the usage would not be incorrect in their native tongues. These differences result from the students' reliance on their native languages while still learning how to use English. Ask students how to express given ideas in their native languages. This practice will help you understand their errors better, and they might appreciate your interest.

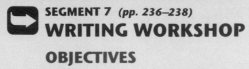
TEACHING THE LESSON

Begin by talking about cause and effect. Discuss some effects that students deal with on a daily basis and ask students to identify the causes of these effects. Bring in some newspaper articles that discuss current events and their effects. For example, you could bring articles about legislation currently being debated and discuss the possi-

RESOURCES

WRITING WORKSHOP
- Listing Steps and Materials
- Writing Your Introduction
- Writing a "How-to" Paper

QUOTATION FOR THE DAY

"Shallow men believe in luck. . . . Strong men believe in cause and effect." (Ralph Waldo Emerson, 1803–1882, American poet, essayist, and philosopher)

Ask students if they believe in luck. Do things happen randomly, or is there a cause for every situation? Have volunteers explain what they think Emerson means by his statement.

MEETING INDIVIDUAL NEEDS

LEP/ESL

Korean, Japanese, and Turkish. English grammar has variable orders for causes and effects, but in Korean and Japanese the order is cause-because-effect, and the order is effect-because-cause in Turkish. You may wish to have students practice with cause-and-effect sentences and then have them work with cause-and-effect relationships from the textbook.

236

WRITING WORKSHOP

The Cause-and-Effect Paper

The "how-to" paper you just wrote gives information. It answers the question *How do you do that?* Another kind of paper that informs is a cause-and-effect paper. It answers the question *Why does that happen?* or *What is the result?* When you write a cause-and-effect paper, you start with an event or situation. Then you explain the causes for it (*Why?*) or its effects (*What's the result?*).

Here's an example. Teenagers often have messy rooms. You could explore the causes of this situation: Teenagers are too busy to keep their rooms looking neat. Or, you could write about the effects of teenagers' messy rooms: Homework—and many other things—get lost forever in them.

Causes and effects are sometimes obvious. But usually you do some thinking—exploring—to discover them. In this passage, astronaut Sally Ride writes about the effects of weightlessness that she discovered in space. Would you have guessed that these effects would happen?

Weightless in Space
by Sally Ride with Susan Okie

The best part of being in space is being weightless. It feels wonderful to be able to float without effort; to slither up, down, and around the inside of the shuttle just like a seal; to be upside down as often as I'm right side up and have it make no difference. On Earth being upside down feels different because gravity is pulling the blood toward my head. In space I feel exactly the same whether my head is toward the floor or toward the ceiling.

When I'm weightless, some things don't change. My heart beats at about the same rate as it does on Earth. I can still

ble effects that this legislation would have if it were passed. If students are not ready for this type of discussion, you could talk about the purposes of school rules and the effects on the students and the school when those rules are broken.

Have the class work together to explore possible topics for cause-and-effect papers. After students have selected topics, have them follow the suggestions in the textbook to complete the writing process. Check the rough drafts for clear statements of the causes and specific examples of the effects.

swallow and digest food. My eyes, ears, nose, and taste buds work fine; I see, hear, smell, and taste things just as I do at home.

I *look* a little different, though—all astronauts do. Since the fluid in our bodies is not pulled toward our feet as it is on Earth, more of this fluid stays in our faces and upper bodies. This makes our faces a little fatter and gives us puffy-looking cheeks. We are also about an inch taller while in orbit because in weightlessness our spines are not compressed. Unfortunately (for me, anyway), we shrink back to normal height when we return to Earth. . . .

In weightlessness the slightest touch can start an astronaut's body floating across the room or drifting over in a slow-motion somersault. The only way to stop moving is to take hold of something that's anchored in place. . . .

Some astronauts are uncomfortable while their bodies are adjusting to weightlessness. Almost half of all shuttle crew members are sick for the first day or two. . . .

By the third day of a week-long shuttle flight, though, all the astronauts are feeling fine. Weightlessness is pure fun, once everyone gets the hang of it.

from *To Space & Back*

LESS-ADVANCED STUDENTS

To help students understand the relationships in a cause-and-effect essay, illustrate the possible relationships on the chalkboard. Here are some possibilities:

1.
```
CAUSE
         EFFECT
CAUSE
```

2.
```
            EFFECT
CAUSE
            EFFECT
```

3.
```
CAUSE  EFFECT  EFFECT  EFFECT
      NEW CAUSE   NEW CAUSE
```

LEARNING STYLES

Kinetic Learners. Have students work with note cards to study causes and effects. Have each student write the cause he or she has chosen on one note card and each of the effects of that cause on separate cards. Suggest that students arrange the cards in the order that best shows the relationships.

SELECTION AMENDMENT
Description of change: excerpted and title changed
Rationale: to focus on the concept of cause and effect presented in this chapter

CLOSURE
Have students identify differences and similarities between cause-and-effect papers and process papers. Write these differences on the chalkboard for students.

EXTENSION
Have students keep lists of cause-and-effect relationships that they see and experience at school. Have students compare lists after a predetermined period of time. ■

238

ANSWERS
Thinking It Over

1. The three effects of weightlessness are being able to float, to slither like a seal, and to be upside down.

2. No gravity is pulling blood toward the head, so being upside down feels the same as being right side up. Because more fluid stays in the upper body, people in space have puffy-looking cheeks. The spine is not compressed by gravity, so astronauts are about an inch taller in orbit.

3. Students might like the idea of floating, having effortless motion, or being taller.

⚡ TIMESAVER
Tell students to circle the causes and to underline the effects in their essays. Their marks will give you the opportunity to glance quickly at the papers to see if students understand cause-and-effect relationships.

Thinking It Over

1. What three effects of weightlessness does Sally Ride mention in the first paragraph?
2. Ride doesn't just list effects. She also explains them for readers. Find details that explain these effects: feeling the same whether upside down or right side up, the changed look of astronauts' faces, and being taller.
3. If you were in orbit, which effect would you like best?

Writing a Cause-and-Effect Paper

 Prewriting. Like Sally Ride, you will write about effects in this paper. So think about something that makes you want to ask *What's the result of that?* Use one of the following ideas or think of one of your own. Just choose a situation you really want to explore, and then brainstorm all the effects you can.

- the effects of being an only child
- the effects of having a disability
- the effects of a hurricane on your town
- the effects of a school volunteer project

 Writing, Evaluating, and Revising. Briefly describe the event or situation in your introduction. A good way to organize your effects is from most important to least important, or the reverse. To tell about effects that happened over a period of time, you may use chronological order. When you evaluate and revise, make sure you have explained your effects with details (as Sally Ride did).

 Proofreading and Publishing. Before you share your paper, check your capitalization, spelling, and punctuation. Think about these possible audiences for your cause-and-effect essay: your family, an older friend, and the school or local newspaper.

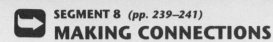
PROCESS ACROSS THE CURRICULUM OBJECTIVE

• To analyze and write a riddle that involves a process

239

MAKING CONNECTIONS

PROCESS ACROSS THE CURRICULUM

Folk Tales, Riddles, and Brainteasers

Here's a brainteaser in the form of an old folk tale. It's about a crow who has an idea for a process that will let him get a drink of water. Exactly what does the crow do? Can you figure out his process?

A Drink for Crow
told by George Shannon

Once there was a crow who had grown so thirsty he could barely caw. He flew down to a big pitcher where he had gotten a drink of water the day before, but there was only a little bit of water remaining at the bottom. He tried and tried to reach it with his beak, but the pitcher was too deep and his beak was too short. But just as he was about to give up, he knew what to do. He flew back and forth from the garden to the pitcher until he was able to drink easily from the pitcher while sitting on its edge.

What did the crow do?

Answer: The crow dropped the pebbles in the pitcher, and the water level rose.

PROCESS ACROSS THE CURRICULUM
Teaching Strategies

Allow students time to figure out the process in **"A Drink for Crow."** You may want to include other brainteasers as examples and to spend time working through them with the class. Discuss with they why this riddle is also a process paper. After they write their own riddles or brainteasers, have students share their work with the class.

GUIDELINES

Each student's riddle should include a process. You may want to suggest that students illustrate their riddles.

SELECTION AMENDMENT
Description of change: excerpted
Rationale: to focus on the concept of process writing presented in this chapter

SPEAKING AND LISTENING
OBJECTIVE
• To create a treasure map that includes
directions to the treasure

240

Make up or find other riddles or brainteasers that involve figuring out a process. (Remember *What am I?* riddles? They sometimes describe a process.) Ask your parents and relatives, too. They may know other folk-tale riddles. Then try to stump your classmates.

SPEAKING AND LISTENING

Teaching Strategies

This activity lends itself to cooperative learning by allowing students to work together to develop maps. Creative students are also given an opportunity to develop unusual maps.

Remind students that their maps are effective only if they give clear directions for finding the treasure. After the maps have been used, talk about the elements of good listening. Discuss the difference between good listeners and good communicators.

SPEAKING AND LISTENING

Process in Social Studies: Mapping and Directions

Giving clear directions is important. Here's a way to practice this skill by making a treasure map.

First, you need to decide what you're going to use for your "treasure." The value of the treasure doesn't matter, because the fun comes from looking for it. Your treasure can be anything small that's easily hidden. It could be a plastic figure or a key ring. Hide the treasure somewhere in your neighborhood.

Next, draw a map of the neighborhood. You can put real names of things on your map (pine tree, garbage cans, Fourth Street). Or you can pretend that the neighborhood is an imaginary place. Then you'd give imaginary names to real things. The pine tree might become "Giant's Tower," the garbage cans "Smelly Swamp," and Fourth Street, "Dragon's Lair." Use an arrow to mark a starting point. Use an *X* to mark the spot where the treasure is. Then, figure out five or six directions that would lead someone to the treasure and write them down.

Give your map to a friend who's going to hunt for the treasure. Then, go together to the starting point. Read your first direction—for instance, "Walk straight ahead to Smelly Swamp, turn left, and stop at the blinking light." Then, give the next direction. Read each one *only once*. (You can try to trick your friend a little, but make the directions accurate.) When your friend finds the treasure (or gets lost), talk about what was good and bad about the map. It might be the directions or your friend's listening powers.

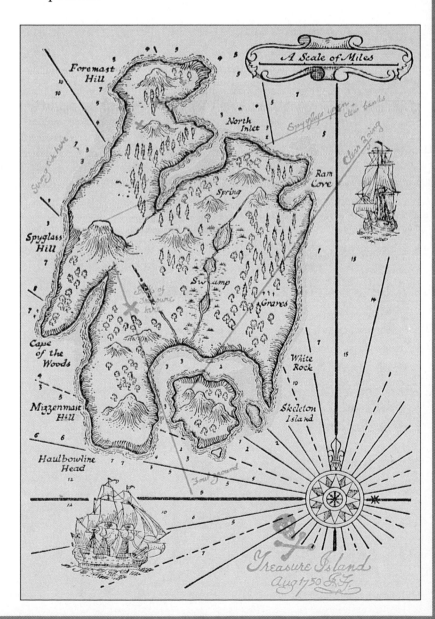

GUIDELINES

You may want to evaluate this activity on two different aspects — the clarity of the instructions and the students' performances as listeners and communicators. Have the class decide on the criteria for giving instructions and listening for information. Here are some possibilities:

1. Giving instructions
   a. State the purpose.
   b. Give complete instructions in order.
   c. Use transition words such as *first, second,* and *last.*

2. Following instructions
   a. Keep the speaker's intent in mind.
   b. Try to remember only key points.
   c. Listen for key points and watch for gestures.

Chapter 8
WRITING TO PERSUADE

Motivation

To motivate students for persuasive writing, begin by discussing how persuasive writing affects their everyday lives. For example, ask students the following questions and discuss responses with the class:

1. Think about the last product you bought because of an advertisement. What attracted you to the product?

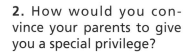

2. How would you convince your parents to give you a special privilege?

3. How do politicians turn voters against their opponents?

Point out to students that they use persuasive techniques every day.

Introduction

As students share their experiences, help them understand that convincing people is not an easy task. To persuade others to agree with an opinion, a person needs strong arguments that listeners will accept. The arguments must be carefully planned and clearly communicated. Convincing others often involves appealing to their emotions.

Integration

To show students how persuasion is employed across the curriculum, explain that famous political speeches by past and present presidents are persuasive. Also, individuals in the past have had to persuade people to believe in their inventions and discoveries. Some of these people include Albert Einstein, George Washington Carver, Galileo, and Alexander Graham Bell. You may want to ask students to research what these people contributed to their fields and to explain the obstacles they had to overcome to convince others they had worthwhile ideas or products.

Students will learn about common mistakes in logic and reasoning in **Critical Thinking: Evaluating Reason,** p. 254. Students can apply these thinking skills to economics.

The chart on the next page illustrates the strands of language arts as they are integrated into this chapter. For vocabulary study, glossary words are underlined in some writing models.

INTEGRATING THE LANGUAGE ARTS

Selection	Reading and Literature	Writing and Critical Thinking	Language and Syntax	Speaking, Listening, and Other Expression Skills
National Dairy Board advertisement **244** **"One Day a Month, Go Without Meat"** by Marjorie Lamb **257-259**	Distinguishing fact from opinion **249, 259** Recognizing how advertisers can manipulate language for specific purposes **245, 269, 272** Identifying the audience for an advertisement **245** Analyzing opening sentence **257, 259** Identifying how emotional language is used **254, 256-259, 264** Examining supporting reasons and details in an essay **256-259, 264** Identifying common persuasive techniques in writing **245, 255, 259, 269, 272** Examining supporting details **245, 256-259** Analyzing the intent of persuasive writing **245** Examining persuasion in a letter to the editor **272-273**	Brainstorming vivid words **245** Choosing an issue to write about **250, 273** Evaluating persuasive statements **245, 256-259, 265, 269, 272** Using facts and reasons to support opinions **255, 259, 273** Using a thesis statement and a chart of supporting information to write a draft for a persuasive essay **255, 261** Evaluating and revising a persuasive essay **262, 265** Analyzing a writer's revisions **264** Publishing a persuasive essay **266** Writing and publishing an advertisement by using persuasive-writing techniques **270** Writing a letter to an editor **273**	Identifying and using the comparative forms of adjectives **265**	Responding to an argument **262** Comparing persuasion in different forms **272**

SEGMENT PLANNING GUIDE

Whether you are planning for a quick review of a writing concept or preparing an extended lesson on composition you can use the following Planning Guide to adapt the chapter material to the individual needs of your class.

SEGMENT	PAGES	CONTENT	RESOURCES
1 Taking a Stand	243-245		
Advertising Model	244	Guided reading: evaluating an advertisement	
Reader's Response/ Writer's Craft	245	Model evaluation: responding to an ad and analyzing persuasive writing	
2 Ways to Persuade	246		
3 Prewriting	247-255		Writing a Persuasive Paper
Choosing a Topic	247	Introduction: expressing an opinion on an issue	Interviewing to Gather Information
Find an Issue That Matters	247	Guidelines: choosing an appropriate issue	
Identifying Your Opinion	248	Guidelines: writing a statement of opinion	
Exercise 1	249	Cooperative learning: distinguishing fact from opinion	
Exercise 2	250	Cooperative learning: exploring possible topics	
Writing Assignment: Part 1	250	Applied practice: choosing an issue and writing a thesis statement	
Planning Your Paper	251	Introduction: planning a persuasive paper	
Thinking About Purpose and Audience	251	Guidelines: focusing on readers	
Supporting Your Opinion	252	Guidelines: finding information and using emotional appeals	
Finding Information to Support Your Opinion	252	Guidelines: finding reasons, facts, or opinions	
Using Emotional Appeals	253	Guidelines: creating emotions in an audience	
Critical Thinking: Evaluating Reasoning	254	Explanation: evaluating reasoning	
Chart: Statements Masquerading as Reasons	254	Guidelines: explaining persuasive methods	
Critical Thinking Exercise	255	Cooperative learning: evaluating persuasive statements	
Writing Assignment: Part 2	255	Applied practice: charting support	
4 Writing	256-261		Writing the Body Paragraph
Combining the Elements	256	Explanation: using basic persuasive elements	
A Good Beginning	256	Guidelines: getting a reader's attention	
Clearly Organized Support	256	Guidelines: using order of importance	
A Good Ending	256	Guidelines: writing the punch line	

SEGMENT	PAGES	CONTENT	RESOURCES
Literary Model from **"One Day a Month Without Meat"**	257-259	Guided reading: examining a model of persuasive writing	
Exercise 3	259	Cooperative learning: analyzing persuasive writing	
Using a Basic Framework	259	Introduction: examining framework in a model	
Writer's Model	260	Guided reading: examining a sample essay	
Chart: Framework for Persuasive Writing	261	Guidelines: structuring a persuasive essay	
Writing Assignment: Part 3	261	Applied practice: writing a first draft	
5 *Evaluating and Revising*	*262-265*		Writing a Persuasive Paper
Evaluating and Revising	262	Guidelines: rehearsing a paper	
Exercise 4	21	Cooperative learning: responding to an argument	
Chart: Evaluating and Revising Persuasive Writing	263	Guidelines: applying evaluation and revision techniques	
Exercise 5	264	Applied practice: analyzing a writer's revisions	
Grammar Hint	265	Writing suggestion: using comparatives	
Writing Assignment: Part 4	265	Cooperative learning: evaluating and revising	
6 *Proofreading and Publishing*	*266-267*		Writing a Persuasive Paper
Publishing	266	Publishing ideas: reaching an audience	
Writing Assignment: Part 5	266	Applied practice: proofreading and publishing	
Student Model	267	Sample: analyzing effectiveness of persuasion	
7 *Writing Workshop*	*268-270*		All the resources in this chapter may be used in this segment.
A Newspaper or Magazine Ad	268-269	Applied practice: examining advertising techniques	
Writing an Ad	270	Applied practice: applying skills to the writing process	
8 *Making Connections*	*271-273*		
Speaking and Listening: Comparing Persuasion in Different Forms	271-272	Guidelines: using criteria to evaluate an ad Cooperative learning: comparing ads in different forms	
Persuasion in Action: Letters to the Editor	272-273	Guidelines: writing a letter to the editor Applied practice: writing a letter to the editor	
Writer's Model	272-273	Sample: examining persuasion in a model	

WHOLE-CHAPTER RESOURCES
A Writing Process Log, A Writing Prompt, Holistically Graded Models, Assessment Portfolio Materials

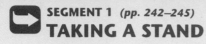

SEGMENT 1 *(pp. 242–245)*
TAKING A STAND
OBJECTIVES
- To analyze a persuasive argument in the form of an advertisement
- To write a journal entry based on an advertisement
- To create an ad slogan using persuasion

MOTIVATION
You may want to focus on how persuasion affects the lives of students. For example, ask students to list at least two things they have attempted to convince their parents to let them do in the last week.

VISUAL CONNECTIONS
Exploring the Subject. In ancient Greece, the Olympics honored Zeus, king of the Greek gods, for over eight hundred years. After the Roman Empire conquered Greece, the games lost their religious meaning and declined in quality until they were finally discontinued. Later, the stadium where the Olympics were held was buried under a landslide, and the games were mostly forgotten until the ruins were discovered in 1875.

A French teacher, Baron Pierre de Coubertin, hearing about the find and feeling that a modern Olympic games would promote world peace, presented his ideas to the international amateur sports community. The International Olympic Committee was formed in 1894, and the first modern Olympic games were held in Athens, Greece, in 1896.

Related Expression Skills. Posters like this one have been effective persuasive tools throughout American history. Discuss with students the elements of this poster, and have them work individually or in groups to create persuasive posters that follow the model of this illustration.

8 WRITING TO PERSUADE

SUPPORT the U.S.

To present this lesson, post a copy of the ad on p. 244 before students arrive. After you have introduced persuasion by following the steps in **Motivation,** have a volunteer read the introduction. Then discuss the persuasiveness of the advertisement by addressing such elements as the picture, word choice, and color. Discuss the importance of audience so that students understand that an advertiser usually has a specific audience in mind when creating an advertisement. Explain that advertisers may have several advertisements for the same product, but will aim each ad at a different audience.

To guide students through the first sample of persuasive writing, discuss **Reader's Response** questions 1 and 2 and

Taking a Stand

When John Parker's Minutemen stood facing the advancing British troops at Lexington in 1775, Parker said, "Stand your ground." And they did. It's often important to **take a stand**—to have a belief you're willing to argue and defend. Doing so won't usually result in a revolution. But you may be able to persuade others that you're right.

Writing and You. Persuasion comes into every part of your life. You might try to talk your classmates into having a class picnic. You might write a speech persuading others how to vote in a school election. You might convince your big brother to lend you his radical shirt. Have you tried to persuade someone lately? Did it work?

As You Read. Advertisers often try to persuade us. Look at the ad on the next page. What is its purpose? Who is it trying to convince? Why?

QUOTATION FOR THE DAY

"Promise, large promise, is the soul of an advertisement." (Samuel Johnson, 1709–1784, British writer)

Write the quotation on the chalkboard and ask students to freewrite for a few minutes about advertisements they remember. Ask students to write about what the ads promised and whether those promises persuaded the readers to buy the products.

LEP/ESL

General Strategies. Some students could find the ADA advertisement difficult to read because they might not understand the puns involved in *need a bunch* and *slip-ups*. You may wish to explain briefly what puns are, give some examples, and point out the humor in them.

Students can answer **Reader's Response** question 3 and **Writer's Craft** questions 6 and 7 as independent practice. These questions check students' understanding of several elements of the persuasive aim.

To assess students' mastery, read through responses to **Writer's Craft** questions 6 and 7 and evaluate the journal writing. You could also discuss responses in class to check for students' comprehension.

MEETING INDIVIDUAL NEEDS

AT-RISK STUDENTS

If students do not have access to television, radio, or other sources where persuasive writing is used, they might have difficulty with **Reader's Response** and **Writer's Craft**. To help them overcome this problem, bring magazines and newspapers to class and allow students to browse through the advertisements. Or, you could let students look for examples of persuasion in the periodical section of the school library.

ADVANCED STUDENTS

Students might work in groups of three or four to evaluate ads for competitive products to determine which ad is more persuasive. For example, they might examine magazine or newspaper advertisements for two different brands of popcorn, laundry detergent, toothpaste, dog food, or fruit juice. Ask students to list reasons why a particular advertisement is more persuasive than a competitor's advertisement.

244

When your potassium comes with dairy calcium, you don't need a bunch.

An 8-ounce glass of milk has about as much potassium as the average banana. And an 8-ounce cup of yogurt has even more. Dairy foods can be an excellent source of potassium. And many other essential nutrients as well. Including, of course, calcium.

Milk and yogurt, like all dairy foods, also come in a variety of lower fat alternatives. So build your family's diet on a firm foundation of dairy foods. It's the perfect way to avoid nutritional slip-ups.

© 1990 N.D.B.
National Dairy Board
America's Dairy Farmers

Dairy Foods. The Basics of Good Nutrition.

CLOSURE

To close this segment, have students discuss the following questions as a class:

1. Why should a person be aware of audience in persuasive writing? [One must use reasons that will appeal to a specific audience if he or she wants to convince that audience.]

2. Name at least three places to find persuasive writing [radio, television, newspapers, and billboards].

3. Describe the persuasive aim. [The persuasive aim attempts to influence a reader's opinion or to convince the reader to do something.] ■

READER'S RESPONSE

1. Does this ad persuade you that milk and other dairy foods are "the perfect way to avoid nutritional slip-ups"? Why or why not?

2. Which part of the ad did you look at first? What part of the ad do you find the most convincing? Why?

3. What's your favorite food? Is it as good as ads for it say it is? In your journal, brainstorm some vivid words to describe it. Create your own ad slogan; for instance, "Scrumptious Smithers' soup—steaming, zesty, robust."

WRITER'S CRAFT

4. Who is the audience for the ad for dairy foods? How can you tell? What kind of magazine do you think it appeared in?

5. What advantages does the ad writer claim for milk and other dairy products?

6. Milk has many nutrients, not just potassium. Why would the Dairy Board compare milk with bananas? [Hint: Have you seen any banana ads?]

7. What does the ad try to get the reader to do?

"Advertising is what you do when you can't go see somebody. That's all it is."

Fairfax Cone

ANSWERS

Reader's Response

Answers to questions 1–3 will vary. Students should support their opinions with sound reasons.

Writer's Craft

4. The audience is parents (probably mothers in particular), because of the words "So build your family's diet on a firm foundation " Possibly it appeared in a women's magazine or in a magazine specifically for parents.

5. Dairy products are excellent sources of nutrients, in particular potassium, and they are low in fat.

6. Advertisements for bananas emphasize how high they are in potassium and how good potassium is for one's heart.

7. The ad tries to get the reader to buy dairy products.

WAYS TO PERSUADE

TEACHING THE MODES
Explain that the modes are the strategies used to achieve a writer's aim. Allow students to work in pairs to practice using each mode. Tell the groups they will have one minute each to speak using narration, description, classification, or evaluation in a persuasive aim. After each group speaks, ask the class to identify the mode used. ■

CRITICAL THINKING
Synthesis
To give students practice in using the modes for persuasion, ask each student to create an example of at least one mode for the class to identify. Students can use the suggestions in the text as models.

A DIFFERENT APPROACH
You may want to quiz students over what they have learned about persuasive modes. For example, ask students to identify which mode is being used in the following situations:

1. defining cooperation to convince your best friend to share a candy bar [classification]
2. deciding an autobiography of Babe Ruth is interesting and convincing your friends to read the book [evaluation]
3. describing your skateboard to a friend to convince the friend to buy it so you can buy a new one [description]
4. trying to convince your parents that the chores associated with owning a puppy will teach you responsibility [narration]

Ways to Persuade

Persuasive writing tries to convince you to *do* something or *believe* something. Advertising comes in many forms—radio, television, newspapers, and billboards. And there are many kinds of persuasion besides advertising—editorials, speeches, sermons, and even songs. Here are some forms that persuasion can take.

Narration: telling what happened to a homeless family to convince classmates they should volunteer at a shelter; trying to convince your parents that a trip to the lake will result in a better grade on your paper about turtles.

Description: describing your school's gymnasium to persuade the school board to buy new bleachers; describing your cat's new kittens to convince a friend to take one.

Classification: comparing two television shows to convince your brother that yours is more entertaining; defining *sacrifice* to convince your sister to loan you her new sweater.

▶ **Evaluation:**   deciding that a new local band is great and getting your friends to go hear them at the art festival; forming an opinion about safe bicycling and writing a letter to the editor, calling for adding bike lanes to streets.

LOOKING AHEAD

In the main assignment in this chapter, you'll be writing a persuasive paper. In your paper you will use the strategy of evaluation. As you work, keep in mind that an effective persuasive paper

- states the writer's opinion about the issue
- provides information to support the opinion
- may appeal to the reader's emotions

SEGMENT 3 *(pp. 247–255)*

PREWRITING

OBJECTIVES

- To distinguish between fact and opinion
- To brainstorm possible topics
- To write an opinion statement for persuasive writing
- To plan support for persuasive writing

MOTIVATION

Initiate a discussion of fact and opinion by asking students to complete the following statements:

1. My favorite food is ____.

2. The biggest city in this state is ____.

Ask students to explain the difference between the answers. [The first one can be

Prewriting **247**

Writing a Persuasive Paper

Choosing a Topic

You may not realize how often you use persuasion. Think about it. Have you ever tried to convince your parents to increase your allowance? Have you ever tried to get a friend to try out for a team? Have you ever tried to persuade someone to go to a movie with you? All these situations involve persuasion. And just think   the more persuasive you are, the better your chances of having things go your way.

In this chapter, you'll get to practice your powers of persuasion. You'll be writing about an *issue,* a topic or idea that people have different opinions about.

Finding an Issue That Matters. It's important to choose an issue that matters to you. It should also be one that people around you think is important. Why try to convince people of something that neither you nor they have any interest in? Look for things that are happening in your school or neighborhood that you feel strongly about. For example, is your school setting up a new

dress code you dislike? Should your community build a hockey rink? Does air pollution upset you? Is there too much violence in movies? Any one of these would be a good issue for persuasive writing. Just be sure it really matters to you.

RESOURCES

PREWRITING
- Interviewing to Gather Information

QUOTATION FOR THE DAY

"The act of writing is an act of optimism. You would not take the trouble to do it if you felt that it didn't matter." (Edward Albee, 1928– American playwright)

As students begin work on their persuasive papers, use the quotation to encourage students to select topics they feel strongly about.

MEETING INDIVIDUAL NEEDS

LEP/ESL

General Strategies. You may want to give a brief discussion of the tradition of taking a stand in the United States so that ESL students can see that this form of expression is permitted in this country. Individual freedom and standing up for what one believes even in the face of societal and familial opposition are traditional values in American society. Some of your students might be reluctant to take a stand—because they are not used to doing so or because it seems rude.

answered based on feelings (subjectively) and is a statement of opinion, but the second can be answered based on thought (objectively) and is a statement of fact.] Explain that the first step in writing a persuasive paper is identifying the opinions that later will be supported by facts to achieve the persuasive aim.

TEACHING THE LESSON

After a volunteer reads the introductions on **Choosing a Topic** on p. 247, discuss the prewriting steps with the class. To help students find issues that matter to them, suggest that they read their school newspaper or think about improvements they believe their school should make.

MEETING INDIVIDUAL NEEDS

LESS-ADVANCED STUDENTS

Students might need more detailed instructions on how to begin their sentences in **Writing Assignment: Part 1**. Explain that most opinion statements include the word *should* or *must*. Give several example statements.

ADVANCED LEARNERS

You may want to encourage students to write about topics that require more in-depth research. Here are some possible topics:

1. prison overcrowding
2. the national debt
3. the depletion of the ozone layer
4. teen marriages
5. coeducational athletic teams

INTEGRATING THE LANGUAGE ARTS

Library Link. Students could use the library to help create their charts of supporting evidence for **Writing Assignment: Part 2**. Have a library session to focus on helping students locate current information in newspapers or in the vertical file. You may need to explain the various parts of a newspaper and the basic structure and content of most newspapers.

Identifying Your Opinion. Your *opinion* is something you believe. It isn't something that can be proven true. For example, it's your opinion that Nolan Ryan is the greatest baseball pitcher of all time. You believe it, but others may disagree. A *fact,* on the other hand, can be proven true. It's a fact that Nolan Ryan pitched seven no-hit games. No one can deny it. As the famous baseball manager Casey Stengel used to say, "You could look it up."

Putting your opinion down in black and white is the first step in writing a persuasive paper. You can do this by writing a *statement of opinion* that tells your topic and what you believe about it. Here are some examples of statements of opinion:

Driving a motorboat should require a license.
The city schools should set up tutoring classes for
  students who don't speak English.
Too many movies today use violence as entertainment.

When you discuss subjective and objective statements, reinforce the idea that subjective statements cannot be proved true or false, while objective statements can be proved.

You will also need to emphasize that audience is critical in developing a persuasive paper. For example, explain to students that arguments to convince their parents to let them attend a concert must be appealing to the parents, not the students. Use suggestions from the textbook for ways to locate support for students' papers. The examples in the **Here's How** chart on p. 254 should help students understand the differences between logical and emotional appeals.

You can guide students as they work to complete **Exercise 1** by working through ☞

When choosing a topic for persuasive writing

- brainstorm, listen to television and radio, and look through newspapers and magazines to find an issue you care about
- write a sentence identifying your issue and telling your opinion about it

---

EXERCISE 1 ▶ Distinguishing Fact from Opinion

With a small group, decide which of the following statements is a *fact* and which is an *opinion*. Keep in mind that a fact can be proven true while an opinion is a belief. Be ready to explain your reasoning about each statement.

1. Our school really should celebrate Harriet Tubman's birthday. **1.** opinion
2. Some of the largest cities in the United States have Spanish names. **2.** fact
3. New York City is the largest city in the United States. **3.** fact
4. I. M. Pei, the architect, is the greatest American of Chinese descent. **4.** opinion

ANSWERS
Exercise 1

1. Other students may want to celebrate other peoples' birthdays.

2. The statement can be checked in a reference source.

3. The statement can be checked in a reference source.

4. The statement presents what one person thinks.

VISUAL CONNECTIONS

Exploring the Subject. Helping more than three hundred slaves reach freedom during the Civil War, Harriet Tubman (1820–1913) was one of the Underground Railroad's most active conductors. She was widely known as the Moses of her people.

After the Civil War, Tubman made her home in Auburn, New York. She died there on March 10, 1913.

Exploring the Subject. Ieoh Ming Pei (1917–   ) is a Chinese American architect who has won several awards for excellence in design. One of his major works includes the glass pyramid shown in the photograph. The pyramid was completed in 1989 and is situated in front of the Louvre Museum in Paris, France.

an example set of facts and opinions such as "The best vacation spot is Alaska," and "Santa Fe is the capital of New Mexico." For **Exercise 2** and **Writing Assignment: Parts 1** and **2**, model the required skills on the chalkboard by giving a persuasive topic you would use, the statement of opinion, and possible logical and emotional appeals to support the opinion.

Using the brainstorming from **Exercise 2**, each student should work on **Writing Assignment: Part 1** independently to write a sentence naming the issue and stating an opinion. Have students design charts similar to the one in the textbook to help them build supporting evidence for these opinion statements.

ANSWERS
Exercise 2

Answers will vary. Students' five issues should involve matters of opinion, not fact. For example: Should the designated hitter be abolished in baseball? Should the United States give foreign aid to dictatorships? Should schools have dress codes? Should communities enforce traffic laws more strictly?

CRITICAL THINKING
Synthesis

You may want to discuss how a particular opinion could be presented persuasively for different audiences. Students should list at least three convincing reasons for each audience. Here are some example opinions and audiences:

1. Teenagers should be able to choose their bedtimes. (audiences: parent, teacher, teen)
2. Students should have at least one all-school assembly a month covering topics of interest to students. (audiences: principal, teacher, student)

EXERCISE 2 ▶ Exploring Possible Topics

With a small group of classmates, brainstorm possible topics for persuasive writing. Talk about what's going on at school. Think about issues you have heard about on television or radio. Look through copies of magazines such as *Sports Illustrated* or *Time* in your library. Make a list of at least five issues.

WRITING ASSIGNMENT

PART 1:
Choosing an Issue to Write About

Pick an issue for persuasive writing. Perhaps you'll stay with one you came up with in Exercise 2. Or you may want to take a stand on something else. Should we have a new national anthem because "The Star-Spangled Banner" is too hard to sing? Should all experiments on animals be outlawed? When you've decided what you want to write about, write a sentence that names the issue and states your opinion about it.

ASSESSMENT

Because **Writing Assignment: Part 1** requires a one-sentence answer, you could have students read aloud their opinion sentences. For **Writing Assignment: Part 2**, display a few of the students' charts on overhead transparencies. Then you can lead a class discussion of the strongest supporting facts and expert opinions.

RETEACHING

If you find that students are having difficulty with **Writing Assignment: Part 1**, provide them with the following simple formula to help them write sentences that name the issues and state their opinions: subject (issue) + opinion = thesis statement.

Prewriting   **251**

Planning Your Paper

Have you ever set out to get something you wanted—and succeeded? Then you probably gave your "plan of action" some careful thought. Persuading on paper takes the same planning.

Thinking About Purpose and Audience

Your *purpose* in persuasive writing is to make readers think a certain way or act a certain way. You can't do that without paying pretty close attention to *them*—to your *audience.* On your issue, what will be their interests and concerns? How can you appeal to your readers?

Suppose you want your classmates to support a city hockey rink. They'll be interested in being able to watch good teams play. Suppose you want to convince the city council. They'll worry about building costs. So to have the right appeal and answers, think ahead about audience.

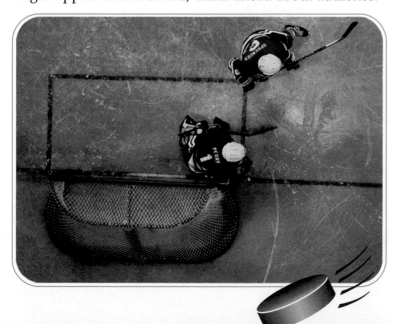

TIMESAVER

Ask students to read aloud answers for **Writing Assignment: Part 1.** The assignment requires a one-sentence answer. Students will benefit from hearing a variety of opinions and issues.

A DIFFERENT APPROACH

You may want to invite guests to your classroom to speak on persuasion. Many professions focus on selling ideas or products. Even teachers must be persuasive at times. Guests might include salespeople, stockbrokers, advertising agents, marketing analysts, lawyers, politicians, newspaper columnists, or broadcast journalists. You could even allow a student to become a host for a panel of professionals. Be sure students prepare questions in advance. The other students in the class can ask questions about how persuasion is used in the working world.

Explain that the thesis sentence is the core of a persuasive paper, just as an apple core is the center of an apple.

CLOSURE

A discussion of the following questions may be used as a summary of this lesson:

1. What is the first step in writing a persuasive essay? [The first step is finding an issue that matters to the writer.]

Supporting Your Opinion

Do you always accept what other people say just because they seem to believe their own words? Probably not. You have opinions of your own that may be completely different from theirs. How, then, do you go about changing other people's opinions? It *can* be done. You just have to give convincing *support,* or proof, for what you believe.

Finding Information to Support Your Opinion. There are several ways to find support for your opinions. Here are three.

1. Talk to friends and others interested in the issue.
2. Talk to experts—people who are knowledgeable about the issue.
3. Look in books, magazines, and newspapers.

As you use these methods, look for *reasons, facts,* or *opinions* from knowledgeable sources. The more support you find, the more likely you are to sway your readers. For example, one writer needed to support his opinion that everyone in Fresno, California, should be required to ration water. He found facts and the opinion of a knowledgeable source.

> Support/Opinion of an expert: According to Water Commissioner Carol Main, "Some people are cutting their water use, but not enough are doing it to save the amount of water we need."

> Support/Fact: In Fresno, people were asked to cut their water use voluntarily by 25 percent. They cut their use by only 11 percent.

WRITING NOTE As you talk to people and read about the issue, you may find your opinion changing. That's okay. It simply means you've become better informed and better able to explain and defend your true point of view.

To give students practice in persuasion, have them work in groups of four. Give students one minute each to convince their peers to believe something. After each student has finished speaking, the other group members will list two reasons why the argument was convincing and two ways that the argument could be more convincing. After every student has had a chance to speak, allow group members to give feedback on the persuasive speaking. Here are some ideas for subjects to discuss:

1. the best music group
2. the messiest food to eat
3. the most enjoyable sport to watch

2. What is the difference between fact and opinion? [Opinions cannot be proven true, even if one believes they are true, and facts can be proven true.]

3. How can a writer find information to support opinions? [A writer can find support by talking to friends who are interested in the issue, by talking to experts, and by looking in books, magazines, and newspapers.] ■

Using Appeals to the Emotions. Not all the support in good persuasive writing is factual. Some is emotional. You want to appeal to people's hearts as well as to their minds.

An organization is raising money to save California's redwood trees. You've been asked to write the appeal for donations. Will you just tell them how many trees will be saved? No. You'll describe a family enjoying a hike through a redwood forest. Then you'll say that a forest just like this one is being logged less than a hundred miles away. You'll describe the ugly, treeless landscape after the logging.

As you write, you'll consider how *you* feel about the issue. Do you feel fear? concern? hope? anger? Then you'll try to create the same emotions in your audience. Draw vivid word pictures. Use a powerful quotation. Tell about a sad incident. Make the audience feel the rightness of your cause.

Emotional appeals alone aren't enough, though. The best persuasion has a base of solid information. Then you can add feelings.

When you're gathering support, you can use a chart like the one on the next page.

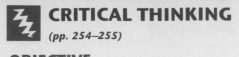
OBJECTIVE

- To evaluate persuasive statements for misleading and faulty reasoning

TEACHING *EVALUATING REASONING*

You may want to begin this lesson by asking students to think of how a candidate's reputation is sometimes ruined in an election. Ask students how this can happen. [Candidates can reveal undesirable behavior from their opponents' past; they can incorrectly blame their opponents for

LEP/ESL

General Strategies. Because some students may not understand the English terms *cause and effect, technique, strategy,* and *attack,* give several examples to illustrate the concepts behind these words. Possibilities are political problems and resolutions for *cause and effect,* ways of cooking or repairing for *technique,* plans for tackling environmental cleanup of some place in your city for *strategy,* and newspaper advertisements that demean a politician for an *attack.*

ADVANCED STUDENTS

Let students spend a class period in the library finding and analyzing at least three examples of faulty or misguided persuasion in magazine or newspaper articles. Students could then mount their findings on cardboard and present them to the class.

---

254   *Writing to Persuade*

 HERE'S HOW

OPINION:	Athletes shouldn't charge for autographs.
AUDIENCE:	Junior high school students
SUPPORT:	1. The most popular players already earn millions.
	2. Fans will think less of their favorite players if they have to pay for autographs.
	3. Players in the past didn't ask fans to pay for autographs. Today's players should be more like them.

CRITICAL THINKING
Evaluating Reasoning

Sometimes what seems like support for an opinion isn't support at all. Some reasons aren't really reasonable (logical), and some emotional appeals are tricks, not truth. Unsuspecting readers and listeners can be fooled by these "statements masquerading as reasons."

So be careful. If you use misleading support, some readers will spot it. Those who do won't be convinced.

STATEMENTS MASQUERADING AS REASONS		
TECHNIQUE	**STRATEGY**	**EXAMPLE**
False Cause and Effect	Assumes that one event caused another just because one came before the other	"Not sending the band to out-of-town games put the team on a losing streak."
Attacking the Person	Ignores the issue by attacking the person instead of the person's view on the topic	"Supporters of this leash law are cat haters at heart."
Bandwagon	Asks you to believe or do something because many other people do	"Don't be the only family in your neighborhood without a Pereira tape deck."

creating bad situations; or they can exaggerate their opponents' weaknesses.] Explain to students that this is a type of faulty reasoning because the supporting evidence does not relate to the issue being discussed. These techniques ignore the issues and attack the person.

Students are asked to work in small groups to complete **Critical Thinking**

Exercise: Evaluating Persuasive Statements. Monitor groups and offer help when necessary. Then have students evaluate the statements they have gathered for their writing.

CRITICAL THINKING EXERCISE:
Evaluating Persuasive Statements

With a small group, study each statement below. Why is the statement misleading? Which technique from page 254 is being used? Be prepared to explain.

1. Everyone is buying Bright-O toothpaste. The stores can hardly keep it on the shelves. Buy yours today!
2. After the principal shortened the homeroom period, many students got poorer grades.
3. Since he is an active deer hunter, it's no wonder that Bob says hunting helps conserve deer.
4. The kids at Del Rio Middle School who started skateboarding lost their A and B averages. Skateboarding definitely eats up study time.

ANSWERS
Critical Thinking Exercise

1. The statement suggests that you should buy a product because others buy it. (bandwagon)
2. It may be coincidence that students got poorer grades when homeroom was shortened. (false cause and effect)
3. The statement ignores the issue of deer conservation. (attacking the person)
4. This is an assumption that skateboarding caused the lower grades. (false cause and effect)

| WRITING ASSIGNMENT | PART 2: **Finding Support for Your Opinion** |

You'll need information and perhaps emotional appeals to support the opinion statement you wrote for your paper. Use a chart like the one on page 254, and start backing up your belief. What reasons or facts can you think of? Whose expert opinion can you quote? What feelings can you tap—and how? Line up some strong support.

WRITING YOUR FIRST DRAFT

OBJECTIVES

- To analyze a professional model for persuasive elements
- To write a draft of a persuasive essay

MOTIVATION

Begin by reading examples of effective persuasion from papers of students you have previously taught or from professional works such as Edith Hamilton's discussion of Norse mythology in her book *Mythology*.

Writing Your First Draft

Combining the Elements of Persuasion

You've seen that the basic elements of persuasive writing are (1) a clear statement of your opinion and (2) support for that opinion. Now that you have both, you need to put them together in a way that's really convincing—in a way that gets your audience to think or to act as you'd like.

A Good Beginning.   You need to try to grab your readers' attention from the start. You could begin with a question that creates strong feelings: "Would you want a nuclear waste dump across the street from your house?" Or you might begin with an interesting *anecdote* (little story): "Yesterday I walked out of a movie and asked for my money back. I got it." Once you have everyone's attention, you can state your opinion. With a good beginning, you've made the first step toward convincing your readers.

Clearly Organized Support.   One way to organize support in persuasion is *order of importance.* Go from your most important reason to your least important, or the opposite. In other words, you try to capture your readers' sympathy at the start, or you build up to a powerful punch at the end. Either way can work. Just be sure to decide what's most important to *your readers*, not only to you.

A Good Ending.   Leave your audience convinced that you're right. Your best ending might be a strong restatement of your opinion. Or it might be a *call to action,* a specific suggestion about something the audience can do.

The writer of the following chapter from a book wants readers to go without meat one day a month. Notice how she uses both information and emotion to support her opinion. Does she put it all together in a strong, persuasive package?

WRITING YOUR DRAFT
- Writing the Body Paragraph

QUOTATION FOR THE DAY

"To believe in your own thought, to believe what is true for you in your private heart is true for all men,—that is genius." (Ralph Waldo Emerson, 1803–1882, American poet and essayist)

Share the quotation with students as they begin writing first drafts. Encourage students to remember that the purpose of each of their papers is to convince an audience to believe or to act in a way the student wants.

MEETING
INDIVIDUAL
NEEDS

LEP/ESL

General Strategies. Several words from Lamb's chapter might be difficult for some students, for example, *hideous, protein, livestock, minuscule, tropical, rainforest, grazing,* and *deteriorates.* Explain that it is not necessary to look up all the new words, a practice that discourages readers. Students could read for the general sense of the article and guess at the meanings of new words from their contexts.

Discuss the suggested structure of a persuasive essay by using the framework given in the textbook as an illustration. You may want to expand the textbook's definition of *anecdote* to "a short, entertaining account of some happening, usually personal or biographical." Then have a volunteer read Lamb's model so that you can note the labels and discuss any questions about beginnings, support, endings, or vocabulary. Students might find the **Framework for Persuasive Writing** chart on p. 261 too confining; however, encourage them to use the framework for the first persuasive essay. Explain that after they have experience in writing to persuade, they can be more flexible. ☞

Writing Your First Draft **257**

A CHAPTER FROM A BOOK

Title/Call to action

One Day a Month, Go Without Meat
by Marjorie Lamb

BEGINNING

Many North Americans are eating less meat than we used to, partly for our health, and partly out of the knowledge that meat consumption wastes our planet's resources.

Statement of opinion

SUPPORT

Expert opinion

Frances Moore Lappé, in her wonderful book, *Diet For a Small Planet* (Ballantine Books), documents the <u>hideous</u> waste of protein fed to livestock compared to the <u>minuscule</u> amount of protein we receive from livestock

Reason

in return. We could easily supply the human population of the Earth with enough protein if we stopped feeding it to our livestock. Cattle consume more than 15 pounds of grains for every pound of beef they give us in return.

Reason

The demand for beef also means the clearing of vast <u>tracts</u> of tropical <u>rainforest</u>

Facts

for cattle grazing. The land rapidly <u>deteriorates</u>, the soil <u>erodes</u> and becomes <u>infertile</u>.

LEARNING STYLES

Visual Learners. Some students might benefit from using colored pens to label their papers according to the framework in the textbook. For example, the beginning could be written in blue ink, the attention grabber could be written in red ink, and so on. Students might also label each colored section. As they follow the framework and use different-colored pens to add each component of the framework, students should get a visual image of each essay part. This illustration will facilitate clear, concise organization and smoother transitions between sections because students will clearly see where each section of the framework begins.

Auditory Learners. Students might want to compose their drafts orally by recording them. Then they can play the material back to transcribe and revise it.

GUIDED PRACTICE

Before students work on **Exercise 3** and **Writing Assignment: Part 3**, analyze the structure of the **Writer's Model** with the class and demonstrate how you would begin writing your own essay.

INDEPENDENT PRACTICE

Students will work independently on **Exercise 3** and write drafts of a persuasive essay for **Writing Assignment: Part 3**. Using the suggested framework as a guide, students should look at their charts of information to write their supporting arguments.

INTEGRATING THE LANGUAGE ARTS

Literature Link. Have students read Borden Deal's short story "Antaeus." After the class has read the selection, discuss the persuasive powers of T. J. in convincing the other boys to make a roof garden. Then have students analyze the techniques T. J. uses to convince the other boys that the garden is a worthwhile effort.

COOPERATIVE LEARNING

You may want to use **Exercise 3** as a cooperative-learning activity. In heterogeneous ability groups, students can discuss the professional model and answer the questions. Assign each group member a particular question and ask students to share their answers with the rest of the group. All group members will be responsible for knowing all answers.

258

---

258   *Writing to Persuade*

Emotional appeal

Then more acreage must be cleared for cattle grazing. Land which once supported farmers in tropical countries now grows <u>soya</u>—not to feed the people, but for export as livestock feed. Some fast food chains get their beef from tropical lands such as Costa Rica. Ask your fast food outlet where their beef comes from.

Facts
Reason

As cattle digest, they give off <u>methane</u>, a <u>greenhouse</u> gas. The world's cattle population, along with large areas of rice <u>paddies</u>, account for nearly half the global release of methane. More beef means more global warming.

Reason

Finally, livestock grazing requires tremendous amounts of water to irrigate pasture land. California alone uses enough water to meet the domestic needs of 22 million people, just to turn the desert into grassland for cattle and sheep grazing.

Fact and emotional appeal

To assess students' comprehension, ask them to answer the following questions and to attach the answers to their drafts for you to check:

1. Who is your audience?
2. What is your opinion statement?

3. What technique are you using to open your paper?
4. What different supporting arguments does your paper contain?

At this stage of the writing process, reinforce as many positive elements as possible and explain that there will be time later for revisions.

Writing Your First Draft **259**

ENDING
Summary of reasons

If we all reduced our meat consumption, we'd make a significant impact on the protein available for the rest of the world, save water for more reasonable uses and help preserve our tropical rainforests, which we desperately need for the health and survival of the planet.

Emotional appeal

from *2 Minutes a Day for a Greener Planet*

EXERCISE 3 ▶ **Analyzing Persuasive Writing**

After you read the excerpt from *2 Minutes a Day for a Greener Planet*, discuss it with some classmates. Use these questions to guide your analysis.

1. Many people who read Marjorie Lamb's book already believe we need a "greener planet." If her readers *did not*, do you think her opening sentence would be different? What opening would you write?
2. What words and phrases make the expert opinion of Frances Moore Lappé also an emotional appeal?
3. How much information does Lamb give compared to her emotional appeals? Do you think the balance is good?
4. Lamb's title contains her call to action because each chapter of her book gives a "quick and simple" act to save the earth. How does she conclude her chapter?
5. Does Lamb convince you of her opinion? Will you do what she asks? Why or why not?

Using a Basic Framework

The excerpt from Lamb's book shows you effective persuasion in action, but it's different from the composition you'll write. You'll probably be writing a simpler paper, with less extensive support—and of course you're not writing a whole book! On the next page is a framework you can use when you're learning to write persuasion.

ANSWERS
Exercise 3

Answers may vary.

1. Yes, it would. A possible alternative is "If we don't consume less meat, we face destruction."
2. "hideous waste" and "miniscule amount"
3. Lamb relies more on information than on emotional appeals. The balance seems good.
4. She summarizes main elements in her argument and again appeals to the reader's emotions.
5. Most people would say they were convinced before they read the essay. Answers will vary on second part of the question, but be sure students support their opinions.

SELECTION AMENDMENT
Description of change: excerpted and title punctuated differently
Rationale: to focus on the concept of drafting a persuasive essay presented in this chapter

CLOSURE

Ask students to provide the answers to the following questions in a class discussion:

1. What are the basic elements of a persuasive paper? [a clear statement of an opinion and support for that opinion]

2. What are two ways that a good paper might begin? [a question that creates strong feeling, an interesting anecdote]

3. How are persuasive papers usually organized? [order of importance]

4. How can you write a good ending? [strong restatement of the opinion, call to action]

CRITICAL THINKING
Analysis

Although the structures of the two models—"One Day a Month, Go Without Meat" and A Writer's Model—differ, they have many similarities. You may want to lead students in a discussion of the similarities between the models.

Both have strong openings—one with emotional appeals, the other with an anecdote—followed by background information; both give facts and expert opinions as evidence; both conclude with statements of opinion and calls to action.

TIMESAVER

Ask students to label the right margins of their drafts with the corresponding framework terminology. You can then quickly assess students' use of the framework in the organization of their papers. Labeling will also give students a visual way to check their papers' structure.

260

260   *Writing to Persuade*

A WRITER'S MODEL

BEGINNING
Attention grabber—anecdote

Last week at a baseball card show, I asked a well-known baseball player for his autograph. Imagine my surprise when a man standing next to him said I would have to pay fourteen dollars before the player would sign his name!

Opinion
SUPPORT
Fact

Emotional appeals

Athletes shouldn't charge fans for autographs. The fans help many athletes get huge salaries in the first place. The most popular players—the ones fans ask for autographs most often—already earn millions of dollars. They don't really need this extra money. And how can you have respect for a player who won't even take a minute to sign his name for you? Babe Ruth was flattered just to have kids look up to him. He wouldn't have dreamed of asking people to pay for his autograph.

ENDING
Call to action
Restatement of opinion

Don't cave in and pay for an autograph. Players should see that an autograph is a way of saying "thank you" to loyal fans, and they shouldn't charge money.

You can use the following framework as a guide. The paper about athletes' autographs uses this framework.

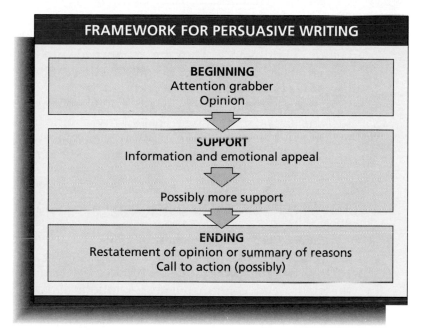

FRAMEWORK FOR PERSUASIVE WRITING

BEGINNING
Attention grabber
Opinion

SUPPORT
Information and emotional appeal

Possibly more support

ENDING
Restatement of opinion or summary of reasons
Call to action (possibly)

WRITING NOTE As you write the draft of your paper, remember to grab your audience's attention. When you're trying to persuade, you may be able to get their attention just by stating your opinion: "I think seventh-grade students should have a class party." But most of the time you'll need to do something special to make your audience want to read on.

| **WRITING** ASSIGNMENT | PART 3: **Writing Your First Draft** |

It's time to start writing. Look back at your statement of opinion and your chart of supporting information. Use the framework as a guide, and don't forget your audience.

CRITICAL THINKING
Synthesis

Students could listen to radio and television ads and read newspaper and magazine ads to compile a master list of persuasive words and phrases with emotional appeal. Have students use this master list to create collages of persuasive language for a wall display.

EVALUATING AND REVISING

OBJECTIVES

- To analyze and evaluate a writer's opinion and supporting details
- To analyze a persuasive model's revision strategies
- To evaluate and revise a persuasive paper

MOTIVATION

Write the word *revise* on the chalkboard and explain that the word literally means "to see again." Tell students that in this stage of the writing process, they will look at their work again to find ways to improve their papers.

RESOURCES

EVALUATING AND REVISING
- Writing a Persuasive Paper

QUOTATION FOR THE DAY

"Great writers leave us not just their works, but a way of looking at things." (Elizabeth Janeway, American author and editor)

Write the quotation on the chalkboard and ask students in small groups to discuss books, stories, television programs, or experiences that have changed their ways of looking at things. Encourage your students to remember Janeway's remark as they evaluate and revise their persuasive papers.

ANSWERS
Exercise 4

Caution students here that they must be very honest, especially about the third question, if they want to help one another. Listeners especially need to pay careful attention.

Evaluating and Revising

By now you know that your drafts are like rehearsals before a performance. They are a chance to "run through" everything from beginning to end. In a first draft, you can try things out to see if they work.

Remember that, in persuasion, you want your readers to *think* or *do* something. That's why a little rehearsal before a preview audience is an excellent idea. You get to see how a real, live audience either accepts or rejects your ideas.

Exercise 4 is a chance to do a preview with a peer. You'll see firsthand how powerful (you hope!) your persuasion is.

Then you can use the chart on page 263 to evaluate all the parts of your paper. The questions in the left-hand column will help you judge each part. The techniques in the right-hand column suggest solutions if you find a problem.

EXERCISE 4 ▶ **Speaking and Listening: Responding to an Argument**

Try out your draft—out loud—with a partner. The listener will use the questions below to take notes as you speak. You can read your draft twice so your partner has a chance to catch everything. After you finish, look at your partner's responses to the questions. Jot down anything you want to keep in mind for your revising. Then change roles. You might even want to get another partner and repeat the process.

1. Can I state the speaker's issue and opinion in my own words?
2. Did the speaker grab my attention right from the start?
3. What supporting point really stood out for me?
4. Did my opinion change by the end? Why or why not?
5. What helpful suggestions can I give the speaker?

TEACHING THE LESSON

To lead students through evaluating and revising, have a student read the introductory explanations. Then coordinating each step to an example in the student model, discuss the **Evaluation Guide and Revision Technique** chart.

GUIDED PRACTICE

You will probably want to guide students through **Exercise 5** to help them understand when revisions are necessary before they peer-evaluate and work on their own papers.

EVALUATING AND REVISING PERSUASIVE WRITING

EVALUATION GUIDE	REVISION TECHNIQUE
1 Does the beginning grab the reader's attention?	**Add** an interesting question or brief story.
2 Is the writer's opinion clearly stated early in the paper?	**Add** a sentence giving your opinion, or **replace** the statement of opinion with a clearer one.
3 Is there enough support to convince the audience?	**Add** reasons, facts, or opinions from experts. **Add** a sentence that will appeal to your reader's feelings.
4 Does the writer include any incorrect or misleading statements?	**Cut** statements that depend on false cause and effect, attacking the person, or bandwagon.
5 Is the ending strong?	**Add** a sentence that restates your opinion or calls your reader to action.

"Just get it down on paper, and then we'll see what to do with it."

Maxwell Perkins

MEETING INDIVIDUAL NEEDS

LEP/ESL

General Strategies. You may expect ESL students to make some mistakes in forming comparatives, as many languages differ from English in the formation of comparatives. For example, German has *–er* and *–erst* but not *more* and *most,* while Spanish has the opposite. Speakers of such languages might have trouble knowing when to use *er* and when to use *more.* Because Arabic has only a single comparison form, the elative, such as in the word *asghar,* meaning "smaller" or "small est," some students may be unsure when to use the comparative or when to use the superlative. Similarly, Japanese and Malay do not have distinct comparative or superlative forms, although comparisons are still possible; speakers of these languages may use a simple form, such as *big,* instead of *bigger* or *biggest.* Help your students by reviewing the forms and rules for comparison of adjectives.

SELECTION AMENDMENT
Description of change: excerpted
Rationale: to focus on the concept of evaluating and revising presented in this chapter

INDEPENDENT PRACTICE

Students can work independently to complete **Exercise 4** and use the notes from their peers to evaluate their papers. Students can use the revision chart in the textbook to evaluate their own papers and to make necessary revisions for **Writing Assignment: Part 4.**

ASSESSMENT

You may want to ask students to highlight all the changes to make it easier for you to evaluate students' mastery.

264   *Writing to Persuade*

| EXERCISE 5 ▶ | **Analyzing a Writer's Revisions** |

Study the writer's revisions of the middle paragraph of the composition on page 260. Then answer the questions that follow.

Athletes shouldn't charge fans for
(The fans help many athletes get huge salaries in the first place⊙)   **add**
autographs. The most popular players—
the ones fans ask for autographs most
often—already earn millions of dollars.
They don't really need this extra money.
And how can you have respect for a
                  take a minute to
player who won't even ∧ sign his name for   **add**
            Babe Ruth
you? A good player in the past was   **replace**
flattered just to have kids look up to him.
He wouldn't have dreamed of asking
people to pay for his autograph. Anyone   **cut**
who pays for an autograph is pretty dumb.

1. What's the writer's reason for adding a new sentence after the first sentence?
2. What do you think the phrase *take a minute to* adds to the fourth sentence?
3. Why does the writer replace *A good player in the past* with *Babe Ruth*?
4. Do you see a good reason to cut the last sentence?

ANSWERS

Exercise 5

Answers may vary slightly, but students should be able to support answers that are not similar to the ones provided.

1. The new sentence introduces one of the strongest reasons for not paying for autographs.
2. The words indicate how little time and effort the baseball player expends in signing his autograph.
3. *Babe Ruth* is a specific detail, and many fans consider him one of the best players ever to play baseball.
4. The last sentence insults the reader instead of trying directly to get the reader to agree. It would antagonize some readers.

264

Summarize what students have learned by discussing the following questions:

1. Why does it help to read your persuasive essay to a partner? [reveals how convincing the essay is]
2. How could you revise a weak beginning? [by beginning with an anecdote or a question]
3. How do you revise a paper that lacks supporting details? [by going back to the prewriting step to gather more details]
4. How could you correct misleading statements? [by not attacking the person and by not using bandwagon techniques and faulty cause-effect relationships] ■

GRAMMAR HINT

Using Comparatives

In writing persuasion, you will sometimes want to compare one person or thing to another. You may want to show that your candidate for class president is *more experienced* than the other candidate. You may want to say that one brand of sneaker feels *better* than another. Be sure not to use the word *more* if the modifier is already in the comparative form (*longer*).

INCORRECT   Powermax batteries last more longer than batteries from other manufacturers.
CORRECT   Powermax batteries last **longer** than batteries from other manufacturers.

INCORRECT   Super Crunchies cereal will make your breakfast more better every day!
CORRECT   Super Crunchies cereal will make your breakfast **better** every day!

 REFERENCE NOTE: For more information on using comparatives, see pages 629–635.

 **WRITING ASSIGNMENT**

PART 4:
Evaluating and Revising Your Persuasive Paper

Do you have your notes from the "peer listening" in Exercise 4? Keep them in mind as you use the chart on page 263 to evaluate your paper. Start by exchanging papers with another student. Using the questions, write an evaluation of each other's work. Then evaluate your essay yourself. Revise it to correct any problems you or your partner has found.

MEETING INDIVIDUAL NEEDS

LESS-ADVANCED STUDENTS

Students might need help following the revision chart. To give them a simple way to recognize what elements the evaluation questions address, have students assign a number or a color to each element. For example, have them highlight all supporting details in a paragraph with a blue marker or mark a number to the side of each detail.

INTEGRATING THE LANGUAGE ARTS

Technology Link. Encourage students who have access to home computers or computer labs at school to revise on the computer. After students have clearly marked the revisions on their first draft printouts, they can revise their documents on their word processors. Have students critique each other's work using strikeouts for deletions and underlining for all insertions.

SEGMENT 6 *(pp. 266–267)*

PROOFREADING AND PUBLISHING

OBJECTIVES

- To proofread an essay carefully
- To correct errors in an essay before publishing it

TEACHING THE LESSON

You may want to discuss the value of good proofreading skills. Explain that mistakes can cost money because a document must be reprinted if there are errors. Point out that simple mistakes are also embarrassing and can destroy the credibility of the author. You can use the explanations in the textbook on proofreading and publishing.

RESOURCES

PROOFREADING AND PUBLISHING
- Writing a Persuasive Paper

QUOTATION FOR THE DAY

"A writer doesn't know what his intentions are until he's done writing." (Robert Penn Warren, 1905–1989, American author and poet)

As students begin proofreading and publishing, write the quotation on the chalkboard. You may wish to ask them to write brief journal entries discussing the truth of this statement. [Students might explain what they've learned while writing persuasively, or they might discuss whether their opinions have changed or grown stronger while working on their papers.]

MEETING INDIVIDUAL NEEDS

LEP/ESL

General Strategies. Many students miss errors when proofreading because mistakes in English are not errors in their native languages. For example, Spanish speakers might not capitalize days of the week or proper adjectives because this is not done in Spanish. Some languages, such as Chinese, Korean, Thai, and Arabic, do not have capital letters, so speakers of these

266

266   *Writing to Persuade*

Proofreading and Publishing

Proofreading.   Proofreading is the last step before you share your work with others. And it's an important one. You need to find and correct any mistakes in spelling, capitalization, punctuation, or usage. If your readers see such mistakes, they may suspect you've made errors in your thinking, too.

Publishing.   Here are two ways you can publish your writing.

- Join with three of your classmates to make an attractive bulletin-board display with your four papers. Use photographs and drawings to illustrate your papers.
- Find someone in class who disagrees with your opinion. Present the ideas from your persuasive paper as part of a debate.

WRITING ASSIGNMENT

PART 5:
Proofreading and Publishing Your Persuasive Paper

Proofread your writing carefully. Correct any errors you find. Then publish or share your work with others.

You may want to discuss techniques to help students proofread, asking students what personal strategies they use. Suggest that students read their papers backwards, checking spelling as they go.

Students could publish essays by displaying them on a bulletin board. You may want to set up another area of the room where students also display the prewriting and writing stages of their essays to emphasize that writing is a process.

For closure, ask each student to share one thing he or she changed in the paper during this stage. ■

A STUDENT MODEL

Kathy Bobek attends Henry David Thoreau Intermediate School in Vienna, Virginia. She says the hardest thing about writing her persuasive paper was "trying to find words, strong ones, to express my thoughts." As you read her paper, you'll probably agree that she did find strong words to express herself. Does she convince you of her opinion on school dances?

School Dances
by Kathy Bobek

I feel that our school should let the seventh- and eighth-grade classes have their own dances. Wouldn't you and your friends love to have dances with just your friends and peers of only your grade? I'm sure most people want to socialize with friends who are in the same grade. They would want to do this and not have to worry about being made fun of by people of a higher or lower grade. The dances wouldn't have mixed grades, so more people would come to the dances, which would bring in more money. I also think there would be fewer people at each individual dance, which would also bring more order. Last but not least, I feel that the dances would be decorated more to the liking of the students. Each grade could have different people from their grade decorate each dance. What one grade might think is stupid or babyish, another might like. For these reasons, I think that having individual school dances for each grade would be a very good idea.

languages might fail to capitalize the first letter of a sentence or a name. Ask students to talk about writing in their native languages as a way to lead into talking about writing in English. It may interest your other students, too, to see how to write without letters (Chinese) or to write from right to left (Arabic).

A STUDENT MODEL
Evaluation
1. Kathy begins her paper with an interesting question to grab the reader's attention.
2. Kathy's opinion is clearly stated in the first sentence.
3. With specific supports such as not "being made fun of" and dances "would bring in more money," Kathy gives reasons to convince her audience.
4. The last sentence presents a strong ending by restating Kathy's opinion.

WRITING WORKSHOP

OBJECTIVES

- To analyze an advertisement
- To write an advertisement using at least one of the four advertising techniques

MOTIVATION

You may want to mount several advertisements on cardboard for student observation and then discuss with the class the ads' appeals.

RESOURCES

WRITING WORKSHOP

- Interviewing to Gather Information
- Writing the Body Paragraphs
- Writing a Persuasive Paper

QUOTATION FOR THE DAY

"Those who stand for nothing fall for anything." (Alex Hamilton, British journalist)

Write the quotation on the chalkboard and discuss with students how the quotation applies to advertising. Lead students to see the importance of being an informed reader.

MEETING INDIVIDUAL NEEDS

LEP/ESL

Speakers of Asian Languages. The great differences in grammar, punctuation, word order, and vocabulary between some students' languages and English may make it very difficult to avoid noticeable errors and still be able to produce an interest-catching text. Students might benefit from critiquing each other's ad material in small groups before handing in the assignment.

268

WRITING WORKSHOP

A Newspaper or Magazine Ad

Advertising is everywhere. Television and radio ads bombard your eyes and ears. Magazine and newspaper ads draw you in with pictures and bold words. All these ads have one aim—to grab your attention and convince you to buy or do something.

How do ads do it? They use certain techniques that have proved successful. Here are four.

1. *"We're the best."* The ad claims its product or service is better than that of its competitors. The ad may give facts to support the claim.
2. *"You'll feel or look better."* The ad promises you health, comfort, or beauty.
3. *"We'll solve your problem."* The ad suggests a problem (maybe one you never thought of) and offers to solve it.
4. *"A famous athlete says . . ."* The ad quotes a famous person who uses or recommends the product or service.

The Far Side cartoon by Gary Larson is reprinted by permission of Chronicle Features, San Francisco, CA.

"Do you know me? I have to deal with lions, wolves, and saber-toothed tigers . . . That's why I carry one of THESE."

THE GOLD CLUB
John Q Caveman
123 456 7890

TEACHING THE LESSON

If your students know the four advertising techniques, ask them to use the following questions to help them analyze ads:

1. Do you think this is a good product, based on the advertisement? Why or why not?
2. How will this product make you feel? What makes you think this?
3. How will this product help you?
4. Does the ad quote a famous person? If so, how does this make you feel about the product?

Guide students through the questions following the Double Oats ad, but allow students to express their opinions.

Students will independently use the writing process to write their advertisements.

These techniques aren't always so obvious in an ad. Advertisers can use them in very clever ways. But if you look closely, you can usually figure out which techniques are being used. What does this cereal ad promise you?

Every round a winner...
and every triangle, too!

Spelling bee champion Pia Sanchez says,
"I start every day with Double Oats. They're simply supercalifragilisticexpialidocious."

Introducing Double Oats

Who says a health-packed cereal can't be a taste sensation? Try this great new treat—toasty oat triangles and hearty oat puffs. With twelve essential vitamins and minerals. Extra low in sugar. Extra high in crunchy goodness.

TOASTED **DOUBLE OATS**
Crisp, Wholesome, Delicious! New Nifty Shapes!

Ideal Source of Oat Bran

Thinking It Over

1. Which of the four techniques does the ad use to make you want to try Double Oats? (More than one is possible.) Does the ad persuade you?
2. How does the ad's headline connect the spelling bee with Double Oats?
3. Does the ad use any facts to support the claim that Double Oats is "a winner"? If so, identify them.
4. Why do you think the illustration includes the spelling-bee scene? Why wouldn't a picture of the cereal box be enough? Explain.

ADVANCED STUDENTS

Instead of having students write and publish advertisements, suggest that they write magazine or newspaper ads for a candidate in a past presidential election. Explain that they must use sound persuasive reasoning and refrain from employing any propaganda techniques. You will probably need to allow library time for students to research the candidates.

ANSWERS
Thinking It Over

Answers may vary.

1. It uses techniques 2 and 4. Answers will vary as to its effectiveness.
2. The headline promises every round (and triangle) is a "winner"; Pia Sanchez is a winner of a spelling bee.
3. Although the ad mentions "twelve essential vitamins and minerals," low sugar, and high oat bran, none of these facts directly supports the claim that the cereal is "a winner."
4. The illustration shows the spelling bee to emphasize the idea of being a winner. A picture of the cereal box alone would not have this emphasis.

For closure, ask students to explain the connection between persuasive writing and advertising.

270

EXTENSION

Ask students to choose advertisements for their least favorite products and to design new advertisements that might convince people to buy the product. ■

INTEGRATING THE LANGUAGE ARTS

Technology Link. Students might want to use the school computer lab to generate advertisements. If a simple desktop publishing program is available, you may want to encourage students to use it. Students might also focus on font and point size. Remind them that attractive advertisements sell products. Encourage creativity and experimentation with the advertisements' appearance.

Writing an Ad

Prewriting. You're going to create an ad of your own. What will you sell? A new shampoo? A bicycle? Sneakers? List some possible products for your ad and choose one. Give it a good name. To plan your ad, think about the four advertising techniques. Which will you use? Jot down ideas for words and pictures. Also decide what audience you'll be trying to persuade.

Writing, Evaluating, and Revising. All three parts of an ad must work together—the headline, the information (a short paragraph), and the illustration. Keeping that in mind, write your headline. Make it short, direct, and catchy. Think about the ad techniques as you write your paragraph. What will appeal to your audience? Why will they want to buy the product? You can sketch your illustration, or clip it from a magazine. Arrange your ad on a sheet of paper. Then look it over carefully with a partner. Would you stop to read it in a magazine? Could you make it stronger?

Proofreading and Publishing. Since ads are brief and eye-catching, any mistakes in spelling, capitalization, or punctuation jump out at readers. Errors will take away from your message. Proofread carefully. Consider publishing your ad as part of a bulletin-board display or class album. Or put together a class magazine. Your persuasion papers from this chapter can be the articles. Ads can then be placed throughout the magazine. You may also want to include other writing—stories and poems, for instance.

SPEAKING AND LISTENING OBJECTIVES

- To compare and contrast different forms of advertising
- To determine which form of advertising is more convincing

271

MAKING CONNECTIONS

SPEAKING AND LISTENING

Comparing Persuasion in Different Forms

Join with two or three classmates in an ad hunt. Find one product that is advertised in two or more forms.

- Some *products* to consider are toothpaste, soap, cereal, shoes, clothing, cameras, and watches.
- Some *forms of advertising* to consider are television, magazines, newspapers, radio, and direct mail (ads that come in the mail).

LUXURY in a car is as much a matter of engine building as it is of upholstery. Luxury as expressed in a Pierce-Arrow means efficiency first, attractive design second, a perfectly appointed car, built around a thoroughly tried-out machine.

THE PIERCE-ARROW MOTOR CAR COMPANY, BUFFALO, N. Y.
Licensed under Selden Patent

SPEAKING AND LISTENING
Teaching Strategies

Explain to students that forms of advertising are directly related to audience. For example, if a cereal cartoon is on television on Saturday morning, it should be obvious that the targeted consumer is a child or a parent of a child. If an advertisement for the same product is on a billboard on a busy freeway, the targeted consumer could be a commuter who is old enough to drive a car and who does grocery shopping. Explain to students that the intended audience determines where an advertiser places an ad and how the ad is developed.

GUIDELINES

Each group should easily be able to find a particular product advertised in a number of different forms. Students may want to cut out or photocopy ads from newspapers and magazines. They may want to videotape ads from TV or record them from radio, if possible. Then they'll be able to refer to the ads easily. Sometimes, students will find the same ad used on radio and TV, although the radio version will not have pictures. Students might want to consider what effect the lack of pictures has. Does the listener's mind supply the pictures? What if the listener has not yet seen the TV ad?

272

You may want to divide the forms among yourselves. That way, everybody won't be searching in the same places. Try to find your product advertised in as many different forms as possible. (You probably won't find it in all forms.) Cut out or record the ads if possible. Otherwise, take notes.

When the group gets together, ask yourselves:

1. How are the ads alike, and how are they different? Describe the ads. [Hint: What do you notice about words, pictures, color, sound, and motion?]
2. Which ad in which form is the most convincing to you? Why?

Report your findings to the class. Use the ads you've collected in your report.

PERSUASION IN ACTION

Letters to the Editor

Almost all newspapers and magazines have a "Letters to the Editor" section. It gives readers a chance to say what's on their minds. They may respond to a news item or an editorial. Or they may bring up a whole new issue.

The audience is really all the newspaper or magazine's readers, not just the editor. And the purpose often is to persuade. Here's a letter from a writer who wants readers to be aware that wild plants can be useful.

CURES FROM THE JUNGLE

I really enjoyed reading "In Search of Jungle Secrets" in the February 1990 issue of *Ranger Rick.* When I was nine years old, I got a very rare type of blood cancer. One of the drugs that was used to cure me came from the *rosy periwinkle.* This flower grows in Madagascar, an island off the African coast.

PERSUASION IN ACTION
Teaching Strategies

Ask students to focus on presenting issues that are timely and appropriate for the publication that will receive the letter. For example, explain to students that they would not submit an article on the pleasures of saltwater fishing to a tennis magazine.

Tell students that they are more likely to get their letters published if they write to school, neighborhood, or community newspapers. Explain to students that even if they do get letters published in magazines like *Time* and *Newsweek,* the letters will not appear until long after they are sent, sometimes many months later.

I am 15 years old now and very happy to be alive. I'm thankful for tropical plants that can be used to make medicines like the one that cured me.

Please tell everyone how important it is to save wild plants and other living things. Not only are they beautiful, but they also might contain some "secret" medicines that can save other people's lives too.

Whitney Hair, Cary, NC
Ranger Rick

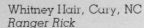

Read a few more letters to the editor, and write one of your own. Think of an issue that concerns you, and choose a specific magazine or newspaper to write to.

Use the elements you've learned in this chapter: opinion statement, supporting information, emotional appeal (not overexcited, though), and perhaps a call to action. But be very brief. Editors often shorten long letters.

Then mail your letter. If it's published, bring the clipping to class.

A DIFFERENT APPROACH

You could have students exchange their letters with partners to write responses. Explain to students that they should assume the role of editor and complete these tasks when answering their partners' letters:

1. Comment about the writer's evidence.
2. Refute or agree with the writer's specific supports.
3. Explain whether you agree or disagree with a proposed suggestion.

GUIDELINES

Students should state their concerns and get the reader's attention at the beginning. Opinions should be supported by reasons and evidence.

Chapter 9
WRITING ABOUT LITERATURE

Motivation

Without telling the others what the role will be, ask one of your students to play the part of a playground bully for the rest of the class and ask one or two other students to play the bully's victims. The situation can be a decision about what game to play. After the actors play their parts, ask the class to identify the part the bully was playing. Then ask students to tell you how they identified the bully. [The answers to this question will vary, but essentially students should list the character traits they noticed. Bullies are generally bossy, tough, mean, physically dominant, and uncooperative.] You can point out to the class that they will be identifying character traits as they did in the discussion when they write their character analyses.

Introduction

This chapter takes students through the process of writing a composition about a short story. The aim of the assignment is to inform and the writing mode is evaluation.

The prewriting segment includes Virginia Driving Hawk Sneve's story **"The Medicine Bag."** Students will practice identifying and analyzing the literary elements of characters, plot, setting, and theme in the story. They will then apply these elements to another story, either one selected by you or one of their own choosing. Finally, they will learn how to write a character analysis.

After students finish their character analyses, the **Writing Workshop** feature asks students to write brief compositions comparing and contrasting two characters. Finally, in **Making Connections**, the students can practice analysis by writing restaurant reviews and analyzing characters from history.

Integration

The chapter is suited for use in the study of literature, especially short stories, novels, and plays. In fact, this chapter could serve as a culmination for a longer literature unit. After students have read all of the short stories you select for the unit, ask each student choose one and to analyze a character in the story.

If you teach a unit on journalism, the material on writing reviews at the beginning and the end of the chapter may be useful in pointing out what a good review should contain.

The chart on the next page illustrates the strands of language arts as they are integrated into this chapter. For vocabulary study, glossary words are underlined in some writing models.

QUOTATIONS

All **Quotations for the Day** are chosen because of their relevance to instructional material presented in that segment of the chapter and for their usefulness in establishing student interest in writing.

INTEGRATING THE LANGUAGE ARTS

Selection	Reading and Literature	Writing and Critical Thinking	Language and Syntax	Speaking, Listening, and Other Expression Skills
"A Review of Lois Lowry's *Number the Stars***"** by Louise L. Sherman **276-277** **"The Medicine Bag"** by Virginia Driving Hawk Sneve **280-291**	Finding the main idea **298** Finding details **298** Evaluating a short story **291** Analyzing the elements of a short story **292-293**	Analyzing and responding to a book review **278** Evaluating a writer's effectiveness **291** Writing a personal response to a short story **291** Taking notes about a character in a short story **291, 294** Analyzing a character in a short story **291, 294, 296, 297, 298, 299** Making a character wheel **296, 297** Creating and analyzing a character **296, 305-306** Developing a writing plan **298** Stating the main idea of a character analysis **297, 298, 299** Writing a first draft of a character analysis **299** Evaluating and revising a draft of a character analysis **303, 304** Analyzing a writer's revisions **303-304** Publishing a character analysis **305-306** Comparing and contrasting two characters **309, 310** Writing a comparison and contrast of two characters **310** Proofreading and publishing a comparison of two characters **310** Writing a restaurant review **312** Writing an analysis of a character in history **313**	Analyzing a character's use of language **296**	Making a character wheel **296, 297** Participating in a group discussion **296, 303, 310** Creating a movie poster about a story **305** Discussing a character in a group setting **296, 303, 305, 306**

SEGMENT PLANNING GUIDE

Whether you are planning for a quick review of a writing concept or preparing an extended lesson on composition you can use the following Planning Guide to adapt the chapter material to the individual needs of your class.

SEGMENT	PAGES	CONTENT	RESOURCES
1 Reading and Responding	*275-278*		
Literary Model **"A Review of Lois Lowry's Number the Stars"**	276-277	Guided reading: a model of a literary analysis	
Reader's Response/ Writer's Craft	278	Model evaluation: responding to literature and analyzing a literary review	
2 Purposes for Writing About Literature	*279*		
3 Prewriting	*280-293*		Writing About a Character
Reading and Responding	280	Introduction: responding personally to literature	Analyzing a Character
Literary Model **"The Medicine Bag"**	280-291	Guided reading: responding to a short story	
Exercise 1	291	Applied practice: writing a journal entry	
Reading for Understanding	292	Explanation: learning the basic parts of a story	
Chart: Basic Elements of Stories	292	Guidelines: identifying the four elements of a short story	
Exercise 2	292-293	Cooperative learning: analyzing the elements of a story	
Writing Assignment: Part 1	293	Applied practice: reading and responding to a story	
Planning a Character Analysis	294-295	Guidelines: identifying a character analysis	
Critical Thinking: Analyzing a Character	295	Guidelines: analyzing details that show character traits	
Critical Thinking Exercise	296	Cooperative learning: analyzing a character and making a character wheel	
Exercise 3	296	Cooperative learning: creating and analyzing a character	
Writing Assignment: Part 2	297	Applied practice: writing details about characters	
Developing a Writing Plan	297-298	Introduction: developing a plan	
Thinking About Purpose and Audience	297	Guidelines: choosing appropriate character for purpose and audience	
Stating Your Main Idea	297	Guidelines: describing main character traits	
Organizing Your Information	298	Guidelines: organizing character traits	
Writing Assignment: Part 3	298	Applied practice: developing a writing plan	
4 Writing	*299-302*		Introducing a Character Analysis
The Parts of a Character	299	Guidelines: organizing a character analysis	

SEGMENT	PAGES	CONTENT	RESOURCES
Writer's Model	299-301	Guided reading: analyzing a character analysis	
A Framework for a Character Analysis	301	Introduction: organizing a character analysis	
Chart: Framework for a Character Analysis	302	Guidelines: organizing details of character traits	
Writing Assignment: Part 4	302	Applied practice: writing a first draft	
5 *Evaluating and Revising*	*303-304*		Writing a Character Analysis
Chart: Evaluating and Revising a Character Analysis	303	Guidelines: applying evaluation and revision techniques	
Exercise 4	303-304	Cooperative learning: analyzing a writer's revisions	
Writing Assignment: Part 5	304	Applied practice: evaluating and revising	
6 *Proofreading and Publishing*	*305-307*		Writing a Character Analysis
Mechanics Hint	305	Writing suggestion: using quotation marks correctly	
Writing Assignment: Part 6	306	Applied practice: proofreading and publishing	
Writer's Model	306-307	Sample: examining a literary analysis	
7 *Writing Workshop*	*308-310*		All the resources in this chapter may be used in this segment.
A Comparison of Two Characters	308	Guidelines: organizing and writing a paper that compares two characters	
Model/Questions	308-310	Examining techniques: analyzing a model	
Writing a Comparison of Two Characters	310	Applied practice: applying skills to the writing process	
8 *Making Connections*	*311-313*		
Informing Through Evaluation: Writing a Review	311	Guidelines: analyzing and evaluating a restaurant Applied practice: writing a restaurant review	
Writer's Model	311-312	Guided reading: analyzing a review of a restaurant	
Writing Across the Curriculum: Analyzing Great Characters in History	312-313	Guidelines: writing an analysis of a great character in history Applied practice: illustrating a character trait	

WHOLE-CHAPTER RESOURCES
A Writing Process Log, A Writing Prompt, Holistically Graded Models, Portfolio Assessment Materials

SEGMENT 1 *(pp. 274–278)*
READING AND RESPONDING

OBJECTIVE

- To analyze and respond to a book review

TEACHING THE LESSON

Some students might not understand what is meant by the word *responding*. You can tell them that most writing causes an emotional reaction. It might be as simple as liking or disliking the story. Responding to a story means putting the reader's feelings into words. The next step is to analyze why the reader feels that way. What in the story

9 WRITING ABOUT LITERATURE

VISUAL CONNECTIONS
Book Objects

About the Artist. Steven Cortright has been using books as his medium since 1973. His alterations to the printed volumes often give visual puns. An example of this technique is a book titled *The Span of Life,* in which the pages have been treated so that each page appears more worn and aged than the previous pages. Cortright uses various techniques in his transformations of books: adding or removing ink, illustrating, writing, and even sometimes carving through the pages.

Related Expression Skills. Give students a list of titles of short stories, poems, and essays. Have them work in groups of four to brainstorm, each group using four of the titles as a starting point. For each title, have students note their impressions, free associations, and whatever else comes to mind. Then ask each student to choose a title, read the selection, and write an expressive paragraph in response to it. In a class discussion, compare the paragraphs of response to the prereading notes. Ask students how the brainstorming session affected their reading process.

274

caused the feeling? Was the feeling caused by something within the reader? A previous experience? A close friend? The questions in **Reader's Response** are for students to express their feelings. The questions in **Writer's Craft** aim at analysis. Before assigning both sets of questions, model answering both types of questions by using your response to question 1 and by discussing the side annotations. You can use students' performance on these questions for assessment.

Reading and Responding

Every day you spend time **reading and responding.** You read your favorite comic strips and laugh. You put a book down because it's so boring you can't stay awake. You have feelings and thoughts about almost everything you read.

Writing and You. People often put their responses in writing. Newspaper and TV critics respond to movies, books, and TV shows. Your friend may write in her journal about a movie she liked. Your teacher may ask you to respond in writing to a poem you read. Or you may be asked to write an in-depth book report. Did you realize that all these were responses?

As You Read. Following is a response about a book you may have read—*Number the Stars*, by Lois Lowry. As you read, think about the reviewer's opinion. Does she like the book? If so, why does she?

QUOTATION FOR THE DAY

"Some books are undeservedly forgotten; none are undeservedly remembered." (W.H. Auden, 1907–1973, British poet)

Write the quotation on the chalkboard and ask students to write reading histories in their journals by recording the very first books they remember reading through the books they have read most recently. Explain that although many books will not be recalled, the lists they come up with will contain the titles that most affected them.

MEETING
INDIVIDUAL
NEEDS

LEP/ESL

General Strategies. Louise Sherman's review contains vocabulary that may be problematic for students. You may want to create a word list that includes *heroism, persecution, smuggling, inspirational,* and *idealism.* Have LEP/ESL students write definitions for each of these words. With the help of peer tutors, they should use these words to create original sentences. If possible, have students engage in this activity prior to a class discussion of Sherman's review.

275

Ask a volunteer to explain the connection between responses to literature and reviewing a literary work.

Bring to class as many copies of Lois Lowry's *Number the Stars* as you can find. Pass them around the room so students can look at them, and then let any students who want to check them out. In a few days volunteers can report to the class on their responses to the novel. ■

A DIFFERENT APPROACH

You can explain to students that writing isn't the only way to express responses to a literary work. They can respond to a story or poem by drawing a picture or creating some other art work, acting out a scene, choreographing a dance that expresses how they feel about what they've read, or singing a song that the literary work calls to mind.

CRITICAL THINKING
Comparing and Contrasting

Bring a movie review to class and share it with your students. Explain that a book review and a movie review have the same function: They not only tell what the work is about, but also help a person decide whether to see the movie or to read the book.

Using the following movie review guidelines, discuss with your class what the corresponding points would be in a book review:

1. includes film's title
2. has an overall judgment
3. explains plot concisely
4. addresses specific film elements such as plot or acting
5. supports judgments with specific evidence from the film

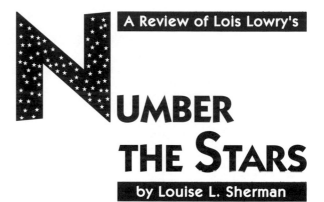

A Review of Lois Lowry's

NUMBER THE STARS
by Louise L. Sherman

Annemarie's life in <u>occupied</u> <u>Copenhagen</u> in 1943 seemingly is not much changed by the war—until the Nazi <u>persecution</u> of Danish Jews begins. Annemarie's family becomes

1   involved in the <u>Resistance</u> effort, helping a Jewish friend by having her pose as Annemarie's dead sister Lise. When an important packet must be taken to the captain of one of the ships

2   smuggling Jews to neutral Sweden, Annemarie finds the courage needed to deliver it despite grave danger to herself. Later her Uncle Henrik tells her that *brave* means "not thinking about the dangers. Just thinking about what you must do." Lowry's story is not just of Annemarie; it is also of Denmark and the Danish people, whose Resistance was so effective in saving their Jews. Annemarie is not just a symbol, however. She is a very real child who is equally involved in playing with a new kitten and running races at school as in the dangers of the occupation. *Number the Stars* brings the war to a child's level of understanding, sug-

3   gesting but not detailing its horrors. It is well plotted, and period

4   and place are convincingly recreated. An afterword answers the questions that readers will have and <u>reiterates</u> the inspirational <u>idealism</u> of the young people whose courage helped win the war.

"...brave

means 'not thinking about the dangers.

Just thinking about what you must do.'"

USING THE SELECTION
A Review of Lois Lowry's
Number the Stars

1
Resistance effort: the underground forces in Denmark that fought against the Nazi occupation of their land

2
Notice the reviewer gives only a hint of what happens.

3
well plotted: the related incidents of the story build realistically as the story develops

4
An afterword is usually written by someone other than the author.

ANSWERS

Reader's Response

1. Responses will vary. Most students will probably say yes because Annemarie seems to be an interesting person who has many adventures and does good things for people. Some boys might think the book unappealing because it's about a girl.

2. Responses will vary. Students should support their reactions with specific evidence.

Writer's Craft

3. The reviewer has a very high opinion of the book. She calls it "moving and satisfying" and says the author convincingly recreates the setting. The story is "well plotted," and the author relates "the inspirational idealism of the young people whose courage helped win the war."

4. She likes the book because it shows Annemarie's bravery (delivering the packet) and the Danish people's bravery. It also presents Annemarie as a believable character (playing with a kitten) and includes an afterword that addresses questions readers might have.

READER'S RESPONSE

1. Does *Number the Stars* seem like a book you'd want to read? Explain why or why not.
2. If you've read this book, tell why you think it is or is not a good story.

WRITER'S CRAFT

3. What is the reviewer's opinion of *Number the Stars*? Does she like or dislike it? What sentences tell you this?
4. The reviewer uses details from the book to support her opinion about it. What does she say about why she likes or dislikes *Number the Stars*?

"She is a very real child who is equally involved in playing with a new kitten and running races at school as in the dangers of the occupation."

TEACHING THE AIMS

You can help students understand the purposes for writing about literature by linking this segment to the process of responding to a literary work. After students have read the explanations of purposes in the textbook, divide the class into four groups to correspond to the four aims. Ask the groups to jot down ideas they might include to achieve their aims. Let one member of each group share the group's ideas with the class. ■

279

Purposes for Writing About Literature

The purpose of a review, like the one about *Number the Stars,* is to tell whether or not others should read a story, poem, or book. You might also write about literature in your journal or in a letter to friends, or make a poster showing your responses to a book. Then your purpose for writing about literature might be different—just to give your own feelings, or to persuade someone else to read something. When you write about literature, you usually have one of these four purposes.

Self-Expressive: writing in your journal about a short story character that seems just like you; writing to a friend about your favorite TV show.

Persuasive: in a note, writing about a movie to persuade your parents to let you see it; on a poster, writing about a book to persuade other students to read it.

▶ **Informative:**   telling a pen pal in Mexico about a film you saw about that country; explaining in a letter to a friend what happens in a movie your friend missed.

Creative: writing a journal entry as though you were a character in a story; imagining what happens to the character ten years after the story ends.

LOOKING AHEAD

In the main assignment in this chapter, your purpose for writing about literature will be informative. You'll be analyzing a character in a story and telling about him or her. Keep in mind that a good character analysis

- tells about two or three character traits
- gives story details to support the analysis

 A DIFFERENT APPROACH

Some students may not be familiar with the term *book review.* They may tend to confuse it with the more familiar term *book report.* You can explain that both book reviews and book reports have in common the fact that they're responses to literary works. However, a review always has the purpose of evaluating, or, as the text puts it, "to tell whether or not others should read" the book. A report, on the other hand, can be a summary of the plot, an analysis, an interpretation, or an evaluation.

CRITICAL THINKING
Analysis

Bring to class book reviews from current newspapers and magazines. Let each student read one to decide which parts of the review are persuasive and which parts are informative. Is any part of the review self-expressive or creative?

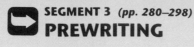

OBJECTIVES

- To write a personal response to a short story
- To analyze the elements of a story
- To read and respond to a story of choice
- To create a character
- To share a created character in a group setting
- To make a character wheel for a character chosen for analysis
- To develop a main idea statement and a writing plan for a character analysis

RESOURCES

PREWRITING
- Analyzing a Character

QUOTATION FOR THE DAY

"Man is like an iceberg—the more important part is hidden under the water. It interests me to dive down to the most hidden places." (Fernando Arrabal, 1922–   , Spanish playwright)

You could use the quotation to help prepare students to analyze a fictional character. Encourage students to look for more than just the obvious facts about a character: his age or grade at school. Challenge the class to notice how the character looks and behaves and what the character says and thinks.

Writing a Character Analysis

 *Prewriting*

Reading and Responding to Stories

Before you can write about literature, you have to read it, respond to it, and think about it. You start with the story or poem itself and your reactions to it. Then you try to understand it.

Starting with a Personal Response

A personal response usually happens automatically. You know right away whether you like a movie or not. You walk out of the theater saying, "Those battle scenes were great!" or "What a boring movie!" You respond to literature—a poem, a novel, or a story—in the same way.

There is no right or wrong way to respond to literature. That's why it's called a "personal" response.

The following story is about a young boy who is embarrassed about the way his great-grandfather looks and acts. As you read, think about your personal response. Can you understand how the boy feels?

A SHORT STORY

The Medicine Bag
by Virginia Driving Hawk Sneve

My kid sister Cheryl and I always bragged about our <u>Sioux</u> grandpa, Joe Iron Shell. Our friends, who had always lived in the city and only knew about Indians from movies and TV, were impressed by our stories. Maybe we exaggerated and made

Ask students to name their favorite film characters and to explain why they like them. For example, students might like Luke Skywalker because he's brave, calm, and decisive. After they name the traits they admire, ask for examples to support their reasons. [Luke is willing to put his life in jeopardy to defend the princess, he handles emergencies without losing his nerve, and he makes life-or-death decisions.] Tell students that the process of choosing a character, naming his or her traits, and finding examples to support their observations is the purpose of this segment.

Prewriting   **281**

Grandpa and the reservation sound glamorous, but when we'd return home to Iowa after our yearly summer visit to Grandpa we always had some exciting tale to tell.

1   We always had some authentic Sioux article to show our listeners. One year Cheryl had new moccasins that Grandpa had made. On another visit he gave me a small, round, flat, rawhide drum which was decorated with a painting of a warrior riding a horse. He taught me a real Sioux chant to sing while I beat the drum with a leather-covered stick that had a feather on the end. Man, that really made an impression.

We never showed our friends Grandpa's picture. Not that we were ashamed of him, but because we knew that the glamorous tales we told didn't go with the real thing. Our friends would

2   have laughed at the picture, because Grandpa wasn't tall and stately like TV Indians. His hair wasn't in braids, but hung in stringy, gray strands on his neck and he was old. He was our great-grandfather, and he didn't live in a <u>tepee</u>, but all by himself in a part log, part tar-paper shack on the Rosebud Reservation in South Dakota. So when Grandpa came to visit us, I was so ashamed and embarrassed I could've died.

There are a lot of yippy poodles and other fancy little dogs in our neighborhood, but they usually barked singly at the mailman from the safety of their own yards. Now it sounded as if a whole pack of mutts were barking together in one place.

I got up and walked to the curb to see what the commotion was. About a block away I saw a crowd of little kids yelling, with

This is a long segment, so you'll probably want to take several days to teach it. You may want to have students read the introductory material and the short story ("**The Medicine Bag**") orally in class and complete **Exercise 1** as a class activity. Discuss the plot of the story in class to make sure that everyone understands what happens in the story. Misreadings can interfere with meaningful responses to the story.

You may want to incorporate the questions from **Exercise 2** into your discussion of the material on story elements and let students use the exercise in conjunction with the stories they choose to write about.

3

Walking down the middle of the street shows Grandpa's inexperience and resourcefulness.

4

Grandpa shows he is proud of who he is.

5

Martin is confused by his embarrassment and his love for his grandpa.

6

Mom's behavior shows her concern for Grandpa.

282

282   *Writing About Literature*

3 the dogs yipping and growling around someone who was walking down the middle of the street.

I watched the group as it slowly came closer and saw that in the center of the strange <u>procession</u> was a man wearing a tall black hat. He'd pause now and then to peer at something in his hand and then at the houses on either side of the street. I felt cold and hot at the same time as I recognized the man. "Oh, no!" I whispered. "It's Grandpa!"

I stood on the curb, unable to move even though I wanted to run and hide. Then I got mad when I saw how the yippy dogs were growling and nipping at the old man's baggy pant legs and how wearily he poked them away with his cane. "Stupid mutts," I said as I ran to rescue Grandpa.

When I kicked and hollered at the dogs to get away, they put their tails between their legs and scattered. The kids ran to the curb where they watched me and the old man.

"Grandpa," I said and felt pretty dumb when my voice cracked. I reached for his beat-up old tin suitcase, which was **4** tied shut with a rope. But he set it down right in the street and shook my hand.

"*Hau, Takoza,* Grandchild," he greeted me formally in Sioux.

All I could do was stand there with the whole neighborhood watching and shake the hand of the leather-brown old man. I saw how his gray hair straggled from under his big black hat, which had a drooping feather in its crown. His rumpled black suit hung like a sack over his stooped frame. As he shook my hand, his coat fell open to expose a bright-red, satin shirt with a beaded <u>bolo tie</u> under the collar. His get-up wasn't out of place on the reservation, but it sure was here, and I wanted to sink right through the pavement.

5 "Hi," I muttered with my head down. I tried to pull my hand away when I felt his bony hand trembling, and looked up to see <u>fatigue</u> in his face. I felt like crying. I couldn't think of anything to say so I picked up Grandpa's suitcase, took his arm, and guided him up the driveway to our house.

6 Mom was standing on the steps. I don't know how long she'd been watching, but her hand was over her mouth and she looked as if she couldn't believe what she saw. Then she ran to us.

"Grandpa," she gasped. "How in the world did you get here?"

The students' choice of a short story is crucial to how well they will be able to handle the writing assignment. If you're using this chapter as part of a literature unit and you want to use students' writing to assess how well they can analyze a character, you'll probably want them to use stories you haven't studied in class. If you do allow students to use stories they've already read and discussed, you can focus your evaluation on how well students organize their papers and use details to support their points. In either case, each story should be engaging and should contain at least one fully developed character.

☞

She <u>checked</u> her move to embrace Grandpa and I remembered that such a display of affection is unseemly to the Sioux and would embarrass him.

"*Hau,* Marie," he said as he shook Mom's hand. She smiled and took his other arm.

7   As we supported him up the steps the door banged open and Cheryl came bursting out of the house. She was all smiles and was so obviously glad to see Grandpa that I was ashamed of how I felt.

"Grandpa!" she yelled happily. "You came to see us!"

Grandpa smiled and Mom and I let go of him as he stretched out his arms to my ten-year-old sister, who was still young enough to be hugged.

"*Wicincala,* little girl," he greeted her and then collapsed.

He had fainted. Mom and I carried him into her sewing room, where we had a spare bed.

After we had Grandpa on the bed Mom stood there helplessly patting his shoulder.

"Shouldn't we call the doctor, Mom?" I suggested, since she didn't seem to know what to do.

"Yes," she agreed with a sigh. "You make Grandpa comfortable, Martin."

I reluctantly moved to the bed. I knew Grandpa wouldn't want to have Mom undress him, but I didn't want to, either. He was so skinny and frail that his coat slipped off easily. When I loosened his tie and opened his shirt collar, I felt a small leather

7
Martin's shame shows that he knows his feelings for his grandpa and his Indian heritage are in conflict.

283

My character has long, shaggy ears that drag the ground. She sleeps a lot during the day, but when she hears me, her eyes pop open like a firecracker going off. She loves to run and jump, and her tail is never still when I'm around. She'd lick my hands and face if I let her, and she pokes her cold, wet nose into every corner of the house. My character is my cocker spaniel Inky.

---

284   *Writing About Literature*

8

thong: a narrow strip of leather used as a strap to hold the medicine bag

8   pouch that hung from a thong around his neck. I left it alone and moved to remove his boots. The scuffed old cowboy boots were tight and he moaned as I put pressure on his legs to jerk them off.

I put the boots on the floor and saw why they fit so tight. Each one was stuffed with money. I looked at the bills that lined the boots and started to ask about them, but Grandpa's eyes were closed again.

Mom came back with a basin of water. "The doctor thinks Grandpa is suffering from heat exhaustion," she explained as she bathed Grandpa's face. Mom gave a big sigh, "*Oh hinh,* Martin. How do you suppose he got here?"

9   We found out after the doctor's visit. Grandpa was angrily sitting up in bed while Mom tried to feed him some soup.

9

Grandpa is probably angry because his dignity is offended.

"Tonight you let Marie feed you, Grandpa," spoke my dad, who had gotten home from work just as the doctor was leaving. "You're not really sick," he said as he gently pushed Grandpa back against the pillows. "The doctor said you just got too tired and hot after your long trip."

Grandpa relaxed, and between sips of soup he told us of his journey. Soon after our visit to him Grandpa decided that he would like to see where his only living <u>descendants</u> lived and what our home was like. Besides, he admitted <u>sheepishly</u>, he was lonesome after we left.

10

Why does Martin feel guilty? [Perhaps he feels his family should have visited more than once a year.]

10   I knew everybody felt as guilty as I did—especially Mom. Mom was all Grandpa had left. So even after she married my

INDEPENDENT PRACTICE

Writing Assignment:**Parts 2** and **3** should provide ample opportunity for independent practice. If you assign the parts as homework, you may want to give students a few minutes to begin their work in class so that they can ask you questions if they have any.

ASSESSMENT

The journal entry in **Exercise 1** is a good opportunity to assess whether or not students are able to elaborate on their responses with details from the story. The questions in this exercise could technically be answered with one word each, but the directions call for two or three sentences. These sentences ☛

dad, who's a white man and teaches in the college in our city, and after Cheryl and I were born, Mom made sure that every summer we spent a week with Grandpa.

I never thought that Grandpa would be lonely after our visits, and none of us noticed how old and weak he had become. But Grandpa knew and so he came to us. He had ridden on buses for two and a half days. When he arrived in the city, tired and stiff from sitting for so long, he set out, walking, to find us.

11 He had stopped to rest on the steps of some building downtown and a policeman found him. The cop, according to Grandpa, was a good man who took him to the bus stop and waited until the bus came and told the driver to let Grandpa out at Bell View Drive. After Grandpa got off the bus, he started walking again. But he couldn't see the house numbers on the other side when he walked on the sidewalk so he walked in the middle of the street. That's when all the little kids and dogs followed him.

I knew everybody felt as bad as I did. Yet I was proud of this eighty-six-year-old man, who had never been away from the reservation, having the courage to travel so far alone.

"You found the money in my boots?" he asked Mom.

"Martin did," she answered, and <u>roused</u> herself to scold. "Grandpa, you shouldn't have carried so much money. What if someone had stolen it from you?"

Grandpa laughed. "I would've known if anyone tried to take the boots off my feet. The money is what I've saved for a long 12 time—a hundred dollars—for my funeral. But you take it now to buy groceries so that I won't be a burden to you while I am here."

"That won't be necessary, Grandpa," Dad said. "We are honored to have you with us and you will never be a burden. I am only sorry that we never thought to bring you home with us this summer and spare you the discomfort of a long trip."

Grandpa was pleased. "Thank you," he answered. "But do not feel bad that you didn't bring me with you, for I would not have come then. It was not time." He said this in such a way that no one could argue with him. To Grandpa and the Sioux, he once told me, a thing would be done when it was the right time to do it and that's the way it was.

11
Why does Grandpa think the cop is good? [The cop was kind and helpful.]

12
This behavior shows Grandpa's sensitivity to others.

should explain why students have responded as they have.

Because the questions in **Exercise 2** ask students to identify the four main literary elements in **"The Medicine Bag,"** you can also use these questions to assess how well students can identify the elements in the story they will write about.

You'll probably want to take a close look at the character wheels your students develop for **Writing Assignment: Part 2**, so you will know whether they can identify character traits and use details that support those traits. Performing these skills is an essential step in writing this paper, and you'll want to make sure your students can do this correctly.

13

Martin is afraid he'll be teased if his friends ever see him wearing the bag.

14

He doesn't want to take the bag but will out of duty.

15

It is not time for what? [possibly Grandpa's death or Martin's acceptance]

16

What makes Grandpa's appearance more imposing? [beaded vest and moccasins, brushed hat, brighter feather]

"Also," Grandpa went on, looking at me, "I have come because it is soon time for Martin to have the medicine bag."

We all knew what that meant. Grandpa thought he was going to die and he had to follow the tradition of his family to pass the medicine bag, along with its history, to the oldest male child.

"Even though the boy," he said still looking at me, "bears a white man's name, the medicine bag will be his."

13   I didn't know what to say. I had the same hot and cold feeling that I had when I first saw Grandpa in the street. The medicine bag was the dirty leather pouch I had found around his neck. "I could never wear such a thing," I almost said aloud. I thought of having my friends see it in gym class, at the swimming pool, and could imagine the smart things they would say.

14   But I just swallowed hard and took a step toward the bed. I knew I would have to take it.

15   But Grandpa was tired. "Not now, Martin," he said, waving his hand in dismissal, "it is not time. Now I will sleep."

So that's how Grandpa came to be with us for two months. My friends kept asking to come see the old man, but I put them off. I told myself that I didn't want them laughing at Grandpa. But even as I made excuses I knew it wasn't Grandpa that I was afraid they'd laugh at.

Nothing bothered Cheryl about bringing her friends to see Grandpa. Every day after school started there'd be a crew of giggling little girls or round-eyed little boys crowded around the old man on the patio, where he'd gotten in the habit of sitting every afternoon.

Grandpa would smile in his gentle way and patiently answer their questions, or he'd tell them stories of brave warriors, ghosts, animals, and the kids listened in <u>awed</u> silence. Those little guys thought Grandpa was great.

Finally, one day after school, my friends came home with me because nothing I said stopped them. "We're going to see the great Indian of Bell View Drive," said Hank, who was supposed to be my best friend. "My brother has seen him three times so he oughta be well enough to see us."

When we got to my house Grandpa was sitting on the patio.

16   He had on his red shirt, but today he also wore a fringed leather

RETEACHING

The first concept you may need to reteach is expressing personal responses to literary works. You can do this by asking students to respond to a movie or TV show. Ask them if they liked it or not and why some students might think there's only one right answer to questions of this type. You can help them overcome this tendency by emphasizing that people's opinions are valuable, and that while others may disagree, everyone has a right to express his or her views. The idea of reader-response discussions is to help people discover what their emotional reactions really are and to find words to express those reactions accurately. Emphasize that it's all right for students to change their minds when they hear the ideas ☛

Prewriting   **287**

vest that was decorated with beads. Instead of his usual cowboy boots he had solidly beaded moccasins on his feet that stuck out of his black trousers. Of course, he had his old black hat on—he was seldom without it. But it had been brushed and the feather in the beaded headband was proudly erect, its tip a brighter white. His hair lay in silver strands over the red shirt collar.

I started just as my friends did and I heard one of them murmur, "Wow!"

17   Grandpa looked up and when his eyes met mine they twinkled as if he were laughing inside. He nodded to me and my face got all hot. I could tell that he had known all along I was afraid he'd embarrass me in front of my friends.

"*Hau, hoksilas,* boys," he greeted and held out his hand.

My buddies passed in a single file and shook his hand as I introduced them. They were so polite I almost laughed. "How, there, Grandpa," and even a "How-do-you-do, sir."

"You look fine, Grandpa," I said as the guys sat on the lawn chairs or on the patio floor.

18   "*Hanh,* yes," he agreed. "When I woke up this morning it seemed the right time to dress in the good clothes. I knew that my grandson would be bringing his friends."

"You guys want some lemonade or something?" I offered. No one answered. They were listening to Grandpa as he started telling how he'd killed the deer from which his vest was made.

17
What does this say about Grandpa's character? [It shows that Grandpa understands Martin's feelings and is sensitive to his pain.]

18
This statement shows Grandpa's Sioux belief that there is a correct time to do things.

287

of others in the class. People often gain inspiration from others' ideas.

In reteaching the elements of a literary work, you can again use a TV show, especially a show that doesn't have a subplot, to illustrate the elements. Literary analysis may be very new to your seventh-graders, and sometimes the visual aspects of a play or a TV show are easier for them to work with.

If your students haven't done much academic writing of this type, you may have to reteach the material on developing a writing plan. The information on outlining and graphic organizers in **Chapter 1** may help students structure their work. Mapping or clustering might be especially helpful.

Grandpa did most of the talking while my friends were there. I was so proud of him and amazed at how respectfully quiet my buddies were. Mom had to chase them home at suppertime. As they left they shook Grandpa's hand again and said to me:

"Martin, he's really great!"

"Yeah, man! Don't blame you for keeping him to yourself."

"Can we come back?"

But after they left, Mom said, "No more visitors for a while, Martin. Grandpa won't admit it, but his strength hasn't returned. He likes having company, but it tires him."

19 That evening Grandpa called me to his room before he went to sleep. "Tomorrow," he said, "when you come home, it will be time to give you the medicine bag."

20 I felt a hard squeeze from where my heart is supposed to be and was scared, but I answered, "OK, Grandpa."

All night I had weird dreams about thunder and lightning on a high hill. From a distance I heard the slow beat of a drum. When I woke up in the morning I felt as if I hadn't slept at all. At school it seemed as if the day would never end and, when it finally did, I ran home.

Grandpa was in his room, sitting on the bed. The shades were down and the place was dim and cool. I sat on the floor in front of Grandpa, but he didn't even look at me. After what seemed a long time he spoke.

"I sent your mother and sister away. What you will hear today is only for a man's ears. What you will receive is only for a man's hands." He fell silent and I felt shivers down my back.

21 "My father in his early manhood," Grandpa began, "made a vision quest to find a spirit guide for his life. You cannot understand how it was in that time, when the great Teton Sioux were first made to stay on the reservation. There was a strong need for guidance from *Wakantanka*, the Great Spirit. But too many of the young men were filled with despair and hatred. They thought it was hopeless to search for a vision when the glorious life was gone and only the hated confines of a reservation lay ahead. But my father held to the old ways.

"He carefully prepared for his quest with a purifying sweat bath and then he went alone to a high butte top to fast and pray.

22 After three days he received his sacred dream—in which he

19

What does Grandpa know here? [He shows that his strength is failing.]

20

What is Martin afraid of? [the unknown, growing up, or Grandpa's dying]

21

A vision quest is part of a young man's initiation into adulthood. He goes on a journey alone, with few tools and supplies, to discover his true identity. Often this identity was revealed in a dream.

22

The vision foreshadows increasing influence of the white culture.

Cut out pictures of people from newspapers and magazines and bring the pictures to class. Show a picture to your students and ask them to write down a character trait they think the person in the picture might have. Then have each student create at least one reason why the person might have this trait. Point out there are no right or wrong answers and discuss with students the clues they used in making their judgments. Point out that an author creates a word picture of a character and often gives only very subtle clues about the character's traits.

found, after long searching, the white man's iron. He did not understand his vision of finding something belonging to the white people, for in that time they were the enemy. When he came down from the butte to cleanse himself at the stream below, he found the remains of a campfire and the broken shell of an iron kettle. This was a sign which reinforced his dream. He took a piece of the iron for his medicine bag, which he had made of elk skin years before, to prepare for his quest.

"He returned to his village, where he told his dream to the wise old men of the tribe. They gave him the name Iron Shell, but neither did they understand the meaning of the dream. This first Iron Shell kept the piece of iron with him at all times and believed it gave him protection from the evils of those unhappy days.

"Then a terrible thing happened to Iron Shell. He and several other young men were taken from their homes by the soldiers and sent far away to a white man's boarding school. He was angry and lonesome for his parents and the young girl he had wed before he was taken away. At first Iron Shell resisted the

MEETING INDIVIDUAL NEEDS

LEP/ESL

General Strategies. Although mainstream students might readily perceive that **"The Medicine Bag"** concerns the experience of a Native American, LEP/ESL student might require additional historical or cultural background information. They might need answers to the following questions:

1. What are the naming traditions of Native Americans?
2. What are some spiritual beliefs of Native Americans?
3. Why are there allusions to The Great Spirit?
4. What is the role of the medicine man?
5. What are the traditional roles of men? Of women?
6. How important are ceremonies and rituals?

Have students research the customs and beliefs of the Sioux Indians. Virginia Driving Hawk Sneve has written several books about Indian life that students might use. They include *Jimmy Yellow Hawk, High Elk's Treasure,* and *When Thunder Spoke.*

Authors often use names to convey character. For example, Charles Dickens created Mr. McChokumchild in *Hard Times* as the teacher in a school where the students are choked on facts. Ask your students to come up with names that reveal traits of the following kinds of characters. Creativity and cleverness are the criteria for these.

290   *Writing About Literature*

teachers' attempts to change him and he did not try to learn. One day it was his turn to work in the school's blacksmith shop. As he walked into the place he knew that his medicine had brought him there to learn and work with the white man's iron.

"Iron Shell became a blacksmith and worked at the trade when he returned to the reservation. All of his life he treasured the medicine bag. When he was old, and I was a man, he gave it to me, for no one made the vision quest anymore."

23   Grandpa quit talking and I stared in disbelief as he covered his face with his hands. His shoulders were shaking with quiet sobs and I looked away until he began to speak again.

"I kept the bag until my son, your mother's father, was a man and had to leave us to fight in the war across the ocean. I gave him the bag, for I believed it would protect him in battle, but he did not take it with him. He was afraid that he would lose it. He died in a faraway place."

Again Grandpa was still and I felt his grief around me.

"My son," he went on after clearing his throat, "had only a daughter and it is not proper for her to know of these things."

He unbuttoned his shirt, pulled out the leather pouch, and lifted it over his head. He held it in his hand, turning it over and over as if memorizing how it looked.

24   "In the bag," he said as he opened it and removed two objects, "is the broken shell of the iron kettle, a pebble from the butte, and a piece of the sacred <u>sage</u>." He held the pouch upside down and dust drifted down.

"After the bag is yours you must put a piece of prairie sage within and never open it again until you pass it on to your son." He replaced the pebble and the piece of iron, and tied the bag.

I stood up, somehow knowing I should. Grandpa slowly rose from the bed and stood upright in front of me, holding the bag before my face. I closed my eyes and waited for him to slip it over my head. But he spoke.

25   "No, you need not wear it." He placed the soft leather bag in my right hand and closed my other hand over it. "It would not be right to wear it in this time and place where no one will understand. Put it safely away until you are again on the reservation. Wear it then, when you replace the sacred sage."

23

Martin's disbelief reflects Grandpa's unusual show of emotion.

24

The medicine bag is a symbol of their heritage, and it binds the generations.

25

Why doesn't Grandpa require Martin to wear the bag? [He understands the ridicule Martin might face, and the medicine bag is too sacred an object to subject to disrespect.]

1. a playground superintendent who doesn't like kids
2. a mean dentist
3. a kind older lady who takes in stray animals
4. a policeman who is always smiling
5. Hansel and Gretel's wicked stepmother
6. the giant in "Jack and the Beanstalk" ■

Grandpa turned and sat again on the bed. Wearily he leaned his head against the pillow. "Go," he said, "I will sleep now."

"Thank you, Grandpa," I said softly and left with the bag in my hands.

26   That night Mom and Dad took Grandpa to the hospital. Two weeks later I stood alone on the lonely prairie of the reservation and put the sacred sage in my medicine bag.

 **Responding to a Story**

What's your personal response to "The Medicine Bag"? How many stars would you give it? (Use four stars as the highest rating and one star as the lowest.) Draw the number of stars in your journal. Then write two or three sentences in your journal about your personal response to the characters and story events. Did you like Martin? How did you feel about the way he treated his great-grandfather? Did events in the story keep your interest? Would you like to read another story like this one?

26
Martin has finally resolved the problems with his heritage.

INTEGRATING THE LANGUAGE ARTS

Literature Link. The poem "Those Winter Sundays" by Robert Hayden is an interesting comparison to **"The Medicine Bag."** Both works deal with a young man's feelings for a family member.

Ask students to read Hayden's poem and to use character wheels to analyze the speaker in the poem. Then students can write informative/classificatory paragraphs comparing the speaker in the poem and Martin.

ANSWERS
Exercise 1

Sentences will vary. Each sentence should express a complete thought, include specific reasons why students did or did not like Martin, tell why the events of the story did or did not keep their interest, and tell why students would or would not like to read another story like this one.

A DIFFERENT APPROACH

Many students often don't understand why they're asked to write about works of literature, particularly because this type of writing doesn't appear to have a direct relationship to a career. You can point out that even though they have a response to everything they read, many times students aren't aware of what that response is until they write it down. Writing about their responses helps them because it forces them to think about how they really feel. Also, if they ask themselves why they responded as they did, they can often gain insights about themselves that they wouldn't otherwise know.

Reading for Understanding

After reading some stories, you may stop at your personal response. But sometimes you need to go beyond it. For instance, you may want to explain to a friend why you want him or her to read a story. Or, you may have a school assignment to read a story and analyze it. Then you'll need to have some understanding of the basic parts, or elements, of a story. These are the characters, the plot, the setting, and the meaning.

BASIC ELEMENTS OF STORIES

CHARACTERS. The *characters* of a story are its actors—the people, animals, or creatures who play parts. You get to know characters in a story the same way you get to know people in real life. You observe what they say, what they think, and what they do. You also notice how they look and how other people respond to them.

PLOT. *Plot* is what happens in the story—the events that unfold from the beginning to the end. The plot almost always presents a *conflict,* or problem, that the main character has to overcome.

SETTING. Where and when a story's events occur make up its *setting.* In some stories, the setting causes things to happen. In others, the events might happen anywhere.

MEANING. The *meaning,* or main idea, of a story is what it tells you about people or life. The meaning of a story about a village hit by an earthquake could be "Hard times can bring out the best in people."

EXERCISE 2 ▶ **Analyzing the Elements of a Story**

How well do you understand the basic parts of a story? Read back over "The Medicine Bag" on pages 280–291. Then, with two or three classmates, answer the following questions.

1. Who are the two main characters? Imagine telling a friend about them. What word or two would you use to describe each one?
2. What conflict, or problem, does Martin face?
3. Briefly describe what happens at the most exciting point (the climax) in the story.
4. What is the setting? Why does this setting cause events in the story to happen?
5. The meaning of this story focuses on the way a boy reacts to his great-grandfather. Tell the meaning of the story in your own words.

WRITING ASSIGNMENT

PART 1:
Reading and Responding to a Story

Choose a story, either one that you would like to read or one your teacher suggests. First, read it and check your own response. How do you feel about this story? Then, look at it more closely. Use the questions in Exercise 2 to analyze the story's basic elements.

ANSWERS
Exercise 2

1. The two main characters are Martin and Grandpa. Martin is confused, insightful, and observant. Grandpa is wise, dignified, and understanding.

2. He must decide if he can accept his heritage.

3. At the climax, Grandpa presents the medicine bag to Martin, who accepts it.

4. The setting is a large city. This setting is a crucial element in the story because Martin hasn't had to tell his friends the real story of his grandpa, who has lived on a South Dakota reservation.

5. Cultural traditions and one's heritage are important to the identity of a person.

INTEGRATING THE LANGUAGE ARTS

Vocabulary Link. Students studying the elements of fiction often need help in developing vocabulary to talk about literary elements. You can explain that the main character is the protagonist. The character or circumstance that works against the main character is the antagonist. Encourage students to use terms like *antagonist* and *protagonist* in their character analyses.

Another term, *theme,* is used to discuss the elements related to the element of meaning. You can tell students that they might make references to meaning by using this term.

COOPERATIVE LEARNING

One way to handle **Writing Assignment: Parts 1–3** is to assign students to groups of four and to let them work together on all parts of the assignment. All of the members of each group should work on the same story, although they don't necessarily have to work on the same character. By having all members of the group use the same story, students will have someone with whom they can discuss ideas and can ask questions.

Prewriting

Planning a Character Analysis

In a literature class, you are often asked to analyze a story or some part of it. A *character analysis* is one type of story analysis.

Studying a Character

When you analyze a character in a story, you try to find out what makes that character "tick." In your everyday life, you do this all the time. You pick up clues about the people around you by noticing what they do and say. To pick up clues about a character in a story, you do the same thing. These are the things you should especially watch for.

- Notice how the character **looks.** Does his or her appearance affect what happens?
- Watch how the character **behaves.** Does he or she take action to face the conflict? What do the character's actions show about what the character feels inside? Are the character's actions and feelings related in any way?
- Listen to what the character **says.** Does the character say how he or she feels? What kind of language does the character use?
- Notice the character's **thoughts.** What goes on in the character's mind? What does that tell you about him or her? Do any thoughts keep popping up over and over again?

As you read a story closely, take notes. Write down details that show how a character feels or thinks. Beside each note, write your own reaction or evaluation (for example: "he's embarrassed"; "cares what his friends think"; "shows honesty"; "proud"). On the next page are some notes one writer made about Martin.

OBJECTIVE

- To analyze a character by making a character wheel containing the student's personal character traits, details about his or her words, and actions to support the traits

TEACHING *ANALYZING A CHARACTER*

You may want to give students a demonstration of character analysis on the chalkboard by using yourself or the mythical teacher whose character analysis follows. Trait 1: messy —I never hang up my clothes when I change after school. I leave books

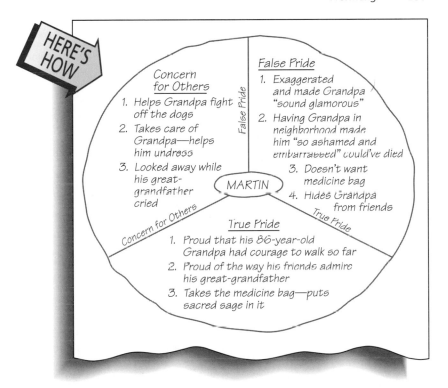

HERE'S HOW

Concern for Others
1. Helps Grandpa fight off the dogs
2. Takes care of Grandpa—helps him undress
3. Looked away while his great-grandfather cried

False Pride
1. Exaggerated and made Grandpa "sound glamorous"
2. Having Grandpa in neighborhood made him "so ashamed and embarrassed" could've died
3. Doesn't want medicine bag
4. Hides Grandpa from friends

MARTIN

True Pride
1. Proud that his 86-year-old Grandpa had courage to walk so far
2. Proud of the way his friends admire his great-grandfather
3. Takes the medicine bag—puts sacred sage in it

MEETING **INDIVIDUAL** NEEDS

LEP/ESL

General Strategies. The Critical Thinking Exercise offers a good opportunity for ESL students to share cultural experiences with the class. Encourage students to draw upon their cultures as they choose their traits and details for their character wheels.

LESS-ADVANCED STUDENTS

You could use the acronym SEAT to help students remember how writers reveal what lies at the heart, or "seat," of a character's personality.

Speech
Effects on others
Actions and **A**ppearance
Thoughts

CRITICAL THINKING
Analyzing a Character

When you *analyze* something, you look at its parts. This analysis helps you understand something better. When you analyze a character, you think about what the character says, does, thinks, and so on.

One way to analyze a character is to create a character wheel. To make one, first think about the character overall. What are his or her *major traits*, or characteristics? Choose two or three traits that you think are the most important. Then, look back through the story to find details that show those traits.

The Here's How above is an example of an analysis using a character wheel. Here are the parts of the wheel.

and papers all over the house.
Trait 2: energetic—I work out three times a week. I play softball in the teachers' league.
Trait 3: generous—I share my lunch with teachers who forget theirs almost every day. I contribute to the United Way every year.

You can emphasize that students should list traits for their characters that readers can see from what the characters say and do or from what other characters say about them.

 INTEGRATING THE LANGUAGE ARTS

Vocabulary Link. Have students look up *trait* in a dictionary to study the etymology of the word [from a French word meaning "a line or mark made with a pencil"]. How is the modern English meaning ["a personality quality or characteristic"] related to the word's original meaning? [A character trait is a kind of mark on the personality of an individual; it marks the person as being of a certain type.]

ANSWERS
Critical Thinking Exercise

Traits will vary. However, all of their traits should be based on specific words and actions that are obvious and that the students could say or do at school or at home. The details should support the traits.

CRITICAL THINKING EXERCISE:
Analyzing a Character

Work with some classmates to analyze a character—perhaps Grandpa in "The Medicine Bag," a character in another story, or a character from one of your favorite TV shows. Work together to make a character wheel. Identify two or three character traits. Then have one person draw the wheel and write the traits on the spokes. As the group identifies details to go with each trait, one person can write them in the wheel between the spokes. What kind of person is this character? Can you write one or two sentences to summarize what you think?

 **Speaking and Listening: Creating and Analyzing a Character**

ANSWERS
Exercise 3

Characters will vary. Students should include enough detail in their descriptions to enable their listeners to have a sense of what the characters are like.

Make up your own character. Then tell a small group of classmates about your character. What does your character look like? How does he or she speak? walk? dress? Suppose the character takes your place at school today. How does he or she behave? Do your classmates like the character? Tell why. Now, listen to your classmates speak. What do you learn about their characters?

PART 2:
Choosing a Character to Analyze

Choose a character from the story you read for Writing Assignment, Part 1 (page 293). The character should be one you either liked or disliked very much. Next, make a character wheel like the one on page 295. Find two or three traits for your character to put on the wheel. Between the spokes, write details that support those traits.

Developing a Writing Plan

Thinking About Purpose and Audience. The *purpose* of a character analysis is to find out what kind of person a story character is. You do this so that you and your readers can understand a character better. When you know a story character in this way, you can often understand yourself or others better. The *audience* for the analysis is usually your teacher and classmates. You may also want to share your analysis with a friend or family member.

Stating Your Main Idea. Think about how you describe someone new in school to friends who have never met him or her. Usually, you describe a few major traits of that person. You may say, for example, that the person seems lonely or cheerful or very shy. In a character analysis, these traits become your *main idea*.

For your character analysis, choose one or two, perhaps three, major traits about your character. (It's better to look at fewer traits and explain them clearly.) Then write a sentence about them. That sentence is your *main idea statement*. If your character changes, you may need two or more sentences to express your main idea. Here's the main idea statement for the character wheel on page 295. The writer uses only two of the traits on his wheel.

EXAMPLE   At first, Martin feels false pride. However, it becomes a true pride after he learns more about his great-grandfather and his heritage.

 CRITICAL THINKING
Inference

The way characters look, behave, talk, and think are means by which the author communicates indirectly what the characters are like. It is the job of readers to interpret this indirect communication by drawing conclusions on the basis of what the author tells them. This requirement is one of the major differences between fiction and nonfiction: The author shows in fiction but tells in nonfiction.

Write the following description on the chalkboard or pass it out in handout form:

The man's eyes were red and his eyelids were droopy. He yawned every few seconds, and he needed a shave.

Ask students why the man looks this way. [He needs sleep or he's been up all night.] Is there a single word that communicates this information? [No.] How do you know he needs sleep? [All of the details paint a picture of a person who's been awake for a long time.]

Point out to students that they will have to do this kind of thinking when they analyze their characters.

A DIFFERENT APPROACH

Instead of having your students merely describe the characters they make up in **Exercise 3,** try having each student deliver a monologue as his or her character would deliver it. Another approach is to let students work in pairs to prepare dialogues. Each member of the pair would be a different character.

MEETING INDIVIDUAL NEEDS

LESS-ADVANCED STUDENTS

Your less-advanced students might benefit from group work on **Writing Assignment: Part 2.** They will all have to use the same story but not necessarily the same character. If three or four students work together to develop character wheels, let them initial their contributions to make sure everyone is involved in the project.

Organizing Your Information.   One way to organize a character analysis is to decide which trait is most important and start or end with it. Another way is to treat the traits chronologically, in the order in which they appear in the story. Just be sure that you don't mix the details that support one trait with the details for another trait.

To develop a plan for your character analysis

- think about your purpose and audience
- identify some traits of the character
- look for details from the story to explain the traits
- decide what traits you will discuss in your paper
- write a main idea statement about those traits

WRITING ASSIGNMENT
PART 3:
Developing a Writing Plan

Think about the character you chose for Writing Assignment, Part 2 (page 297). Review the traits on your character wheel and choose one or two that you think are very important. Write a main idea statement about them. Then decide how you will organize your analysis. List the traits and supporting details in the order you will use them.

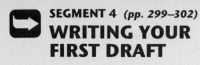

OBJECTIVE

• To write a first draft of a character analysis

TEACHING THE LESSON

Be sure students use the character wheels and the main idea statements they've already developed to guide them as they write. Emphasize that a first draft doesn't have to be perfect in grammar, usage, and mechanics, and remind students that they can take care of problems in these areas later in the writing process. ☜

Writing Your First Draft

The Parts of a Character Analysis

Now it's time to write your character analysis and turn your notes into sentences and paragraphs. Your paper should be four or five paragraphs long. It will be organized like a composition.

- First paragraph: Name the title and author of the story and tell what character you're analyzing. State your main idea in one or two sentences.
- Middle (or body) paragraphs: In each paragraph, write about one trait and the details that explain it. Start a new paragraph for each trait.
- Last paragraph: Sum up the main points of your paper and restate your main idea.

☞ **REFERENCE NOTE:** For more information on the parts of a composition, see pages 104–110.

Here's a model character analysis of Martin, the main character of "The Medicine Bag." It tells about two of Martin's character traits. As you read, notice how each trait has details to support it.

A WRITER'S MODEL

The Discovery of True Pride

INTRODUCTION
Author/Title
Character
Main idea

The main character in Virginia Driving Hawk Sneve's "The Medicine Bag" is a young boy named Martin. One of the strongest traits of this character is his pride. At the beginning of the story it is a false, bragging kind of pride. But at the end of the story it is a true pride—in his heritage.

RESOURCES

WRITING YOUR FIRST DRAFT
• Introducing a Character Analysis

QUOTATION FOR THE DAY

"Writing is a difficult trade which must be learned slowly by reading great authors . . ." (André Maurois, 1885–1967, French writer)

Write the quotation on the chalkboard to initiate a discussion about how reading, analyzing, or responding to good stories or books helps readers learn about writing. Explain that each time a student reads, he or she is also gathering ideas about how another author works with words. Writing about literature allows the student to take an even closer look at a story or book.

The model character analysis of Martin is a clear example of what a character analysis should be. You'll probably want to read it to the class and spend some time pointing out the aspects of the paper that are labeled to the left of the essay. Studying the model closely with your class is a way of providing guided practice. Emphasize that the use of third person in the model focuses attention on the character being analyzed and not on the writer or the reader.

Have students use the **Framework for a Character Analysis** on p. 302 as a blueprint for the structure of their papers.

MEETING
INDIVIDUAL
NEEDS

LEP/ESL

General Strategies. Writing a first draft may be the most difficult part of the writing process for some students. If possible, work closely with students, helping them choose stories that readily lend themselves to character analysis. Review students' notes and character wheels to make sure students are recording necessary details. Discuss the main idea statements, and ask students about purpose and audience to ensure they understand what is expected in the analysis. Once the rough drafts are written, review each paper before having the class evaluate and revise.

BODY
First trait
Details—
Martin's actions

Details—
Martin's words and actions

Details—
Martin's thoughts

Details—
Martin's actions

Second trait
Details—
Martin's thoughts

Details—
Martin's thoughts and actions

At the beginning of the story, Martin admitted that he and his sister had always bragged about their Sioux "grandpa," who was actually their great-grandfather. For Martin, though, this pride in a way wasn't sincere. He exaggerated and made his great-grandfather sound like Indians in the movies and on TV.

When Grandpa actually walked into his neighborhood, Martin was embarrassed. He said that he felt hot and cold all over and was "so ashamed and embarrassed" he could have died. When Martin held his head down and pulled his hand away, he showed how his pride in his great-grandfather was not real. He was proud only of his pretend "grandpa," not the real one.

How Martin felt about the medicine bag also showed his false pride. His great-grandfather had come to give the medicine bag to Martin. But Martin didn't want it. He didn't want his friends to see him wearing it.

He didn't even want them to see his great-grandfather. They asked to, but Martin wouldn't let them. But one day they went right into Martin's house anyway. Grandpa seemed to have known they were coming. He had put on his best clothes, and he was impressive in his beaded vest and moccasins. When Martin saw that his friends thought Grandpa was great, he began to feel a true pride.

The next day, Grandpa told Martin about the medicine bag. He explained how his father had passed it on to him. Then he asked Martin to find a piece of sacred sage to add to the medicine bag and save it for his own son. As Martin listened to the story, he began to understand his heritage and be proud of it. Soon after that Grandpa died. At the end of the story, Martin stood alone on the prairie and put the sacred sage in his medicine

ASSESSMENT

Your assessment of the first drafts can be based on whether students follow the guidelines given in the framework. A question that can guide your assessment is "Did students put together clearly and logically the parts of their papers they developed during prewriting?"

CLOSURE

Bring closure to this lesson by copying some of the better drafts and allowing students to share them. Not only will this reinforce the work of students who give permission for their papers to be used, but also will provide additional models to students who are still struggling. ∎

Writing Your First Draft   **301**

bag. He was now proud of the medicine bag and what it meant to his family.

CONCLUSION

Main idea in different words

Martin always had pride. But as he came to know his great-grandfather, that pride changed. It went from a false pride to a sincere pride and feeling of honor in his heritage.

WRITING NOTE Use details from the story to support the traits of your character. But don't just tell your readers what happens in the story. Many of your readers may already know the story, and it's boring to read something you already know.

PEANUTS reprinted by permission of UFS, Inc.

A Framework for a Character Analysis

On the following page is a framework for a character analysis like the one about Martin. You may want to use this framework when you write your own analysis.

STUDENTS WITH SPECIAL NEEDS

Writing reviews can be challenging for learning disabled students because of the difficulty in differentiating between the various parts of the literary work while determining what passages students like and what they dislike. To help strengthen students' analytical skills, have each student read a story and choose a character. Next, instruct students to write each character trait on an index card and to list examples of the characters' displaying that trait on the back of the card. Finally, have students use their indexed observations to support their opinions as they write the compositions. A summation of the opinion can be used as the conclusion for each essay.

 CRITICAL THINKING
Analysis

You may want to point out to students that the writer of the model character analysis informs readers in the first paragraph that the paper will be structured chronologically with the phrase "At the beginning of the story . . . ." Remind students that this is one way to structure their essays but that they can also use the order of importance.

INTEGRATING THE LANGUAGE ARTS

Mechanics Link. Students might not be familiar with how the ellipsis can be used to show that words have been left out of a quotation. Explain to students that they are free to leave out parts of quotations from their stories (if they don't change the meaning of the quotation) by using three periods to show each time they've left something out. If an ellipsis comes at the end of a sentence, students should use the three periods of the ellipsis and another period to show the end of the sentence.

TIMESAVER

You can save yourself some time grading first drafts by having students underline the character traits in red and the details that support the traits in another color. When you read the papers, the underlined material should stand out.

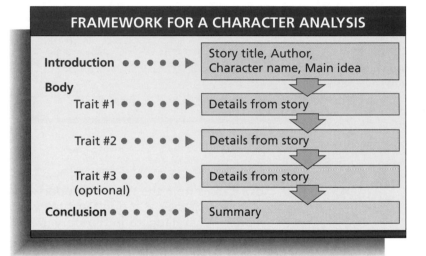

FRAMEWORK FOR A CHARACTER ANALYSIS

Introduction ••••• ▶	Story title, Author, Character name, Main idea
Body	
Trait #1 ••••• ▶	Details from story
Trait #2 ••••• ▶	Details from story
Trait #3 ••••• ▶ (optional)	Details from story
Conclusion ••••• ▶	Summary

 **Writing Your First Draft**

You've already done most of the work for your analysis. Now, use your main idea statement and the details on your character wheel to write a rough draft of a character analysis. Remember that you'll have a chance to make changes in your analysis later. It doesn't have to be perfect on the first try.

EVALUATING AND REVISING

OBJECTIVES

- To analyze a writer's revisions
- To evaluate and revise the first draft of a character analysis

TEACHING THE LESSON

This segment contains two important features. The first is the guidelines in the **Evaluating and Revising a Character Analysis** chart, and the second is **Exercise 4**, which deals with analyzing a writer's revisions.

The chart contains specific guidelines for evaluating and revising, and you'll ☞

Evaluating and Revising

To evaluate your analysis, use the following guide. Ask yourself each question in the left-hand column. If you find a problem, use the ideas in the right-hand column to fix it.

EVALUATING AND REVISING A CHARACTER ANALYSIS

EVALUATION GUIDE	REVISION TECHNIQUE
1 Does the introduction identify the story's author and title? Does it name the character who is analyzed?	**Add** the missing information.
2 Does the introduction state the main idea?	Review your character wheel and **add** a main idea statement.
3 Does the body have enough details from the story to support each character trait?	**Add** direct quotations and other story details that describe the words, thoughts, actions, and appearance of the character.
4 Does the conclusion sum up the main points and restate the main idea?	**Add** one or two sentences or rewrite sentences in the conclusion.

EXERCISE 4 ▶ **Analyzing a Writer's Revisions**

On the next page is a first draft of the first paragraph of the analysis of Martin. With two or three classmates, figure out why the writer made the changes. Then answer the questions that follow.

RESOURCES

EVALUATING AND REVISING
- Writing a Character Analysis

QUOTATION FOR THE DAY

"I am under the spell of language, which has ruled me since I was 10." (V.S. Pritchett, 1900–   , British critic)

After writing the quotation on the chalkboard, ask students to freewrite about its meaning. A few volunteers might read aloud from their responses. Explain to students that the purpose of evaluation and revision is to make their papers as clear and powerful as the work of the professional authors they admire.

MEETING INDIVIDUAL NEEDS

LEP/ESL

General Strategies. It is difficult for LEP/ESL students to critique their own work and to maneuver through the evaluating process independently. It is crucial that students receive individual attention and input from the teacher. Although peer tutors may be able to perceive mechanical or usage weaknesses in their classmates' compositions, it is likely that they will not be able to convey effectively how to revise content.

probably want to have students study its contents and use it when they evaluate and revise their papers. You can also use it in your assessment of their revisions. Use **Exercise 4** to guide students as they analyze why certain revisions have been made. Students can then complete **Writing Assignment: Part 5** independently.

CLOSURE

Bring to class a revised draft of a paper you've written so students can see extensive revision. Ask students to discuss some of the revisions by telling why and how they think the changes were made. ■

The main character in Virginia Driving Hawk Sneve's ~~story~~ "The Medicine Bag" is a young boy. named Martin. One of the strongest traits of this   **replace**
    add

character is his pride. At the beginning of

the story it is a false, bragging kind of

pride. But at the end of the story it is a

true pride—in his heritage. ~~That's because~~   **cut**

~~he'd gotten to know his great-grandfather~~

~~and learned about the medicine bag.~~

1. Why does the writer replace the word *story* with *"The Medicine Bag"*?
2. In the same sentence, what words does the writer add after the word *boy*? What important information do the new words add to the paragraph?
3. Why does the writer cut out the last sentence? [Hint: Where does this information belong?]

PART 5:
Evaluating and Revising Your Character Analysis

A first draft is like a caterpillar; a revision is the butterfly. Reread your own first draft, and think of ways to "make it fly." The questions from the evaluating and revising chart on page 303 will help you.

ANSWERS
Exercise 4

1. The writer identifies the title of the story.
2. The writer added the words "named Martin." The new information identifies the character being analyzed.
3. The new sentence states information that should be analyzed in the body of the paper.

 **INTEGRATING THE LANGUAGE ARTS**

Technology Link. Word processors have simplified revision, especially when rearranging information. Students can copy passages to the clipboards of most word processors and insert these passages wherever they're needed. Encourage students who use word processors to make their revisions on hard copy, rather than directly on screen, so they can get a better idea of what their essays look like.

PROOFREADING AND PUBLISHING

OBJECTIVE

- To proofread and publish a character analysis

TEACHING THE LESSON

You can deal with this segment as two separate but related tasks. First, have your students read the material on proofreading. If you have emphasized some aspect of grammar, usage, or mechanics before you started this chapter, remind students of the concept and encourage them to apply their knowledge in their proofreading.

Proofreading and Publishing

Proofreading. You've "given wings" to your paper. Now it's time to take care of the finishing details. Read carefully over your paper at least twice to check for mistakes.

MECHANICS HINT

Using Quotation Marks

Use quotation marks around the title of the story. And when you quote directly from a story, put quotation marks around the words. Do this even when a character isn't speaking.

EXAMPLES　The main character in Virginia Driving Hawk Sneve's **"The Medicine Bag"** is a young boy named Martin.
He said that he felt hot and cold all over and was **"so ashamed and embarrassed"** he could have died.

☞ REFERENCE NOTE: For more information on quotation marks, see pages 737–744.

Publishing. With your teacher's help, plan some special ways to share your papers. Here are two ideas:

- Create a "movie poster" to go with your paper, spotlighting the most exciting point of the story. Place the posters around the room.
- Find a "friend" for your character. Get together with three or four classmates and share your papers. Decide

RESOURCES

PROOFREADING AND PUBLISHING

- Writing a Character Analysis

QUOTATION FOR THE DAY

"Publications are useful and lovely—there is no motivation quite like the glory of being published." (Meredith Sue Willis, 1946–   , American author and writing teacher)

Have students copy this quotation and freewrite their opinions of Willis' thoughts. Is publication as important as she thinks? Why? Why not?

For example, you may want to remind students to check spelling, to begin each sentence with a capital letter, to correct any sentence fragments and run-on sentences, and so on. Because this may be the first time your students have written papers on works of literature, you may want to emphasize the **Mechanics Hint** (p. 305) about using quotation marks.

After the papers have been proofread and recopied, if necessary, you can let your students publish their papers by using one of the suggestions in the text or in the side margin.

which of your classmates' characters would make the best friend for your character. Write a short dialogue between the two characters.

PART 6:
Proofreading and Publishing Your Character Analysis

You're at the finish line. Proofread your paper and make sure it has no errors and is clear to your readers. Use one of the ideas on page 305 and above, or another idea of your own, to share your paper with others.

A STUDENT MODEL

David Street, a student at West Ridge Middle School in Austin, Texas, writes about a well-known short story in his paper. David recommends "asking yourself questions about the story" and "working through many drafts before the final copy." As you read his paper, ask yourself if David makes you want to read O. Henry's story, "After Twenty Years."

Evaluation of "After Twenty Years"
by David Street

I enjoyed reading the story "After Twenty Years" by O. Henry because of the surprising twist at the end. My attention was quickly absorbed when the policeman, Jimmy Wells, noticed his old friend Bob and started carrying on a conversation with him. Bob's quick talking in the beginning

MEETING
INDIVIDUAL
NEEDS

LEP/ESL

Spanish. Proofreading provides an excellent opportunity for students to focus on one grammatical feature at a time. Because description generally plays a key role in character analysis, ask students to focus on the use of adjectives. In Spanish, an adjective follows the noun it modifies. For example, *the rich man* translates as *el hombre rico*. Students might tend to transfer this rule to English. Another interference problem lies in the fact that, in Spanish, an adjective agrees with the accompanying noun in both number and gender. For example, the Spanish speaker might express *las muchachas altas* (the tall girls) as *the talls girls*. Pair Spanish-speaking students with peer tutors. Have them review their character analyses for correct usage of adjectives.

To assess students' proofreading, read their papers and focus on the errors in the aspects of grammar, usage, and mechanics you've emphasized. You can call these to students' attention by circling them or by making comments in the margin.

CLOSURE

On the last day of the lesson, have each student volunteer one element of the paper that was corrected during proofreading. ■

of the conversation caught my attention, and his unusual and suspicious story kept me listening. O. Henry set up the meeting with an appropriate setting, which helped to attract my attention. He described the weather as "chilly gusts of wind with a taste of rain in them," and he made the streets nearly vacant. This scenery gave an eerie feeling to help elaborate on the mystery. The characters were described enough to set up the reader but not too much. He described Bob as having "a pale, square-jawed face with keen eyes, and a little white scar near his right eyebrow." Then he told how his "scarfpin was a large diamond, oddly set." These details give the reader a subtle clue that Bob might be some sort of a gangster. The plot was well thought out and fairly easy to follow. It gave the reader many clues that led up to the surprise ending. Overall, I enjoyed "After Twenty Years" because of the suspense and the ending. I would recommend it to anyone who enjoys unexpected twists in stories.

INTEGRATING THE LANGUAGE ARTS

Vocabulary Link. The words *quotation* and *quote* are often incorrectly used as synonyms for one another. You can point out to students that *quotation* is a noun and means "a group of words spoken or written by someone else and later used by another speaker or writer." The word *quote* is a verb that means "to use the words of someone else."

A STUDENT MODEL
Evaluation

1. David includes both the story's author and the title in his introduction.
2. With his second sentence, David names the character he is analyzing and then states his main idea.
3. Several direct quotations and specific details support the character's traits; for example, Bob has "a pale, square-jawed face with keen eyes."
4. The last sentences sum up the main points by restating David's main idea.

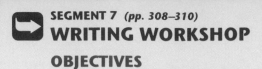

WRITING WORKSHOP

OBJECTIVES

- To analyze a comparison/contrast essay
- To write a comparison and contrast of two characters

TEACHING THE LESSON

You can present several alternatives students can choose from in writing their papers. First, they can use the characters they wrote about in their character analyses and find characters from other stories to compare and contrast. Second, they can each find two new stories and compare characters from each. Third, they can each find one story

WRITING WORKSHOP
- Analyzing a Character
- Introducing a Character Analysis
- Writing a Character Analysis

QUOTATION FOR THE DAY

"The reader will be drawn into our stories if we are drawn into characters." (Lucy M. Calkins, American author, speaker, and professor of writing at Columbia University)

Share this quotation with your students and discuss its meaning with them. Why would an author have to be involved with a character he or she creates? How would this make the reader see the character better?

308

308

WRITING WORKSHOP

A Comparison of Two Characters

Sometimes you write an analysis of one character. But many times you can understand one character better by comparing him or her to another character.

When you compare two characters, you start by looking at their similarities. How are they alike? Sometimes you may also contrast them. How are they different?

When you write a paper or paragraph comparing two characters, you can organize it in one of two ways.

1. Present everything you have to say about one character, and then present everything you have to say about the other character, or
2. Present one detail about both characters, then a second detail about both characters, then a third detail about both characters, and so on.

Here's a writer's model comparing Martin in "The Medicine Bag" with the main character in "The All-American Slurp."

Martin, a young boy whose ancestry is part Native American, is the main character in Virginia Driving Hawk Sneve's "The Medicine Bag." At the beginning of the story, he is embarrassed by his family background. Because his great-grandfather, called "Grandpa," doesn't look like the Indians in the movies, Martin is afraid his friends will laugh at him. The Chinese American girl in Lensey Namioka's "The All-American Slurp" is also embarrassed by her family background. At the beginning of the story she and her family are invited out to their first dinner in America. She feels her family has "disgraced" themselves because they don't know how to eat American food.

with two comparable characters and compare and contrast them.

Use this segment as an independent lesson (after your class has studied the chapter) when you study stories that have comparable characters.

Your assessment should address whether students considered all of the similarities and differences and if students have supported their analyses with textual proof.

Both Martin and the Chinese American girl learn to be proud of their own families and heritage. Martin discovers that his friends really think Grandpa is great. He also listens to Grandpa tell about the medicine bag and begins to understand his heritage. The Chinese American girl learns that their American friends have as much trouble with chopsticks as her family had with the celery. She even discovers that the embarrassing sounds her family make when they eat soup, "Shloop, shloop," aren't so unusual. Her friend Meg makes the same sound when she drinks a milkshake. The Chinese American girl, like Martin, is no longer embarrassed by her heritage.

Thinking It Over

1. In what ways are Martin and the Chinese American girl alike?
2. When you compare two things, you sometimes contrast (show differences) as well. Does this paper show any differences between the two characters? Can you think of any obvious differences?
3. How is this comparison paper organized? Did the writer use the first method or the second one (page 298)?

MEETING INDIVIDUAL NEEDS

LEP/ESL

General Strategies. The Writing Workshop segment suggests having students read each other's first drafts to offer input. Be sure to pair LEP/ESL students with mainstream classmates who have demonstrated strong cognitive and interpersonal skills. These students must speak slowly and clearly and remain sensitive to the LEP/ESL students' special needs. Otherwise, the interactive process may not prove particularly useful.

ANSWERS
Thinking It Over

1. They both are embarrassed by their families' cultural backgrounds but learn to accept and admire their heritages.

2. The biggest difference is that Martin's family has lived in America much longer than the Chinese American family.

3. The writer uses the second method.

If your students are having problems gathering and organizing details for their comparison/contrast papers, show them an example of a Venn diagram and explain how this type of graphic organizer can help to identify the similarities and differences.

Lead the class in a discussion of the traits that occur most often in the characters they have analyzed. Focus on such traits as courage, fearfulness, inventiveness, kindness, and truthfulness. ■

PREWRITING

If any student has trouble finding a story with a character comparable to the character he or she wants to write about, suggest using the theme index at the back of the class literature book. The student might have to skim several stories to find a character to use, but the theme index is a place to begin.

🔗 INTEGRATING THE LANGUAGE ARTS

Literature Link. If you have each of your students choose two new stories for this activity, you may want to suggest that someone compare and contrast the father in "One-Shot Finch" taken from Harper Lee's novel *To Kill a Mockingbird* and the mother in Edna St. Vincent Millay's story "The Courage That My Mother Had." Both works deal with parents' courage when their children are threatened. Students could also compare and contrast the two dogs in Eric Knight's "Lassie Come Home" and James Thurber's "The Dog That Bit People."

Writing a Comparison of Two Characters

Prewriting. Choose a character from another story to compare with the character in your analysis. The two characters should have something in common. They may face a similar conflict or be about the same age. For example, in the writer's model, both characters learn to be proud of their heritage.

Develop a chart like the one below. List the main traits the characters have in common. If there are important differences between them, list those too.

Martin	Chinese American girl
1. embarrassed by great-grandfather (false pride)	1. embarrassed by family
2. accepted his heritage (sincere pride)	2. accepted her heritage

Writing, Evaluating, and Revising. Follow the model on pages 308–309 to write your paper. First, compare one quality of each character. Then, compare the next quality. If you feel it is important, you can also discuss any major difference between the two characters. Be sure to include details from each story to support your main points.

When you finish your draft, ask a classmate to read it. Have your reader tell you in his or her own words how your two characters are alike. Listen carefully. Take notes about anything your reader seems confused about. Then, make changes in your paper to help readers understand those points.

Proofreading and Publishing. Correct any mistakes in your paper, and then share it with your classmates. Did anyone else write about either of your characters?

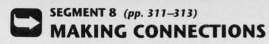

SEGMENT 8 *(pp. 311–313)*
MAKING CONNECTIONS

INFORMING THROUGH
EVALUATION
OBJECTIVE

• To write a review of a restaurant

311

MAKING CONNECTIONS

INFORMING THROUGH EVALUATION

Writing a Review

You have learned to analyze a story character by looking closely at his or her actions and words. People who write reviews of movies, books, or restaurants use similar methods. For example, a restaurant reviewer analyzes the quality of the food and service and makes an evaluation.

McHenry's Steak House

Subject

When you enter McHenry's Steak House, you're greeted warmly. The hosts make you

Detail 1
feel as though you're a friend who has come to eat in their home. It's obvious from the

Main idea
start: This restaurant delivers more than just excellent food.

Detail 2
And the food *is* excellent. Especially good are the fresh swordfish and thick, juicy burgers. They are seasoned well and served with a big tossed salad and fresh vegetable. And if you aren't in the mood for these, try McHenry's special pizza for one. It's delicious!

Detail 3
Prices at McHenry's are low. My meal came to only $8.95. This is a restaurant that

Summing up
you'll return to again and again. The people at McHenry's serve great food in a friendly way, without taking a big bite out of your budget.

INFORMING THROUGH EVALUATION
Teaching Strategies

You can remind students that they review restaurants, including the school cafeteria, every time they comment to a friend about the food or some other aspect of the restaurant. Students can take this assignment as an opportunity to put some of their ideas in writing.

The sample review can serve as a model of what students' reviews should contain. Suggest that students give specific details about the cleanliness of the restaurant, the variety of foods it serves, the atmosphere it has, and so on.

If your school doesn't have a cafeteria and your students aren't familiar with any other restaurants, they can write about the food at home and pretend they're writing about a restaurant.

GUIDELINES

Students should identify the restaurants they're writing about by name. Each review should contain a statement of a main idea that expresses the overall evaluation of the restaurant. (For example, "Addie's Kitchen is the place to go when you're hungry and in a hurry.") It should contain reasons to support the main idea, details to support the reasons, and a summary that restates the main idea. In addition, the review should have a title, be written in complete sentences, and be fairly free of grammar, usage, and mechanics errors.

WRITING ACROSS THE CURRICULUM

Teaching Strategies

You can start by having your students brainstorm, either individually or with the whole class, names of historical characters. After each student has selected a character, you may need to plan a visit to the school library so students can find information. If that isn't possible, ask the librarian to pull some books and encyclopedia volumes for your students to use in the classroom.

Remind students that the assignment calls for writing about one important character trait, not necessarily the most important trait. Students should understand that they have to find details for support; therefore, the number of available details might determine which traits students choose.

312

Now, try your hand at writing a restaurant review. Pick a restaurant that you know well. It doesn't have to be a fancy one. You might write about a fast-food restaurant or even the school cafeteria!

Think of details to support your opinions. Be specific about the food, the service, the prices, and the appearance of the restaurant itself. Your audience will be your classmates. Give them a good "picture" of the restaurant. Through your writing, persuade them either to go to this restaurant or to avoid it!

WRITING ACROSS THE CURRICULUM

Analyzing Great Characters in History

You can use what you have learned about analyzing characters in literature to learn more about real people in history. You usually don't have any way of finding out what historical figures were thinking because you can't read their minds. But you can find out some of the things they said and did, as well as what other people said or wrote about them.

Pick some historical figure you have always been interested in—Abraham Lincoln, Pocahantas, Cleopatra, Martin Luther King. It's your decision. Then use your history book, encyclopedia articles, and biographies to catch up on the figure's personality. Was honesty really one of Lincoln's important character traits? Was Cleopatra a strong leader? Was Eleanor Roosevelt (pictured below) really one of the most active first ladies of all time? Decide which character trait seems to stand out or be most interesting in the figure you've chosen. Then choose one of the following ways to illustrate that trait:

1. Draw a picture showing the historical figure doing something that shows the trait.
2. Pretend you are the historical figure and write an entry in your diary. Use the figure's thoughts to show his or her character trait.
3. Write a dialogue between the historical figure you've chosen and someone else. Have your figure say something that shows the character trait.
4. Write a paragraph identifying the trait and telling about something the historical figure did that illustrates the trait.

You can use this activity as a conclusion to the chapter or in conjunction with a literature unit on biography. You can also share this material with your students' history or science teachers for a lesson in writing across the curriculum.

GUIDELINES

Each paragraph should state in the first or second sentence the trait being analyzed. All of the details in the paragraph should be directly related to that trait, and the paragraph should end with a sentence restating the main idea.

VISUAL CONNECTIONS
Exploring the Subject. Anna Eleanor Roosevelt was born into a prominent New York City family in 1884. Her parents died when she was young, so she was raised by her grandmother. When she married her distant cousin Franklin Delano Roosevelt, her father's brother, President Theodore Roosevelt, gave away the bride.

In addition to her social and political activities, Mrs. Roosevelt was a prolific author. She wrote a number of books and articles, and she also wrote a syndicated newspaper column called "My Day."

Chapter 10

WRITING A REPORT

OBJECTIVES

- To select an appropriate topic for a report and to make a list of questions about the topic
- To locate and list sources and to take notes from those sources for a report
- To write an outline for a report
- To write the first draft of a report
- To list sources for a report on a Works Cited page
- To evaluate and revise the first draft of a report
- To proofread a report and to prepare it for publication
- To write a book report
- To prepare a group report about a city's history
- To write and present a weather report

Motivation

Initiate a class discussion about the kinds of writing students have done in school up to this time. Begin by asking students to talk about reports or compositions they've already written. Ask whether students find writing reports difficult and boring or challenging and interesting. If they find writing reports difficult, explain that writing reports, like most things, becomes easier with practice. If students feel that writing reports is boring, tell them they can avoid boredom by choosing topics that are interesting to them.

Introduction

From the beginning, impress upon students that they will be dealing with facts when writing reports. Tell them that they will be finding, sorting, analyzing, and writing facts. Tell students that a fact is a piece of information that can be tested and proven.

Then help students place report writing in relation to other aims of discourse. Tell students that the aim of a report is informative—the writer wants to inform readers about a topic. Other aims of writing—expressive, literary, and persuasive—may also use facts, but only to achieve another purpose.

Integration

This chapter is designed to give students insight into preparing reports across the curriculum. For example, they learn by following the preparation of a report on killer bees, by studying the techniques for gathering information about a city's history, and by collecting facts for a weather report.

In addition, students will find it easier to produce any type of composition if they are able to find appropriate sources, recognize and locate facts, synthesize notes, and arrange researched information in a logical and orderly way.

The chart on the next page illustrates the strands of language arts as they are integrated into this chapter. For vocabulary study, glossary words are underlined in some writing models.

QUOTATIONS
All **Quotations for the Day** are chosen because of their relevance to instructional material presented in that segment of the chapter and for their usefulness in establishing student interest in writing.

INTEGRATING THE LANGUAGE ARTS

Selection	Reading and Literature	Writing and Critical Thinking	Language and Syntax	Speaking, Listening, and Other Expression Skills
"Meet-a-Cheetah" by Fred Johnson **316-317**	Identifying facts in a report **318** Experiencing vicariously the situations and events in a selection **318** Analyzing a model book report **347-349** Inferring an author's opinion **349**	Writing facts about a subject **318** Writing a journal entry **318** Choosing a topic **322** Deciding about audience and purpose **324-325** Asking questions about a topic **326, 328** Writing interview questions **328** Finding sources for a topic **330, 352** Listing sources for a topic **330, 352** Taking notes for a report **332, 352** Writing an outline for a report **334** Synthesizing notes and using them to write sentences and a paragraph **337** Writing a first draft **342** Analyzing a writer's revisions **344** Evaluating and revising a report **345** Writing a book report by following the stages of the writing process **350** Writing a report about a city's history **352** Writing a weather report **353**	Proofreading for errors in spelling, capitalization, usage, and punctuation **346**	Discussing suitable topics with others **322** Interviewing a classmate about a topic **328** Answering questions about a topic during an interview **328** Listening to a partner's sentences **337** Reading sentences to a partner **337** Planning a history report with others **352** Presenting a weather report **353**

SEGMENT PLANNING GUIDE

Whether you are planning for a quick review of a writing concept or preparing an extended lesson on composition you can use the following Planning Guide to adapt the chapter material to the individual needs of your class.

SEGMENT	PAGES	CONTENT	RESOURCES
1 *Exploring Your World*	*315-318*		
Literary Model from **"Meet-a-Cheetah"**	316-317	Guided reading: a model of a research report	
Reader's Response/ Writer's Craft	318	Model evaluation: responding to literature and analyzing a report	
2 *Ways to Develop a Report*	*319*		
3 *Prewriting*	*320-334*		Narrowing Your Subject
Choosing and Narrowing a Subject	320-321	Introduction: selecting a suitable report topic	Asking Questions
Exercise 1	322	Applied practice: choosing a topic for a report	Finding and Listing Sources
Writing Assignment: Part 1	323	Applied practice: choosing a report topic	
Planning Your Report	324	Introduction: planning a report	
Thinking About Audience and Purpose	324	Guidelines: selecting information	
Exercise 2	324-325	Applied practice: selecting information	
Asking Questions	325	Guidelines: using the *5W-How?* questions	
Writing Assignment: Part 2	326	Applied practice: listing the *5W-How?* questions	
Finding Sources	326-327	Introduction: reading and interviewing	
Reading and Viewing	326	Guidelines: using print and nonprint sources	
Interviewing	327	Guidelines: using the *5W-How?* questions	
Exercise 3	328	Cooperative learning: writing and using the *5W-How?* questions for interviewing	
Listing Sources	329	Guidelines: crediting sources	
Chart: MLA Guide for Listing	329	Guidelines: examining MLA guidelines	
Writing Assignment: Part 3	330	Applied practice: finding and listing report sources	
Taking Notes	330-331	Guidelines: examining criteria for taking notes	
Writing Assignment: Part 4	332	Applied practice: taking notes for a report	
Organizing and Outlining Your Information	333-334	Guidelines: examining criteria and a model outline	
Writing Assignment: Part 5	334	Applied practice: writing a report outline	
4 *Writing*	*335-342*		Using Note Cards
Writing Your First Draft	335	Introduction: writing a report	

SEGMENT	PAGES	CONTENT	RESOURCES
Understanding the Parts of a Report	335-336	Guidelines: understanding the parts of a report	
Critical Thinking: Synthesizing Information	336-337	Guidelines: synthesizing information from notes	
Critical Thinking Exercise	337	Cooperative learning: synthesizing notes	
Writing Your Report	338	Guidelines: using an outline as a guide	
Writer's Model	338-341	Guided reading: examining a sample report	
Mechanics Hint	342	Writing suggestion: punctuating titles	
Writing Assignment: Part 6	342	Applied practice: writing a first draft	
5 *Evaluating and Revising*	*343-345*		Writing a Report
Chart: Evaluating and Revising Your Report	343	Guidelines: applying evaluation and revision techniques	
Exercise 4	344	Cooperative learning: analyzing a writer's revisions	
Exercise 5	345	Cooperative learning: evaluating a paragraph	
Writing Assignment: Part 7	345	Cooperative learning: evaluating and revising	
6 *Proofreading and Publishing*	*346*		Writing a Report
Publishing	346	Publishing ideas: reaching an audience	
Writing Assignment: Part 8	346	Applied practice: proofreading and publishing	
7 *Writing Workshop*	*347-350*		All the resources in this chapter may be used in this segment.
A Book Report	347	Guidelines: examining criteria for evaluation	
Model/Questions	348-349	Examining techniques: analyzing a book report	
Writing a Book Report	350	Applied practice: applying skills to the writing process	
8 *Making Connections*	*351-353*		
Research Across the Curriculum: History	351-352	Guidelines: examining research questions Cooperative learning: writing a report about a city's history	
Speaking and Listening: Reporting on the Weather	352-353	Guidelines: writing and presenting a weather report Cooperative learning: writing and presenting a weather report	

WHOLE-CHAPTER RESOURCES
A Writing Process Log, A Writing Prompt, Holistically Graded Models, Assessment Portfolio Materials

EXPLORING YOUR WORLD

OBJECTIVES

- To record personal responses to a report
- To identify facts and an expert's opinion in a literary model

TEACHING THE LESSON

After students have read the introduction to this segment, invite them to discuss other reports they've recently read, heard, or seen. Ask them what facts or details they remember from these reports.

Read the report on cheetahs aloud, and encourage class discussion afterward. Focus the discussion on the author's use of

VISUAL CONNECTIONS

Ideas for Writing. This poster, commissioned for the National Forum on BioDiversity, focuses on some of the ecosystems that are currently endangered. To get students started on prewriting for their research reports, have them brainstorm as a class or in groups to ask questions about this picture. Possible questions are "What ecosystems are in danger?" and "What can be done to change the situation?" Interested students can take the prewriting notes and develop topics related to endangered ecosystems; others can use the brainstorming technique to ask questions about other subjects that interest them and can develop suitable topics from those notes.

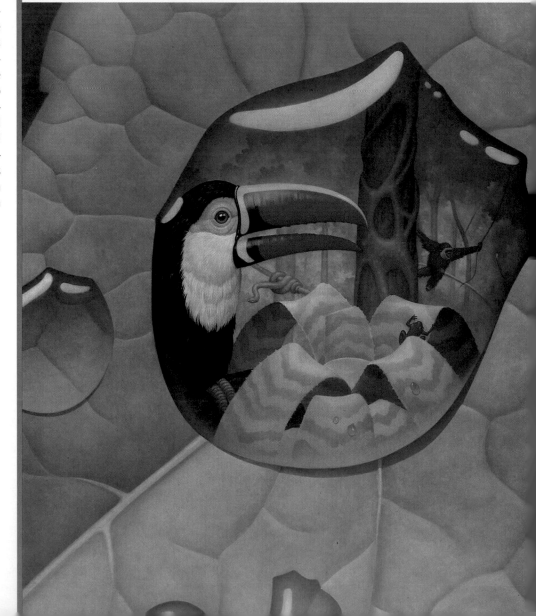

10 WRITING A REPORT

facts to create the report. Use the **Reader's Response** questions for class discussion and assign the **Writer's Craft** questions to be done independently. Assess students' understanding from their written answers to the **Writer's Craft** questions.

CLOSURE

Ask students to tell you what kind of information provides the basis for reports [facts]. Then ask students to explain what facts are [information that experts have checked and believe to be true].

Detail of poster commissioned for the National Forum on BioDiversity, Robert Goldstrom (1986).

Exploring Your World

The **world** around you is full of things to **explore** and learn about. Many of these wonders you'll be able to explore for yourself. Others you'll explore through the eyes of someone who wrote about them.

Writing and You. Reports are written summaries of someone's experience or knowledge. They allow scientists to tell us what they know about animals and the environment. Travel writers share their knowledge about distant lands in written reports. And we learn about the most distant planets in what is written about them. Reports are everywhere—in books, magazines, newspapers. What is the last thing you read a report about?

As You Read. Reports are based on fact. As you read the following report about the cheetah, look for the facts that help you learn more about this great animal.

QUOTATION FOR THE DAY

"I do hold literature accountable for the *truth*, but that is quite different from facts." (Richard Rodriguez, Mexican American writer)

Give students an example of a statement that is figuratively accurate but that is not a literal fact, such as "Cheetahs run like the wind." Ask students what the factual equivalent of such a statement might be. Point out to students that it is possible for statements to be true figuratively, but not factually.

MEETING **INDIVIDUAL** NEEDS

LEP/ESL

General Strategies. To ensure that students fully comprehend the form and content of the reports they will be expected to produce, give them photocopies of good student reports to use as references.

INTEGRATING THE LANGUAGE ARTS

Speaking Link. A few days before you begin this chapter, ask a few students to select brief reports that interest them from newspapers or magazines. As part of your introduction to reports, ask students to read aloud the reports they've selected and to tell what facts in the reports especially interest them.

To get students to start thinking about different uses of research, have them bring in published materials for which the writers have done research. Explain that most articles in newspapers and magazines are informative and require research. Persuasive writing such as an editorial may be partly informative and may require research.

Self-expressive writing does not require research, but creative writing sometimes requires research for accuracy of details in background and setting.

Have students share with the class the titles and topics of their articles. After discussing with students the ways research is used in the articles, have them speculate on how the writers conducted their research. ■

316

from MEET-A-

Cheetah

BY FRED JOHNSON

USING THE SELECTION

from **Meet-a-Cheetah**

1

Other members of the cat family include the lion, tiger, leopard, jaguar, puma, and snow leopard. These animals are often called big cats. Different kinds of big cats live throughout the world, except in Europe, Australia, and Antarctica.

2

Afghanistan is in central Asia.

3

Why does the author ask the reader a direct question? [He wants to relate the facts to the reader's world and thus more closely involve the reader in the report.] Give an earlier example of the author's relating the facts to the reader. [He compares the cheetah's claw to "your thumb."]

1   **A**ll members of the cat family can move fast when they really want to. But there is one who can easily leave all the others far behind. In fact, he can leave any animal far behind. Nothing can outrun a cheetah (CHEE-tuh).

2   Cheetahs are found in Africa, in India, Afghanistan, and Arabia. Some scientists think that the cheetah is between the cat and dog families. They have the body build of dogs rather than cats.

Their claws, like dogs', are dull. And they cannot be pulled back into the paw. Their claws are of little use in fighting or killing. But like all cats, cheetahs have one claw that is very sharp and dangerous. This is a claw on the inside of the foreleg, something like your thumb. It can be pulled into the paw.

The cheetah's sense of smell is poor, but its eyesight is keen. Its fur is brownish-yellow with black or brown "polka dots." A clear black line runs from the inside corner of each eye down the side of the nose. A full-grown cheetah may measure as much as

3   7 feet long with his tail outstretched. How tall is the door to your room? A cheetah may be as long as your door is tall.

4   One surprising fact about the cheetah is that it can be tamed easily. Once it has become used to people, it seems to enjoy being a member of a human family.

5   The cheetah is also one of the few big cats which purrs when happy, just as a pet cat does. However, its purr is far louder and sounds more like an engine.

But the most amazing thing about cheetahs is their speed.
6   They have been timed at speeds up to 80 miles an hour! Daniel P. Mannix is an animal owner and trainer. He tells of a cheetah which saw a man going down the road on a motorcycle. The cheetah went out to look at this strange, noisy animal. The man speeded up to 60 miles an hour—and the cheetah ran along beside him!

4

Dating back to ancient Egypt, cheetahs have been favored pets for thousands of years. They've always been a favorite of royalty and movie stars.

5

The cheetah, like the puma and the snow leopard, doesn't roar.

6

The cheetah is fast but is best as a short-distance runner. A cheetah can run at top speed for only a few hundred yards.

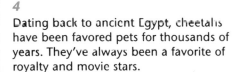

LEARNING STYLES

   Visual and Auditory Learners. If time allows, show a brief documentary about cheetahs or big cats. Afterward, discuss the facts mentioned in the documentary. Have students compare the facts given by the report to the facts presented in the documentary.

SELECTION AMENDMENT
Description of change: excerpted
Rationale: to focus on the concept of research presented in this chapter

ANSWERS

Reader's Response

Responses will vary.

1. The facts students list should be drawn from the report. Students should give specific reasons why they would or would not like to read more about the cheetah.

2. Some students might not have had any pets. Give students the option of noting a fact they know about any animal.

3. Students should give reasons to support their answers.

Writer's Craft

4. A cheetah can be up to seven feet long. No animal can outrun a cheetah in a short race. It has been timed at speeds up to eighty miles an hour.

5. He tells about a cheetah that ran sixty miles an hour beside a motorcycle.

READER'S RESPONSE

1. What facts about the cheetah seem unusual or surprising to you? Would you like to read more about the animal? Why?
2. A *fact* can be something you observe directly—for example, that your cat has gray fur and likes milk. In your journal jot down some facts you know about a cat, dog, or some other pet.
3. Would you like to have a cheetah for a pet? Why?

WRITER'S CRAFT

4. What facts did you learn about the cheetah's length? about its speed?
5. One source for this report is an animal expert named Daniel P. Mannix. What information does he give about the cheetah?

"Nothing can outrun a cheetah...."

TEACHING THE MODES

Help students define *narration, description, classification,* and *evaluation.* Then ask the class to give further examples of how each mode might be used in developing a report. You may want to bring some reports to class and work with students to identify the modes that the reports use. Reinforce that more than one mode can appear in a report.

Assess students' understanding of the modes by calling on individual students to name one mode and to give a specific example of how it might be used in a report. ■

319

Ways to Develop a Report

Reports come in many forms. You will read them in magazines and newspapers. You'll see them when you watch a television news show or a science program like *NOVA.* And you can even get them by telephone if you call for a weather report. All these kinds of reports give you information, developed in different ways. Here are some ways to develop a report.

▶ **Narration:** telling about how the Spanish settled Saint Augustine; telling about the life of a civil rights leader.

Description: describing the Anasazi cliff dwellings; describing how the ruby-throated hummingbird looks.

▶ **Classification:** comparing cheetahs with house cats; reporting on a member of the skink (a type of lizard) family.

Evaluation: reporting on the quality of various brands of portable radios; reporting on a series of tests about the durability of certain bicycles.

In this chapter, you'll learn how to gather information about a subject. Tons of information—much more than a human brain can hold—are stored away every week in sources like books and tapes. Writing a report lets you use those storehouses of information.

LOOKING AHEAD

In the main assignment in this chapter, you will write a short, informative report. You'll use the strategy of narration or classification. Remember that a report

- gives information about a subject
- uses a variety of sources
- lists the sources of the information

 INTEGRATING THE LANGUAGE ARTS

Literature Link. Tell students that each of these modes also appears in literature. Point out, though, that usually the modes are mixed—a paragraph of description followed by a paragraph of narration, or an integration of the two in one paragraph.

Ask students to read short stories and to find examples of at least two of the modes in the stories. A good choice is Eva-Lis Wuorio's "You Can't Take It With You." Discuss with students why different modes are used in one story. [All of the modes contribute to the development of the story. Description reinforces character and setting, and narration furthers the plot.]

SEGMENT 3 *(pp. 320–334)*
PREWRITING
OBJECTIVES
- To analyze the suitability of topics for a report
- To select an appropriate topic for a report and to ask questions about that topic
- To choose information for a particular audience and purpose
- To make a list of questions about a topic and to use them to interview a classmate
- To locate and list sources for a report and to take notes on the sources
- To write an outline for a report

Writing a Report

 *Prewriting*

Choosing and Narrowing a Subject

What causes earthquakes? Do vampire bats really exist? When did dogs first become pets? Who invented tab-top cans for carbonated soda? Writing a report is your chance to learn about an interesting subject.

Choosing Your Subject

To choose a subject, think about your interests. What kinds of books or magazines do you like to read? What kinds of subjects do you like hearing about on television programs like *NOVA* or *National Geographic World*? Do you have special collections of things like stamps or insects? What subjects do you enjoy talking, thinking, and wondering about?

Here are some ideas for general subjects. Try to think of three or four other subjects you'd like to learn more about.

dinosaurs	ancient kingdoms
pyramids	bats
early explorers of the United States	Native Americans the Old West
the Civil War	exploring space

Narrowing Your Subject

You probably realize that there's a great deal of information about a broad subject like dinosaurs—hundreds of books, articles, and TV programs. That's way too much information to try to sift through and include in a short report. You need to narrow broad subjects by focusing on just one part. The subjects you've just read include many smaller *topics*. On the next page you'll find some of them.

You may want to make it clear that this segment actually begins the writing process and leads toward a finished report. To make sure students know their goals, provide them with copies of well-written, short reports produced by other seventh-grade students.

Next, guide students through the lengthy prewriting process step by step. Ask students to name some subjects that especially interest them, and write those subjects on the chalkboard. Then help students narrow the subjects to manageable topics.

Once topics have been generated, choose one to use for a discussion of 👉

---

why dinosaurs
    disappeared
the pyramids
    of Egypt
the Spanish explorer
    Ponce de León
photography in
    the Civil War

the ancient kingdom
    of Kush
vampire bats
the Cherokee
    "Trail of Tears"
African American cowboys in the Old West
the first moon landing

As you narrow your subject, remember that any broad subject includes many smaller topics. For example, the subject "dinosaurs" also includes these topics: renaming the brontosaurus, famous dinosaur discoveries, and forms of protection against enemies.

MEETING INDIVIDUAL NEEDS

LESS-ADVANCED STUDENTS

Have students who are not ready to write individual reports write group reports instead. Ask members in each group to collaborate to choose a subject, find a limited topic, and ask research questions. Each student in the group might then be assigned to find the answer to one of the research questions. Another way to divide the work is to have each person in the group find one source and take notes on that source. Each group should then cooperatively write, evaluate, revise, and proofread its report.

AT-RISK STUDENTS

Encourage students to talk to their parents or guardians about their interests and about possible resources from their homes or communities. You may want to send a notice home to students' parents or guardians telling them when each writing assignment will be due. Interest from their homes might help less-motivated students meet assignment deadlines.

audience and purpose. Decide on an audience and then have students help you generate answers to the three questions in the section **Thinking About Audience and Purpose** on p. 324. Help students decide what information should be included in a report about a topic for a certain audience.

Next, keeping the intended audience in mind, model the development of *5W-How?*

questions for the same topic. Discuss with students what sources might be useful for finding answers to the *5W-How?* questions you have developed, and show students what a listing of one of these sources should look like. Finally, model for students the creation of an outline.

 *Reminder*

Not all topics work equally well for a report. Here are some questions that will help you figure out if your topic will work for a report.

- Can you find facts about your topic? (*Facts* are information that experts have checked and believe is true.)
- Can you find enough information about your topic? (If your topic is *too* narrow, you may not find enough information.)
- Will you have enough time to find the information you need? (If you write a letter to get information, how long will it take to get an answer?)
- Is your topic interesting enough to hold your attention? (You'll put a great deal of time and effort into your report. If you like your topic, you'll be more willing to put the time and effort into it.)

EXERCISE 1 ▶ **Choosing Topics for a Report**

What's a good topic? Here are some topics for a report. Get together with one or two classmates and discuss each topic. Try to decide which topics are suitable for a short report. Can you find facts about the topic from sources like books or videotapes? Is it narrow enough? Is it appropriate for a report?

1. robots for surgery **1. suitable**
2. why I like soccer
3. space—the final frontier
4. Egyptian mummies **4. suitable**
5. Sarah Winnemucca, a Native American hero **5. suitable**
6. the history of horses
7. Mexican birthday customs **7. suitable**
8. my most exciting birthday
9. the killer fish—the piranha **9. suitable**
10. schools in Japan

INDEPENDENT PRACTICE

Have students complete **Exercises 1–3** and **Writing Assignment: Parts 1–5** independently.

ASSESSMENT

Assess students' mastery through their performance on **Writing Assignment: Parts 1–5.** Be sure that students have mastered each assignment before assigning the next one. Emphasis here should be on completion rather than on correctness.

☞

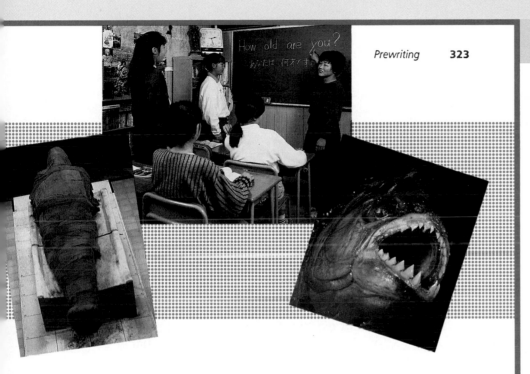

Prewriting **323**

 A DIFFERENT APPROACH

After students have read and discussed narrowing subjects, introduce a game called Topic Bee. Choose a subject that will be familiar to students, perhaps from an earlier activity. Let each student take turns giving you a topic related to the subject. Allow thirty seconds for a response. If no topic is given, the student is out of the game, and play proceeds to the next student. The game continues until students run out of topics and one player remains.

You could ask a student who is out of the game early to write on the chalkboard all of the topic ideas. After the game, have students copy the ideas. Point out the topics that are appropriate for reports.

WRITING ASSIGNMENT

PART 1:
Choosing a Topic for Your Report

What would you like to know more about? Think of a subject you're interested in. Then narrow it to a topic for your report. Check your library to be sure it's a topic you can find facts about.

WRITING NOTE

Writing a report takes more time than one or two days. Don't try to do most of your report in one weekend. To do a good job in the time you have, make a schedule now. Then, stick to it. In your schedule, allow time to do five things:

1. Find information about your topic.
2. Take notes about the information.
3. Write your first draft.
4. Evaluate and revise your draft.
5. Proofread and publish your report.

RETEACHING

Give students copies of a brief report (one or two pages) from a magazine. Read the report aloud or have a student read it aloud. Work with students to identify the subject and the limited topic, to label important facts about the topic, to write at least one possible source beside each fact, to generate *5W-How?* questions answered by the report, and to write an outline for the report.

LEARNING STYLES

Kinetic Learners. Have interested students choose topics for reports for a first-grade audience. Then have each student draw or find three illustrations that would be appropriate for the topic and audience and one that would not be appropriate. Have students explain why they think each illustration is or isn't appropriate for the topic and audience.

Planning Your Report

When is the last time you planned a surprise for someone? You probably planned it carefully ahead of time so that it would work out just right. If you plan your report ahead, it should work out right, too.

Thinking About Audience and Purpose

The purpose for writing a report is to discover information and share it with other people. Most of the information in a report is made up of facts. Some information may be the opinions of experts on the topic.

Your teacher and classmates will probably be the first readers of your report. (On page 346, you'll find ideas you can use to share your report with other readers.) As you write your report, think about three things.

1. What information will interest your readers?
2. What do your readers already know?
3. What information do your readers need?

Reports are boring to readers if they already know all the facts you give, so look for new or unusual information about your topic. Try to give your readers all the information they need to understand the topic. If you think they may not know a word, tell them what it means. If they may not understand how something works, explain it to them.

EXERCISE 2 ▶ **Deciding About Audience and Purpose**

On the next page is some information you might put in a report on giant snakes. You are writing this report to give both your teacher and classmates facts about the snakes. Which information would you put in your report? Why wouldn't you include the other information?

CLOSURE

Ask students to tell you the most important steps involved in the prewriting stage of a report. [Some important steps are choosing a topic, considering audience and purpose, asking questions, finding and listing sources, taking notes, and writing an outline.]

ENRICHMENT

Have students provide art to accompany their reports. Students could illustrate their reports themselves or select appropriate pictures from magazines or other sources. Either way, encourage students to provide art that suits the purpose and audience of their reports.

☞

Prewriting **325**

1. *Giant* means "big."   **1.** wouldn't—audience already knows
2. One giant snake, the anaconda, can be as long as twenty-five feet.   **2.** would
3. I hate snakes.   **3.** wouldn't—no need for information
4. Boa constrictor babies are born live; python babies are hatched from eggs.   **4.** would
5. There are many kinds of snakes.   **5.** wouldn't—audience already knows

▲ **boa constrictor** babies are born live

python babies are hatched from eggs ▼

Asking Questions

What would you like to know about your topic? What would your readers like to know? Make a list of questions that will help you find this information. First try the *5W-How?* questions—*Who? What? When? Where? Why? How?* Which questions you ask will depend on your topic. For a report on Africanized honeybees, also called "killer" bees, you might ask these questions.

> *What* are Africanized honeybees?
> *When* will they come here?
> *Where* do they come from?
> *Why* are they called "killer" bees?
> *How* are they different from native bees?
> *How* can they be stopped?

 CRITICAL THINKING
Analysis

Tell students that to analyze something is to break it down into its parts. Point out to students that they are analyzing a subject when they think of topics and that they are analyzing a topic when they ask the *5W-How?* questions about it.

325

Explain to students that to include accurate and vivid details in a short story or a novel, writers often must do considerable research. If a description of a time period, a place, or a profession contains inaccurate details, readers will find the work less credible.

Have students read "The Wild Duck's Nest" by Michael McLaverty, a story in which the author describes the setting, an island off the northern coast of Ireland, with accurate and vivid details. Picking out at least one detail from categories such as geography, weather, flora, or fauna, students should check the accuracy of McLaverty's writing. ■

---

326   *Writing a Report*

If you don't know much about your topic, you may want to get some general information about it first. You can read one or two encyclopedia articles about your topic, or you can watch a videotape about it. You might also talk to other people who know about the topic. Then make your list of questions.

PART 2:
Asking Questions About Your Topic

What do you want to know about your topic? What do you think your readers will want to know? Make a list of *5W-How?* questions that you'll answer in your report.

Finding Sources

Reading and Viewing. It's generally a good idea to have at least three sources of information for your report. If you use only one or two sources, you'll only be repeating what someone else has already said. When you use more sources, you can combine facts and opinions in new ways.

The library is a good place to start your hunt for information. It's full of *print sources* like encyclopedias, books, magazines and newspapers, and pamphlets. And don't forget about *nonprint sources* like videotapes, audiotapes, slides, and even CDs. (For help in finding and using library sources, see pages 816–823.)

Other places to look for information depend on your topic. You might check radio and TV guides for programs that will give you some information. You can also find videotapes about many science and history topics in local video stores. Here are some ideas for other places to look for sources.

museums	hospitals	bookstores
government offices	planetariums	zoos

INTEGRATING THE LANGUAGE ARTS

Library Link. To help students locate information about their topics, ask the school librarian to give a talk about the library's nonfiction resources. Before you go to the library, ask students to make up *5W-How?* questions to ask the librarian about finding information in the library. Here are some examples of questions students might ask:

1. *What* nonfiction information is available?
2. *When* is the library open?
3. *Where* are the nonfiction resources?
4. *Why* do I need nonfiction material?
5. *How* can I find the information I need?

LEP/ESL

General Strategies. Although including nonprint sources is recommended, you may want to steer students in the direction of print sources for their reports. Listening and taking notes while listening can be difficult and frustrating for students because the listening experience is difficult to control. Except in an interview situation, a student cannot ask the speaker to slow down and, therefore, is likely to miss important information.

Interviewing. Here's an idea for a nonprint source. Interview someone who's an expert on your topic, perhaps a teacher, someone at a zoo or museum, or even a parent or high school student. It's only important that this person know a great deal about your topic. Suppose your topic is "mountain bikes." Your expert might be a bike store owner or a high school student who has taken trips on a mountain bike.

Before the interview do some reading about your topic. Make a list of questions to ask. Write each question at the top of a sheet of paper. To avoid *yes* or *no* answers, ask questions that begin with *Who, What, When, Where, Why,* and *How.* (For more information about interviewing, see page 811.)

WRITING NOTE   Not all sources will be helpful to you. To judge how useful a source is, ask yourself these questions about it.

■ *Is the information up-to-date?* Some topics simply need more up-to-date information than others. If your topic is "Ponce de León, early sixteenth-century Spanish explorer," you may not need many recent books and articles. If your topic is "robots and people who have disabilities," you will need new information.

■ *Can you trust the information?* Some sources give a truer picture of the facts than others. You can usually trust reference books more than the magazines you buy at the grocery store checkout stand. Can you tell why?

E X E R C I S E **3** ▶   **Speaking and Listening: Interviewing**

Practice your interviewing skills with a classmate. Ask a classmate to name a special interest, such as soccer, collecting stamps, or horror movies. Make out a list of *5W-How?* questions about the topic. Then interview your classmate about that topic. When you finish, change places and let your classmate interview you.

ANSWERS
Exercise 3

Questions will vary. Be sure that the questions are appropriate for the topics and that each student asks a complete set of *5W-How?* questions.

Listing Sources

The next step is to list each of your sources. Then, give each source a number. You'll use these *source numbers* later when you take notes. There are several different ways to list sources. The following chart shows the way the Modern Language Association recommends.

MLA GUIDE FOR LISTING SOURCES

Books. Give this information: author, title, city of publication, publisher, and copyright year.
 	
    Pringle, Laurence. Here Come the Killer Bees.
        New York: William Morrow, 1986.

Magazines and Newspapers. Give this information: author, title of article, name of magazine or newspaper, date, and page numbers.
 	
    Alper, Joseph. "The Big Sting." Health Apr. 1989:
        53–54.
    Sidener, Jonathan. " 'Killer Bees' May Reach
        Arizona Within a Year." Arizona Republic
        25 Oct. 1990: A1.

Encyclopedia Articles. Give this information: author, title of article, name of encyclopedia, year and edition (ed.).
 	
    Heinrich, Bernd. "Bee." The World Book Encyclopedia.
        1990 ed.

Interviews. Give this information: expert's name, the words *Personal interview* or *Telephone interview,* and date.   Hardy, Ann. Telephone interview. 12 Dec. 1990.

Television or Radio Programs. Give this information: the title of the program, the producer or director if available, the network, the local station call letters and city, and the date of broadcast.
 	
    Living With Killer Bees. Prod. Tony Burden. PBS.
        KUHT, Houston. 24 Nov. 1991.

TIMESAVER
You may not want to go over **Listing Sources** in class. Instead, you could instruct students to use this section of the chapter as a handbook. Emphasize that students need not memorize these conventions for listing sources; rather, they should keep the information handy to serve as a reference.

PART 3:
Finding and Listing Sources for Your Report

Where can you find information? What books and articles does your library have? Can you find a videotape about your topic? Do you know someone you can interview? Find three or four different sources of information about your topic. Then use the forms you've just read about on page 329 to list them.

Taking Notes

Now you're ready to start gathering information from your sources. Be sure to keep your list of questions in mind as you work. Your questions will help keep you focused on gathering the information you need to write about your topic. Here are some other tips for taking good notes.

- Write your notes on 4″ × 6″ cards or on sheets of paper.
- Use abbreviations and short phrases. You can also make lists of details and ideas. You don't have to write complete sentences.
- Use your own words unless the exact words in the source are especially interesting.
- Put quotation marks around an author's or interviewee's exact words. (Not using quotation marks around someone else's words is called *plagiarism.* Plagiarizing is not identifying the source of ideas and words that are not your own.)
- Write the source number you're using at the top of the note card or piece of paper. You'll use that number later when you try to recall where you got your information.
- Give each note a short label telling what the note is about. Write each label at the top of each card or piece of paper.
- At the bottom of the card, write the page number(s) where you found the information.

COOPERATIVE LEARNING
You may want to give students practice taking notes. Divide the class into groups of four or five and give each group copies of a paragraph from a nonfiction book. Instruct students to take notes on the paragraphs they've been given. When they've finished taking notes, have students compare what they have written with the original paragraphs and with notes other group members have taken. Then ask students to discuss within their groups how note-taking styles varied.

These two examples show you how to take notes.

How Different	*2*
Africanized bees chase 1/2 mi.	
Native bees lose interest	
after a few yds.	
	p. 54

- label/source number
- note written in your own words
- page number(s)

This note is from the second source (see page 329), a magazine article titled "The Big Sting," by Joseph Alper. Notice how the card includes a label, a source number, and a page number. This information will come in handy later when the writer is planning and writing the report.

Where They'll Go	*1*
Where there are mild winters:	
Fla., Ga., Miss., La., Tex., Ariz.,	
Calif., Va., N.C., S.C.	
	p. 35

- label/source number
- note written in your own words
- page number(s)

This note is from the first source (see page 329), a book titled *Here Come the Killer Bees,* by Laurence Pringle. Notice how the writer uses abbreviations. This simplifies note taking. (Just be sure you understand the abbreviations you use!)

INTEGRATING THE LANGUAGE ARTS

Library Link. Even your advanced students may not know how to utilize the nonprint resources available at your school. Your librarian may be willing to present a short session to explain how such sources are used. Students might want to look at public television programming, video programs, and filmstrips, or they may want to attend local lectures, if possible.

Technology Link. Many databases are now available for all types of computers and for all levels of skill. You may want to check the computer facilities available in your district to see if computers could function as a research tool for your students.

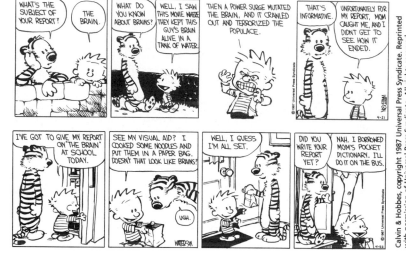

Reminder

To keep from getting confused

- don't put notes from different sources on the same card or sheet of paper
- don't place notes in your own words and quotations on the same card or sheet of paper
- do use a new card or sheet of paper whenever you write a new label

 **REFERENCE NOTE:** For more help with taking notes, see pages 854–855.

WRITING ASSIGNMENT

PART 4:
Taking Notes for Your Report

What interesting information can you gather about your topic? Take notes from the sources you listed for Writing Assignment, Part 3 (page 330). Use half-sheets of paper if you don't have note cards. Save your notes to use in writing your report.

Organizing and Outlining Your Information

By now you've found most of the information you will use in your report. The next step is to organize your notes into groups, like an *early plan* (see pages 100–101), and to make an *outline*. First, sort through your note cards or sheets of paper. (You want to figure out what note cards deal with the same or similar information.) Make several stacks. In each stack put notes that have the same or similar labels. Then, decide on a heading for each stack.

The headings of your stacks are the main ideas for your report. Decide how you will arrange these ideas in your report. Which ones will come first? last? What order of ideas will help your readers understand your topic? The writer of the killer bee report arranged headings this way, making an *early plan* for the report.

> Nature of the bees
> History of the bees
> Africanized bees in the United States
> Attempts to stop the bees
> Ways to protect people

Next, make an *outline* for your report. You already have the main headings. These directions can help you with the rest of the outline.

1. Go through each stack of notes. Take out notes that aren't about the heading.
2. Put the rest of the notes in the order you'll discuss them in your report.
3. Use these notes to make subheadings for your outline.

The example on the next page shows how you might write your outline.

ADVANCED STUDENTS

You may want to give students some examples of different ways to organize main ideas. Provide copies of brief reports from newspapers or magazines. Then ask students to identify the main ideas in the reports and to analyze and explain how the ideas are organized. Possible methods of organization include chronological order, cause and effect, comparison and contrast, and order of importance.

A DIFFERENT APPROACH

Give students the option of using other organizational techniques such as webbing, clustering, or a spider map. The following organizer is a spider map:

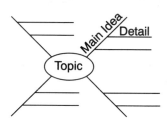

The Invasion of the Killer Bees

I. Nature of the bees
   A. Behavior of United States bees and killer bees
      1. Gentleness of United States bees
      2. Fierceness of Africanized bees
   B. Danger of United States bees and killer bees
      1. Little danger of United States bees
      2. Great danger of Africanized bees

II. History of Africanized bees
   A. Import of African bees to Brazil in 1956
   B. Escape of queen bees
   C. Spread of bees

III. Africanized bees in the United States
   A. Movement to western and southern states
   B. Effects on honey industry
   C. Effects on agriculture

IV. Attempts to stop Africanized bees
   A. Attempts to crossbreed bees
   B. Attempts to kill bees

V. Ways to protect people
   A. Knowledge about bees
   B. Advice from beekeeper

👉 **REFERENCE NOTE:** For more help with making an early plan and outlining, see pages 100–102.

PART 5:
Writing an Outline for Your Report

You probably have many pieces of information for your report. Now you need to organize these pieces into groups and put them in order by writing an outline. You don't need to include everything in your outline. Just use headings and subheadings that will guide you when you write.

OBJECTIVES

- To use notes and an outline as a guide for writing the first draft of a report
- To list sources for a report on a Works Cited page

TEACHING THE LESSON

You could read **A Writer's Model** on pp. 338–341 in class and discuss the annotations in the margin that refer to the various parts of the report. Or you may prefer to discuss the parts of a report in the order presented in the chapter, and then have students read the model independently.

Cont. on p. 338

Writing Your First Draft

In one way, a report is not very different from other compositions you write. Like them, it has an introduction, a body, and a conclusion. The difference is that you use information from outside sources in your report. At the end of the report, you write a list of your sources to show readers where you found the information. That way, interested readers can look up your sources if they want to.

Understanding the Parts of a Report

Title Page. A report printed in a newspaper or magazine doesn't need a title page; it just needs a title. But reports that stand alone, like a school report or a business report, often need a cover page. On the cover page you put your name, the title of your report, the date, and any other information your teacher recommends.

Introduction. The *introduction* of the report isn't in your outline. It's a short opening paragraph where you do two things:

- catch your reader's attention
- tell what the report is about

Notice the introduction in the sample report on page 338. The writer first catches the reader's attention with a vivid example of attacking bees. At the same time, she introduces the topic of her report—Africanized honeybees, also known as "killer" bees.

Body. The *body* of the report contains paragraphs that discuss the information on your note cards and outline. The body of the sample report on pages 338–341 has nine paragraphs. Your own report may be shorter. Each paragraph should have enough information to inform readers about the main idea of each paragraph.

RESOURCES

WRITING YOUR FIRST DRAFT
- Using Note Cards

QUOTATION FOR THE DAY

"Truth is never strengthened by exaggeration." (John Kenneth Galbraith, 1908– , Canadian-born American economist, diplomat, and writer)

Ask students why exaggeration is not acceptable in a report. [Reports should be based on facts, and exaggerations are not facts.]

COOPERATIVE LEARNING

Copy two or three informative articles from a school or local newspaper. Try to find articles about issues that students will consider important. Divide the class into groups of three or four and have each group analyze a different article. Ask students to identify and label the introductions, bodies, and conclusions of the articles.

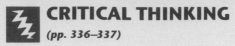
TEACHING *SYNTHESIZING* **INFORMATION**

You may want to use the notes from the report on killer bees to model synthesis. Show students other ways that these notes could be synthesized to create a paragraph. On the chalkboard, write one or two alternative paragraphs developed from the same sample notecard. Stress the fact that synthesis

LEP/ESL

General Strategies. In some cultures, copying without using either quotation marks or citations is allowed. You may need to convey to students how important it is either to quote or to paraphrase, and to remind them to always give credit to sources.

AT-RISK STUDENTS

You may want to borrow a few reports from local businesses or organizations to show to students. Or, if possible, invite a local businessperson to come to your classroom and discuss the role that reports play in business. This strategy can demonstrate that writing reports is a part of real life and that many people write reports as part of their jobs.

336

---

336 *Writing a Report*

Conclusion. The *conclusion* is the final paragraph of your report, where you sum up your ideas. You may want to state the main idea of your report in a new way. Without writing the words *The End*, make sure your readers know your report is finished.

REFERENCE NOTE: For more information on how to write the introduction, body, and conclusion, look at Chapter 3, "Learning About Compositions," pages 104–110.

List of Sources. What if your readers want to know where they can find out more about your topic? They can turn to your *list of sources*, the place where you list the information about the sources you've used. After your conclusion, begin a new page. At the top of the paper, write the words *Works Cited*. (Some people use the word *Bibliography*, but it refers only to print sources like books.) List your sources in alphabetical order by the author's last name. If there is no author, alphabetize by the first word in the title.

List your sources in the way described on page 329. The Works Cited page of the sample report on page 341 shows you how to do this.

CRITICAL THINKING

Synthesizing Information

To *synthesize* means "to combine different things in a new way." A green plant synthesizes light, water, carbon dioxide, and certain minerals to make food. A music video synthesizes music, dance, and special effects to make a "mini-movie." When you write a report, you synthesize the information in your notes. You use other people's ideas, but you put them together in a new way.

On the next page there are some notes for the report on killer bees.

is a creative process and tell students that it is unlikely that two people's syntheses of the same notes would be exactly alike. You could test this hypothesis by having students write paragraphs based on a sample notecard and then having students compare their paragraphs. ⚡

Bees in the United States   1

Where they'll go depends on mild winters.
Could live year-round in parts of the U.S.: as
far north as San Francisco and S. Maryland,
all Ala., Miss., La., Tex., Ariz., Va., N.C. & S.C.

pp. 34-35

This paragraph from the sample report on page 340 shows how this information is put into the writer's own words. This is a synthesis of the information.

> Killer bees can live where the winters are mild. They will be year-round residents as far north as San Francisco and southern Maryland. They will also live all year in southern Texas and in Arizona, Alabama, Mississippi, Louisiana, Virginia, North Carolina, and South Carolina. In the summer, killer bees will live even in the northern states. They will die off there when it gets cold.

⚡ CRITICAL THINKING EXERCISE:
Synthesizing Your Notes

Go over your notes under one heading of your outline. Try out different ways of putting the notes into your own words. Make up sentences that include the information you found. Next, get together with a partner and read your paragraph aloud as he or she listens and makes suggestions for changes. Then, exchange places with your partner and do the same with your partner's notes. ⚡

ANSWERS
Critical Thinking Exercise

Responses will vary. Students should not simply recopy their notes, but should use them to discuss a part of a topic in their own words.

Cont. from p. 335
GUIDED PRACTICE

Using the topic and outline generated during the lesson cycle in the prewriting segment, model on the chalkboard or on an overhead transparency the process of writing a first draft. Rather than modeling an entire report, you could model the title page, the introduction, one paragraph from the body, the conclusion, and a few examples of how to cite sources.

Because you are modeling a first draft, your sample need not be perfect. In fact, it might be useful for students to see that first drafts are never flawless.

Writing Your Report

Use your outline as a guide while you write. You may want to turn each of the main headings in your outline into a topic sentence for a paragraph. (Be sure that each sentence has a subject and a verb.) The subheadings can become the details for each paragraph.

You can use the following sample report as a model for your own. Remember that your report doesn't have to be this long. Writing a good, short report can teach you just as much as writing a longer one.

A WRITER'S MODEL

The Invasion of the Killer Bees

INTRODUCTION
Main idea

Very soon, much of the United States may be invaded by fierce Africanized honeybees from Brazil called "killer" bees. The invasion seems like a horror movie. In such a movie, millions of bees are attacking the people. They try to run, but there are so many bees that they can't see. They are stung over and over and over!

Attention grabber

👁 VISUAL CONNECTIONS

Ideas for Writing. Ask students if they have ever seen a horror film, such as *Jaws, The Birds,* or *Arachnaphobia,* in which some type of animal is portrayed as a monster.

Have students use what they have learned about Africanized bees to develop ideas for horror films about "killer" bees. Then have students write brief descriptions of the characters, settings, and plots of the films. You could have students work independently or in small groups.

INDEPENDENT PRACTICE

Have students complete **Writing Assignment: Part 6** independently. Tell them that because they will be able to revise their first drafts, their efforts don't have to be perfect.

ASSESSMENT

Students should be assessed on the basis of whether or not they have produced a piece of writing that includes a Works Cited page and that reflects the work they have done during the prewriting stage.

Writing Your First Draft **339**

BODY
Nature of the bees

The Africanized bees are very different from native bees that live in the United States. These bees, which first came from Europe, live mostly in hives and hollow trees. They have few enemies and are usually gentle. In Africa, honeybees build their nests in the open because the weather is so warm. To protect their nests, they have become very fierce.

Killer bees are extremely nervous, and they are also fighters. Native bees chase people for a yard or so when they are bothered. Africanized bees, however, will chase for more than half a mile. Their poison is not different from the poison of ordinary bees, but they come after people in a big swarm. No one can survive a hundred or more stings. Dr. Kenneth Schuberth of the Johns Hopkins Medical Institutions says, "When you get that much venom in your system at once, it's like receiving a giant snake bite."

History of killer bees

The invasion of the killer bees began in 1956. In that year a scientist in Brazil imported seventy-five fierce queen bees from Africa. He wanted to crossbreed them with peaceful European bees. Twenty-six of these African bees accidentally escaped in 1957. They began attacking and killing animals and people.

ADVANCED STUDENTS

Some students might be interested in researching other animals that have been introduced to the United States and that have caused problems for humans and agriculture. Ask students to locate information about the animals and to prepare brief oral reports to deliver to the class. Tell students to note similarities and differences between the problems Africanized bees have caused and the problems caused by the animals they research.

SELECTION AMENDMENT
Description of change: excerpted
Rationale: to focus on the concept of research presented in this chapter

339

RETEACHING

Show a short documentary film or video and work with students to identify its introduction, its main ideas, and its conclusion.

CLOSURE

Ask students to identify the principal parts of a report.

340   *Writing a Report*

The descendants of the African bees are the killer bees. They spread all over South America, flying seven thousand miles in thirty years. Some of them have already crossed the United States' border. Many more of them will be here by the early 1990s.

Killer bees in the United States

Killer bees can live where the winters are mild. They will be year-round residents as far north as San Francisco and southern Maryland. They will also live all year in southern Texas and in Arizona, Alabama, Mississippi, Louisiana, Virginia, North Carolina, and South Carolina. In the summer killer bees will live even in the northern states. They will die off there when it gets cold.

The invasion of the killer bees is serious. They kill people and animals, and they could ruin the honey industry. This industry is worth 150 million dollars a year. Wherever killer bees have gone, many beekeepers have changed jobs. Also, many crops cannot be grown without the pollinating that native bees do. After killer bees get here, fruits and vegetables may become much more expensive.

Attempts to stop the bees

Scientists have tried to tame the killer bees. The United States Department of Agriculture has tried to mate them with the European bees, which are much more peaceful. The results have not been too good because the resulting bees are still very fierce. There has also been an attempt to kill the bees. So far, the USDA has trapped and destroyed 13,700 swarms of killer bees in Mexico.

Ways to protect people

There is some hope. Most deaths from killer bees happen in the first four years after they come to a new place. Then people learn how to avoid them. Also, killer bees may become more peaceful in cool weather.

In an interview, a beekeeper had some advice about preparing for killer bees. She pointed out

Tell students that a writer's particular way of writing, including the choice and arrangement of words, is called his or her style. Ask each student to find a short report from a magazine or a newspaper and to evaluate the writer's style. Students might consider these questions:

1. What is appealing or unusual about the writer's use of language?
2. How has the writer arranged facts in an interesting way?
3. Is the writing as interesting as or more interesting than the topic? ■

Writing Your First Draft **341**

that people who live in South America have learned how to deal with African bees. Only strangers to these bees and their ways get killed.

According to the beekeeper, here's what to do once the killer bees get here. She said, "When you see a bee, run as far and as fast as you can. Run behind things that block the bee's vision. Run to a house. Then call the fire department."

CONCLUSION
Restatement of main idea

The fierce killer bees are on their way through the United States. If people are not ready for them, they can cause great harm to the honey industry and to agriculture. Killer bees can seriously hurt or even kill people. Will this country be ready for them?

Works Cited

Alper, Joseph. "The Big Sting." Health Apr. 1989: 53–54.
Hardy, Ann. Telephone interview. 12 Dec. 1990.
Kerby, Mona. Friendly Bees, Ferocious Bees. New York: Franklin Watts, 1987.
Patoski, Joe Nick. "Killer Buzz." Texas Monthly Dec. 1990: 104.
Pringle, Laurence. Here Come the Killer Bees. New York: William Morrow, 1986.

MEETING INDIVIDUAL NEEDS

LEARNING STYLES

Kinetic and Visual Learners. You may want to ask some students to work either independently or in groups to make poster-sized Works Cited pages for display in the classroom.

STUDENTS WITH SPECIAL NEEDS

Before writing their lists of sources, students might need extra practice with the format. Create several versions of the "killer" bee report's Works Cited page. In one version, scramble the entries alphabetically. In another version, make sure that neither book titles nor journals are underlined. A third version could have the necessary dates or punctuation omitted. Have students correct the three versions by comparing them to the original.

WORKS CITED

The MLA calls for a 5–space indent. For the typeface used in this book, the 5–space indent translates into a printer's measure which is slightly different.

MECHANICS HINT

Punctuating Titles

In a printed book or magazine, italics are used to identify titles of books and magazines. In a handwritten or typewritten report, underlining does the same thing. In your report or list of sources, underline the title of each book, magazine, or encyclopedia. Notice this, however: don't underline the title of your own report or the titles of articles. Put quotation marks around the titles of articles in magazines or encyclopedias.

EXAMPLES **Book:**

Pringle, Laurence. <u>Here Come the Killer Bees</u>. New York: William Morrow, 1986.

Magazine:

Alper, Joseph. "The Big Sting." <u>Health</u> Apr. 1989: 53–54.

Encyclopedia:

Heinrich, Bernd. "Bee." <u>The World Book Encyclopedia</u>. 1990 ed.

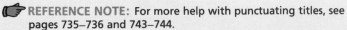 **REFERENCE NOTE:** For more help with punctuating titles, see pages 735–736 and 743–744.

 **WRITING ASSIGNMENT**

PART 6:
Writing Your First Draft

Using your notes and outline as a guide, write your first draft. Remember that it doesn't have to be as long as the sample report. At the end of your report, list your sources on a Works Cited page.

SEGMENT 5 (pp. 343–345)

EVALUATING AND REVISING

OBJECTIVES

- To analyze a writer's revisions
- To evaluate a paragraph from a report
- To evaluate and revise the first draft of a report

TEACHING THE LESSON

Tell students that evaluating and revising is an important part of the writing process. Point out that professional writers constantly evaluate and revise their work before giving it to editors who evaluate and revise it even more.

You may want to use **Exercises 4** and **5** for guided practice of evaluation and ☞

Evaluating and Revising

After you've written your first draft, put it away for a day. Then use the chart below to evaluate and improve it. Ask yourself each question at the left. Whenever you answer a question no, use the technique in the right-hand column to revise your report.

EVALUATING AND REVISING REPORTS

	EVALUATION GUIDE	REVISION TECHNIQUE
1	Does the report use at least three different sources?	**Add** sources. Try to use at least one nonprint source.
2	Does the report have enough information?	**Add** facts or the ideas of an expert.
3	Does the report give credit to an author's words?	**Add** quotation marks where you use someone's words.
4	Is information in the report clearly organized?	**Reorder** paragraphs so that the order of ideas is clear.
5	Does an interesting introduction give the report's topic?	**Add** (or rewrite) a sentence that tells your main idea.
6	Does a conclusion let readers know the report is over?	**Add** eye-catching details. **Add** a paragraph that summarizes or restates the main idea.
7	Does a list of sources in the correct form end the report?	**Add** a list of your sources. Use the form on page 341.

EVALUATING AND REVISING
- Writing a Report

QUOTATION FOR THE DAY

". . . Plato is said to have written the introduction to his *Republic* seven times, differently modified." (Arthur Schopenhauer, 1788–1860, German philosopher)

Write this quotation on the chalkboard and tell students that Plato was a Greek philosopher and writer who lived from about 428 to 347 B.C. Ask students whether they have ever done anything seven times to get a certain result.

MEETING INDIVIDUAL NEEDS

ADVANCED STUDENTS

Ask students to work in groups to write short reports that need major revision. For example, the paragraphs should not be clearly organized and the introductions should not tell what the reports are about. Then have groups display their reports and lead a class discussion on how to improve the reports.

INDEPENDENT PRACTICE

Students can use what they've learned to revise their first drafts for **Writing Assignment: Part 7** independently. Have students show you any major revisions they've made so you can assess their evaluation and revision techniques.

EXERCISE 4 ▶ Analyzing a Writer's Revisions

Before you revise your own draft, look at the changes another writer made. Working with a partner, study the writer's changes to one paragraph in the report on killer bees. Then answer the questions that follow. You and your partner might compare your answers to another pair's answers. Do your answers agree?

> No one can survive a hundred or more **reorder**
> stings. Killer bees are extremely nervous,
> and they are also fighters. Native bees
> (for a yard or so)
> chase people when they are bothered.   **add**
> Africanized bees, however, will chase for
> more than half a mile. Their poison is not
> different from the poison of ordinary bees,
> but they come after people in a big swarm.
> ~~I wouldn't want them chasing after me!~~   **cut**
> Dr. Kenneth Schuberth of the Johns
> Hopkins Medical Institutions says, "When   **add**
> you get that much venom in your system at
> once, it's like receiving a giant snake bite."   **add**

1. Why did the writer move the first sentence to a new place in the paragraph? Where does it make more sense?
2. Why did the writer add the words *for a yard or so* to the third sentence? [Hint: Does the reader need this information?]
3. Why did the writer cut the sentence *I wouldn't want them chasing after me!*? [Hint: Does this sentence give a fact or an expert's ideas? How does this sentence change the way the paragraph sounds?]
4. Why did the writer add quotation marks to the last sentence?

INTEGRATING THE LANGUAGE ARTS

Technology Link. If students are creating their reports on word processors, remind them to use the search feature to locate words that they think may be overused in their reports, and tell them to replace these words with synonyms. Tell students that sometimes writers unconsciously repeat words. For example, writers often overuse the adjective *very*. Ask students to think of other words often overused by writers.

ANSWERS
Exercise 4

1. The information was out of place. It logically follows the fact that bees "come after people in a big swarm."
2. The information is necessary to contrast Africanized bees with native bees.
3. The sentence states the writer's opinion rather than a fact or an expert's ideas. It makes the paragraph sound too informal.
4. The quotation marks show words that are not the writer's.

EXERCISE 5 ▶ Evaluating a Report

Have you ever heard the song "Swing Low, Sweet Chariot"? It's a spiritual, a song first sung by slaves. Here's a paragraph from a report on spirituals. Get together with one or two classmates, and evaluate the paragraph. What are its weaknesses? What changes should be made? Use the evaluating and revising chart on page 343 to decide.

> Spirituals were sung by slaves on southern plantations. Frederick Douglass, a former slave, said, Slaves are generally expected to sing as well as to work. Most of the songs were very sorrowful. Many of these spirituals are still sung today. They were often about a better life to come. Some of the spirituals had codes in them.

PART 7:
Evaluating and Revising Your Report

What changes will you make in your first draft to improve it? Read your report to a small group of classmates. Listen carefully to their suggestions. You might even want to take notes on what they like and dislike about your report. Then use the chart on page 343 to evaluate and revise the draft by yourself.

ANSWERS
Exercise 5

Responses will vary. The introduction could be more interesting. Quotation marks are needed to show the exact words of Frederick Douglass. "Many of these spirituals are still sung today" should be moved to become the last sentence. The sentence about codes could be deleted because codes could be discussed in a separate paragraph.

MEETING
INDIVIDUAL
NEEDS

LEP/ESL

General Strategies. Many students will need individual attention at this stage of the writing process. If feasible, meet with students privately and have them read their reports aloud. Your immediate feedback will more than likely bolster their confidence and give them the information necessary to make effective revisions. Have students make written notations concerning aspects of their reports that need further work.

PROOFREADING AND PUBLISHING

OBJECTIVES

- To produce a clean, proofread report
- To share a report

TEACHING THE LESSON

On the chalkboard, write a paragraph that contains several grammar, usage, and mechanics errors and guide students through the process of proofreading it. As closure, discuss with students various ways of publishing their reports. ■

RESOURCES

PROOFREADING AND PUBLISHING
- Writing a Report

QUOTATION FOR THE DAY

"Any man can make mistakes, but only an idiot persists in his error." (Cicero, 106–43 B.C., Roman orator, philosopher, politician, and writer)

You could use this quotation to initiate a discussion of common errors. Ask students to try to remember what kinds of mistakes they have made in other papers and assignments. Suggest that students try especially hard to eliminate the kinds of mistakes they have made before.

◾ TIMESAVER

Appoint a student-publications committee to be in charge of publishing the reports. The committee can decide how best to publish the reports (perhaps several different ways) and then make publishing arrangements by preparing bulletin boards, contacting other teachers, and so on.

---

346   Writing a Report

Proofreading and Publishing

Read your report carefully to make sure it has no mistakes in spelling, capitalization, usage, and punctuation. Then, think of a way to share your report. Here are two ideas.

- Bind all the reports in your class on similar subjects (such as animals or ancient cultures) into a book. (You can use staples or different kinds of report binders.) Number the pages in order from first to last page in the book. Make up a table of contents page and add it to the binder. Then decide on a title for the book of reports. Give a copy of the book to your school library.
- If your topic is about science or history, volunteer to give an oral report in your science or history class. Use the information in your report to prepare your talk.

WRITING ASSIGNMENT   PART 8:
Proofreading and Publishing Your Report

Now you're ready for the final touches. Make a clean copy of your report and proofread it carefully. Then use one of the ideas above or one of your own to share your report. Give a copy of your report to anyone you interviewed for information. (It's the courteous thing to do.)

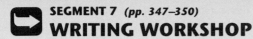
OBJECTIVES
- To analyze the content and form of a book report
- To write a book report

MOTIVATION

Ask students if any of them have read any books lately. Ask students to tell whether they enjoyed the books or not and to explain what made the books good or bad. Tell students that in this segment they'll learn how to evaluate a book for a written report.

👉

WRITING WORKSHOP

347

A Book Report

You and your friends probably talk about the movies you've seen. When you do, you usually say whether the movie is worth seeing. What you're doing is giving a movie review. One kind of book report is like a movie review. It evaluates (judges) the book and tells whether the writer thinks the book is worth reading.

How do you evaluate a book? You can start with whether or not you liked it. But most readers want a little more information. Here are some questions you can ask yourself to evaluate a book.

1. *Do the characters seem like real people?*
2. *Do they change or grow in some way?*
3. *Why do events in the novel happen? Is there a reason, or do they happen by accident?*
4. *What's the novel's main idea, or theme? Does it apply to real life?*
5. *Does the book have suspense? Did it keep my interest?*

If you answer most of these questions yes, the book is probably very good. It's worth reading. If you answer most of them no, you probably shouldn't recommend the book to others.

Now back to your book report. How do you put it together? First, you have to get your readers' attention. Then, you have to let them know what book you are writing about. (Tell them the book's author and title.) After that you can begin to let them know your recommendation as you tell a little about the plot and characters. Don't tell too much, though. You don't want to spoil the suspense for someone who might read the book.

A sample book report appears on the next page. As you read it, look for the writer's recommendation.

RESOURCES

WRITING WORKSHOP
- Narrowing Your Subject
- Asking Questions
- Finding and Listing Sources
- Using Note Cards
- Writing a Report

QUOTATION FOR THE DAY

"Readers of novels are a strange folk, upon whose probable or even possible tastes no wise book-maker would ever venture to bet." (E. V. Lucas, 1868–1938, English novelist, journalist, and essayist)

Ask students if they have ever disagreed with someone about a novel or film and what they think accounts for such differences of opinion.

TEACHING THE LESSON

Stress that a book report should develop an evaluation of a book that can be supported with specific details from the book itself. Have students read the sample book report and use the three **Thinking It Over** questions to initiate a class discussion.

To guide students through the process of evaluating a book, use the five evalua- tion questions on p. 347 to evaluate a novel or film with which the class is familiar. Then have students write their book reports independently. Use students' completed book reports to assess their mastery.

MEETING INDIVIDUAL NEEDS

LEP/ESL

General Strategies. The sample book report, **"Carlota, a Woman of Courage,"** contains idioms that may prove problematic for students. Prior to asking them to read this report, pair ESL students with students whose first language is English and have the pairs cooperate to write definitions for each of the following expressions:

1. to take place
2. to get along with
3. to stand up to (someone)
4. to stand up for (something)
5. to make one's way
6. to go on to (do something)
7. a close call

 ## INTEGRATING THE LANGUAGE ARTS

Literature Link. Ask students to read a short story such as Shirley Jackson's "Charles," and then have them use the five questions on p. 347 to evaluate it. You could answer these questions during a class discussion, divide the class into groups to answer them, or have students work individually. Finally, have students say whether they would recommend the short story. Be sure that students support their answers with specific examples from the story.

Carlota, a Woman of Courage

Have you ever dived for sunken treasure? Ridden in a horse race? Faced a hostile army? The main character of Carlota, by Scott O'Dell, does all these things and more. Carlota is a good, exciting novel that readers will enjoy.

Carlota is about a young woman named Carlota de Zubarán, who lives with her grandmother and her father in California. The novel takes place in the last part of the 1848 war between the United States and Mexico. At that time, California was still a part of Mexico. Carlota's family, whose Spanish ancestors settled Mexico, is on the side of Mexico.

In many ways Carlota is like my friends and me. Sometimes she does not get along with the adults around her. For example, Carlota enjoys riding her horse out on the ranch with her father. This bothers her grandmother who wants her to dress and behave like a young woman. Later, in a serious incident, Carlota stands up to her father. Not knowing the war is over, some American soldiers are making their way to California. Carlota's father and some other ranchers track the soldiers and attack them. Carlota wounds one of the soldiers with her lance and then insists on taking care of him. This makes her father very angry.

The main idea of this novel is that sometimes courage means standing up for what you believe. This is harder to do when other people do not feel the same way you do. At first, Carlota hates the Americans because her father does. Then she realizes that the American she has wounded is also a

349

human being, and she takes care of him. To do this, she must show courage and stand up against her father. As Carlota says, "I was ashamed, now, of what I had tried to do. The shame gave me courage" (125). In real life, there are many times when you must show this kind of courage.

Carlota is very suspenseful; it holds the reader's interest. Carlota has many adventures and many close calls. One of these adventures is the horse race at her sister's wedding. She has a dangerous fall from her horse, but she goes on to win a close and exciting victory. To share in these adventures and to enjoy a good book, read Carlota.

Thinking It Over

1. In the first two paragraphs, what information do you learn about the novel *Carlota*?
2. Does the writer think *Carlota* is a good or bad novel?
3. Give two reasons why the writer feels this way about *Carlota*.

INTEGRATING THE LANGUAGE ARTS

Library Link. After students have read the sample book report, plan a visit to the school or community library. Ask the librarian to show students the section where novels are shelved and to give them an overview of the library's novels. You and the librarian may want to help some students select appropriate novels. If students want to write about books they have read previously, stress that they must reread the books to gather the specific information necessary for their reports.

ANSWERS
Thinking It Over

1. Responses will vary. In the first two paragraphs, the reader learns the writer's opinion of the novel, the name of the novel's main character, the setting, and other background information.

2. good

3. Responses will vary. The writer likes *Carlota* because its main character, Carlota, is like the writer and her or his friends and because the novel is suspenseful.

SELECTION AMENDMENT
Description of change: excerpted
Rationale: to focus on the concept of the book report presented in this segment

After students have taken notes about their books, divide the class into groups of three or four for discussion. Encourage group members to tell each other about their books and to share their opinions of the books.

You may want to monitor each group's discussion. Give students freedom to explore ideas generated from discussion of the content of their books.

Afterward, ask representatives from the groups to summarize their groups' discussions. Ask students if, during the discussions, they heard about a book that they would like to read.

Writing a Book Report

Prewriting. For your report choose a novel that you feel strongly about. It may be one that you think is very good—or one that you think is very bad. After you've read the book, take notes on it. To evaluate the book, answer the questions on page 347.

Writing, Evaluating, and Revising. In the first part of your report, use some interesting details to get your readers' interest. Give the title and author of the book. Then, tell briefly what the novel is about and when and where it takes place. Give your evaluation of the novel. Is it good or bad? When you revise, make sure you've given examples from the book. If you like, include a quotation from the book. Just be sure to give the author's exact words in quotation marks and the page number for the quotation in parentheses.

Proofreading and Publishing. Proofread your book report and correct any errors. Be sure that you've underlined the name of the book whenever it appears. Don't underline your own title for the report. Put a copy of your report into a file with other students' reports. You may even want to illustrate your report with drawings of events or people from the novel. Your teacher may keep the file for other students to use when they select books.

SEGMENT 8 *(pp. 351–353)*
MAKING CONNECTIONS

**RESEARCH ACROSS
THE CURRICULUM
OBJECTIVE**

- To research, write, and illustrate a report
  about a city's history

351

MAKING CONNECTIONS

RESEARCH ACROSS THE CURRICULUM

History

Do you ever wonder what your city (or a nearby city) looked like many years ago? What the place looked like even before a city was there? You can find out by doing some research, perhaps about the following things.

1. What's the history of the city? How old is it? Who first settled it? Why was a city started here? Who were some of the first families? What's the oldest building?
2. What was here two hundred years ago? Did Native Americans live here? Who were they, and how did they live? What happened to them?
3. Who is the oldest living resident of the city? Could you interview this person?
   In what ways has the town changed since this person was a child?

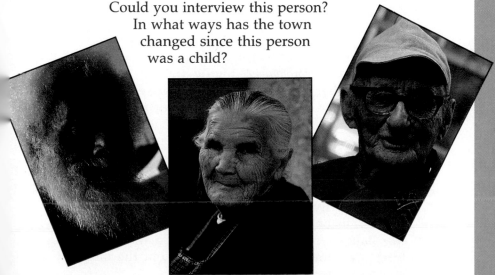

RESEARCH ACROSS THE CURRICULUM
Teaching Strategies

Before dividing the class into groups, have students read and discuss the sample questions in the textbook. Then ask students if they can think of other questions to ask about their city or a nearby city.

At the beginning of this project, try to arrange for a local historian to talk to the class to give students some ideas about how to go about their research.

Encourage students to include as many visual aids as possible in their reports. You could place copies of the finished reports in the school library or have students present oral reports to other classes or to the local historical society.

GUIDELINES

Reports will vary. Students' reports should reflect research corresponding to the amount of time you allowed for the project. Reports should include visual aids.

4. What natural resources made the area a good place to live? What are the native plants and animals? How might this place have looked before people arrived?
5. What ethnic groups from other countries settled in the city? When did they arrive? What part of the city did they settle in?
6. How do people earn their living in your city? Have the jobs changed since the city was started?

Get together with several of your classmates and find out about the history of the place where you live. Divide the questions, and decide on a research job for each classmate. The library is a good place to start your research. Other sources might be your local newspaper or a historical society or museum.

Take careful notes from your sources. Then, prepare a group report on the history of your city. Include drawings of important events, or of buildings, plants, and animals that have made your city an interesting place to live.

SPEAKING AND LISTENING

Reporting on the Weather

You've probably seen weather forecasters on TV. Some read reports put out by the National Weather Service. But others are *meteorologists*, highly trained scientists who study weather and report on it. They base their reports on facts collected from a vast network of weather stations. They also check records of weather patterns from earlier years. Then they make a forecast, a prediction of future weather.

Here's your chance to gather weather information and present a weather report to your class. You may want to do this activity with a partner.

First, listen to the TV or radio meteorologist on at least two stations. Notice the kind of information they report. Also pay attention to how they present the information they've gathered.

Next, take notes on the weather information that has been in your local paper for the past week. At the library, find last year's newspapers for that week. Read what the weather was like at this time last year. What, if anything, do you find is unusual about this year's rainfall, wind, or temperature?

Now gather information on this year's weather. Keep a record of your town's weather for at least three days. To collect your own data, record the temperature three times each day. Note the amount of precipitation (rain or snow). Describe the type and quantity of clouds. If you prefer, you can get this information from the National Weather Service. The closest airport will also have it.

Finally, make some weather charts:

- one chart comparing the weather last week to the weather at the same time last year
- one chart showing what the weather has been like for the past three days
- one chart showing what the weather will be like tomorrow

Then, make notes on the information you want to present along with your charts. Practice your weather report out loud until you can present your report in an interesting way.

Chapter 11

WRITING EFFECTIVE SENTENCES

OBJECTIVES

- To identify and revise sentence fragments and run-on sentences
- To combine sentences by inserting words and phrases, by creating compound subjects and verbs, and by using subordinate clauses
- To revise stringy and wordy sentences
- To reconstruct a message by supplying missing words

Motivation

One way to handle this chapter is to include it in a general treatment of the revision stage of the writing process. Students usually learn best when they have some reason to know the material, and you can help create this reason by emphasizing one or more of the first three segments of the chapter during revision.

After students have written first drafts for one of the other composition chapters, collect the papers and read them to find examples of fragments, run-on sentences, and stringy and wordy sentences.

Introduction

This chapter consists of three independent segments, and it's possible to use them in different ways. First, you can treat the chapter as a unit. For some seventh-graders, this might be their first exposure to concepts such as sentence fragments and run-on sen-

tences. Second, you can treat the chapter as a resource for students who have specific problems with one or more of the areas the chapter covers. Third, you can emphasize each of the segments as part of the revision stage of the writing process when you teach the other composition chapters.

Because revision is an essential component of the writing process for any writing aim on mode, this chapter will help sharpen students' skills in writing to express, to inform, to persuade, and to create literature. Also, the material in this chapter will help improve their narration, description, classification, and evaluation skills.

Integration

Most of the examples and exercises in this chapter are based on subjects seventh-graders study. For example, there are examples and exercises that discuss flying squirrels, desert plants, dolphins, pearls, and starfish, all of which relate to biology. Features dealing with literature include several biographies, two stories from Greek mythology, and a movie review. Features based on social studies include material on Native American peoples. All of these could be linked to lessons in other classes or could serve as springboards for oral and written reports on these and related subjects.

The chart on the next page illustrates the strands of language arts as they are integrated into this chapter. For vocabulary study, glossary words are underlined in some writing models.

BEST SENTENCE

QUOTATIONS

All **Quotations for the Day** are chosen because of their relevance to instructional material presented in that segment of the chapter and for their usefulness in establishing student interest in writing.

Selection	Reading and Literature	Writing and Critical Thinking	Language and Syntax	Speaking, Listening, and Other Expression Skills
	Making judgments about clarity **361** Evaluating the effectiveness of sentences **372, 377**	Identifying complete sentences **357, 361** Identifying and revising sentence fragments **358, 361** Identifying and revising run-on sentences **360, 361** Combining sentences by inserting words **363** Combining sentences by inserting phrases **365-366** Combining sentences by creating compound subjects, verbs, and sentences **367-368, 369, 372** Combining sentences by using a subordinate clause **371, 372** Revising stringy sentences **373-374, 377** Revising wordy sentences **376-377** Reconstructing a message by adding missing words **378**	Identifying components of a complete sentence **357, 361, 378** Using coordinating conjunctions to revise run-on sentences **360, 361** Identifying phrases **365-366** Identifying compound subjects and verbs **367-368, 369, 372** Identifying clauses **371, 372** Identifying independent and subordinate clauses **371, 372** Identifying relative and adverbial clauses without using terminology **371, 372** Revising stringy (rambling) sentences **373-374** Identifying wordy sentences **376-377**	Using commas with two independent clauses **369** Using commas to set off nonrestrictive phrases **371** Using a comma after an introductory adverbial clause **371, 373-374** Using a comma between two independent clauses joined by a coordinating conjunction **373-374**

SEGMENT PLANNING GUIDE

Whether you are planning for a quick review of a writing concept or preparing an extended lesson on composition you can use the following Planning Guide to adapt the chapter material to the individual needs of your class.

SEGMENT	PAGES	CONTENT	RESOURCES
1 *Writing Clear Sentences*	*354-361*		Sentence Fragments
Writing Clear Sentences	354-355	Guidelines: writing clear sentences	Run-on Sentences
Sentence Fragments	355-356	Guidelines: identifying and revising sentence fragments	
Grammar Hint	356	Writing suggestion: identifying fragments	
Exercise 1	357	Applied practice: identifying sentence fragments	
Exercise 2	358	Applied practice: identifying and revising sentence fragments	
Run-on Sentences	358-59	Guidelines: identifying and revising run-on sentences	
Mechanics Hint	359	Writing suggestion: using commas correctly	
Revising Run-on Sentences	360	Guidelines: examining ways to revise run-on sentences	
Exercise 3	360-361	Applied practice: identifying and revising run-on sentences	
Review Exercise A	361	Applied practice: identifying and revising sentence fragments and run-on sentences in a paragraph	
2 *Combining Sentences*	*361-372*		Inserting Words and Phrases
Combining Sentences	361-362	Guidelines: examining paragraph revisions	Combining with *And, But,* or *Or*
Combining Sentences by Inserting Words	362-363	Guidelines: combining sentences by inserting a key word from one sentence into another	Adding a Subordinate Clause
Exercise 4	363	Applied practice: combining sentences by inserting words	
Combining Sentences by Inserting Phrases	364	Guidelines: combining sentences by inserting a phrase from one sentence into another	
Mechanics Hint	364-365	Writing suggestion: using commas with phrases	
Exercise 5	365-366	Applied practice: combining sentences by inserting phrases	
Combining Sentences by Using *And, But,* or *Or*	366-367	Guidelines: combining sentences using *and, but,* or *or* to make compound subjects, verbs, and sentences	
Grammar Hint	367	Writing suggestion: checking for subject-verb agreement	
Exercise 6	367-368	Applied practice: combining sentences by creating compound subjects and verbs	
Writing Note	368	Writing suggestion: combining closely related sentences	

WRITING CLEAR SENTENCES

OBJECTIVES

- To identify and revise sentence fragments
- To identify and revise run-on sentences

TEACHING THE LESSON

If students already have a solid grasp of the grammatical terms *subject* and *verb,* you can probably have them read the material, study the examples, and work the exercises. However, if their grasp of the terminology is weak, you may first want to spend some time reviewing these terms.

QUOTATION FOR THE DAY

"When people will not weed their own minds, they are set to be overrun with nettles." (Horace Walpole, 1717–1797, Fourth Earl of Oxford)

Write the quotation on the chalkboard and have students freewrite for a few minutes about what the quotation means. You may then wish to explain that sentences, too, sometimes need to be "weeded." Tell students that in this section they will learn to distinguish run-ons and fragments, two enemies of clarity.

11 WRITING EFFECTIVE SENTENCES

LOOKING AHEAD

In this chapter, you will learn how to make your sentences clearer and more interesting by

- writing complete sentences
- combining sentences
- improving your sentence style

Writing Clear Sentences

One of the best ways to make your writing clear is to use *complete sentences.* A complete sentence

- has a subject
- has a verb
- expresses a complete thought

If you're using this segment as part of a larger lesson on revision, you may not want to review grammar. One way to avoid a review is to teach students to read the examples in such a way as to make it clear they aren't acceptable. Read fragments as though they were introductory clauses or phrases. At the end of each fragment, your voice should clearly indicate that more of the sentence is coming. For example, in the fragment "Because it was raining . . .," the last syllable should remain at a high pitch so that your listeners' mental response would be something like, "Well, what happened?"

You can teach run-on sentences in the same way. For example, in the run-on "He served pumpkin pie, Tina ate two pieces," read the sentence so that the first part comes ☞

EXAMPLES   Some birds can imitate human speech.
Parrots and myna birds are great mimics.
Listen to that bird talk!

Each of the example word groups expresses a complete thought. Each has a verb. The last example may not appear to have a subject in it, but it actually has the unstated subject *you:* (You) Listen to that bird talk!

There are two common errors that get in the way of writing complete sentences: *sentence fragments* and *run-on sentences.* Once you learn how to recognize fragments and run-ons in your writing, you can revise them to form clear, complete sentences.

Sentence Fragments

A *sentence fragment* is a part of a sentence that has been punctuated as if it were a complete sentence. Because it is incomplete, a sentence fragment sends a confusing message.

FRAGMENT   Was the first black man to win the Wimbledon tennis championship. [The subject is missing. *Who* was the first black man to win Wimbledon?]

SENTENCE   Arthur Ashe was the first black man to win the Wimbledon tennis championship.

MEETING
INDIVIDUAL
NEEDS

LEP/ESL

General Strategies. Students who are just learning to speak English will probably need help with this segment. If ESL students speak a Romance language like Spanish or French, you can capitalize on the fact that the grammar of those languages has many similarities to the grammar of English. For example, you could ask students to write simple English sentences such as "The man hit the ball" in their native languages. Then students could write the equivalent English sentences below the others and point out the subject and the verb in each. Emphasize that in English, both a subject and a verb must be present for a statement to be a complete sentence. You can use a similar activity for run-on sentences.

out, "He served pumpkin pie Tina." Let your voice trail off on "ate two pieces." Then read the sentence correctly with a conjunction. Other run-ons can also be presented this way.

GUIDED PRACTICE

Fragments and run-ons from students' writing can be used to provide guided practice. Read two or three examples of each type of sentence fault and emphasize their faulty nature by exaggerating your reading. Let students supply revisions.

COOPERATIVE LEARNING

You may want to have students work in pairs or groups of three on **Exercise 2.** The sentence fragments in the exercise can be revised in a number of ways. Have each group come up with as many different revisions as there are members and then have the group select the best version. This procedure will ensure that everyone in the group participates.

FRAGMENT	Ashe the Wimbledon singles title in 1975. [The verb is missing. What's the connection between Ashe and the singles title?]
SENTENCE	Ashe won the Wimbledon singles title in 1975.

FRAGMENT	While he was a student at the University of California. [This has a subject and a verb, but it doesn't express a complete thought. *What happened* while Ashe was a student?]
SENTENCE	Ashe also won several championships in college tennis while he was a student at the University of California.

As you can see from the first two examples, you can correct some sentence fragments by adding a subject or verb. Other times a sentence fragment just needs to be attached to the sentence next to it. You may have accidentally separated it from the sentence it belongs with by putting in a period and a capital letter too soon.

FRAGMENT	The crowd cheered wildly. **When Leon scored the winning touchdown.**
SENTENCE	The crowd cheered wildly when Leon scored the winning touchdown.

GRAMMAR HINT

Identifying Fragments

Some words look like verbs but really aren't. These "fake" verbs can fool you into thinking a group of words is a sentence when it is really a fragment. A word that ends in *–ing* can't stand as a verb unless it has a helping verb (such as *is, are, were*) with it.

FRAGMENT	The children playing on the swings. [Without the helping verb, this isn't a complete thought.]
SENTENCE	The children **were playing** on the swings.

You may want to assign and check **Exercise 1** before you assign the other two exercises. If you don't think students can identify sentence fragments well enough after they've done **Exercise 1**, you may want to do some reteaching before assigning the other exercises.

If students need more independent practice than the exercises provide, make up practice exercises by rewriting exercises from a different part of this textbook. **Chapter 18: "The Clause"** has exercises that can be rewritten to create fragments, and **Chapter 19: "The Kinds of Sentence Structure"** should prove useful for creating run-ons.

☞

Writing Clear Sentences   **357**

EXERCISE 1▶   **Identifying Sentence Fragments**

Decide which of the following groups of words are sentence fragments and which are complete sentences. This simple three-part test will help you.

1. Does the group of words have a subject?
2. Does it have a verb?
3. Does it express a complete thought?

If you answer *no* to any of the questions, write *F* to show that the group of words is a fragment. If the group of words is a complete sentence, write *S*. (Remember, the subject "you" isn't always stated directly in a sentence.)

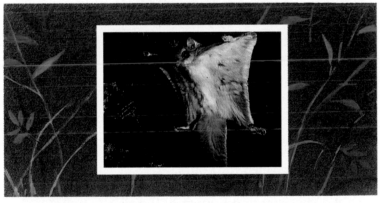

1. A flying squirrel a squirrel that can glide through the air.   **1. F**
2. Some Asian flying squirrels four feet long.   **2. F**
3. Leaps from one tree to another.   **3. F**
4. The squirrel glides downward, then straight, and finally upward.   **4. S**
5. Some flying squirrels more than fifty feet.   **5. F**
6. If they use a higher starting point.   **6. F**
7. Flying squirrels live in the forests of Asia, Europe, and North America.   **7. S**
8. Eat berries, birds' eggs, insects, and nuts.   **8. F**
9. Nest in the hollows of trees.   **9. F**
10. Notice how this squirrel stretches out its legs to help it glide.   **10. S**

VISUAL CONNECTIONS
Exploring the Subject. Nocturnal creatures with excellent night vision, flying squirrels eat berries, seeds, nuts, and insects. They have pouches in their cheeks that let them hold large amounts of food until they have an opportunity to store it.

Flying squirrels get their name from the folds of skin that connect their hind legs to their tails. These folds enable them to glide long distances.

EXERCISE 2 ▶ **Finding and Revising Fragments**

Some of the following groups of words are sentence fragments. Revise each fragment by (1) adding a subject, (2) adding a verb, or (3) attaching the fragment to a complete sentence. You may need to change the punctuation and capitalization, too. If the word group is already a complete sentence, write *S*.   Revisions will vary.

EXAMPLE   **1.** As soon as we finished eating breakfast.
　　　　　　1. *We left for our camping trip as soon as we finished eating breakfast.*

1. The whole family ˄ into the car.   **1.** got
2. We traveled for hours.   **2.** S
3. When we arrived at the campground ˄   **3.** , we unpacked.
4. My sister and I ˄ down to the river.   **4.** ran
5. ˄ Took our fishing gear with us.   **5.** We   **6.** S
6. We cast our lines the way our aunt had taught us.
7. ˄ Because we didn't have the best bait.   **7.** We didn't catch any fish
8. We headed back to the campsite at sunset.   **8.** S
9. Dad ˄ cooking bean soup over the fire.   **9.** was
10. Mom and my sister ˄ the tent.   **10.** pitched

Run-on Sentences

A *run-on sentence* is actually two complete sentences punctuated like one sentence. In a run-on, the thoughts just run into each other. The reader can't tell where one idea ends and another one begins.

To help students eliminate run-ons, have them try one or more of the following suggestions:

1. Read sentences orally; if you hesitate or stop at certain places, you may need a conjunction and comma.

2. Watch for changes in ideas.
3. Check for especially long sentences.

☞

Writing Clear Sentences **359**

RUN-ON	Edna Ferber was a novelist and playwright she wrote about American life in the 1800s.
CORRECT	Edna Ferber was a novelist and playwright. She wrote about American life in the 1800s.
RUN-ON	Ferber's novel *Show Boat* was made into a musical play, some of her other novels were made into movies.
CORRECT	Ferber's novel *Show Boat* was made into a musical play. Some of her other novels were made into movies.

To spot run-ons, try reading your writing aloud. As you read, you will usually pause where one thought ends and another begins. If you pause at a place where you don't have any end punctuation, you may have a run-on sentence.

MECHANICS HINT

Using Commas Correctly

A comma does mark a brief pause in a sentence, but it doesn't show the end of a sentence. If you use just a comma between two sentences, you create a run-on sentence.

RUN-ON	Clogging is a lively kind of dancing, the dancers wear special shoes to tap out the rhythm.
CORRECT	Clogging is a lively kind of dancing. The dancers wear special shoes to tap out the rhythm.

VISUAL CONNECTIONS

Exploring the Subject. Clogging is a popular form of folk dancing in the American South. Its origins are uncertain, but it probably began in the mountains of western North Carolina in the 1920s or 1930s in association with the Asheville Mountain Dance and Folk Festival. Clogging is a group dance that synthesizes square dancing and "buck and wing" dancing, a type of tap dance.

Precision clogging is the kind that is most often performed. Developed in the 1950s, it involves the dancers' performing the same steps at the same time. Freestyle clogging is an older form in which the dancers make up steps in time with the music.

REVIEW A

OBJECTIVE

• To identify and revise sentence fragments and run-on sentences

ADVANCED STUDENTS

Some students might practice correcting run-on sentences in ways other than those given in the textbook. For example, a run-on can also be joined by a semicolon without a coordinating conjunction. If two independent clauses are joined by a conjunctive adverb such as *however, therefore,* or *consequently,* the correct punctuation is a semicolon before the conjunctive adverb plus a comma after it. An example is, "I enjoyed the meal; however, I didn't taste everything."

Have students revise the sentences in **Exercise 3** by using semicolons and conjunctive adverbs.

360   *Writing Effective Sentences*

Revising Run-on Sentences

There are several ways you can revise run-on sentences. Here are two of them.

1. You can make two sentences.

RUN-ON   Asteroids are tiny planets they are sometimes called planetoids.

CORRECT   Asteroids are tiny planets**.** They are sometimes called planetoids.

2. You can use a comma and the coordinating conjunction *and, but,* or *or.*

RUN-ON   Some asteroids shine with a steady light, others keep changing in brightness.

CORRECT   Some asteroids shine with a steady light**, but** others keep changing in brightness.

EXERCISE 3 ▶   **Identifying and Revising Run-ons**

Decide which of the following groups of words are run-ons. Then revise each run-on by (1) making it into two separate sentences or (2) using a comma and a coordinating conjunction. If the group of words is already correct, write *C.*   Revisions will vary.

1. Saturn is a huge planet‸it is more than nine times larger than Earth.   **1.** ⊙
2. Saturn is covered by clouds‸it is circled by bands of color.   **2.** and
3. The clouds at the equator are yellow‸the clouds at the poles are green.   **3.** but
4. Saturn has ten moons‸Phoebe is the smallest moon.   **4.** ⊙
5. Most of Saturn's moons orbit the planet from west to east‸Phoebe travels in the opposite direction.   **5.** but
6. Saturn's most striking feature is a group of rings that circles the planet.   **6.** C
7. The rings of Saturn are only about ten miles thick‸ they spread out from the planet for a great distance.   **7.** and

COMBINING SENTENCES

• To combine sentences using subordinate clauses

OBJECTIVES

- To combine sentences by inserting words and phrases
- To combine sentences by creating compound subjects and verbs and compound sentences

☞

8. The rings are made up of billions of tiny particles. **8.** C
9. Some of the rings are dark, but others are brighter. **9.** C
10. Saturn is a beautiful planet͵you need a telescope to **10.** , but see it.

REVIEW A ▶

The following paragraph is confusing because it contains some fragments and run-ons. First, identify the fragments and run-ons. Then, revise each fragment and run-on to make the paragraph clearer.   Revisions will vary.

> Many deserts have no plant life,͵some desert regions   but
> have a variety of plants. Many plants can survive,͵Where
> the climate is hot and dry. Cacti, Joshua trees, palm trees,
> and wildflowers grow in deserts. These plants͵Do not grow
> close together.͵Are spread out, each plant gets water and
> minerals from a large area.   Because they

Combining Sentences

Short sentences can sometimes express your ideas well. But if you use only short sentences, your writing will sound choppy and dull. For example, read the following paragraph, which has only short sentences.

QUOTATION FOR THE DAY

"Real writers revise to make their meaning come through the form in the best possible way." (Marian M. Mohr, American author and teacher/consultant with the Northern Virginia Writing Project)

Share this quotation with the class and discuss the importance of revision. Explain that sentence combining is just one of the skills used in revision.

Tell students that they have been combining sentences without realizing it since they learned to talk. Show examples by writing the following sentences on the chalkboard:

1. I bought a car.
2. I bought a little car.

3. I bought a red car.
4. I bought an American car.

Ask students how they could make these four sentences become one. Point out that the work of this segment is much the same as the work students did in the previous segment.

MEETING INDIVIDUAL NEEDS

LEP/ESL

General Strategies. ESL students can benefit from sentence combining because the process helps build fluency by breaking down the complex skills of writing into smaller components. Work with students individually or pair them with native English speakers to work through the exercises. Consider letting students use the **Combining with *And, But,* or *Or*** resource for additional practice.

ADVANCED STUDENTS

Ask advanced students to further combine the sentences in the example paragraph about Thomas Edison. Their answers will vary, but an example follows:

Most people know that Thomas Edison invented the electric light and the phonograph, but many people don't know that he also experimented with robots. For example, he created a very popular talking doll that recited "Mary Had a Little Lamb" when a crank in its back was turned. He opened a factory that made five hundred of the dolls every day.

Thomas Edison invented the phonograph. He also experimented with robots. A lot of people don't know this. Edison created a talking doll. He created the talking doll in 1894. The doll said the words to "Mary Had a Little Lamb." It said the words when a crank in its back was turned. The talking doll was very popular. Edison opened a factory. The factory made five hundred of the dolls every day.

Now read the revised paragraph. Notice how the writer has combined some of the short sentences to make longer, smoother sentences.

Thomas Edison invented the phonograph. A lot of people don't know that he also experimented with robots. Edison created a talking doll in 1894. When a crank in its back was turned, the doll said the words to "Mary Had a Little Lamb." The talking doll was very popular, and Edison opened a factory that made five hundred of the dolls every day.

As you can see from the revision, sentence combining has also helped to reduce the number of repeated words and ideas. The revised paragraph is clearer, shorter, and more interesting to read.

Combining Sentences by Inserting Words

One way to combine short sentences is to take a key word from one sentence and insert it into the other sentence.

ORIGINAL   The Easter lily is a flower. It is a white flower.
COMBINED   The Easter lily is a **white** flower.

Sometimes you'll need to change the form of the key word before you can insert it. You can change the forms of some words by adding an ending such as *–ed, –ing, –ful,* or *–ly*. In its new form, the key word can be used to describe another word in the sentence.

ORIGINAL	Easter lily plants have leaves. The leaves have points.
COMBINED	Easter lily plants have **pointed** leaves.

EXERCISE 4 ▸ **Combining Sentences by Inserting Words**

Each of the following items contains two sentences. To combine the two sentences, take the italicized key word from the second sentence and insert it into the first sentence. The directions in parentheses will tell you how to change the form of the key word if you need to do so.

EXAMPLE   **1.** Peanuts are the tiny fruit of the peanut plant. They have a good *taste.* (Change *taste* to *tasty.*)

   1. *Peanuts are the tiny, tasty fruit of the peanut plant.*

1. This picture shows peanuts∧underground. ~~They grow underground.~~ (Add *–ing.*)   **1.** growing
2. Peanuts are a∧crop of many warm regions. ~~They are a major crop.~~   **2.** major
3. Peanuts are a∧food for snacking. ~~Peanuts are good for your *health.*~~ (Add *–ful.*)   **3.** healthful
4. The oil from peanuts is used in many∧dressings. ~~The dressings are for *salad.*~~   **4.** salad
5. ∧Grades of peanut oil are used to make soap and shampoo. ~~The *low* grades are used for these products.~~   **5.** Low

GUIDED PRACTICE

The examples within the text and at the beginning of **Exercises 5–8** offer opportunities for guided practice. Make sure students pay close attention to these examples as they read the material. You may even want to put the sentences on the chalkboard to make sure students understand how elements have been combined.

Combining Sentences by Inserting Phrases

A *phrase* is a group of words that doesn't have a subject and a verb. You can combine sentences by taking a phrase from one sentence and inserting it into the other sentence.

ORIGINAL   Arachne is a famous figure. She is a figure in Greek mythology.
COMBINED   Arachne is a famous figure **in Greek mythology.**

INTEGRATING THE LANGUAGE ARTS

Grammar Link. The phrases that students are most likely to use in sentence combining are prepositional phrases. Some students might find it helpful to identify phrases by first picking out the prepositions that start them. You can refer students to **Chapter 15** for more information about prepositions.

Mechanics Link. Combining sentences by inserting words often results in two or more adjectives preceding a noun. Remind students that if the word *and* would make sense between the adjectives, a comma is needed between them. Write the following sentences on the chalkboard and have students determine where commas are needed:

1. Poe was a great fiction writer.
2. Poe led a short tragic life.

When *and* is inserted, the sentences become "Poe was a great and fiction writer" and "Poe led a short and tragic life." The first sentence does not make sense, so no comma is needed. The second sentence makes sense, so a comma should separate the adjectives.

MECHANICS HINT

Using Commas with Phrases

Some phrases need to be set off by commas. Before you insert a phrase into a sentence, ask yourself whether the phrase renames or explains a noun or pronoun. If it does, set it off with a comma (or two commas if the phrase is in the middle of the sentence).

ORIGINAL   Arachne challenged Athena to a weaving contest. Athena was the goddess of wisdom.
COMBINED   Arachne challenged Athena**, the goddess of wisdom,** to a weaving contest.

👉 REFERENCE NOTE: For more information about phrases that need to be set off by commas, see pages 713–720.

Sometimes you can change the verb in a sentence to make a phrase. Just add *–ing* or *–ed* to the verb or put the word *to* in front of it. You can then use the phrase to describe a noun or pronoun in a related sentence. Be sure to place the phrase near the word(s) it modifies.

ORIGINAL   The name *Eskimo* refers to several groups of people. These people live in and near the Arctic.
COMBINED   The name *Eskimo* refers to several groups of people **living in and near the Arctic.**

You may also want to guide students through the first problem in each of the exercises. You can talk students through the solution, or you can write the problems on the chalkboard and demonstrate how to solve them.

INDEPENDENT PRACTICE

The exercises should provide enough independent practice for most students. If you think they need more, have students work on their own compositions to combine sentences. If you use this segment as part of the revision stage of the writing process, let students work through their current compositions. If you're using this chapter as an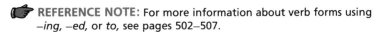

ORIGINAL   Early Eskimos had to follow a special way of life. They had to do this so they could survive in a harsh environment.

COMBINED   **To survive in a harsh environment,** early Eskimos had to follow a special way of life.

👉 **REFERENCE NOTE:** For more information about verb forms using *—ing, —ed,* or *to,* see pages 502–507.

EXERCISE 5 ▶   **Combining Sentences by Inserting Phrases**

Each of the following items contains two sentences. Combine the two sentences by taking the italicized word group from the second sentence and inserting it into the first sentence. The hints in parentheses tell you when and how to change the forms of words. Remember to insert commas where they are needed.

EXAMPLE   **1.** Eskimo peoples followed their traditional way of life. They followed this way of life *for thousands of years.*
   1. *Eskimo peoples followed their traditional way of life for thousands of years.*

1. ₍ᴧ₎Eskimos could build winter shelters in a few hours. ~~They *stacked blocks of snow.*~~ (Change *stacked* to *stacking.*)   **1.** Stacking blocks of snow,
2. They used harpoons₍ᴧ₎ ~~This is how they *hunted seals.*~~ (Change *hunted* to *to hunt.*)   **2.** to hunt seals⊙

👁 **VISUAL CONNECTIONS**
   Ideas for Writing. You may want to have students research how and why the names commonly used for groups of people may differ from the names those groups use for themselves. (The term *Eskimo* was first used by rival tribes to name the people who live near the Arctic Circle. The term literally means "eaters of raw flesh," and it was used to show contempt. The name the Eskimos give themselves is *Inuit* or *Inupik,* which means "the real people.")

Some terms students might consider include *American* (for people who live in the United States, but not for people who live in other countries of North and South America), *Negro/Black/African American, Caucasian/White/Anglo,* and *Indian/Native American.*

independent lesson, return an older composition for further revision, or ask students to
write paragraphs and then to revise them by
applying the sentence-combining skills from
this segment.

ASSESSMENT

You can assess students' sentence-
combining abilities by evaluating how well
they complete the exercises. **Review B** is
especially well suited for assessment because
it requires students to use all of the skills that
are taught in the segment.

You can create another assessment tool
by finding a paragraph in a newspaper or a

![INTEGRATING THE LANGUAGE ARTS logo]

INTEGRATING THE LANGUAGE ARTS

Grammar Link. One way students can make sure they've correctly
used plural verbs with compound subjects is to substitute mentally the word
they for any compound subject. If the
verb agrees with the subject *they*, the
verb is correct.

366 *Writing Effective Sentences*

3. Eskimos also hunted and ate caribou, ~~Caribou are a~~
   ~~type of deer.~~ **3.** , a type of deer⊙   **4.** in the 1800s
4. Whalers and fur traders came to the region, and
   affected the Eskimo way of life. ~~They arrived in the~~
   ~~region~~ *in the 1800s.*   **5.** Like these Canadian Eskimos,
5. ‸Most Eskimos today follow a modern way of life.
   ~~They are~~ *like these Canadian Eskimos.*

Combining Sentences by Using *And, But,* or *Or*

You can also use the conjunctions *and, but,* and *or* to combine sentences. With these connecting words, you can
make a *compound subject*, a *compound verb*, or a *compound
sentence.*

Compound Subjects and Verbs

Sometimes two sentences have the same verb with different subjects. You can combine the sentences by linking
the two subjects with *and* or *or*. You will end up with a
compound subject.

ORIGINAL   Dolphins look a little like fish. Porpoises look a
            little like fish.
COMBINED   **Dolphins and porpoises** look a little like fish.

Two sentences can also have the same subject with different verbs. You can use *and, but,* or *or* to connect the two
verbs. The result is a *compound verb.*

ORIGINAL   Dolphins swim like fish. They breathe like other mammals.
COMBINED   Dolphins **swim** like fish **but breathe** like other mammals.

GRAMMAR HINT

Checking for Subject–Verb Agreement

When you use the conjunction *and* to link two subjects, your new compound subject will be a plural subject. Don't forget to make the verb agree with the subject in number.

ORIGINAL   Harry likes visiting the sea mammals at the aquarium. Dorothy likes visiting the sea mammals at the aquarium.
REVISED   **Harry and Dorothy like** visiting the sea mammals at the aquarium. [The plural subject *Harry and Dorothy* takes the verb *like*.]

🖝 **REFERENCE NOTE:** For more information about agreement of subjects and verbs, see pages 551–569.

GRAMMAR HINT

You may need to explain to students that a compound subject does not always take a plural verb. For example, when using the conjunctions *either. . .or* and *neither. . .nor*, one part of the compound subject can be singular and one part can be plural. Remind students that the verb always agrees with the subject that is closer. Here are some examples:

1. Neither yeast nor <u>nuts were</u> used in the cake.
2. Neither nuts nor <u>yeast was</u> used in the cake.

EXERCISE 6▶ **Combining Sentences by Creating Compound Subjects and Verbs**

Combine each of the following pairs of short, choppy sentences by using *and, but,* or *or*. If the two sentences have the same verb, make a compound subject. If they have the same subject, make a compound verb. Remember to check your combined sentences for subject–verb agreement.

1. Dolphins can't smell‿things as people do. ~~They can't taste things as people do.~~   **1. or taste**
2. Dolphins hunt‿fish. ~~Dolphins eat fish.~~   **2. and eat**

tences that are the result of combining and ask students to break them down into their separate parts. Then work back through the process with students to produce the original sentence.

CLOSURE

Ask a volunteer to list the four ways to combine sentence elements.

INTEGRATING THE LANGUAGE ARTS

Grammar Link. Remind students that when they combine two sentences into a compound sentence, they have to consider the tense of the verbs. For example, two sentences like "Mary ate the pie" and "I eat ice cream" can't be combined because the verb tenses differ. Changing the tense of a verb would change the meaning of one of the sentences.

3. Baby dolphins catch‸waves near the beach. ~~Baby dolphins ride waves near the beach.~~   **3.** and ride
4. Sharks sometimes attack‸porpoises. ~~Sharks sometimes kill porpoises.~~   **4.** and kill
5. A porpoise‸could outswim most sharks. ~~A tuna could outswim most sharks.~~   **5.** or a tuna

Compound Sentences

Sometimes you will want to combine two sentences that express equally important ideas. You can connect two closely related, equally important sentences by using a comma plus the coordinating conjunction *and, but,* or *or.* This creates a *compound sentence.*

ORIGINAL	My brother entered the Annual Chili Cook-off. His chili won a prize.
COMBINED	My brother entered the Annual Chili Cook-off**,** **and** his chili won a prize.
ORIGINAL	I didn't help him cook the chili. I helped him clean up the kitchen.
COMBINED	I didn't help him cook the chili**, but** I helped him clean up the kitchen.
ORIGINAL	We can help cook the meal. We can help wash the dishes.
COMBINED	We can help cook the meal**, or** we can help wash the dishes.

WRITING NOTE A compound sentence tells the reader that the two ideas are closely related. If you combine two short sentences that are not closely related, you will confuse your reader.

UNRELATED	Fernando mowed the grass, and I brought a broom.
RELATED	Fernando mowed the grass, and I swept the sidewalk.

One of the important benefits of sentence combining is that it can teach students to vary sentence beginnings. This is especially true when students use introductory subordinate clauses. Ask students to look through newspaper and magazine articles to make lists of the sentences that begin with subordinate clauses. You may want to let students work in groups of three or four on this part of the activity so they can check each other's accuracy.

Next, have students select the two or three strongest sentences and write these on the chalkboard or on an overhead transparency for the class to consider and "uncombine." Finally, work through the process of how the uncombined sentences

EXERCISE 7▶ **Combining Sentences by Forming a Compound Sentence** Conjunctions may vary.

Each of the following pairs of sentences is closely related. Make each pair into a compound sentence by adding a comma and a coordinating conjunction (*and, but,* or *or*).

EXAMPLE   **1.** The Pueblo Indians have lived in the same location for a long time. They have strong ties to their homeland.

     1. *The Pueblo Indians have lived in the same location for a long time, and they have strong ties to their homeland.*

1. Some Pueblos built villages in the valleys. Others settled in desert and mountain areas.   **1.** , but
2. Desert surrounded many of the valleys. The people could grow crops with the help of irrigation systems.   **2.** , but
3. Women gathered berries and other foods. Men hunted game.   **3.** , and
4. Their adobe homes had several stories. The people used ladders to reach the upper levels.   **4.** , and
5. Today, each Pueblo village has its own government. The Pueblo people still share many customs.   **5.** , but

Combining Sentences by Using a Subordinate Clause

A *clause* is a group of words that contains a subject and verb. Some clauses can stand alone as a sentence. We call

VISUAL CONNECTIONS

Exploring the Subject. The word *pueblo* is Spanish for *village* or *town*. This term is now capitalized to refer to Native Americans of several ancestral groups that live in New Mexico, Arizona, Colorado, and Utah. The main ancestral groups include the Hopis, Zunis, Keresans, Tiwas, Tewas, and Jemezes.

ENRICHMENT

To help students understand the link between sentence complexity and the maturity level of writing, bring a few children's books to class and have students work in groups of two or three to combine simple sentences from the stories. Then the students can take turns reading their revised stories to the class. ■

370   *Writing Effective Sentences*

them *independent.* Other clauses can't stand alone as a sentence because they don't express a complete thought. We call them *subordinate.*

| INDEPENDENT CLAUSE | Gertrude Ederle swam the English Channel. [can stand alone] |
| SUBORDINATE CLAUSE | when she was nineteen years old [can't stand alone] |

If two sentences are closely related, you can combine them by using a subordinate clause. Just turn one of the sentences into a subordinate clause and attach it to the other sentence (the independent clause). The subordinate clause will give information about a word or idea in the independent clause.

| TWO SENTENCES | Gertrude Ederle swam the English Channel. She was nineteen years old at the time. |
| ONE SENTENCE | Gertrude Ederle swam the English Channel **when she was nineteen years old.** |

Clauses Beginning with *Who, Which,* or *That*

You can make a short sentence into a subordinate clause by inserting *who, which,* or *that* in place of the subject.

| ORIGINAL | The Everglades are huge swamps. They cover the southern part of Florida. |
| COMBINED | The Everglades are huge swamps **that cover the southern part of Florida.** |

Clauses Beginning with Words of Time or Place

Another way to turn a sentence into a subordinate clause is to add a word that tells time or place at the beginning. Some words that can begin this type of clause are *after, before, where, wherever, when, whenever,* and *while.* You may also need to delete some words before you can insert the clause into another sentence.

| ORIGINAL | No humans lived in the Everglades until 1842. In 1842, the Seminole Indians fled to the area. |
| COMBINED | No humans lived in the Everglades until 1842, **when the Seminole Indians fled to the area.** |

MECHANICS HINT

Using Commas with Introductory Clauses

If you put your time or place clause at the beginning of the sentence, use a comma after the clause.

ORIGINAL   People began draining the swamps to make farmland. The Everglades were in danger.

COMBINED   **When people began draining the swamps to make farmland,** the Everglades were in danger.

👉 REFERENCE NOTE: For more about the use of commas with subordinate clauses, see pages 713 and 720.

EXERCISE 8 ▶ **Combining Sentences by Using a Subordinate Clause**

Combine each sentence pair by making the second sentence into a subordinate clause and attaching it to the first sentence. The hints in parentheses tell you how to begin the subordinate clause. You may need to delete a word or two from the second sentence.

1. The pearl is a gem. It is made by certain kinds of oysters and clams. (Use *that.*)   1. that
2. Beautiful pearls are found in tropical seas. The best pearl oysters live there. (Use a comma and *where.*)   2. , where
3. A valuable pearl has a shine. The shine comes from below its surface. (Use *that.*)   3. that
4. A pearl becomes round. It is formed in the soft part of the oyster. (Use *when.*)   4. when
5. Pearls should be wiped clean with a soft cloth. They are worn as jewelry. (Use *after.*)   5. after

371

🖐 COOPERATIVE LEARNING

After students complete **Exercise 8**, have them work in groups of three or four to compare answers and to work on combining the sentences in different ways to produce the same meanings. You could require a different revision from each group member. To assure that everyone participates, ask that each group member initial the versions he or she contributes.

REVIEW B

OBJECTIVE

- To use a variety of methods to combine sentences in paragraphs

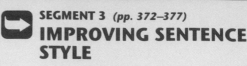

SEGMENT 3 *(pp. 372–377)*

IMPROVING SENTENCE STYLE

OBJECTIVES

- To identify and revise stringy sentences
- To identify and revise wordy sentences

372   *Writing Effective Sentences*

R E V I E W **B** ▶   **Revising a Paragraph by Combining Sentences**

Revisions will vary.

These paragraphs sound choppy because they have too many short sentences. Use the methods you've learned in this section to combine sentences in the paragraphs. The revised paragraphs should sound much better.

, winged

, the Greek

, caught and tamed Pegasus.

Only/or

After

Pegasus, is a winged horse. He is a beautiful, horse. He is a horse from Greek mythology, Pegasus was created by Poseidon. Poseidon, was the god of the sea. He was a Greek god. Athena caught Pegasus. Athena tamed Pegasus. Athena, was the goddess of wisdom,

A hero, could ride Pegasus. A true poet could ride Pegasus. These were the only kinds of people who could ride him. The first person to ride the winged horse was a Greek youth, The youth was sent by a king to kill a monster, The youth destroyed the monster, He became a hero.

Improving Sentence Style

When you combine short, choppy sentences, your writing is easier and more interesting to read. You can also make your writing more effective by avoiding *stringy* and *wordy sentences*. You can revise stringy and wordy sentences to make them shorter and clearer.

Revising Stringy Sentences

A *stringy sentence* is made up of several independent clauses strung together with words like *and* or *but*. Stringy sentences just ramble on and on. They don't give the reader a chance to pause before each new idea.

To fix a stringy sentence, you can

- break the sentence into two or more sentences
- turn some of the independent clauses into phrases or subordinate clauses

QUOTATION FOR THE DAY

"This is one of the most important things a teacher can share with students: that a piece of writing can be manipulated and molded like clay." (Meredith Sue Willis, 1946–   , American author and teacher)

Share this quotation with the class and ask your students to discuss how clay and writing could be comparable. Emphasize that writing, like a sculpture, has to go through many stages before it is finished.

The two distinct but related concepts in this segment will probably be new to many students. If you are using this segment as part of a lesson on revision, you may first have to review phrases and clauses. Ask a volunteer to read the explanation for revising stringy and wordy sentences and then use the examples for illustration.

The hardest thing for most students to learn will probably be how to identify stringy and wordy sentences. In either case, emphasize close, careful reading as the main tool for identifying these problem sentences.

You may find it useful to develop a bank of stringy and wordy sentences from students' writing to supplement the examples in the text. You can present these

Improving Sentence Style   **373**

STRINGY   Martina climbed the stairs of the haunted house and she knocked on the door several times but no one answered and she braced herself and then she opened the door.

REVISED   Martina climbed the stairs of the haunted house. She knocked on the door several times, but no one answered. Bracing herself, she opened the door.

MECHANICS HINT

Punctuating Compound Sentences

When you revise a stringy sentence, you may decide to keep *and* or *but* between two closely related independent clauses. If you do this, remember to add a comma before the *and* or *but*.

ORIGINAL   She knocked on the door several times but no one answered.

REVISED   She knocked on the door several times, but no one answered.

☞ REFERENCE NOTE: For more about compound sentences, see pages 536–538.

 **EXERCISE 9** ▶ **Revising Stringy Sentences**

Some of the following sentences are stringy and need to be improved. First, identify the stringy sentences. Then, revise them by (1) breaking each sentence into two or more sentences or (2) turning some of the independent clauses into phrases or subordinate clauses. If the sentence is effective and doesn't need to be improved, write *C*.

Revisions will vary.

1. Mercedes O. Cubria was born in Cuba, ~~but~~ her mother died, ~~and~~ she moved to the United States, ~~and she moved~~ with her two sisters.   1. ⊙When

---

GUIDED PRACTICE

You can provide guided practice by using the first two or three items in **Exercises 9** and **10**. Write the sentences on the chalkboard or an overhead transparency and ask volunteers to point out why each sentence is stringy or wordy. Then work with the class to suggest revisions.

CRITICAL THINKING
Analysis

You may want to have your students make a density analysis of the **Review C** paragraph. First, have them count the total number of words. Next, they should count the total number of essential words. (Prepositions, conjunctions, articles, pronouns, vague references, and trite expressions are not considered essential in terms of density analysis.)

When students have these two totals, they should divide the essential count by the total count to arrive at a percentage. After they have revised the paragraph, ask them to do the analysis again and to compare the percentages. The second percentage should be higher.

If this type of analysis proves helpful for your students, you may want to have them apply it to their writing during future assignments.

---

374   *Writing Effective Sentences*

2. ∧S̶h̶e̶ ̶w̶o̶r̶k̶e̶d̶ as a nurse, a̶n̶d̶ ̶t̶h̶e̶n̶ she joined the Women's Army Corps∧, a̶n̶d̶ s̲he soon became an officer͵i̶n̶ ̶t̶h̶e̶ ̶a̶r̶m̶y̶.   **2.** After working/⊙

3. Cubria was the first Cuban-born woman to become an officer in the U.S. Army.   **3.** C

4. Her job during World War II was to put important government papers into a secret code.   **4.** C

5. ∧T̶h̶e̶ ̶w̶a̶r̶ ̶e̶n̶d̶e̶d̶,̶ ̶a̶n̶d̶ she was promoted to captain∧, a̶n̶d̶ later her official rank rose to major.   **5.** After the war,/⊙

6. ∧T̶h̶e̶n̶ ̶t̶h̶e̶r̶e̶ ̶w̶a̶s̶ the Korean War, a̶n̶d̶ she worked as an intelligence officer,͵ a̶n̶d̶ ̶s̶h̶e̶ ̶s̶t̶u̶d̶i̶e̶d̶ information about the enemy.   **6.** During/studying

7. Cubria retired from the army in 1953 but was called to duty again in 1962.   **7.** C

8. After the Castro revolution, thousands of Cubans fled to the United States⊙, a̶n̶d̶ Cubria interviewed many of these refugees⁄ and s̶h̶e̶ also prepared reports on Cuba.

9. In her spare time, she helped people from Cuba find jobs and housing.   **9.** C

10. She retired again in 1973∧, a̶n̶d̶ s̲he settled in Miami, Florida,͵a̶n̶d̶ she was surrounded by friends and family͵t̶h̶e̶r̶e̶.   **10.** ⊙/where

The two exercises in this segment offer good material for independent practice. Students can also practice independently by revising their writing to eliminate stringy and wordy sentences.

How well students perform on the exercises should indicate whether they can identify and revise stringy and wordy sentences. However, to determine their understanding of these concepts, you may also want to evaluate how well they eliminate stringy and wordy sentences in their writing. ☞

Revising Wordy Sentences

Sometimes you may use more words in a sentence than you really need. Extra words don't make writing sound better or more impressive. They just get in the reader's way. You can revise *wordy sentences* in three different ways.

1. Replace a phrase with one word.

   WORDY   In the event that we win this game, our team will go to the playoffs.

   REVISED   **If** we win this game, our team will go to the playoffs.

   WORDY   In a state of exhaustion, Tony slumped across the bus seat and fell asleep.

   REVISED   **Exhausted,** Tony slumped across the bus seat and fell asleep.

2. Take out *who is* or *which is*.

   LENGTHY   Yesterday I went for a hike with Sonya, who is my best friend.

   REVISED   Yesterday I went for a hike with Sonya, **my best friend.**

   LENGTHY   Afterward, we drank some apple juice, which is a good thirst quencher.

   REVISED   Afterward, we drank some apple juice, **a good thirst quencher.**

3. Take out a whole group of unnecessary words.

   WORDY   What I mean to say is that I am going to work on my model airplane tonight.

   REVISED   I am going to work on my model airplane tonight.

   WORDY   I spend a lot of time building model airplanes because it is my favorite hobby, and I like model building better than any other hobby I've tried.

   REVISED   I spend a lot of time building model airplanes because it is my favorite hobby.

COOPERATIVE LEARNING

Have students work in pairs to complete **Exercise 10.** One student can be responsible for the odd-numbered items and the other for the even-numbered ones. One student can identify the wordy part of his or her sentence, and the other student can suggest a revision.

RETEACHING

Bring in two or three ads from magazines or newspapers and ask students to revise them to make them purposely stringy and wordy. Discuss with students which version is more effective and why. Make the point that even though it's hard to be concise, concise writing is more effective writing.

CLOSURE

Put an example of a stringy sentence and a wordy sentence on the chalkboard. Ask for volunteers to label and revise the sentences. ■

376   *Writing Effective Sentences*

Here is a list of some common wordy phrases and their shorter, simpler replacements. Be on the lookout for these wordy phrases as you revise your writing.

WORDY	SIMPLER
at the point at which	when
by means of	by
due to the fact that	because, since
in spite of the fact that	although
in the event that	if
the fact is that	actually

EXERCISE 10 ▶   Revising Wordy Sentences

Some of the following sentences are wordy and need improving. Decide which of the sentences are wordy; then, revise them. You can (1) replace a phrase with one word, (2) take out *who is* or *which is,* or (3) take out a whole group of unnecessary words. If a sentence is effective as it is, write C.   Revisions will vary.

1. Our science class has been learning about the ~~starfish, which is a~~ strange and beautiful ̭fish.   **1.** starfish
2. ~~What I want to say is that~~ starfish are fascinating creatures.
3. A starfish has little feet tipped with ̭suction cups⊙ ~~that have suction power.~~   **3.** powerful
4. At the end of each arm is a sensitive "eyespot."   **4.** C
5. ̭~~In spite of the fact that~~ the eyespot cannot really see things, it can tell light from dark.   **5.** Although
6. The starfish's mouth is in the middle of its body.   **6.** C
7. ̭~~When it uses~~ its arms, it can pull at the shells of clams.   **7.** Using
8. ̭~~At the point at which~~ the clam's shell opens, the starfish can feed on the clam.   **8.** When
9. Starfish come in a variety of colors, shapes, and sizes⊙ ~~and some are bigger than others.~~

REVIEW C

OBJECTIVE

To identify and revise stringy and wordy sentences in a paragraph

10. This photograph shows a candy cane starfish holding onto a soft coral ~~by holding it~~ with its suction cups.

REVIEW C ▶

The following paragraph is hard to read because it contains stringy and wordy sentences. First, identify the stringy and wordy sentences. Then, revise them by using the methods you've learned. Notice how your revisions improve the style of the paragraph. **Revisions will vary.**

The movie *The Dark Crystal* features a lot of strange characters, ~~and the characters~~ are actually puppets, ~~and~~ **that** ~~they were~~ designed by Jim Henson, ~~and he was~~ the man who created the Muppets. The puppets used in *The Dark Crystal* were different from the original Muppets, ~~having things about them that were different. One thing is that~~ they weren't as brightly colored as the TV Muppets. They also had legs and could move through a scene with their whole bodies showing. Some of the *Dark Crystal* characters were radio-controlled, ~~and~~ others were operated by ~~puppeteers, and the~~ puppeteers **who** were hidden under the movie set.

MAKING CONNECTIONS

FILL IN THE MISSING PIECES
OBJECTIVE

- To reconstruct a message by supplying missing words

FILL IN THE MISSING PIECES
Teaching Strategies

This activity is a variation of the traditional cloze technique and is useful in assessing reading comprehension. One way of approaching this activity is to have students work in pairs. One student reads the message aloud, sentence by sentence. The other student notes where words or phrases are missing. After the reading, they work together to supply the missing items. You can evaluate the reconstructed messages on their sense and their avoidance of fragments, run-ons, and stringy or wordy sentences.

When students are finished, let them decorate the reconstructed messages as they think the messages might have appeared in bottles.

GUIDELINES

Messages will vary. Here is a possibility:

To whoever finds this message: My name is Claudia. I live at the northern end of the bay. I was walking by a small cave when I saw a mysterious shadow near the cave opening. I thought could it be some kind of dangerous monster or even a ghost? I walk by the cave almost every day. I can't get anyone to help me explore the cave. Leave a message near the cave if you want to help me.

MAKING CONNECTIONS

Fill in the Missing Pieces

You are fishing in a bay when you suddenly spot a corked bottle bobbing in the water near the pier. You guess that the bottle has floated over from the summer camp across the bay. You pull the bottle out of the water and take out the cork. Inside is a piece of paper with a mysterious message. But some water has leaked into the bottle, and parts of the sentences have been washed away. Try to reconstruct the message by adding the missing words.

ENGLISH: ORIGINS AND USES

OBJECTIVES

- To decode Old English words
- To identify the origins of words
- To identify dialects and to rewrite a passage in the student's own dialect
- To write a formal and an informal thank-you letter
- To analyze the connotations of words
- To make a list of tired words and clichés
- To define words with specialized meanings
- To identify and list dated words and expressions

Motivation

Start a discussion with your students by asking them what parts of English are particularly hard for them to learn or remember. Many of students' problems will probably involve spelling, pronunciation, irregular verbs, and subject-verb agreement. You can explain that English has been an identifiable language since 1500 A.D. and that it has a rich history of dynamic change. Point out that there are historical reasons for most of the unusual spellings and pronunciations and other irregularities that they will study in the chapter. Emphasize that many English words are borrowed from other languages and thus are exceptions to certain spelling rules. Students might be interested to learn that English and Chinese are considered by linguists to be the most difficult languages to learn.

Introduction

This chapter contains basic information on the origins of English and explains how changes over the years have caused problems for the students of English today. It also covers dialects, connotations of words, formal and informal language, slang, clichés, and jargon.

Initiate a discussion with your students by noting that there is often a difference between the way that people speak and write and what is considered standard English. Explain that this anomaly might be caused by the different dialects that people speak.

Tell your students that studying the origins of English, how English has evolved, and how these changes affect modern English might help them improve their reading, listening, writing, and speaking skills.

Integration

You may want to cover the information in **Chapter 32: "The Dictionary"** before you begin this chapter, because students will be called on to investigate etymologies of words throughout the chapter.

Before students write thank-you letters in **Exercise 5**, you could review **Chapter 34: "Letters and Forms"** so that students will use the proper letter form.

Also, you may want to refer to information learned in this chapter when teaching **Chapter 28: "Spelling"** and **Chapter 29: "Speaking."**

Refer to **Exercise 6** on word connotations when you teach **Chapter 8: "Writing to Persuade,"** because connotations are very important in persuasive writing. Also, the results of **Exercise 7** can be used in all writing assignments to alert students to tired words and phrases that they need to avoid.

The chart on the next page illustrates the strands of language arts as they are integrated into this chapter. For vocabulary study, glossary words are underlined in some writing models.

QUOTATIONS

All **Quotations for the Day** are chosen because of their relevance to instructional material presented in that segment of the chapter and for their usefulness in establishing student interest in writing.

INTEGRATING THE LANGUAGE ARTS

Selection	Reading and Literature	Writing and Critical Thinking	Language and Syntax	Speaking, Listening, and Other Expression Skills
from *The Octopus* by Frank Norris **382** from *The Prehistory of the Far Side* by Gary Larson **384** from *I Wish I Could Give My Son a Wild Raccoon* by Eliot Wigginton **386**	Recognizing colloquialisms in reading **386**	Inferring meanings of Old English words to determine the modern-day counterparts **382** Comparing the connotations of pairs of words with similar meanings **390** Evaluating pairs of words with similar meanings but differing connotations to decide which of the pair is preferable **390** Making a list of tired words and expressions **392** Combining lists of tired words and clichés to create a composition guide **392**	Enlarging vocabulary through study of the evolution of words **382** Answering word riddles by looking up etymologies **383** Studying etymologies of words to understand meanings **383** Identifying origins of English words from foreign languages **383-384** Applying knowledge of parts of a dictionary by looking up the etymologies of words **383-384** Explaining and comparing regional dialects **386** Understanding the nature of dialect and recognizing differences **386** Writing letters in formal and informal English **390**	Reading dialect aloud **386** Recognizing colloquialisms in reading **392** Defining examples of jargon **392** Using mass media to obtain information **393**

CHAPTER 12

SEGMENT PLANNING GUIDE

Whether you are planning for a quick review of a writing concept or preparing an extended lesson on composition you can use the following Planning Guide to adapt the chapter material to the individual needs of your class.

SEGMENT	PAGES	CONTENT	RESOURCES
1 *A Changing Language*	*379-385*		How Language Changes
A Changing Language	379-380	Introduction: learning the origins of English	Where Words Come From
The Growth of English	380	Explanation: understanding that language changes	
How Do You Spell It?	381	Guided practice: comparing present-day spellings of words with their original spellings	
How Do You Say It?	381	Explanation: relating Old English pronunciation to modern-day spelling	
Exercise 1	382	Applied practice: decoding Old English	
What Does It Mean?	382-383	Guided practice: recognizing changes meanings of words	
Literary Model from *The Octopus*	382	Guided reading: examining word meanings	
Exercise 2	383	Applied practice: answering word-origin riddles	
Where Does It Come From?	383	Explanation: recognizing borrowed words from other languages	
Looking at Language	384	Example: examining the word *phobia*	
Literary Model from *The Prehistory of the Far Side*	384	Guided reading: examining word usage in a model	
Exercise 3	384-385	Applied practice: researching word origins	
2 *Dialects of America English*	*385-387*		Dialects of American English
Dialects of American English	385	Introduction: learning about dialects	
Regional Dialects	385	Explanation: recognizing that words are pronounced differently according to the speaker's region	
Ethnic Dialects	386	Explanation: recognizing that words are pronounced differently according to the speaker's ethnic group	
Exercise 4	386	Guided practice: reading and translating a dialect	
Literary Model from *I Wish I Could Give My Son a Wild Raccoon*	386	Guided reading: examining dialect in a model	
Standard American English	387	Explanation: learning appropriate use of standard and nonstandard English	

SEGMENT	PAGES	CONTENT	RESOURCES
3 *Choosing Your Words*	*388-392*		Formal and Informal English
Choosing Your Words	388	Introduction: using clear, effective, and appropriate words	Denotation and Connotation
Formal and Informal English	388	Guided practice: using appropriate style	Tired Words and Expressions
Uses of Informal English	389	Explanation: examining colloquialisms and slang	The Conclusion
Style Note	390	Writing suggestion: using slang appropriately	
Exercise 5	390	Applied practice: writing a formal and an informal thank-you letter	
Denotation and Connotation	390	Explanation: understanding the importance of connotation	
Exercise 6	390	Applied practice: analyzing the connotations of words	
Tired Words and Expressions	391	Explanation: examining tired words and clichés	
Style Note	391	Writing suggestion: using synonyms	
Exercise 7	392	Cooperative learning: listing tired words and expressions	
Jargon	392	Explanation: using jargon appropriately	
Exercise 8	392	Applied practice: translating jargon	
4 *Making Connections*	*393*		
Identify Dated Language	393	Applied practice: identifying dated words and expressions from 1970s television reruns	

WHOLE-CHAPTER RESOURCES
Review Form A, Review Form B

SEGMENT 1 *(pp. 379–385)*
A CHANGING LANGUAGE

OBJECTIVES

- To decode Old English words
- To answer word riddles by finding the earliest meaning of the italicized words in the riddles
- To identify the original languages of borrowed words and to tell when the words entered the English language

12 ENGLISH: ORIGINS AND USES

RESOURCES

A CHANGING LANGUAGE
- How Language Changes
- Where Words Come From

QUOTATION FOR THE DAY

"Every living language, like the perspiring bodies of living creatures, is in perpetual motion and [extension]. . . ." (Richard Bentley, 1662–1742, English clergyman)

Write the quotation on the chalkboard and ask students to use their own words to tell what the quotation says about language. To help students understand that language is always changing, discuss with students words or expressions they have used that are now out of style.

LOOKING AHEAD

In this chapter, you will take a close look at the English language—where it comes from, how it has grown, and how it is used today. You will also examine your own use of language with an eye for style, learning

- what kinds of language are appropriate for particular situations
- how to improve your writing by choosing clearer, more effective words

A Changing Language

Languages have ancestors just as people do. English and dozens of other languages come from a single early language that was spoken thousands of years ago on the other side of the globe.

To create interest in the different influences on the English language, write the words *tomato*, *humor*, *address*, and *thug* on the chalkboard and ask students which of these words comes from English. [None. They originate from the Spanish, Latin, French, and Hindustani languages.]

Then ask students to suggest other languages that may have influenced American English. [Some possibilities are Italian, German, Irish, and Chinese.]

MEETING INDIVIDUAL NEEDS

LEP/ESL

Spanish. Have students bring lists of other words borrowed from Spanish to share with their classmates. Some examples are *tortilla, patio, siesta, fiesta, rodeo,* and *vista.* To show the relationships between languages and to help students increase their vocabulary, you could include cognates from Latin and other languages in the list. The students can combine all their lists into one, but they should also use a dictionary to avoid false cognates such as *pan* (bread), *fabrica* (factory), *exito* (success), *ordinario* (common, vulgar), and *sano* (healthy).

A TRANSLATION OF *BEOWULF*

The following translation may be helpful if any student inquires about the meaning of this passage:

He that is a strong and savage fighter took the goblet from Wealtheow and, desiring to go to battle, Beowulf, Ecgtheow's son, declared:

SELECTION AMENDMENT
Description of change: excerpted
Rationale: to focus on the concept of the changing English language as presented in this chapter

---

Although each language is unique, you can still see the family resemblance among words with the same meaning in related languages.

ENGLISH	GERMAN	FRENCH	SPANISH
new	neu	nouveau	nuevo
nose	Nase	nez	nariz
salt	Salz	sel	sal
young	jung	jeune	joven

No one knows exactly when English branched off as a separate language. However, we do know that a form of English was being spoken by tribes of people in the fifth century. These tribes migrated to the island of Britain and conquered the area that is now England. Their language is the ancestor of modern-day English.

The earliest known English writings date back about 1,300 years. This early form of English is so different from our English that it looks like a foreign language to us.

> He þæt ful geþeáh
> wæl-reow wíga, æt Wealhþeówe,
> and þá gyddode, gúðe gefýsed.
> Beowulf maðelode, bearn Ecgþeówes:
>
> from Beowulf

The Growth of English

English didn't grow up all at once. If you had a time machine, you could stop off in England every few hundred years and witness gradual changes taking place in people's language. You would hear and see new pronunciations, forms, and meanings of words. You would also notice many new words being added to the language. By about 1500, you would probably be able to understand the English of the time. However, it would still sound strange to you.

How Do You Spell It?

Some English words have traveled through the centuries with only small changes in spelling. Others have undergone greater change. Here are some examples of present-day English words and their original forms.

PRESENT-DAY	red	three	summer	sheep	fish
ORIGINAL	read	threo	sumor	sceap	fisc

Even today, the spellings of words vary. Different spellings of a word can be standard in different places. For example, compare standard American and standard British spellings of some everyday words.

AMERICAN	color	flavor	theater	tire
BRITISH	colour	flavour	theatre	tyre

How Do You Say It?

By the 1300s, written English looked similar to the English we use. But English-speaking people of that time still pronounced words differently from the way we do. For example, they pronounced *meek* like *make*, *boot* like *boat*, and *mouse* like *moose*.

Changes in pronunciations help account for many of the English words that aren't spelled like they sound. For example, the word *knight* used to be pronounced with a strong *k* sound at the beginning. The letter remained part of the spelling even though the *k* sound was eventually dropped.

You could model **Exercise 1** orally or just read the first pair of words and then have volunteers read the other words. Next, you may want to model the skills required in **Exercise 2** by answering the first question with the students. Do the same for **Exercise 3** and explain to students that if the etymologies of words are in a dictionary, these word histories will be found immediately before or after the definitions of the words. Then read the entry for the first word of **Exercise 3** to show students how to locate information about word origin.

LESS-ADVANCED STUDENTS

Some students might have trouble reading the dictionary entries for words with several meanings and multiple origins. A review of dictionary usage might be useful. Then have each student copy a word entry and label its parts. After they have completed the entries, you could have students compile them to create a class dictionary.

ADVANCED STUDENTS

Explain to students that Geoffrey Chaucer (born sometime between 1339–1346) lived in medieval England and created one of the more important works in Middle English. Have students seek out copies of Chaucer's *The Canterbury Tales*. Tell them to attempt to translate a short passage from any of the tales. Students can turn in their findings in the form of a report, or you could have them present small passages to the class by writing the originals on transparencies and translating them for the class.

SELECTION AMENDMENT
Description of change: excerpted
Rationale: to focus on the concept of a changing language as presented in this chapter

---

382   *English: Origins and Uses*

EXERCISE 1 ▶ **Giving Present-Day Forms of Words**

Here are five sets of English words written with their original spellings. See if you can figure out what the words are in present-day English.

1. bryht, deorc   1. bright/dark
2. sealt, mete   2. salt/meat
3. muth, lippa   3. mouth/lip
4. docga, hors   4. dog/horse
5. plante, saed   5. plant/seed

What Does It Mean?

Read the following sentence:

> Without reply, the typewriter rose and withdrew, thrusting her pencil into the coil of her hair. . . .
>
> Frank Norris, *The Octopus*

When people read Frank Norris's sentence in the early 1900s, they didn't see anything strange about it. In those days, it wasn't unusual for a typewriter to get up and walk out of a room. The word *typewriter* could mean "typist" as well as "typewriting machine."

The meaning of *typewriter* has changed only slightly. But some words have ended up with meanings entirely different from their original ones. Nine hundred years ago, *awful* meant "awe-inspiring, very impressive." Today, it usually means "terrifying" or "very bad." Another good example is the word *nice*. In the 1300s, *nice* didn't mean "pleasant"; it meant "lazy" or "foolish."

INDEPENDENT PRACTICE

Exercises **2** and **3** allow independent dictionary practice. Discuss the example in **Exercise 2**, especially how the word *villain* has changed over the years. **Exercise 3** can be handled the same way.

ASSESSMENT

The assessment for **Exercise 1** is strictly oral. Checking **Exercise 2** in class will give an opportunity for a lively discussion of how each of the words has changed over the years. **Exercise 3** can also be checked in class.

A Changing Language **383**

The meanings of words are still changing today. For example, the word *bad* can now mean "good" in informal English. And *bonnet* means only "a hat" in the United States but also "the hood of a car" in Great Britain.

EXERCISE 2 ▶ Answering Word-Origin Riddles

See if you can answer each of the following riddles. First, look up the italicized word in a dictionary that gives word origins. (*Webster's New World Dictionary* is one.) The earliest meaning listed for the word will be your clue to the riddle. Give this meaning along with your answer.

EXAMPLE   **1.** Where should a *villain* work?
          1. on a farm (villain *meant "farm tenant"*)

1. Why do *silly* people smile all the time?
2. What should you do with a *brat*?
3. Why do *comets* need shampoo?
4. Why is cheese a good food for your *muscles*?
5. What should you buy with your *salary*?

Where Does It Come From?

Have you ever *munched* a *burrito* or *feasted* on *chop suey*? If so, then you haven't just eaten foods from different cultures. You've also used words from different languages.

About 15 percent of the words we use are native to English. The rest have been borrowed or adapted from other languages. Many nonnative words were borrowed as English people came into contact with people from other cultures and lands. Here are a few examples of words that have been borrowed in the past one thousand years.

NORSE	leg, fellow, get
LATIN	area, candle, decorate, joke
FRENCH	beauty, dance, study
SPANISH	chili, hurricane, mustang
NATIVE AMERICAN LANGUAGES	bayou, chipmunk, squash
AFRICAN LANGUAGES	jazz, okra, gumbo

CLOSURE

Have students summarize briefly what has happened to English from its earliest days to the present. Be sure to remind them about changes in spelling, pronunciation, and meaning. ■

INTEGRATING THE LANGUAGE ARTS

Literature Link. Have students read and analyze how the language of Washington Irving's "Rip Van Winkle," written in the nineteenth century, differs from the language of a modern story. Point out the old-fashioned words and phrases and the complicated sentence structures found in the story. To illustrate that English is a dynamic, changing language, explain that Irving's story bridges a gap between an earlier, more British English and today's modern American English. Have students find examples of complicated sentences in the story to share with the class.

LOOKING AT

Name Your Phobia

Can you catch *brontophobia* from a brontosaurus? Has someone with *anthophobia* been bitten by ants? Neither of these words means what it sounds like. For each, the key to the meaning is the ending *–phobia*, which comes from the Greek word *phobos*, "fear."

The ending *–phobia* is added to Greek and Latin root words to describe all kinds of fears. *Brontophobia*, from *bronte*, "thunder," means "fear of thunder." *Anthophobia*, from *anthos*, "flower," means "fear of flowers." Some better-known phobias include *claustrophobia*, "fear of closed-in spaces," and *arachnophobia*, "fear of spiders."

See how Gary Larson came up with the *–phobia* word that he used in the following cartoon. Why would his made-up word look familiar to an *ornithologist*, someone who studies birds?

Anatidaephobia: The fear that somewhere, somehow, a duck is watching you.

Far Side, by permission of Universal Press Syndicate

In coming up with the name for the phobia, I played around with words like "quackaphobia" and "duckalookaphobia" and so on. But then I got the bright idea to look up the scientific name for ducks, and discovered their family name is *Anatidae*. And so, I ended up coining a word that twelve ornithologists understood and everyone else probably went, "Say what?"

Gary Larson,
The Prehistory of the Far Side

EXERCISE 3 ▶ Researching Word Origins

Each of the following words came into English from another language. Using a dictionary that gives word

DIALECTS OF AMERICAN ENGLISH

OBJECTIVE

- To read a passage in Appalachian dialect, to identify how it is different from one's own, and to rephrase the passage in one's own dialect

MOTIVATION

Have students brainstorm odd-sounding words they've heard other people pronounce. Write these words on the chalkboard. Then ask students why they think different people might pronounce the same word in different ways.

---

origins, find out what language each word was borrowed from. Give a date for the word's entry into English if your dictionary lists one.

1. tea   1. Chin
2. sketch   2. Du/Ger < It
3. shawl   3. Pers
4. parade   4. Fr
5. census   5. L

6. same   6. ME < ON
7. school   7. ME < OE < L < Gr
8. command   8. ME < OF
9. salsa   9. Am Sp < Sp < L
10. skunk   10. Am E < Algonquin

ANSWERS

Exercise 3

Answers may vary depending on the dictionary used.

1. 1655
2. 1668
3. 1662
4. 1656
5. 1613

6. 13th cent.
7. around 1000
8. 14th cent.
9. 1846
10. 1634

RESOURCES

DIALECTS OF AMERICAN ENGLISH
- Dialects of American English

QUOTATION FOR THE DAY

"My bosses said we should all sound alike. They said we should all sound as if we'd grown up in the same place." (Linda Ellerbee, 1944–   , American broadcast journalist and author)

Ask students to think about people they know whose English is different from theirs. Then discuss where these people originally lived.

Dialects of American English

You probably know people whose English is different from yours. Maybe they pronounce words strangely, or maybe they use words in unfamiliar ways. Your English probably sounds as "funny" to them as theirs sounds to you.

Because ways of speaking vary so widely, the English of one group of people is bound to sound "funny" to another group. There are many different forms of English, and no form is better or worse than another. The variety of English used by a particular group of people is called a *dialect.* In this section, you'll learn about two types of American English dialects, *regional dialects* and *ethnic dialects.*

Regional Dialects

Do you carry a *pail* or a *bucket*? Do you *wash* (or *warsh*) the *car* (or *cah*)? Do you stand *on* line or *in* line? Where you come from can help determine what words you use, how you pronounce words, and how you put words together. A dialect shared by people from the same area of the United States is called a *regional dialect.*

Not everyone who lives in a region uses that region's dialect. Someone from Alabama or Georgia won't necessarily say *y'all,* and someone from Boston may not pronounce *farm* like *fahm.* When people move from place to place, they often lose some of their old dialect and learn a new one.

TEACHING THE LESSON

Generate a discussion about dialects students have heard on television and note the regions in which the television shows supposedly take place.

The segment's only exercise should be used as guided practice and can be read by either you or a skilled student reader. It may need to be read more than once. List any difficult words or phrases on the chalkboard and discuss them with your students before reading the passage.

To give students independent practice, have them translate a passage, such as one from Mark Twain's *The Adventures of Tom Sawyer*, into their own dialects.

MEETING INDIVIDUAL NEEDS

LEP/ESL

General Strategies. In China, speakers of different dialects of Mandarin Chinese often cannot understand each other. Similarly, in Mexico there are many dialects of Spanish whose speakers cannot understand one another. Students from these and other countries often question whether the speakers of English dialects can understand one another. You may want to address these questions for the benefit of your ESL students.

SELECTION AMENDMENT
Description of change: excerpted
Rationale: to focus on the concept of dialect as presented in this chapter

---

Ethnic Dialects

People who share the same cultural heritage may share a dialect of English, too. The English used by a particular cultural group is called an ***ethnic dialect.*** Widely used American ethnic dialects include the Black English of many African Americans and the Spanish-influenced English of many people whose families come from Mexico, Central America, Cuba, and Puerto Rico.

Many words that are now part of general English usage originally came from ethnic dialects. For example, the words *afro, jazz,* and *jukebox* were originally Black English dialect words, and *arroyo, mesa,* and *taco* were originally from Hispanic English.

EXERCISE 4 ▶ **Reading a Dialect**

In the following excerpt, the speaker, Stanley Hicks, is describing some happy memories from his childhood. He is from Sugar Grove, North Carolina, and speaks Appalachian dialect. Read the passage aloud to hear the sounds of Hicks's dialect. Try to pronounce the words as the writer has spelled them. Is Stanley Hicks's dialect different from yours? If it is, tell how you would say the same things in your own words. **Responses will vary. Words and phrases that students might revise are underscored.**

> And we used to play fox and goose. You've got two red foxes—you know, red grains of corn—and the rest of them is white. Play on a board like a checkerboard. And then the geese tries to hem these foxes up. Dad'd get 'em hemmed up and he'd say, "Que-e-e-e-e-e-e! Listen to her wheeze!" He'd say, "Watch her wiggle her tail, boys! She's a-dying!" It'd made us so cussed mad, you know. He was good on it. And then every time he'd jump one of our geese, he'd go "Quack!" Make like a goose a-hollering, you know.
>
> Eliot Wigginton,
> *I Wish I Could Give My Son a Wild Raccoon*

Standard American English

Every variety of English has its own set of rules and guidelines. No variety is the best or the most correct. However, one kind of English is more widely used and accepted than others in the United States. This variety is called *standard American English.*

Standard American English is the one variety that belongs to all of us. Because it's commonly understood, it allows people from many different regions and cultures to communicate with one another clearly. It is the variety of English used most often in books and magazines, on radio and television. It is the variety people are expected to use in most school and business situations.

The **Handbook** in this textbook gives you some of the rules and guidelines for using standard American English. To identify the differences between standard American English and other varieties of English, the **Handbook** uses the labels *standard* and *nonstandard. Nonstandard* doesn't mean wrong language. It means language that is inappropriate in situations where standard English is expected.

☞ REFERENCE NOTE: For more about standard English, see page 653.

Calvin & Hobbes, copyright 1987 Universal Press Syndicate. Reprinted with permission. All rights reserved.

 INTEGRATING THE LANGUAGE ARTS

Literature Link. Engage your students in a discussion of the dialects of the Ozark Mountains and of Native American words used in the novel *Where the Red Fern Grows.* Remind students that the novel's author, Wilson Rawls, grew up on Cherokee land in the Ozark Mountains of Oklahoma and did not attend public school until he was in his teens. He destroyed his first draft of the novel because he was very aware of his lack of education. He rewrote the novel after he married, with his wife helping to put it into standard American English. Point out that Billy Coleman, the young hero of the novel, lives in a rural area. Have your students find examples of both standard and informal language in the novel.

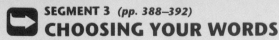

SEGMENT 3 *(pp. 388–392)*

CHOOSING YOUR WORDS

OBJECTIVES

- To use appropriate formal or informal English to write two thank-you notes, one to a recently visited friend and the other to his or her parents

- To choose between pairs of synonyms with differing connotations

- To compile a list of tired words and expressions

- To translate jargon into standard English

QUOTATION FOR THE DAY

"Slang is a language that rolls up its sleeves, spits on its hands and goes to work." (Carl Sandburg, 1878–1967, American poet)

Share the quotation with the class and pretend that you don't understand it. Ask students to explain it to you.

MEETING INDIVIDUAL NEEDS

LEP/ESL

General Strategies. ESL students often use slang because they learned it from peers early in the development of their second-language skills. You may want your students to make and keep lists of slang expressions. They can refer to these lists during the revising stage of writing.

Choosing Your Words

Because English offers you many different ways to say the same thing, you have to make decisions every time you speak and write. Sometimes you make these choices naturally. For example, you probably don't think much about word choice when you're talking with a friend. But at other times, especially when you write, you need to give some thought to the words you use. You need to make sure your words are clear, effective, and appropriate.

Formal and Informal English

Read the following sentences:

> I really enjoyed that story about the men who climbed Mount Everest.
> I really got into that story about the guys who climbed Mount Everest.

Just a few words have been changed from the first sentence to the second, but the effect of each sentence is different. One is written in *formal English* and the other in *informal English.*

Different levels of formality in language are appropriate for different situations. You might use the more formal language of the first example sentence if you were telling a teacher how you liked a story. But if you were talking about the story to a classmate, you might use informal expressions like *got into* and *guys.*

MOTIVATION

Write the words *plump, robust,* and *rotund* on the chalkboard. Ask students what common word is a synonym for these words [fat]. Using these examples, explain that words have much influence and should be chosen carefully.

TEACHING THE LESSON

Students might have trouble understanding how colloquialisms, slang, and clichés differ. Model the differences by putting several examples on the chalkboard and by discussing them with the class. Then have the class brainstorm colloquialisms.

☞

Choosing Your Words **389**

Uses of Informal English

There are two kinds of informal English that you should be familiar with: *colloquialisms* and *slang*.

Colloquialisms are the casual, colorful expressions that we use in everyday conversation. Many colloquialisms aren't meant to be taken literally. They have understood meanings that are different from the basic meanings of the words.

EXAMPLES The band **brought down the house** with the last number.
The plot of that movie was **hard to swallow.**
We'll order some sandwiches **to go.**

Slang consists of made-up words or old words used in new ways. Slang words are usually the special language of a particular group of people, such as teenagers or musicians. You and your friends probably use slang that's unique to your generation.

Although slang words seem up-to-date when they're first used, they tend to fall out of style very quickly. Some of the slang words in the following sentences probably seem dated to you.

EXAMPLES That's a **cool** set of **wheels, dude.**
That last scene really **broke me up.**
Where did you get those **neat** shoes?
Tim just got a **rad** new haircut.

STYLE NOTE Don't use slang in essays, test answers, or reports. If you use slang in a formal speaking or writing situation, your audience may think you are not serious about your subject. However, you may want to use slang in short stories. For example, if one of your characters is a teenager, slang will help make the character's dialogue seem realistic.

LESS-ADVANCED STUDENTS

To help students gain a deeper understanding of the differences between formal and informal English, write the following sentences on the chalkboard:

1. He was into it totally.
2. We got a gig Sunday.
3. Would you guys just cool it?
4. I got to get me some shoes.

Ask a student to read the first sentence. Discuss what the sentence means and ask how that sentence could be stated using formal English. Repeat the process with the other sentences. Then ask students to state various colloquialisms and slang words that they know.

AT-RISK STUDENTS

Use **Exercise 6** to initiate a discussion about self-esteem and the connotation of words. Ask students to describe situations in which words with bad connotations are used, such as with peers, siblings, and authority figures. You can extend this activity into a writing exercise by using it as the topic for journal entries.

EXERCISE 5 ▶   **Writing Letters in Formal or Informal English**

You've just returned from visiting a friend in another state. You want to write letters to your friend and your friend's parents telling them what a good time you had.

Write the thank-you note you would send to your friend's parents and the letter you would send to your friend. In each letter, mention some parts of your visit that you especially enjoyed—for example, a sightseeing trip, a day at an amusement park, or a family barbecue. Use the formal or informal English that you think is appropriate for each letter.

Denotation and Connotation

Suppose you heard someone say, "Cara is beautiful and scrawny." You'd probably wonder whether the person meant to compliment or insult Cara. *Scrawny* is another way of saying "thin." That is the word's basic meaning, or ***denotation.*** But *scrawny* and *thin* create very different pictures of a person. *Scrawny* suggests that Cara is bony and looks underfed. This is the emotional association, or ***connotation,*** of the word.

It's important to think about the connotations of the words you use. If you use a word without knowing its connotations, you may send the wrong message to your audience.

EXERCISE 6 ▶   **Responding to Connotations**

Which of the words in each pair would you prefer if someone were describing you? Why?

1. stubborn, determined
2. serious, grim
3. eccentric, weird
4. wishy-washy, undecided
5. sensitive, touchy

Exercise 7 should begin as a guided practice. Initiate the activity by brainstorming a few examples of tired words and clichés and listing them on the chalkboard. After students have seen a few examples, you can assign the rest of **Exercise 7** as homework.

INDEPENDENT PRACTICE

Exercises **5** and **7** can be accomplished independently. Use **Exercise 8** as a short in-class activity to evaluate students' comprehension.

Choosing Your Words   **391**

Tired Words and Expressions

A tired word is a dull, worn-out word. It has been used so often and so carelessly that it has become almost meaningless. Tired words like *nice, fine, great,* and *wonderful* are common in everyday conversation, but they are too dull and vague to be effective in writing.

Tired expressions are often called *clichés.* Many clichés were striking and vivid the first time they were used. But after a while, they lost their originality and their expressiveness. Here are some examples of clichés; you can probably think of many more.

break the ice	easier said than done
busy as a bee	eat like a horse
the crack of dawn	on top of the world
clear as a bell	sadder but wiser

STYLE NOTE Most writers have a few favorite words that they tend to overuse. If a word appears too often in your writing, find *synonyms* for it— words that have a similar meaning. You can look up synonyms in a *thesaurus,* a dictionary of synonyms. Here are just a few of the words that *Roget's International Thesaurus* lists as synonyms for *interesting: appealing, captivating, intriguing, thought-provoking.*

Keep in mind, though, that no two words have exactly the same meaning. Before you use a synonym, look up the word in a dictionary to make sure it has the meaning you intend.

COOPERATIVE LEARNING

Divide the class into groups of three or four students and have each group compile a list of at least five examples for each of the categories in this segment (colloquialisms, slang, tired words, clichés, and jargon). Have groups make a large flashcard for each word or phrase with the identification of its category on the back of the card. Remind your students that some words or phrases may belong to more than one category.

You could encourage students to make the flashcards colorful and interesting if art materials are available. Students can use flashcards for extra practice, or they can invent games to play with the cards.

Have your students suggest different types of social situations to list, such as parties or family dinners. After you have listed as many situations as possible, ask students whether they would use formal or informal English for each one. ■

ANSWERS
Exercise 7

Lists will vary. Students may have more difficulty with clichés than you expect. Students who don't read very much may not be aware of phrases that you have seen dozens of times.

ANSWERS
Exercise 8

Answers may vary according to the dictionary used.

1. a large fancy marble used for shooting

2. a pitched ball that is counted against a batter, typically one swung at and missed or one considered to be in the strike zone, often defined as being over the plate and between the batter's armpits and knees

3. to move a motion picture or television camera to follow a moving object or to create a panoramic effect by moving over a large area

4. any of several wrestling holds in which a wrestler has a firm grip on the opponent's body

5. a trial print

392

EXERCISE 7 ▶   Identifying Tired Words and Clichés

Make a list of all the tired words and expressions you can think of. You may want to spend a few days watching and listening for them, jotting down words and expressions as you hear them. Then compare your list with those of your classmates. By combining lists, you'll have a handy collection of words and expressions to avoid when you write.

Jargon

Jargon is special language that is used by a particular group of people, such as people who share the same profession, occupation, sport, or hobby. For example, the word *set* is used as theater jargon for "the props and scenery arranged on a stage" or "the act of arranging scenery on a stage." The same word is also printer's jargon for "put a piece of writing into print." Like *set*, many jargon words are ordinary words that have been given special meanings.

Jargon can be practical and effective because it reduces many words to just one or two. However, don't use jargon when you are writing or speaking for a general audience who may not be familiar with the terms.

 REFERENCE NOTE: For an example of how dictionaries label special uses of words, see page 826.

EXERCISE 8 ▶   Translating Jargon

Look up each of the following words in a dictionary to find out what the word means for the group indicated. For help with looking up special uses of words, see page 26.

1. *taw*—marble players
2. *strike*—baseball players
3. *pan*—filmmakers
4. *lock*—wrestlers
5. *proof*—photographers

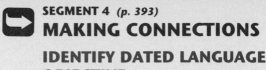
393

MAKING CONNECTIONS

Identify Dated Language

When you watch reruns of old television shows, you probably notice that the people's clothes and cars seem out of style. But have you ever noticed that their way of talking seems dated, too? By watching a television show from twenty years ago, you can get a good sense of how people's everyday language has changed over time.

Watch at least one rerun of a situation comedy from the 1970s. Listen to the characters' language—especially that of teenage characters. Jot down any words and expressions that seem dated or unfamiliar to you.

Which of the words and expressions on your list are colloquialisms or slang? What words and expressions do you and your friends use today to mean the same things?

IDENTIFY DATED LANGUAGE
Teaching Strategies

Discuss television shows from the 1970s with your students and make a list of titles. If students have difficulty, provide them with examples from your local television guide. Many old shows are found only on cable channels, so if a student does not have cable television, he or she may have to work with another student.

You could also ask students about such things as clothing styles and the portrayal of relationships (parent—child, peer—group, and so on) to illustrate that language reflects life and that both are constantly changing.

GUIDELINES

Answers depend on the programs students watched. Most of the dated expressions will probably be slang. After students view the programs, they could engage in a comparison of their current slang to that of the characters in the situation comedies from the 1970s.

PART TWO

HANDBOOK

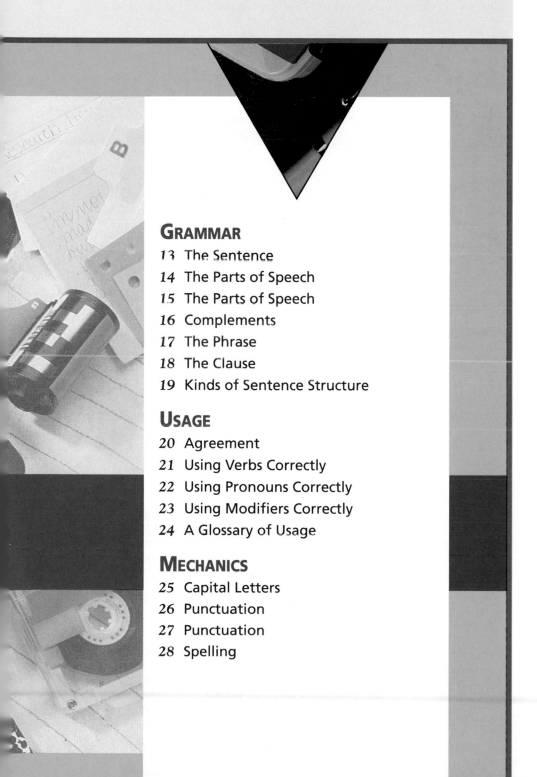

DIAGNOSTIC TEST

OBJECTIVES

- To identify sentences and fragments
- To add capital letters to the beginnings of sentences
- To add correct punctuation at the ends of sentences
- To identify simple subjects and simple predicates in sentences

GRAMMAR

CHAPTER OVERVIEW

This chapter begins by contrasting complete sentences with sentence fragments. It identifies and explains the subject and the predicate and, following a discussion of complete and simple subjects and predicates, explores compound subjects, compound verbs, verb phrases, and sentence classification. In the **Writing Application,** students use their knowledge of complete sentences to write friendly letters.

An understanding of subject and predicate will enable students to understand related grammatical ideas and to solve problems with usage and sentence structure in their writing.

GRAMMAR

13 THE SENTENCE

Subject and Predicate, Kinds of Sentences

Diagnostic Test

A. Identifying Sentences

Some of the following groups of words are sentences; others are not. If a group of words is a sentence, add a capital letter at the beginning and an appropriate punctuation mark at the end. If a group of words is not a sentence, write *sentence fragment.*

EXAMPLES **1.** revised the paper and then proofread it
1. *sentence fragment*

2. we can meet you at the bus stop after school
2. *We can meet you at the bus stop after school.*

1. one day this week or maybe next week **1.** frag.
2. will you lend me that book**?**
3. on her vacation she met her pen pal for the first time⊙
4. his favorite meal, cheese enchiladas with refried beans
5. lock the door on your way out⊙ **4.** frag.

B. Identifying Simple Subjects and Simple Predicates

Identify each *simple subject* and *simple predicate* in the following sentences. [Hint: Be on the alert for compound subjects, compound verbs, and verb phrases.]

EXAMPLE **1.** Foods and beverages with large amounts of sugar can contribute to tooth decay.
1. *Foods, beverages—simple subject; can contribute—simple predicate*

6. The lava from a volcano can be very dangerous.
7. The earthquake survivors camped on blankets in the streets.
8. In Beijing, cyclists pedal on the sidewalks and weave expertly through the busy streets.
9. Between 1896 and 1899, gold prospectors rushed to Alaska.
10. The weather during an Alaskan summer can be very hot.
11. Have you read this collection of Claude McKay's poems?
12. In the center of the table was a huge bowl of fruit.
13. Linked forever in legend are Paul Bunyan and Babe the Blue Ox.
14. Many famous racehorses have been raised or trained in Kentucky.
15. The bright lights and the tall buildings amaze and delight most visitors to New York City.

C. Classifying and Punctuating Sentences

For each of the following sentences, add the correct end mark of punctuation. Then label each sentence *declarative*, *interrogative*, *imperative*, or *exclamatory*.

EXAMPLE **1.** Has anyone guessed the right number
1. *Has anyone guessed the right number?—interrogative*

USING THE DIAGNOSTIC TEST

If you notice that students are writing sentence fragments or are having other problems with sentence structure in their writing, you can use the **Diagnostic Test** to pinpoint error patterns and specific strengths and weaknesses. **Part A** relates to the material in **Segment 2** of this chapter; **Part B** relates to the material in **Segments 3** and **4**; and **Part C** relates to the material in **Segment 5**.

GRAMMAR

OBJECTIVES
- To identify sentences and fragments
- To add capital letters to the beginnings of sentences
- To add correct punctuation to the ends of sentences

398 *The Sentence*

16. We celebrate our parents' anniversary every year⊙ **16.** decl.
17. Don't tell them about our surprise⊙ **17.** imp.
18. Our cousins are coming all the way from Hawaii⊙ **18.** decl.
19. Who is in charge of decorations**?** **19.** int.
20. What a beautiful Navajo blanket that is**!** **20.** excl.

Sentence Sense

13a. A *sentence* is a group of words that expresses a complete thought.

A sentence begins with a capital letter and ends with a period, a question mark, or an exclamation point.

EXAMPLES **A**lice Walker won a prize for her book**.**
Please fasten your seat belt**.**
Why did you stop running**?**
Watch out for the car**!**

When a group of words looks like a sentence but does not express a complete thought, it is a *sentence fragment*.

SENTENCE FRAGMENT **After they pitched the tent.** [This is not a complete thought. What happened after they pitched the tent?]
SENTENCE **After they pitched the tent, they built a campfire.**

SENTENCE FRAGMENT **Sailing around the world.** [The thought is not complete. Who is sailing around the world?]
SENTENCE **Some marine biologists are sailing around the world.**

SENTENCE FRAGMENT **Her hike through the Grand Canyon.** [The thought is not complete. What about her hike?]
SENTENCE **Sheila enjoyed her hike through the Grand Canyon.**

RESOURCES

SENTENCE SENSE
• The Sentence

🦉 QUICK REMINDER
Write the following groups of words on the chalkboard and ask your students to identify them as complete sentences or as fragments:

1. they stop
2. the broken elevators
3. the full moon looked enormous
4. trees swaying

Ask students to add the necessary capital letters and end marks to the complete sentences.

◄ **MEETING**
INDIVIDUAL
NEEDS ►

LEARNING STYLES
Auditory Learners. If students are having trouble distinguishing complete sentences from sentence fragments, you may want to give them oral examples. Some students are better at hearing the differences between sentences and fragments than they are at recognizing them in print.

13a

▶ EXERCISE 1   **Identifying Sentences**

Tell whether each of the following groups of words is a _sentence_ or a *sentence* _fragment_. If a group of words is a sentence, use a capital letter at the beginning and add a mark of punctuation at the end.

EXAMPLES   [1] during her vacation last summer
1. *sentence fragment*

[2] my friend Michelle visited Colorado
2. *sentence—My friend Michelle visited Colorado.*

[1] she took an exciting boat trip on the Colorado River [2] running the rapids [3] at first her boat drifted calmly through the Grand Canyon [4] then the river dropped suddenly [5] and became foaming rapids full of dangerous boulders [6] which can break a boat [7] Michelle's boat was small, like the one in this picture [8] with one guide and four passengers [9] some people prefer large inflatable boats with outboard motors [10] that can carry eighteen passengers

1. sent.
2. frag.
3. sent.
4. sent.
5. frag.
6. frag.
7. sent.
8. frag.
9. sent.
10. frag.

A DIFFERENT APPROACH
Students may have difficulty determining whether or not a group of words expresses a complete thought. The term *complete thought* is very abstract. You may want to wait until after students have learned the definitions of *subject* and *predicate* to assign **Exercise 1.**

MEETING
INDIVIDUAL
NEEDS

LEARNING STYLES
Kinetic Learners. Cut out sentences from magazines, and then cut the sentences in half to make sentence fragments. Give these fragments to students and have students piece the fragments together to form sentences.

GRAMMAR

THE SUBJECT AND THE PREDICATE
- Subject and Predicate
- Complete Subject and Simple Subject
- Complete Predicates and Verbs

 QUICK REMINDER

After writing the following sentences on the chalkboard, ask students to identify the complete subject and the complete predicate of each sentence:

1. Raul sold us these tamales.
2. The yellow book belongs to Martha.
3. Bootsey had her kittens last Tuesday.

MEETING
INDIVIDUAL
NEEDS

LEP/ESL

Asian Languages. In some Asian languages, verbs always appear at the ends of sentences. Consequently, speakers of such languages may have difficulty locating subjects and verbs, especially when verbs appear at the beginnings of sentences.

Make sure students are aware of the fact that verbs in English can appear at the beginnings, middles, or ends of sentences. Give students examples of the various possibilities.

THE SUBJECT AND THE PREDICATE
Rules 13b–13e

OBJECTIVES
- To identify simple and complete subjects in sentences
- To complete sentences by adding subjects and end marks and by capitalizing first words

The Subject and the Predicate

Every sentence has two parts: a *subject* and a *predicate*.

The Subject

13b. The *subject* tells whom or what the sentence is about.

EXAMPLES   **Nicholasa Mohr** is a writer and an artist.
The girls on the team were all good students.

To find the subject, ask *who* or *what* is doing something, or *whom* or *what* is being talked about. The subject may come at the beginning, middle, or end of a sentence.

EXAMPLES   **The pitcher** struck Felicia out. [*Who* struck Felicia out? *The pitcher* did.]
After practicing for hours, **Timmy** bowled two strikes. [*Who* bowled two strikes? *Timmy* did.]
Hiding in the tall grass was **a baby rabbit**. [*What* was hiding? *A baby rabbit* was.]

▶ EXERCISE 2   **Identifying Subjects**

Identify the <u>subject</u> of each of the following sentences.

EXAMPLE   **1.** Have you read a book by N. Scott Momaday?
1. *you*

1. Born in 1934 in Oklahoma, <u>Momaday</u> lived on Navajo and Apache reservations in the Southwest.
2. <u>Both</u> of Momaday's parents were Native Americans.
3. As a young man, <u>Momaday</u> attended the University of New Mexico and Stanford University.
4. In *The Way to Rainy Mountain*, <u>Momaday</u> tells about the myths and history of the Kiowa people.
5. The <u>book</u> includes poems, an essay, and stories about the Kiowa people.
6. *<u>The Way to Rainy Mountain</u>* was published in 1969.

- To identify verbs, verb phrases, and complete predicates in sentences
- To complete sentences by adding predicates

7. After Momaday's book came other <u>works</u> by Native American writers.
8. <u>William Least Heat-Moon</u> traveled in a van across the United States and wrote about his journey.
9. Was <u>he</u> inspired to write by his travels?
10. <u>Readers</u> of this Osage writer enjoy his beautiful descriptions of nature.

▶ EXERCISE 3 **Writing Subjects and Punctuating Sentences**

Add subjects to fill in the blanks in the following sentences. Begin each sentence with a capital letter, and end it with a mark of punctuation. **Subjects will vary.**

EXAMPLE **1.** ____ is very heavy
1. *This bag of cement is very heavy.*

1. ____ is a difficult game to play⊙ **1.** Soccer
2. ____ works in the post office⊙ **2.** Jack
3. Luckily for me, ____ was easy to read⊙ **3.** this book
4. Tied to the end of the rope was ____⊙ **4.** a calf
5. Did ____ help you**?** **5.** anyone

Complete Subject and Simple Subject

The *complete subject* consists of all the words needed to tell *whom* or *what* a sentence is about.

13c. The *simple subject* is the main word or words in the complete subject.

EXAMPLES **The four new students** arrived early.
Complete subject The four new students
Simple subject students

A round walnut table with five legs stood in the middle of the dining room.
Complete subject A round walnut table with five legs
Simple subject table

A DIFFERENT APPROACH
Because *subject* is a familiar word in other contexts, you may want to ask your class what the word means in an expression like *subject of a book.* When students arrive at a working definition (perhaps, the subject is what the book is about), suggest that their definition might also apply to the subject of a sentence.

GRAMMAR

GRAMMAR

A DIFFERENT APPROACH

Divide the class into two groups. Have students in one group write complete subjects and have students in the other group write complete predicates. Pair students at random, one from each group, and have them read their joint sentences aloud. Ask the class to decide whether each subject-predicate combination forms a sentence.

If you leave out the simple subject, a sentence does not make sense.

EXAMPLES   The four new . . . arrived early.
A round walnut . . . with five legs stood in the middle of the dining room.

A simple subject may consist of one word or several words.

EXAMPLES   **Jets** break the sound barrier. [one word]
Does **Aunt Carmen** own a grocery store? [two words]
On the library shelf was ***The Island of the Blue Dolphins.*** [six words]

NOTE: In this book, the term *subject* refers to the simple subject unless otherwise indicated.

EXERCISE 4   **Identifying Complete Subjects and Simple Subjects**

Identify the complete subject in each of the following sentences. Then, underline the simple subject.

EXAMPLES   **1.** Stories about time travel make exciting reading.
1. *Stories about time travel*
2. Samuel Delany writes great science fiction.
2. *Samuel Delany*

1. [Ray Bradbury] is also a writer of science fiction.
2. [*The Golden Apples of the Sun*] is a collection of his short stories.
3. [My favorite story in that book] is "A Sound of Thunder."
4. [The main character in the story] is called Mr. Eckels.
5. For ten thousand dollars, [Mr. Eckels] joins Time Safari, Inc.
6. [He] is looking for the dinosaur *Tyrannosaurus rex*.
7. With four other men, [Bradbury's hero] travels over sixty million years back in time.
8. On the safari, [trouble] develops.

9. Because of one mistake, [the <u>past</u>] is changed.
10. [The <u>results</u> of that mistake] affect the future.

The Predicate

13d. The *predicate* of a sentence is the part that says something about the subject.

EXAMPLES   Old Faithful **is a giant geyser in Yellowstone National Park.**
Jade Snow Wong **wrote about growing up in San Francisco's Chinatown.**

Like the subject, the predicate may be found anywhere in a sentence.

EXAMPLES   **Outside the tent was** a baby bear.
Late in the night we **heard a noise.**

▶ EXERCISE 5   **Identifying Predicates**

Identify the <u>predicate</u> in each of the sentences in the following paragraph.

EXAMPLE   **[1] My favorite sports poster is this one of Roberto Clemente.**
1. *is this one of Roberto Clemente*

[1] <u>Also among my treasures is</u> a book about Clemente. [2] Clemente <u>played right field for the Pittsburgh Pirates</u>. [3] <u>During his career</u>, he <u>won four National League batting titles</u>. [4] <u>In 1966</u>, he <u>was named the league's Most Valuable Player</u>. [5] <u>Twice</u> Clemente <u>helped lead the Pirates to World Series victories</u>. [6] <u>In fourteen World Series games</u>, Clemente

ANSWERS
Exercise 6

Predicates will vary. Here are some possibilities:

1. My favorite food is spinach.
2. A course in first aid is offered here.
3. In the sunlight our car looks purple.
4. Rock climbing is fun.
5. Spanish explorers in the Americas were looking for gold.
6. Several computers were given to our school.
7. In the box was a new pair of roller skates.
8. The skyscrapers of New York City loomed above us.
9. Some dogs chase cars.
10. In June my family is going to Mississippi.

 CRITICAL THINKING
Synthesis

Synthesizing complete subjects and complete predicates from their component parts can help students understand how to distinguish simple subjects and predicates from complete subjects and predicates. Ask each student to write a simple subject on a sheet of paper. Then have each student add modifiers to make a complete subject. Have students do the same thing with simple predicates. You may want to ask students to repeat the process for additional practice.

---

never went without a hit. [7] Roberto Clemente died in a plane crash off the coast of his homeland, Puerto Rico. [8] The crash occurred on a flight to Nicaragua to aid earthquake victims. [9] After his death, Clemente was elected to the National Baseball Hall of Fame. [10] In New York, a park has been named for this beloved ballplayer.

> EXERCISE 6 **Writing Predicates**

Make a sentence out of each of the following groups of words by adding predicates to fill the blank or blanks.

EXAMPLES **1.** A flock of geese ____.
  1. *A flock of geese flew high overhead.*

  2. ____ a poster of Nelson Mandela.
  2. *Over Kim's desk hung a poster of Nelson Mandela.*

1. My favorite food ____.
2. A course in first aid ____.
3. ____ our car ____.
4. Rock climbing ____.
5. Spanish explorers in the Americas ____.
6. Several computers ____.
7. ____ a new pair of roller skates.
8. The skyscrapers of New York City ____.
9. Some dogs ____.
10. ____ my family ____.

Complete Predicate and Simple Predicate

The *complete predicate* consists of all the words that say something about the subject.

13e. The *simple predicate,* or *verb,* is the main word or group of words in the complete predicate.

EXAMPLES The pilot broke the sound barrier.
  Complete predicate broke the sound barrier.
  Simple predicate (verb) broke

13e

We should have visited the diamond field in Arkansas.

Complete predicate	should have visited the diamond field in Arkansas.
Simple predicate (verb)	should have visited

NOTE: In this book, the simple predicate is usually referred to as the *verb.*

▶ EXERCISE 7 **Identifying Complete Predicates and Verbs**

Identify the <u>complete predicate</u> of each of the following sentences. Then, underline the <u>verb</u>.

EXAMPLE 1. Nobody knows the creator of the U.S. flag.
1. *knows the creator of the U.S. flag*

1. Scholars <u>are unsure about the history of the Stars and Stripes</u>.
2. The Continental Congress <u>approved a design for the flag</u>.
3. The design <u>included thirteen red stripes and thirteen white stripes</u>.
4. The top inner quarter of the flag <u>was a blue field with thirteen white stars</u>.
5. The name of the designer <u>remains a mystery</u>.
6. <u>During the American Revolution</u>, the colonists <u>needed a symbol of their independence</u>.
7. George Washington <u>wanted flags for the army</u>.
8. <u>Unfortunately</u>, the flags <u>did not arrive until after the Revolutionary War</u>.
9. <u>According to legend</u>, Betsy Ross <u>made the first flag</u>.
10. Historians <u>doubt the Betsy Ross story</u>.

The Verb Phrase

Some verbs consist of more than one word. Such a verb is called a *verb phrase.*

GRAMMAR

GRAMMAR

TIMESAVER
To save time, go over the odd-numbered problems in **Exercise 7** orally. Students who need additional practice could do the even-numbered problems as homework.

A DIFFERENT APPROACH
With your students' help, generate a list of five words that can be used in sentences as either nouns or verbs, such as *run, picnic,* and *skate.* Write the list on the chalkboard. Have students write ten sentences that include each of the words as the simple subject of a sentence and as the simple predicate of another sentence.

INTEGRATING THE LANGUAGE ARTS

Literature Link. Have students read and discuss Randall Jarrell's poem "The Chipmunk's Day." Ask students to identify the simple predicate of each sentence in the poem. Then ask why the poet places all the simple predicates that express the chipmunk's actions at the ends of the sentences in the first three stanzas. [In the first three stanzas, Jarrell emphasizes the chipmunk's rapid movements by placing the verbs at the ends of the sentences.] Ask students why the simple predicates in the last two stanzas are not placed at the ends of the sentences. [The focus of the poem shifts in the last two stanzas from the chipmunk's quick activity to his hole.]

EXAMPLES   Kathy **is riding** the Ferris wheel.
The carnival **has been** in town for two weeks.
Bernice **should have been** here sooner.

NOTE: The words *not* and *never* are not verbs. They are never part of a verb or verb phrase.

EXAMPLES   She **has** not **written** to me recently.
I **will** never **forget** her.

▶ EXERCISE 8   **Identifying Verbs and Verb Phrases**

Identify the <u>verb or verb phrase</u> in each of the following sentences.

EXAMPLES   **1.** Look at these beautiful pictures of Hawaii.
1. *Look*

2. They were taken by our science teacher.
2. *were taken*

1. Hawaii <u>is called</u> the Aloha State.
2. It <u>was settled</u> by Polynesians around the year 750.
3. The musical heritage and rich culture of the original Hawaiians <u>have contributed</u> much to the islands' popularity.
4. Hawaii <u>has</u> the largest, most active volcanoes in the world.
5. These volcanoes <u>may be viewed</u> by tourists in Hawaii Volcanoes National Park.

Finding the Subject

Sometimes it's difficult to locate the subject of a sentence. In such cases, it can help to find the verb first and then to ask yourself *whom* or *what* the verb is referring to.

EXAMPLES **In high school we will have more homework.** [The verb is *will have. Who* will have? *We* will have. *We* is the subject of the sentence.]
Can you untie this knot? [*Can untie* is the verb. *Who* can untie? *You* can untie. *You* is the subject of the sentence.]
The peak of Mount Everest was first reached by Sir Edmund Hillary and Tenzing Norgay. [The verb is *was reached. What* was reached? The answer is *peak. Peak* is the subject of the sentence.]
Ahead of the explorers lay a vast wilderness. [The verb is *lay. What lay?* The answer is *wilderness. Wilderness* is the subject of the sentence.]

NOTE: The subject of a sentence is never part of a prepositional phrase.

EXAMPLE **The papayas on the table look tasty.** [*What* look tasty? *Papayas.* To say *table look tasty* doesn't make sense.]

WRITING APPLICATION

Using Complete Sentences in a Letter

Sometimes a thought or an impression is so clear in your mind that you forget that others do not see it as clearly. Where you express such thoughts and expressions, you may be tempted to use a single word or phrase rather than a complete statement.

COMMON ERROR

Problem. In sentences with prepositional phrases, students frequently identify the objects of the prepositions as the subjects of the sentences.

Solution. Suggest that students identify and bracket prepositional phrases before they try to identify subjects in sentences.

WRITING APPLICATION

Because some students may not have had the experience of going to a birthday party, you may want to provide alternative topics for students' descriptive letters.

For an example of descriptive writing, refer students to **A Student Model** on page 172.

407

CRITICAL THINKING
Synthesis

Have students brainstorm various activities, games, refreshments, and emotions that they associate with birthday parties. Tell students that when they are brainstorming, they should jot down words and fragments. Give students ample time to brainstorm.

Then have students synthesize the words and fragments that they generated into complete sentences.

SENTENCE FRAGMENTS	What a great birthday party! All my friends. Good eats—popcorn, roasted peanuts, lots of goodies. Playing games. Music. Dancing.
COMPLETE SENTENCES	I had a great birthday party. All my friends were there. My mom and I made popcorn, roasted peanuts, and made lots of other goodies. Everybody had fun playing games, listening to music, and dancing.

To make sure that others can clearly understand you, use complete sentences.

▶ WRITING ACTIVITY

Yesterday, you went to a birthday party. Write a letter to a friend or relative who lives far away. In your letter, describe where the party was held, how long it lasted, and what refreshments were served. Also include details about the activities you enjoyed and about the other people who were there. Use complete sentences to make sure your thoughts are clear.

Prewriting Make a list of the details that you'd like to include in your letter. At this stage, you don't have to use complete sentences—just jot down your thoughts as they come to you.

Writing Use your prewriting list of details as you write your rough draft. Choose details that would be interesting to your friend or relative. You might organize your letter chronologically (telling about events in the order they occurred). Or you might want to tell about one or two important events.

Evaluating and Revising Read your letter aloud. As you read, mark any parts of the letter that seem unclear. Add, cut, or rearrange details to make your letter clear and interesting to your reader. (See pages 361–371 for information on combining sentences.) Check your work once again to make sure you have used only complete sentences.

COMPOUND SUBJECTS AND COMPOUND VERBS Rules 13f, 13g

OBJECTIVES

- To identify compound subjects, compound verbs, and verb phrases in sentences
- To create sentences by adding compound subjects to predicates

---

The Subject and the Predicate **409**

13f

GRAMMAR

Proofreading Read over your letter for errors in spelling and punctuation. Be sure that you have capitalized the first word of each sentence and have ended each sentence with correct punctuation.

Compound Subjects and Compound Verbs

Compound Subjects

> **13f.** A *compound subject* consists of two or more connected subjects that have the same verb. The usual connecting word is *and* or *or*.

EXAMPLES **Paris** and **London** remain favorite tourist attractions. [The two parts of the compound subject have the same verb, *remain.*]
Nelson Mandela or **Bishop Desmond Tutu** will speak at the conference. [The two parts of the compound subject have the same verb phrase, *will speak.*]
Among my hobbies are **reading, snorkeling,** and **painting.** [The three parts of the compound subject have the same verb, *are.*]

 EXERCISE 9 **Identifying Compound Subjects**

Identify the <u>compound subject</u> in each of the following sentences.

EXAMPLE **1.** The shapes and sizes of sand dunes are determined by the wind.
    1. *shapes, sizes*

1. The national <u>parks</u> and <u>monuments</u> of the United States include many of the world's most spectacular landforms.

 **QUICK REMINDER**
Write the following sentences on the chalkboard and ask students to identify the subject and verb of each sentence:

1. Manuel and Rosa played their guitars.
2. Rosa played her guitar and sang for us.
3. Manuel and Rosa played their guitars and sang for us.

MEETING
INDIVIDUAL
NEEDS

STUDENTS WITH SPECIAL NEEDS

To help your learning disabled students grasp the concepts in this segment, involve as many of their senses as possible. Give magazines to students and ask them to find photographs that depict action involving several objects or people. Then have students use compound subjects and compound verbs to write sentences that describe the photographs. Suggest that students read their sentences aloud and listen to determine whether they used compound subjects and compound verbs correctly.

409

INTEGRATING THE LANGUAGE ARTS

Literature Link. Have your students read and discuss "in Just-" by E. E. Cummings, and ask them to identify the compound subjects in the poem [*eddieandbill, bettyandisbel*]. Ask students to explain how Cummings treats the compound subjects. [He combines them.] Ask students what he could be implying by this treatment. [Students may say that Cummings is implying that the pairs are inseparable friends.]

Ask students whether they've ever had friends from whom they were inseparable. Tell the students to write sentences about things they have done with their friends and to combine compound subjects as E. E. Cummings does. Students might also want to unite compound verbs in a similar way, as in *annieandgina* or *skippedandjumped.*

VISUAL CONNECTIONS

Exploring the Subject. The geographical features shown here were caused by normal, geologic erosion. There is another type of erosion, however. It is called soil erosion. Soil erosion occurs when the soil from land used for agriculture is carried away by wind or water. Erosion of this type has accelerated rapidly in many regions due to mismanagement of the land. Globally, hundreds of millions of acres of once-productive land have been damaged or ruined by soil erosion. In response, many nations have implemented conservation programs to confront the problem.

2. The <u>Grand Canyon</u> and the <u>waterfalls</u> of Yosemite are examples of landforms shaped by erosion.
3. <u>Water</u> and other natural <u>forces</u> are continuing the age-old erosion of landforms.
4. On the Colorado Plateau, for example, natural <u>bridges</u> and <u>arches</u> like the ones shown below have been produced by erosion.
5. Likewise, <u>Skyline Arch</u> and <u>Landscape Arch</u> in Utah are two natural arches formed by erosion.
6. Underground, <u>caves</u> and immense <u>caverns</u> are created by rushing streams and waterfalls.
7. <u>Stalagmites</u> and <u>stalactites</u> such as the ones in the photo on the right are formed by lime deposits from drops of water seeping into these caverns.
8. In river systems throughout the world, <u>canyons</u> and <u>gorges</u> are cut into the earth by erosion.
9. Many <u>rapids</u> and <u>waterfalls</u> have also originated through erosion.
10. Do steep <u>areas</u> with heavy rainfall or dry <u>regions</u> with few trees suffer more from erosion?

13g

▶ EXERCISE 10 **Writing Compound Subjects**

Add a compound subject to each of the following predicates. Use *and* or *or* to join the parts of your compound subjects.

EXAMPLE **1.** ____ were at the bottom of my locker.
  1. *My bus pass and a pair of gym socks were at the bottom of my locker.*

1. Yesterday ____ arrived in the mail.
2. ____ make loyal pets.
3. On the beach ____ spotted a dolphin.
4. ____ will present their report on Álvar Núñez Cabeza de Vaca.
5. In the attic were piled ____.

Compound Verbs

13g. A *compound verb* consists of two or more connected verbs that have the same subject. A connecting word—usually *and, or,* or *but*—is used to join the verbs.

EXAMPLES The basketball team **played** well but **lost** the game anyway.
  The rain **has fallen** for days and **is** still **falling** in some areas.

A sentence may have both a *compound subject* and a *compound verb*. Notice in the following example that both subjects carry out the action of both verbs.

EXAMPLE A few **vegetables** and many **flowers sprouted** and **grew** in the rich soil. [The vegetables sprouted and grew, and the flowers sprouted and grew.]

▶ EXERCISE 11 **Identifying Compound Verbs**

Identify each <u>compound verb or verb phrase</u> in the following sentences.

ANSWERS
Exercise 10

Compound subjects will vary. Here are some possibilities:

1. Yesterday, four letters and a magazine arrived in the mail.
2. Dogs and birds make loyal pets.
3. On the beach Daniel and Chandra spotted a dolphin.
4. My sister and her friend will present their report on Álvar Núñez Cabeza de Vaca.
5. In the attic were piled suitcases and old picture albums.

A DIFFERENT APPROACH
  Ask students to help you generate a list of nouns and a list of verbs. Write the lists on the chalkboard. Have each student write three sentences, each of which must contain at least two of the nouns and two of the verbs in compound subjects and verbs.

COMMON ERROR
  Problem. Students often have trouble with subject-verb agreement in sentences with compound subjects that are connected by *or*.
  Solution. Tell students that verbs in sentences in which a compound subject is connected by *or* can be singular or plural, depending on whether the subject closest to the verb is singular or plural. Here is a strategy students can use to check subject-verb agreement in sentences in which a compound subject is connected by *or*:

1. Cover the part of the compound subject that is farther from the verb.
2. Determine whether or not the remaining part of the compound subject agrees with the verb.

412 *The Sentence*

EXAMPLE **1.** Just like children today, children in ancient Egypt played games and enjoyed toys.
      1. *played, enjoyed*

1. <u>Have</u> you <u>heard</u> of the game Serpent or <u>learned</u> the game Senet?
2. For the Egyptian board game Serpent, players <u>found</u> or <u>carved</u> a serpent-shaped stone.
3. Players <u>placed</u> the serpent in the center of the board and then <u>began</u> the game.
4. They <u>used</u> place markers and <u>threw</u> bones or sticks as dice.
5. The players <u>took</u> turns and <u>competed</u> with one another in a race to the center.
6. Senet <u>was</u> another ancient Egyptian board game and <u>was played</u> by children and adults alike.
7. Senet <u>looked</u> like an easy game but <u>was</u> actually quite difficult.
8. Players <u>moved</u> their playing pieces toward the ends of three rows of squares but sometimes <u>were stopped</u> by their opponents.
9. Senet boards <u>were</u> complex and <u>had</u> certain squares for good luck and bad luck.
10. These squares <u>could help</u> players or <u>could block</u> their playing pieces.

▶ EXERCISE 12 **Writing Appropriate Compound Verbs**

Where in the solar system are you? That's what you—the captain of this spaceship—want to find out. To do so, you've called up on your viewing screen the map shown on the next page. Look at the map and find your spaceship among the planets. Then use the map and the accompanying notes you've made in your log to write your official report for the last three days of June. (Be as imaginative as you want.) Use at least five sentences that have compound verbs.

EXAMPLE *We then landed on Jobel's Dark Spot and captured Shelzan, king of the Noidles.*

AT-RISK STUDENTS

    Because cooperative learning is an effective instructional method for at-risk students, you might want to have students work in pairs to complete **Exercise 12.** You could either encourage pairs of students to share ideas and to exchange papers for proofreading, or you could have each pair collaborate to produce one report.

ANSWERS
Exercise 12

Students' sentences will vary. To save grading time, have students underline the compound verbs in their reports.

GRAMMAR

LOG NOTES

FRIDAY
JUNE
28

rough trip through Banzoi Asteroid Belt
contacted Intergalactic Command for
instructions   Dark Spot on Jobel   captured
Shelzan—king of the Noidles

SATURDAY
JUNE
29

surveyed Prog   strange light   spotted
ancient satellite Voyager I   lost gravity field
crater creature

SUNDAY
JUNE
30

ship's fuel low   sighted Bittzer's Comet
landing on Grepinak   took on supplies
frozen fog   plan next course

MONDAY
JULY

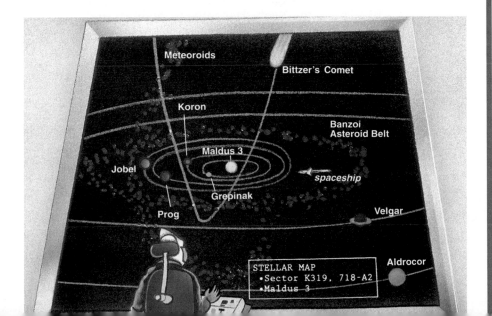

Meteoroids

Bittzer's Comet

Koron

Banzoi
Asteroid Belt

Maldus 3

Jobel

spaceship

Grepinak

Prog

Velgar

STELLAR MAP
•Sector K319, 718-A2
•Maldus 3

Aldrocor

INTEGRATING THE LANGUAGE ARTS

Technology Link. If your class has access to computers with graphics programs, ask students to create illustrations to accompany their reports.

413

INTEGRATING THE LANGUAGE ARTS

Grammar and Speaking. You may want to ask students to research and present brief oral reports about Australia. The reports could focus on one of the subjects discussed in **Review A**—Australia's native peoples, its economy, or perhaps the unusual animals found there. Students should incorporate verb phrases, compound subjects, and compound verbs in their reports. Encourage students to enhance their reports by including original drawings or pictures from magazines.

414

REVIEW A

OBJECTIVE

• To identify the complete subjects, simple subjects, complete predicates, and verbs or verb phrases in sentences

414 *The Sentence*

 EXERCISE 13 **Identifying Subjects and Verbs**

Identify the <u>subject</u> and <u>verb</u> in each of the following sentences. Some of the subjects and verbs are compound.

EXAMPLE **1.** American pioneers left their homes and traveled to the West.
   1. *pioneers—subject; left, traveled—verbs*

1. <u>Settlers</u> <u>faced</u> and <u>overcame</u> many dangers.
2. <u>Mount McKinley</u> and <u>Mount Whitney</u> <u>are</u> two very high mountains.
3. <u>Sacagawea</u> of the Shoshones <u>helped</u> open the West.
4. Every winter many <u>skiers</u> <u>rush</u> to the Grand Tetons.
5. Few Hollywood <u>stars</u> <u>have been</u> both <u>born</u> and <u>raised</u> in California.
6. Broad <u>valleys</u> and dense <u>forests</u> <u>cool</u> and <u>refresh</u> travelers through the Appalachian Mountains.
7. On Beartooth Highway in Montana, excellent <u>campgrounds</u> and scenic <u>overlooks</u> <u>provide</u> many views of distant glaciers.
8. <u>Mount Evans</u> <u>is</u> west of Denver and <u>can be reached</u> by the highest paved road in America.
9. The <u>view</u> from the top slopes of Mount Evans <u>is</u> breathtaking.
10. The <u>name</u> *Kentucky* <u>comes</u> from an Iroquois word and <u>means</u> "meadowland."

 REVIEW A **Identifying Subjects and Predicates**

Write the following sentences. Underline the <u>complete subjects</u> once and the <u>complete predicates</u> twice. Then, circle each (simple subject) and each (verb or verb phrase)

EXAMPLE **1.** The seven continents are divisions of the earth's land.
   1. *The seven (continents) (are) divisions of the earth's land.*

1. The entire (continent) of Australia (is occupied) by a single nation.
2. (Can) (you) (name) the capital of Australia?

KINDS OF SENTENCES Rules 13h–13k

OBJECTIVES

- To write a concert review that includes each of the four types of sentences—declarative, imperative, interrogative, and exclamatory
- To classify sentences as declarative, imperative, interrogative, or exclamatory

3. Australia is a federation of six states and two territories.
4. The continent was claimed for Britain by Captain James Cook.
5. The native people of Australia live mainly in the desert regions and have a very close bond to their environment.
6. British colonists settled in cities on the coast.
7. Many ranchers raise sheep and export wool.
8. In addition, large quantities of gold and uranium are mined in Australia.
9. The country is also highly industrialized and produces a variety of goods, ranging from shoes to airplanes.
10. Among Australia's unusual animals are the platypus and the anteater.

GRAMMAR

Kinds of Sentences

13h. A *declarative sentence* makes a statement. It is always followed by a period.

EXAMPLES   Amy Tan was born in San Francisco.
I couldn't hear what Jason said.

13i. An *imperative sentence* gives a command or makes a request. It is usually followed by a period. A strong command is followed by an exclamation point.

EXAMPLES   Be quiet during the play.
Please give me another piece of melon.
Stop!

The subject of a command or a request is always *you*, although *you* doesn't appear in the sentence. In such cases, *you* is called the *understood subject*.

RESOURCES

KINDS OF SENTENCES
- Kinds of Sentences

QUICK REMINDER

Write the following sets of words on the chalkboard. Ask each student to write a declarative, an imperative, an exclamatory, and an interrogative sentence by using each of the following phrases as complete subjects. After everyone is finished, ask for volunteers to read their sentences aloud.

1. the thirteenth floor
2. scary Halloween costumes
3. the blue album cover
4. westerly winds

GRAMMAR

LEARNING STYLES

Auditory Learners. Read the example sentences from this segment aloud to students. Inflect your voice to indicate the purpose of each sentence.

PICTURE THIS

You may want to give students a little more information about what a Beatles' concert might have been like by sharing any relevant personal experiences or knowledge. Encourage students to use their imaginations to decide what rock concerts of the twenty-third century might be like. Conduct a brainstorming session to help students generate ideas.

EXAMPLES (You) Be quiet during the play.
          (You) Please give me another piece of melon.
          (You) Stop!

The word *you* is the understood subject even when the person spoken to is addressed by name.

EXAMPLE Miguel, (you) please answer the door.

13j. An *interrogative sentence* asks a question. It is followed by a question mark.

EXAMPLES When did Thurgood Marshall retire from the
          Supreme Court?
          Did the surfboard cost much?

13k. An *exclamatory sentence* shows excitement or expresses strong feeling. It is followed by an exclamation point.

EXAMPLES Gabriella won the match!
          How terrifying that movie was!

PICTURE THIS

The time is the 1960s. The young men on stage are the Beatles. You are a reporter for *Rock Roots,* a music databank that is popular in the twenty-third century. You've been transported back in time to write a short review of this Beatles' concert. You find the Beatles' hair styles and clothes most unusual, and you're amazed at the number of police on the scene to protect the group from the crowd. As you watch the concert, you compare it with rock concerts of the twenty-third century. Because space is limited on the databank, your review must be no longer than ten sentences. In your review, use at least one example of each of the four kinds of sentences (declarative, imperative, interrogative, and exclamatory).

GRAMMAR

Subject: Beatles concert
Audience: users of music history databank *Rock Roots*
Purpose: to inform

 EXERCISE 14 **Classifying Sentences by Purpose**

Label each of the following quotations as *declarative*, *imperative*, *interrogative*, or *exclamatory*.

EXAMPLE **1.** Lead me from darkness to light!

Brihadaranyaka Upanishad

1. *exclamatory*

1. The only thing we have to fear is fear itself.

Franklin Delano Roosevelt, 1933 Inaugural Address **1. decl.**

2. Push yourself.

from an interview with Nikki Giovanni **2. imp.**

3. Do any human beings ever realize life while they
   live it?

Thornton Wilder, *Our Town* **3. int.**

4. I am beginning, just beginning, to find out who I am.

Gloria Steinem, "Sisterhood" **4. decl.**

5. I have yet to meet a man who, on observing his own
   faults, blamed himself!

Confucius, *The Sayings of Confucius* **5. excl.**

INTEGRATING THE LANGUAGE ARTS

Grammar and Diction. Slang sometimes enters mainstream culture through song lyrics. For example, the Beatles introduced the slang term *heavy* (meaning "serious") to mainstream American culture through the song lyric "She's so heavy."

Share this information with students and ask them whether or not they think the slang used in the twenty third century will be the same as the slang they use today. You might want to suggest that students make their reviews more authentic by including some twenty-third century slang. You could get students started by brainstorming for twenty-third century replacements for current slang.

A DIFFERENT APPROACH

To help students differentiate among types of sentences, give students a declarative sentence and ask them to use the declarative sentence as a departure point to form the other three types of sentences. For example, "The test was hard" could become "Was the test hard?" (interrogative); "Please tell me if the test was hard" (imperative); "That test was really hard!" (exclamatory).

SELECTION AMENDMENT
Description of change: excerpted
Rationale: to focus on the concept of sentence classification
presented in this chapter

GRAMMAR

LESS-ADVANCED STUDENTS

Assign **Review B** to pairs of students. Group less-advanced students with students who have a good grasp of the material. Encourage students to talk about the sentences and the problems they have in classifying the sentences. You may want to monitor the groups to verify that students are interacting to complete the review.

418 *The Sentence*

▶ REVIEW B   **Classifying and Punctuating Sentences**

Add the correct end mark of punctuation to each of the following sentences. Then, label each sentence as *declarative*, *imperative*, *interrogative*, or *exclamatory*.

EXAMPLE   **1.** Are prairie dogs social creatures
           1. *Are prairie dogs social creatures?—interrogative*

1. Many of these small mammals live together in underground "towns" like the one shown below⊙ **1.** decl.
2. As you can see, American prairie dogs dig family burrows⊙ **2.** decl.
3. These burrows sometimes cover several acres⊙ **3.** decl.
4. Have you ever seen a prairie dog**?** **4.** int.
5. These creatures can usually be seen at night or in the early morning⊙ **5.** decl.
6. What alert animals prairie dogs are**!** **6.** excl.
7. At least one prairie dog always keeps a constant lookout for threats to the community⊙ **7.** decl.
8. Look at how it sits up to see better⊙ **8.** imp.
9. It will make a shrill whistle of alarm at the first sign of danger⊙ **9.** decl.
10. It then dives headfirst into the burrow and alerts the entire colony⊙ **10.** decl.

SEGMENT 6 *(pp. 419–421)*
REVIEW: POSTTESTS 1 and 2
OBJECTIVES
- To identify sentences and fragments
- To add capital letters and end marks to sentences
- To identify simple subjects and verbs in sentences
- To classify sentences as declarative, interrogative, imperative, or exclamatory and to add end marks accordingly ☛

Review: Posttest 1

A. Identifying Sentences

Label each of the following groups of words as a *sentence* or a *sentence fragment*. Write each sentence, using a capital letter at the beginning and an end mark of punctuation.

EXAMPLES **1.** having forgotten their homework
    1. *sentence fragment*

    2. how strong the wind is
    2. *sentence—How strong the wind is!*

1. after we visit the library and gather information for the report **1.** frag.
2. are you ready for the big game next week**?** **2.** sent.
3. listen closely to our guest speaker⊙ **3.** sent.
4. have read the first draft of my paper **4.** frag.
5. an excellent short story, "The Medicine Bag," is in that book⊙ **5.** sent.

B. Identifying Simple Subjects and Verbs

Identify the <u>simple subject</u> and the <u>verb</u> in each of the following sentences.

EXAMPLE **1.** A computer can be a wonderful tool for people with disabilities.
    1. *computer—simple subject; can be—verb*

6. Specially designed <u>machines</u> <u>have been developed</u> in recent years.
7. <u>Have</u> <u>you</u> ever <u>seen</u> a talking computer?
8. <u>It</u> <u>is used</u> by both visually impaired people and sighted people.
9. Its electronic <u>voice</u> <u>speaks</u> the words typed into the machine.
10. Most <u>computers</u> <u>show</u> their writing on a screen.

420   *The Sentence*

11. However, these special <u>models</u> <u>can give</u> information by voice.
12. Close-captioned <u>television</u> <u>is</u> another interesting invention.
13. <u>Subtitles</u> <u>appear</u> on the television screens of hearing-impaired viewers.
14. These <u>viewers</u> <u>can read</u> the subtitles and <u>enjoy</u> their favorite shows.
15. Many new <u>inventions</u> <u>make</u> life easier and more enjoyable nowadays.

C. Classifying and Punctuating Sentences

Add the correct end mark of punctuation after the last word in each of the following sentences. Then, label each sentence <u>*declarative*</u>, <u>*interrogative*</u>, <u>*imperative*</u>, or <u>*exclamatory*</u>.

EXAMPLE   **1.** Flowers and insects depend on one another for life
       1. *life.—declarative*

16. Have you ever watched a bee in a garden**?**   **16.** int.
17. The bee flies busily from one flower to another.   **17.** decl.
18. Notice the pollen on the legs and body of the bee.   **18.** imp.
19. The bee is carrying pollen from flower to flower.   **19.** decl.
20. What a remarkable insect the bee is**!**   **20.** excl.

Review: Posttest 2

Writing Sentences

Identify each of the following sentence parts as a <u>*complete subject*</u> or a <u>*complete predicate*</u>. Then, use each sentence part in a sentence. Begin each sentence with a capital letter and end it with the correct mark of punctuation.

EXAMPLE   **1.** the tides of the oceans
          1. *complete subject*
              Are the tides of the oceans influenced by the moon?

1. the path through the woods **1.** comp. subj.
2. the city of San Juan **2.** comp. subj.
3. found a four-leaf clover **3.** comp. pred.
4. my favorite television show **4.** comp. subj.
5. can call a meeting and take a vote on the matter **5.** comp. pred.
6. splashed happily in the shallow water **6.** comp. pred.
7. one of the nurses **7.** comp. subj.
8. our broken VCR **8.** comp. subj.
9. will represent us at the meeting **9.** comp. pred.
10. mentioned rain and high winds **10.** comp. pred.

GRAMMAR

ANSWERS
Review: Posttest 2

Sentences will vary. Here are some possibilities:

1. The path through the woods was dark and mysterious.
2. The city of San Juan is fascinating.
3. My sister found a four-leaf clover.
4. My favorite television show is starting.
5. The club can call a meeting and take a vote on the matter.
6. The children splashed happily in the shallow water.
7. One of the nurses took the patient's temperature.
8. Among the missing items was our broken VCR.
9. Jorge will represent us at the meeting.
10. The weather forecaster mentioned rain and high winds.

GRAMMAR

GRAMMAR

CHAPTER OVERVIEW

This chapter first explains nouns and classifies nouns as common or proper and concrete or abstract. The chapter next focuses on pronouns and their antecedents, discussing various types of pronouns—personal, reflexive, intensive, demonstrative, interrogative, indefinite, and relative. The **Writing Application** calls on students to integrate their knowledge of pronouns with writing. Finally, students are introduced to modifiers of nouns and pronouns—adjectives. Several types of adjectives are discussed in this chapter—articles, nouns used as adjectives, demonstrative adjectives, and proper adjectives.

USING THE DIAGNOSTIC TEST

The **Diagnostic Test** can help you pinpoint error patterns and specific strengths and weaknesses in students' use of nouns, pronouns, and adjectives. Based on the results of the test, you may want to spend more time on some parts of this chapter and less on others.

GRAMMAR

14 THE PARTS OF SPEECH

Noun, Pronoun, Adjective

Diagnostic Test

Identifying Nouns, Pronouns, and Adjectives

Identify each italicized word in the following paragraph as a *noun*, a [*pronoun*] or an *adjective*.

EXAMPLE The mangrove [1] *tree* grows in [2] *coastal* areas, and [3] *it* sends down roots from its branches.
1. *noun*
2. *adjective*
3. *pronoun*

In [1] *this* country [2] *mangroves* grow along the coasts of [3] *Florida*. [4][*They*] form a [5] *wonderland* where land, water, and [6] *sky* blend. [7] *The* lush, green [8] *mangrove* islands and [9] *shoreline* are both beautiful and valuable. Mangroves are [10] *important* to [11][*our*][12] *environment*. They produce [13] *tons* of valuable [14] *vegetable* matter and are an essential part of [15] *tropical* biology. So far as [16][*we*] know, the

11. [*or* <u>our</u>]

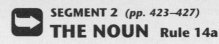
THE NOUN Rule 14a

OBJECTIVES

- To identify the nouns in a paragraph
- To classify nouns as common or proper
- To revise sentences by substituting proper nouns for common nouns ☞

[17] *first* reference to mangroves was in early [18] *Egyptian* times. A [19] *South African* expert has also discovered evidence of mangrove islands along the [20] *Red Sea*.

The Eight Parts of Speech			
noun	adjective	adverb	conjunction
pronoun	verb	preposition	interjection

The Noun

14a. A *noun* is a word that names a person, place, thing, or idea.

PERSONS	Jessye Norman, teacher, Dr. Ling, first baseman
PLACES	Grand Canyon, city, Nigeria, kitchen
THINGS	lamp, canary, Nobel Prize, Empire State Building
IDEAS	happiness, self-control, democracy, bravery

Notice that some nouns are made up of more than one word. Such nouns are called *compound nouns.* They may be written as one word, as a hyphenated word, or as two or more words.

ONE WORD	grandmother
HYPHENATED WORD	great-grandmother
TWO WORDS	grand piano

▶ EXERCISE 1 **Identifying Nouns**

Identify the twenty-five <u>nouns</u> in the following paragraph. Some nouns will be used more than once.

RESOURCES

THE NOUN
- The Noun
- Types of Nouns

🦉 QUICK REMINDER

Put the following sentences on the chalkboard. Then ask students to underline the nouns and to classify them as the names of persons, places, things, or ideas.

1. On the weekends Frank and Joe like to go to the mall.
2. We must take responsibility for saving our planet.
3. Mathematics is difficult for some students.

MEETING INDIVIDUAL NEEDS

LESS-ADVANCED STUDENTS

Have each student name something in the room that could be labeled as either a common or a proper noun. Have students name the thing as a common noun and then as a proper noun. For example, a student might say, "book, *Elements of Writing."*

• To classify nouns as concrete or abstract and then to use each noun in a sentence

EXAMPLE   [1] We have been reading about patriotic heroines in our textbook.
   1. *heroines, textbook*

[1] <u>Rebecca Motte</u> was a great <u>patriot</u>. [2] During the <u>Revolutionary War</u>, British <u>soldiers</u> seized her <u>mansion</u> in <u>South Carolina</u>. [3] <u>General Harry Lee</u> told <u>Motte</u> that the <u>Americans</u> would have to burn her <u>home</u> to smoke out the <u>enemy</u>. [4] <u>Motte</u> supported the <u>plan</u> and was glad to help her <u>country</u>. [5] She even supplied fire <u>arrows</u> and a <u>bow</u> for the <u>attack</u>. [6] But the <u>enemy</u> raised the white <u>flag</u> of <u>surrender</u>, and the <u>house</u> was saved. [7] Afterward, <u>Motte</u> invited <u>soldiers</u> from both <u>sides</u> to <u>dinner</u>.

Proper Nouns and Common Nouns

A *proper noun* names a particular person, place, thing, or idea. It always begins with a capital letter. A *common noun* names any one of a group of persons, places, or things. It is not capitalized.

COMMON NOUNS	PROPER NOUNS
girl	Kay O'Neill
writer	Octavio Paz
country	Panama
monument	Eiffel Tower
team	Atlanta Braves
book	*Tiger Eyes*
religion	Buddhism

EXERCISE 2   **Identifying Common and Proper Nouns**

Identify the nouns in the following paragraph as <u>common</u> or <u>proper</u>. [Note: Some nouns are used more than once.]

EXAMPLE   [1] Mark visited an interesting museum in Colorado last month.
   1. *Mark—proper; museum—common; Colorado—proper; month—common*

[1] <u>Mark</u> and his <u>parents</u> went to the <u>Black American West Museum and Heritage Center</u> in <u>Denver</u>. [2] The

INTEGRATING THE LANGUAGE ARTS

Literature Link. Have students read a poem such as Robert Frost's "Stopping by Woods on a Snowy Evening" that uses only common nouns, and ask students to consider why the poet uses common nouns. Discuss with students how the poem would be different if the poet had used proper nouns to name specific places, people, and things. [The use of proper nouns might make the poem less universal.]

Grammar and Vocabulary. Share with students the fact that some common nouns were originally proper nouns. For example, the word *sandwich* was derived from the name of the man who reputedly came up with the concept of layering bread and meat to make a meal—John Montague, the fourth Earl of Sandwich. Other such common nouns are *cardigan* and *jodphurs,* which both originated from the names of places. Ask interested students to research common nouns that were originally proper nouns and to present their findings to the class.

museum displays many <u>items</u> that <u>cowboys</u> used. [3] These <u>items</u> are from the <u>collection</u> of <u>Paul Stewart</u>, the <u>man</u> who founded the <u>museum</u>. [4] <u>Mark</u> saw <u>saddles</u>, <u>knives</u>, <u>hats</u>, and <u>lariats</u>. [5] He also saw many <u>pictures</u> of African American <u>cowboys</u>. [6] The <u>museum</u> is located in an old <u>house</u> that is listed in the <u>National Register of Historic Places</u>. [7] The <u>house</u> once belonged to <u>Dr. Justina L. Ford</u>. [8] She was the first black woman <u>physician</u> in <u>Colorado</u>. [9] <u>Mark</u> was amazed by all of the old medical <u>instruments</u> in one <u>display</u>. [10] He said he was glad <u>doctors</u> don't use <u>equipment</u> like that any more.

 EXERCISE 3 **Revising Sentences by Using Proper Nouns**

Revise the following sentences by substituting a proper noun for each common noun. You may need to change some other words in each sentence. You may also make up proper names to use.

EXAMPLE **1.** An ambassador visited a local school and spoke about his country.
   1. *Ambassador Rios visited Jackson High School and spoke about Brazil.*

1. That painting is in a famous museum.
2. The police officer directed us to the building on that street.
3. My relatives, who are from a small town, now live in a large city.
4. The librarian asked my classmate to return the book.
5. That newspaper is published daily; this magazine is published weekly.
6. The girl read a poem for the teacher.
7. That state borders on the ocean.
8. The owner of that store visited two countries during a spring month.
9. A man flew to a northern city one day.
10. The mayor visited our school and talked about our city.

ANSWERS
Exercise 3

Proper nouns will vary. Here are some possibilities:

1. The *Mona Lisa* is in the Louvre.
2. Officer Martinez directed us to the Federal Building on Main Street.
3. Aunt Sally and Uncle Bill, who are from Butte, now live in Chicago.
4. Mr. Ellman asked Jerry to return *A Wizard of Atuan.*
5. The *Daily Bugle* is published daily; *Newsweek* is published weekly.
6. Iris read "The Highwayman" for Mr. Hodge.
7. Maine borders on the Atlantic Ocean.
8. Ms. Jensen, owner of Jensen's Dive Shop, visited Vietnam and China during the month of May.
9. Mr. Anoki flew to New York City last Friday.
10. Mayor Arlene James visited Newark Junior High and talked about Newark, New Jersey.

LEP/ESL

Spanish. In Spanish, abstract nouns are always accompanied by definite articles, as in *la democracia* (democracy), *la justicia* (justice), and *la inflación* (inflation). Therefore, students might construct sentences such as "*The* freedom is our goal." Scan students' writing for errors of this type and offer extra practice if necessary.

ANSWERS
Exercise 4

Sentences will vary. Here are some possibilities:

1. concrete—Soy sauce is my favorite sauce.
2. abstract—A spirit of brotherhood among peoples of the earth might bring world peace.
3. concrete—Laughter is contagious.
4. concrete—I like to put ice in my water.
5. abstract—The crowd's excitement mounted as the players were introduced.

REVIEWS A and B
OBJECTIVES
- To identify nouns and to classify them as proper or common
- To use specified kinds of nouns to complete a poem

Concrete Nouns and Abstract Nouns

A *concrete noun* names a person, place, or thing that can be perceived by one or more of the senses (sight, sound, taste, touch, smell). An *abstract noun* names an idea, a feeling, a quality, or a characteristic.

CONCRETE NOUNS	poster, music, beans, heat, Florida
ABSTRACT NOUNS	love, fun, freedom, pride, beauty

EXERCISE 4 **Writing Sentences with Concrete and Abstract Nouns**

Identify each noun in the following list as *concrete* or *abstract*. Then, use each noun in an original sentence.

EXAMPLE **1.** truth
1. *abstract—My mother said I should always tell the truth.*

1. soy sauce   3. laughter   5. excitement
2. brotherhood   4. ice

REVIEW A **Identifying and Classifying Nouns**

Identify the twenty nouns in the following paragraph. Then tell whether each noun is a *common noun* or a *proper noun*. Be sure to capitalize all proper nouns.

EXAMPLE [1] Lillian evanti sang operas in europe, latin america, and africa.
1. *Lillian Evanti—proper noun; operas—common noun; Europe—proper noun; Latin America—proper noun; Africa—proper noun*

[1] Evanti was the first African American woman to sing opera anywhere in the world. [2] Her talent was recognized early, when at the age of four, she gave a solo concert in washington, d.c. [3] As an adult, she performed in a special concert at the white house for president franklin roosevelt and his wife. [4] Evanti also composed a

musical <u>piece</u> titled "<u>*himno latinoamericano*</u>," which was a great <u>success</u>. [5] Her <u>career</u> inspired many other African American <u>singers</u>.

▶ REVIEW B **Using the Different Kinds of Nouns**

Complete the following poem based on this picture. Add common, proper, concrete, or abstract nouns as directed. Choose nouns that you think will help describe or explain the picture. For proper nouns, you'll need to make up names of people and places. Nouns will vary.

Jacob Lawrence, *Strong Man*, gouache on paper, 22 × 17", photo by Chris Eden, Francine Seders Gallery

Hanging Around

Meet my [1] <u>*(common)*</u> , the really amazing,
Truly tremendous [2] <u>*(proper)*</u> , that's who.
You can see what [3] <u>*(abstract)*</u> he gives
His fans who hang on him like glue.
        1. friend **2.** Lou **3.** joy **4.** gym
The walls of his [4] <u>*(concrete)*</u> on [5] <u>*(proper)*</u> **5.** Sycamore Street
Are covered with [6] <u>*(concrete)*</u> that show **6.** posters
The muscled, tussled [7] <u>*(common)*</u> aplenty, **7.** athletes
Who work out there, come rain or come snow.

Eduardo, [8] <u>*(proper)*</u> , and I really enjoy **8.** Janelle
The [9] <u>*(abstract)*</u> of hanging on tight **9.** fun
Way above the [10] <u>*(concrete)*</u> and swinging, **10.** sidewalk
Held up by the muscle man's might.

STUDENTS WITH SPECIAL NEEDS

Students might understand the distinction between abstract nouns and concrete nouns more easily if they associate the terms with familiar words. Have students supply words to fill in the following charts:

CONCRETE NOUNS

PERSON	PLACE	THING

ABSTRACT NOUNS

IDEA	FEELING	CHARACTERISTIC

Students might need some help filling in the abstract nouns.

VISUAL CONNECTIONS
Strong Man

About the Artist. Jacob Lawrence, born in 1917 in Atlantic City, New Jersey, is an African American painter noted for his use of stylized patterns, abstract design, and bright colors. Like *Strong Man*, most of Lawrence's paintings have human subjects. In addition to commissioned illustrations for magazines, Lawrence has painted several historical series, including *Migration of the Negro* and *War*. Some people have seen the strength of the human spirit despite adversity as the theme of many of Lawrence's works.

SEGMENT 3 *(pp. 428–434)*
THE PRONOUN Rule 14b

OBJECTIVES
- To identify pronouns and their antecedents
- To rewrite sentences by replacing nouns with pronouns
- To write a descriptive letter that includes pronouns
- To identify pronouns and their antecedents in an original letter

RESOURCES

THE PRONOUN
- The Pronoun
- Types of Pronouns

QUICK REMINDER
Put the following sentences on the chalkboard. Ask students to identify the pronouns and to tell which words they stand for or refer to.

1. James gave Jill his book.
2. Carlos himself served the meal.
3. These are the books Mei Lee needs.

MEETING
INDIVIDUAL
NEEDS

LEP/ESL

Asian Languages. In English, the single second-person pronoun *you* suffices when talking to any person, deity, animal, or inanimate object. However, many Asian languages, such as Indonesian, Japanese, and Vietnamese, have a collection of nouns and pronouns that mean *you*. Consequently, some of your Asian students might avoid using *you* because it seems impolite or awkward to use the same word to address respected elders, peers, both men and women, and animals. Remind students that in English it is acceptable to use *you* in nearly all situations.

---

428 *The Parts of Speech*

The Pronoun

| 14b. | A *pronoun* is a word used in place of a noun or more than one noun. |

EXAMPLES After Lois borrowed the book, Lois lost the book.
After Lois borrowed the book, **she** lost **it**.

Ask Dan if Dan has done Dan's homework.
Ask Dan if **he** has done **his** homework.

The word that a pronoun stands for (or refers to) is called its *antecedent.*

    antecedent   pronoun   pronoun
EXAMPLE **Frederick,** have **you** turned in **your** report?

Sometimes the antecedent is not stated.

    pronoun
EXAMPLE **It** was hot outside today.

Personal Pronouns

A *personal pronoun* refers to the one speaking (*first person*), the one spoken to (*second person*), or the one spoken about (*third person*).

PERSONAL PRONOUNS		
	SINGULAR	**PLURAL**
First person	I, me, my, mine	we, us, our, ours
Second person	you, your, yours	you, your, yours
Third person	he, him, his, she, her, hers, it, its	they, them, their, theirs

NOTE: Some teachers prefer to call possessive pronouns (such as *my, your,* and *their*) possessive adjectives. Follow your teacher's directions in labeling these words.

Reflexive and Intensive Pronouns

A *reflexive pronoun* refers to the subject and directs the action of the verb back to the subject. An *intensive pronoun* emphasizes a noun or another pronoun.

REFLEXIVE AND INTENSIVE PRONOUNS	
FIRST PERSON	myself, ourselves
SECOND PERSON	yourself, yourselves
THIRD PERSON	himself, herself, itself, themselves

REFLEXIVE   Tara enjoyed **herself** at the party.
The band members prided **themselves** on their performance.
INTENSIVE   I **myself** cooked that delicious dinner.
Did you redecorate the room **yourself?**

 If you are not sure whether a pronoun is reflexive or intensive, use this test. Read the sentence aloud, omitting the pronoun. If the meaning of the sentence stays the same, the pronoun is intensive. If the meaning changes, the pronoun is reflexive.

EXAMPLES   The children enjoyed **themselves** all morning. [Without *themselves,* the sentence doesn't make sense. The pronoun is reflexive.]
Mark repaired the car **himself.** [Without *himself,* the meaning stays the same. The pronoun is intensive.]

Demonstrative Pronouns

A *demonstrative pronoun* points out a person, a place, a thing, or an idea.

Demonstrative Pronouns			
this	that	these	those

LEARNING STYLES

Kinetic Learners. Because kinetic learners learn by doing, you may want to have them do exercises that require physically connecting pronouns with their antecedents. Having students circle pronouns and draw lines to their antecedents may help students understand the relationship between the two parts of speech.

INTEGRATING THE LANGUAGE ARTS

Literature Link. In her poem "I'm Nobody," Emily Dickinson includes pronouns of many different types. Tell students to read the poem and to identify and classify each pronoun. Ask students how the use of the indefinite pronouns *nobody* and *somebody* serves the theme of the poem. [The use of the indefinite pronouns reinforces the poem's theme of anonymity.]

A DIFFERENT APPROACH

Write the following awkwardly written paragraph on the chalkboard:

The boys and girls were excited about the boys' and girls' first day in junior high. The boys and girls got lost and wandered around the huge building. The boys and girls asked some ninth-graders to help the boys and girls find the boys' and girls' way to class.

Ask students to revise the paragraph by replacing the repeated nouns with the appropriate personal pronouns.

COMMON ERROR

Problem. Many students have trouble using the indefinite pronouns *some, any, none, all,* and *most* correctly.

Solution. Remind students that these particular pronouns may be singular or plural, depending on their antecedents. For example, *none* is singular in the sentence "None of the milk is sour." However, *none* is plural in the sentence "None of the grapes are sweet."

---

430   *The Parts of Speech*

EXAMPLES   **This** is the book I told you about.
Are **these** the kinds of plants that bloom at night?

NOTE: Demonstrative pronouns can also be used as adjectives. When they are used in this way, they are called *demonstrative adjectives*.

DEMONSTRATIVE PRONOUN   **Those** are very sturdy shoes.
DEMONSTRATIVE ADJECTIVE   **Those** shoes are very sturdy.

Interrogative Pronouns

An *interrogative pronoun* introduces a question.

Interrogative Pronouns				
what	which	who	whom	whose

EXAMPLES   **What** is the best brand of frozen yogurt?
Who wrote *Barrio Boy*?

Indefinite Pronouns

An *indefinite pronoun* does not refer to a definite person, place, thing, or idea.

Common Indefinite Pronouns				
all	both	few	nobody	other
any	either	more	none	several
anyone	everything	much	no one	some

EXAMPLES   **Both** of the girls forgot their lines.
I would like **some** of that chow mein.

NOTE: Indefinite pronouns can also be used as adjectives.

PRONOUN   **Some** are bored by this movie.
ADJECTIVE   **Some** people are bored by this movie.

Relative Pronouns

A *relative pronoun* introduces a subordinate clause.

Relative Pronouns				
that	which	who	whom	whose

EXAMPLES   Thomas Jefferson, **who** wrote the Declaration of Independence, was our country's third president.

Exercise is one of several methods **that** people use to control their weight.

REFERENCE NOTE: For more information about subordinate clauses, see pages 516–525.

EXERCISE 5   Identifying Pronouns

Identify each <u>pronoun</u> and its <u>antecedent</u> in the following sentences. [Note: A sentence may have more than one pronoun.]

EXAMPLE   **1.** The drama coach said he would postpone the rehearsal.

           1. *he—coach*

                            1. I—Ms. Gaines/you—class

1. "<u>I</u> want <u>you</u> to study," <u>Ms. Gaines</u> said to the <u>class</u>.
2. The <u>firefighter</u> carefully adjusted <u>her</u> oxygen mask.
3. The <u>children</u> made lunch <u>themselves</u>.
4. <u>Jenny</u> and <u>Rosa</u> decided <u>they</u> would get <u>popcorn</u>, but Amy didn't want <u>any</u>.
5. <u>Dad</u> said to let <u>him</u> know when Tamisha came home.

EXERCISE 6   Writing Appropriate Pronouns

Rewrite each sentence, replacing the repeated nouns with pronouns.

1. Put the flowers in water before the flowers' petals droop.   **1.** their
2. The canoe capsized as the canoe neared the shore.   **2.** it

3. The players convinced ˄ the players that ˄ the players would win the game.   **3.** themselves/they
4. Lorraine oiled the bicycle before ˄ Lorraine put ˄ the bicycle in the garage.   **4.** she/it
5. Tim said, "˄ Tim answered all six questions on the quiz."   **5.** I

▷ EXERCISE 7   **Writing Sentences with Pronouns and Antecedents**

Your pen pal in another country has written you to ask about the American pastimes of roller-skating and in-line skating. In your next letter, you send this photograph along with a written description of these types of skating. In your letter, use at least five pronouns. Underline each pronoun and draw an arrow to its antecedent.

EXAMPLE   *The skater slowly increases his speed.*

ANSWERS
Exercise 7

Letters will vary. Suggest that students use several types of pronouns in their letters. For an example of descriptive writing, refer students to **A Student Model** on p. 172.

WRITING APPLICATION
OBJECTIVE
• To use pronouns clearly in a report

WRITING APPLICATION

Using Pronouns Clearly

When you write about people, you nearly always use pronouns for variety. Sometimes, though, pronouns can be confusing.

CONFUSING   Joel wrote to Mark while he was on vacation.
                      [Who was on vacation, Joel or Mark?]
    CLEAR   While Joel was on vacation, **he** wrote to Mark.
                      or
    CLEAR   While Mark was on vacation, Joel wrote to **him**.

When you use a pronoun, make sure that it refers clearly to its antecedent. If the pronoun reference is not clear, change the order of the sentence or reword parts of the sentence.

WRITING ACTIVITY
Your class is creating a bulletin board display for the school's Special People Day. For the display, write a brief report about someone you think is special. Tell why you think so. Be sure that the pronouns you use refer clearly to their antecedents.

Prewriting First, you'll need to select your subject. Someone special—perhaps a friend, a neighbor, or a relative—may come to mind immediately. If not, make a list of the different people you know. Which of these people really stands out? After you choose a subject, freewrite about that person. What makes this person special? Tell what that person has done to earn your respect and admiration.

Writing As you write your first draft, refer to your freewriting notes. In your first paragraph, catch the reader's attention and identify your subject. Your thesis statement should briefly state what is special about your subject. In the rest of your paragraphs, give specific examples that illustrate why the person is special.

WRITING APPLICATION
Remind students that when they use pronouns they will need to modify the structure of their sentences to ensure clarity of reference. For an example of descriptive writing, refer students to **A Student Model** on p. 172. In the model, student Matt Harris describes his dog and tells why his dog is special.

 CRITICAL THINKING
Comparison and Contrast
To be special is to be different or unique. Consequently, to describe how someone is special is to contrast that person with others. Tell students to consider how their special people are different from other people they know. Have students consider whether their special people are more generous, more talented, less critical, or more courageous than others.

GRAMMAR

GRAMMAR

433

PROOFREADING AND PUBLISHING

For the publishing stage, students might want to obtain photographs or create portraits of their subjects to display with their reports.

THE ADJECTIVE
• Adjectives
• Types of Adjectives

 QUICK REMINDER

Put the following sentences on the chalkboard. Ask students to underline the adjectives and to draw arrows to the words they modify.

1. Angry students boycotted the cafeteria.
2. Fifteen horses pranced in the Memorial Day parade.
3. Some cars can go three hundred miles on a full tank of gas.
4. A big, yellow dog barred my way.
5. The school bus was late.

THE ADJECTIVE Rule 14c

OBJECTIVES

• To identify adjectives and the words they modify in a paragraph
• To complete a story by inserting appropriate adjectives
• To identify common and proper adjectives in a paragraph

 Evaluating and Revising Now, read through your report and imagine that you don't know the subject. What do you think about him or her? Does the person sound special? If not, you may want to add or cut details or rearrange your report. Read your report aloud to hear whether it sounds choppy. Combine short, related sentences by inserting prepositional phrases or appositive phrases. For more about combining sentences, see pages 361–371. Look closely at your use of pronouns. Be sure that each pronoun has a clear antecedent. You may need to revise some sentences to make the antecedents clear.

Proofreading and Publishing Check to see that you have spelled and capitalized all proper names correctly. You and your classmates may want to use your reports to make a classroom bulletin board display. If possible, include pictures or drawings of your subjects. You may also wish to send a copy of your report to the person you wrote about.

The Adjective

14c. An *adjective* is a word that modifies a noun or a pronoun.

To *modify* a word means to describe the word or to make its meaning more definite. An adjective modifies a noun or a pronoun by telling *what kind, which one, how much,* or *how many*.

WHAT KIND?	WHICH ONE OR ONES?	HOW MANY OR HOW MUCH?
happy children	seventh grade	full tank
busy dentist	these countries	five dollars
sunny day	any book	no marbles

Sometimes an adjective may come after the word that it modifies.

EXAMPLES **The box is empty.** [The adjective *empty* modifies *box.*]

A woman, kind and helpful, gave us directions. [The adjectives *kind* and *helpful* modify *woman*.]

Articles

The most commonly used adjectives are *a, an,* and *the.* These adjectives are called **articles.** *A* and *an* are called **indefinite articles** because they refer to someone or something in general. *The* is called a **definite article** because it refers to someone or something in particular.

Nouns Used as Adjectives

When a noun modifies another noun or a pronoun, it is considered an adjective.

NOUNS	NOUNS USED AS ADJECTIVES
bean	**bean** soup
spring	**spring** weather
gold	**gold** coin
football	**football** game

LEP/ESL

General Strategies. In English, descriptive adjectives usually precede the nouns they modify, as in *big house.* However in many languages, such as Khmer, Portuguese, Spanish, and Vietnamese, adjectives usually follow the nouns, as in *house big.* Speakers of these languages may have difficulty identifying adjectives in English. Stress the adjective-noun order in English by writing several adjective noun pairs on the chalkboard and by having students read the words aloud and correctly label the parts of speech.

VISUAL CONNECTIONS

Related Expression Skills. Ask students to create cartoons that mention any of the parts of speech discussed in this chapter. Then have the class use the cartoons to make a display for the classroom.

INTEGRATING THE LANGUAGE ARTS

Literature Link. Have students read a story such as "Three Skeleton Key" by George G. Toudouze in which description is used to create a mood. Then discuss with students what mood is created and which adjectives serve to reinforce the mood. For example, in "Three Skeleton Key" description serves to create a mood of horror and suspense. Some of the adjectives that contribute to this mood are *terrifying, nauseating, horrible, foul, maniacal,* and *weird.*

Grammar and Vocabulary. Tell students that well-chosen adjectives can make their writing more colorful and descriptive. Write the following sentences on the chalkboard. Have students replace the underscored adjectives with vivid, descriptive adjectives that do not change the meanings of the sentences.

1. The hot sun had made us thirsty.
2. We saw a cute panda at the zoo.
3. Everybody thinks she is such a nice girl.
4. What a pretty day!

Demonstrative Adjectives

This, that, these, and *those* can be used both as adjectives and as pronouns. When they modify a noun, they are called *demonstrative adjectives.* When they are used alone, they are called *demonstrative pronouns.*

DEMONSTRATIVE ADJECTIVES	Did Jennifer draw **this** picture or **that** one? Let's take **these** sandwiches and **those** apples on our picnic.
DEMONSTRATIVE PRONOUNS	**This** is mine and **that** is his. **These** are much more expensive than **those** are.

☞ **REFERENCE NOTE:** For more information about demonstrative pronouns, see pages 429–430.

▶ EXERCISE 8   **Identifying Adjectives**

Identify the twenty underlined adjectives in the following paragraph and give the noun or pronoun each modifies. Do not include the articles *a, an,* and *the.*

EXAMPLE   **[1]** Why don't you take the local bus on cold days?
            1. *local—bus; cold—days*

[1] On winter afternoons, I sometimes walk home after basketball practice rather than ride on a crowded, noisy bus. [2] I hardly notice the heavy traffic that streams past me. [3] The wet sidewalk glistens in the bright lights from the windows of stores. [4] The stoplights throw green, yellow, and red splashes on the pavement. [5] After I turn the corner away from the busy avenue, I am on a quiet street, where a jolly snowman often stands next to one of the neighborhood houses. [6] At last, I reach my peaceful home. [7] There I am often greeted by my brother and sister. [8] I know they are glad to see me. [9] Delicious smells come from the kitchen. [10] This walk home always makes me feel tired but happy.

▶ EXERCISE 9   **Writing Appropriate Adjectives**

Complete the following story by writing an appropriate adjective to fill each blank.   Adjectives will vary.

EXAMPLE   [1] ____ parks have [2] ____ trails for hikers.
　　　　　1. *National*
　　　　　2. *many*

1. dark **2.** thick **3.** several

The hikers went exploring in the [1] ____ woods. Some-times they had difficulty getting through the [2]____ undergrowth. On [3]____ occasions they almost turned back. Yet they kept going and were rewarded for their [4] ____ effort. During the [5] ____ hike through the woods, they discovered [6]____ kinds of [7]____ animals. In the afternoon the [8] ____ hikers pitched camp in a [9] ____ clearing. They were [10] ____ for supper and rest.

4. huge
5. long
6. ten
7. small
8. tired
9. beautiful **10.** ready

INTEGRATING THE LANGUAGE ARTS

　　Technology Link. Many software programs have thesauruses in addition to spell-check features. If your school has the facilities and the appropriate software for computer-assisted instruction, encourage students to use the thesaurus to find synonyms for stale, overused adjectives. Caution students to check the meanings of words in a dictionary to avoid using a word with inappropriate connotations.

Proper Adjectives

A *proper adjective* is formed from a proper noun.

PROPER NOUNS	PROPER ADJECTIVES
Thanksgiving	**Thanksgiving** dinner
Catholicism	**Catholic** priest
Middle East	**Middle Eastern** country
Africa	**African** continent

Notice that a proper adjective, like a proper noun, always begins with a capital letter.

▶ EXERCISE 10   **Identifying Common and Proper Adjectives**

Identify the ten adjectives in the following paragraph. Then tell whether each is a <u>*common*</u> or a <u>*proper*</u> adjective. Do not include the articles *a, an,* and *the.*

438 *The Parts of Speech*

EXAMPLE   [1] We have been studying how various animals protect themselves.
   1. *various—common*

[1] <u>Many</u> <u>small</u> animals defend themselves in <u>clever</u> ways. [2] For example, <u>South American</u> armadillos wear suits of armor that consist of <u>small</u>, <u>bony</u> scales. [3] As you can see from the photograph, armadillos seem <u>delicate</u>, with their <u>narrow</u> faces. [4] However, their <u>tough</u> armor protects them well. [5] Likewise, the <u>Asian</u> anteater has scales that overlap like the shingles on a roof.

armadillos

▶ EXERCISE 11   **Using Proper Adjectives in Sentences**

Change the following proper nouns into proper adjectives. Then use each proper adjective in a sentence. Use a dictionary to help you spell the adjectives.

EXAMPLE   **1.** Spain
   1. *Spanish—Those Peace Corps volunteers take Spanish lessons every Tuesday.*

1. Mexico   3. Memorial Day   5. Congress
2. Hawaii   4. Korea

👁 **VISUAL CONNECTIONS**
Ideas for Writing. Ask students to think of other small animals that defend themselves in clever or unusual ways. [The porcupine, the opossum, and the skunk are good examples.] Have each student (1) choose an animal, (2) find information about it, and (3) write a short informative paragraph about the animal's method of self-defense. [Porcupines have sharp spines, opossums feign death, and skunks spray a foul-smelling liquid.]

ANSWERS
Exercise 11

Sentences will vary. Here are some possibilities:

1. Mexican—Mexican food is sometimes hot and spicy.

2. Hawaiian—The Hawaiian landscape is lush with tropical plants and trees.

3. Memorial Day—The Memorial Day parade featured marching bands playing patriotic music.

4. Korean—Professor Park showed us photographs of the Korean countryside.

5. Congressional—Tomorrow, candidates from the Sixth Congressional District will debate the issues of concern to the voters.

PICTURE THIS

You're a mobile reporter for a radio station, and you travel around looking for interesting stories. You just received a call about something strange happening at the beach. When you arrive, this is the amazing scene you see! Of course, you immediately call the station and start a live broadcast from the beach. Write at least five sentences that you would use in your broadcast. In your sentences, use a variety of adjectives that appeal to the senses. Remember, your radio listeners have only your words to help them visualize this scene.

Subject: unusual beach scene
Audience: radio listeners
Purpose: to inform

Kenny Scharf, *Feliz a Praia*, 1983–84, Acrylic and Spraypaint on Canvas, 6'10½" × 12'2", Collection: Mr. Tony Shafrazi, NY, Photo: Ivan Dalla Tana

GRAMMAR

PICTURE THIS

As a prewriting activity, students could work in groups to discuss what they see in the beach scene and to brainstorm about ways to appeal to a radio audience. For an example of descriptive writing that appeals to the senses, refer students to **A Student Model** on p. 172.

VISUAL CONNECTIONS
Feliz a Praia

Related Expression Skills. Give students the opportunity to present the radio broadcasts they wrote for the **Picture This** activity. You may want to obtain a recording of Orson Wells' radio broadcast of an adaptation of the science fiction novel *War of the Worlds*. Listening to the recording will give students a better idea of how a radio broadcast of such a strange event might sound.

GRAMMAR

COOPERATIVE LEARNING
Divide the class into groups of four, and tell each group to generate a list of four words that can be used as both nouns and adjectives. Have groups write sentences using each word as a noun once and as an adjective once. Here is an example using the word *red:*

Red is my favorite color.
Cherie has three *red* sweaters.

ADVANCED STUDENTS
There are a few words that can be used as nouns, adjectives, and verbs. Challenge students to generate as many such words as possible (individually or in small groups). You could ask students to write sentences that use each of their words as all three parts of speech, or you could simply ask students to share their lists with the class. [Possibilities include *black, calm, cut, marble, quiet, silver, snap,* and *yellow.*]

440 *The Parts of Speech*

Changing Parts of Speech

The way that a word is used in a sentence determines what part of speech it is. Some words may be used as nouns or as adjectives.

NOUN	The helmet is made of **steel.**
ADJECTIVE	It is a **steel** helmet.

Some words may be used as pronouns or as adjectives.

PRONOUN	**That** is a surprise.
ADJECTIVE	**That** problem is difficult.

REVIEW C **Identifying Nouns, Pronouns, and Adjectives**

Identify all of the <u>nouns,</u> [pronouns], and <u>adjectives</u> in the following paragraph. Do not include the articles *a, an,* and *the.*

EXAMPLE　**1.** We walked along the empty beach at sundown.

　　　1. *We—pronoun; empty—adjective; beach—noun; sundown—noun*

[1] When the <u>tide</u> comes in, [it] brings a <u>variety</u> of <u>interesting</u> <u>items</u> from the <u>sea</u>. [2] When [it] ebbs, [it] leaves behind <u>wonderful</u> <u>treasures</u> for the <u>watchful</u> <u>beachcombers</u>. [3] <u>Few</u> <u>creatures</u> live here, but [you] almost certainly will find <u>several</u> <u>animals</u> if [you] try. [4] [Some] live in <u>shallow</u> <u>burrows</u> under the <u>wet</u> <u>sand</u> and emerge in the <u>cool</u> <u>evening</u> to dine on <u>bits</u> of <u>plants</u> and <u>other</u> <u>matter</u>. [5] A <u>number</u> of <u>different</u> <u>species</u> of <u>beetle</u> like <u>this</u> <u>part</u> of the <u>beach</u>. [6] Around [them] [you] can find <u>bristly</u> <u>flies</u> and <u>tiny</u> <u>worms</u>. [7] [You] might also come across <u>old</u> <u>pieces</u> of <u>wood</u> with <u>round</u> <u>holes</u> and <u>tunnels</u> in [them]. [8] <u>These</u> <u>holes</u> are produced by <u>shipworms</u>. [9] If [you] watch the <u>shoreline</u> carefully, [you] will see <u>many</u> <u>signs</u> of <u>life</u> that <u>casual</u> <u>strollers</u> miss. [10] <u>Low</u> <u>tide</u> is a <u>marvelous</u> <u>time</u> to search along the <u>shore</u>.

REVIEW: POSTTESTS 1 and 2

OBJECTIVES

- To identify nouns, pronouns, and adjectives in paragraphs
- To write sentences that use the same words as different parts of speech

"Now! ... *That* should clear up a few things around here!"

Review: Posttest 1

Identifying Nouns, Pronouns, and Adjectives

Identify each italicized word in the following paragraphs as a <u>*noun,*</u> a <u>*pronoun,*</u> or an <u>*adjective.*</u>

EXAMPLE   The [1] *achievements* of the [2] *native* peoples of
North America have sometimes been overlooked.
1. *noun*
2. *adjective*

Recent [1]<u>*studies*</u> show that the Winnebago people developed a [2] <u>*calendar*</u> based on careful observation of the [3] <u>*heavens.*</u>

An [4]<u>*archaeologist*</u> has found that the markings on an old [5] <u>*calendar*</u> stick are the precise records of a [6] <u>*lunar*</u> year and a solar year. These records are remarkably accurate, considering that at the time the [7] <u>*Winnebagos*</u> had neither a [8] <u>*written*</u> language nor a [9] <u>*mathematical*</u> system.

GRAMMAR

ADVANCED STUDENTS

Make **Posttest 2** both more interesting and more challenging for students by involving their creativity. Have each student write a short story in which five words are used as both nouns and adjectives. Students could use the five words from the exercise or choose five other words, provided the words can be used as both nouns and adjectives.

ANSWERS

Review: Posttest 2

Sentences will vary. Here are some possibilities:

1. This is a delicious casserole. — pronoun
   This casserole is delicious. — adjective

2. I would like a new radio for my birthday. — noun
   Grandma prefers listening to radio programs. — adjective

3. Only a few know what really happened that fateful day. — pronoun
   Few people know what really happened that fateful day. — adjective

4. The light in the eastern sky was faint when Lupe left for work. — noun
   Lupe's doctor told her to do only light work for three weeks. — adjective

5. April is a glorious month. — noun
   April days are usually sunny and mild. — adjective

---

[10] _The_ calendar stick is a carved [11] _hickory_ branch with [12] _four_ sides. [13]**[**_If_**]**is worn along the [14]_edges_ and shows other signs of frequent use. A [15] _similar_ stick appears in a portrait of an early chief of the Winnebagos. In it, the chief

16. [or his] holds a calendar stick in [16]**[**_his_**]**right hand. [17]**[**_Our_**]**current

17. [or Our] theory is that the chief went out at [18] _sunrise_ and sunset to observe the sun and the moon. [19]**[**_He_**]**then marked on the stick what he saw. According to one researcher, this is the [20] _first_ indication that native North American peoples recorded the year day by day.

Review: Posttest 2

Using Words as Different Parts of Speech

Write ten sentences using each of the following words first as a noun or pronoun and then as an adjective. Underline the word and give its part of speech after the sentence.

EXAMPLE **1.** silk
        1. _Leonie's scarf is made of silk.—noun_
        May I borrow your silk scarf?—adjective

        2. that
        2. _That is a silly idea!—pronoun_
        That idea is very silly!—adjective

1. this   **2.** radio   **3.** few   **4.** light   **5.** April

OBJECTIVE

- To identify words or phrases in paragraphs as either verbs, adverbs, prepositions, conjunctions, or interjections

THE PARTS OF SPEECH
- Chapter Review Form A
- Chapter Review Form B
- Assessment Portfolio
  Grammar Pretest
  Grammar Mastery Test 1
  Grammar Mastery Test 2

15 THE PARTS OF SPEECH

Verb, Adverb, Preposition, Conjunction, Interjection

Diagnostic Test

Identifying Verbs, Adverbs, Prepositions, Conjunctions, and Interjections

Identify each numbered, italicized word or word group in the following paragraphs as a *verb*, an *adverb*, a *preposition*, a *conjunction*, or an *interjection*.

EXAMPLES   [1] *Tomorrow,* we [2] *will order* equipment [3] *for* our summer camping trip.

     1. *adverb*
     2. *verb*
     3. *preposition*

                              1. v.

Have you ever [1]*hiked* into the wilderness [2]*with* a **2.** prep.
pack on your back and [3]*camped* under the stars? Back- **3.** v.
packing [4]*was* once popular mainly with hardy moun- **4.** v.
taineers, [5]*but* now almost anyone who loves the **5.** conj.
outdoors [6]*can become* a backpacker. **6.** v.

CHAPTER OVERVIEW

This chapter teaches students to recognize and understand the functions of verbs, adverbs, prepositions, conjunctions, and interjections. It can be referenced when teaching any of the writing chapters but will be of special help with **Chapter 11**, which deals specifically with sentence construction.

USING THE DIAGNOSTIC TEST

You may wish to use the **Diagnostic Test** to gauge students' familiarity with verbs, adverbs, prepositions, conjunctions, and interjections. You may also wish to evaluate students' writing to determine whether students use these five parts of speech proficiently.

If students are having difficulty using these parts of speech in their writing, you can use the **Diagnostic Test** to pinpoint error patterns and specific strengths and weaknesses.

GRAMMAR

THE VERB Rule 15a

OBJECTIVES

- To identify action verbs in sentences
- To write a letter that includes action verbs
- To identify verbs in sentences as transitive or intransitive
- To write sentences that include both transitive and intransitive verbs

---

7. v.   First, however, you [7] *must be* able to carry a heavy
8. prep.   pack long distances [8] *over* mountain trails. To get in
9. adv.   shape, start with short walks and [9] *gradually* increase
10. conj. them to several miles. Doing leg exercises [10] *and* going on
11. adv.   organized hikes can [11] *further* help build your strength.
12. prep. [12] *After* a few hikes, you [13] *should be* ready.
13. v.   **14.** itj. [14] *Oh*, you [15] *may be thinking*, what equipment and
15. v.   food should I take? Write [16] *to* the International Back-
16. prep. packers Association [17] *for* a checklist. The first item on
17. prep. the list will [18] *usually* be shoes with rubber [19] *or* synthetic
18. adv.   soles. The second will [20] *certainly* be a sturdy backpack.
19. conj. **20.** adv.

QUICK REMINDER

Write the following sentence on the chalkboard and have students copy it. Then tell students to identify an action verb, a linking verb, a verb phrase, and a helping verb.

The pony seems frightened and is running toward the forest. [action verb — *is running;* linking verb — *seems;* verb phrase — *is running;* helping verb — *is*]

MEETING INDIVIDUAL NEEDS

STUDENTS WITH SPECIAL NEEDS

Because this segment includes many terms, you may want to repeat important ideas frequently and begin each lesson with a summary of material covered the previous day. This repetition will help learning disabled students who have poor recall.

The Verb

15a. A *verb* is a word that expresses an action or a state of being.

EXAMPLES We **celebrated** the Chinese New Year yesterday.
The holiday **is** usually in February.

Action Verbs

(1) An *action verb* is a verb that expresses physical or mental action.

EXAMPLES The owls **hooted** all night.
Gloria **plays** with the children.
She **thought** about the problem.
I **believe** you.
Finish your work by three o'clock, please.

▶ EXERCISE 1 **Identifying Action Verbs**

Identify the <u>action verb</u> in each of the following sentences.

EXAMPLE **1.** I saw that movie last week.
1. *saw*

• To identify linking verbs in sentences
• To identify verbs in sentences and to label them as either action verbs or linking verbs
• To write sentences that include action verbs and linking verbs
• To identify verb phrases and helping verbs in sentences
• To write sentences that include verb phrases

The Verb **445**

15a

1. For a science project, Elena <u>built</u> a sundial.
2. Mr. Santos carefully <u>explained</u> the problem again.
3. I <u>enjoy</u> soccer more than any other sport.
4. This waterfall <u>drops</u> two hundred feet.
5. Mike's bicycle <u>skidded</u> on the pavement.
6. Mrs. Karras <u>showed</u> us how to make stuffed grape leaves.
7. <u>Mix</u> the ingredients slowly.
8. The heavy traffic <u>delayed</u> us.
9. For the Jewish holiday of Purim, Rachel <u>gave</u> a costume party
10. The early Aztecs <u>worshiped</u> the sun.

▶ EXERCISE 2   **Writing Action Verbs**

Your pen pal in another country wants to know what students at your school do at school dances. To explain, you send this photograph to your pen pal. In addition, you write a letter describing the things that people do at school dances. In your letter, use at least ten action verbs. Include at least three verbs that express actions that can't be seen. Then underline the action verbs in your letter.

EXAMPLES   **1.** *Everyone* <u>*dances*</u> *to the fast songs.*
2. *Darnell and I sometimes* <u>*invite*</u> *the chaperone to dance.*

ANSWERS
Exercise 2

Letters will vary. Follow the guidelines in the textbook for evaluating answers: A minimum of ten action verbs should appear in each letter, and three of these should name actions that can't be seen. All action verbs in the letters should be underlined.

EXERCISE 2

   Teaching Note. For a variety of reasons (school policy, personal preference, or parental rules, for example) students might not have any personal experience of school dances to draw on for **Exercise 2.** You may wish to give students the option of writing a letter about a sporting event, a musical concert, or a family celebration. If students write on an alternative topic, allow them extra time to brainstorm ideas because they will not have the assistance of a photograph.

LEARNING STYLES

Kinetic and Visual Learners. Write the following sentences on the chalkboard:

1. Melanie ate a potato.
2. Hector and Tom are reading.
3. They painted the house blue.
4. Did you carry his suitcase?
5. My plant grows quickly.

Have students come to the chalkboard and draw arrows from the verbs in the sentences to the persons or things that receive the actions of the verbs. Students will find that this can be done only for sentences 1, 3, and 4. Tell students that sentences 1, 3, and 4 contain transitive verbs, while sentences 2 and 5 contain intransitive verbs.

Transitive and Intransitive Verbs

(2) A *transitive verb* is an action verb that expresses an action directed toward a person or thing.

EXAMPLES   Derrick **greeted** the visitors. [The action of *greeted* is directed toward *visitors.*]
             Felicia **painted** her room. [The action of *painted* is directed toward *room.*]

With transitive verbs, the action passes from the doer—the subject—to the receiver of the action. Words that receive the action of a transitive verb are called *objects.*

☞ **REFERENCE NOTE:** For more information about objects and their uses in sentences, see pages 474–477.

An *intransitive verb* expresses action (or tells something about the subject) without passing the action to a receiver.

EXAMPLES   The train **stopped.**
             Last night we **ate** on the patio.

A verb may be transitive in one sentence and intransitive in another.

EXAMPLES   The children **play** checkers. [transitive]
             The children **play** quietly. [intransitive]

             Mr. Lopez **is baking** bread. [transitive]
             Mr. Lopez **is baking** this afternoon. [intransitive]

▶ EXERCISE 3   **Identifying Transitive and Intransitive Verbs**

In each of the following sentences, identify the <u>italicized action verb</u> as <u>*transitive*</u> or <u>*intransitive*</u>.

EXAMPLE   **1.** She *runs* early in the morning.
            1. *intransitive*

1. If you do different kinds of exercises, you <u>*are*</u> <u>*exercising*</u> in the correct way.   **1.** itr.

2. When you exercise to improve endurance, flexibility, and strength, your body *develops*.   **2.** itr.
3. Aerobic exercise *builds* endurance.   **3.** tr.
4. When you *walk* quickly, you do aerobic exercise.   **4.** itr.
5. Many people *attend* classes in aerobic dancing.   **5.** tr.
6. They *enjoy* the fun of exercising to music.   **6.** tr.
7. Exercises that *improve* flexibility require you to bend and stretch.   **7.** tr.
8. *Perform* these exercises slowly for maximum benefit.   **8.** tr.
9. Through isometric and isotonic exercises, your muscle strength *increases*.   **9.** itr.
10. These exercises *contract* your muscles.   **10.** tr.

▶ EXERCISE 4 **Writing Sentences with Transitive and Intransitive Verbs**

For each verb given below, write two sentences. In one sentence, use the verb as a *transitive* verb and underline its object. In the other, use the verb as an *intransitive* verb. You may use different tenses of the verb.

EXAMPLE **1.** write
  1. *Alex is writing a research report. (transitive)*
  Alex writes in his journal every day.
  (intransitive)

1. fly   **2.** leave   **3.** return   **4.** draw   **5.** drive

Linking Verbs

(3) A **linking verb** is a verb that expresses a state of being. A linking verb connects the subject of a sentence with a word in the predicate that explains or describes the subject.

EXAMPLES **Howard Rollins is an actor.** [The verb *is* connects *actor* with the subject *Howard Rollins.*]
  The children remained quiet during the puppet show. [The verb *remained* links *quiet* with the subject *children.*]

ANSWERS
Exercise 4
Sentences will vary. Here are some possibilities:

1. I flew a kite.
  The kite flew overhead.

2. She left the club.
  We left yesterday.

3. Sharika returns library books.
  Sharika returns from her trip tomorrow.

4. Draw a monster.
  You draw very well.

5. Gabriel drives a motorcycle.
  Gabriel drove here.

CRITICAL THINKING
Analysis and Synthesis

You could integrate the study of linking verbs with a lesson on figurative language. Tell students that the linking verb *to be* is often used to create metaphors. Then write the following sentences on the chalkboard:

1. He has bright eyes.
2. His eyes are small suns.

Ask students which sentence they think is more descriptive. Tell them that the second sentence is an example of the type of figurative language called a metaphor and that writers often use metaphors to create vivid images.

Challenge students to create two original metaphors with the linking verb *to be.*

Linking Verbs Formed from the Verb *Be*		
am	has been	may be
is	have been	might be
are	had been	can be
was	will be	should be
were	shall be	would have been

Other Linking Verbs			
appear	grow	seem	stay
become	look	smell	taste
feel	remain	sound	turn

Some words may be either action verbs or linking verbs, depending on how they are used.

ACTION   Amy **looked** through the telescope.
LINKING   Amy **looked** pale. [The verb links *pale* with the subject *Amy.*]

ACTION   **Remain** in your seats until the bell rings.
LINKING   **Remain** quiet. [The verb links *quiet* with the understood subject *you.*].

☞ **REFERENCE NOTE:** For more about understood subjects in imperative sentences, see pages 415–416.

▶ EXERCISE 5   **Identifying Linking Verbs**

Identify the <u>linking verb</u> in each sentence in the following paragraphs.

EXAMPLE   [1] A radio station can be the voice of a community.
         1. *can be*

[1] "Good morning, listeners! This <u>is</u> Roberto Martínez, your weather forecaster. [2] Unfortunately, the forecast <u>looks</u> bad today. [3] Outside the window here at Station

WOLF, the skies <u>appear</u> cloudy. [4] It certainly <u>felt</u> rainy earlier this morning. [5] And, according to the latest information, it <u>should be</u> a damp, drizzly day with an 85 percent chance of rainfall. [6] Now, for the latest scores, our sportscaster this morning <u>is</u> Marta Segal."

[7] "Well, Roberto, things <u>have been</u> quiet here around Arlington for the past few days. [8] But <u>stay</u> alert for sports action tonight. [9] It <u>should be</u> a great game between our own Arlington Angels and the visiting Jackson City Dodgers. [10] The team <u>looked</u> great at practice today, and I predict a hometown victory."

 EXERCISE 6   **Identifying Action Verbs and Linking Verbs**

Identify the <u>verb</u> in each of the following sentences. Then label each verb as either an *action <u>verb</u>* or a *linking <u>verb</u>*. If the verb is a linking verb, give the two <u>words that it connects</u>.

EXAMPLES   **1.** We sent our dog to obedience school.
1. *sent—action verb*

2. Some breeds are extremely nervous.
2. *are—linking verb; breeds, nervous*

1. <u>Everyone</u> <u>felt</u> <u>sorry</u> about the misunderstanding.   **1.** l.v.
2. In daylight, this <u>sweater</u> <u>looks</u> <u>blue</u>.   **2.** l.v.
3. The temperature <u>plunged</u> to almost ten degrees below zero.   **3.** a.v.
4. The museum <u>exhibited</u> Inuit sculptures of whales and seals.   **4.** a.v.
5. Loretta <u>felt</u> her way carefully through the dark, quiet room.   **5.** a.v.
6. The <u>city</u> almost always <u>smells</u> <u>musty</u> after a heavy summer storm.   **6.** l.v.
7. <u>Dakar</u> <u>is</u> the <u>capital</u> of Senegal.   **7.** l.v.
8. The firefighter cautiously <u>smelled</u> the burned rags.   **8.** a.v.
9. <u>Antonia Novello</u> <u>is</u> the <u>Surgeon General</u> of the United States.   **9.** l.v.
10. <u>They</u> <u>looked</u> <u>handsome</u> in their party clothes.   **10.** l.v.

TIMESAVER
Because **Exercises 6** and **7** both give students practice identifying action verbs and linking verbs, you may want to have students complete only one of the exercises, or you could use one for guided practice and one for independent practice.

EXERCISE 6

Teaching Note. The ninth sentence in this exercise contains two compound nouns. Before they begin the exercise, you may want to remind students of the existence of compound nouns.

Give students examples of compound nouns, such as *Jane Smith* and *prime minister,* and tell them to expect to find compound nouns in **Exercise 6.**

INTEGRATING THE LANGUAGE ARTS

Literature Link. Have students read the poem "Living Tenderly," by May Swenson, and ask them to identify its speaker. Then direct students' attention to the first four lines of the poem, and point out that in the first and third lines the verbs are understood. Ask students what they think the understood verbs might be—action verbs or linking verbs. Then ask students what effect the absence of verbs has on the meaning of those lines of the poem. [Responses will vary. Students might say that, without verbs between them, the subjects of the lines and the words that describe them seem more closely connected.]

ANSWERS
Exercise 8

Sentences will vary. Students' sentences should be based on the photographs. Five of the sentences should contain action verbs and five should contain linking verbs. All verbs should be underlined. You could ask students to underline action verbs once and linking verbs twice.

For an example of descriptive writing, refer students to **A Student Model** on page 172.

 EXERCISE 7

Identifying Action Verbs and Linking Verbs

Identify the twenty verbs in the following paragraphs. Then label each verb as either an *action verb* or a *linking verb*.

EXAMPLE   [1] I always enjoy field trips.
        1. *enjoy—action verb*

[1] Last spring, our class <u>visited</u> the Hayden Planetarium. [2] It <u>is</u> a wonderful place, full of amazing sights. [3] We <u>wandered</u> through the various displays and <u>saw</u> a collection of fascinating exhibits. [4] One <u>showed</u> a space vehicle. [5] Another <u>displayed</u> a thirty-four-ton meteorite. [6] When this meteorite <u>fell</u> to earth many years ago, it <u>made</u> a huge crater.

[7] After lunch, we <u>went</u> to the show in the observatory. [8] As the room <u>became</u> darker, the picture of a galaxy <u>appeared</u> on the dome above us. [9] The lecturer <u>said</u> that the galaxy <u>is</u> so far away from here that its light <u>reaches</u> us centuries after its first appearance. [10] When we <u>look</u> at such stars, we actually <u>see</u> the ancient past! [11] I still <u>feel</u> a little strange when I <u>think</u> about the galaxy and its history. [12] We really <u>live</u> in a universe that <u>is</u> full of wonders.

EXERCISE 8

Writing Sentences with Action Verbs and Linking Verbs

The circus is in town! Unfortunately, your best friend is sick and can't go. So that your friend won't miss out entirely, you take some photographs. Using the pictures on the next page and your imagination, write ten sentences describing the circus to your friend. In five of the sentences, use action verbs. In the other five, use linking verbs. Underline each verb that you use.

EXAMPLES   **1.** *The trapeze artist <u>leaps</u> from the trapeze into the air.*
        2. *He probably <u>feels</u> nervous, but he certainly <u>looks</u> brave!*

451 The Verb **451**

Helping Verbs

A *verb phrase* contains one main verb and one or more helping verbs.

EXAMPLES   Many people in Africa **can speak** more than one language.
Kansas **has been named** the Sunflower State.
The ball **should have been caught** by the nearest player.

(4) A *helping verb* helps the main verb to express action or a state of being.

EXAMPLES   **can** speak
has been named
should have been caught

Helping Verbs				
am	be	do	might	shall
is	been	does	must	should
are	has	did	can	will
was	have	may	could	would
were	had			

MEETING INDIVIDUAL NEEDS

LESS-ADVANCED STUDENTS

Helping verbs and verb phrases might be confusing to students. Provide examples of helping verbs that can also be main verbs—either action verbs or linking verbs (have, was). Point out the words on the **Helping Verbs** chart that are different forms of the same verb.

LEP/ESL

Spanish. In Spanish, helping verbs are not used as frequently as they are in English. Consequently, students might need extra help identifying and using helping verbs. You may want to have students write sentences using each of the helping verbs listed in the chart.

451

A DIFFERENT APPROACH

To review this segment on verbs, create a humorous or exciting story that uses all five types of verbs (action, transitive, intransitive, linking, and helping) many times, but instead of writing these words, leave blanks labeled according to the type of verb needed to fill them in.

As a class, have students supply the correct type of verb for each blank in the story. Encourage students to make interesting word choices. When every blank is filled, read the story aloud.

For homework, you could have students create their own stories, leave blanks for the five types of verbs, and label the blanks as you did.

ANSWERS
Exercise 10

Sentences will vary. At least five of students' sentences should contain verb phrases. Each verb phrase should be underlined and each helping verb should be circled.

452

Sometimes a verb phrase is interrupted by another part of speech, such as an adverb or a pronoun.

EXAMPLES   Ken **does** not **have** a new desk.
Our school **has** always **held** a victory celebration.
Did you **hear** César Chávez's speech?

EXERCISE 9 **Identifying Verb Phrases and Helping Verbs**

Identify the verb phrases in the following paragraphs. Underline the (helping verbs).

EXAMPLE [1] **You can recognize redwoods and sequoias by their bark.**
    1. *can recognize*

[1] (Have) you ever visited Redwood National Park? [2] The giant trees there (can) be an awesome sight. [3] For centuries, these trees (have) been an important part of the environment of the northwest United States. [4] Surely, these rare trees (must be) saved for future generations.

[5] More than 85 percent of the original redwood forest (has been) destroyed. [6] Because of this, the survival of the forest (is being) threatened. [7] With proper planning years ago, more of the forest (might) already (have been) saved. [8] Unfortunately, redwood forests (are) still shrinking rapidly. [9] According to some scientists, all forests outside the park (will have) disappeared by the year 2000. [10] However, according to other experts, the redwood forests (can) still (be) saved!

EXERCISE 10 **Writing Sentences with Verb Phrases**

You are a member of the city planning board. Your job is to figure out what kind of traffic control is needed at the busy street corner shown on the next page. Does the intersection require stoplights, stop signs, or a traffic police officer? After you investigate the street corner, you will make your recommendation to the rest of the planning board. Using this photograph, make some notes about what is happening at the intersection. Write at least five sentences containing verb phrases. Then, underline each verb phrase and circle the helping verb.

EXAMPLE   **1.** *The number of crosswalks (can) confuse people.*

▶ REVIEW A   **Identifying Action Verbs and Linking Verbs**

Identify the verbs in the following paragraphs. Then, label each verb as an *action verb* or a *linking verb*. [Note: A sentence may contain more than one verb.]

EXAMPLE   **[1] Have you ever seen a play in Spanish?**
          1. *Have seen—action verb*

[1] The Puerto Rican Traveling Theatre <u>presents</u> plays about Hispanic life in the United States. [2] Over the past twenty years, this group <u>has become</u> a leader in Hispanic theater. [3] Sometimes, a production <u>has</u> two casts—one that <u>performs</u> in English and one that <u>speaks</u> in Spanish. [4] In this way, speakers of both languages <u>can enjoy</u> the play.

[5] In recent years many young Hispanic playwrights, directors, and actors <u>have begun</u> their careers at the Traveling Theatre. [6] Some <u>became</u> well-known at the Puerto Rican Traveling Theatre and then <u>moved</u> on to

STUDENTS WITH SPECIAL NEEDS

   Students with learning disabilities might be overwhelmed by the dense text of **Review A.** To make this exercise less threatening, reproduce the sentences and leave spaces between each of them so that students can focus on one sentence at a time.

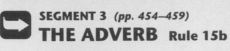

OBJECTIVES

- To identify adverbs and the words they modify in sentences and in paragraphs
- To supply adverbs to complete a paragraph
- To write a brief informative description that includes adverbs

454 *The Parts of Speech*

Broadway or Hollywood. [7] Others <u>remain</u> happy at the Traveling Theatre, where they <u>enjoy</u> the warm, supportive atmosphere.

[8] Each production by the Traveling Theatre <u>has</u> its own style. [9] Some shows <u>are</u> musicals, full of song and dance, while other plays <u>seem</u> more serious. [10] Light or serious, Puerto Rican Traveling Theatre productions <u>present</u> a lively picture of Hispanic life today.

The Adverb

15b. An *adverb* is a word that modifies a verb, an adjective, or another adverb.

An adverb answers the following questions:

Where?	How often?	To what extent?
When?	*or*	*or*
How?	How long?	How much?

EXAMPLES **The sprinter ran swiftly.** [*Swiftly* is an adverb modifying the verb *ran;* it tells *how.*]

Jolene was comforting a very small child. [*Very* is an adverb modifying the adjective *small;* it tells *to what extent.*]

The fire blazed too wildly for anyone to enter. [*Too* is an adverb modifying the adverb *wildly;* it tells *to what extent. Wildly* is an adverb modifying the verb *blazed;* it tells *how.*]

Dad often quotes from Bishop Desmond Tutu's speech. [*Often* is an adverb modifying the verb *quotes;* it tells *how often.*]

Put the apples there, and we'll eat them later. [*There* is an adverb modifying the verb *put;* it tells *where. Later* is an adverb modifying the verb *eat;* it tells *when.*]

QUICK REMINDER

Write the following paragraph on the chalkboard and have students identify the adverb in each sentence:

Detergent breaks down *slowly* in the environment. It *often* contaminates the air and water. Vinegar and baking soda clean *effectively* and do not harm the environment.

WORDS OFTEN USED AS ADVERBS	
Where?	away, here, inside, there, up
When?	ago, later, now, soon, then
How?	clearly, easily, quietly, slowly
How often? or *How long?*	always, usually, continuously, never, forever, briefly
To what extent? or *How much?*	almost, so, too, more, least, extremely, quite

NOTE: The word *not* is nearly always used as an adverb to modify a verb. When *not* is part of a contraction, as in *hadn't, aren't,* and *didn't,* the *–n't* is still an adverb and is not part of the verb.

Adverbs and Adjectives

Many adverbs end in *–ly.* These adverbs are formed by adding *–ly* to adjectives.

> **Adjective + –ly = Adverb**
> clear   + –ly = clearly
> quiet   + –ly = quietly

However, some words ending in *–ly* are used as adjectives.

> **Adjectives Ending in –ly**
> daily   friendly   lonely
> early   kindly   timely

If you aren't sure whether a word is an adjective or an adverb, ask yourself what it modifies. If a word modifies a noun or a pronoun, it is an adjective.

MEETING **INDIVIDUAL** NEEDS

LEP/ESL

General Strategies. You may discover that students use the adverbs *very* and *too* interchangeably. Explain that *very* means extremely, whereas *too* means excessively. You could offer extra practice to help students distinguish between these two adverbs. Work with students to complete the following sentences by supplying either *very* + an adjective or *too* + an adjective:

1. Pepperoni pizza is ____.
2. I find English class ____.
3. My best friend is ____.
4. Rock music is ____.
5. Summer weather can be ____.

COOPERATIVE LEARNING
Explain to students that in addition to words that end in *–ly,* there are other words that can be used both as adjectives and as adverbs. For example, the words *hard, high, late,* and *deep* can be used as both adjectives and adverbs. Have students work in groups of three or four and hold a contest to see which group can generate the longest list of words that can be used both as adjectives and as adverbs.

COOPERATIVE LEARNING

Divide the class into an even number of small groups and assign each group an equal number of words that can be used as both adverbs and adjectives.

Have each group work to generate two sentences for each word—one using the word as an adjective and one using the word as an adverb. Then have groups exchange sentences and label words as adjectives or adverbs.

COMMON ERROR

Problem. Students searching for adverbs may be confused by prepositional phrases.

Solution. Tell students that even though prepositional phrases can answer the same questions as adverbs, they can only be adverbs if they use only one word to answer each question.

EXAMPLES She gave us a **friendly** hello. [*Friendly* modifies the noun *hello,* so it is an adjective.]
Were you **lonely** yesterday? [The word *lonely* modifies the pronoun *you,* so it is an adjective.]

☞ REFERENCE NOTE: For more about adjectives, see pages 434–437.

If a word modifies a verb, an adjective, or an adverb, then it's an adverb.

EXAMPLES People from many nations have come to the United States **recently.** [The adverb *recently* modifies the verb *have come.*]
English can be a **fairly** difficult language to learn. [The adverb *fairly* modifies the adjective *difficult.*]
Newcomers study **incredibly** hard to learn the language. [The adverb *incredibly* modifies the adverb *hard.*]

NOTE: The adverb *very* is overused. In your writing, try to use adverbs other than *very* to modify adjectives.

EXAMPLE Arnold Schwarzenegger is very strong.
Arnold Schwarzenegger is **amazingly** strong.

▶ EXERCISE 11 **Identifying Adverbs**

Identify the <u>adverb</u> and the <u>word or words it modifies</u> in each sentence in the following sentences.

EXAMPLE **1.** Many Cherokees still live in the mountains of North Carolina.
1. *still—live*

1. <u>Today</u>, many Cherokee people <u>make</u> their homes in Oklahoma.
2. This area <u>was</u> <u>not</u> the Cherokees' original home.
3. These people <u>once</u> <u>lived</u> in Georgia, North Carolina, Alabama, and Tennessee.
4. In 1815, a small boy <u>excitedly</u> <u>reported</u> the discovery of gold in Georgia.
5. Many white settlers of the region <u>fought</u> <u>greedily</u> for the gold.

6. These settlers <u>totally</u> <u>ignored</u> the Cherokees' right to the land.
7. In fact, many Cherokees <u>had fought</u> <u>bravely</u> for the settlers against the British.
8. <u>Still</u>, the Cherokee <u>were forced</u> by the government to leave their land.
9. The people <u>were</u> <u>hardly</u> <u>given</u> a chance to collect their belongings.
10. Many Cherokees <u>will</u> <u>never</u> <u>forget</u> the "Trail of Tears" that led their ancestors to Oklahoma.

The Position of Adverbs

One of the characteristics of adverbs is that they may appear at various places in a sentence. Adverbs may come before, after, or between the words they modify.

EXAMPLES   We **often** study together.
We study together **often.**
Often we study together.

When an adverb modifies a verb phrase, it frequently comes in the middle of the phrase.

EXAMPLE   We have **often** studied together.

An adverb that introduces a question, however, must be placed at the beginning of a sentence.

EXAMPLES   **When** does your school start? [The adverb *when* modifies the verb phrase *does start.*]
How did you spend your vacation? [The adverb *how* modifies the verb phrase *did spend.*]

▶ EXERCISE 12   **Identifying Adverbs**

Identify the twenty <u>adverbs</u> and the <u>words they modify</u> in the following paragraphs.

EXAMPLE   [1] "To Build a Fire" is a dramatically suspenseful short story.
1. *dramatically—suspenseful*

ADVANCED STUDENTS

As a supplementary activity, you may wish to have students write an answer to the question at the end of **Exercise 12.** Encourage students to read the story as a follow-up.

ANSWERS

Exercise 13

Responses will vary. Only adverbs that answer certain questions can go in each blank.

1. how or how often
2. to what extent or how often
3. where or how
4. to what extent or how
5. how or when or how often
6. how or to what extent
7. how
8. how or when
9. where or how
10. how or to what extent

458

---

3. completely—alone/alone—is traveling

[1] "To Build a Fire" <u>is</u> probably one of Jack London's best stories. [2] In this story, a nameless character <u>goes</u> <u>outdoors</u> on a <u>terribly</u> <u>cold</u> day in the Yukon. [3] Except for a dog, he is traveling completely alone to a mining camp. [4] <u>Foolishly</u> <u>confident</u> of his ability to survive the <u>unusually</u> <u>harsh</u> cold, he <u>does</u> <u>not</u> <u>understand</u> the dangers of the northern wilderness. **6.** fearfully—slinks/along—slinks

[5] The dog <u>knows</u> <u>instinctively</u> that they <u>are</u> <u>certainly</u> in a bad situation. [6] It <u>slinks</u> <u>fearfully</u> <u>along</u> at the man's heels and seems to question his every movement. [7] <u>Soon</u> both the dog's muzzle and the man's beard <u>are frosted</u> with ice.

[8] Along the way, the man <u>accidentally</u> <u>falls</u> into a hidden stream. [9] <u>Desperately</u>, he <u>builds</u> a fire under a tree to avoid frostbite. [10] The flames <u>slowly</u> <u>grow</u> stronger. [11] <u>Unfortunately</u>, he <u>has built</u> his fire in the wrong place. [12] A pile of snow <u>suddenly</u> <u>falls</u> from a tree limb and kills the fire. [13] Unable to relight the fire, the man <u>again</u> <u>finds</u> himself in serious trouble. [14] Based on what you <u>now</u> <u>know</u> about the story, what kind of ending would you write for "To Build a Fire"?

▶ EXERCISE 13 **Writing Adverbs**

Supply ten different adverbs to fill the blanks in the following paragraph.

EXAMPLE [1] I have ____ been a real music lover.
    1. *always*

Every Friday I [1]____ go to the record store. I can [2] ____ wait to see what new cassettes and CDs have arrived. As soon as school is out, I bicycle [3] ____ to the store and join other [4] ____ enthusiastic customers. [5] ____ I stroll through the aisles and [6] ____ study the selections. I listen [7]____ as the loudspeaker announces the day's specials. When I have decided what I want, I [8] ____ figure out which items I can afford. Then I walk [9]____ to the cash register. I grin [10]____ as I think of how much I will enjoy the music.

PICTURE THIS

You are part of an important deep-sea expedition. Your job is to record what you see down in the ocean. The other members of your team lower your diving bell into the water. The diving bell is a heavy steel cabin with thick windows. When you reach the right depth, you switch on the outside light. Through the window in front of you, you see this scene. Write a brief report describing your observations. In your report, use at least five adverbs. Underline each adverb that you use.

Subject: underwater observations
Audience: scientists and others interested in undersea
            exploration
Purpose: to inform

GRAMMAR

PICTURE THIS

You could take this opportunity to discuss the aims and the modes of writing with students. Ask them what the aim for their reports will be [to inform] and what modes they will use [description and narration]. Then ask students to generate a different prompt, related to the picture, that would call for another aim and mode of writing.

For prewriting, have students brainstorm as a class for verbs and adjectives to describe what they see in the picture. Next, have students brainstorm for adverbs to modify the verbs and the adjectives they listed.

For an example of descriptive writing, refer students to **A Student Model** on page 172.

GRAMMAR

RESOURCES

THE PREPOSITION
• Prepositions and Prepositional Phrases

QUICK REMINDER

Write the following paragraph on the chalkboard and have students identify the preposition(s) in each sentence:

He keeps his collection *of* shells *on* a shelf. He found the shells *at* the beach. If you hold the conch shell *over* your ear, you can hear the ocean.

MEETING INDIVIDUAL NEEDS

LEP/ESL

Spanish. In Spanish, the single preposition *a* is used to denote *in, on,* and *at.* Therefore, Spanish-speaking students might have difficulty deciding which English preposition is appropriate in sentences.

Go over the definitions of these three prepositions with students and give several examples of how each is used. You may want to give examples that can be demonstrated in the classroom, such as *on the desk, in the desk,* and *at the chalkboard.*

THE PREPOSITION Rule 15c

OBJECTIVES

• To supply prepositions to complete sentences
• To identify prepositional phrases in paragraphs
• To identify prepositions and their objects in prepositional phrases
• To identify words in paragraphs as adverbs or as prepositions

---

460 *The Parts of Speech*

The Preposition

15c. A *preposition* is a word that shows the relationship between a noun or pronoun and another word in the sentence.

Notice how changing the preposition in the following sentences changes the relationship of *cat* to *door* and *kite* to *tree.*

The cat walked **through** the door.
The cat walked **toward** the door.
The cat walked **past** the door.

The kite **in** the tree is mine.
The kite **beside** the tree is mine.
The kite **above** the tree is mine.

Commonly Used Prepositions

aboard	before	for	off	toward
about	behind	from	on	under
above	below	in	out	underneath
across	beneath	in front of	out of	unlike
after	beside	inside	over	until
against	between	instead of	past	up
along	beyond	into	since	up to
among	by	like	through	upon
around	down	near	throughout	with
as	during	next to	till	within
at	except	of	to	without

▶ EXERCISE 14 **Writing Prepositions**

In each of the following sentences, a preposition is missing. Choose two prepositions that would make sense in each sentence.

EXAMPLE **1.** The car raced ____ the highway.
     1. *along, across*

15c

1. We watched television ____ dinner.
2. She ran ____ the park.
3. A boat sailed ____ the river.
4. The dog crawled ____ the fence.
5. The runner jogged ____ the gym.

The Prepositional Phrase

A preposition is always followed by at least one noun or pronoun. This noun or pronoun is called the *object of the preposition.* The preposition, its object, and the object's modifiers make up a *prepositional phrase.*

EXAMPLES   You can press those leaves **under glass.** [The preposition *under* relates its object, *glass,* to *can press.*]
The books **in my pack** are heavy. [The preposition *in* relates its object, *pack,* to *books.*]

A preposition may have more than one object.

EXAMPLE   Thelma's telegram **to Nina and Ralph** contained **good news.** [The preposition *to* relates its objects, *Nina* and *Ralph,* to *telegram.*]

The objects of prepositions may have modifiers.

EXAMPLE   It happened **during the last examination.** [*The* and *last* are adjectives modifying *examination,* which is the object of the preposition *during.*]

NOTE: Be careful not to confuse a prepositional phrase beginning with *to* (*to the park, to him*) with a verb form beginning with *to* (*to sing, to be heard*). Remember that a prepositional phrase always ends with a noun or a pronoun.

▶ EXERCISE 15   **Identifying Prepositional Phrases**

Identify the <u>prepositional phrases</u> in the following paragraphs. Underline the (preposition) once and its <u>object</u> twice. [Note: A sentence may contain more than one prepositional phrase.]

ANSWERS
Exercise 14

Responses will vary. Here are some possibilities:

1. during, after
2. by, to
3. down, along
4. under, through
5. around, near

LEARNING STYLES

Kinetic and Visual Learners. To help students understand the different relationships named by different prepositions, have students draw pictures to illustrate them. For example, a student could illustrate *above* by drawing a cat sitting in a tree above a dog. You could then display the drawings around the classroom.

WRITING APPLICATION

OBJECTIVE

• To write a "how-to" composition that includes prepositional phrases

GRAMMAR

A DIFFERENT APPROACH

Find or draw a large picture of a dangerous animal such as a shark. Post it in the room and write the following sentence on the chalkboard:

I don't want to be ＿＿ the (name of animal) ＿＿.

Have students suggest prepositions that tell where (in relationship to the animal) they don't want to be.

WRITING APPLICATION

Before students begin the **Writing Application** you may want to review adverbs that indicate the sequence of events (*first, next, then, afterwards,* and so on).

CRITICAL THINKING
Analysis

Tell students that to avoid skipping a necessary stage, they should break their processes down into as many steps as possible. To illustrate the importance of this advice, have a student give you oral directions for performing an activity, such as tying your shoe. Assume that you have never tied a shoe before, and follow the student's directions precisely. It is likely that students will see the importance of including all necessary steps.

462

---

462   *The Parts of Speech*

EXAMPLE   [1] Lieutenant Robert Peary and Matthew Henson reached the North Pole in 1909.

    1. *in 1909*

[1] Lieutenant Peary looked for the North Pole for many years. [2] Matthew Henson traveled with him on every expedition except the first one. [3] However, for a long time, Henson received no credit for his role.

[4] Peary had hired Henson as his servant on a trip to Nicaragua. [5] There, Peary discovered that Henson had sailing experience and could also chart a path through the jungle. [6] As a result, Peary asked Henson to join his Arctic expedition. [7] The two explorers became friends during their travels in the North. [8] On the final push to the North Pole, Henson was the only person who went with Peary.

[9] Yet because Peary was white, he received all the credit for the discovery. [10] Finally, after many years, Henson was honored by Congress, Maryland's state government, and two U.S. presidents.

WRITING APPLICATION

Using Prepositional Phrases to Write Directions

You have probably given directions many times. They may have been directions telling how to get somewhere or how to do something. Using prepositional phrases can help you give directions that are clear and complete.

INCOMPLETE Walk straight ahead a little bit. Then turn and keep going. You will see the house.

COMPLETE Walk straight ahead *for four blocks, to the first stoplight.* Turn *to the right at that corner* and go *for two more blocks.* The house is *at the end of the driveway with the mailbox with flowers on it.*

▶ WRITING ACTIVITY

Your class has decided to provide a "how-to" manual for seventh-graders. The manual will have chapters on crafts and hobbies, personal skills, school skills, and other topics. Write an entry for the manual, telling someone how to do a particular activity. You may use one of the following ideas or one of your own. In your entry, be sure to use prepositional phrases to make your directions clear and complete. Underline the prepositional phrases that you use.

1. how to keep a bicycle in good condition
2. how to care for houseplants
3. how to study for an essay test
4. how to bathe a cat or a dog
5. how to make friends at a new school
6. how to amuse a younger child

Prewriting First, picture yourself doing the activity you are describing. As you imagine doing the activity, jot down each thing that you do. Then put each step in the order that you do it. If necessary, change the order or add steps to make your directions clear and complete.

Writing Refer to your prewriting notes as you write your first draft. You may find it necessary to add or rearrange steps to make your directions clear and complete.

Evaluating and Revising Ask a friend or a classmate to read your paragraph. Then have your reader repeat the directions in his or her own words. If any part of the directions is unclear, revise your work.

Proofreading and Publishing Read over your entry again to check your spelling, grammar, and punctuation. Make sure you have used prepositional phrases correctly. (See pages 640–643 for more about the correct placement of phrase modifiers.) You and your classmates may wish to photocopy your manual entries or input them on a computer. You could then share your how-to hints with other students.

INTEGRATING THE LANGUAGE ARTS

Literature Link. Have students read a selection that describes a process, such as "The Rattlesnake Hunt" by Marjorie Kinnan Rawlings. Then have students analyze how the author uses prepositional phrases to reinforce her detailed, accurate description of a process.

LEARNING STYLES

Kinetic Learners. For prewriting, encourage students to act out the processes they are explaining.

Visual Learners. Have students draw diagrams to accompany their entries for their "how-to" manual.

Prepositions and Adverbs

Some words may be used as prepositions or as adverbs. Remember that a preposition always has an object. An adverb never does. If you can't tell whether a word is used as an adverb or a preposition, look for an object.

ADVERB I haven't seen him **since.**
PREPOSITION I haven't seen him **since** Thursday. [*Thursday* is the object of the preposition *since.*]

ADVERBS The bear walked **around** and then went **inside.**
PREPOSITIONS The bear walked **around** the yard and then went **inside** the cabin. [*Yard* is the object of the preposition *around. Cabin* is the object of *inside.*]

▶ EXERCISE 16 **Identifying Adverbs and Prepositions**

Identify the italicized word in each sentence in the following paragraphs as either an *adverb* or a *preposition*.

EXAMPLE [1] He watches uneasily as the hunter brings the pistol *up.*
  1. *up—adverb*

[1] "The Most Dangerous Game" is the story of Rainsford, a famous hunter who falls *off* a boat and swims to a strange island. [2] Rainsford knows that this island is feared by every sailor who passes *by.* [3] In fact, *among* sailors, the place is known as "Ship-Trap Island."

[4] After looking *around* for several hours, Rainsford can't understand why the island is considered so dangerous. [5] Finally, he discovers a big house *on* a high bluff. [6] A man with a pistol *in* his hand answers the door. [7] Putting his pistol *down,* the man introduces Rainsford to the famous hunter General Zaroff. [8] Zaroff invites Rainsford *inside.* [9] Soon, however, Rainsford wishes he could get *out* and never see Zaroff again. [10] Rainsford has finally discovered the secret *about* the island—Zaroff likes to hunt human beings!

THE CONJUNCTION Rule 15d

OBJECTIVES

- To identify conjunctions and the words they join in sentences
- To complete sentences by providing appropriate conjunctions
- To write sentences that include conjunctions

The Conjunction

 15d. A *conjunction* is a word that joins words or groups of words.

Coordinating conjunctions connect words or groups of words used in the same way.

Coordinating Conjunctions						
and	but	for	nor	or	so	yet

EXAMPLES Jill **or** Anna [two nouns]
strict **but** fair [two adjectives]
over the river **and** through the woods [two prepositional phrases]
Alice Walker wrote the book, **yet** she did not write the movie script. [two complete ideas]

The word *for* may be used either as a conjunction or as a preposition. When *for* joins groups of words that are independent clauses or sentences, it is used as a conjunction. Otherwise, it is used as a preposition.

CONJUNCTION He waited patiently, **for** he knew his ride would be along soon.
PREPOSITION He waited patiently **for** his ride.

NOTE: When *for* is used as a conjunction, there should always be a comma in front of it.

EXAMPLE I'll be home late**,** **for** I have basketball practice today.

Reprinted by permission of UFS, Inc.

THE CONJUNCTION
- Types of Conjunctions

 **QUICK REMINDER**
Write the following sentence on the chalkboard:

Grandma bought not only a feather duster but also a chimpanzee, a pumpkin, a mountain bike, and a laptop computer.

Have students identify the conjunctions in the sentence.

MEETING INDIVIDUAL NEEDS

LEP/ESL

General Strategies. Students commonly make the mistake of using the coordinating conjunction *and* when *or* is called for, as in the following sentence:

Hilary didn't bring the dog and the hat.

To help students avoid this mistake, make sure they know that when a verb is negative, its objects should usually be joined by *or*, rather than *and*, as in "Hilary didn't bring the dog or the hat."

GRAMMAR

Correlative conjunctions are pairs of conjunctions that connect words or groups of words used in the same way.

Correlative Conjunctions	
both . . . . . . and	not only . . . . but also
either . . . . or	whether . . . . or
neither . . . . . nor	

EXAMPLES   **Both** Bill Russell **and** Larry Byrd have played for the Celtics. [two nouns]
She looked **neither** to the left **nor** to the right. [two prepositional phrases]
Not only did Wilma Rudolph overcome her illness, **but** she **also** became an Olympic athlete. [two complete ideas]

▶ EXERCISE 17 **Identifying Conjunctions**

Identify the <u>conjunction</u> in each of the following sentences. Be prepared to tell what <u>words or groups of words each conjunction joins</u>.

EXAMPLES   **1.** Both she and her mother enjoy sailing.
         1. *Both . . . and*

1. <u>I wanted to see Los Lobos in concert</u>, <u>but</u> <u>I didn't have the money</u>.
2. Our class is recycling <u>not only</u> <u>newspapers</u> <u>but also</u> <u>aluminum cans</u>.
3. He set the table with <u>chopsticks</u> <u>and</u> <u>rice bowls</u>.
4. Have you seen <u>either</u> <u>Whitney Houston</u> <u>or</u> <u>Janet Jackson</u> in person?
5. We learned to use <u>neither</u> <u>too many adjectives</u> <u>nor</u> <u>too few</u>.
6. <u>That diet is dangerous</u>, <u>for</u> <u>it does not meet the body's needs</u>.
7. <u>Both</u> <u>the Mohawk</u> <u>and</u> <u>the Oneida</u> are part of the Iroquois Confederacy.
8. <u>It rained all day</u>, <u>yet</u> <u>we enjoyed the trip</u>.
9. Shall we <u>walk home</u> <u>or</u> <u>take the bus</u>?
10. <u>Revise your paper</u> <u>and</u> <u>proofread it carefully</u>.

OBJECTIVE

• To write sentences that include interjections

15e

 EXERCISE 18 **Writing Conjunctions**

For each blank in the following sentences, choose an appropriate conjunction. Answers may vary except in sentence **2**.

EXAMPLE **1.** _____ solve the problem yourself _____ ask your teacher for help.
   1. *Either—or*

1. We will visit _____ the Johnson Space Center _____ AstroWorld. **1.** both/and
2. Alaska _____ Hawaii were the last two states admitted to the Union. **2.** and
3. Those two students are twins, _____ they do not dress alike. **3.** but
4. They were _____ hungry _____ thirsty. **4.** both/and
5. _____ turn that radio down _____ take it into your room.
   5. Either/or

EXERCISE 19 **Writing Sentences with Conjunctions**

Follow the directions given below to write sentences using conjunctions.

EXAMPLE **1.** Use *and* to join two verbs.
   1. *Jessye Norman smiled at the audience and bowed.*

1. Use *and* to join two adverbs.
2. Use *or* to join two prepositional phrases.
3. Use *for* to join groups of words that are sentences.
4. Use *but* to join two linking verbs.
5. Use *either . . . or* in an imperative sentence.

The Interjection

15e. An *interjection* is a word that expresses strong emotion.

An interjection has no grammatical relationship to the rest of the sentence. Usually an interjection is followed by an exclamation point.

GRAMMAR

GRAMMAR

ANSWERS
Exercise 19

Sentences will vary. Here are some possibilities:

1. He sang merrily and loudly.
2. The spy may be hiding in the attic or behind the wardrobe.
3. I will run to school, for I am late.
4. He seems frightening but is actually very sweet.
5. Either wash the dishes or sweep the floor.

RESOURCES

THE INTERJECTION
• The Interjection

QUICK REMINDER
Write the words *oh, gee,* and *wow* on the chalkboard. Have students write sentences using each interjection.

467

OBJECTIVES

- To identify italicized words in sentences as verbs, adverbs, prepositions, conjunctions, or interjections
- To write sentences that include specified words as two different parts of speech

LEP/ESL

General Strategies. Most languages include interjections. You could ask students who speak other languages to share interjections from their languages with the class. Often, interjections such as *ouch* are similar in many different languages.

ANSWERS
Exercise 20

Sentences will vary. Students' responses should include five sentences, each using a different interjection. Interjections should be underlined. All sentences should relate to the picture provided.

---

468 *The Parts of Speech*

EXAMPLES   **Ouch!** That hurts!
           Goodness! What a haircut!
           Aha! I know the answer.

Sometimes an interjection is set off by a comma.

   Oh, I wish it were Friday.
   Well, what have you been doing?

▶ EXERCISE 20   **Writing Interjections**

The people at this video arcade need your help. To express their excitement, they want to use some interjections—but they don't know any. Write five sentences that might be spoken by these people. In each sentence, use a different interjection from the list below. Underline the interjections you use. (Remember that an interjection may be followed by either an exclamation point or a comma.)

gee	yay	oh	wow
darn	no	oops	yes

EXAMPLE   *Wow! That's the highest score ever!*

▶ REVIEW B   **Identifying Parts of Speech**

For the following sentences, identify the part of speech of each <u>italicized word</u> as either a <u>*verb*</u>, an <u>*adverb*</u>, a <u>*preposition*</u>, a <u>*conjunction*</u>, or an <u>*interjection*</u>.

EXAMPLE   **1.** *Both* otters *and* owls hunt *from* dusk to dawn.
             1. *both . . . and—conjunction; from—preposition*

1. *Oh!* I *just* spilled soup on the new white tablecloth!   **1.** itj./ adv.
2. Luis Alvarez *closely* studied atomic particles *for* many years.   **2.** adv./prep.
3. *Did* Toni Morrison *or* Toni Cade Bambara *write* that book?   **3.** v./conj./v.
4. The Inuit hunters *ate* their meal *inside* the igloo.   **4.** v./prep.
5. They were tired, *yet* they did *not* quit working.   **5.** conj./adv.

Determining Parts of Speech

Remember that you can't tell what part of speech a word is until you know how it is used in a particular sentence. A word may be used in different ways.

NOUN	The **play** had a happy ending.
VERB	The actors **play** their roles.

NOUN	The **outside** of the house needs paint.
ADVERB	Let's go **outside** for a while.
PREPOSITION	I saw the birds' nest **outside** my window.

▶ REVIEW C   **Writing Sentences**

Write ten sentences that meet the requirements in the following directions. Underline the given word in each sentence, and identify how it is used.

EXAMPLE   **1.** Use *yet* as an adverb and as a conjunction.
             1. *Are we there yet?—adverb*
                  The sky grew brighter, yet the rain continued falling.—conjunction

1. Use *walk* as a verb and a noun.
2. Use *like* as a preposition and a verb.
3. Use *well* as an interjection and an adverb.
4. Use *inside* as an adverb and a preposition.
5. Use *fast* as an adjective and an adverb.

ANSWERS
Review C

Sentences will vary. Here are some possibilities:

1. Don't *walk* on the grass. — verb
   The *walk* helped her headache. — noun

2. That smells *like* spaghetti. — preposition
   I *like* fresh vegetables. — verb

3. *Well,* do you want to go? — interjection
   She writes *well.* — adverb

4. I'm staying *inside.* — adverb
   He keeps his marbles *inside* a jar. — preposition

5. Who needs a *fast* car? — adjective
   He drives too *fast.* — adverb

REVIEW: POSTTEST

OBJECTIVES

- To identify italicized words in sentences as verbs, adverbs, prepositions, conjunctions, or interjections
- To write sentences that include words used as adverbs and as prepositions

GRAMMAR

 A DIFFERENT APPROACH

Hold a contest in which you challenge each student to write one sentence that includes, as many times as possible, all of the parts of speech discussed in this chapter. To be considered, a sentence should use each part of speech at least once. Run-on sentences should be automatically disqualified. Here is a sample entry:

Oh, I forgot that tomorrow we are going to walk slowly to the park and picnic together under the trees. [one interjection, three verbs (verb phrases count as one verb), three adverbs, two prepositions, one conjunction]

ANSWERS

Review: Posttest B

Sentences will vary. Here are some possibilities:

1. The balloon sailed *up.* — adverb
Katie climbed *up* the oak tree. — preposition

2. Stay *near!* — adverb
The bus stops *near* my house. — preposition

3. They came *over.* — adverb
Tennis balls were flying *over* my head. — preposition

4. You have to come *through.* — adverb
A comet blazed *through* the sky. — preposition

5. His old car crept *by.* — adverb
I walk *by* your house every day. — preposition

470

---

470 *The Parts of Speech*

Review: Posttest

A. Identifying Verbs, Adverbs, Prepositions, Conjunctions, and Interjections

Identify the part of speech of each italicized word in the following paragraphs. v. = verb adv. = adverb prep. = prepostion
conj. = conjunction   itj. = interjection

EXAMPLES   Some [1] *very* unusual words [2] *are used* [3] *in* crossword puzzles.
1. *adverb*
2. *verb*
3. *preposition*

1. prep.

2. v. **3.** prep.

4. conj.

5. adv. **6.** v.

7. prep.

8. adv. **9.** adv.

10. adv.

11. adv.

12. v.

13. v. **14.** adv.

15. prep.

16. conj.

17. adv. **18.** v.

19. itj.

20. conj.

The first crossword puzzle was published [1] *in* 1913. It [2] *appeared* on the Fun Page [3] *of* a New York City newspaper, [4] *and* readers [5] *immediately* [6] *asked* the editors [7] *for* more. [8] *Almost* every newspaper in the United States [9] *now* publishes a daily crossword puzzle.

About fifty million Americans [10] *faithfully* work crossword puzzles. Many people take their puzzles [11] *quite* seriously. For many, solving puzzles [12] *is* a competitive game.

I [13] *do* puzzles [14] *strictly* for fun. Best of all, I can work on them [15] *by* myself. That way, no one knows whether I succeed [16] *or* fail. I [17] *occasionally* [18] *brag* about my successes. [19] *"Aha!"* I exclaim. "That was a tough one, [20] *but* I filled in every space."

B. Writing Sentences Using Words as Different Parts of Speech

Write ten sentences, using each of the following words first as an adverb and then as a preposition. Underline the word, and give its part of speech after the sentence.

EXAMPLE   **1.** around
1. *We walked <u>around</u>.—adverb*
We walked <u>around</u> the mall.—preposition

1. up   **2.** near   **3.** over   **4.** through   **5.** by

SUMMARY OF PARTS OF SPEECH

Rule	Part of Speech	Use	Examples
14a	noun	names	**Marie** had a good **idea**.
14b	pronoun	takes the place of a noun	Bill had an idea, but **he** would't tell **it** to **anyone**.
14c	adjective	modifies a noun or pronoun	I have **two Mexican** bowls, and both are **large** and **heavy**.
15a	verb	shows action or a state of being	Ada **has met** you, but she **is** not sure where.
15b	adverb	modifies a verb, an adjective, or another adverb	We left **early** when the sky was **almost completely** dark.
15c	preposition	relates a noun or a pronoun to another word	We looked **for** you **next to** the gate **at** the game.
15d	conjunction	joins words or groups of words	Bill **or** she will call us later **and** give us directions.
15e	interjection	shows strong feeling	**Ouch!** My arm is caught.

DIAGNOSTIC TEST

OBJECTIVE

• To identify complements as direct objects, indirect objects, predicate nominatives, or predicate adjectives

COMPLEMENTS
• Chapter Review Form A
• Chapter Review Form B
• Assessment Portfolio
  Grammar Pretest
  Grammar Mastery Test 1
  Grammar Mastery Test 2

GRAMMAR

CHAPTER OVERVIEW

This chapter explains how complements can be added to the subject and verb of a sentence base to complete the meaning of a sentence. The first part of this chapter focuses on identifying direct and indirect objects in sentences. The second part of the chapter addresses predicate nominatives and predicate adjectives following linking verbs. Composition is integrated with the concept of complements in the **Writing Application.** Students are asked to use subject complements to write riddles.

USING THE DIAGNOSTIC TEST

Use the **Diagnostic Test** to determine students' mastery of complements. After students have finished the test, you may want them also to identify their own use of complements at the revision stage of a writing assignment so that you can determine how much time to spend on this chapter.

GRAMMAR

16 COMPLEMENTS

Direct and Indirect Objects, Subject Complements

Diagnostic Test

Identifying Complements

Identify the <u>complement or complements</u> in each of the following sentences. Then, label each complement as a *direct object*, an *indirect object*, a *predicate nominative*, or a *predicate adjective*.

EXAMPLE   **1.** My mother bought us some tamales.
            1. *us—indirect object; tamales—direct object*

1. Native American peoples taught the English <u>colonists</u> many useful <u>skills</u> for survival.   **1.** i.o./d.o.   **2.** p.n.
2. Rhode Island is the smallest <u>state</u> in the United States.
3. A hurricane of immense power lashed the Florida <u>coast</u>.   **3.** d.o.

4. They became very <u>anxious</u> during the final minutes of the game. **4.** p.a.
5. This winter was <u>colder</u> and <u>drier</u> than normal. **5.** p.a./p.a.
6. My aunt showed <u>us</u> <u>pictures</u> of her new puppy. **6.** i.o./d.o.
7. The new homeowners found some rare <u>photographs</u> in the attic. **7.** d.o.
8. Although many eggshells are <u>white</u>, others are <u>brown</u>, and still others are bluish <u>green</u>. **8.** p.a./p.a./p.a.
9. Some consumers prefer <u>eggs</u> with brown shells. **9.** d.o.
10. At the end of May, Mars is too <u>close</u> to the Sun to be seen easily from Earth. **10.** p.a.
11. Congress gave the <u>president</u> its <u>support</u> on the bill. **11.** i.o./d.o
12. The movers carried the heavy <u>sofa</u> up the stairs. **12.** d.o.
13. I found a <u>dollar</u> in the pocket of my jeans. **13.** d.o.
14. That gigantic reflector is the world's most powerful <u>telescope</u>. **14.** p.n.
15. Did Henry Cisneros lead the state <u>delegation</u> at the convention last month? **15.** d.o.
16. *A Raisin in the Sun* was Lorraine Hansberry's most successful <u>play</u>. **16.** p.n.
17. Why do animals seem <u>nervous</u> during a storm? **17.** p.a.
18. The manager will pay <u>all</u> of the ushers an extra five <u>dollars</u> this week. **18.** i.o./d.o.
19. Luis Alvarez won a <u>Nobel Prize</u> for his research into nuclear power. **19.** d.o.
20. Our neighbor has offered my <u>mother</u> a good <u>price</u> for her car. **20.** i.o./d.o.

Recognizing Complements

16a. A *complement* is a word or a group of words that completes the meaning of a verb.

Every sentence has a subject and a verb. In addition, the verb often needs a complement to complete its meaning.

RECOGNIZING COMPLEMENTS

You may want to use the term *completer* instead of *complement* and tell the class that there are two types of complements—*object completers* and *subject completers*.

Put four short sentence bases on the chalkboard. Two of them should be complete thoughts without complements, and two of them should require complements. Read the examples aloud and lead students to see the necessity of adding complements to complete the thoughts in two of the sentences. Here are some possibilities:

1. Stephano ran.
2. The teacher spoke loudly.
3. Our class likes ____.
4. The movie was ____.

OBJECTIVE
• To identify direct objects in sentences

474 *Complements*

		S	V	
INCOMPLETE	Dr. Charles Drew researched [*what?*]			

	S	V	C
COMPLETE	Dr. Charles Drew researched blood **plasma.**		

	S	V	
INCOMPLETE	Medical societies honored [*whom?*]		

	S	V	C
COMPLETE	Medical societies honored **him.**		

	S	V	
INCOMPLETE	Dr. Drew's research was [*what?*]		

	S	V	C
COMPLETE	Dr. Drew's research was **important.**		

Direct Objects

The *direct object* is one type of complement. It completes the meaning of a transitive verb.

👉 **REFERENCE NOTE:** Transitive verbs are discussed on page 446.

16b. A *direct object* is a noun or a pronoun that receives the action of the verb or shows the result of that action. A direct object answers the question *Whom?* or *What?* after a transitive verb.

EXAMPLES **Today, I met Dr. Mason.** [*Dr. Mason* receives the action of the verb *met* and tells *whom* I met.]
That shop makes small parts for jet engines. [*Parts* tells *what* results from the action of the verb *makes.*]

A direct object can never follow a linking verb because a linking verb does not express action. Also, a direct object is never in a prepositional phrase.

LINKING VERB **Augusta Savage was a sculptor during the Harlem Renaissance.** [The verb *was* does not express action; therefore, it has no direct object.]

▼ **RESOURCES**

DIRECT OBJECTS
• Direct Objects

🦉 **QUICK REMINDER**
Ask students to fill in the blanks in the following sentences with direct objects. Explain to students that the verbs in the sentences are action verbs, and the words added in the blanks complete the action as direct objects.

1. It was a rainy night, and Lei (subject) threw (verb) a ____ (threw what?).
2. Shouldn't we (subject) buy (verb) new ____ (shouldn't buy what?)?
3. An architect (subject) builds (verb) the ____ (builds what?).

474

PREPOSITIONAL PHRASE	**She worked with clay.** [*Clay* is not the direct object of the verb *worked*; it is the object in the prepositional phrase *with clay.*]

☞ **REFERENCE NOTE:** For more about linking verbs, see pages 447–448. For more about prepositional phrases, see pages 491–497.

Direct objects may be a compound of two or more objects.

EXAMPLE	**We bought ribbon, wrapping paper, and tape.** [The compound direct object of the verb *bought* is *ribbon, wrapping paper,* and *tape.*]

▶ EXERCISE 1   **Identifying Direct Objects**

Identify the <u>direct object</u> in each of the following sentences. [Remember: A direct object may be compound.]

EXAMPLE	**1.** Many sports test an athlete's speed and agility.
	1. *speed, agility*

1. However, long-distance, or marathon, swimming requires <u>strength</u> and <u>endurance</u> from an athlete.
2. A swimmer in training may swim five or six <u>miles</u> every day.
3. Marathon swimmers smear <u>grease</u> on their legs and arms for protection against the cold water.
4. During a marathon, some swimmers may lose seventeen <u>pounds</u>.
5. Fatigue, pain, and huge waves challenge marathon <u>swimmers</u>.
6. As they swim, they endure extreme <u>isolation</u> from the rest of the world.
7. Toward the end of the marathon, swimmers hear the loud <u>applause</u> and <u>shouts</u> of encouragement from their fans.
8. Spectators can watch only the <u>finish</u> of a marathon.
9. Nevertheless, they know the long <u>distance</u> that the athletes have traveled.
10. Emerging from the water, exhausted swimmers have successfully completed another <u>marathon</u>.

GRAMMAR

MEETING INDIVIDUAL NEEDS

LEP/ESL

    Spanish. You may want to give students extra practice using pronouns as complements. In Spanish, the pronoun complement generally comes before the verb. For example, "Carlos told me" translates as "Carlos me dijo." To reinforce common English syntax, give students a worksheet with scrambled sentences, such as the ones listed below. Ask students to place the subjects, verbs, and pronouns in correct order so that the sentences make sense.

1. me/my friend/likes
2. know/we/them
3. found/I/it
4. her/Manuel/called
5. married/Lisa/him

LESS-ADVANCED STUDENTS

    Less-advanced students may initially try to locate direct objects in prepositional phrases. To help students avoid this problem, review phrases with students. Explain that prepositional phrases do not contain direct objects, subjects, or verbs. Model the sentences below, filling in the blanks with different-colored chalk. Then ask students to write three original sentences using both a direct object and a prepositional phrase in each sentence.

1. Kim called ＿＿ (direct object) to invite her ＿＿ (prepositional phrase).
2. Mario lifted the ＿＿ (direct object) ＿＿ (prepositional phrase).
3. Carl gave the ＿＿ (direct object) to the coach ＿＿ (prepositional phrase).

GRAMMAR

MEETING
INDIVIDUAL
NEEDS

ADVANCED STUDENTS

To extend this lesson for advanced students, teach them how to identify and use retained objects. Explain to students that retained objects are objects that are retained after a verb has changed from active to passive voice. Point out that retained objects can be either direct or indirect. You may need to review active and passive voice with students. After you have discussed the following models, ask students to write three sentences in the active voice. Then have students rewrite the sentences in passive voice with retained objects. Use the following models as a guide:

1. The audience gave me applause. [I was given applause by the audience.]
2. My mother fixed me a snack. [I was fixed a snack by my mother.]
3. Romeo gave Juliet a letter. [A letter was given Juliet by Romeo.]

LEARNING STYLES

Kinetic Learners. Have students write the following sentences on the chalkboard and draw arrows from the verbs to the direct objects:

1. She wrote me a letter.
2. He gave his dog a bone.
3. Tom brought us the newspaper.
4. Sue sang her sister a lullaby.

Then have students create sentences of their own and label the new sentences in the same way.

EXERCISE 2 **Identifying Direct Objects**

Identify the ten <u>direct objects</u> in the following paragraph. If a sentence does not contain a direct object, write <u>*no direct object*</u>. [Remember: Objects follow action verbs only.]

EXAMPLES [1] **Have you ever flown a hang glider?**
1. *hang glider*

[2] **Hang gliding has become a popular sport.**
2. *no direct object*

[1] Many adventurous people enjoy the <u>thrill</u> of gliding through the air. [2] As you can see, a hang glider can carry a full-grown <u>person</u> in its harness. [3] The hang glider has a lightweight <u>sail</u> with a triangular control bar underneath. [4] At takeoff, the pilot lifts the <u>glider</u> shoulder-high and runs hard down a slope into the wind. [5] The wind lifts the <u>glider</u> and carries the <u>pilot</u> off the ground.

6. no d.o. [6] Because of the wind currents, takeoffs from a hilltop or a cliff are the easiest. [7] Once airborne, the pilot directs the <u>path</u> of flight. [8] He or she also controls the glider's <u>speed</u> by pushing or pulling on the control bar. [9] For example, a gentle pull increases <u>speed</u>. [10] To land, the pilot stalls the <u>glider</u> near the ground and drops lightly to his or her feet.

INDIRECT OBJECTS Rule 16c

OBJECTIVES

- To identify direct objects and indirect objects in sentences
- To write a story using three direct objects and two indirect objects

Indirect Objects

The *indirect object* is another type of complement. Like a direct object, an indirect object helps to complete the meaning of a transitive verb. If a sentence has an indirect object, it always has a direct object also.

> **16c.** An *indirect object* is a noun or pronoun that comes between the verb and the direct object. It tells *to whom* or *to what,* or *for whom* or *for what,* the action of the verb is done.

EXAMPLES **The waiter gave her a smile.** [The pronoun *her* is the indirect object of the verb *gave*. It answers the question "*To whom* did the waiter give a smile?"]

Pam left the waiter a tip. [The noun *waiter* is the indirect object of the verb *left*. It answers the question "*For whom* did she leave a tip?"]

NOTE: Linking verbs do not have indirect objects, because they do not show action. Also, an indirect object is never in a prepositional phrase.

INDIRECT OBJECT	Vinnie made **us** some lasagna.
PREPOSITIONAL PHRASE	Vinnie made some lasagna **for us.**

Like a direct object, an indirect object can be a compound of two or more objects.

EXAMPLE **Felicia threw Jane and Paula slow curve balls until they had warmed up.** [*Jane* and *Paula* are the indirect objects of the verb *threw*. They answer the question "*To whom* did Felicia throw curve balls?"]

 EXERCISE 3 **Identifying Direct Objects and Indirect Objects**

Identify the <u>direct object</u> and the <u>indirect object</u> in each of the following sentences.

RESOURCES

INDIRECT OBJECTS
- Indirect Objects

🦉 QUICK REMINDER

To show students how easily indirect objects can be found in sentences, write the following sentences on the chalkboard, and circle in colored chalk the verbs and direct objects. Explain to students that the indirect object will tell *to whom, to what, for whom,* or *for what* the action of the verb is done.

1. James gave Mary an apple.
2. Maria took her mother a message.
3. Kunio brought his sister a souvenir from the ocean.

GRAMMAR

MEETING INDIVIDUAL NEEDS

LEP/ESL

Spanish. Students might have difficulty positioning direct and indirect object pronouns within the sentence. An object pronoun comes before the verb in Spanish. For example, "Lalo gave it to me" is translated in Spanish as "Lalo me lo dio." A small group activity can reinforce the sentence order used in English. Asking students to sit in a circle, hand a book to one student. Then ask another, "Did I give the book to Delia?" The student should respond, "Yes, you gave it to her." Then hand the same book to the student who just spoke and ask him or her, "Did I give the book to you?" He or she responds, "Yes, you gave it to me." There are numerous variations on this theme that use both singular and plural object pronouns.

LEARNING STYLES

Auditory Learners. It might be easier for some students to hear the direct and indirect objects than for them to recognize the objects visually. You could group students together and have them take turns reading aloud the example sentences and the sentences in the exercises.

EXAMPLE **1.** Did you buy Mom a calculator for her birthday?
  1. *Mom—indirect object; calculator— direct object*

1. The usher found <u>us</u> <u>seats</u> near the stage.
2. I'll gladly lend <u>you</u> my <u>typewriter</u>.
3. The Nobel Committee gave <u>Octavio Paz</u> the <u>Nobel Prize</u> for literature.
4. Please show <u>me</u> your beaded <u>moccasins</u>.
5. Mai told the <u>children</u> <u>stories</u> about her family's escape from Vietnam.
6. Our teacher taught <u>us</u> some English <u>words</u> of Native American origin.
7. I fed the <u>horse</u> some <u>hay</u>.
8. My secret pal sent <u>me</u> a birthday <u>card</u>.
9. They owe <u>you</u> an <u>apology</u>.
10. Will you please save <u>Ricardo</u> a <u>seat</u>?

▶ EXERCISE 4   **Identifying Objects of Verbs**

All of the following sentences contain <u>direct objects</u>. Some sentences contain <u>indirect objects</u>, too. Identify the object or objects in each sentence.

EXAMPLE **1.** My parents gave me a choice of places to go on our camping vacation.
  1. *me—indirect object; choice—direct object*

1. I told <u>them</u> my <u>answer</u> quickly.
2. I had recently read a magazine <u>article</u> about the Flathead Indian Reservation in Montana.
3. We spent five <u>days</u> of our vacation there.
4. We liked the friendly <u>people</u> and the rugged <u>land</u>.
5. Two tribes, together known as the Flathead Nation, govern the huge <u>reservation</u>.
6. I especially liked the beautiful <u>mountains</u> and twenty-eight-mile long <u>Flathead Lake</u>.
7. My parents assigned <u>me</u> the <u>job</u> of putting up our tent beside the lake.

8. Someone gave my <u>father</u> <u>directions</u> to the National Bison Range, and we went there one day.
9. We also attended the <u>Standing Arrow Pow-Wow</u>, which was the highlight of our stay.
10. The performers showed <u>visitors</u> traditional Flathead <u>dances</u> and <u>games</u>.

PICTURE THIS

The year is 1924, and you're a customer in this toy store. You are looking for gifts for your friends and family, but your attention soon turns to the conversations at the counter. The two salesmen seem to be having some trouble with their customers. As you watch the conversations, you decide to record this amusing incident. This year, in addition to a toy, your gift to everyone will be a copy of your story about what happened at the toy store. Write down your observations. Include as many details as you can so that your readers can imagine the scene. In your writing use at least three direct objects and two indirect objects.

Subject: customers in a toy store
Audience: friends and family
Purpose: to entertain

PICTURE THIS

To help you grade this activity, ask students to circle and label direct objects and indirect objects. You may want to ask students to read their stories aloud. Give the class an opportunity to locate direct and indirect objects in the stories. Ask the class to write down the objects on paper while the students are speaking, and after students have finished presenting their stories, compare notes to make sure that all students can identify direct and indirect objects in speech.

SUBJECT COMPLEMENTS Rules 16d–16f

OBJECTIVES

- To identify linking verbs and predicate nominatives in sentences
- To identify linking verbs and predicate adjectives in sentences
- To write a description that includes five predicate adjectives and five predicate nominatives

---

RESOURCES

SUBJECT COMPLEMENTS
- Predicate Nominatives

QUICK REMINDER

To help the class distinguish between direct objects and subject complements, ask students to identify the subject, action verb or linking verb, direct object, predicate nominative, or adjective in each of these sentences:

1. Mario [subject] broke [action verb] the handle [direct object] on the suitcase.
2. Amy [subject] became [linking verb] captain [predicate noun] of the cheerleading squad.

MEETING
INDIVIDUAL
NEEDS

LEP/ESL

Spanish. Because English and Spanish use the same syntax in sentences with predicate adjectives and predicate nominatives, you may want to take advantage of this comfort zone by introducing students to new and more challenging vocabulary (nouns and adjectives) for them to use in original sentences.

---

480 *Complements*

Subject Complements

16d. A ***subject complement*** completes the meaning of a linking verb and identifies or describes the subject.

EXAMPLES   Julio has been **president** of his class since October. [*President* identifies the subject *Julio.*]
Was it **you**? [*You* identifies the subject *it.*]
Barbara looks **sleepy** this morning. [*Sleepy* describes the subject *Barbara.*]

☞ REFERENCE NOTE: For more information about linking verbs, see pages 447–448.

There are two kinds of subject complements—the *predicate nominative* and the *predicate adjective*.

Predicate Nominatives

16e. A ***predicate nominative*** is a noun or pronoun that follows a linking verb and explains or identifies the subject of the sentence.

EXAMPLES   **A good dictionary is a valuable tool.** [*Tool* is a predicate nominative following the linking verb *is.* It explains the subject *dictionary.*]
This piece of flint may be an old arrowhead. [*Arrowhead* is a predicate nominative following the linking verb *may be.* It identifies the subject *piece.*]
The winner of the race was she. [*She* is a predicate nominative following the linking verb *was.* It identifies the subject *winner.*]

NOTE: Expressions such as *It is I* and *That was he* sound awkward even though they are correct. In conversation, you would probably say *It's me* and *That was him.* Such nonstandard expressions may one day become acceptable in writing as well as in speech. For now, however, it is best to follow the rules of standard English in your writing.

Like other sentence complements, a predicate nominative may be compound.

EXAMPLE   The discoverers of radium were **Pierre Curie** and **Marie Sklodowska Curie.**

Be careful not to confuse a predicate nominative with a direct object. A predicate nominative always follows a linking verb. A direct object always follows an action verb.

PREDICATE NOMINATIVE   We are the **delegates** from our school.
DIRECT OBJECT   We elected the **delegates** from our school.

The predicate nominative is never part of a prepositional phrase.

PREDICATE NOMINATIVE   Bill Russell became a famous basketball **coach.**
PREPOSITIONAL PHRASE   Bill Russell became famous **as coach** of the Boston Celtics.

▶ EXERCISE 5   **Identifying Predicate Nominatives**

Identify the <u>linking verb</u> and the <u>predicate nominative</u> in each of the following sentences.

EXAMPLE   **1.** Are whales mammals?
          1. *Are—mammals*

1. Mount Kilimanjaro <u>is</u> the tallest <u>mountain</u> in Africa.
2. The kingdom of Siam <u>became</u> modern-day <u>Thailand</u>.
3. Dandelions <u>can be</u> a <u>problem</u>.
4. Sue Mishima <u>is</u> a <u>lawyer</u>.
5. When <u>will</u> a woman <u>be</u> <u>president</u> of the United States?
6. Reuben <u>has become</u> a fine <u>pianist</u>.
7. Variety <u>is</u> the <u>spice</u> of life.
8. At the moment, she <u>remains</u> our <u>choice</u> for mayor.
9. Alaska <u>is</u> the largest <u>state</u> in the United States.
10. *Philately* <u>is</u> another <u>name</u> for stamp collecting.

GRAMMAR

LESS-ADVANCED STUDENTS

Students might need to review linking verbs before studying subject complements. You may wish to provide newspapers and assign articles and ask students to underline any linking verbs. Have students put the sentences with linking verbs on the chalkboard. Using these examples, explain that any noun, pronoun, or adjective that follows a linking verb is a subject complement. Have volunteers circle the subject complements.

AT-RISK STUDENTS

To help students visualize the relationship of a predicative nominative or predicate adjective to the subject, write the following sentences on the chalkboard. Have students draw an arrow from each subject to its subject complement.

1. The two families were proud of their heritage.
2. The long road was hazardous.
3. She might be the winner.

GRAMMAR

INTEGRATING THE LANGUAGE ARTS

Literature Link. To illustrate how subject complements can affect writing, show the class how predicate nominatives and predicate adjectives often signal the classificatory mode. For example, you may want to examine and discuss the classificatory mode in Ogden Nash's "The Germ." In this poem Nash uses predicate nominatives and predicate adjectives several times to add to his descriptions. Ask students to identify some of Nash's sentences that use subject complements, such as "A mighty creature is the germ." You may want to suggest that students try writing a short poem using subject complements and a classificatory mode.

ANSWERS
Exercise 7

Sentences will vary. You may want to have students draw an arrow from the subject to the subject complement in each sentence to check that they have used subject complements instead of direct objects.

482

Predicate Adjectives

16f. A *predicate adjective* is an adjective that follows a linking verb and describes the subject of the sentence.

EXAMPLES   Cold milk tastes **good** on a hot day. [*Good* is a predicate adjective that describes the subject *milk.*]

The pita bread was **light** and **delicious.** [*Light* and *delicious* form a compound predicate adjective that describes the subject *bread.*]

 EXERCISE 6   **Identifying Predicate Adjectives**

Identify the <u>linking verb</u> and the <u>predicate adjective</u> in each of the following sentences.

EXAMPLE   **1.** The crowd became restless.
            1. *became—restless*

1. Everyone <u>felt</u> <u>good</u> about the decision.
2. That container of milk <u>smells</u> <u>sour</u>.
3. <u>Don</u>'t the Cuban black <u>beans</u> mixed with rice and onions <u>taste</u> <u>delicious</u>?
4. The situation <u>appears</u> <u>complicated</u>.
5. Everyone <u>remained</u> <u>calm</u> during the emergency.
6. Why <u>does</u> the water in that pond <u>look</u> <u>green</u>?
7. During Barbara Jordan's speech, the audience <u>grew</u> <u>thoughtful</u>, then <u>enthusiastic</u>.
8. Jan <u>stays</u> <u>cheerful</u> most of the time.
9. She <u>must be</u> <u>happy</u> with the results.
10. From here, the drums <u>sound</u> too <u>loud</u>.

 EXERCISE 7   **Using Predicate Adjectives and Predicate Nominatives**

You want to write an adventure story, but you aren't sure how to begin. You remember reading about a professional writer who gets ideas from watching people and making

REVIEW A

OBJECTIVE

- To identify and label direct objects, indirect objects, predicate nominatives, and predicate adjectives in sentences

up interesting identities for them. You decide to try this method of writing while you are sitting in this waiting room. Write a brief description of the other patients in the waiting room. Imagine the patients' jobs, families, backgrounds, and personalities. In your description, use five predicate adjectives and five predicate nominatives. Underline each predicate adjective once. Underline each predicate nominative twice. You may want to use your description to write the whole adventure story.

EXAMPLES   *The woman next to the coats is <u>Julia Johnson</u>.*

She looks <u>friendly</u>, but she is really an international <u>spy</u>.

REVIEW A   **Identifying Complements**

Identify the <u>complement or complements</u> in each of the following sentences. Then label each complement as a *direct object*, an *indirect object*, a *predicate nominative*, or a *predicate adjective*.

EXAMPLES   **1.** Our teacher read us stories from the Leatherstocking Tales.
1. *us—indirect object; stories—direct object*
2. James Fenimore Cooper was the author of these tales.
2. *author—predicate nominative*

COMMON ERROR

Problem. Students might have difficulty in determining if a subject complement is a predicate adjective or a direct object.

Solution. To avoid or correct this problem, ask students to think of the verb as an equal sign or as an unequal sign. If the sentence makes sense with the equal sign, the adjective is a predicate adjective; if not, the word is probably a direct object. Use the following examples as an illustration:

1. Tom likes sports. [Tom does not equal sports.]
2. Skiing is dangerous. [Skiing does equal dangerous.]

INTEGRATING THE LANGUAGE ARTS

Grammar and Usage. Students might be tempted to use constructions such as "It is me" and "that was him" when using pronouns as complements. Explain to students that subjects of verbs and predicate nominatives are always in the nominative case. Therefore, "It is I" and "that was he" are correct forms. In addition, tell students they can check for correct usage by making the predicate nominative the subject of the sentence. If the correct case is used, the predicate nominative could be used as the subject of the sentence.

WRITING APPLICATION

OBJECTIVE

- To use the writing process to write riddles with subject complements

WRITING APPLICATION
This writing assignment will give students practice in writing subject complements in original riddles. Each student will think of a person, place, or thing and then, using subject complements, write two descriptions in riddle form .

CRITICAL THINKING
Synthesis
Students will be applying critical-thinking skills to create riddles. They must decide what characteristics of the persons, places, or things described by the riddles can be used cleverly to keep the audience guessing. You may want to discuss with students how riddles often rely on plays on words to divert the listeners. Encourage students to use plays on words to describe their subjects accurately, but in such a way that the audience will have to think of all possible word meanings to solve the riddles.

484

484 *Complements*

1. Leatherstocking was a fictional <u>scout</u> in Cooper's Leatherstocking Tales.   **1.** p.n.
2. He was also a <u>woodcrafter</u> and a <u>trapper</u>.   **2.** p.n./p.n.
3. He could not read, but he understood the <u>lore</u> of the woods.   **3.** d.o.
4. To generations of readers, this character has become a <u>hero</u>.   **4.** p.n.
5. He could face any <u>emergency</u>.   **5.** d.o.
6. He always remained <u>faithful</u> and <u>fearless</u>.   **6.** p.a./p.a.
7. Leatherstocking loved the <u>forest</u> and the open <u>country</u>.   **7.** d.o./d.o.
8. In later years he grew <u>miserable</u>.   **8.** p.a.
9. The destruction of the wilderness by settlers and others greatly disturbed <u>him</u>.   **9.** d.o.
10. He told <u>no one</u> his <u>views</u> and retreated from civilization.   **10.** i.o./d.o.

WRITING APPLICATION

Using Subject Complements to Write Riddles

Popcorn pops, flashlights light, and linking verbs link. Like popcorn and flashlights, linking verbs do just what their name suggests. They link subjects with subject complements, which identify or describe the subject. Notice how the subject complements in the following riddle give clues to the identity of the subject *I*.

RIDDLE | I feel **smooth** to the touch.
I can be **white** or **brown.**
I am a **box** without a lid.
Inside me, you'll find gold.
What am I?
ANSWER | an egg

▶ WRITING ACTIVITY

A magazine for young people is sponsoring a riddle-writing contest. Whoever writes the best riddle will win the most advanced video game system on the market. You are determined to write the best riddle and win. Write two riddles to enter in the contest. In each one, use at least two subject complements.

Prewriting The best way to make up a riddle is to begin with the answer. List some animals, places, and things that suggest funny or hidden meanings. For instance, the example riddle plays on the idea that an egg is like a box of treasure. For each animal, place, or thing, jot down a description based on a funny or hidden meaning. Then choose the four animals, places, or things that you think will make the best riddles.

Writing Use your prewriting notes as you write your first draft. In each riddle, make sure that your clues will help your audience guess the answer. Be sure that you use a subject complement (a predicate nominative or a predicate adjective) in the riddle.

Evaluating and Revising Ask a friend to read your riddles. If the riddles are too difficult or too simple, revise them. You may want to add details that appeal to the senses. Linking verbs such as *appear, feel, smell, sound,* and *taste* can help you add such details. (For a longer list of linking verbs, see page 448.)

Proofreading and Publishing Read through your riddles again to check for errors in spelling, punctuation, and capitalization. Pay special attention to the capitalization of proper nouns. You and your classmates may want to publish a book of riddles. Collect your riddles and draw or cut out pictures as illustrations. Make photocopies for all the members of the class.

PREWRITING

You may want to stress the importance of brainstorming for riddle ideas before students begin jotting down descriptions. Explain to students that brainstorming is a necessary part of prewriting because it allows them to think of many ideas and to choose the best ones to write about.

WRITING

In the writing step, students can experiment with how words can be manipulated to confuse a reader. Encourage students to think of how they can make plays on words or purposefully select words that might have double meanings. Point out that all descriptions must accurately describe the subjects, even though students are trying to distract the reader from solving the riddles.

EVALUATING AND REVISING

To help students evaluate and revise, suggest they ask friends to read the riddles to see if the riddles are too difficult or too simple. You may want to caution students to be careful when using the sense verbs mentioned in the text. Most of these can be used both as linking verbs and as action verbs.

INTEGRATING THE LANGUAGE ARTS

Technology Link. If students have access to computers, they might want to use the computers to write their riddles. You could encourage students to use the computer program's thesaurus to help them write plays on words.

REVIEW B

OBJECTIVE

• To identify and label complements in sentences as direct objects, indirect objects, predicate nominatives, or predicate adjectives

486 *Complements*

 REVIEW B **Identifying Complements**

Identify the <u>complement or complements</u> in each sentence in the following paragraphs. Then label each complement as a *direct object*, an *indirect object*, a *predicate nominative*, or a *predicate adjective*. [Remember: A complement may be compound.]

EXAMPLE [1] **Sean, my brother, won three medals at the Special Olympic games.**
1. *medals—direct object*

1. p.n.
2. d.o.
3. d.o.
4. p.n.
5. i.o./d.o.
6. p.n.
7. p.a./p.a.
8. p.a.
9. p.a./p.a.
10. d.o.
11. d.o.
12. p.n.
13. i.o./d.o.
14. p.n.
15. d.o.
16. i.o./d.o.
17. d.o.
18. p.n.
19. p.n.
20. d.o.

[1] Sean was <u>one</u> of more than one hundred special-education students who competed in the regional Special Olympics last month. [2] The games brought <u>students</u> from many schools to our city. [3] The highlights of the games included track <u>events</u> such as sprints and relay races. [4] These were the closest <u>contests</u>. [5] Sean's excellent performance in the relays gave <u>him</u> <u>confidence</u>. [6] The softball throw and high jump were especially challenging <u>events</u>. [7] Sean looked <u>relaxed</u> but <u>determined</u> as he prepared for the high jump. [8] He certainly felt <u>great</u> after making the best jump.

[9] The Special Olympics are <u>exciting</u> and <u>inspiring</u>. [10] Many of the contestants have physical <u>impairments</u>; some cannot walk or see. [11] Teachers and volunteers train <u>contestants</u> in the different events. [12] However, the young athletes themselves are the <u>force</u> behind the program. [13] The pictures on the next page give <u>you</u> a <u>glimpse</u> of the excitement at the Special Olympics. [14] The two smiling girls on the left are <u>winners</u> of a sprint. [15] On the right, this determined boy gains the <u>lead</u> in the wheelchair race.

[16] Mrs. Duffy, one of the coaches, told <u>us</u> the <u>history</u> of the Special Olympics. [17] Eunice Kennedy Shriver founded the <u>program</u> in 1961. [18] To begin with, the program was a five-week <u>camp</u>. [19] Several years later, however, the camp became an international sports <u>event</u> with contestants from twenty-six states and Canada. [20] Today, the organizers of the Special Olympics sponsor regional and international <u>games</u>.

REVIEW: POSTTESTS 1 and 2

OBJECTIVES

- To identify and label direct objects, indirect objects, and subject complements in sentences
- To write original sentences that feature a variety of complements

STUDENTS WITH SPECIAL NEEDS

You may want to provide students with an organizational strategy for **Review: Posttest 1.** List the following steps on the chalkboard, and suggest that students follow the sequence in analyzing each sentence in the exercise:

1. Bracket the prepositional phrases (as a reminder that essential parts cannot be within the brackets).
2. Locate the verb.
3. Find the subject.
4. Find the complement that receives the action or renames the subject.

Review: Posttest 1

Identifying Complements

Identify the <u>complement or complements</u> in each of the following sentences. Label each complement as a *direct object*, an *indirect object*, a *predicate nominative*, or a *predicate adjective*.

EXAMPLE   **1.** A respirator pumps oxygen into the lungs.
   1. *oxygen—direct object*

1. Our cat avoids <u>skunks</u> and <u>raccoons</u>.   **1.** d.o./d.o.
2. Jim Thorpe was a famous Native American <u>athlete</u>.   **2.** p.n.
3. The teacher showed <u>us</u> a <u>film</u> about drug abuse.   **3.** i.o./d.o.
4. The television commercials for that new product sound <u>silly</u>.   **4.** p.a.
5. Who put the <u>roses</u> in that vase?   **5.** d.o.
6. I sent my <u>grandparents</u> a <u>card</u> for their anniversary.   **6.** i.o./d.o.
7. During her interview on television, Zina Garrison appeared <u>relaxed</u> and <u>confident</u>.   **7.** p.a./p.a.
8. At first the colt seemed <u>frightened</u>.   **8.** p.a.
9. Mrs. Karas offered <u>us</u> <u>olives</u> and stuffed grape <u>leaves</u>.   **9.** i.o./d.o./d.o.

488 *Complements*

10. The DJ played <u>songs</u> by Freddie Jackson, Gloria Estefan, and Paula Abdul.   **10.** d.o.
11. The newspaper story prompted an <u>investigation</u> by the mayor's office.   **11.** d.o.   **12.** p.n.   **13.** d.o./d.o.
12. My sister has become a computer repair <u>technician</u>.
13. Write your <u>name</u> and <u>address</u> on the envelope.
14. The weather forecasters haven't issued a tornado <u>warning</u>.   **14.** d.o.
15. Before long, the mistake became <u>obvious</u> to nearly everyone.   **15.** p.a.
16. The sky looked <u>gray</u> and <u>stormy</u>.   **16.** p.a./p.a.
17. The Egyptian writer Naguib Mahfouz won the <u>Nobel Prize</u> for literature in 1988.   **17.** d.o.   **18.** i.o./d.o.
18. The consumer group wrote the <u>senator</u> a <u>letter</u>.
19. *Barrio Boy* is the <u>autobiography</u> of Ernesto Galarza.
20. The candidate seems <u>ambitious</u> but <u>sincere</u>.   **19.** p.n.
   20. p.a./p.a.

ANSWERS
Posttest 2

Sentences will vary. Here are some possibilities.

1. I met the <u>teacher</u> and the <u>principal</u> in the cafeteria.
2. Send <u>me</u> your <u>answer</u> as soon as you can.
3. The young soldier was a <u>hero</u>.
4. The cake seemed <u>stale</u>.
5. The icy wind feels <u>strong</u> and <u>bitter</u>.

Review: Posttest 2

Writing Sentences with Complements

Write two sentences for each of the following kinds of complements. Underline each complement.

EXAMPLE   **1.** a direct object
   1. *We heard the president's <u>speech</u>.*
   Both of my parents enjoy <u>novels</u> set in ancient Rome.

1. a compound direct object
2. an indirect object followed by a direct object
3. a predicate nominative after a form of *be*
4. a predicate adjective after a form of *become* or *seem*
5. a compound predicate adjective after a linking verb other than *be*, *become*, or *seem*

SEGMENT 1 *(pp. 489–490)*

DIAGNOSTIC TEST

OBJECTIVES

- To identify phrases in sentences
- To identify and classify prepositional phrases as either adjective phrases or adverb phrases

17 THE PHRASE

Prepositional and Verbal Phrases

Diagnostic Test

A. Identifying Phrases

Identify the <u>phrase</u> in each of the following sentences.

EXAMPLES **1.** Payat drew a picture of his adobe house.
 1. *of his adobe house*

 2. Returning her library books, Janelle chose two more.
 2. *Returning her library books*

1. <u>Organized in 1885</u>, the first black professional baseball team was the Cuban Giants.
2. The jacket <u>with a blue collar</u> is mine.
3. My goal is <u>to become a forest ranger</u>.
4. <u>On the sidelines</u>, the coach paced nervously.
5. The student, <u>frowning slightly</u>, erased the title.
6. Guillermo hopes <u>to visit us soon</u>.
7. The charity received donations <u>for the hungry</u>.
8. Immediately <u>after school</u>, we left.

RESOURCES

THE PHRASE
- Chapter Review Form A
- Chapter Review Form B
- Assessment Portfolio
   Grammar Pretest
   Grammar Mastery Test 1
   Grammar Mastery Test 2

CHAPTER OVERVIEW

The first part of the chapter defines and explains prepositional and verbal phrases. Prepositional phrases are further classified as adjective or adverb phrases, and verbal phrases are further classified as participial or infinitive phrases. Exercises and the **Writing Application** give students practice in including phrases in informative writing.

This information can be incorporated into the study of any of the composition chapters. Knowledge of phrases can help in the revision stage of the writing process to subordinate ideas or in the proofreading stage to correct fragments.

USING THE DIAGNOSTIC TEST

The **Diagnostic Test** is in two parts. **Part A** will determine if students can recognize each phrase. **Part B** focuses on prepositional phrases. Students who have mastered adjective and adverb modifiers in **Chapter 15: "The Parts of Speech"** should have no problem differentiating between adjective and adverb phrases. You may want to use the results of the test to determine which students may be having difficulty in identifying and using phrases.

489

OBJECTIVES

- To identify phrases and their modifiers
- To identify prepositional phrases in sentences

GRAMMAR

490 *The Phrase*

9. I practice my Japanese calligraphy <u>on Mondays,</u> <u>Wednesdays, and Saturdays</u>.
10. Several <u>of my friends</u> are absent today.

B. Identifying and Classifying Prepositional Phrases

Identify the <u>prepositional phrase</u> in each sentence, and classify the phrase as an *adjective phrase* or an *adverb phrase*. Then, give the <u>word or words that the phrase modifies</u>.

EXAMPLE **1. Harvest festivals are celebrated throughout the world.**
        1. *throughout the world—adverb phrase; are celebrated*

11. adj. **11.** The <u>view</u> <u>from Mount Fuji</u> is spectacular.
12. adv. **12.** <u>Has</u> the search party <u>returned</u> <u>to the campsite</u> yet?
13. adv. **13.** <u>After the game</u>, we <u>got</u> something to eat.
14. adj. **14.** We heard <u>stories</u> <u>about our Cherokee ancestors</u>.
15. adj. **15.** An umbrella tent has <u>supports</u> <u>on the outside</u>.
16. adj. **16.** The second-longest <u>river</u> <u>in Africa</u> is the Congo.
17. adv. **17.** The magician <u>pulled</u> a rabbit <u>out of her hat</u>.
18. adj. **18.** Boulder Dam was the original <u>name</u> <u>of Hoover Dam</u>.
19. adj. **19.** The Hudson River was once the chief trading <u>route</u> <u>for the western frontier</u>.
20. adv. **20.** Hearing a loud noise, Mr. Cárdenas stopped his car, got out, and <u>looked</u> <u>underneath it</u>.

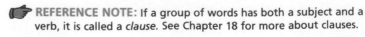

17a. A *phrase* is a group of related words that is used as a single part of speech and does not contain both a subject and a verb.

EXAMPLES **in the kitchen** [phrase; no subject or verb]
          played the guitar [phrase; no subject]

☞ **REFERENCE NOTE:** If a group of words has both a subject and a verb, it is called a *clause*. See Chapter 18 for more about clauses.

GRAMMAR

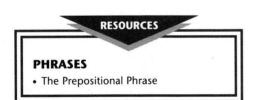 **QUICK REMINDER**
Write the following sentences on the chalkboard. Ask for volunteers to explain the advantages, if any, of using the sentence with a phrase.

1. Alice ordered a hamburger.
2. Alice ordered a hamburger with lettuce, tomatoes, pickles, onions, and mustard, on a toasted bun.

[Alice is more likely to get what she wants because her use of a prepositional phrase allows her to add details to her order.]

17 a–b

> ▶ EXERCISE 1   **Identifying Phrases**

Identify each of the following groups of words as a *phrase* or *not* a *phrase*.   v. = verb   adv. = adverb   part. = participial

EXAMPLES **1.** on the paper
1. *phrase*

2. after we eat
2. *not a phrase*

1. when you know **1.** not phr.
2. as they walked in **2.** not phr.
3. in the garden **3.** phr.
4. is sleeping **4.** phr.
5. remembered suddenly
    5. not phr. — v. and adv.

6. smiling brightly **6.** phr.
7. to the supermarket **7.** phr.
8. with a warm smile **8.** phr.
9. to laugh at myself **9.** phr.
10. if he says so **10.** not phr.
    [or phr. — part.]

Prepositional Phrases

17b. A *prepositional phrase* is a phrase that begins with a preposition and ends with a noun or a pronoun.

EXAMPLES   under the umbrella
among good friends
for ourselves

Notice that an article or another modifier may appear in a prepositional phrase. The first example contains the article *the*. In the second example, *good* modifies *friends*.

☞ REFERENCE NOTE: See page 460 for a list of commonly used prepositions.

The noun or pronoun that ends a prepositional phrase is called the *object of the preposition.*

EXAMPLES   **Linh Phan has the lead in the school play.** [The noun *play* is the object of the preposition *in.*]
They divided the prize between them. [The pronoun *them* is the object of the preposition *between.*]

GRAMMAR

LEP/ESL

Asian Languages. In the Japanese and Korean languages, prepositions follow their objects; for example, "in the house" would be "house in." Also, some languages such as Vietnamese do not always use prepositions. For example, "I went to the train station" would be "I go arrive train station." If you notice the incorrect use of prepositions in students' writing, you could ask them how they say the phrases in their native languages. Then point out the differences between their usage and English usage.

LESS-ADVANCED STUDENTS

For extra practice, bring in a picture that would elicit prepositional phrases and ask students to describe where certain things are in the picture. Objects found in the classroom could also be used. For example, "The plant is on the file cabinet." Have one student write a number of these class-generated sentences on the chalkboard. Follow up by having students come to the chalkboard to circle the prepositions and underline their objects.

GRAMMAR

COMMON ERROR

Problem. Some students might use nominative case pronouns as objects of prepositions, especially with compound objects.

Solution. Write the following sentences on the chalkboard, and ask students which is correct:

1. Wait for Susie and I.

2. Wait for Susie and me.

Show students that by omitting the first object of the preposition (Susie), they can determine more easily whether *I* or *me* is right.

▶ EXERCISE 2 **Identifying Prepositional Phrases**

Identify each <u>prepositional phrase</u> in the following sentences. [Note: A sentence may contain more than one prepositional phrase.]

EXAMPLE   [1] Many soldiers fought bravely during the Vietnam War.

       1. *during the Vietnam War*

[1] One <u>of these soldiers</u> was Jan C. Scruggs. [2] When the war was over, he and other veterans wondered why there was no national memorial honoring those who had served <u>in Vietnam</u>. [3] Scruggs decided he would raise funds <u>for a Vietnam Veterans Memorial</u>. [4] The memorial would include the names <u>of all American soldiers</u> who had died or were missing <u>in action</u>. [5] Organizing the project took years <u>of great effort</u>. [6] Many different people contributed their talents <u>to the project</u>. [7] Maya Ying Lin, a college student, designed the memorial that now stands <u>in Washington, D.C.</u> [8] This picture shows the V-shaped, black granite wall that was built <u>from Lin's design</u>. [9] Inventor Larry Century developed a way to stencil each name <u>on the shiny granite</u>. [10] Now, the men and women who fought and died <u>in Vietnam</u> will never be forgotten <u>by the American people</u>.

SEGMENT 3 *(pp. 493–495)*
ADJECTIVE PHRASES Rule 17c
OBJECTIVES
- To identify adjective phrases and the words they modify
- To create adjective phrases

Prepositional Phrases **493**

17c

Adjective Phrases

A prepositional phrase used as an adjective is called an *adjective phrase.*

> ADJECTIVE   Rosa chose the **blue** one.
> ADJECTIVE PHRASE   Rosa chose the one **with blue stripes.**

17c. An *adjective phrase* modifies a noun or a pronoun.

Adjective phrases answer the same questions that single-word adjectives answer.

> *What kind?*   *Which one?*
> *How many?*   *How much?*

EXAMPLES   The music store is the one **with the neon sign.** [The prepositional phrase *with the neon sign* is used as an adjective modifying the pronoun *one.* The phrase answers the question *Which one?*]

We bought a tape **by Janet Jackson.** [*By Janet Jackson* is used as an adjective modifying the noun *tape.* The phrase answers the question *What kind?*]

▶ EXERCISE 3   **Identifying Adjective Phrases**

Identify the <u>adjective phrase</u> in each of the following sentences, and give the <u>word that each phrase modifies</u>.

EXAMPLE   **1.** Marie Sklodowska Curie, a scientist from Poland, was awarded the Nobel Prize.
        1. *from Poland—scientist*

1. While still a student, Marie became <u>friends</u> <u>with Pierre Curie</u>.
2. Pierre had already gained <u>fame</u> <u>as a scientist</u>.
3. Paris, France, was where the <u>two</u> <u>of them</u> met.

GRAMMAR

GRAMMAR

🦉 **QUICK REMINDER**
Write the sentences below on the chalkboard, and ask for volunteers to underline the adjective phrases. Ask other volunteers to draw arrows to the words the phrases modify.

1. Who left the umbrella with the broken clasp? [with the broken clasp—umbrella]
2. The antique shop sells dozens of old tables. [of old tables—dozens]
3. Marie writes poetry about romance. [about romance—poetry]
4. Farsighted people may need glasses with bifocal lenses. [with bifocal lenses—glasses]

◆ **MEETING INDIVIDUAL NEEDS** ◆

LEP/ESL

General Strategies. You may want to preview the more difficult vocabulary in **Exercise 4** and give students a list of words that they can look up in the dictionary. Examples are *compression, swelling, elastic,* and *hamstring.*

A DIFFERENT APPROACH

Tell students that many well-known sayings contain examples of nouns and adjective phrases. Give students clues and see if they recognize these sayings. Ask volunteers to write their answers on the chalkboard. Give the following clues:

1. an easy task [piece of cake]
2. an incident that is past and forgotten [water under the bridge]
3. a discreet warning [bug in his ear]
4. solve a problem with reason [mind over matter]

After students guess, have volunteers write the phrases on the chalkboard, circle the noun, and make a box around the phrase. Then see if students have modern equivalents for these older sayings.

COMMON ERROR

Problem. Misplaced modifiers will show up more often as students begin to use multiple modifiers, especially lengthy phrases.

Solution. Tell students to check their sentences for misplaced adjective-phrase modifiers by circling the phrases and drawing arrows to the words they modify. Modifiers should be as close as possible to the words they modify.

4. Their <u>enthusiasm</u> <u>for science</u> brought them together.
5. The <u>marriage</u> <u>between the two scientists</u> was a true partnership.
6. The <u>year</u> <u>after their marriage</u> another scientist discovered natural radioactivity.
7. The Curies began researching the <u>radiation</u> <u>in certain substances</u>.
8. Their <u>theories</u> <u>about a new element</u> were proved to be true.
9. Their <u>research</u> <u>on the mineral pitchblende</u> uncovered a new radioactive element, radium.
10. The Curies won a <u>Nobel Prize</u> <u>for their discovery</u>.

More than one adjective phrase may modify the same noun or pronoun.

EXAMPLE   The sign **with neon letters near my house** flashes on and off all night long. [The two phrases, *with neon letters* and *near my house,* both modify the noun *sign.*]

An adjective phrase may also modify the object in another adjective phrase.

EXAMPLE   A majority **of the mammals in the world** sleep during the day. [The adjective phrase *of the mammals* modifies the noun *majority.* The adjective phrase *in the world* modifies the noun *mammals,* which is the object of the preposition in the first phrase.]

▶ EXERCISE 4   **Identifying Adjective Phrases**

Each numbered sentence in the following paragraph contains at least one <u>adjective phrase</u>. Identify each phrase and give the <u>word that it modifies</u>.

EXAMPLE   [1] R.I.C.E. is the recommended treatment for minor sports injuries.
          1. *for minor sports injuries—treatment*

[1] The first <u>letters</u> of the words *Rest, Ice, Compression, and Elevation* form the abbreviation *R.I.C.E.* [2] Total rest is

not necessary, just <u>rest</u> <u>for the injured part</u> <u>of the body</u>. [3] Ice helps because it deadens pain and slows the <u>loss</u> <u>of blood</u>. [4] Ice also reduces <u>swelling</u> <u>in the injured area</u>. [5] <u>Compression</u> <u>with a tight bandage</u> <u>of elastic cloth</u> prevents further <u>strain</u> <u>on the injury</u>. [6] This photograph shows a compression bandage treating the pulled <u>hamstring</u> <u>of Carl Lewis</u>. [7] The last <u>step</u> <u>in the treatment</u> is <u>elevation</u> <u>of the injury</u>. [8] The <u>effect</u> <u>of gravity</u> helps fluid drain away. [9] If pain continues, <u>someone</u> <u>with medical training</u> should be called. [10] Even <u>injuries</u> <u>of a minor</u> nature need proper attention.

▶ EXERCISE 5 **Using Adjective Phrases**

In the following sentences, insert an adjective phrase for each blank. Then, give the word that the phrase modifies. Remember that an adjective phrase must modify a noun or a pronoun.

EXAMPLE **1.** A flock ____ flew overhead.
          1. *A flock of small gray birds flew overhead.—flock*

1. The sound ____ suddenly filled the air.
2. The theater ____ often shows kung-fu movies.
3. I would like to know more ____.
4. Our vacation ____ was relaxing.
5. Her photograph ____ looks like a prizewinner.
6. Baki found the answer ____.
7. He put the flowers in a vase ____.
8. A boy ____ hung a piñata in the tree.
9. The nest is in the top branch ____.
10. Someone ____ shouted for quiet.

GRAMMAR

GRAMMAR

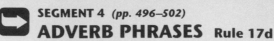
ADVERB PHRASES Rule 17d

OBJECTIVES

- To identify adverb phrases and the words they modify
- To write an informative paragraph containing adjective and adverb phrases

GRAMMAR

 **QUICK REMINDER**
Write the following sentences on the chalkboard. Then ask the class to add adverb phrases that will answer such questions as *When?, Where?, How?, How often?,* or *To what extent?*

1. The hikers rested.
   [The hikers rested beside the stream. The hikers rested on a large rock beside the stream. The hikers rested at noon on a large rock beside the stream.]
2. The plane landed
   [The plane landed in a storm. The plane landed on runway three in a storm. The plane landed at night on runway three in a storm.]

496 *The Phrase*

Adverb Phrases

A prepositional phrase used as an adverb is called an *adverb phrase.*

ADVERB The cavalry **soon** reached the fort.

ADVERB PHRASE **By noon** the cavalry reached the fort.

17d. An *adverb phrase* modifies a verb, an adjective, or another adverb.

Adverb phrases answer the same questions that single-word adverbs answer.

When?	How often?
Where?	To what extent?
How?	

EXAMPLES Our puppy often barks early **in the morning.**
[The adverb phrase *in the morning* modifies the adverb *early,* telling *when.*]
We got our new puppy **at the animal shelter.**
[The adverb phrase *at the animal shelter* modifies the verb *got,* telling *where.*]
A puppy is always ready **for a game.** [The adverb phrase *for a game* modifies the adjective *ready,* telling *how.*]

Unlike adjective phrases, which usually follow the word or words they modify, adverb phrases may appear at various places in sentences.

EXAMPLES We planted elm seedlings **along the driveway.**
Along the driveway we planted elm seedlings.

At our house we have dinner early.
We have dinner early **at our house.**

> EXERCISE 6   **Identifying Adverb Phrases**

Identify the <u>adverb phrase</u> in each of the following sentences, and give the <u>word that each phrase modifies</u>. [Note: Do not list adjective phrases.]

EXAMPLE   **1. Pecos Bill will live forever in the many legends about him.**

     1. *in the many legends—will live*

1. When he was only a baby, Pecos Bill <u>fell</u> <u>into the Pecos River</u>.
2. His parents <u>searched</u> <u>for him</u> but couldn't find him.
3. He <u>was saved</u> <u>by coyotes</u>, who raised him.
4. He <u>thought</u> <u>for many years</u> that he was a coyote.
5. <u>After a long argument</u> a cowboy <u>convinced</u> him that he was not a coyote.
6. <u>During a drought</u> he <u>dug</u> the bed of the Rio Grande.
7. <u>On one occasion</u> Bill <u>rode</u> a cyclone.
8. A mountain lion once <u>leaped</u> <u>from a ledge</u> above Bill's head.
9. Bill had the mountain lion tamed <u>soon</u> <u>after the leap</u>.
10. Stories like these about Pecos Bill <u>are</u> common <u>in the West</u>.

Like adjective phrases, more than one adverb phrase may modify the same word.

EXAMPLES   She drove **for hours through the storm.** [Both adverb phrases, *for hours* and *through the storm*, modify the verb *drove.*]
The library is open **during the day on weekends.** [Both adverb phrases, *during the day* and *on weekends*, modify the adjective *open.*]

NOTE: An adverb phrase may be followed by an adjective phrase that modifies the object in the adverb phrase.

    EXAMPLE   The boat landed **on an island near the coast.**
        [The adverb phrase *on an island* modifies the verb *landed.* The adjective phrase *near the coast* modifies the noun *island.*]

MEETING
INDIVIDUAL
NEEDS

LEP/ESL

    General Strategies. You may want to give students two or three sets of adverb phrases and main clauses (similar to the examples on p. 496) and help them write three sentences for each set by manipulating the placement of the adverb phrases. It would also be helpful to point out to students the sentences in **Exercise 6** in which the adverb phrases cannot be moved.

LEARNING STYLES

    Visual Learners. It might be easier for students to understand how placement of adverb phrases can be varied if they see the same sentence with two variations placed side by side. You may want to copy sentences 5, 6, and 7 of **Exercise 6** onto the chalkboard. Have student volunteers rewrite the sentences on the chalkboard by moving each adverb phrase to a new location to show the contrast.

COOPERATIVE LEARNING

For a learning game, divide the class into pairs. Have one student in each pair select a preposition from the paragraphs in **Exercise 7** and use it to write a prepositional phrase that can be used as an adverb. The partner should then use the phrase as an adverb in a sentence. That partner will then select another preposition, turn it into a phrase, and pass it back to his or her partner, and so on.

ANSWERS
Exercise 8

Paragraphs will vary. The following paragraph is a possibility:

When you walk in the woods or in the fields, avoid poison oak and poison ivy. Hunt for plants with leaves growing in clusters of threes. On poison ivy, the leaves are glossy green, oval-shaped, and smoothly textured. On poison oak, the leaves are similar, but thicker and smaller, with ends rounded rather than pointed. If you come into contact with these plants, wash the skin thoroughly with soap and water. If itching, swelling, and redness of the skin develop, see your doctor.

VISUAL CONNECTIONS
Related Expression Skills.
You may want to ask students to design covers for their pamphlets. The titles could have a prepositional phrase. Remind students that the text will cover other topics besides poison ivy and poison oak.

498

 EXERCISE 7 **Identifying Adverb Phrases**

Identify the ten <u>adverb phrases</u> in the following paragraph. Then, give the <u>word or words that each phrase modifies</u>. [Note: Do not list adjective phrases.]

EXAMPLE [1] **Never before had a blizzard struck the coastal area with such force.**
1. *with such force—had struck*

[1] The raging wind <u>blew</u> eleven-year-old Andrea <u>over a sea wall</u> near her home and <u>trapped</u> her <u>in a deep snowdrift</u>. [2] No one <u>could hear</u> her shouts <u>over the howling wind</u>. [3] Suddenly, Andrea's dog <u>charged</u> <u>through the snow toward the beach</u>. [4] He <u>plunged</u> <u>into the snow</u> around Andrea and licked her face, warming the skin. [5] Then the huge dog <u>walked</u> <u>around Andrea</u> until the snow was packed down. [6] The dog <u>pulled</u> her <u>to an open area</u> on the beach. [7] <u>With great effort</u>, Andrea and her dog <u>made</u> their way home. [8] <u>Later</u> <u>in the evening</u>, the heroic dog was served a special steak dinner.

 EXERCISE 8 **Writing a Paragraph Using Adjective and Adverb Phrases**

You are working with a park ranger for the summer. Together you are writing a safety pamphlet for campers. One part of the pamphlet will explain how to avoid coming into contact with poison ivy and poison oak. Using these drawings the ranger has given you and the notes on the next page, write a paragraph informing campers about these plants. Use at least two adjective phrases and three adverb phrases in your paragraph.

REVIEWS A and B

OBJECTIVES

- To identify and classify prepositional phrases
- To write sentences containing prepositional phrases

> ## Notes
>
> poison ivy and poison oak—plants can cause an
> allergic reaction when touched
>
> some people react worse than others—some not at all
>
> reaction includes itching and blistering of the skin
>
> best method to deal with these plants—learn to
> recognize and avoid them
>
> poison ivy—leaf made up of three leaflets that are
> glossy green, oval-shaped, and smoothly textured
>
> poison oak—similar to poison ivy, but leaflets are
> thicker and smaller, and the ends are rounded
> rather than pointed
>
> first aid—wash the area thoroughly with soap and
> water; visit a doctor if itching, swelling, and
> redness develop

▶ REVIEW A   **Identifying and Classifying Prepositional Phrases**

In the following sentences, identify each <u>prepositional phrase</u> and classify it as an *adjective phrase* or an *adverb phrase*. Then, give the <u>word or words the phrase modifies</u>.

EXAMPLE   **1.** Here is some information about sharks.
            1. *about sharks—adjective phrase; information*

1. Did you know that there are 350 <u>types</u> <u>of them</u>?   **1.** adj.
2. Scientists <u>group</u> these different types <u>into thirty large families</u>.   **2.** adv.
3. <u>Sharks</u> <u>within the same family</u> share many traits.   **3.** adj.
4. The body shape, tail shape, and teeth determine the <u>differences</u> <u>between families</u>.   **4.** adj.

GRAMMAR

499

GRAMMAR

5. adv. **5.** Sharks <u>are found</u> <u>throughout the world's oceans</u>.

6. adv. **6.** As the chart shows, some sharks prefer cold waters, and others <u>live</u> mostly <u>in warm tropical oceans</u>.

7. adj. **7.** Only twenty-five <u>kinds</u> <u>of sharks</u> are dangerous.

8. adv. **8.** The huge whale shark, however, <u>falls</u> <u>under the "not dangerous" category</u>.

9. adj. **9.** Divers can even hitch a <u>ride</u> <u>on its fins</u>.

10. adv. **10.** Beautiful yet fearsome, sharks <u>are</u> widely <u>regarded</u> <u>as the world's most awesome creatures</u>.

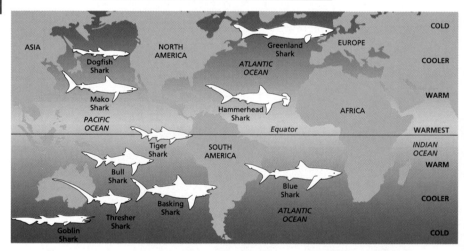

 REVIEW B

Writing Sentences with Prepositional Phrases

Write five sentences of your own. In each sentence, use a different prepositional phrase from the following list. After each sentence, label the phrase as an *adjective phrase* or an *adverb phrase*.

EXAMPLE **1.** through the toll booth
  1. *A car passed through the toll booth.—adverb phrase*

1. in the movie theater
2. for the Cinco de Mayo party
3. along the water's edge
4. about General Colin Powell
5. into the crowded department store

GRAMMAR

VISUAL CONNECTIONS

Exploring the Subject. Tiger sharks, one of the sharks shown on the chart, are not finicky feeders and will eat almost anything. Tiger sharks following ships have been known to swallow whatever has been thrown overboard, including paper, tin cans, and clothing.

ANSWERS

Review B

Sentences will vary. Here are some possibilities:

1. We sat in the movie theater.—adverb phrase

2. The decorations for the Cinco de Mayo party were donated.—adjective phrase

3. The dog raced along the water's edge.—adverb phrase

4. Have you read any articles about Gen. Colin Powell recently?—adjective phrase

5. They pushed into the crowded department store.—adverb phrase

WRITING APPLICATION

OBJECTIVE

- To use both adjective and adverb phrases to write instructions

WRITING APPLICATION

Using Prepositional Phrases to Add Detail to Your Writing

Prepositional phrases add information to a sentence. Adjective phrases give details about *what kind, which one,* and *how many.* Adverb phrases tell details about *when, where, how, how much,* and *to what extent.*

WITHOUT PHRASES We fed the cat.
WITH PHRASES In the morning we fed the cat from the blue box of dry Kitty Bits.

▶ WRITING ACTIVITY

You are writing a note to a friend explaining how to care for your pet while you are away on vacation. In your note, use a combined total of at least ten adjective phrases and adverb phrases to give detailed instructions to your friend.

Prewriting Begin by thinking about a pet you have or would like to have. Then, make a chart or list of the pet's needs. If you need more information about a particular pet, ask a friend or someone else who owns such a pet.

Writing As you write your first draft, focus on giving information about each of your pet's needs. Tell your friend everything he or she needs to know to care for your pet properly.

Evaluating and Revising Ask a family member or friend to read your note. Add any missing information and take out any unnecessary instructions. Be sure that you have used both adjective phrases and adverb phrases and that you have used a total of at least ten phrases.

Proofreading Read over your note again to check the grammar, punctuation, and spelling. Be sure that your prepositional phrases are properly placed. Remember that

GRAMMAR

✎ WRITING APPLICATION

The **Writing Application** gives students practice in using prepositional phrases to convey essential details through written instructions.

🗡 CRITICAL THINKING
Evaluating

In prewriting, students might include more information than is necessary for writing the instructions. Tell students that in the writing stage, they should omit any procedures not essential to accomplishing the task. For example, while they will need to tell where to find can openers or food and water dishes, it is not necessary to include instructions to open the can or to place the contents in a dish.

Tell students to keep in mind what information their friends will need and what knowledge any person would already have.

PREWRITING

Tell students to visualize themselves going through the procedure. They should stop after each imagined action and write exactly what they did.

WRITING

Tell students to look at their lists of steps when they begin writing to make sure that all procedures are in the correct sequence.

EVALUATING AND REVISING

Have students exchange papers. Students should be able to tell their partners whether they would be able to take care of the pets by following the instructions given.

GRAMMAR

501

SEGMENT 5 (pp. 502–506)
THE PARTICIPLE Rules 17e, 17f

OBJECTIVES

- To identify present and past participles and the words they modify
- To identify participial phrases and the words they modify
- To use participial phrases to write sentences

---

502 *The Phrase*

an adjective phrase follows the noun or pronoun it modifies. An adverb phrase may occur at various places in a sentence. (See page 720 for information on when to use commas with introductory prepositional phrases.)

Verbals and Verbal Phrases

A *verbal* is a word that is formed from a verb but is used as a noun, an adjective, or an adverb.

The Participle

17e. A *participle* is a verb form that can be used as an adjective.

There are two kinds of participles: *present participles* and *past participles*.

(1) Present participles end in —ing.

EXAMPLES   Mr. Sanchez rescued three people from the **burning** building. [*Burning* is the present participle of the verb *burn.* The participle modifies the noun *building.*]
Chasing the cat, the dog ran down the street. [*Chasing* is the present participle of the verb *chase.* The participle acts as an adjective modifying the noun *dog.*]

(2) Past participles usually end in —d or —ed. Some past participles are irregularly formed.

EXAMPLES   Well **trained** in gunnery, the soldier successfully carried out her mission. [The past participle *trained* modifies the noun *soldier.*]
We skated on the **frozen** pond. [The irregular past participle *frozen* modifies the noun *pond.*]

QUICK REMINDER

To give students practice in recognizing participles, write the following sentences on the chalkboard. Have students first find the prepositional phrase, and then identify the participle within it.

1. Sally sat on the broken chair. [on the broken chair—broken]
2. Mother gave us a party after our winning game. [after our winning game—winning]
3. The coach took the entire team to a widely publicized track meet. [to a widely publicized track meet—publicized]

17e

GRAMMAR

☞ **REFERENCE NOTE:** For a list of irregular past participles, see pages 583–586.

NOTE: Be careful not to confuse participles used as adjectives with participles used in verb phrases. Remember that the participle in a verb phrase is part of the verb.

| PARTICIPLE | **Discouraged,** the fans went home. |
| VERB PHRASE | The fans **were discouraged** and went home. |

| PARTICIPLE | **Singing** cheerfully, the birds perched in the trees. |
| VERB PHRASE | The birds **were singing** cheerfully in the trees. |

▶ EXERCISE 9 **Identifying Participles and the Nouns They Modify**

Identify the <u>participles used as adjectives</u> in the following sentences. After each participle, give the <u>noun that the participle modifies</u>.

EXAMPLE **1.** The deserted cities of the Anasazi are found in the Four Corners area of the United States.
 1. *deserted—cities*

1. Utah, Colorado, New Mexico, and Arizona are the <u>bordering states</u> that make up the Four Corners.
2. Because of its natural beauty, Chaco Canyon is one of the most <u>visited sights</u> in this region of the Southwest.
3. Among the <u>remaining ruins</u> in Chaco Canyon are the houses, public buildings, and plazas of the Anasazi.
4. What <u>alarming event</u> may have caused these people to leave their valley?
5. Historians are studying the <u>scattered remains</u> of the Anasazi culture to learn more about these mysterious people.

▶ EXERCISE 10 **Identifying Participles and the Nouns or Pronouns They Modify**

Identify the <u>participles used as adjectives</u> in the following sentences. Then, give the <u>noun or pronoun the participle modifies</u>.

GRAMMAR

LEP/ESL

 Asian Languages. Because some Asian languages such as Vietnamese do not have participles, students might have difficulty identifying and using participles. You could use the following activity to help clarify the concept:

 First, list the verbs *jump, howl, march, polish, iron,* and *trust* on the chalkboard. Ask students to add *–ing* to the first three verbs and *–ed* to the last three verbs and to add nouns to these newly formed participles. [jumping frogs, howling dogs, marching band, polished floor, ironed shirt, trusted friend]

LESS-ADVANCED STUDENTS

 To reinforce the use of participles and to show how often they are used, bring in some pictures that might elicit the use of participles for description. First, have a short discussion about the subject of each picture. Then ask students to describe what is happening and encourage them to use participles as adjectives. These descriptions can be written on the chalkboard, and the participles can be identified along with the pronouns they modify. To follow up, you may want to give students a cloze exercise the next day. Use these same sentences and give students two answer choices, the present or past participial form.

ADVANCED STUDENTS

To help students understand that prepositional phrases can be a part of participial phrases, try an exercise in which students combine participles and prepositional phrases to make participial phrases. Write the following prepositional phrases on the chalkboard and ask students to supply participles. Possible participles are listed in brackets.

1. by the police officer [prevented]
2. with milk and sugar [eaten]
3. about the Civil War [reading]

Next, ask students to use the phrases in sentences. [Here are some possibilities:

1. A serious crime was prevented by the police officer.
2. Breakfast cereal sometimes is eaten with milk and sugar.
3. The class has been reading about the Civil War.]

 ## INTEGRATING THE LANGUAGE ARTS

Technology Link. If available, computers would be of use to students in completing **Exercise 12.** Tell students to create a sentence with the given participle, then enter this sentence into a thesaurus program on the computer to find synonyms for it. Ask students how they will need to change the form of the thesaurus words before they can use them. [Words appearing on the screen will be present-tense verbs, which they must change to participle form.] Have students print out **Exercise 12** along with the synonymous participles.

504

EXAMPLE   **1.** Buzzing mosquitoes swarmed around me.
           1. *Buzzing—mosquitoes*

1. <u>Annoyed</u>, <u>I</u> went inside to watch TV.
2. I woke my <u>sleeping</u> <u>father</u> to ask about mosquitoes.
3. <u>Irritated</u>, <u>he</u> directed me to the encyclopedia.
4. I learned that some <u>flying</u> <u>insects</u> carry diseases.
5. <u>Biting</u> <u>mosquitoes</u> put liquid poison into the skin.
6. The <u>swollen</u> <u>skin</u> itches.
7. <u>Sucking</u> blood for food, <u>mosquitoes</u> survive in many different climates.
8. Sometimes you can hear <u>mosquitoes</u> <u>humming</u>.
9. Their <u>vibrating</u> <u>wings</u> make the sound.
10. <u>Mosquitoes</u>, <u>living</u> only a few weeks, may go through as many as twelve generations in a year.

The Participial Phrase

17f.   A *participial phrase* consists of a participle together with its modifiers and complements. The entire phrase is used as an adjective.

EXAMPLE   **Stretching slowly,** the cat jumped down from the windowsill. [The participle *stretching* is modified by the adverb *slowly.*]

The tornado **predicted by the weather forecaster** did not hit our area. [The participle *predicted* is modified by the prepositional phrase *by the weather forecaster.*]

Reading the assignment, she took notes carefully. [The participle *reading* has the direct object *assignment.*]

A participial phrase should be placed close to the word it modifies. Otherwise the phrase may appear to modify another word, and the sentence may not make sense.

 REFERENCE NOTE: For information on how to place participial phrases correctly, see pages 642–643.

17f

▶ EXERCISE 11 **Identifying Participial Phrases and the Nouns or Pronouns They Modify**

Identify the <u>participial phrases</u> in the following sentences. Then, give the <u>word or words each phrase modifies</u>.

EXAMPLE   **1.** Living over four hundred years ago, Leonardo da Vinci kept journals of his many ideas and inventions.

        1. *Living over four hundred years ago—Leonardo da Vinci*

1. The <u>journals</u>, <u>written in a secret code</u>, are more than five thousand pages long.
2. Leonardo drew many <u>pictures</u> <u>showing birds in flight</u>.
3. <u>Based on his sketches of birds</u>, his <u>design</u> for a helicopter was the first one in history.
4. <u>Shown here</u>, this <u>design</u> gives the viewer a sense of motion.

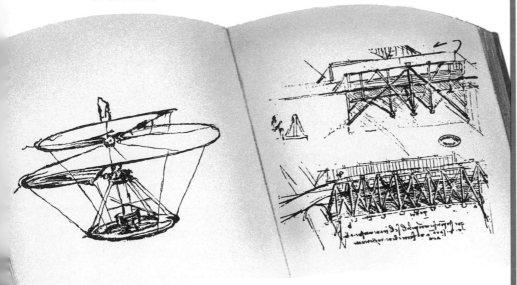

5. <u>Studying the eye</u>, <u>Leonardo</u> understood the sense of sight.
6. <u>He</u> worked hard, <u>filling his journals with sketches like the one above for a movable bridge</u>.

GRAMMAR

GRAMMAR

ANSWERS
Exercise 12

Sentences will vary. Here are some possibilities:

1. Confused by the directions, we couldn't locate the street.
2. The boy gathering information on the Hopi went to the library.
3. Practicing my part in the play, I bowed to the audience.
4. Followed closely by my younger brother, the cat climbed the tree.
5. Searching through the crowd, the drummer located the singer.

RESOURCES

THE INFINITIVE
• Infinitives and Infinitive Phrases

 QUICK REMINDER

Write the following pairs of sentences on the chalkboard. Ask students to identify which underlined words are infinitive phrases and which are prepositional phrases.

1a. You can lead a horse *to water,* but you cannot make it drink. [prepositional phrase]
  b. Dad got up early *to water the lawn.* [infinitive]
2a. The old man lifted a lantern *to light the path.* [infinitive]
  b. The moth flew *to the light.* [prepositional phrase]
3a. The chief told the firefighter to hook the hose *to the pump.* [prepositional phrase]
  b. Wind is needed for the windmill *to pump water.* [infinitive]

506

SEGMENT 6 *(pp. 506–511)*
THE INFINITIVE Rules 17g, 17h
OBJECTIVES
• To identify infinitives and infinitive phrases in sentences
• To write a story using infinitive phrases and participial phrases

506 *The Phrase*

7. The <u>solutions</u> <u>reached in his journals</u> often helped Leonardo when he created his artworks.
8. The <u>hands</u> <u>sketched in the journals</u> helped him paint the hands of the *Mona Lisa.*
9. <u>Painting on a large wall,</u> <u>Leonardo</u> created *The Last Supper.*
10. <u>Leonardo,</u> <u>experimenting continually,</u> had little time to paint in his later years.

▶ EXERCISE 12 **Writing Sentences with Participial Phrases**

Write five sentences, using in each sentence a different participial phrase from the following list. [Note: Place a comma after a participial phrase that begins a sentence.]

EXAMPLE **1.** cheering for the team
1. *Cheering for the team, we celebrated the victory.*

1. confused by the directions
2. gathering information on the Hopi
3. practicing my part in the play
4. followed closely by my younger brother
5. searching through the crowd

The Infinitive

17g. An *infinitive* is a verb form, usually preceded by *to,* that can be used as a noun, an adjective, or an adverb.

INFINITIVES	
USED AS	**EXAMPLES**
Nouns	**To succeed** is my goal. [*To succeed* is the subject of the sentence.] My ambition is **to teach** Spanish. [*To teach* is a predicate nominative.] She tried **to win.** [*To win* is the direct object of the verb *tried.*]

(continued)

17g

INFINITIVES *(continued)*	
USED AS	**EXAMPLES**
Adjectives	The place **to meet** tomorrow is the library. [*To meet* modifies the noun *place.*] **She is the one to call.** [*To call* modifies the pronoun *one.*]
Adverbs	Tamara claims she was born **to surf.** [*To surf* modifies the verb *was born.*] This math problem will be hard **to solve** without a calculator. [*To solve* modifies the adjective *hard.*]

NOTE: *To* plus a noun or a pronoun (*to Washington, to her*) is a prepositional phrase, not an infinitive.

PREPOSITIONAL PHRASE	I am going **to the mall** today.
INFINITIVE	I am going **to shop** for new shoes.

▶ EXERCISE 13   **Identifying Infinitives**

Identify the <u>infinitives</u> in the following sentences. If a sentence does not contain an infinitive, write *none.*

EXAMPLE   **1.** I would like to go to New York City someday.
          1. *to go*

1. My first stop would be <u>to visit</u> the Statue of Liberty.
2. Thousands of people go <u>to see</u> the statue every day.
3. They take a boat to Liberty Island.   **3.** none
4. The statue holds a torch <u>to symbolize</u> freedom.
5. The idea of a statue <u>to represent</u> freedom came from a French historian.   **6.** none
6. France gave the statue to the United States in 1884.
7. It was a gift <u>to express</u> the friendship between the two nations.   **8.** none
8. The statue was shipped to this country in 214 cases.
9. In the 1980s, many people helped <u>to raise</u> money for repairs to the statue.
10. The repairs were completed in time <u>to celebrate</u> the statue's 100th anniversary on October 28, 1986.

MEETING **INDIVIDUAL** NEEDS

LEP/ESL

General Strategies. Infinitives in some languages such as Spanish and French are marked by a suffix, while English infinitives are not. Also, some languages such as Japanese and Vietnamese do not have infinitives. You may want to give students extra help with additional oral and written practice similar to **Exercise 13.**

A DIFFERENT APPROACH

To emphasize the different uses of infinitive phrases, use the same infinitive in three different ways—as a noun, as an adjective, and as an adverb—in three different sentences. Write the sentences on the chalkboard, and ask students to pick out the infinitive phrases. Then discuss whether these phrases are used as nouns, adjectives, or adverbs. Here are some examples using the infinitive *to keep*:

1. To keep the peace is the role of the military. [To keep the peace—noun]
2. A locker is a place to keep books and pencils. [to keep books and pencils—adjective]
3. To keep his desk in order, John needs an extra drawer. [To keep his desk in order—adverb]

CRITICAL THINKING
Analysis

To help students differentiate between infinitive phrases and prepositional phrases, you could try this activity, that involves a newspaper. Have students form groups of three. Make one person responsible for finding all infinitive phrases in a specified number of newspaper pages and make another person responsible for finding all prepositional phrases beginning with *to* in those same pages. The third group member will list the findings. This procedure can involve some competition if the group with the most phrases is offered some reward.

The Infinitive Phrase

17h. An *infinitive phrase* consists of an infinitive together with its modifiers and complements. It may be used as a noun, an adjective, or an adverb.

EXAMPLES **To be a good gymnast** takes hard work. [The infinitive phrase is used as a noun. The infinitive *to be* has a complement, *a good gymnast.*]

The first person **to fly over both the North Pole and the South Pole** was Richard Byrd. [The infinitive phrase is used as an adjective modifying the noun *person*. The infinitive *to fly* is modified by the prepositional phrase *over both the North Pole and the South Pole.*]

We would like **to eat supper on the porch.** [The infinitive phrase is used as an adverb modifying the verb *would like.* The infinitive *to eat* has the object *supper* and is modified by the prepositional phrase *on the porch.*]

▶ EXERCISE 14 **Identifying Infinitive Phrases**

Identify the <u>infinitive phrase</u> in each of the following sentences.

EXAMPLE **1.** We went to the park to watch birds.
1. *to watch birds*

1. A bird is able <u>to control each of its feathers</u>.
2. Birds use their feathers <u>to push their bodies through the air</u>.
3. Human beings learned <u>to build aircraft by studying birds</u>.
4. A bird sings <u>to claim its territory</u>.
5. <u>To recognize the songs of different birds</u> takes practice.
6. By molting (or gradual shedding), birds are able <u>to replace their feathers</u>.

7. Eagles use their feet <u>to catch small animals</u>.
8. Since they have no teeth, birds have <u>to swallow their food whole</u>.
9. Both parents usually help <u>to build a nest</u>.
10. Most birds feed their young until the young are ready <u>to fly from the nest</u>.

PICTURE THIS

Wow! Whoever drew this sketch is a good artist. You found this sketch on the bus this morning, and you wish you knew who lost it. What is the artist like? Who is the person in the sketch? You find yourself thinking about these things and making up stories. You decide to write a short story about the artist or about the person in the sketch. Use at least three participial phrases and two infinitive phrases in your story. Underline the phrases you use.

Subject: sketch by an unidentified artist
Audience: classmates
Purpose: to entertain

PICTURE THIS

As a prewriting assignment, ask students to generate a list of details about the subjects of their short stories and to make notes somewhat like those on p. 499, in the assignment on poison ivy and poison oak. Students can then use these prewriting notes to construct their stories.

MEETING
INDIVIDUAL
NEEDS

LEARNING STYLES

Auditory Learners. To help students with the **Picture This** activity, you could use an auditory model as a prompt. One effective way to do this is by playing some music for the students and then discussing with them what scene or event they feel the composer might have been thinking about. From this discussion, write a story with the help of the class about the composer. You may have to elicit the participial and infinitive phrases by asking questions. Students will then be better prepared to write their descriptions of the artist or the sketch.

ANSWERS
Exercise 15

Sentences will vary. Here are some possibilities:

1. I want to sing with the Harlem Boys Choir.
2. The class was allowed to ask a question about the test.
3. He tried to write a poem to his girlfriend.
4. I am beginning to understand the assignment.
5. We volunteered to give a report on the Spanish exploration of California.

 COOPERATIVE LEARNING
For a round-robin learning game, divide the class into teams of three. The first member of each team writes an infinitive on a sheet of paper and then passes it along to the second member of the team, who turns the infinitive into a phrase. Then the paper is passed to the third member of the team, who will use the phrase in a complete sentence. Finally, the third team member passes the paper back to the first member, who writes the completed sentence on the chalkboard. Keep track of the time it takes each team to complete the process. The team who has the best time with correct responses wins.

Here is an example:

1. to be
2. to be in England
3. The poet wanted to be in England in April.

510

REVIEW C

OBJECTIVE
• To identify and classify phrases as participial or infinitive

510 *The Phrase*

▶ EXERCISE 15 **Writing Sentences with Infinitive Phrases**

Write five sentences, using in each sentence a different infinitive phrase from the following list. Try to vary your sentences as much as possible.

EXAMPLE **1.** to see the carved masks of the Haida people
1. *Terry wants to see the carved masks of the Haida people.*

1. to sing with the Harlem Boys Choir
2. to ask a question about the test
3. to write a poem to his girlfriend
4. to understand the assignment
5. to give a report on the Spanish exploration of California

▶ REVIEW C **Identifying and Classifying Participial Phrases and Infinitive Phrases**

Identify the <u>participial phrase</u> or the <u>infinitive phrase</u> in each sentence of the following paragraph. Label each phrase as a *participial phrase* or an *infinitive phrase*.

EXAMPLES [1] My family is proud to celebrate our Jewish holidays.
1. *to celebrate our Jewish holidays—infinitive phrase*

[2] Observing Jewish traditions, we celebrate each holiday in a special way.
2. *Observing Jewish traditions—participial phrase*

1. part.   [1] During Rosh Hashanah we hear the Torah <u>read in</u>
2. part.   <u>our synagogue</u>. [2] <u>Celebrated in September or October,</u>
3. inf.   Rosh Hashanah is the Jewish New Year. [3] On this holiday, the rabbi at our synagogue chooses <u>to wear white</u>
4. part.   <u>robes instead of the usual black robes</u>. [4] <u>Representing</u>
<u>newness and purity</u>, the white robes symbolize the new
5. part.   year. [5] My favorite food of Rosh Hashanah is the honey
6. part.   cake <u>baked by my grandmother</u>. [6] During this holiday
everyone eats a lot, <u>knowing that Yom Kippur, a day of</u>

REVIEW: POSTTEST 1 and 2

OBJECTIVES

- To identify prepositional phrases and to classify them as either adjective or adverb
- To identify verbal phrases and to classify them as either participial or infinitive
- To add specified phrases to sentences

fasting, is only ten days away. [7] Yom Kippur, <u>considered the holiest day of the Jewish year</u>, is a serious holiday. [8] <u>To attend services like the one you see below</u> is part of my family's Yom Kippur tradition. [9] I am always pleased <u>to see many of my friends and neighbors there</u>. [10] Sunset, <u>marking the end of the day</u>, brings Yom Kippur to a peaceful close.

7. part.

8. inf.

9. inf.

10. part.

GRAMMAR

INTEGRATING THE LANGUAGE ARTS

Literature Link. You may want to select several paragraphs from Charles Dickens' "A Christmas Carol" to discuss with students how extensively Dickens uses descriptive phrases. Explain to students that many 19th-century writers used elaborate descriptions containing many phrases because literature was the television of their day. The more descriptive the passages were, the more easily readers could visualize the scenes.

Ask students to analyze other paragraphs in Dickens' story for his use of descriptive phrases. Tell them to find at least one adjective phrase, one adverbial phrase, one participial phrase, and one infinitive phrase.

GRAMMAR

Review: Posttest 1

A. Identifying and Classifying Prepositional Phrases

Identify each <u>prepositional phrase</u> in the following sentences and classify it as an *adjective phrase* or an *adverb phrase*. Then, give the <u>word that the phrase modifies</u>.

EXAMPLE   **1.** The chairs in the kitchen need new cushions.
     1. *in the kitchen—adjective phrase; chairs*

1. Cathy Guisewite is the <u>creator</u> of the cartoon strip "Cathy." **1.** adj.
2. The Rio Grande is the <u>boundary</u> between Texas and Mexico. **2.** adj.

3. Those totem poles <u>come</u> <u>from Washington State</u>. **3. adv.**
4. The official <u>name</u> <u>for the United States flag</u> is the Stars and Stripes. **4. adj.**
5. Heu Feng was a <u>finalist</u> <u>at the international violin competition</u>. **5. adj.**
6. <u>Through the window</u> <u>crashed</u> the baseball. **6. adv** **7. adv.**
7. Do you want <u>to order</u> a pizza <u>instead of a sandwich</u>?
8. <u>During the Persian Gulf Conflict</u>, we <u>watched</u> the news often. **8. adv.**
9. The first United States space shuttle <u>was launched</u> <u>in 1981</u>. **9. adv.**
10. <u>Outside the door</u> the hungry cat <u>waited</u> patiently. **10. adv.**

B. Identifying and Classifying Verbal Phrases

Identify the <u>verbal phrase</u> in each of the following sentences. Then, tell whether it is a *participial phrase* or an *infinitive phrase*.

EXAMPLE **1.** The snow, falling steadily, formed huge drifts.
1. *falling steadily—participial phrase*

11. We expect <u>to do well on the test</u>. **11. inf.**
12. The bus, <u>slowed by heavy traffic</u>, arrived later than it usually does. **12. part.**
13. <u>Breaking the eggs into the wok</u>, he made egg foo yong. **13. part.**
14. <u>To remain calm</u> is not always easy. **14. inf.**
15. She wants <u>to study Spanish in high school</u>. **15. inf.**
16. The magazine <u>featuring that article</u> is in the school library. **16. part.**
17. <u>Chilled to the bone</u>, the children finally went inside. **17. part.**
18. Who are the candidates that they plan <u>to support in the election</u>? **18. inf.**
19. Bethune-Cookman College, <u>founded by Mary McLeod Bethune</u>, is in Daytona Beach, Florida. **19. part.**
20. Teresa called <u>to ask about tonight's homework assignment</u>. **20. inf.**

Review: Posttest 2

Writing Phrases for Sentences

For each of the following sentences, write the kind of phrase that is called for in parentheses.

EXAMPLE **1.** ____ , the audience cheered Yo-Yo Ma's performance. (*participial phrase*)

1. *Clapping loudly, the audience cheered Yo-Yo Ma's performance.*

1. We walked slowly ____. (*adverb phrase*)
2. The people ____ applauded Barbara Jordan's speech. (*adjective phrase*)
3. I finished my report ____. (*adverb phrase*)
4. The water ____ dripped steadily. (*adjective phrase*)
5. ____ we saw many beautiful Navajo rugs. (*adverb phrase*)
6. ____, the principal entered the classroom. (*participial phrase*)
7. Suddenly, ____, the lion pounced. (*participial phrase*)
8. My friends and I like ____. (*infinitive phrase*)
9. ____ is my one ambition. (*infinitive phrase*)
10. She wrote a poem ____. (*participial phrase*)

ANSWERS
Review: Posttest 2

Phrases will vary. Here are some possibilities:

1. We walked slowly toward the car.
2. The people in the auditorium applauded Barbara Jordan's speech.
3. I finished my report in the morning.
4. The water from the faucet dripped steadily.
5. On our trip we saw many beautiful Navajo rugs.
6. Trying to catch his breath, the principal entered the room.
7. Suddenly, using all his strength, the lion pounced.
8. My friends and I like to go to the movies.
9. To climb Mount Everest is my one ambition.
10. She wrote a poem praising her mother.

SEGMENT 1 *(pp. 514–515)*
DIAGNOSTIC TEST

OBJECTIVES
- To identify a group of words as a clause or not a clause
- To classify subordinate clauses as adjective clauses or adverb clauses

▼ **RESOURCES** ▼

THE CLAUSE
- Chapter Review Form A
- Chapter Review Form B
- Assessment Portfolio
  Grammar Pretest
  Grammar Mastery Test 1
  Grammar Mastery Test 2

CHAPTER OVERVIEW

This chapter should help students understand how to structure sentences. The first part of the chapter explains the difference between independent and subordinate clauses and asks students to write sentences using subordinate clauses. The rest of the chapter provides a thorough discussion of adjective and adverb clauses. In the **Writing Application,** students are asked to apply their knowledge of clauses to explain a process. For more help on how to write a process paper, refer students to **Chapter 7: "Writing to Inform."**

Knowledge of independent and subordinate clauses will also be important when studying **Chapter 11: "Writing Effective Sentences."**

USING THE DIAGNOSTIC TEST

You may want to use the **Diagnostic Test** to determine students' understanding of clauses and phrases, especially if you are working on sentence combining in the revision stage of compositions. You will also be able to assess students' comprehension of the characteristics of adjective and adverb clauses. You may want to see if students can identify clauses as they work with their own writing.

18 THE CLAUSE

Independent and Subordinate Clauses

Diagnostic Test

A. Identifying Clauses

Label each of the following groups of words as a *clause* or *not a clause*.

EXAMPLES **1.** last winter we ice-skated
  1. *clause*

  2. on the frozen pond
  2. *not a clause*

1. until tomorrow **1.** not cl.
2. for lunch they had tacos **2.** cl.
3. their pictures in the newspaper **3.** not cl.
4. waiting at the corner for the bus **4.** not cl.

5. because they are twins **5.** cl.
6. neither answer is right **6.** cl.
7. after the concert last Saturday **7.** not cl.
8. that honors Rosa Parks **8.** cl.
9. which happened before I was born **9.** cl.
10. playing first base **10.** not cl.

B. Classifying Subordinate Clauses

Label each italicized clause in the following sentences as an *adjective clause* or an *adverb clause*. Then give the <u>word or words each clause modifies</u>.

EXAMPLES **1.** Manuel's paper route has doubled *since he took it over.*

    1. *adverb clause—has doubled*

    2. The present *that I bought for Mother's Day* is in my closet.

    2. *adjective clause—present*

11. <u>Everyone</u> *who signed up for the marathon* should meet at 8:00 A.M. tomorrow in the parking lot. **11.** adj. cl.
12. Tuesday we went to the <u>Mardi Gras Parade</u>, *which is held every year in New Orleans.* **12.** adj. cl.   **13.** adv. cl.
13. <u>Can</u> you <u>go</u> to the park *when school is over today*?
14. The <u>CD</u> *that I wanted to buy* was out of stock. **14.** adj. cl.
15. Loretta <u>stayed</u> home today *because she has a bad case of the flu.* **15.** adv. cl.
16. I <u>play</u> soccer *so that I will get more exercise.* **16.** adv. cl.
17. We <u>met</u> the García family *as we were leaving the grocery store.* **17.** adv. cl.
18. My older <u>sister</u>, *who is on the varsity basketball team,* practices after school every day. **18.** adj. cl.
19. *Since it was such a beautiful evening,* we <u>decided</u> to take a long walk. **19.** adv. cl.
20. The <u>students</u> *whose families observe the Jewish Sabbath* will be excused early on Friday. **20.** adj. cl.

GRAMMAR

INTEGRATING THE LANGUAGE ARTS

Literature Link. Ask students to read and analyze the structure of Edgar Allan Poe's poem "Annabel Lee." Work with students to identify the subordinate clauses they find and to locate the words that the clauses modify. As a class, discuss the effects of Poe's use of clauses in this poem. [Poe's use of the word *that* and his placement of adjective clauses help sustain his rhythm.]

GRAMMAR

INDEPENDENT AND SUBORDINATE CLAUSES Rules 18a–18c

OBJECTIVES

- To identify independent and subordinate clauses in sentences
- To write sentences using independent and subordinate clauses

INDEPENDENT AND SUBORDINATE CLAUSES
- Independent and Subordinate Clauses

 **QUICK REMINDER**

Ask students to finish the following sentences by providing the designated clauses:

1. . . . . (independent) before coming to school.
2. The students . . . . (subordinate) will arrive at the football game early.
3. I went to the store . . . . (subordinate).
4. Since I had forgotten my lunch . . . . (independent).
5. We went to the mall . . . . (subordinate).

MEETING INDIVIDUAL NEEDS

LESS-ADVANCED STUDENTS

Students may need extra practice distinguishing between independent and subordinate clauses. After pairing them with peer tutors, give students ten strips of paper—five strips containing independent clauses, and five containing subordinate clauses. When the ten clauses are joined appropriately and the resulting sentences are strung together, a paragraph is formed. This puzzlelike exercise offers students a chance to manipulate individual pieces of expression so that they form a logical whole.

516

---

516 *The Clause*

 18a. A *clause* is a group of words that contains a verb and its subject and is used as a part of a sentence.

Every clause contains a subject and a verb. However, not all clauses express complete thoughts. Clauses that do express a complete thought are called *independent clauses*. Clauses that do not make complete sense by themselves are called *subordinate clauses*.

The Independent Clause

18b. An *independent* (or *main*) *clause* expresses a complete thought and can stand by itself as a sentence.

EXAMPLES I woke up late this morning.
The alarm clock never rang.

When an independent clause stands alone, it is called a sentence. Usually, the term *independent clause* is used only when such a clause is joined with another clause.

SENTENCE **My mother drove me to school.**
INDEPENDENT CLAUSE Since I missed the bus, **my mother drove me to school.**

The Subordinate Clause

18c. A *subordinate* (or *dependent*) *clause* does not express a complete thought and cannot stand alone.

A subordinate clause must be joined with at least one independent clause to make a sentence and express a complete thought.

SUBORDINATE CLAUSES   since the day we met
that the veterinarian recommended
if the dress is too long

SENTENCES   I have liked you **since the day
we met.**
We give our hamster the food **that
the veterinarian recommended.**
If the dress is too long, we will
hem it.

Notice that words such as *since*, *that*, and *if* signal the beginning of a subordinate clause.

▶ EXERCISE 1 **Identifying Independent and Subordinate Clauses**

For each of the following sentences, label the italicized clause as *independent* or *subordinate*.

EXAMPLE   **1.** *If you know any modern music history,* you are probably familiar with the Motown sound.
    1. *subordinate*

1. Do you recognize any of the entertainers *who are shown in the photographs on the next page*?
2. These performers all had hit records in the 1950s and 1960s *when the music business in Detroit (the Motor City, or "Motown") was booming*.
3. Berry Gordy, *who founded the Motown record label*, began his business in a small office in Detroit.
4. He was a songwriter and producer, and *he was able to spot talent*.
5. Gordy went to clubs to hear local groups *whose sound he liked*.
6. The Miracles, *which was the first group he discovered*, had a lead singer named Smokey Robinson.
7. *Robinson was also a songwriter*, and Gordy included him in the Motown team of writers and musicians.
8. Gordy carefully managed all aspects of the Motown sound, *which is a special combination of rhythm and blues and soul*.

GRAMMAR

COOPERATIVE LEARNING
To give students practice in using subordinate clauses, divide the class into groups of four or five. Write on a large piece of posterboard the following word groups for students to complete with the types of clauses indicated.

1. . . . (subordinate) I went to summer camp.
2. Because I was so young . . . (independent).
3. I had a lot of fun that summer, mainly . . . (subordinate).
4. My best friend at camp . . . (subordinate).

After groups have finished, two group members will face the class, one holding the poster board and the other reading the story. The listeners will be responsible for determining if the correct clauses have been used. To help students avoid using phrases, ask that each group circle the subject and verb in each clause.

GRAMMAR

LEARNING STYLES

Kinetic and Visual Learners.
Students might benefit from the following hands-on exercise. Divide the class into six groups, and ask for one student volunteer from each group to hold one of the following word groups on a cardboard sign. Each group of students should decide whether its member is holding a phrase, an independent clause, or a subordinate clause. The class should evaluate whether groups have labeled their word groups correctly.

1. when we arrived [sub. clause]
2. around the world [phrase]
3. the block of wood [phrase]
4. Because they played well [sub. clause]
5. She was the leader [ind. clause]
6. by the lake [phrase]

9. Diana Ross and the Supremes, Stevie Wonder, Marvin Gaye, the Four Tops, the Temptations, Gladys Knight and the Pips, and Michael Jackson are just some of the performers *that Gordy discovered*.
10. *As you look at the photographs again*, can you recognize more of these modern music legends?

▶ EXERCISE 2 **Identifying Subordinate Clauses**

Identify the <u>subordinate clause</u> in each of the following sentences.

EXAMPLE **1.** When you get up in the morning, do you look at your sleepy face in a mirror?
1. *When you get up in the morning*

1. A mirror is a piece of polished metal or glass <u>that is coated with a substance such as silver</u>.

2. The most common type of mirror is the plane mirror, <u>which is flat</u>.
3. The image <u>that is reflected in a plane mirror</u> is reversed.
4. <u>As you look into a mirror</u>, your left hand seems to be the image's right hand.
5. <u>When an image is reversed</u>, it is called a mirror image.
6. A sailor <u>who looks through the periscope of a submarine</u> is using a system of lenses and mirrors to see above the water's surface.
7. Right-hand rear-view mirrors on cars, <u>which show a wide area of the road behind</u>, are usually convex, or curved outward.
8. Drivers must be careful <u>because convex mirrors make reflected objects appear far away</u>.
9. <u>Because the mirror in a flashlight is concave, or curved inward</u>, it strengthens the light from a small light bulb.
10. <u>When you look in a concave mirror</u>, you see a magnified reflection.

▶ EXERCISE 3 **Writing Sentences with Subordinate Clauses**

Write five sentences by adding an independent clause to each of the following subordinate clauses. Underline the independent clause in each of your sentences. Make your sentences interesting by adding a variety of independent clauses.

EXAMPLE **1.** who lives next door to us
      1. <u>The woman</u> who lives next door to us <u>is a computer programmer</u>.

1. when I bought the CD
2. who won the contest
3. if my parents agree
4. as Jessye Norman began to sing
5. because we are going to a fiesta

GRAMMAR

 COMMON ERROR

Problem. Students are sometimes unable to see that subordinate clauses are incomplete thoughts even though the clauses contain subjects and verbs. The problem may become worse if students often use subordinate clauses as complete thoughts when they write and speak.

Solution. To help students identify subordinate clauses incorrectly used as sentences, ask students to bracket each sentence in each of their paragraphs. This process will help isolate each sentence for examination. Ask students to circle the subjects and the verbs. Then ask students to answer the following question about each clause: "Does the clause make a complete thought?" If it does, the clause is a complete sentence.

ANSWERS
Exercise 3

Sentences will vary. You may want to require that students vary the position of the independent clauses in their sentences.

GRAMMAR

THE ADJECTIVE CLAUSE Rule 18d

OBJECTIVES

- To identify adjective clauses and relative pronouns
- To write appropriate adjective clauses
- To design a greeting card that includes adjective clauses

RESOURCES

THE ADJECTIVE CLAUSE
- The Adjective Clause

QUICK REMINDER

Write the following sentences on the chalkboard, and ask students to identify which words modify each underlined word. Explain that these sentences show how a group of words can do the job of an adjective.

1. The <u>girl</u> who hit the home run is a freshman.

2. The gray <u>squirrel</u>, which can leap more than <u>twenty feet</u>, is common in both rural and urban areas.

520 *The Clause*

The Adjective Clause

18d. An *adjective clause* is a subordinate clause that modifies a noun or a pronoun.

Like an adjective or an adjective phrase, an adjective clause may modify a noun or a pronoun. Unlike an adjective phrase, an adjective clause contains a verb and its subject.

ADJECTIVE | a **blue** flower
ADJECTIVE PHRASE | a flower **with blue petals** [does not have a verb and its subject]
ADJECTIVE CLAUSE | a flower **that has blue petals** [does have a verb and its subject]

An adjective clause usually follows the noun or pronoun it modifies and tells *which one* or *what kind*.

EXAMPLES | Emma Willard was the one **who founded the first women's college in the United States.** [The adjective clause modifies the pronoun *one*, telling *which one.*]
I want a bicycle **that I can ride over rough ground.** [The adjective clause modifies the noun *bicycle*, telling *what kind.*]

The Relative Pronoun

An adjective clause is almost always introduced by a *relative pronoun.*

Relative Pronouns				
that	which	who	whom	whose

These words are called *relative pronouns* because they *relate* an adjective clause to the noun or pronoun that the clause modifies.

18d

EXAMPLES   A snorkel is a hollow tube **that lets a diver breathe underwater.** [The relative pronoun *that* begins the adjective clause and relates it to the noun *tube.*]

The team's mascot, **which is a horse,** is called Renegade. [The relative pronoun *which* begins the adjective clause and relates it to the noun *mascot.*]

Gwendolyn Brooks is the writer **who is the poet laureate of Illinois.** [The relative pronoun *who* begins the adjective clause and relates it to the noun *writer.*]

Those **whose library books are overdue** must pay fines. [The relative pronoun *whose* begins the adjective clause and relates it to the pronoun *Those.*]

EXERCISE 4   Identifying Adjective Clauses

Identify the <u>adjective clause</u> in each of the following sentences. Underline the <u>relative pronoun</u> that begins the clause.

EXAMPLE   **1.** The person who wrote the Declaration of Independence was Thomas Jefferson.
        1. *who wrote the Declaration of Independence*

1. In his later years, Jefferson lived at Monticello, <u>which he had designed</u>.
2. Jefferson planned a daily schedule <u>that kept him busy all day</u>.
3. He began each day by making a note <u>that recorded the morning temperature</u>.
4. Then he did his writing, <u>which included letters to friends and businesspeople</u>.
5. Afterward, he ate breakfast, <u>which was served promptly at 9:00 A.M</u>.
6. Jefferson, <u>whose property included stables as well as farm fields</u>, went horseback riding at noon.

LEP/ESL

Spanish. Students may have difficulty with adjective clauses that end with a verb, such as "I like the book *that Maria is reading.*" In Spanish, it is considered awkward to end a clause with a verb. The Spanish speaker will invert the subject and the verb, producing the following sentence: "Me gusta el libro *que lee Maria.*" Inverting the word order in this manner may show up when students write in English. You will need to check students' work carefully to determine if this is a problem.

LESS-ADVANCED STUDENTS

Students may need practice determining which words are modified by an adjective clause. To help students more readily see the function of adjective clauses, work with them to draw an arrow from the adjective clauses to the nouns or pronouns that are being modified.

ADVANCED STUDENTS

Explain to students that adjective clauses should not be used where a single adjective would suffice. Suggest that students examine previously written paragraphs and revise them for wordiness by substituting precise adjectives where possible.

ANSWERS
Exercise 5

Sentences will vary. You may want students to label the subjects and verbs of their clauses and to draw arrows from the adjective clauses to the words they modify.

PICTURE THIS

Ask students to brainstorm about where they could send their greeting cards. After students have determined where they might send their cards (nursing homes, daycare centers, hospitals), they can create cards appropriate for their audiences. You may want to spend some time discussing audience and explaining how writing should be done with a specific audience in mind.

522

522 *The Clause*

7. Dinner was a big meal, <u>which began about 4:00 P.M.</u>
8. From dinner until dark, he talked to friends and neighbors <u>who came to visit</u>.
9. He also spent time with his family, <u>which included twelve grandchildren</u>.
10. Jefferson, <u>whose interests ranged from art and architecture to biology and mathematics</u>, read each night.

▶ EXERCISE 5　**Writing Appropriate Adjective Clauses**

Complete each of the following sentences by adding an adjective clause that will make sense in the blank. Then, underline the relative pronoun. Remember that a clause must contain a verb and its subject.

EXAMPLE　**1.** We read the Greek legend ____.
　　　　　1. *We read the Greek legend <u>that</u> tells the story of the Trojan horse.*

1. You should proofread every composition ____.
2. My friend ____ is a good student.
3. Mrs. Echohawk ____ was my fifth-grade teacher.
4. We heard a sound ____.
5. Our neighbors ____ are from Fez, Morocco.

PICTURE THIS

You are visiting a small company that creates greeting cards. The artist shown on the next page is a family friend, and she designs cards that will be marketed to young people. She has asked you to help her write messages for the cards that she illustrates. For example, she might design a card with a rabbit on the cover, and you might write *This is a bunny who has something to say: Have a Hoppy Birthday!* Write messages for at least five greeting cards. Use an adjective clause in each message, and circle

OBJECTIVE
• To identify adverb clauses in sentences

each relative pronoun. Following each message, write a brief description of a photo or illustration to go with your message.

Subject: greeting card messages
Audience: people your age
Purpose: to entertain

RESOURCES

THE ADVERB CLAUSE
• The Adverb Clause

QUICK REMINDER
Write the following sentences on the board, and ask students to determine if the underlined words are prepositional phrases used as adverbs or adverb clauses.

1. I will be leaving before tomorrow.
2. If I could go, I would.
3. Since first grade, I have always wanted to be an astronaut.
4. Since you are going to the movies, you will need some extra money.
5. After I raked the leaves, I relaxed and read a book.

MEETING INDIVIDUAL NEEDS

LEP/ESL

General Strategies. Most languages have structures similar to adverb clauses; however, often the order of the subject and the verb is inverted. You may want to have students practice saying and writing sentences with adverb clauses by using the **Common Subordinating Conjunctions** list on p. 524. Emphasize the subject-verb pattern that is most common in English by having students identify the subject and the verb of each clause they write.

The Adverb Clause

> **18e.** An *adverb clause* is a subordinate clause that is used as an adverb.

Like an adverb or an adverb phrase, an adverb clause may modify a verb, an adjective, or an adverb. Unlike an adverb phrase, an adverb clause contains a verb and its subject.

ADVERB **Bravely,** Jason battled a fierce dragon.
ADVERB PHRASE **With great bravery,** Jason battled a fierce dragon. [does not have a verb and its subject]
ADVERB CLAUSE **Because Jason was brave,** he battled a fierce dragon. [does have a verb and its subject]

523

ADVANCED STUDENTS

To help students see how they can use adverb clauses to clarify idea relationships and to increase coherence in paragraphs, write this paragraph on the chalkboard:

Last year we visited several antique shops. We were looking for an old radio to use in the spring play. We came to a small shop. We were sure it didn't have what we wanted. It had one radio—just the one we needed.

Ask students to revise the sentences using adverb clauses to subordinate some of the ideas. [Here is one possible revision: Last year, while we were looking for an old radio to use in the spring play, we came to a small shop. Although we were sure it didn't have what we wanted, it had just the radio we needed.]

COMMON ERROR

Problem. Students are often hesitant to vary the positions of adverb clauses in sentences they write. For example, if students are learning to use adverb clauses, they may have a tendency to place all adverb clauses in the same position in their sentences.

Solution. Encourage students to experiment with the placement of adverb clauses. To allow students to see this variety more easily, ask them to bracket any independent clauses in their writing and to try to switch the positions of the adverb clauses and the main clauses.

An adverb clause answers the following questions: *How? When? Where? Why? To what extent? How much? How long?* or *Under what conditions?*

EXAMPLES I feel **as though I will never catch up.** [The adverb clause tells *how* I feel.]
After I finish painting my bookcases, I will call you. [The adverb clause tells *when* I will call you.]
I paint **where there is plenty of fresh air.** [The adverb clause tells *where* I paint.]
I have more work to do today **because I didn't paint yesterday.** [The adverb clause tells *why* I have more work to do.]
I will paint **until Mom comes home;** then I will clean my brushes and set the table for supper. [The adverb clause tells *how long* I will paint.]
If I paint for two more hours, I should be able to finish. [The adverb clause tells *under what conditions* I should be able to finish.]

Notice in these examples that adverb clauses may be placed in various positions in sentences. When an adverb clause comes at the beginning, it is usually followed by a comma.

☞ REFERENCE NOTE: For more about punctuating introductory adverb clauses, see page 720.

Subordinating Conjunctions

Adverb clauses begin with *subordinating conjunctions.*

Common Subordinating Conjunctions			
after	as soon as	in order that	until
although	as though	since	when
as	because	so that	whenever
as if	before	than	where
as long as	how	though	wherever
as much as	if	unless	while

Some subordinating conjunctions, such as *after, as, before, since,* and *until,* may also be used as prepositions.

PREPOSITION	**Before** sunrise, we left for the cabin.
SUBORDINATING CONJUNCTION	**Before** the sun had risen, we left for the cabin.
PREPOSITION	In the nineteenth century, buffalo skins were used **as** blankets and clothing.
SUBORDINATING CONJUNCTION	Around 1900, **as** the buffalo became nearly extinct, conservationists fought for its protection.

▶ EXERCISE 6   **Identifying Adverb Clauses**

Identify the <u>adverb clause</u> in each sentence in the following paragraph. Then write whether the clause tells *when, where, how, why, how much,* or *under what condition.*

EXAMPLE   [1] Long before they had a written history, the Chinese were making kites.
   1. *Long before they had a written history— when*

[1] <u>Although this story is only a legend</u>, many people believe that a kite like the one pictured on the next page may have saved the people of China's Han Dynasty. [2] The Chinese were about to be attacked by an enemy army <u>when an adviser to the emperor came up with a plan</u>. [3] <u>As the adviser stood beside an open window</u>, his hat was lifted off by a strong wind. [4] He immediately called for a number of kites to be made <u>so that they might be used to frighten the enemy</u>. [5] The kite makers had no trouble finding lightweight bamboo for their kite frames <u>because bamboo is native to China</u>. [6] <u>As soon as each frame was completed</u>, silk was stretched over it. [7] The emperor's adviser attached noisemakers to the kites <u>so that they would produce an eerie sound</u>. [8] He ordered his men to fly the kites in the darkest hour of night <u>because then the enemy would hear the kites but not see them</u>. [9] <u>Unless the adviser had misjudged the enemy,</u>

COOPERATIVE LEARNING

After dividing the class into groups of four, give each student a newspaper article and ask students to circle all the adverb clauses they can find. Point out that in newspaper writing, adverb clauses are extremely important because they tell us when, where, how, why, how much, or under what condition. After students have had a chance to discuss the adverb clauses in the newspaper articles, ask groups to work collectively to write their own newspaper articles. Groups should include adverb clauses as they write a news story, a sports story, and a feature story that all pertain to upcoming school activities. After the stories are written, ask students' underline all adverb clauses. You may want to display stories for students' enjoyment or to combine all stories to form newspaper pages for display.

ANSWERS
Exercise 6
  1. under what condition
  2. when
  3. when
  4. why
  5. why
  6. when
  7. why
  8. why
  9. under what condition
  10. how

REVIEW A

OBJECTIVE

• To identify subordinate clauses and to label them as adjective clauses or adverb clauses

VISUAL CONNECTIONS

Ideas for Writing. Ask students to imagine that they are in the enemy army and to record the feelings of the fleeing soldiers. Have students write their accounts in short expressive paragraphs that include adverb clauses. Ask students to circle all adverb clauses in their paragraphs.

INTEGRATING THE LANGUAGE ARTS

Grammar and Mechanics. As they proofread papers containing adverb clauses, students should locate subordinating conjunctions to make sure that they have used commas to separate introductory adverb clauses from the rest of the sentences. Suggest that students highlight with a colored marker all subordinating conjunctions so that they can more readily see the positions of the adverb clauses in their sentences.

526 *The Clause*

they would be fooled into thinking that the kites were gods warning them to retreat. [10] According to the legend, the enemy retreated <u>as if they were being chased by a fire-breathing dragon</u>.

Chinese Kites, How to Make and Fly Them,
David F. Jue, Charles E. Tuttle Co., Inc. of

 REVIEW

Identifying and Classifying Subordinate Clauses

Identify the subordinate clause in each of the following sentences. Then, label each clause as an *adjective clause* or an *adverb clause*.

EXAMPLES
1. American history is filled with stories of people who performed heroic deeds.
   1. *who performed heroic deeds—adjective clause*
   2. As the American colonists struggled for independence, women played important roles.
   2. *As the American colonists struggled for independence—adverb clause*

1. <u>When you study the American Revolution</u>, you may learn about the adventures of a woman known as Molly Pitcher.

WRITING APPLICATION

OBJECTIVE

- To write a composition that explains a process and that includes subordinating conjunctions

2. Molly, <u>whose real name was Mary Ludwig</u>, was the daughter of farmers.
3. <u>Although she was born in New Jersey</u>, she moved to Pennsylvania.
4. There she married John Hays, <u>who was a barber</u>.
5. Hays joined the colonial army <u>when the Revolution began</u>.
6. Mary Ludwig Hays went to be with her husband in Monmouth, New Jersey, <u>which was the site of a battle on a hot June day in 1778</u>.
7. At first, she carried water to the soldiers <u>so that they would not be overcome by the intense heat</u>.
8. The soldiers nicknamed her "Molly Pitcher" <u>because she carried the water in pitchers</u>.
9. Later, <u>when her husband collapsed from the heat</u>, she took over his cannon.
10. George Washington, <u>who was the commander of the Continental Army</u>, made Molly an honorary sergeant.

GRAMMAR

WRITING APPLICATION

Using Subordinating Conjunctions to Explain a Process

Subordinating conjunctions don't just connect ideas. They show the relationships between ideas. Notice how the subordinating conjunctions in the following examples show the different time relationships between the two clauses.

1. Squeeze the trigger of the fire extinguisher **before** you aim the nozzle.
2. Squeeze the trigger of the fire extinguisher **as** you aim the nozzle.
3. Squeeze the trigger of the fire extinguisher **after** you aim the nozzle.

WRITING APPLICATION

This writing assignment gives students practice in clarifying the relationships between clauses and the logical order of ideas within sentences. Because students will be writing to inform other students of a process, you may wish to review the guidelines in **Chapter 7: "Writing to Inform."**

CRITICAL THINKING
Synthesis

To help students think critically about creating a safety manual, ask them to prepare a poster depicting noteworthy instructions that tell what to do in a particular emergency. For example, a student might depict a fire extinguisher being used and write the following caption beneath the picture: "Squeeze the trigger of the fire extinguisher after you aim the nozzle." During the publishing stage of the writing process, students can present their posters with their instructions.

PREWRITING

You may want to remind students that their audience will probably not be familiar with all of the steps in their emergency instructions. Therefore, students' prewriting notes, as the basis for their writing, must contain accurate and specific details. Encourage students to seek the help of professionals or to use their library to help in listing the correct steps.

EVALUATING AND REVISING

To help students decide if they have explained all unfamiliar terms and have used appropriate subordinating conjunctions to make the order of the steps clear, ask them to read their papers to two other students.

Which of the instructions on the previous page would help you put out a fire efficiently?

Clearly showing relationships between clauses in your writing is always important. However, it is particularly necessary when you are giving instructions or explaining a process.

▶ WRITING ACTIVITY

Your class project for National Safety Week is to write a safety manual. Each class member will write one page of instructions telling what to do in a particular emergency. You may write about a major emergency, such as a fire, an earthquake, or a tornado. Or you may write about a minor emergency, such as a brief power outage, a sprained ankle, or a case of poison ivy. Use subordinating conjunctions to show the relationships between your ideas.

Prewriting Think of a specific emergency that you know how to handle. List the steps that someone should follow in this emergency. Number the steps in order. If you aren't sure of the order or don't know a particular step, stop writing and get the information you need. A health teacher, the school nurse, or an organization such as the Red Cross should be able to provide information. [Remember: Readers will rely on your manual in an emergency. *The information you present must be accurate.*]

Writing Use your prewriting list to begin your first draft. As you write, make your instructions as clear as possible. Define or explain terms that might be unfamiliar to your readers. Be sure that your instructions are in the right order.

Evaluating and Revising Read over your instructions to be sure that you've included all necessary information. Add, cut, or rearrange steps to make the instructions easy to follow. Be sure to use appropriate subordinating conjunctions to make the order of the steps clear. You may want to present your instructions in a numbered list rather than in a paragraph.

SEGMENT 5 *(pp. 529–531)*
REVIEW: POSTTESTS 1 and 2
OBJECTIVES
- To identify and classify independent and subordinate clauses
- To identify and classify subordinate clauses
- To write sentences that include subordinate clauses

PROOFREADING AND PUBLISHING

You may want to encourage students to present their posters and paragraphs orally, or you may prefer to let students display their work somewhere in the classroom.

INTEGRATING THE LANGUAGE ARTS

Technology Link. If students have access to computers, ask them to prepare their papers in parallel columns, with the left column for the composition and the right column for your comments. Also, encourage students to use the grammar-check program to ensure correct comma placement for introductory adverb clauses.

REVIEW: POSTTEST 1

Teaching Note. You may want to put sample sentences on the board for items 8 and 10 so that students can see how these word groups could be either independent clauses (as questions) or subordinate clauses.

 Proofreading and Publishing Check your work carefully for any errors in grammar, punctuation, or spelling. For information on punctuating introductory adverb clauses, see page 720. To publish your class safety manual, gather all the pages and input them on a computer or make photocopies. Organize your topics alphabetically, or group them by kinds of emergencies.

Review: Posttest 1

A. Identifying and Classifying Independent and Subordinate Clauses

Label each of the following clauses as either *independent* or *subordinate*.

EXAMPLES **1.** when I was eleven years old
1. *subordinate*

2. he was eleven years old
2. *independent*

1. because I have lived in Chile and Ecuador **1.** sub.
2. his writing has improved **2.** ind.
3. although Gullah is still spoken on South Carolina's Sea Islands **3.** sub.
4. when the Philadelphia Phillies won the National League pennant **4.** sub.
5. she served as Secretary of Labor **5.** ind.
6. that we brought to the Juneteenth picnic **6.** sub.
7. everyone laughed **7.** ind.
8. who heard the Navajo story about Coyote **8.** sub. [*or* ind.]
9. during the storm the power failed **9.** ind.
10. which seemed to be the reason for the delay **10.** sub. [*or* ind.]

STUDENTS WITH SPECIAL NEEDS

For learning disabled students with a visual processing deficit, oral work either with the class as a whole or with student helpers may be beneficial. After a class discussion outlining the differences between subordinate clauses and independent clauses, ask student helpers to repeat the following subordinate clauses to their partners and have the partners create independent clauses to make them into complete sentences:

1. as Mark rode his bike
2. who liked music
3. if we like football
4. when we get home
5. who flew airplanes

B. Identifying and Classifying Subordinate Clauses

Identify the subordinate clause in each of the following sentences. Then, label each clause as either an *adjective clause* or an *adverb clause*.

EXAMPLE 1. Today is the day that you are having dinner at my house.
 1. *that you are having dinner at my house—adjective clause*

 2. I will give you a map so that you can find my house easily.
 2. *so that you can find my house easily—adverb clause*

11. <u>If you have never eaten Caribbean food</u>, you are in for a big treat.
12. My mother, <u>who was born and raised in Jamaica</u>, really knows how to cook.
13. <u>Whenever I have a chance</u>, I help her in the kitchen to learn her secrets.
14. My grandmother, <u>whose cooking is even better than my mother's</u>, is making her special sweet potato pone for dessert.
15. Some of the fruits and vegetables <u>that grow in Jamaica</u> are hard to find in the markets around here.
16. Today we are shopping for coconuts, avocados, and callaloo greens, <u>which were introduced to the Caribbean by Africans</u>.
17. We must also remember to buy fresh hot peppers, onions, and spices <u>that are needed for seasoning the meat</u>.
18. <u>Although my mother never uses measuring spoons</u>, she seems to know just how much of each spice to add.
19. <u>As soon as we pay for these items</u>, let's take them to my house.
20. Part of your treat will be to sniff the delicious smells from the kitchen <u>before you even begin eating</u>.

Review: Posttest 2

Writing Sentences with Subordinate Clauses

Write ten different sentences of your own. In each sentence, include a subordinate clause that begins with one of the following words. Underline the subordinate clause. After the sentence, label the subordinate clause as an *adjective clause* or an *adverb clause*.

EXAMPLES
1. so that
1. *We hurried so that we wouldn't miss the bus.—adverb clause*

2. whom
2. *Jim Nakamura, whom I met at summer camp, is now my pen pal.—adjective clause*

1. which	4. who	7. as though	9. that
2. before	5. than	8. although	10. if
3. since	6. whose		

GRAMMAR

ANSWERS
Review: Posttest 2

Sentences will vary. Here are some possibilities:

1. The soup which is creamy is the best. — adjective clause

2. Before we can leave, we must put air in the tires. — adverb clause

3. I haven't seen her since we were in the third grade. — adverb clause

4. The person who fights for a cause must understand his or her rights. — adjective clause

5. She can run faster than I can. — adverb clause

6. The teacher whose class is best wins a prize. — adjective clause

7. The puppy barked as though it were a huge dog. — adverb clause

8. Although I can't swim, I love going to the beach. — adverb clause

9. The team played with a spirit that was inspirational. — adjective clause

10. If we want to stop pollution, we all must do our part. — adverb clause

GRAMMAR

OBJECTIVES

- To identify independent and subordinate clauses
- To classify sentences as simple, compound, or complex

RESOURCES

KINDS OF SENTENCE STRUCTURE
- Chapter Review Form A
- Chapter Review Form B
- Assessment Portfolio
  Grammar Pretest
  Grammar Mastery Test 1
  Grammar Mastery Test 2

CHAPTER OVERVIEW

The chapter discusses the three types of sentences (simple, compound, and complex) in terms of independent and subordinate clauses. Identification of subjects and verbs within the different types of sentences is stressed.

Refer to this chapter when teaching any of the composition chapters, especially **Chapter 11: "Writing Effective Sentences."** You may choose to observe how students vary sentence structure after they have completed the **Writing Application.**

USING THE DIAGNOSTIC TEST

Part A of this **Diagnostic Test** examines students' ability to differentiate between independent and subordinate clauses. **Part B** of the test requires students to classify sentences by structure. You may wish to use this test to determine students' knowledge of the different types of sentences. However, you can monitor students' writing to gauge how well they incorporate the different types of sentences into their compositions, especially during revision.

19 KINDS OF SENTENCE STRUCTURE

Simple, Compound, and Complex Sentences

Diagnostic Test

A. Identifying Independent and Subordinate Clauses

Identify each clause in the following sentences as either an *independent clause* or a *subordinate clause*.

EXAMPLES　**1.** I waved to them, but they didn't see me.
1. *I waved to them—independent clause; they didn't see me—independent clause*

2. All tennis players who are renting rackets should pay their rental fees today.
2. *All tennis players should pay their rental fees today—independent clause; who are renting rackets—subordinate clause*

1. She raked the leaves, and I mowed the lawn.
2. Lupe and Ben rode their bicycles to the park so that they could watch the fireworks.

3. We chose tacos instead of sandwiches from the cafeteria's menu.
4. The new camp that offers instruction in computer programming will be in session from August 17 through August 28.
5. The rain changed to snow mixed with sleet.
6. At the beach, Mei-Ling and her parents practiced their tai chi exercises.
7. My grandparents, who enjoy exciting vacations, are planning to visit Nepal this year.
8. Since last year I have grown three inches, but I still can't reach the top shelf in the kitchen.
9. Uncle Martin gave me this book by Jamaica Kincaid because he enjoyed it.
10. She wants to be a veterinarian, for she likes to be around animals.

B. Classifying Sentences by Structure

Classify each of the following sentences as a *simple sentence*, a *compound* sentence, or a *complex* sentence.

EXAMPLES   **1.** The religion of the Muslims is called Islam, and it is based on a belief in one God.
   1. *compound sentence*

11. Muslims live in various parts of the world, though mostly in Africa, the Middle East, and Malaysia. **11.** simp.
12. In recent years many Muslims have come to the United States, and they have brought their religion with them. **12.** cd.
13. In April 1991, a mosque was built in New York. **13.** simp.
14. When the mosque was opened, religious leaders and other Muslims went there to pray. **14.** cx.
15. Some worshipers wore the traditional clothing of their homelands, and others were dressed in typical American clothes. **15.** cd.
16. Muslims were particularly pleased that the new mosque opened in the spring. **16.** cx.

THE SIMPLE SENTENCE Rule 19a

OBJECTIVE

• To identify subjects and verbs in simple sentences

RESOURCES

THE SIMPLE SENTENCE

• The Simple Sentence

QUICK REMINDER

Write "The grass is" on the chalkboard. Explain that a subject and verb are essential to every sentence, but tell students that they can include other words. Then have students supply an appropriate adjective [green]. Next, have students add further description to the same sentence by using compound subjects and compound verbs. [The grass and the trees are green and fresh.]

MEETING

INDIVIDUAL

NEEDS

LEP/ESL

General Strategies. Students might need a review of the terms *compound subject, compound verb, independent clause,* and *subordinate clause.* You may want to give a definition and an example of each on the chalkboard. Then give the class several clauses and ask students to classify them as independent or subordinate.

---

534 *Kinds of Sentence Structure*

17. The month of fasting called Ramadan had just ended, so the holiday after Ramadan could be celebrated in the new house of worship.   **17. cd.**
18. Although Muslims share a common religion, their languages differ.   **18. cx.**
19. Many Muslims speak Arabic, but those in Iran, Turkey, and neighboring countries, for example, speak other languages, too.   **19. cd.**
20. Of course, Muslims in the United States speak English, or they are learning it as a new language.
     20. cd.

The Simple Sentence

19a. A *simple sentence* has one independent clause and no subordinate clauses.

| | S | V |
EXAMPLES   A good **rain helps** the farmers.

| | V | S |
Up for the rebound **leaped Kareem.**

A simple sentence may have a compound subject, a compound verb, or both.

| | S | | S | V |
EXAMPLES   **Burritos** and **fajitas are** two popular Mexican dishes. [compound subject]

| | S | V |
Susan read *The Planet of Junior Brown* and
| | V |
reported on it last week. [compound verb]

| | S | | S | V |
The huge **dog** and the tiny **kitten lay** down in
| | V |
the sunshine and **napped.** [compound subject and compound verb]

▶ EXERCISE 1

Identifying Subjects and Verbs in Simple Sentences

Identify the <u>subject</u>(s) and the <u>verb</u>(s) in each sentence of the following paragraph. [Note: Some sentences have a compound subject, a compound verb, or both.]

EXAMPLE   [1] I enjoy urban life but need to escape from the city once in a while.
1. *I—subject; enjoy, need—verbs*

[1] My favorite <u>escape</u> from city life <u>is</u> the green world of Central Park in New York City. [2] Its beautiful <u>woods</u> and relaxing outdoor <u>activities</u> <u>are</u> just a few minutes from our apartment. [3] The enormous <u>size</u> of the park, however, <u>can</u> sometimes <u>be</u> a problem. [4] Often, <u>I</u> <u>take</u> this map along with me for guidance. [5] Using the map, <u>I</u> <u>can</u> easily <u>find</u> the zoo, the bandshell, and the Lost Waterfall. [6] In the summertime my <u>brothers</u> and <u>I</u> <u>row</u> boats on the lake, <u>climb</u> huge rock slabs, and <u>have</u> picnics in the Sheep Meadow. [7] <u>I</u> also <u>watch</u> birds and often <u>wander</u> around the park in search of my favorite species. [8] Last month a pair of purple <u>finches</u> <u>followed</u> me along the pond. [9] Near Heckscher Playground, the <u>birds</u> <u>got</u> tired of the game and <u>flew</u> off. [10] In Central Park my <u>family</u> and <u>I</u> <u>can enjoy</u> a little bit of nature in the middle of a bustling city.

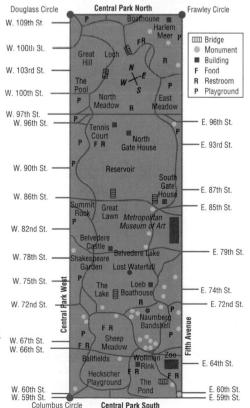

COMMON ERROR

Problem. Because simple sentences can have compound subjects, compound verbs, or both, students might mistakenly view them as compound sentences.

Solution. Tell students to place a box around the subject and a circle around the verb in any questionable sentence. Explain that sometimes they will have two or more boxes or circles, but that unless the boxes or circles go together, that part of the sentence is not an independent clause. The following two sentences can be used as examples:

1. [Lieutenant Sulu] and [Mr. Spock] (saved) Captain Kirk.
2. [Bill] and [Ted] (had) an excellent adventure, and then [they] (had) another one.

COOPERATIVE LEARNING

Ask students to work in groups of three to brainstorm eight to ten examples of television or print advertising. It may be necessary to supply current magazines from the library. Next, have one member in each group identify the subject and verb of each slogan in each of the advertisements. Another group member can read the examples to the class, and the third group member can explain why the examples were identified as simple or compound.

THE COMPOUND SENTENCE

RESOURCES

THE COMPOUND SENTENCE
• The Compound Sentence
• Compound Sentences and Sentence Parts

QUICK REMINDER

Students might be confused about the difference between compound sentences and simple sentences with compound subjects, compound verbs, or both. Write the following sentences on the chalkboard:

1. John and Maria rode the bus.
2. Mary left the party and drove her new car to the park.
3. Realizing the time, Suzanne and Bernice grabbed their helmets, and they rode their bikes to the mall.

Have students practice using coordinating conjunctions to create compound sentences. Point out the use of commas before conjunctions.

MEETING INDIVIDUAL NEEDS

LEP/ESL

Spanish. Spanish-speaking students may have problems identifying subjects and verbs in sentences, because Spanish word order is variable and often different from English. Additional practice may be helpful. Start with several simple sentences, and when students are able to identify the subjects and verbs correctly, move to compound sentences.

536

THE COMPOUND SENTENCE   Rule 19b

OBJECTIVES

• To identify subjects, verbs, and coordinating conjunctions in compound sentences
• To distinguish between compound sentences and simple sentences
• To write a letter using different sentence structures

536 *Kinds of Sentence Structure*

The Compound Sentence

> **19b.** A *compound sentence* has two or more independent clauses and no subordinate clauses.

INDEPENDENT CLAUSE	Melvina wrote about her mother's aunt
INDEPENDENT CLAUSE	Leroy wrote about his cousin from Jamaica
COMPOUND SENTENCE	Melvina wrote about her mother's aunt, and Leroy wrote about his cousin from Jamaica.

The independent clauses of a compound sentence are usually joined by a comma and a coordinating conjunction (*and, but, or, nor, for, so,* or *yet*).

EXAMPLES   A variety of fruits and vegetables should be a part of everyone's diet, **for** they supply many important vitamins.
No one was injured in the fire, **but** several homes were destroyed, **and** many trees burned down.

The independent clauses of a compound sentence may be joined by a semicolon.

EXAMPLE   Pedro Menéndez de Avilés founded Saint Augustine, the first permanent settlement in the United States; he also established six other colonies in the Southeast.

▶ EXERCISE 2   **Identifying Subjects and Verbs in Compound Sentences**

Identify the <u>subject</u> and <u>verb</u> in each independent clause. Then, give the coordinating conjunction.

EXAMPLE   1. A newspaper reporter spoke to our class last week, and we learned about careers in journalism.
1. *reporter—subject; spoke—verb; we—subject; learned—verb; and*

1. Ruth Benedict <u>was</u> a respected anthropologist, and Margaret Mead <u>was</u> one of her students.   **1. and**
2. An area's <u>weather</u> <u>may change</u> rapidly, but its <u>climate</u> <u>changes</u> very slowly.   **2. but**
3. Linh Phan <u>lived</u> in Vietnam for many years, so <u>he</u> <u>was</u> able to tell us about Vietnamese foods such as *nuoc mam*.   **3. so**
4. Students <u>may type</u> their reports, or <u>they</u> <u>may write</u> them neatly.   **4. or**
5. Our <u>landlord</u> <u>is</u> kind, yet <u>she</u> <u>will</u> not <u>allow</u> pets in the building.   **5. yet**
6. Daniel Boone <u>had</u> no formal education, but <u>he</u> <u>could</u> <u>read</u> and <u>write</u>.   **6. but**
7. Sofia's favorite <u>dance</u> <u>is</u> the samba, and <u>Elena</u> <u>enjoys</u> the merengue.   **7. and**
8. Benjamin Franklin <u>was</u> one of the members of the Constitutional Convention, yet <u>none</u> of his proposals <u>were adopted</u>.   **8. yet**
9. Sheena <u>did</u> not <u>play</u> soccer this week, for <u>she</u> <u>had</u> <u>sprained</u> her ankle.   **9. for**
10. They <u>did</u> not <u>watch</u> the shuttle take off, nor <u>did</u> <u>they</u> <u>watch</u> it land.   **10. nor**

Distinguishing Compound Sentences from Compound Subjects and Compound Verbs

A simple sentence has only one independent clause. It may have a compound subject or a compound verb or both. A compound sentence has two or more independent clauses. Each independent clause has its own subject and verb. Any of the independent clauses in a compound sentence may have a compound subject, a compound verb, or both.

SIMPLE SENTENCE   **Kim** and **Maureen read** each other's stories and **made** suggestions for improvements. [compound subject and compound verb]

TIMESAVER

You could have students work in pairs to complete **Exercise 2.** One student would be responsible for the odd-numbered questions and the other for the even. When you go over the answers or write them on the chalkboard, students can exchange papers and check one another's work. By doing the exercise this way, students will be exposed to all the questions, and you can assess students' progress by looking at the corrected papers.

COMMON ERROR

Problem. Students often fail to place a comma before a coordinating conjunction used to join independent clauses.

Solution. Tell students that a comma is needed because more than one clause is involved. Explain that if they can remove the conjunction and see two clauses, they must include a comma before the conjunction.

INTEGRATING THE LANGUAGE ARTS

Literature Link. Have students read Emily Dickinson's poem "I'm Nobody! Who are you?" and discuss the sentence types used. Ask students to explain why the author chooses to vary sentence types so seldom. [Students might say that the repetition of short, simple sentences creates a feeling of fright, or they might say that because the poem is supposed to be spoken by a child, the sentence type reinforces the mood.]

	S S V
COMPOUND SENTENCE	**Kim** and **Maureen read** each other's
	S V
	stories, and **they gave** each other suggestions for improvements. [The first independent clause has a compound subject and a single verb. The second independent clause has a single subject and a single verb.]

NOTE: When a subject is repeated after a coordinating conjunction, the sentence is compound.

	S V
SIMPLE SENTENCE	**We studied** about the artist
	V
	Romare Bearden and **went** to an exhibit of his paintings.

	S V
COMPOUND SENTENCE	**We studied** about the artist
	S V
	Romare Bearden, and **we went** to an exhibit of his paintings.

EXERCISE 3 Distinguishing Compound Sentences from Compound Subjects or Compound Verbs

Identify each of the following sentences as either *simple* or *compound*. Then identify the <u>subject</u>(s) and <u>verb</u>(s) in each sentence.

EXAMPLES **1.** A rain forest is a tropical evergreen forest and has heavy rains throughout the year.
  1. *simple; forest—subject; is, has—verbs*

  2. The trees and other plants in a rain forest grow close together, and they rise to different heights.
  2. *compound; trees, plants—subjects; grow—verb; they—subject; rise—verb*

  1. The <u>Amazon River</u> <u>is located</u> in South America and <u>is</u> one of the longest rivers in the world. **1.** simp.

2. The <u>Amazon</u> <u>begins</u> in Peru, and <u>it</u> <u>flows</u> across Brazil to the Atlantic Ocean.   **2. cd.**

3. This <u>river</u> <u>drains</u> about one fifth of the earth's fresh water and <u>carries</u> more water than any other river in the world.   **3. simp.**

4. The <u>Amazon</u> <u>is</u> actually a network of several rivers, but most <u>people</u> <u>think</u> of these combined rivers as only one river.   **4. cd.**

5. These <u>rivers</u> <u>drain</u> the largest rainy area in the world, and during the flood season, the main <u>river</u> often <u>overflows</u> its banks.   **5. cd.**

6. Unlike many rivers, the <u>Amazon</u> <u>does</u> not <u>twist</u> and <u>curve</u>.   **6. simp.**

7. Instead, <u>it</u> <u>follows</u> a fairly straight course and <u>flows</u> at an average rate of about one and one-half miles an hour.   **7. simp.**

8. The Amazonian rain <u>forest</u> <u>is</u> only two hundred miles wide along the Atlantic, but <u>it</u> <u>stretches</u> to twelve hundred miles wide at the foot of the Andes Mountains in Peru.   **8. cd.**

9. The <u>variety</u> of plant life in the Amazonian rain forest <u>is</u> remarkable; in fact, the <u>area</u> <u>may contain</u> a greater number of species of plants than any other rain forest.   **9. cd.**

10. Raw <u>materials</u> <u>are shipped</u> directly from ports deep in the rain forest, for oceangoing <u>ships</u> <u>can sail</u> more than two thousand miles up the Amazon.   **10. cd.**

PICTURE THIS

Your community has been given the abandoned theater shown on the next page. Now the local citizens' council must decide what to do with the building. They could sell the theater, they could restore it, or they might find some other use for it. Write a letter to the council, giving your opinion on what should happen to the theater. To make

INTEGRATING THE LANGUAGE ARTS

Technology Link. If possible, have students use a computer program designed to check for grammatical and stylistic errors. Relevant grammar mistakes that such programs identify include comma splices, run-on sentences, and sentence fragments. Common mistakes such as forgetting commas before coordinating conjunctions and joining two subordinate clauses into an incomplete sentence will be highlighted immediately for the student.

Some programs also evaluate students' ability to vary sentence types and, therefore, help to increase the readability of writing. If possible, have students run such a program on samples of their writing.

PICTURE THIS

Consider having members of the class role-play positions on the local citizens' council. Some could suggest reasons why the building should be sold. Other students might suggest reasons why it should be restored. One final group of students could suggest other uses for the building. Then the groups' ideas could be listed on the chalkboard for class use.

GRAMMAR

GRAMMAR

THE COMPLEX SENTENCE Rule 19c

OBJECTIVES

- To identify subordinate clauses
- To identify subordinate conjunctions and relative pronouns

540 *Kinds of Sentence Structure*

your letter more interesting, vary your sentence structure. Use at least three simple sentences and two compound sentences.

Subject: an abandoned theater
Audience: community leaders
Purpose: to persuade

The Complex Sentence

19c. A *complex sentence* has one independent clause and at least one subordinate clause.

Two kinds of subordinate clauses are adjective clauses and adverb clauses. Adjective clauses usually begin with relative pronouns such as *who, whose, which,* and *that.* Adverb clauses begin with subordinating conjunctions such as *after, as, because, if, since,* and *when.*

☞ **REFERENCE NOTE:** For more information on adjective clauses, see pages 520–521. For more information on adverb clauses, see pages 523–525.

 QUICK REMINDER

Write the following sentence on the chalkboard:
    Thomas wrote a song.
    Have students compose separate sentences with clauses that answer the questions *When?* and *Why?*
    [*When?* —Thomas wrote a song after his grandmother bought him a songbook. *Why?* —Thomas wrote a song because he was happy.]

19c

GRAMMAR

EXAMPLES Patricia Roberts Harris, **who served as President Carter's Secretary of Housing and Urban Development,** was the first African American woman Cabinet member. [complex sentence with adjective clause]

When I hear ukulele music, I think of my cousin Alani. [complex sentence with adverb clause]

One interesting annual event **that is held in the Southwest** is the Inter-Tribal Ceremonial, **which involves many different Native American peoples.** [complex sentence with two adjective clauses]

☞ **REFERENCE NOTE:** For help in deciding when to use commas with subordinate clauses, see pages 713 and 720.

▶ EXERCISE 4   **Identifying Subordinate Clauses**

Identify the <u>subordinate clause</u> in each of the following sentences. Then, circle the ⬭subordinating conjunction⬮ or the ⬭relative pronoun⬮ that begins the subordinate clause.

EXAMPLES **1.** Helen Keller, who overcame severe handicaps, showed courage and determination.
　1. ⬭*who*⬮ *overcame severe handicaps*
　2. Keller was fortunate because she had such a skillful and loving teacher.
　2. ⬭*because*⬮ *she had such a skillful and loving teacher*

1. Helen Keller, ⬭who⬮ <u>is shown in the photographs on the next page,</u> became very ill as a small child.
2. ⬭After⬮ <u>she recovered from the illness,</u> she could no longer see or hear.
3. ⬭Because⬮ <u>she could not hear,</u> she also lost her ability to speak.
4. Helen's parents asked Alexander Graham Bell, ⬭who⬮ <u>trained teachers of people with hearing impairments,</u> for his advice about the child's education.
5. Upon Bell's suggestion, a special teacher, ⬭whose⬮ <u>name was Annie Sullivan,</u> stayed at the Kellers' home to teach Helen.

MEETING
INDIVIDUAL
NEEDS

LEP/ESL

　General Strategies. You may want to explain that subordinate clauses are used to stress one idea more than another. You can use the sentences in **Exercise 4** to illustrate how emphasis is given to one part of the sentence.

LESS-ADVANCED STUDENTS

　Have students draw two circles and label them *Tree Island* and *Desert Island.* Then have each student compose a short sentence about what is on Tree Island and one about what is on Desert Island. [Tree Island has a lot of trees. Desert Island does not have many trees.] Tell students to write the sentences under the appropriate circles.

　Next, have each student draw a bridge between the two islands and write the word *but* on the bridge. Ask a student to read the new sentence. Repeat this exercise by first having students create new sentences, and then having them change these sentences by using subordinating conjunctions.

GRAMMAR

WRITING APPLICATION

OBJECTIVE

• To use a variety of sentence structures to write a letter

542 *Kinds of Sentence Structure*

6. Sullivan spelled words into Helen's hand (as) the
child touched the object represented by the word.
7. From this basic understanding of language, Helen
went on to learn Braille, (which) is the alphabet used
by people with visual impairments.
8. Sullivan, (who) had been partly cured of blindness
herself, remained with Helen for many years.
9. (Because) she had triumphed over her handicaps,
Helen Keller was awarded the Presidential Medal of
Freedom.
10. Her autobiography, (which) is titled *The Story of My
Life*, tells about her remarkable achievements.

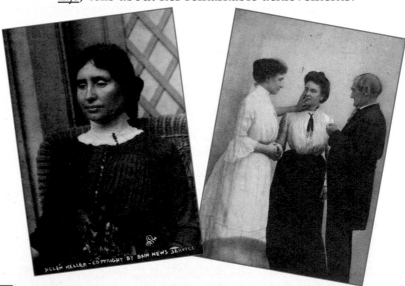

HELEN KELLER - COPYRIGHT BY BAIN NEWS SERVICE

WRITING APPLICATION
You could have students develop
lists of things they dislike about houses
as well as lists of things they like.
Because their letters must be about the
good things in their dream houses, tell
them that they should identify the oppo-
sites of the things they dislike about
houses.

542

WRITING APPLICATION

Using a Variety of Sentence Structures in Your Writing

"I'm bored!" That's how a reader responds to writing that
uses the same kind of sentence structure over and over
again. Using a variety of sentence structures can make your
writing more interesting to read.

SIMPLE SENTENCES	Josh and I went to the supermarket. Josh watched the lobsters in the fish tank. I picked out some flowers to surprise Mom. We got everything on our shopping list. We paid for our groceries. We walked home.
SENTENCE VARIETY	Josh and I went to the supermarket. [simple] While Josh watched the lobsters in the fish tank, I picked out some flowers to surprise Mom. [complex] We got everything on our shopping list. [simple] Then we paid for our groceries, and we walked home. [compound]

▶ WRITING ACTIVITY

Anyone can enter the "Win Your Dream Home" Contest. All you have to do is describe your ideal house. Write a letter to the contest judges, describing where your dream house would be and what it would look like. Use a variety of sentence structures to make your letter interesting for the judges to read.

Prewriting Make a list of the special features of the house you want to describe. To help you think of ideas, you may want to look through magazines or books to find pictures of interesting homes. You may also find it helpful to draw a rough diagram of the rooms, yard, and other features you would want. Take notes for details you want to include.

Writing As you write your first draft, use your notes to include vivid details that will give the contest judges a clear picture of your dream house.

Evaluating and Revising Read over your letter to make sure it is interesting and clear. Also, check to see whether you can combine similar ideas by using either compound or complex sentences. Ask an adult to read your letter. Does he or she think your description would impress the contest judges?

CRITICAL THINKING
Synthesis

Have students list adjectives or short descriptions next to the features they identify in the prewriting stage.

Then have students look over their lists of adjectives to brainstorm about what kinds of pictures those adjectives or descriptions might give to a judge. [Students might find that a bright, happy, open, and green house could be compared to an open field or a clear ocean.] Encourage students to describe their houses in terms of these other images by comparing the houses to the images in compound or complex sentences.

EVALUATING AND REVISING

Have students role-play in pairs to evaluate their work. Have them act as loan officers in a bank and explain who should or should not receive a loan for the house.

PROOFREADING AND PUBLISHING

When students publish the letters, have them design covers for their dream house entries. You may want students to draw pictures of their dream houses, to choose quotations about the houses, or just to write their names and the titles of their contest entries on the covers.

GRAMMAR

A DIFFERENT APPROACH

Have students build a quick reference chart such as the one below that they can refer to as they do **Reviews A and B:**

Kinds of Sentence Structure	Independent Clauses	Subordinate Clauses
Simple	1	0
Compound	2 or more	0
Complex	1	1 or more

REVIEWS A and B

OBJECTIVE

• To classify sentences as simple, compound, or complex

 Proofreading Check over the grammar and spelling in your letter. Also, make sure that you have used commas correctly in compound sentences and complex sentences. (For information on using commas, see pages 706–722.)

▶ REVIEW A   **Classifying Simple, Compound, and Complex Sentences**

Classify each of the following sentences as *simple*, *compound*, or *complex*.

EXAMPLE   **1.** The Mississippi River, which is the longest river in the United States, begins in the town of Lake Itasca, Minnesota.
1. *complex*

1. I drew an illustration for a poem that was written by Robert Hayden. **1.** cx.
2. The Olympic skaters felt anxious, but they still performed their routine perfectly. **2.** cd.
3. Kamehameha Day is an American holiday that **3.** cx. honors the king who united the islands of Hawaii.
4. For the first time in his life, José saw the ocean. **4.** simp.
5. If you had a choice, would you rather visit China or Japan? **5.** cx.
6. The bull was donated to the children's zoo by the people who bought it at the auction. **6.** cx.
7. Lookout Mountain, which is in Tennessee, was the site of a battle during the Civil War. **7.** cx.
8. The guide led us through Mammoth Cave, and she explained the difference between stalactites and stalagmites. **8.** cd.
9. Wilhelm Steinitz of Austria became famous after he was officially recognized as the first world champion of chess. **9.** cx.
10. Amy Tan is the author of the book *The Joy Luck Club*. **10.** simp.

▶ REVIEW B

Classifying Simple, Compound, and Complex Sentences

Classify each sentence in the following paragraphs as *simple*, *compound*, or *complex*.

EXAMPLE
[1] The Iroquois people traditionally held a Green Corn Festival in August when their crops were ready for harvesting.
1. *complex*

[1] For the early Iroquois, the Green Corn Festival was a celebration that lasted several days. [2] During the celebration, all children who had been born since midwinter received their names. [3] Tribal leaders made speeches, and adults and children listened to them carefully. [4] In one traditional speech, the leader would give thanks for the harvest. [5] After they had heard the speeches, the people sang and danced until dawn.

[6] On the second day of the festival, the people performed the special dance pictured here, and during the dance they gave thanks for the sun, the moon, and the stars. [7] On the third day, the Iroquois gave thanks for the helpfulness of their neighbors and for good luck. [8] The festival ended on the fourth day when teams of young people would play a bowling game. [9] During the festival the people renewed their friendships and rejoiced in their harmony with nature. [10] This Iroquois festival resembles the U.S. Thanksgiving holiday, which has its roots in similar Native American celebrations.

1. cx.
2. cx.
3. cd.
4. simp.
5. cx.
6. cd.
7. simp.
8. cx.
9. simp.
10. cx.

THE CORN DANCE.

GRAMMAR

LEARNING STYLES

Visual Learners. To illustrate the relationships of subjects and verbs in compound and complex sentences, draw the following tree diagrams for students:

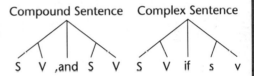

You could point to the different parts of the diagrams as you discuss the two types of sentences, and students can also use the diagrams to analyze sentences.

GRAMMAR

545

OBJECTIVES

- To identify and classify clauses
- To identify sentences as simple, compound, or complex
- To write simple, compound, and complex sentences

MEETING INDIVIDUAL NEEDS

ADVANCED STUDENTS

To give students more practice with sentence structure, have them develop compound-complex sentences. First, create groups of three students each. One student will write a simple sentence and then pass the piece of paper with this sentence to the next student, who will add a subordinate clause. This second student will pass the paper along to the final group member, who will add a coordinating conjunction and another independent clause. Each group can repeat this exercise after switching roles.

GRAMMAR

Review: Posttest 1

A. Identifying and Classifying Clauses

Label each clause in the following sentences as an *independent clause* or a *subordinate clause*.

EXAMPLE 1. We did warm-up exercises before we practiced the difficult routine.
1. *We did warm-up exercises—independent clause; before we practiced the difficult routine—subordinate clause*

1. Students <u>who are interested in attending the science fair at the community college</u> <u>should sign up now</u>.
2. <u>The musical *West Side Story* is a modern version of the story of Romeo and Juliet</u>.
3. <u>The first poem in the book is about spring</u>, and <u>the second one is about autumn</u>.
4. <u>Molasses</u>, <u>which is made from sugar cane</u>, <u>is a thick brown liquid used in human food and animal feed</u>.
5. <u>Before the test</u> <u>we studied the chapter and did the review exercises</u>.
6. <u>We took notes</u> <u>while our teacher discussed the formation of the African nation of Liberia</u>.
7. <u>It rained Saturday morning</u>, but <u>the sun came out in time for the opening of the Special Olympics</u>.
8. <u>The player</u> <u>whose performance is judged as the best</u> <u>receives the Most Valuable Player Award</u>.
9. <u>The tourists went to the Japanese exhibit</u> <u>after they had reached the museum</u>.
10. <u>Not all stringed instruments sound alike</u>, for <u>their shapes and the number of their strings vary</u>.

B. Identifying Simple, Compound, and Complex Sentences

Identify each of the following sentences as *simple*, *compound*, or *complex*.

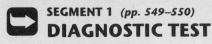

OBJECTIVES

- To identify and correct errors in subject-verb agreement
- To identify and correct errors in pronoun-antecedent agreement

20 AGREEMENT

Subject and Verb, Pronoun and Antecedent

USAGE

CHAPTER OVERVIEW

The chapter first reviews the basic concept of number and then moves to subject-verb agreement. Special problems in agreement such as prepositional phrases appearing between subjects and verbs are discussed. Indefinite pronouns, compound subjects and other agreement problems are presented. Additionally, an explanation of pronoun-antecedent agreement is presented.

The **Writing Application** requires standard agreement to be used in a formal report. In addition to this assignment, students should employ the rules discussed in this chapter for any composition. Suggest that students refer to these agreement rules in the revision stage of their writing.

Diagnostic Test

A. Identifying and Correcting Errors in Subject-Verb Agreement

If the underlined verb in each sentence does not agree with its subject, write the correct form of the verb. If the verb does agree with its subject, write C.

EXAMPLE **1.** A car with five forward gears <u>cost</u> extra.
    1. *costs*

1. ~~Don't~~ anybody know how to make egg rolls? **1.** Doesn't
2. "Those Winter Sundays" <u>was</u> written by Robert Hayden. **2.** C
3. Mathematics <u>are</u> taught every morning at 9:00 A.M. **3.** is

USING THE DIAGNOSTIC TEST

Use the **Diagnostic Test** to evaluate your students' mastery of agreement. The test is constructed in two parts; the focus of **Part A** is subject-verb agreement, and the focus of **Part B** is pronoun-antecedent agreement. The results of this test will indicate if students need extra practice to understand the correct use of agreement in their writing.

Students with learning problems often have difficulty understanding directions. Read the directions for the **Diagnostic Test** to students while they follow in their books. Then have students repeat the directions to you before they attempt the test.

550 *Agreement*

4. Seventy dollars˄seem like a high price for a pair of skates. **4.** seems
5. Here˄is your tickets for tomorrow's basketball game, Jennifer. **5.** are
6. Dolores and Frank wear glasses only for reading. **6.** C
7. One of the batteries˄do not work. **7.** does
8. Everyone except us˄know some Spanish. **8.** knows
9. My family˄are originally from Thailand. **9.** is
10. Neither of these cassette recorders˄have automatic reverse. **10.** has

B. Identifying and Correcting Errors in Pronoun-Antecedent Agreement

If the underlined pronoun in each of the following sentences does not agree with its antecedent, write the correct form of the pronoun. If the pronoun does agree with its antecedent, write *C*.

EXAMPLE   **1.** Someone left their skis here.
                    1. *his or her*

11. Neither of these plants should have˄their roots disturbed. **11.** its
12. Did anyone forget˄their CDs? **12.** his or her
13. Either Maria or Louise will receive˄their award today. **13.** her
14. Everybody should know˄their ZIP code. **14.** his or her
15. Each student has given˄their report on an African American folk tale. **15.** his or her
16. Every one of the dogs obeyed its owner. **16.** C **17.** C
17. Each of the components has its own on-off switch.
18. Will either Hector or Tony read his paper aloud? **18.** C
19. Not one of the students had finished˄their science project on time. **19.** his or her
20. She borrowed my Navajo silver jewelry and forgot to return˄them. **20.** it

NUMBER AND AGREEMENT OF SUBJECT AND VERB Rules 20a, 20b

OBJECTIVES

- To classify nouns and pronouns by number
- To identify verbs that agree in number with their subjects

Number

Number is the form of a word that indicates whether the word is singular or plural.

20a. When a word refers to one person, place, thing, or idea, it is *singular* in number. When a word refers to more than one, it is *plural* in number.

SINGULAR	igloo	she	one	child	joy
PLURAL	igloos	they	some	children	joys

 REFERENCE NOTE: For more information about forming plurals, see pages 754 and 773–776.

 EXERCISE 1 **Classifying Nouns and Pronouns by Number**

Classify each of the following words as *singular* or *plural*.

EXAMPLES **1.** girl
1. *singular*

2. rivers
2. *plural*

1. evening **1.** sing.
2. wolves **2.** pl.
3. women **3.** pl.
4. leaf **4.** sing.
5. they **5.** pl.
6. teeth **6.** pl.
7. tacos **7.** pl.
8. we **8.** pl.
9. thief **9.** sing.
10. armies **10.** pl.

Agreement of Subject and Verb

20b. A verb agrees with its subject in number.

Two words *agree* when they have the same number. The number of a verb must always agree with the number of its subject.

▼ **RESOURCES**

NUMBER AND AGREEMENT OF SUBJECT AND VERB
- Singular and Plural

QUICK REMINDER

Take a few minutes to have your students examine the relationship of subjects and verbs. Write the following lists of subjects and verbs on the chalkboard or display them on an overhead projector. Ask the class to duplicate the lists on paper and to draw lines connecting the subjects to their verbs.

SUBJECT	VERB
horse	speed
monkey	climbs
racers	gallops
students	study

Students should explain their choices. Or you may prefer to ask them to write an original sentence for each subject-verb combination.

LEP/ESL

Chinese and Vietnamese. Speakers of these languages and of several others that do not show number in nouns or verbs might have difficulty with the concept of agreement. Students should be reminded that in written English proper agreement is essential in every sentence—not only the first one.

USAGE

AFRICAN AMERICAN

Many students use singular verbs with both singular and plural subjects. For example, one might hear "Where is they at?" Explain that students need to use plural verbs with plural subjects in writing, and then provide an oral drill in which you give two alternatives such as "They goes there" and "They go there." Ask which should be used in writing.

USAGE

---

552 *Agreement*

(1) Singular subjects take singular verbs.

EXAMPLES   The **lightning fills** the sky. [The singular verb *fills* agrees with the singular subject *lightning.*]
Jan begins her vacation today. [The singular verb *begins* agrees with the singular subject *Jan.*]

(2) Plural subjects take plural verbs.

EXAMPLES   **Cheetahs run** fast. [The plural verb *run* agrees with the plural subject *cheetahs.*]
New **families move** into our neighborhood frequently. [The plural verb *move* agrees with the plural subject *families.*]

When a sentence contains a verb phrase, the first helping verb in the verb phrase agrees with the subject.

EXAMPLES   The **motor is** running.
The **motors are** running.

The **girl has** been delayed.
The **girls have** been delayed.

Is anyone filling the piñata?
Are any **students** filling the piñata?

👉 **REFERENCE NOTE:** Most nouns ending in *–s* are plural (*cheetahs, families*). Most verbs that end in *–s* are singular (*fills, begins*). For more about spelling the plural forms of nouns, see pages 773–776.

▶ EXERCISE 2   **Identifying Verbs That Agree in Number with Their Subjects**

Choose the <u>form of the verb</u> in parentheses <u>that agrees with the given subject.</u>

EXAMPLE   **1.** wind (*howls, howl*)
1. *howls*

1. people (*talks*, *talk*)
2. rain (*splashes*, *splash*)
3. birds (*flies*, *fly*)
4. we (*helps*, *help*)
5. it (*appears*, *appear*)

6. geese (*hisses*, *hiss*)
7. night (*falls*, *fall*)
8. roofs (*leaks*, *leak*)
9. baby (*smiles*, *smile*)
10. tooth (*aches*, *ache*)

EXERCISE 3 **Identifying Verbs That Agree in Number with Their Subjects**

For each of the following sentences, choose the <u>form of the verb</u> in parentheses <u>that agrees with the subject</u>.

EXAMPLE　**1.** Special tours (*is, are*) offered at the National Air and Space Museum, Washington, D.C.

　　　　　1. *are*

1. This museum (<u>*has*</u>, *have*) been called the best of all the Smithsonian museums.
2. The huge building (<u>*covers*</u>, *cover*) three blocks.
3. Twenty-seven showrooms (*offers*, <u>*offer*</u>) visitors information and entertainment.
4. The different showrooms (*deals*, <u>*deal*</u>) with various aspects of air and space travel.
5. As you can see, the exhibits (*features*, <u>*feature*</u>) antique aircraft as well as modern spacecraft.
6. In another area, a theater (<u>*shows*</u>, *show*) films on a five-story-high screen.
7. A planetarium (<u>*is*</u>, *are*) located on the second floor.
8. Projectors (*casts*, <u>*cast*</u>) realistic images of stars on the ceiling.
9. Some tours (*is*, <u>*are*</u>) conducted by pilots.
10. In addition, the museum (<u>*houses*</u>, *house*) a large research library.

 INTEGRATING THE LANGUAGE ARTS

Literature Link. Explain to students that a writer may avoid standard English to create a special tone in a work. Have students read and discuss "Madam and the Rent Man" by Langston Hughes, or assign some other piece that employs dialect. Tell the students that Hughes uses special language to give the reader a clear picture of the characters' personalities and backgrounds. Have the class pick out the lines in which Hughes purposefully uses subjects and verbs that do not agree in number [lines 12, 17, and 29]. Ask students to rewrite each example. How is the effect of the poem changed? [The reader is less sympathetic.] How is the image of Madam changed? [She seems more educated.]

 VISUAL CONNECTIONS
Related Expression Skills. You may want to form groups of two or three students each. Ask them to study the picture of the *USS Enterprise* carefully. Then you could suggest that they design original spaceships. These designs could be followed by short expressive/ descriptive paragraphs about their designs.

SEGMENT 3 *(pp. 554–556)*
PROBLEMS IN AGREEMENT Rule 20c

OBJECTIVES
- To choose the verb form that agrees in number with the subject
- To write sentences with correct subject-verb agreement

---

554 *Agreement*

▶ EXERCISE 4   **Proofreading for Errors in Subject-Verb Agreement**

Most of the following sentences contain errors in subject-verb agreement. If a verb does not agree with the subject, write the correct form of the verb. If a sentence is correct, write C.

EXAMPLE   **1.** More than nineteen million people lives in and around Mexico's capital.
1. *live*

1. Located in an ancient lake bed, Mexico City ∧have been built on Aztec ruins.   **1.** has
2. Visitors admire the murals of Diego Rivera at the National Palace.   **2.** C
3. In one of the city's subway stations, an Aztec pyramid still ∧stand.   **3.** stands
4. Sculptures grace the Alameda, which is Mexico City's main park.   **4.** C
5. Atop the Latin-American Tower, an observatory ∧offer a great view on a clear day.   **5.** offers
6. At the National University of Mexico, the library's outer walls ∧is famous as works of art.   **6.** are
7. Juan O'Gorman's huge mosaics ∧shows the cultural history of Mexico.   **7.** show
8. Usually, tourists ∧is fascinated by the Great Temple of the Aztecs.   **8.** are
9. Many fiestas ∧fills Mexico City's social calendar.   **9.** fill
10. In addition, the city has one of the largest soccer stadiums in the world.   **10.** C

Problems in Agreement

Prepositional Phrases Between Subject and Verb

20c. The number of a subject is not changed by a phrase following the subject.

PROBLEMS IN AGREEMENT
- Agreement of Subject and Verb
- Agreement and Prepositional Phrases

🦉 QUICK REMINDER
Write the following sentences on the chalkboard or on an overhead transparency. Have students copy and underline each subject once and each verb twice. Also have them check to see if the subjects and verbs agree and to fill in the blank in each sentence with a prepositional phrase.

1. The glass ___ topples over easily. [of orange juice]
2. The attorney ___ always sits near the witness. [in the flannel suit]
3. The girl ___ earned a scholarship. [by the bookshelf]

20c

EXAMPLES   The **hero** of those folk tales **is** Coyote. [The verb *is* agrees with the subject *hero.*]
The successful **candidate,** along with two of her aides, **has** entered the auditorium. [The helping verb *has* agrees with the subject *candidate.*]
Scientists from all over the world **have** gathered in Geneva. [The helping verb *have* agrees with the subject *Scientists.*]

☞ **REFERENCE NOTE:** If the subject is an indefinite pronoun, its number may be determined by a prepositional phrase that follows it. See page 430 for a discussion of indefinite pronouns.

▶ EXERCISE 5   **Identifying Verbs That Agree in Number with Their Subjects**

In the following sentences, choose the <u>form of the verb</u> in parentheses <u>that agrees with the subject</u>.

EXAMPLE   **1.** The water in the earth's oceans (*cover, covers*) much of the planet's surface.
1. *covers*

1. A tidal wave, despite its name, (<u>*is*</u>, *are*) not caused by the tides.
2. An eruption beneath the sea (<u>*causes*</u>, *cause*) a tidal wave.
3. A network of warning signals (*alert,* <u>*alerts*</u>) people in coastal areas of an approaching tidal wave.
4. The tremendous force of tidal waves (<u>*causes*</u>, *cause*) great destruction.
5. Walls of earth and stone along the shore (*is,* <u>*are*</u>) often too weak to protect coastal villages.

▶ EXERCISE 6   **Using Correct Subject-Verb Agreement**

What do you notice first about the painting shown on the next page? Is it the floating people? the upside down train? the multicolored cat? Look at the painting closely, and identify at least five features you notice. Then, write five sentences about the unusual features you find. Be sure

USAGE

USAGE

ANSWERS
Exercise 6

Sentences will vary. Here are some possibilities:

1. The cat sitting on the window ledge has a human face.
2. A man is floating in the sky.
3. A man and a woman are lying on the ground.
4. The train is upside down.
5. The building behind the cat's head looks like a wedge of cheese.

555

INDEFINITE PRONOUNS Rules 20d–20f

OBJECTIVE

• To choose verb forms that agree in number with their subjects

556 *Agreement*

VISUAL CONNECTIONS
Paris through the Window

Ideas for Writing. Ask your students to select one of the unusual objects or people in the painting. Have them write expressive/descriptive paragraphs to explain the reason for the odd situation. How did the person or object get into the predicament? How does he, she, or it feel about the circumstance? Some students may want to personify inanimate objects. Tell the students to check for correct subject-verb agreement in all sentences.

RESOURCES

INDEFINITE PRONOUNS
• Agreement with Indefinite Pronouns

QUICK REMINDER

Write the following sentence on the chalkboard:

____ wanted ____ to have ____ toys, but ____ was interested in ____ of the food.

Ask your students to fill in the blanks with indefinite pronouns. [Possible answers are *Neither, anyone, some, each,* and *most.*] Then ask students to create original sentences with blanks where indefinite pronouns should go.

556

that each of your sentences has correct subject-verb agreement. You may want to compare your findings with those of other students.

EXAMPLE **1.** *The man in the painting has two faces.*

Marc Chagall, *Paris through the Window*, 1913, Oil on canvas, 53¾ x 55¼ inches, Solomon R. Guggenheim Museum, New York. Gift, Solomon R. Guggenheim, 1937. PHOTO: David Heald copyright Solomon R. Guggenheim Foundation, New York. FN 37.438

Indefinite Pronouns

You may recall that personal pronouns refer to specific people, places, things, or ideas. A pronoun that does not refer to a definite person, place, thing, or idea is called an *indefinite pronoun.*

PERSONAL PRONOUNS	we	you	she	them
INDEFINITE PRONOUNS	anybody	both	either	everyone

20d. The following indefinite pronouns are singular: *each, either, neither, one, everyone, everybody, no one, nobody, anyone, anybody, someone, somebody.*

EXAMPLES **Each** of the newcomers **was** welcomed to the city.
Neither of these papayas **is** ripe.
Does anybody on the bus speak Arabic?

▶ EXERCISE 7   **Choosing Verbs That Agree in Number with Their Subjects**

In the following sentences, choose the <u>form of the verb</u> in parentheses <u>that agrees with the subject</u>. Remember that the subject is never part of a prepositional phrase.

EXAMPLE **1.** One of these books (*is, are*) yours.
1. *is*

1. Neither of the movies (<u>*was*</u>, *were*) especially funny.
2. Everybody in those classes (<u>*gets*</u>, *get*) to see the Balinese dancers.
3. Someone among the store owners (<u>*donates*</u>, *donate*) the trophy each year.
4. Each of the Washington brothers (<u>*studies*</u>, *study*) with a Zulu dance instructor.
5. No one on either team (<u>*was*</u>, *were*) ever in a playoff before.
6. Everyone with an interest in sports (<u>*is*</u>, *are*) at the tryouts.
7. Anybody with binoculars (<u>*is*</u>, *are*) popular at a large stadium.
8. Each of our neighbors (<u>*has*</u>, *have*) helped us plant the community garden.
9. One of the Spanish teachers (<u>*supervises*</u>, *supervise*) the language lab.
10. Nobody in our family (<u>*is*</u>, *are*) able to speak Greek well, but we all can speak a little bit.

20e. The following indefinite pronouns are plural: *both, few, many, several.*

EXAMPLES **Few** of our neighbors **have** parakeets.
Many of them **keep** dogs as pets.

MEETING INDIVIDUAL NEEDS

LEP/ESL

Spanish. In English, singular pronouns such as *everyone* are used to refer to many people. In Spanish, people usually use the plural *todos,* meaning "all," to express the same idea. Also, English uses a singular verb with *either* and *neither,* as in "Either goes on that shelf." In Spanish, the verb would be singular in some cases, but more often plural. Thus, some of your Spanish-speaking students may think that it is safe to use the plural verb if the subject refers to more than one person or thing. You may wish to remind them that the singular form is needed in standard English.

TIMESAVER
If you use **Exercise 7** for reteaching, review only the even-numbered items. You will save instructional time and will be able to assess students' progress quickly. For students who still need additional practice, assign the odd-numbered items as written work.

20f. The indefinite pronouns *all, any, most, none,* and *some* may be either singular or plural.

The number of the pronouns *all, any, most, none,* and *some* is determined by the number of the object in the prepositional phrase following the subject. If the pronoun refers to a singular object, it is singular. If the pronoun refers to a plural object, it is plural.

EXAMPLES **All** of the fruit **looks** fresh. [*All* is singular because it refers to one thing—*fruit*. The verb *looks* is singular to agree with the subject *All*.]
All of the pears **are** ripe. [*All* is plural because it refers to more than one thing—*pears*. The verb *are* is plural to agree with the subject *All*.]

Some of the crowd **has** left. [*Some* is singular because it means "a part" of the crowd. The helping verb *has* is singular to agree with the subject *Some*.]
Some of the fans **are** getting autographs. [*Some* is plural because it refers to more than one fan. The helping verb *are* is plural to agree with the subject *Some*.]

▶ EXERCISE 8 **Choosing Verbs That Agree in Number with Their Subjects**

For each of the following sentences, choose the form of the verb in parentheses that agrees with the subject.

EXAMPLE **1.** All of the new research on dreams (*is, are*) fascinating.
1. *is*

1. Most of our dreams (*occur*, occurs) toward morning.
2. Few of us really (*understand*, understands) the four cycles of sleep.
3. During the cycle known as rapid eye movement (REM), some dreams (is, *are*) very clear.
4. None of my dreams ever (*make*, makes) sense to me.
5. Many of them (is, *are*) about what happened that day.

OBJECTIVE

- To select verbs that agree in number with their subjects

20f

  REVIEW A

Identifying Verbs That Agree in Number with Their Subjects

For each sentence in the following paragraph, choose the <u>verb form</u> in parentheses <u>that agrees with the subject</u>.

EXAMPLE   [1] These flying objects probably (*look, looks*)
familiar to you.
   1. *look*

[1] Many people throughout the world (*claims, <u>claim</u>*) to have seen objects like these. [2] However, no one (*know, <u>knows</u>*) for sure what they are. [3] They (*resembles, <u>resemble</u>*) huge plates or saucers. [4] Not surprisingly, everyone (*call, <u>calls</u>*) them "flying saucers." [5] Since 1947, they (*has, <u>have</u>*) been officially called unidentified flying objects, or UFOs. [6] The U.S. government (*<u>is</u>, are*) conducting investigations into many UFO sightings. [7] The Air Force's Project Blue Book (*<u>has</u>, have*) investigated more than thirteen thousand reported UFOs. [8] The project (*cover, <u>covers</u>*) a seventeen-year period. [9] Most reported sightings (*turns, <u>turn</u>*) out to be fakes, but others remain unexplained. [10] None of the official reports (*offers, <u>offer</u>*) proof that UFOs are real.

USAGE

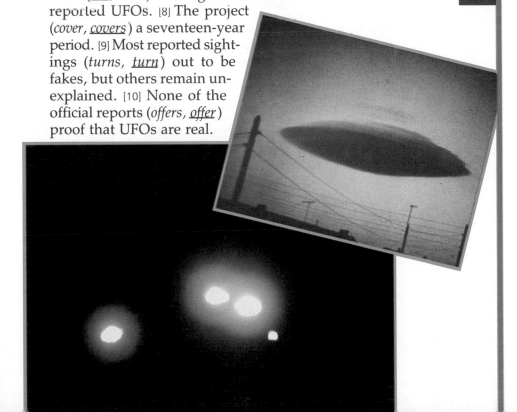

MEETING
INDIVIDUAL
NEEDS

LESS-ADVANCED STUDENTS

Some students may benefit from doing **Review A** when paired with other students who understand the material. Assign the exercise to groups of two or three. Encourage them to read the sentences aloud and to evaluate the problems they have in comprehending the sentences. You may want to walk about the room to listen to conversations and to verify that the information is being explained adequately.

USAGE

COMPOUND SUBJECTS Rules 20g–20i

OBJECTIVE

* To choose verbs that agree with their compound subjects

RESOURCES

COMPOUND SUBJECTS
* Agreement with Compound Subjects

QUICK REMINDER

To encourage your class to think about subjects and their verbs, write the following lists of subjects and verbs on the chalkboard:

SUBJECTS	VERB
blanket	are
cats	lie
fan	link
marshmallow	were

Ask students to compose sentences with any combination of subjects and verbs. The subjects of the sentences must be compound. [Example: A marshmallow and two calico cats link the suspect to the crime.]

LEP/ESL

Spanish. The rules for agreement with compound subjects in Spanish are complex. Whether the Spanish verb should be singular or plural can be influenced by three things—the applicability of the verb to both elements of the compound subject, the relative distance of the subject and the object from the verb, and the importance of the predicate nominative, if there is one. You may want to emphasize the agreement rules of English and to give extra practice to any students who have trouble with agreement.

560

---

560 *Agreement*

Compound Subjects

20g. Subjects joined by *and* usually take a plural verb.

EXAMPLES **Our dog and cat get** baths in the summer.
Mr. Duffy and his **daughter have** gone fishing.

A compound subject that names only one person or thing takes a singular verb.

EXAMPLES **A famous singer and dancer is** going to speak at our drama club meeting. [One person is meant.]
Macaroni and cheese is my favorite supper. [One combination is meant.]

▶ EXERCISE 9 **Identifying Verbs That Agree in Number with Their Subjects**

For each of the following sentences, choose the <u>correct form of the verb in parentheses</u>. If you choose a singular verb with any of these compound subjects, be prepared to explain why.

EXAMPLE **1.** Chris and her sister (*is, are*) in the school band.
1. *are*

1. (*Is, <u>Are</u>*) the brown bear and the polar bear related?
2. Fruit and cheese (*tastes, <u>taste</u>*) good together.
3. My guide and companion in Bolivia (*<u>was</u>, were*) Pilar, a high school student. **3.** One person is meant.
4. New words and new meanings for old words (*is, <u>are</u>*) included in a good dictionary.
5. Mrs. Chang and her daughter (*rents, <u>rent</u>*) an apartment in San Francisco's Chinatown.
6. Both iron and calcium (*needs, <u>need</u>*) to be included in a balanced diet.
7. Mr. Marley and his class (*has, <u>have</u>*) painted a wall-size map of the Caribbean islands.
8. A horse and buggy (*<u>was</u>, were*) once a fashionable way to travel.

9. Tornadoes and hurricanes (*is*, <u>*are*</u>) dangerous storms.
10. Wind and water (*erodes*, <u>*erode*</u>) valuable farmland throughout the United States.

20h. Singular subjects joined by *or* or *nor* take a singular verb.

EXAMPLES   The chief **geologist or** her **assistant is** due to arrive tonight. [Either one is due, not both.]
Neither a **rabbit nor** a **mole does** that kind of damage in a garden. [Neither one does the damage.]

Plural subjects joined by *or* or *nor* take a plural verb.

EXAMPLES   **Either mice or squirrels are** living in our attic.
Neither the **senators nor** the **representatives want** the bill to be vetoed by the president.

20i. When a singular subject and a plural subject are joined by *or* or *nor*, the verb agrees with the subject nearer the verb.

EXAMPLE   A **book or flowers** usually **make** an appropriate **gift**. [The verb agrees with the nearer subject, *flowers.*]
Flowers or a **book** usually **makes** an appropriate **gift**. [The verb agrees with the nearer subject, *book.*]

Compound subjects that have both singular and plural parts can sound awkward even though they are correct. Whenever possible, revise a sentence to avoid such constructions.

AWKWARD   Two small boards or one large one is what we need to patch that hole.
REVISED   We need two small boards or one large one to patch that hole.

AWKWARD   Neither the lights nor the microwave is working.
REVISED   The lights aren't working, and neither is the microwave.

USAGE

A DIFFERENT APPROACH
Tell your students that they will write an expressive paragraph together. Ask them to think of a verb and a compound subject that agree in number and to write these words. Have the first student at the beginning of each row write a topic sentence with a compound subject and verb. If students have trouble getting started, suggest topics for their paragraphs, such as "snow," "football," or "hound dogs." As the first writer finishes writing, he or she will pass the paper to the next student in line, who will compose a sentence with another compound subject and verb and then pass the paper back. When all rows have finished writing, the paper will be passed back to the first student, who will read the paragraph aloud.

USAGE

REVIEW B

OBJECTIVE

• To proofread sentences for subject-verb agreement

 EXERCISE 10

Identifying Verbs That Agree in Number with Their Subjects

Choose the <u>correct form of the verb</u> in parentheses in each of the following sentences. Be able to explain the reason for your choice.

EXAMPLE   **1.** The club president or the officers (*meets, meet*) regularly with the sponsors.
1. *meet*

1. Neither pens nor pencils (*is, <u>are</u>*) needed to mark the ballots.
2. Either my aunt or my uncle (*<u>is</u>, are*) going to drive us to the lake.
3. That table or this chair (*<u>was</u>, were*) made by hand in Portugal.
4. (*Has, <u>Have</u>*) the sandwiches or other refreshments been served?
5. Index cards or a small tablet (*<u>is</u>, are*) handy for taking notes.   **5.** Closer subject is singular.
6. Neither that clock nor my watch (*<u>shows</u>, show*) the correct time.
7. One boy or girl (*<u>takes</u>, take*) the part of the narrator.
8. During our visit to Jamaica, a map or a guidebook (*<u>was</u>, were*) my constant companion.
9. The dentist or her assistant (*<u>checks</u>, check*) my braces.
10. Either Japanese poetry or Eskimo myths (*is, <u>are</u>*) going to be the focus of my report.   **10.** Closer subject is plural.

REVIEW B

Proofreading Sentences for Subject-Verb Agreement

Identify each verb that does not agree with its subject in the following sentences. Then supply the correct form of each incorrect verb.

EXAMPLE   **1.** The players in the photograph on the next page is competing in the most popular sport in the world—soccer.
1. *is—are*

1. One expert in the field of sports, ~~have~~ described soccer as the world's favorite type of football.   **1.** has

2. Some sports writers, ~~has~~ estimated that there are over thirty million registered soccer players around the globe.   **2.** have

3. Youth leagues and coaching clinics, ~~has~~ helped make soccer the fastest-growing team sport in America.   **3.** have

4. For example, in Dallas, Texas, neither baseball nor American football, ~~attract~~ as many young players as soccer does.   **4.** attracts

5. Also, more colleges now, ~~has~~ varsity soccer teams than football teams.   **5.** have

6. This increase in soccer fans, ~~are~~ a trend that started in 1967, when professional teams began playing in the United States.   **6.** is

7. Additional interest, ~~were~~ generated when the U.S. Youth Soccer Association was formed.   **7.** was

8. Both males and females, ~~enjoys~~ playing this sport.   **8.** enjoy

9. In fact, by the 1980s, many of the soccer teams in the country, ~~was~~ women's teams.   **9.** were

10. In the past, professional soccer, ~~were~~ mostly a foreign game, but the United States competed for the World Cup in 1990.   **10.** was

VISUAL CONNECTIONS

Ideas for Writing. Have your students write five-sentence expressive paragraphs describing favorite sports or hobbies. They should not name their topics, and three of the five sentences should contain compound subjects. Ask volunteers to read their paragraphs aloud. The class will then have the opportunity to guess the subject of each writer's paragraph.

OTHER PROBLEMS IN AGREEMENT
Rules 20j–20o

OBJECTIVES
- To identify subjects of sentences and the verbs that agree with them
- To choose correct verb forms in sentences

RESOURCES

OTHER PROBLEMS IN AGREEMENT
- Other Problems in Agreement

🦉 QUICK REMINDER

Write the following sentences on the chalkboard. Tell students to copy the sentences and to use only the correct verbs. Then they should identify each subject as plural or singular. Ask volunteers to explain why choosing the right verb is a challenge.

1. The football team (is riding, are riding) the bus together.
2. Here (is, are) the list of students for Mr. Howell.
3. Two hours (is, are) too long to wait.

MEETING
INDIVIDUAL
NEEDS

LEP/ESL

General Strategies. Many languages have similar rules governing agreements between collective-noun subjects and verbs. For example, British English, which is learned by many Asian students, uses the plural more frequently than American English, as in "The Government have decided to . . . ." In Spanish, a verb is often singular if it is in the same clause as the collective subject. It is either singular or plural otherwise. You may wish to give your ESL students additional examples of sentences that use collective nouns and to explain whether each reference is to a unit or to its members.

564

---

564 *Agreement*

Other Problems in Subject-Verb Agreement

20j. Collective nouns may be either singular or plural.

A *collective noun* is singular in form but names a group of persons, animals, or things.

Common Collective Nouns			
audience	committee	group	swarm
class	family	herd	team
club	flock	jury	troop

A collective noun takes a singular verb when the noun refers to the group as a unit. A collective noun takes a plural verb when the noun refers to the individual parts or members of the group.

EXAMPLES The **class were** divided in their opinions of the **play.** [The members of the class were divided in their opinions.]
The **class has** decided to have a science fair in **November.** [The class as a unit has decided.]

My **family are** coming from all over the state for **the reunion.** [The members of the family are coming.]
My **family plans** to attend Beth's graduation. [The family as a unit plans to attend.]

20k. When the subject follows the verb, find the subject and make sure that the verb agrees with it. The subject usually follows the verb in sentences beginning with *here* or *there* and in questions.

EXAMPLES Here **is** my **umbrella.**
Here **are** our **umbrellas.**

**20
j–k**

There **is** a scary **movie** on TV.
There **are** scary **movies** on TV.

Where **was** the **cat**?
Where **were** the **cats**?

Does Jim know the Chens?
Do the **Chens** know Jim?

NOTE: When the subject of a sentence follows the verb, the
word order is said to be *inverted.* To find the subject of a
sentence with inverted order, restate the sentence in
normal word order.

INVERTED   Here **are** your **gloves.**
NORMAL   Your **gloves are** here.

INVERTED   **Were you** late, too?
NORMAL   **You were** late, too?

INVERTED   In the pond **swim** large **goldfish.**
NORMAL   Large **goldfish swim** in the pond.

The contractions *here's, there's,* and *where's* contain the
verb *is* and should be used only with singular subjects.

EXAMPLES   There**'s** our new **neighbor.**
Where**'s** my lunch **money**?

☞ REFERENCE NOTE: For more information about contractions, see
pages 749–750.

▶ EXERCISE 11   **Identifying Verbs That Agree in
Number with Their Subjects**

Identify the <u>subject</u> in each of the following sentences.
Then, choose the <u>correct form of the verb</u> in parentheses.

EXAMPLE   **1.** That flock of geese (*migrates, migrate*) each
year.
1. *flock—migrates*

1. There (*is, <u>are</u>*) at least two <u>solutions</u> to this Chinese
puzzle.
2. The Austrian Olympic <u>team</u> (*was, <u>were</u>*) all getting
on different buses.

MEETING
INDIVIDUAL
NEEDS

LEARNING STYLES

Visual Learners. Seeing the
subject of a sentence in relation to its
verb may help students clarify potential
problems with agreement. Write the following sentences on the chalkboard.
First, ask for volunteers to illustrate these
sentences. Then, ask your students to
label each subject as acting as one group
or as several individuals. Finally, have the
class tell whether the verbs are correct.

1. The herd of horses in the south
pasture runs together. [subject—one
group *herd*, singular; verb—*runs*,
singular]
2. Ten dollars is the fee. [subject—one
amount *dollars*, singular; verb—*is*,
singular]
3. The basketball team members won
the trophy. [subject—several individuals *members*, plural; verb—*won*,
plural]

If any students can think of other
example sentences to label, have the students come to the chalkboard to write
the sentences.

INTEGRATING THE LANGUAGE ARTS

Technology Link. If computers are available to your classes, you could have students make a file of agreement rules found in this chapter. They can then access this file during evaluation and revision. This file will give students a quick way to check the rules, and applying rules in this way will reinforce students' understanding.

USAGE

USAGE

566 *Agreement*

3. (*Is, Are*) <u>both</u> of your parents from Korea?
4. Here (*comes, come*) the six <u>members</u> of the dance committee.
5. Here (*is, are*) some <u>apples</u> and <u>bananas</u> for the picnic basket.
6. There (*is, are*) neither <u>time</u> nor <u>money</u> for that project.
7. (*Here's, Here are*) the social studies <u>notes</u> I wrote about Mohandas Gandhi.
8. At the press conference, there (*was, were*) several <u>candidates</u> for mayor and two for governor.
9. The <u>family</u> (*has, have*) announced its plans to celebrate Grandma's promotion.
10. Here (*is, are*) some <u>masks</u> carved by the Haida people in Alaska.

20l. Words stating amounts are usually singular.

A word or phrase stating a weight, measurement, or an amount of money or time is usually considered one item. Such a word or phrase takes a singular verb.

EXAMPLES   Sixteen **ounces equals** one pound.
Ten **feet is** the height of a regulation basketball hoop.
Seventy-five **cents is** enough money for my lunch today.
Two **weeks** never **seems** long enough for vacation.

20m. The title of a book, or the name of an organization or a country, even when plural in form, usually takes a singular verb.

EXAMPLES   ***World Tales*** **is** a collection of folk tales retold by Idries Shah. [one book]
The **United Nations has** its headquarters in New York City. [one organization]
The **Philippines is** an island country that is located in the southwest Pacific Ocean. [one country]

▶ EXERCISE 12   **Identifying Verbs That Agree in Number with Their Subjects**

Choose the <u>correct form of the verb</u> in parentheses in each of the following sentences.

EXAMPLE   **1.** Three inches (*is, are*) a great deal to grow in one year.
        1. *is*

1. *The Friends* (<u>*is*</u>, *are*) a book about a girl from the West Indies and a girl from Harlem.
2. Two cups of broth (<u>*seems*</u>, *seem*) as if it is too little for that recipe.
3. Fifteen feet (<u>*was*</u>, *were*) the length of the winning long jump.
4. Navarro and Company (<u>*is*</u>, *are*) selling those jackets.
5. The National Council of Teachers of English (<u>*is*</u>, *are*) holding its convention in our city this year.
6. The United States (<u>*is*</u>, *are*) home to many different peoples.
7. Three hours of practice (<u>*is*</u>, *are*) not unusual for the band.
8. *Arctic Dreams* (<u>*was*</u>, *were*) written by Barry Lopez.
9. Two weeks of preparation (<u>*has*</u>, *have*) been enough.
10. Seventy-five cents (<u>*is*</u>, *are*) the cost of a subway ride.

20n. *Don't* and *doesn't* must agree with their subjects.

The words *don't* and *doesn't* are contractions of *do not* and *does not*. Use *don't* with all plural subjects and with the pronouns *I* and *you*.

EXAMPLES   The children **don't** seem nervous.
        I **don't** understand.
        You **don't** remember.

Use *doesn't* with all singular subjects except *I* and *you*.

EXAMPLES   Kim **doesn't** ride the bus.
        He **doesn't** play tennis.
        It **doesn't** snow here.

USAGE

ANSWERS
Exercise 13

Sentences will vary. Here are some possibilities:

1. My flat football doesn't hold air.

2. This picture made with glue and beans doesn't look attractive.

3. The t-shirt with a cartoon on the front doesn't fit anymore.

4. This stuffed toy dinosaur doesn't have a tail.

5. One red tennis shoe and one green tennis shoe don't make a pair.

6. I don't have interest in this bug collection anymore.

7. I don't read *Cricket* magazine anymore.

8. These jigsaw puzzles don't have all their pieces.

9. This brown sock doesn't have a match.

10. These dried-up paint brushes don't have any useful purpose.

▶ ORAL PRACTICE   **Using *Don't* and *Doesn't***

Read the following sentences aloud, stressing the italicized words.

1. My friend *doesn't* understand the problem.
2. *Doesn't* she want to play soccer?
3. The tomatoes *don't* look ripe.
4. Our school *doesn't* have a gymnasium.
5. Italy *doesn't* border Germany.
6. The geese *don't* hiss at Mr. Waverly.
7. Our Muslim neighbors, the Nassers, *don't* eat pork.
8. He *doesn't* play chess.

▶ EXERCISE 13   **Writing Original Sentences with *Don't* and *Doesn't***

You're cleaning out your closet and deciding what to do with the things you don't want any more. You plan to give reusable items to a thrift store, but some things just can't be saved. Here are some of the items you've found:

> a flat football
> a picture made with glue and beans
> a t-shirt with a cartoon on the front
> a stuffed toy dinosaur
> one red and one green tennis shoe
> a bug collection
> several *Cricket* magazines
> pieces of jigsaw puzzles
> a brown sock
> dried-up paint brushes

Write five sentences telling why you're getting rid of some of these items. Use *don't* or *doesn't* to agree with a different subject in each sentence.

EXAMPLE   **1.** *This stuffed toy dinosaur doesn't have all its stuffing any more.*

20o. A few nouns, though plural in form, take a singular verb.

OBJECTIVES

- To select verbs that agree in number with their subjects
- To proofread for errors in subject-verb agreement

Problems in Agreement **569**

20o

EXAMPLES **Mathematics seems** easier this year.
Civics is being taught by Ms. Gutierrez.
Mumps is the most uncomfortable disease I've ever had.
The **news was** not encouraging.

▶ REVIEW C **Identifying Verbs That Agree in Number with Their Subjects**

For each of the following sentences, choose the <u>verb form</u> in parentheses <u>that agrees with the subject</u>.

EXAMPLE **1.** New wheelchairs with lifts (*help, helps*) many people reach objects up high.
1. *help*

1. Twenty-five cents (<u>*is*</u>, *are*) not enough money to buy that newspaper.
2. Everyone in her company (<u>*prefers*</u>, *prefer*) to take winter vacations.
3. Allen and his parents (<u>*enjoy*</u>, *enjoys*) the Puerto Rican Day Parade in New York City.
4. Jan (*don't*, <u>*doesn't*</u>) know the rules for volleyball.
5. Neither the cassette player nor the speakers (<u>*work*</u>, *works*) on my stereo.
6. There (*is*, <u>*are*</u>) 130 islands in the state of Hawaii.
7. Many of the place names in California (*comes*, <u>*come*</u>) from Spanish words.
8. The principal or her assistant (<u>*is*</u>, *are*) the one who can help you.
9. Home economics (<u>*is*</u>, *are*) a required course in many schools.
10. A flock of sheep (<u>*was*</u>, *were*) grazing on the hill.

▶ REVIEW D **Proofreading Sentences for Subject-Verb Agreement**

Most of the sentences in the following paragraph contain errors in subject-verb agreement. If a verb does not agree with its subject, give the correct form of the verb. If a sentence is correct, write C.

USAGE

USAGE

569

EXAMPLE [1] Here is two pictures of Wang Yani and her artwork.

  1. *are*

1. are

2. regards

3. C

4. doesn't

5. change

6. C

7. feature

8. pictures

9. are

10. fills

[1] There surely∧is few teenage artists as successful as Yani. [2] In fact, the People's Republic of China∧regard her as a national treasure. [3] She has shown her paintings throughout the world. [4] A painter since the age of three, Yani∧don't paint in just one style. [5] Her ideas and her art naturally∧changes over the years. [6] The painting on the left shows one of Yani's favorite childhood subjects. [7] Many of her early paintings∧features monkeys. [8] In fact, one of her large works∧picture 112 monkeys. [9] However, most of her later paintings∧is of landscapes, other animals, and people. [10] As her smile suggests, Yani∧fill her paintings with energy and life.

WRITING APPLICATION

Using Subject-Verb Agreement in Formal Writing

You would probably write a thank-you note more neatly than you would write a grocery list. Like penmanship, English usage depends upon the situation. A formal piece of writing calls for special care with language. In formal writing, standard usage, like good penmanship, helps you make a good impression on your audience. Subject-verb agreement is one of the basic rules of standard usage.

| NONSTANDARD | The last two governors of the state has been highly respected. |
| STANDARD | The last two **governors** of the state **have** been highly respected. |

▶ WRITING ACTIVITY

If you could be any person in history, who would you be? Why? Your social studies teacher has asked you to answer these questions in a short composition. Be sure to use correct subject-verb agreement in explaining your choice.

Prewriting First, decide what historical person you would like to be. You can be someone out of ancient history or someone who is alive today. List some types of people such as heads of government, inventors, military leaders, explorers, writers, and artists. Then write the names of people you admire under each type. Select the person you would most like to be and freewrite about that person. As you write, think about why the person is noteworthy and why you would want to be him or her.

Writing Use your freewriting ideas to write your first draft. Begin with a sentence that states the purpose of your composition and identifies your historical figure. Then, give your main reasons for wanting to be that person. If you have

 WRITING APPLICATION
This writing assignment provides students with an opportunity to develop persuasive essays with subject-verb agreement. Students will be focusing their attention on subject-verb agreement, so you may want to review rules and examples from the textbook before the students begin to write.

CRITICAL THINKING
Evaluation

Because students are often hypercritical of their writing, they may suffer from writer's block or stifled creativity. When they begin the evaluation step of this assignment, you could suggest that they read their work aloud and listen to the rhythm of the written language. If awkward sentences exist, students will be able to hear the problems.

WRITING

Remind students that the most important aspect of this stage of writing is simply to get their thoughts on paper. Tell them to write on every other line of notebook paper so that they will have sufficient space for revisions.

USAGE

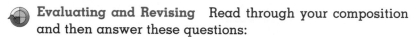

USAGE

USAGE

572 *Agreement*

several main reasons, you may want to write about each reason in a separate paragraph. Summarize your main points in a conclusion.

Evaluating and Revising Read through your composition and then answer these questions:

- Is it clear what person from history I want to be? If not, revise your main idea statement. For more about writing main ideas, see pages 64–66 and 98.
- Is it clear why I want to be that person? If not, explain your reasons in more detail. See page 69 for more about using supporting details.

Make sure that all subjects and verbs agree in number. Pay special attention to the subject-verb agreement in subordinate clauses. For more about subordinate clauses, see pages 516–525.

Proofreading and Publishing Check your composition for errors in spelling, capitalization, and punctuation. Your class may want to create a display using the compositions and pictures of the people written about. One type of display is a time line. Arrange the compositions and pictures to show where each subject fits in time—from ancient to recent. Another type of display requires a large world map. Use straight pins and yarn to connect each composition to the place on the map where that person lived.

RESOURCES

AGREEMENT OF PRONOUN AND ANTECEDENT

• Agreement of Pronoun and Antecedent

Agreement of Pronoun and Antecedent

A pronoun usually refers to a noun or another pronoun called its *antecedent.* Whenever you use a pronoun, make sure that it agrees with its antecedent.

 REFERENCE NOTE: For more information about antecedents, see page 428.

20p

20p. A pronoun agrees with its antecedent in number and gender.

Some singular personal pronouns have forms that indicate gender. Feminine pronouns refer to females. Masculine pronouns refer to males. Neuter pronouns refer to things (neither male nor female) and sometimes to animals.

Feminine	she	her	hers
Masculine	he	him	his
Neuter	it	it	its

EXAMPLES   **Carlotta** said that **she** found **her** book.
Aaron brought **his** skates with **him**.
The **plant** with mold on **it** is losing **its** leaves.

The antecedent of a personal pronoun can be another kind of pronoun. In such cases, you may need to look in a phrase that follows the antecedent to determine which personal pronoun to use.

EXAMPLES   **Each** of the **girls** has offered **her** ideas.
One of the **men** lost **his** key.

Some antecedents may be either masculine or feminine. In such cases, use both the masculine and the feminine forms.

EXAMPLES   Every **one** of the parents praised **his or her** child's efforts.
No one in the play forgot **his or her** lines.

NOTE: In conversation, people often use a plural personal pronoun to refer to a singular antecedent that may be either masculine or feminine. This form is becoming more common in writing, too, and it may someday be considered standard written English.

EXAMPLES   **Everybody** brought **their** swimsuit.
Each **member** of the club sold **their** tickets.

USAGE

USAGE

COMMON ERROR

Problem. Some students may be able to hear the awkwardness of repetitive *his or her* constructions in their writing, yet not know how to communicate a point without using this construction.

Solution. In sentences with indefinite pronouns that refer to mixed groups of males and females, students may find it helpful to reword sentences to eliminate the *his or her* construction.

 REFERENCE NOTE: For lists of the different kinds of pronouns, see pages 428–431.

(1) Use a singular pronoun to refer to *each, either, neither, one, everyone, everybody, no one, nobody, anyone, anybody, someone,* **or** *somebody.*

EXAMPLES   **Someone** in the class left behind **his or her** pencil.
Each of the snakes escaped from **its** cage.

(2) Use a singular pronoun to refer to two or more singular antecedents joined by *or.*

EXAMPLES   Either **Ralph or Carlos** will display **his** baseball card collection.
Nina or Mary will bring **her** CD player.

Sentences with singular antecedents joined by *or* can sound awkward if the antecedents are of different genders. If a sentence sounds awkward, revise it to avoid the problem.

AWKWARD   Odessa or Raymond will bring her or his road map.
REVISED   Either **Odessa** will bring **her** road map, or **Raymond** will bring **his.**

NOTE: Rules (1) and (2) are often ignored in conversation; however, they should be followed in writing.

(3) Use a plural pronoun to refer to two or more antecedents joined by *and.*

EXAMPLES   **Isaac and Jerome** went to the playground so that **they** could practice shooting baskets.
Elena and Roberto sent letters to **their** cousin in Costa Rica.

NOTE: Be sure that any pronoun referring to a collective noun has the same number as the noun.

EXAMPLES   The **cast** is giving **its** final performance tonight.
The **cast** are trying on **their** costumes.

REVIEW E

OBJECTIVE

- To proofread a paragraph for correct pronoun-antecedent agreement

> **EXERCISE 14** **Identifying Antecedents and Writing Pronouns That Agree with Them**

For each blank in the following sentences, give a pronoun that will complete the meaning of the sentence. Then identify the <u>antecedent or antecedents</u> for that pronoun.

EXAMPLE   **1.** Dominic or Martin will show ___ slides.
   1. *his—Dominic, Martin*

1. A <u>writer</u> should proofread ___ work carefully.   **1.** his or her
2. The store sent <u>Paula</u> and <u>Eric</u> the posters that ___ had ordered.   **2.** they
3. <u>Mark</u> or <u>Hector</u> will arrive early so that ___ can help us prepare the dim sum.   **3.** he
4. <u>One</u> of the students raised ___ hand.   **4.** his or her
5. <u>Each</u> of the dogs ate the scraps that we gave ___.   **5.** it
6. The <u>principal</u> and the Spanish <u>teacher</u> announced ___ plans for the Cinco de Mayo fiesta.   **6.** their
7. <u>Everyone</u> in my class has ___ own writer's journal.   **7.** his or her
8. <u>Neither</u> recalled the name of ___ first-grade teacher.   **8.** his or her
9. <u>Anyone</u> may join if ___ collects stamps.   **9.** he or she
10. Either <u>Vanessa</u> or <u>Marilyn</u> was awarded the blue ribbon for ___ design.   **10.** her

> **REVIEW E** **Proofreading a Paragraph for Correct Pronoun-Antecedent Agreement**

Most of the following sentences contain errors in pronoun-antecedent agreement. Identify each error and give the correct pronoun. If a sentence is correct, write C.

EXAMPLE   **[1]** At the meeting, each member of the Small Business Council spoke about their concerns.
   1. *their—his or her*

[1] Everybody had a chance to express ~~their~~ opinion about the new shopping mall. [2] Mrs. Gomez and Mr. Franklin are happy about ~~his or her~~ new business locations at the mall. [3] Both said that ~~his~~ profits have increased significantly. [4] Neither Mr. Chen nor Mr. Cooper, however, feels that ~~their~~ customers find parking

1. his or her
2. their
3. their
4. his

USAGE

 INTEGRATING THE LANGUAGE ARTS

Literature Link. May Swenson uses many pronouns but only a few referents in her poem "Cat & the Weather." Ask your students to read the poem carefully and to examine closely how all the pronouns and their antecedents are used.

Ask students to tell you how Swenson uses placement to avoid confusing the reader with so many pronouns. [All pronouns referring to the cat are masculine, and other pronouns are placed near their antecedents.] The pronoun *it's* (line 26) does not have a stated antecedent. Ask your students if they know what the pronoun refers to [personal world/life]. Have your students write short poems in which they use pronouns. Like Swenson, they may want to incorporate several pronouns and only a few antecedents. Ask volunteers to read their poems in class.

USAGE

575

5. his or her
convenient enough. [5] Anyone shopping at the mall has to park ∧their car too far from the main shopping area.

6. C
[6] Several members of the council said that the mall has

7. her
taken away many of their customers. [7] One of the new women on the council then presented ∧their own idea

8. they
about creating a farmers' market on weekends. [8] Many members said ∧he or she favored the plan, and a proposal

9. his or her
was discussed. [9] Each farmer could have ∧their own spot near the town hall. [10] The Small Business Council then

10. its
agreed to take ∧their proposal to the mayor.

PICTURE THIS

You are a sportswriter for the school newspaper and are covering this bicycle race. As the cyclists zoom by, you quickly take notes. Write several sentences that describe this exciting moment in the race. In your sentences, use five of the following pronouns: *her, nobody, his, each, its, one, their, anyone, they.* Remember that a pronoun should agree with its antecedent in number and gender.

Subject: bicycle race
Audience: school newspaper readers
Purpose: to inform

USAGE

PICTURE THIS

If students have difficulty starting, suggest they outline the events of the race. Then have them arrange the outline in chronological order. After students have a clear idea of how the race happened, they can write their sentences. Ask students to underline pronouns and to draw arrows to the antecedents during proofreading so that you can check student mastery.

VISUAL CONNECTIONS

Ideas for Writing. You may want to ask your students to write brief, informative essays about a fictional cyclist in this picture. Have them make up facts about the cyclist's life, training, accomplishments, latest race, and so on. Ask volunteers to read their essays aloud.

REVIEW: POSTTEST

OBJECTIVES

- To identify correct subject-verb and pronoun-antecedent agreement
- To proofread sentences for subject-verb and pronoun-antecedent agreement

Review: Posttest

A. Identifying Correct Subject-Verb and Pronoun-Antecedent Agreement

Choose the <u>correct word in parentheses</u> in each of the following sentences.

EXAMPLE **1.** Some of the paintings (*is, are*) dry now.
      1. *are*

1. Three hours of work (<u>*is*</u>, *are*) needed for a charcoal drawing.
2. Everybody has offered (<u>*his or her*</u>, *their*) advice.
3. *Harlem Shadows* (<u>*is*</u>, *are*) a collection of poems by Claude McKay.
4. Either Stu or Ryan can volunteer (<u>*his*</u>, *their*) skill in the kitchen.
5. Black beans, rice, and onions (*tastes*, <u>*taste*</u>) good together.
6. Not one of them has offered (<u>*his or her*</u>, *their*) help.
7. Sometimes my family (*disagrees*, <u>*disagree*</u>) with one another, but usually we all get along fairly well.
8. There (*is*, <u>*are*</u>) a beaded belt and a pair of moccasins in that box.
9. (*Doesn't*, <u>*Don't*</u>) too many cooks spoil the broth?
10. One of my aunts gave me (<u>*her*</u>, *their*) silk kimono.

B. Proofreading Sentences for Subject-Verb and Pronoun-Antecedent Agreement

Most of the following sentences contain an agreement error. For each error, identify the incorrect verb or pronoun, and supply the correct form. If the sentence is correct, write *C*.

EXAMPLE **1.** Most stargazers has seen points of light shooting across the night sky.
      1. *has—have*

USAGE

LESS-ADVANCED STUDENTS

If your students need additional review before taking the **Review: Posttest**, you may want to give them a little extra study time. Form study groups of two or three students each and assign the even-numbered items. Go over the answers orally to identify students who are struggling with the material. Then assign the odd-numbered items as a test.

USAGE

11. These points of light,~~is~~ commonly called shooting stars.   **11.** are

12. Scientists who study outer space,~~calls~~ these points of light meteors.   **12.** call

13. A meteor is a piece of an asteroid that exploded long ago.   **13.** C

14. Each of these pieces,~~are~~ still flying through space on the path of the original asteroid.   **14.** is

15. Most nights, a person is lucky if,~~they~~ can see a single meteor now and then.   **15.** he or she

16. Throughout the year, however, there,~~is~~ meteor "showers."   **16.** are

17. None of these showers are as big as the ones in August and November.   **17.** C

18. These large showers come at the same time each year.   **18.** C

19. In November 1833, one of the largest meteor showers in history,~~were~~ recorded.   **19.** was

20. Two hundred forty thousand meteors in nine hours ~~are~~ a record that has never been matched!   **20.** is

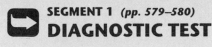

DIAGNOSTIC TEST

OBJECTIVE

- To choose the correct past or past participle form of an irregular verb

21 USING VERBS CORRECTLY

Principal Parts, Regular and Irregular Verbs, Tense

USAGE

CHAPTER OVERVIEW

This chapter explains the use of regular and irregular verbs and emphasizes past and past participle forms. Tense and the consistency of tense in paragraphs are also covered. **Segment 5** focuses on six irregular verbs that are often used incorrectly. In the **Writing Application**, students will have the opportunity to use verb tenses correctly when writing adventure stories.

Students can refer to the charts in this chapter during the proofreading stage of writing when they are uncertain about the correctness of a verb.

USAGE

Diagnostic Test

Using the Past and Past Participle Forms of Verbs

For each of the following sentences, give the correct form (past or past participle) of the verb in parentheses.

EXAMPLE   **1. The mayor has (*speak*) at our school's assemblies several times.**
       1. *spoken*

1. The sun (*rise*) over the pyramids of Giza in Egypt.   **1.** rose
2. We have (*swim*) only three laps.   **2.** swum
3. Vera was (*choose*) captain of the volleyball team.   **3.** chosen
4. I have (*go*) to visit the Grand Canyon twice with my family.   **4.** gone
5. The tiny tree frog (*sit*) motionless.   **5.** sat
6. Joan has (*write*) a story about aliens from Venus.   **6.** written
7. During lunch hour, Jorge (*do*) his impersonation of Ruben Blades.   **7.** did
8. Someone (*lay*) a mysterious package on my desk.   **8.** laid

USING THE DIAGNOSTIC TEST

This test will show which students have problems using correct verb forms in sentences. Some students will make errors because they do not recognize the auxiliary verbs that determine verb forms. Others will have problems using the correct forms of the irregular verbs and of the six troublesome verbs discussed in this chapter.

OBJECTIVES
- To use the correct verb forms when reading sentences aloud
- To form correctly the present participle, past, and past participle forms of regular verbs

USAGE

QUICK REMINDER

To give students a review of the forms of the principal parts of regular verbs, write the following sentences on the chalkboard:

1. Cynthia ____ today
2. She ____ yesterday.
3. She has ____ before.

Have volunteers supply several verbs for each sentence. You can then explain that all the suggested verbs have something in common: They are forms of regular verbs, known as the principal parts. Reinforce that the past forms never require helping verbs, but that past participle forms always require helping verbs.

580

USAGE

580 *Using Verbs Correctly*

9. This summer's heat wave has (*break*) all records.   **9.** broken
10. Have you (*drink*) all of the tomato juice?   **10.** drunk
11. The log slowly (*sink*) into the quicksand.   **11.** sank
12. The old postcards have (*lie*) in the box for years.
13. Have you ever (*drive*) across the state of Texas?
14. Our local PBS station (*begin*) its fund-raising drive yesterday.   **12.** lain   **13.** driven   **14.** began
15. Have you (*set*) the paper plates and napkins on the picnic table?   **15.** set   **16.** threw
16. Who (*throw*) the ball to first base?   **17.** known
17. I have (*know*) some of my classmates for six years.
18. Kadeem Niles (*take*) the part of Frederick Douglass in the play.   **18.** took   **19.** raised
19. The supermarket has (*raise*) the price of eggs.
20. We (*come*) close to winning the tournament.   **20.** came

Principal Parts

The four basic forms of a verb are called the ***principal parts*** of the verb.

21a. The principal parts of a verb are the ***infinitive,*** the ***present participle,*** the ***past,*** and the ***past participle.***

Here are the principal parts of two familiar verbs.

INFINITIVE	PRESENT PARTICIPLE	PAST	PAST PARTICIPLE
talk	(is) talking	talked	(have) talked
draw	(is) drawing	drew	(have) drawn

Notice that the present participle and the past participle require helping verbs (forms of *be* and *have*).

The principal parts of a verb are used to express time.

PRESENT TIME   He **draws** excellent pictures.
                Susan **is drawing** one now.
PAST TIME   Last week they **drew** two maps.
                She **has** often **drawn** cartoons.
FUTURE TIME   Perhaps she **will draw** one for you.
                By next Thursday, we **will have
                drawn** two landscapes.

© 1992 by Sidney Harris

Because *talk* forms its past and past participle by adding –*ed*, it is called a *regular verb*. *Draw* forms its past and past participle differently, so it is called an *irregular verb*.

Regular Verbs

21b.   A *regular verb* forms its past and past participle by adding –*ed* or –*d* to the infinitive form.

INFINITIVE	PRESENT PARTICIPLE	PAST	PAST PARTICIPLE
clean	(is) cleaning	cleaned	(have) cleaned
hope	(is) hoping	hoped	(have) hoped
inspect	(is) inspecting	inspected	(have) inspected
slip	(is) slipping	slipped	(have) slipped

☞ **REFERENCE NOTE:** Most regular verbs that end in –*e* drop the –*e* before adding –*ing*. Some regular verbs double the final consonant before adding –*ing* or –*ed*. For a discussion of these spelling rules, see pages 770–771.

One common error in forming the past or the past participle of a regular verb is to leave off the –*d* or –*ed* ending.

NONSTANDARD   Our street use to be more quiet.
   STANDARD   Our street **used** to be more quiet.

☞ **REFERENCE NOTE:** For a discussion of standard and nonstandard English, see page 387.

USAGE

LEP/ESL

General Strategies. The past-tense suffixes *–ed* and *–d* often result in groups of final consonant sounds that do not occur in many other languages. For example, the sound groups *skt* in *asked* and *gd* in *logged* do not occur in Chinese, Indonesian, Korean, Japanese, Portugese, Spanish, Turkish, or Vietnamese. Speakers of such languages often simplify such unpronounceable groups by omitting the last sounds, a practice that might lead to omitting the final consonants in writing as well. You could model **Oral Practice 1** for students to emphasize the past-tense suffixes.

VISUAL CONNECTIONS

Ideas for Writing. Have students write expressive/descriptive paragraphs describing early experiences with dance classes, recitals, or sports. Ask students to underline all the verbs and to exchange papers with partners to check the verb forms. Because students are writing about past experiences, most verbs will have the past or past participle form.

▶ ORAL PRACTICE 1 **Using Regular Verbs**

Read each of the following sentences aloud, stressing the italicized verbs.

1. We are *supposed* to meet at the track after school.
2. The twins *happened* to buy the same shirt.
3. They have already *called* me about the party.
4. Do you know who *used* to live in this house?
5. I *hoped* they could go to the concert with us.
6. The chairs have been *moved* for the dance.
7. That salesclerk has *helped* my mother before.
8. Eli may not have *looked* under the table for the cat.

▶ EXERCISE 1 **Writing the Forms of Regular Verbs**

For each of the following sentences, fill in the blank with the correct present participle, past, or past participle form of the verb given.

EXAMPLE **1.** *learn* Many people today are _____ folk dances from a variety of countries.
1. *learning*

1. *practice* These Spanish folk dancers must have _____ for a long time. **1.** practiced
2. *perform* Notice that they are _____ in colorful, native costumes. **2.** performing
3. *wish* Have you ever _____ that you knew how to do any folk dances? **3.** wished

OBJECTIVES

- To use the correct irregular verb forms when reading sentences aloud
- To form the past and past participle forms of irregular verbs

RESOURCES

IRREGULAR VERBS
- Principal Parts of Irregular Verbs

Principal Parts **583**

21c

4. *use*   Virginia reels ____ to be popular dances in the United States.   **4.** used   **5.** promised

5. *promise*   Mrs. Stamos, who is from Greece, ____ to teach her daughter the Greek chain dance.

6. *lean*   The Jamaican dancer ____ backward before he went under the pole during the limbo competition.   **6.** leaned   **7.** starting

7. *start*   The group from Estonia is ____ a dance about a spinning wheel.   **8.** requested

8. *request*   Someone in the audience has ____ an Irish square dance called "Sweets of May."

9. *dance*   During the Mexican hat dance, the girl ____ on the rim of the sombrero.   **9.** danced

10. *fill*   The Jewish wedding dance ____ the room with music and movement.   **10.** filled

USAGE

Irregular Verbs

21c. An *irregular verb* forms its past and past participle in some other way than by adding *–d* or *–ed* to the infinitive form.

Irregular verbs form their past and past participle in three ways:

- by changing vowels *or* consonants

INFINITIVE	PAST	PAST PARTICIPLE
ring	rang	(have) rung
make	made	(have) made

- by changing vowels *and* consonants

INFINITIVE	PAST	PAST PARTICIPLE
do	did	(have) done
go	went	(have) gone

USAGE

QUICK REMINDER
Write the following irregular verbs on the chalkboard:

begin	run	swing
drive	speak	think
go	swim	write

Ask the class to supply the correct forms in the following sentences for each verb:

1. Today I ____.
2. Yesterday I ____.
3. Often I have ____.

583

LEP/ESL

General Strategies. Some strategies for adding suffixes in English require familiarity with the sounds of English. For example, to know when to double the final consonant of a one-syllable verb before adding *–ing* necessitates being able to recognize the short vowel sounds of English. Some ESL students might not yet be able to distinguish some of the sounds of English, especially vowels that sound similar, such as short *e* and short *a*. Try reviewing the long and short vowels of English, the stress patterns in English words, and the sound pairs that are problematic for ESL students.

STUDENTS WITH SPECIAL NEEDS

Learning disabled students may have limited vocabularies or experience difficulties with abstract concepts. It is helpful to read all instructions for exercises aloud and to explain any concepts and terms used.

Have each student make a chart of verb tenses. Then have students focus on a limited number of activities. For example, it may be effective to have students highlight the verbs and work with partners to correct problems. If necessary, ask students to write both forms and to underline the correct one.

USAGE

USAGE

584 *Using Verbs Correctly*

■ by making no changes

INFINITIVE	PAST	PAST PARTICIPLE
hurt	hurt	(have) hurt
put	put	(have) put

NOTE: If you are not sure about the principal parts of a verb, look in a dictionary. Entries for irregular verbs list the principal parts of the verb. If the principal parts are not given, the verb is a regular verb.

COMMON IRREGULAR VERBS			
INFINITIVE	PRESENT PARTICIPLE	PAST	PAST PARTICIPLE
begin	(is) beginning	began	(have) begun
bite	(is) biting	bit	(have) bitten
blow	(is) blowing	blew	(have) blown
break	(is) breaking	broke	(have) broken
bring	(is) bringing	brought	(have) brought
build	(is) building	built	(have) built
burst	(is) bursting	burst	(have) burst
catch	(is) catching	caught	(have) caught
choose	(is) choosing	chose	(have) chosen
come	(is) coming	came	(have) come
cost	(is) costing	cost	(have) cost
do	(is) doing	did	(have) done
draw	(is) drawing	drew	(have) drawn
drink	(is) drinking	drank	(have) drunk
drive	(is) driving	drove	(have) driven
eat	(is) eating	ate	(have) eaten
fall	(is) falling	fell	(have) fallen
feel	(is) feeling	felt	(have) felt
freeze	(is) freezing	froze	(have) frozen
get	(is) getting	get	(have) got *or* gotten

(continued)

COMMON IRREGULAR VERBS *(continued)*			
INFINITIVE	**PRESENT PARTICIPLE**	**PAST**	**PAST PARTICIPLE**
give	(is) giving	gave	(have) given
go	(is) going	went	(have) gone
grow	(is) growing	grew	(have) grown
know	(is) knowing	knew	(have) known
lead	(is) leading	led	(have) led

▶ ORAL PRACTICE 2   **Using Irregular Verbs**

Read each of the following sentences aloud, stressing the italicized verbs.

1. Ellen's sister *drove* her to the mall this afternoon.
2. My parents *came* to the spelling bee last year.
3. I should have *known* the test would be difficult.
4. He's *going* to Cape Canaveral this summer.
5. Maya has been *chosen* to play Emily in *Our Town*.
6. The water pipe *burst* during the ice storm.
7. *Did* you see the northern lights last night?
8. Wyatt *brought* his new computer game to the party.

▶ EXERCISE 2   **Writing the Past and Past Participle Forms of Irregular Verbs**

For each of the following sentences, give the past or past participle form of the verb that will fit correctly in the blank.

EXAMPLE   **1.** *choose* Sara has _____ her song for the recital.
            1. *chosen*

1. *drive* Last summer we _____ to Denver, where we visited the U.S. Mint. **1.** drove
2. *begin* The concert _____ an hour ago. **2.** began
3. *break* Mike Powell _____ the world long jump record by jumping 29 feet, $4\frac{1}{2}$ inches. **3.** broke
4. *blow* The wind has _____ the tent down. **4.** blown

CRITICAL THINKING
Analysis

Have each student listen to five friends or relatives to make notes on which verbs are used most often. Suggest that students each choose one person to analyze each day for a school week. Tell each student to keep a log, to list all the verbs that occur in each conversation, and to categorize the verbs as regular or irregular. Students can then conclude the assignment by writing summaries about how people speak, including information about verb choices and correctness.

USAGE

USAGE

MEETING
INDIVIDUAL
NEEDS

ADVANCED STUDENTS

To help students improve their writing, explain that they should choose vibrant verbs whenever possible. Let them work in groups of three to practice doing this. In each group, the first person will write a common verb on a piece of paper. The next group member, possibly using a thesaurus, will think of a more interesting synonymous verb. The final group member will create a sentence with the more effective verb. Ask volunteers to share their verbs and sentences with the class.

586 *Using Verbs Correctly*

5. gotten   **6.** fallen

5. *get*   We've ____ tickets to ride *The Silverton.*
6. *fall*   People have ____ over that log several times.
7. *do*   Mother ____ her best, and she got a promotion.
8. *drink*   According to legend, the Aztec emperor Montezuma ____ chocolate.   **7.** did   **8.** drank
9. *build*   People in Africa ____ large cities hundreds, even thousands, of years ago.   **9.** built   **10.** gone
10. *go*   You've never ____ to Puerto Rico, have you?

MORE COMMON IRREGULAR VERBS			
INFINITIVE	**PRESENT PARTICIPLE**	**PAST**	**PAST PARTICIPLE**
lend	(is) lending	lent	(have) lent
lose	(is) losing	lost	(have) lost
make	(is) making	made	(have) made
meet	(is) meeting	met	(have) met
ride	(is) riding	rode	(have) ridden
ring	(is) ringing	rang	(have) rung
run	(is) running	ran	(have) run
say	(is) saying	said	(have) said
see	(is) seeing	saw	(have) seen
sell	(is) selling	sold	(have) sold
send	(is) sending	sent	(have) sent
shrink	(is) shrinking	shrank	(have) shrunk
sing	(is) singing	sang	(have) sung
sink	(is) sinking	sank	(have) sunk
speak	(is) speaking	spoke	(have) spoken
stand	(is) standing	stood	(have) stood
steal	(is) stealing	stole	(have) stolen
swim	(is) swimming	swam	(have) swum
swing	(is) swinging	swung	(have) swung
take	(is) taking	took	(have) taken
tell	(is) telling	told	(have) told
throw	(is) throwing	threw	(have) thrown
wear	(is) wearing	wore	(have) worn
win	(is) winning	won	(have) won
write	(is) writing	wrote	(have) written

▶ ORAL
PRACTICE 3   **Using Irregular Verbs**

Read each of the following sentences aloud, stressing the italicized verbs.

1. When the bell *rang*, we hurried out of the building.
2. The audience was quiet as the acrobats *swung* from the trapeze.
3. That dress *shrank* because it was washed in hot water.
4. Otherwise, Lily would have *worn* it to the dance.
5. Have you *met* the foreign exchange student this year?
6. We were late to the picnic because I *lost* the map.
7. My father *lent* me the money to buy a new watch.
8. Would you believe that Raymond *took* singing lessons?

▶ EXERCISE 3   **Writing the Past and Past Participle Forms of Irregular Verbs**

For each of the following sentences, give the past or past participle form of the verb that will fit correctly in the blank.

EXAMPLE **1.** *see* I have ____ that movie twice already.
           1. *seen*

1. *run*   Carl Lewis ____ the 100-meter dash in record-breaking time. **1.** ran
2. *sell*   My aunt has ____ more houses than any other real estate agent in the city. **2.** sold
3. *speak* The director of the state health department ____ to our class today. **3.** spoke
4. *win*   Mexican poet Octavio Paz ____ the Nobel Prize for literature. **4.** won
5. *write* I have ____ some poems, but I am shy about showing them to anyone. **5.** written
6. *ride*   Tamisha's whole family ____ on mules to the bottom of the Grand Canyon. **6.** rode
7. *sing*   At the concert, the group ____ my favorite song. **7.** sang

USAGE

REVIEWS A–C

OBJECTIVES

- To choose the past or past participle forms of irregular verbs to complete sentences
- To use the correct past or past participle forms of given irregular verbs to write ten sentences

USAGE

USAGE

588 *Using Verbs Correctly*

8. thrown

8. *throw*   This trash must have been ____ from a car.
9. *swim*   Two swans ____ across the lake.   9. swam
10. *sink*   King Arthur's sword Excalibur ____ slowly to the bottom of the lake.   10. sank

▶ REVIEW A   **Writing the Past and Past Participle Forms of Irregular Verbs**

For each of the following sentences, give the past or past participle form of the verb that will fit correctly in the blank.

EXAMPLE   **1.** *tell*   Has Alameda ____ you about the book *The Indian Tipi: Its History, Construction, and Use*?
1. *told*

1. *write*   Reginald and Gladys Laubin ____ that book and several others about Native American culture.   1. wrote
2. *come*   The word *tepee,* or *tipi,* has ____ into English from the Sioux language.   2. come
3. *stand*   Tepees of various sizes once ____ all across the plains.   3. stood
4. *see*   I have ____ pictures of camps full of decorated tepees.   4. seen   5. made
5. *make*   For many years, Native Americans have ____ tepees out of cloth rather than buffalo hides.
6. *build*   The Laubins ____ their own tepee and lived in it.   6. built
7. *draw*   On the outside of their tepees, the Sioux and Cheyenne peoples ____ designs like the ones shown on the next page.   7. drew
8. *take*   Because the Plains peoples followed the animal herds, they needed housing that could be ____ from place to place.   8. taken
9. *know*   Even before reading the book, I ____ that tepee covers weren't painted inside.   9. knew
10. *do*   Women ____ all the work of making tepees and putting them up.   10. did

LEP/ESL

General Strategies. Some ESL students might not understand the idea of irregular verbs if their native languages, such as Indonesian, Japanese, Korean, Turkish, and Vietnamese, have few or no irregular verbs. Students might write the present-tense forms of these verbs when they should use the past tense. Give students copies of a comprehensive list of irregular verbs with blank spaces left for the past tense. Tell students to fill in the past tense forms of the verbs and to keep the lists in their notebooks.

> REVIEW B

Writing the Past and Past Participle Forms of Irregular Verbs

For each of the following sentences, give the past or past participle form of the verb that will fit correctly in the blank.

EXAMPLE   **1.** *write*   I ___ a report on Jim Thorpe.
1. *wrote*

1. *blow*   Yesterday the wind ___ the leaves into our yard.   **1.** blew
2. *break*   My pen pal from Australia has never ___ his promise to write once a week.   **2.** broken
3. *bring*   I ___ the wrong book to class.   **3.** brought
4. *burst*   The children almost ___ with excitement.
5. *choose*   The director ___ James Earl Jones to star in the new series.   **4.** burst   **5.** chose
6. *come*   My aunt and her friend ___ to dinner last night.   **6.** came

INTEGRATING THE LANGUAGE ARTS

Grammar and Library Skills.
To help students complete **Review C**, ask them to create lists of ten *What?* questions and ten *Why?* questions to ask their celebrities. They can then research the ten most interesting questions.

Students might need to use a resource such as *Current Biography*. They can find addresses and write letters to the celebrities. To reinforce the verb tenses, ask students to use the present tense to describe themselves and the past tense to explain their interest in the celebrities.

ANSWERS
Review C

Sentences will vary. Be sure students use complete sentences. You might consider having students underline the verbs and circle any auxiliary verbs that are used. Remind students that the past participle requires an auxiliary verb.

7. *do*   I have always ____ my homework right after supper. **7.** done **8.** drank

8. *drink*   The guests ____ four quarts of fruit punch.

9. *fall*   One of my Russian nesting dolls has ____ off the shelf. **9.** fallen

10. *freeze*   Has the pond ____ yet? **10.** frozen

11. *go*   We have never ____ to see the Parthenon in Nashville, Tennessee. **11.** gone **12.** known

12. *know*   Had I ____, I would have called you sooner.

13. *ring*   Suddenly the fire alarm ____. **13.** rang **14.** ran

14. *run*   Joan Samuelson certainly ____ a good race.

15. *see*   I ____ you in line at the movies. **15.** saw

16. *shrink*   We dried apples in the sun, and they ____.

17. *speak*   After we had ____ to George Takai, who plays Mr. Sulu, we went to the *Star Trek* convention banquet. **16.** shrank **17.** spoken

18. *throw*   You shouldn't have ____ the ball to second base. **18.** thrown **19.** written

19. *write*   She has ____ me several long letters.

20. *swim*   We ____ out to the float and back. **20.** swam

 REVIEW C   **Using Past and Past Participle Forms of Irregular Verbs**

You've won a radio contest called "Ask a Star." Now you get to interview the celebrity of your choice. You name the star, and the radio station will arrange the interview. Pick a celebrity to interview, and write ten questions to ask him or her. In your questions, use the past or past participle forms of ten of the following verbs. Underline each verb you use.

begin	cost	know	sing
break	do	meet	tell
build	drive	ride	throw
catch	feel	say	wear
choose	get	sell	write

EXAMPLE   **1.** *Have you really underline{ridden} a camel down Hollywood Boulevard?*

PICTURE THIS

The year is 2030. Just ten years ago scientists made great advances in time travel. Now, time-travel booths like this one are common in malls and shopping centers. For a small fee, you can travel to any place at any time in history. You sit down in the booth, fasten your seat belt, and set the dials for the time and place of your choice. When the machine stops, you get out and begin to explore your surroundings. You take notes about what you see so that you won't forget anything when you tell your family and friends about your trip. In your notes, describe how life in this time and place is similar to or different from life as you know it. Use at least ten irregular verbs, underlining each one you use.

Subject: a journey to a different place and time
Audience: your family and friends
Purpose: to inform and entertain

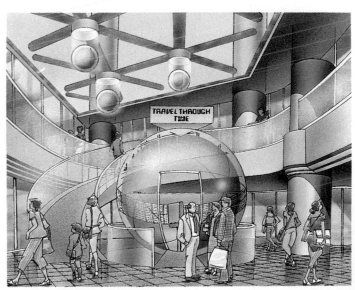

USAGE

PICTURE THIS

Students can go to the library to research their topics. If they have difficulty choosing settings, offer them two lists of choices, one of years and one of locations. Each student needs to use at least ten facts or details about the people, places, and events he or she might see or hear. Students should strive for specific and important details concerning their chosen times.

COOPERATIVE LEARNING

As a prewriting activity for the **Picture This** assignment, form groups of four students who will develop statements on time travel. The following guidelines might help them:

1. People being visited should be able to see and talk to time travelers.
2. Time travelers should be able to participate in the events that are occurring in the past or future.
3. Time travelers should discuss cultural similarities with the people they visit.

After they meet, the groups can report the results of their discussions to the class.

USAGE

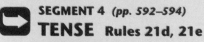

TENSE
• Verb Tense

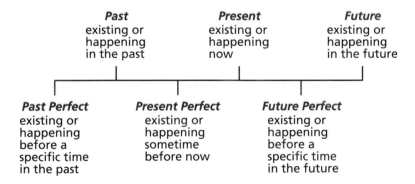

QUICK REMINDER
Write the following sentences on the chalkboard, and have students convert them to the verb tenses specified:

1. Kilroy runs faster than anyone else in his class. (past) [Kilroy ran . . .]
2. Samantha is a lifeguard at the beach. (future) [Samantha will be . . .]
3. Keesha wants to be a doctor. (present perfect) [Keesha has wanted . . .]
4. The weight lifter really pressed fifty pounds of weight. (past perfect) [The weight lifter had really pressed . . .]
5. Stopping an oil-well fire costs over a billion dollars. (future perfect) [Stopping an oil-well fire will have cost . . .]

592 *Using Verbs Correctly*

Tense

21d. The *tense* of a verb indicates the time of the action or of the state of being expressed by the verb.

Every verb has six tenses.

Present	Past	Future
Present Perfect	Past Perfect	Future Perfect

The following time line shows the relationship between the six tenses.

Past	***Present***	***Future***
existing or happening in the past	existing or happening now	existing or happening in the future

Past Perfect	***Present Perfect***	***Future Perfect***
existing or happening before a specific time in the past	existing or happening sometime before now	existing or happening before a specific time in the future

Listing all the forms of a verb is called *conjugating* the verb.

CONJUGATION OF THE VERB *SEE*	
PRESENT TENSE	
SINGULAR	**PLURAL**
I see	we see
you see	you see
he, she, or it sees	they see

(continued)

**21
d–e**

CONJUGATION OF THE VERB *SEE* (continued)	
PAST TENSE	
SINGULAR	**PLURAL**
I saw	we saw
you saw	you saw
he, she, or it saw	they saw
FUTURE TENSE	
SINGULAR	**PLURAL**
I will (shall) see	we will (shall) see
you will see	you will see
he, she, or it will see	they will see
PRESENT PERFECT TENSE	
SINGULAR	**PLURAL**
I have seen	we have seen
you have seen	you have seen
he, she, or it has seen	they have seen
PAST PERFECT TENSE	
SINGULAR	**PLURAL**
I had seen	we had seen
you had seen	you had seen
he, she, or it had seen	they had seen
FUTURE PERFECT TENSE	
SINGULAR	**PLURAL**
I will (shall) have seen	we will (shall) have seen
you will have seen	you will have seen
he, she, or it will have seen	they will have seen

Consistency of Tense

21e. Do not change needlessly from one tense to another.

When writing about events that take place in the present, use verbs that are in the present tense. When writing

USAGE

LEP/ESL

Asian Languages. Some languages, such as Chinese, Lao, Indonesian, and Vietnamese, do not use verb tenses to indicate time. Instead, a speaker will use either context or an adverb to establish the time of the events being discussed. The idea of specifying tense repeatedly in every sentence might seem redundant to some students; therefore, they might use only the present tense. Emphasize that in English the correct tense must be used in every sentence.

 INTEGRATING THE LANGUAGE ARTS

Literature Link. Have students read "Guess What? I Almost Kissed My Father" by Robert Cormier. Both present tense and past tense are used in the story. Have students work in groups of four to divide the story into parts and to list all the verbs in their sections. Then ask students to determine how the verb tenses change and what effect the changes have on the story. Each group should write an informative/descriptive paragraph supporting the group's interpretation of Cormier's tense choices. Tell groups to use specific lines from the story to illustrate their opinions.

USAGE

ANSWERS
Exercise 4

Students can choose either present or past tense, but they must be consistent throughout their paragraphs. Verbs in direct quotations and in statements of general truth (an example of which is sentence 6) should not be changed. In the following answers, the present tense is given first and the past tense is in parentheses:

1. strikes, run (struck, ran)
2. exclaim (exclaimed)
3. has gone (had gone)
4. light, play (lighted *or* lit, played)
5. discover, keeps (discovered, kept)
6. asks (asked)
7. tell (told)
8. nods (nodded)
9. start, doesn't, am talking, walks (started, didn't, was talking, walked)
10. are, shines, works (were, shone, worked)

---

about events that occurred in the past, use verbs that are in the past tense.

INCONSISTENT	**When we go to the movies, we bought some popcorn.** [*Go* is in the present tense, and *bought* is in the past tense.]
CONSISTENT	**When we go to the movies, we buy some popcorn.** [Both *go* and *buy* are in the present tense.]
CONSISTENT	**When we went to the movies, we bought some popcorn.** [Both *went* and *bought* are in the past tense.]

▶ EXERCISE 4 **Revising a Paragraph to Make the Tenses of the Verbs Consistent**

Read the following paragraph and decide whether it should be rewritten in the present or past tense. Then rewrite the paragraph, changing the verb forms to make the verb tense consistent.

EXAMPLE [1] I picked up the telephone receiver, but the line is still dead.

1. *I picked up the telephone receiver, but the line was still dead.*

or

I pick up the telephone receiver, but the line is still dead.

[1] Lightning struck our house, and I run straight for cover. [2] "Oh, no!" I exclaim. [3] The electricity had gone out! [4] My parents light candles, and we played a game by candlelight. [5] We discover that the lightning had struck our answering machine, because it keeps playing the same message over and over. [6] My younger brother asks me what lightning is. [7] "Lightning is a big spark of electricity from a thundercloud," I tell him. [8] He nods. [9] I started to tell him about positive and negative charges creating lightning, but he doesn't understand what I'm talking about and walks away. [10] In the morning, we were all glad when the sun shone and our phone works again.

OBJECTIVES

- To use the correct verb forms when reading sentences aloud
- To choose the correct forms of *sit* or *set* to complete sentences
- To choose the correct forms of *rise* or *raise* to complete sentences
- To choose the correct forms of *lie* or *lay* to complete sentences

Six Troublesome Verbs

Sit and *Set*

The verb *sit* means "to be seated" or "to rest." *Sit* seldom takes an object.

The verb *set* means "to place" or "to put (something)." *Set* usually takes an object. Notice that *set* has the same form for the infinitive, past, and past participle.

INFINITIVE	PRESENT PARTICIPLE	PAST	PAST PARTICIPLE
sit	(is) sitting	sat	(have) sat
set	(is) setting	set	(have) set

EXAMPLES   **Three girls sat** on the platform. [no object]
Set those geraniums in a sunny place. [Set what? *Geraniums* is the object.]

I **will sit** here for a while. [no object]
I **will set** your dinner on the table. [I will set what? *Dinner* is the object.]

 ORAL PRACTICE 4   **Using the Forms of *Sit* and *Set* Correctly**

Read each of the following sentences aloud, stressing the italicized verbs.

1. Darnell and I *sat* down to play a game of chess.
2. After he had been *sitting* for a while, Darnell decided to make banana bread.
3. I *set* the pan on the table.
4. Darnell *set* out the ingredients; then he mixed them.
5. We returned to our game but could not *sit* still for long.
6. We had not *set* the pan in the oven.
7. Then we almost *sat* too long.
8. The pan had been *set* on the wrong rack, and the bread was beginning to burn.

USAGE

USAGE

 QUICK REMINDER

Write the following verb forms on the chalkboard:

Pres.	Past	Past Part.	Meaning
lie	lay	(have) lain	to rest
lay	laid	(have) laid	to put

Stress to students that although these two verbs are similar in appearance, they have different meanings. Then have students determine which of these words belongs in the blank in each of the following sentences. Have them tell you why they chose these words.

1. I ____ the book on the table yesterday.
2. The dog ____ beside the fireplace last night.

LEP/ESL

General Strategies. Many speakers will use confusing verbs incorrectly because many of their role models speak this way. Students, therefore, think that standard usage sounds incorrect. You could emphasize that writers will use standard English because it is clear, and speakers can use either formal or informal English, depending on the audience.

COOPERATIVE LEARNING

Place students in groups of four to create verses that will help them to remember the correct usage of these six verbs. Suggest a rap beat or a humorous rhyme. For example:

While I sat,
He set the bat
On my hat
On my head.
Ouch!

Encourage students to recite their rhymes or to put them on posters.

▶ EXERCISE 5 **Writing the Forms of *Sit* and *Set***

For each blank in the following sentences, supply the correct form of *sit* or *set*.

EXAMPLE **1.** I ____ my suitcase on the rack.
1. *set*

1. On the train to Boston, I ____ next to a middle-aged woman wearing a shawl. **1.** sat **2.** set
2. She ____ a large basket on the floor by her feet.
3. When the conductor asked her if she would like to ____ it in the baggage rack, she refused. **3.** set
4. She insisted that the basket must ____ by her feet.
5. As I ____ beside her, I wondered what was in the basket. **4.** sit **5.** sat
6. I ____ my book down and tried to see inside the tightly woven basket. **6.** set
7. Perhaps I was ____ next to a woman with a picnic lunch to share. **7.** sitting
8. Maybe she had ____ next to me because I looked hungry. **8.** sat
9. As the woman ____ her packages down, I watched the basket. **9.** set **10.** sat
10. A sudden movement of the train caused the basket to open, and inside it ____ a small white rabbit.

Rise and *Raise*

The verb *rise* means "to move upward" or "to go up." *Rise* never takes an object.

The verb *raise* means "to lift (something) up." *Raise* usually takes an object.

INFINITIVE	PRESENT PARTICIPLE	PAST	PAST PARTICIPLE
rise	(is) rising	rose	(have) risen
raise	(is) raising	raised	(have) raised

EXAMPLES Coretta **has** already **risen** from the bench. [no object]
My brother **has raised** the curtain. [My brother has raised what? *Curtain* is the object.]

The fans **were rising** to sing the national anthem. [no object]
Passing cars **were raising** clouds of dust. [Cars were raising what? *Clouds* is the object.]

 ORAL PRACTICE 5 **Using Forms of *Rise* and *Raise***

Read each of the following sentences aloud, stressing the italicized verbs.

1. Mount Everest *rises* over 29,000 feet.
2. The flag was *raised* at sunrise.
3. The TV reporter *raised* her voice to be heard.
4. She *rose* from her seat and looked out the window.
5. The constellation Orion had not yet *risen* in the southern sky.
6. They had *raised* the piñata high in the tree.
7. I hope the bread is *rising*.
8. He will be *raising* the bucket from the well.

EXERCISE 6 **Identifying the Correct Forms of *Rise* and *Raise***

For each of the following sentences, choose the <u>correct verb</u> of the two in parentheses.

EXAMPLE **1.** After the storm, Diana (*rose, raised*) the window.
   1. *raised*

1. The audience (*<u>rose</u>, raised*) for the "Hallelujah Chorus."
2. They used a jack to (*rise, <u>raise</u>*) the car so that they could change the tire.
3. The fire juggler is (*rising, <u>raising</u>*) two flaming batons over his head to signal the start of the show.
4. Some people have trouble remembering that the sun (*<u>rises</u>, raises*) in the east.

LEP/ESL

General Strategies. The vowel sounds in the six verbs in this section sound rather similar—especially to students who speak other languages. This similarity can cause confusion for students who do not have these sounds in their languages. Spanish, for example, does not use the vowel sounds in *sit, set,* and *sat,* so trying to differentiate these words by sound is very difficult; a Spanish speaker might not know what sounds the vowel letters in these words represent. You could dictate the words for any students who have difficulty, and they could write these words.

AT-RISK STUDENTS

Have each student choose two television shows to view and analyze. Tell each student to watch one scene and to write down the verbs that one of the characters uses. Students should then repeat this with another scene and character. Then have students use the following questions as the basis for a summary of their findings:

1. Were the characters' choices standard or nonstandard?
2. Why are these characters appealing?
3. Describe the scene in which these verbs were used.
4. Is there a connection between the scene and the choice of language?

5. He gently (*rose*, *raised*) the injured duckling from the lake.
6. Only half of Mauna Kea, a mountain on the island of Hawaii, (*rises*, *raises*) above the ocean.
7. The proud winner has (*risen*, *raised*) her trophy so that everyone can see it.
8. The guests have (*risen*, *raised*) from their seats to see the bride enter.
9. Yeast makes the pizza dough (*rise*, *raise*).
10. They will (*rise*, *raise*) the couch while I look under it for the hamster.

Lie and *Lay*

The verb *lie* means "to recline," "to be in a place," or "to remain lying down." *Lie* never takes an object.

The verb *lay* means "to put (something) down," "to place (something)." *Lay* usually takes an object.

INFINITIVE	PRESENT PARTICIPLE	PAST	PAST PARTICIPLE
lie	(is) lying	lay	(have) lain
lay	(is) laying	laid	(have) laid

EXAMPLES **Rocky Ridge lies** twenty miles east of here. [no object]
Aunt Martha lays her apple dolls in the sun to dry. [Aunt Martha lays what? *Dolls* is the object.]

That bicycle has lain in the driveway for a week. [no object]
Dad has laid your clean shirts on the bed. [Dad has laid what? *Shirts* is the object.]

 ORAL PRACTICE 6   **Using Forms of *Lie* and *Lay* Correctly**

Read each of the following sentences aloud, stressing the italicized verbs.

1. If you are tired, *lie* down for a while.
2. *Lay* your pencils down, please.
3. Two huge dogs *lay* by the fire.
4. The cat has been *lying* on the new bedspread.
5. Mr. Cortez *laid* the map of Puerto Rico on the table.
6. In our state, snow usually *lies* on the ground until early spring.
7. *Lay* your coats on the bed in my room.
8. After the baby had *lain* down for a nap, she wanted to play.

▷ EXERCISE 7 **Identifying the Correct Forms of *Lie* and *Lay***

For each of the following sentences, choose the <u>correct verb</u> of the two in parentheses.

EXAMPLE **1.** Marc (*lay, laid*) his new tennis shoes on the floor.
      1. *laid*

1. The islands of American Samoa (<u>lie</u>, lay) about 4,800 miles southwest of San Francisco.
2. We quickly (lay, <u>laid</u>) the crab down when it began to pinch.
3. I don't know where I have (lain, <u>laid</u>) my copy of *Chinese Proverbs* by Ruthanne Lum McCunn.
4. Cattle often (<u>lie</u>, lay) under trees during sunny days.
5. Many visitors (lie, <u>lay</u>) flowers and wreaths at the Vietnam Veterans Memorial in Washington, D.C.
6. My brother, who is sick, has been (<u>lying</u>, laying) in bed all day.
7. The postal employee (lay, <u>laid</u>) the small package on the scales.
8. (Lie, <u>Lay</u>) your backpack down and come see my new comic books.
9. Those clothes will (<u>lie</u>, lay) on the floor until you pick them up.
10. You're sore because you've been (<u>lying</u>, laying) in one position too long.

LESS-ADVANCED STUDENTS

Have students work in pairs to use the problem verbs in original cartoon strips. One person in each pair could be the illustrator, while the other partner could write the dialogue. These comic strips could be displayed on a bulletin board to highlight the troublesome verbs for other students.

USAGE

USAGE

REVIEW D

Identifying the Correct Forms of *Sit* and *Set*, *Rise* and *Raise*, *Lie* and *Lay*

For each of the following sentences, choose the <u>correct verb</u> of the two in parentheses.

EXAMPLE **1.** The bricklayer (*rose, raised*) from the patio floor and dusted himself off.
1. *rose*

1. These rocks have (<u>*lain*</u>, *laid*) here for centuries.
2. (<u>*Sit*</u>, *Set*) there until your name is called.
3. The nurse (*lay*, <u>*laid*</u>) her cool hand on the sick child's brow.
4. The cows are (<u>*lying*</u>, *laying*) in the pasture.
5. The senator and her advisers (<u>*sat*</u>, *set*) around the huge conference table.
6. After the picnic, everyone (<u>*lay*</u>, *laid*) on blankets to rest.
7. Smoke (<u>*rose*</u>, *raised*) from the chimney.
8. The farmhands (*sat*, <u>*set*</u>) their lunch pails under a tree.
9. Have you been (<u>*sitting*</u>, *setting*) there all afternoon?
10. The sun has already (<u>*risen*</u>, *raised*).

 REVIEW E

Proofreading a Paragraph for Correct Verb Forms

Most sentences in the following paragraph contain incorrect verb forms. If a sentence contains the wrong form of a verb, write the correct form. If a sentence is correct, write *C*.

EXAMPLE **[1]** During the 1800s, many German settlers choosed to live in the Hill Country of central Texas.
1. *chose*

1. built   [1] These hardy, determined pioneers ˄builded towns
2. gone   and cleared land for farming. [2] I have ˄went to this town, Fredericksburg, several times. [3] This interesting town
3. lies   ˄lays about eighty miles west of Austin. [4] Fredericksburg

A DIFFERENT APPROACH
In groups of four, students can create tests in the format of **Review E** from descriptive sentences they write about their town. Ask students to picture a particular street in their city. Then ask them to write sentences to describe the street and to incorporate the six troublesome verbs they have studied.

WRITING APPLICATION

OBJECTIVES

- To use different verb forms and tenses correctly and consistently in writing
- To use descriptive words to write a suspenseful and believable scene

4. used ‸~~use~~ to be in Comanche territory.

5. C [5] Early on, German settlers made peace with the Comanche chiefs.

6. grew [6] The town then ‸~~growed~~ rapidly. [7] German-style houses, churches, and public buildings like these

7. rose ‸~~raised~~ along the town's central street. [8] On one of our visits,

8. sat my family ‸~~set~~ and talked about the town with a woman who was

9. C born there. [9] She said that she had spoken German all

10. C her life. [10] When we left, she raised a hand and said, "*Auf Wiedersehen*" (until we meet again).

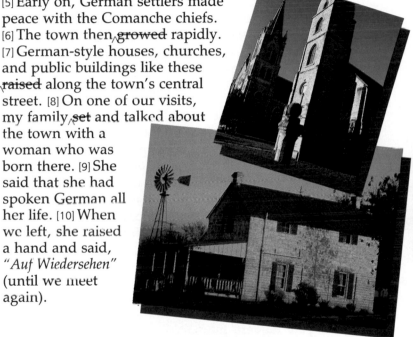

WRITING APPLICATION

Using Different Verb Forms and Tenses in a Story

When you write a story, you use verbs to express the action. The use of correct verb forms and consistent tense helps show your readers the order of events.

INCORRECT FORM AND INCONSISTENT TENSE	The gale wind blowed the tiny boat off course. Huge waves batter the craft. The weary crew will bail out the water.
CORRECT FORM AND CONSISTENT TENSE	The gale wind **blew** the tiny boat off course. Huge waves **battered** the craft. The weary crew **bailed** out the water.

WRITING APPLICATION

Review short stories that students have read from the literature textbook to give students some examples and ideas for descriptive writing. Tell students to envision their scenes before they begin writing to help them think of descriptive words.

CRITICAL THINKING
Synthesis

To help students use irregular verbs in their assignments, have them choose which words they think they will include. Then, tell each student to write three sentences with each verb and to use a different tense for each sentence. Next, explain that these sentences can be used as prewriting and may be included in the paragraphs.

EVALUATING AND REVISING

You could divide the class into groups of four and ask students to proofread and comment on one another's papers. Here are some guidelines to help students with their evaluations:

1. Give examples of five irregular verbs used correctly.
2. What tense does the writer use? Is the verb tense consistent throughout?
3. Give three examples of specific, descriptive verbs and other words used effectively.
4. How does the writer build suspense to an exciting ending?

Students should make suggestions that will improve the paragraphs and state what they thought was very good and effective about the writing.

INTEGRATING THE LANGUAGE ARTS

Technology Link. Many word-processing programs have thesauruses that will aid in finding synonyms for overused words. Some programs even have the ability to count the number of times a word has been used in a document. If available, have students use one of these programs before they turn in their assignments.

▶ WRITING ACTIVITY

A local writers' club is sponsoring a contest for the best "cliffhanger" opening of an adventure story. Write an exciting paragraph to enter in the contest. Your paragraph should leave readers wondering, "What happens next?" In your paragraph, use at least five verbs from the lists of **Common Irregular Verbs** on pages 584–585 and 586.

Prewriting First, you'll need to imagine a suspenseful situation to describe. Maybe your characters will actually be hanging on the edge of a cliff, or maybe they'll be in another type of life-or-death situation. Jot down several ideas for your story opening. Then, choose the one you like best. With that situation in mind, scan the lists of irregular verbs. Note down at least ten verbs that you might be able to use. (You can weed out some of them later.) Include some lively action verbs like *burst, swing, throw*.

Writing As you write your rough draft, think of your readers. Choose words that create a suspenseful, believable scene. Remember that you have only one paragraph to catch your readers' interest.

Evaluating and Revising Ask a friend to read your paragraph. Does your friend find it interesting? Can he or she picture the scene clearly? If not, you may want to add, delete, or revise some details. Check to see if you've used any tired words like *great* or *bad* that you can replace with more specific ones. For more about replacing tired words, see page 391.

Proofreading Check over your spelling, usage, punctuation, and grammar. Be sure that you've used at least five irregular verbs from the lists on pages 584–586. Use your textbook or a dictionary to check the spellings of these verbs. Also, check to make sure the forms are correct and the tenses are consistent.

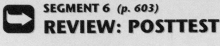

REVIEW: POSTTEST

OBJECTIVE

- To proofread and correct verb forms in sentences

Review: Posttest

Proofreading Sentences for Correct Verb Forms

If a sentence contains an incorrect past or past participle form of the verb, write the correct form. If a sentence is correct, write *C*.

EXAMPLE **1.** Melissa drunk the medicine in one gulp.
1. *drank*

1. We ~~swum~~ in the lake last weekend. **1.** swam
2. Carlos ~~come~~ from the Dominican Republic. **2.** came
3. The crow just ~~set~~ there on the barbed wire fence and wouldn't move. **3.** sat
4. I ~~seen~~ that magician on television. **4.** saw
5. The balloon burst with a loud pop. **5.** C
6. The gypsy raised his tambourine to begin the dance. **6.** C
7. You should have ~~went~~ with me to the Native American celebration in Gallup, New Mexico. **7.** gone
8. The block of ice ~~shrunk~~ to half its original size. **8.** shrank
9. Meanwhile, the water level has ~~rose~~. **9.** risen
10. I would have ~~wrote~~ to you much sooner, but I lost your address. **10.** written
11. Sandra ~~throwed~~ the ball to the shortstop. **11.** threw
12. Ms. Lopez has ~~spoke~~ before many civic groups. **12.** spoken
13. All of these photographs were taken in Florida's Everglades National Park. **13.** C
14. The bell has ~~rang~~ for fourth period. **14.** rung
15. While visiting Los Angeles, I ~~run~~ into an old friend in the city's Little Tokyo district. **15.** ran
16. I ~~laid~~ down under a tree to rest. **16.** lay
17. I ~~done~~ everything asked of me. **17.** did
18. It ~~begun~~ to rain shortly after dusk. **18.** began
19. Sue ~~lay~~ her pen down and studied the question again. **19.** laid
20. Some of the saucers were broken. **20.** C

USAGE

REVIEW: POSTTEST

Teaching Note. There are some verbs that have alternate past-tense forms. Some of these are *dived* or *dove*, *shone* or *shined*, *rang* or *rung*, and *shrank* or *shrunk*. Explain that these alternatives have recently evolved in the language, and students may encounter them on this and other tests. If students give alternative forms, make them show evidence of the forms' acceptability in a dictionary.

USAGE

603

SEGMENT 1 *(pp. 604–605)*

DIAGNOSTIC TEST

OBJECTIVES
- To choose the correct forms of pronouns to complete sentences
- To identify standard forms of reflexive pronouns

USAGE

CHAPTER OVERVIEW

This chapter concentrates on the specific uses of the nominative and objective cases of personal pronouns. Also included is a look at three special pronoun problems: the use of *who* and *whom,* the use of pronouns before appositives, and the use of reflexive pronouns. In the **Writing Application,** students are asked to write informative paragraphs and to pay special attention to clear pronoun reference.

USAGE

22 USING PRONOUNS CORRECTLY

Nominative and Objective Case Forms

Diagnostic Test

A. Identifying the Correct Forms of Pronouns

For each of the following sentences, choose <u>the correct form of the pronoun</u> in parentheses.

EXAMPLE   **1.** Mrs. Boyd gave Jeff and (*I, me*) a ride to school.
        1. *me*

1. The closing procession of the powwow will be led by (*he, <u>him</u>*) and the other Dakota dancers.
2. May (<u>*we*</u>, *us*) choir members leave science class a few minutes early today?
3. (<u>*Who*</u>, *Whom*) do you think you are, anyway?
4. Please hand out these copies of Consuela's report to (*she, <u>her</u>*) and the committee members.
5. (<u>*He*</u>, *Him*) and his cat relaxed in the easy chair and listened to the rain.

6. Darnell certainly seemed to enjoy (*himself*, *hisself*) at the African Heritage Festival last night.
7. The last tennis player to beat Martina Navratilova in straight sets was (*her*, *she*).
8. (*Who*, *Whom*) have you asked to help you with your math homework?
9. Mom, will you take (*we*, *us*) tired yard workers out for dinner tonight?
10. Collect about a dozen colorful leaves, and then brush (*they*, *them*) with a thin coat of shellac.

B. Identifying the Correct Forms of Pronouns

For each of the following sentences, choose the correct form of the pronoun in parentheses.

EXAMPLE   **1.** The most loyal sports fans at our school are Glenn and (*I*, *me*).
              1. *I*

11. (*We*, *Us*) baseball fans are going to the playoff game on Saturday.
12. (*Who*, *Whom*) will we see at the game?
13. Mario's mother will be driving (*we*, *us*) and Elena to the stadium.
14. Elena and (*he*, *him*) volunteered to design a banner.
15. "Tell Jennifer and (*I*, *me*) your slogan," Glenn said to Mario.
16. "Neither Elena nor (*I*, *me*) can decide which one we like best," Mario answered.
17. "Well, (*who*, *whom*) are the two best slogan inventors in the whole school?" I boasted, pointing at Glenn and myself.
18. Last year, the biggest banner was designed by the twins and (*she*, *her*).
19. They really outdid (*theirselves*, *themselves*)!
20. You should see the banner designed by (*we*, *us*) four fans this year, though!

USAGE

USING THE DIAGNOSTIC TEST
Use the **Diagnostic Test** in conjunction with assessments of students' writing to gauge their understanding of how to use pronouns correctly. If you find students are having trouble using pronouns correctly in their writing, you can use the **Diagnostic Test** to pinpoint error patterns and specific strengths and weaknesses.

USAGE

OBJECTIVES

- To read sentences aloud to reinforce correct pronoun use
- To choose the correct forms of pronouns to complete sentences
- To complete sentences by adding the correct forms of pronouns

▼ **RESOURCES**

CASE

- The Nominative Case
- The Objective Case
- Nominative or Objective?

USAGE

🦉 **QUICK REMINDER**

Write the following sentences on the chalkboard. Ask students to provide a pronoun to fill in each blank.

1. You and ___ are studying pronouns.
2. The pronoun experts in this class will be ___.
3. Please don't tell ___ which pronouns to use.
4. I can choose ___ correctly.
5. The teacher asked Carol and ___ first.

USAGE

Case

Case is the form of a noun or pronoun that shows its use in a sentence. There are three cases:

- nominative
- objective
- possessive

The form of a noun is the same for both the nominative and the objective cases. For example, a noun used as a subject (nominative case) will have the same form when used as a direct object (objective case).

NOMINATIVE CASE   That Ming **vase** is very old. [subject]
  OBJECTIVE CASE   Who bought the **vase?** [direct object]

A noun changes its form only in the possessive case, usually by adding an apostrophe and an *s*.

POSSESSIVE CASE   The Ming **vase's** new owner is pleased.

☞ **REFERENCE NOTE:** For more information about forming the possessive case of nouns, see pages 746–748.

Unlike nouns, most personal pronouns have different forms for all three cases.

PERSONAL PRONOUNS		
SINGULAR		
NOMINATIVE CASE	**OBJECTIVE CASE**	**POSSESSIVE CASE**
I	me	my, mine
you	you	your, yours
he, she, it	him, her, it	his, her, hers, its
PLURAL		
NOMINATIVE CASE	**OBJECTIVE CASE**	**POSSESSIVE CASE**
we	us	our, ours
you	you	your, yours
they	them	their, theirs

NOTE: Some teachers prefer to call possessive forms of pronouns (such as *our, your,* and *their*) adjectives. Follow your teacher's instructions regarding possessive forms.

Drawing by Ziegler; © 1988 The New Yorker Magazine, Inc.

The Nominative Case

22a. The subject of a verb is in the nominative case.

EXAMPLES **They** made candles from antique molds. [*They* is the subject of *made.*]

We admired the Navajo rugs. [*We* is the subject of *admired.*]

He and **I** mowed lawns. [*He* and *I* are used together as the compound subject of *mowed.*]

To help you choose the correct pronoun in a compound subject, try each form of the pronoun separately.

EXAMPLE: The guide and (*I, me*) looked for tracks.
I looked for tracks.
Me looked for tracks.
ANSWER: The guide and **I** looked for tracks.

EXAMPLE: (*She, Her*) and (*I, me*) found them.
She found them.
Her found them.
I found them.
Me found them.
ANSWER: **She** and **I** found them.

- To write sentences that include pronouns as objects of prepositions
- To write a brief story that includes pronouns used in various ways

LEP/ESL

General Strategies. English pronouns have three cases. Other languages vary in their number of cases, such as Korean (nine), Russian (six), Arabic (three), and Vietnamese (zero). Students who speak languages with several cases may wonder what cases to use in the situations where the variety of cases in their languages comes into play. Those who speak caseless languages may have trouble understanding what case is, why it is important, and what to do with it. You may wish to hold individual or small group sessions with students to field any questions they might have.

AT-RISK STUDENTS

As an alternative to one of the exercises or as a supplementary activity, have students bring articles from their favorite magazines or newspapers to class. Then ask students to identify which of the pronouns used in the articles (or parts of the articles) are in the objective and nominative cases.

INTEGRATING THE LANGUAGE ARTS

Literature Link. Help students to understand the important role personal pronouns play in English by having the class read a literary selection such as Isaac Bashevis Singer's short story "Zlateh the Goat." Ask students what the story would be like if the author did not use any personal pronouns. [Students will probably say that without personal pronouns the repetition of the names (Zlateh and Aaron) would become very tedious, perhaps detracting from the story. Also, the use of personal pronouns adds to the cohesiveness of the story. Each time a personal pronoun is used it refers the reader to its noun referent, thus tying two ideas together.]

USAGE

 ORAL PRACTICE 1 **Using Pronouns in Compound Subjects**

Read each of the following sentences aloud, stressing the italicized pronouns.

1. Dr. Chen and *they* discussed the usefulness of herbal medicines.
2. *He* and *I* live next door to each other.
3. *They* and *we* should try to get along better.
4. Yesterday *she* and *they* gave their reports on African American poets.
5. You and *she* left the party early.
6. Since the third grade, you and *I* have been friends.
7. *He* and his family are moving to Puerto Rico.
8. *She* and *I* will miss them.

 EXERCISE 1 **Identifying Correct Pronoun Forms**

For each sentence in the following paragraph, choose the correct form of the pronoun in parentheses.

EXAMPLE **1.** My friends and (*I, me*) like to spend time outdoors.
1. *I*

[1] Lou and (*I, me*) asked my mother to drive us to a nearby state park. [2] There (*he and I, him and me*) set out on a marked trail through a wooded area. [3] Before long, (*he and I, him and me*) were exploring a snowy area off the beaten track. [4] At dusk Lou and (*I, me*) reluctantly followed our tracks back to the path. [5] (*We, Us*) had had the best time of our lives.

22b. A predicate nominative is in the nominative case.

A *predicate nominative* follows a linking verb and identifies or explains the subject of the verb. A pronoun used as a predicate nominative usually follows a form of the verb

USAGE

be (such as *am, are, is, was, were, be, been,* or *being*) and identifies the subject.

EXAMPLES **The candidates should have been he and she.**
[*He* and *she* follow the linking verb *should have been* and identify the subject *candidates.*]
The members of the debating team are they.
[*They* follows the linking verb *are* and identifies the subject *members.*]

NOTE: Expressions such as *It's me* and *That's her* are acceptable in everyday speaking. However, such expressions should be avoided in writing.

REFERENCE NOTE: For more information about predicate nominatives, see pages 480–481.

▶ ORAL **Using Pronouns as Predicate**
PRACTICE 2 **Nominatives**

Read each of the following sentences aloud, stressing the italicized pronouns.

1. Were the only Spanish-speaking people you and *they*?
2. The caller could have been *she*.
3. The leaders will be my mother and *he*.
4. The three candidates for class president are you and *we*.
5. That must be the pilot and *he*.
6. The three winners were Frank, May, and *I*.
7. The first ones on the scene were our neighbors and *they*.
8. The speakers at the rally were *she* and Jesse Jackson.

▶ EXERCISE 2 **Identifying Correct Pronoun Forms**

For each of the following sentences, choose the correct form of the pronoun in parentheses.

EXAMPLE **1. Could it be (*they, them*)?**
1. they

1. It must be (*them, they*).
2. Two witnesses claimed that the burglar was (*him, he*).

 INTEGRATING THE LANGUAGE ARTS

Usage and Writing. Although predicate nominatives are considered standard usage, they usually sound stilted or awkward to most native speakers of American English. Tell students that to make their writing flow more smoothly, they can rewrite sentences by using predicate nominatives as subjects. For example, in **Oral Practice 2** the second sentence could be rephrased as "She could have been the caller."

USAGE

USAGE

REVIEW A

OBJECTIVE

- To respond to questions with sentences that use pronouns in specified ways

610 *Using Pronouns Correctly*

3. Is the last performer (*her*, *she*)?
4. The next speaker will be (*him*, *he*).
5. Among the invited guests are Luther and (*us*, *we*).
6. I knew it was (*her*, *she*), of course.
7. The hardest workers are Susan, Tranh, and (*me*, *I*).
8. Can that be (*her*, *she*) in that Mexican sombrero?
9. The next batter should be (*her*, *she*).
10. Our newest neighbors are the Blumenthals and (*them*, *they*).

▶ REVIEW A **Writing Sentences That Contain Pronouns in the Nominative Case**

The busy scene you see on the next page was painted by the Mexican American artist Carmen Lomas Garza. It shows one of her childhood birthday parties. The fish-shaped object is a piñata, full of gifts and treats for the children. Carmen is getting ready to take a swing at the piñata. Answer each of the following questions by writing a sentence. Follow the directions after each question.

EXAMPLE **1. What are the kneeling boys in the lower left-hand corner doing?** (*Use a plural personal pronoun as the subject.*)
1. *They are getting ready to play marbles.*

1. What is Carmen using to hit the piñata? (*Use a singular personal pronoun as the subject.*)
2. Whom are the presents on the table for? (*Use a plural personal pronoun as the subject.*)
3. Who will get the gifts and treats inside the piñata? (*Use a person's name and a plural personal pronoun as the compound subject.*)
4. Have you and your classmates ever played a game that requires a blindfold? (*Use a plural and a singular personal pronoun as the compound subject.*)
5. Why does the boy at the far right have presents in his hand? (*Use a singular personal pronoun as the subject.*)

ANSWERS

Review A

Sentences will vary. Here are some possibilities:

1. She is using a bat.
2. They are for Carmen.
3. Carmen and they will get the gifts and treats.
4. They and I have played a game that requires a blindfold.
5. He is going to give the presents to Carmen.
6. "The birthday girl is I."
7. Yes, it was they and she.
8. Yes, she and the baby are having a good time.
9. No, that is not he.
10. The ones enjoying the birthday party now are we.

6. What would Carmen say if you asked her, "Who's the birthday girl?" (*Use a singular personal pronoun as a predicate nominative.*)
7. Did Carmen's parents and her grandmother plan the party? (*Use a plural and a singular personal pronoun as a compound predicate nominative.*)
8. Are the baby and his mother standing near the table having a good time? (*Use the baby and a singular personal pronoun as the compound subject.*)
9. Is Carmen's father the man holding the piñata rope? (*Use a singular personal pronoun as a predicate nominative.*)
10. Who are the ones now enjoying Carmen Lomas Garza's long-ago birthday party? (*Use a plural personal pronoun as a predicate nominative.*)

Reprinted by permission of GRM Associates, Inc., Agents for Children's Book Press, from the book *Family Pictures* by Carmen Lomas Garza, copyright 1990 by Carmen Lomas Garza

The Objective Case

22c. *Direct objects* and *indirect objects* of verbs are in the objective case.

A *direct object* follows an action verb and tells *whom* or *what* receives the action of the verb.

VISUAL CONNECTIONS

About the Artwork. This painting of a birthday party is one of Carmen Lomas Garza's *monitos*. *Monitos* are paintings of traditional Mexican American activities and events such as gathering *nopalitos* (prickly pear cactuses), attending a *feria* (carnival), and participating in a cakewalk. Inspired by Mexican folk art, such as *altares* (homemade religious altars), *retablos* (paintings on tin), and *colchas* (quilts), Lomas Garza's *monitos* are syntheses of imagination and memory that tell stories about Mexican Americans and their vibrant culture.

Related Expression Skills. Carmen Lomas Garza's work expresses the assumption that all peoples share similar values and experiences. Reinforce this idea for students by asking them to draw or paint pictures that depict activities or events from their cultures that are similar to those depicted in Lomas Garza's work. Have students focus on details, as Lomas Garza does in her *monitos*.

LEARNING STYLES

Kinetic and Visual Learners. Have students write each of the sixteen personal pronouns in the nominative and objective cases on separate sheets of paper or on index cards. Then write a sentence on the chalkboard and leave a blank where a personal pronoun should go. Allow the student who raises his or her hand first to come to the chalkboard to tape a pronoun over the blank. If the pronoun correctly completes the sentence, it should remain taped to the chalkboard. Repeat this process until a student runs out of pronouns—that student is the winner.

EXAMPLES   Mom called **me** to the phone. [*Me* tells *whom* Mom called.]

Julia bought sweet potatoes and used **them** to fill the *empanadas.* [*Them* tells *what* she used.]

An *indirect object* comes between an action verb and a direct object and tells *to whom* or *to what* or *for whom* or *for what*.

EXAMPLES   The hostess handed **her** a name tag. [*Her* tells *to whom* the hostess handed the name tag.]

Mr. Tanaka raises large goldfish; he often feeds **them** rice. [*Them* tells *to what* Mr. Tanaka feeds rice.]

To help you choose the correct pronoun in a compound object, try each form of the pronoun separately in the sentence.

EXAMPLE: The teacher chose Luisa and (*I, me*).
The teacher chose *I.*
The teacher chose *me.*
ANSWER: The teacher chose Luisa and **me.**

☞ **REFERENCE NOTE:** For more information about direct and indirect objects, see pages 474–477.

▶ ORAL PRACTICE 3   **Using Pronouns as Direct Objects and Indirect Objects**

Read each of the following sentences aloud, stressing the italicized pronouns.

1. I took Joe and *her* to a performance by French mimes.
2. The bus driver let Melba, Joe, and *me* off at the next corner.
3. An usher gave *us* programs.
4. Another usher guided *them* and *me* to our seats.
5. The performers fascinated Melba and *me*.
6. Their costumes delighted the crowd and *her*.
7. No one else impressed Joe and *me* as much as the youngest mime.
8. We watched *her* explore the walls of an invisible room.

REVIEW B

OBJECTIVE

- To choose the correct forms of personal pronouns to complete sentences

▶ EXERCISE 3

Writing Pronouns Used as Direct Objects and Indirect Objects

For each blank in the following sentences, give an appropriate pronoun. Use a variety of pronouns, but do not use *you* or *it*. Responses will vary.

EXAMPLE **1.** Have you seen Kim and ____?
1. *her*

1. The manager hired Susana and ____. **1.** me
2. Lana sent ____ and ____ invitations. **2.** them/us
3. We gave Grandpa López and ____ round-trip tickets to Mexico City. **3.** her
4. The firefighters rescued ____ and ____. **4.** them/me
5. Aunt Coretta showed my cousins and ____ a carved mask from Nigeria. **5.** him
6. The show entertained the children and ____. **6.** me
7. The waiter served ____ and ____ a variety of dim sum dumplings. **7.** her/him
8. Our team chose ____ and ____ as representatives. **8.** her/me
9. The election committee nominated Gerry and ____. **9.** her
10. The clerk gave Misako and ____ the receipt for the paper lanterns. **10.** me

▶ REVIEW B

Identifying Correct Pronoun Forms

For each sentence in the following paragraph, choose the correct form of the pronoun in parentheses.

EXAMPLE **1.** Paul told Ms. Ésteban that (*he, him*) and (*I, me*) need a topic for our report.
1. *he, I*

[1] Some of the other students and (*he*, *him*) thought that there should be more reports on women in American history. [2] (*They*, *Them*) and their achievements are sometimes overlooked. [3] The picture on the next page, showing Amelia Earhart looking cheerful and confident, interested Paul and (*I*, *me*). [4] Both (*he*, *him*) and (*I*, *me*) were eager to find out more about her contribution to aviation. [5] We learned that it was (*she*, *her*) who made the

Have students rewrite the ten sentences in **Review B** by using the opposite cases for the pronouns. Sentences should retain their original meanings as much as possible. For example, sentence 10 calls for the nominative case, *we.* The sentence could be rewritten to use the objective case, *us.* [This mystery is still puzzling to Ms. Ésteban and *us,* as it is to many people.]

VISUAL CONNECTIONS

Ideas for Writing. Have students imagine that they have been assigned to write a screenplay for a new movie. The movie will tell the story of what happened to Amelia Earhart and her navigator after they lost contact with radio operators. Tell students to imagine that the movie's producer wants each student to leave a brief synopsis or summary of the screenplay on her desk tomorrow. Each summary should be no more than two or three paragraphs in length and should include personal pronouns used in both the objective and the nominative cases.

first solo flight by a woman across the Atlantic. [6] The fact that Amelia Earhart was the first pilot to fly from Hawaii to California surprised the rest of the class and (*we, us*), too. [7] In 1937, her navigator and (*she, her*) took off in a twin-engine plane for a trip around the world. [8] After (*they, them*) had completed two thirds of the trip, Earhart an her navigator lost contact with radio operators. [9] Neither the plane nor (*they, them*) were ever sighted again. [10] Ms. Ésteban and (*we, us*) are among the many people still puzzling over this mystery.

22d. The *object of a preposition* is in the objective case.

A *prepositional phrase* begins with a preposition and ends with a noun or pronoun, called the *object of the preposition.*

EXAMPLES   **We waited for them.** [*Them* is the object of the preposition *for.*]

The secret is between him and me. [*Him* and *me* are the compound object of the preposition *between.*]

 REFERENCE NOTE: For a list of prepositions, see page 460.

**INTEGRATING THE
LANGUAGE ARTS**

Usage and Grammar. As your class studies pronouns as objects of prepositions, you may want to help the class identify and understand prepositions. Begin by giving students this definition: A preposition is a word that shows the relationship between a noun or a pronoun and some other word in the sentence.

Write the following sentences on the chalkboard. Ask students to identify the prepositions and to explain which words in each sentence they relate to.

1. Jesse walks toward them. [*Toward* shows the relationship of *Jesse* to *them.*]
2. The dog with her is playful. [*With* shows the relationship of *the dog* to *her.*]

ORAL PRACTICE 4   **Using Pronouns as Objects of Prepositions**

Read each of the following sentences aloud, stressing the italicized pronouns.

1. Mr. Torres divided the burritos *among them* and *us*.
2. At the game Maria sat *near him* and *her*.
3. Rose walked *toward* Nell and *me*.
4. Sam stood *between him* and *me*.
5. Mom ordered sandwiches *for* Hannah and *her*.
6. "*Without* Squanto and *me*, the Pilgrims won't last through another winter," thought Samoset.
7. I have read biographies *about him* and Martin Luther King, Jr.
8. David's parents gave a bar mitzvah party *for him*.

EXERCISE 4   **Choosing Correct Pronouns Used as Objects of Prepositions**

For each of the following sentences, choose the <u>correct form of the pronoun</u> in parentheses.

EXAMPLE   **1.** Of all the people who traveled with Lewis and Clark, Sacagawea was particularly helpful to (*them, they*).
   1. *them*

1. Sacagawea's husband, a guide named Toussaint Charbonneau, joined the expedition with (*her, she*) and their newborn baby.
2. The Shoshone were Sacagawea's people, and she longed to return to (*them, they*).
3. Captain Clark soon realized how important she would be to Lewis and (*he, him*).
4. The land they were traveling through was familiar to (*she, her*).
5. Luckily for (*she, her*) and the expedition, they met a group of friendly Shoshone.
6. From (*they, them*), Sacagawea obtained the ponies that Lewis and Clark needed.

7. Sacagawea's baby boy delighted the expedition's leaders, and they took good care of (*he*, *him*).
8. In fact, Captain Clark kept a promise to (*she*, *her*) and Charbonneau that he would give the boy a good education.
9. However, after the boy turned sixteen, no one knows what became of (*him*, *he*).
10. In 1875, a very old Shoshone woman who said she was Sacagawea told stories of traveling with Lewis and Clark, and many people listened to (*she*, *her*).

EXERCISE 5

Writing Sentences That Include Pronouns as Objects of Prepositions

A day in the life of a guide dog is full of responsibilities. A guide dog leads its owner safely *around* obstacles, *through* traffic, *among* crowds, *up* and *down* stairs, *onto* buses, *into* stores, *under* low-hanging awnings, and *along* busy sidewalks. Write five sentences describing the actions of Duchess as she guides Michael through this busy downtown area. In each sentence, use at least one pronoun as the object of a preposition. In two of your sentences, use a pronoun as part of a compound object.

EXAMPLE   1. *Duchess noticed a group of teenagers in front of a store and guided Michael around them and their bicycles.*

ANSWERS
Exercise 5

Sentences will vary. Here are some possibilities:

1. Michael does not follow Duchess; he walks beside her.
2. Crowds are tricky, so Duchess helps Michael navigate through them.
3. When they get to a street, Duchess guides Michael across it.
4. Steps and curbs are especially daunting to him and her, but they manage to get up and down them.
5. When people or an object gets in the way, Duchess leads Michael around them or it.

REVIEW C

OBJECTIVES

- To choose the correct forms of personal pronouns to complete sentences
- To label personal pronouns in sentences as subjects, predicate nominatives, direct objects, indirect objects, or objects of prepositions

Case **617**

 REVIEW C   **Identifying Correct Pronoun Forms**

For each of the following sentences, choose the <u>correct form of the pronoun</u> in parentheses. Then tell what part of the sentence each pronoun is: *subject, predicate nominative, direct object, indirect object,* or *object of a preposition.*

EXAMPLE   1. My brother Pete and (*I, me*) wanted to know more about Elizabeth Blackwell.
        1. *I—subject*

1. Mom told Pete and (*I, <u>me</u>*) that Elizabeth Blackwell was the first woman ever to graduate from medical school in the United States.   **1.** i.o.
2. Geneva College granted (*she, <u>her</u>*) a degree in 1849.   **2.** i.o.
3. At first, no male doctor would let her work for (*he, <u>him</u>*) because she was a woman.   **3.** o.p.
4. Pete and (*<u>I</u>, me*) admire Elizabeth Blackwell for not giving up.   **4.** s.
5. She wanted to help the poor and opened her own clinic for (*they, <u>them</u>*).   **5.** o.p.
6. Wealthy citizens were soon supporting (*she, <u>her</u>*) and the clinic with donations.   **6.** d.o.
7. Before long, one of the most talked-about topics in medical circles was (*<u>she</u>, her*) and the excellent work she was doing for the poor.   **7.** p.n.
8. Mom and (*<u>we</u>, us*) read more about Dr. Blackwell, and we learned that she opened a medical school just for women.   **8.** s.
9. Dr. Blackwell set high standards for students and gave (*they, <u>them</u>*) hard courses of study to complete.   **9.** i.o.
10. Her teaching helped (*they, <u>them</u>*) to become excellent physicians, and she was proud of their success.   **10.** d.o.

GRAMMAR INVADERS

"It's a new concept in teaching machines. You get 50 points for every grammatical error you blast away!"

GLASBERGEN

USAGE

A DIFFERENT APPROACH

List the possible uses of pronouns on the chalkboard: subject, predicate nominative, direct object, indirect object, and object of a preposition. Start a game in which you assign each student a pronoun and one of the pronoun uses. Tell each student to create a sentence that uses a pronoun in a specific way. For example, if a student were directed to use the pronoun *me* as the object of a preposition, a possible response would be "The fish swam around me."

Set a time limit for responses. Any student who doesn't respond within the allotted time is out of the game. Play continues until only one student remains.

USAGE

PICTURE THIS

If students are having a hard time getting started, you might want to suggest that they ignore the specifications for using pronouns as they write their first drafts. Students can then revise their drafts to include the specified pronouns. Assess students' stories on the basis of how well the directions were followed. Give extra points for creativity. To save grading time, you could have students underline pronouns and identify their uses.

PICTURE THIS

You and your family are spending the weekend in a large, unfamiliar city. Too excited to sleep, you watch the traffic and the city lights from the hotel window. As you're watching, you notice this person climbing into a taxi on the street below. You wonder why he is out in the rain on such a dark, chilly night. Is he rushing to meet someone? Is he a doctor called to an emergency? Perhaps he is a spy who must get to the airport in a hurry. You decide to write a brief story based on this scene. Imagine who the man is, where he is coming from, and where he is going. In your story, use pronouns in each of the following ways: as a subject, as a predicate nominative, as a direct object, as an indirect object, or as an object of a preposition.

Subject: a man climbing into a taxi
Audience: yourself
Purpose: to write a story about the man

Yvonne Jacquette, Three Taxis, 1983, Oil on Canvas, Courtesy Brooke Alexander, New York.

SPECIAL PRONOUN PROBLEMS

OBJECTIVES

- To reinforce the correct use of *who* and *whom* by reading sentences aloud
- To choose the correct forms of pronouns to complete sentences
- To choose the standard forms of reflexive pronouns

Special Pronoun Problems

Who and Whom

The pronoun *who* has different forms in the nominative and objective cases. *Who* is the nominative form; *whom* is the objective form.

> **NOTE:** In spoken English, the use of *whom* is becoming less common. In fact, when you are speaking, you may correctly begin any question with *who* regardless of the grammar of the sentence. In written English, however, you should distinguish between *who* and *whom.*

When you need to decide whether to use *who* or *whom* in a question, follow these steps:

STEP 1: Rephrase the question as a statement.
STEP 2: Decide how the pronoun is used in the statement—as subject, predicate nominative, object of the verb, or object of a preposition.
STEP 3: Determine the case of the pronoun according to the rules of standard English.
STEP 4: Select the correct form of the pronoun.

EXAMPLE: (*Who, Whom*) is she?
STEP 1: The statement is *She is* (*who, whom*).
STEP 2: The subject is *she,* the verb is *is,* and the pronoun is the predicate nominative: *She is* (*who, whom*).
STEP 3: A pronoun used as a predicate nominative should be in the nominative case.
STEP 4: The nominative form is *who.*
ANSWER: **Who** is she?

EXAMPLE: (*Who, Whom*) will you invite to the dance?
STEP 1: The statement is *You will invite* (*who, whom*) *to the dance.*
STEP 2: The subject is *you,* and the verb is *will invite.* The pronoun is the direct object of the verb: *You will invite* (*who, whom*).
STEP 3: A pronoun used as a direct object should be in the objective case.
STEP 4: The objective form is *whom.*
ANSWER: **Whom** will you invite to the dance?

USAGE

QUICK REMINDER

Write the following sentences on the chalkboard and ask students to choose the correct forms of the pronouns to complete the sentences:

1. (Who, Whom) do you want to represent you in the Senate?
2. (We, Us) voters must take action now.
3. Our candidate speaks for (himself, hisself) on the issues.
4. (Who, Whom) will win the election?
5. Only the voters (themselves, theirselfs) can decide.

MEETING INDIVIDUAL NEEDS

LEP/ESL

General Strategies. You may have students in your class who speak languages such as Japanese, Korean, Turkish, and Vietnamese, which do not normally use the relative pronouns *who, whom, which,* and *that.* For example, the phrase *the boy who is reading the book* would be rendered as *boy reading book* in Japanese, Korean, and Turkish and *boy read book* in Vietnamese. To help students, give numerous oral and written examples of these relative pronouns.

USAGE

ORAL
PRACTICE 5   **Choosing *Who* or *Whom***

Read each of the following sentences aloud, stressing the italicized pronouns.

1. *Who* is captain of the football team this year?
2. To *whom* did you give your old skateboard?
3. *Whom* will you call to come and pick us up after band practice?
4. *Who* were the first Americans?
5. In the last play of the game, *who* passed the ball to *whom?*
6. *Who*'s that woman in the green kimono?
7. For *whom* did you buy those flowers?
8. *Who* painted that beautiful still life?

Pronouns with Appositives

Sometimes a pronoun is followed directly by a noun that identifies the pronoun. Such a noun is called an *appositive.* To help you choose which pronoun to use before an appositive, omit the appositive and try each form of the pronoun separately.

EXAMPLE: On Saturdays, (*we, us*) cyclists ride to Mount McCabe and back. [*Cyclists* is the appositive identifying the pronoun.]
         We ride to Mount McCabe.
         Us ride to Mount McCabe.

ANSWER: On Saturdays, **we** cyclists ride to Mount McCabe and back.

EXAMPLE: The speaker praised (*we, us*) volunteers. [*Volunteers* is the appositive identifying the pronoun.]
         The speaker praised *we.*
         The speaker praised *us.*

ANSWER: The speaker praised **us** volunteers.

☞ REFERENCE NOTE: For more information about appositives, see page 715.

EXERCISE 6   **Choosing Correct Pronouns**

For each of the following sentences, choose the <u>correct form of the pronoun</u> in parentheses.

EXAMPLE   **1.** Hanukkah is always an exciting holiday for (*we, us*) Feldmans.

     1. *us*

1. The famous golfer Lee Trevino is a symbol of pride to (*we*, <u>*us*</u>) Mexican Americans.
2. (*Who*, <u>*Whom*</u>) will your brother invite to his birthday party?
3. (<u>*Who*</u>, *Whom*) will be our substitute teacher while Mr. Chen is away?
4. Miss Jefferson, (<u>*we*</u>, *us*) students want to thank you for all your help.
5. (*Who*, <u>*Whom*</u>) has Ms. Spears chosen to serve on the Kite Festival committee?
6. Of the three candidates, (*who*, <u>*whom*</u>) do you have the most confidence in?
7. (<u>*We*</u>, *Us*) contestants shook hands warmly.
8. To (*who*, <u>*whom*</u>) do you wish these flowers sent?
9. (*Who*, <u>*Whom*</u>) do you admire?
10. (*Who*, <u>*Whom*</u>) is the leftover macaroni and cheese for?

Reflexive Pronouns

The reflexive pronouns *himself* and *themselves* can be used as objects. Do not use the nonstandard forms *hisself* and *theirselfs* or *theirselves* in place of *himself* and *themselves*.

NONSTANDARD	The secretary voted for hisself in the last election.
STANDARD	The secretary voted for **himself** in the last election.

NONSTANDARD	The cooks served theirselves some of the won-ton soup.
STANDARD	The cooks served **themselves** some of the won-ton soup.

USAGE

COOPERATIVE LEARNING

Divide the class into groups of three or four. Tell each group to think of a person about whom it can write questions using *who* and *whom*. For example, a group that chooses Elvis Presley might ask, "Who has been called the king of rock 'n' roll?" Each group member should write and initial at least one question.

When the questions have been formulated, ask a representative from each group to read the group's questions to the class. Students should try to guess the names of the other groups' subjects.

USAGE

REVIEW D

OBJECTIVES

- To choose the correct forms of personal pronouns to complete sentences
- To choose the standard forms of reflexive pronouns to complete sentences

LEARNING STYLES

Auditory Learners. Changing some of the pronouns to incorrect forms, read students a paragraph or a brief excerpt from an article or a composition. Students should listen and write down any incorrect pronoun forms that they hear used. Then read through the selection again to note and correct each incorrect pronoun usage.

USAGE

USAGE

622 *Using Pronouns Correctly*

 EXERCISE 7 **Identifying Correct Pronoun Forms**

For each of the following sentences, choose the <u>correct form of the pronoun</u> in parentheses.

1. Before he started to read, Zack asked (*hisself*, <u>*himself*</u>) three questions to set his purpose.
2. My little brother often falls down, but he never seems to hurt (*hisself*, <u>*himself*</u>).
3. The guests helped (*theirselves*, <u>*themselves*</u>) to the nuts and raisins.
4. John Yellowtail enjoys (<u>*himself*</u>, *hisself*) making fine silver jewelry.
5. If the early settlers wanted cloth, they had to spin it (*theirselves*, <u>*themselves*</u>).

 REVIEW D **Identifying Correct Pronoun Forms**

For each of the following sentences, choose the <u>correct form of the pronoun</u> in parentheses.

EXAMPLE **1.** To me, the two most interesting explorers are (*he, him*) and Vasco da Gama.
1. *he*

1. The team captains will be Jack and (<u>*he*</u>, *him*).
2. Was the joke played on you and (*he*, <u>*him*</u>)?
3. We were warned by our parents and (*they*, <u>*them*</u>).
4. The Washington twins and (<u>*I*</u>, *me*) belong to the same club.
5. Who are (<u>*they*</u>, *them*)?
6. Pelé and (<u>*he*</u>, *him*) both played soccer for the New York Cosmos.
7. "What do you think of (*he and I*, <u>*him and me*</u>)?" I asked.
8. "You and (<u>*he*</u>, *him*) are improving," they replied.
9. When Miriam Makeba and the troupe of African musicians arrived, we gave (*she and they*, <u>*her and them*</u>) a party.
10. Do you remember my sister and (*I*, <u>*me*</u>)?
11. The coach spoke to (*we*, <u>*us*</u>) players before the game.

12. The finalists in the talent contest are Alfredo, Sylvia, and (*I, me*).
13. Are you and (*she, her*) going to celebrate Kwanzaa this year?
14. Père Toussaint taught my brother and (*I, me*) to play a Cajun fiddle tune.
15. Mom, Andy gave (*himself, hisself*) the biggest piece of banana bread.
16. Both (*he and she, her and him*) have promised to write us this summer.
17. They congratulated (*themselves, theirselves*) on a job well done.
18. Don't leave without (*he and I, him and me*).
19. (*We, Us*) skiers had a beautiful view from the lift.
20. (*Who, Whom*) were you expecting?

USAGE

WRITING APPLICATION

Using Nouns to Make the Meaning of Pronouns Clear

Using pronouns to take the place of nouns helps you avoid repeating the same nouns over and over. However, it's important not to use so many pronouns that your reader gets confused.

CONFUSING	Steve brought two dog biscuits for Duke. As he walked up the steps, he threw them to him. He lay down happily on some towels and ate them. (*Who walked up the steps? What was thrown? To whom was it thrown? Who lay down? What did he eat?*)
CLEAR	Steve brought two dog biscuits for Duke. As Steve walked up the steps, he threw both biscuits to the dog. Duke lay down happily on some towels and ate the biscuits.

Be sure that the pronouns you *do* use refer clearly to their antecedents.

WRITING APPLICATION Take this opportunity to review antecedents with your class. Explain that every pronoun refers to or stands for a noun that is called its antecedent. You may want to write some sentences that contain pronouns on the chalkboard and guide students through the process of identifying each pronoun's antecedent.

CRITICAL THINKING
Analysis

A successful radio show must address the concerns and interests of its intended audience. Explain to students that to write proposals for radio shows that young people will enjoy, they will need to analyze the concerns and interests of young people.

You may want to help students generate a list of analysis questions such as the following ones:

1. Are young people more interested in international news or music news?
2. What times of day are young people most likely to be listening to the radio?
3. Would young people prefer a radio show with a serious tone or with a lighthearted, or even zany, tone?

LEARNING STYLES

Kinetic and Visual Learners. Write on the chalkboard the beginning for a story. Have students take turns writing additional sentences on the chalkboard to complete the story. The first student should use a pronoun in the objective case, while the second should use a pronoun in the nominative case, and so on. The story could continue as long as time permits. After the story is completed, discuss any unclear pronoun references that may have been made.

 WRITING ACTIVITY

Your favorite radio station is having a "Create a Radio Show" contest. The show will be produced by and for young people. The station has set aside a half-hour of prime time each week for the winning program. Write a letter to the manager of the station explaining what you would like to include in a radio show. The show can have any format you like. It can be like an existing radio show, or it can be something completely new. In your letter, use a variety of pronouns in the nominative case and the objective case. Be sure to include enough nouns so that the meaning of all your pronouns is clear.

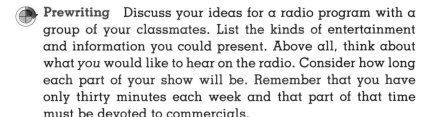 **Prewriting** Discuss your ideas for a radio program with a group of your classmates. List the kinds of entertainment and information you could present. Above all, think about what *you* would like to hear on the radio. Consider how long each part of your show will be. Remember that you have only thirty minutes each week and that part of that time must be devoted to commercials.

Writing As you write your first draft, follow the format for a business letter. (You will find information about business letters on pages 838–842.) Give specific examples of what you want to do on the show, and give reasons for your choices. Remember that even though your ideas may be very creative, your writing must be formal.

Evaluating and Revising Ask the other group members to read your letter to see if your ideas sound interesting and are clearly stated. Ask them if the relationship between each pronoun and its antecedent is clear. If your meaning is not clear, revise your letter. You may need to include more nouns.

Proofreading and Publishing Reread your letter, and correct any remaining errors in usage, spelling, punctuation, or capitalization. Be sure that you have followed the correct format for a business letter. Also, make sure that you have used all pronouns according to the rules for standard written

REVIEW: POSTTEST

OBJECTIVES

- To identify and correct errors in the use of nominative and objective case pronouns in sentences
- To identify and correct nonstandard forms of reflexive pronouns

English. Your class might want to create a bulletin-board display of the letters, titled "WISH—Imagination Radio." With your teacher's permission, the class might vote on the best idea for a show and then produce and tape the pilot episode.

Review: Posttest

Correcting Errors in Pronoun Forms

Most of the following sentences contain errors in the use of pronoun forms. For each sentence, identify the error and give the correct pronoun form. If a sentence is correct, write C.

EXAMPLE **1.** The Garcia children and them grew up together in Texas.
1. *them—they*

1. Omar and ~~him~~ offered us some *pita,* a Middle Eastern bread. **1.** he
2. ~~Us~~ basketball players know the value of good sneakers. **2.** We
3. The computer experts in our class are Rosalinda and ~~her~~. **3.** she
4. There's more than a three-year age difference between Edward and ~~I~~. **4.** me
5. Pablo and ~~me~~ are planning to visit the Andes Mountains someday. **5.** I
6. At Passover, my grandparents make gefilte fish and other traditional foods for my cousins and ~~I~~. **6.** me
7. Give Suki and him this invitation to the Japanese tea ceremony. **7.** C
8. Josh made ~~hisself~~ a bookcase in industrial arts class.
8. himself

MEETING INDIVIDUAL NEEDS

STUDENTS WITH SPECIAL NEEDS

Students with visual-processing deficits such as dyslexia might have trouble reading the twenty sentences of the **Review: Posttest** in a limited amount of time. To ensure that the testing situation is fair to these students, engage student helpers to read the sentences to them. Student helpers should read the sentences slowly and pause after each sentence to allow their partners to record their answers.

9. Two angry hornets chased Earline and ∧she̶ all the way home. **9.** her

10. The first actors on stage were Jesse and ∧him̶. **10.** he

11. Mr. Mendez and ∧u̶s̶ organized a debate about the rights of students. **11.** we

12. Will you attend the rally with Dominick and me? **12.** C

13. I helped Kimberly and ∧they̶ with their play about Hiawatha. **13.** them

14. Jeannette and ∧her̶ know a great deal about Greek myths. **14.** she

15. The hickory smoke smelled good to ∧we̶ campers. **15.** us

16. The only seventh-graders in the marching band are Bianca and ∧me̶. **16.** I

17. Liang was telling them and me about his birthplace in Hong Kong. **17.** C

18. Julia and ∧them̶ learned how to use hot wax to make batik patterns on cloth. **18.** they

19. During most of the marathon, Lionel ran just behind Jim and ∧she̶. **19.** her

20. Thomas asked Marvella and ∧he̶ if they wanted to join a gospel chorus. **20.** him

OBJECTIVE

- To revise sentences to correct errors in the use of modifiers

▼ RESOURCES ▼

USING MODIFIERS CORRECTLY
- Chapter Review Form A
- Chapter Review Form B
- Assessment Portfolio
  - Usage Pretest
  - Usage Mastery Test 1
  - Usage Mastery Test 2

23 USING MODIFIERS CORRECTLY

Comparison and Placement

USAGE

CHAPTER OVERVIEW

This chapter teaches the correct use of modifiers, an essential component of clear written communication. The concept of comparison is discussed, as are the terms *positive, comparative,* and *superlative.* The chapter also explains common errors in the use of adjectives and adverbs and deals with the correct placement of modifiers—prepositional phrases, participial phrases, and adjective clauses.

The **Writing Application** requires students to use comparative and superlative forms of adjectives and adverbs in letters. Refer students to **Chapter 34** if they need help on letter form.

USAGE

Diagnostic Test

A. Correcting Errors in the Use of Modifiers

The following sentences contain errors in the use of modifiers. Rewrite each sentence, correcting the misuse of the modifier in that sentence. Revisions of sentences with double negatives may vary.

EXAMPLE   **1.** Linen feels more rougher than silk.
             1. *Linen feels rougher than silk.*

1. **don't have any**
1. These Hawaiian shirts ~~don't have no~~ pockets.
2. This ring is the ~~most~~ expensive of the two. **2. more**
3. That striped tie would go ~~good~~ with a white shirt. **3. well**
4. Is a ticket to Mexico ~~more~~ cheaper than a ticket to Canada?
5. Orange juice tastes ~~more sweetly~~ than grapefruit juice. **5. sweeter**

627

USING THE DIAGNOSTIC TEST

If students are using modifiers incorrectly in their writing, you can use the **Diagnostic Test** to pinpoint error patterns and specific strengths and weaknesses. Your assessment of students' performances on the **Diagnostic Test** may indicate that it will be necessary to spend more time on some parts of the chapter and less on others.

6. What is the ~~most~~ funniest thing that ever happened to you?
7. I ⌃can't hardly take another step.   **7.** can
8. My uncle thinks that Stevie Wonder sings⌃~~more well~~ than Michael Jackson does.   **8.** better
9. No one is⌃~~courteouser~~ than Rosa.   **9.** more courteous
10. Ted felt⌃~~calmly~~ during the test on Greek mythology.
    10. calm

B. Correcting Misplaced Modifiers

Each of the following sentences contains a misplaced modifier. Revise each sentence so that it is clear and correct.   **Revisions may vary.**

EXAMPLE   **1.** Hidden in his back pocket, Delbert found the missing ticket.
  1. *Delbert found the missing ticket hidden in his back pocket.*

11. In today's assembly,   **12.** Looking through the microscope,

11. ⌃The famous explorer described being attacked by a baboon ~~in today's assembly.~~
12. ⌃Pam examined a plant cell ~~looking through the microscope.~~   **13.** that he had found
13. Juan read the poem ⌃to the class ~~that he had found.~~
14. My sister promised ~~on Sunday~~ she would take me fishing⌃   **14.** on Sunday.
15. Black Hawk ⌃was a chief of the Sauk people ~~born in Illinois.~~   **15.** , born in Illinois,
16. The plums ~~are drying in the sun~~ that we picked yesterday morning⌃   **16.** are drying in the sun.
17. In this African folk tale, my favorite character ⌃who outwits all his enemies ~~is a rabbit.~~   **17.** is a rabbit
18. A bird ⌃landed on the window sill ~~with a bright red beak.~~   **18.** with a bright red beak
19. ~~Skateboarding down the street,~~ a large dog chased my brother⌃   **19.** , who was skateboarding down the street.
20. The books ⌃are now used by many young readers ~~that we donated to the library.~~   **20.** that we donated to the library

COMPARISON OF ADJECTIVES AND ADVERBS Rule 23a

OBJECTIVE
• To form the degrees of comparison of modifiers correctly

23a

Comparison of Adjectives and Adverbs

A *modifier* is a word, a phrase, or a clause that describes another word or limits the meaning of the word. The two kinds of modifiers—adjectives and adverbs—may be used to compare things. In making comparisons, adjectives and adverbs take different forms. The specific form that is used depends upon how many things are being compared. The different forms of comparison are called *degrees of comparison.*

23a. The three degrees of comparison of modifiers are the *positive*, the *comparative*, and the *superlative.*

(1) The **positive degree** is used when only one thing is being described.

EXAMPLES   This suitcase is **heavy.**
Luís **cheerfully** began the job.

(2) The **comparative degree** is used when two things are being compared.

EXAMPLES   My suitcase is **heavier** than yours.
He began to talk **more cheerfully** about his plans.

(3) The **superlative degree** is used when three or more things are being compared.

EXAMPLES   Sylvia's suitcase is the **heaviest** of all.
Of all the boys, Luís worked at the task **most cheerfully.**

NOTE: In conversation, you may hear and use expressions such as *Put your best foot forward* and *May the best team win.* This use of the superlative is acceptable in spoken English. However, in your writing for school and other formal occasions you should generally follow rule (3) above.

USAGE

RESOURCES

COMPARISON OF ADJECTIVES AND ADVERBS
• Degrees of Comparison
• Regular Comparison
• Irregular Comparison

QUICK REMINDER
Write the following sentences on the chalkboard. Tell students to write the form of the italicized adjective or adverb that correctly fills the blank in each sentence.

1. *large*
Of the three cats, Fluffy is the ____.
2. *lively*
George's dog, King, is ____ than Ginger's dog, Sport.
3. *young*
Of the two children in his family, James is the ____.

USAGE

LEP/ESL

General Strategies. The practice of counting the syllables of an adjective in order to determine how to form its comparative and superlative degrees is found in few if any other languages. In many languages, syllables have nothing to do with grammar. Consequently, some of your ESL students may be unaccustomed to thinking about syllables or may be unsure what syllables are. If students have trouble with the exercises in this segment, be sure they know how to consult a dictionary to check syllabication.

A DIFFERENT APPROACH

Have three fairly tall students stand in front of the chalkboard in order from shortest to tallest. Then have the rest of the class give forms of the word *tall* to compare the standing students with one another [*tall, taller, tallest*].

Regular Comparison

Most one-syllable modifiers form their comparative and superlative degrees by adding *–er* and *–est*.

POSITIVE	COMPARATIVE	SUPERLATIVE
close	closer	closest
slow	slower	slowest
straight	straighter	straightest
sly	slier	sliest

Notice that both adjectives and adverbs form their degrees of comparison in the same way.

Some two-syllable modifiers form their comparative and superlative degrees by adding *–er* and *–est*. Other two-syllable modifiers form their comparative and superlative degrees by using *more* and *most*.

POSITIVE	COMPARATIVE	SUPERLATIVE
simple	simpler	simplest
easy	easier	easiest
jealous	more jealous	most jealous
swiftly	more swiftly	most swiftly

When you are unsure about which way a two-syllable modifier forms its degrees of comparison, look up the word in a dictionary.

 REFERENCE NOTE: For guidelines on how to spell words when adding *–er* or *–est*, see page 771. For a discussion of the information included in dictionary entries, see pages 824–826.

Modifiers that have three or more syllables form the comparative degree by using *more* and the superlative degree by using *most*.

USAGE

630

POSITIVE	COMPARATIVE	SUPERLATIVE
powerful	more powerful	most powerful
illegible	more illegible	most illegible
joyfully	more joyfully	most joyfully
attractively	more attractively	most attractively

 EXERCISE 1 **Forming the Degrees of Comparison of Modifiers**

Give the forms for the comparative and superlative degrees of the following modifiers. Use a dictionary if necessary.

EXAMPLE **1.** light
1. *lighter; lightest*

1. near
2. proud
3. carefully
4. honestly
5. small
6. tiny
7. timidly
8. enthusiastically
9. safe
10. shady

To show decreasing comparisons, all modifiers form the comparative degree by using *less* and the superlative degree by using *least*.

POSITIVE	COMPARATIVE	SUPERLATIVE
sharp	less sharp	least sharp
costly	less costly	least costly
often	less often	least often
frequently	less frequently	least frequently

Irregular Comparison

Some modifiers do not form their comparative and superlative degrees by using the regular methods.

INTEGRATING THE LANGUAGE ARTS

Literature Link. Have students read the poem "Stopping by Woods on a Snowy Evening" by Robert Frost to analyze his use of modifiers. Ask students why the poet uses the word *darkest* in the eighth line, rather than *dark* or *darker.* [Because Frost is comparing the evening to many evenings, the superlative degree is called for.] Then ask students how the use of *darkest* affects the mood of the poem. [The use of *darkest* in the eighth line, rather than *dark* or *darker,* reinforces the idea that this night is different from any other and it also conveys a suspenseful mood.]

ANSWERS
Exercise 1

1. nearer, nearest
2. prouder, proudest
3. more carefully, most carefully
4. more honestly, most honestly
5. smaller, smallest
6. tinier, tiniest
7. more timidly, most timidly
8. more enthusiastically, most enthusiastically
9. safer, safest
10. shadier, shadiest

USAGE

TIMESAVER

Because **Exercise 1** and **Review A** cover the same material, you could give students a key and allow them to check their own answers for **Exercise 1**. You could then use **Review A** for assessment purposes.

INTEGRATING THE LANGUAGE ARTS

Usage and Dictionary Skills. If students don't know how a word forms its comparative and superlative degrees, encourage them to look up the word in a dictionary. You might give students a list of adjectives and adverbs not used as examples in this chapter, and ask them to find the words in a dictionary and to write their comparative and superlative forms. Tell students that if the comparative and superlative forms are not given in a dictionary, they are often formed by adding *more* and *most,* respectively.

USAGE

632 *Using Modifiers Correctly*

POSITIVE	COMPARATIVE	SUPERLATIVE
bad	worse	worst
far	farther	farthest
good	better	best
well	better	best
many	more	most
much	more	most

▶ REVIEW A   **Writing Comparative and Superlative Forms of Modifiers**

Write the form of the italicized adjective or adverb that will correctly fill the blank in each of the following sentences. You may use a dictionary.

EXAMPLE   **1.** *unusual*   The Corn Palace in Mitchell, South Dakota, is one of the ____ buildings in the United States.
1. *most unusual*

1. *big*   The Corn Palace is ____ than I thought it would be.   **1. bigger**   **2. prettier**   **3. freshest**

2. *pretty*   People in Mitchell try to make each year's Corn Palace ____ than the one before.

3. *fresh*   The building looks the ____ in September after new corn and grasses are put on it.

4. *easy*   Some workers find it ____ to saw and nail the corn to panels while others prefer to hang the panels on the building.   **4. easier**

5. *good*   Which of the huge corn murals on the Corn Palace do you like ____?   **5. best**

6. *mysterious*   The enlarged mural of the dancing figure was the ____ to me.   **6. most mysterious**

7. *famous*   These murals feature Native American scenes designed by Mitchell's ____ artist, Oscar Howe.   **7. most famous**

8. *interesting*   The life of this Sioux artist is the ____ story I've ever heard.   **8. most interesting**

OBJECTIVES

- To decide when to use adjectives and when to use adverbs in sentences ☞

9. more slowly

9. *slowly*   My parents walked ___ around the Corn Palace than I did and studied every design.

10. *far*   The family from Mexico traveled ___ than we did to see the Corn Palace.   **10.** farther

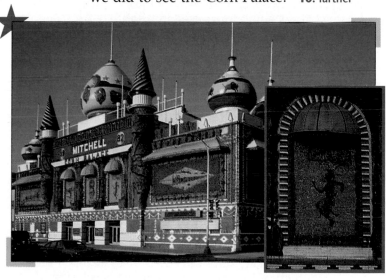

Special Problems in Using Modifiers

23b. Use *good* to modify a noun or a pronoun. Use *well* to modify a verb.

EXAMPLES   **The weather was good on the day of the match.** [*Good* modifies the noun *weather.*]
If you like pears, here is a good one. [*Good* modifies the pronoun *one.*]
The trees are producing well this fall. [*Well* modifies the verb phrase *are producing.*]

Good should not be used to modify a verb.

NONSTANDARD   **Both teams played good.**
STANDARD   **Both teams played well.**

☞ REFERENCE NOTE: For a discussion of standard and nonstandard usage, see page 387.

USAGE

👁 VISUAL CONNECTIONS

About the Artist. Oscar Howe, a Yanktonai Sioux, was born in 1915 on the Crow Creek Indian Reservation in South Dakota. Several of his murals are among the permanent interior panels of the Corn Palace in Mitchell, South Dakota. Howe's work is characterized by bright colors and stylized forms that depict Native American subjects.

▼ **RESOURCES** ▼

SPECIAL PROBLEMS IN USING MODIFIERS

- Special Problems with Modifiers
- Double Comparisons and Double Negatives

🦉 QUICK REMINDER

Put the following sentences on the chalkboard and have students revise the sentences to eliminate errors in the use of modifiers:

1. Joey's new haircut is the most weirdest haircut I have ever seen.
2. I didn't want no bologna after I read the ingredients.
3. Janet felt nervously as she waited to kick the field goal.

USAGE

INTEGRATING THE LANGUAGE ARTS

Literature Link. At the beginning of *Flowers for Algernon,* the main character, Charlie, makes many mistakes in grammar, usage, and mechanics, including using *good* to modify a verb. After the experiment has begun to work, however, Charlie makes fewer and fewer mistakes in his writing. He even learns to use *well* rather than *good,* when appropriate. Have students read *Flowers for Algernon* and discuss with them how the changes in Charlie's language arts skills serve the plot and character development of the story.

A DIFFERENT APPROACH

The incorrect use of adverbs after linking verbs often creates absurd images. For example, "The flower smelled well" creates the image of a flower sniffing at something. Have students generate as many amusing errors of this type as possible. You could have students draw cartoons to illustrate examples.

USAGE

---

634 *Using Modifiers Correctly*

Well may be used as an adjective meaning "in good health" or "pleasing in appearance."

EXAMPLES   Mom feels quite **well** today. [Meaning "in good health," *well* modifies *Mom.*]
Damon looks **well** in bright colors. [Meaning "pleasing in appearance," *well* modifies *Damon.*]

23c.   Use adjectives, not adverbs, after linking verbs.

Linking verbs are often followed by predicate adjectives modifying the subject.

EXAMPLES   Ingrid looked **sleepy** (not *sleepily*) this morning. [The predicate adjective *sleepy* modifies the subject *Ingrid.*]
Kadeem felt **uncertain** (not *uncertainly*) about the race. [The predicate adjective *uncertain* modifies the subject *Kadeem.*]

NOTE: Some linking verbs can also be used as action verbs. As action verbs they may be modified by adverbs.

EXAMPLES   Ingrid looked **sleepily** at the clock. [*Sleepily* modifies the action verb *looked.*]
Kadeem felt his way **uncertainly** along the hall. [*Uncertainly* modifies the action verb *felt.*]

REFERENCE NOTE: For a list of linking verbs, see page 448.

▶ EXERCISE 2   **Using Adjectives and Adverbs Correctly**

Choose the <u>adjective or adverb</u> in parentheses <u>that will make the sentence correct</u>.

EXAMPLE   **1.** John seems (*nervous, nervously*) about his speech.
1. *nervous*

1. When we came into the house after ice-skating, the fire felt (<u>*good*</u>, *well*).
2. The wind blew (*fierce*, <u>*fiercely*</u>) all night.

3. Tino looked (*good, well*) after his trip to Mexico.
4. We moved (*slow, slowly*) along the trail.   **3.** [or well—used as an adj.]
5. Venus looks (*beautiful, beautifully*) tonight.
6. Liang cooked a (*good, well*) meal of vegetables, shrimp, and noodles.
7. We (*sure, surely*) enjoyed seeing you again.
8. We checked the boat (*close, closely*) for leaks.
9. A cup of soup tastes (*good, well*) on a cold day.
10. The ball was caught (*easy, easily*) by the shortstop.

23d. Avoid double comparisons.

A **double comparison** is the use of both *–er* and *more* (less) or *–est* and *most* (least) to form a comparison. When you make a comparison, use only one form, not both.

NONSTANDARD	This is Kathleen Battle's most finest performance.
STANDARD	This is Kathleen Battle's **finest** performance.

NONSTANDARD	His hair is more curlier than his sister's.
STANDARD	His hair is **curlier** than his sister's.

▶ EXERCISE 3 **Revising Sentences to Eliminate Double Comparisons**

For each of the following sentences, identify the incorrect modifier. Then give the correct form of the modifier.

EXAMPLES **1.** I have been studying more harder lately.
  1. *more harder—harder*

  2. Frederick Douglass was one of the most brilliantest speakers against slavery.
  2. *most brilliantest—most brilliant*

1. Sunday was ~~more~~ rainier than Saturday.
2. That is the ~~most~~ saddest story I have ever heard.
3. Are you exercising ~~more~~ longer than you used to?
4. Native arctic peoples have learned to survive in the ~~most~~ coldest weather.
5. He has a ~~more~~ stronger backhand than his brother.

USAGE

USAGE

USAGE

Double Negatives

23e.   Avoid the use of double negatives.

A *double negative* is the use of two negative words to express one negative idea.

Common Negative Words			
barely	never	none	nothing
hardly	no	no one	nowhere
neither	nobody	not (–n't)	scarcely

NONSTANDARD   We couldn't hardly move in the subway car.
STANDARD   We **could** hardly move in the subway car.

NONSTANDARD   Yolanda didn't eat no breakfast this morning.
STANDARD   Yolanda didn't eat **any** breakfast this morning.
STANDARD   Yolanda ate **no** breakfast this morning.

▶ EXERCISE 4   **Revising Sentences by Eliminating Double Negatives**

Revise each of the following sentences to eliminate the double negative.   **Revisions will vary.**

EXAMPLE   **1.** I couldn't find no one to go camping with.
           1. *I couldn't find anyone to go camping with.*
                      or
           I could find no one to go camping with.

1. I didn't see ~~no one~~ I knew at the game.   **1. anyone**
2. Early Spanish explorers searched for gold, but they didn't find ~~none.~~   **2. any.**   **3. could**   **4. anything**
3. We ~~couldn't~~ hardly hear the guest speaker.
4. The cafeteria didn't serve ~~nothing~~ I like today.
5. Double negatives don't have ~~no~~ place in standard English.   **5. any**

WRITING APPLICATION
OBJECTIVE
• To use clear comparisons in a letter to school administrators

WRITING APPLICATION

Using Clear Comparisons in a Letter

You use comparisons every day to describe changes in the world and in yourself. For instance, your hairstyle may be *shorter* (or *longer*) this year than it was last year. An intersection near your school may be *more dangerous* in the morning than in the afternoon. Complete comparisons help you express your thoughts and observations clearly.

INCOMPLETE   The library seems noisier today. [noisier than what?]

COMPLETE   The library seems noisier today than it was yesterday.

▶ WRITING ACTIVITY

An anonymous donor has given a large sum of money for improvements to your school. The school's administrators have invited students to suggest practical uses for the money. Write a letter to the administrators describing the improvements you'd like to see. Use at least three comparative and two superlative forms of adjectives and adverbs in your writing.

Prewriting What facilities, equipment, or supplies would make your school a better place? Does your school need a computer lab? more athletic equipment? a bigger library? List all the improvements you can think of. You may want to discuss your ideas with a classmate or a teacher before you select the ones to include in your letter. Also note *why* the improvements are needed. List some ways that these improvements would change life at your school.

Writing As you write your first draft, use your list to help you make clear and accurate comparisons. Keep your audience in mind. The administrators need practical suggestions for how to spend the money. Let them know exactly what improvements your school needs and why. For more about writing persuasion, see Chapter 8.

USAGE

 WRITING APPLICATION
This assignment gives students practice writing business letters, writing clear comparisons, and writing in the persuasive aim. Students must consider their audience (the school administrators) and their purpose (to influence administrators' decisions about how the money given to the school should be spent).

For an example of persuasive writing, refer students to **A Student Model** on page 267. In her paper, Kathy Bobek writes persuasively in favor of a particular change that she would like to see at her school.

CRITICAL THINKING
Analysis

Discuss with students the basic elements of persuasive writing:
1. an opinion or opinions (opinions about what improvements their school needs)
2. a purpose (to convince administrators to make certain improvements)
3. reasons and evidence (reasons why administrators should make certain changes)
4. credibility (reasons why administrators should listen to students)

PREWRITING

Divide the class into groups of four or five students. Ask each group to brainstorm for supplies, equipment, and facilities that they would like to have at the school. Then have students discuss why these improvements would be beneficial.

USAGE

Evaluating and Revising Read your letter to a parent or other adult to see if your arguments are convincing. Add, delete, or rearrange details to make your letter more interesting and effective. Finally, be sure you've used the correct comparative and superlative forms of adjectives and adverbs.

 Proofreading Check the form of your letter to make sure it follows the guidelines for business letters (see pages 838–842). Be sure you've used at least three comparative and two superlative forms of adjectives and adverbs. Read through your letter a final time to catch any errors in spelling, grammar, usage, or punctuation.

 REVIEW B **Using Modifiers Correctly**

Most of the following sentences contain errors in the use of modifiers. Revise each incorrect sentence to eliminate the error. If a sentence is correct, write *C*.   **Revisions of sentences with double negatives may vary.**

EXAMPLE   **1.** My cold is worst today than it was yesterday.
          1. *My cold is worse today than it was yesterday.*

1. She is the funnier of the two comedians.   **1.** c
2. Kendo, a Japanese martial art, is more ~~gracefuller~~ than many other sports.   **2.** graceful
3. No one in our class can play chess as ~~good~~ as Sylvia Yee.   **3.** well
4. Time passes too ~~slow~~ during the summer.   **4.** slowly
5. After a long swim, she felt good.   **5.** c
6. I ~~wasn't hardly able~~ to hear you.   **6.** was hardly able
7. Which of the twins is ~~strongest~~?   **7.** stronger
8. Some people ~~don't seem to have no~~ control over their tempers.   **8.** don't seem to have any
9. He hardly ever visits us.   **9.** c
10. Of all the folk dances my grandfather taught me, the polka is the ~~most funnest.~~   **10.** most fun.

REVIEWS B and C
OBJECTIVES
• To revise sentences to eliminate incorrect use of modifiers
• To write sentences that use specified forms of modifiers correctly

REVIEW C

Writing Sentences with Correct Forms of Modifiers

When you watch television, you probably don't think about how a show is created. This diagram of a TV studio shows some of the jobs and equipment involved in producing a show. Which of these jobs might you be interested in doing? Would you rather be in front of the camera or behind the scenes? Imagine that you are working in this studio. Write five sentences describing what you do or telling about the show or your coworkers. Use five of the following items correctly in your sentences. Underline each one you use.

- the superlative of *new*
- the comparative of *good*
- a linking verb and a predicate adjective
- *barely* to express a negative idea
- the positive of *well*
- the superlative of *loud*
- the comparative of *popular*
- a decreasing comparison of *costly*

EXAMPLE   **1.** *The new spotlight is <u>better</u> than the old one.*

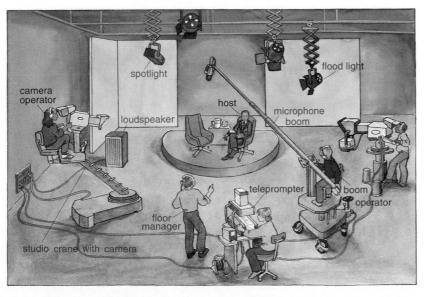

spotlight

flood light

camera operator

loudspeaker

host

microphone boom

teleprompter

boom operator

floor manager

studio crane with camera

USAGE

ANSWERS

Review C

Responses will vary. Here are some possibilities:

1. These cameras are our <u>newest</u> pieces of equipment.
2. We like them <u>better</u> than our old cameras.
3. Joe Ready, the host for our six and ten o'clock news programs, <u>is</u> very <u>professional</u> in dealing with the public.
4. Some of our documentaries have brought in <u>barely</u> enough money to cover the cost of producing them.
5. Most of my coworkers perform <u>well</u> under pressure.
6. The <u>loudest</u> program we present is *Saturday Night Rock.*
7. Our six o'clock news program is <u>more popular</u> than our ten o'clock program.
8. It is <u>less costly</u> to buy programs offered by the television networks than to produce our own.

USAGE

PLACEMENT OF MODIFIERS Rule 23f

OBJECTIVES

- To revise sentences to eliminate misplaced prepositional phrases
- To add prepositional phrases to sentences
- To revise sentences to eliminate misplaced or dangling participial phrases

PLACEMENT OF MODIFIERS

- Misplaced Prepositional Phrases
- Misplaced and Dangling Participle Phrases
- Misplaced Adjective Clauses

QUICK REMINDER

Remind students that modifying phrases and clauses should be placed as close as possible to the word(s) they modify. Then ask students to revise the following sentences to eliminate errors in the placement of modifying phrases and clauses:

1. The representative returned to Capitol Hill after a long illness on Wednesday.
2. Carla's Deli delivered two submarine sandwiches to Keesha wrapped in foil.
3. Forrest read that Ernie Benchpress's new movie was opening in the newspaper.

USAGE

USAGE

640 *Using Modifiers Correctly*

Placement of Modifiers

Notice how the meaning of these sentence changes when the position of the phrase *from Cincinnati* changes.

EXAMPLES The basketball player **from Cincinnati** gave a TV interview for his fans. [The phrase modifies *player.*]
The basketball player gave a TV interview for his fans **from Cincinnati**. [The phrase modifies *fans.*]
From Cincinnati, the basketball player gave a TV interview for his fans. [The phrase modifies *gave.*]

23f. Place modifying phrases and clauses as close as possible to the words they modify.

Prepositional Phrases

A *prepositional phrase* begins with a preposition and ends with a noun or a pronoun.

REFERENCE NOTE: For more information about prepositions, see pages 460–464. For more about prepositional phrases, see pages 491–497.

A prepositional phrase used as an adjective should be placed directly after the word it modifies.

MISPLACED The hat belongs to that girl with the green feather.
CLEAR The hat **with the green feather** belongs to that girl.

A prepositional phrase used as an adverb should be placed near the word it modifies.

MISPLACED She read that a new restaurant had opened in today's newspaper.
CLEAR **In today's newspaper** she read that a new restaurant had opened.

23f

Avoid placing a prepositional phrase so that it seems to modify either of two words. Place the phrase so that it clearly modifies the word you intend it to modify.

MISPLACED	Manuel said in the afternoon he would call Janet. [Does the phrase modify *said* or *would call*?]
CLEAR	Manuel said he would call Janet **in the afternoon.** [The phrase modifies *would call.*]
CLEAR	**In the afternoon** Manuel said he would call Janet. [The phrase modifies *said.*]

> EXERCISE 5 **Revising Sentences with Misplaced Prepositional Phrases**

The meaning of each of the following sentences is not clear and sensible because the modifying phrase is misplaced. Decide where the phrase belongs; then revise the sentence. **Revisions will vary.**

EXAMPLE 1. In the United States, Zora Neale Hurston grew up in the first self-governed black township.
1. *Zora Neale Hurston grew up in the first self-governed black township in the United States.*

1. That woman ~~was out walking her dog~~ in high heels and a tweed suit this morning. **1.** was out walking her dog
2. The poster caught my eye ~~on the wall.~~ **2.** on the wall
3. Hoy taught us ~~with chopsticks~~ how to scoop up rice. **3.** with chopsticks.
4. Our teacher said ~~on Monday~~ the class would put on a play. **4.** on Monday.
5. Don't forget to take the box to the store ~~with the empty bottles.~~ **5.** with the empty bottles

> EXERCISE 6 **Placing Prepositional Phrases Correctly**

Rewrite each of the following sentences, adding the prepositional phrase given in parentheses. Be careful to place each prepositional phrase near the word or words it modifies.

USAGE

LEP/ESL

General Strategies. You may have students in your class who speak languages, such as Korean and Turkish in which nearly all modifiers precede the words modified. Other students may speak languages, such as Indonesian, Spanish, and Tagalog, in which nearly all modifiers follow the words modified. Errors may occur as the rules of placement of modifiers in other languages get confused with those in English. You may wish to give students extra practice in correct placement of English modifiers.

After students have completed the exercises in this segment, you could supply additional modifiers to be inserted in the sentences in **Exercises 5, 6, 7,** and **9.** For example, for the second sentence in **Exercise 5** the prepositional phrase *in the dining room* could be supplied to students. Students could then add that phrase to form the sentence, "The poster on the wall in the dining room caught my eye."

USAGE

VISUAL CONNECTIONS
The Green Violinist

About the Artwork. Marc Chagall's choice of subject matter was influenced by his love for Russian and Jewish folklore, and he was also inspired by the Fauvists to use bright colors and by the Cubists to experiment with space. Chagall often ignored traditional treatment of perspective in his paintings. For example, in *The Green Violinist,* the houses in the background are roughly the same size as those in the foreground (traditional artists draw background figures smaller and foreground figures larger to give the illusion of depth), and the animal at the bottom left of the painting is as large as the dwelling by its side.

MEETING INDIVIDUAL NEEDS

LEARNING STYLES

Kinetic Learners. To reinforce the concept that modifying phrases and clauses need to be as close as possible to the words they modify, write sentences on strips of paper. Then for each sentence, write a modifying phrase or clause that could be added to the sentence without any rewording. Ask students to cut the sentence strips where appropriate and to insert the corresponding phrase and clause strips.

642

EXAMPLE **1.** Many paintings show strange, fantastical scenes. (by Marc Chagall)
1. *Many paintings by Marc Chagall show strange, fantastical scenes.*

1. Chagall's *The Green Violinist* contains many delightful mysteries and surprises. (for the eye and mind)
2. As you can see in the painting, a gigantic violinist sits among the buildings of a small village. (with a green face and hand)
3. Dark windows look just like the windows of the houses. (on the musician's pants)
4. A man waves to the violinist, and a dog taller than a house seems to smile at the music it hears. (above the clouds)
5. As you look at the painting's bright colors, perhaps you can almost hear the enchanting music. (of the green violinist)

Marc Chagall, *The Green Violinist,* 1923–24, Oil on canvas, 78 × 42¾ inches, Solomon R. Guggenheim Museum, New York. Gift, Solomon R. Guggenheim, 1937. Photo: David Heald copyright Solomon R. Guggenheim Foundation, New York. FN 37.446

Participial Phrases

A *participial phrase* consists of a verb form—either a present participle or a past participle—and its related words. A participial phrase modifies a noun or a pronoun.

☞ **REFERENCE NOTE:** For more information about participial phrases, see page 504.

Like a prepositional phrase, a participial phrase should be placed as close as possible to the word it modifies.

EXAMPLES **Walking to school,** Celia and James found a wallet. [The participial phrase modifies *Celia* and *James.*]
I. M. Pei, **born in China,** is a gifted architect. [The participial phrase modifies *I. M. Pei.*]

REFERENCE NOTE: For more about using commas with participial phrases, see page 713 and 720.

A participial phrase that is not placed next to the noun or pronoun that it modifies is a *misplaced modifier.*

MISPLACED **Stolen from the media center,** the deputies found the video recorder. [Were the deputies stolen from the media center?]
CLEAR The deputies found the video recorder **stolen from the media center.**

MISPLACED **Sleeping on the roof,** I saw the neighbor's cat. [Was I sleeping on the roof?]
CLEAR I saw the neighbor's cat **sleeping on the roof.**

MISPLACED We're used to the noise **living by the airport.** [Was the noise living by the airport?]
CLEAR **Living by the airport,** we're used to the noise.

A participial phrase that does not clearly and sensibly modify a word in the sentence is a *dangling participle.*

DANGLING **Cleaning the attic,** an old trunk was found.
CLEAR **Cleaning the attic, we** found an old trunk.

EXERCISE 7 **Revising Sentences with Misplaced or Dangling Participial Phrases**

Revise all sentences that contain misplaced or dangling participial phrases. [Hint: You will need to add, delete, or rearrange some words.] Participial phrases that begin or interrupt sentences should be set off by commas. If a sentence is correct, write *C.*

EXAMPLE **1.** Made from matzo meal, Rachel shapes tasty dumplings.
1. *Rachel shapes tasty dumplings made from matzo meal.*

INTEGRATING THE LANGUAGE ARTS

Usage and Mechanics. If students are having trouble revising sentences due to uncertainty about comma usage, give them the following rules:

1. When a clause or phrase is unessential to the meaning of a sentence, it should be set off by commas; for example, "My brother, who is a vegetarian, loves tofu."
2. Introductory phrases are usually followed by a comma; for example, "Feeling excited about the first cool weather, she decided to take her dog for a walk."

ADVANCED STUDENTS

Have students conduct a scavenger hunt in newspapers and magazines for sentences with misplaced or dangling modifiers. At the end of the hunt, ask students to read their sentences to the class and then to suggest revisions.

ANSWERS
Exercise 7

Revisions may vary.

1. I watched the lion pacing in its cage.

2. C

3. While exploring the cave, we discovered a new tunnel.

4. The circus featured a clown wearing a bright orange suit and floppy yellow shoes.

5. The girls walked through the field filled with daisies.

6. C

7. The turkey stuffed with sage and bread crumbs was large enough for three families.

8. Tired from the long walk through the snow, we welcomed food and rest.

9. C

10. We saw the young birds perched in their nest.

ANSWERS
Exercise 8

Sentences will vary. Here are some possibilities:

1. Alarmed by the noise, I peeked through the miniblinds to see what was causing it.

2. I saw a figure creeping closer to the door.

3. I remained hidden from view as I watched it approach the house.

4. A large bird perched in the tree outside the window shrieked so loudly that I nearly jumped out of my skin.

5. Shaking like a wet dog, I stood there until I caught my breath.

---

644 *Using Modifiers Correctly*

1. Pacing in its cage, I watched the lion.
2. Talking on the telephone, Lori did not hear the doorbell.
3. Exploring the cave, a new tunnel was discovered.
4. Wearing a bright orange suit and floppy yellow shoes, the circus featured a clown.
5. Filled with daisies, the girls walked through the field.
6. Reading his part, the actor felt nervous.
7. The turkey was large enough for three families stuffed with sage and bread crumbs.
8. Tired from the long walk through the snow, food and rest were welcomed.
9. Checking the shelves, Judy found the books she needed.
10. Perched in their nest, we saw the young birds.

▶ EXERCISE 8 ### Writing Sentences with Participial Phrases

What's going on at the neighbors' house? You were on your way inside your house when loud voices caught your attention. You look next door and see this scene.

Write five sentences about what you see and what happens next. In your sentences, use five of the following

Placement of Modifiers **645**

participial phrases correctly. Use two of the phrases at the beginning of sentences and three within sentences. [Note: Make sure you use each phrase as a modifier, not as part of a verb phrase.]

- alarmed by the noise
- shaking like a wet dog
- hidden from view
- creeping closer to the door
- lying on the sidewalk
- laughing at the shadow
- perched in the tree
- blinded by the sudden light

EXAMPLE **1.** *The shadow creeping closer to the door frightened me, too.*

Adjective Clauses

An *adjective clause* modifies a noun or a pronoun. Most adjective clauses begin with a relative pronoun—*that, which, who, whom,* or *whose.*

☞ **REFERENCE NOTE:** For more information about adjective clauses, see pages 520–521.

Like adjective phrases, adjective clauses should be placed directly after the words they modify.

MISPLACED The picnic in the park **that we had** was fun. [Did we have the park?]
CLEAR The picnic **that we had** in the park was fun.

MISPLACED The girls are from my school **who won the relay race.** [Did the school win the relay race?]
CLEAR The girls **who won the relay race** are from my school.

▶ EXERCISE 9 **Revising Sentences with Misplaced Clause Modifiers**

Revise each of the following sentences by placing the adjective clause near the word it should modify.

LEARNING STYLES

Visual and Kinetic Learners. Write five sentences containing adjective clauses on the chalkboard. Have student volunteers come to the chalkboard, circle the adjective clauses, and draw arrows from the clauses to the words they modify.

Here are some sentences that you could use:

1. Akeem, who is very good at math, helped me study.
2. I enjoyed the movie that we saw.
3. The man whose books you borrowed wants them back.
4. The class to whom Ms. Yamamoto spoke was interested in her presentation.
5. The bicycle that she rides to school is broken.

645

PICTURE THIS

You might begin this activity by asking students if they have ever witnessed an accident. Ask them to describe what they saw. Then ask students who have been involved in accidents to tell what happened. Listening to accounts should give students some ideas for writing their descriptions.

EXAMPLE   **1.** I showed the fabric to my sister that was made in Kenya.

            1. *I showed the fabric that was made in Kenya to my sister.*

1. The students ~~received an A~~ who made the first presentation͡ **1.** received an A.
2. The kitten ~~belongs to my neighbor~~ that is on the branch͡ **2.** belongs to my neighbor.
3. My friend Beverly,~~visited me~~ who lives in Sarasota, Florida͡ **3.** , visited me.
4. The doctor͡said that the triplets were healthy͡~~who examined them.~~ **4.** who examined them
5. The cleanup program ~~was supported by all of the students~~ that the president of the seventh-grade class suggested͡ **5.** was supported by all of the students.

PICTURE THIS

You have just witnessed this accident. No one has been hurt, but both drivers are very upset. Each driver insists that the other is to blame. Because you are a witness, the police would like you to describe what happened. Write a brief description of what you saw up to the time of the accident and when the accident occurred. In your description, use at least five adjective clauses.

Subject:	traffic accident
Audience:	police officers
Purpose:	to give an accurate description

 REVIEW D **Identifying and Correcting Errors in the Use of Modifiers**

Each of the following sentences contains an error in the form or placement of a modifier. Revise each sentence by changing the form of a modifier or by adding, deleting, or rearranging words.

EXAMPLE   **1.** The record was the sound track of the movie that we heard.
   1. *The record that we heard was the sound track of the movie.*

1. My stepsister plays both soccer and softball, but she likes soccer ~~best.~~   **1.** better.
2. The waiter brought plates ~~to Terrell and me~~ piled high with spaghetti and meat sauce∧   **2.** to Terrell and me.
3. Janet's cartoon is ~~more~~ funnier than yours.
4. ~~Barking and growling,~~ the stranger was frightened by the∧dogs.   **4.** barking and growling
5. The German cuckoo clock still runs∧~~good~~ after all these years.   **5.** well
6. I didn't do too∧~~bad~~ on the geography quiz this morning.   **6.** badly
7. Our puppy is much∧~~more playfuller~~ than our older dog is.   **7.** more playful
8. We drove∧~~slow~~ past the duck pond to see if any new ducklings had hatched.   **8.** slowly
9. They never did find∧~~no~~ sponsor for their team.   **9.** a
10. I have never been ~~more~~ happier in my life.

TIMESAVER

You could make an answer key for **Exercises 5–9** and **Reviews D** and **E** and have students check their work and correct their errors. The **Review: Post-test** could then be used for assessment purposes.

USAGE

USAGE

USAGE

Proofreading Sentences for Correct Use of Modifiers

Each of the following sentences contains an error in the form or placement of a modifier. Revise each sentence by changing the form of a modifier or by adding, deleting, or rearranging words.

EXAMPLE　**1.** Of all the actors on the TV series *Life Goes On*, Chris Burke is the one I admire more.

　　　　　1. *Of all the actors on the TV series* Life Goes On, *Chris Burke is the one I admire the most.*

1. Born with Down's syndrome, Chris is the younger of four children.
2. Chris decided that he would be a TV star at the age of eight.
3. He plays a character on the show whose name is Corky.
4. Chris's acting impressed the director in the pilot show for the series.
5. I read that *Life Goes On* is one of the most popular TV shows in the newspaper.
6. In the picture below, Chris (the most farthest person on the left) takes a break during filming.
7. As you can see, Chris doesn't hardly seem nervous about being a TV star.

USAGE

ANSWERS
Review E

Revisions may vary.

1. Born with Down's syndrome, Chris is the youngest of four children.
2. At the age of eight, Chris decided that he would be a TV star.
3. On the show, he plays a character whose name is Corky.
4. Chris's acting in the pilot show for the series impressed the director.
5. I read in the newspaper that *Life Goes On* is one of the most popular TV shows.
6. In the picture below, Chris (the person on the far left) takes a break during filming.
7. As you can see, Chris hardly seems nervous about being a TV star.
8. Chris, who says he has "Up Syndrome," usually has a positive attitude.
9. When he reads his fan mail, especially letters from other people with Down's syndrome, Chris feels really good.
10. Fans of the show agree that an actor who has overcome many obstacles is a great role model.

OBJECTIVE

- To revise sentences to correct errors in the use of modifiers

8. Saying he has "Up Syndrome," Chris's attitude is usually positive.
9. Chris feels really well when he reads his fan mail, especially letters from other people with Down's syndrome.
10. Fans of the show agree that an actor is a great role model who has overcome many obstacles.

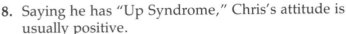

Review: Posttest

A. Revising Sentences by Correcting Errors in the Use of Modifiers

Most of the following sentences contain errors in the form or placement of modifiers. If a sentence has an error, rewrite the sentence correctly. If a sentence is correct, write *C*. **Revisions of sentences 4, 8, and 9 may vary.**

EXAMPLE **1.** There wasn't nothing missing.
1. *There wasn't anything missing.*
or
There was nothing missing.

1. Weigh both packages to see which is ~~heaviest.~~ **1. heavier.**
2. With care, this car will run ~~good~~ for years. **2. well**
3. Did you read that Eduardo Mata received an award**?** ~~in the newspaper?~~ **3. in the newspaper**
4. We always pass a Czech bakery ~~walking to school.~~ **4. Walking to school,**
5. The bean soup tasted good. **5. C**
6. I think the play *Fiddler on the Roof* is better than the movie. **6. C**
7. Who is the ~~most~~ smartest person you've ever met?
8. Jason tried to push the huge desk but ~~couldn't hardly~~ move it. **8. could hardly**
9. The balloons startled the younger children ~~when they burst.~~ **9. When they burst,**
10. A jet taking off can sound ~~more~~ noisier than a jackhammer.

STUDENTS WITH SPECIAL NEEDS

Students might be especially interested in the information about Chris Burke given in **Review E.** Encourage them to find out more about Chris Burke or about another well-known person who has overcome a disability. If students feel comfortable doing so, have them present their findings to the class.

B. Revising Sentences by Correcting Errors in the Use of Modifiers

Most of the following sentences contain errors in the form or placement of modifiers. If a sentence has an error, rewrite the sentence correctly. If a sentence is correct, write C. Revisions of sentences with double negatives will vary.

EXAMPLE **1.** This gold and silver-colored French franc is the most prettiest coin I've seen.

    1. *This gold and silver-colored French franc is the prettiest coin I've seen.*

11. A coin dealer ~~looked at my collection~~ that has a shop near my house∧ **11.** looked at my collection.

12. He examined two old Greek coins but∧~~couldn't see no~~ date. **12.** could see no

13. The shinier coin looked newer. **13.** C **14.** older

14. It turned out to be the ∧~~oldest~~ of the two, however.

15. I showed∧one coin ~~to the dealer~~ valued at nearly twenty dollars. **15.** the dealer

16. He said he ~~couldn't hardly pay~~ more than fifteen dollars for it. **16.** could hardly pay **17.** well

17. If I could bargain∧~~good~~, I might get more for it.

18. Those two coins ~~come from Ireland~~ that have harp designs on them∧ **18.** come from Ireland.

19. Collecting coins∧ my knowledge about other countries and peoples∧~~increases.~~ **19.** increases

20. I polished my Saudi Arabian fifty-halala piece∧~~good~~ so that I could see the Arabic writing on it. **20.** well

USAGE

OBJECTIVES

- To identify correct usage of words and expressions
- To use standard English to rewrite sentences

▼ RESOURCES

A GLOSSARY OF USAGE
- Chapter Review Form A
- Chapter Review Form B
- Assessment Portfolio
  Usage Pretest
  Usage Mastery Test 1
  Usage Mastery Test 2

24 A GLOSSARY OF USAGE

Common Usage Problems

Diagnostic Test

Revising Sentences by Correcting Errors in Usage

In each of the following sets of sentences, one sentence contains an error in usage. Choose the letter of the <u>sentence that contains an error</u>. Revise the sentence, using standard English.

EXAMPLE   **1. a.** Bring the books here.
       b. I was somewhat embarrassed.
       c. Please return these here books.
     1. *c. Please return these books.*

1. **a.** <s>Who's</s> book is it?   **1.** Whose
  b. There is your hat.
  c. He is the man who owns the shop.
2. **a.** I would <s>of</s> gone with you.   **2.** have
  b. You're my friend.
  c. They're here.

CHAPTER OVERVIEW

The chapter includes commonly misused words and expressions as well as certain expressions that are regarded as nonstandard. Guidelines and examples are given for understanding the differences between formal and informal speech and writing. Exercises cover many common usages that students will encounter in their own speaking and writing. The chapter also demonstrates the importance of precision in word choice.

The **Writing Application** requires the use of formal English in a persuasive speech. For an example of persuasive writing, see the student model written by Kathy Bobek in **Chapter 8,** on p. 267.

USAGE

USING THE DIAGNOSTIC TEST

The **Diagnostic Test** will help to determine students' familiarity with the most commonly misused words and phrases as well as students' abilities to choose alternatives for better expression. You may find that even though students have knowledge of many of these words and phrases, they fail to apply them, especially when speaking.

You may wish to examine the test results to determine which students may have developed habits of misuse in speaking and writing. Your assessment will help you pinpoint error patterns and specific strengths and weaknesses.

3. **a.** These kinds of games are challenging.
    b. They bought themselves new shoes.
    c. Can you fix this ~~here~~ shelf?
4. **a.** I ~~use~~ to know the title of this song.   **4.** used
    b. That headdress looks as if it is genuine.
    c. Set the bucket down on the porch.
5. **a.** We sat on straw mats called *tatami*.
    b. That fruit salad is ~~real~~ tasty.   **5.** really
    c. You ought to try it.
6. **a.** If we had liked it, we would have bought it.
    b. The cat jumped off ~~of~~ the chair.
    c. Please wait outside the office.
7. **a.** She looks like her sister.
    b. They went somewhere together.
    c. He acts ~~like~~ he is tired.   **7.** as if
8. **a.** I made ~~less~~ mistakes this time.   **8.** fewer
    b. My brother is learning how to dive.
    c. Jack is somewhat nervous.
9. **a.** I like this type of pen.
    b. I know ~~how come~~ he won.   **9.** why
    c. Marco served himself some meatloaf.
10. **a.** The monkey scratched its head.
    b. It's not here.
    c. We ~~had~~ ought to check the weather report.
11. **a.** Our chorus sang ~~good~~.   **11.** well
    b. Clog dancing gives you a good workout.
    c. Sofía plays the castanets well.
12. **a.** I looked everywhere.
    b. The balloon burst.
    c. Bring the box over ~~there~~.   **12.** here
13. **a.** You should have been there.
    b. Tom and Sabrena ~~they~~ are in my English class.
    c. It's been a cold winter.
14. **a.** We shared the popcorn among the three of us.
    b. From here she looks like Karen.
    c. Where is the lake ~~at~~?
15. **a.** Bill looks as if he is upset.
    b. The milk smells ~~badly~~.   **15.** bad
    c. We had scarcely enough books for everyone.

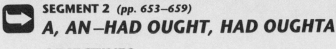

OBJECTIVES

- To recognize nonstandard usage and to select correct usage
- To rewrite sentences by using standard English

A Glossary of Usage **653**

16. **a.** They sang a lot of ballads.
     b. The meal was ~~alright~~.   **16.** all right
     c. Alan had already left.
17. **a.** Everyone can go ~~accept~~ Ramón.   **17.** except
     b. She worked for half an hour.
     c. I rode an elephant.
18. **a.** Marco grew up in Honduras.
     b. The musicians were ~~already~~ to begin playing.   **18.** all ready
     c. They divided the task among the six workers.
19. **a.** Use less water in the mixture.
     b. Music makes me feel good.   **19.** everywhere
     c. We looked ~~everywheres~~ for red suede shoes.
20. **a.** That kimono looks good on you.
     b. Where did you get ~~them~~ shoes?   **20.** those
     c. They raised the price of stamps.

This chapter contains an alphabetical list, or glossary, of many common problems in English usage. You will notice throughout the chapter that some examples are labeled *standard* or *nonstandard*. **Standard English** is the most widely accepted form of English. It is used in *formal* situations, such as speeches and compositions for school, and in *informal* situations, such as conversations and everyday writing. **Nonstandard English** is language that does not follow the rules and guidelines of standard English.

☞ REFERENCE NOTE: For more discussion of standard and nonstandard English, see page 387.

a, an   *Use a* before words beginning with a consonant sound. Use *an* before words beginning with a vowel sound. Keep in mind that the *sound,* not the actual letter, that a word begins with determines whether *a* or *an* should be used.

EXAMPLES   They are building **a** hospital near our house.
I bought **a** one-way ticket.
I would like **an** orange.
We worked for **an** hour.

USAGE

QUICK REMINDER

Write *all ready* and *already* on the chalkboard. As you read the following sentences aloud to students, have them write one of the two forms for each sentence:

1. When I got there, she was already gone.
2. When I got there, she was all ready to go.

Point out to students that although *all ready* and *already* sound the same, they have different spellings and different meanings. When students are writing, they need to distinguish between the forms to follow standard usage.

USAGE

USAGE

LEP/ESL

General Strategies. The distinction between *a* and *an* might be lost on many of your ESL students because many languages, such as Korean and Russian, do not have articles; some, such as Arabic, do not have indefinite articles as English does; and virtually none have articles that vary in form depending on the following sound. You may need to remind students that in English the use of *a* and *an* is determined by the sound of following nouns.

COMMON ERROR

Problem. *Ain't* may have come into nonstandard usage in an effort to form a contraction of *am not.* Contractions can be formed with all forms of the verb *to be* and *not* except for *am* (*isn't, aren't, wasn't, weren't, won't*).

Solution. To help students avoid awkward contractions with *am not,* suggest that they form contractions with the pronoun and the verb rather than with the verb and *not.*

---

accept, except *Accept* is a verb; it means "to receive." *Except* may be either a verb or a preposition. As a verb, it means "to leave out." As a preposition, *except* means "excluding."

EXAMPLES Ann **accepted** the gift.
No one will be **excepted** from writing a research paper.
All my friends will be there **except** Jorge.

ain't Avoid this word in speaking and writing; it is nonstandard English.

all right Used as an adjective, *all right* means "satisfactory" or "unhurt." Used as an adverb, *all right* means "well enough." *All right* should always be written as two words.

EXAMPLES Your science project looks **all right** to me.
[adjective]
Judy cut her toe, but she is **all right** now.
[adjective]
I did **all right** in the drama club tryouts.
[adverb]

a lot *A lot* should always be written as two words.

EXAMPLE I have read **a lot** of Native American folk tales.

already, all ready *Already* means "previously." *All ready* means "completely prepared."

EXAMPLES By the time my mother came home, I had **already** cooked dinner.
The students were **all ready** for the trip.

among See **between, among.**

anywheres, everywheres, nowheres, somewheres Use these words without the final *–s.*

EXAMPLE Did you go **anywhere** [not *anywheres*] today?

as See **like, as.**

as if See **like, as if.**

at Do not use *at* after *where.*

> NONSTANDARD   Where are the Persian miniatures at?
> STANDARD   Where are the Persian miniatures?

bad, badly *Bad* is an adjective. It modifies nouns and pronouns. *Badly* is an adverb. It modifies verbs, adjectives, and adverbs.

> EXAMPLES   **The fruit tastes bad.** [The predicate adjective *bad* modifies *fruit.*]
> **Don't treat him badly.** [The adverb *badly* modifies the verb *do treat.*]

NOTE: The expression *feel badly* has become acceptable, though ungrammatical, informal English.

> INFORMAL   Carl felt badly about losing the race.
> FORMAL   Carl felt **bad** about losing the race.

▶ EXERCISE 1   **Identifying Correct Usage**

Choose the <u>correct word or words</u> in parentheses in each of the following sentences.

> EXAMPLE   **1.** Navajo people came to the Southwest from (*somewhere, somewheres*) in the North.
> **1.** *somewhere*

1. One group of Navajos settled in the region where the Pueblo people (*lived, lived at*).
2. Pueblo artists (*already, all ready*) used powdered paint to make sacred, or religious, pictures on the earth floors of their lodges.
3. The Navajos (*excepted, accepted*) the idea of sacred painting, but they changed the ceremony into sand painting.
4. When the Navajo artists were (*all ready, already*) to begin the ceremony, they gathered in a circle, as shown in the picture on the next page.
5. (*A, An*) artist skilled in sand painting knew which designs to use for different purposes.

MEETING INDIVIDUAL NEEDS

LESS-ADVANCED STUDENTS

It may be especially difficult for students to choose between *a* and *an* when a word begins with *h*. When writing, it may help students to choose correctly if they form the habit of pronouncing any word modified by *a* or *an*.

To give students practice, write the following words and expressions on the chalkboard. Then ask students to pronounce each word silently and to select the correct article, *a* or *an*.

1. hornet [a]
2. honest man [an]
3. horror movie [a]
4. helper [a]
5. honor [an]

USAGE

USAGE

655

USAGE

656

USAGE

6. For example, he might make a certain design when things were not (*all right, alright*) in the community.
7. If someone were injured or feeling (*badly, bad*), the Navajo sand painter would use his art to help heal that person.
8. The ceremony sometimes lasted for several days— (*anywheres, anywhere*) up to nine days, in fact.
9. The traditional art of sand painting (*ain't, hasn't*) disappeared, and artists still take part in the ceremonies.
10. At sunset, the sand paintings are carefully swept away, and the designs are recorded nowhere (*accept, except*) on Navajo blankets, in photographs, and in the artist's imagination.

between, among Use *between* when referring to two things at a time, even though they may be part of a group consisting of more than two.

EXAMPLES Who sits **between** you and Sue?

Between the last three track meets, I trained very hard. [Although there were more than two meets, the training occurred between any two of them.]

There isn't much difference **between** these three brands of juice. [Although there are more than two brands, each one is being compared with the others separately.]

Use *among* when referring to a group rather than to separate individuals.

EXAMPLES   We divided the tacos and burritos **among** the five of us.
There was much disagreement **among** the governors about the new tax plan. [The governors are thought of as a group.]

bring, take   *Bring* means "to come carrying something." *Take* means "to go carrying something." Think of *bring* as related to *come*, *take* as related to *go*.

EXAMPLES   **Bring** that chair here.
Now **take** this one over there.

bust, busted   Avoid using these words as verbs. Use a form of either *burst* or *break*.

EXAMPLES   The pipe **burst** [not *busted*] after the storm.
The Japanese raku ware vase **broke** [not *busted*] when it fell.

can't hardly, can't scarcely   The words *hardly* and *scarcely* are negative words. They should never be used with another negative word.

EXAMPLES   I **can** [not *can't*] **hardly** wait to hear your new CD.
We **had** [not *hadn't*] **scarcely** enough food for everyone at the Juneteenth picnic.

REFERENCE NOTE: For more on double negatives, see page 636.

could of   Do not write *of* with the helping verb *could*. Write *could have*. Also avoid *ought to of, should of, would of, might of,* and *must of*.

EXAMPLES   Abdul could **have** [not *of*] helped us.
You should **have** [not *of*] hung the piñata higher.

don't, doesn't   See page 567.

except   See **accept, except**

USAGE

USAGE

USAGE

everywheres See **anywheres,** etc.

fewer, less *Fewer* is used with plural words. *Less* is used with singular words. *Fewer* tells "how many," *less* tells "how much."

> EXAMPLES　We had expected **fewer** guests.
> Please use **less** salt.

good, well *Good* is always an adjective. Never use *good* to modify a verb; use *well,* which is an adverb.

> NONSTANDARD　The steel-drum band played good.
> STANDARD　The steel-drum band played **well.**

Although it is usually an adverb, *well* may be used as an adjective to mean "healthy."

> EXAMPLE　I did not feel **well** yesterday.

NOTE: *Feel good* and *feel well* mean different things. *Feel good* means "to feel happy or pleased." *Feel well* simply means "to feel healthy."

> EXAMPLES　Helping others makes me feel **good.**
> I went home because I didn't feel **well.**

had of See **of.**

had ought, hadn't ought The verb *ought* should never be used with *had.*

> NONSTANDARD　You had ought to learn to dance the polka.
> You hadn't ought to be late for class.
> STANDARD　You **ought** to learn to dance the polka.
> You **oughtn't** to be late for class.
> *or*
> You **should** learn to dance the polka.
> You **shouldn't** be late for class.

▶ EXERCISE 2　**Identifying Correct Usage**

Choose the <u>correct word or words</u> in parentheses in each of the following sentences.

REVIEW A

OBJECTIVES

- To identify errors in English usage
- To rewrite sentences by choosing the correct usage

EXAMPLE   **1.** Bike riders (*had ought, ought*) to know some simple rules of safety.
   1. *ought*

1. Just about (*everywheres*, *everywhere*) you go these days you see people riding bikes.
2. Riders who wear helmets have (*fewer*, *less*) major injuries than riders who don't.
3. When my aunt came for a visit, she (*brought*, *took*) her bicycle with her.
4. In choosing clothes, cyclists (*can hardly*, *can't hardly*) go wrong by wearing bright, easy-to-see colors.
5. On busy streets, groups of cyclists should ride in single file and leave space (*among*, *between*) their bikes in case of sudden stops.
6. Members of cycling clubs may decide (*between*, *among*) themselves on special communication signals.
7. A cyclist who is involved in an accident should not try to ride home, even if he or she seems to feel (*well*, *good*).
8. If possible, call a family member or friend who can (*bring*, *take*) both the rider and the bike home.
9. A tire that is punctured can usually be patched, but you may not be able to fix one that has (*burst*, *busted*).
10. Many of the cycling accidents that happened last year (*could of*, *could have*) been avoided if cyclists and motorists had been more careful.

USAGE

▶ REVIEW A   **Proofreading a Paragraph for Correct Usage**

Each sentence in the following paragraph contains an error in English usage. Identify each error. Then write the correct usage.

EXAMPLE   [1] I should of known that the painting on the next page was done by Grandma Moses.
   1. *should of—should have*

MEETING INDIVIDUAL NEEDS

LEP/ESL

General Strategies. Some of the usage errors studied in this chapter appear in many American dialects. For example, many speakers of dialects say *a* for both *a* and *an*, *bad* for *bad* and *badly*, *don't* for *don't* and *doesn't*, *less* for *less* and *fewer*, and *good* for *good* and *well*. These appear in such spoken sentences as "Have a apple," "She don't like spinach," and "You did good." Tell your students that in standard English, which they will use in writing assignments, such distinctions are needed so that any speaker of English can easily read what they have written.

STUDENTS WITH SPECIAL NEEDS

Many learning disabled students have difficulty in working with large blocks of text because they tend to lose their place with unnumbered lines. With **Review A** and other paragraphs, you could have students break the paragraphs into individual sentences. Tell students first to number their papers to correspond with the sentences. Next, have them use spare sheets of paper to uncover one sentence at a time.

USAGE

OBJECTIVES

- To identify correct usage of words and expressions in sentences
- To write a letter to a friend, correctly using five words or expressions from the glossary

USAGE

VISUAL CONNECTIONS
Rockabye

About the Artist. Art critics refer to Grandma Moses as a modern primitive or folk artist. She first began expressing herself artistically by doing needlework, but failing eyesight forced her to abandon her yarn pictures. She then began painting with oils, a skill which didn't require the close concentration needed for needlework. Many of her paintings have been reproduced on Christmas cards.

RESOURCES

HE, SHE, THEY–TYPE
- Common Usage Problems B

QUICK REMINDER

Tell students that *like* is frequently used incorrectly for *as*. For an exercise, write the following sentences or phrases on the chalkboard, and ask students to choose the correct expressions:

1. This soup tastes salty, (*as if/like*) someone salted it twice.
2. Marian looks (*as though/like*) she might be asleep.
3. She is late in coming, (*as/like*) you are.

---

660 *A Glossary of Usage*

USAGE

1. an
2. have

4. already
5. fewer
6. except
7. good

8. between
9. can
10. all ready

[1] My art teacher gave me ∧ a̶ assignment to write a report about any artist I chose. [2] Of all the artists that I could ∧ o̶f̶ chosen, Grandma Moses appealed to me the most. [3] I went to the library and looked for a quiet place where I could do my research ∧ a̶t̶. [4] I learned that Anna Mary Robertson Moses didn't start painting until she was ∧ a̶l̶l̶ ̶r̶e̶a̶d̶y̶ in her seventies. [5] By then, her children were grown, and she had ∧ l̶e̶s̶s̶ responsibilities. [6] Grandma Moses had no art teacher ∧ a̶c̶c̶e̶p̶t̶ herself. [7] As you can see in the self-portrait *Rockabye*, Grandma Moses felt ∧ w̶e̶l̶l̶ about her role as a grandmother. [8] She holds one baby in her lap while the other one rocks in a cradle ∧ a̶m̶o̶n̶g̶ the artist and the dog. [9] You ∧ c̶a̶n̶'̶t̶ hardly help feeling that she really loves these children. [10] My report is ∧ a̶l̶r̶e̶a̶d̶y̶ for class now, and I can't wait to tell my classmates about this remarkable artist.

Grandma Moses: *Rockabye*. Copyright 1987, Grandma Moses Properties Co., New York

he, she, they Do not use an unnecessary pronoun after a noun. This error is called the *double subject*.

NONSTANDARD Isiah Thomas he was named Most Valuable Player.

STANDARD Isiah Thomas was named Most Valuable Player.

hisself, theirself, theirselves These words are nonstandard English. Use *himself* and *themselves*.

EXAMPLES Bob hurt **himself** [not *hisself*] during the game.
They served **themselves** [not *theirselves*] last.

how come In informal English, *how come* is often used instead of *why*. In formal English, *why* is always preferred.

INFORMAL I know how come he's upset.
FORMAL I know **why** he is upset.

its, it's *Its* is a personal pronoun in the possessive case. *It's* is a contraction of *it is* or *it has*.

EXAMPLES The kitten likes **its** new home. [possessive pronoun.]
We have Monday off because **it's** the Rosh Hashanah holiday. [contraction of *it is*]
It's been a long day. [contraction of *it has*]

kind, sort, type The words *this, that, these,* and *those* should agree in number with the words *kind, sort,* and *type. This* and *that* are singular. *These* and *those* are plural.

EXAMPLES **That kind** of watch is expensive. [singular]
Those kinds of jokes are silly. [plural]

kind of, sort of In informal English, *kind of* and *sort of* are often used to mean "somewhat" or "rather." In formal English, *somewhat* or *rather* is preferred.

INFORMAL I feel kind of tired.
FORMAL I feel **somewhat** tired.

learn, teach *Learn* means "to acquire knowledge." *Teach* means "to instruct" or "to show how."

EXAMPLES My brother is **learning** how to drive.
The driving instructor is **teaching** him.

less See **fewer, less.**

lie, lay See page 598.

USAGE

LEP/ESL

General Strategies. Many languages, such as Portuguese and Spanish, do not require a subject pronoun in a sentence when there is no noun subject. Also, some languages, such as Korean and Japanese, make a point of avoiding the use of subject pronouns. Learning that subject pronouns are necessary in English, as in "He went there," instead of "Went there," students might think they are necessary in all sentences in English and might try to use them when a subject noun is present—as in "That man he went there." Remind students to write subject pronouns only when subject nouns are not present.

LESS-ADVANCED STUDENTS

To help review the proper use of pronouns, you could have students create a pronoun collage. You will need to provide old magazines and newspapers, glue, scissors, and construction paper.

First, tell students to think about all the items that they own or that friends or family own. Then have them divide their papers into sections and label the sections with the possessive pronouns that will show who owns the items. For example, "Mine," "His," or "Theirs" could be categories. Last, have students cut out pictures that represent items for each category, arrange the pictures, and glue them to the paper.

USAGE

COMMON ERROR

Problem. Many students use *less* in sentences that require the use of *fewer*.

Solution. Tell students that *fewer* is used for things that can be counted, as in "Fewer than ten students passed the test," and *less* is used in situations in which precise units of measure are omitted, as in "There is less water in the lake since the dam broke." Remind students that *fewer* is used with plural nouns and *less* with singular.

INTEGRATING THE LANGUAGE ARTS

Usage and Library Skills. To increase students' familiarity with glossary use, use this library exercise. Tell students that many books, especially those about specialized subjects, have glossaries of difficult or specialized words that occur within the text. Ask them to find several books with glossaries; then have students compare the definitions in the glossaries with definitions in dictionaries.

like, as *Like* is a preposition and therefore introduces a prepositional phrase. In informal English, *like* is often used as a conjunction meaning "as." In formal English, *as* is always preferred.

EXAMPLES Your uncle's hat looked **like** a sombrero. [*Like* introduces the phrase *like a sombrero.*]
Marcia trained every day **as** the coach had suggested. [*As the coach had suggested* is a clause and needs the conjunction *as* (not the preposition *like*) to introduce it.]

☞ **REFERENCE NOTE:** For more information about prepositional phrases, see pages 491–497. For more information about clauses, see Chapter 18.

like, as if, as though In formal written English, *like* should not be used for the subordinating conjunction *as if* or *as though*.

EXAMPLES The Swedish limpa bread looks **as if** [not *like*] it is ready.
The car looks **as though** [not *like*] it needs to be washed.

might of, must of See **could of.**

nowheres See **anywheres,** etc.

▶ EXERCISE 3 **Identifying Correct Usage**

Choose the <u>correct word or words</u> in parentheses in each of the following sentences.

EXAMPLE **1.** Young rattlesnakes (*learn, teach*) themselves to use their rattles by imitating their parents.
1. *teach*

1. (*Its, It's*) a sound that most people have learned to dread.
2. As you can see on the next page, the snake's rattle consists of "buttons" of flesh at the end of (*its, it's*) tail, which are shaken against rings of loose skin.

3. The rings of skin (*themselves*, *theirselves*) are fragile and can break.
4. (*As*, *Like*) zookeepers have discovered, snakes that rattle at visitors all day may damage their rattles.
5. (*These kind*, *These kinds*) of snakes are highly poisonous, but they do not attack unless threatened.
6. Not all scientists agree about (*how come*, *why*) certain snakes have rattles.
7. According to many scientists, rattlesnakes (*they use*, *use*) the rattling sound to frighten enemies.
8. Other scientists believe that the rattles may act (*like*, *as*) signals allowing snakes to communicate with each other.
9. As the photograph shows, snakes don't have ears; however, they are (*sort of*, *rather*) sensitive to sound vibrations.
10. When people hear a rattlesnake, they react (*like*, *as if*) the situation is an emergency—and it is.

of Do not use *of* with prepositions such as *inside*, *off*, and *outside*.

> EXAMPLES   We waited **outside** [not *outside of*] the theater for the ticket window to open.
> The glass fell **off** [not *off of*] the table.
> Only Muslims are allowed **inside** [not *inside of*] the city of Mecca in Saudi Arabia.

USAGE

USAGE

Of is also unnecessary with *had*.

EXAMPLE If we **had** [not *had of*] tried harder, we would have won.

ought to of See **could of.**

real In informal English, the adjective *real* is often used as an adverb meaning "very" or "extremely." In formal English, *very* or *extremely* is preferred.

INFORMAL Basenji puppies are real quiet because they don't bark.
FORMAL Basenji puppies are *very* quiet because they don't bark.

rise, raise See pages 596–597.

she, he, they See **he,** etc.

should of See **could of.**

sit, set See page 595.

some, somewhat Do not use *some* for *somewhat* as an adverb.

NONSTANDARD I like classical music some.
STANDARD I like classical music **somewhat.**

PICTURE THIS

The year is 2045. You are a new crew member on a space station. The amazing view shown on the next page is your first glimpse of Earth from your new quarters. Write a letter to a friend back home describing what you see and explaining how the view makes you feel. In your letter, correctly use five of the following words or expressions.

already	hardly	ought	real
as if	good	its	except
like	less	it's	well

PICTURE THIS

As a prewriting exercise, you may wish to divide students into research teams of four or five to search through magazines for additional information about space travel. Suggest that students incorporate some of this data into their letters.

Subject: the view of Earth from space
Audience: a friend
Purpose: to describe the view and your reaction to it

somewheres See **anywheres,** etc.

sort See **kind,** etc.

sort of See **kind of,** etc.

take See **bring, take.**

teach See **learn, teach.**

than, then *Than* is a conjunction. *Then* is an adverb.

> EXAMPLES   I sing better **than** I act.
> We'll eat first, and **then** we'll ride our bikes.

that See **who,** etc.

that there See **this here, that there.**

their, there, they're *Their* is the possessive form of *they*. *There* is used to mean "at that place" or to begin a sentence. *They're* is a contraction of *they are*.

> EXAMPLES   Do you have **their** CDs?
> The lake is over **there**.
> **There** are five movie theaters in town.
> **They're** writing a report on the poet Américo Paredes.

TIMESAVER
Have students list on the back of their papers the glossary words they included in their letters. To check whether they accomplished the activity, look first for the sentences containing these words. Then you can score the rest of the writing holistically.

USAGE

LEP/ESL

Asian Languages. Several Asian languages, such as Chinese, Japanese, and Korean, have a common sentence form in which one first states the topic (usually a noun) and then comments on it, such as in the nonstandard English sentence "My aunt, she's coming to visit tomorrow." It is very natural for speakers of such languages to transfer this structure into English sentences, resulting in double subjects. Remind students that only one noun or pronoun is permitted before the verb in English, unless there is a conjunction to form a compound subject or there is a reflexive pronoun.

USAGE

theirself, theirselves See **hisself,** etc.

them *Them* should not be used as an adjective. Use *these* or *those.*

EXAMPLE   Where did you put **those** [not *them*] papers?

they See **he,** etc.

this here, that there The words *here* and *there* are not needed after *this* and *that.*

EXAMPLE   I like **this** [not *this here*] Chinese dragon kite, but I like **that** [not *that there*] one better.

this kind, sort, type See **kind,** etc.

try and In informal English, *try and* is often used for *try to.* In formal English, *try to* is preferred.

INFORMAL   I will try and be there early.
FORMAL   I will **try to** be there early.

type See **kind,** etc.

▶ EXERCISE 4   **Identifying Correct Usage**

Choose the <u>correct word or words</u> in parentheses in each of the following sentences.

EXAMPLE   **1.** The Amish people (*try and, try to*) maintain a simple, traditional way of life.
1. *try to*

1. In the early 1700s, the Amish were not allowed to practice (*<u>their</u>, they're, there*) religion in Germany and Switzerland.
2. Hearing that there was more freedom in North America (*<u>than</u>, then*) in Europe, the Amish came to the New World.
3. Since that time, they have remained (*outside of, <u>outside</u>*) the mainstream of American life.
4. The Amish work (*real, <u>very</u>*) hard at producing organically grown crops.

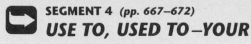

OBJECTIVE

• To identify correct usage of words and expressions in sentences

5. In Amish communities such as (*this*, *this here*) one, modern conveniences such as telephones, cars, and televisions are not used.

6. The closeness of Amish family life is evident in the way (*these*, *them*) people build their homes.

7. (*They're*, *There*, *Their*) are often three generations—grandparents, parents, and children—living in a large compound made up of several houses.

8. Pictures and photographs are not allowed (*inside of*, *inside*) Amish homes, but the Amish brighten their plain houses with colorful pillows, quilts, and rugs.

9. If an Amish person gets sick, he or she is almost always cared for by family members rather (*than*, *then*) by a doctor.

10. The Amish way of life might surprise you (*somewhat*, *some*), yet Amish communities have thrived in North America for nearly four hundred years.

use to, used to Be sure to add the *–d* to *use*. *Used to* is in the past form.

EXAMPLE Gail **used to** [not *use to*] be on the softball team.

way, ways Use *way*, not *ways*, in referring to a distance.

EXAMPLE Do we have a long **way** [not *ways*] to go?

USAGE

VISUAL CONNECTIONS
Ideas for Writing. After students have completed **Exercise 4**, have them pretend that they have been invited to spend a weekend with an Amish family on their farm. Ask students to write an expressive/descriptive paragraph about the visit. You could have students find more information in the library first. They can explain what work they may have observed, what they ate, what their hosts wore, what recreational activities they may have experienced, and how many generations of family members may have lived at the farm.

RESOURCES

> ***USE TO, USED TO–YOUR***
> • Common Usage Problems C

QUICK REMINDER
Tell students that *that* is most often used to introduce clauses that are essential to the meaning of a sentence. *Which*, on the other hand, most often introduces clauses that could be omitted without changing the meaning of the sentence. Write the following sentences on the chalkboard, and ask for volunteers to fill in the blanks:

1. This is the house ____ Jack built. [that]
2. This house, ____ Jack built, is very cold. [which]

USAGE

LEP/ESL

General Strategies. Many of the points of usage covered in this chapter are problems that native speakers of English have, such as using *like* for *as,* or *ways* instead of *way.* Native speakers will be familiar with such usages, while ESL students might wonder why certain points of usage are emphasized. Explain that many of the problems outlined in this chapter are derived from the differences in usage between dialect, which many Americans use, and standard English, which is used in writing.

USAGE

USAGE

well See **good, well.**

when, where Do not use *when* or *where* incorrectly in writing a definition.

NONSTANDARD	A *homophone* is when a word sounds like another word but has a different meaning and spelling.
STANDARD	A *homophone* is a word that sounds like another word but has a different meaning and spelling.

where Do not use *where* for *that.*

EXAMPLE Did you read in the newsletter **that** [not *where*] the teen center is closing?

who, which, that The relative pronoun *who* refers to people only. *Which* refers to things only. *That* refers to either people or things.

EXAMPLES Jolene is the one **who** called. [person]
Here is the salad, **which** is my favorite part of the meal. [thing]
The book **that** you want is here. [thing]
He is the salesperson **that** helped me choose the gift. [person]

who, whom See pages 619–620.

whose, who's *Whose* is the possessive form of *who. Who's* is a contraction of *who is* or *who has.*

EXAMPLES **Whose** book is this? [possessive pronoun]
Who's the new student? [contraction of *who is*]
Who's read "A Walk to the Jetty"? [contraction of *who has*]

without, unless Do not use the preposition *without* in place of the conjunction *unless.*

EXAMPLE I can't go **unless** [not *without*] I ask Dad.

would of See **could of.**

your, you're *Your* is the possessive form of *you. You're* is the contraction of *you are.*

> EXAMPLES **Your** Saint Patrick's Day party was great!
> **You're** a good friend.

▶ EXERCISE 5   **Identifying Correct Usage**

Choose the <u>correct word or words</u> in parentheses in the following sentences.

> EXAMPLE   **1.** Last week I received a letter from Sandra,
> (*who's, whose*) a good friend of mine.
> **1.** *who's*

1. When I opened the envelope, I saw (*where, <u>that</u>*) she had sent me these chopsticks and these instructions.

2. "I thought you'd like (*you're, <u>your</u>*) own pair of chopsticks, with instructions for how to use them," Sandra wrote.
3. Instructions like the ones Sandra sent me are helpful because chopsticks can be hard to use (<u>*unless*</u>, *without*) you are shown how.

USAGE

USAGE

REVIEW B

OBJECTIVE

- To compose five original sayings by using five standard words or expressions from the glossary

670 *A Glossary of Usage*

4. In the letter, Sandra told me (*that*, *where*) she and her family had taken a trip to visit her grandparents in New York City.
5. Because Sandra lives in a small town, she wasn't (*use*, *used*) to the crowds.
6. She especially enjoyed visiting Chinatown, (*which*, *who*) is located on Manhattan Island.
7. While her family was eating in a Chinese restaurant, one of the servers, (*which*, *who*) was very helpful, showed her how to use chopsticks.
8. "(*Your*, *You're*) not going to believe this," she wrote, "but by the end of the meal, I was using chopsticks quite well."
9. *Etiquette* is (*when you use good manners*, *the use of good manners*), and Sandra claimed, "It was only proper etiquette to use chopsticks to eat Chinese food."
10. I'll write Sandra that I have a long (*ways*, *way*) to go before I'm an expert in using chopsticks.

▶ REVIEW B **Writing Original Sayings with Correct Usage**

People throughout the world pass knowledge along from one generation to another. In many cases, such knowledge is stated in a sentence or two called a *folk saying*. While these sayings express bits of wisdom, they are also often humorous. You've probably heard some of the following folk sayings:

If you carry a light, you'll not fear the dark.
It is easier to hear a secret than to keep it.
Learn to behave from those who cannot.
Don't count your chickens before they're hatched.
Slow and steady wins the race.
A penny saved is a penny earned.
Lost time is never found again.

Write five sayings of your own. Base each saying on your own experiences or on things you've been told. In your

ANSWERS

Review B

Sayings will vary. Here are some additional examples:

1. It's better to be safe than sorry.

2. You can't teach an old dog new tricks.

3. Early to bed, early to rise makes a man healthy, wealthy, and wise.

4. There's more than one way to skin a cat.

5. You can't make an omelet without breaking a few eggs.

WRITING APPLICATION

OBJECTIVE
• To use formal standard English to write a five-minute television speech that expresses an opinion about a community issue

sayings, include the correct use of one of the words in five of the following items. Underline each of these words that you use.

good, well	like, as	who, which, that
its, it's	rise, raise	whose, who's
kind, sort, type	than, then	without, unless
learn, teach	way, ways	your, you're

EXAMPLE   **1.** *A horse that keeps walking can go a long <u>way</u>, as long as it doesn't walk in circles.*

WRITING APPLICATION

Using Formal English in a Speech

At formal occasions, you probably wear your best clothes and use your best manners. That's expected. In formal writing and speaking situations, people expect you to "dress up" your language. Of course, you can't put a report or a speech in a tuxedo, but you can express your ideas in formal standard English.

INFORMAL /
NONSTANDARD   I'm real upset that the mayor's Clean Air Commission ain't come up with a plan for shutting down that there incinerator.

FORMAL /
STANDARD   I am extremely upset that the mayor's Clean Air Commission has not thought of a plan for shutting down that incinerator.

▶ WRITING ACTIVITY
A local television station has started a new program called *Sound-Off*. Each speaker on the program gets five minutes on the air to express an opinion about a community issue. Some of the issues that have been addressed are crime prevention, pet leash laws, and the addition of more leagues

 WRITING APPLICATION
Suggest that students begin by stating their hypotheses as forcefully as possible. After students research the topics and before they make their rough outlines, suggest they list supporting arguments in ascending order of impact.

⚗ CRITICAL THINKING
Analysis
Before writing, students might want to ask classmates to argue against their supporting points so that they can test the strength of their conclusions.

Remind students that the purpose of this prewriting stage is to eliminate any weak points in their presentations and to expose any gaps in their arguments. Therefore, they must listen critically, analyze the two opposing points of view, and be prepared to reinforce their own supporting points with further research, if necessary. Once students are satisfied with their arguments, they can begin writing.

EVALUATING AND REVISING

Tell students to double-check their usage, grammar, and style. Because this is a speech, they will want to read the piece aloud. Phrases, clauses, and sentences should be arranged so that pauses in speaking can coincide with the punctuation of the sentences. Tell students to time their speeches so that the five-minute time limit is not exceeded.

📚 A DIFFERENT APPROACH

As a way of publishing this assignment, you may want to arrange a simulation of a television newscast or public affairs program during which students can present their papers. Design the format so that the audience (other students) can ask questions of the speakers or can provide other feedback.

for youth sports. Choose a topic that you think is important, and write a speech to submit to the TV station. Use only formal standard English in your speech.

Prewriting First, choose a specific topic that interests you. You might ask friends, classmates, or relatives to help you brainstorm some ideas. After you've selected your topic, jot down some notes about it. List important facts and information about the issue. Do you have all the information you need? If not, do some research at your school or local library. Also be sure to include your own feelings and opinions about your topic. Finally, make a rough outline of what you want to say.

Writing Use your notes and outline to help you write a draft of your speech. Try to write a lively introduction that will grab your listeners' attention. In your introduction, give a clear statement of opinion. (For more about statements of opinion, see page 262.) Then discuss each supporting point in a paragraph or two. Conclude your speech by restating your main point.

Evaluating and Revising Ask a friend to time you as you read your speech aloud. Then, ask your friend the following questions:

- Is the main idea clear?
- Does the speech give useful information?
- Is the speech convincing?
- Did you hear any informal expressions?

Use the **Glossary of Usage** in this chapter to help you revise any informal or nonstandard usages. If your speech runs longer than five minutes, you'll need to cut or revise some information.

Proofreading Read your speech slowly to check for any errors in grammar, spelling, or punctuation. Be sure that you have correctly spelled the names of people and organizations. (For more about capitalizing proper names, see pages 676–678.)

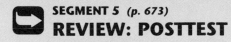

OBJECTIVE

- To recognize errors in usage and to revise sentences, using standard formal English

Review: Posttest

Revising Sentences by Correcting Errors in Usage

Each of the following sentences contains an error in usage. Write each sentence correctly, using standard formal English.

EXAMPLE   **1.** They did they're best to help.
         1. *They did their best to help.*

1. We are ∧already for our trip to Washington, D.C.   **1.** all ready
2. Can you tell the difference ∧among these three baseball mitts?   **2.** between
3. Please ∧take those packages to me.   **3.** bring
4. Elena had a cold, but she is feeling ∧good now.   **4.** well
5. Mr. Chang he is my t'ai chi instructor.
6. Will you ∧learn me how to throw a baseball?   **6.** teach
7. May I borrow that there collection of Cheyenne folk tales?
8. Tara might ∧of come with us, but she had to baby-sit.   **8.** have
9. We ∧use to live in Karachi, Pakistan.   **9.** used
10. She is the woman ∧which owns the Great Dane.   **10.** who
11. I dropped the pictures, but I think they're ∧alright.   **11.** all right
12. I read in the newspaper ∧where Mayor Alvarez will visit our school.   **12.** that
13. ∧Their the best players on the team.   **13.** They're
14. The pipes ∧busted last winter.   **14.** burst
15. We cannot go sailing ∧without we wear life jackets.   **15.** unless
16. Her new apartment is bigger ∧then her last one.   **16.** than
17. The group went ∧everywheres together.   **17.** everywhere
18. Lydia acted ∧like she was bored.   **18.** as if
19. *Antonyms* are when words ∧are opposite in meaning.   **19.** that
20. I hope that you will ∧except my apology.   **20.** accept
21. Have you played ∧you're new Natalie Cole CD?   **21.** your
22. Do you know ∧how come the library is closed today?   **22.** why
23. They ∧can't hardly wait for their vacation.   **23.** can
24. I feel ∧well when I am with my friends.   **24.** good
25. Those ∧kind of movies make me laugh.   **25.** kinds

USAGE

CHAPTER OVERVIEW

Basic rules of capitalization are outlined in this chapter. Students receive instruction for capitalizing the first words of sentences, the pronoun *I*, and school subjects. Detailed information is also given on capitalizing proper nouns, proper adjectives, and titles. In the **Writing Application**, students are called upon to apply their knowledge of correct capitalization to writing a friendly letter. The entire chapter or specific rules could provide a helpful review in the proofreading stage of writing assignments.

USING THE DIAGNOSTIC TEST

This test contains items relating to almost all of the rules in this chapter; therefore, you can use the test to determine which rules to focus on if you teach this chapter as a whole.

MECHANICS

MECHANICS

25 CAPITAL LETTERS

Rules for Capitalization

Diagnostic Test

Proofreading Sentences for Correct Capitalization

For each of the following sentences, find the <u>words that should be capitalized</u> but are not. Write the words correctly.

EXAMPLE **1.** The Mississippi river lies west of illinois.
            1. *River, Illinois*

1. At the <u>crossbay</u> <u>supermarket</u>, <u>i</u> bought a can of <u>jensen's</u> soup, a loaf of <u>garfield</u> bread, and a box of <u>zoom</u> soapflakes.
2. Aunt <u>janice</u>, who lives in <u>holbrook</u>, <u>arizona</u>, took me to visit <u>petrified</u> <u>forest</u> <u>national</u> <u>park</u>.
3. The <u>rosenbach</u> <u>foundation</u> in <u>philadelphia</u> is open to the public on <u>tuesday</u> and <u>friday</u> afternoons.
4. The <u>bijou</u> <u>theater</u> is next to my junior high school.
5. In world history class, we learned about <u>queen</u> <u>elizabeth</u> I, the defeat of the <u>spanish</u> <u>armada</u>, and the <u>age</u> of <u>exploration</u>.

SEGMENT 2 *(pp. 675–685)*
FIRST WORDS, PRONOUN *I*, PROPER NOUNS Rules 25a–25c

OBJECTIVES

- To proofread and revise sentences and paragraphs for correct capitalization of the first words of sentences or quotations, the pronoun *I*, and proper nouns ☞

Diagnostic Test **675**

25a

6. Ares, <u>hera</u>, and <u>zeus</u> are <u>greek</u> gods whose <u>roman</u> names are <u>mars</u>, <u>juno</u>, and <u>jupiter</u>.
7. *The <u>wind</u> in the <u>willows</u>* is a famous children's book.
8. Dave's <u>housewares</u> <u>store</u> has moved from <u>sixteenth</u> <u>avenue</u> to <u>front street</u>. **8.** [or housewares store]
9. The <u>lozi</u> people in <u>africa</u> live near the Zambezi <u>river</u>.
10. "Stopping by <u>woods</u> on a <u>snowy</u> <u>evening</u>" is by <u>robert</u> <u>frost</u>, an <u>american</u> poet from <u>new</u> <u>england</u>.
11. Do you know when <u>david</u> <u>souter</u> was appointed to the <u>supreme</u> <u>court</u>?
12. Next <u>monday</u> is <u>memorial</u> <u>day</u>.
13. When we traveled through the <u>south</u>, we visited the <u>antietam</u> <u>national</u> <u>battlefield</u> at <u>sharpsburg</u>, <u>maryland</u>.
14. Shirley <u>ling</u> came from <u>hong</u> <u>kong</u> last year, and she is teaching us about <u>chinese</u> culture.
15. Cayuga <u>lake</u> stretches north from <u>ithaca</u>, <u>new</u> <u>york</u>.
16. The main religion in <u>indonesia</u> is <u>islam</u>, but there are many <u>indonesian</u> <u>buddhists</u> and <u>hindus</u>.
17. My older sister, who goes to <u>lincoln</u> <u>high</u> <u>school</u>, is taking <u>spanish</u>, history, <u>mathematics</u> II, and art.
18. Carlos and <u>i</u> had sandwiches made of <u>polish</u> ham with <u>german</u> mustard on <u>french</u> bread.
19. We turned west onto <u>route</u> 95 and stayed on it for five miles.
20. George <u>copway</u>, who was born in <u>canada</u>, wrote about his people, the <u>ojibwa</u>.

25a. Capitalize the first word in every sentence.

EXAMPLES **That** dog knows several tricks. **It** will shake hands or roll over when **I** tell it to.

The first word of a direct quotation should begin with a capital letter, whether or not the quotation starts the sentence.

EXAMPLE Mrs. Hernandez said, **"Don't** forget to bring your contributions for the bake sale."

MECHANICS

QUICK REMINDER

Ask students the following questions and have them answer orally:

1. What pronoun is always capitalized? [*I*]

2. When should a common noun be capitalized? [first word of a direct quotation or of a sentence, as part of a title]

3. What are some types of geographical names that should be capitalized? [continents, countries, cities, towns, states, islands, bodies of water, streets, parks, mountains, sections of the country]

MEETING INDIVIDUAL NEEDS

LEP/ESL

General Strategies. Many languages, such as Chinese, Japanese, Korean, Lao, Thai, Hindi, Arabic, and Hebrew, have no capital letters. Not having grown up seeing the interplay of capital and small letters, some students who speak these languages may have trouble understanding the importance of capital letters in English. Make sure that students know that speakers of English consider the correct use of capital letters important. You may also want to give students extra practice using capital letters. Have them focus on capitalization when they are proofreading their writing.

676

---

676 *Capital Letters*

Traditionally, the first word of every line of poetry begins with a capital letter.

EXAMPLE
In the night
The rain comes down.
Yonder at the edge of the earth
There is a sound like cracking,
There is a sound like falling.
Down yonder it goes on slowly rumbling.
It goes on shaking.

A Papago poem, "In the Night"

NOTE: Some modern poets do not follow this style. If you are quoting from a poem, be sure to follow the capitalization that the poet uses.

☞ **REFERENCE NOTE:** For information about using capital letters in quotations, see pages 737–738.

25b. Capitalize the pronoun *I*.

EXAMPLE   This week **I** have to write two papers.

25c. Capitalize proper nouns.

A *proper noun* names a particular person, place, thing, or idea. Such a word is always capitalized. A *common noun* names a kind or type of person, place, thing, or idea. A common noun is not capitalized unless it begins a sentence or is part of a title.

PROPER NOUNS	COMMON NOUNS
Central High School	high school
Saturday	day
Barbara Jordan	woman
Cambodia	country
Lassie	dog
USS *Nautilus*	submarine

REFERENCE NOTE: For information about using capital letters in abbreviations, see pages 703–704.

Some proper nouns consist of more than one word. In these names, short prepositions (those of fewer than five letters) and articles (*a, an, the*) are not capitalized.

EXAMPLES   **House of Representatives
Ivan the Terrible**

 REFERENCE NOTE: For more discussion of proper nouns, see page 424.

(1) Capitalize the names of persons.

EXAMPLES   **Monica Sone, Aaron Neville, Mrs. Abrams,
Charlayne Hunter-Gault**

(2) Capitalize geographical names.

TYPE OF NAME	EXAMPLES	
Continents	Europe Antarctica	South America Asia
Countries	Australia El Salvador	Egypt Finland
Cities, Towns	Miami Los Angeles	Indianapolis Manila
States	Tennessee Rhode Island	Delaware Wyoming
Islands	Aleutian Islands Crete	Long Island Isle of Pines
Bodies of Water	Amazon River Chesapeake Bay Suez Canal	Lake Ontario Jackson's Pond Indian Ocean
Streets, Highways	Main Street Eighth Avenue	Canary Lane Ventura Highway

NOTE: In a hyphenated street number, the second part of the number is not capitalized.

EXAMPLE   West Thirty-fourth Street

MECHANICS

MECHANICS

INTEGRATING THE LANGUAGE ARTS

Literature Link. You may want to direct students to some examples of poems that begin every line with a capital letter and to other poems that do not. You can find many suitable examples in literature anthologies. For example, Emily Dickinson begins each line with a capital letter in "I'm Nobody," while Carl Sandburg does not begin each line in "Fog" with a capital letter. Ask students if they think such a style difference matters, and discuss how the flow of a poem such as "Fog" would be different if each line did begin with a capital letter.

ADVANCED STUDENTS

You could have students choose countries that interest them and write short, informative reports about those countries. Have students underline and correctly capitalize all proper nouns in their reports.

Other students might like to make detailed maps of countries and label all important cities, regions, bodies of water, parks, and mountains. Remind students to capitalize all geographical names.

LEARNING STYLES

Kinetic, Auditory, and Visual Learners. You might go through the chapter with students by reading each rule aloud. This procedure will give students an overview of capitalization use. Call students' attention to the **Summary Style Sheet** at the end of the chapter; students can use this summary in the proofreading stage of writing assignments. You could also have students create similar style sheets to display on a bulletin board as your class studies the chapter.

TYPE OF NAME	EXAMPLES	
Parks and Forests	Yosemite Park Sherwood Forest	Everglades National Park
Mountains	Catskills Mount Fuji	Mount Everest Alps
Sections of the Country	New England the West	Corn Belt the Southeast

NOTE: Words such as *east, west, north,* or *south* are not capitalized when the words merely indicate *direction.*

EXAMPLES   A car was going **west** on Oak Street. [direction]
The **S**outh has produced some of America's great writers. [section of the country]

EXERCISE 1   **Correcting Errors in Capitalization**

Each of the following sentences contains <u>errors in capitalization</u>. Correct these errors by either changing capital letters to small letters or by changing small letters to capital letters.   Words that should be capitalized or lower-cased are underscored.

EXAMPLE   **1.** The original Settlers of hawaii came from the marquesas islands and tahiti.
1. *settlers, Hawaii, Marquesas Islands, Tahiti*

1. <u>our</u> <u>Class</u> is studying about <u>hawaii</u>.
2. The Hawaiian <u>islands</u> are located in the <u>pacific ocean</u>, nearly three thousand miles <u>West</u> of <u>san francisco</u>, <u>california</u>.
3. Hawaii became the fiftieth <u>State</u> in the <u>united</u> <u>states</u> in 1959.
4. Our teacher, <u>ms</u>. Jackson, explained that the <u>Capital City</u> is <u>honolulu</u>, and it is located on the southeast <u>Coast</u> of <u>oahu</u> <u>island</u>.
5. The largest of the <u>Islands</u> is <u>hawaii</u>.
6. On the southeast shore of <u>hawaii</u> <u>island</u> is <u>hawaii</u> <u>volcanoes</u> <u>national</u> <u>park</u>.
7. Ms. Jackson asked, "<u>can</u> anyone name one of the <u>Volcanoes</u> there?"

MECHANICS

MECHANICS

8. Since i have been reading about <u>National</u> <u>Parks</u>, i raised my hand.
9. "The <u>Park</u> has two active volcanoes, <u>mauna</u> Loa and <u>kilauea</u>," I answered.

10. "This picture shows how lava from <u>kilauea's</u> 1989 eruption threatened everything in its path," I added.

(3) Capitalize names of organizations, teams, businesses, institutions, and government bodies.

TYPE OF NAME	EXAMPLES	
Organizations	Drama Club Girl Scouts	Modern Language Association
Teams	Boston Celtics Dallas Cowboys	Los Angeles Dodgers
Businesses	Sears, Roebuck and Co.	Fields Department Store
Institutions	Westside Regional Hospital	Roosevelt Junior High School
Government Bodies	United Nations Peace Corps York City Council	Office of Management and Budget

NOTE: Do not capitalize such words as *hotel, theater,* or *high school* unless they are part of the name of a particular building or institution.

EXAMPLES **Capital Theater**   a theater
Lane Hotel   the hotel
Taft High School   this high school

MECHANICS

AT-RISK STUDENTS

   Provide a questionnaire for students that personalizes the application of the capitalization rules for proper nouns.

   Here are some questions that you could include:

1. What are the full names of your parents or guardians?
2. Name the schools that you have attended.
3. Name the state, county, and city in which you live.
4. What is your full address?
5. What are the names of some shops or restaurants that you like to visit?
6. What is your birth date and on what day of the week were you born?
7. What brands of cereals do you like?

MECHANICS

679

MECHANICS

ANSWERS
Exercise 2

Before students begin this exercise, you may want to specify a length for their short stories. Students' short stories should include at least five words from the map, and students should follow **Rules 25a–25c.**

 A DIFFERENT APPROACH
Have each student (or small group of students) write one sentence, which may be quite long, that illustrates as many of the subrules of **Rules 25a–25c** as possible.

MECHANICS

 EXERCISE 2 **Using Capitalization Correctly**

Mark Twain and his famous character Huckleberry Finn had many adventures on the Mississippi River. It's a big, long river with room for many adventures! Write your own short story about traveling on the Mississippi. Use the map below to tell about the journey. In your story, use at least five words from the map. Remember to capitalize all names of persons and geographical names.

EXAMPLE *Early on the fourth day, Jason and she knew they were in Kentucky.*

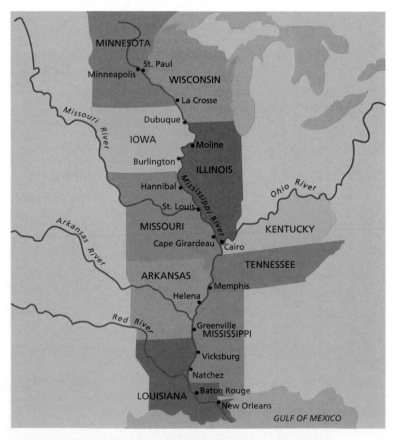

(4) Capitalize the names of historical events and periods, special events, and calendar items.

TYPE OF NAME	EXAMPLES	
Historical Events and Periods	Revolutionary War Middle Ages Renaissance	United States Bicentennial Age of Reason
Special Events	Texas State Fair Special Olympics	Super Bowl Festival of States
Calendar Items	Monday February	Memorial Day Thanksgiving Day

NOTE: Do *not* capitalize the name of a season unless it is part of a proper name.

EXAMPLES the **f**all semester
     the Quebec **W**inter Carnival

(5) Capitalize the names of nationalities, races, and peoples.

EXAMPLES **M**exican, **N**igerian, **C**aucasian, **I**roquois

NOTE: The words *black* and *white* may or may not be capitalized when they refer to races.

EXAMPLE In the 1960s, both **B**lacks and **W**hites [*or* blacks and whites] worked to end segregation.

(6) Capitalize the brand names of business products.

EXAMPLES **L**ux soap, **G**eneral **E**lectric stove, **P**epsi **C**ola **b**ottle [Notice that the names of the types of products are not capitalized.]

(7) Capitalize the names of ships, trains, airplanes, and spacecraft.

TYPE OF NAME	EXAMPLES	
Ships	*Queen Elizabeth 2*	*Kon Tiki*
Trains	*City of New Orleans*	*Orient Express*
Airplanes	*Air Force One*	*Spruce Goose*
Spacecraft	*Voyager II*	*Sputnik*

MECHANICS

MECHANICS

A DIFFERENT APPROACH

Make up some broad categories based on the eleven subrules of **Rule 25c**, such as names of female singers, businesses in a well-known mall, holidays, and heavenly bodies. Divide the class into two teams and, at random, choose one of the categories to begin the game. Then tell one of the teams to select a specific, capitalized name to fit the category and write that name on the chalkboard. The next team does the same, and play using that category continues until one team cannot give a name. The team with the last answer gets a point. Then, at random, choose another category. The game can continue as long as time and categories permit; the team with the most points wins.

(8) Capitalize the names of buildings and other structures.

EXAMPLES Sydney Opera House, World Trade Center, Aswan Dam, Eiffel Tower, Brooklyn Bridge

(9) Capitalize the names of monuments and awards.

TYPE OF NAME	EXAMPLES	
Monuments	Statue of Liberty Lincoln Memorial	Tomb of the Unknown Soldier
Awards	Emmy Award Nobel Prize	Distinguished Service Medal

(10) Capitalize the names of religions and their followers, holy days, sacred writings, and specific deities.

TYPE OF NAME	EXAMPLES	
Religions and Followers	Judaism Hinduism	Christian Muslim
Holy Days	Easter Ramadan	Yom Kippur Christmas Eve
Sacred Writings	Koran Bible	Talmud Upanishads
Specific Deities	God Allah	Jehovah Krishna

NOTE: The word *god* is not capitalized when it refers to a god of ancient mythology. The names of specific gods *are* capitalized.

EXAMPLE The king of the Norse gods was Odin.

(11) Capitalize the names of planets, stars, and other heavenly bodies.

EXAMPLES Mercury, Venus, Sirius, Andromeda, Ursa Major

NOTE: The word *earth* is not capitalized unless it is used along with the names of other heavenly bodies. The words *moon* and *sun* are not capitalized.

EXAMPLES   Oceans cover three fourths of the **earth's** surface.
Which is largest—Saturn, **Earth**, or the **moon**?

▶ EXERCISE 3   **Proofreading Sentences for Correct Capitalization**

For each of the following sentences, supply capital letters where they belong. Words that should be capitalized are underscored.

EXAMPLE   **1.** Each arbor day the students at franklin junior high school plant a tree.
1. *Arbor Day, Franklin Junior High School*

1. The golden gate bridge is a suspension bridge that spans san francisco bay.
2. Yosemite national park in california has the nation's highest waterfall.
3. The peace corps became an agency of the federal government by an act of congress.
4. On august 4, 1984, upper volta, a nation in africa, changed its name to burkina faso.
5. Thousands of cherokee people live in the smoky mountains in and around cherokee, north carolina.
6. To stop flooding in the south, the tennessee valley authority, a government agency, built twenty-six dams on the tennessee river and the streams that flow into it.
7. The first two states to be admitted to the united states were delaware and pennsylvania.
8. On new year's day, many fans crowd into football stadiums for the annual bowl games.
9. The rose bowl is the oldest of these annual football bowl games.
10. A noted scholar, thomas jefferson, founded the university of virginia.

MECHANICS

INTEGRATING THE LANGUAGE ARTS

Technology Link. You may want to have students call up information on capitalization using a style- and grammar-checking computer program. As students ask questions and receive information from the program, point out how the information in the computer program reinforces the rules in the textbook. Discuss possible reasons for any differences between the two.

MECHANICS

EXERCISE 4   **Proofreading Paragraphs for Correct Capitalization**

In the following paragraphs all capital letters have been omitted. Rewrite the paragraphs, using capitals wherever they are needed.   Words that should be capitalized are underscored.

the branford mall is the largest in melville county. it is on jefferson parkway, two miles north of duck lake state park and the big bridge that crosses duck lake. across the parkway from the mall is the new branford high school with its parking lots, playing fields, and stadium, home of the branford panthers. near the mall are the american legion hall, bowlerama, and king skating rink.

the mall has two jewelry stores, nicholson's department store, the palace cinema, and thirty-five other businesses. they range from small stationery stores to the finest restaurant in the midwest. the restaurant larue is run by marie and jean larue, who are from france. also in the mall is the american paper box company, which sells boxes for every packaging need. an outlet store for northwestern leather goods of chicago sells uffizi purses and wallets.

 REVIEW A   **Correcting Errors in Capitalization**

Each of the following sentences contains errors in capitalization. Correct these errors by either changing capital letters to small letters or changing small letters to capital letters.   Words that should be capitalized or lower-cased are underscored.

EXAMPLE   **1.** African americans in massachusetts have played an important part in american history.
       1. *Americans, Massachusetts, American*

1. In Boston, the Crispus attucks monument is a memorial to attucks and the other men who died in the boston Massacre.
2. According to many Historians, attucks was a former slave who fought against the british in the american Revolution.

685

W.E.B. Du Bois

Jan Ernst Matzeliger

Amherst
Northampton
• Great
Barrington
Springfield
Worcester
Lynn
Cambridge
Boston
ATLANTIC
OCEAN
Plymouth
Rock
Cape
Cod
New Bedford
Martha's
Vineyard
Nantucket
Island

Crispus Attucks

3. The <u>department</u> of the Interior has made the <u>Home</u> of <u>maria</u> <u>baldwin</u> a historic building in <u>cambridge</u>.
4. Baldwin was a <u>Leader</u> in the <u>league</u> for Community Service, an <u>Organization</u> to help the <u>Needy</u>.
5. One of the founders of the National <u>association</u> for the Advancement of <u>colored</u> <u>people</u>, <u>w</u>.<u>e</u>.<u>b</u>. Du Bois, was born in <u>great</u> Barrington, Massachusetts.
6. A marker stands on the <u>Spot</u> where Du Bois lived.
7. Jan <u>ernst</u> <u>matzeliger</u>, who lived in <u>lynn</u>, invented a machine that made <u>Shoes</u> easier and cheaper to manufacture.
8. The <u>nantucket</u> <u>whaling</u> Museum has information about Peter <u>green</u>, a <u>Sailor</u> and <u>Second</u> <u>Mate</u> on the ship *john* Adams.
9. During a storm at sea, Green saved the <u>Ship</u> and crew after the <u>Captain</u> and <u>First</u> <u>Mate</u> had drowned.
10. Use the <u>Map</u> of Massachusetts shown above to locate the <u>Towns</u> and <u>Cities</u> in which these notable <u>african</u> Americans lived.

MEETING
INDIVIDUAL
NEEDS

ADVANCED STUDENTS

Students who have a firm grasp of **Rules 25a–25c** might want to examine some works by modern writers who use capitalization in creative, unusual ways (such as poet E. E. Cummings). Tell students to find examples of creative capitalization and to write short analyses that give their opinions about why the authors chose to break or bend the rules.

LEARNING STYLES

Visual Learners. Have students read magazine or newspaper articles and list all the proper nouns they can find. Then have students cite the subrule of **Rule 25c** that governs the capitalization of each of the proper nouns on their lists.

MECHANICS

MECHANICS

685

PROPER ADJECTIVES, COURSE NAMES
• Using Capital Letters B

QUICK REMINDER

Write these proper nouns on the chalkboard, and ask students to tell you the proper adjectives that can be formed from them:

1. France [French]
2. Alaska [Alaskan]
3. Egypt [Egyptian]
4. Spain [Spanish]
5. Victoria [Victorian]
6. China [Chinese]

MEETING
INDIVIDUAL
NEEDS

LEP/ESL

General Strategies. In many languages, adjectives derived from proper nouns are not capitalized. For example, *French,* used as an adjective as in *French food,* translates as *ranskalainen* in Finnish, *français* in French, *frankisch* in German, *frantsuzskiy* in Russian, *francuski* in Serbo-Croatian, and *frances* in Spanish. You may want to let students tell you about capitalization rules in their languages and how they differ from English rules. Discussion of this sort may help students remember English capitalization rules.

PROPER ADJECTIVES, COURSE NAMES
Rules 25d, 25e

OBJECTIVES

- To proofread and revise sentences for correct capitalization of proper adjectives and the names of school subjects
- To write a fictional letter that includes at least three proper nouns and two proper adjectives

686 *Capital Letters*

25d. Capitalize proper adjectives.

A *proper adjective* is formed from a proper noun and is always capitalized.

PROPER NOUN	PROPER ADJECTIVE
Greece	Greek theater
Mars	Martian moons
Darwin	Darwinian theory
Japan	Japanese tea ceremony

25e. Do *not* capitalize the names of school subjects, except course names followed by a number and languages.

EXAMPLES   history, typing, mathematics, English, Spanish, Latin, History 101, Music III, Art Appreciation I

EXERCISE 5   Proofreading Sentences for Correct Capitalization

In each of the following sentences, find the word or words that should be capitalized but are not. Write the words correctly.

EXAMPLE   **1.** Rosa said we were eating real mexican *fajitas.*
    1. *Mexican*

1. The program featured russian ballet dancers.
2. The european Common Market helps improve international trade.
3. The scandinavian countries include both Norway and Sweden.
4. In geography, we learned about the platypus and the koala, two australian animals.
5. Many great english plays were written during the elizabethan age.

6. I am planning to take <u>computer</u> I next year.
7. On the floor was a large <u>persian</u> rug.
8. England, France, Scotland, Russia, and the United States played important roles in <u>canadian</u> history.
9. The back yard was decorated with <u>chinese</u> lanterns.
10. Have you ever tasted <u>indian</u> rice pudding?

PICTURE THIS

The year is 1845. You and your family are pioneers traveling west in one of these covered wagons. You are using this map to find your way from St. Louis to Los Angeles. Write a letter describing your journey to a friend back in St. Louis. You may want to tell about your fellow pioneers, the towns you've passed through, or the rivers and stretches of land you've crossed. You may also want to mention some of the people, places, and things you miss back home. In your letter, use at least three proper nouns and two proper adjectives.

Subject: heading west in a covered wagon
Audience: a friend
Purpose: to describe your journey

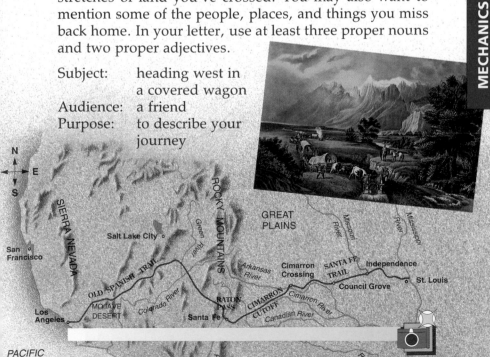

MECHANICS

PICTURE THIS

It might help spark students' imaginations to read about subjects related to this assignment. To give students an understanding of what it would be like to move constantly, have them read Francisco Jiménez's short story "The Circuit," which is about the young son of migrant workers. To help students visualize the countryside along the way, have them read Nina Otero's "The Wind in the Mountains," a nonfiction selection about the area around Santa Fé.

For an example of descriptive writing, refer students to **A Student Model** on page 172.

MECHANICS

OBJECTIVE

• To proofread and revise sentences for correct capitalization of titles

 **QUICK REMINDER**

Write the following sentences on the chalkboard. Have students copy the sentences and correct any errors in capitalization.

1. The principal, mrs. Lopez, asked my Mother to sing "The star-spangled banner" at the assembly.
2. Did you see aunt Evelyn's picture in the *Arkansas gazette,* doctor?
3. I think her Uncle Rick is reading *a Tale Of Two Cities.*

MEETING INDIVIDUAL NEEDS

LEP/ESL

Spanish. In Spanish, only the first letter of the first word of the title of a book, article, or movie is capitalized, as in the title of the Mexican novel *Los de abajo* (*The Ones from Below*). Consequently, when using English, students might have difficulty determining which words in titles to capitalize. Help them by showing a variety of titles, so that they get a sense of which words in titles are capitalized in English.

MECHANICS

688

MECHANICS

688 *Capital Letters*

25f. Capitalize titles.

(1) Capitalize the title of a person when the title comes before a name.

EXAMPLES **President Lincoln**   **Mrs. Wendell**
Mayor Bradley   **Commissioner Rodriguez**

☞ **REFERENCE NOTE:** For more information about abbreviations, see pages 703–704.

(2) Capitalize a title used alone or following a person's name only when you want to emphasize the title of someone holding a high office.

EXAMPLE The **S**ecretary of Defense held a news conference. Lien Fong, class **s**ecretary, read the minutes.

A title used by itself in direct address is usually capitalized.

EXAMPLES Is it very serious, **D**octor? How do you do, **S**ir [*or* sir]?

(3) Capitalize a word showing a family relationship when the word is used before or in place of a person's name.

EXAMPLES We expect **U**ncle **F**red and **A**unt **H**elen soon. We always go to **G**randma **L**owery's house for Thanksgiving dinner. Both **M**om and **D**ad work at the hospital.

Do not capitalize a word showing a family relationship when a possessive comes before the word.

EXAMPLE We asked Pedro's **m**other and his **a**unt Celia to be chaperons.

(4) Capitalize the first and last words and all important words in titles of books, magazines, newspapers, poems, short stories, movies, television programs, works of art, and musical compositions.

25f

Unimportant words in titles include

- articles (*a, an, the*)
- coordinating conjunctions (*and, but, for, nor, or, so, yet*)
- prepositions of fewer than five letters (such as *by, for, on, with*)

TYPE OF NAME	EXAMPLES	
Books	*The Mask of Apollo* *Mules and Men* *The Foxfire Book*	*Chicano Authors:* *Inquiry by* *Interview*
Magazines	*Popular Mechanics* *Ebony*	*Seventeen* *Sports Illustrated*
Newspapers	the *Miami Herald* the *Houston Post*	the *Wall Street* *Journal*
Poems	"Season at the Shore"	"In Time of Silver Rain"
Short Stories	"The Night the Bed Fell"	"Zlateh the Goat"
Movies	*Dances with Wolves*	*It's a Wonderful* *Life*
Television Programs	*Life Goes On* *In Living Color*	*Star Trek: The* *Next Generation*
Works of Art	*Mona Lisa* *David*	*The Old Guitarist* *Mankind's Struggle*
Musical Compositions	"America the Beautiful"	*The Marriage* *of Figaro*

NOTE: The article *the* before a title is not capitalized unless it is the first word of the title.

EXAMPLES   My father reads the *Wall Street Journal.*
Does she work for *The Georgia Review*?

☞ **REFERENCE NOTE:** For guidelines on what titles are italicized, see pages 735–736. For guidelines on what titles are enclosed in quotation marks, see pages 743–744.

MECHANICS

 INTEGRATING THE LANGUAGE ARTS

Mechanics and Listening. Have students interview at least five people to get answers to the following questions:

1. What is your favorite book?
2. What is your favorite magazine?
3. What is your favorite movie?
4. What is your least favorite movie?
5. What is your favorite television show?

Remind students to capitalize titles correctly as they record responses.

MECHANICS

INTEGRATING THE LANGUAGE ARTS

Capitalization and Punctuation. Some students may be confused about when to use underlining (italics) with titles and when to use quotation marks with titles. Be sure that students understand that they should use underlining (italics) for titles of books, periodicals, movies, television programs, and works of art, and that they should use quotation marks to enclose the titles of short works such as articles, short stories, poems, and songs.

TIMESAVER

Since **Reviews B–D** and the **Posttest** cover the same material (**Rules 25a–25f**), you may not want to assign all of them. You could make assignments based on students' understanding and their application of the rules in previous exercises and activities.

REVIEWS B and C

OBJECTIVE

- To proofread and revise sentences for correct capitalization of the first words of sentences, proper nouns, proper adjectives, school subjects, and titles

▶ EXERCISE 6 **Proofreading Sentences for Correct Capitalization**

Write the following sentences, using capitals wherever they are needed. Words that should be capitalized are underscored.

EXAMPLE **1.** The series *all creatures great and small* is being rerun on public television.
1. *The series* All Creatures Great and Small *is being rerun on public television.*

1. While waiting to interview <u>mayor</u> <u>ward</u>, I read an article in *<u>newsweek</u>*.
2. Have you read <u>leslie</u> <u>marmon</u> <u>silko's</u> poem "<u>story</u> from <u>bear</u> <u>country</u>"?
3. You have probably seen a picture of *<u>the</u> <u>thinker</u>*, one of <u>rodin's</u> best-known sculptures.
4. On television last night we saw a movie called *<u>the</u> <u>three</u> <u>faces</u> of <u>eve</u>*.
5. This year voters will elect a president and several <u>united</u> <u>states</u> senators.
6. Uncle <u>nick</u> read aloud from <u>francisco</u> <u>jiménez's</u> short story "<u>the</u> <u>circuit</u>."
7. The reporter asked, "Can you tell us, <u>senator</u> <u>inouye</u>, when you plan to announce the committee's final decision?"
8. The main speaker was <u>dr</u>. <u>andrew</u> <u>holt</u>, a former president of the <u>university</u> of <u>tennessee</u>.
9. Besides <u>uncle</u> <u>don</u>, our visitors included <u>aunt</u> <u>pat</u>, <u>aunt</u> <u>jean</u>, both of my grandmothers, and my great-grandfather.
10. The <u>president</u> met with his advisers before he spoke to the nation.

▶ REVIEW B **Proofreading Sentences for Correct Capitalization**

Each of the following sentences contains at least one error in capitalization. Write correctly the <u>words that require capital letters</u>.

EXAMPLE   **1.** The waters of the caribbean are pleasantly warm.
           1. *Caribbean*

1. The greeks believed that zeus, the king of the gods, lived on mount olympus.
2. The *titanic* sank after hitting an iceberg off the coast of newfoundland.
3. My cousin collects scandinavian pottery.
4. Stephanie is taking english, math II, biology, and world history.
5. On friday we were cheered by the thought that monday, memorial day, would be a holiday.
6. that chair is made of teakwood.
7. I wanted to name my persian cat after the chief justice of the supreme court.
8. In *roots*, alex haley, a famous journalist, traces the history of his family.
9. She usually travels to boston on american airlines.
10. The quaker oats company has introduced a new corn cereal.

▶ REVIEW C   **Proofreading a Paragraph for Correct Capitalization**

Each sentence in the following paragraph contains at least one error in capitalization. Write correctly the words that require capital letters.

EXAMPLE   [1] Before the thanksgiving holidays, i learned some interesting facts about africa in my history II class.
           1. *Thanksgiving, I, Africa, History II*

[1] My teacher, mr. davidson, told us about the mighty kingdoms and empires that existed for hundreds of years in africa. [2] some of these kingdoms dated back to the time of the roman empire. [3] Others rose to power during the period known as the middle ages in europe. [4] For many years, the people in the kingdom of cush did ironwork and traded along the nile river. [5] Later, the cush

MECHANICS

were defeated by the people of <u>axum</u>, led by <u>king ezana</u>. [6] As you can see in the map below, kingdoms in <u>west africa</u> developed between <u>lake chad</u> and the <u>atlantic ocean</u>. [7] Three of these kingdoms were <u>ghana</u>, <u>mali</u>, and <u>songhai</u>. [8] These kingdoms established important trade routes across the <u>sahara desert</u>. [9] Mali's famous university attracted <u>egyptian</u> and other <u>arab</u> students. [10] I read more about these <u>african</u> kingdoms and empires in our textbook, <u>*world*</u> <u>*history: people*</u> and <u>*nations*</u>.

VISUAL CONNECTIONS
Exploring the Subject. The kingdom of Cush (also spelled *Kush*) was founded sometime before 2000 B.C. and continued until about A.D. 350. Cush was important as a center for the exchange of ideas and as a center for trade. People from other African civilizations and from the Mediterranean and the Near East shared knowledge of metals, farming, art, politics, and religion. These people also came to Cush to trade slaves, cattle, gold, and ivory.

MECHANICS

MECHANICS

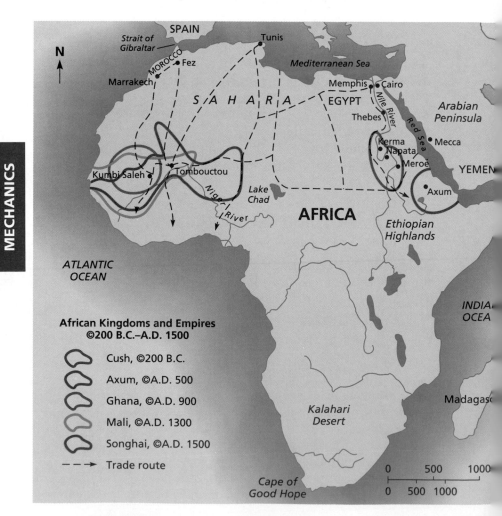

African Kingdoms and Empires
©200 B.C.–A.D. 1500

Cush, ©200 B.C.
Axum, ©A.D. 500
Ghana, ©A.D. 900
Mali, ©A.D. 1300
Songhai, ©A.D. 1500
- - -> Trade route

WRITING APPLICATION

Using Capital Letters to Make Your Writing Clear

Used correctly, capital letters help your readers understand your writing. Capital letters signal that you mean a particular person, place, thing, or idea. Compare the following sentences:

I'd like to see the white house.
I'd like to see the White House.

The capital letters in the second sentence completely change the meaning of the sentence. The second sentence refers to the home of the President of the United States, not to just any "white house."

WRITING ACTIVITY

Students in your class have become pen pals with students in another country. You have been given the name of someone to write to. Write a letter to your pen pal introducing yourself and telling about your school and your community. In your letter, be sure to use capitalization correctly.

 Prewriting Note down the information you want to give in your letter. You may wish to include some of the following information:

- your age
- a description of yourself
- your favorite books, movies, actors, or musicians
- the name of your school
- the courses you are taking in school this year
- some clubs, organizations, or special activities you participate in
- a description of your community
- some special places, events, or attractions in your community or state

 WRITING APPLICATION

If students are unclear about the form for a friendly letter, refer them to **Chapter 34, "Writing Letters and Completing Forms."**

CRITICAL THINKING
Inference

Tell students that because they do not know the people they are writing to, they will have to make inferences about what might be interesting to them. Tell students that they will need to think about what sorts of letters they would like to receive from foreign pen pals. Students can then infer from their own experiences what information their pen pals might find interesting.

It might also be helpful to have students decide what countries their pen pals are from. Knowing their pen pals' nationalities should help students to make inferences about what types of information would be of interest. For example, a pen pal from a tropical country might be interested in reading about snow—how it looks and feels and what sorts of games people play with it.

MECHANICS

MECHANICS

REVIEW D

OBJECTIVE

- To proofread and revise sentences for correct capitalization of the first words of sentences, proper nouns, proper adjectives, school subjects, and titles

694 *Capital Letters*

 Writing As you write your draft, keep in mind that your pen pal may not recognize names of some people, places, and things in the United States. For example, he or she may not recognize the names of your favorite movies or musical groups. Be sure to use correct capitalization and even brief explanations to make your meaning clear.

Evaluating and Revising Read through your letter carefully. Have you left out any important information? Are any parts of your letter confusing? If so, you may want to add, cut, or revise some details. Is the tone of your letter friendly? Have you followed the correct form for a personal letter? (For more about personal letters, see page 836.)

Proofreading Read over your letter carefully to check for any errors in grammar, spelling, or punctuation. Use the rules in this chapter to help you double-check your capitalization.

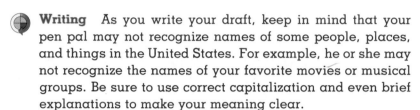 REVIEW D **Correcting Errors in Capitalization**

Each of the following sentences contains errors in capitalization. Correct these errors by either changing capital letters to small letters or changing small letters to capital letters. Words that should be capitalized or lower-cased are underscored.

EXAMPLE **1.** On june 25, 1876, the Sioux and cheyenne warriors defeated general george a. Custer and his Troops.
1. *June, Cheyenne, General George A., troops*

1. The <u>Defeat</u> of <u>gen</u>. <u>custer</u> occurred at the <u>battle</u> of the <u>little</u> <u>bighorn</u>.
2. In <u>december</u> of 1890, many Sioux were killed by the <u>Soldiers</u> in a battle at <u>wounded</u> Knee <u>creek</u> in <u>south</u> Dakota.

MECHANICS

MECHANICS

3. Both <u>Battles</u> have become part of <u>american</u> <u>History</u>, remembered by artists, writers, and filmmakers.
4. In the late nineteenth century, the <u>sioux</u> <u>Artist</u> Kicking <u>bear</u> painted the *Battle Of The little Bighorn*.
5. The painting, done on muslin <u>Cloth</u>, is shown below.

Kicking Bear (Sioux), *Battle of the Little Big Horn*, 1898, Courtesy of the Southwest Museum, Los Angeles. Photo #184.

6. Kicking <u>bear</u>, who himself fought in the <u>Battle</u>, painted at the <u>pine</u> Ridge <u>agency</u> in <u>south</u> Dakota, where he lived.
7. <u>soldiers</u> who fought against <u>kicking</u> Bear described him as courageous.
8. The well-known American <u>Poet</u> Stephen <u>vincent</u> <u>benét</u> wrote about the <u>battle</u> of <u>wounded</u> <u>knee</u> in a <u>Poem</u> called "<u>american</u> <u>names</u>."
9. More recently, the author Dee <u>brown</u> wrote about the <u>native</u> <u>americans</u> of the <u>west</u> in her book *<u>bury</u> <u>my</u> Heart at Wounded <u>knee</u>*.
10. In 1970, the movie *Little big Man* told the story of a 121-year-old man who survived the <u>Battle</u> against <u>general</u> Custer.

MECHANICS

 VISUAL CONNECTIONS
Battle of the Little Big Horn

Exploring the Subject. With long yellow hair and a mustache, General Custer was a flamboyant leader who sometimes purposely took his troops into dangerous battles. But the general apparently didn't know what he was leading his troops into as they marched to the Little Bighorn River in Montana. Custer's cavalry numbered 264 men. The Sioux and Cheyenne numbered between 2,500 and 4,000. Warriors from the two tribes were led by Crazy Horse and Rain-in-the-Face; the great Sioux chief Sitting Bull helped plan the battle. It took only half an hour for the Sioux and the Cheyenne to defeat Custer's troops.

About the Artist. Kicking Bear was a Sioux medicine man as well as an artist. He led the first Ghost Dance to be held at Sitting Bull's camp. The Ghost Dance is a religious dance performed with the belief that Native Americans' former, natural way of life will be restored to them and that they should continue to perform ceremonies and dances.

MECHANICS

OBJECTIVE

• To identify and correct errors in capitalization in sentences

STUDENTS WITH SPECIAL NEEDS

This **Review: Posttest**, with its twenty-five lengthy sentences, might be overwhelming to students with learning disabilities. Here are some steps you can take to help them:

1. Isolate each sentence so that students can focus on one sentence at a time.
2. For students with visual processing deficits, have student helpers read the sentences to students.
3. Suggest that students first check only for errors in the application of **Rule 25a.** Next, students should look for errors in the application of **Rule 25b,** and so on.

MECHANICS

696

MECHANICS

Review: Posttest

Proofreading Sentences for Correct Capitalization

For each of the following sentences, write the <u>words</u> in the sentence <u>that require capitalization</u>. If a sentence is correct, write C.

EXAMPLE   **1.** Next saturday rachel and i will get to watch the filming of our favorite TV show.
   1. *Saturday, Rachel, I*

1. The <u>curtiss</u> <u>soap</u> <u>corporation</u> sponsors the television show called *<u>three</u> <u>is</u> <u>two</u> <u>too</u> <u>many</u>.*
2. The show's theme song is "<u>you</u> and <u>i</u> <u>might</u> <u>get</u> <u>by</u>."
3. My favorite actor on the show is <u>joe</u> <u>fontana</u>, <u>jr.</u>, who plays the lovable <u>dr.</u> <u>mullins</u>.
4. The female lead, <u>janelle</u> <u>bledsoe</u>, used to go to our junior high school right here in <u>houston</u>, <u>texas</u>.
5. The action takes place out <u>west</u>, just after the <u>civil</u> <u>war</u> ended.
6. The program is on <u>monday</u> nights, except during the summer.
7. One episode took place at a <u>fourth</u> of <u>july</u> picnic, where <u>dr.</u> <u>mullins</u> challenged the local sheriff to a pie-eating contest.
8. Ms. Bledsoe plays a teacher who is married to Mr. <u>reginald</u> <u>wilson</u> <u>foster</u> II, president of the <u>flintsville</u> National <u>bank</u>.
9. Mrs. <u>foster</u> teaches <u>latin</u>, home economics, and <u>arithmetic</u> I at <u>flintsville's</u> one-room school.
10. One local character, <u>uncle</u> <u>ramón</u>, once played a practical joke on <u>judge</u> <u>grimsby</u> right outside the mayor's office.
11. Some people, including my mother, think that the program is silly, but my father enjoys watching it occasionally. **11. C**
12. Even <u>i</u> don't think it will receive an <u>emmy</u> from the <u>academy</u> of <u>television</u> <u>arts</u> and <u>sciences</u>.

13. When <u>grandma</u> <u>murray</u> and <u>aunt</u> <u>edna</u> from <u>mobile</u>, <u>alabama</u>, visited us, they watched the program.

14. In that <u>monday</u> night's show, an alien named <u>romax</u> from the planet <u>zarko</u> came to town and stayed at the <u>sidewinder</u> <u>hotel</u>.

15. The <u>alien</u>, who looked like United States <u>president</u> <u>zachary</u> <u>taylor</u>, spoke <u>english</u> perfectly and could read people's minds.

16. He settled a dispute between the <u>union</u> <u>pacific</u> <u>railroad</u> and the <u>flintsville</u> <u>ranchers'</u> <u>association</u>.

17. In another show a <u>united</u> <u>states</u> senator and <u>romax</u> discussed their views of justice.

18. In the silliest show, the people in the next town, <u>longview</u>, thought that a sea monster was living a few miles north in <u>lake</u> <u>cranberry</u> and reported it to the <u>national</u> <u>bureau</u> of <u>endangered</u> <u>species</u>.

19. A week later, <u>mayor</u> <u>murdstone</u> lost his only copy of his secret recipe for <u>irish</u> stew and saw the recipe in the next issue of the *<u>flintsville</u> <u>weekly</u> <u>gazette</u>*.

20. One time a mysterious stranger appeared, claiming he had sailed to the <u>east</u> around <u>cape</u> <u>horn</u> on the ship *<u>the</u> <u>gem</u> of the <u>ocean</u>*.

21. Another time, wealthy landowner <u>mabel</u> <u>platt</u> hired the law firm of <u>crum</u>, <u>lockwood</u>, and <u>tarr</u> to sue <u>mayor</u> <u>murdstone</u> and threatened to take the case all the way to the <u>united</u> <u>states</u> <u>supreme</u> <u>court</u>.

22. In the next episode, a <u>buddhist</u> priest, who just happened to be traveling through the <u>west</u> on his way back to <u>china</u>, stopped off in <u>flintsville</u> and gave some of the townsfolk a few lessons in manners.

23. Once, when someone mistakenly thought he had found gold down at <u>cutter's</u> <u>creek</u>, thousands of prospectors flocked to <u>flintsville</u>, including three bank-robbing members of the feared <u>gumley</u> gang.

24. The programs are taped before an audience in the <u>universal</u> <u>theater</u> in <u>los</u> <u>angeles</u>, <u>california</u>.

25. You can get tickets to be in the audience by writing to <u>curtiss</u> <u>soap</u> <u>corporation</u>, 151 <u>holly</u> <u>avenue</u>, <u>deerfield</u>, <u>michigan</u> 49238.

MECHANICS

COMMON ERROR

Problem. Writers frequently make mistakes in capitalization because they don't proofread their work. This situation is also true of students working on exercises.

Solution. Tell students to take their time to complete the **Review: Posttest** and to proofread their answers carefully.

INTEGRATING THE LANGUAGE ARTS

Mechanics and Writing. After students have completed the **Review: Posttest**, they may be intrigued by the strange happenings on the television show *Three Is Two Too Many*. You could have students write their own plot summaries for future episodes of the show. Tell students to include in their plot summaries examples of the six rules of capitalization from this chapter. You may want to have students read their plot summaries to the class. Interested students could also illustrate their plot summaries.

MECHANICS

SUMMARY STYLE SHEET

Names of Persons

Emilio Estevez	an actor
Marie Curie	a scientist
Crazy Horse	a leader

Geographical Names

Fifty-first Street	a dead-end street
Little Rock	the capital of Arkansas
Hidalgo	a county in New Mexico
in the South	traveling south
Kenya	a country in Africa
Galápagos Islands	a group of islands
Indian Ocean	the ocean between Africa and Australia
Everglades National Park	a park in Florida
Appalachian Mountains	hiking in the mountains

Names of Heavenly Bodies

Jupiter, Venus, Earth	the surface of the earth
Ursa Minor	a constellation
Milky Way	a spiral galaxy

Names of Teams, Organizations, Businesses, Institutions, Government Bodies

Overton Owls	a softball team
Westboro Writers' Club	the members of the club
American Printing Company	the company she works for
East Side High School	the local high school
Department of Energy	a department of the government

Names of Historical Events and Periods, Special Events, Calendar Items

Battle of the Little Bighorn	a fierce battle
Ice Age	at an early age
Travis County Fair	a large fair
Veterans Day	a national holiday
June	summer

(continued)

MECHANICS

MECHANICS

SUMMARY STYLE SHEET *(continued)*

Names of Nationalities, Races, Religions

Turkish	a nationality
Caucasian	a race
Judaism	a religion
God	a god of Greek mythology

Names of Buildings, Monuments, Awards

Copley Hotel	a fancy hotel
the General Assembly Building	a United Nations building
Washington Monument	a national monument

Names of Trains, Ships, Airplanes, Spacecraft

Super Chief	a train
Titanic	a ship
Air Force One	an airplane
Challenger	a space shuttle

Brand Names

Nike shoes	red shoes
Fab detergent	laundry detergent

Names of Languages, School Subjects

English, Dutch, Cree, Spanish	a foreign language
Algebra I, Biology II, Music 104	algebra, biology, music

Titles

Senator Suarez	a senator from my state
President of the United States	the president of the club
Aunt Martha	my aunt
How are you, Aunt?	
Up from Slavery	a book
Teen	a magazine
the *New York Times*	a newspaper
"Hector the Collector"	a poem
"The House on Mango Street"	a short story
Teenage Mutant Ninja Turtles	a movie, a play
A Different World	a television program
The Pumpkin Patch	a painting
"The Star-Spangled Banner"	a national anthem

MECHANICS

DIAGNOSTIC TEST

OBJECTIVE

• To rewrite and punctuate sentences using end marks, commas, semicolons, and colons correctly

CHAPTER OVERVIEW

This chapter allows students to review and build on past knowledge of the four basic types of punctuation. First, the chapter discusses end marks and abbreviations. Then, several rules about commas are presented, including how they are used in conventional situations, complex sentences, appositives, parenthetical expressions, and introductory words, phrases, and clauses. Finally, the chapter covers the use of semicolons and colons. The **Writing Application** gives students the opportunity to incorporate knowledge of correct punctuation into an original news announcement. For more information on audience and purpose, direct students to **Chapter 1: "Writing and Thinking."**

The material in this chapter will be of help to students during the proofreading stage of any of the composition chapters in this textbook, especially **Chapters 4–9.**

MECHANICS

26 PUNCTUATION

End Marks, Commas, Semicolons, Colons

Diagnostic Test

Using End Marks, Commas, Semicolons, and Colons to Punctuate Sentences Correctly

The following sentences lack necessary punctuation. Write each sentence, inserting the correct punctuation.

EXAMPLE **1.** After I read my history assignment I did my other homework but I did not finish it

1. *After I read my history assignment, I did my other homework, but I did not finish it.*

1. The following students gave their reports yesterday: Carlos, Sue, and Alan.
2. Tanay's grandfather carved this beautiful soapstone cooking pot.
3. Have you met Ellen, who has recently transferred to our school?
4. Calling Simon's name, I ran to the door.

END MARKS Rules 26a–26e

OBJECTIVES

- To rewrite sentences by adding the appropriate end marks
- To create abbreviations and to write sentences that illustrate the meaning of the abbreviations
- To use end marks correctly in a description of an event

End Marks **701**

5. Her new address is 151 Mesa Drive, El Paso, TX 79912.
6. Have you listened to that Bill Cosby tape, Felix?
7. You will let me know, of course, if you can't attend.
8. Mia will conduct the meeting, Gary, recently elected secretary, will take the minutes.
9. Looking out at the harsh, bright glare, Angela closed the curtains.
10. Carlos Montoya picked up the guitar, put his fingers on the fingerboard just before the frets, and strummed a few chords of a flamenco song.
11. If you hurry, you can get home before 9:00 P.M.
12. Help! This is an emergency!
13. By the way, Rosalinda, have you seen any of the re-releases of Alfred Hitchcock's old movies?
14. Dave hit a long fly ball toward the fence, but Phil was there to make the catch.
15. *El Norte*, which is one of my favorite movies, is about a brother and sister fleeing Central America.
16. Performed in Spanish, the movie that we saw had English subtitles.
17. Nicaragua, Panama, and Honduras are in Central America; Peru and Chile are in South America.
18. One of our cats, Gypsy, scooted through the door, across the room, and out the window.
19. The Lock Museum of America, a fascinating place in Terryville, Conn., has over twenty thousand locks on display.
20. Could the surprise gift be in-line skates or a new football or tickets to a concert?

End Marks

An *end mark* is a mark of punctuation placed at the end of a sentence. *Periods, question marks,* and *exclamation points* are end marks.

USING THE DIAGNOSTIC TEST

The **Diagnostic Test** can analyze your students' mastery of the basics of punctuation. Then using that knowledge, you may choose to concentrate on the students' weakest concepts and use the others as review. If you are working with an honors class, you may want to use the results of the test to decide which segments to teach directly and which to assign to cooperative learning groups.

MECHANICS

MECHANICS

RESOURCES

END MARKS
- Using End Marks

QUICK REMINDER

Write the four types of sentences on the chalkboard. Then define them, and ask students what end punctuation would be appropriate for each kind of sentence. Ask students to compose a sentence of each type on their own paper.

LEP/ESL

General Strategies. In most languages, punctuation is generally the same as in English, but some differences do exist. For example, a period is a vertical line in Hindi, a circle in Japanese, and four dots in Aramaic. In many languages such as Greek, Korean, Persian, and Arabic, the period is slightly raised. The Greek question mark looks like an English semicolon, and Spanish interrogative and exclamatory sentences have end marks at both ends of the sentence, with the first mark inverted. Differences such as these could create confusion for some ESL students when they write.

STUDENTS WITH SPECIAL NEEDS

Students with language problems need to learn to identify and to generate statements, questions, exclamations, and commands orally before being required to use end marks.

Before you assign **Exercise 1,** you may want to provide several examples of each kind of sentence. These examples should be presented orally. Include as much body language and as many facial expressions as you can to reinforce the meaning of each sentence.

26a. Use a period at the end of a statement.

EXAMPLES The chess player considered his next move.
Tea is grown in Sri Lanka.

26b. Use a question mark at the end of a question.

EXAMPLES Did you see the exhibit of Benin bronzes?
What time is it?

26c. Use an exclamation point at the end of an exclamation.

EXAMPLES What a high bridge!
Look at how bright the moon is!

26d. Use either a period or an exclamation point at the end of a request or a command.

EXAMPLES Please call the dog. [a request]
Call the dog! [a command]

▶ EXERCISE 1 **Adding End Marks to Sentences**

Rewrite each of the following sentences, adding the necessary end marks.

EXAMPLE **1.** Did you know that a choreographer is a person who creates dance steps
    1. *Did you know that a choreographer is a person who creates dance steps?*

1. Why is Katherine Dunham called the mother of African American dance?
2. She studied anthropology in college and won a scholarship to visit the Caribbean⊙
3. In Haiti, she was inspired by the dances she saw⊙
4. When Dunham returned to the United States, she started one of the first all-black professional dance companies in the nation⊙

5. How I admire such a talented person**!**
6. Look at the beautiful costume and jewelry worn by Dunham in the photograph below⊙
7. How many honors has Dunham's creativity won her**?**
8. She was named to the Hall of Fame of the National Museum of Dance in Saratoga, New York⊙
9. She was also given the National Medal of Arts Award for exploring Caribbean and African dance⊙
10. The editors of *Essence* magazine praised Dunham for helping to break down racial barriers⊙

26e. Use a period after most abbreviations.

TYPES OF ABBREVIATIONS	EXAMPLES
Personal Names	F. Scott Fitzgerald Livie I. Durán W.E.B. Du Bois
Titles Used with Names	Mr. Mrs. Ms. Jr. Sr. Dr.
Organizations and Companies	Co. Inc. Corp. Assn.

NOTE: Abbreviations for government agencies and some widely used abbreviations are written without periods. Each letter of the abbreviation is capitalized.

EXAMPLES   UN, FBI, PTA, NAACP, PBS, CNN, YMCA, VHF

MECHANICS

Point out that sentences beginning with *what* and *how* that are obviously not interrogative sentences are usually exclamatory sentences as in "What a beautiful day!" or "How beautiful that flower is!" Then work with students to write exclamatory sentences that begin with the words *how* or *what*. Have students illustrate the sentences. The illustrations could then be used for a bulletin board.

LEARNING STYLES
Auditory Learners. To help students recognize the need for appropriate end marks, read a paragraph to them and omit the punctuation. Then show the paragraph to students on an overhead projector and have them decide what end marks should be inserted.

COMMON ERROR
Problem. Students often have trouble deciding whether to use a period or an exclamation point at the end of an imperative sentence.
Solution. Advise your students to analyze the urgency of the sentence. For example, "Feed the dog" would not carry the weight of "Don't drop the baby!"

MECHANICS

COOPERATIVE LEARNING

Divide the class into groups of three to four students. Each group will compose a short story without any end punctuation. The stories should include all sentence types and end marks. Then have the groups exchange stories. Using the appropriate editing marks, the next group should add end marks where needed. Each story will then go to a third group for recopying and to a final group for proofreading. After each story has been completed, the original group should check to see that the end marks were placed appropriately. Finally, the stories should be read aloud to the class.

TYPES OF ABBREVIATIONS	EXAMPLES
Addresses	Ave. St. Rd. Blvd. P.O. Box
States	Tex. Penn. Ariz. Wash.

NOTE: A two-letter state abbreviation without periods is used only when it is followed by a ZIP code. Both letters of the abbreviation are then capitalized.

EXAMPLE   Orlando, **FL** 32819

TYPES OF ABBREVIATIONS	EXAMPLES
Times	A.M. P.M. B.C. A.D.
Units of Measure	oz. lb. in. ft. yd. mi.

NOTE: Abbreviations for metric units of measure are usually written without periods and are not capitalized.

EXAMPLES   mm, kg, dl

If you're not sure whether to use periods with abbreviations, look in a dictionary.

NOTE: When an abbreviation with a period ends a sentence, another period is not needed. However, a question mark or an exclamation point is used as needed.

EXAMPLES   We will arrive by 3:00 P.M.
Can you meet us at 3:30 P.M.?

EXERCISE 2   Creating and Writing Abbreviations

Abbreviations provide a quick way to express information. Think of how inconvenient it would be to have to write 10 ante meridiem instead of 10 A.M. Create five abbreviations that you think would be handy timesavers. Use each one in a sentence that tells what it stands for. Be sure to use periods after each letter in your abbreviations.

EXAMPLE   *I.A.F. means "I'm almost finished," an abbreviation students use when they've nearly completed their homework.*

ANSWERS
Exercise 2

Abbreviations will vary. There must be five abbreviations, and they must be defined in the context of a sentence. Abbreviations should be punctuated correctly.

MECHANICS

PICTURE THIS

Suddenly last night, monster tomatoes began attacking your town! They're so huge that they have crushed cars, knocked down buildings, and caused general panic. When the attack started, you grabbed your camera and got this amazing shot of one of the giant tomatoes chasing two friends of yours. But now your camera won't work because it is drenched with tomato juice. You remember that you have a small notebook in your pocket. Jot down a description of the attack so that the rest of the world will know what happened. Use all three types of end marks in your description.

Subject: monster tomatoes attacking your town
Audience: people who haven't seen the attack
Purpose: to inform by giving a clear description

PICTURE THIS

Assessment should be based on the correct use of end marks. You may want to specify the number of sentences students should create. It might be helpful to brainstorm a list of appropriate adjectives and leave these on the chalkboard for students to reference.

A DIFFERENT APPROACH

In a variation of a spelling bee, divide the class into two teams. Read sentences to each team and ask for the appropriate end marks. Limit the time each team has per sentence. If a team member gives the correct answer, he or she takes another turn. If a team member answers incorrectly, the opposing team may try the sentence.

MECHANICS

MECHANICS

SEGMENT 3 *(pp. 706–724)*

COMMAS Rules 26f–26k

OBJECTIVES

- To proofread sentences, adding commas when necessary
- To create a restaurant menu, using commas in a series of adjectives describing the meals
- To identify and add commas to compound sentences

▼ **RESOURCES**

COMMAS
- Commas with Items in a Series
- Commas with Compound Sentences
- Commas with Interrupters
- Commas with Introductory Elements
- Other Uses of Commas

QUICK REMINDER

Commas not only reinforce a natural break in a sentence, they also help make complicated sentences clearer. Put the following sentences on the chalkboard, and have your students suggest places where commas should be added:

1. We bought chips deviled ham spread bread mayonnaise and pickles for the picnic.
2. The students drew dinosaurs colored them in and framed them for display.
3. The most talented charming beautiful and intelligent girl will win this beauty contest.

MEETING
INDIVIDUAL
NEEDS

LEP/ESL

General Strategies. In some languages such as Japanese, Persian, and Arabic, the comma is raised above the line of writing and inverted or reversed. You may find that some of your ESL students will do this in English. You could remind students that they should put the comma level with the bottom of the letters and with the tail opening down and curving left.

706

---

706 *Punctuation*

Commas

End marks are used to separate complete thoughts. *Commas,* however, are used to separate words or groups of words within a complete thought.

Items in a Series

26f. Use commas to separate items in a series.

A series is a group of three or more items written one after another. The items in a series may be words, phrases, or clauses.

WORDS IN A SERIES
December, January, and February are all summer months in the Southern Hemisphere. [nouns]
The engine rattled, coughed, and stalled. [verbs]
The baby was happy, alert, and active after her nap. [adjectives]
PHRASES IN A SERIES
There were fingerprints at the top, on the sides, and on the bottom. [prepositional phrases]
Cut into pieces, aged for a year, and well dried, the wood was ready to burn. [participial phrases]
To pitch in a World Series game, to practice medicine, and to run for mayor are all things I hope to do some day. [infinitive phrases]
CLAUSES IN A SERIES
We sang, we danced, and we played trivia games. [short independent clauses]

NOTE: Only *short* independent clauses in a series may be separated by commas. Independent clauses in a series are usually separated by semicolons.

- To identify and add commas to sentences containing appositives or appositive phrases and to compose sentences using a stated group of words as an appositive in the sentence
- To proofread sentences for the correct use of commas with expressions that interrupt
- To use commas correctly with certain introductory elements
- To proofread sentences for the correct use of commas in conventional situations

Always be sure that there are at least three items in the series; two items do not need a comma between them.

INCORRECT   You will need a pencil, and plenty of paper.
CORRECT   You will need a pencil and plenty of paper.

NOTE: In your reading, you will find that some writers omit the comma before the *and* joining the last two items of a series. Nevertheless, you should form the habit of always including this comma. Sometimes a comma is necessary to make your meaning clear. Notice how the comma affects the meaning in the following examples.

EXAMPLES   Mom, Jody and I want to go to the movies.
[Mom is being asked for her permission.]
Mom, Jody, and I want to go to the movies.
[Three people want to go to the movies.]

Including a comma before the last item in a series is never incorrect; therefore, it is usually best to do so.

When all the items in the series are joined by *and* or *or,* do not use commas to separate them.

EXAMPLES   Take water **and** food **and** matches with you.
I will take a class in karate **or** judo **or** aikido next year.

MECHANICS

▷ EXERCISE 3   **Proofreading Sentences for the Correct Use of Commas**

Some of the following sentences need commas; others do not. If a sentence needs commas, write the <u>word before each missing comma</u> and add the comma. If a sentence is correct, write *C.*

EXAMPLE   **1.** Seal the envelope stamp it and mail the letter.
1. *envelope, it,*

1. The mountains and valleys of southern Appalachia were once home to the Cherokee people.   **1.** c
2. <u>Cleveland Toledo</u> and Dayton are three large cities in Ohio.

LEARNING STYLES

Kinetic Learners. When going over the exercises orally, you may want to use a signaled-response system. For example, instruct students that if a comma is needed in a sentence, they should make a comma with a finger. If none is needed, they should make a zero, and if they are unsure of the answer, they should raise a thumb.

3. The captain entered the <u>cockpit</u>,checked the <u>instruments</u>,and prepared for takeoff.
4. Luisa bought mangos and papayas and oranges. **4.** C **5.** C
5. The speaker took a deep breath and read the report.
6. My dog Rover can roll <u>over</u>,walk on his hind <u>feet</u>, and catch a tennis ball.
7. The neighbors searched behind the <u>garages</u>,in the <u>bushes</u>,and along the highway.
8. Ruben Blades is an <u>attorney</u>,an <u>actor</u>,and a singer.
9. Eleanor Roosevelt's <u>courage</u>,her <u>humanity</u>,and her service to the nation will always be remembered.
10. Rivers overflowed in Virginia and North Carolina. **10.** C

26g. Use a comma to separate two or more adjectives that come before a noun.

EXAMPLES   Jupiter is a large, strange planet.
Zina Garrison played a powerful, brilliant game.

Do not place a comma between an adjective and the noun immediately following it.

INCORRECT   My spaniel is a fat, sassy, puppy.
CORRECT   My spaniel is a fat, sassy puppy.

Sometimes the final adjective in a series is closely connected to the noun. When the adjective and the noun are linked in such a way, do not use a comma before the final adjective.

EXAMPLES   A huge **horned owl** lives in those woods. [not *huge, horned owl*]
An unshaded **electric light** hung from the ceiling. [not *unshaded, electric light*]

To see whether a comma is needed, insert *and* between the adjectives (*unshaded and electric*, for example). If *and* sounds awkward there, don't use a comma.

☞ REFERENCE NOTE: When an adjective and a noun are closely linked, they may be considered one word. Such a word is called a *compound noun*. For more about compound nouns, see page 423.

EXERCISE 4

Proofreading Sentences for the Correct Use of Commas

Most of the following sentences need commas. If a sentence needs any commas, write the <u>word before each missing comma</u> and add the comma. If a sentence is correct, write *C.*

EXAMPLE **1.** Juanita Chen and I are making enchiladas.
1. *Juanita, Chen, and I are making enchiladas.*
or
Juanita, Chen and I are making enchiladas.

1. In judo class I learned that <u>skill</u>ˌ<u>balance</u>ˌand timing are more important than strength.
2. Among Robert Fulton's interests were a steam warship and the submarine. **2. C**
3. Smoking is a <u>costly</u>ˌdangerous habit.
4. In the human ear, the <u>hammer</u>ˌ<u>anvil</u>ˌand stirrup carry sound waves to the brain.
5. Buffalo Bill was a Pony Express <u>rider</u>ˌa <u>scout</u>ˌand a touring stunt performer.
6. "The Masque of the Red Death" is a famous horror story by Edgar Allan Poe. **6. C**
7. According to Greek mythology, the three Fates spin the thread of <u>life</u>ˌmeasure <u>it</u>ˌand cut it.
8. LeVar Burton plays the <u>intelligent</u>ˌlikable character Jordi on *Star Trek: The Next Generation.*
9. Burton also starred in the <u>popular</u>ˌaward-winning miniseries *Roots.*
10. Falstaff begged for mercy in a <u>fight</u>ˌran <u>away</u>ˌand later bragged about his bravery in battle.

PEANUTS reprinted by permission of UFS, Inc.

MECHANICS

COMMON ERROR

Problem. Many students use *etc.* Therefore, it is important that they use it appropriately.

Solution. Remind your students that when *etc.* ends a series, it should be preceded and followed by a comma; for example, "The girl made bread, rolls, pies, etc., in her kitchen." Also, students should not put the word *and* before *etc.* because *etc.* is the abbreviation for *et cetera* and *et* means *and.*

A DIFFERENT APPROACH

Have your students write informative/descriptive paragraphs about endangered animals. Tell students to use vivid, colorful adjectives. Remind them to use commas correctly when separating adjectives in their descriptions. Have students edit each other's papers and look only for the proper use of adjectives and commas.

ANSWERS
Exercise 5

Menu descriptions will vary. They should include the use of commas in a series, and students should create the required minimum of five items.

A DIFFERENT APPROACH

Clauses can add spice to sentences, but for clarity they must be punctuated correctly. Write the following scrambled sentences on the chalkboard, and have your students unscramble and punctuate them correctly:

1. Who ran away to the circus my aunt clowns around.
2. Is very large the circus which travels to the great cities of the world.
3. Becoming extinct in Africa elephants which are love to show off in the circus.

▶ EXERCISE 5 **Creating Menu Descriptions**

Your parents have opened a restaurant, and they are eager to attract customers. Your job is to list today's specials on a sign outside the restaurant. List at least five food items and give a short description of each one. Try to make the foods sound appealing. Be sure to use commas between a series of adjectives. [Remember: Do not use a comma between an adjective and the noun it modifies.]

EXAMPLE *Delicious, homemade chicken soup served with a fresh garden salad and refreshing iced tea —$2.75*

Compound Sentences

26h. Use a comma before *and, but, for, or, nor, so,* and *yet* when they join independent clauses in a compound sentence.

EXAMPLES Tamisha offered to get tickets, and I accepted.
They had been working very hard, but they didn't seem especially tired.
The twins were excited, for they were going to day care for the first time.

NOTE: *So* is often overused. If possible, try to reword a sentence to avoid using *so.*

EXAMPLE It was late, so we went home.
REVISED Because it was late, we went home.

When the independent clauses are very short, the comma before *and, but,* or *or* may be omitted.

EXAMPLES It rained and it rained.
She's going but I'm not.
Come with us or meet us there.

NOTE: Always use a comma before *nor, for, so,* or *yet* joining independent clauses.

EXAMPLE I don't know much about modern art, yet I enjoy the work of Mark Rothko.

Don't be confused by a simple sentence with a compound verb. A simple sentence has only one independent clause.

SIMPLE SENTENCE
WITH COMPOUND VERB

Usually we **study** in the morning and **play** tennis in the afternoon.

COMPOUND SENTENCE

Usually we study in the morning, and we play tennis in the afternoon. [two independent clauses]

👉 REFERENCE NOTE: For more about compound sentences, see pages 536–538. For more about simple sentences with compound verbs, see page 534.

EXERCISE 6 **Correcting Compound Sentences by Adding Commas**

Some of the following sentences are compound and need additional commas. If a sentence needs a comma, write the word before the missing comma and add the comma. If the sentence is correct, write C.

EXAMPLE **1.** Native American artists have a heritage dating back thousands of years and many of them use this heritage to create modern works.
1. *years,*

1. Today's artists may work with many nontraditional materials, but they use traditional techniques.
2. In the photograph on the next page, you can see the work of the Tohono O'odham artist Mary Thomas and begin to appreciate this basket-weaver's skill. **2.** C
3. The baskets in the photograph are woven in the "friendship design" and show a circle of human figures in a prayer ceremony. **3.** C
4. Yucca, banana yucca root, and devil's claw are used to make these baskets, and each plant's leaves are a different color.
5. The Navajo artist Danny Randeau Tsosie learned about his heritage from his grandmother. **5.** C
6. She taught him songs and explained the meaning of the different ceremonies. **6.** C

MECHANICS

MECHANICS

INTEGRATING THE LANGUAGE ARTS

Mechanics and Writing. Caution your students against overusing adjective clauses, as this tendency leads to wordiness. Have students rewrite sentences that contain adjective clauses to make them more concise. Students should check to make sure they have used commas correctly. Here are some example sentences:

1. The day, which was rainy and cold, dampened their spirits. [The rainy, cold day dampened their spirits.]

2. The girl, who was smart, helped the new boy in class. [The smart girl helped the new boy in class.]

7. Christine Nofchissey McHorse learned the skill of pottery making from her <u>grandmother</u>,and she can make beautiful bowls.
8. McHorse has an unusual <u>style</u>,for her designs combine traditional Navajo and Pueblo images.
9. Native American jewelry makers often use pieces of turquoise and coral found in North <u>America</u>,but they also use other stones from around the world.
10. Native American art may look very <u>modern</u>,yet some of its symbols and patterns are quite old.

Interrupters

26i. Use commas to set off an expression that interrupts a sentence.

Two commas are needed if the expression to be set off comes in the middle of the sentence. One comma is needed if the expression comes first or last.

EXAMPLES   Our neighbor, Ann Myers, is a fine golfer.
Naturally, we expect to win.
My answer is correct, I think.

(1) Use commas to set off nonessential participial phrases or nonessential subordinate clauses.

A *nonessential* (or *nonrestrictive*) phrase or clause adds information that isn't needed to understand the meaning of the sentence. Such a phrase or clause can be omitted without changing the main idea of the sentence.

NONESSENTIAL PHRASES	My sister, **listening to her radio,** did not hear me.
	Paul, **thrilled by the applause,** took a bow.
NONESSENTIAL CLAUSES	*Out of Africa,* **which I saw again last week,** is my favorite movie.
	I reported on *Secret of the Andes,* **which was written by Ann Nolan Clark.**

Do not set off an *essential* (or *restrictive*) phrase or clause. Since such a phrase or clause tells *which one(s),* it cannot be omitted without changing the meaning of the sentence.

ESSENTIAL PHRASES	The people **waiting to see Arsenio Hall** whistled and cheered. [Which people?]
	A bowl **made by Maria Martínez** is a collector's item. [Which bowl?]
ESSENTIAL CLAUSES	The dress **that I liked** has been sold. [Which dress?]
	The man **who tells Navajo folk tales** is Mr. Platero. [Which man?]

NOTE: A clause beginning with *that* is usually essential.

☞ **REFERENCE NOTE:** For more about phrases, see Chapter 17. For more about subordinate clauses, see pages 516–525.

▶ EXERCISE 7 **Adding Commas with Nonessential Phrases and Clauses**

Some of the following sentences need commas to set off nonessential phrases and clauses. Other sentences are correct without commas. If a sentence needs commas,

COOPERATIVE LEARNING

Separate the class into groups of three or four students. Give each group a set of index cards containing clauses. Have each group write a correctly punctuated story using the clauses. One member of each group should read the group's story to the class. Here are some possible clauses:

1. who stole a million dollars
2. while they had nothing to lose
3. with no hope in sight
4. putting on her make-up
5. which made them scream

MECHANICS

MECHANICS

A DIFFERENT APPROACH

Bring several newspapers to class and have each student pick an article to read. Then have the students copy and evaluate the punctuation of any compound sentences, phrases, or clauses. As an optional activity, each student could summarize his or her article for the class.

ANSWERS
Exercise 7

1. Island,
2. C
3. buildings, years,
4. Island, museum,
5. C
6. lobby, baggage,
7. C
8. Room, floor,
9. immigrants, countries,
10. C

write the <u>word that comes before each missing comma</u> and add the comma. If the sentence is correct, write C.

EXAMPLE   **1.** This photograph which was taken near Ellis Island shows a family of immigrants from Eastern Europe.
1. *photograph, Ellis Island,*

1. Millions of immigrants who came to the United States between about 1892 and 1924 stopped at Ellis <u>Island</u>∧which is in Upper New York Bay.
2. Families arriving from Europe were examined and interviewed there.   **2.** C

3. The island and its <u>buildings</u>∧which were closed to the public for many <u>years</u>∧are now part of the Statue of Liberty National Monument.
4. In 1990, Ellis <u>Island</u>∧rebuilt as a <u>museum</u>∧was officially opened to the public.
5. Visitors who wish to see the museum can take a ferry ride from Manhattan Island.   **5.** C
6. The museum's <u>lobby</u>∧crowded with steamer trunks and other old <u>baggage</u>∧is the visitors' first sight.
7. One special attraction in the museum consists of audiotapes and videotapes that describe the immigrants' experiences.   **7.** C

8. The Registry Room which is on the second floor sometimes held more than eleven thousand people.
9. The immigrants who came from many countries hoped to find freedom and a happier life in America.
10. Immigrants who came to the United States brought with them the value of hard work and a variety of skills that helped to make our country great.

(2) Use commas to set off appositives and appositive phrases that are nonessential.

An *appositive* is a noun or a pronoun used to explain or identify another noun or pronoun.

EXAMPLES   Vernon, **my cousin,** was born in Jamaica.
             Jamaica, **a popular island for tourists,** is in the Caribbean Sea.

Do not use commas to set off an appositive that is essential to the meaning of a sentence.

EXAMPLES   My sister **Alicia** is at basketball practice. [The speaker has more than one sister and must give a name to identify which sister.]
             My sister, **Alicia,** is at basketball practice. [The speaker has only one sister and is giving her name as added information.]

▶ EXERCISE 8 **Proofreading Sentences for the Correct Use of Commas with Appositives**

For each of the following sentences, identify the <u>appositive or appositive phrase</u>. Supply commas where needed. [Hint: Not all of the appositives require commas.]

EXAMPLE   **1.** Mars one of the closest planets can be seen without a telescope.
           1. *Mars, one of the closest planets,*

1. The whole class has read the novel <u>*Old Yeller*</u>.
2. Shana Alexander, <u>a former editor of *McCall's*,</u> was the main speaker.

COMMON ERROR

Problem. Students may not recognize when appositives have become part of a proper name.

Solution. Explain to your students that only in some historical cases has an appositive become part of a proper name, as in *Ivan the Great, Eric the Red,* or *William the Conqueror.*

3. Do you own a thesaurus, a dictionary of synonyms and antonyms?

4. The Galápagos Islands, a group of volcanic islands in the Pacific Ocean, were named for the Spanish word meaning "tortoise."

5. Rubber, an elastic substance, quickly restores itself to its original size and shape.

6. This bowl is made of clay found on Kilimanjaro, the highest mountain in Africa.

7. The North Sea, an arm of the Atlantic Ocean, is rich in fish, natural gas, and oil.

8. Jamake Highwater, a Blackfoot/Eastern Band Cherokee, writes about the history of his people.

9. At Gettysburg, a town in Pennsylvania, an important battle of the Civil War was fought.

10. My friend Juanita is teaching me to make tortillas.

 EXERCISE 9   **Writing Sentences with Appositives**

In this painting by Frederic Remington, cowboys break for a midday meal at the chuck wagon. If you'd worked hard on the ranch all morning, you'd gladly join them! Write

Frederick Remington, *The Midday Meal*, Remington Art Memorial Museum, Ogdensburg, New York.

MECHANICS

ANSWERS
Exercise 9

Sentences will vary. The sentences should include the provided appositives and should indicate by the correct use of commas students' comprehension of the concept of essential or nonessential clauses.

VISUAL CONNECTIONS
The Midday Meal

About the Artist. Frederic Remington (1861–1909) is well known for his paintings of horses, cowboys, and Indians of the Old West. Remington also sculpted scenes from the Old West and wrote books and articles about it, including *Pony Tracks* and *The Way of an Indian*.

five sentences about these cowboys and their meal. In your sentences, use five of the following groups of words as appositives. Be sure that you insert commas wherever they are needed.

EXAMPLE   **1.** *The new cook, Jake Thompson, makes great chili.*

the last day on the trail
a terrible cook
our two visitors
the newest ranch hand
the wildest horse in the territory
Jake Thompson
an unusual feast
a good place to eat chow
beans and cornbread again
my partner

(3) Use commas to set off words that are used in direct address.

EXAMPLES   **Ben,** please answer the doorbell.
Mom needs you, **Francine.**
Would you show me, **Kadeem,** where the craft store is?

 EXERCISE 10   **Correcting Sentences by Adding Commas with Words Used in Direct Address**

Identify the <u>words in direct address</u> from the following sentences. Insert commas before, after, or both before and after the words, as needed.

EXAMPLE   **1.** Listen folks to this amazing announcement!
            1. , *folks,*

1. <u>Andrea</u>‚when are you leaving for Detroit?
2. Pay attention now‚<u>class</u>.
3. Let us‚<u>my sisters and brothers</u>‚give thanks.
4. Please‚<u>Dad</u>‚may I use your computer?
5. <u>Senator</u>‚please summarize your tax proposal.

 INTEGRATING THE LANGUAGE ARTS

Technology Link. Have students work in groups and use televisions and VCRs to tape several small portions of dialogue that they will then transcribe. (Or students could use radios and tape recorders.) Then have students punctuate their dialogues. (To shorten this assignment, specify that each group concentrate on only one dialogue.) Groups can then present their tapes and punctuated transcriptions to the class. Ask if others in the class can suggest variations.

TIMESAVER

When students complete the exercises in this chapter, you could have them write the sentences in blue and then use a different color for punctuation marks. Or have students alternate pencil and ink in the same manner. This procedure will make the punctuation more visually striking and easier for grading.

(4) Use commas to set off parenthetical expressions.

A *parenthetical expression* is a side remark that adds information or relates ideas.

EXAMPLES Carl, **on the contrary,** prefers soccer to baseball.
To tell the truth, Jan is one of my best friends.

Common Parenthetical Expressions		
by the way	in fact	of course
for example	in my opinion	on the contrary
however	I suppose	on the other hand
I believe	nevertheless	to tell the truth

Some of these expressions are not always used as parenthetical expressions.

EXAMPLES **Of course** it is true. [not parenthetical]
That is, **of course,** an Indian teakwood screen. [parenthetical]

I suppose we ought to go home now. [not parenthetical]
He'll want a ride, **I suppose.** [parenthetical]

EXERCISE 11 **Correcting Sentences by Adding Commas with Expressions That Interrupt**

The following sentences contain parenthetical expressions that require commas. Write the <u>parenthetical expressions</u>, inserting commas as needed.

EXAMPLE **1.** As a matter of fact even a small refracting telescope gives a good view of Saturn's rings.
1. *As a matter of fact,*

1. You don't need a telescope, however, to see all the beautiful sights in the night sky.
2. <u>For instance,</u> on a summer night you can view the Scorpion, the Serpent, and the Serpent Bearer.

3. <u>By the way,</u> you should not overlook the Milky Way.
4. The Milky Way, <u>in fact,</u> is more impressive in the summer than at any other time of year.
5. Hercules, <u>of course,</u> is an interesting constellation.
6. Studying the constellations is, <u>in my opinion,</u> a most interesting hobby.
7. It takes an active imagination, <u>however,</u> to spot some constellations.
8. The Archer, <u>for example,</u> is hard to see unless you're familiar with a constellation map like this one.
9. The Scorpion, <u>on the other hand,</u> is quite clearly outlined.
10. Astronomy is a fascinating science, <u>I think</u>.

NORTHERN   SOUTHERN

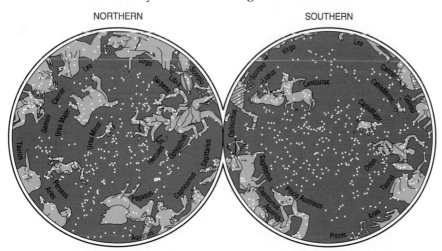

Introductory Words, Phrases, and Clauses

26j. Use a comma after certain introductory elements.

(1) Use a comma after *yes, no,* or any mild exclamation such as *well* or *why* at the beginning of a sentence.

EXAMPLES   **Yes,** you may borrow my bicycle.
              Why, it's Lena!
              Well, I think you are wrong.

(2) Use a comma after an introductory participial phrase.

EXAMPLES **Beginning a new school year,** Zelda felt somewhat nervous.

Greeted with applause from the fans, Rashid ran out onto the field.

(3) Use a comma after two or more introductory prepositional phrases.

EXAMPLE **At the bottom of the hill,** you will see the baseball field.

Use a comma after a single introductory prepositional phrase only when the comma is necessary to make the meaning of the sentence clear.

EXAMPLES **In the morning they left.** [clear without a comma]

In the morning, sunlight streamed through the window. [The comma is needed so that the reader does not read "morning sunlight."]

(4) Use a comma after an introductory adverb clause.

EXAMPLE **After I finish my homework,** I will go to the park.

An adverb clause that comes at the end of a sentence does not usually need a comma.

EXAMPLE I will go to the park **after I finish my homework.**

▶ EXERCISE 12 **Adding Commas with Introductory Elements**

If a comma is needed in a sentence, <u>write the word before the missing comma</u> and add the comma. If a sentence is punctuated correctly, write C.

EXAMPLE **1.** Walking among the lions the trainer seemed unafraid.

1. *lions,*

MECHANICS

MECHANICS

26k

1. At our school students eat lunch in the cafeteria.　**1.** c
2. Although Jesse Jackson did not win the 1984 or 1988 Democratic presidential <u>nomination,</u>he raised many important issues.
3. On the desk in the <u>den,</u>you will find your book.
4. <u>Yes,</u>I enjoyed the fajitas that Ruben made.
5. Walking home from <u>school,</u>Rosa saw her brother.
6. When I go to bed <u>late,</u>I have trouble waking up in the morning.
7. <u>Well,</u>we can watch *True Colors* or play checkers.
8. Seeing the calculators in the store <u>window,</u>George decided to go in and buy one.
9. At the stoplight on the corner of the next <u>block,</u>they made a right turn.
10. Because pemmican remained good to eat for several <u>years,</u>it was a practical food for many Native American peoples.

Conventional Situations

26k. Use commas in certain conventional situations.

(1) Use commas to separate items in dates and addresses.

EXAMPLES　She was born on January 26, 1981, in Cheshire, Connecticut.
A letter dated November 26, 1888, was found in the old house at 980 West Street, Davenport, Iowa.

Notice that a comma separates the last item in a date or in an address from the words that follow it. However, a comma does *not* separate a month and a day (*January 26*) or a house number and a street name (*980 West Street*).

NOTE: Use the correct ZIP code on every envelope you address. The ZIP code follows the two-letter state abbreviation without any punctuation between it and the state.

EXAMPLE　Fargo, ND 58101

MECHANICS

INTEGRATING THE LANGUAGE ARTS
Mechanics and Writing. Have your students write letters to pen pals. (You can get the names of pen pal organizations from your school library.) Remind students to use correct letter format—using a comma after the salutation and after the closing of the letter. Also, remind your students to use commas appropriately when addressing the envelopes to their pen pals.

MECHANICS

CRITICAL THINKING
Analysis

One outside reading source that students may find interesting to analyze for punctuation in dialogue is comic books. For this activity, have students provide old comic books. You can sometimes find them at garage sales if you want to acquire a collection for class use.

Put students into groups of four, and provide each group with two comic books. Have two students in each group be the compilers and the other two be the researchers. The objective is for the groups to analyze different ways commas are used in the pages they will read.

Suggest that the groups review the **Summary of the Uses of the Comma** found at the end of the chapter and create a table or chart that contains these rules. Students could report their findings by placing marks in each column. Tell the groups to rank the comma usages from most often used to least often used.

REVIEW A and B

OBJECTIVES

- To identify where commas should be used in a sentence
- To use commas correctly in a sentence

 EXERCISE 13 **Using Commas Correctly**

Rewrite each of the following sentences, inserting commas wherever they are needed.

EXAMPLE **1.** I received a package from my friend who lives in Irving Texas.
1. *I received a package from my friend who lives in Irving, Texas.*

1. On May 25₁1935₁Jesse Owens tied or broke six world track records.
2. The American Saddle Horse Museum is located at 137 West Muhammed Ali Boulevard₁Louisville₁KY 40202.
3. Marian Anderson was born on February 27₁1902₁in Philadelphia₁Pennsylvania.
4. Our ZIP code address is Ames₁IA 50010.
5. Ocean City₁New Jersey₁is a popular seaside resort.

(2) Use a comma after the salutation of a friendly letter and after the closing of any letter.

EXAMPLES Dear Dad,   Dear Sharon,
With love,   Yours truly,

 REVIEW A   **Proofreading Sentences for the Correct Use of Commas**

Write each <u>word</u> in the following sentences <u>that should be followed by a comma</u> and add the comma after the word.

EXAMPLE **1.** The substitute's name is Mr. Fowler I think.
1. *Fowler,*

1. What time is your <u>appointment</u>₁Kevin?
2. My aunt said to forward her mail to 302 Lancelot <u>Drive</u>₁<u>Simpsonville</u>₁SC 29681.
3. George Washington <u>Carver</u>₁a famous <u>chemist</u>₁was mostly self-educated.
4. <u>Quick</u>₁violent flashes of lightning cause approximately 27,500 forest fires a year in the United States alone.

5. My cousin Lono sent me a note on a postcard from Pahala, Hawaii.
6. A single branch stuck out of the water, and the beaver grasped it in its paws.
7. The beaver, by the way, is a rodent.
8. This hard-working mammal builds dams, lodges, and canals.
9. The lodges of American beavers, built with their entrances underwater, are marvels of engineering.
10. The beaver uses its large tail, which is flattened, as a rudder.

▶ REVIEW B **Proofreading Sentences for the Correct Use of Commas**

For the following sentences, write each word that should be followed by a comma and add the comma.

EXAMPLE **1.** Kyoto's palaces shrines and temples remind visitors of this city's importance in Japanese history.
1. *palaces, shrines,*

1. The Procession of the Eras, celebrated every autumn, takes place in Kyoto.
2. Kyoto, a beautiful city, was Japan's capital for more than one thousand years.
3. The Procession of the Eras festival, which celebrates Kyoto's history, begins on October 22.
4. The beautiful, solemn procession is a remarkable sight.
5. At the beginning of the festival, priests offer special prayers.
6. Portable shrines are carried through the streets, and thousands of marchers follow.
7. The photograph on the next page, for example, shows marchers dressed as ancient warriors.
8. Because the marchers near the front represent recent history, they wear costumes from the nineteenth-century Royal Army Era.

MECHANICS

OBJECTIVE

- To identify sentences needing semicolons and to use semicolons correctly

724 *Punctuation*

9. Marching at the end of the <u>procession</u>,archers wear costumes from the eighth-century Warrior Era.
10. The procession <u>is</u>,in <u>fact</u>,a rich memorial to Kyoto's long and varied history.

Semicolons

A *semicolon* looks like a combination of a period and a comma, and that is just what it is. A semicolon separates complete thoughts as a period does. A semicolon also separates items within a sentence as a comma does.

26l. Use a semicolon between independent clauses if they are not joined by *and, but, or, nor, for, so,* or *yet.*

EXAMPLES   Jimmy took my suitcase upstairs; he left his own in the car.

After school, I went to band practice; then I studied in the library for an hour.

🦉 QUICK REMINDER

Write the following sentences on the chalkboard, and have your students indicate where semicolons should be used:

1. The new comedy series pilot was a flop it didn't appeal to teenagers. [flop;]
2. The network tried it out on prime time it was a flop there too. [time;]
3. After school, teenagers wanted to relax then they wanted to watch television before they started their homework. [relax;]

26m. Use a semicolon rather than a comma before a coordinating conjunction to join independent clauses that contain commas.

CONFUSING   I wrote to Ann, Ramona, and Mai, and Jean notified Latoya and Sue.

CLEAR   I wrote to Ann, Ramona, and Mai**;** and Jean notified Latoya and Sue.

NOTE: Semicolons are most effective when they are not overused. Sometimes it is better to separate a compound sentence or a heavily punctuated sentence into two sentences rather than to use a semicolon.

ACCEPTABLE   In the tropical jungles of South America, it rains every day, sometimes all day**;** the vegetation there, some of which is found nowhere else in the world, is lush, dense, and fast-growing.

BETTER   In the tropical jungles of South America, it rains every day, sometimes all day**.** The vegetation there, some of which is found nowhere else in the world, is lush, dense, and fast-growing.

▶ EXERCISE 14   **Using Semicolons Correctly**

Most of the following sentences have a comma where there should be a semicolon. If the sentence needs a semicolon, write the <u>words before and after the missing semicolon</u> and insert the punctuation mark. If the sentence does not need a semicolon, write *C*. **Carets indicate placement of semicolons.**

EXAMPLE   **1.** Human beings have walked on the moon, they have not yet walked on any of the planets.
     1. *moon; they*

1. Miyoko finished her <u>homework</u>ʌ <u>then</u> she decided to go outside.
2. Each January some people predict the major events of the upcoming year, but they are seldom accurate.
3. Tie these newspapers together with <u>string</u>ʌ <u>put</u> the aluminum cans in a bag.

MECHANICS

LEP/ESL

General Strategies. In English, two independent clauses are not separated with only a comma; a semicolon or a comma plus a conjunction is needed. However, in some other languages such as Arabic, Russian, and Turkish, a comma may set off two independent clauses. You may find that some of your ESL students will use a comma where they should use a semicolon. Give them extra practice with this punctuation mark.

LEARNING STYLES

Auditory Learners. It is often easier to identify the two complete thoughts in a run-on sentence when the sentence is heard. When you introduce run-on sentences, read them to students and elicit from them where they think one complete thought ends and another begins. Point out that the semicolon would go at that point.

Kinetic Learners. Have students come to the chalkboard and punctuate sentences using large cardboard punctuation marks that have magnets affixed to them.

You can use sentences from the textbook, such as those found in different exercises in other grammar chapters, and omit the punctuation.

MECHANICS

SEGMENT 5 *(pp. 726–730)*
COLONS Rules 26n–26q
OBJECTIVE
• To write sentences using either a list or a time of day, using colons and commas where needed

MECHANICS

726

MECHANICS

726 *Punctuation*

4. I called Tom, Paul, and <u>Francine</u>ₐ <u>and</u> Fred called Amy, Carlos, and Brad.
5. Reading is my favorite <u>pastime</u>ₐ I love to begin a new book.
6. In 1991, Wellington Webb was elected mayor of <u>Denver</u>ₐ <u>he</u> was the first African American to hold that office.
7. The two companies merged, and they became the largest consumer goods firm in the nation. **7.** c
8. Your grades have <u>improved</u>ₐ <u>you</u> definitely will pass the course.
9. I want to work with animals <u>someday</u>ₐ I might even become a veterinarian.
10. We haven't seen the movie, for it hasn't come to our town yet. **10.** c

Colons

26n. Use a colon before a list of items, especially after expressions such as *the following* or *as follows.*

EXAMPLES You will need these items for map work**:** a ruler, colored pencils, and tracing paper.
Jack's pocket contained the following items**:** a key, half an apple, a piece of gum, and two rusty nails.
The primary colors are as follows**:** red, blue, and yellow.

Never use a colon directly after a verb or a preposition. Omit the colon or reword the sentence.

INCORRECT This marinara sauce is made of: tomatoes, bay leaves, onions, oregano, and garlic.
CORRECT This marinara sauce is made of the following ingredients**:** tomatoes, bay leaves, onions, oregano, and garlic.

INCORRECT My stepsister's favorite sports are: basketball, tennis, swimming, and bowling.

CORRECT My stepsister's favorite sports are basketball, tennis, swimming, and bowling.

CORRECT My stepsister's favorite sports are the following ones: basketball, tennis, swimming, and bowling.

26o. Use a colon between the hour and the minute.

EXAMPLES 8:30 A.M., 10:00 P.M.

26p. Use a colon after the salutation of a business letter.

EXAMPLES Dear Sir or Madam: Dear Mrs. Foster:
      To Whom It May Concern: Dear Dr. Christiano:

26q. Use a colon between chapter and verse in referring to passages from the Bible.

EXAMPLE John 1:1
     Ruth 1:15–17

▶ EXERCISE 15 **Using Colons and Commas Correctly**

Make each of the following word groups into a complete sentence by supplying an appropriate list or time. Insert colons and commas where they are needed.

EXAMPLE **1.** The test will begin at *[time]*
     1. *The test will begin at 9:30 A.M.*

1. My classes this year are as follows *[list]*
2. You will need these supplies for your project *[list]*
3. So far we have studied the following punctuation marks *[list]*
4. Meet me at the mall at *[time]*
5. My favorite foods are *[list]*

MECHANICS

ANSWERS
Exercise 15

Sentences will vary. The following examples are possibilities:

1. My classes this year are as follows: geometry, biology, English, American history, and gym.
2. You will need these supplies for your project: paper, glue, and scissors.
3. So far we have studied the following punctuation marks: period, comma, semicolon, and colon.
4. Meet me at the mall at 3:00.
5. My favorite foods are okra, pickles, olives, and spinach.

MECHANICS

COMMON ERROR

Problem. Students often do not know whether or not to capitalize the first word following a colon.

Solution. Tell students to capitalize the first word following a colon only when it introduces an independent clause or introduces a sentence as in "The teacher gave these instructions: 'Come into class quietly, take a seat, and get out your book.'"

728 *Punctuation*

▶ REVIEW C

Using End Marks, Commas, Semicolons, and Colons Correctly

The sentences in the following paragraph lack necessary end marks, commas, semicolons, and colons. Write each sentence, inserting the correct punctuation.

EXAMPLE   [1] What an unusual clever caring way to help animals

1. *What an unusual, clever, caring way to help animals!*

[1] Animal lovers, have you heard about the Sanctuary for Animals? [2] Founded by Leonard and Bunny Brook, the sanctuary is a safe home for all kinds of animals. [3] Through the years, hundreds of stray, unwanted, and abused animals have found a home at the sanctuary. [4] It is located on the Brooks' land in Westtown, New York. [5] On their two hundred acres, the Brooks take care of the following animals: camels, lions, elephants, even this Australian kangaroo, as well as dogs and cats. [6] Of course, Mr. and Mrs. Brook also raise chickens, keep horses, and look after their other farm animals. [7] The Brooks, their family, and their friends care for animals, like this baby cougar; they also let

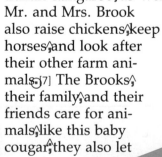

Colons **729**

the animals work for themselves. [8] How do the animals work? [9] The Brooks formed the Dawn Animal Agency, and their animals became actors and models. [10] You may have seen this camel or some of the other animals in magazines, movies, television shows, and commercials.

WRITING APPLICATION

Using Punctuation to Make Your Meaning Clear

When you talk, you have many different ways to make your meaning clear. You pause between ideas, raise and lower your voice, and gesture with your hands. When you write, your words and punctuation have to do all the work. Punctuation helps separate your ideas and show the relationships between them. Notice how changing punctuation changes the meaning in the following sentences.

EXAMPLES   We'll hold the carwash on Saturday, and on
            Monday we'll be able to buy the new baseball
            uniforms.
            We'll hold the carwash on Saturday and on
            Monday. We'll be able to buy the new
            baseball uniforms.

            I'll help wash cars with Jeff and Carla, and Susan
            will put up flyers around town.
            I'll help wash cars with Jeff, and Carla and Susan
            will put up flyers around town.

▶ WRITING ACTIVITY

Your class is sponsoring a carwash to raise money for a special project or trip. You've been chosen to write an announcement about the carwash for publication in a community newsletter. Write a brief announcement telling when and where the carwash will be, how much it will cost,

MECHANICS

 WRITING APPLICATION
Announcements must include enough information to be clear about the event. You may want to specify how many sentences students should write. Assessment can be based on correct use of punctuation and creativity.

CRITICAL THINKING
Analysis

Students could study effective presentation of information by examining different advertisements. Have them search through magazines and newspapers and find three advertisements that are appealing to them.

Have students write a sentence describing each advertisement. Then they can list all the information that particular ad contains.

Model this activity for students first. Depending upon your supply of materials, you could allow students to work in groups of four, with two sharing a magazine and two sharing a newspaper. Each pair could then switch media after a specified number of minutes.

MECHANICS

729

OBJECTIVES
- To identify what punctuation marks are needed in sentences and where they are needed
- To use all kinds of punctuation marks correctly in sentences

A DIFFERENT APPROACH

Volunteers can submit their announcements for a special bulletin board display.

what the money will be used for, and any other important details. In your announcement be sure to use end marks, commas, semicolons, and colons correctly.

Prewriting List the information that you'll include in your announcement. Clearly state the purpose of the carwash—what your class will spend the money on. You may also want to tell how much money the class needs to raise. Make sure you've included all the facts people will need to know about the time, location, and cost of the carwash.

Writing As you write your draft, remember that the purpose of your announcement is to attract customers. Write an attention-grabbing first sentence that explains the purpose of the carwash. Be sure to present all your information in clear, complete sentences. Add any important details that you didn't list earlier.

Evaluating and Revising Ask a friend to read your announcement. Is it clear and straightforward? Does it convince your friend that the carwash is for a good cause? If not, revise, rearrange, or add details.

Proofreading As you proofread your announcement, pay special attention to your use of punctuation. Remember to check the placement of colons in expressions of time.

Review: Posttest

Using End Marks, Commas, Semicolons, and Colons Correctly

The following sentences lack necessary end marks, commas, semicolons, and colons. Write each sentence, inserting the correct punctuation.

MECHANICS

EXAMPLE   **1.** Snakes lizards and crocodiles are reptiles
            1. *Snakes, lizards, and crocodiles are reptiles.*

1. Toads and frogs, on the other hand, are amphibians.
2. Some turtles live on land; others live in lakes, streams, or oceans.
3. Although turtles have no teeth, they can bite with their strong, hard beaks.
4. The terms *turtle* and *tortoise* are interchangeable, but *tortoise* usually refers to a land dweller.
5. The African pancake tortoise, which has a flat, flexible shell, has a unique means of defense.
6. Faced with a threat, it takes the following precautions: it crawls into a narrow crack in a rock, takes a deep breath, and wedges itself in tightly.
7. Because some species of tortoises are endangered, they cannot be sold as pets.
8. Three species of tortoises that live in the United States are the desert tortoise, the gopher tortoise, and the Texan tortoise.
9. The gopher tortoise lives in the Southeast, but the desert tortoise comes from the Southwest.
10. The Indian star tortoise, now an endangered species, is very rare.
11. As this kind of tortoise grows older, its shell grows larger, the number of stars increases, and their pattern becomes more complex.
12. The Indian star tortoise requires warmth, sunlight, and a diet of green vegetables.
13. Living in fresh water, soft-shelled turtles have long, flexible noses and fleshy lips.
14. Their shells are not really soft, however, but are covered by smooth skin.
15. Wanda, may I introduce you to my pet turtle, Pokey?
16. Pokey, who has been part of our family for years, is a red-eared turtle.
17. When my parents got Pokey, he was only two inches in diameter.

MECHANICS

LEP/ESL

     General Strategies. There are words in the **Review: Posttest** that some of your ESL students might not be familiar with such as *lizard, crocodile, tortoise, endangered,* and *species.* You may wish to review these words with them before giving assignment.

MECHANICS

18. Pokey has been in my family for fifteen years‚and he could easily live to be fifty⊙
19. If you look at the design on Pokey's shell‚you can get a good idea of his age⊙
20. Don't you agree with me‚Wanda‚that a turtle makes a good pet**?**

SUMMARY OF USES OF THE COMMA

26f	Use commas to separate items in a series—words, phrases, and clauses.
26g	Use a comma to separate two or more adjectives that come before a noun.
26h	Use a comma before *and*, *but*, *for*, *or*, *nor*, *so*, and *yet* when they join independent clauses.
26i	Use commas to set off an expression that interrupts a sentence.
	(1) Use commas to set off nonessential participial phrases and nonessential subordinate clauses.
	(2) Use commas to set off appositives and appositive phrases that are nonessential.
	(3) Use commas to set off words used in direct address.
	(4) Use commas to set off parenthetical expressions.
26j	Use a comma after certain introductory elements.
	(1) Use a comma after *yes*, *no*, or any mild exclamation such as *well* or *why* at the beginning of a sentence.
	(2) Use a comma after an introductory participial phrase.
	(3) Use a comma after two or more introductory prepositional phrases.
	(4) Use a comma after an introductory adverb clause.
26k	Use a comma in certain conventional situations.
	(1) Use commas to separate items in dates and addresses.
	(2) Use a comma after the salutation of a friendly letter and after the closing of any letter.

MECHANICS

MECHANICS

OBJECTIVE

- To proofread and revise sentences for the correct use of underlining (italics), quotation marks, apostrophes, hyphens, parentheses, and dashes

RESOURCES

PUNCTUATION
- Chapter Review Form A
- Chapter Review Form B
- Assessment Portfolio
    Mechanics Pretest
    Mechanics Mastery Test 1
    Mechanics Mastery Test 2

27 PUNCTUATION

Underlining (Italics), Quotation Marks, Apostrophes, Hyphens, Parentheses, Dashes

MECHANICS

Diagnostic Test

Using Underlining (Italics), Quotation Marks, Apostrophes, Hyphens, Parentheses, and Dashes

The following sentences contain errors in the use of underlining (italics), quotation marks, apostrophes, hyphens, parentheses, or dashes. Write each sentence correctly.

Hyphens are indicated by the ⋏ symbol.

EXAMPLE   **1.** My mother's note said, "Please buy celery, rye bread, and milk.

    1. *My mother's note said, "Please buy celery, rye bread, and milk."*

1. Sharon(she's my youngest cousin)asked me to tell her a bedtime story.

2. "Did you know," asked Kathy, "that the novel *Don Quixote* has seventy⋏four chapters?

CHAPTER OVERVIEW

This chapter introduces several marks of punctuation that seventh-graders must master: underlining (italics), quotation marks, apostrophes, hyphens, parentheses, and dashes. Explanations of each punctuation mark are followed by exercises that provide students the opportunity to practice newly learned skills as well as to integrate those skills with the writing process. The **Writing Application** challenges students to use quotation marks correctly in reports based on interviews.

USING THE DIAGNOSTIC TEST

If students are having problems using these punctuation marks in their writing, you can use the **Diagnostic Test** to pinpoint error patterns and specific strengths and weaknesses. Your assessments of students' performance on this test, in conjunction with your assessments of students' writing, will help you determine which rules students need to review.

MECHANICS

3. "Have you ever read Robert Hayden's poem 'Those Winter Sundays?" asked Jorge.

4. "Who's your favorite professional baseball player?" asked Don.

5. Randall Jarrell wrote both fiction and nonfiction, but he's best known for his poetry.

6. Many people misspell the word *accommodate* by leaving out one <u>c</u>.

7. "Meet me at 2:30 sharp; don't be late," my mother's note read.

8. The reading list included the novel <u>Island of the Blue Dolphins</u>.

9. My complaint was that the sandwiches we ate at the beach were three-fourths sand.

10. In English class today, we read the poem "Sisters," which was written by Lucille Clifton.

11. "Can you volunteer just two hours' worth of your time a week?" asked Mrs. Jackson.

12. The bearded man, you probably guessed, is really the jewel thief in disguise.   **12. dash/dash**

13. "A group of twenty-one students is not a two-thirds majority of our class," Stan stated.

14. This coupon is for a free enchilada at Pedro's Lunch Palace on Oak Street.

15. The librarian told me that the only copy of the book *Children's Songs* had been checked out for more than two weeks.

16. Ms. Liu said, "Turn to Chapter 7, 'Multiplying Fractions.'"

17. "What is the origin of the word <u>inoculate</u>?" Derrick asked Dr. Jackson.

18. "The state of Massachusetts was named after a Native American people that lived in that area," Jessica said.

19. She added, "The word *Massachusett* also refers to that people's language."

20. Aunt Rosie and Uncle Fred went to the Bahamas on the cruise ship <u>Princess</u>.

MECHANICS

UNDERLINING (ITALICS) Rules 27a, 27b

OBJECTIVE

- To identify words in sentences that should be italicized and to underline them

Underlining (Italics)

Italics are printed letters that lean to the right—*like this.* When you write or type, you show that a word should be *italicized* by underlining it. If your composition were to be printed, the typesetter would set the underlined words in italics. For example, if you type

> Madeleine L'Engle wrote <u>A Wrinkle in Time</u>.

the sentence would be printed like this:

> Madeleine L'Engle wrote *A Wrinkle in Time*.

NOTE: If you use a personal computer, you can probably set words in italics yourself. Most word-processing software and many printers can produce italic type.

27a. Use underlining (italics) for titles of books, plays, periodicals, films, television programs, works of art, long musical compositions, ships, aircraft, and spacecraft.

TYPE OF NAME	EXAMPLES	
Books	*A Wind in the Door*	*Watership Down* *Mules and Men*
Plays	*Our Town* *Hamlet*	*I Never Sang for My Father*
Periodicals	the *Houston Post* *Essence*	*National Geographic*
Films	*The Maltese Falcon*	*Cry Freedom*
Television Programs	*The Golden Girls*	*In Living Color*
Works of Art	*Starry Night* *The Dream*	*Watson and the Shark*
Long Musical Compositions	*Carmen* *An American in Paris*	*Music for the Royal Fireworks*
Ships	the *Titanic* the *Pequod*	the USS *Eisenhower*
Aircraft	the *Silver Dart* the *Hindenburg*	the *Deperdussin Racer*
Spacecraft	*Soyuz XI*	*Atlantis*

MECHANICS

RESOURCES

UNDERLINING (ITALICS)
- Underlining and Italics

QUICK REMINDER

Put the following sentences on the chalkboard. Then ask students to identify the word or words in the sentences that should be italicized or underlined.

1. My favorite episode of Star Trek is "The Trouble with Tribbles."
2. Teresita loves Bless Me, Ultima because the novel reminds her of her grandmother.
3. The Magic Flute was the first opera Mozart wrote.

RULE 27a

Individual newspapers and magazines may have house styles for the punctuation of titles. For example, some publications use quotation marks rather than italics for the titles of films.

MECHANICS

MECHANICS

MECHANICS

736 *Punctuation*

NOTE: The article *the* before the title of a magazine or a newspaper is neither italicized nor capitalized when it is written within a sentence.

EXAMPLE   Would you like to subscribe to **the** *Dallas Morning News*?

☞ REFERENCE NOTE: For examples of titles that are not italicized but are enclosed in quotation marks, see page 744.

27b.   Use underlining (italics) for words, letters, and figures referred to as such.

EXAMPLES   I often confuse the words *accept* and *except.*
Don't forget to double the final *n* before you add *–ing* in words like *running.*
Can you tell whether he wrote a *4* or a *9*?

▷ EXERCISE 1   **Using Underlining (Italics) Correctly**

For each of the following sentences, write each <u>word or item that should be italicized</u> and underline it.

EXAMPLE   1. Mike Royko writes a column for the Chicago Tribune.
          1. *Chicago Tribune*

1. The British spell the word <u>humor</u> with a <u>u</u> after the <u>o</u>.
2. In Denmark, you might see the spelling *triatlon* for the word <u>triathlon</u>.
3. The current <u>Newsweek</u> has an informative article on the famine in Africa.
4. Our school paper, the <u>Norwalk Valley News</u>, is published weekly.
5. Luis Valdez wrote and directed <u>La Bamba</u>, a movie about the life of Richie Valens.
6. The <u>Oceanic</u> is one of the ocean liners that sails to the Caribbean.
7. The movie <u>Dances with Wolves</u> has some of the most beautiful photography that I have ever seen.
8. Our local theater group is presenting <u>The Time of Your Life</u>, a comedy by William Saroyan.

OBJECTIVES

- To proofread and revise sentences for the correct use of quotation marks, commas, end marks, and capital letters
- To revise indirect quotations to create direct quotations
- To write correctly punctuated dialogue

9. Lindbergh's <u>Spirit of St. Louis</u> is on display at the museum, along with the Wright brothers' <u>Flyer</u> and <u>Gemini IV</u>.

10. The best novel that I read during vacation was <u>The Summer of the Swans</u>.

Quotation Marks

27c. Use quotation marks to enclose a ***direct quotation***—a person's exact words.

Be sure to place quotation marks both before and after a person's exact words.

EXAMPLES   Emma Lazarus wrote the famous quotation on the Statue of Liberty, which begins with the words "Give me your tired, your poor. . . ."
"When the bell rings," said the teacher, "leave the room quietly."

Do not use quotation marks for an ***indirect quotation***—a rewording of a direct quotation.

DIRECT QUOTATION   Tom predicted, "It will be a close game." [Tom's exact words]
INDIRECT QUOTATION   Tom predicted that it would be a close game. [not Tom's exact words]

27d. A direct quotation begins with a capital letter.

EXAMPLES   Maria said, "The *carne asada* isn't ready yet, but please help yourself to the guacamole."
While he was in prison, Richard Lovelace wrote a poem containing the well-known quotation "Stone walls do not a prison make."

27e. When the expression identifying the speaker interrupts a quoted sentence, the second part of the quotation begins with a small letter.

▼ **RESOURCES**

QUOTATION MARKS
- Direct and Split Quotations
- Punctuating Quotations
- Other Uses of Quotation Marks

QUICK REMINDER
Write the following sentences on the chalkboard and ask students to insert periods, commas, and quotation marks where they are needed:

1. Do you want to go watch the fireworks? Alice asked.
2. No, I had enough fireworks this weekend Andy said. I'm going to stay home and read.
3. Well, I didn't said Alice I never pass up a chance to watch fireworks.

STUDENTS WITH SPECIAL NEEDS

Students with learning disabilities may find it difficult to use quotation marks in conjunction with other punctuation marks. For an activity that engages all three learning modalities (an effective teaching strategy for students with learning disabilities), write visual cues in the form of patterns on the chalkboard. For example, a pattern for a quoted statement could be presented like this:

____ said, "____."

Similarly, the pattern for a quoted question and exclamation could be presented like this:

____ asked, "____?" *and* ____ exclaimed, "____!"

Ask students to fill in the blanks and to read their sentences aloud.

EXAMPLES   "Lightning has always awed people," explained Mrs. Worthington, "and many of us are still frightened by it."

"The time has come," insisted the speaker, "to improve our educational program."

A quoted sentence that is divided in this way is called a *broken quotation*. Notice that each part of a broken quotation is enclosed in a set of quotation marks.

When the second part of a divided quotation is a sentence, it begins with a capital letter.

EXAMPLE   "I can't go today," I said. "**A**sk me tomorrow."

27f.   A direct quotation is set off from the rest of the sentence by a comma, a question mark, or an exclamation point, but not by a period.

Set off means "to separate." If a quotation comes at the beginning of a sentence, a comma follows it. If a quotation comes at the end of a sentence, a comma comes before it. If a quoted sentence is interrupted, a comma follows the first part and comes before the second part.

EXAMPLES   Bernie said, "Science is more interesting than history."

"I especially like to do experiments," Velma commented.

"Yes," Juan added, "Bernie loves to do experiments, too."

When a quotation ends with a question mark or an exclamation point, no comma is needed.

EXAMPLES   "Is that a good video game?" Jane wanted to know.

"I'll say it is!" Debbie exclaimed.

▶ EXERCISE 2   **Punctuating Quotations**

For each of the following sentences, insert commas, quotation marks, and capital letters where they are needed. If a sentence is correct, write C.

EXAMPLE **1.** Let's go to a horror movie this afternoon, said Bob.

> **1.** *"Let's go to a horror movie this afternoon," said Bob.*

1. When I shrieked in fear, the usher warned me to be quiet. **1.** C
2. At the same time, Bob whispered "It's only a movie—calm down!"
3. He pointed out that the people around us were getting annoyed. **3.** C
4. I quietly replied "I'm sorry."
5. "You shouldn't have screamed," he complained.
6. "From now on," I said to him, "I promise I'll try to be quiet."
7. When the lights came on, Bob said, "It's time to go."
8. Outside the theater he muttered something about people who shouldn't go to horror movies. **8.** C
9. "But I can't help it," I explained.
10. "You were even afraid," Bob protested, "during the credits!"

27g. A period or a comma should always be placed *inside* the closing quotation marks.

EXAMPLES "The Ramses exhibit begins over there," said the museum guide.
Darnell replied, "I'm ready to see some ancient Egyptian jewelry and art work."

27h. A question mark or an exclamation point should be placed inside the closing quotation marks when the quotation itself is a question or an exclamation. Otherwise, it should be placed outside.

EXAMPLES "How far have we come?" asked the exhausted man. [The quotation is a question.]
Who said, "Give me liberty or give me death"? [The sentence, not the quotation, is a question.]

MECHANICS

INTEGRATING THE LANGUAGE ARTS

Literature Link. Select a story that contains plenty of dialogue, such as "Charles" by Shirley Jackson, and have students read the story. During a class discussion of the story, ask students to consider how difficult it would be to read the story without correct use of quotation marks. To illustrate this point, copy a portion of dialogue from the story on the chalkboard. Leave out the quotation marks or use them incorrectly. Students will then be able to see how important the correct use of quotation marks is to the readers of a piece of writing.

A DIFFERENT APPROACH

Designate sounds to represent each punctuation mark. For example, quotation marks could be represented by the sound *blip,* commas by *ping,* and periods by *pop.* Write the punctuation marks and their corresponding sounds on the chalkboard. Then ask student volunteers to read their answers for **Exercise 2** aloud. Have them indicate the appropriate punctuation marks as they read by making the designated sounds. The example sentence for **Exercise 2** would sound like this: *blip* Let's go to a horror movie this afternoon *ping blip* said Bob *pop*

MECHANICS

739

"Jump!" ordered the firefighter. [The quotation is an exclamation.]

I couldn't believe it when he said, "No, thank you"! [The sentence, not the quotation, is an exclamation.]

When both the sentence and the quotation at the end of the sentence are questions (or exclamations), only one question mark (or exclamation point) is used. It is placed inside the closing quotation marks.

EXAMPLE   Did Josh really say, "What's Cinco de Mayo?"

EXERCISE 3   **Punctuating and Capitalizing Quotations**

For each of the following sentences, insert capital letters, quotation marks, and other marks of punctuation where needed.

EXAMPLE   **1.** Ashley Bryan wore traditional African clothes when he came to our school Elton said

1. *"Ashley Bryan wore traditional African clothes when he came to our school," Elton said.*

1. "Oh, like the clothes Mr. Johnson showed us in class!" Janell exclaimed.

2. Elton asked, "have you read any of Ashley Bryan's books about African culture?"

3. "I've read," Janell quickly replied, "the one titled *Beat the Story-Drum, Pum-Pum.*"

4. "I'd like to read that again," Elton said, "those African folk tales are wonderful."

5. "Mrs. Ray thinks *Walk Together Children* is excellent," Janell said.

6. "Isn't that," Elton asked, "about Negro spirituals?"

7. "You're right," Janell answered, "and Bryan wrote that spirituals are America's greatest contribution to world music."

8. She added, "he grew up in New York City and began writing stories and drawing when he was still in kindergarten."

9. "Did you know," Elton asked, "that he illustrated his own books?"

10. "This is one of the woodcuts Bryan made to illustrate *Walk Together Children,*" he added.

Reprinted with permission of Atheneum Publishers, an imprint of Macmillan Publishing Company from WALK TOGETHER CHILDREN selected and illustrated by Ashley Bryan. Copyright © 1974 Ashley Bryan.

▶ EXERCISE 4 **Revising Indirect Quotations to Create Direct Quotations**

Revise each of the following sentences by changing the indirect quotation to a direct quotation. Be sure to use capital letters and punctuation wherever necessary.

EXAMPLE 1. I asked my grandmother if she would like to help us paint our float.

1. *"Grandma," I asked, "would you like to help us paint our float?"*

1. Mayor Alaniz announced that he would lead the parade this year.
2. Ms. Feldman asked me what my plans for the big parade were.
3. I answered that my brother and I were building a float.
4. She exclaimed that she thought that was terrific.
5. Ron remarked that our float probably had something to do with sports.

VISUAL CONNECTIONS
About the Artist

In kindergarten, Ashley Bryan began illustrating books to give to his friends. Since that time, Bryan has illustrated and written many children's books based on African, American, and Caribbean folktales.

Mr. Bryan was born in New York, in 1923, and grew up in the Bronx, where he attended public schools. He then majored in philosophy at Columbia University and went on to teach at Queens College of the City University of New York, Lafayette College, the Dalton School, and the Brooklyn Museum. Mr. Bryan has also worked with Head Start and other community programs.

ANSWERS
Exercise 4

1. Mayor Alaniz announced, "I will lead the parade this year."
2. Ms. Feldman asked me, "What are your plans for the big parade?"
3. I answered, "My brother and I are building a float."
4. She exclaimed, "That's terrific!"
5. Ron remarked, "Your float probably has something to do with sports."

MECHANICS

---

742 *Punctuation*

MECHANICS

27i. When you write dialogue (conversation), begin a new paragraph every time the speaker changes.

EXAMPLE   The young man smiled, and said, "My old master, now let me tell you the truth. My home is not so far away. It is quite near your temple. We have been old neighbors for many years."

The old monk was very surprised. "I don't believe it. You, young man, will have your joke. Where is there another house round here?"

"My master, would I lie to you? I live right beside your temple. The Green Pond is my home."

"You live in the pond?" The old monk was even more astonished.

"That's right. In fact," said Li Aiqi, in a perfectly serious tone, "I'm not a man at all. I am a dragon."

from "Green Dragon Pond," a Bai folk tale

☞ REFERENCE NOTE: For more information on writing dialogue, see pages 140 and 194.

27j. When a quotation consists of several sentences, put quotation marks only at the beginning and the end of the whole quotation.

EXAMPLE   "Mary Elizabeth and I will wait for you at Robertson's Drug Store. Please try to get there as soon as you can. We don't want to be late for the concert," Jerome said before he rushed off down the hall.

27k. Use single quotation marks to enclose a quotation within a quotation.

EXAMPLES   Brandon added, "My mom always says, 'Look before you leap.'"

"Did Ms. Neuman really say, 'It's all right to use your books and your notes during the test'?" asked Sakura.

PICTURE THIS

Watch out! You and a friend are making sure that no one gets hurt at your little sister's birthday party. If this child hits the piñata hard enough, it will break open. Then all the small toys and treats inside will fall out, and the children will rush for them. Breaking open piñatas, which are papier-mâché figures like this one, is a Latin American party custom. It's also popular in the United States. As you watch the children, you and your friend talk about the scene. Write a short conversation about what you see and hear. Be sure to use quotation marks and punctuation correctly.

Subject: a piñata contest
Audience: a friend
Purpose: to talk about what's happening

> **27l.** Use quotation marks to enclose the titles of short works such as short stories, poems, articles, songs, episodes of television programs, and chapters and other parts of books.

MECHANICS

PICTURE THIS

As a prewriting activity, ask students who have attended a piñata party to describe the rules of the game and the kinds of toys and treats piñatas hold. You could divide the students into pairs and have them collaborate to write short conversations.

COOPERATIVE LEARNING

Divide the students into groups of four and assign each group a category of titles that need to be underlined (italicized) or enclosed in quotation marks. Have groups generate examples of titles within their categories. Then have each group create a bulletin-board display that shows the list of titles generated by the group.

MECHANICS

743

INTEGRATING THE LANGUAGE ARTS

Mechanics and Writing.
Have students create guides they can keep in their notebooks to use as references when punctuating titles in their writing. List on the chalkboard all the categories of titles in the examples for **Rules 27a** and **27l.** Have the class brainstorm other categories to add to the list. Then alphabetize the list and designate beside each category whether it requires italics or quotation marks. Have students copy the list and illustrate their guides with pictures or icons if they like.

TYPE OF NAME	EXAMPLES
Short Stories	"A Day's Wait" "The Medicine Bag" "The Circuit"
Poems	"In Time of Silver Rain" "Birdfoot's Grampa" "Annabel Lee"
Articles	"Rooting for the Home Team" "Annie Leibovitz: Behind the Images" "The Storytelling Renaissance"
Songs	"La Cucaracha" "The Star-Spangled Banner" "Swing Low, Sweet Chariot"
Episodes of Television Programs	"Cheap Is Cheap" "This Side of Paradise" "Growing Up Hispanic"
Chapters and Other Parts of Books	"The Natural World" "The Myths of Greece and Rome" "The Double Task of Language"

REFERENCE NOTE: For examples of titles that are italicized, see page 735.

▶ EXERCISE 5   **Punctuating Quotations**

Insert quotation marks where they are needed in each of the following items. If a sentence is correct, write C.

EXAMPLE   1. Let's sing 'The Ballad of Gregorio Cortez,' suggested Jim.
      1. *"Let's sing 'The Ballad of Gregorio Cortez,'" suggested Jim.*

1. "Lani, have you seen my clarinet?" asked Rob. "It was on this table. I need it for my lesson this afternoon."
2. The most interesting chapter in *The Sea Around Us* is "The Birth of an Island."
3. "Didn't Benjamin Franklin once say, 'Time is money?'" asked Myra.
4. "My favorite Langston Hughes poem is 'As I Grew Older,'" said Mom.

REVIEW A

OBJECTIVES

- To proofread and revise paragraphs for the correct use of quotation marks, commas, and end marks
- To revise a passage for correct indentation of paragraphs

TIMESAVER
You could provide keys for **Exercises 2–5** and allow students to check their answers independently and to correct their errors. Then you could use **Review A** to evaluate students' mastery of the material in this segment.

5. Lea Evans said, "One of the greatest changes in architecture has been in the design of churches. They no longer follow traditional forms. Churches have been built that are shaped like stars, fish, and ships."
6. The latest issue of *Discover* has a fascinating picture of a shark that swallowed an anchor. **6. C**
7. "Do you know the speech that begins 'What's in a name?' from *Romeo and Juliet*?" I asked.
8. "Yes," answered Li. "My mother used to say that to me when I was a little girl. That's how I first heard of Shakespeare."
9. "A human hand has more than twenty-five bones and twenty-five muscles!" exclaimed Marcus. "No wonder it can do so much."
10. There is an article called "The Customers Always Write" in today's newspaper.

▶ REVIEW A **Punctuating Paragraphs**

Revise the following paragraphs, using quotation marks and other marks of punctuation wherever necessary. Remember to begin a new paragraph each time the speaker changes. If a sentence is correct, write C. [Note: The punctuation marks that are already included in the exercise are correct.] Carets indicate paragraph breaks.

EXAMPLE [1] **Mr. Brown asked Can you baby-sit tonight?**
  1. *Mr. Brown asked, "Can you baby-sit tonight?"*

[1] Last night I baby-sat for the Browns, a new family **1. C** on our block. [2] "Come in," Mrs. Brown greeted me. [3] "You must be Lisa." "Hello, Mrs. Brown," I replied. [5] "I'm looking forward to meeting the children." [6] "First," Mrs. Brown explained, "I want you to meet Ludwig." [7] "Is he a member of the family?" I asked. [8] "In a way," replied Mrs. Brown as she led me to the kitchen and pointed to an aging dachshund. [9] "That is Ludwig. [10] He rules this house and everyone in it."

[11] Mr. Brown entered the kitchen and introduced himself. [12] "I see that you've met Ludwig," he said. [13] "Yes,

APOSTROPHES Rules 27m–27s

OBJECTIVES

- To add necessary apostrophes to words in a passage
- To revise expressions by using the possessive case
- To write sentences that include plural possessives
- To write possessives of indefinite pronouns
- To add necessary apostrophes to contractions

---

746 *Punctuation*

Mrs. Brown answered for me. [14]"Why don't you give Lisa her instructions while I go find the children?"

[15]"If Ludwig whines," said Mr. Brown, "give him a dog biscuit." [16]"Should I take him for a walk?" I asked. [17]"No," replied Mr. Brown. [18]"Just let him out into the yard."

[19] Mrs. Brown came back into the kitchen with the children. [20]"Did my husband remind you to cover Ludwig when he falls asleep?" she asked. [21]"I'll remember," I promised. [22]"But what should I do for the children?" [23]"Don't worry," said Mr. Brown. [24]"They'll behave themselves and go to bed when they're supposed to." [25]"As I told you," laughed Mrs. Brown, "Ludwig rules this house and everyone in it, even the sitter!"

Apostrophes

Possessive Case

The *possessive case* of a noun or a pronoun shows ownership or relationship.

OWNERSHIP	RELATIONSHIP
Kathleen's desk **his** bat **their** car	**anybody's** guess an **hour's** time **horse's** mane

27m. To form the possessive case of a singular noun, add an apostrophe and an *s*.

EXAMPLES   a boy's cap   Cleon's pen
           the baby's toy   Charles's opinion

NOTE: A proper noun ending in *s* may take only an apostrophe to form the possessive case if the addition of *'s* would make the name awkward to say.

EXAMPLES   Philippines' government
           Ms. Rodgers' cat

RESOURCES

APOSTROPHES
- Apostrophes to Show Possession
- Apostrophes in Contractions
- Contractions and Possessive Pronouns
- Apostrophes in Plurals

QUICK REMINDER

Put the following paragraph on the chalkboard and ask students to insert apostrophes where they are needed:

My dog Dash loves the cats food more than his own. If I leave it on the floor, he thinks its his. Ive even caught him with his front paws on the counter-top trying to reach the cats dish.

27m

▶ EXERCISE 6 **Using Apostrophes for Singular Possessives**

For each sentence in the following paragraph, identify the <u>word that needs an apostrophe</u>. Then, write the word correctly punctuated.

EXAMPLE [1] The Prado in Madrid, Spain, is one of the worlds greatest museums.

1. *worlds—world's*

[1] Shown here is one of the <u>Prados</u> paintings by Diego Velázquez, *Las Meninas*. [2] <u>Velázquezs</u> painting is known in English as The Maids of Honor. [3] In the center of the canvas is Princess Margarita, the royal <u>couples</u> daughter. [4] To the <u>princesss</u> right, a kneeling maid of honor offers her something to drink. [5] To the royal <u>childs</u> left, another maid of honor curtsies. [6] On the far left of the canvas, you can see the <u>artists</u> own image, for he has painted himself! [7] The <u>palaces</u> other important people, such as the chamberlain and a court jester, also appear. [8] The faces of <u>Margaritas</u> parents are reflected in the mirror on the back wall. [9] In the foreground, the royal dog ignores a young <u>guests</u> invitation to play. [10] This <u>paintings</u> fame has grown since it was painted in 1656, and each year millions of people see it while visiting the Prado.

Diego Velázquez, *Las Meninas*, Prado, Madrid, Scala/Art Resource.

MECHANICS

 **MEETING INDIVIDUAL NEEDS**

LEP/ESL

General Strategies. There are many ways to express possession in the world's many languages. For example, *the man's coat* would be *the coat of the man* in Spanish, *man of coat* in Japanese, *coat man* in Indonesian and Russian, and *coat the man* in Arabic. Students who speak these and other languages may be completely unfamiliar with showing possession by using an apostrophe. Ask students to tell you how possession is indicated in their languages and discuss with students the differences between those methods and the English method of showing possession with punctuation.

👁 **VISUAL CONNECTIONS**
Las Meninas

About the Artist. Diego Velázquez, thought to be one of the world's greatest artists, was born in Seville, Spain, in 1599. When Velázquez was only twelve, he was apprenticed to a painter named Francisco Pacheco, who influenced the development of his early naturalistic style. In 1622, Velázquez traveled to Madrid, and in 1623, he was appointed court painter. One of Velázquez's most famous paintings, done only four years before his death in 1660, is *Las Meninas* ("Maids of Honor"). *Las Meninas* portrays a casual glance into Velázquez's studio, where he is painting a portrait of the king and queen.

MECHANICS

27n. To form the possessive case of a plural noun that does not end in *s*, add an apostrophe and an *s*.

EXAMPLES mice's tracks   men's hats
          children's games teeth's enamel

27o. To form the possessive case of a plural noun ending in *s*, add only the apostrophe.

EXAMPLES cats' basket   four days' delay
          brushes' bristles the Carsons' bungalow

NOTE: Do not use an apostrophe to form the *plural* of a noun. Remember that the apostrophe shows ownership or relationship.

INCORRECT Three girls' lost their tickets.
  CORRECT Three **girls** lost their tickets. [plural]
  CORRECT Three **girls'** tickets were lost. [plural possessive]

▶ EXERCISE 7 **Writing Possessives**

Rewrite each of the following expressions by using the possessive case. Be sure to insert an apostrophe in the right place.

EXAMPLE **1.** food for the dog
         1. *the dog's food*

1. the nominee of the party
2. the clothes of the babies
3. the grades of my sister
4. the name tags of the guests
5. the dish for the cat

▶ EXERCISE 8 **Writing Sentences with Plural Possessives**

Write the plural form of each of the following words. After each plural form, write a sentence using the plural form as a possessive.

1. dog
2. plumber
3. goose
4. friend
5. woman

ANSWERS
Exercise 7

1. the party's nominee

2. the babies' clothes

3. my sister's grades

4. the guests' name tags

5. the cat's dish

ANSWERS
Exercise 8

Sentences will vary. Here are some possibilities:

1. *dogs*
The dogs' toys were scattered all over the back yard.

2. *plumbers*
George tripped over the plumbers' tools.

3. *geese*
The geese's migration took almost two weeks.

4. *friends*
Jamie is always willing to baby-sit his friends' dogs and cats.

5. *women*
The women's meeting featured a speech by the governor of Texas.

27p. Do not use an apostrophe with possessive
personal pronouns.

EXAMPLES Is that sticker **yours** or **mine**?
Our cat is friendlier than **theirs**.
His report on Cherokee folk tales was as good
as **hers**.

☞ REFERENCE NOTE: For more about possessive personal pronouns,
see pages 606–607 and 749.

27q. To form the possessive case of some indefinite
pronouns, add an apostrophe and an *s*.

EXAMPLES neither**'s** homework
everyone**'s** choice
somebody**'s** jacket

☞ REFERENCE NOTE: For more about indefinite pronouns in the
possessive case, see page 749.

▶ EXERCISE 9 **Writing Possessives of Indefinite
Pronouns**

Rewrite each of the following expressions by using the
possessive case of each indefinite pronoun. Be sure to
insert an apostrophe in the right place.

EXAMPLE **1.** the park for everyone
1. *everyone's park*

1. the stereo that belongs to somebody **1.** somebody's stereo
2. the footprints of anyone **2.** anyone's footprints
3. the fault of nobody **3.** nobody's fault
4. the turn of either **4.** either's turn
5. the opinion of another **5.** another's opinion

Contractions

27r. Use an apostrophe to show where letters have
been omitted (left out) in a contraction.

COMMON ERROR
Problem. Students may have
difficulty distinguishing between possessives and contractions when reading
sentences.

Solution. Encourage students
to read the sentences aloud. Often their
ears will catch the sense of the sentence
when their eyes are confused.

MEETING
INDIVIDUAL
NEEDS

AT-RISK STUDENTS
An exercise that uses possessive
case nouns and pronouns to describe
objects in students' lives might make the
usage more personally relevant for them.
Have each student write down three
things that belong to the student, three
things that belong to someone they
know, and three things that are shared
by two people. Then have the student
write in the possessive case the name of
the owner or owners in front of each
object listed. Have students exchange
lists with partners to check each other's
punctuation.

MECHANICS

LEARNING STYLES

Kinetic Learners. Have students write on strips of paper word combinations that can be made into contractions, such as *cannot, have not, should have,* and *who is.* Students should also write apostrophes on several strips. Have students cut and rearrange the strips to change the words and phrases into contractions.

A *contraction* is a shortened form of a word, a number, or a group of words. The apostrophe in a contraction shows where letters or numerals have been left out.

Common Contractions	
I am . . . . I'm	they had . . . . they'd
1993 . . . . '93	where is . . . . where's
let us . . . . let's	we are . . . . we're
of the clock . . . . . o'clock	he is . . . . he's
she would . . . . she'd	you will . . . . you'll

The word *not* can be shortened to *n't* and added to a verb, usually without any change in the spelling of the verb.

EXAMPLE	is not . . . . isn't	has not . . . . hasn't
	are not . . . . aren't	have not . . . . haven't
	does not . . doesn't	had not . . . . hadn't
	do not . . . . . don't	should not . . shouldn't
	was not . . . . wasn't	would not . . wouldn't
	were not . . weren't	could not . . . . couldn't
EXCEPTIONS	will not . . . . **won't**	cannot . . . . **can't**

Be careful not to confuse contractions with possessive pronouns.

CONTRACTIONS	POSSESSIVE PRONOUNS
It's Friday. [*It is*] **It's** been a pleasure. [*It has*]	**Its** nest is over there.
Who's your server? [*Who is*] **Who's** been practicing the piano? [*Who has*]	**Whose** backpack is this?
You're late. [*You are*]	**Your** mom called
They're arriving soon. [*They are*] **There's** the path. [*There is*]	**Their** parakeet is friendly. That rose bush is **theirs**.

INTEGRATING THE LANGUAGE ARTS

Mechanics and Writing. Remind students that while contractions are handy in everyday speech and writing, good usage dictates that they not be used in formal writing. Help your students understand that because of its audience and purpose, formal writing often requires different usage.

▶ EXERCISE 10 **Using Apostrophes in Contractions Correctly**

For each of the following sentences, write the <u>word or words requiring an apostrophe</u> and insert the apostrophe. Be sure to spell the word correctly. If a sentence is correct, write *C.*

EXAMPLE **1.** Arent you going with us at one oclock?
1. *Aren't; o'clock*

1. <u>We'd</u> better chain our bicycles to the rack.
2. That old <u>car's</u> seen better days, <u>hasn't</u> it?
3. She <u>wasn't</u> too happy to see us.
4. <u>Whose</u> ringing the doorbell? **4.** Who's
5. We <u>won't</u> forget how helpful <u>you've</u> been.
6. <u>I'm</u> certain <u>you'll</u> be invited.
7. Whose turn is it to take attendance? **7.** C
8. <u>Ann's</u> an excellent swimmer, but she <u>can't</u> dive.
9. <u>It's</u> almost time to leave, <u>isn't</u> it?
10. <u>I'm</u> sure <u>they'll</u> show up before <u>it's</u> over.

▶ EXERCISE 11 **Punctuating Contractions**

For each sentence in the following paragraph, identify the <u>word that needs an apostrophe</u> to indicate a contraction. Then, write the word correctly.

EXAMPLE [1] Whats the best route from Lawrenceville, New Jersey, to Newtown, Pennsylvania?
1. *What's*

[1] <u>There's</u> one especially pretty route you can take to get there. [2] I think <u>you'll</u> enjoy the drive. [3] You <u>shouldn't</u> go due west directly. [4] <u>You've</u> got to go north or south first. [5] <u>It's</u> easier to go south on Route 206 to Route U.S. 1, cross the Delaware River, and then go north on Route 32 to Yardley. [6] From Yardley, turn left on Route 332, and in a little while <u>I'm</u> sure you will find yourself in Newtown. [7] If <u>you'd</u> prefer a different route, go south on Route 206 to Route 546 and make a right turn to go west. [8] After you cross the Delaware River and the road becomes 532, <u>don't</u>

MECHANICS

MECHANICS

turn until Linton Hill Road. [9] When you turn left onto Linton Hill Road, it <u>won't</u> be long before you arrive in Newtown. [10] <u>Here's</u> a map you can use to help you find your way.

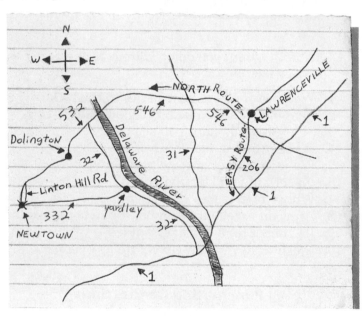

▶ EXERCISE 12 **Writing Contractions**

For each sentence in the following paragraph, write the contraction of the underlined word or words.

EXAMPLE [1] If you think it <u>should have</u> been easy to visit the building shown on the next page, guess again!

1. *should've*

1. It's   [1] <u>It is</u> the Potala Palace in Lhasa, Tibet, which my par-
2. couldn't   ents and I visited last year. [2] The city of Lhasa is two miles high in the Himalaya Mountains, and we <u>could not</u> move around much because the lack of oxygen made us tired. [3] The Potala Palace is the former residence of the
3. who's   Tibetan spiritual leader, <u>who has</u> been living in exile in

India. [4] Because it is the holiest shrine in Tibet, pilgrims <u>do not</u> mind traveling on foot from all over the country to worship there. [5] After <u>they have</u> bought yak butter in the city square, they take it to the palace as an offering. [6] From the photograph, you <u>cannot</u> imagine how steep those stairs on the right are! [7] Because it <u>would have</u> taken us hours to climb them, our bus driver took us directly to the rear entrance on the left. [8] Once inside, we spent hours exploring the palace, but we <u>were not</u> able to visit most of its more than one thousand rooms! [9] <u>I am</u> sure we would never have found our way out without our guide, who led us to an exit on the right. [10] Walking down the stairs <u>was not</u> too hard, and soon we were in the beautiful central square in the Himalayan sunshine!

4. don't

5. they've

6. can't

7. would've

8. weren't

9. I'm

10. wasn't

MECHANICS

VISUAL CONNECTIONS
Exploring the Subject. The fifth Dalai Lama of Tibet (1617–1682) ordered the construction of the Potala; however, the Dalai Lama died before the Potala was completed.

The Dalai Lama's death was concealed for fourteen years by his regent, who wanted to solidify power and complete the Potala. After the Potala was finished in 1695, the regent announced the death of the fifth Dalai Lama and the discovery of the sixth. (According to Tibetan Buddhism, when a Dalai Lama dies, his soul is reincarnated. The reincarnation of the old Dalai Lama—usually a young boy—must then be found and instated as the new Dalai Lama.)

MECHANICS

754 *Punctuation*

▶ EXERCISE 13   **Writing Contractions**

Write a suitable contraction for the blank in each of the following sentences.   Contractions will vary.

1. Where's
2. We're
3. can't

4. Isn't
5. haven't

1. ___ my sweater?
2. ___ lying on the beach.
3. We ___ help you right now.

4. ___ dinner ready?
5. They ___ played that game before.

Plurals

27s.   Use an apostrophe and an *s* to form the plurals of letters, numerals, and signs, and of words referred to as words.

EXAMPLES   Your *o*'s look like *a*'s, and your *u*'s look like *n*'s.
There are three *5*'s in his telephone number.
One sign of immature writing is too many *and*'s.
There are two *o*'s, two *k*'s, and three *e*'s in the word *bookkeeper*.

▶ REVIEW B   **Using Underlining (Italics) and Apostrophes Correctly**

For each of the following sentences, add underlining or apostrophes as necessary. The punctuation already supplied is correct.

EXAMPLE   **1.** One of my brothers college textbooks is History of Art by H. W. Janson.
1. *brother's;* History of Art

1. Who's the painter who inspired the musical play Sunday in the Park with George?
2. He's Georges Seurat, one of France's greatest painters.
3. "The young children's reactions to Jacob Lawrence's paintings were surprising," Angie said.
4. Didn't you read the review in Rolling Stone of the movie Vincent & Theo?

5. It's about Vincent van Gogh and his brother, who often supported him.
6. "I like Jasper Johns," Rick said, "but I can't tell if that is one of Johns's paintings."
7. Have you ever tried counting all the 2's or 4's in his <u>Numbers in Color</u> painting?
8. On a class trip to Chicago, we saw the bronze statue <u>The Great Horse</u> by Duchamp-Villon.
9. In our group, everybody's favorite painting is <u>Cow's Skull: Red, White and Blue</u> by Georgia O'Keeffe.
10. "I've seen an <u>American Playhouse</u> program on PBS about O'Keeffe's life," Joyce said.

Hyphens

27t. Use a hyphen to divide a word at the end of a line.

EXAMPLES   In my opinion, what this salad needs is some cu-
cumber slices.
Will you and Marguerite help me put the silver-
ware on the table?

When dividing a word at the end of a line, remember the following rules:

(1) Divide a word only between syllables.

INCORRECT   Mr. Morrison looked around with a bewild-
ered expression.
CORRECT   Mr. Morrison looked around with a bewil-
dered expression.

(2) Do not divide a one-syllable word.

INCORRECT   Exercises like push-ups help to develop strength of the arm muscles.
CORRECT   Exercises like push-ups help to develop
strength of the arm muscles.

LEP/ESL

General Strategies. Very few languages use hyphens between parts of numbers as is done in English. To provide students extra practice in using hyphens to write numbers, give students a list of twenty popular albums, films, and television shows and have students rate each item from one (least favorite) to one hundred (most favorite). Have students write out their ratings and remind students to use hyphens correctly.

AT-RISK STUDENTS

Give students a list of dollar amounts written in numerals and have them write out the amounts as they would on a check or money order. Emphasizing the practical applications of **Rule 27u** might help students to learn and remember it.

REVIEW C

OBJECTIVE

- To proofread and revise sentences for the correct use of underlining, quotation marks, commas, apostrophes, and hyphens

(3) Do not divide a word so that one letter stands alone.

INCORRECT   The seating capacity of the new stadium is e-
             normous.

CORRECT   The seating capacity of the new stadium is
             enormous.

27u.   Use a hyphen with compound numbers from *twenty-one* to *ninety-nine* and with fractions used as modifiers.

EXAMPLES   During a leap year, there are twenty-nine days in February.

            Congress may override a president's veto by a two-thirds majority. [*Two-thirds* is an adjective that modifies *majority.*]

            The pumpkin pie was so good that only one sixth of it is left. [*One sixth* is not used as a modifier. Instead, *sixth* is a noun modified by the adjective *one.*]

▶ EXERCISE 14   **Using Hyphens Correctly**

Write a number—using words, not numerals—to fit the blank in each sentence. Use hyphens where they are needed. Hyphens are indicated by the ⌃ symbol. Responses will vary.

EXAMPLE   **1.** The sum of ten and fifteen is ____.
           1. *twenty-five*

1. thirty⌃one   2. One half

1. January, March, May, July, August, October, and December are the months that have ____ days.
2. ____ of the moon is visible from the earth, but the other half can be seen only from outer space.
3. In twenty years I will be ____ years old.   3. thirty⌃three
4. I used ____ cup, which is 25 percent of the original one cup.   4. one⌃fourth
5. Our seventh-grade class has ____ students, fifteen boys and twelve girls.   5. twenty⌃seven

PARENTHESES AND DASHES Rules 27v, 27w

OBJECTIVES

- To correct sentences by adding parentheses
- To correct sentences by adding dashes

 REVIEW C · **Punctuating Sentences Correctly**

Rewrite the following sentences, inserting underlining, quotation marks, commas, apostrophes, and hyphens as necessary. Hyphens are indicated by the ∧ symbol.

EXAMPLE   **1. For the talent show, Leila recited Poes poem
The Raven.**

1. *For the talent show, Leila recited Poe's poem
"The Raven."*

1. Queen Hatshepsut seized the throne of Egypt in 1503 B.C. and ruled for twenty‸one years.
2. "Who's borrowed my scissors?" demanded Jean.
3. It's hard to decide which author's story I should read first.
4. A week's vacation never seems long enough.
5. After we'd eaten supper, we decided to watch an old episode of Star Trek.
6. The driver shouted, "Move to the rear of the bus!"
7. We didn't eat any salmon during our visit to Oregon.
8. "I wasn't sorry," admitted the clerk, "to see those picky customers leave."
9. "Very Short on Law and Order" is my favorite chapter in Andrew Garcia's autobiographical book Tough Trip Through Paradise.
10. Our new phone number starts with two 6's and ends with two 4's.

Parentheses

27v. Use parentheses to enclose material that is added to a sentence but is not considered of major importance.

EXAMPLES   Emilio Aguinaldo **(**1869–1964**)** was a Filipino patriot and statesman.
Mom and Dad bought a kilim **(**ki lēm'**)** rug from our Turkish friend Ali.

 A DIFFERENT APPROACH
To reinforce the practice of looking up words to check for syllable divisions, give each student a dictionary. (If there are not enough dictionaries available to give one to each student, use words from the glossary of this textbook.) Then call out a word from the dictionary or glossary. The first student to find the word and to show how to divide its syllables correctly wins a point. At the end of the game, the student with the most points wins.

MECHANICS

MECHANICS

RESOURCES

PARENTHESES AND DASHES
- Using Parentheses
- Using Dashes

QUICK REMINDER

Write the following sentences on the chalkboard and ask students to add parentheses or dashes where needed:

1. Seattle named after a Native American chief is a city in Washington.
2. The Indianapolis Colts formerly the Baltimore Colts had a losing season.
3. What would we do if alien beings real Martians were to come to earth?

MEETING
INDIVIDUAL
NEEDS

LEARNING STYLES

Auditory Learners. Encourage students to read sentences aloud and to listen for the drop in their voices when they read parenthetical expressions.

Material enclosed in parentheses may be as short as a single word or as long as a short sentence. A short sentence in parentheses may stand alone or be contained within another sentence. Notice that a sentence within a sentence is not capitalized and has no end mark.

EXAMPLES   Please be quiet during the performance. **(Take crying babies to the lobby.)**
Jack Echohawk **(he's Ben's cousin)** told us about growing up on a reservation.

▷ EXERCISE 15   **Correcting Sentences by Adding Parentheses**

Insert parentheses where they are needed in the following sentences.

EXAMPLE   **1.** My bicycle I've had it for three years is a ten-speed.
1. *My bicycle (I've had it for three years) is a ten-speed.*

1. At the age of thirteen, Jennifer Capriati began playing tennis (my favorite sport) professionally.
2. Elijah McCoy (1843–1929) invented a way to oil moving machinery.
3. I had to buy a new pocket calculator. (My old one stopped working.)
4. Charlemagne (shär′lə mān′) was one of Europe's most famous rulers.
5. Lian Young (she's a friend of mine) told our class about her school in China.

Dashes

A *parenthetical expression* is a word or phrase that breaks into the main thought of a sentence. Parenthetical expressions are usually set off by commas or parentheses.

27w

EXAMPLES   Grandma Moses**, for example,** started painting
in her seventies.
The butler **(Theo Karras)** was the detective's
first suspect.

☞ REFERENCE NOTE: For more about using commas with
parenthetical expressions, see page 718. For more about using
parentheses, see pages 757–758.

Some parenthetical elements need stronger emphasis.
In such cases, a dash is used.

27w. Use a dash to indicate an abrupt break in
thought or speech.

EXAMPLES   The right thing to do—I know it'll be hard—is
to apologize.
"Do you think Ann will mind—I really hope she
won't—if I borrow her sunglasses?" asked
Melody.

▶ EXERCISE 16   **Correcting Sentences by Adding
Dashes**

Insert dashes where they are needed in the following
sentences.   Carets indicate placement of dashes.

EXAMPLE   **1.** The school lunchroom it was a dull green has
been painted a cheery yellow.
1. *The school lunchroom—it was a dull green—
has been painted a cheery yellow.*

1. Fireflies͜I can't remember where I read this͜make
what is called cold light.
2. Roberto has always wanted to be͜can't you guess?͜
an astronaut.
3. Randy Travis͜I really want to see his concert͜has a
new song out.
4. Do you mind͜I don't͜if Jill and Mandy go to the mall
with us?
5. The best way to learn how to swim͜that is, after
you've learned the basic strokes͜is to practice.

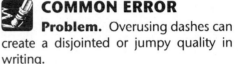

**INTEGRATING THE
LANGUAGE ARTS**

Mechanics and Writing. You
may want to stress to students that the
use of parentheses and dashes should be
limited in formal writing.

COMMON ERROR

Problem. Overusing dashes can
create a disjointed or jumpy quality in
writing.

Solution. Have students read
their writing aloud so that they can listen
for the breathiness created by too many
dashes.

MECHANICS

MECHANICS

WRITING APPLICATION
You may want to videotape a couple of sample interviews to show to your class. After students have watched the interviews, use the questions at the end of **Prewriting** to initiate discussion.

You could allow students to videotape their interviews and to show them to the class. However, students who videotape interviews should still be required to complete written reports.

For an example of how one student incorporates quotations into his writing, refer students to **A Student Model** on pp. 306—307.

MECHANICS

WRITING APPLICATION

Using Quotations in Reports

In persuasive and informative essays, a direct quotation can sometimes be more effective than a secondhand paraphrase. However, a quotation can be confusing and misleading if it isn't correctly capitalized and punctuated.

CONFUSING   Inés Torro, manager of the Waste Disposal Department, said by the end of December, weekly recycling pickup will be available in all areas of the city.

CLEAR   Inés Torro, manager of the Waste Disposal Department, said, "By the end of December, weekly recycling pickup will be available in all areas of the city."

▶ **WRITING ACTIVITY**
Your social studies class is taking a survey of people's attitudes toward recycling. Interview at least three people from different households in your community. Ask them specific questions to find out

- whether they think recycling is important
- what items, if any, they recycle
- whether they find it easy or difficult to recycle
- how they think recycling could be made easier for people in the community

Based on the information you gather, write a brief report about recycling in your community. In your report, quote several people's exact words.

Prewriting First, think of several questions to ask. Word your questions so that they can't be answered with a simple *yes* or *no*. Next, decide whom you want to interview. You might interview friends, family members, or neighbors. Begin each interview by recording the person's name, age, and occupation. During the interview, write down or tape-

MECHANICS

record what the person says. (If you want to tape the interview, make sure you have the person's permission first.) If you write down the interview, be sure to write the person's answers word for word. (You may need to ask the person to speak slowly.) When all your interviews are completed, compare your interviewees' responses. How are they similar? How are they different? What conclusions can you draw about attitudes toward recycling in your community? Jot down some notes to help you organize your information.

Writing In the first paragraph of your draft, give a statement that sums up the main idea of your report. Then, use your interviewees' answers to support your main idea. Since you can't quote every word, you'll need to choose your quotations carefully. Quote words and sentences that accurately represent each person's answers and attitudes. Clearly identify each person that you quote. Conclude your report by restating your main idea.

Evaluating and Revising After you've completed your first draft, reread your main idea. Does the body of your report support that idea? If not, rethink and revise your main idea. Make sure the body of your report follows a logical order. As you organize your report, you may need to add, cut, or rearrange details. Be sure that all direct quotations are correctly quoted. Also, be sure that you have not used a person's words or ideas without giving him or her credit.

Proofreading and Publishing As you proofread your report, check your quotations against your notes. Be sure you've spelled people's names correctly. Finally, make sure that you've put quotation marks around direct quotations and that you've capitalized and punctuated all quotations correctly. You and your classmates can share your findings and suggestions with the person or agency in charge of recycling in your community. As a class, write a letter that summarizes your findings.

MECHANICS

CRITICAL THINKING
Synthesis

To complete this assignment, students will need to draw conclusions. Remind students that the conclusions they draw should not be based on their feelings about recycling but on the data collected during their interviews. You may want to put the following chart on the chalkboard to help students draw conclusions:

HOW TO DRAW CONCLUSIONS	
Gather all the evidence.	What facts or details have you learned about the subject?
Evaluate the evidence.	What do the facts and details tell you about the subject?
Make appropriate connections.	What can you reasonably conclude from the evidence?

MECHANICS

MECHANICS

SEGMENT 7 *(pp. 762–763)*
REVIEW: POSTTEST

OBJECTIVE

• To proofread and revise sentences for the correct use of apostrophes, quotation marks, underlining (italics), hyphens, parentheses, and dashes

A DIFFERENT APPROACH

Conduct a scavenger hunt for uses of italics, quotation marks, apostrophes, hyphens, parentheses, and dashes that exemplify all of the rules in this chapter. Students should hunt through newspapers and magazines for examples. The first student to find an example of each rule in the chapter wins.

---

762 *Punctuation*

Review: Posttest

A. Proofreading Sentences for the Correct Use of Apostrophes, Quotation Marks, Underlining (Italics), Hyphens, Parentheses, and Dashes

Revise each of the following sentences so that apostrophes, quotation marks, underlining, hyphens, parentheses, or dashes are used correctly. [Note: A sentence may contain more than one error.] Hyphens are indicated by the ⌃ symbol.

EXAMPLE   **1.** "May I borrow your copy of 'Life' magazine? Phil asked Alan.

      1. *"May I borrow your copy of Life magazine?" Phil asked Alan.*

1. Boris Karloff (his real name was William Henry Pratt) played the monster in the original movie version of <u>Frankenstein</u>.
2. "I've never known—do you?⌃what the word <u>kith</u> means," Phil said. **2.** dash
3. "It's just a simple word," Anna said, "that refers to family and friends."
4. I've heard that the program's announcer and inter⌃viewer will be Connie Chung⌃(a favorite of mine).
5. Alan said that "Norma couldn't understand why twenty⌃two people had voted against having the dance on a Friday night.
6. "A two⌃thirds majority of the men's team hadn't played before" Shawn said.
7. Fred said, "This magazine article titled *Luxury Liners of the Past* is interesting." **7.** 'Luxury . . . Past'
8. "Does the public library have copies of the <u>Lakota Times</u> or any other Native American newspapers?" Tanya asked.
9. My sisters like to read folk tales in books such as <u>Two Ways to Count to Ten</u> by Ruby Dee.
10. The Lopezes' cat⌃I don't think they know⌃is living in our garage," Mary said. **10.** dash/dash

B. Punctuating Quotations Correctly

For each of the following sentences, add quotation marks where they are needed.

EXAMPLE **1.** I wonder why so many people enjoy collecting things, said J. D.
1. *"I wonder why so many people enjoy collecting things," said J. D.*

11. "I know I do!"Julia exclaimed.
12. Tomás said,"My grandmother once said,"It's the thrill of the hunt.""
13. "Do you collect anything as a hobby?"Josh asked Marsha, who had just entered the room.
14. "No,"Marsha answered,"but I know a person who collects old cameras and antique costume jewelry."
15. "My aunt collects John McCormack's records,"Kevin said."Do you know who he is?"
16. "I'm not sure,"Julia said,"but I think that he was an Irish singer."
17. "Yes, he sang in the opera; he also sang popular Irish songs such as"The Rose of Tralee,"Kevin said.
18. "My stepbrother has a collection of arrowheads. He hasn't been collecting them very long,"Sydney said.
19. "You should see Mrs. Webb's collection of Chinese jade carvings,"J. D. said."It's great!"
20. "Some people—I'm sure you know—have unusual collections,"Josh said."For instance, my aunt collects old shoelaces."

MECHANICS

SEGMENT 1 *(pp. 764–773)*

GOOD SPELLING HABITS Rules 28a–28g

OBJECTIVES

- To divide words correctly into syllables
- To spell correctly words that contain the letters *ei* or *ie*
- To proofread a paragraph to correct spelling errors
- To add prefixes and suffixes to words correctly

CHAPTER OVERVIEW

The chapter begins with an introduction to the basic rules and techniques of spelling. After gaining an understanding of these rules and techniques, students can proceed confidently when proofreading writing assignments. Exercises can help reinforce the understanding of the spelling rules. The final segment of the chapter also contains lists of homonyms and other confusing words.

Understanding spelling rules and techniques will help students improve their writing by increasing their fluency. This chapter can be used for reference purposes also.

MECHANICS

MECHANICS

28 SPELLING

Improving Your Spelling

Good Spelling Habits

Practicing the following techniques can help you spell words correctly.

1. **To learn the spelling of a word, pronounce it, study it, and write it.** Pronounce words carefully. Mispronunciation can cause misspelling. For instance, if you say *ath • a • lete* instead of *ath • lete,* you will probably spell the word wrong.

   - First, make sure that you know how to pronounce the word correctly, and then practice saying it.
   - Second, study the word. Notice any parts that might be hard to remember.
   - Third, write the word from memory. Check your spelling.
   - If you misspelled the word, repeat the three steps of this process.

2. **Use a dictionary.** When you find that you have misspelled a word, look it up in a dictionary. Don't guess about the correct spelling.

3. **Spell by syllables.** A *syllable* is a word part that can be pronounced by itself.

EXAMPLE   thor • ough [two syllables]
sep • a • rate [three syllables]

Instead of trying to learn how to pronounce and spell a whole word, break it up into its syllables whenever possible. It's easier to learn a few letters at a time than to learn all of them at once.

☞ REFERENCE NOTE: For information on using the dictionary to determine the syllables in a word, see page 825.

▶ EXERCISE 1   **Spelling by Syllables**

Look up the following words in a dictionary, and divide each one into syllables. Pronounce each syllable correctly, and learn to spell the word by syllables.

1. legislature
2. perspire
3. modern
4. temperature
5. probably
6. similar
7. library
8. definition
9. recognize
10. awkward

4. **Proofread for careless spelling errors.** Reread your writing carefully, and correct any mistakes and unclear letters. For example, make sure that your *i*'s are dotted, and your *t*'s crossed, and your *g*'s don't look like *q*'s.

5. **Keep a spelling notebook.** Divide each page into four columns:

COLUMN 1   Correctly spell the word you missed. (Never enter a misspelled word.)
COLUMN 2   Write the word again, dividing it into syllables and marking its accents.
COLUMN 3   Write the word once more, circling the spot that gives you trouble.
COLUMN 4   Jot down any comments that might help you remember the correct spelling.

MECHANICS

MECHANICS

LEP/ESL

General Strategies. English spelling is complicated, with many irregularities; spelling in most other languages is fairly simple because a letter generally stands for one and only one sound. You could help your ESL students remember English spelling rules by explaining them and then giving informal, oral mini-quizzes from time to time so that students will think about the rules repeatedly.

LESS-ADVANCED STUDENTS

Some long words may confuse students when students see the words written. Explain that many long words are made up of letter combinations that by themselves may also be words. Write the following words on the chalkboard and ask students to copy them. Then have the students find the small words in the longer words by covering parts of the longer word one syllable, or even one letter, at a time.

1. peppermint [pep, pepper, mint]
2. breakfast [break, fast]
3. another [an, other, her]
4. careless [car, are, care, less]

MECHANICS

766

Here is an example of how you might make entries for two words that are often misspelled.

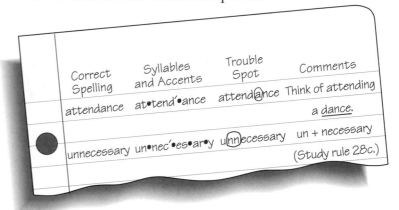

Correct Spelling	Syllables and Accents	Trouble Spot	Comments
attendance	at•tend´•ance	attend@nce	Think of attending a *dance*.
unnecessary	un•nec´•es•ar•y	u(nn)ecessary	un + necessary (Study rule 28c.)

Spelling Rules

ie and *ei*

28a. Write *ie* when the sound is long *e*, except after *c*.

EXAMPLES   **chief, brief, believe, yield, receive, deceive**
EXCEPTIONS   **seize, leisure, either, neither, weird**

Write *ei* when the sound is not long *e*, especially when the sound is long *a*.

EXAMPLES   **sleigh, veil, freight, weight, height, foreign**
EXCEPTIONS   **friend, mischief, ancient, pie**

You may find this time-tested verse a help.

I before *e*
Except after *c*,
Or when sounded like *a*,
As in *neighbor* and *weigh*.

If you use this rhyme, remember that "*i* before *e*" refers only to words in which these two letters stand for the sound of long *e*, as in the examples under rule 28a.

▶ EXERCISE 2　**Writing Words with *ie* and *ei***

Add the letters *ie* or *ei* to correctly spell each of the following words.

EXAMPLE　**1.** conc . . . t
　　　　　1. *conceit*

1. dec . ei . ve
2. n . ei . ther
3. rec . ei . ve
4. h . ei . ght
5. fr . ie . nd
6. l . ei . sure
7. misch . ie . f

8. w . ei . ght
9. . ei . ght
10. sl . ei . gh
11. fr . ei . ght
12. n . ei . ghbor
13. c . ei . ling
14. shr . ie . k

15. rec . ei . pt
16. p . ie . ce
17. r . ei . gn
18. th . ei . r
19. s . ei . ze
20. br . ie . f

▶ EXERCISE 3　**Proofreading a Paragraph to Correct
Spelling Errors**

The following paragraph contains ten spelling errors
involving the use of *ie* and *ei*. For each sentence, write the
misspelled word or words correctly. If a sentence has no
spelling error, write *C*.

EXAMPLE　[1] Last summer I recieved an airline ticket as a
　　　　　　birthday gift.
　　　　　1. *received*

[1] I used the ticket to fly to Puerto Rico with my freind
Alicia to see my grandmother and other relatives. [2] We
flew to San Juan, where my grandmother's nieghbor, Mr.
Sanchez, met us and drove us to my grandmother's
house. [3] When we got there, all of my relatives—aunts,
uncles, cousins, neices, nephews—came to welcome us.
[4] They couldn't beleive that niether of us had ever been
to Puerto Rico before, so the next day, they took us
sightseeing. [5] First we went to Humacao, which, as you
can see on the map on the next page, is located on the
Caribbean. [6] Then we drove along the coast to Ponce, the
island's cheif city after San Juan. [7] Continuing north from
Ponce, we thought that we'd take a liesurely drive on this
mountain road, *Ruta Panoramica,* which means "Panoramic

1. ie
2. ei
3. ie
4. ie/ei
5. C
6. ie
7. ei

MECHANICS

MECHANICS

Auditory Learners. You may want to conduct a modified spelling bee for students by asking them to pronounce and spell the words below. Call out each word (enunciate normally) and ask a student to pronounce it syllable by syllable before spelling it. The student should pause slightly after each syllable.

Ask each student who spells a word correctly to stand in front of the class. To continue this contest beyond the provided words, appoint other students to use their dictionaries to find challenging words.

1. abhorrence [ab hor rence]
2. clearance [clear ance]
3. examination [ex am i na tion]
4. improbable [im prob a ble]
5. characteristic [char ac ter is tic]
6. dilate [di late]
7. powerful [pow er ful]
8. stripe [stripe]

MECHANICS

Road." [8] However, the road turned and twisted so much
8. ie that I was relieved to get back on the main road. [9] After
9. ie we had a breif rest, we explored the western part of the island. [10] Within two days, Puerto Rico no longer seemed
10. ei foriegn to us.

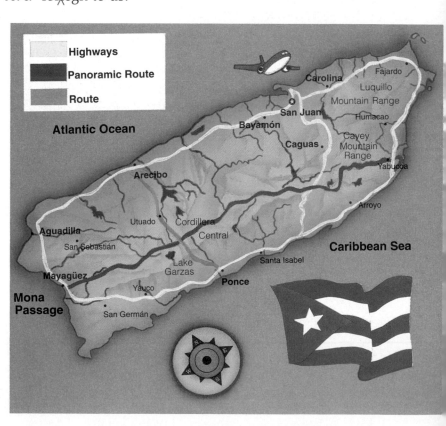

—cede, —ceed, and —sede

28b. The only word ending in —*sede* is *supersede*. The only words ending in —*ceed* are *exceed*, *proceed*, and *succeed*. All other words with this sound end in —*cede*.

EXAMPLES   con**cede**, re**cede**, pre**cede**

28
b–d

Prefixes and Suffixes

A *prefix* is a letter or a group of letters added to the beginning of a word to change its meaning. A *suffix* is a letter or a group of letters added to the end of a word to change its meaning.

28c. When adding a prefix to a word, do not change the spelling of the word itself.

EXAMPLES il + legal = **il**legal
un + natural = **un**natural
dis + appear = **dis**appear
mis + spent = **mis**spent

EXERCISE 4 Spelling Words with Prefixes

Spell each of the following words, adding the prefix given.

EXAMPLE 1. semi + circle
1. *semicircle*

1. il + legible
2. un + necessary
3. im + partial
4. in + offensive
5. im + mortal
6. mis + spell
7. dis + satisfy
8. dis + approve
9. mis + understand
10. over + rule

28d. When adding the suffix *–ness* or *–ly* to a word, do not change the spelling of the word itself.

EXAMPLES sudden + ness = sudden**ness**
truthful + ly = truthful**ly**
still + ness = still**ness**
final + ly = final**ly**

EXCEPTION For most words that end in *y,* change the *y* to *i* before *–ly* or *–ness.*

EXAMPLES kindly + ness = kindl**iness**
day + ly = da**ily**

MECHANICS

COMMON ERROR

Problem. Words with double letters that are not related to prefix- or suffix-formation rules may cause confusion in spelling.

Solution. Tell students that double letters within words often indicate a certain pronunciation rule. The double consonant usually indicates a short vowel sound, as in *latter.* Call out the pairs of words below and tell students that one of each pair will have double letters somewhere within it. Ask students to write the words side by side. After you have gone through the list, write the pairs on the chalkboard so students can check their spelling.

1. bone, bonnet
2. bore, borrow
3. coma, comma
4. diner, dinner
5. filer, filler
6. cuter, cutter

ANSWERS

Exercise 4

1. illegible
2. unnecessary
3. impartial
4. inoffensive
5. immortal
6. misspell
7. dissatisfy
8. disapprove
9. misunderstand
10. overrule

MECHANICS

INTEGRATING THE LANGUAGE ARTS

Literature Link. Have students read aloud Shel Silverstein's "Sarah Cynthia Sylvia Stout Would Not Take the Garbage Out" and look at the word at the end of each line. Ask students if any of these words conform to the spelling rules they have just studied [*ceiling, pie*]. Next, ask students to look at the words at the ends of lines 40 through 45; ask if a pronunciation rule could be derived from the spellings of these words. [An *a* coming between two consonants will usually have a long sound if the second consonant is followed by an *e.*]

To test the rule, divide the class into two teams and give each a dictionary. Ask one team to list as many words as it can find that follow the rule, and ask the other to find as many exceptions as it can [*cadet, dare, mare,* and *soon*]. If the team looking for exceptions finds as many or almost as many words as the other team, the rule must be declared invalid or must be further qualified.

ANSWERS
Exercise 5

1. hopefully
2. happiness
3. sincerely
4. writing
5. desirable
6. changeable
7. crossing
8. advancement
9. truly
10. easily

28e. Drop the final silent *e* before a suffix beginning with a vowel.

Vowels are the letters *a, e, i, o, u,* and sometimes *y.* All other letters of the alphabet are *consonants.*

EXAMPLES	nice + est = nic**est**
	love + able = lov**able**
EXCEPTION	Keep the silent *e* in words ending in *ce* and *ge* before a suffix beginning with *a* or *o.*

EXAMPLES   notice + able = notic**eable**
           courage + ous = courag**eous**

28f. Keep the final *e* before a suffix beginning with a consonant.

EXAMPLES	care + less = care**less**
	plate + ful = plate**ful**
	false + hood = false**hood**
EXCEPTIONS	argue + ment = argu**ment**
	true + ly = tru**ly**

F W WNT T TLK RLLY GD, W'LL HV T NVNT VWLS.

FRANK & ERNEST reprinted by permission of NEA, Inc.

 EXERCISE 5   **Spelling Words with Suffixes**

Spell each of the following words, adding the suffix given.

EXAMPLE   **1.** joy + ful
          1. *joyful*

1. hopeful + ly	**5.** desire + able	**9.** true + ly
2. happy + ness	**6.** change + able	**10.** easy + ly
3. sincere + ly	**7.** cross + ing	
4. write + ing	**8.** advance + ment	

28g. For words ending in *y* preceded by a consonant, change the *y* to *i* before any suffix that does not begin with *i.*

EXAMPLES   friendly + er = friendl**ier**
            beauty + ful = beaut**iful**
            carry + ing = carry**ing**

Words ending in *y* preceded by a vowel do not change their spelling before a suffix.

EXAMPLES   key + ed = ke**yed**
            pay + ment = pay**ment**

EXCEPTIONS   lay—laid   say—said

28h. Double the final consonant before adding *–ing, –ed, –er,* or *–est* to a one-syllable word that ends in a single consonant preceded by a single vowel.

EXAMPLES   sit + ing = si**tting**
            hop + ed = ho**pped**
            dim + er = di**mmer**

With a one-syllable word ending in a single consonant that is *not* preceded by a single vowel, do not double the consonant before adding *–ing, –ed, –er,* or *–est.*

EXAMPLES   reap + ed = rea**ped**   neat + est = nea**test**
            cold + er = col**der**   hold + ing = hol**ding**

 EXERCISE 6   **Spelling Words with Suffixes**

Spell each of the following words, adding the suffix given.

EXAMPLE   **1.** beauty + ful
            1. *beautiful*

1. bay + ing   5. pity + less   9. tap + ing
2. silly + ness   6. swim + er   10. clean + er
3. drop + ed   7. sly + est
4. deny + ing   8. hurry + ed

MECHANICS

MECHANICS

ANSWERS
Exercise 6
1. baying
2. silliness
3. dropped
4. denying
5. pitiless
6. swimmer
7. sliest *or* slyest
8. hurried
9. tapping
10. cleaner

MECHANICS

772

REVIEW A

OBJECTIVE

- To proofread a paragraph, identifying and correcting misspelled words

772   *Spelling*

▷ REVIEW A   **Proofreading a Paragraph for Correct Spelling**

Most of the following sentences contain words that have been misspelled. Write each misspelled word correctly. If a sentence is correct, write *C*.

EXAMPLE   [1] Remember the beautyful bonsai trees in the *Karate Kid* movies?
　　　　　1. *beautiful*

　　　　　　　　　　　　　　　　1. C   **2.** Simply

[1] Bonsai trees can live to be hundreds of years old, yet you can quickly create one of your own in an afternoon. [2] use these pictures as you proceed through the following steps.

MECHANICS

FORMING THE PLURAL OF NOUNS Rule 28h

OBJECTIVE

- To spell the plural forms of nouns

3. inexpensive **4.** choosing **5.** careful

[3] First, you'll need an ⌃~~inxpensive~~ plant, like a juniper, some soil and moss, as well as a shallow bowl. [4] When you are ⌃~~chooseing~~ a plant, try to get one with a trunk that has some of its roots showing so that your tree will look old. [5] Make a ⌃~~carful~~ study of your plant, and decide how you want the bonsai to look in the bowl. [6] Then, cut or pinch away ⌃~~undesireable~~ branches and leaves until the plant looks like a tree. [7] After ⌃~~triming~~ your plant, remove most of the large roots so that the plant can stand in the bowl. [8] Cover the remaining roots with soil, and, if the weather is mild, put your bonsai in a shaded place outside. [9] You don't have to water your plant ⌃~~dayly~~, but you should keep the soil moist. [10] After your plant has ⌃~~healled~~, you will have many years of enjoyment from your bonsai. **6.** undesirable **7.** trimming **8.** C **9.** daily **10.** healed

Forming the Plural of Nouns

28i. Observe the following rules for spelling the plural of nouns:

(1) To form the plural of most nouns, add –s.

SINGULAR	girl	cheese	task	monkey	banana
PLURAL	girl**s**	cheese**s**	task**s**	monkey**s**	banana**s**

☞ **REFERENCE NOTE:** Make sure that you do not confuse the plural form of a noun with its possessive form. For a discussion of possessive forms of nouns, see pages 746–748.

(2) Form the plural of nouns ending in *s, x, z, ch,* or *sh* by adding –*es*.

SINGULAR	moss	wax	waltz	birch	dish
PLURAL	moss**es**	wax**es**	waltz**es**	birch**es**	dish**es**

NOTE: Proper nouns usually follow this rule, too.

EXAMPLES   the Nuñez**es**
the Williams**es**

MECHANICS

▼ **RESOURCES**

FORMING THE PLURAL OF NOUNS
- Forming the Plural of Nouns

MECHANICS

🦉 **QUICK REMINDER**

Write on the chalkboard the following plural nouns that are never, or almost never, used in the singular:

1. scissors
2. pliers
3. shears (as noun)

Ask students to think of other examples and add them to the list. [Some possibilities are *forceps, trousers,* and *handlebars.*] Remind students that words denoting multiple items (collective nouns) don't count.

LEP/ESL

General Strategies. Some of your ESL students might speak languages that have no plural forms, such as Chinese or Vietnamese. Others might speak languages with very regular plurals, such as Portuguese, Spanish, or Turkish. Periodically remind students of the importance of the rules by reviewing different rules on different days.

LESS-ADVANCED STUDENTS

Students might confuse collective nouns with noun plurals. To demonstrate the difference, draw several goats or other stick figures on the chalkboard. Draw a circle around one goat and write the word *goat* next to it. Then have a volunteer draw a circle around the smallest number of goats that would denote the plural of *goat.* [The student should circle two goats.] Write *goats* on the chalkboard.

Now draw a circle around all the goats and write the word *herd* on the chalkboard. Ask the class if *herd* is singular or plural [singular]. Ask a volunteer to draw circles to make the word *herd* plural. [At least two circles dividing the herd should be drawn.] Write *herds* on the chalkboard.

 EXERCISE 7 **Spelling the Plural of Nouns**

Spell the plural form of each of the following nouns.

EXAMPLE **1.** match
1. *matches*

1. boxes	**3.** wrenches	**5.** churches	**7.** Gómezes	**9.** misses
1. box	**3.** wrench	**5.** church	**7.** Gómez	**9.** miss
2. crash	**4.** address	**6.** index	**8.** ditch	**10.** tax
2. crashes	**4.** addresses	**6.** indexes	**8.** ditches	**10.** taxes

(3) Form the plural of nouns ending in *y* preceded by a consonant by changing the *y* to *i* and adding *–es.*

SINGULAR   lady   hobby   county   strawberry
 PLURAL   lad**ies**   hobb**ies**   count**ies**   strawberr**ies**

EXCEPTION   With proper nouns, simply add *–s.*
 EXAMPLES   **the Applebys, the Trilbys.**

(4) Form the plural of nouns ending in *y* preceded by a vowel by adding *–s.*

SINGULAR   toy   journey   highway   Wednesday
 PLURAL   toy**s**   journey**s**   highway**s**   Wednesday**s**

(5) Form the plural of most nouns ending in *f* by adding *–s.* The plural of some nouns ending in *f* or *fe* is formed by changing the *f* to *v* and adding either *–s* or *–es.*

SINGULAR   gulf   belief   knife   loaf   wolf
 PLURAL   gulf**s**   belief**s**   kni**ves**   loa**ves**   wol**ves**

NOTE: When you are not sure about how to spell the plural of a noun ending in *f* or *fe,* look in a dictionary.

(6) Form the plural of nouns ending in *o* preceded by a vowel by adding *–s.* The plural of many nouns ending in *o* preceded by a consonant is formed by adding *–es.*

SINGULAR   patio   ratio   veto   hero
 PLURAL   patio**s**   ratio**s**   veto**es**   hero**es**

EXCEPTIONS   Eskimo—Eskimo**s**   silo—silo**s**

Form the plural of most musical terms ending in *o* by adding *–s.*

SINGULAR	piano	alto	solo	trio
PLURAL	pianos	altos	solos	trios

NOTE: To form the plural of some nouns ending in *o* preceded by a consonant, you may add either *–s* or *–es.*

SINGULAR	banjo	mosquito	flamingo
PLURAL	banjos	mosquitos	flamingos
	or	*or*	*or*
	banjoes	mosquitoes	flamingoes

(7) The plural of a few nouns is formed in irregular ways.

SINGULAR	man	mouse	foot	ox	child
PLURAL	men	mice	feet	oxen	children

▶ EXERCISE 8   **Spelling the Plural of Nouns**

Spell the plural form of each of the following nouns.

EXAMPLE   **1.** industry
　　　　　　1. *industries*

1. turkey
2. studio
3. chief
4. soprano
5. puppy
6. self
7. chimney
8. baby
9. tomato
10. echo

(8) Form the plural of compound nouns consisting of a noun plus a modifier by making the modified noun plural.

SINGULAR	sister-in-law	coat-of-arms
PLURAL	sisters-in-law	coats-of-arms
SINGULAR	Chief of State	editor in chief
PLURAL	Chiefs of State	editors in chief

☞ REFERENCE NOTE: For more on compound nouns, see
page 423.

MECHANICS

MECHANICS

CRITICAL THINKING
Synthesis

Many people might feel that the spelling of some words should be simplified to more closely follow the words' pronunciations. There may be practical reasons for simplifying the spellings of some words. For example, highway signs display the simplified spelling of *through,* as in *thruway* and *thru street,* because it is easier and quicker to read from a moving vehicle.

Ask students to think of one word that could be spelled more simply and then to write a short explanation of why the simplified spelling would work.

ANSWERS
Exercise 9

1. side-wheelers
2. moose
3. mothers-in-law
4. 1930s (*or* 1930's)
5. *m*'s
6. thirteen-year-olds
7. trout
8. governors-elect
9. Chinese
10. commanders in chief

MECHANICS

(9) The plural of a few compound nouns is formed in irregular ways.

SINGULAR   eight-year-old   tie-up   drive-in
   PLURAL   eight-year-old**s**   tie-up**s**   drive-in**s**

(10) Some nouns are the same in the singular and the plural.

SINGULAR AND PLURAL   deer   sheep   salmon   Sioux

(11) Form the plural of numerals, letters, signs, and words referred to as words by adding an apostrophe and –*s*.

SINGULAR   1800   *B*   &
   PLURAL   1800**'s**   *B***'s**   &**'s**

NOTE: In your reading you may notice that some writers do not use apostrophes to form the plurals of numerals, letters, signs, and words referred to as words. However, using an apostrophe is never wrong. Therefore, it is best always to use the apostrophe.

 EXERCISE 9   **Spelling the Plural of Nouns**

Spell the plural form of each of the following nouns.

EXAMPLE   **1.** push-up
   1. *push-ups*

1. side-wheeler
2. moose
3. mother-in-law
4. 1930
5. *m*

6. thirteen-year-old
7. trout
8. governor-elect
9. Chinese
10. commander in chief

1. side-wheelers   **2.** moose   **3.** mothers-in-law
4. 1930's [*or* 1930s]   **5.** *m*'s [*or* *m*s]
6. thirteen-year-olds   **7.** trout
8. governors-elect   **9.** Chinese   **10.** commanders in chief

Shoe, by Jeff MacNelly, reprinted by permission: Tribune Media Services.

➡ **WORDS OFTEN CONFUSED**

OBJECTIVES

- To identify often-confused words to complete sentences
- To identify misspelled words and correct their spellings
- To write sentences that correctly use often-confused words

Words Often Confused

People often confuse the words in each of the following groups. Some of these words are ***homonyms,*** which means that their pronunciations are the same. However, these words have different meanings and spellings. Other words in the following groups have the same or similar spellings yet have different meanings.

accept	[verb] *to receive; to agree to* The Lanfords would not *accept* our gift.
except	[preposition] *with the exclusion of; but* Everyone *except* Lauren agreed.
advice	[noun] *a recommendation for action* What is your mother's *advice*?
advise	[verb] *to recommend a course of action* She *advises* me to take the camp job.
affect	[verb] *to act upon; to change* Does bad weather *affect* your health?
effect	[noun] *result; consequence* What *effect* does the weather have on your health?
already	*previously* We have *already* studied the customs of the Navajo people.
all ready	*all prepared* or *in readiness* The crew is *all ready* to set sail.

▶ EXERCISE 10 **Choosing Between Words Often Confused**

From each pair in parentheses, choose the <u>word or words that will make the sentence correct</u>.

RESOURCES

WORDS OFTEN CONFUSED
- Words Often Confused A
- Words Often Confused B
- Words Often Confused C
- Commonly Misspelled Words

🦉 **QUICK REMINDER**

Write the following words and corresponding parts of speech on the chalkboard:

1. affect — verb; effect — noun
2. accept — verb; except — preposition
3. advice — noun; advise — verb

Then list these sentences. Ask some students to supply the parts of speech called for by the blanks; then ask others to select appropriate words from the list.

1. I must get mother's ___ before I ___ the job. [noun — advice; verb — accept]
2. The coach had high praise for the team, ___ for its blocking, but his opinion will not ___ me at all. [preposition — except; verb — affect]
3. ___ Helen that if she does well on the test, the ___ on her final grade will be positive. [verb — Advise; noun — effect]

MECHANICS

MECHANICS

MEETING INDIVIDUAL NEEDS

LEP/ESL

General Strategies. Among the complexities of English are homonyms, words that can be spelled differently and yet have the same pronunciation. Homonyms may seem strange to many ESL students whose languages lack or have few such homonyms. A game might help students to become more confident in the use of homonyms.

Divide the class into three teams and give each team a different list of ten words. Then challenge the teams to find the homonyms of the words on their lists. Allow students to use dictionaries. The team that finishes first wins.

LESS-ADVANCED STUDENTS

Students might need extra help to become proficient with homonyms. Write the following pairs of words on the chalkboard and ask volunteers to circle the syllables or letters that differentiate each pair. Next, ask students to copy the circled syllables or letters and to write the definition of the words next to them.

1. compliment, complement [i, e]
2. stationary, stationery [a, e]
3. their, there [ir, re]
4. threw, through [ew, ough]
5. weak, week [a, e]
6. capital, capitol [a, o]

MECHANICS

778 *Spelling*

EXAMPLE   **1.** Everyone (*accept, except*) Josh forgot their tickets.
              1. *except*

1. By the time Melba arrived, Roscoe had (<u>*already*</u>, *all ready*) baked the sweet potatoes.
2. One of the purposes of the Cabinet is to (*advice*, <u>*advise*</u>) the president.
3. The soft music had a soothing (*affect*, <u>*effect*</u>) on the tired child.
4. The girls were (*already*, <u>*all ready*</u>) for the sleigh ride.
5. The arrival of Buddhism in Japan had an enormous (*affect*, <u>*effect*</u>) on Japanese culture.
6. The snow has melted everywhere (*accept*, <u>*except*</u>) in the mountains.
7. The doctor's (<u>*advice*</u>, *advise*) was to drink plenty of fluids and to rest.
8. Sarita was happy to (<u>*accept*</u>, *except*) the invitation to the party.
9. Reading the newspaper usually (<u>*affects*</u>, *effects*) my ideas about current events.
10. What do you (*advice*, <u>*advise*</u>) me to do?

altar	[noun] *a table or stand at which religious rites are performed* There was a bowl of flowers on the *altar*.
alter	[verb] *to change* Another hurricane may *alter* the shoreline near our town.
altogether	*entirely* It is *altogether* too cold for swimming.
all together	*everyone in the same place* Will our class be *all together* at the Ramses exhibit?

brake	[noun] *a device to stop a machine* I used the emergency *brake* to prevent the car from rolling downhill.
break	[verb] *to fracture; to shatter* Don't *break* that mirror!

capital	*a city, the location of a government* What is the *capital* of this state?
capitol	*building; statehouse* The *capitol* is on Congress Avenue.

cloths	*pieces of cloth* I need some more cleaning *cloths*.
clothes	*wearing apparel* I decided to put on warm *clothes*.

▶ EXERCISE 11   **Choosing Between Words Often Confused**

From each pair in parentheses, choose the <u>word or words</u> <u>that will make the sentence correct</u>.

EXAMPLE   **1.** If it rains, we will (*altar, alter*) our plans.
          1. *alter*

1. My summer (*cloths,* <u>*clothes*</u>) are loose and light.
2. In England, you can still see remains of (<u>*altars*</u>, *alters*) built by early tribes.
3. A bicyclist can wear out a set of (<u>*brakes*</u>, *breaks*) going down a steep mountain.
4. You should use soft (<u>*cloths*</u>, *clothes*) to clean silver.
5. The cold weather did not (*altar,* <u>*alter*</u>) Ling's plans for the Chinese New Year celebration.
6. Lagos is the (<u>*capital*</u>, *capitol*) of Nigeria.
7. Put the pieces of the vase (*altogether,* <u>*all together*</u>), and I will try to repair it.

MECHANICS

After students have completed any of the exercises, you may want to have them exchange papers to mark corrections as you write on the chalkboard the answers to the exercises.

8. Did he (*brake*, <u>*break*</u>) his promise?
9. On the dome of the (*capital*, <u>*capitol*</u>) stands a large bronze statue.
10. The audience was (<u>*altogether*</u>, *all together*) charmed by the mime's performance.

coarse	[adjective] *rough, crude, not fine* The *coarse* sand acts as a filter.
course	[noun] *path of action; series of studies* [also used in the expression *of course*] What is the best *course* for me to take? You may change your mind, *of course*.
complement	[noun] *something that completes* Red shoes are a good *complement* to that outfit.
compliment	[verb] *to praise someone;* [noun] *praise from someone* Mrs. Katz *complimented* Jean on her speech. Thank you for the *compliment*.
council	*a group of people who meet together* The mayor's *council* has seven members.
councilor	*a member of a council* The mayor appointed seven *councilors*.
counsel	[noun] *advice;* [verb] *to give advice* He needs legal *counsel* on this matter. His attorney will *counsel* him before the hearing.
counselor	*one who advises* Mr. Jackson is the guidance *counselor* for the seventh grade.

> **des′ert** [noun] *a dry, barren, sandy region;*
> *a wilderness*
> This cactus grows only in the *desert.*
> **desert′** [verb] *to abandon; to leave*
> Good sports do not *desert* their
> teammates.
> **dessert′** [noun] *the final course of a meal*
> Let's have fresh peaches for *dessert.*

EXERCISE 12 — **Choosing Between Words Often Confused**

From each pair in parentheses, choose the word that will make the sentence correct.

EXAMPLE **1.** At the end of dinner, we ate (*desert, dessert*).
1. *dessert*

1. The city (*council, counsel*) will not meet unless seven of the ten (*councilors, counselors*) are present.
2. The patient received (*council, counsel*) from the doctor on the best (*coarse, course*) to a speedy recovery.
3. Chutney and yogurt are often the (*complements, compliments*) of Indian food.
4. When we visited Cairo, we saw the Nile River, of (*coarse, course*).
5. Juan is preparing the enchiladas, and I'm making *piedras* for (*desert, dessert*) tonight.
6. Marilyn made a hand puppet out of (*coarse, course*) burlap.
7. The major would not (*desert, dessert*) her regiment.
8. I want your (*council, counsel*), not your (*complements, compliments*).
9. My mother and father both took part in Operation (*Dessert, Desert*) Storm.
10. Our camp (*councilor, counselor*) suggested that we eat fruit for (*desert, dessert*).

MECHANICS

INTEGRATING THE LANGUAGE ARTS

Spelling and Writing. For an exercise in researching confusing pairs of words, divide the class into teams of two to four students and assign each team a pair of confusing words from the exercises in this section. This exercise ideally should be conducted in the library, where students can consult as many dictionaries as possible. If the exercise is conducted in the classroom, provide several dictionaries, including an unabridged edition if possible.

Each team will find its words in the dictionaries and compose original definitions. Tell teams to keep the definitions brief but to include at least one usage example per word.

MECHANICS

COOPERATIVE LEARNING

Divide the class into teams of two or three students and assign each team confusing words from this chapter.

Give each team a stack of index cards. Instruct teams to write one word on each card, followed by as many synonyms from memory as possible. Then have students augment their lists by consulting dictionaries, usage books, and thesauruses.

Once the cards have been completed, proofread, and corrected, the words can be entered on a word processor. Each member of the class could then have a copy of the compiled list. Suggest that students keep the lists in their notebooks as a reference guide for future writing assignments.

782 *Spelling*

formally	*with dignity; following strict rules or procedures* We must behave *formally* at the reception.
formerly	*previously; at an earlier date* *Formerly*, people thought travel to the moon was impossible.
hear	[verb] *to receive sounds through the ears* You can *hear* a whisper through these walls.
here	[adverb] *in this place* How long have you lived *here?*
its	[possessive form of *it*] That book has lost *its* cover.
it's	[contraction of *it is* or *it has*] *It's* the coldest winter anyone can remember. *It's* not rained for two months.
lead	[verb, present tense, rhymes with *feed*] *to go first, to be a leader* Can she *lead* us out of this tunnel?
led	[verb, past tense of *lead*] *went first* Elizabeth Blackwell *led* the movement for hospital reform.
lead	[noun, rhymes with *red*] *a heavy metal; graphite used in a pencil* There is no *lead* in a *lead* pencil.
loose	[adjective, rhymes with *moose*] *not tight* This belt is too *loose.*
lose	[verb] *to suffer loss* Fran will *lose* the argument if she doesn't check her facts.

> **passed** [verb, past tense of *pass*] *went by*
> He *passed* us five minutes ago.
> **past** [noun] *that which has gone by*; [preposition]
> *beyond*; [adjective] *ended*
> Good historians make the *past* come alive.
> We rode *past* your house.
> That era is *past*.

▶ EXERCISE 13 **Choosing Between Words Often Confused**

From each pair in parentheses, choose the <u>word that will make the sentence correct</u>.

EXAMPLE **1.** Kaya (*lead, led*) us to the ceremonial lodge.
1. *led*

1. The woman who (*formally, <u>formerly</u>*) (*lead, <u>led</u>*) the band moved to Alaska.
2. We do not expect to (*loose, <u>lose</u>*) any of our backfield players this year.
3. We (*<u>passed</u>, past*) three stalled cars this morning on our way to school.
4. "Why did you (*<u>lead</u>, led*) us (*hear, <u>here</u>*)?" the angry group demanded.
5. Can you (*<u>hear</u>, here*) the difference between the CD and the album?
6. The workers removed the (*<u>lead</u>, led*) pipes from the old house.
7. How did the ship break (*<u>loose</u>, lose*) from both of its anchors?
8. The guests are to dress (*<u>formally</u>, formerly*) for the inauguration ball.
9. "I think (*<u>it's</u>, its*) time for a pop quiz," announced Mrs. Ferrari.
10. Has the school bus already gone (*passed, <u>past</u>*) our street, Tiffany?

MECHANICS

INTEGRATING THE LANGUAGE ARTS

Technology Link. After completing any of the exercises in this segment, you may want to ask students to enter their answers in the thesaurus program of a word processor to see if the synonyms from the thesaurus agree with the sense of the sentences.

784 *Spelling*

peace	*quiet order and security* World *peace* is the goal of the United Nations.
piece	*a part of something* Lian bought that *piece* of silk in Hong Kong.
plain	[adjective] *unadorned, simple, common;* [noun] *a flat area of land* Jeans were part of his *plain* appearance. A broad, treeless *plain* stretched before them.
plane	[noun] *a flat surface; a tool; an airplane* Use an inclined *plane* to move that couch. I have just learned how to use a carpenter's *plane*. Have you ever flown in a *plane*?
principal	[noun] *the head of a school;* [adjective] *chief, main* The *principal* spoke of the *principal* duties of students.
principle	[noun] *a rule of conduct; a fundamental truth* Action should be guided by *principles*.
quiet	[adjective] *still and peaceful; without noise* The forest was very *quiet*.
quite	[adverb] *wholly or entirely; to a great extent* Some students are already *quite* sure of their career plans.
shone	[verb, past tense of *shine*] *gleamed; glowed* The moon *shone* softly over the grass.
shown	[verb, past participle of *show*] *revealed* Tamisha has *shown* me how to crochet.

EXERCISE 14   **Choosing Between Words Often Confused**

From each pair in parentheses, choose the <u>word that will make the sentence correct</u>.

EXAMPLE   **1.** Mr. Ramírez used a (*plain, plane*) to smooth the board.
   1. *plane*

1. Each drop of water (<u>*shone*</u>, *shown*) like crystal.
2. Motor vehicles are one of the (<u>*principal*</u>, *principle*) sources of air pollution in our cities.
3. If you don't hurry, you'll miss your (*plain*, <u>*plane*</u>).
4. The (*principal*, <u>*principle*</u>) of trust can lead to world (<u>*peace*</u>, *piece*).
5. Jan has (*shone*, <u>*shown*</u>) me how to change a tire.
6. It is clear that Luisa is acting on (*principal*, <u>*principle*</u>), not from a personal motive.
7. On Christmas Eve we always sing carols and have a (*peace*, <u>*piece*</u>) of fruitcake.
8. "What a (<u>*quiet*</u>, *quite*) Fourth of July," said Gloria.
9. "For once," the (<u>*principal*</u>, *principle*) announced with a smile, "you don't have to be (<u>*quiet*</u>, *quite*)."
10. (<u>*Plain*</u>, *Plane*) fruits and vegetables can provide a delicious and nutritious meal.

 EXERCISE 15   **Proofreading for Words Often Confused**

In the following paragraph, identify the ten misspelled words. Then give the correct spelling of each word.

EXAMPLE   [1] Some portraits are quiet striking.
   1. *quiet—quite*

[1] The painting on the next page is by Rembrandt, one of the~ ~~principle~~ painters of the seventeenth century. [2] The portrait, probably of a rabbi in Amsterdam, is~quiet lovely even though it is relatively~ ~~plane~~. [3] The painting illustrates one of Rembrandt's main artistic~~~principals~~, the strong contrast between light and dark. [4] Light is shown

MECHANICS

ANSWERS
Exercise 15
1. principal
2. quite, plain
3. principles
4. piece
5. quite, plane
6. shown, peace, quiet

only on the rabbi's face, hands, and a ~~peace~~ of his clothing. [5] The rest of the painting is ~~quiet~~ dark, making it look almost like a flat ~~plain~~. [6] The rabbi is ~~shone~~ in a state of ~~piece~~, and the lack of detail in the painting gives an impression of ~~quite~~ elegance.

Van Rijn Rembrandt, *Portrait of an Old Man*, Florence, Uffizi, Scala/Art Resource

stationary	[adjective] *in a fixed position* Is that chalkboard *stationary*?
stationery	[noun] *writing paper* Do you have any white *stationery*?
than	[a conjunction used in comparisons] Alaska is bigger *than* Texas.
then	[adverb] *at that time* If she will see me after class, we can talk about it *then*.

VISUAL CONNECTIONS
Portrait of an Old Man

About the Artist. Rembrandt's full name is Rembrandt Harmensz van Rijn. Many famous people during Rembrandt's era, especially artists, were known by only their first names.

Rembrandt learned how to paint and draw by serving as an apprentice to several successful artists, including Jacob van Swanenburgh and master artist Pieter Lastman.

Rembrandt moved to Amsterdam at the age of twenty-five and remained there for the rest of his life. His paintings are highly prized by museums and collectors, and reproductions of them appear in many books.

MECHANICS

their	[possessive form of *they*]
	Can you understand *their* message?
there	[adverb] *a place*; [also used to begin a sentence]
	Let's meet *there*.
	There are toys hidden inside the piñata.
they're	[contraction of *they are*]
	They're all from Guam.

threw	[verb, past tense of *throw*] *hurled*
	Ted *threw* me the mitt.
through	[preposition]
	I can't see *through* the lens.

▶ EXERCISE 16   **Choosing Between Words Often Confused**

From each pair or group in parentheses, choose the <u>word that will make the sentence correct</u>.

EXAMPLE   **1.** When will we arrive (*their, they're, there*)?
           1. *there*

1. That noise is from a jet plane going (*threw*, <u>*through*</u>) the sound barrier.
2. The stars appear to be (<u>*stationary*</u>, *stationery*), but we know that (*their, there,* <u>*they're*</u>) moving at very high speeds.
3. Thailand is much larger (<u>*than*</u>, *then*) South Korea.
4. The pitcher (<u>*threw*</u>, *through*) a curve ball.
5. A (*stationary,* <u>*stationery*</u>) store usually sells paper, pencils, and other supplies.
6. We started our trip in Barcelona and (*than,* <u>*then*</u>) traveled north to Madrid.
7. The girls brought (<u>*their*</u>, *there, they're*) displays for the science fair.
8. A moving target is much harder to hit (<u>*than*</u>, *then*) a (<u>*stationary*</u>, *stationery*) one.

MECHANICS

MECHANICS

MEETING
INDIVIDUAL
NEEDS

LEP/ESL

General Strategies. Some ESL students might be unsure of how to spell a word they hear or how to pronounce a word they see. Native English speakers who have not memorized spellings will make educated guesses based on the usual spellings of certain sounds or by similarities to other words they know. Some ESL students, however, might not be able to distinguish subtle differences between some English sounds, know which spellings are more frequent, or have the vocabularies to make analogies. Pointing out the various ways to spell certain sounds and giving practice with comparing similar words may help students minimize mistakes.

9. Iola can't get her call (*threw, through*) to Fargo, North Dakota, because the circuits are busy.
10. (*Their, They're, There*) first rehearsal will be after school today.

to	[preposition] We are going *to* Mexico.
too	[adverb] *also; more than enough* Audrey is going, *too.* Kazuo used *too* much miso; consequently, the soup was very salty.
two	*one plus one* We bought *two* sets of chopsticks.
weak	[adjective] *feeble; not strong* Melinda's illness has left her very *weak.*
week	[noun] *seven days* Let's practice again next *week.*
weather	[noun] *the condition of the atmosphere* The *weather* seems to be changing.
whether	[conjunction] *if* We don't know *whether* to expect rain or snow.
who's	[contraction of *who is* or *who has*] *Who's* going to the museum? "*Who's* been eating my porridge?" asked Papa Bear.
whose	[possessive form of *who*] *Whose* report was the most original?
your	[possessive form of *you*] What is *your* middle name?
you're	[contraction of *you are*] *You're* my best friend.

▶ EXERCISE 17 **Choosing Between Words Often Confused**

From each pair or group in parentheses, choose the <u>word that will make the sentence correct</u>.

EXAMPLE **1.** What are (*your, you're*) plans for celebrating Juneteenth?
1. *your*

1. (<u>*Who's*</u>, *Whose*) the present Secretary of State of the United States?
2. My stepsister and I built (*to, too,* <u>*two*</u>) snow forts on our front lawn.
3. "(*Your,* <u>*You're*</u>) late," my friend complained.
4. Would you be able to stand the (<u>*weather*</u>, *whether*) in Alaska?
5. That sounds like a (<u>*weak*</u>, *week*) excuse to me.
6. (<u>*Your*</u>, *You're*) dog is (*to,* <u>*too*</u>, *two*) sleepy to learn any new tricks.
7. "(*Who's,* <u>*Whose*</u>) boots and mittens are these?" Mrs. Allen asked.
8. The pilot must quickly decide (*weather,* <u>*whether*</u>) to parachute to safety or try to land the crippled plane.
9. Spring break starts next (*weak,* <u>*week*</u>).
10. My family is going (*too,* <u>*to*</u>, *two*) New Orleans for the holidays.

▶ EXERCISE 18 **Writing Sentences with Words Often Confused**

You are the new meteorologist for a local television station. Tonight is your first broadcast, and you still haven't written your script. Using the weather map on the next page, write five sentences for your script. In each sentence, use one of the words from the following list. Underline each one you use.

to	weak	whose
two	weather	your
too	whether	you're
week	who's	

MECHANICS

ANSWERS
Exercise 18

Sentences will vary. Words must be used correctly, and sentences should be suitable for a weather broadcast.

MECHANICS

OBJECTIVE

- To identify and choose often-confused words to complete sentences

790 *Spelling*

EXAMPLE **1.** *I'll let you know whether you'll need an umbrella this weekend, right after these messages.*

Bands separate high temperature zones for the day.

| −10s | −0s | 0s | 10s | 20s | 30s | 40s | 50s | 60s | 70s | 80s | 90s | 100s | 110s |

Cold Front | Warm Front | Stationary Front | L Low Pressure | H High Pressure | Showers | Rain | T-Storms | Flurries | Snow | Ice | Sunny | Pt. Cloudy | Cloudy

▶ REVIEW B

Choosing Between Words Often Confused

From each pair or group in parentheses, choose the <u>word or words that will make the sentence correct</u>.

EXAMPLE My parents asked my [1] (*advice, advise*) about where we should spend our vacation.
1. *advice*

Last March, my family could not decide [1] (*weather, <u>whether</u>*) to visit Boston or Philadelphia. Finally, we decided on Boston, the [2] (<u>*capital*</u>, *capitol*) of Massachusetts. We drove [3] (<u>*to*</u>, *too, two*) the city in three days. Even

MECHANICS

MECHANICS

my parents could not conceal [4] (*their*, *there*, *they're*) excitement. We did not [5] (*loose*, *lose*) a moment. Boston [6] (*formally*, *formerly*) was "the hub of the universe," and we discovered that [7] (*it's*, *its*) still a fascinating city.

Everyone in my family [8] (*accept*, *except*) me had eaten lobster, and I ate my first one in Boston. I was not [9] (*altogether*, *all together*) certain how to eat the lobster, but my doubt did not [10] (*affect*, *effect*) my appetite. My parents insisted that pear yogurt was a strange [11] (*desert*, *dessert*) to follow lobster, but I would not [12] (*altar*, *alter*) my order. After the pear yogurt, I asked for a small [13] (*peace*, *piece*) of pie, but my father told me to be [14] (*quiet*, *quite*).

While in Boston, we walked up and down the streets just to [15] (*hear*, *here*) the strange accent of the Bostonians. [16] (*Their*, *There*, *They're*) especially noted for [17] (*their*, *there*, *they're*) pronunciation of *a*'s and *r*'s.

We had not been in Boston long before the [18] (*weather*, *whether*) bureau predicted a big snowstorm for the area. Since we had not taken the proper [19] (*cloths*, *clothes*) for snow, we decided to return home. On the way back, we were [20] (*already*, *all ready*) making plans for another visit to Boston.

50 Commonly Misspelled Words

As you study the following words, pay particular attention to the letters in italics. These letters generally cause the greatest difficulty in correctly spelling the words.

ach*e*	colo*r*	fr*ie*nd	re*a*dy	ti*r*ed
ag*ai*n	cou*gh*	*gu*ess	s*ai*d	toni*gh*t
a*l*ways	cou*l*d	ha*l*f	s*a*ys	tr*ie*s
answ*e*r	c*ou*ntry	h*ou*r	sense	tr*ou*ble
bel*ie*ve	d*ai*ly	inste*a*d	sh*oe*s	*u*pon
b*ui*lt	docto*r*	l*ai*d	since	us*i*ng
b*u*sy	do*e*sn't	min*u*te	speci*a*l	we*a*r
b*u*y	do*n*'t	of*t*en	s*t*rai*gh*t	wom*e*n
ca*nn*ot	*ea*rly	*o*nce	thou*gh*	wo*n*'t
ca*n*'t	easy	p*ai*d	throu*gh*	*w*rite

MEETING INDIVIDUAL NEEDS

ADVANCED STUDENTS

Students can integrate their spelling and dictionary skills with a lesson for another discipline. Tell students to choose a chapter in one of their textbooks and to scan the chapter for new or especially challenging words. Then tell students to use dictionary symbols to write these words phonetically in one column. The other column will contain the definitions of the words. Tell students to write the correctly spelled words on a separate list.

You could coordinate this lesson with another teacher. The students' products would be useful learning material for both classes.

MECHANICS

MECHANICS

200 Spelling Words

absence	brilliant	excellent
absolutely	bureau	execute
acceptance	business	existence
accommodate	candidate	experience
accumulate	career	experiment
achieve		explanation
acquire	careless	extremely
across	carrying	familiar
advertisement	ceased	favorite
against	ceiling	February
	choice	
aisles	college	field
among	committee	fierce
announce	completely	finally
anxiety	conceive	foliage
apologize	conscience	foreign
apparent		fortunately
appreciation	conscious	forty
arctic	control	fourth
arguing	correspondence	genius
argument	courteous	genuine
	criticize	
arithmetic	curiosity	government
assistance	decision	governor
associate	definite	grammar
attacked	describe	guarantee
attendance	description	height
attitude		heir
attorney	desirable	humorous
audience	discipline	hungrily
basis	divine	icicles
beginning	efficiency	imaginary
	eighth	
benefit	eliminate	immediately
bicycle	embarrass	independent
bough	equipment	intelligence
bouquet	especially	interest
brief	exactly	interpret

jealous
judgment
knowledge
laboratory
leisure

license
liquor
loneliness
losing
luxury
magazine
marriage
mathematics
meant
medicine

mischief
muscle
museum
necessary
nervous
nineteen
ninety
occasion
occur
occurrence

opinion
opportunity
opposite
originally
particularly
patience
perceive
performance
permanent
personal

physical
picnic
possess
preferred
privilege
probably
professor
pursue
realize
receive

recommend
referred
religion
repetition
rhythm
safety
satisfy
scene
schedule
seize

separate
shining
similar
society
speech
strength
studying
succeed
success
surprise

suspicion
sympathy
teammates
technique
temperament

temporary
theory
thorough
tomorrow
tongue

tournament
tragedy
transferred
treasury
uncomfortable
university
unnecessary
unusually
vacuum
vague

various
veil
vicinity
villain
violence
warrior
wholly
whose
writing
yield

MECHANICS

MECHANICS

PART THREE

RESOURCES

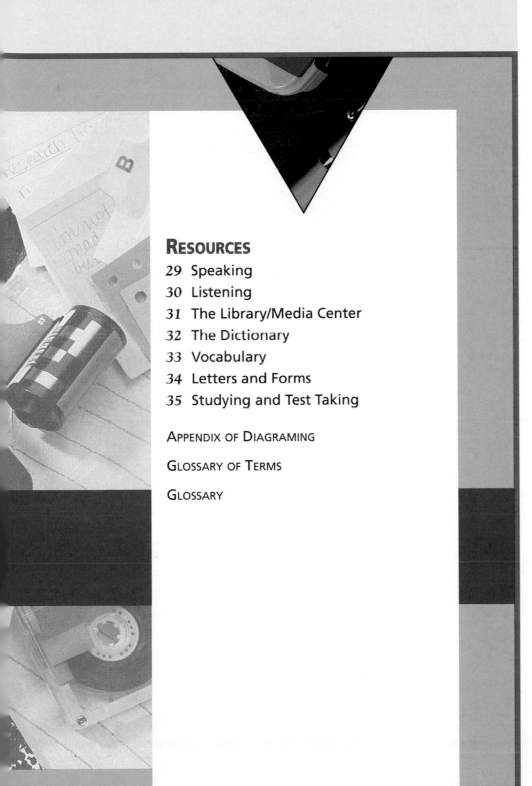

RESOURCES

OBJECTIVES

- To explain how to handle conversations in given situations
- To write an announcement for an upcoming event
- To prepare and deliver a speech
- To participate in a group discussion

CHAPTER OVERVIEW

In this chapter, students will receive instruction for both formal and informal speaking situations. Guidelines are presented for using the telephone, giving directions and instructions, and making introductions. The chapter also presents extensive guidelines for formal speaking situations, including speeches, announcements, introductions, group discussions, and oral interpretations. Students are given opportunities to practice following these guidelines in the **Review** section at the end of the chapter.

29 SPEAKING

Skills and Strategies

Effective speaking takes a little practice. Fortunately, you can learn some simple techniques that will allow you to speak confidently in almost any speaking situation. Whenever you speak, you can improve your effectiveness if you think about

- your purpose (What are you trying to say?)
- your topic (What are you speaking about?)
- your audience (Who are your listeners?)

The Communication Cycle

Communicating is a two-way process. First, a speaker communicates feelings or ideas to the listeners. Then the listeners respond to the speaker's message. This response is called *feedback.*

• To prepare and present an oral interpretation of a literary selection

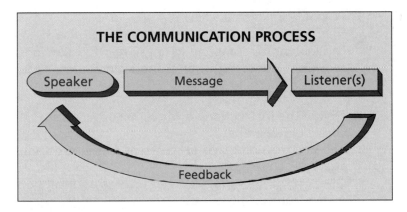

THE COMMUNICATION PROCESS

Speaker → Message → Listener(s)

Feedback

Speaking Informally

Impromptu Speaking

At times you will need to speak to a group of people without having time to plan what you will say. This is called an *impromptu speech*. Here are some suggestions.

1. *Think about your purpose.* (Do you want to give information to your audience? to persuade them?)
2. *Think about your topic.* (What's the main thing you need to say? If you have time, add details to explain your main ideas.)
3. *Think about your audience.* (Does what you're saying suit the time, the place, and the people that you are speaking to?)

Speaking Socially

In most social situations, you need to remember to speak clearly and politely.

Speaking on the Telephone

1. Call people at times that are convenient for them.
2. Identify yourself; then state your reason for calling.

QUICK REMINDER
Have students identify the following statements as either true or false:

1. When giving directions, don't worry about giving each necessary step. [false]
2. When giving a speech, you should mumble. [false]
3. During a group discussion, listen carefully to others. [true]
4. When giving a speech or an oral interpretation, consider your audience. [true]

MEETING
INDIVIDUAL
NEEDS

STUDENTS WITH SPECIAL NEEDS
Students with learning disabilities and students with attention deficit disorder will more readily remember the guidelines for speaking socially if they are given the opportunity to dramatize each situation discussed. Pair students and have them create and perform short skits that illustrate the guidelines presented under **Speaking Socially.** (For **Making Social Introductions,** p. 798, combine pairs into groups of four.)

You may want to lead a class discussion about why these guidelines are necessary.

INTEGRATING THE LANGUAGE ARTS

Speaking and Vocabulary. Point out to students that it's helpful to use transitional words when giving directions and instructions. Ask students to tell you some commonly used transitional words. [Words used to make the order of events clear are *first, second, then, next, earlier, later, when,* and *before.* Words and phrases used to show comparison and contrast are *similarly, also, however, on the other hand,* and *but.* Words and phrases that make cause-and-effect relationships clear are *because, as a result, since, therefore, for this reason, so,* and *consequently.*]

MEETING
INDIVIDUAL
NEEDS

ADVANCED STUDENTS

Students may want to research some leading books on manners and then give oral reports on introduction etiquette. Or students could present a historical perspective on proper introductions. Encourage students to offer their opinions on introduction etiquette.

3. Be polite and speak clearly.
4. Keep your call to a reasonable length. It may not be convenient for someone to speak to you early in the morning, late at night, or around mealtimes.

Giving Instructions or Directions

1. Divide the instructions or directions into a series of clear, logical steps.
2. Tell your listener each of the steps in the process, one at a time, in order.
3. Check to be sure your listener understands all of the instructions or directions.
4. Repeat any instructions that are not clear.

Making Social Introductions

1. Have confidence. If no one else introduces you, introduce yourself to other people.
2. When you introduce others, identify them by name.
3. When you are introducing others, it is customary to speak first to

   - a person of higher job position
   - an older person before a younger person
   - the person you know best

Speaking Formally

Preparing a Speech

A formal speech is one that you give at a specific time and place. When you give this kind of speech, you usually have the chance to prepare carefully beforehand.

Planning Your Speech

When you prepare your speech, you will need to consider your purpose for speaking. The following chart shows some common types of speeches, arranged according to their purpose.

SPEECH CONSIDERATIONS

PURPOSE	DESCRIPTION OF SPEECH	EXAMPLES OF SPEECH TITLES
To inform	gives facts or general information or explains how to do something	Dinosaurs Once Lived in West Texas How to Take Good Snapshots
To persuade	attempts to change an opinion or attempts to get listeners to act	Why Everyone Should Recycle How Volunteering Can Make a Difference
To entertain	relates an amusing story or incident	My Most Embarrassing Moment

Considering Your Audience

When you plan your speech, you also need to consider your audience's interests.

THINKING ABOUT YOUR AUDIENCE

QUESTIONS ABOUT AUDIENCE	ANSWER	YOUR SPEECH WILL NEED
What does the audience already know about this subject?	very little	to give background details to listeners
	a little	to give at least some background details
	a lot	to focus only on interesting points
How interested will the audience be in this subject?	very interested	to keep your listeners' interest
	only a little interested	to focus on aspects most interesting to your listeners
	uninterested	to convince your listeners that this topic is important

TIMESAVER

If, while studying writing, your students have studied purpose and audience, as well as the gathering and organizing of information, you may want to proceed directly to **Giving Your Speech**, p. 800. Tell students that the steps for writing a speech are the same steps they would follow when writing any other composition. For review, ask students to describe the stages of the writing process.

LEARNING STYLES

Auditory Learners. Students might benefit from listening to audio recordings of outstanding speeches designed to inform, persuade, or entertain. If you can't locate actual recordings, you may be able to obtain copies of speeches and tape them yourself or have someone else tape them.

RESOURCES

RESOURCES

CRITICAL THINKING
Evaluation

When preparing their speeches, students must evaluate the appropriateness of possible topics. To give students practice, have them evaluate the appropriateness of the following topics for an informative speech to a sixth-grade class:

1. workings of a hydroelectric dam [not appropriate because subject is too complex, requires too much background knowledge, and is probably not of interest to most sixth-grade students]
2. Scandinavian voting practices that give young people the right to vote on some issues [appropriate because subject is relevant to sixth-grade students]

A DIFFERENT APPROACH

To prove to students the importance of nonverbal communication, show—without sound—a videotape of part of a television program. Ask students what they can tell about what is happening and being said by looking at facial expressions, gestures, and body movements.

You also could use a video camera to record students in the classroom for several minutes. Then play the tape for the students and let them comment on each other's nonverbal communications.

800

Organizing Your Speech Notes

The most common type of speech is a speech you give using note cards. First, you prepare an outline of your main points. Next, you make note cards for each of the main points. Then, when you give your speech, you talk directly to the audience. You can refer to your note cards whenever you need to remember your main points.

Here are some suggestions for making note cards.

1. Write each main idea on a separate note card.
2. Make a special note card for anything that you might need to read word for word (such as a quotation, a series of dates, or statistics that are too difficult to memorize).
3. Include a special note card to tell you when to show a chart, diagram, graphic, drawing, model, or other visual materials.
4. Number your completed note cards to help you keep them in the correct order.

Giving Your Speech

Speaking Effectively

To give an effective speech, you'll need to use your voice and your gestures to help express your meaning to your listeners. Here are some pointers to use when you are speaking.

1. *Stand confidently.* Stand up straight and look alert. Use comfortable and appropriate movements to emphasize your words.
2. *Speak clearly.* Speak loudly enough so that everyone can hear you. Pronounce your words carefully.
3. *Look at your audience.* When you speak, look directly at your audience. Speak directly to them.
4. *Use a normal way of speaking.* Your voice gives your audience clues that help them understand what points you want to emphasize.

Speaking in Front of an Audience

It's normal to feel nervous about speaking in front of an audience. But you can use the following suggestions to help you stay in command.

1. *Be prepared.* Organize your material carefully. Practice using your note cards and any special information or visuals you plan to use during your speech.
2. *Practice your speech.* Each time you rehearse, pretend you're actually giving your speech.
3. *Remember your purpose.* Focus on what you want to tell your audience and how you want them to react instead of worrying about yourself.

Special Speaking Situations

Making Announcements

When you make an announcement, your main goal is to provide information. Follow these guidelines.

1. Write out your announcement. Be sure to include all the important facts. Add important details that will interest your listeners.
2. When it's time to give your announcement, first get your audience's attention. Then announce your message slowly and clearly.

Making an Introduction

Sometimes a short introduction is given before a speech or before a dramatic performance. An introduction gets the audience's attention. It also gives an audience any necessary background information. For example, an introduction may explain details about the performance or presentation. (Include information about the speaker or the subject of a speech.) Or, it might include background information about a dramatic work, the actors, or the author of a theatre work being presented.

RESOURCES

COOPERATIVE LEARNING
Before students give their speeches to the entire class, you may want to let them practice speaking in small groups. Divide the class into groups of four. Assign each group a short speech to prepare and deliver. Have group members use the seven guidelines under **Giving Your Speech** to evaluate each other. Tell students to be fair, kind, and helpful in their evaluations. You could walk around the room and monitor the groups' activities. After all students have delivered their speeches, ask volunteers to tell you what the activity taught them about their speaking abilities.

A DIFFERENT APPROACH
Ask students to picture themselves as hosts of an international music awards program. As a host, each student is to write and present an introduction for a favorite singer or musical group. Tell students to follow the guidelines presented in this chapter when writing their introductions. When delivering their introductions, students should follow the guidelines for delivering a speech.

RESOURCES

801

AT-RISK STUDENTS

Invite a local businessperson to tell your class about group discussions at his or her place of work. Ask the speaker to tell why group discussions are important in the business world and to give some tips for holding successful group discussions.

RESOURCES

RESOURCES

802 *Speaking*

Group Discussions

Setting a Purpose

You probably work in groups in many of your classes. The goal of group discussions is to accomplish a specific purpose. This purpose may be

- to discuss and share ideas
- to cooperate in group learning
- to solve a problem
- to arrive at a group decision or to make a group recommendation

To help your group decide about your purpose, find out how much time will be allowed. Then you'll need to identify what your group will be expected to accomplish within the time allowed.

Assigning Roles

Everyone involved in a group discussion should have a specific role. Each role has special responsibilities. For example, your group may choose a chairperson to help keep the discussion moving smoothly. Someone else may be chosen as the secretary, or reporter (recorder), who has the responsibility of taking notes during the discussion.

Usually, a group establishes a plan, or outline, for the order of topics to follow in a discussion. This plan may be established by the chairperson, or sometimes the entire group may discuss and organize the plan for the discussion.

A Chairperson's Responsibilities

1. Announce the topic and establish a plan.
2. Follow the plan.
3. Encourage each member to take part.
4. Help group members stay on track. Avoid disagreements and distractions.

A Secretary's or Reporter's Responsibilities

1. Take notes about important information.
2. Prepare a final report.

A Participant's Responsibilities

1. Take an active part in the discussion.
2. Ask questions and listen attentively to others.
3. Cooperate and share information.

Oral Interpretation

Oral interpretation is more like acting in a play than giving a speech. When you give an oral interpretation, you read a piece of literature expressively to your listeners. To indicate the meaning of the selection, you use facial expressions, your voice, gestures, and movements to interpret the literary work for your listeners.

Choosing a Selection

The purpose of an oral interpretation is to entertain. An oral interpretation is usually planned, so you should have enough time to select your literary piece and practice your presentation.

The material you choose for your presentation depends on several different factors, such as

- who your audience is (what their interests are and how willing they are to be an attentive audience)
- how long a presentation you plan to make (can vary greatly, from very short to very long)
- what the occasion or situation is (material suited to one occasion may not work well in another)
- how expressive an interpretation you want to give (can vary, from readings that require a lot of acting to mildly expressive pieces)

LEP/ESL

General Strategies. You may want to have ESL students present oral interpretations in their native languages. Require that their interpretations be followed by English translations. This procedure will allow ESL students to express themselves in languages they are fluent in and will give the rest of the class the chance to learn about literature from other cultures and the chance to hear foreign languages spoken.

Students could find literature that has already been translated into English, or they could translate selections themselves.

Think about the kind of story you would choose to read to a group of six-year-olds during story hour. You would probably want a story with lots of action, and you would want characters whose voices and movements you could act out to amuse and entertain your young listeners.

Now think about what might be an appropriate reading for a presentation at a parent-teacher banquet near Thanksgiving. Perhaps you would select a literary work that suits the holiday coming up, or that has characters or a situation that would interest your audience. An older audience of enthusiastic parents and teachers will probably be more willing to pay attention to a longer, more serious selection than an audience of six-year-olds would.

Here are suggestions for finding a literary work for an oral interpretation.

SELECTING AN ORAL INTERPRETATION	
TYPE OF LITERATURE	**DESCRIPTION OF POSSIBLE SELECTION**
poem	a poem that tells a story, such as an epic poem
	a poem that has a speaker (using the word *I*) or a conversation between characters
	a poem that is expressive of a particular emotion
short story	a brief story, or portion of a story, that has ■ a beginning, middle, and end ■ either a narrator who tells the story (using *I*) or characters who talk to one another (using dialogue in quotation marks)
play	a short play, or one scene from a play, that has ■ a beginning, middle, and end ■ one or more characters with dialogue

You may need an introduction for your interpretation. This introduction may set the scene, tell something about the author of the piece of literature you're presenting, or give details that tell your audience about important events that have already taken place in the story.

Adapting Material

You may be able to find just the right piece of literature. It may already be the perfect length. It may have just the right number of characters, with dialogue that tells the part of the story you want to tell. But sometimes you need to shorten a short story, a long poem, or a play. This shortened version is called a *cutting*. To make a cutting, follow these suggestions.

1. Decide where the part of the story you want to use should begin and where it should end.
2. Cut out parts that don't contribute to the portion of the story you are telling.
3. From a short story, cut dialogue tags such as *she whispered sadly*. Instead, use these clues to tell you how to act out the characters' words.

Presenting an Oral Interpretation

After you've chosen a piece of literature to present, you can prepare a *reading script.* A reading script is usually typed (double-spaced or written neatly with space between each line). You can then mark this script to help you when you are reading your selection. For example, you can underline words to remind you to use special emphasis when you say them. Or you can mark a slash (/) to show where you plan to take a breath or pause briefly to create suspense. You might write a word or two or a brief note as a reminder of the emotion that you want to express when you say a character's words.

Rehearse your presentation several different ways until you feel that you have found the most effective. Practice in front of your mirror. Then try out your reading on friends, classmates, or relatives.

Use your voice to suit your meaning. Vary your body movements and your voice to show that you are portraying different characters and to show important emotions (such as fear or joy).

LEARNING STYLES

Auditory and Visual Learners. To give students a better idea of what is involved in an oral interpretation, play a recording of a celebrity reading a famous story, show a video of an actor reciting a poem, or prepare a presentation of one of your favorite short works of fiction. Or you might ask a drama teacher to have a student prepare an oral presentation. Afterward, discuss the performance with students.

You could use the following questions to guide the discussion:

1. Was the selection well chosen?
2. If the selection was adapted, was the adaptation effective?
3. Did the person presenting the oral interpretation vary her or his voice and movements to convey the meaning of the selection?

RESOURCES

RESOURCES

ANSWERS
Exercise 1

Responses will vary, but they should correspond with the guidelines given for speaking socially. After you've read the students' responses, you may want to select some to be read aloud or dramatized by students.

ANSWERS
Exercise 2

Announcements will vary, but they should include all necessary information.

ANSWERS
Exercise 3

You may want to approve students' topics before they begin gathering information for their speeches. Students' presentations should reflect thoughtful planning in the prewriting and writing stages and practice in the delivery stage. Speakers should stay within the time limit given in the assignment.

806

Review

▶ EXERCISE 1   **Speaking Socially**

For each of the situations, explain how you might handle the conversation. What would you say to be polite and to be clear?

1. You're calling to congratulate a classmate who has won a science award.
2. You've invited a new classmate to study at your house. Give directions on how to get to your house from the school.
3. You're standing in front of the school, talking to your new teacher. Your mother arrives. Introduce your mother to your teacher.
4. Explain to your classmates how to make or repair something (such as how to bake bread or repair a bicycle tire). Make sure you provide all the necessary information and give the steps in order. Repeat or summarize all necessary instructions.
5. At a baseball game, you realize that the person sitting next to you is a classmate you like but do not know well. Introduce yourself.

▶ EXERCISE 2   **Making an Announcement**

Write an announcement for an upcoming event. The event can be real, or you can make up the details. Give all the necessary information.

▶ EXERCISE 3   **Preparing and Giving a Speech**

Choose a topic for a short, two- to three-minute speech to your English class. Think about your audience and your purpose when choosing your speech topic. Prepare note cards for your speech. Then give your speech to the class, following the guidelines for speaking effectively on page 800.

 EXERCISE 4 **Conducting a Group Discussion**

Select a group chairperson to lead a discussion on a topic your teacher assigns or one of your own choosing. Establish a plan for the discussion and assign roles. The purpose for the discussion is to make a list of the group's findings about the topic. Here are some suggestions for a topic your group might discuss.

1. activities that every community should provide for young people
2. ways to improve teacher-student relationships
3. the most important thing we can do to improve the future
4. leadership qualities and how to develop them
5. how to reduce gang violence

 EXERCISE 5 **Presenting an Oral Interpretation**

Select a literary work or a suitable portion of a piece of literature. Prepare a script for a three-minute oral interpretation to present to your class. Write a brief introduction telling the title and author of the selection. Present your interpretation to your class.

ANSWERS
Exercise 4

Students' discussions should follow the procedures outlined in the chapter. Each student should participate according to his or her role in the group. Students should cooperate to accomplish the goal of making a list of the group's findings about the topic.

ANSWERS
Exercise 5

Each student should follow the procedures given in the chapter for choosing a selection, adapting material, writing an introduction, preparing a reading script, and rehearsing a selection. Each introduction should set the scene, give the title and author of the selection, and provide background information. Students' oral interpretations should stay within the time limit given in the assignment.

RESOURCES

RESOURCES

OBJECTIVES

- To write questions designed to gauge listening accuracy
- To listen and respond to questions designed to gauge listening accuracy
- To prepare questions for an interview

CHAPTER OVERVIEW

Active listening is the focus of this chapter. The chapter begins with a brief look at the communication cycle and at guidelines for polite and effective listening. Next, both the listener's and the speaker's purposes are considered. Suggestions for listening for information, interviewing, and critical listening follow. Students are also told how to recognize five common persuasive techniques. The chapter concludes with four exercises that allow students to apply what they've learned.

QUICK REMINDER

Give students a brief set of instructions to test how well they listen. Ask them to take out sheets of paper, to write their names in the upper left-hand corners, to fold the pages in half, and to pass the papers to the front. Do not repeat the instructions. This exercise will help introduce the importance of listening carefully.

30 LISTENING

Strategies for Active Listening

Listening is not as simple as it sounds. You constantly hear noises and sounds of one kind or another. But you probably don't really *listen* to very many of them. In other words, hearing and listening are not the same thing. Hearing just happens. But listening is an active process. Listening requires that you think as well as hear.

Listening with a Purpose

Keep your purpose in mind as you listen. This will help you be a more effective listener. Common purposes for listening are

- for enjoyment or entertainment
- to gain information
- to understand information or an explanation
- to evaluate or form an opinion

- To listen to a speech and to take notes
- To identify the main ideas and supporting details of a speech
- To distinguish between facts and opinions in a speech
- To identify comparisons and contrasts and cause-and-effect relationships in a speech
- To identify persuasive techniques

Listening for Information

Listening for Details

When you listen for information, you need to listen for details that answer the basic *5W-How?* questions: *Who? What? When? Where? Why?* and *How?* As you listen to whoever is speaking, try to find answers for each of these questions.

Listening to Instructions

Careful listening is important when you are given assignments, instructions, or directions. Follow these guidelines.

1. Identify each separate step. Listen for words that tell you when each step ends and the next one begins. These words may include *first, second, third, next, then,* and *last* or *finally.*
2. Listen to the order of the steps. Take notes whenever it is necessary.
3. Imagine yourself completing each step in order.
4. Make sure you have all the instructions and understand them. Ask questions if you are unclear about any step.

Listening Politely

Follow these guidelines to be a polite and effective listener.

1. Look at the speaker. When you pay attention, the speaker can tell that you are interested in what he or she has to say.
2. Respect the speaker. Be tolerant of individual differences, such as a speaker's accent, customs, race, or religion.
3. Don't interrupt the speaker.

MEETING
INDIVIDUAL
NEEDS

LEP/ESL

General Strategies. Students for whom English is a second language may have an especially hard time listening for information. Suggest that students tape-record speeches and lectures. This will give students more control over the listening experience by enabling them to stop and replay phrases or sentences that they do not understand.

STUDENTS WITH SPECIAL NEEDS

Students with learning disabilities might have difficulty identifying the information that answers *5W-How?* questions. Give students examples of the types of information that answer each of these questions. For example, the phrase *with a hammer* tells how something is done.

When they can generate the types of phrases that answer each of the *5W-How?* questions, have students identify sentences that give this information within short speeches, lectures, or oral instructions.

RESOURCES

RESOURCES

A DIFFERENT APPROACH

To emphasize the fact that listening is an active process, open the doors and windows in your classroom. Instruct students to write down any sounds that they hear coming from outside the classroom. Then have students write as many details as they can about the sounds — descriptions of the sounds, possible origins of the sounds, the meanings of the sounds, and so forth.

After sufficient time has passed for students to identify and write about several sounds, call on volunteers to discuss what they have heard.

4. Pay attention. Don't whisper, fidget, or make other types of noises or actions that could distract other listeners.
5. Try to understand the speaker's point of view. Also, be aware of how your own point of view affects the way you judge what others have to say.
6. Don't judge too soon. Listen to the speaker's entire message before you evaluate the speech.

Using the LQ2R Method

The LQ2R study method is especially helpful when you are listening to a speaker who is giving information or instructions.

L   *Listen* carefully to information as it is being presented. Focus your attention only on the speaker, and don't allow yourself to be distracted.

Q   *Question* yourself as you listen. Make a list of questions as they occur to you.

R   *Recite* in your own words the information as it is being presented. Summarize information in your mind or jot down notes as you listen.

R   *Re-listen* as the speaker concludes the presentation. The speaker may sum up, or repeat, major points of the presentation.

☞ REFERENCE NOTE: For more information about study methods, see pages 845–862.

Taking Notes

You can't write down every word a speaker says. Instead, write only the key words or important phrases the speaker uses. Translate difficult terms into your own words.

☞ REFERENCE NOTE: For more about note taking, see pages 845–855.

Interviewing

An interview is a special listening situation. When you interview someone, you usually ask someone who is an expert or has special knowledge about a subject to speak to you and give you information about what they know. Interviews are good sources for obtaining interesting and up-to-date information. Follow these suggestions to conduct an effective interview.

Preparing for the Interview
- Decide what information that you really want to ask about most.
- Make a list of questions to ask.
- Make an appointment for the interview. Be on time.

Conducting the Interview
- Be courteous and patient. Give the person you are interviewing time to answer each question that you ask. Respect what the person you are interviewing has to say, even if you disagree.
- Listen carefully to each answer that the person you are interviewing gives to the questions you ask. If the person gives you an answer that confuses you, or if you're not sure you understand what the person means, you may want to ask some follow-up questions to be clear about the information the person is giving you.
- It is polite to tell the person you are interviewing how you plan to use the information you are asking for. For example, if you plan to use the person's exact words in a report, it is usually best to tell the person as you begin the interview and ask permission to quote him or her directly.
- Thank the person for granting you the interview.

Following up on the Interview
- Review your notes to be sure they are clear.
- Write a summary of the interview as soon as possible.

RESOURCES

COOPERATIVE LEARNING

You may want to give the class some practice preparing and conducting interviews. Divide the class into three or four groups and give each group the name of a celebrity to interview. Provide time for group members to plan and write their questions. Instruct each member of each group to prepare at least one question.

You could assign a student from each group, perhaps someone with theatrical interests, to act as the person being interviewed. Have students conduct their interviews according to the guidelines in the textbook.

INTEGRATING THE LANGUAGE ARTS

Technology Link. Many professional interviewers use tape recorders during their interviews. Tell students that they can use tape recorders for their interviews, but that they must ask the persons being interviewed for permission to do so at the beginnings of the interviews.

RESOURCES

811

TIMESAVER
If your students have already studied the writing chapters, they might be familiar with identifying details and main ideas and with analyzing information. In that case, you could skip over **Critical Listening** and simply remind students to apply those skills when listening as well as when writing and reading. You could then have students complete **Exercise 3** for practice and review.

INTEGRATING THE LANGUAGE ARTS
Literature Link. Have students listen closely while you read a poem, such as "Annabel Lee" by Edgar Allan Poe, in which sound is especially important. After the reading, ask students how the sounds of the words affect the poem's mood and meaning. You may want to review briefly the sound devices such as repetition, rhyme, and alliteration used by poets.

Critical Listening

When you listen critically, you think carefully about what you hear. You analyze and then evaluate the ideas being presented.

GUIDELINES FOR LISTENING CRITICALLY	
Find main ideas.	What are the most important points? Listen for clue words, such as *major, main, most important,* or similar words.
Identify significant details.	What dates, names, or facts does the speaker use to support main ideas? What kinds of examples or explanations are used to support the main ideas?
Distinguish between facts and opinions.	A *fact* is a statement that can be proved to be true. (May is the fifth month.) An *opinion* is a belief or a judgment about something. It cannot be proved to be true. (Cherry pie is better than apple pie.)
Note comparisons and contrasts.	Are some details compared or contrasted with others?
Understand cause and effect.	Does the speaker say or hint that some events cause others to occur? Or does the speaker suggest that some events are the result of others?
Predict outcomes and draw conclusions.	What reasonable conclusions or predictions can you make from the facts and evidence you have gathered from the speech?

 REFERENCE NOTE: For more information about interpreting and analyzing information, see pages 849–852.

Understanding Persuasive Techniques

To get you to believe in something or to take some action, speakers may use one of the common persuasive techniques listed below. Learning to recognize these techniques can help you understand a speaker's message. It can also help you avoid being "taken in" by arguments that are not based on logic or reason.

COMMON PERSUASIVE TECHNIQUES USED BY SPEAKERS	
Bandwagon	Users of this technique urge you to "jump on the bandwagon" by suggesting that you should do or believe something because "everyone" is doing it. The idea is to make you think you're missing out if you don't join in.
Testimonial	Experts or famous people sometimes give a personal "testimony" about a product or idea. However, the person giving the testimonial may not really know much about that particular product or idea.
Emotional appeals	This technique uses words that appeal to your emotions rather than to your logic or reason.
"Plain folks"	Ordinary people (or people who pretend to be ordinary) are often used to persuade others. People tend to believe others who seem to be similar to themselves.
False cause and effect	This technique is used to suggest that because one event happened first, it caused a second event to occur. However, the two events may not actually have a cause-and-effect relationship.

COOPERATIVE LEARNING

Divide your class into five groups and assign each group a different persuasive technique. Instruct each group to prepare and present a television commercial based on its assigned technique. Each student should have a part in the presentation, as well as in the planning, of her or his group's commercial.

MEETING **INDIVIDUAL** NEEDS

AT-RISK STUDENTS

To show students how **Understanding Persuasive Techniques** relates to the world outside the classroom, ask them to find at least one example of each of the five common persuasive techniques in advertisements or commercials. Suggest that students look for examples in magazines and newspapers, or that they listen for examples on the radio and television. You may want to point out that a speaker or advertiser may use several techniques.

RESOURCES

RESOURCES

Review

▶ EXERCISE 1 **Listening for Information**

Make up five questions similar to those that follow. Read them aloud, pausing briefly to allow your classmates time to jot down their answers. Have listeners check their answers to see how accurately they listened.

Students' questions should be similar to the five examples given.

1. In the series of numbers *6—1—8—3—4*, the fourth number is ____.   **1.** 3
2. In this list, *in—off—but—for—how*, the word beginning with *o* is ____.   **2.** off
3. Here is the order for pairs: first, Josh and Erika; then, Graciella and Cindy; last, Roberto and Quan. Which group is Cindy in?   **3.** the middle group
4. The Colorado River is in Arizona, the Sabine River is in Texas, and the Columbia River is in Oregon. Where is the Sabine River?   **4.** Texas
5. Here are six colors: red, green, yellow, blue, purple, orange. Which color is second?   **5.** green

▶ EXERCISE 2 **Preparing Interview Questions**

Think of an elected official, a celebrity, or an individual from history that you would like to interview. Then prepare ten questions you would like to be able to ask that person in an interview. Follow the steps for preparing for an interview on page 811.

▶ EXERCISE 3 **Listening to a Speech**

Listen to a short speech presented by your teacher in class. Take brief notes. Then respond to the following questions about the speech.

1. What are the main ideas of the speech?
2. Does the speech contain details that support the main points in the speech? If so, identify several of them.

ANSWERS
Exercise 2

Students' questions will vary but should follow the guidelines for preparing for an interview.

ANSWERS
Exercise 3

Students' answers will vary depending on the speech but should prove that students actively listened to the speech and applied the **Guidelines for Listening Critically.**

3. Can you distinguish between facts and opinions mentioned in the speech?
4. Does the speech contain comparisons and contrasts?
5. Do some events in the speech cause other events to happen?

▶ EXERCISE 4 **Identifying Persuasive Techniques**

Identify the persuasive technique used in each of the following items.

1. "You should buy Yummies," says Jo Jo Jackson, champion skeet-shooter. "They'll help start your day off with a bang!" **1.** testimonial
2. "Everyone's joining our crusade for reforming the school system. Sign up to do your part now!" **2.** bandwagon
3. "Those big spenders in Washington are ruining our country!" **3.** emotional appeals
4. "Our candidate for City Council is shown with her husband and two lovely children in front of their attractive, yet modest, home." **4.** "plain folks"
5. Because Jim forgot to wear his lucky bowling shirt, he lost the first three games of the tournament.
5. false cause and effect

MEETING INDIVIDUAL NEEDS

ADVANCED STUDENTS

Have students listen to speeches given by candidates in state or local elections. Tell students to identify the persuasive techniques used by the candidates and to evaluate the effectiveness of these techniques. Ask students to share their findings with the class.

RESOURCES

RESOURCES

OBJECTIVES

- To list book titles in the order they should be shelved in a library
- To use the card catalog or on-line catalog to find information
- To use parts of a book to find information
- To select reference tools for researching topics
- To analyze an entry from the *Readers' Guide*
- To analyze the parts of a newspaper

CHAPTER OVERVIEW

This chapter is designed to assist students in finding information quickly and easily in the library or media center. Classification and arrangement of nonfiction and fiction books are explained. Also, a description and explanation of the card catalog and on-line catalog is provided. Additionally, parts of a book are discussed to give students a basis for locating information more easily. Reference materials such as a verticle file, microforms, a database system, encyclopedias, newspapers, biographical references, and the *Readers' Guide to Periodical Literature* are listed and defined so that your students' library visits might be informative and productive.

31 THE LIBRARY/ MEDIA CENTER

Finding and Using Information

In the library or media center you can find information on many subjects. But you need to know how to find it.

The Arrangement of a Library

Every book in a library has a number and letter code, the book's *call number.* The call number tells you how the book has been classified and where to find it.

DEWEY CLASSIFICATION OF NONFICTION		
NUMBERS	**SUBJECT AREAS**	**EXAMPLES OF SUBDIVISIONS**
000–099	General Works	encyclopedias, handbooks
100–199	Philosophy	psychology, ethics, personality
200–299	Religion	bibles, mythology, theology
300–399	Social Sciences	government, law, economics
400–499	Languages	dictionaries, grammars
500–599	Science	general science, mathematics
600–699	Technology	engineering, inventions
700–799	The Arts	music, theater, recreation
800–899	Literature	poetry, drama, essays
900–999	History	biography, geography, travel

RESOURCES

RESOURCES

In most school libraries nonfiction books are classified and arranged using the Dewey decimal system. The Dewey decimal system assigns a number to each nonfiction book according to its subject.

Biographies are often shelved in a separate section of the library, apart from other nonfiction books with a special call number of their own. Libraries arrange biographies in alphabetical order according to the last name of the person the book is about. Two or more biographies of the same person are put in alphabetical order according to the last name of the author.

Arrangement of Fiction

In most libraries, fiction books are placed in a section separate from the nonfiction books. The books in the fiction section of a library are arranged alphabetically by their author's last name. Two or more books written by the same author are arranged alphabetically by the first word of their titles (not counting *A, An,* or *The*). Sometimes collections of short stories are kept separate from other works of fiction.

The Card Catalog

To find the book you want, find the call number in the library's *card catalog.* The card catalog is a cabinet of small drawers containing cards. These cards are arranged in alphabetical order by title, author, or subject. Books of fiction have at least two cards in the catalog—a *title card* and an *author card*. Or, if a book is nonfiction, it will have a third card—a *subject card*. Occasionally, you may find *"see"* or *"see also"* cards. These cards tell you where to go in the card catalog to find additional information on a subject.

An *on-line catalog* is a version of the card catalog stored on a computer. It contains the same information as a regular catalog. An on-line catalog can display author, title, or subject information just like a regular card catalog.

RESOURCES

RESOURCES

LESS-ADVANCED STUDENTS

To give students hands-on practice with the card catalog, ask them to list on a piece of paper three subjects that interest them. Take students to the subject catalog in the school library, and ask them to locate and write down the title and call numbers of a book for each subject. If they are interested in reading these books, allow students time to locate their choices and check them out.

 INTEGRATING THE LANGUAGE ARTS

Library Skills and Dictionary Skills. From ancient Roman and Greek history and literature, North American founding fathers borrowed names for U.S. cities and towns. For example, Ithaca, New York, comes from the *Odyssey.* Take your students to the library, and ask them to use an atlas index or other geographical reference book to identify the states in which the following cities are located. Ask them to find in an unabridged dictionary whether the original words were Greek or Roman.

1. Alexandria [Louisiana, Minnesota, Virginia; Greek]
2. Athens [Alabama, Georgia, Ohio, Tennessee, Texas; Greek]
3. Naples [Florida, Idaho; Roman]
4. Olympia [Washington; Greek]
5. Rome [Georgia, New York, Oregon; Roman]
6. Syracuse [Kansas, New York; Roman]

818

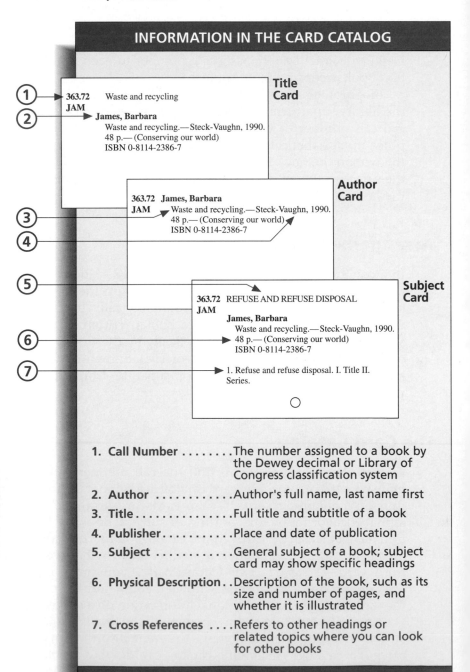

INFORMATION IN THE CARD CATALOG

1. Call Number . . . . The number assigned to a book by the Dewey decimal or Library of Congress classification system

2. Author . . . . Author's full name, last name first

3. Title . . . . Full title and subtitle of a book

4. Publisher . . . . Place and date of publication

5. Subject . . . . General subject of a book; subject card may show specific headings

6. Physical Description . . Description of the book, such as its size and number of pages, and whether it is illustrated

7. Cross References . . . . Refers to other headings or related topics where you can look for other books

Parts of a Book

Information is often easier to find if you know how to use the parts of a book effectively. The title, the table of contents, and the index are examples of the types of information that can be found in the different parts of a book.

INFORMATION FOUND IN PARTS OF A BOOK	
PART	INFORMATION
Title page	gives full title, author, publisher, and place of publication
Copyright page	gives date of first publication and of any revisions
Table of contents	lists titles of chapters or sections of the book and their starting page numbers
Appendix	provides additional information about subjects found in the book; maps and charts are sometimes found here
Glossary	in alphabetical order defines difficult or technical words found in the book
Bibliography	lists sources used to write the book; gives titles of works on related topics
Index	lists topics mentioned in the book and page numbers on which they can be found

Reference Materials

The *Readers' Guide*

The most current information on many topics is found in magazines rather than in books. To find a magazine article, use the *Readers' Guide to Periodical Literature.* The *Readers' Guide* indexes articles, poems, and stories from more

Technology Link. If your school library has an on-line catalog, ask the librarian to show your class how to use the computer. Following this brief lesson, allow each student time to locate in the system and then on the shelves a book for pleasure reading.

LEP/ESL

General Strategies. Books in other languages may not have all the parts listed in this textbook. They may also have book parts arranged differently. For example, books in many languages have the table of contents last, some books don't have them, and many lack an index. Show your ESL students the parts in several books, giving students time to look them over.

RESOURCES

RESOURCES

INTEGRATING THE LANGUAGE ARTS

Literature Link. Explain to students that events and people from writers' lives often influence their fictional works. Discuss with students the reference books that would be helpful in finding biographical information about authors. Then have students choose fictional selections from their literature books and research the lives of the authors of these selections. Students should write an informative paragraph explaining what information they think sheds light on the authors' choices of plot, setting, theme, or characters. A good story to use as an example is Isaac Bashevis Singer's "Zlateh the Goat."

SELECTION AMENDMENT
Description of change: excerpted, boxed, numbers added
Rationale: to focus on the use of the *Readers' Guide* presented in this chapter

than 150 magazines. In the *Readers' Guide,* magazine articles are listed alphabetically by author and by subject. These headings are printed in boldfaced capital letters.

Information in *Readers' Guide* entries is abbreviated. In the front of the *Readers' Guide* these abbreviations are explained.

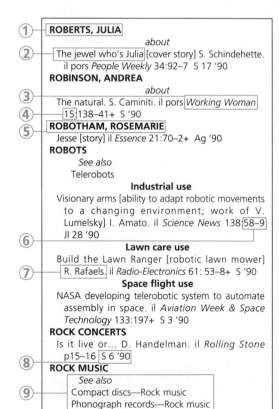

1. **Subject entry**
2. **Title of article**
3. **Name of magazine**
4. **Volume number of magazine**
5. **Author entry**
6. **Page reference**
7. **Author of article**
8. **Date of magazine**
9. **Subject cross-reference**

Special Reference Sources

The *vertical file* is a special filing cabinet containing up-to-date materials. These materials may include newspaper clippings or government and information pamphlets.

Microforms are pages from various newspapers and magazines that are reduced to miniature size. The two most common type are *microfilm* (a roll or reel of film) and *microfiche* (a sheet of film). You view them by using a special projector to enlarge the images to a readable size.

Some libraries store reference sources on computers. Ask your librarian what database systems your library has. A *database* is information that is stored on computer for easy retrieval.

Reference Works

Most libraries devote a section entirely to reference books that contain information on many subjects.

REFERENCE WORKS		
TYPE	**DESCRIPTION**	**EXAMPLES**
Encyclopedias	• multiple volumes • articles arranged alphabetically by subject • source for general information	*Collier's Encyclopedia* *Compton's Encyclopedia* *The World Book Encyclopedia*
General Biographical References	• information about the lives and accomplishments of outstanding people	*Current Biography* *The International Who's Who* *Webster's New Biographical Dictionary*
Atlases	• maps and geographical information	*Atlas of World Cultures* *National Geographic Atlas of the World*
Almanacs	• up-to-date information about current events, facts, statistics, and dates	*The Information Please Almanac, Atlas and Yearbook* *The World Almanac and Book of Facts*
Books of Synonyms	• lists more interesting or more exact words to express ideas	*Roget's International Thesaurus* *Webster's New Dictionary of Synonyms*

RESOURCES

STUDENTS WITH SPECIAL NEEDS

To help learning disabled students gain a better understanding of how to use a library or media center, assign peer helpers for students as they practice using a variety of sources.

Assigning the partners a topic, ask them to find a nonfiction book about their topics. Have them copy the title page, the copyright page, the table of contents, the appendix, two glossary words, two bibliography sources, and two subjects in the index. Next, ask students to find two articles about their topics in the *Readers' Guide* and to copy the title, author, month of publication, and publisher of the articles. Finally, ask them to copy information about their topics from an encyclopedia.

CRITICAL THINKING
Synthesis

You may want to ask your students to design the title page, copyright page, and table of contents of their autobiographies. Have them share these parts of their books with the class.

RESOURCES

COOPERATIVE LEARNING
Use the following activity to expose students to various genres found in the library. First, make a list of subjects and titles (fiction and nonfiction). Then combine these titles and subjects randomly so that each student receives a different list of books to locate. Pair students and take them to the school library. Each student will use the card catalog to find a title for each genre listed and then check the accuracy of his or her partner's work.

INTEGRATING THE LANGUAGE ARTS
Library Skills, Writing, and Literature. You could have students work in groups to create their own newspapers. To incorporate the study of literature into the project, have groups use one or more literary selections — short stories, poetry, plays, or novels — as the basis for the articles. Explain to students that they may have to use their imaginations to fill in any missing details.
Students should include at least one of each of the following elements:

1. news article
2. editorial
3. opinion column
4. feature article
5. entertainment news
6. obituary
7. social news
8. advertisements

Newspapers

Most daily newspapers are divided into sections that contain a wide variety of features and types of writing. Newspaper writers write for different purposes. And readers, like you, read the newspaper for purposes of your own. The following chart shows some of the different contents that you will find in a typical daily newspaper.

WHAT'S IN A NEWSPAPER?		
WRITER'S PURPOSE/ TYPE OF WRITING	READER'S PURPOSE	READING TECHNIQUE
to inform news stories sports	to gain knowledge or information	Ask yourself the *5W-How?* questions (page 33).
to persuade editorials comics reviews ads	to gain knowledge, to make decisions, or to be entertained	Identify points you agree or disagree with. Find facts or reasons the writer uses.
to be creative or expressive comics columns	to be entertained	Identify ways the writer interests you or gives you a new viewpoint or ideas.

 Review

 EXERCISE 1 **Using the Parts of a Book**

Tell which part or parts of a book you would check to find the following information. **1.** table of contents or index
2. glossary, index, or appendix **3.** bibliography
1. a list of page numbers that deal with a specific topic
2. the meaning of a technical term used often in the book
3. a list of the sources used to write the book **4.** title page
4. the place where the book was published **5.** copyright page
5. how many times the book has been revised

▶ EXERCISE 2 **Using the Library**

Answer the following questions to show your understanding of the information resources in the library.

1. In order, which of the following books would be shelved first: *Winter Thunder* by Mari Sandoz, or *Nisei Daughter* by Monica Sone?
2. Use the sample *Readers' Guide* entry on page 820 to find the title of an article written by S. Caminiti about Andrea Robinson. What magazine printed this article?
3. Use the card catalog or the on-line catalog in your library to find a biography of a famous person. Write the book title, the author's name, and the call number.
4. Tell which reference book you might use to find the names of the countries that border Yugoslavia.
5. Tell which reference book might contain recent statistics on the total population of the United States.

▶ EXERCISE 3 **Exploring the Newspaper**

Using a copy of the daily newspaper from home or your library, answer the following questions.

1. Is there a special identification or title for each section of this newspaper? Explain.
2. Find an article that gives you information about a specific event in world news, sports, or entertainment. Find answers to the *5W-How?* questions (*Who? What? Where? When? Why? How?*) in the details of this article.
3. Find an editorial or a letter to the editor. Identify what the writer wants you to think or do. What facts or opinions does the writer use to try to persuade you?
4. Find a comic that you think is intended to persuade you. Find another comic that you think is intended just for fun. Explain your selection.
5. Find an advertisement or classified ad that makes you want to buy the item offered. What do you find most effective about the ad?

ANSWERS
Exercise 2

1. *Winter Thunder*
2. "The Natural" was printed in *Working Woman.*
3. Answers will vary.
4. an atlas
5. an almanac

ANSWERS
Exercise 3

Responses will vary. Check your newspaper to verify students' references.

RESOURCES

RESOURCES

OBJECTIVES

- To use the dictionary to check for capitalization
- To divide words into syllables
- To use the dictionary to find part-of-speech labels and synonyms for words
- To identify usage labels of words in the dictionary

RESOURCES

THE DICTIONARY

CHAPTER OVERVIEW

By explaining features of the dictionary (entry word, pronunciation, part-of-speech labels, etymology, definitions), this chapter clarifies the dictionary's content for students. Additionally, this material describes the different types of dictionaries students might encounter.

QUICK REMINDER

Ask students to look up *bottom* in the dictionary and answer the following questions.

1. How many syllables are in the entry word? [2] Write them [bot • tom].
2. *Bottom* can be used as how many different parts of speech? [3] What are they? [noun, adjective, verb — both transitive and intransitive]
3. In the etymology of *bottom* what does *L* stand for? [Latin]
4. How is the Latin word *fundus* translated? [ground]

RESOURCES

RESOURCES

32 THE DICTIONARY

Types and Contents

Types of Dictionaries

There are many types of dictionaries. Each type contains different kinds of information. However, all dictionaries contain certain general features.

TYPES OF DICTIONARIES		
TYPE AND EXAMPLE	NUMBER OF WORDS	NUMBER OF PAGES
Unabridged *Webster's Third International Unabridged Dictionary*	460,000	2,662
College or Abridged *Webster's Ninth New Collegiate Dictionary*	160,000	1,563
School *The Lincoln Writing Dictionary*	35,000	932
Paperback *The Random House Dictionary*	74,000	1,056

A SAMPLE ENTRY

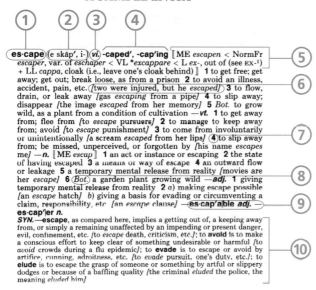

From *Webster's New World Dictionary*. © 1986 by Merriam-Webster Inc., publisher of Merriam-Webster ® Dictionaries. Reprinted by permission of Merriam-Webster Inc.

1. **Entry word.** The entry word shows the correct spelling of a word. An alternate spelling may also be shown. The entry word shows how the word should be divided into syllables, and may also show if the word should be capitalized.
2. **Pronunciation.** The pronunciation of a word is shown using accent marks, phonetic symbols or diacritical marks. Each *phonetic symbol* represents a specific sound. *Diacritical marks* are special symbols placed above letters to show how they sound. Dictionaries provide guides to the meanings and use of diacritical marks or phonetic symbols.
3. **Part-of-speech labels.** These labels are usually abbreviated and show how the entry word should be used in a sentence. Some words may be used as more than one part of speech. In this case, a part-of-speech label is provided before the set of definitions that matches each label.

LEP/ESL

General Strategies. While your native English speakers might have experience with English-language dictionaries, some of your ESL students may be accustomed to using only dictionaries in their native languages and may need extra help. Dictionaries in many languages lack pronunciation sections, because the pronunciation is obvious from the spelling, and many lack etymological sections, because their words do not come from the variety of sources that English words do. Also, students may need help with parts-of-speech labels, because their languages might not have the same parts of speech that English does.

ADVANCED STUDENTS

Ask students to use the *Oxford English Dictionary* and a collegiate dictionary to look up the complete histories of *bugle, cloud, guest, puny,* and *worry* [bugle–ME, O Fr; cloud–ME, OE, IE; guest–ME, ON, OE; puny–Fr, O Fr, L; worry–ME, OE, G, IE]. Then have students write short explanations of how the word entries differ in the two sources.

SELECTION AMENDMENT
Description of change: excerpted and numbers added
Rationale: to focus on the concept of dictionary usage presented in this chapter

RESOURCES

INTEGRATING THE LANGUAGE ARTS

Literature Link. Students might think it odd that O. Henry read the dictionary for pleasure. However, with his expansive working vocabulary, O. Henry skillfully weaves words together in unique ways. In his short story "After Twenty Years," for example, O. Henry writes in the second paragraph, *pacific thoroughfare* for a peaceful street.

Ask students to read the short story "After Twenty Years" noting words they think O. Henry uses in an unusual way or words that they do not know. Some words they might suggest are *beat, habitual, depeopled,* and *intricate.* Have students include five of these words in an expressive paragraph describing a friend.

ANSWERS
Exercise 1

1. president — a presiding officer of a company, club, etc.
   President — the chief executive of a republic having no prime minister

2. roman — the upright style of printing
   Roman — characteristic of ancient or modern Rome

3. arctic — characteristic of or near the North Pole or the region around it
   Arctic — the region around the North Pole

4. Ping-Pong — trademark for table tennis equipment
   ping-pong — table tennis

5. mason — a brick layer
   Mason — a member of the Freemason's secret society

4. **Other forms.** Sometimes your dictionary shows spellings of plural forms of nouns, tenses of verbs, or the comparative forms of adjectives and adverbs.

5. **Etymology.** The *etymology* tells how a word (or its parts) entered the English language. The etymology also shows how the word has changed over time.

6. **Examples.** Your dictionary may demonstrate how a word may be used by giving phrases or sentences containing that word.

7. **Definitions.** If there is more than one meaning for a word, the different definitions are separated by numbers or letters.

8. **Special usage labels.** These labels identify the circumstances in which a word has a special meaning, such as *Bot.* (botany), or how it is used in special ways, such as *Slang* or *Rare*.

9. **Related word forms.** These are other forms of the entry word. For example, another form of the word might be shown that is created by adding suffixes or prefixes. Or a common phrase might be shown in which the entry word appears.

10. **Synonyms and antonyms.** Words that are similar in meaning are *synonyms.* Words that are opposite in meaning are *antonyms.* Dictionaries may list synonyms and antonyms at the end of some word entries.

Review

EXERCISE 1   **Using the Dictionary to Check for Capitalization**

Look up the following words in a dictionary and explain when they are and are not capitalized. Your dictionary may not give capitalized uses for all the words.

1. president
2. roman
3. arctic
4. ping-pong
5. mason

▶ EXERCISE 2   **Dividing Words into Syllables**

Divide the following words into syllables. Use the same method to show syllable division that your dictionary uses.

1. habitat   **1.** hab | i · tat
2. turmoil   **2.** tur · moil
3. diamond   **3.** di | a · mond
4. incomplete   **4.** in · com · plete
5. mediterranean
   5. med | i · ter · ra · ne | an

Answers may vary according to the dictionary used. These are from *Webster's New World Dictionary*, Third College Edition.

▶ EXERCISE 3   **Finding Part-of-Speech Labels**

Look up each of the following words in a dictionary. Give all the parts of speech listed for each word and an example of how the word is used as each part of speech.

EXAMPLE   **1.** elastic   Examples will vary.
                1. *adj.—an elastic waistband*
                    n.—lined with elastic

1. fall   **1.** v.i./v.t./n./adj.
2. interview   **2.** n./v.t./v.i.
3. record   **3.** v.t./v.i./n./adj.
4. mask   **4.** n./v.t./v.i.
5. base   **5.** n./adj./v.t.

▶ EXERCISE 4   **Identifying the Usage Labels of Words**

Look up the following words in a college dictionary and write the usage label or labels given for the word, if any.

1. foul
2. relief
3. grub
4. master
5. degree

▶ EXERCISE 5   **Finding Synonyms for Words**

Write all the synonyms you can think of for each of the following words. Then use a dictionary to check your list and to add to it.

1. fear
2. mix
3. enormous
4. part
5. rich

ANSWERS
Exercise 4

Answers may vary according to the dictionary used. The following answers appear in *Webster's New World Dictionary*, Third College Edition.

1. archaic
2. architecture, sculpture; literature, drama; painting; geology; printing; baseball
3. old slang, slang
4. chiefly British; games, sports; law; now rare
5. algebra; education; grammar; law; math, astronomy, geography; music; physics; chiefly British

ANSWERS
Exercise 5

Synonyms will vary. Here are some possibilities:

1. fear—anxiety, fright, terror, scare
2. mix—join, combine, stir, blend
3. enormous—large, huge, colossal, gigantic
4. part—fraction, piece, section, slice, chunk
5. rich—wealthy, fertile, fortune

RESOURCES

RESOURCES

VOCABULARY *(pp. 828–834)*

OBJECTIVES

- To define words by using prefixes
- To define words by using suffixes
- To define words through context clues
- To use a dictionary to find correct definitions

CHAPTER OVERVIEW

The first part of the chapter explains how understanding word parts can help in defining words. Prefixes, suffixes, base words, and roots are identified. Then students are shown how to use context clues to determine definitions. Students are given specific strategies to use when determining meaning from context. These strategies include using synonyms, antonyms, comparison and contrast, and cause and effect.

The material in this chapter can be referred to anytime you are using reading material in which students might find new words. The material can also be referred to during the revision stage of the writing process when students are seeking precise words.

RESOURCES

RESOURCES

33 VOCABULARY

Learning and Using New Words

You constantly learn new words from your parents and friends, from subjects you study, and from books, television, and games. You can also learn the meanings of word parts and how they are combined to form new words.

Building a Vocabulary

One good way to build your vocabulary is to start a word bank. When you see or hear a new word, write the word and its definition in a section of your notebook. Always check the definition and pronunciation of any unfamiliar words in your dictionary.

Using Word Parts

Many English words can be divided into parts. If you know the meanings of various word parts, you can often determine the meanings of many unfamiliar words.

A word part added to the beginning of a word is called a *prefix.* A word part added to the end of a word is called a *suffix.* Prefixes and suffixes can't stand alone. They must be added to other words or word parts.

A *base word* can stand alone. It is a complete word all by itself, although other word parts may be added to it to make new words.

PREFIX	BASE WORD	SUFFIX	NEW WORD
bi–	week	–ly	biweekly
un–	comfort	–able	uncomfortable

Roots, like prefixes and suffixes, can't stand all alone. Roots can combine with one or more word parts to form words.

WORD ROOT	MEANING	EXAMPLES
–dict–	to speak	dictate, dictionary
–ject–	to throw	project, reject
–voc–	to call	vocation, vocal
–vis–	to see	visual, invisible

COMMONLY USED PREFIXES		
PREFIXES	MEANINGS	EXAMPLES OF PREFIXES + BASE WORDS
anti–	against, opposing	antisocial, antiviral
bi–	two	biannual, bicultural
co–	with, together	codefendant, coordinate
dis–	away, from, opposing	disarm, disconnect
in–	not	inappropriate, ineffective
inter–	between, among	interaction, interstate
mis–	badly, not, wrongly	misconduct, misshape

QUICK REMINDER

Write the word *antidisestablish-mentarianism* on the chalkboard. Have someone try to pronounce it; then ask students to break it down into its word parts. Students might begin with its root word, *establish,* and go from there. Ask several students to look up each word part in a dictionary. Have students share the definitions to see if the class can determine the word's meaning.

MEETING INDIVIDUAL NEEDS

LEP/ESL

General Strategies. Some students will want to look up every word they do not understand when reading a passage of literature. Encourage students to read whole blocks of text without stopping at every unknown word instead. Students should try to comprehend the main idea just as they might have to do in conversation.

LESS-ADVANCED STUDENTS

Suggest that students reinforce the definitions of words by creating pictures from or with the words. For example, for the word *bloated,* students could write the word using big, puffy letters; for *granular,* they could use small dots to make the letters; for *diminuitive,* they could write the word in tiny letters.

COMMONLY USED PREFIXES *(continued)*		
PREFIXES	**MEANINGS**	**EXAMPLES**
non–	not	nonactive, nonfatal
post–	after, following	postdated, postwar
pre–	before	predawn, preview
re–	back, again	replay, restock
semi–	half, partly	semidarkness, semisweet
sub–	under, beneath	subgroup, subplot
trans–	across, beyond	transfer, transform
un–	not, reverse of	uneven, untrue

 REFERENCE NOTE: For guidelines on spelling when adding prefixes, see page 769.

COMMONLY USED SUFFIXES		
SUFFIXES	**MEANINGS**	**EXAMPLES OF BASE WORDS + SUFFIXES**
–able	able, likely	adaptable, changeable
–ate	become, cause	activate, invalidate
–dom	state, condition	freedom, kingdom
–en	make, become	darken, weaken
–ful	full of, characteristic of	joyful, truthful
–hood	condition, quality	childhood, sisterhood
–ion	action, condition	liberation, protection
–ize	make, cause to be	dramatize, Americanize
–ly	in a characteristic way	blandly, swiftly
–ment	result, action	enchantment, payment
–ness	quality, state	peacefulness, sadness
–or	one who	actor, editor
–ous	characterized by	joyous, murderous
–ship	condition, state	friendship, hardship
–y	condition, quality	dirty, jealousy

 REFERENCE NOTE: For guidelines on spelling when adding suffixes, see pages 769–771.

RESOURCES

RESOURCES

Learning New Words from Context

The *context* of a word includes all the other words and sentences that surround it. These surrounding words often provide valuable clues to meaning.

USING CONTEXT CLUES	
TYPE OF CLUE	**EXPLANATION**
Definitions and Restatements	Look for words that define the term or restate it in other words. ■ The university owns a *seismograph,* a machine for measuring the force of earthquakes.
Examples	Look for examples used in context that reveal the meaning of an unfamiliar word. ■ There are many types of literary *genres,* such as novels, short stories, poems, and plays.
Synonyms	Look for clues that indicate an unfamiliar word is similar to a familiar word. ■ For a beginner, the *novice* played well.
Antonyms	Look for clues that indicate an unfamiliar word is opposite in meaning to a familiar word. ■ The speaker was *strident,* not soft-spoken.
Comparison and Contrast	Look for clues that indicate that an unfamiliar word is compared to or contrasted with an unfamiliar word or phrase. ■ A *salvo* of cheers burst, like a sudden thunderstorm, from the onlookers. ■ Unlike Sofía, who is wise and sensible, Pierce is often *fatuous.*
Cause and Effect	Look for clues that indicate an unfamiliar word is related to the cause or the result of an action, feeling, or idea. ■ Since our trip was *curtailed,* we came home early.

INTEGRATING THE LANGUAGE ARTS

Literature Link. To reinforce for students that vocabulary choice is integral to the tone and mood of a story, have them read and analyze passages of Ursula Le Guin's novel *A Wizard of Earthsea* for its exotic words. Ursula Le Guin often includes archaic and creative words to give readers the sense that they are reading a mysterious yet believable language. [Some of her archaic words are *rune, mage,* and *lest.* Examples of her created words are *searim, mage-craft,* and *magewind.*]

Technology Link. There are several brands of electronic dictionaries and thesauruses on the market. If you have one or if you can find someone who does, you might bring it to class for the students to experiment with as they are reading and writing.

RESOURCES

RESOURCES

COOPERATIVE LEARNING
Divide the class into groups of three and ask the groups to compile lists of twenty root or base words that they are familiar with. Give the groups five to seven minutes for this activity. Next, take up the lists and distribute them randomly among the groups, making sure that a group doesn't get its own list. Then the groups should create as many new words as they can by adding prefixes, suffixes, or both. After ten minutes, groups can share their lists and discuss them.

ANSWERS
Exercise 1

Answers may vary according to the dictionary used. Here are some possibilities:

1. *bi–* (two) = able to speak two languages

2. *mis–* (badly, not, wrongly) = to fail to ignite or go off

3. *anti–* (against, opposing) = opposed to labor unions

4. *pre–* (before) = to warm beforehand

5. *non–* (not) = containing no milk or milk products

6. *trans–* (across, beyond) = crossing or spanning the Atlantic

7. *inter–* (between, among) = between, shared by, or involving different religious denominations

8. *post–* (after, following) = of or taking a course of study after graduation, especially after receiving a bachelor's degree

9. *semi–* (half, partly) = designating gems of lower value than those classified as precious

10. *sub–* (under, beneath) = below or less than the expected standard

832

Choosing the Right Word

Since many English words have several meanings, you must look at *all* the definitions given in the dictionary for any particular word. Always think about the context of an unfamiliar word. Then determine the definition that best fits the given context.

Dictionaries sometimes provide sample contexts to show the various meanings of a word. Compare each of the sample contexts given in the dictionary with the context of a new word to make sure you've found the meaning that fits.

Synonyms and Antonyms

Synonyms are words that have nearly the same meaning. For example, here are some pairs of synonyms: happy—glad, big—large, and beautiful—lovely. However, *antonyms* are words that have nearly the opposite meaning. For example, here are some pairs of antonyms: happy—sad, big—small, and beautiful—ugly.

When you look up a word in a dictionary, you will often find several synonyms listed. To help you distinguish between synonyms, some dictionaries give *synonym articles*—brief explanations of a word's synonyms and how they differ in meaning. Dictionaries sometimes also list antonyms at the end of an entry for a word.

 Review

▶ EXERCISE 1 **Using Prefixes to Define Words**

For each of the following words, give the prefix used and its meaning. Give the meaning of the whole word. Use a dictionary if necessary.

1. bilingual	**6.** transatlantic
2. misfire	**7.** interdenominational
3. antilabor	**8.** postgraduate
4. preheat	**9.** semiprecious
5. nondairy	**10.** subnormal

▶ EXERCISE 2   **Adding Suffixes to Words**

To each of the following words add the suffix in parentheses that follows the word. Then give the meaning of each new word and its part of speech. Use a dictionary if necessary to find the meaning or the spelling of each new word. [Note: Be careful. Remember that some words change their spelling when a suffix is added.]

1. appease (–ment)	**6.** state (–hood)
2. official (–dom)	**7.** envy (–ous)
3. like (–able)	**8.** haste (–en)
4. civil (–ize)	**9.** grit (–y)
5. spite (–ful)	**10.** author (–ship)

▶ EXERCISE 3   **Using Context Clues**

Use context clues to choose the word or phrase that best fits the meaning of each italicized word.

a. beautiful	**e.** round
b. entertaining	**f.** reacting
c. considering	**g.** myths
d. dropped sharply	**h.** nicknames

1. Sharria spends as much time *pondering* what to wear to school as she does thinking about her homework.
2. The earth is *spherical*, like a ball.   **1.** c   **2.** e
3. Ludlow was known by various *sobriquets*, including Lumpy and Pokey.   **3.** h
4. Emiliano thought the tiny, blue insect was *exquisite*, not hideous as his aunt believed.   **4.** a
5. Because the temperature *plummeted*, we decided to build a fire.   **5.** d

ANSWERS
Exercise 2

Answers may vary according to the dictionary used. Here are some possibilities:

1. *appeasement* — a giving in to demands or being satisfied (n.)

2. *officialdom* — officials collectively; the domain or position of officials (n.)

3. *likeable* (likable) — able to be enjoyed (adj.)

4. *civilize* — to better the habits or manners of (v.)

5. *spiteful* — full of evil feeling (adj.)

6. *statehood* — the condition or status of being a state (n.)

7. *envious* — characterized by discontent or resentment because of another's advantages or possessions (adj.)

8. *hasten* — to cause to be or come faster (v.)

9. *gritty* — of, like, or containing rough particles of sand or stone (adj.)

10. *authorship* — the state of being a creator (n.)

RESOURCES

RESOURCES

833

STUDENTS WITH SPECIAL NEEDS

Building a working vocabulary can be a challenge for any student, especially one who is learning disabled. To aid students in learning new words, choose five or six words for students to research. (Abstract nouns, adjectives, and verbs are the best choices for this exercise.) Instruct students to write each word on a separate piece of paper after they have looked up the meanings. Next, ask students to look up the opposite for each word in a dictionary of antonyms and to write each of these words on a separate sheet of paper. Tell students to mix up the antonyms and to see if they can match the words with their proper antonyms. If these words are not already part of a word bank, you may want to start one.

 EXERCISE 4 **Selecting the Correct Context**

For each sentence below, write the word from the following list that best fits the sentence. Use a dictionary to find the definition that best fits the context for each word.

flawless	intrude
caliber	eliminate
pummel	moderate
incite	envelop

1. The concert was so long that the director decided to ____ two songs.   **1.** eliminate
2. The dark fog seemed to ____ the cottage.   **2.** envelop
3. On the field trip, the class stopped for lunch at a restaurant that had ____ prices.   **3.** moderate
4. The fiery speaker was able to ____ the crowd.   **4.** incite
5. The final report of the year should be a work of high ____.   **5.** caliber

OBJECTIVES
- To write a social letter
- To write a business letter for a given situation
- To address an envelope
- To complete a form

RESOURCES

LETTERS AND FORMS
- The Parts of a Personal Letter
- Social Letters
- The Parts of a Business Letter
- The Complaint or Adjustment Letter
- The Appreciation or Commendation Letter
- Completing Printed Forms
- Chapter Review Form A
- Chapter Review Form B

34 LETTERS AND FORMS

Style and Contents

Letters are an important form of communication. Everyone likes to get letters. To receive letters, however, you usually have to write your share. It is important to learn how to write effective social and business letters. You will also find there are a few general rules you should follow when you complete printed forms.

Types of Letters

Like all other forms of communication, letters have a purpose and an intended audience.

LETTERS		
TYPE	PURPOSE	AUDIENCE
Personal	to express emotions and ideas	close friends or relatives
Social	to express appreciation or to communicate information about a specific event	close friends or social acquaintances
Business	to inform a business that you need its services, or to tell how well or badly a service was performed	a business or organization

CHAPTER OVERVIEW

This chapter demonstrates and explains the skills necessary for students to write letters and to complete forms. The first part of the chapter explains personal letters and social letters. Later, the various types and parts of business letters are explained. Also included in the chapter are tips for addressing envelopes and completing forms.

The material in this chapter can be referred to when students are writing certain kinds of letters in a literature unit, or it can be used to reinforce a letter-writing unit in which students address real audiences.

QUICK REMINDER

Have students brainstorm all the reasons they might have for wanting to write to someone [to order something, to complain, to obtain information, to express an opinion, to wish someone well].

RESOURCES

RESOURCES

Writing Letters

Personal Letters

A *personal letter* is often the best way to communicate, even with someone you know well. In conversations—face-to-face or on the telephone—other people or time schedules may intrude. Personal letters, however, often get their receiver's complete attention. Unlike conversations, letters last. People often save personal letters and read them many times. A friendly letter is a gesture of friendship, containing a personal message from the sender to the receiver, such as best wishes for an upcoming holiday. When you're writing a personal letter, remember to write about things that interest you and the person you're writing to.

Social Letters

Social letters are usually for a specific purpose or in response to a specific event. The most common types of social letters are thank-you letters, invitations, and letters of regret.

Thank-you Letters

You write thank-you letters when you want to thank someone for taking the time, trouble, or expense to do something for you. Thank the person, then try to add a personal note. For example, if you're thanking someone for a gift, tell why the gift is special to you.

Invitations

An invitation should include specific information about the occasion, such as the time and place and any other special details your guests might need to know (such as that everyone may bring a friend, should dress casually, or is expected to bring food).

Letters of Regret

You write a *letter of regret* when you receive an invitation to an event that you will not be able to attend. You should especially respond in writing to invitations that include the letters *R.S.V.P.* (in French, an abbreviation for "please reply").

You should always respond quickly enough so that the person who is inviting you can accurately count the number of guests to prepare for. If the planned event is very soon, you may want to telephone the person to say that you can't come. But another consideration is politeness. Even if you have telephoned to say you won't attend, it's still polite to send a follow-up letter of regret.

> 5455 Blackstone Street
> Chicago, IL 60615
> March 20, 1992
>
> Dear Felicia,
>
> I was so happy to receive your invitation to your birthday slumber party next Friday evening. I really would like to be there. Unfortunately, my parents had already made plans for the whole family for that night.
> Thank you very much for inviting me. I hope you have a happy birthday and a lot of fun at your party.
>
> Your friend,
>
> Bianca

RESOURCES

RESOURCES

837

A DIFFERENT APPROACH

You may want to teach this letter-writing unit in conjunction with a particular issue such as the environment, nature, aging, or war. Students could research people to whom to write and then compose letters for purposes related to the issues being studied. If students are reading stories about nature, they could write to friends and tell what they have learned from their reading. The class could compose letters inviting several guest speakers to come to class, or they could write business letters requesting information about certain aspects of nature—such as wildlife or endangered species—to various organizations.

Business Letters

The Parts of a Business Letter

Business letters follow a particular form. There are six parts of a business letter; they are

(1) the heading
(2) the inside address
(3) the salutation
(4) the body
(5) the closing
(6) the signature

These six parts are usually arranged in one of the two most common styles used for business letters.

The *block form* places each part of the letter at the left margin of the page. A blank space is left between each paragraph in the body of the letter. Each paragraph is not indented.

The *modified block form* arranges the heading, the closing, and your signature just to the right of an imaginary line that extends down the center of the page. The middle parts of the letter all begin at the left margin. Each paragraph is indented.

Block Style

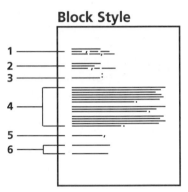

Modified Block Style

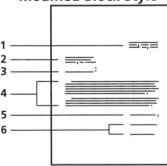

The Heading. The heading usually has three lines:

- your street address
- your city, state, and ZIP code
- the date the letter was written

The Inside Address.   The inside address gives the name and address of the person you are writing.

■ If you're directing your letter to someone by name, use a courtesy title (such as *Mr., Ms., Mrs.,* or *Miss*) or a professional title (such as *Dr.* or *Professor*) in front of the person's name. After the person's name, include the person's business title (such as *Editor, Business Manager,* or *Department Chairperson*).
■ If you don't have a person's name, use a business title or position title (such as *Store Manager* or *Complaints Department*).

The Salutation.   The salutation is your greeting to the person you're writing.

■ In a business letter, the salutation ends with a colon (such as in *Dear Mayor Williams:*). If you are writing to a specific person, use the person's name (such as *Dear Ms. Stokes*).
■ If you don't have the name of a specific person, use a general salutation, such as *Dear Sir or Madam,* or *Ladies and Gentlemen.* Or, you can use a department or a position title (such as *Activity Director* or *Head of Division*), with or without the word *Dear.*

The Body.   The body contains the message of your letter. Leave a blank line between paragraphs in the body of the letter.

The Closing.   You should end your letter politely. There are several standard phrases that are often used to close business letters such as *Sincerely, Respectfully yours,* or *Yours truly.*

The Signature.   Your signature should be handwritten in ink directly below the closing. Your name should be typed or printed neatly just below your signature.

RESOURCES

COOPERATIVE LEARNING

Divide the class into small groups and give each group a number. Put the numbers into a box and have each group draw a number other than its own. Then each group can compose a personal letter to the group whose number it drew. After the letters are written, the groups should deliver their letters and respond to the ones written to them.

CRITICAL THINKING
Synthesis

Ask students to create situations for which they must produce a friendly letter, a social letter, and a business letter. For example, a party could entail writing friendly letters to relatives to describe the event, writing formal letters to issue the invitations, and writing business letters to order decorations or food.

RESOURCES

STUDENTS WITH SPECIAL NEEDS

Many learning disabled students have a difficult time keeping things organized. Remembering to include the six parts of a business letter in the proper places can prove difficult. A helpful approach may be to have the students act out the placement of the parts of a business letter. Write the names of each of the six parts on six sheets of paper, one name on each sheet. Pick out six students, hand each one a sheet, and tell them where to place themselves. Next, hand the sheets to six other students and instruct them to find their proper places.

LEARNING STYLES

Auditory Learners. Allow students to pretend they are having telephone conversations based on the kinds of letters they are to write. Then partners can write down what is said and can ask any necessary questions. This sharing can give auditory learners more ideas for their letters.

Types of Business Letters

The Request or Order Letter. In a *request letter,* you write to request a product or service. For example, you might write to an art museum to request a schedule of hours it is open and any fees that are charged. In an *order letter,* you ask for something specific, such as a free brochure advertised in a magazine. You may also need to write an order letter to ask for a product by mail that appears in a magazine or advertisement without a printed order form.

When you are writing a request or order letter, remember the following points.

1. State your request clearly.
2. If you need to receive information, enclose a stamped envelope addressed to yourself. You are asking a favor of the persons you're writing to, so it's polite not to expect them to pay for the reply.
3. Make your request long before you need whatever you are requesting. Allow the persons to whom you have sent your request enough time to fit their reply into their normal schedule.
4. If you want to order something, include all important information. For example, give the size, color, brand name, or any other specific information. If there are costs involved, add the amount carefully.

The Complaint or Adjustment Letter. When you do not receive services or products that you have reason to expect, you may wish to write a *complaint* or *adjustment letter.* Remember these points.

1. Send your letter as soon as possible.
2. Be specific in your letter. Include the following details:
   - why you are unhappy (with the product or service)
   - how you were affected (lost time or money)
   - what solution you believe will correct the problem
3. Read your letter over to make sure it's calm and courteous.

RESOURCES

RESOURCES

The Appreciation or Commendation Letter. In an *appreciation* or *commendation letter,* you tell some-one—a specific person, a group of people, a business, or an organization—that he, she, or they did a good job with a product or service. Be specific about exactly what action or idea of this person's you are commending. For example, if your city's mayor has just proposed some new summer recreation programs that you feel teenagers need, you might want to write an appreciation letter to thank him or her for being concerned with good recreation facilities and healthful programs for the city's young people.

210 Valley View Place
Minneapolis, MN 55419
March 10, 1993

Sgt. Latrice Jeffreys
Second Precinct Police Station
850 Second Avenue South
Minneapolis, MN 55402

Dear Sgt. Jeffreys:

Thank you very much for coming to speak to our school about safety. We are aware of this issue and how much it can affect our lives. It's good to know that there are so many things we can do ourselves to keep from becoming victims of crime.

I hope you will continue to speak to students about this very important subject. We should all know what our part is in fighting crime.

Sincerely yours,

Ingrid Johansen

Ingrid Johansen

RESOURCES

RESOURCES

INTEGRATING THE LANGUAGE ARTS

Literature Link. Have students read and analyze Andy Rooney's satirical essay "Letter Writing." Students might discuss what Rooney's purpose is and why he is poking fun at letter writing. Then they could write their own satires about some aspect of letter writing. Students could discuss their need to write notes to each other in school, or they could make fun of other types of communication such as the telephone.

Appearance of a Business Letter

Follow these suggestions to give your letter the best possible appearance.

- Use plain, white, unlined $8\frac{1}{2}'' \times 11''$ paper.
- Type your letter if possible (single-spaced, with an extra line between paragraphs). Or, write your letter by hand, using black or blue ink. Be as neat as possible. Try to avoid cross-outs, smudges, erasures, and inkblots. Check your letter for typing errors and misspellings, and correct them neatly.
- Leave equal margins on the sides, top, and bottom of the page.
- Use only the front of each page. If your letter is more than one page, leave a one-inch margin at the bottom of the first page and finish the letter on the next page.

Addressing an Envelope

The return address goes in the top left-hand corner of the envelope. The name and address of the person to whom the letter is written is in the center of the envelope. On the envelope for a business letter, the name and address to which the letter is being sent should exactly match the inside address of the letter.

Tama Wuliton
2703 Bryant Road
Dana Point, CA 92629

Clasprite Paperclip Company
1605 S. Noland Rd., Building 6
Borita, CA 92002

Completing Printed Forms

When you fill out a form, your purpose is to give clear, complete information. The following guidelines will help you complete all types of forms.

HOW TO FILL OUT FORMS

1. Look over the entire form before you begin.
2. Look for, and follow, special instructions (such as "Type or print" or "Use a pencil").
3. Read each item carefully.
4. Supply all the information requested. If a question does not apply to you, write "does not apply," or use either a dash or the symbol *N/A* (meaning "not applicable").
5. When you're finished, make sure nothing is left blank. Also, check for errors and correct them neatly.
6. Mail the form to the correct address or give it to the correct person.

Review

 EXERCISE 1 **Writing a Social Letter**

Write a social letter for one of the following situations, or make up one of your own.

1. A friend's mother baked you cookies for your birthday and sent you a thoughtful card.
2. You have been invited to a friend's house party but cannot attend because your grandparents will be in town for an overnight visit on the date of the party.
3. You are planning a movie-watching party at your house. Write a letter of invitation including all the information your guests would need to know.

RESOURCES

ANSWERS
Exercise 1

Students' letters will vary, but students should include the following points:

1. a heading in the upper right corner that includes the sender's address and the date
2. a salutation that begins under the heading and is placed to the left
3. a body in paragraph form
4. a closing and a signature, both aligned with the heading

RESOURCES

ANSWERS
Exercise 2

Students' letters will vary, but students should follow the guidelines in this chapter for writing business letters and addressing envelopes.

ANSWERS
Exercise 3

Responses will vary, but each should be complete.

INTEGRATING THE LANGUAGE ARTS

Technology Link. Ask students to type their business letters for **Exercise 3** on computers or typewriters. Then the students could experiment with both the block and modified block styles to see which style they prefer. Encourage students to use the document-preview feature, if available, to view how their letters will look when printed.

844

▶ EXERCISE 2　**Writing a Business Letter**

Write a business letter for one of the situations below. Use your own return address, but make up any other information you need to write the letter. Address an envelope for your letter. Fold the letter neatly and place it into the envelope. (Do not mail the letter.)

1. Your parents said you could spend two weeks this summer at the youth camp of your choice. Write to the Circle Q Summer Camp, located at 3333 Route 1, Festus, Missouri 63028.
2. Write a letter of appreciation or commendation to an individual or organization you would like to thank or congratulate for outstanding efforts or performance.

▶ EXERCISE 3　**Completing a Form**

For each numbered blank, write what you would put in that blank if you filled out this form.

INFORMATION FORM

NAME		BIRTHDAY	
	1		2
NICKNAME	3	PHONE #	4
ADDRESS		5	
PARENT OR GUARDIAN	6	WORK #	7

	TEACHER	ROOM #	HOBBIES AND INTERESTS
PERIOD 0	8	9	10
PERIOD 1			
PERIOD 2			
PERIOD 3			
PERIOD 4			
PERIOD 5			
PERIOD 6			
PERIOD 7			

35 STUDYING AND TEST TAKING

Using Skills and Strategies

RESOURCES

STUDYING AND TEST TAKING
- Chapter Review Form A
- Chapter Review Form B

CHAPTER OVERVIEW

Because this chapter teaches study skills and test-taking strategies, you may want to begin the year with it. Applying these techniques may prove to be the difference between success and failure for some students. Moreover, mastering the information in this chapter will allow students to become more independent learners; that is, they will have the means to learn on their own. In addition, through your assessment of students' performances on the exercises in the **Review** section of the chapter, you will gain insight into the needs and abilities of your students.

Good grades are almost always a sign of good study skills. If you develop good study habits, you can earn better grades with less last-minute panic before tests. You might not have to study harder to improve your grades. You might be able to study smarter, instead.

Planning a Study Routine

Plan a study schedule that will help you study successfully. When you map out a schedule, stick to it. Here are some suggestions:

1. *Know your assignments.* Write down all the assignments you have and their due dates. Be sure you understand the instructions for each assignment.
2. *Make a plan.* Break large assignments into small steps. Keep track of when you should be finished with each step.
3. *Concentrate when you study.* Set aside a time and a place to focus your attention on your assignments.

RESOURCES

OBJECTIVES
- To identify reading rates that fit given situations
- To use the SQ3R method to formulate and answer questions about reading material
- To analyze details in a reading passage

QUICK REMINDER

Ask students to explain what is meant by writing to learn, and ask them to name one type of writing to learn. Next, ask students to name three purposes for reading and the reading rates that fit each purpose [for details—scanning; for main points—skimming; to understand and remember—reading for mastery]. Finally, ask students to explain what SQ3R means.

---

846 *Studying and Test Taking*

Strengthening Study Skills

Reading and Understanding

The way you read depends on what you're reading and why you are reading it. Your reading rate should match your purpose for reading. Here are some common purposes for reading.

READING RATES AND THEIR PURPOSE		
READING RATE	PURPOSE	EXAMPLE
Scanning	Reading for specific details	Looking in your math book for the page that has the explanation for solving a problem
Skimming	Reading for main points or important ideas	Looking through the chapter headings, charts, and time lines of your history book to review for a test
Reading for mastery	Reading closely to understand and remember	Reading a new chapter in your science book to plan for an in-class writing assignment

Writing to Learn

Writing can help you learn. When you write, you are forced to put your thoughts in order. You may use writing to analyze a problem, record your observations, or work out all the details of a plan. See the following chart for examples of types of writing that can help you explore and make decisions about your ideas.

- To draw conclusions and make inferences about a reading passage
- To interpret graphic information
- To analyze note-taking methods
- To identify classifications of groups of words
- To create a graphic aid to represent the content of a passage and to use the graphic aid to answer questions about the passage
- To paraphrase a poem

Strengthening Study Skills **847**

TYPE OF WRITING	PURPOSE	EXAMPLE
Freewriting	To help you focus your thoughts	Writing for ten minutes to explore plot ideas for a creative writing assignment
Autobiographies	To help you examine the meaning of important events in your life	Writing about your hopes for the future on the day of your sister's wedding
Diaries	To help you recall your impressions and express your feelings	Writing about your reactions to a speech made by a guest speaker in your history class
Journals and Learning Logs	To help you record your observations, descriptions, solutions, and questions	Jotting down notes for a biology class discussion while watching a bird building its nest
	To help you define or analyze information, or propose a solution	Listing reasons for and against a plan of action to help you decide to do it or not

Using a Word Processor as a Writing Tool

The word processor is a wonderful tool for writing. You can use it to help you plan, draft, and edit your writing. Almost every step of the writing process is easier if you use a word processor.

Prewriting. With a little practice, you can type quickly on a word processor. You can then rewrite your notes or ideas without having to recopy or retype them.

LESS-ADVANCED STUDENTS

You may want to set aside a few minutes of class time each day or each week for silent reading. Ask students to bring their books to class. You could set up a time for visiting the library, so that students can find books they like. Your action—allowing class time for silent reading—will communicate to students the importance you place on reading.

LEP/ESL

General Strategies. The information concerning word processors will be of little practical use unless students can have hands on, one-to-one instruction. Arrange a field trip to your school's computer lab or to a computer facility in the community. LEP/ESL students will probably need individual guidance in the basic steps of opening a file and naming it, creating a document and saving it, and printing out hard copy. Before the trip, discuss with students the terminology that will be used.

Auditory and Kinetic Learners.
The SQ3R method uses visual learning more than auditory or kinetic learning. Discuss with the class ways in which auditory and kinetic learning techniques may be incorporated into SQ3R.

You might construct a chart like the one below to record the adaptions.

	Auditory	Kinetic
S	Replace *look at* with *read aloud*	Photocopy the assignment and replace *look at* with *highlight*
Q	Ask questions aloud	No change
R	Read aloud or into a tape recorder (listen to the tape later)	Be sure to take notes, perhaps using a webbing technique
R	No change	Replace *recite* with *write*
R	Review main ideas, ask questions, and recall answers aloud	Rewrite main ideas, questions, and answers

848

Writing First Drafts. You can write, revise, and rearrange your ideas as often as you want. Then you can use the printer to produce a hard copy, or printout.

Evaluating. The word processor is great for trying out different versions. Just save your original document. Then, on a copy of the document, type in your changes. If you don't like the revisions, you still have the original.

Revising. You can easily type in changes on a word processor. Then you can print a clean copy without having to rewrite or retype the unchanged portions.

Proofreading. Some word processors can check spelling or find errors in punctuation or sentence structure.

Writing the Final Version. It's simple to print a final copy with a word processor. You can even print multiple copies with your printer.

Using the SQ3R Method

SQ3R is the name of a study method that was developed by Francis Robinson, an educational psychologist. The SQ3R study method includes five simple steps.

S   *Survey* the entire assignment. If you're studying a chapter in a textbook, look quickly at the headings, subheadings, terms in boldface and italics, charts, outlines, illustrations, and summaries.

Q   *Question* yourself. List questions that you want to be able to answer after reading the selection.

R   *Read* the material carefully to find answers to your questions. Take notes as you read.

R   *Recite* in your own words answers to each of the questions you wanted to be able to answer.

R   *Review* the material by rereading quickly, looking over your questions, and recalling the answers.

The SQ3R method will help you read material more carefully. When you read actively, you are more likely to remember what you read.

Interpreting and Analyzing Information

Writers of essays, articles, and textbook chapters organize ideas and relate them to one another. If you can interpret and analyze the relationship of ideas, you will understand more of whatever you read.

Stated Main Idea.   The main idea of a passage is the most important point the writer is making. Sometimes the main idea is stated. This means the author may clearly state the main idea in one or two sentences.

Implied Main Idea.   Sometimes the main idea is not stated. There may not be one or two sentences that tell the major point the writer is making. Instead, the main idea may be implied. You may have to figure out for yourself the central idea that ties all the other ideas together.

HOW TO FIND THE MAIN IDEA
■ Skim the passage. (What topic do the sentences have in common?) ■ Identify the general topic. (What is the passage about?) ■ Identify what the passage says about the topic. (What's the message of the passage as a whole?) ■ State the meaning of the passage in your own words. ■ Review the passage. (If you have correctly identified the main idea, all the other ideas will support it.)

 REFERENCE NOTE: For additional information on finding a stated or implied main idea, see pages 64–66.

RESOURCES

LEARNING STYLES

Visual Learners. Some students may find it helpful to use colors to show relationships among details in reading assignments. Make photocopies of the reading passage that begins on this page, and have students identify four categories of information in the passage. Categories might include habitat, feeding habits, and helpful characteristics. Then have students highlight each category with a different color. Caution students to keep the highlighting to a minimum, or it will lose its effectiveness.

Recognizing Relationships Among Details

Sometimes you have to work to understand the meaning of a reading passage. First, you need to understand the main idea. Then you need to look at how the details are related to the main idea and to each other.

FINDING RELATIONSHIPS AMONG DETAILS	
Identify specific details.	What details answer questions such as *Who? What? When? Where? Why?* and *How?* (*5W-How?* questions)?
Distinguish between fact and opinion.	What information can be proved true or false? What statements express a personal belief or attitude?
Identify similarities and differences.	How are the details similar to or different from one another?
Understand cause and effect.	Do earlier events affect later ones?
Identify an order of organization.	In what kind of order are the details arranged? Are they in chronological order, spatial order, order of importance, or some other pattern or order?

Reading Passage

In the story "Rikki-tikki-tavi," by Rudyard Kipling, a young English boy living in India rescues a young mongoose from drowning. Later in the story, the grateful, brave mongoose saves the lives of the boy and his parents by killing two cobras that plan to kill the humans. Kipling's story made mongooses famous.

Sample Analysis

OPINION: How did the mongoose in Kipling's story feel about humans?

ANSWER: *Rikki-tikki-tavi felt grateful to the humans for saving him. He felt brave when he was killing the cobras.*

Scientists who became interested in the mongoose proved that, just as Kipling said, mongooses could kill poisonous snakes. The mongoose is a small animal, similar to a ferret, that makes its home in Africa, Asia, and Southern Europe. Cobras and other poisonous snakes are only part of the mongoose's strange daily menu. Mongooses also feed on rodents, including rats, and insects, including wasps. A mongoose will even eat a scorpion.

Many people think that mongooses are immune to the poisonous venom of a snake. Others believe that mongooses know where to find a plant to eat that will keep a snake's venom from being harmful. But a mongoose only succeeds in killing a poisonous snake because it is faster than the snake. When a mongoose attacks a snake, it bites through the snake's spine right behind its head. The mongoose then holds on to the snake's head until the snake has completely stopped struggling.

In the past, people brought mongooses to Hawaii and the West Indies, hoping that they would kill some of the rats and snakes on those islands. Instead, the mongooses hunted rare birds that were easier to catch and kill than rodents and reptiles. Because of the mongooses' unpredictable eating habits, they are allowed in the United States only for zoos and scientific research.

FACT: What is the mongoose's defense against the venom of a snake?
ANSWER: *The only defense of the mongoose is its quickness.*

DETAILS: Mongooses can be found inhabiting which three continents?
ANSWER: *Mongooses can be found in Africa, Asia, and the southern part of Europe.*

DIFFERENCE: How is the mongoose not like any other animal?
ANSWER: *It is the only animal that has been known to seek out, attack, and kill a cobra.*

CAUSE AND EFFECT: Why did the United States decide that people would not be allowed to import mongooses?
ANSWER: *Mongooses that were imported into Hawaii and the West Indies did not control pests as expected. They did not eat rats and snakes. Instead, they ate rare birds.*

RESOURCES

 INTEGRATING THE LANGUAGE ARTS

Literature Link. First, tell students that personification is a kind of figurative language in which human qualities are attributed to something nonhuman. Then have students read the short story "Rikki-tikki-tavi" by Rudyard Kipling, and tell them to identify instances of personification. Afterward, discuss with students which characters are personified and how this personification is achieved. Ask students how the story would be different if the animal characters had not been personified. [All the animal characters are personified. They are able to speak; they have human emotions; they have human relationships with one another, including familial relationships; they are very intelligent. If the animals had not been personified, the story might have focused more on the activities of the humans in the story; it might have been much shorter.]

RESOURCES

MEETING INDIVIDUAL NEEDS

LESS-ADVANCED STUDENTS

To make **Applying Reasoning Skills** less intimidating to students, tell them that they use these skills every day. Explain that when a person decides to change a light bulb because the light doesn't come on when they flip the switch, he or she is drawing a conclusion—because the light doesn't come on, the light bulb must be burnt out. The conclusion is based on previous experience.

Tell students that if the light still refused to work after the bulb was changed, the person might infer that there was a problem with the electric wiring.

You could ask students to generate more examples of occasions when they draw conclusions and make inferences.

RESOURCES

RESOURCES

Applying Reasoning Skills

To understand what you read, you have to think about the ideas. These ideas are like clues, and you have to act like a detective to analyze evidence that you find in your reading. When you think critically, you may draw *conclusions*. *Conclusions* are decisions based on facts and evidence that are drawn from your reading.

Sometimes, thinking critically means that you must make *inferences*. *Inferences* are decisions based on evidence that is only hinted at, or implied, in what you have read. For example, when you analyze the reading passage on pages 850–851, you might draw these conclusions or inferences.

> Mongooses can survive in many different habitats. (Evidence: Mongooses are found on three continents. Mongooses eat all sorts of animals that live in many types of environments—deserts, mountains, or forests.)

> The cobra is a dangerous creature. (Evidence: Only one animal, the mongoose, will hunt and kill the cobra.)

A *valid conclusion* is firmly established by facts, evidence, or logic. An *invalid conclusion*, however, is one that is not supported by facts or logic. For example, it is invalid to conclude that mongooses are considered pests in their natural habitat. This conclusion is not consistent with facts in the reading passage. In the passage you find that the mongoose's diet in its natural environment consists mainly of animals that are considered pests by humans.

HOW TO DRAW CONCLUSIONS	
Gather all the evidence.	What facts or details have you learned about the subject?
Evaluate the evidence.	What do the facts and details tell you about the subject?
Make appropriate connections.	What can you reasonably conclude from the evidence?

Analyzing Graphics and Illustrations

Many times, a book or article will include visuals such as diagrams, maps, graphs, and illustrations. These visuals often make information clearer and easier to understand than if it is written out.

A paragraph filled with details is often difficult to understand. Graphics and illustrations help you understand relationships between sets of facts. For example, the pie charts below show the distribution of farm work in the United States.

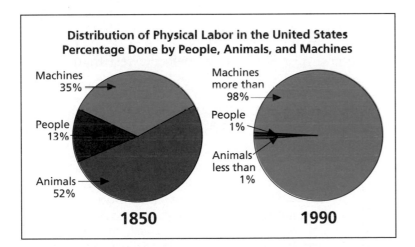

Distribution of Physical Labor in the United States
Percentage Done by People, Animals, and Machines

Machines 35%
People 13%
Animals 52%
1850

Machines more than 98%
People 1%
Animals less than 1%
1990

Looking at these graphs, you can quickly compare the overall amount of farm work performed by machines today with the amount performed by machines in 1850. Graphs like these can help you understand information more easily.

Applying Study Methods

Various study methods are simply different ways of organizing and handling information. The following are some of the most common methods:

RESOURCES

COOPERATIVE LEARNING
Group students in pairs and have them find statistical data that can be presented graphically. Such data could concern the growth or decline of specific populations in a city or state, the growth in revenues for college athletic programs, or the growth or decline in the birthrates of foreign countries. Students could use almanacs, encyclopedias, or specialized reference books. Ask them to make graphs to represent their information and then to present their graphs to the class.

RESOURCES

General Strategies. Taking lecture notes can be especially difficult for students because they cannot control the situation. Because they cannot ask the speaker to slow down, they are likely to miss key information. Furthermore, students often have to concentrate so much on the meanings of individual words that they are unable to absorb main ideas.

You may want to provide situations in which students can practice their note-taking skills. You could also suggest that students tape-record lectures. Taped lectures would allow students to stop to look up unfamiliar words whenever necessary.

- taking notes
- classifying
- organizing information visually
- outlining
- paraphrasing
- summarizing
- memorizing

Taking Notes

Taking accurate notes during a reading assignment or in class is worth the extra effort. Detailed information will be recorded in your notebook, and you will be ready to study for even the most challenging test. It's much easier to review your study notes before a test than to review a whole chapter or series of chapters.

HOW TO TAKE STUDY NOTES

1. Identify and take note of the main ideas in class or your reading. These main ideas should be the headings in your notes. In class, listen for key words and phrases, such as *first, most important,* or *therefore.* These words often introduce main ideas. In a textbook, chapter headings and related subheadings usually contain key ideas.
2. Keep your notes brief. Use abbreviations and summarize material in your own words.
3. Include brief examples or details, if you can. Important examples or details can help you recall the main ideas.
4. Review your notes soon after you have written them to be sure you have included all important information.

Here's an example of careful study notes about the reading passage on pages 850–851. The notes show the main ideas as headings. Underneath these main headings are grouped important details that relate to each heading. You can see that not every detail from the passage appears in these notes. Only the most important details are listed.

Mongooses

"Rikki-tikki-tavi"

- Story written by Rudyard Kipling
- Boy in India saves mongoose from drowning
- Mongoose kills two cobras—saves boy and family
- Story made people interested in mongooses

Characteristics of mongooses

- Small and ferret-like
- Live in Africa, Asia, and Southern Europe
- Eat poisonous snakes, rodents, and insects
  (including wasps and scorpions)

Mongooses and snakes

- Mongooses not immune to snake venom
- Don't seek out special plant to counter venom
- Mongoose's advantage is quickness
- Mongoose bites through snake's spine behind
  its head; holds on until snake dies
- Mongooses brought to Hawaii and West Indies to eat
  poisonous snakes—ate rare birds instead (thus not
  allowed in U.S. except for research and zoos)

Classifying

Classifying is arranging information into categories or groups. All the items that are in a category or group are related to each other. The name or description of the category shows the relationship between the various items in the group. For example, the name *sports* is the label of a category that could include various items, such as *baseball*, *basketball*, *hockey*, or *soccer*.

RESOURCES

RESOURCES

EXAMPLE   **What do the following birds have in common?**
          penguins, chickens, emus, ostriches
ANSWER   **They are all birds that can't fly.**

You also use classification when you identify patterns. For example, look at the relationship between the following sequence of numbers.

What's the next number in the series?

3   6   12   24   48   ?

ANSWER   **The first number in this series, *3,* is doubled to produce the second number, *6.* The second number is then doubled to produce the third number, *12.* This doubling goes on (*12* doubled is *24, 24* doubled is *48*). Then, to produce the next number in the series, you would double *48.* The answer is *96.***

Organizing Information Visually

Sometimes, new information is easier to understand if you organize it visually. A map, diagram, or chart is easier to understand than the same information provided in paragraph form.

For example, the passage that follows compares different poisonous snakes.

There are many kinds of venomous snakes. Rattlesnakes, for example, are found throughout the Western Hemisphere. They range from two to eight feet in length. The likelihood of a human dying as a result of a rattler's bite is low. The same is true for the bite of a cottonmouth. Cottonmouths are found from West Virginia to Texas. They can reach up to five feet in length. The coral snake is smaller, ranging from two to four feet in length. The coral snake, which may be found south of Canada in both North and South

America, is very deadly. King cobras, found throughout southern Asia, may reach a length of sixteen feet. The king cobra's bite is not usually deadly. The Cape cobra, however, is very deadly. This snake reaches up to seven feet in length and is found in southern Africa. One of the largest and most deadly snakes is the black mamba. This snake reaches up to fourteen feet in length and is found in southern and central Africa. Almost all of the people who are attacked by a black mamba die if they do not receive medical treatment immediately after being bitten.

It would be very difficult to identify all the snakes and all of their differences and similarities if you just read this passage and tried to remember all the details. However, if you made a chart like the one below, you would find the information in the paragraph much easier to remember.

VENOMOUS SNAKES			
TYPE OF SNAKE	LENGTH	LIKELIHOOD OF DEATH IF BITTEN (UNTREATED)	LOCATION
rattlesnake	2–8 ft.	low	W. Hemisphere
cottonmouth	up to 5 ft.	low	W. Virginia to Texas
coral snake	2–4 ft.	high	south of Canada; North and South America
king cobra	up to 16 ft.	low	southern Asia
Cape cobra	up to 7 ft.	high	southern Africa
black mamba	up to 14 ft.	very high	southern and central Africa

RESOURCES

MEETING INDIVIDUAL NEEDS

ADVANCED STUDENTS

Ask students to generate topics, such as the number of students participating in extracurricular activities, that concern information that can be represented visually. Have students gather data and present their data by using visual aids such as maps, diagrams, or charts.

A DIFFERENT APPROACH

Students may not be familiar with a method of visual organization called the spider map. Draw the spider map shown below on the chalkboard and have students create their own spider maps to organize information visually.

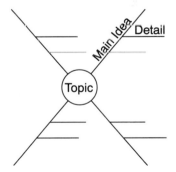

RESOURCES

Outlining

An *outline* helps you organize important information. In an outline, the ideas are arranged in an order and in a pattern that makes their relationship to one another clear.

Sometimes you might want to make a formal outline by using Roman numerals for headings and capital letters for subheadings. For taking notes in your classes, however, you might want to use a faster method. An informal outline helps organize information quickly.

FORMAL OUTLINE FORM

I. Main Point
  A. Supporting Point
    1. Detail
      a. Information
        or detail

INFORMAL OUTLINE FORM

Main idea
  Supporting detail
  Supporting detail
  Supporting detail

Paraphrasing

When you *paraphrase,* you restate someone else's ideas in your own words. A paraphrase often helps explain ideas that are expressed in complicated or unfamiliar terms.

For example, the first part of President Lincoln's Gettysburg Address is: "Fourscore and seven years ago, our fathers brought forth on this continent, a new nation conceived in Liberty, and dedicated to the proposition that all men are created equal." You might paraphrase this as: "Eighty-seven years ago, our ancestors established here in America a new country that was committed to freedom and to the idea that every person is born equal."

When you write a paraphrase, it will usually be about the same length as the original. This means that you will probably not use paraphrasing for long passages of writing. However, you may sometimes be asked (usually in language arts classes) to paraphrase a short passage, such as a poem.

Here is an example of a poem and its paraphrase.

> ### Those Winter Sundays
> #### by Robert Hayden
>
> Sundays too my father got up early
> and put his clothes on in the blueblack cold,
> then with cracked hands that ached
> from labor in the weekday weather made
> banked fires blaze. No one ever thanked him.
>
> I'd wake and hear the cold splintering, breaking.
> When the rooms were warm, he'd call,
> And slowly I would rise and dress,
> fearing the chronic angers of that house,
>
> Speaking indifferently to him,
> who had driven out the cold
> and polished my good shoes as well.
> What did I know, what did I know
> of love's austere and lonely offices?

Here is a possible paraphrase of the poem.

> The speaker in the poem is talking about his father. Each day the father would rise in the early morning, while the house was still cold, to build a fire. The father's hands were cracked and aching from his week's work. He was never thanked for his hard work.
>
> On these cold mornings, the speaker would awake to the sounds of his father splitting wood. When the house had warmed, his father would call him downstairs. The speaker would slowly get dressed.
>
> Unlike the house, which could be warmed, relations between the father and son remained cold and distant. The son expressed no thanks for the fires his father built or the shoes his father polished for him. The son later realizes that he was unaware of the love and commitment that motivated his father's daily routine.

RESOURCES

INTEGRATING THE LANGUAGE ARTS

Literature Link. To emphasize that the specific language used by the poet is important to the total effect of the poem, have one student present a reading of "Those Winter Sundays" and have another student read aloud the sample paraphrase.

After the readings, discuss with students the differences between the poem and the paraphrase. Point out specific word choices, such as *blueblack* (to describe the cold), that affect the mood and meaning of the poem but that are necessarily absent from the paraphrase.

RESOURCES

Follow these guidelines when you write a paraphrase.

HOW TO PARAPHRASE

1. Read the selection carefully before you begin.
2. Be sure you understand the main idea of the selection. Look up unfamiliar words in a dictionary.
3. Determine the tone of the selection. (What is the attitude of the writer toward the subject of the selection?)
4. Identify the speaker in fictional material. (Is the poet speaking, or is it a character in the poem?)
5. Write your paraphrase in your own words. Shorten long sentences or stanzas. Use your own, familiar vocabulary, but follow the same order of events or ideas that is used in the selection.
6. Check to be sure that the ideas in your paraphrase of a selection match the ideas that are expressed in the original selection.

You also use paraphrasing when you write a research report. Make sure to cite the source of whatever you paraphrase. It's important to give credit for someone else's words or ideas.

☞ **REFERENCE NOTE:** For more about giving appropriate credit to sources when writing reports, see pages 330–331.

Summarizing

A *summary* is a brief restatement of the main ideas expressed in a piece of writing. Like a paraphrase, a summary expresses another person's ideas in your own words. However, a summary is shorter than a paraphrase. A summary shortens the original material, presenting only the most important points.

When you summarize, you think critically about the material that you are condensing. You make decisions and draw conclusions about what to include in the summary and what to leave out.

HOW TO SUMMARIZE

1. Skim the selection you wish to summarize.
2. Read the passage again closely. This time, look for the main ideas and notice all of the details that support each main idea.
3. Write your summary in your own words. Include only the main ideas and the most important supporting points.
4. Evaluate and revise your summary, checking to see that you have covered the most important points. Make sure that the information in your summary is clearly expressed and that the person reading your summary can follow your ideas.

Here's a sample summary of the reading passage found on page 316.

> The cheetah is the fastest land animal. It lives in Arabia, Africa, and parts of Asia. The cheetah's body is built more like a dog's than a cat's. Its claws are dull except for the claw on the inside of the foreleg. Cheetahs have a bad sense of smell, but they have good eyesight. A cheetah may be seven feet long from the head to the tip of the tail. Unlike most big cats, it can be easily tamed; a cheetah will even purr when it is happy. Cheetahs have been clocked at amazing speeds of up to 80 miles per hour.

Memorizing

When you take tests and quizzes, you need to memorize the information that you are to be tested on. One long effort to memorize study material the night before a test will not be very effective. Instead, you'll find that frequent, short, focused sessions are more likely to help you remember information. On the following page are some hints for memorizing effectively.

RESOURCES

A DIFFERENT APPROACH

Summarizing a piece of writing is often difficult for students. To give them practice summarizing a short story and to help them distinguish between *summary* and *evaluation,* have students read a short story. After the students have read and discussed the story, have each student write a short review that includes one paragraph of summary and one paragraph of evaluation.

The paragraph of summary should name the title and the author of the story, the main events of the plot, the main characters, and a brief description of the setting. The evaluative paragraph should include three reasons why the story is good (or not good), and it should tell if (and why) the student would or would not recommend the story to a friend.

MEETING
INDIVIDUAL
NEEDS

LEARNING STYLES

Kinetic Learners. Suggest that students move around when they are memorizing. Students could walk in a quiet place or simply squeeze a soft rubber ball as they review material to be memorized.

RESOURCES

SEGMENT 2 *(pp. 862–874)*
IMPROVING TEST-TAKING SKILLS
OBJECTIVES
- To identify key verbs in essay questions
- To briefly explain how to answer specific essay questions

862 *Studying and Test Taking*

HOW TO MEMORIZE	
Memorize key concepts.	Whenever possible, condense the material you need to remember.
Rehearse the material in different ways.	Copy the material by hand or recite the material out loud.
Invent memory games.	Form a word from the first letters of important terms, or make up rhymes to help you remember facts and details.

Improving Test-Taking Skills

Preparing for Different Kinds of Tests

Nervousness before a test is normal. However, you can channel the energy that comes from being nervous to help you do well on the test. Your attitude is the key.

HOW TO PREPARE FOR A TEST
Plan for success. Do everything you can to help you perform your best on the test. Identify the material to be covered on the test. Then make a plan that allows enough time to take notes, study, and review the material.
Be confident. If you have studied thoroughly, you know you are prepared. During the test, pay attention only to reading and answering the test questions.
Keep trying. Be determined to keep improving. Your efforts will help you improve your study effectiveness.

Objective questions and *essay questions* are two basic ways that your knowledge can be tested. There are specific ways to prepare for each type of test.

QUICK REMINDER

Ask students to name three things they do to prepare themselves for tests. Write their responses on the chalkboard, and discuss each one. Afterward, fill in any gaps you see in their responses.

Objective Tests

There are many kinds of objective test questions. Some examples are multiple-choice, true/false, matching, reasoning or logic, or short-answer questions. Objective questions test you on specific information, such as names, terms, dates, or definitions. Most objective test questions have only one correct answer.

To prepare for objective tests, you will need to review specific information from your textbook and your notes. The study skills listed earlier in this chapter will help you prepare for objective tests.

HOW TO STUDY FOR OBJECTIVE TESTS

1. Identify important terms, facts, or ideas in your textbook and class notes.
2. Review the information in more than one form. For example, you may be responsible for defining literary terms. Make flashcards. Practice identifying the definition from the term, then identify the term from its definition.
3. Practice and rehearse factual information. Go over the items you have had difficulty with until you know them well.
4. If possible, briefly review all the information shortly before the actual test.

Your study strategies may be slightly different for each type of objective test. If you have to define key terms, then study using flashcards. If problem-solving questions are on the test, work out practice problems and check your answers with your textbook.

Taking Different Kinds of Objective Tests

Before you begin an objective test, quickly scan the questions. Knowing the number of items on the test helps you decide how to budget your time for each item. Here are

MEETING INDIVIDUAL NEEDS

AT-RISK STUDENTS

One way to allay anxiety about taking tests is to introduce the topic for class discussion. How do students feel about taking tests? What kinds of experiences have contributed to their feelings? Why take tests at all? What's a fair way to test knowledge and understanding of a subject? What can a student do to overcome test anxiety? All of these questions will help students discuss and examine their experiences with testing. From this discussion, lead students to consider what they might do to improve their performances on tests.

STUDENTS WITH SPECIAL NEEDS

Students who have disabilities of any kind may be more prone to suffer from test anxiety. If possible, help students by modifying the way tests are given. For example, visually impaired students might need someone to read questions to them (in person or on tape), and dictation tests may need to be modified for hearing-impaired students. It's important that all students be tested in a manner that is fair and that will allow them to do their best work.

RESOURCES

LESS-ADVANCED STUDENTS

You may want to give students the following additional tips for taking objective tests:

1. multiple choice—Cover the answer choices as you read the questions. An answer may pop into your mind. Now, check to see if the answer that came to you is among the answer choices. If so, it is probably correct.
2. true-false—Do not go back to change any answers unless you have a good reason to do so. Studies show that people's first responses to true-false questions are usually correct.
3. matching—Mark through items you have already matched.
4. short answer—Use other parts of the test to find information and to check the spellings of words.

some strategies for handling specific kinds of objective test questions.

Multiple-Choice Questions. With a multiple-choice question, you select a correct answer from a number of choices.

EXAMPLE   1. Mongooses are effective as hunters of poisonous snakes because
  A mongooses know where to find an herb that acts as an antidote for snake venom.
  B mongooses are quicker than most snakes.
  C mongooses are immune to snake venom.
  D mongooses know when to find snakes sleeping.

HOW TO ANSWER MULTIPLE-CHOICE QUESTIONS	
Read the question or statement carefully.	▪ Make sure you understand the key question or statement you are given before you look at the answer choices. ▪ Look for words such as *not* or *always.* These words limit your choice of answers.
Read all the choices before selecting an answer.	▪ Eliminate choices that you know are incorrect. This improves your chances of choosing correctly among the remainder. ▪ Think carefully about the remaining choices. Select the one that makes the most sense.

True/False Questions. In a true/false question, you are asked to decide whether a certain statement is true or false.

EXAMPLE   1. T Ⓕ In both 1850 and 1990 in the United States, people did less farm work than machines.

HOW TO ANSWER TRUE/FALSE QUESTIONS	
Read the statement carefully.	■ The whole statement is false if any part of it is false.
Look for word clues.	■ Words such as *always* or *never* limit a statement. ■ A statement is true only if it is entirely and always true.

Matching Questions.   Matching questions ask you to match the items in one list with the items in another list.

> Directions: Match the name of the snake in the left-hand column with its natural home in the right-hand column.

C **1.** king cobra   **A** southern Africa
D **2.** black mamba   **B** from West Virginia to Texas
A **3.** Cape cobra   **C** southern Asia
B **4.** cottonmouth   **D** central and southern Africa

HOW TO ANSWER MATCHING QUESTIONS	
Read the directions carefully.	Sometimes you won't use all the items listed in one column. Other items may be used more than once.
Scan the columns.	If you match items you know first, you'll have more time to evaluate items you are less sure about.
Complete the rest of the matching.	Make your best guess on remaining items.

Reasoning or Logic Questions.   This type of question tests your reasoning abilities more than your knowledge of a particular subject. You often find reasoning or logic questions on standardized tests. You may be asked to

RESOURCES

CRITICAL THINKING
Synthesis

Have students work individually or in small groups to create reasoning problems that ask, "What comes next?" Problems should be similar to the sequence of boxes on this page. Students should then present their reasoning problems for the rest of the class to solve.

If students seem to be having trouble with this activity, draw on the chalkboard several more examples. Here is one that you could use:

1. ◯   2. ◎   3. ◉   4. **?**

identify the relationship between several items (usually words, pictures, or numbers).

Reasoning questions might ask you to identify a pattern in a number sequence (as in the example on page 856) or ask you to predict the next item in a sequence.

What comes next?

 1   2   3   4

In this sequence of three drawings, the front of the block is in a different corner of the box each time. Therefore, in its final position the front of the block must be in the lower right corner of the box.

HOW TO ANSWER REASONING OR LOGIC QUESTIONS	
Be sure you understand the instructions.	Reasoning or logic questions are often multiple-choice. On some tests, however, you may need to write a word or phrase, complete a number sequence, or even draw a picture for your answer.
Analyze the relationship implied in the question.	Look at the question carefully to gather information about the relationship of the items.
Draw reasonable conclusions.	Evaluate the relationship of the items to decide your answer.

One special type of reasoning and logic question is an analogy question. In an analogy you recognize the relationship between two words and identify two other words that have a similar relationship.

EXAMPLE **1.** Directions: Select the appropriate pair of words to complete the analogy.

GLASS : MILK :: _____

A glass : cup
B ice : iced tea
C bowl : soup
D cow : grass

In this analogy, you would express the relationship of items in the form of a sentence or question: "A *glass* is used to hold *milk.*" What other pair of words has the same relationship?

You would then test all the choices to see which one fits best. For example, to test the first choice, *A*, you would say, "Does a *glass* hold a *cup*? (No.)" For the second, you'd say, "Does *ice* hold *iced tea*? (No.)" For the third choice, you'd say, "Does a *bowl* hold *soup*? (Yes.)" Now look at the last choice, *D.* "Does a *cow* hold *grass*? (Yes, but only when the cow eats grass.)"

You now have two possibilities for answers, *C* and *D.* To choose between them, you would decide which pair of words is more like the relationship of a *glass* to the *milk* it holds. You might reason that both *milk* and *soup* are foods for humans and a *glass* and a *bowl* are both dishes. Maybe *grass* is food, but not for humans, nor is a *cow* like a *dish.* Therefore, the best choice is *C.*

Short-Answer Questions.   Short-answer questions ask for short, precise responses. Instead of choosing from among a set of choices, you write the answer yourself.

Some short-answer questions (such as labeling a map or diagram, or fill-in-the-blank questions) can be answered with one or a few words. Other types of short-answer questions require you to give a full, written response, usually one or two sentences in length.

EXAMPLE   Describe how a mongoose kills a snake.
ANSWER   *The mongoose bites through the snake's spine right behind its head. The mongoose then holds onto the snake until it stops struggling.*

RESOURCES

HOW TO RESPOND TO SHORT-ANSWER QUESTIONS	
Read the question carefully.	Some questions have more than one part. You will have to include an answer to each part to receive full credit.
Plan your answer.	Briefly decide what you need to include in the answer.
Be as specific as possible in your answers.	Give a full, exact answer.
Budget your time.	Begin by answering those questions you are certain about.

Essay Tests

Essay tests measure how well you understand a subject. Essay answers are usually a paragraph or more in length.

HOW TO STUDY FOR ESSAY TESTS
1. Read assigned material carefully.
2. Make an outline of main points and important details.
3. Create your own essay questions and practice writing answers.
4. Evaluate and revise your practice answers. Check your answers by your notes and textbook. Also check the composition section of this textbook for help in writing.

Taking Essay Tests

There are certain steps you should take before you begin an essay test. Quickly scan the questions. How many questions will you need to answer? Do you need to choose from several items? Which of them do you think you can answer best? After you have determined the

INTEGRATING THE LANGUAGE ARTS

Test Taking and Writing. An essay written during a test should have the same qualities in its content as an essay written outside of class. Have students generate a checklist of qualities that a well-written essay should have. You might list the suggestions on the chalkboard and add any qualities students forget. After completing and organizing the list, have students copy it for their notes.

answers to these questions, plan how much time to spend on each essay answer. Then stay with the schedule.

Read the question carefully. You may be asked for an answer that contains several parts.

Pay attention to important terms in the question. Essay questions on tests usually require specific tasks to be accomplished in the answer. Each task is expressed with a verb. If you become familiar with the key verbs and what kind of response each one calls for, this knowledge can help you to write a more successful essay.

ESSAY TEST QUESTIONS		
KEY VERB	**TASK**	**SAMPLE QUESTION**
argue	Take a viewpoint on an issue and give reasons to support this opinion.	Argue whether or not your school should start a recycling or a landscaping project.
analyze	Take something apart to see how each part works.	Analyze the life cycle of the chicken.
compare	Point out likenesses.	Compare word processors and typewriters.
contrast	Point out differences.	Contrast Cinderella and Snow White.
define	Give specific details that make something unique.	Define the term *divisor* as it is used in math.
demonstrate	Provide examples to support a point.	Demonstrate the importance of a balanced diet to good health.

MEETING INDIVIDUAL NEEDS

LESS-ADVANCED STUDENTS

For each key verb in the **Essay Test Questions** chart give several sample questions that relate to something that students are familiar with. For example, you could create sample questions related to something students have been studying in class or related to a television show or a movie.

COOPERATIVE LEARNING

Group students in threes or fours and give each group one of the key verbs listed on the **Essay Test Questions** chart. Ask each group to choose three topics and to use their key verb to write an essay question for each topic. Then have a representative from each group read the questions and explain how to answer them.

RESOURCES

869

ESSAY TEST QUESTIONS *(continued)*		
KEY VERB	TASK	SAMPLE QUESTION
describe	Give a picture in words.	Describe how Tom Sawyer convinces all his friends to whitewash his fence.
discuss	Examine in detail.	Discuss the term *cause and effect.*
explain	Give reasons.	Explain the need for protecting an endangered species.
identify	Point out specific characteristics.	Identify the types of clouds.
list	Give all steps in order or all details about a subject.	List the steps for opening a lock with a combination.
summarize	Give a brief overview of the main points.	Summarize the tale of Beauty and the Beast.

Take a moment to use prewriting strategies. Consider the key verbs in the question. Then jot down a few notes or an outline to help you decide what you want to say. Write notes or a rough outline on scratch paper.

Evaluate and revise as you write. You probably can't redo your whole essay, but you can edit and improve it.

QUALITIES OF A GOOD ESSAY ANSWER

- The essay is well organized.
- The main ideas and supporting points are clearly presented.
- The sentences are complete and well written.
- There are no distracting errors in spelling, punctuation, or grammar.

Review

▶ EXERCISE 1 **Choosing an Appropriate Reading Rate**

Identify the reading rate that best fits each of the following situations.

1. skimming

1. You are looking at a test just handed to you to decide how much time you need to allot to each section.
2. You are looking in your grammar book for the section on the proper use of a semicolon. **2.** scanning
3. You are reading a chapter in your history book that you will be tested on in two days. **3.** mastery
4. You are reviewing the main points of the same chapter in your history book the night before your test. **4.** skimming
5. You are looking in a textbook chapter for the answer to a question on your review sheet. **5.** scanning

▶ EXERCISE 2 **Applying the SQ3R Method**

Use the SQ3R method while reading a textbook chapter that you need to read for a class. List at least five questions and write a brief answer to each one.

▶ EXERCISE 3 **Analyzing Details in a Passage**

Answer the following questions about the reading passage on pages 850–851.

1. Give two facts or details about mongooses (other than those noted in the sample analysis).
2. Why was the mongoose brought to Hawaii and the West Indies?
3. How did the mongoose in Kipling's story save the lives of the boy and his family?
4. What two myths about the mongoose's ability to kill poisonous snakes are discussed in the reading passage?
5. Under what conditions may a mongoose be brought into the United States?

COOPERATIVE LEARNING

Divide your class into groups of four or five and assign each group the task of creating questions about a reading passage. The questions should be similar to those in **Exercise 3.** You could allow students to choose the reading passage or you could assign one. When the questions have been written, have groups exchange questions and write answers to the questions they have received.

ANSWERS
Exercise 2

Students' questions and answers should reflect a careful reading of the material.

ANSWERS
Exercise 3

1. Mongooses are similar to ferrets and they feed on rodents and insects.
2. to kill rats and poisonous snakes
3. It killed two cobras that were planning to kill him and his family.
4. immune to venom; know where to find a plant that makes the venom harmless
5. for a zoo; for research

RESOURCES

RESOURCES

ANSWERS
Exercise 4

Responses will vary.

1. The mongoose is the only animal that will seek out and kill a cobra.

2. Mongooses can kill poisonous snakes. They know where to strike and they know that they need to hold on to the snake's head until it has stopped struggling.

3. The mongoose kills cobras and other poisonous snakes, as well as rodents and insects.

4. Mongooses will dare to attack a cobra.

5. If the mongoose can kill a cobra, it can kill any kind of snake.

ANSWERS
Exercise 6

Students' notes should include main ideas as headings and supporting details and examples. Notes should be concise and should be summarized in the students' own words.

EXERCISE 4 Drawing Conclusions and Making Inferences

Using the reading passage on pages 850–851, identify the evidence or explain the reasoning that you might use to make the following inferences or draw the following conclusions.

1. The mongoose is important for controlling the cobra population.
2. Mongooses are clever animals.
3. People in Asia, Africa, and southern Europe probably consider the mongoose a very valuable member of the animal kingdom.
4. Mongooses are not timid.
5. The mongoose is able to kill almost any kind of snake in the world.

EXERCISE 5 Interpreting Graphic Information

Using the chart on page 857, answer each of the following questions.

1. What is the longest venomous snake shown on the chart? **1.** king cobra   **2.** black mamba
2. Which snake's bite would be most likely to kill you if you were left untreated after its attack?
3. Which snakes can be found somewhere in North America? **3.** rattlesnake, cottonmouth, and coral
4. Which of the snakes shown on the chart is the smallest? **4.** coral
5. Where are king cobras found? Cape cobras?
   5. king cobra — southern Asia/Cape cobra — southern Africa

EXERCISE 6 Analyzing Your Note-Taking Method

Select a homework assignment in your science, social studies, or English textbook. Take study notes, following the guidelines for how to take effective study notes on page 854. Be prepared to share your notes in class and to explain how you took notes.

> EXERCISE 7 **Identifying Classifications**

For each of the following groups, identify the category.

1. tile, carpet, Oriental rug, linoleum
2. bed, cot, bunk, couch
3. basket, purse, suitcase, shopping bag
4. beagle, dachshund, retriever, Doberman pinscher
5. sandals, tennis shoes, hightops, boots

> EXERCISE 8 **Applying Visual Organization**

After reading the paragraph below, make a chart of its contents. Use your graphic to answer the numbered questions on page 874. [Hint: Your completed chart should have two columns: one labeled "Reptiles" and one labeled "Amphibians."]

Reptiles and amphibians are two of the three classes of cold-blooded vertebrates. Reptiles and amphibians can appear to be very similar, but they are actually very different. First, reptiles are a larger class of animals than amphibians. For example, the largest reptiles, pythons and anacondas, can grow to be over thirty feet long. By contrast, the largest of the amphibians, the Japanese giant salamander, is only five feet long. Second, their appearance is different. The skin of a reptile is scaly, while an amphibian's skin is smooth and sometimes even slimy. Reptiles breathe only with their lungs. Amphibians breathe with gills when they are young and with lungs as adults. Some amphibians retain their gills and have both lungs and gills as adults. In addition, all amphibians take in oxygen through their skins. Third, their mating habits differ. Amphibians mate during rainy periods, while reptiles mate in the spring. Reptiles are born on land, while amphibians are born in water or on moist ground. Reptiles are either hatched from eggs or are born live. Amphibians always hatch from eggs.

ANSWERS
Exercise 7

1. floor coverings
2. furniture to recline or lie on
3. hand-held containers
4. dogs
5. footwear

ANSWERS
Exercise 8

Reptiles	Amphibians
larger (some over 30 ft.)	smaller (largest only 5 ft.)
scaly skin	smooth or slimy skin
lungs	gills when young; lungs, or lungs and gills, as adults; absorb oxygen through skin
mate in the spring	mate during rainy periods
born on land	born in water or on moist ground
hatched or born alive	hatched

RESOURCES

1. How is the skin of a reptile different from the skin of an amphibian? **1.** reptile—scaly/amphibian—smooth and slimy
2. Which is a larger class of animals: reptiles or amphibians? **2.** reptiles
3. What is the difference, in feet, between the largest reptile and the largest amphibian? **3.** over 25 feet
4. Do reptiles breathe differently than amphibians? Explain. **4.** yes—no gills; oxygen not absorbed through skin
5. How do reptiles and amphibians differ in their place of birth? **5.** reptiles—land/amphibians water or moist ground

▶ EXERCISE 9 **Paraphrasing a Poem**

Paraphrase the following excerpt from "A Psalm of Life" by Henry Wadsworth Longfellow.

> Not enjoyment, and not sorrow,
>   Is our destined end or way;
> But to act, that each to-morrow
>   Find us farther than today.
>
>   from "A Psalm of Life"
>   by Henry Wadsworth Longfellow

▶ EXERCISE 10 **Analyzing Essay Questions**

Identify the <u>key verb</u> that states the specific task in each of the following essay questions. Do not write an essay response. Instead, state briefly what you would need to do to answer each question.

1. <u>Contrast</u> the temperaments of Rip and Dame Van Winkle in Washington Irving's "Rip Van Winkle."
2. <u>Explain</u> the importance of the U.S. Constitution at the time it was written.
3. <u>Discuss</u> the importance of setting in the poem "The Highwayman" by Alfred Noyes.
4. <u>List</u> the steps of the rain cycle.
5. <u>Demonstrate</u> the importance of imagery in the poem "A Dream Deferred" by Langston Hughes.

ANSWERS
Exercise 9

Paraphrases will vary. Here is a possibility:
      The speaker of the poem says that a person's goal or path is neither pleasure nor sorrow. Instead, people should take action so that each new day finds them farther along than they were the day before.

ANSWERS
Exercise 10
Responses will vary.

1. point out differences between
2. give reasons for
3. write about
4. give, in order
5. provide examples to support

SELECTION AMENDMENT
Description of change: excerpted
Rationale: to focus on the concept of paraphrasing presented in this chapter

874

DIAGRAMING SENTENCES

A *sentence diagram* is a picture of how the parts of a sentence fit together. It shows how the words in the sentence are related.

Subjects and Verbs (pages 400–411)

To diagram a sentence, first find the simple subject and the simple predicate, or verb, and write them on a horizontal line. Then separate the subject and verb with a vertical line. Keep the capital letters but leave out the punctuation marks, except in cases such as *Mr.* and *July 1, 1992.*

EXAMPLE   **Horses gallop.**

Questions (page 407)

To diagram a question, first make the question into a statement. Then diagram the sentence. Remember that in a diagram, the subject always comes first, even if it does not come first in the sentence.

EXAMPLE   **Are you going?**

The examples on the previous page are easy because each sentence contains only a simple subject and a verb. Now look at a longer sentence.

EXAMPLE **A quiet, always popular pet is the goldfish.**

To diagram the simple subject and verb of this sentence, follow these steps.

Step 1: Separate the complete subject from the complete predicate.

complete subject	complete predicate
A quiet, always popular pet	is the goldfish.

Step 2: Find the simple subject and the verb.

simple subject	verb
pet	is

Step 3: Draw the diagram.

Understood Subjects (pages 415–416)

To diagram an imperative sentence, place the understood subject *you* in parentheses on the horizontal line.

EXAMPLE **Clean your room.**

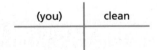

▶ EXERCISE 1 **Diagraming Simple Subjects and Verbs**

Diagram only the simple subject and verb in each of the following sentences. Remember that simple subjects and verbs may consist of more than one word.

EXAMPLE   **1.** Gwendolyn Brooks has been the poet laureate
of Illinois.

Gwendolyn Brooks	has been

1. My friend Angela just returned from Puerto Rico.
2. She was studying Spanish in San Juan.
3. Listen to her stories about her host family.
4. She really enjoyed her trip.
5. Have you ever been to Puerto Rico?

PEANUTS reprinted by permission of UFS, Inc.

Compound Subjects (page 409)

To diagram a compound subject, put the subjects on parallel lines. Then put the connecting word (the conjunction) on a dotted line that joins the subject lines.

EXAMPLE   **Sharks** and **eels** can be dangerous.

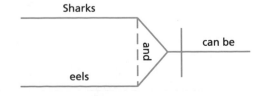

Compound Verbs (page 411)

To diagram a compound verb, put the two verbs on parallel lines. Then join them by a dotted line on which you write the connecting word.

EXAMPLE   The cowboy **swung** into the saddle and **rode** away.

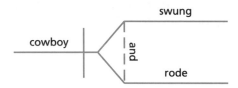

This is how a compound verb is diagramed when it has a helping verb.

EXAMPLE   Alice Walker **has written** many books and **received** several prizes for them.

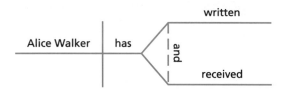

Compound Subjects and Compound Verbs (pages 409–411)

A sentence with both a compound subject and a compound verb combines the patterns for each.

EXAMPLE   **Rosa Parks** and **Martin Luther King, Jr., saw** a problem and **did** something about it.

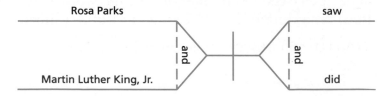

Sometimes parts of a compound subject or a compound verb are joined by correlative conjunctions, such as *both . . . and.* Correlatives are diagramed like this:

EXAMPLE **Both** Luisa **and** Miguel can sing.

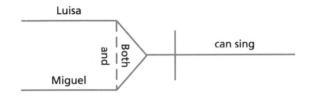

> EXERCISE 2 **Diagraming Compound Subjects and Compound Verbs**

Diagram the simple subjects and the verbs in the following sentences. Include the conjunctions that join the compound subjects or the compound verbs.

EXAMPLE **1.** Both Whitney Houston and Ray Charles are going on tour and cutting new albums.

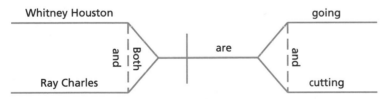

1. Everyone knows and likes Mr. Karras.
2. Hurricanes and tornadoes are frequent during the summer.
3. Julio and Rosa were frying tortillas and grating cheese for the tacos.
4. Both Jade Snow Wong and Amy Tan have written books about their childhoods in San Francisco's Chinatown.
5. Elena and I grabbed our jackets and took the bus to the mall.

Adjectives and Adverbs

Adjectives and adverbs are written on slanted lines connected to the words they modify. Notice that possessive pronouns are diagramed in the same way adjectives are.

Adjectives (pages 434–437)

EXAMPLES **dark** room   **a lively** fish   **my best** friend

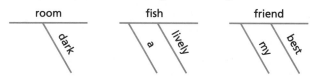

▶ EXERCISE 3   **Diagraming Sentences with Adjectives**

Diagram the subjects, verbs, and adjectives in the following sentences.

EXAMPLE   **1.** A huge silver spaceship landed in the field.

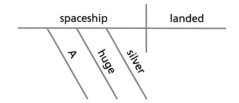

1. The horror movie will soon be finished.
2. The soft, silky kitten played with a shoelace.
3. A tall red-headed woman walked into the room.
4. The funniest television show stars Bill Cosby.
5. A weird green light shone under the door.

Adverbs (pages 454–457)

EXAMPLES walks **briskly**   arrived **here late**

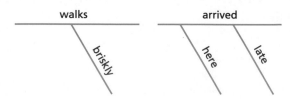

When an adverb modifies an adjective or another adverb, it is placed on a line connected to the word it modifies.

EXAMPLES   a **very happy** child   drove **rather slowly**

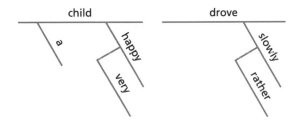

This **extremely rare** record will **almost certainly** cost a great deal.

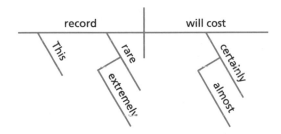

Conjunctions and Modifiers (pages 465–466)

When a modifier applies to only one part of the compound subject, it is diagramed like this:

EXAMPLE   Benjamin Davis, Sr., and **his** son worked **hard** and rose **quickly** through the military.

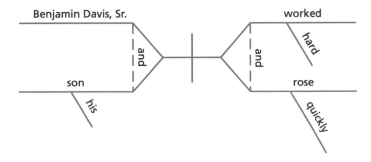

When a conjunction joins two modifiers, it is diagramed like this:

EXAMPLE   The **English** and **American** musicians played **slowly** and quite **beautifully.**

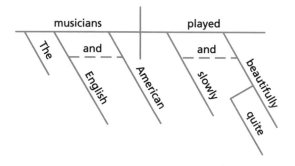

▶ EXERCISE 4   **Diagraming Sentences with Adjectives and Adverbs**

Diagram the subjects, verbs, adjectives, and adverbs in the following sentences.

EXAMPLE   **1.** A relatively unknown candidate won the election easily and rather cheaply.

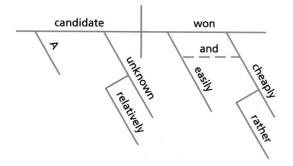

1. The determined young Frederick Douglass certainly worked hard.
2. The talented actress spoke loudly and clearly.
3. Mei-Ling and her younger sister will arrive early tomorrow.
4. The best musicians always play here.
5. Generally that glue does not work very well.

Objects (pages 474–477)

Direct Objects (pages 474–475)

A direct object is diagramed on the horizontal line with the subject and verb. A vertical line separates the direct object from the verb. Notice that this vertical line does not cross the horizontal line.

EXAMPLE   We like **pizza**.

Compound Direct Objects (page 475)

EXAMPLE   Lizards eat **flies** and **earthworms**.

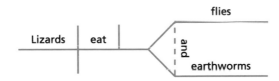

Indirect Objects (page 477)

An indirect object is diagramed on a horizontal line beneath the verb. The verb and the indirect object are joined by a slanting line.

EXAMPLE   Marisol brought **me** a piñata.

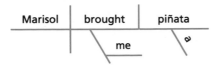

Compound Indirect Objects

EXAMPLE   Tanya gave the **singer** and the **dancer** cues.

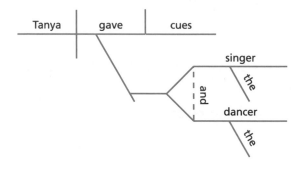

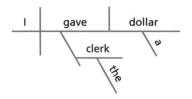 EXERCISE 5   **Diagraming Direct and Indirect Objects**

Diagram the following sentences.

EXAMPLE   **1.** I gave the clerk a dollar.

1. Several businesses bought our school computer equipment.
2. He sent the American Red Cross and Goodwill Industries his extra clothes.
3. My aunt knitted Violet and me sweaters.
4. Kim drew us a quick sketch.
5. Gerardo and Wendie are organizing the play and the refreshments.

Subject Complements (pages 480–482)

A subject complement is diagramed on the horizontal line with the subject and the verb. It comes after the verb. A line slanting toward the subject separates the subject complement from the verb.

Predicate Nominatives (pages 480–481)

EXAMPLE   Barbra Streisand is a famous **singer.**

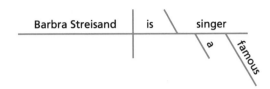

Compound Predicate Nominatives (page 481)

EXAMPLE   Clara is a **student** and a volunteer **nurse.**

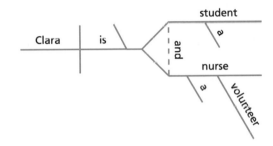

Predicate Adjectives (page 482)

EXAMPLE   She was extremely **nice.**

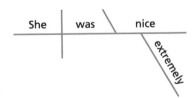

Compound Predicate Adjectives (page 482)

EXAMPLE   We were **tired** but very **happy.**

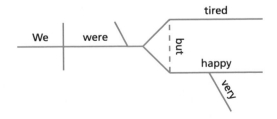

EXERCISE 6   **Diagraming Sentences**

Diagram the following sentences.

EXAMPLE   **1.** The indigo snake is large and shiny.

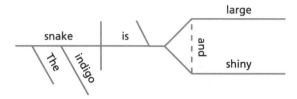

1. Turtles are reptiles.
2. Their tough bills look sharp and strong.
3. Turtles may grow very old.
4. The alligator snapper is the largest freshwater turtle.
5. Few turtles are dangerous.

Prepositional Phrases (pages 491–497)

A prepositional phrase is diagramed below the word it modifies. Write the preposition on a slanting line below the modified word. Then write the object of the preposition on a horizontal line connected to the slanting line.

Adjective Phrases (pages 493–494)

EXAMPLES   traditions **of the Sioux**   gifts **from Nadine and Chip**

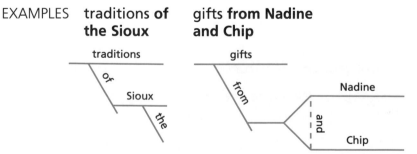

Adverb Phrases (pages 496–497)

EXAMPLES   awoke early **in the morning**

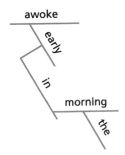

search **for the gerbil and the hamster**

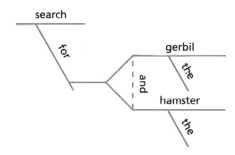

Two prepositional phrases may modify the same word.

EXAMPLE   The tour extends **across the country** and **around the world.**

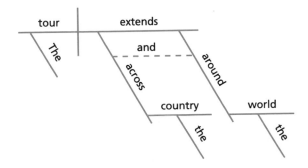

When a prepositional phrase modifies the object of another preposition, the diagram looks like this:

EXAMPLE   Richard Wright wrote one **of the books on that subject.**

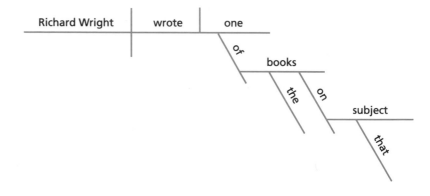

EXERCISE 7 **Diagraming Sentences with Prepositional Phrases**

Diagram the following sentences.

1. The director of that movie about the Civil War was chosen for an Academy Award.
2. A play about Cleopatra will be performed tonight.
3. Leroy practices with his band and by himself.
4. Stevie Wonder has written songs about love and freedom.
5. The scientist worked late into the night.

Subordinate Clauses (pages 516–525)

Adjective Clauses (pages 520–521)

Diagram an adjective clause by connecting it with a broken line to the word it modifies. Draw the broken line between the relative pronoun and the word that it relates to. [Note: The words *who*, *whom*, *whose*, *which*, and *that* are relative pronouns.] The adjective clause is diagramed below the independent clause.

EXAMPLES   The students **whose projects are selected** will attend the regional contest.

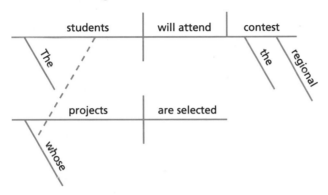

Adverb Clauses (pages 523–525)

Diagram an adverb clause by using a broken line to connect the adverb clause to the word it modifies. Place the subordinating conjunction that introduces the adverb clause on the broken line. [Note: The words *after, because, if, since, unless, when,* and *while* are common subordinating conjunctions.] The adverb clause is diagramed below the independent clause.

EXAMPLE   **If I study for two more hours,** I will finish my homework.

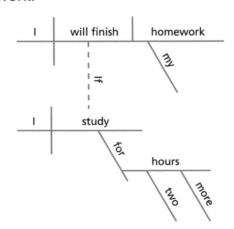

EXERCISE 8   **Diagraming Sentences with Adjective Clauses and Adverb Clauses**

Diagram the following sentences.

EXAMPLE   **1.** Will you stop by my house after you go to the library?

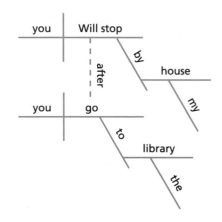

1. Proverbs are sayings that usually give advice.
2. Because the day was very hot, the cool water felt good.
3. The problem that worries us now is the pollution of underground sources of water.
4. If it does not rain tomorrow, we will visit Crater Lake.
5. Janice and Linda found some empty seats as the movie started.

The Kinds of Sentence Structure (pages 534–541)

Simple Sentences (page 534)

EXAMPLE   **Ray showed us his new bike.** [one independent clause]

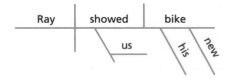

Compound Sentences (pages 536–538)

The second independent clause in a compound sentence is diagramed below the first and is joined to it by a coordinating conjunction. [The coordinating conjunctions are *and, but, for, or, nor, so,* and *yet.*]

EXAMPLE   Ossie Davis wrote the play, and Ruby Dee starred in it. [two independent clauses]

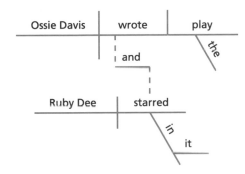

▶ EXERCISE 9   **Diagraming Compound Sentences**

Diagram the following compound sentences.

EXAMPLE   **1.** Lucas likes that new CD, but I have not heard it.

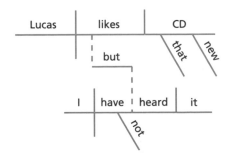

1. We went to the mall, and everyone had a good time.
2. Miriam celebrates Hanukkah, and she told our class about the holiday.
3. Luis Alvarez was an atomic scientist, but his son became a geologist.
4. Do you like basketball, or do you prefer hockey?
5. Sandy Koufax is my baseball hero, but my sister prefers Hank Aaron.

Complex Sentences (pages 540–541)

EXAMPLE   **Altovise has a carving that was made in Nigeria.**
[one independent clause and one subordinate clause]

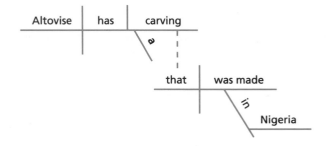

▶ EXERCISE 10   **Diagraming Complex Sentences**

Diagram the following complex sentences.

EXAMPLE   **1.** If you see Lola, you can give her this book.

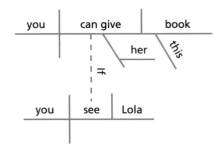

1. Because my cousins live in Toledo, they took a plane to the wedding.
2. Sally Ride was the first American woman who flew in space.
3. Although Wilma Rudolph had been a very sick child, she became a top Olympic athlete.
4. All three of the children screamed as the roller coaster began its descent.
5. The amusement park that we like best offers two free rides to frequent customers.

Glossary of Terms

A

Action verb An action verb is a verb that expresses physical or mental action. (See page 444.)

Adjective An adjective is a word that modifies a noun or a pronoun. (See page 434.)

Adjective clause An adjective clause is a subordinate clause that modifies a noun or a pronoun. (See page 520.)

Adjective phrase An adjective phrase is a prepositional phrase that modifies a noun or a pronoun. (See page 493.)

Adverb An adverb is a word that modifies a verb, an adjective, or another adverb. (See page 454.)

Adverb clause An adverb clause is a subordinate clause that is used as an adverb. (See page 523.)

Adverb phrase An adverb phrase is a prepositional phrase that modifies a verb, an adjective, or another adverb. (See page 496.)

Agreement Agreement refers to the correspondence, or match, between grammatical forms. (See Chapter 20.)

Aim An aim is one of the four basic purposes, or reasons, for writing. (See pages 7 and 24.)

Antecedent An antecedent is a noun or pronoun to which a pronoun refers. (See page 428.)

Antonym An antonym is a word with the opposite meaning of another word. (See page 832.)

Appositive An appositive is a noun or a pronoun that explains or identifies another noun or pronoun. (See page 715.)

B

Body The body of a composition is one or more paragraphs that state and develop the composition's main points. (See page 107.)

Brainstorming Brainstorming is a way a writer finds ideas for writing by making a list of all thoughts about a subject without stopping to judge the ideas. (See page 29.)

C

Case Case is the form of a noun or pronoun that shows its use in a sentence. (See page 606.)

Chronological order Chronological order is a way a writer arranges details in a paragraph or composition according to when events or actions take place. (See page 79.)

Clause A clause is a group of words that contains a verb and its subject and is used as a part of a sentence. (See page 516.)

Cliché A cliché is a vague and over-used expression. (See page 391.)

Clustering Clustering is a way a writer finds writing ideas and gathers information by breaking a large subject into its smaller parts, using circles and lines to create a diagram of his or her thoughts. (See page 31.)

Coherence Coherence, in a paragraph or composition, means that a writer has clearly arranged and connected all ideas. (See pages 74 and 108.)

Colloquialism A colloquialism is a casual, colorful expression used in everyday conversation. (See page 389.)

Comparing Comparing means telling how things are alike. (See page 82.)

Comparative degree Comparative degree is the form a modifier takes when two things are being compared. (See page 629.)

Complement A complement is a word or group of words that completes the meaning of a verb. (See page 473.)

Complex sentence A complex sentence has one independent clause and at least one subordinate clause. (See page 540.)

Compound sentence A compound sentence has two or more independent clauses and no subordinate clauses. (See pages 368 and 536.)

Compound subject A compound subject consists of two or more subjects that are joined by a connecting word and have the same verb. (See pages 366, 409, and 560.)

Compound verb A compound verb consists of two or more verbs that are joined by a connecting word and have the same subject. (See page 411.)

Conclusion (1) A conclusion restates the main idea in different words, sums up the ideas in the composition, and brings it to a definite close. (See pages 109 and 336.) **(2)** A conclusion is a decision reached by reasoning from clearly expressed facts and evidence found in a reading passage or other materials. (See page 852.)

Conflict A conflict is a situation that holds a problem or challenge for a character in a story. (See page 186.)

Conjunction A conjunction is a word that joins words or groups of words. (See page 465.)

Connotation The connotation of a word is the word's emotional meanings suggested by or associated with that word. (See page 390.)

Context The context of a word includes the surrounding words and the way the word is used. (See page 831.)

Contrasting Contrasting means telling how things are different from one another. (See page 82.)

Creative writing Creative writing is writing that aims at creating literature: stories, poems, songs, and plays. (See page 7.)

D

Declarative sentence A declarative sentence makes a statement and is followed by a period. (See page 415.)

Denotation The denotation of a word is its direct, plainly expressed meaning—the meaning a dictionary lists. (See page 390.)

Description Description is a way a writer develops a paragraph or composition by using sensory details to describe something. (See page 77.)

Dialect A dialect is a different variety of a language used by a particular group of people. (See page 385.)

Dialogue Dialogue consists of the words that characters say in a story. (See page 194.)

Direct object A direct object is a noun or pronoun that receives the action of a transitive verb. (See page 474.)

Double negative A double negative is the use of two negative words to express one negative idea. (See page 636.)

E

Essential clause/Essential phrase An essential (or **restrictive**) clause or phrase is one that is necessary to the meaning of the sentence. (See page 713.)

Evaluating Evaluating is the stage in the writing process in which a writer goes over a draft, making judgments about its strengths and weaknesses in content, organization, and style. (See pages 6 and 46.)

Evaluation Evaluation is a way a writer develops a paragraph or composition by making judgments, telling what is good or bad about a subject. (See page 84.)

Exclamatory sentence An exclamatory sentence shows excitement or expresses strong feeling and is followed by an exclamation point. (See page 416.)

Expressive writing Expressive writing is writing that aims at expressing a writer's feelings and thoughts. (See page 7.)

F

Figure of speech A figure of speech is a word or a group of words that have a meaning other than what they actually say. (See page 164.)

5W-How? questions The *5W-How?* questions—*Who? What? Where? When? Why? How?*—are questions a writer uses to collect information about a subject. (See page 33.)

Freewriting Freewriting is a way of finding ideas for writing which a writer writes whatever pops into his or her head. (See page 28.)

H

Helping verb A helping verb helps the main verb to express action or a state of being. (See page 451.)

Homonyms Homonyms are words that are spelled differently and that mean different things, but are pronounced alike. (See page 777.)

"How-to" process writing "How-to" process writing is a form of writing in which a writer tells a step-by-step story of how to do something. (See page 216.)

I

Imperative sentence An imperative sentence gives a command or makes a request and is followed by either a period or an exclamation point. (See page 415.)

Independent clause An independent, or **main,** clause expresses a complete thought and can stand by itself as a sentence. (See page 516.)

Indirect object An indirect object is a noun or pronoun that comes between the verb and the direct object and tells *to whom* or *for whom* the action of the verb is done. (See page 477.)

Inference An inference is a decision that is made based on evidence that is hinted at or implied. (See page 852.)

Infinitive (1) An infinitive is one of the four principal, or basic, parts of a verb. (See page 580.) **(2)** An infinitive is a verbal, usually preceded by *to,* that can be used as a noun, an adjective, or an adverb. (See page 506.)

Infinitive phrase An infinitive phrase consists of an infinitive together with its modifiers and complements. (See page 508.)

Informative writing Informative writing is writing that aims at giving facts or information, or explaining something. (See page 7.)

Interjection An interjection is a word that expresses strong emotion. (See page 467.)

Interrogative sentence An interrogative sentence asks a question and is followed by a question mark. (See page 416.)

Intransitive verb An intransitive verb expresses action (or tells something about the subject) without passing the action to a receiver. (See page 446.)

Introduction An introduction begins a composition and should catch the readers' interest and present the main idea. (See page 104.)

Irregular verb An irregular verb is a verb that forms its past and past participle in some other way than by adding *–d* or *–ed* to the infinitive form. (See page 583.)

Jargon Jargon is special language that is used by a particular group of people. (See page 392.)

Linking verb A linking verb is a verb that expresses a state of being and links, or connects, the subject of a sentence with a word in the predicate that explains or describes the subject. (See page 447.)

List of sources A list of sources, or **Works Cited** list, tells what sources of information were used in a report. (See page 336.)

Logical order Logical order is a way of grouping ideas by what makes sense. (See page 82.)

Main idea A main idea is what a writer wants to say about a topic. It is the idea that a paragraph or composition is organized around. (See pages 64 and 98.)

Metaphor A metaphor is a figure of speech that compares two things directly, without using the words *like* or *as.* A metaphor says that something *is* something else. (See page 165.)

Modifier A modifier is a word, a phrase, or a clause that describes another word or limits the meaning of the word. (See page 629.)

Narration Narration is a way a writer develops a paragraph or composition by telling about events or actions as they change over a period of time. (See page 78.)

Nonessential clause/Nonessential phrase A nonessential (or **nonrestrictive**) clause or phrase adds information that is not needed to understand the meaning of the sentence. It is set off by commas. (See page 713.)

Noun A noun is a word that names a person, place, thing, or idea. (See page 423.)

Number Number is the form of a word that indicates whether the word is singular or plural. (See page 551.)

O

Object of the preposition The noun or pronoun that ends a prepositional phrase is the object of the preposition that begins the phrase. (See page 491.)

Order of importance Order of importance is a way of arranging details in a paragraph or composition according to how important the details are—most to least important, or the opposite. (See pages 84 and 160.)

P

Paraphrase A paraphrase is a restatement of someone's ideas in different words. (See page 858.)

Parenthetical expression A parenthetical expression is a side remark that adds information or relates ideas. (See page 718.)

Participial phrase A participial phrase consists of a participle together with its modifiers and complements. (See page 504.)

Participle A participle is a verb form that can be used as an adjective. (See page 502.)

Personal narrative A personal narrative is a form of writing in which an author explores and shares the meaning of an experience that was especially important to him or her. (See Chapter 4.)

Persuasive essay A persuasive essay is a form of writing in which a writer supports an opinion and tries to persuade an audience. (See Chapter 8.)

Persuasive writing Persuasive writing is writing that aims at persuading people to think or act in a certain way. (See page 7.)

Phrase A phrase is a group of related words that is used as a single part of speech and does not contain a verb and its subject. (See page 490.)

Plot The plot is the series of events that follow each other in a story. (See page 191.)

Positive degree Positive degree is the form a modifier takes when only one thing is being described. (See page 629.)

Predicate The predicate is the part of a sentence that says something about the subject. (See page 404.)

Predicate adjective A predicate adjective is an adjective that follows a linking verb and describes the subject of a sentence. (See page 482.)

Predicate nominative A predicate nominative is a noun or pronoun that follows a linking verb and explains or identifies the subject of a sentence. (See page 480.)

Prefix A prefix is a letter or group of letters added to the beginning of a word to create a new word with a different meaning. (See page 769.)

Preposition A preposition is a word that shows the relationship between a noun or pronoun and another word in the sentence. (See page 460.)

Prepositional phrase A prepositional phrase is a group of words beginning with a preposition and ending with a noun or a pronoun. (See pages 461 and 491.)

Prewriting Prewriting is the first stage in the writing process. In this stage, a writer thinks and plans, decides what to write about, collects ideas and details, and makes a plan for presenting ideas. (See pages 6 and 26.)

Principal parts of a verb The principal parts of a verb are a verb's four basic forms: the *infinitive,* the *present participle,* the *past,* and the *past participle.* (See page 580.)

Pronoun A pronoun is a word used in place of a noun or more than one noun. (See page 428.)

Proofreading Proofreading is the stage of the writing process in which a writer carefully reads a revised draft to correct mistakes in grammar, usage, and mechanics. (See pages 6 and 53.)

Publishing Publishing is the last stage of the writing process. In this stage, a writer makes a final, clean copy of a paper and shares it with an audience. (See pages 6 and 54.)

Purpose Purpose, or **aim,** is the reason for writing or speaking.(See pages 7, 24, and 37.)

Regular verb A regular verb is a verb that forms its past and past participle by adding *–d* or *–ed* to the infinitive form. (See page 581.)

Report A report is a form of writing in which a writer presents factual information that he or she has discovered through reading and asking questions about a topic. (See Chapter 10.)

Revising Revising is the stage of the writing process in which a writer goes over a draft, making changes in its content, organization, and style in order to improve it. (See pages 6 and 49.)

Run-on sentence A run-on sentence is two or more complete sentences run together as one. (See page 358.)

Sensory details Sensory details are words used to describe one of the five senses—sight, sound, touch, taste, and smell. (See page 69.)

Sentence A sentence is a group of words that has a subject and a verb and expresses a complete thought. (See page 398.)

Sentence fragment A sentence fragment is a group of words that looks like a sentence but does not express a complete thought. (See pages 355 and 398.)

Setting The setting is where and when a story takes place. (See page 190.)

Simile A simile is a figure of speech that compares two basically unlike things, using the words *like* or *as.* (See page 164.)

Simple sentence A simple sentence has one independent clause and no subordinate clauses. (See page 534.)

Slang Slang consists of made-up words and old words used in new ways. (See page 389.)

Spatial order Spatial order is a way of arranging details in a paragraph or composition by ordering them according to their location—from near to far, left to right, and so on. (See pages 77 and 160.)

Statement of opinion A statement of opinion is a sentence in which a writer clearly states a topic and his or her opinion about it. (See page 248.)

Subject The subject is the part of a sentence that tells whom or what the sentence is about. (See page 400.)

Subject complement A subject complement completes the meaning of a linking verb and identifies or describes the subject. (See page 480.)

Subordinate clause A subordinate, or **dependent,** clause does not express a complete thought and cannot stand alone as a sentence. (See page 516.)

Subordinating conjunction A subordinating conjunction begins an adverb clause and shows the relationship between the adverb clause and the word or words that the clause modifies. (See page 524.)

Suffix A suffix is a letter or group of letters added to the end of a word to create a new word with a different meaning. (See page 769.)

Summary A summary is a brief restatement of the main ideas expressed in a piece of writing. (See page 860.)

Superlative degree Superlative degree is the form a modifier takes when three or more things are being compared. (See page 629.)

Supporting sentences Supporting sentences are sentences in a paragraph or composition that give details or information to explain or prove the main idea. (See page 69.)

Syllable A syllable is a word part that can be pronounced by itself. (See page 765.)

Synonym A synonym is a word that has a meaning similar to, but not exactly the same as, another word. (See page 832.)

T

Topic sentence A topic sentence is the sentence that states the main idea of a paragraph. (See page 65.)

Transitional expressions Transitional expressions connect ideas in a paragraph or composition by showing why and how ideas and details are related. (See pages 74 and 108.)

Transitive verb A transitive verb is an action verb that expresses an action directed toward a person or thing. (See page 446.)

U

Unity Unity, in a paragraph or composition, means that all the sentences or paragraphs work together as a unit to express or support one main idea. (See pages 71 and 107.)

V

Verb A verb is a word that expresses an action or a state of being. (See page 444.)

Verb phrase A verb phrase contains one main verb and one or more helping verbs. (See pages 405 and 451.)

Verbal A verbal is a form of a verb used as a noun, an adjective, or an adverb. (See page 502.)

W

"What if?" questions Asking "What if?" questions is a way of thinking creatively that can help a writer spark his or her imagination to explore ideas for writing. (See page 34.)

Writer's journal A writer's journal is a written record of what happens in a person's life, and how he or she feels and thinks. The journal can be a sourcebook for writing ideas. (See page 27.)

Writing Writing is the stage in the writing process in which a writer puts his or her ideas into sentences and paragraphs, following a plan for presenting the ideas. (See pages 6 and 44.)

Writing process The writing process is the series of stages or steps that a writer goes through to develop ideas and to communicate them clearly in a piece of writing. (See pages 6 and 24.)

Glossary

This glossary is a short dictionary of words found in the professional writing models in this textbook. The words are defined according to their meanings in the context of the writing models.

Pronunciation Key

Symbol	Key Words	Symbol	Key Words
a	asp, fat, parrot	b	bed, fable, dub, ebb
ā	ape, date, play, break, fail	d	dip, beadle, had, dodder
ä	ah, car, father, cot	f	fall, after, off, phone
e	elf, ten, berry	g	get, haggle, dog
ē	even, meet, money, flea, grieve	h	he, ahead, hotel
i	is, hit, mirror	j	joy, agile, badge
ī	ice, bite, high, sky	k	kill, tackle, bake, coat, quick
ō	open, tone, go, boat	l	let, yellow, ball
ô	all, horn, law, oar	m	met, camel, trim, summer
o͞o	look, pull, moor, wolf	n	not, flannel, ton
o͞o	ooze, tool, crew, rule	p	put, apple, tap
yo͞o	use, cute, few	r	red, port, dear, purr
yoo	cure, globule	s	sell, castle, pass, nice
oi	oil, point, toy	t	top, cattle, hat
ou	out, crowd, plow	v	vat, hovel, have
u	up, cut, color, flood	w	will, always, swear, quick
ur	urn, fur, deter, irk	y	yet, onion, yard
ə	a in ago	z	zebra, dazzle, haze, rise
	e in agent	ch	chin, catcher, arch, nature
	i in sanity	sh	she, cushion, dash, machine
	o in comply	th	thin, nothing, truth
	u in focus	*th*	then, father, lathe
ər	perhaps, murder	zh	azure, leisure, beige
		ŋ	ring, anger, drink

Abbreviation Key

adj.	adjective	*prep.*	preposition
adv.	adverb	*vi.*	intransitive verb
n.	noun	*vt.*	transitive verb
pl.	plural		

A

ag·ate [ag'it] *n.* A marble made of a hard stone, usually striped or clouded in color.

ap·pren·tice [ə pren'tis] *adj.* Beginning.

ar·rest·ing [ə rest'iŋ] *adj.* Attracting immediate and full attention.

at·ta·ché [at' ə shā'] *n.* A person who works for his or her own country in another country.

awed [ôd] *adj.* Feeling respect and wonder.

B

bay·o·net [bā'ə net'] *n.* A kind of blade attached to the barrel of a rifle.

blus·ter·y [blus'tər ē] *adj.* Windy, with clouds; stormy.

bo·lo tie [bō'lō tī] *n.* A cord worn around the neck with a decorated fastener to tighten the neck loop.

braille [brāl] *n.* A system of writing used by the blind in which patterns of raised dots are felt by the fingers.

buck·skin [buk'skin'] *n.* A yellow-gray horse.

bur·dock [bur'däk'] *n.* A plant with large leaves and purple flowers.

butte [byo͞ot] *n.* A lone steep hill in an area of flat land.

C

car·mine (kär'min) *adj.* Red or purplish-red.

check [chek] *vt.* To hold back.

chlo·rine [klôr'ēn] *n.* A chemical used to clean water.

com·mo·tion [kə mō'shən] *n.* Noisy confusion.

com·pe·tent [käm'pə tənt] *adj.* Very capable; skilled.

con·fines [kän'fīns'] *n.* A fenced in or limited area.

con·sume [kən so͞om'] *vt.* To eat up.

Co·pen·hag·en [kō' pən hā'gən] *n.* The capital city of Denmark.

Crazy Horse [krā'zē hôrs] *n. c.* 1842–1877. A famous chief of the Dakotas.

D

dep·re·cat·ing·ly [dep'rə kāt'iŋ lē] *adv.* In a disapproving manner.

de·scend·ant [dē sen'dənt] *n.* One who is the son, daughter, grandchild, great-grandchild, etc., of a certain person.

de·scend [dē send'] *vi.* To come down.

de·te·ri·o·rate [dē tir'ē ə rāt] *vi.* To become poorer in quality.

dor·sal [dôr'səl] *adj.* On the back.

E

en·trance [en trans'] *vt.* To fill with delight.

e·phem·er·al [ē fem'ər əl] *adj.* Short-lived.

e·rode [ē rōd'] *vi.* To wear away until gone.

ex·ten·sive·ly [ek sten'siv lē] *adv.* To a great extent; covering a wide variety.

F

fast [fast] *vi.* To go without food.

fa·tigue [fə tēg'] *n.* Exhaustion; weariness.

for·feit [fôr'fit] *vt.* To lose or give up something in payment for a mistake in a game.

for·mat [fôr'mat'] *n.* Form.

fume [fyo͞om] *vi.* To show annoyance.

great·coat [grāt′kōt′] *n.* A heavy overcoat.

green·house [grēn′hous′] *adj.* Helping to trap the sun's rays in the earth's atmosphere, which causes climates all over the earth to gradually become hotter.

guf·faw [gu fô′] *vi.* To laugh loudly and roughly.

har·assed [hə rasd′] *adj.* Troubled and busy.

ha·ven [hā′vən] *n.* A safe place.

hid·e·ous [hid′ē əs] *adj.* Horrible to see or hear about.

hu·man·oid [hyōō′mə noid] *adj.* A creature with human characteristics.

hyp·not·ic [hip nät′ik] *adj.* Causing a sleep-like condition.

i·de·al·ism [ī dē′əl iz′əm] *n.* Thought based on the way one wishes things to be.

in·di·ca·tion [in′ di kā′shən] *n.* A sign; something that suggests.

in·fer·tile [in furt′′l] *adj.* Not able to grow plants.

ir·i·des·cent [ir′ i des′ənt] *adj.* Showing shiny colors that change when an object is moved.

in·step [in′step′] *n.* The upper part of the arch of the foot.

in·ter·spe·cies [in′tər spē′shēz] *adj.* Between two different kinds of creatures or species.

Ju·bi·lee [jōō′bə lē′] *n.* A cry of joy.

ju·ve·nile [jōō′və nīl′] *adj.* Immature; lacking adult skill or experience.

knead [nēd] *vt.* To mix and work dough or clay by folding and pressing with the hands.

las·so [las′ō] *n.* A long rope with a movable loop on the end for catching cattle.

ma·neu·ver [mə nōō′vər] *n.* A planned movement.

meth·ane [meth′ān′] *n.* A colorless, odorless gas given off by rotting or digested plants.

mi·nus·cule [mi nus′kyōōl′] *adj.* Very small.

Mo·ses [mō′zəz] *n.* A character in the Bible who led his people out of slavery, usually pictured as a tall, old man with a long, white beard.

nat·u·ral·ist [nach′ər əl ist] *n.* A person who studies nature.

Na·zi [nät′sē] *adj.* Done by the political party that controlled Germany under Hitler from 1933 to 1945.

neu·ro·bi·ol·o·gist [nōō′rō bī äl′ə jist] *n.* A scientist who is an expert on the nervous system.

ob·jec·tive·ly [əb jek′tiv lē] *adv.* Without opinion for or against.

oc·cu·pied [äk′yōō pîd] *adj.* Captured and being run by a foreign government.

o·cean·ar·i·um [ō′shə ner′ē əm] *n.* A large aquarium for fish and animals from the ocean.

▼ P

pad · dy [pad'ē] *n.* A rice field, partly under water.

pal · sied [pôl'zēd] *adj.* Paralyzed; often small from lack of use.

perch [purch] *n.* A freshwater fish.

per · se · cu · tion [pur'si kyoo'shən] *n.* The cruel or harsh treatment of someone for believing differently.

pre · ma · ture · ly [prē'mə toor' lē] *adv.* Too early.

pro · ces · sion [prō sesh'ən] *n.* A group moving forward together.

▼ Q

quest [kwest] *n.* A journey in search of something of value.

▼ R

raf · ter [raf'tər] *n.* A board that helps hold up a roof.

rain · forest [rān fôr'ist] *n.* A thick, evergreen forest in a tropical area that receives rain year-round.

re · it · er · ate [rē it'ə rāt'] *vt.* To repeat.

rem · i · nisce [rem'ə nis'] *vi.* To think and talk about memories of past events.

rep · er · toire [rep'ər twär'] *n.* The range of special skills that a performer is familiar with and prepared to demonstrate.

Re · sist · ance [ri zis'təns] *n.* The organized secret work of the people in a captured country fighting against the foreign country that has captured it.

rimed cou · plet [rīmd kup'lit] *n.* Two rhyming lines that are the same length, one written just after the other.

rouse [rouz] *vi.* To cause someone to act.

ru · pee [roo'pē] *n.* The basic money unit of India.

▼ S

sa · cred [sā'krid] *adj.* Holy; spiritually perfect or pure.

sage [sāj] *n.* A plant that is dried and used for seasoning; it was once believed to have healing powers.

sau · ci · ly [sô'si lē] *adv.* In a bright, lively way.

sheep · ish · ly [shēp'ish lē] *adv.* In an embarrassed manner.

sil · ver [sil'vər] *vt.* To cover with a silvery color.

Sioux [soo] *n.* A North American Indian people of the Northern Plains.

so · ber [sō'bər] *vt.* To make someone be serious.

sound · ing [soun'diŋ] *n.* The act of measuring the depth of water using sound.

soy · a [soi'ə] *n.* A plant of the pea family.

spat [spat] *n.* A heavy cloth or leather covering worn over the upper part of a shoe.

▼ T

te · pee [tē' pē] *n.* A cone-shaped tent made of animal skins stretched over poles.

ter · mi · nate [tur'mə nāt'] *vt.* To put an end to.

tract [trakt] *n.* A large area of land.

trem · o · lo [trem'ə lō'] *n.* A trembling sound made by rapidly repeating the same tone.

▼ V

ve · ran · da [və ran'də] *n.* A long, open porch.

vi · cious [vish'əs] *adj.* Intense; mean.

vi · sion [vizh'ən] *adj.* Having to do with seeing unreal, dreamlike images in the mind.

Index

C

INDEX

INDEX

INDEX

INDEX

INDEX

INDEX

INDEX

INDEX

INDEX

INDEX

hyphens, 755–56
incorrect, in fragments and run-on
  sentences, 355–56, 359
interrupters, 712–16
introductory words, phrases, and
  clauses, 719–20
italics (underlining), 735–36
parentheses, 757–58
parenthetical expression, 758–59
period, 702
plurals, 754
possessive case, 746–49
question mark, 702
quotation marks, 737–44
semicolons, 724–25
sentence within a sentence, 758
Purpose. *See also* Aims for writing.
  character analysis, 297
  creative, 7, 24
  description, 155
  expressive, 7, 24
  formal speech, 798–99
  group discussions, 802
  impromptu speech, 797
  informative, 7, 24
  letters, 835
  of literary review, 279
  oral interpretation, 803–804
  personal narrative, 125
  persuasive, 7, 24
  persuasive paper, 251
  for reading, 846
  report, 324
  short story, 185
  for writing, 7, 24
  writing process, 37
Put, principal parts of, 584

Question mark
  and abbreviation, 704
  as end mark, 398, 702
  and closing quotation marks, 739–40
  and direct quotation, 738
Questions
  analogy, 866–67
  asking, as part of writing process,
    33–35
  diagraming, 875
  essay test, 869–70
  5W-How?, 33–34, 325, 809
  in introduction, 104

matching, 865
multiple-choice, 864
punctuating, 702
reasoning or logic, 865–67
report, 325
short-answer, 867–68
true/false, 864–65
"What if?," 34–35
"Questions and Answers," 20–22
Quiet, quite, 784
Quotation marks, 737–44
  in character analysis, 305
  closing, 739–40
  and commas, 739
  for direct quotation, 305, 737–42
  and end marks, 738–40
  and note taking, 330
  not for indirect quotation, 737
  placement of, 737
  for several sentences, 742
  single, 742
  for titles of short works, 305, 342,
    743–44
Quotations
  broken, 737–38
  capitalizing, 675
  direct, 737–42
  indirect, 737
  in a personal narrative, 127
  quotation within a quotation, 742

R

Raise, principal parts of, 596–97
Raise, rise, 596–97
Randall, Dudley, 20–22
Rawlings, Marjorie Kinnan, 164
Reader's Guide to Periodical Literature,
  819–20
Reader's interest
  in introduction, 104
  in a personal narrative, 130
  in process paper, 217
  in a short story, 193
Reading
  focused, 36
  for mastery, 846
  purpose of, 846
  rate of, 846
  scanning, 846
  skimming, 846
  as a study skill, 846
Reading script, for oral interpretation,
  805

INDEX

INDEX

INDEX

S

INDEX

INDEX

Y

Z

Acknowledgments

For permission to reprint copyrighted material, grateful acknowledgment is made to the following sources:

American Way: From "Dream of the Blue Dolphins" by Michael DiLeo from *American Way,* the magazine of American Airlines. Copyright © 1991 by American Airlines.

Andrews and McMeel, A Universal Press Syndicate Company: Excerpt from *The Pre-History of the Far Side, A 10th Anniversary Exhibit* by Gary Larson. Copyright © 1980, 1981, 1982, 1983, 1984 by the Chronicle Publishing Company; copyright © 1984, 1985, 1986, 1987, 1988, 1989 by Universal Press Syndicate.

Arte Público Press: From "The Jacket" from *Small Faces* by Gary Soto. Copyright © 1986 by Gary Soto.

Bradbury Press, an Affiliate of Macmillan, Inc.: From *Hatchet* by Gary Paulsen. Copyright © 1987 by Gary Paulsen.

Broadside Press: From "Questions and Answers" by Dudley Randall from *A Capsule Course in Black Poetry Writing* by Gwendolyn Brooks, Keorapetse Kgositsile, Haki R. Madhubuti, and Dudley Randall. Copyright © 1975 by Gwendolyn Brooks Blakely, Keorapetse Kgositsile, Haki R. Madhubuti, and Dudley Randall.

Carlinsky & Carlinsky, Inc.: From "Kites" by Dan Carlinsky from *Boy's Life,* May 1974. Copyright © 1974 by Dan Carlinsky.

The Christian Science Monitor: Quote by Fairfax Cone from *The Christian Science Monitor,* March 20, 1963. Copyright © 1963 by The Christian Science Monitor.

Dial Books for Young Readers, a division of Penguin Books USA Inc.: From *Roll of Thunder, Hear My Cry* by Mildred D. Taylor. Copyright © 1976 by Mildred D. Taylor.

Doubleday, a division of Bantam, Doubleday, Dell Publishing Group, Inc.: From *Mighty Hard Road: The Story of Cesar Chavez* by James P. Terzian and Kathryn Cramer. Copyright © 1970 by Doubleday & Company, Inc. From "I'm from Out of the Beech" from *I Wish I Could Give My Son a Wild Raccoon* by Eliot Wigginton. Copyright © 1976 by Reading is Fundamental.

Dutton, a division of Penguin Books USA, Inc.: From *Insects, The Creeping Conqueror and Human History* by Carson I. A. Ritchie. Copyright © 1979 by Carson I. A. Ritchie.

Harcourt Brace Jovanovich, Inc.: "The Marble Champ" from *Baseball in April and Other Stories* by Gary Soto. Copyright © 1990 by Gary Soto.

HarperCollins Publishers: From "Hard Times" from *Black Elk: The Secret Ways of a Lakota* by Wallace H. Black Elk and William S. Lyon. Copyright © 1990 by Wallace H. Black Elk and William S. Lyon. From "One day a month, go without meat" from *Two Minutes a Day for a Greener Planet* by Marjorie Lamb. Copyright © 1990 by Marjorie Lamb.

Henry Holt and Company, Inc.: From "A Runaway Slave" from *Chariot In the Sky: A Story of the Jubilee Singers* by Arna Bontemps. Copyright 1951 by Arna Bontemps. Copyright © 1979 by Mrs. Arna (Alberta) Bontemps. "Stopping by Woods on a Snowy Evening" from *The Poetry of Robert Frost,* edited by Edward Connery Lathem. Copyright 1923, © 1969 by Holt, Rinehart and Winston. Copyright 1951 by Robert Frost.

Houghton Mifflin Company: From *Carlota* by Scott O'Dell. Copyright © 1977 by Scott O'Dell. All rights reserved.

Gary L. Johnson: From "A Son's Challenge" by Gary L. Johnson from *Reader's Digest,* September 1991. Copyright © 1991 by Gary L. Johnson.

Kalmbach Publishing Company: From "The Spaceport Mermaids" by Greg Walz-Chojnacki from *Odyssey*, vol. 12, no. 10, October 1990. Copyright © 1990 by Kalmbach Publishing Co.

Lion Books, Publishers, Scarsdale, NY: "Ubuhlali and Umnaka-Beaded Necklaces and Bangles" from *African Crafts.* Published by and copyright © Lion Books, Publisher, Scarsdale, NY.

Little, Brown and Company: From *Nisei Daughter* by Monica Sone. Copyright © 1953 and copyright renewed © 1981 by Monica Sone.

Liveright Publishing Corporation: "Those Winter Sundays" from *Collected Poems* by Robert Hayden, edited by Frederick Glaysher. Copyright © 1985 by Erma Hayden.

Lothrop, Lee and Shepard Books: From "Green Dragon Pond" from *The Spring of Butterflies*, translated by He Liyi. Copyright © 1985 by William Collins Sons & Co. Ltd.

Macmillan Publishing Company: From "My Aunt" from *Meet My Folks* by Ted Hughes. Copyright © 1961, 1973 by Ted Hughes.

Margaret K. McElderry Books, an imprint of Macmillan Publishing Company: From *A Jar of Dreams* by Yoshiko Uchida. Copyright © 1981 by Yoshiko Uchida.

William Morrow and Company, Inc./ Publishers, New York: From *Willie Bea and the Time the Martians Landed* by Virginia Hamilton. Copyright © 1983 by Virginia Hamilton Adoff. From *To Space and Back* by Sally Ride with Susan Okie. Copyright © 1986 by Sally Ride and Susan Okie. "A Drink for Crow" from *Stories to Solve: Folktales from Around the World*, told by George Shannon. Copyright © 1985 by George W. B. Shannon.

National Dairy Board, America's Dairy Farmers: Ad, "When your potassium comes with dairy calcium, you don't need a bunch." Copyright © 1990 by the National Dairy Board.

National Wildlife Federation: "Cures from the Jungle" by Whitney Hair from "Dear Ranger Rick" from *Ranger Rick* magazine, vol. 24, no. 8, August 1990. Copyright © 1990 by National Wildlife Federation. From "Meet-a-Cheetah" by Fred Johnson from *Ranger Rick* magazine, January 1969. Copyright © 1969 by National Wildlife Federation.

New American Library, a division of Penguin Books USA Inc.: From *The Sayings of Confucius* by James R. Ware. Copyright © 1955, 1983 by James R. Ware.

New York Magazine: Quote by Barbara Costikyan from "Holiday Entertaining" from *New York*, October 22, 1984. Copyright © 1984 by New York Magazine.

Newsweek, Inc.: From "A Doll Made to Order" from *Newsweek*, December 9, 1985. Copyright © 1985 by Newsweek, Inc. All rights reserved.

Omni International, Ltd.: From "The Dinner Party" by Mona Gardner from *Saturday Review*, January 31, 1942. Copyright © 1942 by Saturday Review.

Philomel Books, a division of The Putnam Publishing Group: From *A White Romance* by Virginia Hamilton. Copyright © 1987 by Virginia Hamilton.

The Pushcart Press: From a quote by Maxwell Perkins from *The Writer's Quotation Book, a literary companion*, edited by James Charlton. Copyright © 1980 by The Pushcart Press.

Marian Reiner: Haiku by Basho from *Cricket Songs: Japanese haiku*, translated by Harry Behn. Copyright © 1964 by Harry Behn.

The Saturday Evening Post, a division of The Benjamin Franklin Literary and Medical Society, Inc.: From "Kachinas: Sacred Drama of the Hopis" by Lonnie Dyer from *Young World* magazine. Copyright © 1976 by The Saturday Evening Post.

School Library Journal: From a book review by Louise L. Sherman on *Number the Stars* by Louis Lowry from *School Library Journal*, vol. 35, no. 7, March 1989. Copyright © 1989 by Reed Publishing, USA.

Charles Scribner's Sons, an imprint of Macmillan Publishing Company: From "Jody's Discovery" from *The Yearling* by Marjorie Kinnan Rawlings. Copyright © 1938 by Marjorie Kinnan Rawlings, copyright renewed © 1966 by Norton Baskin.

Virginia Driving Hawk Sneve: "The Medicine Bag," by Virginia Driving Hawk Sneve from *Boy's Life*, 1975. Copyright © 1975 by Virginia Driving Hawk Sneve.

Texas A & M University Press: From *Journal of an Indian Trader: Anthony Glass and the Texas Trading Frontier, 1790–1810,* edited by Dan L. Flores. Copyright © 1985 by Dan L. Flores.

Universal Press Syndicate: From "Coyote Places the Stars" from *Giving Birth to Thunder, Sleeping With His Daughter: Coyote Builds North America* by Barry Lopez. Copyright © 1977 by Barry Holstun Lopez.

University of California Press: From "In the Night" from *Singing for Power: The Song Magic of the Papago Indians of Southern Arizona* by Ruth Murray Underhill. Copyright © 1938, 1966 by Ruth Murray Underhill.

University of Nebraska Press: From "Across the Big Water" from *Black Elk Speaks: Being the Life Story of a Holy Man of the Oglala Sioux* as told through John G. Neihardt (Flaming Rainbow). Copyright © 1932, 1959, 1972 by John G. Neihardt. Copyright © 1961 by John G. Neihardt Trust.

Viking Penguin, a division of Penguin Books USA Inc.: "How to Eat Like a Child" from *How to Eat Like a Child and Other Lessons in Not Being a Grown-up* by Delia Ephron. Copyright © 1977, 1978 by Delia Ephron.

Webster's New World Dictionaries, A Division of Simon & Schuster, New York, NY: From the entry "escape" from *Webster's New World Dictionary of American English,* Third College Edition. Copyright © 1988 by Simon & Schuster, Inc.

Westminister/John Knox Press: From *Winter Thunder* by Mari Sandoz. Copyright © 1951 by The Curtis Publishing Company. Copyright © 1954 by Mari Sandoz. From *My Diary - My World* by Elizabeth Yates. Copyright © 1981 by Elizabeth Yates.

H. W. Wilson Company: Entries for "Roberts, Julia" through "Rock Music" from *Readers' Guide to Periodical Literature,* October 25, 1990, Vol. 90, No. 12. Copyright © 1991 by The H.W. Wilson Company.

PHOTO CREDITS

Abbreviations used: (t)top, (c)center, (b)bottom, (l)left, (r)right.

COVER: Ralph J. Brunke Photography

TABLE OF CONTENTS: Page xxxv(r), Ed Crabtree; xxxv(l), Courtesy Dudley Randall; xxxii, Bob Daemmrich/The Image Work; xxii(r), Michael Ochs Archives/Venice CA; x, Kobal Collection/SuperStock; xxii(l), Michael Ochs Archives/Venice CA; vi, Nawrocki Stock Photo; xv(c), HRW Photo by Russell Dian; xvi(b), Christopher Arenc/AlaskaPhoto Collection/Allstock; xv(b), Bev Rehkop/Unicorn Stock Photo; xii, NASA; xv(t), Ted Horowitz/The Stock Market; xxi, Norma Morrison; xvii, The Granger Collection; vii, David Young-Wolff/PhotoEdit; xxv, Camerique; xxiv, HBJ Photo by Stephanie Maize; xix(t), Mary Messenger; xix(b), UPI/Bettmann Newsphotos; xvi(t), James Balog/Black Star; viii, Archive Photos; xiii, Culver Pictures.

CHAPTER 0: Page 2, Mitchell B. Reibel/Sportschrome East/West; 4, Blair Seitz/Seitz & Seitz; 5, Mark Antman/The Image Works; 6, Marc Deville/Gamma-Liaison; 7, Bonnie Kamin/Comstock.

CHAPTER 1: Page 21, Courtesy Dudley Randall; 27(l), 27(r), Myrleen Ferguson/PhotoEdit; 29(l), 29(r), Prettyman/PhotoEdit; 31, David R. Razier Photolibrary; 33, HRW Photo by Ken Lax; 34(l), Lorraine Rorke/The Image Works; 34(r), Rosebush Vision/Phototake NY; 37, 38(l), David R. Frazier Photolibrary; 38(r), Ric Noyle/Visual Impact Hawaii; 40, Paolo Koch/Photo Researchers Inc.; 42(l), 42(r), 45, 50, Nawrocki Stock Photo; 52(l), Focus on Sports; 52(r), Arnold Michlin/PhotoEdit; 52(c), Usman Khan; 57, Michael & Barbara Reed/Animals, Animals.

CHAPTER 2: Page 60, Smithsonian Institution; 61, The Bettmann Archive; 62, Topham/The Image Works; 64(l), Tom Bean/DRK Photo; 64(r), David Young-Wolff/PhotoEdit; 65, Culver Pictures, Inc.; 66, HRW Photo by Eric Beggs/Shoes courtesy RunTex, Austin, Texas; 68, Charles Palek/Animals Animals; 70, Tony Freeman/PhotoEdit; 71, People Weekly © 1986 Richard Howard; 72, R. Hamilton Smith/FPG; 73, David R. Frazier Photolibrary; 75(l), Shostal Associates/SuperStock; 75(r), Jim Cartier/Photo Researchers, Inc.; 76, Lawrence Migdale; 78, Myrleen Ferguson/PhotoEdit; 79, 81, Runk/Schoenberger/Grant Heilman; 83, Aaron Haupt/David R. Frazier Photolibrary; 85(r), Lee Kuhn/FPG; 85(l), Stan Osolinski/FPG; 87(r), Phil Schermeister/Photographers Aspen; 87(l), Grant Heilman/Grant Heilman Photography; 89(r), M. Richards/PhotoEdit; 89(l), Reuters/Bettmann Newsphotos.

CHAPTER 3: Page 95(t), Pat and Rae Hagan/Bruce Coleman Inc.; 95(b), Jeff Foott/Bruce Coleman Inc.; 96, Pat and Rae Hagan/Bruce Coleman Inc.; 97(tl), FourByFive/SuperStock; 98, Archive Photos; 99(l), David R. Frazier Photolibrary; 99(r), Tony Freeman/PhotoEdit; 101, 103(l), 103(r), M. Richards/PhotoEdit; 105, Hans Reinhard/Bruce Coleman Inc.; 109(l), 109(r), Runk/Schoenberger/Grant Heilman; 111, Shostal Associates/SuperStock; 112(l), FourByFive/SuperStock; 112(r), Shostal Associates/SuperStock; 113, The Photo Source/SuperStock.

CHAPTER 4: Page 123, Tom McCarthy/Unicorn Stock Photo; 124(l), Richard Hutchins/PhotoEdit; 124(r), David Young-Wolff/PhotoEdit; 125, Tony Freeman/PhotoEdit; 126, Walter Chandoha; 128, George D. Lepp/Comstock; 131, David E. Kennedy/TexaStock; 132, DiMaggio/Kalish/Peter Arnold Inc.; 134, Tom Murphy/SuperStock; 142, Ed Crabtree; 144(l), Tony Freeman/PhotoEdit; 144(r), Bob Daemmrich/The Image Works.

CHAPTER 5: Page 154(t), David DeLossy/The Image Bank; 157, Kobal Collection/SuperStock; 159, Tony Freeman/PhotoEdit; 161, Alfred B. Thomas; 162, Chuck O'Rear/Westlight; 163, HRW Photo Library; 164, Gary W. Friffen/Animals, Animals; 171, Richard Hutchings/PhotoEdit; 175(t), 175(l), 175(r), HRW Photo by Eric Beggs; 176, SuperStock.

CHAPTER 6: Page 185(l), 185(r), Walt Disney Pictures/Shooting Star; 187(l), Shostal Associates/SuperStock; 187(r), FourByFive/SuperStock; 188, Richard Hutchings/PhotoEdit; 190(r), S. Chester/Comstock; 190(l), Spectrum/Vavaria/Viesti Associates, Inc.; 194, Comstock; 199, FourByFive/SuperStock; 200, Neal and Molly Jansen/Shostal Associates/SuperStock; 205, David Young-Wolff/PhotoEdit; 207(t), Shostal Associates/SuperStock; 207(b), Geffen 1986/Kobal Collection/SuperStock.

CHAPTER 7: Page 217(l), David R. Frazier Photolibrary; 217(r), Lawrence Migdale; 220, Bob Daemmrich/The Image Works; 221, HRW Photo by Eric Beggs; 223, Camerique; 224, Robert Frerck/Odyssey, Chicago; 226, SuperStock; 229, FourByFive/SuperStock; 237, NASA; 238, Larry Kolvoord/Viesti Associates, Inc.; 241, Treasure Island, R.L. Stevenson, J.B. Lippincott Company.

CHAPTER 8: Page 247, Grant Heilman/Grant Heilman Photography; 248, Culver Pictures; 249(l), UPI/Bettmann Newsphotos; 249(r), Witt/Sipa-Press; 251, Dan Helms/Duomo; 251, Tony Freeman/PhotoEdit; 253, Jack S. Grove/Tom Stack & Associates; 255, Eric Sander/Gamma-Liaison; 257, Grant Heilman Photography; 258, R. Azoury/Sipa-Press; 260, Al Tielemans/Duomo; 264, UPI/Bettmann; 266, Norma Morrison; 271, Culver Pictures, Inc.; 273, Richard Shiell/Earth Scenes.

CHAPTER 9: Page 293, Elena Rooraid/PhotoEdit; HBJ Photo by Stephanie Maize; 304(l), D. Cavagnaro/DRK Photo; 304(r), John Shaw/Tom Stack & Associates; 309, HRW Photo by John Langford; 312, Jerry Howard/Positive Images; 313, UPI/Bettmann.

Illustration Credits

Acknowledgments

For permission to reprint copyrighted material in the Annotated Teacher's Edition, grateful acknowledgment is made to the following sources:

Edward Albee: Quotation by Edward Albee from *Evening Standard*, 1970. Copyright © 1970 by Edward Albee.

Anchor Press, an imprint of Doubleday, a division of Bantam Doubleday Dell Publishing Group, Inc.: From "Getting It Down" from *Write to the Point* by Bill Stout. Copyright © 1984 by Bill Stout.

The Christian Science Monitor: Quotation by John Cheever from *The Christian Science Monitor*, October 24, 1970. Copyright © 1970 by The Christian Science Publishing Society. All rights reserved. Quotation by Virgil Thomson in an article by Daniel B. Wood from *The Christian Science Monitor*, February 12, 1985. Copyright © 1985 by The Christian Science Publishing Society.

Clarendon Press, an imprint of Oxford University Press Inc.: Quotation from "On Authorship and Style" (1851), translated by E.F.J. Payne (1974), II. 545, from *Parerga and Paralipomena* by Arthur Schopenhauer. Copyright © 1974 by E.F.J. Payne.

Cosmopolitan Magazine: Quotation by John Steinbeck from "Interview with a Best-Selling Author: John Steinbeck" by Robert van Gelder from *Cosmopolitan*, April 1947. Copyright © 1947 by Cosmopolitan Magazine.

John Kenneth Galbraith: Quotation by John Kenneth Galbraith from *Perspectives on Galbraith: Conversations and Opinions* by Frederick J. Pratson. Copyright © 1978 by John Kenneth Galbraith.

Mavis Gallant: Quotation by Mavis Gallant from *Contemporary Novelist*, 1976. Copyright © 1976 by Mavis Gallant.

Harcourt Brace Jovanovich, Inc.: Quotation by E. M. Forster. From "The Raison d'Etre of Criticism in the Arts" from *Two Cheers for Democracy* by E. M. Forster. Copyright 1951 by E. M. Forster; copyright renewed © 1979 by Donald Parry.

HarperCollins Publishers, Inc.: From *Reading, Writing and Remembering* by E. V. Lucus. Copyright 1932 by E. V. Lucus.

Harvard University Press: From *One Writer's Beginnings* by Eudora Welty, Cambridge, Mass.: Harvard University Press. Copyright © 1983, 1984 by Eudora Welty.

Heinemann–Boynton/Cook on behalf of Marian M. Mohr: From *Revision: The Rhythm of Meaning* by Marian M. Mohr. Copyright © 1984 by Boyton/Cook, Publishers, Inc., Portsmouth, NH.

Heinemann Educational Books, Ltd.: From *The Art of Teaching Writing* by Lucy McCormick Calkins. Copyright © 1986 by Lucy McCormick Calkins.

Henry Holt and Company, Inc.: From "The Figure A Poem Makes" from *Complete Poems of Robert Frost 1949*. Copyright 1930, 1939, 1943, 1947, 1949 by Henry Holt and Company, Inc. Copyright 1936, 1942, 1945, 1948, by Robert Frost.

Alfred A. Knopf, Inc.: From "Miss Jewett" from *Not Under Forty* by Willa Cather.

Andre Maurois: Quotation by Andre Maurois from *New York Journal-American*, July 31, 1963. Copyright © 1963 by Andre Maurois.

More: Quotation by Ronald Ribman from *More*, 7:31, July/August 1977. Copyright © 1977 by More.